Dana Facaros and Michael Pauls

SPAIN

'...not a melting pot but a *paella*, in which each ingredient retains its integrity and flavour while enhancing the whole.'

CADOGANguides

Contents

Introducing

The Guide

Reference

Maps

About the authors

Dana Facaros and **Michael Pauls** have written over 30 books for Cadogan Guides. They have lived all over Europe, but have recently hung up their castanets in a farmhouse surrounded by vineyards in the Lot Valley.

About the updaters

Various people updated this guide: **Kristina Cordero** (Madrid); **Adam Coulter** (Andalucía); **Mary-Ann Gallagher** (Catalunya; València and the Levante); **Leonie Loudon** (Andorra); **Susannah Sayler** (Barcelona); **David Stott and Helen Laird** (The Basque Lands, Navarra and La Rioja; Cantabria, Asturias and Galicia; Northern Castile and Léon); **Catherine Weiss** (Aragón; Around Madrid; Castilla La Nueva; Southern Castile and León). Acknowledgements and details about the updaters can be found after the Index.

Cadogan Guides
Network House, 1 Ariel Way, London W12 7SL
cadoganguides@morrispub.co.uk
www.cadoganguides.com

The Globe Pequot Press
246 Goose Lane, PO Box 480, Guilford, Connecticut 06437–0480

Cover and photo essay design by Kicca Tommasi
Book design by Andrew Barker
Cover photographs: John Ferro Sims, Kicca Tommasi
Maps © Cadogan Guides, drawn by Map Creation Ltd
Editorial Director: Vicki Ingle
Series Editor: Linda McQueen
Editor: Justine Montgomery
Art direction: Sarah Rianhard-Gardner
Proofreading: Susannah Wight
Indexing: Isobel McLean
Production: Book Production Services

Printed in Italy by Legoprint
A catalogue record for this book is available from the British Library
ISBN 1-86011-848-8

The publishers would like to thank the Fundación del Museo Guggenheim Bilbao for permission to use the image of the Guggenheim Museum.

The author and publishers have made every effort to ensure the accuracy of the information in this book at the time of going to press. However, they cannot accept any responsibility for any loss, injury or inconvenience resulting from the use of information contained in this guide.

Please help us to keep this guide up to date. We have done our best to ensure that the information in this guide is correct at the time of going to press. But places and facilities are constantly changing, and standards and prices in hotels and restaurants fluctuate. We would be delighted to receive any comments concerning existing entries or omissions. Authors of the best letters will receive a copy of the Cadogan Guide of their choice.

Spain
a photo essay

01

RETABLO SIENDO CVRA

PINCHOS MORUNOS
SERRANITO

HIJOS DE AGUSTIN BLAZQUEZ
JEREZ
12 MEDALLAS DE ORO Y
7 GRANDES DIPLOMAS DE HONOR
RAFAEL
EXPORTADOR DE
BODEGAS

Santa María de Naranco, Oviedo, Asturias

Guadalupe monastery

13th-century west portal, Zamora

Roman statue, Mérida

Pineas Pinea, Segovia

coast near Nerja

Badajoz vineyards

Bardenas Reales

San Esteban, Salamanca

Verula monastery, Tarazona

Sala de las Dos Hermanas, the Alhambra

Picos de Europa

Sagrada Família, Barcelona

Retiro Gardens, Madrid

public gardens, Almería

Peñafiel Castle

market scene, León

flamenco dancing, Córdoba

Ronda

white village, Andalucía

The Alhambra, Granada

La Mezquita, Córdoba

bar, Bilbao

Madrid

tile bar, Madrid

Bilbao

Guadalupe

Guggenheim, Bilbao

Introduction

Spain is a vivid country, one that catalyzes the imagination. All of us, perhaps, carry around a certain picture of the particular Spain that once caught our fancy. It could be the Spain of blood and sand in the bullring, of medieval crusades and troubadours, or of Moorish gardens full of roses; the seed of it may have been planted by Cervantes or Hemingway, Gil Blas or Washington Irving. All of these Spains can still be still be found if you seek them out, but they hardly exhaust the list of treasures and pleasures of this inexhaustible country. You must also see the lush valleys of the Atlantic coast, the snow-capped Pyrenees, the orange groves around Valencia, the weird dream landscapes of Old Castile. In between are 3,000 castles, great cathedrals, gardens, villages, palaces, rare works of art, and cities so lively they bounce.

Another attraction of the country is the Spaniards themselves. A remarkably lucid people, they are friendly, sane, enthusiastic, democratic in the widest sense of the word, and more awake than anyone in Europe – and not only because they regard going to bed before 3am as a kind of personal dishonour. They are in throes of creating something brand new, a novel kind of federal state: not a melting pot but a *paella*, in which each ingredient retains its integrity and flavour while enhancing the whole. To know Spain you must visit its 17 autonomous regions, most of them born out of once-independent kingdoms: the Galicians and Asturians, the Basques, Aragonese and Catalans, the Andalucíans and Riojans, and so on, all proud (and free now, since Franco) to express their differences through language, music, dance, cuisine, and traditions. Gone are the black and white, wrong and right days that lingered well past their sell-by date into the '70s. The Spain of today comes in all hues. Paradoxes and contradictions abound, and are savoured like different plates of tapas.

Keep your eyes open. Spain is a subtler country than many people think, and reveals itself in surprising ways. You may catch it in the moon reflected in a pool of the Alhambra, in the face of a Velázquez *infanta*, in a fond medieval jest such as the cats and rats chiselled into the cloister in Tarragona, or in a lone eagle coasting over a fortified castle in Extremadura. Travel on a train through a sparse Andalucían district in the spring, and all at once your glance may take in more colour than you've ever seen: pink and white almond blossoms, oranges on the trees, red poppies and yellow daffodils along the track bed. In a second it will be gone, but you will have seen Spain.

We can't pretend to be opening up a new territory. Spain is, after all, Europe's biggest holiday playground, last year playing host to some 50 million foreign visitors. We suspect that many more who would like to go have been discouraged, thinking the tourist tide has spoiled it all. Nothing could be further from the truth. Spain is not the kind of place that would ever let such a trivial phenomenon change its ways.

A Guide to the Guide

After the visual stimulus of the **photo essay**, the early chapters of this guide provide all the background information you need to get to grips with Spain. **History**, **Art and Architecture**, **Food and Drink** (including a menu decoder) and **Sketches of Spain** offer

Chapter Divisions

an incisive glimpse into Spain's many-faceted cultural identity, while the **Travel** and **Practical A–Z** sections ensure you have the practical support you need to set you on your way.

The guide then covers the country by region, from Catalunya and 'Green Spain' in the north, through the central plains around Madrid, then south to the sunshine coast of Andalucía. You'll find any practical information you need on site in the grey boxes that are interspersed throughout the narrative chapters, complete with considered hotel, restaurant and nightlife recommendations.

At the end of the guide are easy-reference chapters: a smattering of Spanish language, a glossary of architectural, artistic and historical terms used in the guide, and suggestions for further background reading if your interest is piqued.

Below, a brief resumé of Spain's many and diverse regions highlights their key characteristics, to help you in choosing your holiday.

Spain's Regions At A Glance

Andalucía: Guitars, sherry, flamenco, bullfights, Carmen, Figaro, Don Juan, olive and orange groves and masses of sunshine.

Aragón: With the Pyrenees, medieval villages and sombre plans dotted with towns with skylines of exotic *mudéjar* towers.

Around Madrid: A ring of fascinating cities and attractions within an easy day trip from the capital.

Asturias: Cider-guzzling Asturias has Atlantic beaches, but also the enchanting Picos de Europa range.

Cantabria: Lovely and rural, with emerald hills and stone houses, and the resorts of the Costa Esmeralda.

Castilla la Nueva and **La Mancha**: Valdepeñas wine, Manchego cheese, memories of Cervantes – and lots of space.

Catalunya: the wealthiest and most dynamic region in Spain.

Euskadi: Europe's oldest nation, the Basques, are the beginning of 'Green Spain' facing the Atlantic.

Extremadura: Black bulls grazing in groves of cork oaks, fine Roman monuments and famous shrines.

Galicia: Famous for the best seafood and Santiago de Compostela, goal of the great medieval pilgrimage.

Madrid: A hopeless jumble with exciting nightlife and Spain's greatest art treasures.

Murcia: its own autonomous community, with beautiful beaches.

Navarra: has some of Spain's most striking medieval sites, as well as the explosive July Sanfermines.

Old Castile and León: Striking landscapes of the *meseta* decorate this oldest part of Castile.

La Rioja: vineyards and *bodegas*, of course, but Rioja has some first-rate medieval monuments too.

València: the land of *paella* and oranges, ceramics and Las Fallas.

History, Art and Architecture

03

History

Prehistory

Evidence of culture in Spain goes back to remotest antiquity. Some 50,000 years ago, when Spain was a cooler, more forested place and glaciers iced the Pyrenees, Neanderthal man minded his business in the mountains and in the caves of Gibraltar. Surprisingly, no low-brow skulls have been found in between. The next players on the Iberian stage arrived around 25000 BC, during the Palaeolithic age; the peninsula's caves began to fill up with Palaeospaniards, living well enough off deer and bison to create impressive art works on cave walls. Scholars divide these people into the earlier Aurignacian and later Magdalenian cultures. The latter peaked around 15000 BC and created some of the Stone Age's finest art in the caves of Altamira in Cantabria.

The Neolithic era, the age of settled agriculture, begins in the peninsula at an uncertain date. The Iberians may have arrived as early as 7000 BC and are believed to have come from North Africa. Physical and linguistic clues suggest that they may have been the precursors of the Basques, the oldest nation of western Europe, but they had little to show for themselves until around 2500 BC. Even then the anonymous culture that built the big dolmen burial chambers at Antequera, north of Málaga, is an exception to the rule. Indeed, so little is known about these millennia that speculation is useless. Linguists believe the language of the Iberians to be related to modern Basque, but they learned their letters later from the Phoenicians. A mere 500 inscriptions have been found. Ancient Greek and Roman writers hint at links between Iberia and Greece, and also the British Isles; Iberians colonized parts of Ireland and south-west Britain, and the Irish bards may have learned their alphabet by way of Spain. But while their cousins in the Balearic Islands were building *talayot* fortresses and trading across the Mediterranean, the mainland Iberians produced little architecture or art.

In about 800 BC they were joined by other peoples, notably the Celts from over the Pyrenees. They got along well enough; in many cases the tribes gradually merged, creating a new people, the Celtiberians, who occupied the centre of the country. Little is known about these people. The great mystery of this era is the fabled kingdom of Tartessos (modern Andalucía), the only place where the anarchistic Iberians founded a state. Archaeologists are still looking for the city of Tartessos; some place it near modern Cádiz, others somewhere on the coast further east.

1100 BC–AD 50: Phoenicians, Greeks and, inevitably, Romans

If Iberians, Celts and Basques were unwilling to coalesce into states and empires, others were happy to do it for them. In this period, when trade boomed all over the Mediterranean, Spain was an 'undeveloped' country where ambitious foreigners with technology came as traders and conquerors. The Phoenician merchant capital of Tyre 'discovered' Spain in about 1100 BC, founding Gades (Cádiz). The Phoenicians were after Spain's mineral resources, and their exploitation of Spain made them economic masters of the Mediterranean. Their rivals, the Greeks, arrived later; expanding from the colony of Massilia (Marseilles) they founded trading towns on Spain's eastern coast, notably Saguntum, Emporion, and Dianion (Dénia), in the 7th and 6th centuries.

By this time Tyre was in decline, and Carthage, its western outpost, was building an empire out of the occupied coasts in Spain and North Africa. In about 500 BC the Carthaginians gobbled up the remains of Tartessos and halted the Greek infiltration. Along the eastern coast, Iberian culture now reached its height, developing important towns such as Ullastret on the Costa Brava. The Carthaginians maintained the status quo until 264–241 BC when Rome drubbed them in the First Punic War. Losing much of its commercial empire made Carthage dependent on Spanish men and resources. The famous leaders, Hamilcar Barca, his son-in-law Hasdrubal and his son Hannibal, consolidated their Spanish lands, and it was a largely Spanish army that Hannibal led over the Alps to ravage Italy in the Second Punic War of 218. The Romans kept him at bay long enough for their legions to conquer Spain (210) in his absence. The defeat of Carthage in 202 made Rome the master of Spain and the western Mediterranean. The Romans were never content to control just a part of Spain. Relentlessly, they slogged over the peninsula, subjugating one Celtic or Iberian tribe after another.

AD 50–406: Roman Hispania

For all the trouble they caused Rome at first, the Spanish soon became some of the Empire's most useful citizens. In the more civilized south, especially, they assumed the Romans' language, religion and customs in short order. New cities grew up to join Cádiz, Saguntum and New Carthage (Cartagena). Of these the most important were Hispalis (Sevilla), Corduba (Córdoba), Tarraco (Tarragona), Augusta Emerita (Mérida) and Caesar Augusta (Zaragoza). The last two were founded for pensioned-off Roman veterans, an important aspect of the policy of Romanization. Another new population element was the Jews, whom Rome settled here in the Diaspora; They were to play a constructive role in Spanish life for the next 1,500 years.

Roman Hispania, like Gaul, was divided into three parts: Lusitania included Portugal and Galicia, home of the vanquished Celts; Baetica (named after the Baetis, or the Guadalquivir) occupied Andalucía, the richest and most cultured Roman province west of Tunisia; the rest made up the sparsely settled province of Tarraconensis. Rome gave Spain bridges and aqueducts, roads and theatres, landlords and tax collectors; Spain in turn contributed soldiers, metals, wheat and oil, Andalucían dancing girls and fish guts (fish *garum* was the most prized gourmet delicacy in the empire, and an important export for Baetica). Spain also gave Rome three of its best emperors: Trajan, Hadrian and Theodosius, and many great figures of the 'silver age' of Latin literature: Lucan, both Senecas, Martial and Quintilian. While Roman Hispania lagged far behind the eastern half of the empire in terms of wealth and civilization, it was streaks ahead of Gaul, Britain, Africa and, eventually, in the last days of the Empire, even Italy itself.

406–711: Roman Twilight and the Visigoths

Even before the western frontiers of the empire crumbled in the fatal year of 406, civilization in Spain and western Europe was in a bad way. In 264 Franks and Alemanni devastated the peninsula in a decade of raids. After their repulse, the crushing burden of the defence budget and government bureaucracy sent Spain's economy into long-term regression. Cities declined and, in the countryside, landowners squeezed the population into serfdom or outright slavery. Thus, when the bloody, anarchic Vandals arrived in the 5th century, they found bands of rural guerrillas, or *bagaudae*, ready to help them smash up the remnants of the Roman system. The Vandals moved on to Africa in 428, leaving nothing behind but the name Andalucía (originally *Vandalusia*).

Here again Spain's history becomes complicated. Up north, the Asturians and Basques achieved independence. The south was occupied intermittently by imperial Byzantine troops. The Visigoths came down from Gaul in 412 to occupy the centre, a military aristocracy of semi-Romanized Teutons. Roving bands of Suebi, Alans and Vandals marauded at will, not so much tribes as mobile protection rackets.

The Visigoths were illiterate, selfish and bloody-minded, but persistent. There weren't many of them; only in the region between Burgos and Toledo did they form a substantial part of the population. They depended on the landowners, who had made a slow but logical transition from Roman *senatores* to feudal lords. Visigothic princes knifed each other in the back at the merest pretext and, when dynastic intrigue failed, there was always religion to keep the pot boiling. The Visigoths were Arian Christians, while the old Roman élite was orthodox in faith; most of the population had probably not converted at all, and looked on bewildered as the two factions anathematized and ambushed each other. The Visigoths ruled from Toledo, maintaining a provisional authority elsewhere. Despite all the troubles, Andalucía was doing well – better than anywhere in western Europe – and there was even a modest revival of learning in the 6th century, the age of St Isidore, famous scholar of Sevilla. This helped to improve the manners of the Visigothic overlords. King Leovigild (573–86) was an able leader; his son Reccared converted to orthodox Christianity in 589, and brought the state to the height of its power as much by internal reform as military victories. Allowing the Church a share of power, however, proved fatal to the Visigoths. As the clerics grew wealthy, they joined with the old Roman nobility in checking the power of the kings. Depredations against the populace and persecutions of Jews and heretics had made the Visigoths as many enemies within their borders as they ever had beyond them.

711–756: The Muslim Conquest

The great wave of Muslim Arab expansion that began in Prophet Muhammad's lifetime was bound to wash up on Spain's shores sooner or later. An unlikely protagonist of the Muslim conquest was Count Julián of Ceuta, lonely ruler of the westernmost bastion of the Byzantine Empire, who nominally was cooperating with the Visigoths. Legend states that Julián's daughter had been violated by the last Visigothic king, Roderick; the Count ferried a small Arab force over to Spain in 710 led by a certain Tarif, who gave his name to today's Tarifa. Tarif came back to tell the tale of a rich land, in disarray and ripe for the plucking, and in the following year Julián assisted in taking over a larger army – still only about 7,000 men – under Tariq ibn-Ziyad, who quickly defeated the Visigoths near Zarbate. Within three years, the Arabs had conquered most of the peninsula, driving northwards as far as Narbonne in France. The conquest was easy, as the majority of the population was delighted to welcome the Arabs and their Berber allies. The persecuted Jews supported them from the first. The final extinction of Roman law made free men of all country people. Religious tolerance was guaranteed under the Muslims; historians suggest that their campaign was more a financial speculation than a holy war and, since the largest share of taxes fell on non-believers, the Arabs were happy to refrain from seeking converts.

This conquest, however, was never complete. In 718, a legendary prince named Pelayo in the tiny kingdom of Asturias defeated the Muslims at an obscure skirmish the Spaniards call the Battle of Covadonga, opening the way for Alfonso I of Asturias to recover much of northwestern Iberia. The Arabs barely noticed; they were busy elsewhere. By 732 their armies had penetrated as far as Poitou in northern France, where Charles Martel whipped them so soundly that their advance was halted. Muslim control of Spain was solid, but hampered by dissension between the haughty Arabs and the neglected Berbers, and between the various Arab tribes.

756–1031: The Emirate of al-Andalus

Far away in Damascus, the political struggles of the Caliphate were being resolved by a massacre of the princes of the Umayyad dynasty, the successors of Muhammad, as the rival tribe of Abbasids replaced them on the throne. One Umayyad, Abd ar-Rahman, escaped: he fled to Córdoba,beyond the reach of the usurping Caliphs, and established himself there as the first leader of an independent Emirate of al-Andalus. Under this new government, Muslim Spain grew strong and prosperous. Political unity was maintained with difficulty, but trade, urban life and culture flourished. The Umayyad emirs referred to all their domain, stretching as far as the Pyrenees, as al-Andalus. Andalucía was its heartland and Córdoba, Sevilla and Málaga its greatest cities, unmatched in western Europe. Toledo and Zaragoza in the north prospered too.

Much nonsense has been written about 'Moorish' Spain. Too often the age has been approached as if it were a foreign occupation, but it cannot be emphasized too strongly that al-Andalus was a *Spanish* culture. Somehow the arrival of Islam, Islamic art and Arab poetry energized the intact, though slumbering, culture of Roman Andalucía. Spaniards, Arabs, Berbers and Jews all made their contributions, living in relative harmony; it would be impossible to disentangle them even if there were reason to try. For its wealth and sophistication, poetry and scholarship, and art and architecture we may take medieval al-Andalus as the height of Spanish civilization.

The political foundation for this achievement was provided by Abd ar-Rahman III, who turned the emirate into the Caliphate of Córdoba in 929. When the boy Caliph Hisham II came to the throne in 976, effective power was seized by his chamberlain Muhammad ben Abd-Allah, better known as al-Mansur ('the victorious'), who recaptured León, Pamplona and Barcelona from the Christians, and raided Compostela, stealing its bells to hang up as trophies in the Great Mosque of Córdoba.

The military superiority of the Moors was great enough for them to have finally erased the tiny Christian kingdoms of the northwest had they cared to do so. If lack of determination was one flaw, another was an anarchic inability to create a modern state. Directly upon al-Mansur's death in 1002, the Caliphate entered a fatal period of factional struggles and civil war. By 1031 the central authority had vanished for ever, and al-Andalus broke up into a patchwork of petty kingdoms called the *taifas*. The Christian states of the north were better organized. Despite their relative weakness, they laid the foundations of reconquest. Three small states appeared, each of which would one day be an important Christian kingdom. Under Alfonso I 'the Catholic' (d. 757) and Alfonso II 'the Chaste' (d. 842), little Asturias grew into the Kingdom of León. The Basques, independent for centuries, developed the Kingdom of Navarre, reaching its height under Sancho the Great (d. 1035). The northeastern corner of the peninsula, the 'Spanish march' of Charlemagne's empire that today is Catalunya, attained its independence as the County of Barcelona, and began its career as a mercantile power in the Mediterranean under Ramón Berenguer II (d. 1131).

1031–1284: The Reconquista

With al-Andalus divided, the Christian kingdoms had their chance. A son of Sancho the Great conquered the border county of Castile in 1037 and made a kingdom of it, installing himself as Ferdinand I. He later annexed León and made the Muslim states of Toledo and Zaragoza his vassals. This new state of Castile and León at once became the scene of permanent civil war, but it was still strong enough to advance under a strong leader. Alfonso VI, with the help of the legendary warrior El Cid, captured Toledo in 1085. The loss of this key fortress-city alarmed the kings of the *taifas* enough for them to invite in the Almoravids from North Africa, fanatical Muslim Berbers with a new empire stretching from Morocco to Senegal. The Almoravid leader Yusuf crossed the straits and defeated Alfonso in 1086. He liked al-Andalus so much he decided to keep it, and Almoravid domination lasted until 1147 when it was replaced by that of the Almohads, a nearly identical military state, also from Africa, which grew up around the reforming fundamentalist zeal of a mystic named ibn-Tumart.

Like the Almoravids, the Almohads went quickly through the cycle of conquest, decadence and decay. The end for them, and for al-Andalus, came with the Battle of Las Navas de Tolosa in 1212 at the hands of a united Christian Spanish and Portuguese army under Alfonso VIII. Alfonso's son, Ferdinand III, reunited Castile and León for the last time, captured Córdoba (1236) and Sevilla (1248), and was made a saint for his trouble. Alfonso X 'the Wise', noted for his poetry and brilliant court, completed the conquest of western Andalucía in the 1270s and 1280s, leaving the newly formed Nasrid Kingdom of Qarnatah (Granada) as the only Muslim state in Spain. At the same time, the growing Kingdom of Aragón, incorporating the County of Barcelona, was completing the Reconquista in the east. Alfonso I 'the Battler' had taken Zaragoza in 1118 but it was left to the greatest Aragonese ruler, Jaume I 'the Conqueror'(d. 1276), to expand Aragón's rule to València, the Balearic Islands and Alicante.

It would be a mistake to see the early days of the Reconquista as a simple crusade; that myth was invented in the reign of Isabel and Ferdinand. The age is as fascinating as it is complex. Before the fanatical Almoravids and Almohads, and the growth of the crusading idea in the Christian Church, Spanish Christians and Muslims had too much respect for each other to lapse into the kind of bigotry of an Isabel or Philip II. Intermarriage was common; all the Castilian and Aragonese kings had some Moorish blood, and the mother of Abd ar-Rahman III was a Basque. Alfonso the Wise and many kings of Aragón were as much at home in Arabic as in their own language, and a warrior like El Cid was as happy serving the Muslim Emir of Zaragoza as Alfonso VI.

Above all, it was a great age for culture. León and Toledo were beginning their cathedrals at about the same time as the Almohads were building La Giralda in Sevilla.

1284–1476: Aragón and Castile

The states of Aragón and Castile came to dominate the new Christian Spain. Of the two, Aragón was the more spectacular. Out of Barcelona's trade connections and navy it built an empire that included Sicily, Sardinia and even parts of Greece. As a rival to Genoa, Pisa and Venice, Barcelona dominated the western Mediterranean until a long stretch of bad luck after 1330 – plagues, bank collapses and class strife directed against the big merchants – sent the city into a long economic decline that enabled Castile to gain the upper hand on the peninsula.

Castile itself, having swallowed up León, Galicia, and most of the reconquered lands, was an aggressive society of ever-greater importance in European affairs. The civil wars between Pedro I 'the Cruel' (d. 1369) and his brother Enrique de Trastámara brought foreign intervention. The English backed Pedro, the French Enrique, and the Black Prince and Bertrand du Guesclin carried out a sideshow to the Hundred Years' War on Spanish soil. Dynastic feuds were still common, but none seriously damaged the kingdom. Castile based its prosperity on the *Honrado Concejo de la Mesta*, a crown-chartered cooperative of sheep farmers that supplied Europe with much of its wool; the annual trade fairs at Medina del Campo were the busiest on the continent. Because of the experience of the Reconquista, when new hands were always needed to settle newly conquered lands, economic feudalism ended in Castile long before anywhere else in western Europe. Still, the nobility flourished, exempt from taxes and loaded with privileges. The Reconquista had seen the creation of three new knightly orders, those of Santiago, Calatrava, and Alcántara, created to replace the heretical Templars who were dissolved in 1312. The new orders, cooperating with an arrogant and worldly Church, gained great power and wealth in this period.

On the whole, the Reconquista seems to have had a negative effect on both kingdoms, particularly Castile. Religious bigotry became widespread in the 13th and 14th centuries: the first pogroms against the Jews occurred in 1391. The years of constant warfare coarsened Castile, creating a pirate ethos which scorned honest labour. In 1474, yet another civil war broke out upon the death of Henry IV 'the Impotent', between partisans of his (likely) daughter Juana 'la Beltraneja' and his sister Isabel.

1476–1516: The Catholic Kings

Isabel had already married Ferdinand, heir to the throne of Aragón, and when Ferdinand defeated Juana and her Portuguese allies in the 1476 Battle of Toro, the way was open to unite their two realms. Ferdinand and Isabel reigned together, collaborating in all decisions; both were capable and intelligent, though Isabel, representing the stronger kingdom, had the final say. Ferdinand, a subtle statesman and excellent campaigner, did all the work. Under these two, the new Spain reached the height of its glory. In the unforgettable year of 1492, Columbus initiated the Age of Discovery by reaching Hispañola, and Ferdinand conquered Muslim Granada, finally completing the Reconquista. Later in their reign Ferdinand would annex Navarra, and the great general Gonzalo de Córdoba, 'El Gran Capitán', would conquer Naples and make Spain for the first time a leading player in European affairs. Also in 1492, the Catholic Kings expelled some 150,000 Jews from Spain. Soon after, they created the Inquisition, in an age when most European countries were disbanding it. They also broke the agreements they had made with the Moors of Granada, instituting a policy that was little better than genocide. Ferdinand and Isabel's fierce bigotry was popular enough in the nation as a whole – there was plenty of confiscated property to be handed out to loyal supporters – and it set the tone for Spain's grisly history in the next two centuries.

1516–1700: The Age of Rapacity

Or, as historians once called it, Spain's 'Golden Age'. Modern historians remind us that any golden age is in the eye of the beholder. In the 16th century Spain fought for hegemony over three continents, and succeeded only in destroying itself.

In an effort to build up their alliances against France, Ferdinand and Isabel had married their daughter Juana to the Habsburg Archduke Philip, son of the Holy Roman Emperor. The death of their other two children made Juana and Philip heirs to the throne, but Philip 'the Handsome' died, and Juana became deranged with grief. It is not known if she became truly insane. Her son Charles arrived from Flanders in 1517, stayed just long enough to force her to sign papers of abdication, and locked her up in a windowless cell for the next 40 years. Spain had suffered invasions and civil wars, plagues and famines, but never had it been subjected to anything like the Habsburgs. The family married into half the thrones of Europe, and Charles inherited them all: Spain, its colonies, the Netherlands, Austria, half of Italy and a smattering of German principalities. To top it off, he bought himself election as Holy Roman Emperor, making him the most powerful ruler in Europe since Charlemagne. (In Spain he is Carlos I, though we know him better under his imperial title, Charles V.)

To Europe, Charles meant unending war, serving his megalomaniac ambitions and his opposition to Protestantism. To Spain, a country he had never seen, Charles meant economic ruin. He and his Flemish minions emptied the royal treasury and shipped it overseas to bribe the German electors. This and other outrages occasioned the Comunero Revolt of 1520–21 in which the cities of Old Castile rose to defend their liberties – and their purses – but were crushed by Charles' foreign troops. It was the start of Castile's decline, and 36 more years of expensive Habsburg imperialism ended all hope of recovery. Charles' wars came to nothing, and in 1556 he chucked it all in for retirement at the monastery of Yuste in Extremadura.

The mess was inherited by his intelligent, pious and neurotic son, Philip II (one-time husband of Mary I of England), whose reign began with a national bankruptcy in 1556, the first of three. Silver from America kept Spain afloat, but little stayed in the country long enough to do any good. Philip had his successes, notably the great naval victory of his brother Don Juan over the Turks at Lepanto in 1571, but most news was bad. The revolt in the Netherlands resulted in Dutch independence, and the failure of the Great Armada against England in 1588 put an end to Habsburg designs in the north.

At home, too, things were going wrong. Philip's religious mania turned Spain into the picture of a modern totalitarian state. The Inquisition shut down intellectual life.

Book-burnings (parodied in *Don Quixote*) were common, and Spaniards forbidden to study overseas. The national movement towards *limpieza de sangre* ('purity of blood') resulted in a manhunt for clerics and officials with a taint of Jewish ancestry, and oppression of the remaining Moors was ferocious. Spanish behaviour in the New World was even more brutal; in the 16th century 80 per cent of the native population of Mexico and Peru died from disease and overwork in the fields and mines.

One Habsburg family tradition was incest. Philip's fourth wife, Anne of Austria, was at once his niece and the daughter of his first cousin. Not surprisingly, their son Philip III was an imbecile, entirely under the influence of a favourite, the Duke of Lerma. His reign was distinguished by the final expulsion of the Moors in 1609. Most of them lived in València, perhaps the most prosperous region in Spain at the time; the departure of its most skilled farmers ruined it. Philip III married another cousin, and the result was Philip IV. This Philip fared slightly better: not quite an idiot, he also chose his favourite better. The Conde Duque de Olivares was a flamboyant, tireless and confident reformer, but 20 years of hard work (1621–43) brought no significant accomplishment. The opposition of the Catalans and the nobility, combined with national exhaustion, made reform impossible. In 1640 Catalunya and Portugal (annexed by Philip II in 1580) revolted. The Portuguese secured their independence, and crushing defeats at the hands of the Dutch, English and French (notably at Rocroy (1643) in the Thirty Years' War) put an end to the age when Spain was taken seriously as a European power. Olivares went mad and died soon after.

Spain was dying with him. Under the Habsburgs, Spaniards had made contributions to European culture despite the terror of the times. The last great generation of Spanish artists, poets and dramatists, including Velázquez, Calderón and Lope de Vega, were contemporaries of Philip IV, but when they died there were no more to replace them. Economically, a wasteland had appeared. Spain's agriculture had been ruined, its mountains deforested, its manufacturers bankrupted. In the Middle Ages the plains of Castile had been the most densely populated part of Spain; by 1650 they had become as lonely and empty as you see them today, their once thriving cities reduced to relics of the past. We cannot blame the Habsburgs for it all: they could not have wrecked Spain so utterly without the help of a grasping Church and nobility. Both enriched themselves at every Spanish reverse, adding nought to the national life. These institutions had once created the expansive, crusading ethos of medieval Castile; later they conspired to assist in a national suicide. To close the book on the Habsburgs, there's drooling, staring Charles II, who lasted 35 years. He spent the last few in trances and convulsions, while the police combed Madrid's back alleys to find the 'sorceress' whom a priest said had enchanted him. Surrounded by a cabal of exorcists, clairvoyants and witch-doctors, Charles passed on in 1700, fortunately childless.

1700–1931: Bourbons, on the Rocks

A vacant throne attracted suitors, and prostrate Spain watched while they fought over it. England backed the Austrian Archduke Charles, while the French schemed for Philip of Anjou, a Bourbon; the result was a general European commotion, the War of the Spanish Succession. The English agitated madly, and the Duke of Marlborough won great victories, but in the end they abandoned their Spanish and Austrian allies for possession of Gibraltar (seized in 1704), and a promise that the Spanish and French thrones would never be united. The new king, Philip V, was put out at not being able to live in Paris, but he knew what Spain needed: more palaces. He and his successors spent Spain's revenues on a dozen mock-Versailles around Castile, and beyond that did their best not to offend the grandees or the Church. The one bright exception was Charles III, who came to the throne in 1759. Charles, with his ministers Floridablanca and Jovellanos, tried to reform everything, but most of his efforts went down the drain with the succession of his son Charles IV, as useless and stupid as any Habsburg.

The aftershocks of the French Revolution disrupted the Bourbons' Rococo daydream. Napoleon first threatened Spain, then enticed it into cooperating with his campaigns. The result was the 1805 Battle of Trafalgar, where nearly the entire Spanish fleet was destroyed under incompetent French leadership. Every Spaniard did his duty, however, and today, with an invincible concept of personal honour, the Spaniards still count it as a kind of victory. Napoleon finessed Charles IV into abdication in 1808 and when French troops kidnapped the heirs to the throne in Madrid, the citizens responded with the famous revolt of the Dos de Mayo, brutally suppressed by General Murat.

In the Peninsular War that followed, French troops occupied all of Spain, and distinguished themselves by stealing as much gold and art as they could carry and blowing up historic buildings just for sport. British forces, under Moore and later the Duke of Wellington, arrived in 1809, won most of their battles, and behaved disgracefully towards the population. The Spanish themselves recovered some self-respect by heroically resisting the French, notably at the Siege of Zaragoza under Palafox in 1809. In 1812 a group of Spanish liberals met in Cádiz to declare a Constitution, and under this the Spanish fitfully conducted what they call their War of Independence. Victory came with the restoration of the Bourbons in 1814. The new king, Ferdinand VII, turned out to be a black-hearted reactionary who restored the Inquisition and invited back the Jesuits. A successful revolt against him in 1820 was suppressed by the French in 1823.

In this decade most of Spain's American colonies achieved their independence; the mother country could do little to stop them. Ferdinand 's death in 1833 occasioned the First Carlist War, in which liberals supporting the rights of the Infanta, Isabel II, fought the Church, reactionaries and the Basques under pretender Don Carlos. The liberals won, but their succeeding dictatorships accomplished little of value apart from the expropriation of the monasteries and the final extinction of the Inquisition.

Spain, by now, had become a banana monarchy, where any ambitious general could issue a *pronunciamiento* and strive for power. Under a Catalan, General Prim, the First Republic was declared in 1868 but it soon succumbed to anarchy in Andalucía and a second, futile, Carlist War. A *pronunciamiento* by General Martínez Campos restored the Bourbons in 1876. Liberal and conservative politicians cut a cynical deal under which they would alternate in power. Frustration with this arrangement encouraged the growth of new left-wing groups: Communists, Socialists, and the Anarchist CNT.

The outstanding feature of Spanish life in the late 19th century was the economic and spiritual blossoming of Catalunya. While the long-oppressed Catalans were rediscovering their language and culture, Barcelona attained the position of Spain's biggest and most modern city, its artistic leader and the stronghold of Anarchism. The heavily industrialized Basque provinces began to assert themselves, too, and even Anarchist Andalucía began to change. Once more regionalism became a political issue, as thriving peripheral areas began to challenge the moribund Castilian centre.

A crisis for Spanish life came with embarrassing defeat in the 1898 Spanish-American War, and the loss of Spain's last important colonies. An informal group of truculent intellectuals, the 'Generation of '98', whose most famous members were Miguel de Unamuno and José Ortega y Gasset, began to examine their country's curious destiny closely. Spain was once a force in European culture, producing Picasso, Gaudí and a host of others. After hibernation, the creative juices were flowing once more. Spain stayed neutral in the First World War. After it, King Alfonso XIII entrusted the government to a genial, though repressive, dictator, Miguel Primo de Rivera, who brought the country's economy into the modern world in the optimistic decade of the 1920s. A newly-confident Spain demanded better; Primo de Rivera was dismissed with the onset of the Depression, and when municipal elections in 1931 showed an overwhelming victory for parties favouring a republic, Alfonso agreed to abdicate.

1931–9: The Second Republic and Civil War

In the beginning, the Second Republic was greeted with euphoria, but the reforms of the leftist government under Manuel Azaña simply brought the underlying conflicts of Spanish politics to the surface. To the reactionary upper classes, any reform was 'Bolshevik', while the Marxists and Anarchists saw the new government as a prelude to revolution. Political violence ranged from an attempted coup by General Sanjurjo in Sevilla in 1932, to a series of peasant revolts and land seizures in the poorest areas of Andalucía. Basques and Catalans took advantage of central weakness to declare their autonomy. Reaction came when the abstention of leftists in the 1933 elections brought the radical right into power. Moderate leaders like Azaña ended up in jail, and an epic miners' revolt in Asturias was brutally crushed in 1934. The alarmed Left formed a Popular Front to regain power in 1936, but street fighting and assassinations occurred daily, and the new government was unable to halt the slide into anarchy. Most trouble was caused by rightist provocateurs from the violent new Fascist party, the Falange Española, led by José Antonio Primo de Rivera, son of the dictator. The Left responded in kind, seizing aristocrats' property, burning churches and forming armed militias. At this point the army decided to step in.

Spain's creaky military, with one officer for every six soldiers, had a long tradition of interfering in politics, dating from the scores of *pronunciamientos* (coups) of the 19th century. On 17 July 1936 simultaneous uprisings occurred across Spain, orchestrated by Generals Francisco Franco and Emiliano Mola. The government was panicked into inaction, but workers' militias took control of the situation in many areas. A substantial part of the army remained loyal to the Republic, and instead of a quick coup the generals got a Spain divided into two armed camps. The balance was swung by the Army of Africa, the only effective fighting force, made up of mercenary Moors who had campaigned in Spain's colonial wars in its North Moroccan protectorate. They quickly captured eastern Andalucía and Extremadura, and their presence made their commander, Franco, first among equals (Mola died in a car crash). The insurgents' hope for an early victory was thwarted by the militia's heroic defence of Madrid.

Almost from the start the Civil War became an international affair. Fascist Portugal, Italy and Germany sent hundreds of aeroplanes and some 200,000 troops. Only Russia helped the Republic (all arms to be paid for in cash, though; the Fascists were a little more liberal to Franco). The Communists organized the famous International Brigade, in fact made up of only a handful of fighters. The list of notable foreigners who participated in the war is endless: Ernest Hemingway and George Orwell came as war-tourists; André Malraux organized an air squadron; Willy Brandt helped to keep the peace among the leftist factions while reporting for a Norwegian newspaper. Among the Communists, arrangements for volunteers were handled from Paris by Josep Broz (Marshal Tito), while future national Communist leaders like Walter Ulbricht of East Germany and Palmiro Togliatti of Italy were agents in Spain.

The imbalance in foreign help favouring Franco decided the war. British governments pursued an appeasement policy, setting up a 'Non-Intervention Committee', pressing the French into going along with it and ignoring German and Italian intervention, while blocking aid to the Republic. Internal Republican dissension did not help. With Russia the sole arms supplier and Communist-run divisions the best disciplined troops, the Communists dominated. In late 1937 the Republic finally found a capable leader in Dr Juan Negrín, but it was already too late.

Franco's careful tactics probably dragged the war on longer than was necessary. The first serious Republican reverse was the fall of Málaga in February 1937, losing them Andalucía once and for all. Spaniards on both sides chuckled when an Italian attempt to mount a blitzkrieg on Guadalajara in the same month lost them most of a division as prisoners. The Germans introduced terror bombing at Gernika (Guernica), in April, in a campaign in which Franco took the Basque provinces and Asturias. In December, the Republicans mounted an offensive in southern Aragón and in July 1938 another across the Ebro, where the Nationalists had reached the sea to cut the Republican zone in two. Both failed for lack of artillery and air support. After these last efforts, the Republic was finished; Franco conquered Catalunya in January 1939 and only token resistance continued in the centre. Madrid surrendered in March.

1939–75: Franco's Dictatorship

Some 500,000 Spaniards died in the war, more in mass killings behind the lines than in battle. When it was over, Franco proved more interested in revenge than reconciliation; even moderate Republican supporters found themselves in jail or forced labour camps. Franco was by now calling himself *Caudillo* (leader) and dressing in full Fascist regalia at public functions. By no means, though, did he convert Spain into a real Fascist state. Since the death of Primo de Rivera in a Republican jail in 1936 the Falangists had been leaderless, though they increased their numbers during and after the war. Franco manipulated them carefully: they were allowed to organize Fascist-style vertical trade unions and 'syndicates', but were gradually excluded from power when Franco guessed the Fascists would lose the Second World War. Franco's relations with the Axis were difficult from the start. Hitler came down from a 1941 meeting at Hendaye, intending to bully Spain into the war, but afterwards stated he would 'rather have his teeth pulled' than ever again talk to such a stubborn character.

Even had Franco been more willing, Spain was capable of little help. Industry and communications were in ruins, and parts of the country knew famine several times in the 1940s. Conditions did not improve until after 1953 when Franco signed a treaty with the United States, exchanging military base sites for a measure of international respectability and a huge transfusion of dollars. To please his new friends and avoid bankruptcy, Franco dismantled the cumbersome Fascist organization of the economy and encouraged a new generation of technocrats (many of whom were members of the secret Catholic society Opus Dei). Their reforms and the American loans began to pay off in the 1960s, when Spain experienced an industrial take-off that provided it with the highest economic growth rate in the world, really just making up for lost time. The growth of tourism and remittances from half a million Spaniards working abroad helped as much as any new industry.

Economic advance meant social changes. Possibly the greatest was the mass migration of rural people from the south to the industrial cities. Between their experience in the cities and the influx of tourists, millions of Spaniards were exposed to foreign ideas and influences for the first time. Such things usually mean trouble for dictators, but Franco proved stubborn enough to resist all pressure for change. As always, his regime depended entirely on Spain's three evil stepsisters: the Church, the Army and the landowners. All legal political factions, Falangists, Carlists and Monarchists were combined in the toothless Movimiento Nacional, but what Franco really wanted was to eliminate politics for ever. The Spaniards had other ideas. All the leftist groups had maintained clandestine organizations, even setting up a network of underground trade unions. Most groups were simply waiting for the old man finally to die; one exception was the Basques, who evolved the terrorist group ETA. This first became prominent in 1973, when their master blasters assassinated Admiral Carrero Blanco, sending his limousine over the roof of a Madrid church where he was coming to attend Mass. Carrero Blanco had been the ageing dictator's strongman and best hope for the continuity of the regime. Franco found no one hard enough to replace him.

1975 to the Present: The Restoration of Democracy

Franco was a monarchist at heart, and back in 1969 he had declared Juan Carlos I, grandson of Alfonso XIII, to be his successor. In doing so he passed over Juan Carlos' democratically minded father Don Juan; Juan Carlos seemed pliable enough and both Franco and the opposition expected him to carry on the old order. Franco died in 1975 and for a while the new King did nothing to excite anyone's suspicions.

Those who underestimated Juan Carlos, however, received a big surprise when he confidently began to move Spain back to democracy. His choice for Prime Minister, Adolfo Suárez, initiated a political reform bill that would establish a democratically elected *Cortes*. On 18 November 1977, the nation watched spellbound on television while the disorganized Francoists in the old *Cortes* committed political suicide by approving it. In the months that followed, the trade unions and the Socialist and Communist parties were legalized, and the Francoist Movimiento disbanded. Press censorship was ended, and the first free elections in 32 years were held, returning Suárez and his centralist party, the UCD, to power. The speed and orderliness of the transition astounded the world. Somehow, the long years of Franco's grey dictatorship had created a new maturity among the vast majority who desired democracy. They had been waiting for this opportunity for years, and no one did anything to ruin it. In the words of one perceptive foreign correspondent, Spain was 'a country whose society was open and democratic long before its institutions were'.

A new Constitution followed, one of the most liberal in Europe. More remarkably still, the long heritage of Castilian centralism was undone once and for all by measures creating regional autonomy, making Spain a federal state like Germany or the USA. The new democracy easily survived the old guards' last hurrah, when Civil Guards under Colonel Antonio Tejero attempted a coup by occupying the *Cortes* in February 1981. Elements in the army were behind it, but they backed down when ordered to do so by the King. In 1982 came the real transition, when general elections were won overwhelmingly by the Socialists under Philip González, a charmer from Sevilla with a chipmunk smile, called by some the 'best politician in Europe'.

Throughout the '80s, González maintained his popularity by staying as close as possible to the centre, while carefully nurturing the economy. In 1986, he overcame all the opposition by steering Spain into the European Community, winning a national referendum over NATO membership (something he had opposed four years earlier), and keeping his majority in two general elections. In the late '80s the rightist parties merged to form a common opposition, the Partido Popular (PP), led by a young, economically conservative, former tax inspector named José María Aznar, while the Communists, finding their support dwindling with each election, reformed into the professedly democratic United Left (IU). Under González and the Socialists, Spanish prosperity increased steadily, growing closer to that of the other major nations of western Europe. The big problem was, and remains, unemployment consistently over 20 per cent, the highest in the EU.

The magic year 1992 – the 500th anniversary of national unification and Columbus' voyage – was a chance for the Spaniards to show off the new Spain to the world, with Sevilla's World's Fair and the Barcelona Olympics. In 1996, after 14 years in power, González's Socialists found themselves suffering the usual lethargy that comes with a long term of office, besides suffering serious scandals over corruption and the GAL, so-called 'death squads' in the security forces that are accused of murdering Basque separatist (ETA) officials involved with terrorism. Spain takes her new democracy with admirable seriousness, and she can put on as fine a spectacle in politics as those in her fiestas. After the most recent attack, Madrid witnessed a silent, monster demonstration at night, led by González, Aznar and the other party chiefs marching together – in the middle of an electoral campaign. In 1999 ETA ended a 14-month ceasefire, starting up a campaign of violence across Spain and the Basque region, to which the government is, for the moment, taking a security-first approach rather than seeking a political solution. After steering a respectable course for four years, the general elections in 2000 saw Aznar's Partido Popular win a second term, gaining an absolute majority in Parliament.

Art and Architecture

Pre-Roman

Early examples of Spanish art are among the oldest yet found anywhere – most notably the Upper Palaeolithic (12000 BC) cave paintings at Altamira, near **Santander**. Prehistoric architectural remains are less remarkable. Neolithic cultures constructed dolmens along the coasts, especially in Galicia and Asturias; the best on the mainland are the three huge dolmen-chambers in **Antequera**, Andalucía, along with the site of Los Millares, near **Almería**. Galicia and Asturias are rich in foundations of Celtic *castros*, the best preserved being in **A Garda**. The Celts brought with them a talent for jewellery and metalwork, and under Roman rule sculpted the stone bulls and boars called *verracos* that are found throughout Ávila province. The most interesting works can be found in the archaeological museums of **Córdoba**, **Sevilla** and, above all, **Madrid**, where you can see the masterpiece of Iberian sculpture, the *Dama de Elche*.

Roman and Visigothic

Considering the literary and political figures Spain gave the Roman world, it's surprising that Roman Spain comes up so short in art. In the museums of **Madrid**, **Córdoba**, **Mérida** and **Barcelona** you'll see the usual copies of Greek sculpture, statues of emperors, and mosaics; some lovely mosaics have recently been uncovered at the Roman villa of Olmeda at **Pedrosa de la Viga** (Palencia province). Among Roman cities **Mérida** is by far the best preserved, although rivalled by **Tarragona** for interest. The aqueduct of **Segovia**, still intact, is one of the largest engineering works left from antiquity; the lofty **Alcántara** bridge in Cáceres province is also impressive. Other Roman ruins may be seen at **Itálica** near Sevilla; there's also a reconstructed temple colonnade in **Córdoba** and an intact belt of Roman walls around **Lugo**.

Art under the Visigoths, what there is of it, was derivative of the Roman with a touch of barbaric dash. The Spanish rediscovered their talent for gaudy, intricate jewellery, best seen in the Archaeological Museum of **Madrid** ('the Treasure of Gurrazar') and the Museo de los Concilios y del Arte Visigótico in **Toledo**. A few churches survive, with the characteristic horseshoe-arch later adopted by the Moors: the most extraordinary is at **Quintanilla de las Viñas**, south of Burgos, **San Pedro de las Naves**, near Zamora, the martyrium in **Palencia** cathedral, King Recesvinto's church at **Baños de Cerrato** (south of Palencia) and the churches at **Terrassa** near Barcelona.

Moorish

The renaissance of culture in Spain began in the 9th century, with the reign of the great Abd ar-Rahman. Its inspirations were surprisingly varied: floral arabesques and detail from late Roman art, architectural forms from Syria, mosaics from Byzantium (often crafted by Greek artists), and the perfection of the already impressive Spanish heritage in metalwork and jewellery. The catalyst that made these disparate elements come together so brilliantly was Islam itself. Prohibiting figurative art, the religion led men to contemplate rhythms and patterns in nature. Islamic art carried on, without decadence or revolutions, until 1492 and beyond, shifting slowly like a kaleidoscope, constantly finding new forms to delight the eye and declare the unity of creation. In the time of the caliphate, before 1009, Moorish Spain excelled in architecture (as in the Great Mosque of **Córdoba**), and its artists became the consummate masters of the minor arts: elaborate woodcarving, metalwork and ceramics, including the *azulejo* tiles used in architectural decoration that have been a Spanish speciality ever since. The best collections are in the museums of **Granada** and **Córdoba**.

The age of the Almohads was a great time for architecture, exemplified by the Torre de Oro and La Giralda in the Almohad capital, **Sevilla**. Islamic art had its last efflorescence in Nasrid **Granada**, where the marriage of art and architecture was raised to a level of perfection in the Alhambra, built in stages throughout the 14th century. Granadan artists also worked for the Christian King Pedro in the Alcázar of **Sevilla**. Much Moorish work was wantonly destroyed after the Reconquista but, besides the sites mentioned above, many castles remain, notably the Alcazabas in **Málaga** and **Almería**. In the north, the Cristo de la Luz church (a former mosque) in **Toledo** and the Aljafería in **Zaragoza** are the outstanding buildings.

Asturian and Mozarabic Pre-Romanesque

In the 9th century, as the Moors in the south were beginning their golden age, the small Christian principalities of the north were developing an architecture as sophisticated and original as anything else in western Europe. Though they are referred to as 'Pre-Romanesque', the monuments of the Kingdom of Asturias are in fact Romanesque, a century ahead of anything elsewhere. Having the cultured Moor for a neighbour and an enemy undoubtedly provided the Asturians with their impetus to build; lacking precedents, they created a new architecture from Roman survivals, along with Celtic decorative motifs and Islamic elements, such as latticework screen windows. The greatest monuments are the Asturian churches in and around **Oviedo**. From the same period, there are interesting Mozarabic churches in the villages of **Soria** province (San Baudelio), **León** (San Miguel de Escalada), **Aragón** and especially at **Melque** (Santa María de Melque), near Toledo. This was also the period of the first great illuminated manuscripts: beautifully coloured copies of the *Commentaries on the Apocalypse*, written by Beato of the Mozarabic monastery of Santa María de Lebeña (Asturias), survive in **Girona**.

Romanesque

Romanesque, the first 'international style' of European art, anticipated in Asturias, took shape across the Pyrenees in the 11th century. A strong French influence came back to Spain along the pilgrimage road to Santiago de Compostela, where you can see scores of examples: **Jaca** cathedral in Aragón, **Santa María de Eunate**, **Sangüesa** and **Estella**, all in Navarra; the 'perfect Romanesque church' at **Frómista**; the Pantheon of St Isidore in **León**; the great cathedral of **Santiago** itself. The Catalans were among the first to develop their own brand of Romanesque: their style was straightforward and solid, distinguished by elegant square belltowers set with ranks of paired windows. **Ripoll**, **San Cugat** and most of the villages in the Pyrenees have impressive churches. Many churches acted as part of a town's defences, such as the cathedrals at **Ávila**, **Tarragona** and **Sigüenza**. As elsewhere in Europe, this was an era of great creative freedom, and there are many regional styles besides Catalunya's: **Segovia**'s, for instance, features side porches, while Byzantine cupolas add character in **Zamora** and **Toro**.

Sculpture, integrated in the architecture of a religious building, was an essential feature of the Romanesque. The Catalans excelled at it (especially at **Ripoll**), and there are many fine capitals, tympana and tombs to be seen along the pilgrimage road (Santo Domingo de Silos, near **Burgos**, has the best cloister), but the finest of all Spanish sculpture from the 12th century is Master Mateo's tremendous Pórtico de la Gloria at **Santiago de Compostela**. The Catalans also had a head start when it came to painting: in **Barcelona**, the Museu Nacional d'Art de Catalunya contains a magnificent collection of frescoes salvaged from tiny churches in the Pyrenees. The finest Romanesque frescoes remaining *in situ* are in the Panteón de los Reyes in San Isidoro, in **León**.

Mudéjar

In parts of the north, in the first lands of the Reconquista, Moorish influence and Moorish artisans survived, developing a new and unique art in the 12th century. One critic has called *mudéjar* the 'national style of Spain', combining the best of Moorish decorative arts – brickwork and *azulejo* tiles – and their love of elaborate geometric patterns with elements from the Romanesque and Gothic. The cloisters of San Juan de Duero at **Soria** and the brick churches at **Sahagún** near León are among the earliest examples, while **Toledo** has the best collection: several parish churches, town gates, and two lovely synagogues. Perhaps the grandest *mudéjar* works are the four great church towers of **Teruel**. Many other towns in southern Aragón – **Zaragoza**, **Calatayud** and **Tarazona** – have good examples. In the south, the Alcázar in **Sevilla**, built for Pedro the Cruel, is *mudéjar* at its most extravagant.

Gothic

The increasing bitterness of the Reconquista broke off many cultural relations between Christian and Moorish Spain; one result was that Moorish influences in architecture ended in Castile and León, allowing the growth of a Gothic aesthetic highly dependent on French originals. The three greatest Gothic cathedrals are in **León**, **Burgos** and **Toledo**. Catalan Gothic is another story altogether, emphasizing width and strength rather than height. The cathedrals of **Girona**, **Tarragona** and **Barcelona** are textbook examples. Barcelona also has Santa María del Mar, Catalan Gothic at its most sublime, and the Barri Gòtic, Europe's greatest concentration of secular Gothic architecture. Gothic penetrated Andalucía with the progress of the Reconquista, as the triumphant Spaniards refused to permit any continuity with the artistic legacy of the Moors. The results range from the simple parish churches of **Córdoba** to the ponderous cathedral in **Sevilla**, the biggest Gothic church ever built. The style lingered in Spain longer than the rest of Europe; the last Gothic cathedrals are those of **Salamanca** and **Segovia**, built in the 16th century. Isabelline Gothic, late

15th-century Spain's ornate contribution to the style, corresponds roughly to the French Flamboyant or English Perpendicular, but it is a distinctive product of a young, confident nation. You can see Isabelline Gothic at its best in San Juan de los Reyes in **Toledo**, San Gregorio in **Valladolid**, Santa María in **Aranda del Duero** (Burgos province) and Enrique Egas' Capilla Real in **Granada**. At the Cartuja of Miraflores in **Burgos**, Gil de Siloé's tombs mark the summit of Isabelline Gothic sculpture.

The 14th and 15th centuries were the first important age of Spanish painting, again mainly in Catalunya but also in València. Works by a score of talented but little-known painters like Ferrer Bassá (d. 1348), Bernat Martorell (d. 1452), Jaume Huguet (d. 1492) and Bartolomé Bermejo (d. 1498) can be seen in the cathedral and museums of **Barcelona**, as well as in the museums of **Vic** and **València**.

Renaissance and the 'Golden Age'

Out of Isabelline Gothic came the early Renaissance style known as Plateresque ('silversmith-like') in the early 16th century, characterized by lavish sculptural decoration, especially elaborate façades, unrelated to the rest of the building. The best Plateresque is all over **Salamanca**, the University in **Alcalá de Henares**, the façades of the Hostel de los Reyes in **Santiago de Compostela** and the Hospital de San Marcos in **León**. Plateresque coincided with the height of Spanish sculpture. Many great works are anonymous, such as the *Doncel* in **Sigüenza** cathedral; Gil de Siloé's son Diego (d. 1563) deftly combined sculpture and architecture in the cathedrals of **Granada** (where he was the master builder) and **Burgos** (tombs and the *Escalera Dorada*). High Renaissance grandiosity arrived with Italian-trained Pedro Machuca in 1527 (Palace of Charles V, **Granada**). The new trend eventually led to something well suited to the grim age of conquest and Counter-Reformation, exemplified in Juan de Herrera's great **El Escorial** near Madrid and in the Ayuntamientos of **Madrid** and **Toledo**. In Andalucía, Herrera and Diego de Siloé had a worthy follower in Andrés de Vandelvira, whose work can be seen in **Úbeda** and **Jaén**.

Spanish painting developed in the 16th century under the influence of the Italian Renaissance and the Flemish painters brought over by Charles V; both styles can be seen in the work of Pedro Berruguete (d. 1504) in **Madrid** (in the Prado) and in **Paredes de Navas**, near Palencia. His son, Alonso Berruguete (d. 1561) went a step further and introduced the emotional intensity of Italian Mannerism in painting and sculpture (works in **Valladolid** and **Toledo**). Alonso Berruguete was succeeded in Toledo by El Greco (d. 1614), a Cretan whose ecstatic Mannerist style may have been *sui generis*, but properly begins the history of a distinctively Spanish painting (works in the Prado, **Madrid** and in **Toledo**). The 17th century was the 'golden age' of Spanish painting. The clarity, virtuosity and naturalistic perfection of the Spanish school's greatest master, Diego Velázquez (d. 1660), stand out head and shoulders above the others. By the end of his career, in his masterpiece *Las Meninas*, he achieved a miraculous subtlety and shimmering vividness, more real than real: examined close up, however, the forms magically dissolve into blurs, as if Velázquez were making a statement on the nature of matter itself (Prado, **Madrid**). The restrained, direct, monumental spirituality of the saints of Francisco de Zurbarán (d. 1664) can be seen in the museums of **Cádiz**, **Sevilla**, the Prado and the cathedral of **Guadalupe**. Other painters limited themselves to orthodox religious commissions: either grim and disquieting (Ribalta, d. 1628; Ribera, d. 1652; and the outrageous Váldez Leal, d. 1690), or saccharine mariolatry with floating angels (Murillo, d. 1682, many works in **Sevilla**; and architect-painter Alonso Cano, d. 1667, of **Granada**).

Baroque

Architecture in the 17th and 18th centuries followed two increasingly divergent strains, havering between the plain and the fancy, as if Spain could not make up its mind whether to laugh or cry over the troubles of the age. The Baroque, as Italy and other nations knew it, never really caught on, although Spaniards often borrowed ideas from it while inventing many original forms. The plainer faction, loath to give up the ideas or the Renaissance, is shown in such works as the Basílica del Pilar in **Zaragoza** and Alonso Cano's façade for **Granada** cathedral. The real interest is with the more decorative party; their amazing creations maintained the freshness and originality of Spanish architecture in the 1700s, when almost every other nation was losing its own. The ornate early works of this school were inspired by the earlier Plateresque (San Pablo at **Valladolid**, 1601). Later, influences were to come from such disparate sources as the *mudéjar* and the wild Mexican Baroque (as seen in the towers of **Jerez de los Caballeros**). The 18th century spawned the extravagant forms of the 'Churrigueresque', named after the sculptor and architect José Churriguera (d. 1723). The finest Churrigueresque creations are the Plaza Mayor in **Salamanca**, Vicente Acero's cathedral in **Guadix**, the Cartuja in **Granada**, churches in **Priego de Córdoba**, the Convento de Merced in **Córdoba**, the 'Transparente' in the cathedral of **Toledo** and the sublime, flaming Obradoiro façade of the cathedral at **Santiago de Compostela** by Fernando Casas y Novoa.

Good Spanish painting died suddenly and completely after the 1660s; real art would have to wait for the luminosity of Goya (d. 1828), ranking with Velázquez as one of Spain's greatest (in **Madrid**, the Prado and La Florida church). Goya had no worthy followers, but the works of 19th-century Romantic realists such as Fortuny, Casas, de Madrazo, Zuloaga and Sorolla fill the museums of **Madrid** and **Barcelona**. Similarly, in architecture eclectism took hold, resulting in neo-Moorish bullrings and Roman-style public buildings.

The 20th Century

The first sign of a rebirth in Spanish architecture occurred in Catalunya, with the advent of Barcelona's Universal Exhibition of 1888 and the first works of the specifically Catalan *modernista* style. The *modernistas* were part of the great Art Nouveau movement at the turn of the century, although in Catalunya the artists had another agenda: Catalan nationalism. All the members of the *modernista* triumvirate – Lluis Domènech i Montaner, Josep Puig i Cadafalch and Antoni Gaudí – made references back to the Middle Ages, when Catalunya possessed its own Mediterranean empire, but expressed their medievalism in the newest techniques in iron and brick and swirling asymmetrical decoration based on stylized natural forms. Gaudí (d. 1926), the most imaginative of the *modernistas*, has been recognized as a key architectural genius of the 20th century (most works, including the Park Güell, the Pedrera, the Colonia Güell crypt and Sagrada Família, are in or near **Barcelona**, others in **Comillas** (Cantabria), **Astorga** and **León**). Gaudí's co-worker Josep Maria Jujol was responsible for most of the magnificent tile mosaic-collages that decorate the buildings; his work and that of scores of other architects and decorators make wandering the streets of Barcelona a delight.

Barcelona's *modernista* movement became a hothouse for some of the greatest artists of the 20th century. Pablo Picasso (d. 1973), was born in Málaga but spent his early manhood in Barcelona (many works are in the Reina Sofía museum in **Madrid**, others in the Picasso Museum in **Barcelona**). In Paris, Picasso met his fellow Cubist Juan Gris (d. 1927) as well as Barcelona natives Julio González (d. 1942) and Joan Miró (d. 1983). Another surreal Catalan, the irascible painter Salvador Dalí (d. 1989), made his whole life a masterpiece of performance art and left his native **Figueres** a delightful museum. The Catalan, Antoni Tàpies (d. 1994), was an important innovator, noted in particular for his use of everyday objects (Fundació Tàpies, **Barcelona**).

The coming of the Civil War and Franco put an abrupt end to Spain's prominence in the arts, and if recovery after Franco has come in fits and starts it hasn't been for lack of good will. The Museum of Contemporary Art in **Cuenca** was built to house works by Spanish abstract artists, beginning with Antonio Saura; another showcase is the new Centro de Arte Reina Sofía in **Madrid**. Elsewhere, look out for the works of the Basque Eduardo Chillida, the greatest living sculptor in Spain (**San Sebastián** and **Vitoria**). **Barcelona** in particular has sought to recapture its old prominence, beginning in 1975 with the construction of Josep-Lluis Sert's beautiful Fundació Miró. Since then, no city anywhere has commissioned more works of public art (over 70 squares have been handed over to artists from around the world) and architecture (Norman Foster's Collserola tower for the Olympics, Isozaki's Palau Sant Jordi, or native Barcelonan Ricardo Bofill's airport terminal and Sport University) or has set up more galleries and museums to digest it all (most recently, Richard Meier's Museu d'Art Contemporani de Barcelona in the Barri Xinès). Barcelona's modern art status is now seriously challenged by Bilbao, seat of the fabulous new Guggenheim Museum, a sublime work of art in itself, designed by Frank Gehry.

Sketches of Spain

04

Air and Light

We can tell you everything about cathedrals and palaces, cities and resorts, but setting the scene for them will prove somewhat harder. One of the delights of all the Mediterranean lands is the endless variety of qualities and colour in the sea and sky. Nowhere, perhaps, will they grab your attention as in Spain.

On the high central plains, where the air is thin, the sun becomes a manifest power. At noon, even on a cool day, it can seem like some diabolical ray, probing deep inside your brain. Always, it illuminates Spain with a merciless brilliance; Spanish writers recall it when trying to explain their country's literature and history. 'Spain', according to one, 'is a country where things can be seen all too clearly.' Spanish art could not be what it is without this light. In the Prado, you'll look at Goya paintings set under an impossibly lovely pale blue sky with clouds like the breath of angels. You'll probably blame the artist for picturesque excess – and then walk outside to find that same Castilian sky, and those same clouds, reproduced over your head. Madrid's air is equally renowned, though with somewhat less lyricism: 'it is like quick lime, drying and consuming a corpse in a trice', as one 18th-century traveller noted. Doctors believed the air was so potent that it would be toxic unless humans were there to dilute it with fetid exhalations. One worried doctor did a census and estimated that 10,000 turds a day (there was no sanitation) hit the streets of Madrid, much to everyone's relief. 'That which one shits in the winter, one drinks in the summer,' they used to say.

The winds, too, will make you take notice: each has its name and characteristics, and when the less gracious of them visit they seize the land like a conquering army. Andalucía and the south annually endure the African *sirocco*; walking into it is like opening the oven door. The *tramontana*, when it's angry, roars over the Pyrenees and knocks the Catalans' houses down. And springtime Cádiz is sometimes plagued with an utterly bizarre wind called the *solano* that gets under your skin like a scalpel. The effect it has on the female population is legendary: in the old days, they would converge on the beach en masse when the *solano* hit, taking off their clothes and jumping in the sea for relief while the local cavalry regiment stood guard. Today, ask the ladies of Cádiz about it and they'll just laugh.

Castrum

In laying out their military camps, as in anything else, the Romans liked to go by the book. From Britain to Babylonia, they established hundreds of permanent forts (*castrum* in Latin) all seemingly stamped out of the same press, with a neatly rectangular circuit of walls and two straight streets, the *cardo* and *decumanus*, crossing in the middle. Many of these grew into towns; any place in Britain, for example, that ends in -chester or -caster.

In Spain, where the Roman wars of conquest went on for 200 years, there are perhaps more of these than anywhere else, and it's interesting to try and trace the outlines of the Roman *castrum* as you're exploring a Spanish city. In Barcelona's Barri Gòtic, the plan is obvious, and in Ávila and Cáceres the streets and walls have hardly changed since Roman times. With a little practice and a good map, you can find the *castra* hiding inside Córdoba, Mérida, León, Zaragoza, Tarragona, Lugo and a score of other towns.

Dr Fleming

Ask a Spaniard to name one famous Scot, and if you get more than a blank stare, it will likely be a mention of the inventor of penicillin. To the Spaniards he is one of the titans of science; there is a street in his name in almost every large town. Fleming has also become a sort of patron saint for two special groups in Spanish society. There are two monuments to the good doctor in Spain; one in front of the Madrid's Ventas bull-ring, and another in the Barri Xinés, the old red-light district of Barcelona.

Bullfights

In Spanish newspapers, you will not find accounts of the bullfights (*corridas*) on the sports pages; look in the 'arts and culture' section, for that is how Spain has always thought of this singular spectacle. Bullfighting combines elements of ballet with the primal finality of Greek tragedy. To Spaniards it is a ritual sacrifice without a religion, and it divides the nation irreconcilably between those who find it brutal and demeaning and those who couldn't live without it. Its origins are obscure. Some claim it derives from Roman circus games, others that it started with the Moors, or in the Middle Ages, when the bull faced a mounted knight with a lance.

There are bullrings all over Spain, and as far afield as Arles in France and Guadalajara, Mexico, but modern bullfighting is quintessentially Andalucían. The present form had its beginnings around the year 1800 in Ronda, when Francisco Romero developed the basic pattern of the modern *corrida*; some of his moves and passes, and those of his celebrated successor, Pedro Romero, are still in use today. The first royal *aficionado* was Ferdinand VII, the reactionary post-Napoleonic monarch who also brought back the Inquisition. He founded the Royal School of Bullfighting in Sevilla, and promoted the spectacle across the land.

In keeping with its ritualistic aura, the *corrida* is one of the few things in Spain that begins strictly on time. The show commences with the colourful entry of the *cuadrillas* (teams of bullfighters or *toreros*) and the *alguaciles*, officials dressed in 17th-century costume, who salute the 'president' of the fight. Usually three teams fight two bulls each, the whole spectacle taking only about two hours. Each of the six fights, however, is a self-contained drama performed in four acts. First, upon the entry of the bull, the members of the *cuadrilla* tease him a bit, and the *matador*, the team leader, plays him with the cape to test his qualities. Next comes the turn of the *picadores*, on padded horses, whose task is to wound the bull slightly in the neck with a short lance or *pica*, and the *banderilleros*, who agilely plant sharp darts in the bull's back while avoiding the sweep of his horns. The effect of these wounds is to weaken the bull physically without diminishing any of his fighting spirit, and to force him to keep his head lower for the third and most artistic stage of the fight, when the lone *matador* conducts his *pas de deux* with the deadly, if doomed, animal. Ideally, this is the transcendent moment, the *matador* leading the bull in deft passes and finally crushing its spirit with a tiny cape called a *muleta*. Now the defeated bull is ready for 'the moment of truth'. The kill must be clean and quick, a sword thrust to the heart. The corpse is then dragged out to the waiting butchers.

More often than not the job is botched. Most bullfights, in fact, are a disappointment, especially if the *matadores* are beginners, or *novillos*, but to the *aficionado* the chance to see one or all of the stages performed to perfection makes it all worthwhile. When a *matador* is good, the band plays and the hats and handkerchiefs fly; a truly excellent performance earns a reward from the president: one of the bull's ears, or both; or, rarely, for an exceptionally brilliant performance, both ears and the tail. Nowadays, you may be lucky to see a bullfight at all; there are only about 500 each year in Spain, mostly coinciding with holidays or a town's fiesta. During Sevilla's *feria* a a bullfight takes place every afternoon at the famous Maestranza ring, while other major venues include the rings in Málaga and Puerto de Santa María near Cádiz. **Tickets** can be astronomically expensive and hard to come by, especially for a well-known *matador*; sometimes touts buy out the lot. Ideally, get them in advance from the office in the *plaza de toros*, so as to avoid any hefty commission charges. Prices vary according to the sun; the most expensive seats are entirely in the shade.

Churros

The Spanish breakfast is as deplorable as the French.

H. V. Morton

As James Michener wrote: 'Any nation that can eat *churros* and chocolate for breakfast is not required to demonstrate its courage in other ways.' These long, fluted wads of fried dough, looking like some exotic variety of garden slug, are an essential part of the Spanish experience; sooner or later every serious traveller will have to step into a *churrería* and face up to them. Properly made, they're as greasy as a oil slick and drowned in sugar. The hot chocolate that comes with them should be quite thick to offer some small degree of protection by coating the stomach lining. Spaniards down billions of them each year.

Pablo Picasso, who as a small boy in Málaga had trouble learning how to count because he could not believe that a figure 7 was not an upside-down nose, recalled that *churros* had always fascinated him, and were in fact the first thing he ever tried to draw – which proves that *churros* are just as subversive aesthetically as they are in your stomach.

El Cid

In the Spanish pantheon El Cid Campeador comes in a close second to Santiago (*see* below) but, unlike Arthur, Siegfried, Roland and other heroes of national medieval epics, El Cid, Rodrigo Díaz de Vivar (1043–99), was entirely flesh and blood. Born in Vivar near Burgos, his unique title is derived from the Arabic *sayyidi* ('my lord'). Campeador means 'Battler', and his fame spread widely among both Moors and Christians (during his career he served both Alfonso VI of Castile and the Emir of Zaragoza); even before his death ballads celebrated his prowess. The greatest achievement of his life, the capture of Valencia from the Moors in 1095, took place when he was already 52 years old.

Through modern eyes, Rodrigo was little better than a gangster, but for the warrior class of the Reconquista, he served as a model of virtue: fearless, with an exaggerated sense of honour, devoutly Catholic and wholly pragmatic, a generous conqueror, devoted to his family, and a man who nearly always kept his word. The Cid was the perfect man for his time, living in the frontier society among Christians, Moors and Jews, where a king's powers were limited, and the main issues of the day were the simple pleasures of turf and booty.

For all that, 'O Born in a Happy Hour' – Rodrigo's other nickname – would not have had such a long shelf life, inspiring such diverse spirits as Corneille and Hollywood (where he was played, inevitably, by Charlton Heston) if there wasn't something more to his character. This comes through in the epic *Poem of the Cid*, composed around 1140, less than half a century after his death. For 500 years the actual poem was lost, until 1779, when the royal librarian, through some literary detective work, located a copy from 1307, appropriately enough in Vivar, El Cid's home town. Not a single ounce of the magical or marvellous touches the text; the Rodrigo Díaz that emerges lies and cheats, but he has a rustic sense of humour and a certain generous charm, always ready to praise another, and happy to have his wife and daughters watch him 'earn his bread' fighting the Moors. You can't help liking the guy. His saga, though somewhat repetitive to read, is also the first known example of the Spanish gift for realism that would reach its climax in *Don Quixote*.

Santiago

No saint on the calendar has as many names as Spain's patron: Iago, Diego, Jaime, Jacques, Jacobus, Santiago, or in English, James the Greater. James the fisherman was one of the first disciples chosen by Jesus, who nicknamed him Boanerges, 'the son of thunder', for his booming voice. After the Crucifixion, he seems to have been a rather ineffectual proselytizer for the faith; in the year 44 Herod Agrippa beheaded him and threw his body to the dogs.

But Spain had another task in store for James: nothing less than posthumously leading a 700-year-old crusade against the peninsula's infidels. The first mention of the Apostle's relics in Spain appear in an 830 annex to the *Martirologio de Florus*, written in 806 in Lyon. From this, a new history of James emerged: after his martyrdom, two of his disciples gathered his remains and sailed off with them in a stone boat (faith works wonders) to Iria Flavia in remote Galicia, where the disciples buried Boanerges in the nearby cemetery of Compostela. In 814, a shower of shooting stars guided a hermit shepherd named Pelayo to the site of James' tomb. Another legend identifies Charlemagne (who died in 814) with the discovery of James' relics: in the Emperor's tomb at Aachen you can see the 'Vision of Charlemagne', with a scene of the Milky Way, the *Via Lactea*, a common name for the pilgrims' road.

In 844, not long after the discovery of the relics, James was called into active duty in the battle of Clavijo, appearing on a white horse to help Ramiro I of Asturias defeat the Moors. This new role as Santiago Matamoros, the Moor-Slayer, was a great morale booster for the forces of the Reconquista, who made 'Santiago!' their battle cry. Ramiro was so pleased by his divine assistance that he made a pledge, the *voto de Santiago*, that ordained an annual property tax for St James' church at Compostela.

Never mind that the bones, the battle and the *voto* were all humbug; the story struck deep spiritual, poetic, and political chords that fitted in perfectly with the great cultural awakening of the 10th and 11th centuries. The medieval belief that a few holy bones or teeth could serve as a hotline to heaven made the discovery essential. After all, the Moors could claim some powerful juju of their own: an arm of the Prophet Muhammad in the Great Mosque of Córdoba (possession of it was Abd ar-Rahman's justification for declaring himself Caliph in 929). Another factor in the early 9th century was the Church's need for a focal point to assert its control over the newborn kingdoms of Spain. A third factor was the desire to reintegrate Spain into Europe – and what better way to do it than to increase commercial and cultural traffic over the Pyrenees? Pilgrimages to Jerusalem and Rome were already in vogue; after the Dark Ages, the Church was keen to re-establish contacts across the old Roman empire it had inherited for Christianity.

The French were the great promoters of the *Camino de Santiago* (the Way to Santiago); so great in fact that the most commonly tramped route became known as the *camino francés*. The first official pilgrim was Gotescalco, bishop of Le Puy, in 950; others followed, including Mozarab Christians from Andalucía, who founded some of the first churches and monasteries along the road in the province of León. In the next century, especially once the Moors were pushed over the south bank of the Duero, the French monks of the reforming abbey of Cluny did more than anyone to popularize the pilgrimage, setting up sister houses and hospitals along the way. Nor were the early Spanish kings slow to pick up on the commercial potential of the road; Sancho the Great of Navarra and Alfonso VI of Castile founded a number of religious houses and hostels along the way, and invited down French settlers to help run them.

The 12th century witnessed a veritable boom along the *camino francés*: the arrival of new monastic and military orders, including the Templars, the Hospitallers, and the Knights of Santiago; all vowed to defend the pilgrim from dangers en route. In 1130, Cluny commissioned Aymeric Picaud, a priest from Poitou, to write the *Codex Calixtinus*, the world's first travel guide, chock full of practical advice for pilgrims: tips on where not to drink the water, where to find the best lodging, where to be on guard against 'false pilgrims' who came not to atone for crimes but to commit them. The final bonus for Compostela came in 1189, when Pope Alexander III declared it a Holy City on equal footing with Jerusalem and Rome, offering a plenary indulgence – a full remission from Purgatory – to pilgrims on Holy Years (should you need one, the next holy year will be 2004).

From the Tour de Saint-Jacques in Paris, the traditional gathering point for groups of pilgrims (there was more safety in numbers), the return journey was over 1,280 kilometres and took a minimum of four months on foot. It was not something to go into lightly, but for many it was more than an act of faith; it was a chance to get out and see the world. Many pilgrims were ill (hence the large number of hospitals), hoping to make it before they died. Not a few were thieves, murderers and delinquents condemned by the judge to make the journey for penance. Dangerous cons had to do it in chains. To keep them from cheating or stealing someone else's indulgence (the *Compostelana* certificate), pilgrims had to have their documents stamped by the clergy at various points along the route, just as today (as a nice touch, the old stamps and seals have recently been revived).

An estimated half a million people a year made the trek in the Middle Ages (out of a European population of about 60 million), and even in the 18th century the pass at Roncesvalles still counted 30,000 pilgrims a year. But in the 19th century numbers fell dramatically; most of the monasteries and churches disappeared forever in the confiscation of church lands in 1837, either converted into stables or pillaged for their building stone. Yet in the 1970s, just when it seemed as defunct as a dodo, the pilgrimage made a remarkable revival, due to a number of factors: the modern world's disillusionment with conventional religion; the search for something beyond what over-organized day-to-day life and church attendance can offer; and, more prosaically, the growth of ecological and alternative tourism. In 1985, UNESCO declared it the 'Foremost Cultural Route in Europe', and set about helping to fund the restoration of the Romanesque churches that punctuate the trail. Although modern roads have changed the face of the pilgrimage forever, efforts have been made to create alternative paths for pedestrians, marked every 500m with a stylized scallop shell; a number of free or inexpensive *hostales* have sprouted along the way for walkers or cyclists. The pilgrims' quest is back in business.

Templars

One of the most provocative chapters of medieval history was written by the Order of the Knights Templar, founded during the First Crusade in 1118 by Hugues de Paynes. The 'Temple' of the knights, generally believed to be the Temple of Solomon, was actually the octagonal Temple of the Dome of the Rock, rebuilt by the Muslims in the 10th century; an octagonal design the Templars recalled in the construction of their own temples in London and in Spain, where the Order spread within a few years of its foundation.

The Order was both religious and military, and assisted the crusades, in Spain as well as in the Holy Land. They soon grew more powerful than the kings and popes they ostensibly served, and in 1307, France's King Philip the Fair and Pope Clement V conspired to dissolve the troublesome Order, Clement declaring it heretical and Philip coordinating the secret orders sent throughout Europe for all the Templars to be seized simultaneously at midnight on a certain date; a ploy necessary to ensure their defeat. The conspiracy succeeded and the Templars were captured unawares, imprisoned and made to face trumped-up charges of sorcery, black masses, orgies and sodomy. Some recanted to save their skins, but many, including the Grand Master, remained silent and were burned at the stake. Their immense worldly goods were, naturally, inherited by their enemies, as well as by the newer Order of the Knights of St John.

The dissolution of the Templars was a great loss for Spain, where they did their most important work, attempting a kind of syncretism between the peninsula's three great religions. In return for military services performed for the various kingdoms of Spain, the Templars would request castles and land, nearly always in the *juderías* (Jewish quarters) or among the Moriscos, to learn from their ancient traditions and to defend them from grabbing Christians. Their other land requests frequently corresponded with holy sites connected to the peninsula's oldest religions, and their surviving castles and churches are often fascinating for their mysterious symbolism and hints of the rites of initiation they once held.

Flamenco

For many people, flamenco is the soul of Spain and, like bullfighting, an essential part of the culture that sets it apart from the rest of the world. Good flamenco, with that ineffable quality of *duende*, has a primitive, ecstatic allure that draws in its listeners until they feel as if their very hearts were pounding in time with its relentless rhythms, their guts seared by its ululating Moorish wails and the sheer drama of the dance. Few modern experiences are more cathartic.

As traditional music goes, however, flamenco is relatively newborn. It began in the 18th century in Andalucía, where its originators, the gypsies, called one another 'flamencos'; a derogatory term dating back to the days when Charles V's Flemish (*flamenco*) courtiers bled Spain dry. These gypsies, especially those living in the Guadalquivir delta cities of Sevilla, Cádiz and Jerez, sang songs of oppression, lamentation and bitter romance, a kind of blues that by the 19th century began to catch on among all the other downtrodden inhabitants of Andalucía.

Despite flamenco's relatively recent origins, Andalucían intellectuals such as Lorca and de Falla have always insisted that it was deeply rooted in the south's soil and soul, and many musicologists now believe they're right. According to a 7th-century archbishop, the first Sevillian guitar was shaped like the human breast, with chords 'that signified the pulsations of the heart'. The Moors of Andalucía based their instruments on these heartstrings and traditionally coloured the first string yellow, symbolic of bile. In 820, the famous Córdoba school of music and poetry was founded by Abu al-Hassan Ali Ibn Nafi, better known as Ziryab, the 'Blackbird'; Ziryab also added a fifth string to the guitar and coloured it red, for blood. The half-tonal notes and lyrics of futility of the *cante jondo*, or deep song, the purest flamenco, seem to go back to the Arab troubadours who followed Ziryab, but it's impossible to prove; the Arabs knew of musical notation, but disdained it in their preference for improvisation.

In the Middle Ages, the gypsies, in their migration from India, arrived in Andalucía bringing ecstatic rhythms and a few new tunes, met the *cante jondo* and the heart string guitar and flamenco was born. But just how faithfully the music of al-Andalus was preserved among the gypsies and others to be reincarnated as flamenco will never be known.

By the late 19th century, flamenco had gone semi-public, performed in the back rooms of cafés in Sevilla and Málaga. Its very popularity in Spain, and the enthusiasm set off by Bizet's *Carmen* abroad, began seriously to undermine its harsh, true quality. At the same time, flamenco's influence spread into the popular and folk repertories to create a happier, less intense genre called the *sevillana* (often songs in praise of you-know-where). When schoolchildren at a bus stop in Cádiz burst into an impromptu dance and hand-clapping session, or when some old cronies in Málaga's train-station bar start singing and reeling, you can bet they're doing a *sevillana*. In the 1920s attempts were made to establish some kind of standards for the real thing, especially *cante jondo*, though without lasting results; the 'real, original flamenco' was never meant to be performed as such, and will only be as good as its 'audience'. This should ideally be made up of other musicians and flamenco *aficionados*, whose participation is essential in the spontaneous, invariably late-night combustion of raw emotion, alcohol, drugs and music, to create *duende*.

With so many intangible factors, your chance of getting in on some genuine soul-stirring flamenco are about as rare as getting in on a genuine soul-stirring bullfight. But perhaps it is this very fleeting, hard-to-pin-down quality that makes both arts so compelling in the midst of a programmed, homogenized world.

The Inquisition

What a day, what a day for an auto-da-fé!

Bernstein's *Candide*

Besides bullfighting and flamenco, it's one of the things Spain is most famous for, an essential part of the 'Black Legend' of the dark days of Philip II. There's nothing to debunk and no need for a historical re-examination; the Inquisition was just as bloody and stupid and horrible as the Protestant propagandists of the day said it was. But what made them do it? Not surprisingly, the original motives were largely political. Ferdinand and Isabel reintroduced the Inquisition in 1480 as an institution entirely under the control of the crown, and they used it as a means to suppress dissent; with their powers strictly limited under the secular laws, they turned to the

Church courts as a way to get at their enemies. Originally, under the direction of a passionate ascetic, the famous Torquemada, the Inquisition's victims were nearly all *conversos*: baptized Jews with wealth or important positions in government or church. Any of them found guilty of backsliding in the faith would have their property confiscated – if they weren't burned at the stake. Much of this booty went to finance the wars against the Moors of Granada.

In the decades that followed, though, the Inquisition took on a life of its own. From the 1530s on, with the Catholic powers in a panic over the onset of the Reformation, a succession of Inquisitors much worse than Torquemada expanded the Holy Office to every city, with a corps of secret agents and investigators estimated at 20,000. Though terror of it spread to every household, application was crazily inconsistent: the Inquisition saw nothing wrong with the opinions of Copernicus, but it sent hundreds of poor souls to the stake for reading the Bible in Spanish instead of Latin. Neither did the learned inquisitors care much for witch-hunting after the late 1500s. The following century saw an estimated 30,000 poor souls burned for witchcraft in Britain, against almost none in Spain. Whatever this says about human nature, it seems that by refusing to take witchcraft seriously, the Spaniards never allowed the hysteria a chance to take root. Still, there were victims enough to be found among the Christians. The first decade of the renewed Inquisition (after 1478) was thorough: 5,200 victims in Toledo alone in a single year, 1486. After the Jews and freethinkers were dealt with, the Inquisition began to look for new targets just to keep itself in business. Blasphemy went under their jurisdiction in the 1490s, and some secular crimes in 1517. At its height, the Holy Office became a state within the state, responsible to no one and dependent on continuous terror to keep its members in jobs.

Despite its cumbersome bureaucracy and a great pretence of legalism, the Inquisition was little better than a kangaroo court. Anyone denounced (even if it were by playful children) had a good chance of spending several years in solitary confinement while the Holy Office decided his or her case. Few were ever cleared, and even if they were, both they and their families were tainted forever. Torture was almost universal – as everywhere else in Europe in that grim age – and after it the accused would be lucky to get let off with a public recantation, a flogging and the loss of all his property. *Autos-da-fé* ('works of faith') were colourful public spectacles, preceded by much pageantry and preaching, where sentences were given out, before the unlucky ones, dressed in capes decorated with flames and devils and bearing signboards explaining their crimes, were led off to the stake. The last, and biggest, was a 14-hour affair with 120 victims, personally staged in Madrid's Plaza Mayor in 1680 by the insane Charles II.

Food and Drink

Read an old guidebook to Spain, and when the author gets around to the local cooking, expressions like 'eggs in a sea of rancid oil' and 'mysterious pork parts' pop up with alarming frequency. One traveller in the 18th century fell ill from a local concoction and was given a purge 'known on the comic stage as angelic water. On top of that followed four hundred catholic pills, and a few days later...they gave me *escordero* water, whose efficacy or devilry is of such double effect that the doctors call it ambidexter. From this I suffered agony.'

You'll fare better; in fact, the chances are you'll eat some of the tastiest food you've ever had, at half the price you would have paid for it at home.

Eating Out

Learning to Eat the Spanish Way

Going to Spain, you may have to learn to eat all over again; dining is a much more complex affair here than in many countries. It may seem as if they eat at absurd hours, but the essential fact to learn is that Spaniards like to eat *all day long*; this scheme spreads the gratification evenly through the day, and it facilitates digestion, which in Spain can be problematic. Give it some consideration. Start out with a big coffee, a *doble in vaso* and a pastry (mostly French clones, with extra sugar) or find a progressive-looking **bar** where you might find a more fitting breakfast: a glass of wine or brandy, and a salami sandwich or *pincho*, or maybe a glazed American doughnut. These bars will be around all day, their piles of treats under the glass cases on the bar growing by the hour, an eternal alternative to a heavy sit-down dinner. Ask around for the one that does seafood tapas. As if the bars weren't enough, there are ***pastelerías*** serving all sorts of savoury pastries in the towns, ***merenderos*** (snack stands) in the countryside, and **ice cream** everywhere. For a mid-morning or mid-afternoon energizer, there are sweet 'n' greasy *churros* (*see* **Sketches of Spain**, p.54), sold in bars and *churrerías* and dipped in cups of thick, rich chocolate – for most non-Spaniards a once-in-a-lifetime gut-gurgling experience.

Spanish cooking as a whole still tends to come a bit on the heavy side, but at the upmarket end of the scale you'll find plenty of modern **restaurants** creating innovative dishes, many of them inspired by *nouvelle cuisine* from over the border in France. There are, however, still thousands of old-fashioned restaurants around – and many of the sort that travellers have been complaining about for centuries. Spain has its share of poor restaurants, and you will need luck as well as judgement, but the worst offenders are often those with the little flags and 10-language menus found in very touristy areas, and common sense will warn you off these. If you dine where the locals do, you'll be assured of a good deal, if not necessarily a good meal.

One step down from a restaurant are ***comedores*** (literally, dining-rooms), often tacked on to the backs of bars, where the food and décor are usually drab but cheap, and ***cafeterías***, usually those places that feature photographs of their offerings of *platos combinados* (combination plates) to eliminate any language problem. ***Asadores*** specialize in roast meat or fish; ***marisqueras*** serve only fish and shellfish – you'll usually see the sign for '*pescados y mariscos*' on the awning. Keep an eye out for ***ventas***, usually modest, family-run establishments offering excellent *menús del día* for working people. Try and visit one on a Sunday lunchtime when all the Spanish families go out and make merry.

There are also many Chinese restaurants in Spain which are fairly good and inexpensive (though all pretty much the same), and American fast-food outlets in the big cities and resort areas; while Italian restaurants are 98 per cent dismal in Spain, you can get a good pizza in many places. Don't neglect the rapidly disappearing shacks on the beach; they often serve up roast sardines that are out of this world. Vegetarians are catered for in the cities, which always manage to come up with one or two veggie restaurants, and usually rather good ones at that. In the countryside and away from the main resorts, proper vegetarians and vegans will find it hard going, though tapas make life easier than it would be in some other southern European countries. Fish-eaters will manage just about everywhere.

Throughout the guide, restaurants in the 'Eating Out' sections are grouped together according to how expensive they are. For a guide to these price categories and more practical advice on eating out, *see* **Practical A–Z**, 'Food and Drink', pp.83–4.

Tapas Bars

If you are travelling on a budget, you may want to eat one of your daily meals at a **tapas bar** or ***tasca***. *Tapas* means 'lids'; they started out simply as little saucers of goodies served on top of a drink, and have evolved over the years to play a major role in the world's greatest snack culture. Bars that specialize in them have platter after platter of delectable titbits, from shellfish to slices of omelette, mushrooms baked in garlic, or vegetables in vinaigrette or stews. All you have to do is pick out what looks best and order a *pincho* or *tapa* (an hors d'oeuvre) or a *ración* (a big helping) if it looks really good. It's hard to generalize about prices, but on average about €6 of tapas and wine or beer will keep you going. You can always save money in bars by standing up; sit at that charming table on the terrace and prices can jump considerably. Another advantage of tapas is that they're available at what most Americans or Britons would consider normal dining hours.

Regional Specialities

The massive influx of tourists has had its effect on Spanish kitchens, but so has the Spaniards' own increased prosperity and, perhaps most significantly, the new federalism. Each region, each town even, has come to feel a new interest and pride in the things that set it apart, and food is definitely one of those. The best restaurants are nearly always those that specialize in regional cuisine, and no regions pride themselves on their own cooking as much as the Basque Lands, Catalunya or Galicia – and with good reason (*see* 'The Three Kings', overleaf).

Along the coast, **seafood** is undoubtedly the star of the show; and in any coastal town or village, you'll find the best seafood restaurants dotted around the harbour. The fancier ones will post set menus, while at the rest you'll find only a chalkboard with prices listed for a plate of grilled fish or whatever else came in that day. On the whole, Spaniards try to keep their seafood simple: **Galicians** like to cook fish with potatoes and garlic; **Basques** do it with simple garlic and parsley sauces; in **Asturias** it's hake in *sidra* (the ubiquitous local cider) or *fabada*, an enchanting mess of pork and beans. Inland, though you'll still find plenty of seafood, the cuisine would seem to come from an entirely different world. In **Castile**, it's almost medieval, and here tureen-sized bowls of soup and roast suckling pig (*cochinillo asado*), lamb or game have pride of place. Over to the east, you can order one of the famous *paellas* or a dozen other rice dishes in **Valencia**, the land of rice, while down in **Andalucía**, several

The Three Kings

Basque Cuisine

By popular acclaim, the champion cooks of Spain are the Basques who, coincidentally, are also the most legendary eaters. Like the Greeks, the well-travelled Basques take their culinary skill with them everywhere. Marseille may have its bouillabaisse, but the Basques stoutly maintain that their version, called *ttoro* (pronounced *tioro*), is the king of them all. A proper one requires a pound of mussels and a mess of crayfish and congers, as well as the head of a codfish and three different kinds of other fish. Basque cuisine relishes imaginative yet simple sauces, including the legendary *pil pil* (named for sound it makes while frying), where olive oil, garlic, and chillies magically meld with the cooking juices of salt cod. Another delight is fresh tuna cooked with tomatoes, garlic, aubergine and spices and *chipirones* (squid) – reputedly the only one in the world that's all black, and better than it sounds. Each Basque chef knows how to work wonders with elvers (*angulas* or *txitxardin*) in garlic sauce, salmon and the famous *txangurro* (spider crab) – flaked, seasoned, stuffed and served in its own shell. Gourmets especially recommend *kokotxas a la Donostiarra*, hake cheeks with a garlic and parsley, green sauce, clams and slightly piquant red guindilla peppers. Peppers are another icon of the Basque kitchen: housewives hang strings of them on the walls of their houses, and they turn up everywhere: in omelettes, in sauces for seafood, or in the common stewed chicken. Basques like to wash it down with *txakoli*, a tangy green wine produced on the coast with just a modicum of sunlight.

Catalan Cuisine

Like the Basque kitchen, the Catalan has enjoyed considerable influence from beyond the Pyrenees and is rated one of the best in Spain. Not surprisingly, seafood is a main ingredient, in such well-known dishes as *zarzuela*, a seafood casserole; lobster with chicken; *suquet* (similar to bouillabaisse); any fish with *romesco* sauce (toasted hazelnuts, wine, nutmeg, paprika, garlic and olive oil) or *xapada*, with dried eels from

varieties of *gazpacho* (chilled tomato, cucumber and onion soup) compete with sizzling fried fish and *rabo de toro* (a spicy concoction of oxtail, tomatoes and onions) for champion status.

Wine and Other Tipples

Wine

No matter how much other costs have risen in Spain, **wine** (*vino*) has remained awesomely inexpensive by northern European or American standards; what's more, it's mostly very good and there's enough variety for you to try something different every day. There are 30 areas in Spain under the control of the *Instituto Nacional de*

the Ebro delta. *Botifarra* – pork sausage, black or white, with beans – is a staple, as is *escudella*, a hearty pork and chicken stew. In the autumn a Catalan's mouth waters for partridge with grapes, or goose with pears, or rabbit cooked with almonds or garlic sauce. Near Tarragona in the very early spring outdoor *calçotada* feasts are the rage, featuring lamb cutlets, sausage, wine and, the star ingredient, tender green onions grilled over the fire, which Catalans, discarding their usual dignity, slurp down dressed in aprons and bibs. Excellent red wine and *cava* (champagne) are also produced in Catalunya.

Galician Cuisine

When it comes to seafood, Galicians claim to have the best of the best, including certain delicacies found nowhere else in the world. The estuaries boast an extraordinary array of riches, from the famous scallops of Santiago to creatures unique to Galicia such as *zamburiñas* scallops, lobster-like *santiaguiños*, and ugly *percebes*, that have no names in English. Quantity is matched by quality: throughout Spain, Gallego restaurants command as much respect as Basque; preparation is kept as simple as possible. In every town you'll come across *empanadas*, large flat flaky pies filled with eels or lamprey (the most sought after; try it before you knock it), sardines, pork, or veal. Turnip greens (*grelos*) are a staple, especially in *caldo gallego*, a broth that also features turnips and white beans; in winter, many opt for the heartier *lacón con grelos*, pork shoulder with greens, sausages and potatoes. Galicia also produces Spain's best veal and good cheeses, such as Roquefort-like *cabrales* and *gamonedo* (both mainly from cow's milk mixed with ewe's or goat's milk); birch-smoked, pear-shaped *San Simón*; or mild, soft *ulloa* or *pasiego*. A tapas meal to make a Gallego weep would include grilled sardines, *pulpo a la gallega* (tender octopus with peppers and paprika), roasted small green peppers (*pimientas de Padrón*), with chewy hunks of bread and lightly salted *tetilla* cheese, washed down with white Ribeira wine. For dessert try *tarta de Santiago* (almond tart) and, to top it all off, a glass of Galician fire water, *aguardiente* – served at night after a meal to ward off evil spirits – properly burned (*queimada*), with lemon peel and sugar.

Denominaciones de Origen (INDO), which acts as a guide to the consumer and keeps a strict eye on the quality of Spanish wine (DO, or *denominación de origen*, is the same as French AOC). A restaurant's *vino del lugar* or *vino de la casa* is always your least expensive option while dining out; it usually comes out of a barrel or glass jug and may be a surprise either way. Much of the inexpensive wine sold throughout the country comes from La Mancha or the neighbouring Valdepeñas DO regions. Anyone with more than a passing interest in wine will want to visit a *bodega* or two. If you take an empty bottle with you, you can usually bring it out filled with the wine that suits your palate that day. A *bodega* can be a bar, wine cellar or warehouse, and is worth a visit whatever its guise. A good place to start would be Haro, the growing and marketing centre for the wines of Rioja Alta (*see* p.335).

What to Drink Where

Each region has its wine and liqueur specialities and nearly every monastery in Spain seems to make some kind of herbal potion or digestive liqueur that tastes more or less like cough syrup.

Catalunya is best known for its wines from Penedés and Priorato, the former producing excellent whites and some fine reds (try Gran Caus '87). One of the most typical Catalunyan whites is Blancs en Noirs and, like the dry white wines of Tarragona, is excellent with fish, or as an *aperitivo*. Spain also produces its own champagne, known as *cava*, which is refined enough to drink alone. The principal house, Cordoniú, is always a safe bet. Some of the best come from Sant Sadurni d'Anoia, near Barcelona; Mestres Mas Vía can rival any standard champagne. **Navarra** has some excellent reds (Magaña Merlot '85), while Navarra's neighbour, **La Rioja**, is the best known and richest area for wine in all Spain (*see* box, opposite). In **La Mancha**, Valdepeñas is Spain's most prolific area; its young, inexpensive table wines are sold everywhere, and make even a potato *tortilla* something special. **Valencia** has some fresh, dry whites and a distinctive rosé (Castillo de Liria). Euskadi is known for its very palatable young 'green' wine called *Txacoli* (in 1994 made a DO or *denominación de origen*), which is poured into the glass with bravura from a height, like cider, while **Galicia**'s excellent Ribeiro resembles the delicate *vinho verde* of neighbouring Portugal; other good wines from the region are *Rías Baixas* (areas on the coast near Pontevedra, and south of Vigo on the Portuguese border), and *Valdeorros* (east of Ourense), pleasant light vintages that complement the regional dishes, seafood in particular. In many parts of **Andalucía** you may have difficulty ordering a simple bottle of white wine, as, on requesting *una botella de vino blanco de la casa*, you will often be served something resembling diluted sherry. To make things clear, specify a wine by name or by region, or ask for *un vino seco*, and the problem should be solved. Some *andaluz* wines have achieved an international reputation for high quality. The best known is *jerez*, or what we in English call **sherry**. When a Spaniard invites you to have a *copita* (glass) it will nearly always be filled with this Andalucían sunshine. It comes in a wide range of varieties: *manzanillas* are very dry; *fino* is dry, light and young (the famous Tío Pepe); *amontillados* are rich and a bit sweeter; *olorosos* are very sweet dessert sherries, and can be either brown, cream, or *amoroso*.

Rioja in the Bottle

Rioja tastes like no other: soft, warm, mellow, full-bodied, with a distinct vanilla bouquet; its *vino de gran reserva* spends three years ageing in American oak barrels, and then another in bottles, before its release to the public. Look for the fine Viña Cumbrero '85 and Monte Real '85, and the aristocratic Marqués de Villamanga '73. It was the Phoenicians who introduced the first vines, which after the various invasions were replanted under the auspices of the Church; the first law concerning wine was decreed by Bishop Abilio in the 9th century. The arrival of masses of thirsty pilgrims proved a big boost to business, much as mass tourism would do in the 1960s and 1970s.

Despite a long pedigree, the Rioja we drink today dates from the 1860s, when growers from Bordeaux, their own vineyards wiped out by phylloxera, brought their techniques south of the border and wrought immense improvements on the native varieties. By the time the plague reached La Rioja in 1899, the owners were prepared for it with disease-resistant stock. During the First World War, when the vineyards of Champagne were badly damaged, the French returned to buy up *bodegas*, sticking French labels on the bottles and trucking them over the Pyrenees. Rioja finally received the respect it deserved after Franco passed on to the great fascist parade ground in the sky. In the last 20 years, *bodegas* have attracted buyers from around the world and prices have skyrocketed. La Rioja's growing area covers 48,000 hectares, comprising three zones: Rioja Alta, home of the best red and white wines, followed by Rioja Alavesa (on the left bank of the Ebro in Alava province) known for its lighter, perfumed wines, and the decidedly more arid Rioja Baja, where the wines are coarse and mostly used for blending – a common practice in La Rioja. The varieties used for the reds are mostly spicy, fruity Tempranillo (alone covering some 24,000 hectares), followed by Garnacha Tinta (a third of the red production, a good alcohol booster) with smaller quantities of Graciano (for the bouquet) and high-tannin Mazuela (for acidity and tone). Traditional Rioja whites, though they remain relatively unknown, are excellent, golden and vanilla-scented like the reds: Viura grapes are the dominant grapes, with smaller doses of Malvasía and Garnacha Blanca. Unlike French wines, Riojas are never sold until they're ready to drink (although you can, of course, keep the better wines for even longer). DOC rules specify that La Rioja's *Gran Reserva*, which accounts for only three per cent of the production, spends a minimum of two years maturing in American oak barrels (six months for whites and rosés) then four more in the *bodega* before it's sold. *Reservas* (six per cent of the production) spend at least one year in oak and three in the *bodega*. *Crianzas* (30 per cent of the production) spends at least a year in the barrel and another in the bottle. The other 61 per cent of La Rioja is *sin crianza* and labelled CVC (*conjunto de varias cosechas*, combination of various vintages): this includes the new young white wines and light red wines (*claretes*) fermented at cool temperatures in stainless steel vats, skipping the oak barrels altogether and losing most of the vanilla tones.

Menu Decoder

Hors d'œuvres (*Entremeses*)

aceitunas olives
alcachofas con mahonesa artichokes with mayonnaise
ancas de rana frogs' legs
caldo broth
entremeses variados assorted hors d'œuvres
gambas pil pil shrimps in hot garlic sauce
gazpacho chilled vegetable soup
huevos de flamenco baked eggs in tomato sauce
huevos al plato fried eggs
huevos revueltos scrambled eggs
sopa de ajo garlic soup
sopa de arroz rice soup
sopa de espárragos asparagus soup
sopa de fideos noodle soup
sopa de garbanzos chickpea soup
sopa de lentejas lentil soup
sopa de verduras vegetable soup
tortilla Spanish omelette, with potatoes
tortilla a la francesa French omelette

Fish (*Pescado*)

acedías small plaice
adobo fish marinated in white wine
almejas clams
anchoas anchovies
anguilas eels
angulas baby eels
ástaco crayfish
atún tuna
bacalao codfish (usually dried)
besugo sea bream
bogavante lobster
bonito tunny
boquerones anchovies
caballa mackerel
calamares squid
cangrejo crab
centollo spider crab
chanquetes whitebait
chipirones cuttlefish
... en su tinta ...in its own ink
chirlas baby clams
escabeche pickled or marinated fish
gambas prawns
langosta lobster
langostinos giant prawns
lenguado sole
lubina sea bass
mariscos shellfish
mejillones mussels
merluza hake
mero grouper
navajas razor-shell clams
ostras oysters
pejesapo monkfish
percebes barnacles
pescadilla whiting
pez espada swordfish
platija plaice
pulpo octopus
rape anglerfish
raya skate
rodaballo turbot
salmón salmon
salmonete red mullet
sardinas sardines
trucha trout
vieiras/veneras scallops
zarzuela fish stew

Meat and Fowl (*Carnes y Aves*)

albóndigas meatballs
asado roast
bistec beefsteak
buey ox
callos tripe
cerdo pork
chorizo spiced sausage
chuletas chops
cochinillo sucking pig
conejo rabbit
corazón heart
cordero lamb
faisán pheasant
fiambres cold meats
filete fillet
hígado liver
jabalí wild boar
jamón de York baked ham
jamón serrano raw cured ham
lengua tongue
lomo pork loin
morcilla blood sausage
paloma pigeon
pato duck
pavo turkey
perdiz partridge
pinchitos spicy mini kebabs
pollo chicken

rabo/cola de toro oxtail with onions and tomatoes
riñones kidneys
salchicha sausage
salchichón salami
sesos brains
solomillo fillet steak
ternera veal

Note: *potajes, cocidos, guisados, estofados, fabadas* and *cazuelas* are all varieties of stew.

Vegetables (*Verduras y Legumbres*)

ajo garlic
alcachofas artichokes
apio celery
arroz rice
arroz marinera rice with saffron and seafood
berenjena aubergine (eggplant)
cebolla onion
champiñones mushrooms
col, repollo cabbage
coliflor cauliflower
endibias endives
ensalada salad
espárragos asparagus
espinacas spinach
garbanzos chickpeas
judías (verdes) French beans
lechuga lettuce
lentejas lentils
patatas potatoes
...fritas ...fried
...salteadas ...sautéed
...al horno ...baked
pepino cucumber
pimiento pepper
puerros leeks
remolachas beetroots (beets)
setas Spanish mushrooms
zanahorias carrots

Fruits (*Frutas*)

albaricoque apricot
almendras almonds
cerezas cherries
ciruelas plums
ciruela pasa prune
frambuesas raspberries
fresas strawberries
...con nata ...with cream
higos figs
limón lemon
manzana apple
melocotón peach
melón melon
naranja orange
pasas raisins
pera pear
piña pineapple
plátano banana
pomelo grapefruit
sandía watermelon
uvas grapes

Desserts (*Postres*)

arroz con leche rice pudding
bizcocho/pastel/torta cake
blanco y negro ice cream and coffee float
flan crème caramel
galletas biscuits (cookies)
helados ice creams
pajama flan with ice cream
pasteles pastries
queso cheese
requesón cottage cheese
tarta de frutas fruit pie
turrón nougat

Drinks (*Bebidas*)

agua water
...con hielo ...with ice
agua mineral mineral water
...sin gas ...still
...con gas ...sparkling
batido de leche milkshake
café coffee
...solo ...black
...con leche ...with milk
cava Spanish champagne
cerveza beer
chocolate hot chocolate
granizado slush, iced squash
jerez sherry
leche milk
té tea
...con limón ...with lemon
vino wine
...tinto ...red
...rosado ...rosé
...blanco ...white
zumo de manzana apple juice
zumo de naranja orange juice

For a list of useful restaurant vocubulary, *see* 'Eating Out' in the **Language** section, p.712.

Beer, Brandy and Other Tipples

Many Spaniards prefer **beer** (*cerveza*), which is also good, though not quite the bargain wine is. The most popular brands are Cruzcampo and San Miguel – most bars sell it cold in bottles or on tap; try Mahón Five Star if you see it. Imported whisky and other spirits are pretty inexpensive, though the versions Spain bottles itself are even cheaper, which may come close to your home favourites.

Spanish **brandy** (mostly from Jerez) is excellent; the two most popular brands, *103* (very light in colour) and *Soberano*, are both drunk extensively by Spanish labourers and postmen about 7am. *Anís* (sweet or dry) is also quite popular. *Sangría* is the famous summertime punch of red wine, brandy, mineral water, orange and lemon with ice, but beware: it's rarely made very well, even when you can find it.

The north of Spain, where apples grow better than vines, produces **cider**, or *sidra*, which can come as a shock to the tastebuds in the first five minutes, and then goes down just fine, though it may leave you wishing it hadn't the morning after.

Gin, believe it or not, is often drunk with Coke. Bacardi and Coke is a popular thirst-quencher but beware, a Cuba Libre is not necessarily a rum and Coke, but Coke with anything, such as gin or vodka – you have to specify; then, with a flourish worthy of a *matador*, the barman will zap an ice-filled tumbler in front of you, and heave in a quadruple measure. No wonder the Costa del Sol has a staggering six chapters of Alcoholics Anonymous.

Soft Options

Coffee, tea, all the international soft-drink brands and *Kas*, the locally made orange drink, round out the average café fare. If you want tea with milk, say so when you order, otherwise it may arrive with a piece of lemon. Coffee comes with milk (*café con leche*) or without (*café solo*). Spanish coffee is good and strong, and if you want a lot of it order a *doble* or a *solo grande*; one of those will keep you awake through the guided tour of any museum. Look out for *Blanco y negros* (coffee and ice cream treats) and *horchata de chufa* (whipped up from ground almonds), which can be wonderfully refreshing, not to say addictive, in the summer heat.

Travel

06

Getting There

By Air from the UK and Ireland

There is an astounding variety of flight options to Spain from the UK.

Scheduled Flights

British Airways flies direct from Heathrow, Gatwick, Manchester and Birmingham to Madrid, Barcelona, Málaga and Gibraltar. BA also flies to Bilbao from Heathrow only and to Murcia, Sevilla and Valencia from Gatwick.

Iberia, Spain's national airline, flies many of the same routes, and also flies direct from the UK to Alicante, Santiago de Compostela, Jerez de la Frontera, Sevilla and the Canaries.

Monarch Airlines flies from Luton to Alicante and Málaga, more frequently in summer. **British Midland (bmi)** flies from Heathrow to Madrid and flies to Málaga weekly from East Midlands Airport.

Low-cost Carriers

The no-frills airlines can offer very cheap flights, but note that the cheapest prices are only available if booked well in advance. Last-minute fares are often no cheaper than regular flights, but if you can be flexible it's worth looking out for deals on the Internet.

Go offers return flights from Stansted to Barcelona and Bilbao for as little as £60, to Málaga for £122 and to Alicante from £195. **EasyJet** flies from Luton to Barcelona and Madrid, and from Liverpool to Málaga for upwards of £40. **Buzz** flies to Girona, Jerez and Murcia from Stansted for £50 one way.

Charter Flights and Special Deals

Charters to Spain can be incredibly cheap, and offer the added advantage of departing from local airports. Companies such as **Thomson**, **Airtours** and **Unijet** offer return flights from as little as £80. The best deals tend to be inflexible once booked, with return dates fixed one week or two after departure. Check the options at any budget travel agent, in local papers or in the Sunday papers. In London, look in the *Evening Standard* and *Time Out*. There are no refunds for missed flights, so take out insurance.

Student and Youth Travel

Besides saving 25 per cent on regular flights, under-26s have the choice of flying on special discount charters. An ISIC card costs about £6.

Major Carriers

British Airways, **t** 0845 773 3377, *www.britishairways.com*.
British Midland (bmi), **t** 0870 607 0555, *www.flybmi.com*.
Iberia, **t** 0845 601 2845, *www.iberia.com*.
Monarch Airlines, **t** (01582) 398 333, *www.fly-crown.com*.

Low-cost Carriers

Buzz, **t** 0870 240 7070, *www.buzzaway.com*.
EasyJet, **t** 0870 600 0000, *www.easyjet.com*.
Go, **t** 0845 605 4321, *www.go-fly.com*.

Charter Flights

Airtours, **t** (01706) 240 033, *www.airtours.com*.
Thomson, **t** 0990 502 555, *www.thomson-holidays.com*.
Unijet, **t** (01444) 255 600, *www.unijet.com*.

Student Flights

STA, 86 Old Brompton Rd, London SW7, UK, **t** (020) 7581 4132, *www.statravel.co.uk*.
Trailfinders, 215 Kensington High Street, London W8, UK, **t** (020) 7937 1234, *www.trailfinders.com*.
Budget Travel, 134 Lower Baggot Street, Dublin 2, Ireland, **t** (01) 661 1866.
United Travel, Stillorgan Bowl, Stillorgan, County Dublin, Ireland, **t** (01) 288 4346/7.

Internet Companies

www.airtickets.co.uk
www.cheapflights.com
www.flightcentre.co.uk
www.lastminute.com
www.skydeals.co.uk
www.sky-tours.co.uk
www.thomascook.co.uk
www.travelocity.com
www.travelselect.com

By Air from the USA and Canada

Scheduled Flights

Several carriers serve Spain from the USA or Canada, flying most frequently to Madrid or Barcelona. **Iberia**, the Spanish national airline, offers fly-drive deals and discounts. Consider flying via London or other European cities.

Charters, Discounts and Special Deals

A charter from New York to Madrid currently varies between $400–700 depending on the season. You may want to check this against competitive transatlantic fares to London, from where you should be able to get a low-cost flight to Spain within a day or two of your arrival. The Sunday *New York Times* usually has the most extensive listings.

Student and Youth Travel

Council Travel are the major US student and charter flight specialists, with branches all over the country (they can also provide Eurail and Britrail passes). **STA** has branches at most university campuses.

Major Carriers (direct to Spain)

Air Canada, **t** (toll-free) 888 247 2262, *www.aircanada.ca*.

American Airlines, **t** (toll-free) 800 433 7300, *www.im.aa.com*.

Continental Airlines, **t** (toll-free) 800 231 0856, *www.continental.com*.

Delta, **t** (toll-free) 800 241 4141, *www.delta.com*.

Iberia, **t** (toll-free) 800 772 4642, *www.iberia.com*; 6100 Blue Lagoon Drive, Suite 200, Miami, FL 33126, **t** (305) 267 7747, reservations and information **t** 800 772 4642; 655 Madison Avenue, New York, NY 10022, **t** (212) 644 8797; 1725 K. Street NW, Washington DC 20006, **t** (202) 293 6970; 102 Bloor Street West, Toronto M5S 1M8, **t** (416) 964 6625; 2020 University Street, Montreal H3A 2A5, **t** (514) 849 3352.

United Airlines, **t** (toll-free) 800 538 2929, *www.ual.com*.

Major Carriers (via other routes)

British Airways, **t** (toll-free) 800 247 9297, *www.britishairways.com*.

KLM, **t** (toll-free) 800 447 4747, *www.klm.com*.

Lufthansa, **t** (toll-free) 800 645 3880, *www.lufthansa.com*.

TAP Air Portugal, **t** (toll-free) 800 221 7370, *www.tap-airportugal.pt*.

Virgin Atlantic, **t** (toll-free) 800 862 8621, *www.virgin-atlantic.com*.

Charters, Discounts and Special Deals

Air Brokers International, **t** (415) 397 1383, **t** (toll-free) 800 883 3273, **f** (415) 397 4767, *www.airbrokers.com*.

Flight Center, **t** 877 967 5347; centres include: Flight Centre California Plaza, Suite D5, 350; Grand Ave, Los Angeles, CA 90071, **t** (213) 346 0230, **f** (213) 346 0260, *www.flightcenter.com*.

Last Minute Travel Club, 132 Brookline Avenue, Boston, MA 02215, **t** 800 527 8646.

Now Voyager, 74 Varick St, Suite 307, New York, NY 10013, **t** (212) 431 1616. For courier flights.

Spanish Heritage Tours: 116–47 Queens Blvd, Forest Hills, NY 11375, **t** (718) 520 1300, *www.shtours.com*. Uses Air Europa.

TFI, 34 West 32nd Street, New York, NY 10001, **t** (212) 736 1140, toll free **t** 800 745 8000.

Student and Youth Travel

Council Travel, 205 East 42nd Street, New York, NY 10017, **t** (212) 822 2700, or **t** 1-800-2COUNCIL, *www.counciltravel.com*.

STA, 10 Downing Street, New York, NY 10014, **t** 800 781 4040, **t** (212) 627 3111; ASUC Building, 2nd Floor, University of California, Berkeley, CA 94720, **t** (510) 642 3000, *www.statravel.com*.

Travel Cuts, 187 College St, Toronto, Ontario M5T 1P7, **t** (416) 979 2406, *www.travelcuts. com*.

Internet Companies

www.air-fare.com
www.expedia.com
www.flights.com
www.orbitz.com
www.priceline.com
www.travellersweb.ws
www.travelocity.com
www.xfares.com (carry-on luggage only)
www.smarterliving.com

By Sea

It's a long haul from the UK to Spain by ferry, and not that cheap, but worth considering if you need your car in Spain and don't fancy the long drive down through France. **Brittany Ferries** operates a car-ferry service from Plymouth to Santander between March and November, making the crossing twice a week and taking an average of 24 hours to cross the notoriously rough Bay of Biscay. Prices vary according to season (it's most expensive from 28 June to 1 September): an adult with a car costs £162–279 (depending on the vehicle size); an adult foot-passenger fare costs £100, dropping to £58 out of season; four to 15-year-olds travel for slightly more than half the adult price. These fares do not include accommodation, which is strongly recommended: in the high season you can pay from £6 for a simple Pullman seat to over £120 for a deluxe twin-berth cabin.

P&O European Ferries operate on the Portsmouth–Bilbao route, with crossings twice weekly except for a three-week break in January. Peak season runs from mid-July to mid-August, when the return fare for an average car and four adults is £765, including accommodation in a four-berth cabin. This drops to £395 in the winter months. Return fare for an adult foot passenger is £150 in peak season, £78 out of season, including accommodation in a two-berth cabin. P&O fares include accommodation on all crossings. Children between four and 15 travel for just over half-price. Good-value five- and eight-day mini-breaks are also available.

Brittany Ferries, t 08705 360 360, *www.brittanyferries.com*.

P&O European Ferries, t 0870 2424 999, *www.ponsf.com*.

By Rail

London to Barcelona is a full day trip, leaving London around 8.30am and arriving in Barcelona at nearly 10pm, after changing trains in Paris (which involves crossing from the Gare du Nord to the Gare de Lyon) and at Port Bou/San Sebastián/La Tour de Carol, Montpellier or Toulouse. The TGV service from Paris to Bordeaux can cut some hours off the trip if the timetable works in your favour. Time can also be saved by taking the **Eurostar** through the Channel Tunnel to Paris. Services are frequent and take just under three hours from London (Waterloo) to Paris (Gare du Nord). Fares are lower if booked at least 14 days in advance. A standard fare is £225.

Rail tickets to Spain from England or vice versa can be obtained from **Rail Europe** (don't forget to take your passport). Tickets for local Spanish services can be obtained from certain UK travel agents, but bookings must be made several weeks in advance.

If you've been resident in Europe for the past six months you might like to consider an **Inter-Rail Pass**, which gives you a month of Europe-wide rail travel for £319 (under-26s, £229), three zones for £275 (£199) or two zones for £239 (£169), as well as half-price discounts on Channel crossings and ferries to Morocco, where the pass is also valid.

Visitors from North America have a wide choice of European rail passes, including **Eurail Pass**, **Saverpass** and **Flexipass**, which can all be purchased in the USA. A one-month Eurail Pass costs around US$918 (US$644 for under-26s). The Eurail Pass, which must be purchased before you leave the States, is a good deal only if you plan to use the trains every day in Spain and elsewhere – although it's not valid in the UK, Morocco or countries outside the European Union.

Note that neither Inter-Rail nor Eurail passes are valid on Spain's numerous narrow-gauge (FEVE) lines and you'll have to pay supplements on any kind of express train.

Rail Travel Agencies

Eurostar, EPS House, Waterloo Station, London SE1, **t** 0345 881 881, *www.eurostar.com*.

Rail Choice, 15 Colman House, Empire Square, High Street, Penge, London SE20 7EX, **t** (020) 8659 7300, *www.railchoice.co.uk*, *www.railchoice.com*.

Rail Europe Travel Centre (UK), 179 Piccadilly, London W1V 0BA, **t** 08705 848 848, *www.raileurope.co.uk*;
(USA) 226 Westchester Ave, White Plains, NY 10064, **t** 800 438 7245, *www.raileurope.com*.

CIT Tours, 342 Madison Avenue, Suite 207, New York 10173, **t** (212) 697 2100, or **t** (toll-free) 800 248 7245.

By Coach

One major company, **Eurolines**, offers departures several times a week in the summer (once a week out of season) from London to Spain, along the east coast as far as Alicante, or to Algeciras via San Sebastián, Burgos, Madrid, Córdoba, Granada and Málaga. Journey times are 24 hours to Barcelona, 33 hours to Alicante, 27 to Madrid, 34 to Málaga and 37 to Algeciras. Fares from London to Málaga start from £139 return (£126 for under-26s). To San Sebastián, fares start from £123 return; to Vitoria and Burgos from £128. APEX fares cost £69 to San Sebastián, and £89 to Vitoria and Burgos. Peak season fares between 22 July and 4 September are slightly higher. There are discounts for anyone under 26, senior citizens and children under 12. In the summer, the coach is the best bargain for anyone over 26; off-season you'll probably find a cheaper charter flight.

Eurolines UK Ltd, 4 Cardiff Road, Luton, LU1 1PP, **t** 08705 143 219, **f** (01582) 400 694, *www.gobycoach.com. Open Mon–Fri 8am–8pm, Sun 10–2.*

By Car

From the UK via France you have a choice of routes. Ferries from Portsmouth cross to Cherbourg, Caen, Le Havre and St Malo. From any of these ports the most direct route takes you to Bordeaux, down the western coast of France to the border at Irún, and on to San Sebastián, Burgos and Madrid. An alternative route is Paris to Perpignan, crossing the border on the Mediterranean side of the Pyrenees, then along the coast to Barcelona. Both routes take on average 1½ days' steady driving. Unless you want to see France en route, you may find it more convenient and less tiring to try the ferry from Plymouth to Santander (*see* above), which cuts out the driving and saves expensive *autoroute* tolls.

For a scenic drive, opt for one of the routes over the Pyrenees, through Puigcerdá, Somport-Canfranc or Andorra, but expect heavy traffic; if you're not in a hurry, take the classic route through Roncesvalles, the Vall d'Arán, or through Tarbes and Aragnouet via the tunnel to Parzán.

To bring a GB-registered car into Spain, you need a **vehicle registration document**, **full driving licence** and **insurance papers** (a Green Card is not necessary), which must be carried at all times when driving. If your driving licence is of the old-fashioned sort without a photograph you are strongly recommended to apply for an international driving permit (available from the AA or RAC). Non-EU citizens should preferably have an **international driving licence**, which has a Spanish translation incorporated. Your vehicle should display a nationality plate indicating its country of registration.

Before travelling, check everything is in perfect order. Two **red hazard triangles**, **headlight converters** and a **spare set of bulbs** are obligatory; it's also recommended that you carry a first-aid kit and a fire extinguisher. For more information on driving in Spain, contact the following organizations:

AA (UK), **t** 0990 500 600, *www.theaa.com*. Offers advice on international driving permits, motorway tolls and travel abroad.

RAC (UK), **t** 0800 550 550, *www.rac.co.uk*. Offers advice on routes and international driving permits, **t** 0906 470 1740 (60p/min).

AAA, (USA) **t** (407) 444 4000.

Moto Europa, *www.ideamerge.com/motoeuropa*. Website detailing all you need to know about driving abroad.

Specialist Tour Operators

The very helpful **Spanish Tourist Office** is located at 22–23 Manchester Square, London W1U 3PX, **t** (020) 7486 8077, **f** (020) 7486 8034, *www.tourspain.co.uk*. It stocks brochures on most main towns in Spain, and information on holiday options. For details of independent and specialist tour operators, *see* pp.76–7.

Entry Formalities

Passports and Visas

Holders of **EU**, **US**, **Canadian**, **Australian** or **New Zealand** passports can enter Spain for up to 90 days without a visa. If you intend to stay longer than three months, you must report to the Foreign Nationals Office (*Oficina de Extranjeros*) at the local police station and

Tour Operators in the UK

General

Cadogan Travel, Cadogan House, 9–10 Portland Street, Southampton SO14 7EB, **t** (01703) 828 300, *www.cadoganholidays.com*. Gibraltar, southern Spain and Morocco.

Kirker Holidays, 3 New Concordia Wharf, Mill Street, London SE1 2BB, **t** (020) 7231 3333, *http://kirker.ping.co.uk*. Tailor-made tours around Madrid, Barcelona, Sevilla and rural Andalucía.

Palmer & Parker, The Beacon, Penn, Buckinghamshire HP10 8ND, **t** (01494) 815411, *www.palmerparker.com*. Self-catering villa holidays to southern Spain.

Unicorn Holidays Ltd, 2–10 Cross Rd, Tadworth, Surrey KT20 5UJ, **t** (01737) 812 255 400. Tailor-made fly-drive and self-drive touring holidays, staying in high-quality character hotels and *paradores*.

Totally Spain, C/ San Prudencio 29, Edificio Ópera, Pl 3, Oficina 62-B, Vitoria 01005, Spain, **t** (UK) 0709 229 6272, **t** (Spain) 945 14 15 38, **f** (UK) 0870 137 2049, *info@totallyspain.com*, *www.totallyspain.com*. Tailor-made and themed itineraries in Bilbao and the Spanish Basque lands, also tours and city breaks.

Cultural Tours

Martin Randall, 10 Barley Mow Passage, London W4 4PH, **t** (020) 8742 3355, *www.martinrandall.com*. Cultural tours with lecturers all over Spain.

Page & Moy Ltd, 136–40 London Road, Leicester LE2 1EN, **t** (0116) 250 7000, *www.page-moy.com*. Cultural guided tours throughout Spain.

Plantagenet Tours, 85 The Grove, Moordown, Bournemouth BH9 2TY, **t** (01202) 521 895, *www.plantagenet-tours.freeserve.co.uk*. Historical tours of medieval Andalucía and of Castile, León, Asturias and Galicia.

Saga Holidays (Discover Europe), The Saga Building, Middelburg Square, Folkestone, Kent CT20 1AZ, **t** 0800 300 500, *www.saga.co.uk*. Guided cultural coach tours for the over-50s.

Specialtours Ltd, 81a Elizabeth Street, London SW1W 9PG, **t** (020) 7730 2297. Fully escorted cultural tours to major cities and sites throughout Spain.

Special-interest Holidays

Andalucían Adventures, Washpool, Horsley, Gloucestershire GL6 0PP, **t** (01453) 834 137, **f** (01453) 835 984, *www.andalucian-adventures.co.uk*. Walking and painting.

Andante Travel, The Old Barn, Old Road, Alderbury, Salisbury, Wiltshire SP5 3AR, **t** (01722) 713 800. Historical study tours of Roman Spain and Altamira cave paintings.

Arblaster & Clarke Wine Tours, Clarke House, The Green, West Liss, Hants GU33 6JQ, **t** (01730) 893 344, *www.winetours.co.uk*. Wine tours to the Rioja, Navarra, Jerez and Penedés regions.

Artscape Holidays, 85 North Street, Wilton, Salisbury, Wiltshire SP2 0HW, **t** (01722) 743 163. Painting holidays in Cataluña.

Cox & Kings Travel Ltd, Gordon House, 10 Greencoat Place, London SW1P 1PH, **t** (020) 7873 5000. Botanical tours of the south and a luxury train trip in Andalucía.

The Dance Holiday Company, 12 Chapel Street North, Colchester, Essex CO2 7AT, **t** (01206) 577 000, **f** (01206) 570 057, *www.danceholidays.com*. The chance to dance in true Andalucìan style on a flamenco, *Sevillanas* or tango holiday. Intensive courses in Córdoba, Granada, Jerez and Sevilla.

Dolphin Safari, Sheppard's Marina, Waterport, Gibraltar, **t** (from outside Spain) (350) 71914, **t** (from Spain) 956 77 19 14, *www.dolphinsafari.gi*. Dolphin-spotting trips (May–Oct).

Pata Negra, 28 Parsons Green, London SW6 4UH, **t** (020) 7736 1959, *www.patanegra.net*. Classy gastronomic holidays, learning to cook Basque, Mediterranean and Arabic dishes from pros.

Walking Tours

Abercrombie & Kent Travel Ltd, Sloane Square House, Holbein Place, London SW1W 8NS, **t** (020) 7730 9600, *www.abercrombiekent.co.uk*. Walking and horse riding in Andalucía.

Alternative Travel Group, 69–71 Banbury Road, Oxford OX2 6PE, **t** (01865) 310 399. Pilgrimage to Santiago de Compostela; walking and mountaineering tours of Andalucía, Catalunya, La Rioja.

Exodus Travel, 9 Weir Road, London SW12 0LT, **t** (020) 8675 5550, **f** (020) 8673 0779, *www.exodus.co.uk*. Walking, cycling and mountaineering holidays.

Explore Worldwide Ltd, 1 Frederick Street, Aldershot, Hants GU11 1LQ, **t** (01252) 344 161, *www.exploreworldwide.com*. Small-group treks in the Picos de Europa, Sierra Nevada and Cazorla regions.

Headwater Holidays, 164 London Road, Northwich, Cheshire CW9 5HH, **t** (01606) 813 333, **f** (01606) 813 334, *www.headwater-holidays.co.uk*. Walking tours in Andalucía and València.

Ramblers Holidays, Box 43, Welwyn Garden City, Herts AL8 6PQ, **t** (01707) 331 133, *www.ramblersholidays.co.uk*. Walking and trekking tours in rural Spain.

Waymark Holidays, 44 Windsor Road, Slough, SL1 2EJ, **t** (01753) 516 477. Guided walks along the Camino de Santiago.

Tour Operators in the USA and Canada

Abercrombie and Kent, 1520 Kensington Road, Oak Brook, IL 60523, **t** 800 323 7208, *www.abercrombiekent.com*. Luxury breaks.

Abreu Tours Inc., 350 Fifth Avenue, Suite 2414, New York, NY 10118-2414, **t** (212) 819 9205, **t** 800 223 1580, **f** (212) 354 1840, *www.abreu-tours.com*. Independent or escorted tours, *parador* and *pousada* itineraries and cruises.

Alta Tours, 870 Market Street, Suite 784, San Francisco CA 94102, **t** (toll-free) 800 338 4191, **f** (415) 434 2684, *www.altatours.com*. Tours.

Cit Tours, 15 West 44th St, New York, NY 10173, **t** (212) CIT-TOUR, *www.cit-tours.com*; 9501 West Devon Avenue, Rosemount, IL 60018, **t** 800 CIT-TOUR; (Canada) 80 Tiverton Ct, Suite 401, Markham, Ontario L3R 0GA, **t** (toll-free) 800 387 0711.

Classic Custom Vacations, **t** (toll-free) 800 221 9748, *www.classiccustomvacations.com*. Customized holiday itineraries.

Contiki Travels, 2300 East Katella Ave 450 , Anaheim, CA 92806, **t** 888 CONTIKI, **f** (714) 935 2556, *www.contiki.com*. In-depth tours of Spain and Portugal, for 18–35s only.

EC Tours, 12500 Riverside Drive, Suite 210, Valley Village, CA 91607-3435, **t** (toll-free) 800 388 0877, *www.ectours.com*. Tours, city packages and breaks in historic *paradores*.

Escapade Vacations, 630 Third Avenue, New York, NY 10017, **t** (toll-free) 800 356 2405, *www.escapadevacations.com*. Personalized outfit offering everything from *parador* itineraries to self-catering vacations.

Heritage Tours, 216 West 18th Street, Suite 1001, New York, NY 10011, **t** (212)206 8400, or **t** (toll-free) 800 378 4555, **f** (212) 206 9101, *www.heritagetoursonline.com*. Customized cultural and historical tours.

Kesher Tours, 347 Fifth Avenue, Suite 706, New York, NY 10016, **t** (212) 481 3721, or **t** (toll-free) 800 847 0700, **f** (212) 481 4212, *www.kesher-tours.com*. Fully escorted kosher tours.

Marketing Ahead Inc., 433 Fifth Avenue, New York, NY 10016, **t** (toll-free) 800 223 1356, **f** (212) 686 0271, *www.marketingahead.com*. The leading US hotel and *parador* agent.

Olé Spain Cultural Walking Tours, 22 Davis Street, Seekonk, MA 02771, **t** (888) 869 7156, **f** (508) 336 8654, *www.olespain.com*. Walking tours of cities and customized itineraries. Andalucían speciality, but they will also do individual trips elsewhere in Spain.

Trafalgar Tours, 11 East 26th Street, New York, NY 10010, **t** (212) 689 8977, *www.trafalgartours.com*. Ten- or eleven-day all-inclusive whirlwind tours of Spain.

Worldwide Classroom, PO Box 1166, Milwaukee, W1 53201, **t** (414) 351 6311, or **t** (toll-free) 800 276 8712, *www.worldwide.edu*. Database of education worldwide.

Tour Operators in Spain

Iberian Adventures, Urb. La Avellaneda 15, Arenas de San Pedro, 05400 Ávila, Spain, **t/f** +34 920 37 25 44, *www.iberianadventures.com*. Activity (walking, mountain biking) and nature (bird-watching, flora and fauna) holidays in central, western and northern Spain.

Madrid & Beyond, Specialists in Spain, Gran Vía 59-8-D, 28013 Madrid, Spain, **t** +34 917 58 00 63, **f** +34 915 42 43 91, *www.madridandbeyond.com*. Bespoke itineraries featuring quality accommodation and ground transport, with the option of personally guided tours, special-interest holidays and walking and cycling tours.

Safari Andalucia, Apartado 20, 29480 Gaucín (Málaga), **t** 952 15 11 48. Walking holidays in the Serranía de Ronda with accommodation in tented camps and hunting lodges.

Spanish Consulates

Canada: 1 West Mount Square, 1456 Montreal H3Z 2P9, **t** (514) 935 5235;
200 Cross Street West, Toronto, Ontario M5R 2A5, **t** (416) 977 1661.

Ireland: 17a Merlyn Park, Ballsbridge, Dublin 4, **t** (1) 269 1640/269 1854.

UK: 20 Draycott Place, London SW3 2RZ, **t** (020) 7589 8989, visa information, **t** 0906 550 8970 (£1 per minute);
63 North Castle Street, Edinburgh EH2 3LJ, **t** (0131) 220 1483.

USA: 180 North Michigan Avenue, Chicago, IL 60601, **t** (312) 782 4588;
6300 Wilshire Blvd, Los Angeles, CA 90036, **t** (323) 938 0158;
150 East 58th Street, New York, NY 10155, **t** (212) 355 4090;
2375 Pennsylvania Ave, NW, Washington, DC 20037, **t** (202) 728 2330.

apply for a community resident's card (*tarjeta de residente comunitario*). There is no trouble getting into Spain if you fly to Gibraltar.

For **Gibraltar** there are no extra visa requirements for US citizens, and EU nationals have the same rights and status as in the UK.

Customs

Duty-free allowances have now been abolished within the EU. Travellers entering the EU from outside may take in some duty-free alcohol and tobacco. Larger quantities can be taken through customs for private consumption if bought locally and as long as taxes have been paid in the country of purchase – and provided you are travelling between EU countries. Our advice is not to bother – alcohol is very cheap on Spain's supermarket shelves.

Pets must be accompanied by a bilingual Certificate of Health from your local Veterinary Inspector.

For residents of Britain and other EU countries, the usual regulations apply regarding what you can carry home. Note that you cannot bring fresh meat, vegetables or plants into the UK. Residents of the USA may each take home US$400 worth of foreign goods without attracting duty, including the tobacco and alcohol allowance. Canadians can bring home CAN$300-worth of goods in a year, plus their tobacco and alcohol allowances.

Getting Around

By Air

Internal flights in Spain are on **Iberia**, **Binter** and **Air Europa**, all part of the Iberia Group and usually sharing an office. Other carriers operate on national routes, such as Alitalia between Málaga and Barcelona. Prices aren't a bargain, although if you are willing to travel at night you can pick up some cheap deals. It's also worth checking the national charters in Spanish travel agencies.

Iberia offices can be found in these cities:

Barcelona: Pza de España, **t** 933 25 73 58.
Bilbao: C/Ercilla 20, **t** 944 24 19 35;
Sondika Airport, **t** 944 71 14 56.
A Coruña: La **Coruña** Airport, **t** 981 18 72 54.
Madrid: Velázquez 130, **t** 915 87 75 36.
Málaga: Molina Larios 13, **t** 952 13 62 94.
San Sebastián: Bengoetxea 3, **t** 943 42 35 86.
Sevilla: Av. de La Buhaira 8, **t** 954 98 82 08.
València: Paz 14, **t** 963 52 75 52.
Gibraltar: Padre San Taella, Primera Izq 04004, **t** 950 23 86 84.

Otherwise call the Iberia 24hr number in Madrid, **t** 902 40 05 00, *www.iberia.com*.

By Sea

The *Trasmediterránea* line operates services from the Spanish mainland to the Balearic Islands, North Africa and the Canary Islands. They can be contacted at the addresses below:

Málaga: Estación Marítima, **t** 952 22 43 93.
UK Agents: Southern Ferries, 179 Piccadilly, London W1V 9DB, **t** (020) 7491 4968.

By Rail

If you're using public transport, there is usually an even choice between bus and train. Trains are slightly cheaper, while buses are a bit faster. Democracy in Spain has made the trains run on time, but western Europe's most eccentric railway, **RENFE**, still has a way to go. The trains themselves are almost always clean and comfortable, and do their best to keep to schedule – but RENFE remains so phenomenally complex that it will foul up your plans at least once if you spend much time in Spain.

Train Types

There are no fewer than 13 varieties of train, each with a different service and price; RENFE ticket vendors and conductors can't always get them straight, and confusion is rampant. They range from the luxury **TEE** (Trans-Europe Express) to the excruciating ***semidirecto*** and ***ferrobús***. Beware of these; they stop at every hamlet to deliver mail. The best are the **Talgo** trains, speedy and stylish beasts in gleaming stainless steel, designed and built entirely in Spain; the Spaniards are justifiably proud of them. **TER** trains are almost as good.

To add to the chaos Spain has two **narrow-gauge railway** lines that operate independently of RENFE: these are **FEVE**, which has tracks along the north coast of Spain, connecting Bilbao to Oviedo via Santander, and a few lines on the east coast (FGV in València); and the **Eusko Trenbideak** (Basque Railways), which connects Bilbao and San Sebastián by way of Zarautz and Zumaya. Both of these show rural Spanish life and scenery at their best, but they're slow, stop everywhere and cost more than the bus.

You'll also come across ***cercanías***, urban or suburban lines rather like the metro, linking places such as Barcelona with its outlying suburbs and beaches, and Málaga with its airport, Torremolinos and Fuengirola.

Fares, Discounts and *Días Azules*

Prices are inconsistent. **Fares** average €6 for every 100km (€9 first class), but there are supplements on the faster trains that can raise the price by as much as 80 per cent.

There are **discounts** for children (under-4s go free; 4–12s pay half), large families, senior citizens (half) and regular travellers, as well as 25 per cent discounts on ***Días Azules*** ('blue days'), for round-trip tickets only. 'Blue days' are posted in RENFE calendars at stations. Interpretations of discounts differ; you may care to undertake protracted negotiations as the Spaniards do.

There is a discount pass for under-26s, the ***tarjeta joven***, and BIGE or BIJ youth fares are available from TIVE offices in the large cities. There is also a ***tarjeta turística***, similar to the Eurail pass, available to anyone resident outside Spain, with unlimited travel for 8, 15 or 22 days but, as with Eurail, it's not worth it unless you intend to do extensive travelling.

RENFE Information

Every city has a **RENFE travel office** in the centre where you can obtain information and tickets. Buy tickets in advance if you can. Don't rely on the list of trains posted up; always ask at the station or travel office. RENFE has plenty of services you'll never hear about such as car transport to all parts of Spain. If you plan to ride the rails much, buy the *Guía RENFE*, an indispensable government publication with all the timetables, tariffs and information, available for a pittance from any station newsagent.

After disappearing for many years because of terrorism, **left luggage** facilities have reappeared in Spanish stations; the word in Spanish is *consigna*.

RENFE: national bookings (in English), **t** 902 24 02 02; international bookings, **t** 934 90 11 22.

Rail Excursions

RENFE has inaugurated a series of tourist trains. The **Transcantábrica** takes in some of the loveliest parts of northern Spain, including the Picos de Europa (contact RENFE for information), while in the south the **Al-Andalus Expreso** takes its passengers on a tour from Sevilla to Córdoba, Granada, Málaga and Jerez – an expensive but memorable trip. These agents deal with the Al-Andalus Expreso:

Cox & King's Travel Ltd, Gordon House, 10 Greencoat Place, London SW1P 1PH, **t** (020) 7873 5000.

Marketing Ahead Inc., 433 Fifth Avenue, New York, NY 10016, **t** (212) 686 9213.

By Bus

Hundreds of companies provide bus services across Spain, and not all cities have central bus stations. Tourist offices are the best sources of information; they almost always know every route and schedule. Like the trains, buses are cheap by northern European standards, but not dirt cheap. Tickets on intercity bus routes are sometimes sold at the last minute; note that advance tickets may only be valid at certain times. Small towns and villages are often linked by bus to their provincial capitals but not each other and, in the middle of Spain, it's almost impossible to get from one town to another without going through Madrid.

City Buses

Every Spanish city has an adequate public transport system, but you won't use it much as, in almost every city except Madrid and Barcelona, all attractions are within walking distance of each other. City buses cost €0.75 and, if you plan to use them often, you can buy books of tickets called ***abonamientos***, or *bono-Bus* or *tarjeta* cards to punch on entry, from tobacco shops. Otherwise buy a ticket on the bus; drivers will give you change if you don't have the correct amount. The route will be displayed on the signs at each stop (*parada*). But don't take it for granted that a bus will stop because you are waiting – nearly every stop seems to be a request stop.

By Taxi

Taxis are cheap enough for Spaniards to use them regularly. The average fare for a ride within a city will be €4.50–6. Taxis are metered, and drivers are honest; they are entitled to surcharges (for luggage, night-time trips, or to the airport) and, if you cross the city limits, they can charge double the fare shown. You can hail a cab from the street, and there are always a few around stations or call the information number (**t** 003) for the number of a **radio taxi**.

By Car

This is the most convenient way of getting about, and often the most pleasurable. Petrol prices are regulated by the government (unleaded: *gasolina sin plomo*; diesel: *gas-oil*); it's about two-thirds cheaper in Spain than in the UK (about twice the US price).

Only a few hotels – the more expensive ones – have garages or parking. In cities, parking is difficult, although a useful tip is that space which appears to be private – e.g. underground car parks of apartment blocks and offices – is often public, and rates are usually modest. Spain's road network is fine, in good repair and sometimes impressive. The system of *autovias* (motorways) is expanding: Spanish road building is remarkable for its speed if not always its durability. Be warned, though, that **tolls** on Spanish motorways are high.

To drive in Spain you'll need registration and insurance documents, and a driving licence (*see* 'Getting There By Car', p.75). Though it's not compulsory, you are advised to extend your car insurance to include a **bail bond**. If you are unlucky enough to have an accident, without a bond your car will be impounded and you may find yourself in jail for the night. Seat belts are mandatory. The speed limit is 100km (62 miles) per hour on national highways, unless otherwise marked, and 120km (75 miles) per hour on motorways. Beware that many Spaniards drive without insurance.

Hitchhiking is likely to involve a long, hot wait. Drivers in Spain are rarely inclined to give lifts and temperatures in midsummer can soar; few Spaniards ever hitchhike.

Car Hire Companies

Auto Europe, t (UK) 1 888 223 5555, **t** (US) 800 223 5555, *www.autoeurope.com*.

Avis, t (UK) 0800 132 781; **t** (US) 800 331 1212, *www.avis.com*.

easyCar, *www.easyCar.com*.

Hertz, UK **t** (020) 8759 2499; Dublin, **t** (01) 660 2255; US **t** (800) 654 3001; Canada **t** (1-800) 263 0600, *www.hertz.com*.

Holiday Autos, t 08705 300 400.

TransHIRE Worldwide Ltd, PO Box 82, Northwood, Middlesex, HA6 3TQ, **t** 0870 789 8000, **f** (01923) 834 919, *www.transhire.com*.

Car Hire

Car hire is slightly cheaper in Spain than elsewhere in Europe. The big international companies are the most expensive; ATESA, the government-owned Spanish firm, is cheaper. Prices for the smallest cars begin at about £90 per week with unlimited mileage, but insurance adds considerably to the costs. Small, local firms can sometimes offer a better deal, but these should be treated with some caution. Local firms also rent **mopeds** and **bicycles**, especially in tourist areas.

If you want to book ahead from abroad, contact your chosen airline or one of the companies listed above.

Practical A–Z

07

Children

Spaniards love children, and they'll welcome yours almost everywhere. Baby foods, etc. are widely available, but don't expect to find babysitters except at the really smart hotels; Spaniards always take their children with them, even if they're up till 4am. Nor are there many special amusements for kids – traditionally Spaniards never thought of their children as separate little creatures who ought to be amused – though these are beginning to spring up with Spain's new prosperity. Ask at a local tourist office for a list of attractions in its area geared towards children.

Climate and When to Go

Spain is hot and sunny in the summer, brisk and sunny in the winter, with little variation among the regions except in the matter of rainfall. The northern coast, especially Euskadi and Galicia, fairly drowns all year, which is why it's so green. Rain is scarce nearly everywhere else, and every locality brags in its brochures about so many 'hours of guaranteed sunshine' each year. Statistically, the champion for the best holiday climate is Alicante, with Europe's warmest winter temperatures and hardly any rain, but most of the southern and eastern coasts are nearly as good.

Spring and autumn are by far the best times to visit; the winter can be pleasant, though it's damp and chill in the north. Teruel and Soria provinces traditionally have the worst winter climate. The chart below shows average temperatures in various places.

Disabled Travellers

Facilities for disabled travellers are limited within Spain and public transport is not particularly wheelchair-friendly, though RENFE usually provides wheelchairs at main city stations. You are advised to contact the Spanish Tourist Office, which has compiled a two-page factsheet and can give general information on accessible accommodation. Alternatively, contact one of the specialist organizations listed below.

Average Maximum Temperatures in °C

	Jan	April	July	Oct
Madrid	17	27	39	29
Barcelona	7	25	33	24
San Sebastián	15	27	34	24
Alicante	21	31	34	29
A Coruña	16	25	27	26
Sevilla	20	31	35	31

Specialist Organizations in Spain

ECOM, Gran Vía de les Corts Catalanas 562 Principal, Barcelona, **t** 934 51 55 50, *www.ecom.es*. Federation of private Spanish organizations offering services for disabled people.

ONCE (Organización Nacional de Ciegos de España), Pso del Prado 24, Madrid, **t** 915 89 46 00, *www.once.es*. The Spanish association for the blind.

Specialist Organizations in the UK

Holiday Care Service, 2 Old Bank Chambers, Station Rd, Horley, Surrey RH6 9HW, **t** (01293) 774 535, *www.holidaycare.org.uk*. For travel information and details of accessible accommodation and care holidays.

RADAR (The Royal Association for Disability and Rehabilitation), 12 City Forum, 250 City Rd, London EC1V 8AF, **t** (020) 7259 3222, *www.radar.org.uk*. Has a wide range of travel information.

Royal National Institute for the Blind, 224 Great Portland St, London W15 5TB, **t** (020) 7388 1266, *www.rnib.org.uk*. Its mobility unit offers a 'Plane Easy' audio-cassette which advises blind people on travelling by plane.

Specialist Organizations in the USA

American Foundation for the Blind, 11 Penn Plaza, Suite 300, New York, NY 10001, **t** 800 232 5463, *www.afm.org*. The best source of information for visually impaired travellers.

Mobility International USA, PO Box 10767, Eugene, OR 97440, **t** (541) 343 1284, **f** (541) 343 6812, *www.miusa.org*. Information on international educational exchange programmes and volunteer services for the disabled.

SATH (Society for Accessible Travel and Hospitality), 347 5th Avenue, Suite 610, New York, NY 10016, **t** (212) 447 7284, **f** (212) 725 8253, *www.sath.org*. Travel and access information; also details other access resources on the web.

Electricity

Current is 225 AC or 220 V, the same as most of Europe. Americans will need converters, and the British will need two-pin adapters for the different plugs. If you plan to stay in the less expensive *hostales*, it may be better to leave your gadgets at home. Some corners of Spain, even some big cities, have pockets of exotic voltage – 150 V for example – guaranteeing a brief display of fireworks. Big hotels have the standard current.

Embassies and Consulates

Australia: Pza Descubridor Diego Ordaz 3, Madrid, **t** 914 41 93 00.

Canada: C/Núñez de Balboa 35, Madrid, **t** 914 23 32 50.

Ireland: Pso de la Castellana 46, Madrid, **t** 915 76 35 00.

New Zealand: Pza de la Lealtad 2, Madrid, **t** 915 23 02 26.

UK: (Embassy) C/de Fernando el Santo 16, Madrid, **t** 913 19 02 00, *www.ukinspain.com*; (Consulate-General) Centro Colon Marqués de la Ensenada 16–2°, Madrid, **t** 913 08 52 01.

USA: C/Serrano 75, Madrid, **t** 915 87 22 00, *www.embusa.es/*. A Consular office for passports is around the corner at Pso de la Castellana 52.

In Gibraltar: The Convent, Main Street, Gibraltar, **t** (350) 45440.

Festivals

One of the most spiritually deadening aspects of Francoism was the banning of many local and regional fiestas. These are now celebrated with gusto, and if you can arrange your itinerary to include one or two you'll be guaranteed an unforgettable holiday. Besides those listed below, there are literally thousands of others, and new ones spring up all the time; local and national tourist offices can provide complete lists.

The big holidays celebrated throughout Spain are *Corpus Cristi* in late May; Holy Week (*Semana Santa*), the week preceding Easter; 15 August, the Assumption of the Virgin and 25 July, the feast day of Spain's patron, Santiago. No matter where you are there are bound to be fireworks or processions on these dates. Do note, however, that dates for most festivals tend to be fluid, flowing towards the nearest weekend; if the actual date falls on a Thursday or a Tuesday, Spaniards 'bridge' the fiesta with the weekend to create a four-day whoopee. If there's a fiesta you want to attend, check the date at the tourist office in advance.

Many village patronal fiestas feature *romerías* (pilgrimages) up to a venerated shrine. Getting there is half the fun, with everyone in local costume, riding on horseback or driving covered wagons full of picnic supplies. Music, dancing, food, wine and fireworks are all necessary ingredients of a proper fiesta, while the bigger ones often include bullfights, funfairs, circuses and competitions.

See the 'Calendar of Events' overleaf for a list of some of Spain's most spectacular festivities.

Food and Drink

See also **Food and Drink** chapter, pp.61–70.

Spaniards are notoriously late diners; in the morning it's a coffee and roll grabbed at the bar, then a huge meal at around 2pm, then after work at 8pm a few tapas at the bar hold them over until supper at 10 or 11pm. After living in Spain for a few months this makes perfect sense, but it's exasperating to the average visitor. On the coasts, restaurants tend to open earlier to accommodate foreigners (some as early as 5pm) but you may as well do as the Spaniards do. Galicians are the early diners of Spain (8 or 9pm), while *madrileños* might think of going for a bite at midnight or

Restaurant Price Categories

In Madrid and Barcelona

Prices are based on a three-course meal without wine.

expensive	over €30
moderate	€15–30
inexpensive	up to €15

Elsewhere in Spain

Prices are based on the set menus or for a three-course meal with drinks, per person.

expensive	over €30
moderate	€18–30
inexpensive	up to €18

Calendar of Events

January

First week Granada: commemoration of the city's capture by the Catholic kings. Bainoa (Pontevedra) and Málaga: epiphany parade of *Los Reyes Magos* (Three Wise Men).

End of month Ituren and Zubieta (Navarra): dances of the *joaldunak* with pointed hats, fur vests and big bells.

February

First weekend Bocairente near València: mock battles between Moors and Christians, and fireworks. Almonacio del Marquesado (Cuenca): *La Endiablada*, a religious rite of pre-Christian origin featuring day-long dances and processions of 'devils' wearing floral costumes and heavy metal bells.

Mid-Feb *Carnaval* is celebrated throughout Spain. Cádiz has perhaps the best in the country, and certainly the oldest: parades, masquerades, music and fireworks in abundance. Other lively celebrations are held at Ciudad Rodrigo, with lots of bull action, and at Solsona, near Lleída, which features the explosive 'marriage of the mad giant'.

Lent During Lent there are Passion Play performances at Ulldecona (Tarragona), Cervera and Esparraguera (Barcelona).

March

15–19 València's *Las Fallas*: one of Spain's great fiestas, with the gaudiest bonfires and the best fireworks west of China (*see* p.213).

Semana Santa The most important celebrations are in Sevilla, with over 100 processions, broken by the singing of *saetas* (weird laments). Cuenca's comes with a week-long festival of religious music. Murcia has the most charming *pasos*.

Easter week Festivities continue in Murcia with Tuesday's *Bando de la Huerta* (a procession of floats dedicated to local agricultural products), jazz concerts and, on Saturday, the *Entierro de la Sardina* (the Burial of the Sardine) and great fireworks. In Avilés (Asturias), Easter and Easter Monday are celebrated with the Fiesta del Bollo, with folklore groups, cake and sailing regattas.

April

23 Barcelona: St Jordi's day, exchange of books and roses. Around the same time Alcoi (València) has the best of the 'battles' between Moors and Christians with pageantry, fireworks and great costumes.

Last week Sevilla's *Feria de Abril*: originally a horse-fair, now the greatest festival of Andalucía. Costumed parades, lots of flamenco, bullfights and drinking. Andújar (Jaén) hosts the *Romería de la Virgin de la Cabeza*, a pilgrimage from all over Andalucía which culminates in a procession to the sanctuary in the Sierra Morena.

May

First week Jerez de la Frontera: much like the April Fair in Sevilla. Almeria: Peña de Taranto Cultural Week. The foremost flamenco singers meet here every year for this prestigious contest. Navas de San Juan (north of Úbeda): in honour of *Nuestra Señora de la Estrella*, one of the most important pilgrimages in the province of Jaén.

1am. A few rounds of tapas – available at what most Americans or Britons would consider normal dining hours – will fill in the gaps.

Almost every restaurant offers a *menú del día*, or a *menú turístico*, featuring an appetizer, a main course, dessert, bread and drink at a set price, always cheaper than if you had ordered the items *a la carta*. These are always posted outside the restaurant, in the window or on the plywood chef at the door; decide what you want before going in if it's a set-price menu, because these bargains are hardly ever listed on the menu the waiter gives you at the table.

Tipping: Unless it's explicitly written on the bill (*la cuenta*), service in most restaurants is not included in the total, although Spaniards generally tip modestly.

Price categories quoted in the 'Eating Out' sections throughout this book are usually based on set menus or for a three-course meal with drinks, per person. However, the price categories in the sections for Madrid and Barcelona (*see* p.83) differ slightly from those used in the rest of the guide; this is because the range of prices in these cities, as in any large city, tends to be more extreme than elsewhere in Spain.

Second week Córdoba: every third year the *Concurso Nacional de Arte Flamenco* takes place on the seventh Sun after *Pentecost*. El Rocío (Huelva): the biggest *romería* in Spain.

Last 2 weeks Madrid: *San Isidro*, with two weeks of entertainment, the best bullfights, parades and concerts.

End of May *Corpus Cristi* initiates four days of festivities, especially in Toledo, Sitges (where the streets are covered with flower carpets), Berga (Barcelona), Zahara de la Sierra (Cádiz), Zamora, Cáceres and Puenteareas.

June

Mid-month Granada: *Festival Internacional de Música y Danza* attracts famous names from around the world; classical music, jazz and ballet; also flamenco competitions in odd-numbered years.

21–4 Alicante celebrates St John's day (*San Juanes*) better than any with a huge *Fallas* bonfire similar to València's. More celebrations for St John are at Prats de Lluçanes (Barcelona); Coria (Cáceres) with bulls in the streets; Segovia, with floats; San Pedro Manrique (Soria) with bonfires and walks on hot coals; León (with parties and bullfights).

End of month Burgos, *San Pedro*: beginning of two weeks of International Folklore Fería. Haro (La Rioja): wine battle. Hita, near Guadalajara: Festival of Medieval Theatre; medieval food, dance, bullfights and falconry, all set to flutes and bagpipes.

July

All month Hecho (Aragón): International Symposium of Contemporary Art and Sculpture, with art work all over the mountain sides. Santander holds its International Music Festival in August.

First 2 weeks Córdoba: International Guitar Festival; classical, flamenco and Latino.

6–7 Nava, Asturias: cider festival.

6–14 Pamplona: the famous running of the bulls and party for San Fermín.

2nd Sunday Olot, near Girona: *Aplec de la Sardana*, big Catalan dance festival.

Second week València, *Feria*: lots of entertainment and the Valencian speciality, fireworks. Segovia has a chamber music festival.

Mid-July–mid-Aug Cadaqués (Girona): International Music and Art Festival.

22 Anguiano (La Rioja): the dance of the *Zancos*, down the streets and steps on stilts.

25 Santiago de Compostela: celebrations for Santiago: national offering to the saint, the swinging of the *Botafumeiro*, burning of a replica of Córdoba's Mezquita, fireworks, etc.

Last week San Sebastián: International Jazz Festival, the biggest in Spain.

29 Santa María de Ribarteme (Pontevedra): pilgrimage made in coffins by people who narrowly escaped death the year before.

End July Jaca, in odd-numbered years, celebrates the International Folklore festival of the Pyrenees; in even numbered years it takes place at Oloron-Ste Marie in France.

August

3–9 Estella (Navarra): ancient fiesta, with giants and the only *encierro* where women can run with the bulls.

4–9 Vitoria: giants, music, bonfires and more for the Virgen Blanca.

Health and Insurance

Ambulance: t 112
Fire Brigade: t 080
Police: t 091

There is a standard agreement for citizens of EU countries, entitling you to a certain amount of free medical care, but it's not straightforward. You must complete all the necessary paperwork before you go to Spain, and allow a couple of months to make sure it comes through. Ask for a leaflet called *Before You Go* from the Department of Health and fill out form E111, which on arrival in Spain you must take to the local office of the *Instituto Nacional de Seguridad Social*, where you'll be given a Spanish medical card and vouchers enabling you to claim free treatment from an INSS doctor. The government is currently trying to implement an easier system. In an emergency, ask to be taken to the nearest *hospital de la seguridad social*. Before resorting to a *médico* (doctor) and his £20 (US$30) fee (ask at the tourist office for a list of English-speaking doctors), go to a pharmacy. *Farmacéuticos* are highly skilled and if there's a prescription medicine that you know will cure you, they'll often supply it without a doctor's note. (The

5 Trevélez (Granada): a midnight pilgrimage up Spain's highest mountain; the pilgrims arrive exhausted for midday prayers.
First week Torrevieja (Alicante): Habaneras International Music Festival. Daroca (Aragón): international Music Festival.
First Sat Arriondas-Ribadesella (Asturias): great kayak race on the Río Sella.
First Sun Gijón: Asturias Day celebrations, with lots of folklore.
11–18 San Sebastián: Fireworks contest.
15–16 Assumption of the Virgin and San Roque festivities at La Alberca (Salamanca), a very ancient festival. Sada (La Coruña): with a big sardine roast. Amer (Girona): with Sardana dancing. Llanes (Asturias): bagpipes and ancient dances. Bilbao: Basque sports and races. Vejar (Cádiz): with flamenco.
15–19 Battle of flowers at Betanzos (A Coruña).
Mid-month Málaga: its *feria* is gaining a reputation as one of the best in Europe, with a week of concerts, bullfights, dancing and singing in the old town.
Third week La Unión (Murcia): festival of *Cante de Las Minas*, flamenco competition, specializing in miners' songs.
Last Sunday Ontentinete (València): four-day Christian and Moor battles.
Last week Sanlúcar de Barrameda (Cádiz): exaltation of the Río Guadalquivir and major flamenco events.
31 Loiola (Euskadi): St Ignatius de Loiola Day.

September
8 Virgin's birthday with celebrations in many places, especially Salamanca, Algemesi (València), Tordesillas. Ronda: 18th-century-style bullfight in its historic ring. Ceremonies at Montserrat.
12 Graus (Aragón): big folklore event, with dances and ancient songs. Murcia: International Mediterranean Music Festival.
19 Oviedo: big *Americas Day* celebration, with floats and bands from all over Latin America. Logroño: *Vendimia* wine festival of La Rioja.
19–28 San Sebastián: The famous International Film Festival.
24 Barcelona: music, human towers and tons of other entertainments for its patroness, the Virgen de la Merced.

October
8–16 Zaragoza: festivities for the Virgen del Pilar, with huge floral offering.
Second week Ávila has an equally big party for Santa Teresa.
18–20 Mondoñedo (Lugo): a big horse fair dating from the Middle Ages.

November
Last Sunday Arcade (Pontevedra): Oyster Festival.

December
First week Martos (Jaén): Fiesta de la Aceituna. Annual four-day olive festival celebrating the olive in all its glory.
21 Santo Tomás fair, with processions, in San Sebastián, Bilbao, Azpeitia.
Last week *Olentzero* processions in many Basque villages.
31 Santiago de Compostela: the National Offering to the Apostle; a major religious ceremony with the *Botafumeiro*.

national newspaper *El País* lists *farmacías* in cities that stay open all night.)

No inoculations are required to enter Spain, though it never hurts to check that your tetanus jab is up to date, as well as some of the more exotic inoculations (typhoid and cholera) if you want to venture on into Morocco. Tap water is safe to drink but bottled stuff is available.

You may want to consider travel insurance, available through most travel agents. Not only is your health insured, but your bags and money as well, and some will even refund a missed charter flight if you're too ill to catch it. But whether you pay on the spot or not, be sure to save all doctors' receipts and police documents (if you're reporting a theft).

Internet

Getting online is easy and cheap. Every city of any size has a couple of places, while heavily visited towns are likely to be infested with *cibers*, as the Spanish call their Internet cafés. Even the most unlikely towns sometimes have Internet facilities – if you can get past the local youths indulging their aggression on digital baddies. The average price in most of the country is €1–2 per hour, though it can be more expensive in the cities.

Maps

Cartography has been an art in Spain since the 12th-century Catalans charted their Mediterranean Empire in Europe's first great school of map-making. The tourist offices hand out beautifully detailed maps of every town; ask for their *Mapa de Comunicaciones*, an excellent general map of the country. The best large-scale maps are produced by *Almax Editores*. Topographical maps for hikers and mountaineers can be obtained in Spain from the following addresses:

Instituto Geográfico Nacional, C/General Ibáñez de Ibero 3, Madrid, **t** 915 33 31 21.

Servicio Geográfico Ejército, C/Dario Gazapo, Madrid, **t** 915 18 11 19.

Librería Quera, Petritoxl 2, Barcelona, **t** 933 18 07 43.

If you can't wait until you get to Spain, specialist shops in the UK and the US include:

UK: Stanford's, 12 Long Acre, London WC2, **t** (020) 7836 1321.

USA: The Complete Traveler, 199 Madison Ave, New York, NY 10022, **t** (212) 685 9007.

Media

The Socialist *El País* is Spain's biggest and best national newspaper. The other big papers are *El Mundo* (a middle-of-the-road challenger that revealed many of the Socialist scandals that *El Pais* daintily overlooked), *Diario 16* (centrist and good for coverage of the *toros*), and *ABC* (conservative). Major British newspapers are widely available, along with the American *International Herald Tribune*, the *Wall Street Journal*, and *USA Today*. Most hit the news stands a day late. There are also publications in English on the major *costas* – notably *Sur*, a translation of a Málaga paper with general items of news; *Lookout*, a glossy monthly general consumer magazine; *The Entertainer*, for local news, events and classified ads; the *Marbella Times*, another slick mag for the expats. In Madrid, two free monthly magazines in English, the *Broadsheet* and the less glossy, *Free In Madrid*, offer insights into the city, listings and ads. All British newspapers are flown daily to Gibraltar.

As for **Spanish TV**, the excessive soaps and adverts are great for honing your Spanish if nothing else. Canal Plus is the only hope for anyone looking for decent movies (European and US), as Spanish television is dominated, generally, by shameless rip-offs of American and British TV programmes. Both channels are state-run, but with satellite dishes outnumbering *bodegas*, who watches them anyway?

There are hundreds of **radio** stations in Spain. For Spanish and international pop music, there is 40 Principales (top 40) at 93.9, Hit Radio at 107, and Cadena Cien at 99.5. Radio Nacional de España is the state-run public radio, and has four stations: RNE 1 at 88.2, with current affairs; Radio Clásica at 96.5 with classical music; Radio 3 at 93.2 with rock and pop music; and RNE 5 with sports and entertainment news. Frequencies vary, and charts can be found in the back of the Cartelera section of *El País*.

Cinema is cheap and the Spaniards love it. *El País* has the best Madrid and regional **film listings**. Some films are subtitled instead of dubbed, and English films are occasionally shown on the Costa del Sol and Costa Blanca in the expatriate communities.

Money

On 1 January 1999, the **euro** (at the rate of €1 = 166.386 pts) became the official currency of Spain, and *peseta* notes and coins became obsolete on 28 February 2002. At the time of writing, the euro is worth UK£0.61, US$0.88 and C$1.34. The notes come in denominations of 5, 10, 20, 50, 100, 200 and 500 euros, and they themselves get bigger as you go up. One euro is divisible by 100 cents, and *céntimo* coins are issued in denominations of 1, 2, 5, 10, 20 and 50. Euro coins are issued in denominations of 1 and 2 euros, and in Spain you get to admire King Juan Carlos's smile on the flip side of both. Until 30 June 2002, you will be able to exchange *pesetas* for Euros in any bank for no charge. From 1 July you will only be able exchange *pesetas* at the Bank of Spain (offices only in major cities).

Spain's city centres seem to have a bank on every street corner, and most of them will exchange money; look for the *cambio* or *exchange* signs and the little flags. There is a slight difference in the rates, though usually not enough to make shopping around worthwhile. Beware exchange offices, as they can charge a hefty commission on all transactions. You can often change money at travel agencies, hotels, restaurants or the big department stores. Even big supermarkets tend to have *telebancos* or automatic bank tellers. There are 24-hour *cambios* at the big train stations in Barcelona and Madrid. A Eurocheque card will be needed to support British Eurocheques, and even then they may not be welcome.

Travellers' cheques, if they are from one of the major companies, will pass at most bank exchanges. Wiring money from overseas entails no special difficulties; just give yourself two weeks to be on the safe side, and work through one of the larger institutions (Banco Central, Banco de Bilbao, Banco Español de Crédito, Banco Hispano Americano, Banco de Santander, Banco de Vizcaya). All transactions have to go through Madrid. **Credit cards** are always helpful, both in towns and in the country. Direct debit cards are also useful ways of obtaining money, though you should check with your bank before leaving to ensure your card can be used in Spain. But do not rely on a hole-in-the-wall machine as your only source of cash; if the machine swallows your card, it may take 10 days to retrieve it.

Opening Hours

Banks: Most are open Mon–Thurs 8.30–4.30, Fri 8.30–2 and Sat (sometimes) 8.30–1.

Churches: Most of the less important ones are always closed. If you're determined to see one, it will never be hard to find the *sacristán* or caretaker. Usually they live close by, and are glad to show you around for a tip.

Shops: Usually open from 9.30am. Except in larger cities, most shops close for 2–3 hours in the afternoon, usually from 1pm or 2pm. In the south, where it's hotter, the siesta can last from 1pm to 5pm. Most establishments stay open until 7pm or 8pm.

Museums and **historical sites**: These tend to follow shop opening hours, though shorter in the winter months; nearly all close on Mondays. Seldom-visited ones have a raffish disregard for their official hours. Don't be discouraged: bang on doors and ask around.

Police Business

Crime is not really a big problem in Spain and Spaniards talk about it perhaps more than is warranted. Pickpocketing and robbing parked cars are the specialities; in Sevilla they like to take the whole car. The big cities (Madrid, Barcelona and especially Málaga and Sevilla) are the places where you should be careful although, except for some quarters of the largest cities, walking around at night is not a problem – primarily because everybody does it. Crime is also spreading to the tourist areas, particularly the Costa del Sol. Even on there, though, you're probably safer than you would be at home: the crime rate is roughly a quarter of that in Britain. Note that in Spain less than 8 grams of marijuana is legal; anything else may easily earn you the traditional 'six years and a day'.

There are several species of **police**, and their authority varies with the area. Franco's old goon squads, the Policía Armada, have been reformed and relatively demilitarized into the *Policía Nacional*. The *Policía Municipal* are responsible for crime control in some cities, while in others they are limited to directing traffic. Mostly in rural areas, there's the *Guardia Civil*, with green uniforms, but minus the sinister black patent-leather tricorn hats of yesteryear. They're most conspicuous as a highway patrol, assisting motorists and handing out tickets (ignoring 'no passing' zones is the best way to get one). Most traffic violations are payable on the spot; the traffic cops have a reputation for upright honesty. The Basques don't want anything to do with any of these. So far, they are the only community to take advantage of the new autonomy laws and set up their own police, the *Ertzantza*. You'll see them looking dapper in their red berets.

Post Offices and Faxes

Every city, regardless of size, seems to have one post office (*correos*) and no more. It will always be crowded, but unless you have packages to post, you may not need ever to visit

Public Holidays

The Spanish, like the Italians, try to have as many as possible. Everything closes on:

1 Jan	Año Nuevo (New Year's Day)
6 Jan	Epifanía (Epiphany)
Mar/April	Viernes Santo (Good Friday)
1 May	Día del Trabajo (Labour Day)
May/June	Corpus Christi
25 July	Santiago Apóstol (St James' Day)
15 Aug	Asunción (Assumption)
12 Oct	Día de la Hispanidad (Columbus Day)
1 Nov	Todos los Santos (All Saints' Day)
6 Dec	Día de la Constitución (Constitution Day)
8 Dec	Inmaculada Concepción (Immaculate Conception)
25 Dec	Navidad (Christmas Day)

one. Most tobacconists sell **stamps** (*sellos*) and they'll usually know the correct postage for whatever you're sending. Send everything air mail (*por avión*) and don't send postcards unless you don't care when they arrive. *Poste restante* is called *lista de correos*, and it is as chancy as anywhere else. **Postboxes**, marked '*Correos y Telégrafos*' are bright yellow and scarce. The post offices also handle **telegrams**, which normally take 4 hours to arrive within Europe but are very expensive. Stationery shops are the best places from which to send **faxes**.

Don't confuse post offices with the *Caja Postal*, the postal savings banks, which look just like them.

Shopping

Notwithstanding the delightfully tacky tourist wares (Toledo 'daggers', plastic bulls and flamenco dolls ad nauseam) there are some high-quality items to be picked up in Spain, notably **leather** from Córdoba, **lace** from Galicia, **inlaid wood** *taracea* work from Granada (chests and chessboards), **jewellery** from Toledo, **woven goods** from nearly every province of Spain, and fine embroidered **linens** available everywhere. Good-quality **antiques** can occasionally be picked up at a **rastro** (flea market), but there aren't the great finds there once were – Spaniards have learned what they're worth and charge accordingly.

The major **department store** chains in Spain, El Corte Inglés and the Galerías Preciadas, often have good selections of crafts and will ship items home. You can also get some good buys at the **weekly markets** where Spaniards do a good deal of their shopping. Local tourist offices will have details. EU citizens are not entitled to tax refunds.

Sports and Activities

Bars, Clubs and Entertainment

Bars take up much of the Spaniards' leisure time. They are wonderful institutions, where you can eat breakfast or linger over a glass of beer until 4 in the morning. Some have music – jazz, rock or flamenco; some have great snacks, or tapas; some have games or pinball machines. **Discos** and **clubs** are easily found in the big cities and tourist spots; most are expensive. Ask around for the favourites. Watch out for posters for **concerts**, **ballets**, and especially **circuses**. The little travelling Spanish troupes with their family acts, tents and tinsel will charm you; they often gravitate to the major fiestas in the summer.

Cycling

Cycling is taken extremely seriously in Spain, though usually by Lycra-clad enthusiasts rather than as a form of transport. If you do want to bring your own bicycle to Spain, you can make arrangements by ferry or train; by air, you'll almost always have to dismantle it and pack it in some kind of crate. Each airline seems to have its own policy.

Maps and information are available from:

Federación Española de Ciclismo, C/Ferraz 16, 28008 Madrid, **t** 915 42 04 21, *www.rfec.com*.

Cyclists' Touring Club, Cotterell House, 69 Meadrow, Godalming, Surrey GU7 3HS, **t** (01483) 417 217.

Fishing

Fishing is a long-standing obsession in Spain, and you'll need to get a licence. Freshwater fishing permits (*permiso de pesca*) are issued on a fortnightly basis from the municipal ICONA office, or from the **Jefatura Provincial del ICONA**, Licencia Nacional de Caza y Pesca, Jorge Juan 39, Madrid (**t** 912 25 59 85).

For a list of the best trout streams, write to the **Spanish Fishing Federation**, Navas de Tolosa 3, 28013 Madrid, **t/f** 915 32 83 52. The **Spanish Agricultural Office** in London, **t** (020) 7235 5005, can also provide information.

Deep-sea fishermen must obtain a five-year licence from the provincial Comandancias de Marina. For details of the best fishing waters and boat rentals, contact the **Directorate General of Sea Fishing**, Subsecretaria de la Marina Mercante, Ministerio de Comercio, C/Ruiz de Alarcón 1, 28071 Madrid.

Football

Soccer is the most popular sport throughout Spain, and the Spaniards play it well: FC Barcelona and Real Madrid are the best teams to watch. The season lasts from September to June, and matches are usually trouble free.

Spanish Football Federation, Alberto Bosch 13, 28014 Madrid, **t** 914 20 33 21, **f** 914 20 20 94.

Golf

Since the advent of Severiano Ballesteros and Jose Maria Olazabal, Spaniards too have gone nuts for the game. The sunny warm winters, combined with greens of international tournament standard, attract golfing enthusiasts from all over the world. Green fees have taken a leap in recent years, and even the humblest clubs charge about €18 – most will hire out clubs. Many hotels cater specifically for golfers and there are numerous specialist tour operators (*see* those listed on pp.76–7).

Royal Spanish Golf Federation, Capitán Haya 9–5°, 28020 Madrid, **t** 914 55 27 57, **f** 915 56 32 90.

Hiking and Mountaineering

Spain's sierras attract thousands of hikers and mountaineers. Los Picos de Europa and the Pyrenees are by far the most popular, though there are also some lovely hikes in the northern Cordillera Cantábrica mountains, in the Sierra Nevada above Granada and Las Hurdes of northern Extremadura. The tourist office or the Spanish Mountaineering Federation provide a list of *refugios*, offering mountain shelter in places. Some are well equipped and can supply food. Most, however, do not, so take a sleeping bag, cooking equipment and food with you. Hiking boots are essential, as is a detailed map of the area.

Spanish Mountaineering Federation, Alberto Aguilera 3, 28015 Madrid, **t** 914 45 13 82.

Pelota

Pelota, the Basque national sport, is a fast, thrilling game, in which contestants wearing long. basket-like gloves propel a hard ball with great force at high walls; rather like squash. The fast action on the *jai-alai* court is matched by the wagering frenzy of the spectators.

Spanish Pelota Foundation, Los Madrazo 11, 28014 Madrid, **t** 915 21 42 99, **f** 915 32 38 79.

Skiing

Spain's ski resorts attract a sizeable number of foreign skiers who come to beat the high costs in France and Switzerland. In the south, an hour from Granada, you can be among the Iberian Peninsula's highest peaks and Europe's southernmost ski resorts; their après-ski can rival anything in the Alps. In Spain, it's easy to arrange all-inclusive ski packages through a travel agent. A typical deal includes six nights' accommodation in a three- or four-star hotel with half board, and unlimited use of ski lifts for the week, at a cost of just under €600. With instruction fees, count on €60–90 extra per week. For information, write to the tourist office, individual resorts listed in this book, or contact:

Spanish Winter Sports Federation, Infanta Maria Teresa 14, 28016 Madrid, **t** 913 44 09 44.

Tennis

There is equal fervour for tennis as for golf, inspired by international champions Arantxa Sánchez Vicario, Conchita Martínez and Carlos Moya. Every resort hotel has its own courts; municipal ones are rare or hard to get to.

Royal Spanish Tennis Federation, Av. Diagonal 618, 08021 Barcelona, **t** 932 01 08 44.

Watersports

Watersports are the most popular activities in the summer. You can rent a windsurfing board and learn how to use it at almost any resort; aficionados head for Tarifa, the continent's southernmost tip and Europe's windsurfing mecca, while along the Atlantic coast of Euskadi and Cantabria there are several places where the waves are suitable for surfing.

Underwater activists flock to the Almería coast in particular for its sparkling water and abundant marine life.

Royal Spanish Sailing Federation, Luis de Salazar 12, 28002 Madrid, **t** 915 19 50 08, **f** 914 16 45 04.

Spanish Sub-Aqua Federation, Santaló 15, 08021 Barcelona, **t** 932 00 67 69.

Federación Española de Esquí Náutico, Sabino de Arana 30, 08028 Barcelona, **t** 933 30 89 03.

Telephones

Spain has a wide network of public phone booths, despite the cellphone craze that has taken over the nation. Local calls are relatively cheap, and it's easy to place international calls from any booth. Many of the old coin-operated phones now only accept phonecards (sold in *estancos* and post offices in denominations of €6 and €12).

There are central telephone offices (*telefónicas*) in every big city, where you call from metered booths (and pay more for the comfort); they are indispensable, however, for reversed charge or collect calls (*cobro revertido*). *Telefónicas* are generally open 9am–1pm and 5–10pm and closed on Sundays.

Overseas calls from Spain are expensive: calls to the UK cost about €1–2 a minute, to the USA substantially more. Expect to pay a big surcharge if you do any telephoning from your hotel. Cheap rate is Mon–Sat 10pm–8am and all day Sunday and public holidays.

For calls to Spain from the UK, dial 00 followed by the country code (34), the area code and the number. To telephone Gibraltar from abroad, dial 00 followed by (350).

For international calls from Spain or Gibraltar, dial 00, wait for the higher tone and then dial the country code (e.g. 00 44 for the UK, 001 for the USA). To call Gibraltar from Spain, dial 9567 followed by the local five-digit number.

All **local calls** now require the 91 before them, which may not appear on lists prior to April 1998 (Spanish phone numbers in this guide are listed as they must be dialled). Telephone numbers in Spain beginning with 900 are free, but those beginning with 901, 902 and 903 carry higher rates; rate information is available by calling **t** 1004 (toll-free).

National directory enquiries: **t** 1003.

International directory enquiries: **t** 025.

Toilets

Outside bus and train stations, public facilities are rare. On the other hand, every bar on every corner has a toilet; don't feel uncomfortable using it without purchasing something – the Spaniards do it all the time. Just ask for *los servicios*. Public lavatories and ones in private commercial establishments have improved tremendously over the last decade.

Tourist Information

After receiving millions of tourists each year for the last two decades, no country has more information offices, or more helpful ones, or more intelligent brochures and detailed maps. Every city will have an office, and about two-thirds of the time you'll find someone who speaks English. Sometimes they'll be less helpful in the big cities in the summer. More often, though, you'll be surprised at how well they know the details of accommodation and transportation. Many large cities also

Spanish National Tourist Offices

Canada: 102 Bloor Street West, 34th Floor, Toronto, Ontario M4W 3E2, **t** (416) 961 3131, **f** (416) 961 1992, *www.tourspain.toronto.on.ca*.

UK/Ireland: 22–3 Manchester Square, London W1U 3PX, **t** (020) 7486 8077, **f** (020) 7486 8034; 24hr brochure request **t** 09063 640 630, *www.tourspain.es*.

USA: Water Tower Place, Suite 915, East 845, North Michigan Avenue, Chicago, IL 60611, **t** (312) 642 1992, **f** (312) 642 9817;
8383 Wilshire Blvd, Suite 960, Beverly Hills, CA 90211, **t** (323) 658 7188, **f** (323) 658 1061;
666 Fifth Avenue, New York, NY 10103, **t** (212) 265 8822, **f** (212) 265 8864, *www.okspain.org*.

Gibraltar Information Bureau

UK: Arundel Great Court, 178–9 The Strand, London WC2R 1EH, **t** (020) 7836 0777, **f** (020) 7240 6612, *www.gibraltar.gov.uk*.

maintain **municipal tourist offices**, though they're not as well equipped as those run by the Ministry of Tourism, better known as **Turismo**. Hours for most offices are Monday to Friday, 9.30–1.30 and 4–7, open on Saturday mornings, closed on Sundays.

Where to Stay

Hotels in Spain are no longer the bargains they once were and have pretty much caught up with the rest of Europe. One thing you can still count on is a consistent level of quality and service; the Spanish government regulates hotels more intelligently, and more closely, than any other Mediterranean country. Room prices must be posted in the hotel lobbies and in the rooms, and if there's any problem you can ask for the complaints book, or *Libro de Reclamaciones*. No one ever writes anything in these; any written complaint must be passed on to the authorities immediately and hotel keepers would always rather correct the problem for you.

The prices given in this guide are for double rooms with bath (unless stated otherwise) in high season but do not include VAT (IVA) charged at 15 per cent on five-star *hoteles*, and 7 per cent on other categories of accommodation. Prices for single rooms will average about 60 per cent of a double, while triples or an extra bed are around 35 per cent more. Prices listed in the 'Where to Stay' sections of the guide have been divided into five categories (*see* box below). Those for Madrid and Barcelona vary a little from those in the rest of the guide; this is because the range of prices found in these cities, as in any large city, tends to be more extreme than elsewhere in Spain.

No government could resist the chance to insert a little bureaucratic confusion, and the wide range of accommodation in Spain is classified in a complex system. Look for the little **blue plaques** next to the doors of all *hoteles*, *hostales* etc., which identify the classification and number of stars.

If you're travelling around a lot, the government publication *Guía de Hoteles* will be a good investment, a great fat book with every classified hotel and *hostal* in Spain, available for about €10 in many bookshops, as well as from Spanish National Tourist Offices. The government also publishes guides to holiday flats (*apartamentos turísticos*) and campsites.

Accommodation Price Ranges

Prices are for a double room with bathroom.

In Madrid and Barcelona

luxury	over €180
expensive	€100–180
moderate	€40–100
inexpensive	€20–40
cheap	under €20

Elsewhere in Spain

luxury	over €132
expensive	€78–132
moderate	€48–78
inexpensive	€30–48
cheap	under €30

Paradores

The government, in its plan to develop tourism in the 1950s, started this nationwide chain of classy hotels to draw attention to little-visited areas. They restored old palaces, castles and monasteries for the purpose, furnished them with antiques and installed fine restaurants featuring local specialities.

Not all are historical landmarks; in resort areas, they are as likely to be cleanly designed modern buildings, usually in a great location with a pool and some sports facilities. As their popularity has increased, so have their prices; in most cases both the rooms and the restaurant will be the most expensive in town. *Paradores* are classed as three- or four-star hotels, and their prices range from €69 (out of season) in remote provincial towns to €200 and upwards (in high season) for the most popular. Many offer out-of-season or promotional weekend rates.

To book a *parador* in advance, contact:

Spain: Head Office, Requena 3, 28013, Madrid **t** 915 16 66 66.

UK: Keytel International, 402 Edgware Road, London W2 1ED, **t** (020) 7402 8182.

USA: Marketing Ahead, 433 Fifth Avenue, New York, NY 10016, **t** (212) 686 9213.

Hoteles

Hoteles (H) are rated from one to five stars, according to the services they offer. These are the most expensive places, and even a one-star hotel will be a comfortable, middle-range establishment. *Hotel Residencias* (HR) are the same, only without a restaurant. Many of the more expensive hotels have rooms available at prices lower than those listed. They won't tell you, though; you'll have to ask.

You can often get discounts in the off season but will be charged higher rates during important festivals. These are supposedly regulated, but in practice hotel-keepers charge whatever they can get. If you want to attend a big event, book your hotel as far in advance as possible.

Hostales and *Pensiones*

Hostales (Hs) and *pensiones* (P) are rated from one to three stars. These are usually more modest, often a floor in an apartment block; a three-star *hostal* is roughly equivalent to a one-star hotel. *Pensiones* may require full or half board; there aren't so many of these.

Hostal Residencias (HsR), like *hotel residencias*, do not offer meals except breakfast, and not always that. Of course, *hostales* and *pensiones* with one or two stars will often have very cheap rooms without private baths, but be warned: small, cheap *hostales* in ports and big cities can be crummy and noisy beyond belief.

Fondas, Casas de Huéspedes and *Camas*

The bottom of the scale is occupied by the *fonda* (F) and *casa de huéspedes* (CH), little different from a one-star *hostal*, though generally cheaper.

Off the scale completely are hundreds of unclassified cheap places, usually rooms in an apartment or over a bar and identified only by a little sign reading *camas* (beds) or *habitaciones* (rooms). You can also ask in bars or at the tourist office for unidentified *casas particulares*, private houses with a room or two; in many villages these will be the best you can do, but they're usually clean – Spanish women are manic housekeepers. The best of these will be in small towns and villages, and around the universities. The worst are found in industrial cities. In cities, it's best to look right in the centre, not around the bus and train stations. Most inexpensive establishments will ask you to pay a day in advance.

Alternative Accommodation

Youth hostels exist in Spain, but they're usually not worth the trouble. Most are open only in the summer; there are the usual inconveniences and silly rules, and they are often in out-of-the-way locations. You'll be better off with the inexpensive *hostales* and *fondas* – sometimes these are even cheaper than youth hostels – or ask at the local tourist office if there are any rooms available in **university dormitories**.

If you fancy some peace and tranquillity, the National Tourist Office has a list of **convents** and **monasteries** that welcome guests (sometimes only in groups). Accommodation starts at around €16 a night, meals are simple and guests are usually permitted to take part in the religious ceremonies.

Camping

Campsites are rated with from one to three stars, depending on their facilities, and in addition to the ones listed in the official government handbook there are always others, rather primitive, that are unlisted. On the whole, camping is a good deal, and facilities in most first-class sites include shops, restaurants, bars, laundries, hot showers, first aid, swimming pools and telephones. Caravans and trailers converge on all the more developed sites, but if you just want to pitch your tent or sleep out in some quiet field, ask around in the bars or at likely farms. Camping is forbidden in many forest areas because of fears of fire, as well as on the beaches. If you're doing any hiking, bring a sleeping bag and stay in the free ***refugios*** along the major trails.

The government handbook *Guía de Campings* can be found in most bookstores and at the Spanish Tourist Office. **Reservations** for sites can be made through the Federación Española de Empresarios de Camping, General Oraa 52, 2° d, 28006 Madrid, **t** 915 62 99 94; or Angel Ganivet 5, 4° a, 18009 Granada, **t** 958 22 14 56. Or contact:

Federación Española de Campings, San Bernardo 97–9, Edificio Colomina, 28015 Madrid, **t** 914 48 12 34.

Camping and Caravan Club, Greenfields House, Westwood Way, Coventry CV4 8JH, **t** (01203) 422 024 (membership £30).

Self-Catering Organizations

In the UK

Casas Cantabricas, 31 Arbury Road, Cambridge, CB4 2JB, **t** (01223) 328 721, **f** 322 711.

Individual Travellers, Bignor, nr Pulborough, West Sussex, RH20 1QD, **t** (01798) 869 461, **f** 869 381. Village and rural accommodation in farmhouses and cottages.

International Chapters, 47–51 St John's Wood High St, London NW8 7NJ, **t** (020) 7722 0722, **f** (020) 7722 9140, *www.villa-rentals.com*. A wide range of high-quality farmhouses, châteaux and villas.

Keytel International, 402 Edgware Road, London, W2 1ED, **t** (020) 7616 0300, **f** 7616 0317, *paradors@keytel.co.uk*.

Magic of Spain, 227 Shepherd's Bush Road, London W6 7AS, **t** (020) 8741 4440. Apartments and hotels along the coast.

Travellers' Way, Hewell Lane, Tardebigge, Bromsgrove, Worcs B60 1LP, **t** (01527) 836 791, **f** 836 159. A choice of self-catering accommodation and hotels along the coast, in mountain villages and in the cities.

In the USA

EC Tours, 10153 1/2 Riverside, Toluca Lake, CA 91602, **t** (800) 388 0877. Pilgrimages and city accommodation.

Ibero Travel, 6924 Loubet Street, Forest Hills, NY 11375, **t** (718) 263 0200. Apartments and fly-drive offers.

Resort Accommodation

Almost everything along the coasts of Spain has been built in the last 25 years, and anonymous high-rise buildings abound. Lately the trend has turned towards low-rise 'villages' or *urbanizaciónes* built around a pool, usually on or near the beach. We've tried to include places that stand out in some way, or which are good bargains for their rating. Most hotels in the big resorts cater for package tours, and may not even answer a request for an individual reservation during the peak season. If you intend to spend a couple of weeks on any of the *costas*, your best bet is to book an all-inclusive package deal from the UK or USA.

Self-Catering Accommodation

With the rise in hotel prices, this has become an increasingly popular way of vacationing in Spain. Write ahead to any provincial tourist office (addresses are listed in the relevant practical information boxes within the regional chapters) for the area you're interested in; most will send you complete listings, with detailed information and often photos. A few firms that arrange self-catering holidays are listed in the box opposite.

Turismo Verde (Rural Tourism)

Self-catering overlaps with the booming industry of rural tourism in Spain, known as *Turismo Rural*, *Turismo Verde*, *Agroturismo* or, in Basque (wait for it), *Nekazalturismoa*. The regional autonomous governments and private sector have responded to the growing demand from Spaniards in particular for rural accommodation, with facilities running the gamut from country cottages to plushed-up cave dwellings to palaces; there are also some modern complexes. These places are often much more characterful than the local hotel or *hostal* and good value. They may also have various outdoor pursuits on offer, such as pony trekking. Again, for more information on rural tourism in any region, contact the Spanish National Tourist Office or the relevant tourist office (*see* the practical information boxes within the regional chapters).

Women Travellers

On the whole, the horror stories of sexual harassment in Spain are a thing of the past, unless you dress provocatively and hang out by the bus station after dark. All Spaniards seem to melt when they see blondes, so if you're fair you're in for a tougher time. Even Spanish women sunbathe topless these days at the international *costa* resorts, but do be discreet elsewhere, especially near small villages. Apart from the coast, it tends to be older men who comment on your appearance as a matter of course. Whether you can understand them or not, they are best ignored.

Catalunya

08

Catalunya

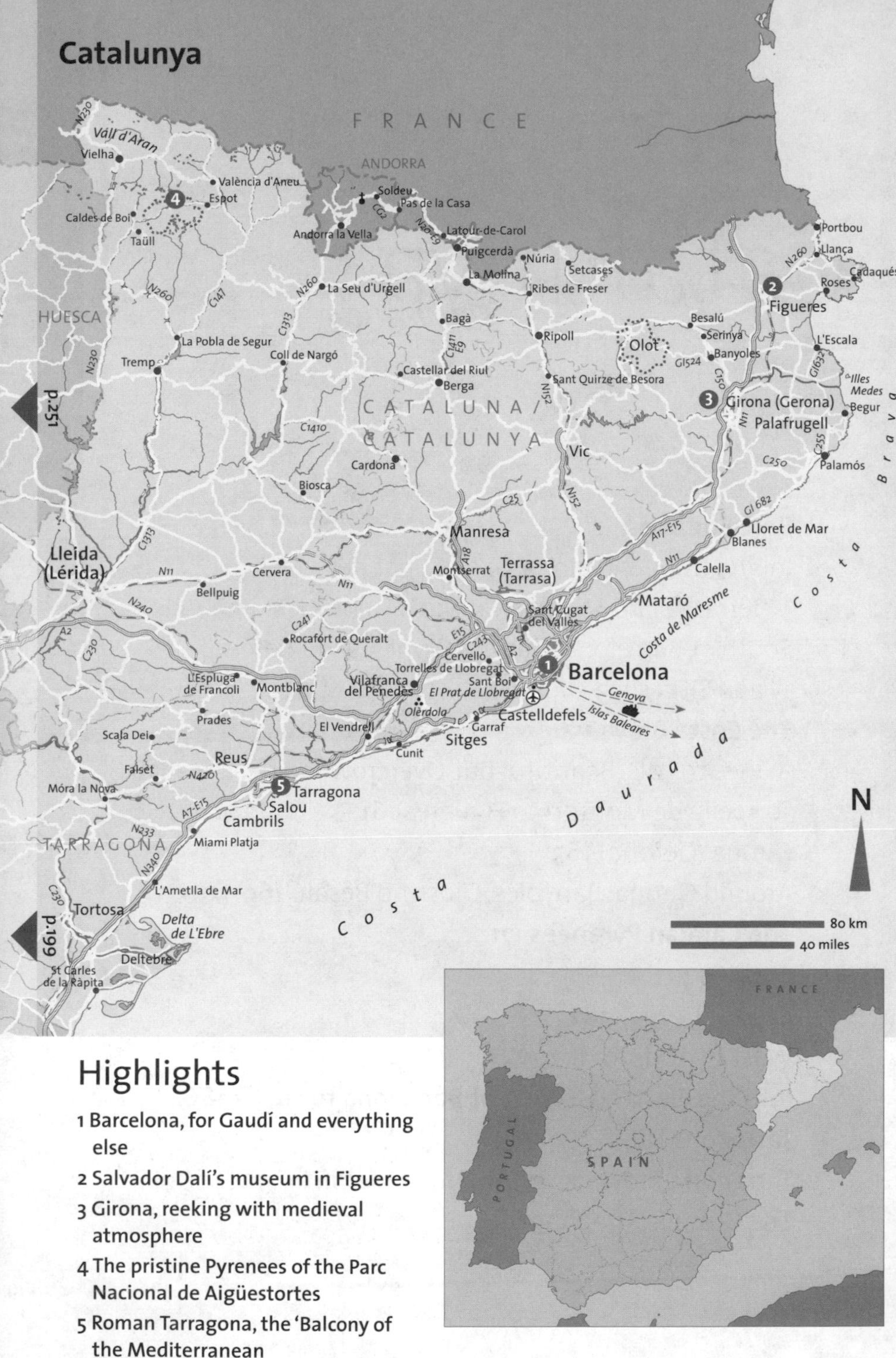

p.251

p.199

Highlights

1 Barcelona, for Gaudí and everything else
2 Salvador Dalí's museum in Figueres
3 Girona, reeking with medieval atmosphere
4 The pristine Pyrenees of the Parc Nacional de Aigüestortes
5 Roman Tarragona, the 'Balcony of the Mediterranean

On the map, Catalunya (in Castilian Spanish, Cataluña; in English Catalonia) occupies a tidy triangle wedged between France, the Mediterranean and the rest of Spain, but that's where the tidiness ends. To the north the Pyrenees stretch down to dip their crooked toes in the sea, forming the fabled Costa Brava; to the south the flat sandy strands of the Costa Daurada peter out at the soggy morasses of the Ebro delta. In between, dead volcanoes and mountains shaped like pipe organs squat inscrutably over a landscape littered with Iberian, Greek, Roman and Romanesque monuments. Enough monsters lurk in Catalunya's medieval cloisters to fill Carnegie Hall. Nowhere else in Spain has early 20th-century architecture (*modernista*, as the Catalans call it) bloomed so furiously, from Gaudí's Barcelona to wine cooperatives in the tiniest village. Spaniards and Hispanophiles tend to warn first-time visitors to Spain away from Catalunya; it's too heady, too 'fizzy', lacking the austere *sol y sombra* of the 'real Spain', whatever that may be. But to visit Spain and miss Barcelona, perhaps the best of its cities, would be to miss the most exciting and dynamic spirit of present day Spain, the vanguard of modern Spanish culture.

In the old days the Spaniards kept Catalunya under an iron heel. Today, they worry that Barcelona's busy entrepreneurs are transforming the nation into a Greater Catalunya. Thirty years ago, flying the Catalan flag was a criminal offence; today it waves proudly over the Catalan Generalitat and also, thanks to an intrepid band of Barcelona alpinists, atop the highest peak of Mt Everest.

Besides Barcelona, Catalunya has two fine provincial capitals: Tarragona with its interesting Roman ruins and Girona with its evocative medieval quarter. The playful Dalí museum, one of the most visited in Europe, is in Figueres, just off the Costa Brava. This is Spain's prettiest coast – if you have magic spectacles that can see through some of the worst speculative *urbanizaciones* anywhere. South of Barcelona, the Costa Daurada lacks such drama, but as compensation there's Sitges, one of the hottest resorts on the Med. Inland, the Pyrenees are the highlight: at their most majestic in Aigüestortes National Park, the secluded Vall d'Aran and the even more secluded Vall de Boí; most commercially in the Catalan principality of Andorra. Enhanced by its fantastic situation, Montserrat is perhaps Spain's best-known monastery; another, Ripoll, is a Romanesque gem. In the wine region, exotic *modernista bodegas* liven up sleepy medieval villages. Besides tripping the *sardana*, Catalans love to stack themselves up in towers, especially during fiestas. For the past two centuries otherwise normal men and boys called *castellers* have climbed on each others' shoulders to the eerie music of the '*grolla*', the best groups, from Valls and El Vendrell, attain eight or nine tiers of bodies.

History

Catalunya has always been a round peg in a square empire; of all the medieval kingdoms that Ferdinand and Isabel wedded together, it had the most illustrious history. Tarragona was the capital of one of the three Roman provinces of Iberia, and Barcelona served as the first Visigothic capital in Spain in the 5th century. But the saga of its separate identity and language really began in 801 when Charlemagne's son Louis reconquered the northern part of 'Gothalanda' or Catalunya. In 874 the

Frankish king Charles the Bald granted independence to Count Wilfred 'the Hairy'. A marriage in 1137, between Count Ramón Berenguer IV and the heiress of Aragón, Queen Petronila, brought the Catalans the crown of Aragón, although each nation jealously retained its own parliaments and privileges, or *usatges*. These were the foundation of Catalunya's unique and extraordinary relationship between sovereign and citizen, manifest in the famous oath of allegiance to the king: 'We who are as good as you swear to you who are no better than we, to accept you as our king and sovereign lord, provided you observe all our liberties and laws; but if not, not.'

The Catalan Golden Age lasted from the 12th century, when the Reconquest of Catalunya was completed and the creative juices of the Catalans ignited in a remarkable burst of Romanesque and Gothic energy, to the 14th century, when Barcelona ruled an empire that included Sicily, Malta, Sardinia and most of modern Greece, not to mention Valencia, the Balearics and the modern French regions of the Cerdagne and Roussillon. Catalan merchants, who so often pop up in Boccaccio's *Decameron*, controlled Mediterranean trade and regulated it by the *Llibre del Consulat del Mar*, Europe's first maritime code, written under the great Jaume I in 1259.

Other nations soon adopted the Consulat, but by the 15th century Catalunya was running out of steam, devastated by plague, spectacular bank crashes, and the Genoese homing in on their Mediterranean markets. The Catalans hoped union with Castile would pump some much-needed vitality into the kingdom, although it soon turned out that subsequent heirs to the crowns of Castile and Aragón were more interested in squeezing all they could from Catalunya to finance their imperial ambitions. Especially grating was the codicil in Isabel's will prohibiting Catalan merchants from any dealings with the New World. For from the Castilians' point of view the Catalans were troublesome hotheads, always insisting on their *usatges* and shirking their share of the increasingly heavy national burden.

Catalan history is a chronicle of revolts and uprisings, both against Madrid and within Catalan society itself. In 1640 Catalunya cut itself loose from the Spanish fold

Català: the Language

Català, or Catalan, is its own proper language, spoken by more than six million people; the classic *faux pas* of the foreigner is to call it a dialect of Spanish. Catalan is a Romance language, closely related to Provençal or Occitan, the medieval languages of southern France. If you read French or Spanish, you'll be able to figure out many of the signs, but just try to understand *spoken* Català. Pronunciation is different from Spanish: the j's and g's are sounded as in French, x sounds like 'sh', ch is 'k' and ll is a pure 'y' (if not, the lls are separated, as in Paral.lel) and -ig at the end of a word is '-tch', as in *puig* (mountain), pronounced 'pootch'. You can usually warm a Catalan's heart by asking *'Com es diu això en català?'* ('How do you say it in Catalan?').

Although Catalunya is officially bilingual, you'll find street signs and shops signs exclusively in Català: here the most important words to know are *obert* (open) and *tancat* (closed), and the days of the week: *Dilluns* (Monday); *Dimarts* (Tuesday); *Dimecres* (Wednesday); *Dijous* (Thursday); *Divendres* (Friday); *Dissabte* (Saturday); *Diumenge* (Sunday).

and threw itself under the protection of France for 12 years. There it learned a lesson about the untrustworthy Bourbons that caused it later to support the claim of the Archduke Charles against Bourbon Philip V in the War of the Spanish Succession. It was a mistake, and hopeless once the English abandoned their cause and made peace with France. Barcelona fell in September 1714, and with it fell away all of Catalunya's privileges and autonomous government.

The Catalan Renaixença and Anarchism

Castilianization proceeded apace, especially among the upper classes who were busy making Catalunya Spain's leading industrial region. Then, in the 1830s, just as literary Catalan was in danger of sinking into oblivion, the Romantic movements of the day played midwife to the Catalan *Renaixença*, or Renaissance, a literary crusade led by such poets as Jacint Verdaguer (1843–1902) and Joan Maragall (1860–1911) who helped to bridge the Catalan of the troubadour poets with the everyday language of the people. Concurrent with the *Renaixença*, a fervent nationalist movement rose up that was embraced by all the parties of the political spectrum and influenced artists from Antoni Gaudí to Pau Casals. Just as Catalan culture began to revive, so did the workers. Catalan industrialists and the Church connived to squeeze factory workers to such a degree that Anarchist doctrines took root in the cities as they did nowhere else in the world. Bombings, riots and church-burnings rocked Catalunya in 1835, 1909 and throughout the 1920s. Barcelona was the most radical city in Europe, 'Anarchism's rose of fire'.

In 1931, as soon as Alfonso XIII had left the country, Catalunya declared itself an independent republic in the Federation of Iberia. Since no such thing existed, the nationalists renamed their government the Generalitat after medieval Catalunya's parliament. Towards the end of the Civil War Catalunya became the Republicans' chief stronghold and, when Valencia fell, Barcelona served as the government's last capital, a time brilliantly evoked in Orwell's *Homage to Catalonia* (1938). And when the war was over, rather than submit to Franco, thousands of Catalans fled over the border to France and Andorra.

Franco dissolved the last remnants of Catalan autonomy, prohibited the public use of Catalan, books in Catalan, and the Catalans' most joyful expression of national unity, a circle dance called the *sardana*. The denizens of Barcelona society put their suits and ties back on – a risky manoeuvre in the heyday of the Republic – and went back to business. Migrants from the south had been flocking to Barcelona's industrial jobs since the turn of the century, and Franco did nothing to discourage them, hoping a tidal wave of poor Andalucians would dilute Catalanism into a harmless eccentricity. In fact, the opposite has happened: second and third generation Andalucians have turned into ardent Catalans. Franco was still warm in his grave when Catalunya burst out of the starting block to recreate itself as a nation. The Generalitat was restored, and Catalan was revived with a vengeance. Yet, when they're not tearing up the place, common sense and clear headed pragmatism, what the Catalans call *seny*, is among their most exalted virtues. Instead of leaving Spain to form an independent Catalunya, modern Catalans are ready to coexist – on their own terms.

Barcelona

Barcelona, the treasure house of courtesy, the refuge of strangers... And although the adventures that befell me there occasioned me no great pleasure, but rather much grief, I bore them the better for having seen that city.

Cervantes, *Don Quixote*, Part II

And so are we all the better for having seen Barcelona, the capital of the Catalans, a city that goes about its business and pleasure with such ballistic intensity that you can't tell whether it's insanely serious or seriously insane or both. In 1975, three million Barcelonans danced in the streets like drunken banshees when they heard of Franco's death; the next day they rolled up their sleeves and channelled their crazed energy into making up for 40 stale, flat years. They've just about done it: modern Barcelona fizzes and sizzles like a bottle of Catalan *cava* spiked with a red pepper. With its superb legacy of *modernista* architecture, its business acumen and ambitious immigrants, its taste for the avant-garde and manic obsession with design, its position as the major publishing centre in both Spanish and Catalan, Barcelona is a little New York – and in many ways the only really successful modern city in old Europe. Nor is it shy about saying so. A compulsive exhibitionist, Barcelona held two great international fairs, in 1888 and 1929, and staged one hell of a show for the 1992 Olympics, bequeathing a festive spirit that colours its incredible edifice complex.

The Barri Gòtic

Barcelona is designed for walking, both through space and time, and there's no better starting point for a pedestrian time-traveller than the ancient heart of the city, the Barri Gòtic, enclosed between the 19th-century Vía Laietana and the curving C/Banys Nous. The Barri Gòtic's gentle hill, **Mons Tàber**, is Barcelona's 'acropolis', where the institutions of medieval Catalunya rose over the ruins of their ancient predecessors. The first of these predecessors was (some say) Hamilcar Barca, father of Hannibal, who founded a Carthaginian colony and named it *Barcino* after himself. The Romans, conquering in 133 BC, renamed it *Faventia Julia Augusta Paterna Barcino* by 15 BC – a mouthful that over the years became simply Barcelona. In the 4th century, the Romans enclosed their colony in lofty walls. They may have failed to keep out the Visigoths in 415, but for the next 1,000 years they held tight to Barcelona's heart. When the city gravitated towards the port in the 16th century, it left behind a time capsule on Mons Tàber. The best introduction to the Barri Gòtic (for map, *see* p.122) is Plaça Angel (***M** Jaume I*). Here the **Roman walls and towers** (some 46ft high) make cameo appearances in a mesh of medieval buildings, especially along C/Sotstinent Navarro; one mighty tower was discovered hidden in a building only in 1968.

The Home of the Count-Kings: Plaça del Rei

Heading into the Barri Gòtic, the first right from Plaça Angel will take you into Plaça del Rei, a handsome architectural ensemble that originally served as the enclosed

A Little Orientation

Barcelona is situated on a plain gently descending to the sea, wrapped in an amphitheatre of hills and mountains that keep its climate mild, protected from the north winds and tempered by the breeze off the Mediterranean. At the south end of the harbour rises its oldest landmark, a smooth-humped mountain called **Montjuïc**, once key to the city's defence and now its pleasure dome and Olympic 'ring'; on the landward side, the highest peak in the **Sierra de Collserola** is **Tibidabo**, with its amusements and priceless views.

Old Catalans may have bewailed their eclipse during the days of Imperial Spain, but moderns may be thankful that the lack of prosperity has left intact the historic centre or **Barri Gòtic**, the greatest concentration of medieval architecture in Europe. This is bounded on the southwest by **Las Ramblas**, Barcelona's showcase promenade; south of the Ramblas and north of Av. Paral.lel, the **Barri del Raval** remains the most piquant, with the remnants of the once notorious red light district, the **Barri Xinès**. The part of the map that looks as if it were stamped by a giant waffle iron is the **Eixample**, the 19th-century extension that quadrupled the size of Barcelona, and coincided with the careers of the *modernista* architects, whose colourful buildings brighten its monotonous chamfered blocks. Las Ramblas, Barri Gòtic and the Eixample meet at an enormous node called **Plaça de Catalunya**.

West of the Eixample the city has digested once independent towns like **Gràcia** and **Sarrià** and spread as far up the hills as gravity permits. Meanwhile, Barcelona has turned its attention to its long neglected seafront: just south of **Barceloneta**, a planned popular neighbourhood from the 18th century, the **Port Vell** (old port), has been transformed into an urban playground, while to the north of Barceloneta the **Vila Olímpica**, founded to house Olympic athletes, has become a swanky address. The rest of the city is hardly being ignored: the Ajuntament (town hall) has filled some 80 public spaces with art and fountains by artists from around the world, many of whom contributed designs for free. Keep your eyes open: you never know when you're going to run into a 15-foot bronze cat or inscrutable post-Modernist froufrou.

courtyard of the Romanesque-Gothic **Palau Reial Major**, home of the counts of Barcelona and later the kings of Aragón. The first residents were the twins, Ramón Berenguer II and Ramón Berenguer, who ruled alternately; the only way to tell them apart was that the first was surnamed the Towhead and the second the Fratricide (so you can guess what finally happened).

The first place to visit, however, is the **Museu d'Història de la Ciutat** (*Plaça del Rei, www.museuhistoria.bcn.es;* **M** *Jaume I; open Oct–June Tues–Sat 10–2 and 4–8, Sun and hols 10–2; July–Sept Tues–Sat 10–8, Sun and hols 10–2; closed Mon; adm; price includes 30 min virtual-reality tour in English*). Occupying a 15th-century Gothic palace, painstakingly moved here to close off the square, the museum offers a fascinating subterranean stroll through Roman and Visigothic *Barcino*, discovered by accident in the 1930s; the houses are directly beneath the modern C/de los Comtes and the 4th-century Paleochristian baptistry and font is directly under the cathedral. A fan-shaped stairway leads up to the Palau Reial and the wonderful **Saló de Tinell** ('Banquet Hall';

To Palau Reial de Pedralbes
To Finca Güell & Monestir de Pedralbes
AVINGUDA DIAGONAL
Maria Cristina
RONDA DEL GENERAL MITRE
VIA AUGUSTA
CARRER DE SANTALÓ
Camp Nou
CARRER DE BORI I FONTESTÀ
Les Corts
CARRER DE JOAN GÜELL
GRAN VIA DE CARLES III
AVINGUDA DIAGONAL
TRAVESSERA DE LES CORTS
PLAÇA DE FRANCESC MACIÀ
TRAVESSERA DE GRÀCIA
CARRER DEL MARQUÈS DE SENTMENAT
AVINGUDA DE MADRID
Plaça del Centre
AVINGUDA DE SARRIÀ
CARRER DEL COMTE D'URGELL
C. DE VILLARROEL
C. DE VILADOMAT
C. DE MUNTANER
AVINGUDA DE JOSEP TARRADELLAS
CARRER DE SANTS
Hospital Clínic
ESQUERRA DE L'EIXAMPLE
Entença
CARRER DEL ROSSELLÓ
CARRER DE BADAL
Mercat de Sants
Plaça de Sants
SANTS
Barcelona Sants
PLAÇA DELS PAÏSOS CATALANES
CARRER DE PROVENÇA
C. D'ANTONI DE CAPMANY
Mercat Nou
CARRER DE SANTS
Parc de l'Espanya Industrial
AVINGUDA DE ROMA
CARRER DE MALLORCA
CARRER DEL COMTE D'URGELL
Tarragona
CARRER DE TARRAGONA
CARRER DE VALÈNCIA
Hostafrancs
CARRER D'ARAGÓ
Parc de Joan Miró
CARRER DEL CONSELL DE CENT
C. DE LA CREU COBERTA
CARRER DE LA DIPUTACIÓ
Les Arenes
Espanya
Rocafort
Urgell
FGC Espanya
PLAÇA D'ESPANYA
GRAN VIA DE LES CORTS CATALANES
GRAN VIA DE LES CORTS CATALANES
CARRER DE SEPÚLVEDA
AVINGUDA DEL PARAL.LEL
PLAÇA DE L'UNIVERS
CARRER DE FLORIDABLANCA
RONDA DE SANT PAU
RONDA DE SAN ANTONI
Poble Espanyol
Font Màgica
Mercatd de Sant Antoni
Sant Antoni
C. DE LLEIDA
Poble Sec
C. SANT ANTONI ABAT
Jardi Botànic
EL RAVAL
Palau Nacional (MNAC)
Institut Nacional d'Educacio Fisica de Catalunya
Museu Etnològic
Museu Arqueològic
C. DE LA RIERETA
AVINGUDA DE L'ESTADI
Jardi d'Aclimatació
Teatre Grec
POBLE
AVINGUDA DEL PARAL.LEL
Paral.lel
Palau Sant Jordi
Palauet Albéniz
Fundació Joan Miró
Estadi Olímpic
AVINGUDA DE MIRAMAR
Funicular
C. NOU DE LA RAMBLA
SEC
PSG OLÍMPIC
MONTJUÏC
Telefèric
N
Parc del Migdia
Parc Atraccions Montjuïc
PLA. DE L'ARMADA
PLA. DE LA SARDANA
Cable Car
Castell de Montjuïc
Museu Militar
CTRA DE MIRAMAR
500 m
500 yards
PASSEIG DE JOSEP CARNER
PASSEIG DE JOSEP CARNER

Barcelona
Parc del Guinardó
Lesseps
Travessera de Dalt
Carrer de Sant Salvador
Carrer de Balcells
Ronda del Guinardó
Alfons X
Fontana
Carrer de l'Or
Carrer de l'Encarnació
Guinardó
FGC Gracia
Gràcia
Joanic
Mercat de la Llibertat
Hospital de la Santa Creu i de Sant Pau
Travessera de Gràcia
Carrer de Sant Antoni Maria Claret
Sagrada Familia
Carrer de la Indústria
Hospital Sant Pau
Avinguda de Gaudí
Plaça de Joan Carles I
Casa Comalat
Carrer de Còrsega
Avinguda Diagonal
Diagonal
L'Eixample
Museu de Música
La Pedrera
Carrer de Provença
Verdaguer
Casa Montaner
Casa Thomas
Carrer de Mallorca
Plaça de Mossèn Jacint Verdaguer
La Sagrada Família
Dreta de l'Eixample
Carrer de València
Encants
Fundació Tàpies
Carrer d'Aragó
Casa Batlló
Casa Amatller
Casa Lleo Morera
Passeig de Gràcia
Carrer del Consell de Cent
Girona
Carrer de la Diputació
Monumental
Plaça de les Glòries Catalanes
Universitat Central
Tetuan
Plaça de Tetuan
Gran Via de les Corts Catalanes
FGC Estació Glòries
Universitat
FGC Catalunya
Teatre Tivoli
Carrer de Casp
Teatre Nacional de Catalunya
Auditori
Ronda de la Universitat
El Triangle
Plaça de Catalunya
Plaça d'Urquinaona
Urquinaona
Carrer d'Ausiàs Marc
CCCB
MACBA
Catalunya
Barri Gotic
p.122
FGC Arc de Triomf
Arc de Triomf
Estacio d'Autobuses del Nord
Sant Pere de les Puelles
Marina
Carrer dels Almogàvers
Palau de Justicia
Carrer de Buenaventura Muñoz
Carrer de Pallars
Hospital Santa Creu
Santa Maria del Pi
Plaça d'Anton i Maura
Cathedral
Bogatell
Liceu
Passeig de Pujades
Sant Agustí
Jaume I
Museu Picasso
Museu de Zoologia
Plaça de Sant Jaume
Parc de la Ciutadella
Museu Textil
Mercat del Born
Museu de Geologia
Santa Maria del Mar
Parlament de Catalunya
Drassanes
Museu de Cera
Basilica de la Mercè
Estació de França
Parc Zoologic
Museu d'Art Modern
Av. del Marquès de l'Argentera
Barceloneta
Ciutadella Vila Olímpica
Vila Olímpica
Ronda del Litoral
Museu Maritim
Moll de la Fusta
Museu d'Historia de Catalunya
B10
Moll de les Drassanes
IMAX
Marina
Barceloneta
Estació Maritima
Maremagnum
Aquarium
Moll de la Barceloneta
Mercat Barceloneta
Parc de la Barceloneta
Port Olímpic
Moll d'Espanya
Cable Car
Passeig Maritim
Port Vell
Platja Barceloneta
World Trade Centre

Getting There

By Air

Barcelona's international airport is **El Prat de Llobregat**, 12km to the south. There are three terminals: **A** for international flights, **B** for domestic and some European flights, and **C** for shuttle flights between Spain's major cities.

There are **banks** in both terminals A and B (*open daily 7am–11pm for currency exchange, and Mon–Fri 8.30–2pm (one also Sat 8.30–1) for bank services*) and also a **post office** (*open Mon–Fri 8.30–2.30pm, Sat 9.30am–1pm*). Both terminals have **tourist offices**, **t** 934 78 47 04 (*open daily 9am–11pm*).

Useful Airport Telephone Numbers:

Customs: **t** 933 70 51 55
Flight information: **t** 932 98 38 28
Lost property: **t** 932 98 33 49
Police station: **t** 933 79 10 16

Airline Offices in Barcelona

Air France: **t** 933 79 74 63
British Airways: **t** 933 79 44 68
Delta: **t** 934 78 23 00
easyJet: **t** 902 29 99 92
Go: **t** 901 33 35 00
Iberia: **t** 902 40 05 00
KLM: **t** 933 79 54 58
TWA: **t** 932 15 81 88
Virgin Express: **t** 900 46 76 12

Getting to and from Aeroport del Prat

Trains link the airport to Plaça de Catalunya and Estació Sants (*6.08am–10.38pm, every 30 mins*). The **A1 Aerobús** connects both domestic and international terminals with Pla de Catalunya, Estació Sants and Pla d'Espanya (*Mon–Fri 5.30am–11.15pm every 15 mins; Sat and Sun 6am–11.20pm every 30 mins*).

By Sea

Barcelona's Estació Marítima is the main port for the Balearic islands. For information, contact **Trasmediterránea**, Estació Marítima de Balears, Moll de Barcelona, **t** 902 45 46 45, *www.trasmediterranea.es*. There is also a ferry three times a week to Genoa in Italy; contact **Agencia Maritima Condeminas**, Pso de Colon 11, 08002 Barcelona, **t** 902 40 12 00, **f** 934 42 40 66, *www.gnv.it*.

By Train

Estació Sants on the south side of town is Barcelona's main station, though many trains also stop at the RENFE stations linked to the more central **M** Passeig de Gràcia. The Estació de França on Av. Marquès de l'Argentera is now served only by a few suburban, intercity lines (Madrid, Valencia, Lleida, Zaragoza) and occasional international trains.

RENFE: **t** 902 24 02 02 (information): **t** 934 90 02 02; **t** 934 90 11 22 (international trains)

Ferrocarrils de la Generalitat de Catalunya (**FGC**) has lines passing through Barcelona to the suburbs and beyond, departing from under Pla de Catalunya (for Sant Cugat and Terrassa, at least one every hour) and from under the Pla d'Espanya (to Montserrat).

FGC: **t** 932 05 15 15.

Getting Around

General Transport Information: **t** 010

By Bus

Barcelona's public transport authority, **TMB**, is efficient, cheap and user-friendly. Its buses run until 11pm. The 14 main lines also have special after-hours '**Nitbuses**' (night, not lice), and at each stop their routes and timetables are clearly posted. The Nitbus costs a bit more; you can pay the fare on board. If you're using one of the day/multiple day passes listed below, remember to get it date-stamped in one of the machines behind the driver.

TMB: **t** 933 18 70 74
Bus information: **t** 932 65 65 08

By Metro (M)

The city also has five underground metro lines with Muzak pumped into the stations, and a sixth underground line operated by the FGC out of Plaça de Catalunya. As stylish as Barcelona is, its metro is not, but it is fast and cheap: trains run until 11pm, or 1am at weekends (€1 a ride).

Metro tickets can be purchased from the window or machines. Passes are available:

T-10: Ten single rides (€5.50). They're very convenient and can be shared.

T-50/30: Fifty single rides within 30 days of buying the pass (€22); can also be shared.

T-Mes: Monthly ticket allowing unlimited trips (€35). This one requires an identity card from the TMB or FGC offices (€1.25).

T-Dia: Unlimited travel for one person for one day (€4).

By Tram and Funicular

TMB also operates the **Tramvia Blau**, a pretty, refurbished old-fashioned streetcar, running from Pla Kennedy to Pla Dr Andreu (*€1.50 one way; running in summer daily 9am–9.35pm; in winter Sat and Sun only 9am–9.35pm*), and Barcelona's **funiculars**. One funicular runs from Pla Dr Andreu to Tibidabo (*€2.10 one way; running end Mar–April and end Sept–Oct Sat, Sun and hols 12–5; May Sat, Sun and hols 12–5 and Thurs 10–6; June Wed–Fri 10–6, Sat, Sun and hols 12–5; July and Aug Mon–Thurs, Sun and hols 12–10, Fri and Sat 12–1am; early Sept Mon–Thurs 12–8, Fri–Sun 12–10*). Another funicular goes from **M** Paral.lel to Montjuïc (*€1.30 one way*). From the latter, you can continue to the Castell de Montjuïc on the **Teleférico de Monjuïc** (*€1.35 one way; open June–mid-Sept Mon–Fri 11.15–8, Sat–Sun 11.15–9; mid-Sept–Oct daily 11.30–2.45 and 4–7.30; Nov–May Sat and Sun only*). Services grind to a halt on weekdays out of season; call TMB on **t** 934 43 08 59.

By Tourist Bus

TMB operates the Barcelona **Bus Turístic**, which has two loops, a red/north one and a blue/south one, taking in the best-known sights of the city. These buses run every 20–30 mins, allowing you to get off and on at will, on either route. A one-day ticket (buy it on the bus) is €12, two days (consecutive) €15, and children cost €10 a day (under-fours free). You get a number of discounts with the ticket (eg. the Poble Espanyol is half-price) that can make it excellent value (and you don't have to use the discount vouchers on the same day).

A bus service for serial shoppers, **TombBus**, plies between Pla de Catalunya and Pla Pius XII on Av. Diagonal (*Mon–Fri 7.30am–9.30pm, Sat and Sun 9.10am–9.20pm*); normal metro and bus passes are not valid on this service.

By Taxi

Taxis are ubiquitous and reasonable. If need be, call **t** 933 57 77 55/934 90 22 22/933 00 11 00; cabs with disabled access, **t** 933 58 11 11.

By Bicycle

Hire a bicycle from one of the following:

Un Cotxe Menys, C/Esparteria 3, **t** 932 68 21 05 (**M** Barceloneta). Arranges guided bike tours.

...al punt de la trobada, C/Badajoz 24, **t** 932 25 05 85 (**M** Barceloneta). They have tandems, too, in case you want to recreate Ramón Casas' famous painting in Els Quatre Gats.

Los Filicletos, Psg de Picasso 38, **t** 933 19 78 75 (**M** Barceloneta). Near the Ciutadella.

By Cable Car

Operates from Torre de Sebastià to Montjuïc, with one stop at the World Trade Centre, **t** 934 43 08 59 (**M** Barceloneta) (*open mid-June–mid-Sept daily 10.30–8; Mar–mid-June and also mid-Sept–mid-Oct daily 10.30–7; mid-Oct–Feb daily 10.30–5.30*). **Tickets** (to Montjuïc): €8.50 rtn, €4.25 one way.

By Balloon

Sway over the city at 492ft for 15 minutes; for information, **t** 934 23 18 00, **f** 934 23 26 49.

Hiring a Car

This is moderately cheaper than elsewhere in Europe, especially if you hire from a local Spanish-owned company. You may get a worthwhile discount with the big international firms if you book along with your flight or from your home country. To hire a car, you need to be at least 21 (some agencies require you to be 23 or 25) and to have held a licence for at least a year; you'll also need to have a credit card or be prepared to pay an enormous cash advance. You can save on parking fees by having the car delivered to your hotel when you're ready to use it.

Atesa/National, C/Muntaner 45, **t** 932 98 34 33; airport, **t** 932 98 34 34.

Avis, C/Casanova 209, **t** 932 09 95 33; C/Aragó 235, **t** 934 87 87 54.

Europcar, Pla Països Catalans, **t** 934 91 48 22, *www.europcar.com*.

Hertz, C/Tuset 10, **t** 932 17 32 48; airport, **t** 932 98 36 36; Estació-Sants, **t** 934 90 86 62.

Vanguard, C/Viladomat 297, **t** 934 39 38 80, *www.vanguardrent.com*.

Guided Tours

The **tourist office** organizes **walking tours** of the Barri Gòtic; they're very popular, so book early. Tours (in English) *Sat and Sun at 10am*; (in Catalan and Castilian) *Sat and Sun at noon* (€6/€3 for 4–12s).

The **Museu d'Història de la Ciutat** organizes a series of tours through the Barri Gòtic; for information call **t** 933 15 11 11 (*'Nit al Museu' tour: June–Sept Tues and Wed at 9pm; 'Ruta del Gòtic' tour: Sat 10am; tickets €6*).

Festivals

Barcelona takes its festivals seriously. Traditional events, especially the *festes majors*, are occasions for a very specialized battery of Catalan folklore and traditional music. In the daytime you'll find processions of *gegants* (tall figures of wood and papier-mâché) and *capogrossos* (demonically grinning 'fat heads', made of the same materials), and the daring construction of human towers by *castellers*. At night, the big event is the *correfoc*, or 'fire-running', when terrifying dragons spit fireworks into the crowds, chased by devils.

Tourist Ofices (*see* opposite) will have additional information and precise dates. The cultural information centre is the Palau de la Virreina on the Ramblas, **t** 933 01 77 75. Some of Barcelona's biggest dates are listed below:

Festa Major, *17 Jan*. Start of a week-long *festa major* in the Barri Sant Antoni.

Festival of Sant Jordi, *23 April*. Day of the Book and Rose (*see* p.125).

Corpus Christi, *late May*. Once the city's biggest festival, now reduced.

L'Ou com Balla, *early June*. Festival of the 'dancing egg', in fountains all around the Barri Gòtic.

Trobada Castellera, *June*. A grand meeting of Catalan *casteller* groups in Pla Sant Jaume.

Nit del Foc or 'Night of Fire', *23 June*. Perhaps the maddest night of all the year. Only a few small fires are tolerated in the city, but non-stop fireworks shake Barcelona throughout the night as everyone downs *cava* and sweet cakes called *cocas de Sant Joan*.

Festival del Grec, *late June–mid-Aug*. A programme of theatre, music and dance in the Teatre Grec and Mercat de les Flors.

Festa Major de Gràcia, *late Aug*. A giant party that draws thousands; there are wonderful street decorations. The *Festa Major de Sants* follows on its heels.

Diada, *11 Sept*. Catalan National Day, with flags, speeches and rallies.

Festa Major, *23 Sept*. A week-long *festa major*, dedicated to Nostra Senyora de la Mercè, all on a huge scale, and culminating in a frenzied *correfoc*.

Fira de Santa Llúcia, *8–24 Dec*. The Christmas market set out in front of the Cathedral, with *caganers*, the defecating figures traditionally shown around Catalan crib.

Tourist Information

Barcelona's tourist offices distribute some excellent detailed maps, transport maps, and a little booklet with useful telephone numbers and addresses called *See Barcelona*. There's an excellent **website**, *www.barcelona-turisme.com*, and a city site at *www.bcn.es*.

Plaça de Catalunya: underground on the Corte Inglés side of the Plaça, **t** 906 30 12 82 (*open daily 9–9*). Has an accommodation booking service (for the same night only, **t** 933 04 32 32), a bank, a gift shop and coin-operated Internet access.

Palau Robert: Psg de Gràcia 107, **t** 932 38 40 00, *www.gencat.es/probert* (*open Mon–Fri 10–7, Sat 10–2.30*). With information on all of Catalunya.

Estació Sants: (*open Oct–May Mon–Fri 8–8, Sat and Sun 8–2; June–Sept daily 8–8*).

Ajuntament: Pla Sant Jaume (*open Mon–Sat 10–8, Sun and hols 10–2*).

Airport: **t** 934 78 47 04/05 65 (*open Mon–Sat 9.30–8, Sun 9.30–3*).

Palau de la Virreina: Ramblas 99, **t** 933 01 77 75, and Palau Moja, Ramblas 7. Both specialize in city cultural information.

There are other **kiosks** open only in the summer in Pla de Catalunya, Psg de Gràcia, by the Sagrada Família, Vila Olímpica and Port Vell. In the summer, a team of '**Red Jackets**', based near the Sagrada Família and other tourist sites, gives on-the-spot information in several languages.

Other Addresses

American Express: C/Rosselló 259 (**M** Diagonal), **t** 932 17 00 70 (*open Mon–Fri 9.30–6, Sat 10–12*); La Rambla 74 (**M** Liceu), **t** 933 01 11 66 (*open April–Sept daily 9am–midnight; Oct–Mar Mon–Fri 9am–8.30pm,*

Sat 10–2 and 3–7). For travellers' cheque emergencies, call freephone **t** 900 99 44 26.

Post Office: Pla d'Antonio López, **t** 933 18 35 07 (*open Mon–Fri 8–10, Sat 8.30–10*).

Medical Emergencies: **t** 061; **fire brigade**: **t** 080; **ambulance**: **t** 932 98 38 38. Go to the nearest *hospital de la seguretat social*, which have 24-hour casualty (*urgències*) departments. Two of these are: **Clínic**, C/Villarroel 170 (**M** Hospital Clinic), **t** 932 27 54 00; and **Santa Creu i Sant Pau**, Av. Sant Antoni María Claret 167 (**M** Hospital de Sant Pau), **t** 932 91 90 00. 24hr ***farmacías*** are listed in local newspapers; alternatively, call **t** 010 or **t** 098.

Lost Property Office: in the Ajuntament on C/Ciutat 9 (**M** Jaume I), **t** 934 02 31 61 (*open Mon–Fri 9–2*).

Police: **t** 091/092; **Tourist police**: **t** 933 01 90 60.

Discount Tickets

The **Barcelona Card**, valid for 24 (€12), 48 (€15) and 72 hours (€18), offers discounts at shops, restaurants, and many major attractions but, best of all, it gives you unlimited use of the metro and bus. It is sold at tourist offices.

A route marked with red roses in the pavement passes Barcelona's foremost *modernista* buildings, and you can get a 50% discount on tickets to the main sights (Palau Güell, Museu d'Art Modern, Palau de la Música, Sagrada Família, La Pedrera, Fundació Antoni Tàpies, Museu de la Música, and Museu de Zoologia), available through the Caixa Catalunya's Tel-Entrada service or at the Centre de la Modernisme, in the lobby of Casa Amatller, Psg de Gràcia 41, **t** 934 88 01 39 (€15; includes a booklet covering these sights and more).

Shopping

Barcelona's new slogan is 'the city of shops'. It may be one of Spain's most expensive cities, but it is also her fashion and design capital. There are roughly three main shopping areas in Barcelona: the **Barri Gòtic** for trendy streetwear, second-hand clothes, interesting junk, and antiques; the centre of the **Eixample** (around Rambla de Catalunya and Psg de Gràcia) for good-quality clothes and jewellery; and **Sant Gervasi** (south of Gràcia and west of Av. Diagonal) for designer boutiques.

Serious shoppers hit Barcelona in January, when everything's on sale; look out for the word *rebaixes* (*rebajas* in Castilian).

Opening Hours: Most shops open Mon–Fri 10–2 and 4.30–8, Sat 10–2, and there are still a traditional few that close in August.

Where to Stay

Barcelona ✉ 08000

There are good places to stay all over the city, with cheaper choices clustered in and around the Barri Gòtic. Sentimental travellers should stay on the Ramblas, 'Barcelona's favourite hotel address for the past century, though exterior rooms may be noisy.

Wherever you stay, it's essential to book in advance: some hotels are fully booked months ahead. If you do arrive without a reservation, there are low-cost booking services in the airport, Estació Sants and at the city's main tourist office on Pla de Catalunya.

Price Categories

The categories listed here and in Madrid differ from those used in the rest of Spain. *See* **Practical A–Z**, 'Where to Stay', p.92, for a note on ranges used in Barcelona.

Luxury

*****__Arts Barcelona__, C/Marina 19–21, **t** 932 21 10 00, **f** 932 21 10 70, *www.ritzcarlton.com*; **M** Ciutadella-Vila Olímpica. Occupies one of the two Olympic towers of the Port Olímpic in a class by itself, offering stunning views of the sea and city and with a fantastic seaside pool. Reduced weekend rates. Parking.

*****__Claris__, C/de Pau Claris 150, Eixample, **t** 934 87 62 62, **f** 932 15 79 70; **M** Urquinaona. Gives luxury a twist, blending refined modern design with a connoisseur's collection of art treasures.

*****__Husa Palace__, Gran Vía de les Corts Catalanes 668, Eixample, **t** 933 18 52 00, **f** 933 18 01 48, *ritz@ritzbcn.com*, *www.ritzbcn.com*; **M** Passeig de Gràcia. Formerly known as the Ritz, this remains Barcelona's classic grand hotel, as it has been since 1919, offering luxury in every sense.

****__Le Meridien Barcelona__, Ramblas 111, **t** 933 18 62 00, **f** 933 18 77 76, *www.meridien-*

barcelona.com; **M** Catalunya or Liceu. Top of the line, imposing, pink, hyper-plush and used to coddling finicky opera and rock stars. A favourite with businessmen. All rooms have a/c and TV and there is parking.

Expensive

★★★★**Avenida Palace**, Gran Vía de les Corts Catalanes 605, **t** 933 01 96 00, **f** 933 18 12 34; **M** Passeig de Gràcia. A favourite older hotel. The rooms from the fourth floor upwards retain some of their older furnishings and offer the best views. It's at the lower end of this price category.

★★★★**Colón**, Av. de la Catedral 7, **t** 933 01 14 04, **f** 933 17 29 15, *info@hotelcolon.es, www.hotelcolon.es*; **M** Jaume I. The grandest hotel in the quarter, in a historic building with fine views of the cathedral. Parking.

★★★★**Condes de Barcelona**, Psg de Gràcia 73, **t** 934 84 22 00, **f** 934 88 06 14, *www.hotelcondesdebarcelona.com*; **M** Passeig de Gràcia. Elegantly designed from twin façades forming an old *modernista* palace; as stylish inside as out, with huge marble bathrooms. Pool, parking, TV and a/c.

★★★★**Majestic**, Psg de Gràcia 68, **t** 934 88 17 17, **f** 934 88 18 80, *reservas@hotelmajestic.es, www.hotelmajestic.es*; **M** Passeig de Gràcia. Three sumptuous buildings, recently knocked into one and dragged back from the 1970s to become one of the city's chicest establishments. There's a pool, parking and two **restaurants**.

★★★★**Regente**, Rambla de Catalunya 76, **t** 934 87 59 89, **f** 934 87 32 27; **M** Passeig de Gràcia. Behind a *modernista* façade, this has an air of stolid stateliness and lots of oak and gilt. Rooms are traditionally stylish, with fabulous views from the upper floors. There is an attractive, if small, rooftop pool with more astounding views and a bar.

★★★★**Rivoli Ramblas**, Rambla dels Estudis 128, **t** 933 02 66 43, **f** 933 17 20 38, *rivoli@alba.mssl.es*; **M** Catalunya. Stylish new Art Deco design throughout, a piano bar, a gym with sauna and Jacuzzi, and a rooftop terrace with great views. TV and a/c in all rooms.

Moderate

★★**Cuatro Naciones**, Ramblas 40, **t** 933 17 36 24, **f** 933 02 69 85, *h4n@h4n.com, www.h4n.com*; **M** Drassanes. Opened its doors at the beginning of the 19th century and for the next 100 years was Barcelona's best hotel; it's not so bad nowadays, either.

★★★**Gaudí**, C/Nou de la Rambla 12, **t** 933 17 90 32, **f** 934 12 26 36, *gaudi@hotelgaudi.es*, www. *hotelgaudi.es*; **M** Liceu. Despite its curly glass and a wrought-iron porch, and the crazy *trencadi* fountain, the newly renovated rooms are modern rather than *modernista*, but there are views of the great roof of the Palau Güell (*see* p.134). There's also a reasonable, if undistinguished, cafeteria. Parking available.

★★★**Gran Vía**, Gran Vía de les Corts Catalanes 642, **t** 933 18 19 00, **f** 933 18 99 97; **M** Passeig de Gràcia. This preserves a touch of 19th-century grace, from its courtyard to its lounge and the antique furnishings.

Marina Folch, C/del Mar, **t** 933 10 37 09, **f** 933 10 53 27; **M** Barceloneta. A charming choice, tucked in Barceloneta's web of streets; only 10 rooms, so be sure to book in advance.

★★**Mesón Castilla**, C/de Valldonzelia 5, **t** 933 18 21 82, **f** 934 12 40 20, *hmesoncastilla@teleline.es, www.hosa.es*; **M** Universitat. This is tucked down a quiet side street near the Museu d'Art Contemporani. It has a delightful interior garden, and spacious, air-conditioned bedrooms; parking.

★★★**Nouvel Hotel**, C/de Santa Anna 20, **t** 933 01 82 74, **f** 933 01 83 70, *www.hotelnouvel.com*; **M** Catalunya. Handy for the shopping district and the Ramblas in a sympathetically renovated *modernista* building with marble floors, gilt mirrors and carved wood. The staff are very friendly and rooms (with a/c) are prettily decorated with ornate tiled floors and large marble bathrooms.

★★★**Oriente**, Ramblas 45, **t** 933 02 25 58, **f** 934 12 38 19; **M** Liceu. A mouldering classic in one of the street's oldest buildings, from 1670. A former monastery, the cloister now gaily serves as the hotel ballroom. Come here for faded grandeur, but rooms overlooking the Ramblas can be noisy.

★★**Peninsular**, C/de Sant Pau 34–6, **t** 933 02 31 38, **f** 934 12 36 99; **M** Liceu. Also nestled in the shell of a convent, with rooms set along curved balconies overlooking a spacious, light-filled inner courtyard filled with flowers. It's good value and fills up quickly.

★★★**San Agustin**, Pla Sant Agustí 3, **t** 933 18 16 58, **f** 933 17 29 28, *hotelsa@hotelsa.com*, *www.hotelsa.com*; **M** Liceu. An elegant and peachy place on a leafy square. All rooms have a/c; try for an attic one with beamed ceilings and views of the old city.

★★★**Suizo**, Pla del Angel 12, **t** 933 10 61 08, **f** 933 10 40 81, *comercial@gargallo-hotels.com*, *www.gargallo-hotels.com*; **M** Jaume I. A relatively small hotel that offers a carefully cultivated 19th-century ambience and a pleasant bar. The nicest and quietest rooms overlook Baixada Llibreteria.

Inexpensive

★★**Barcelona House**, Escudellers 19, **t** 933 17 18 16; **M** Drassanes. Comfortable rooms with TV, and central. Best to reserve in advance as it fills up fast, mostly with young travellers.

Hs Eden, C/de Balmes 55, 1st and 2nd floors, **t/f** 934 52 66 20, *hostaleden@teleline.es*, *www.barcelona-on-line.es/hostaleden*; **M** Passeig de Gràcia. One of the area's pleasant budget surprises, up a staircase in an old Eixample building, with 25 spotless, whitewashed and endearingly eccentric rooms – some have whirlpools set behind beautiful sliding wooden doors, and some have patios. There is coin-operated Internet access. *Closed at Easter and Christmas.*

Las Flores, Ramblas 79, **t** 933 17 16 34; **M** Liceu. Up a narrow white staircase, a spotless *pensión* run by a kindly old couple. It has rooms with bath.

Hs Gat Raval, Joaquin Costa 44, **t** 934 81 66 70, *www.gataccommodation.com*; **M** Universitat. A lovely new *hostal*, perfect for the sophisticated traveller on a moderate budget. Knowledgeable staff are friendly and multilingual. Rooms are modern, clean and bright with fans for the hot months and TV. Free Internet access available for guests.

★★**Hs Jardí**, Pla de Sant Josep Oriol 1, **t** 933 01 59 00, **f** 933 18 36 64; **M** Liceu. Book well in advance. The most popular budget hotel in the area, with scrupulously clean rooms with a/c set around a central courtyard; the nicest overlook the tree-filled Plaça del Pi.

★★**Hs Oliva**, Psg de Gràcia 32, **t** 934 88 01 62; **M** Passeig de Gràcia. Large, airy rooms and great views, and is one of the cheapest in the street that Gaudí made famous.

Paseo de Gràcia, Psg de Gràcia 102, **t** 932 15 58 24, **f** 932 15 37 24; **M** Diagonal. Reasonable for this chi-chi district. Try to get a room on the eighth floor, some of which retain their old *modernista* fittings.

Cheap

P. Ambos Mundos, Pla Reial 10, **t** 933 18 79 70, **f** 934 12 23 63; **M** Liceu. Run by very friendly South Americans. All the prettily tiled rooms have en suite bathrooms.

Maldà, C/del Pi 5, **t** 933 17 30 02; **M** Liceu. Small and cheery, up the stairs in Barcelona's first shopping arcade; its sunny, quiet rooms (none en suite) are very good value.

La Terassa, C/Junta de Comerç 11, **t** 933 02 51 74, **f** 933 01 21 88; **M** Liceu. Run by the same people as the **Jardí**, but slightly less well equipped and cheaper as a result. Breakfast is on the pretty interior patio in summer.

Youth Hostels

Call ahead for these to ensure there's room.

Albergue Kabul, Pla Reial 17, **t** 933 18 51 90, **f** 933 01 40 34; **M** Liceu. A centrally located, privately run youth hostel, with rooms that house from two to 12 people.

Albergue Pere Tarrés, C/Numancia 149–51, **t** 934 10 23 09; **M** Les Corts. Closest if you arrive at Estació Sants. It also has a pretty roof terrace. IYHF cards are required.

Hostel de Joves, Psg de Pujades 29, **t** 933 00 31 04; **M** Arc de Triomf. Probably the nicest of the official IYHF hostels.

Eating Out

Restaurants

Restaurants open at about 8 or 8.30pm and stay open until midnightr. The range is vast: some serve the finest Catalan cuisine, while others feed the masses with more standard fare. Besides the native eateries are numerous restaurants from other regions of Spain and the world. As a rule, book ahead for the more expensive restaurants. These tend to close in August.

Price Categories

The categories listed here differ from those used in the rest of Spain in this guide. Here, prices are for a three-course meal without wine, per person. *See* **Practical A–Z**, 'Food and Drink', p.83, for price ranges in Barcelona.

Expensive

Agut d'Avignon, C/Trinitat 3, **t** 933 02 60 34; **M** Jaume I. Just off C/de Avinyó is one of Barcelona's swankiest restaurants: classic Catalan cuisine prepared with the freshest seasonal ingredients and some imaginative twists of their own. Try the excellent stuffed cabbage leaves or the wild boar with strawberry sauce. *Open daily 1–3.30 and 9–11.30.*

Antigua Casa Solé, C/Sant Carles 4, **t** 932 21 51 12; **M** Barceloneta. With its pretty blue and white tiles, wealth of flowers and astonishing range of seafood, this place has been popular since it opened well over a century ago; Barceloneta locals recommend it despite the multilingual menus. *Open Tues–Sat 1–4 and 8–11, Sun 1–4pm.*

Beltxenea, C/Mallorca 275, **t** 932 15 30 24; **M** Passeig de Gràcia/Diagonal. Charming and romantic, with some of Barcelona's best and most ambitious Basque cuisine served on a garden terrace. *Open Mon–Fri 1.30–3.30 and 8.30–11.30, Sat 8.30–midnight.*

Café de l'Acadèmia, C/Lledo 1, **t** 933 19 82 53; **M** Jaume I. In the summertime you can take in the enchanting Plaça Sant Just from shaded tables on the square; or, if you are with a larger group, from grand rooms on the second floor. The menu boasts over 50 dishes. The emphasis is Catalan, including their renowned *rossejat* (rice cooked in fish broth), but international flourishes also abound. *Open Mon–Fri 9–noon, 1.30–4 and 8.45–11.30; closed 2 weeks in Aug.*

Ca l'Isidre, C/de les Flors 12, **t** 934 41 11 39; **M** Paral.lel. In the music-hall district. This warm, intimate restaurant has long been a favourite of artists as well as King Juan Carlos, and serves lovely food based on the freshest ingredients, accompanied by a magnificent wine list. *Open Mon-Sat 1.30–4 and 8.30–11.30; closed 2 weeks in Aug.*

Can Ramonet, C/de la Maquinista 17, **t** 933 19 30 64; **M** Barceloneta. Set in the oldest tavern in the port (founded 1763) on the edge of a quiet square in Barceloneta, this restaurant serves excellent seafood dishes and a variety of tapas. Outdoor tables are available in the square or you can eat inside surrounded by dark woodwork and stone walls. The enormous barrels in the front contain the restaurant's speciality wine. *Open daily 10–4 and 8–midnight.*

Casa Calvet, C/de Casp 48, **t** 934 13 40 12; **M** Urquinaona. One of the most innovative restaurants, serving creative, imaginative Mediterranean dishes in a house designed by Gaudí. *Open 1.30–4 and 8.30–11.30; closed Sun and last 2 weeks of Aug.*

Els Quatre Gats, C/Montsió 3, **t** 933 02 41 40; **M** Catalunya. In the replica of the famous *modernista* taverna, with a smart, expensive restaurant specializing in upscale Catalan cuisine. Try the salt cod with figs and pine nuts. *Open Mon–Sat 9am–2am, Sun 5pm–2am; closed Sun and 3 weeks in Aug.*

Els Pescadors, Pla Prim 1, **t** 932 25 20 18; **M** Poblenou. Overlooking a peaceful square, this charming out-of-the-way establishments is one of Barcelona's best seafood restaurants. House specialties include the *fideuà* (paella made with noodles, not rice) and *arros negre* (seafood with rice cooked in squid ink). *Open daily 1–3.45 and 8–midnight.*

Espai Sucre, C/Princesa 53, **t** 932 68 16 30; **M** Jaume I. Although full meals are served, Espai Sucre is Barcelona's dessert destination. A cooking school by day, this elegant restaurant specializes in mouth-watering sweets. The romantic dining room is decorated in cream tones and fresh flowers abound. By reservation, there is seating in the back with an ingenious mirror that provides a view of the chefs and chefs-in-training hard at work. *Open Tues–Sat 9pm–11.30pm.*

Hoffman, C/de l'Argenteria 74–8 1°, **t** 933 19 58 89; **M** Jaume I. With a celebrated culinary school next door, offers creative *cordon bleu* dishes served with quiet aplomb in a series of cosy little plant-filled rooms on the first floor. Booking is essential. *Open Mon–Fri; closed Aug and Holy Week.*

Jaume de Provença, C/de Provença 88, **t** 934 30 00 29; **M** Hospital Clinic. Offers Catalan cuisine at its most elaborate – a typical dish is fillet of turbot with saffron lobster. *Open Tues–Sat 1–4 and 9–11.30, Sun 1–4.*

Jean-Luc Figueras, C/Santa Teresa 10, **t** 934 15 28 77; **M** Diagonal. The real deal. If you are going to treat yourself to one truly excellent meal during your stay consider this. Nothing about the food in this 19th century neo-classical palace now named for its artiste-chief is staid or pretentious. Some advice: do not deny yourself dessert. *Open Mon–Fri 1.30–3.30 and 8.30–11.30; Sat 8.30–11.30; closed 2 weeks in Aug.*

Passadís d'en Pep, Pla del Palau 2, **t** 933 10 10 21; **M** Barceloneta. Booking essential. Gourmet heaven, although it's hard to find (down a long unmarked corridor). The prices are fairly hefty but you don't even have to look at a menu: food is simply brought to you, including some of the city's finest seafood. *Open Mon–Sat 1.30–3.30 and 9–11.30.*

Semproniana, C/de Rosselló 148, **t** 934 53 18 20; **M** Hospital Clinic. Prices are a little on the high side for the quality of the food, but the décor does much to justify the price of admission. It's an old printworks: books and pamphlets used to spin through the presses where waiters now bustle with their bottles of wine. The bric-a-brac on the walls, salvaged as if from a hundred fleas markets, are like artifacts fallen from the pages of the mass-produced books, and left behind. *Open Mon–Sat 1.30–4 and 9–11.30.*

Set Portes, 14 Psg d'Isabel II, **t** 933 19 30 33; **M** Barceloneta. One of the city's most famous restaurants, founded in 1836 and now more popular than ever, serving delicious rice and seafood. *Open daily 1–1.*

Moderate

Agua, Psg Marítim de la Barceloneta 30, **t** 932 25 12 72; **M** Barceloneta. An elegant restaurant on the beach, serving very good meat, fish, pasta and rice dishes. *Open Mon–Thurs and Sun 1.30–4pm and 8.30–midnight, Fri and Sat 1.30–4pm and 8.30–1am.*

Agut, C/d'En Gignàs 16, **t** 933 15 17 09; **M** Jaume I. Warm and traditional. It has been serving up succulent Catalan specialities since 1924. *Open 1.30–4 and 9–midnight; closed Aug.*

Ateneu, Pla de Sant Miquel 2, **t** 933 02 11 98, *www.ateneu.com*; **M** Jaume I. This has an adjoining cigar bar, and serves delicious and creative seasonal Catalan cuisine in graceful, romantic surroundings, with contemporary art on the walls. It draws a mixed, animated crowd of artists, politicians and intellectuals. The lunch *menú del día* is superb value. *Open 1–3 and 8–11.30; closed Sun and first 3 weeks of Aug.*

Brasserie Flo, C/de les Jonqueres 10, **t** 933 19 31 02; **M** Urquinaona. Not far from the Palau de la Música Catalana, has an elegant mix of *modernista* and modern décor. The cuisine is French and Catalan with a fabulous array of desserts. *Open daily 1–4 and 8.30–12.45.*

Can Culleretes, C/d'En Quintana 5, **t** 933 17 31 22; **M** Liceu. Book for Sun lunch. Tucked in a little side street off C/de la Boqueria is the city's oldest restaurant. It's friendly and very popular, with photos of local celebrities lining the walls. They serve big platefuls of good-value traditional Catalan dishes. *Open Tues–Sat 1.30–4 and 9–11, Sun 1.30–4.*

Cangrejo Loco, Moll Gregal 29–30, Port Olímpic, **t** 932 21 05 33; **M** Ciutadella-Vila Olímpica. One among the plethora of fish restaurants in the Port Olímpic. This one has excellent seafood and service, and during the summer months has outdoor tableswith fine views of the sea. *Open daily 1–1.*

Can Ros, C/Almirall Aixada 7, **t** 932 21 45 79; **M** Barceloneta. One of the best places for seafood in Barceloneta. While waiting for a main course of *paella* or *arrós negre*, sample some of the fresh seafood hors d'œuvre, or steamed mussels and clams in tomato sauce. *Open Thurs–Tues 1–5 and 8–12.*

El Convent, C/Jerusalem 3, **t** 933 17 10 52; **M** Liceu. This spot has been popular a long while (formerly as Egipte), and word of mouth has conjured a critical mass of the curious and hungry. There is good reason for the hoopla. The food is fresh, with produce culled directly from the adjacent Boqueria market, and expertly prepared. Despite the crowds, the antiqueness and authenticity of the place come through. Best during off-peak hours. *Open 1–4 and 8.30–11.*

Euskal Etxea, Plaçeta de Montcada, **t** 933 10 21 85; **M** Jaume I. Serves up the best Basque food in Barcelona and also does excellent regional tapas (*see* Tapas section below for bar opening hours). *Open Tues–Sat 1–3.30 and 9–11.30; closed Aug.*

El Gran Café, C/de Avinyó 9, **t** 933 18 79 86; **M** Liceu. A grand, old, galleried *modernista* restaurant with dark wooden panelling, elaborate light fittings, chandeliers and long-aproned waiters. The food is deliciously Catalan and the prices extremely reasonable. The service is attentive and excellent. *Open Mon–Sat 1–4 and 9–11.30.*

Habana Vieja, C/Banys Vells 2, **t** 932 68 25 04; **M** Jaume I. Barcelona's only Cuban restaurant is run by a Cuban expat serious about serving the real thing. The diners crowd in to try *mojitos* and traditional Cuban dishes such as *ropa vieja* (shredded beef) served with *arroz congri* (rice with black beans), and fried sweet bananas. The selection is slim for non-meat eaters. *Open Mon–Thurs and Sun 10–4 and 8–midnight; Fri, Sat 10–4 and 8–1.*

La Llotja, Museu Marítim, Av. de les Drassanes, **t** 933 02 64 02; **M** Drassanes. Located in the vast, vaulted 13th-century shipyards. The restaurant is run by a local food critic, who serves very fine Catalan food, including a medieval dish of saffron and chicken to match its setting. *Open Mon–Fri 8–8, Sat–Sun lunch from 2pm and dinner 9–11pm.*

Mamacafé, C/Doctor Dou 10, **t** 933 01 29 40; **M** Catalunya. The name says it all: buxom, booming and welcoming. A terrific variety of dishes with lively music. *Open Mon 9–5, Tues–Fri 9am–1am, Sat 1–1.*

Nou Celler, C/de Princesa 16, **t** 933 10 47 73; **M** Jaume I. Homey old-world artefacts hang from the ceiling and walls lending a warm atmosphere to this busy restaurant. Nou Celler's versions of classic Catalan dishes are so popular that it is difficult to get a seat without a reservation. *Open Sun–Fri 8am–midnight, closed 15 June–15 July.*

L'Olivé, C/Balmes 47, **t** 934 52 19 90; **M** Universitat. A very popular place serving traditional Catalan food, with the emphasis on fish and fresh market ingredients. Try the *fricandó*, a meat and veg stew. *Open 1–4 and 8.30–midnight; closed Sun eve.*

Plaça, C/de Bellafila 5, **t** 934 12 65 52; **M** Jaume I. Tucked down a side street behind the Ajuntament; this is delightful, small and chic. It serves excellent and very creative Catalan cuisine. *Open from 2.30pm; dinner Sun–Thurs 9pm–midnight, Fri– Sat 9pm–1am.*

Salero, C/del Rec 60, **t** 933 19 80 22; **M** Jaume I. This is one of the most fashionable haunts of the Born-district: a beautiful, cool white space serving an imaginative fusion of Mediterranean and Oriental cuisine at lunchtime. *Open Tues–Thurs 1–4 and 9–midnight, Fri and Sat 1–4 and 9–1, Sun 1–4.*

El Salón, C/Hostal del Sol 6, **t** 933 15 21 59; **M** Barceloneta. Just behind the Correus, this place has a lovely, slightly louche Baroque atmosphere, with guttering candles and plush red velvet sofas. The food is rich and excellent with great desserts and bar cocktails. *Open 1.30–5 and 8.30–midnight.*

Senyor Parellada, C/de l'Argenteria 37, **t** 933 10 50 94; **M** Jaume I. Booking essential. Where you can dine on *estofats*, *manitas de cerdo*, fish platters and old-fashioned recipes in a magnificent 18th-century building. *Open Mon–Sat 1–3.30 and 9–11.30.*

Silenus, C/dels Àngels 8, **t** 933 02 26 80; **M** Catalunya. Near the Museu d'Art Contemporani, serves excellent international and Catalan food in a charming, relaxed setting with contemporary art on the walls. Long, light and pretty, with comfortable sofas, it is also a good place to relax over coffee, mornings or afternoons. *Open Mon 1–4pm, Tues–Sat 1–4 and 9–11.30.*

La Targa Florio, C/de Villarroel 190, **t** 934 30 72 79; **M** Hospital Clinic. Filled with heaving crowds, lending weight to the claim that it's the finest Italian restaurant in Spain. *Open 1–4 and 8.30–midnight.*

La Veronica, C/de Avinyó 30, **t** 934 12 11 22; **M** Jaume I. Sleek and new. It's where bright young things chatter over excellent pizzas and Mediterranean dishes; the décor is ultra-modern with tomato-red and white walls and a fabulous sheet of wall lights. *Open Mon–Sat 1pm–2am.*

Inexpensive

Compostela, C/de Ferran 30; **M** Jaume I. Draws crowds for its popular Galician specialities such as *pulpo* and *tetilla* cheese, for a meal or just tapas. *Open Wed–Mon 9am–noon, 1–4 and 8–11.*

L'Hostal de Rita, C/d'Aragó 279, **t** 934 87 23 76; **M** Passeig de Gràcia. Always busy and has long queues, but it's worth it for the hefty portions of Catalan cooking. It's run by the same folks as Les Quinze Nits in Pla Reial. *Open daily 1–3.30 and 8.30–11.30.*

Mesón David, C/de les Carretes 63, **t** 934 41 59 34; **M** Sant Antoni. Authentic Gallego cuisine, with hearty portions at reasonable prices. *Open Mon, Tues, Thurs–Sun 1–4 and 8–midnight; closed Wed and Aug.*

Mesón Jesús, Cecs de la Boquería 4, **t** 933 17 46 98; **M** Liceu. On a street between C/de la Boqueria and Plaça de Sant J. Oriol is an enshrined favourite for good, cheap Catalan fare in a cosy, traditional setting. *Open Mon–Fri 1–4 and 8–11, Sat 1–4; closed Aug.*

Oolong, C/Gignás 25, **t** 933 15 12 59; **M** Jaume 1. With its imaginative blend of Asian and Spanish flavours, cool décor, and steady stream of hip sounds, this mostly vegetarian eatery caters to the groovy. (Oolong, by the way is a type of Chinese tea.) *Open Mon–Sat 8.30am–2.30am, Sun 6pm–2am.*

Plaça dels Angels, C/Ferlandia 23 (opposite MACBA), **t** 934 43 31 03; **M** Universitat. With brightly painted, art-adorned walls and a strange rock garden out the back, this delightful restaurant feels like an extension of the close-by MACBA. Like the décor, the food presentation is imaginative and lively. *Open 1–3 and 8.30–12.30.*

Rodrigo, C/de l'Argenteria 67, **t** 933 10 30 20; **M** Jaume I. Near the Santa María del Mar, offering excellent home cooking at very reasonable prices. Though full meals are served only at lunchtime, a wide selection of sandwiches is available at night. *Open Fri–Tues 1–4 and 8.30–12, Wed 1–4.*

Restaurante Romesco, C/de Sant Pau 28, **t** 933 18 93 81; **M** Liceu. A classic budget favourite just off the Ramblas: noisy and cheerful serving heaped platefuls of fried rice and beans to young foreigners. *Open Mon–Sat 1pm–midnight; closed Aug.*

Sandwich and Friends, Psg del Born 27, **t** 933 10 07 86; **M** Jaume I. This is great for a quick lunch. There are no fewer than 75 kinds of *bocadillos* served up in a modern, colourful café-gallery. *Open Mon–Sat 12.30pm–1.30am.*

Solkai, C/del Palau 5, **t** 933 17 90 94; **M** Jaume I. A sleek, minimalist café with an excellent salad buffet at lunchtimes. *Open Mon–Fri 1–4 and 9–midnight, Sat 1–4 and 9–1.*

Venus, C/de Avinyó 25, **t** 933 01 15 85; **M** Jaume I. A simple, arty café and delicatessen, with a good range of vegetarian dishes and delicious pastries. *Open Mon–Sat 12–12.*

Zoo, C/Escudellers 33, **t** 933 02 77 28; **M** Liceu. Popular and cute, animals set the theme; they line the walls, and the toasted sandwiches that dominate the menu are all named after zoo characters. Not that the portions are kid-sized. *Open daily 6pm–2am, Fri and Sat 6pm–2.30am.*

Vegetarian Restaurants

Barcelona has a surprisingly good range of these. More and more restaurants offer veggie options, and falafels are springing up all over.

Biocenter, C/del Pinto Fortuny 25, Raval, **t** 933 01 45 83; **M** Liceu (*inexpensive*). Has a generous salad bar and various hot dishes to choose from. *Open Mon–Sat 9am–11pm.*

La Buena Tierra, C/de l'Encarnacio 56, Gràcia, **t** 932 19 82 13; **M** Joanic (*moderate*). Cosy, with deliciously imaginative specialities and a garden. *Open Mon and Sun 1.30–4pm, Tues–Sat 1.30–4 and 8.30–12.*

La Flauta Magica, C/de Banys Vells 18, Ribera, **t** 932 68 49 64; **M** Jaume I (*moderate*). One of Barcelona's nicest and most imaginative vegetarian spots, with some organic meat dishes. The atmosphere is young and stylish, the décor a funky blend of peach and violet lit with candles, and the service friendly and welcoming. *Open 9pm–midnight.*

L'Hortet, C/Pintor Fortuny 32, **t** 933 17 61 89; **M** Catalunya. A friendly, 'good-for-lunch' sort of place. Wholly veggie with good juices, and inexpensive set menus. *Open Mon–Thurs and Sun 1.15–4, Fri and Sat 1.15–4 and 9–11.*

Cafés and Tapas

Although there are places that specialize in coffee or cocktails or tapas, most serve all three, along with a selection of sandwiches (*bocadillos*). Tapas are not as essential to the local eating habits as in Madrid, but are usually regarded as warm-ups to the main event. If you're a big fan, however, there is a handful of places, usually Basque or Gallego, that specialize in delicious titbits that can take the place of a light meal.

Coffee drinkers will find their brew everywhere, but tea drinkers may have cause to despair. Traditional breakfast coffee with milk (*café amb llet*) comes in a cup big enough for dunking. If you order a plain *cafè*, you'll get an espresso; for a lashing of milk in it, ask for a *tallat*. If you prefer your coffee more diluted, ask for a *cafè americano*.

Many cafés are linked to cake shops, to cater to the Catalan sweet tooth. *Granjas*, or dairy bars, are an old Catalan institution, favourite places to indulge in a late-afternoon pick-me-up of pastries, curd cheese with honey, *crema catalana*, milkshakes and rich hot chocolate with cream (*suizo*). *Orxaterias/horchaterias* are tiger milk bars, specializing in *orxata* (*horchata* in Castilian), a pale refreshing drink made of crushed tiger nuts.

Cafés

Bauma, C/de Roger de Llúria 124, **t** 934 59 05 66; **M** Verdaguer/Diagonal. A laid-back, welcoming café which attracts the local artists. *Open Mon–Thurs 8am–11pm, Fri–Sat 8am–midnight; closed Aug.*

La Cerería, Baixada de Sant Miquel 3–5, **t** 933 01 85 10; **M** Liceu. Near Pla de Sant Miquel, serving a wonderful range of delicious cakes, pastries and chocolates in its teashop with a tiny terrace.

El Tío Che, Rambla del Poblenou 44–6, **t** 933 09 18 72; **M** Poblenou. Taste *xorchata*, or have a chilled, sugary *granizado* in this famous old *horchateria* in a *modernista* building. *Open Oct–May Mon, Tues, Thurs–Sun, 9–2 and 5–9; closed Wed in winter. May–mid-Sept Mon–Thurs 9am–1am, Fri–Sat 9am–3am.*

Els Tres Tombs, Ronda de Sant Antoni 2, **t** 934 43 41 11; **M** Sant Antoni. A great place to sit outside and watch the world buzz by – what everyone else seems to be doing. It opens at 6am for early birds and night owls staggering from the clubs. *Open daily 6am–1am.*

Granja Dulcinea, C/de Petritxol 2, **t** 933 02 68 24; **M** Liceu. A classic for atmosphere and frothy, sweet dairy delights. *Open daily 9–1 and 5–9; closed Aug.*

Granja Viader, C/d'En Xuclà 4 (near Eglésia de Betlem), **t** 933 18 34 86; **M** Liceu. Going since 1870, this serves luscious milkshakes, hot chocolate, *crema catalana*, *ensaïmades* and curd cheese with honey. *Open Mon 5–8.45pm, Tues–Sat 9–1.45 and 5–8.45.*

Café de l'Hivernacle, Parc de la Ciutadella, **t** 933 10 22 91; **M** Barceloneta. An elegant, light-filled and relaxing café with wicker and palms, near the Museu de Zoologia.

Bar Kasparov, Pla Vicenç Matorell 4, **t** 933 02 20 72; **M** Liceu or Catalunya. This charming café in the Raval is perfect any time of day for a light meal, coffee or drink. *Open winter 9am–10pm, summer 9am–midnight.*

Laie Llibreria Café, C/de Pau Claris 85, **t** 933 02 73 10; **M** Passeig de Gràcia. Barcelona's original and best bookshop-café, with a wonderful interior terrace. *Café open Mon–Fri 9am–1am, Sat 10am–1am; bookshop open Mon–Sat 10.30am–9pm; closed Sun.*

Mesón de Café, C/Llibreteria 16, **t** 933 15 07 54; **M** Jaume I. A classic and is widely reputed to serve the best cup of java in Barcelona. *Open Mon–Sat 7am–11pm; closed Sun.*

Mora, Av. Diagonal 409, **t** 934 16 07 26; **M** Diagonal. Barcelona's most famous cake shop and one of its chicest establishments, a place to linger over a late breakfast and the papers. It also has a restaurant serving inexpensive meals. *Open daily 7.30am–9pm.*

Café de la Opera, Ramblas 74, **t** 933 02 41 89; **M** Liceu. An institution, this is the classiest place on the Ramblas, founded in 1929 opposite Teatre del Liceu. Art Deco opera heroines etched in the mirrors watch clients watch the passing parade from the four corners of the earth. *Open daily 8.30am–2am.*

Café Torino, Psg de Gràcia 59, **t** 934 87 75 71; **M** Passeig de Gràcia. One of the city's most elegant cafés, with a fine selection of pastries and cakes. *Open Mon–Thurs and Sun 8am–11pm, Fri–Sat 9am–1.30am.*

Xocoa, C/de Petritxol 11, **t** 933 01 11 97, *www.xocoa.com*; **M** Liceu. A coffee shop and pâtisserie, serving rich, melt-in-the-mouth chocolate truffle cakes. *Open 7am–9pm.*

Café Zurich, Pla de Catalunya 1, **t** 933 17 91 53; **M** Catalunya. Not the original much-loved Zurich but a shinier clone installed in the same spot in the new Triangle mall, with strategically placed tables. *Open Mon–Fri 8am–1am, Sat 10am–1am, Sun 10am–11pm.*

Tapas Bars

Ambos Mundos, Pla Reial 10, **t** 933 17 01 66; **M** Liceu. Located on the charming Pla Reial, this is a bit touristy but a great people-watch spot. *Open Wed–Mon 9.30am–2am.*

Bar Bodega Fortuny, C/Pintor Fortuny 31, **t** 933 17 98 92; **M** Catalunya. A favourite hang-out for local artists, this feels halfway between a diner and a bar. The décor is well worn but funky and cheerful. *Open Tues–Sun 10am–midnight.*

Bodega La Tinaja, C/Espartería 9, **t** 933 10 22 50; **M** Barceloneta/Jaume I. With dim corners, antique furnishing, candle-lit tables and a fantastic selection of wines, La Tinaja is one of the most romantic spots in the city for tapas. *Open daily 6pm–2am.*

La Bodegueta, Rambla de Catalunya 98, **t** 932 15 48 94; **M** Passeig de Gràcia. Join the rest of Barcelona in the cellar for *cava* and excellent wines, with *pa amb tomàquet* and other snacks to soak it up. *Open daily 7am–1.30am; closed Aug mornings.*

Cal Marques, Psg Joan de Borbo 66, **t** 932 21 56 48; **M** Barceloneta. An exception to the tourist traps that line Psg Joan de Borbo but takes advantage of harbour views to over-price its food. *Open Tues–Sat 11–11, Sun 11–3.*

Cal Pep, Pla de les Olles, **t** 933 10 79 61; **M** Barceloneta. *The* place for excellent grilled fish and seafood, run by the charismatic owner of the pricier Passadis del Pep. There's a restaurant (*expensive*) but most people line up at the bar for the excellent tapas. *Open Mon 8pm–12, Tues–Sat 1–4.30 and 8–12.*

Celta la Pulpería, C/de la Mercè 16, **t** 933 15 00 06; **M** Drassanes. Serves great Gallego seafood tapas; an essential stop along a Mercè bar crawl. *Open Mon–Sat 10am–1am, Sun 10am–midnight.*

El Petit Miau, Moll d'Espanya (Maremagnum), **t** 932 25 81 10; **M** Drassanes. In Art-Deco style, this restaurant on the first floor of the Maremagnum complex has something for everyone: tapas bar, beer hall and restaurant rolled into one. *Open daily 11am–1am.*

Estrella de Plata, Pla del Palau 9, **t** 933 19 60 07; **M** Barceloneta. A long-established port bar now serving gourmet (pricey) tapas, some of which you'll find nowhere else in town. *Open Mon–Sat 11–4 and 8–12.*

Euskal Etxea, Plaçeta de Montcada, **t** 933 10 21 85; **M** Jaume I. Excellent regional tapas (*see* also Restaurant above). *Bar open Tues–Sat 9.30am–11.30pm, Sun 12.45–3.30.*

Irati, C/del Cardenal Casanyes 17; **M** Liceu. Great for exquisite, reasonably priced Basque tapas, *pinchos* and *txacoli* wine. *Food served Tues–Sun 12–12.*

Les Gens Que L'Aime Pub, C/Valencia 286, **t** 932 15 68 79; **M** Passeig de Gràcia. Romantic and dimly lit, decked in red velvet and wood, this tapas bar is worth a visit if only for the atmosphere. *Open Mon–Thurs 6pm–2.30am, Fri and Sat 7pm–3am, Sun 7pm–2.30am.*

Mesón de León, C/de la Barra de Ferro (just off C/de Montcada); **M** Jaume I. Garlic and peppers abound in this small tapas bar. *Open Tues–Sun noon–3 and 8–midnight.*

La Pineda, C/del Pi 16; **M** Liceu. A delightful, old-fashioned delicatessen hung with hams, trotters and the like – vegetarians may wish stay away Try the cured meats, then pay at the ancient till. *Open daily 9–3 and 5–10.*

Bodega la Plata, C/de la Mercè 28, **t** 933 15 10 09; **M** Drassanes or Jaume I. A very popular and characterful neighbourhood bar. Open to the street, it's a key stop for wine and tapas. *Open daily 10–4 and 8–11.*

Qu Qu, Psg de Gràcia 24, **t** 933 17 45 12; **M** Passeig de Gràcia. Though one in a chain of tapas restaurants marketed to tourists, Qu Qu serves surprisingly creative tapas and sandwiches for decent prices. *Open daily 8.30am–1am.*

Quimet & Quimet, C/Poeta Cabañas 25, **t** 934 42 31 42; **M** Paral.lel. From the Raval, cross over Paral.lel to find this delightful wine and tapas bar. Built around 1900, this tavern is run by the fifth generation of Quimets who have preserved the atmosphere and still serve a wide selection of high-quality tapas. *Open Tues–Sat noon–4 and 7–10.30, Sun noon–4; closed Aug.*

Café de la Ribera, C/Consolat de Mar 6, **t** 933 19 50 72; **M** Jaume I. Situated on a lovely quiet square and serving reasonably priced tapas all day. *Open Mon–Sat 8.30am–1am.*

Santa María, C/Comerç 17, **t** 933 15 12 27; **M** Barceloneta/Jaume I. About as sophisticated as a tapas bar comes; its excellent wine list, unusual tapas and décor, fusing old-world comfort with elegant modern details, make it worth the rather high prices. *Open Tues–Sat 1.30–3.30 and 8.30–12.30.*

La Soccarena, C/de la Mercè 21, no phone; **M** Drassanes or Jaume I. Popular Asturian bar with tapas of goats' cheese and cured meat. Asturian cider is poured in the traditional way: over the back of the waiter's head. *Open 1.30–3 and 6pm–3am.*

Taberna del Prior, C/Ample 18, **t** 932 68 74 27; **M** Drassanes. Has a wide range of hams suspended from the ceilings, *cava* and tapas. Try the succulent grilled cuttlefish. They also do reasonably priced sandwiches at lunchtime. *Open 11am–2am; closed Tues.*

Txirimiri, C/Princesa 11, **t** 933 10 18 05; **M** Jaume I. Another Basque tapas bar, serving *pintxos*: bite-sized slices of bread with delicious toppings, usually seafood or sausage. One of the originals, *Txirimiri* is extremely popular. *Pintxos* are put out at 11.30am– 3.30pm and 7pm–11pm. *Open daily 11.30am–1am.*

La Vinateria del Call, C/de Sant Domènec del Call 9, **t** 933 02 60 92; **M** Liceu. The place for some of the best wines and freshest tapas in the city. Sit at one of the old wooden tables and select from the menu – if you're at a loss, the friendly staff are more than happy to advise on what to pick. *Open 6pm–1am; closed Sun.*

Restaurants Outside the Centre

Expensive

Asador de Aranda, Av. Tibidabo 31, Tibidabo, **t** 934 17 01 15; **FGC** Avinguda Tibidabo. Serves Castilian cusine, specializing in roast lamb, served with home-made bread in a beautiful *modernista* setting. *Open Mon–Sat lunch and dinner, Sun lunch.*

Bilbao, C/de Peril 33, Gràcia, **t** 934 58 96 24; **M** Diagonal. Bilbao specializes in seasonal dishes using the freshest ingredients from the region. The food is simple yet excellent and beautifully presented. This restaurant is something of a dining landmark in Gràcia and as such its popularity led to a recent addition in the back. Try to get a table in the front for the best atmosphere. *Open Mon–Sat 1–4 and 9–11.*

Gaig, Psg Maragall 402, Horta, **t** 934 29 10 17; **M** Horta. Old and famous, having been under the culinary care of the Gaig family for four generations. Meals served are of a refined Catalan variety, with such delicacies as *arròs de colomí amb ceps* (pigeon in rice with wild mushrooms). The wine cellar is out of this world. *Open 1.30–4 and 9–11pm.*

Neichel, Av. de Pedralbes 16, Pedralbes, **t** 932 43 84 08; **M** María Cristina. Has an elegant modern dining room, the perfect stage for some of the most creative and refined cuisine in Spain, prepared by French chef Jean-Louis Neichel. The magnificent cheese and pastry chariots that round off the meal are legendary. *Open 1–3.30 and 8.30–11.*

El Raco d'en Freixa, C/de Sant Elíes 22, Gràcia, **t** 932 09 75 59; **FGC** Muntaner. Named after Chef Ramó Freixa, one of Barcelona's new culinary stars, this designer restaurant offers surprising reinterpretations of classics. *Open Tues–Sat 1–4 and 9–11.30, Sun 1–4; closed Aug.*

Tram Tram, C/Major de Sarrià 121, Tibidabo, **t** 932 04 85 18; **FGC** Reina Elisenda. Set in a old farmhouse just up Sarrià, and well worth the trip. It is one of Barcelona's most imaginative restaurants, regularly putting a modern spin on classic dishes. *Open Mon–Sat 1–4 and 8.30–11, Sun 8.30–11.*

Moderate

Friends, Deu i Mata 125, Camp Nou, **t** 934 39 35 56; **M** Les Corts. Reservations advisable. Eva, the warm owner, makes you feel right at home in this welcoming place. Sample from the menu of home-style dishes or ask Eva for a recommendation. *Open Mon–Sat 1pm–1am; closed first 2 weeks of Aug.*

Manolete, C/Laforja 132, Gràcia, **t** 930 0 20 70; **FGC** Muntaner. A romantic little spot if you want to splash out a bit for lunch. It also has an excellent wine çellar. *Open Mon–Fri 1–4 and 9–11.30, Sat 1–4; closed Sun and Aug.*

La Troballa, C/de la Riera de Sant Miquel 69, Gràcia; **FGC** Gràcia. A tiny, quietly stylish establishment with whitewashed walls and wooden floors, serving traditional Catalan dishes such as *magret* of duck with apple, and rabbit paté with caramelized onions.

Inexpensive

Jardí de l'Abadessa, Abadessa Olzet 26, Pedralbes, **t** 932 80 37 54. An oasis-like spot offering simple, home-style food, with some more elaborate dishes. Informal, popular with students, and comfortable. *Open winter Mon–Wed 8–6, Thurs and Fri 8–5 and 8–midnight; summer Mon–Fri 8am–midnight.*

On Li Lu, C/Sant Pere Màrtir, Gràcia, **t** 934 15 72 14; **M** Diagonal. The place for a cheese fest, a pretty and friendly little restaurant with soft candlelight. They offer raclette and fondue along with more classic fare.

Cafés Outside the Centre

Horchateria-Turroneria Sirvent, Ronda de Sant Pau 3, Montjuïc, **t** 934 41 76 16; **M** Sant Antoni. Take a break here for some of their delicious ice cream, cakes and coffee. *Open Mon–Sat 10–10.*

Salambó, C/de Torrijos 51, Gràcia, **t** 932 18 69 66; **M** Joanic. A classy and relaxing two-storey café with an unusual selection of teas and healthy food. There are outdoor tables and billiards, too. *Open 12–3am.*

Tapas Outside the Centre

Café Sol Solet, Pla del Sol, Gràcia, **t** 932 17 44 40; **M** Fontana. Has a faded boho chic, with tiled floors, marble tables and wooden panelling. The tapas include an unusual wholefood and often vegetarian mixture of salads and tortilla.

Casa Fernandez, Santalo 46, Gràcia; **FGC** Muntaner. This well-loved neighbourhood establishment serves various house specialties. Try the *papas arrugadas con mojo picon* (literally wrinkled potatoes with *picon* gravy). *Open daily 1.30pm–1am.*

El Roble, C/Granada de Penedes de Luis Antunes 7, Gràcia, **t** 932 18 73 87; **FGC** Gràcia. A bustling neighbourhood favourite, with big boards listing all the Gallego seafood tapas on offer. *Open Mon–Sat 7am–1am.*

Tapas Bar, Via Augusta 9, Gràcia; **M** Diagonal. This quiet spot is in fact much more than a tapas bar, as it also serves excellent meals in the restaurant. *Open Mon–Thurs 8am–1am, Fri 8am–2am, Sat noon–2am, Sun 7pm–1am.*

Txistulari, C/Doctor Rizal 16, Gràcia, **t** 932 37 13 26; **M** Fontana. Offers Basque cuisine and *pintxos* (crusty French bread with various toppings) at lunch and in the early evenings.

Nightlife

Bars

Barcelona's nightlife cranks up after 11pm and at weekends lasts until breakfast, if you've got the energy (and money) to keep up. Note that bars officially close at 2 or 3am, but if the ambience is good the owner will close the door and let the party continue. Favourite spots for drinks are the Barri Gòtic, the Passeig del Born by Santa María del Mar, Gràcia, in the Eixample around the Passeig de Gràcia, and trendy Sant Gervasi (south of Gràcia), where posing can get in the way of a good time.

All bars serve wine by the glass (*negre* for red, *blanco* for white, *rosado* for rosé) but don't expect anything special unless you go to a wine bar or old-fashioned *bodega*, with big oak barrels. The Damm company sews up the local beer market, with Estrella lager and the heavier Voll-Damm. In summer, it's refreshing to have it on draught (a *caña* is a small one, a *jarra* is a pint).

For bars best known for their tapas, *see* 'Tapas Bars', above.

Abaixadors Deu, C/Abaixadors 10; **M** Jaume I. A hip, fashionable theatre-café and nightclub, on the first floor of an immense *modernista* flat. It offers poetry readings, belly-dancing, classical recitals and jazz concerts, as well as late-night dinners. *Open Wed, Thurs, Sun 11pm–3am, Fri–Sat 11pm–4am.*

Aurora, C/Aurora 7, **t** 934 22 30 44; **M** Liceu. This comfortable colourful bar is a favourite with neighbourhood artists. The laid-back atmosphere makes it a great place to start or end the evening. *Open Sun–Thurs 8pm–3am, Fri–Sat 6am–noon.*

Bar Almirall, C/Joaquim Costa 33, no phone; **M** Universitat. Founded in 1860, Almirall has somehow managed to preserve its beautiful *modernista* woodwork; its laid-back atmosphere makes it a great place to meet friends before going out. *Open Mon–Thurs 7pm–2.30am, Fri–Sat 7pm–3.30am.*

Bar Ra, Pla de la Gardunya 3, **t** 934 23 18 78; **M** Liceu. Behind the Boqueria market, Bar Ra's super-hip (not super-efficient) staff serve drinks as well as an eclectic array of tapas and international fusion dishes. The music ranges from jazz to light drum 'n' bass. *Open Mon–Sat 1.30–4 and 9–midnight.*

Benidorm, C/Joaquim Costa 39, **t** 933 17 80 52; **M** Universitat. With nightly DJs spinning everything from disco to electronic music, this tiny bar in the Raval has a decidedly unpretentious atmosphere for such a cool spot. The décor is very funky and very red. *Open Mon–Thurs, Sun 7pm–2am, Fri–Sat 7pm–2.30am.*

Bier Art, Placeta Montcada 5, **t** 933 15 14 47; **M** Jaume I. Just up from the Santa María del Mar church, this beer garden has an amazing selection of beers from all over the world. *Open Tues–Sun 12.30pm–4.30pm and 7.30pm–12.30am, Mon 7.30pm– 12.30am.*

Boadas, C/dels Tallers 1; **M** Catalunya. A famous Art Deco cocktail bar from 1933 that introduced Cuban drinks to Barcelona. *Open Mon–Thurs noon–2am, Fri–Sat noon–3am; closed Sun.*

Borneo, C/del Rec 49, **t** 932 68 23 89; **M** Arc de Triomf. Just opposite Gimlet, Borneo is another recent addition to the list of super-arty bars in the Born. Jazz is the favoured sound at Borneo, lending an extra laid-back atmosphere. *Open daily 8pm–3am.*

Bosc de les Fades, Psg Banca 5; **M** Drassanes. Just outside the Museu de Cera is a bar kitted out like a fairy-tale grotto. Take the small fry here for a soda pop. *Open Mon–Thurs noon–2.30am, Fri–Sat noon–3.30am.*

Café Royale, C/Nou de Zurbano 3; **M** Liceu. Sleek and relaxed, offering giant comfy sofas in which to sink and soak up the eclectic, groovy rhythms.

Cava Universal, Pla Portal de la Pau 4; **M** Drassanes. A classic bar that has been there forever, in the shadow of Columbus, with outdoor tables for watching the ebb and flow from the Ramblas to the Port Vell. *Open daily 9am–10pm.*

Espai Barroc, C/Montcada 20; **M** Jaume I. On the ground floor of the Palau Dalmases, a place to sit and sip in surroundings of total Baroque excess. An experience. *Open Tues–Sun 4pm–midnight.*

La Fira, C/de Provença 171; **M** Hospital Clinic. A bar of bizarre design, jammed full of fun-house paraphernalia, including a row of warped mirrors in the entrance hall that could throw you off balance as you exit. *Open Tues–Thurs 10pm–3am, Fri and Sat 7pm–4.30am, Sun 6pm–1am.*

El Foro, C/Princesa 53, **t** 933 10 10 20; **M** Jaume I. The sign advertises food, art and culture. During the day there is a café/restaurant on the ground floor, with art exhibitions. At weekends the latest sounds rock the house when the downstairs becomes a funky nightclub called Galaxy. *Open Sun, Wed, Thurs 1.30pm–4.30pm and 9pm–midnight, Fri–Sat 1.30pm–4.30pm and 9pm–4am.*

Gimlet, C/Rec 24, **t** 933 10 10 27; **M** Arc de Triomf. Classic, cool and dark, this cocktail bar serves some of the finest cocktails in town. Word has it that Gimlet is a good spot for celebrities. *Open Mon–Sat 8pm–3am.*

Jordy's Cocktail Bar, C/Casanova 91, **t** 934 51 88 23; **M** Universitat. With décor straight out of a scene from *The Godfather*, a tuxedo-clad bartender shakes up a mean cocktail at Jordy's. Be sure to try the cocktail of the day. *Open Mon–Sat 1.30pm–2.30am.*

Les Gens Que L'aime Pub, C/de Valencia 286; **M** Diagonal. Has dim lights, ancient velvet couches and an incurable romanticism. *Open Mon–Thurs 6pm–2.30am, Fri–Sat 7pm–3am, Sun 7pm–2.30am.*

Lola, C/Asses 20, no phone; **M** Jaume I. This tiny bar on a tiny street only serves wine and beer. The friendly owner and down-to-earth atmosphere are a nice break from some of the Born's slick bars. *Open Mon–Sat 8.30pm–3am.*

Mama Café, C/Doctor Dou 10, **t** 933 01 29 40; **M** Catalunya. Mama Café is colourful and comfortable, serving delicous food to go along with the DJ's ethnic beats and acid jazz. *Open Mon 1pm–5pm, Tues–Sat 1–1.*

Maremagnum, Port Vell; **M** Drassanes. Has a slew of Latin bars on the first floor, including the Mojito Bar (*open daily noon–4.30am*) and the Tropicana Bar.

El Paraigua, Pas de l'Ensenyança 2; **M** Jaume I. On Pla de Sant Miquel, this is the place to tipple to classical music. The setting is a pretty *modernista* umbrella shop of 1902, transferred here piece by piece from the Ramblas. *Open Mon–Fri 8am–2am, Sat 4pm–2am.*

La Pedrera, C/de Provença 261–5; **M** Diagonal. The place to be on summer evenings, on Gaudí's roller-coaster roof terrace. Cocktails are served and live music performed. *Open July–Sept, Fri–Sat 9pm–midnight.*

Pilé 43, C/N'Agla 4, **t** 933 17 39 02; **M** Liceu. Nothing matches and everything is for sale in this new super-hip bar. So if you fall in love with the vintage fake fur seat on which you are sitting, buy it and take it home. *Open Sun–Thurs 7pm–2am, Fri–Sat 7pm–3am.*

Pipa Club, Pla Reial 3, **t** 933 02 47 32; **M** Liceu. The 'Pipe Club' is a real smokers' club and one of the coolest late-night bars in Barcelona, located on the third floor in a corner building overlooking Plaça Reial. You must push the buzzer and sometimes contend with the doorman's eagle eye to gain entry. *Open daily 10pm–6am.*

Pitin Bar, Psg del Born 34, **t** 933 19 50 87; **M** Jaume I. In business for more than 20 years, this is still El Born's original cool. The friendly, efficient staff serve light snacks, desserts, wine and cocktails. *Open daily noon–3am.*

Plàstic Café, Psg del Born 19; **M** Barceloneta. Currently the trendiest bar by far in the Born. It's where shiny young things get warmed up for the long night ahead. *Open Mon–Thurs 4pm–3am, Fri–Sat 4pm–4am.*

Portalón, C/de Banys Nous 20; **M** Liceu. The most atmospheric old *bodega* in the city. *Open Mon–Sat 9am–midnight; closed Aug.*

Salsitas/Club 22, C/Nou de la Rambla 22, **t** 933 18 08 40; **M** Liceu. After midnight from Wed to Sat, Salsitas becomes the super-trendy Club 22 where Barcelona's gorgeous ones flock to dance to the sounds of house music. Best to dine on the early side on club nights to avoid being rushed. *Open (bar) Tues–Sun 11–5 and 8pm–3am; (restaurant) Tues–Sun 1–4pm and 8–11.*

La Vinya del Senyor, Pla de Santa María 5; **M** Jaume I. A fantastic selection of 250 wines by the bottle, 20 by the glass, and tidbits (*platillos*) to accompany them. *Open Tues–Sat noon–1.30am, Sun noon–4pm.*

Bars Outside the Centre

Barcelona Brewing Co., C/de Sant Augustí 14, Gràcia; **M** Diagonal. The place for down-to-earth beer lovers: watch them make the contents of your beer glass. *Open Sun–Thurs 11am–2am, Fri–Sat 11am–3am.*

Café del Sol, Pla del Sol 16, Gràcia; **M** Fontana. The main grandstand for Gràcia's hipsters. *Open Tues–Sun noon–2am.*

Mirablau, Pla Dr Andreu, Tibidabo, **t** 934 18 58 79; **FGC** Tibidabo. A glassed-in bar with one of the very best views in Barcelona. *Open Mon–Thurs and Sun 11am–4am, Fri and Sat 11am–5am.*

Partycular, Av. Tibidabo 61, Tibidabo; Tramvia Blau. A huge fun bar located in a mansion on Tibidabo, with outdoor bars in its gardens during the summer. *Open Mon–Sat 7pm–3am, Sun 7pm–1.30am.*

Torres d'Avila, Poble Espanyol (at entrance), Montjuïc; **M** Espanya. Designed by Mariscal and Arribas, here you'll find amazement at the design and the bill go hand in hand. In a town obsessed with design, it's not surprising to find this completely over-the-top late-night high-tech multi-space music bar. *Open Fri–Sat 12.30am–7am.*

Universal Bar, C/Marià Cubí 182, Sant Gervasi; **M** Fontana. Offers 'drinks and design' (only in Barcelona). *Open Thurs–Sat 11pm–4.30am.*

Clubs

Discos and clubs don't gear up for action until after midnight, and they stay open until 5am or later, especially on Friday and Saturday. Drinks and/or the cover charge cost a bomb.

Bikini, C/Déu i Mata 105; **M** María Cristina. One of the most popular nightspots on the scene. *Open Tues–Thurs midnight–4.30am, Fri and Sat midnight–5.30am.*

Fonefone, C/Escudellers 24, **t** 933 17 14 24; **M** Drassanes. Nightly themes range from drum' n' bass to house. The design is simultaneously modern and retro, making it enjoyable whether you're up for a wild night, or something tamer. *Open Sun–Thurs 10pm–2.30am, Fri and Sat 10pm–3am.*

Fuse, C/Roger de Lluria 40, **t** 933 01 74 99; **M** Girona or Catalunya. A hip restaurant/club serves Japanese/Mediterranean food from 8.30pm. On Fri and Sat nights it becomes a club with techno and house sounds. *Open Fri and Sat midnight–4am.*

Lagota2, Vía Laietana 5; **M** Jaume I. The Caribbean community dances its socks off at the weekend. *Open Fri and Sat 9pm–5am.*

Luz de Luna, C/Comerc 21, **t** 933 10 75 42; **M** Jaume I. A lively, unpretentious salsa club, packed with dancers of all abilities. *Open Tues–Sun 10pm–3am, Thurs 10pm–4.30am, Fri and Sat 10pm–5am.*

Mond Club (in the Sala Cibeles), C/Corsega 363, **t** 932 72 09 10; **M** Diagonal. Mond Bar runs a Friday dance club in a classic old dance hall, regularly bringing in well-known international DJs. *Open Fri 12.30am–6am.*

La Paloma, C/del Tigre 27; **M** Universitat. Serious dancers flock to this ornate 1902 dance hall, where a live band plays anything from salsa to bugaloo until about 1am, and then, on Thurs and Fri, it becomes a hugely popular house, breakbeat and dance club. *Open Thurs–Sat 6pm–9.30pm and 11.30pm–5am, Sun 6pm–9.30pm.*

Row (at Nick Havanna Club), C/del Rosselló 208; **M** Diagonal. Thursdays see a youthful, trendy crowd head in, when it becomes a mecca for international dance DJs. *Open Thurs 11.30pm–5.30am.*

Suborn, C/de la Ribera 18, **t** 933 10 11 10; **M** Barceloneta. Despite the slick décor the atmosphere is upbeat and friendly, mixing various music styles; step outside for tapas overlooking the Park. *Open daily 10pm–3am.*

Out of the Centre

Antilla Barcelona, C/d'Aragó 141–3, Gràcia; **FGC** Muntaner. The hottest place for salsa in all its forms, with superb live bands. *Open Mon–Thurs, Sun 11pm–4am, Fri and Sat 11pm–5am.*

Gràcia Llatina, C/de l'Or 19, Gràcia; **M** Fontana. The spiciest Cuban sounds. *Open Mon–Thurs, Sun 9pm–4am; Fri and Sat 4pm–4am.*

KGB, C/de ca l'Alegre de Dalt 55, Gràcia; **M** Joanic. A classic neo-Barcelona design creation, this one with a Cold War spy theme. It's something of a traditional late-late last stand. *Open Thurs–Sat 9pm–5am.*

Lo-Li-Ta, C/Tuset 13, Gràcia, **t** 932 72 09 10; **M** Diagonal. This newish club doesn't open until 3am – truly for the late birds. Lo-Li-Ta features international and local DJs spinning hypnotic rhythms. *Open Fri and Sat 3am–6am.*

Otto Zutz, C/de Lincoln 15, Gràcia; **FGC** Gràcia. Dress-code police bristling at the door, this calls itself 'the New York-style disco where the beautiful people go'. It's a designer-converted warehouse, sometimes with good live music. *Open Tues–Sat midnight–5.30am.*

Sal de Gràcia, C/de Tordera 42, Gràcia, **t** 607 23 09 52; **M** Joanic. A grungy club playing rock n' roll, largely to expats. *Open Sun–Thurs 9pm–3am, Fri and Sat 6pm– 3.30am.*

Xampanyerias

Barcelona's popular *xampanyerias* serve Catalan champagne, *cava* and elegant titbits from bitter chocolate to raw oysters. Try out:

Casablanca, C/de Bonavista 6, Gràcia; **M** Diagonal. Bogart wouldn't look out of place here; a classic bar, great for cooling off on a hot night. *Open Mon–Sat 6pm–2.30am.*

La Cava del Palau, C/Verdaguer i Callís 10, La Ribera; **M** Uriquinaona. Near Palau de la Música. Pricey, but a must for *cava* enthusiasts. *Open Mon–Sat 7pm–2am; closed Aug.*

Languedoc Roussillon, C/de Pau Claris 77, Eixample; **M** Urquinaona. Barcelona's first oyster bar, featuring the fine bivalves from Bouzigue. *Open Mon–Fri 1–4 and 9–11, Sat 1–4, closed Sun.*

El Xampanyet, C/Montcada 22, Barri Gòtic; **M** Jaume I. A charming old *cava* and cider bar, full of *bonhomie* and a lingering aroma of anchovies. *Open Tues–Sat noon–4pm and 5.30–11.30pm, Sun noon–4pm.*

Entertainment

Barcelona's artistic tendencies don't stop short of performance; it has a plethora of live music venues and over 20 active theatres. News-stands sell the weekly *Guía del Ocio* (€0.75) with detailed events listings; its 'Cine' section lists films shown in their original language (VO) and has information on the excellent **Filmoteca de la Generalitat** (*Cine Aquitania, Av. de Sarrià 33,* **t** *934 10 75 90;* **M** *Hospital Clinic*). The free monthly music calendar *Informatiu Musical* (from tourist offices), lists daily performances of everything from classical to country. *Butxaca* is a free pocket-sized listing magazine orientated toward contemporary art, culture and clubbing, picked up in bars and cafés; check out its website at *www.focus.es*. *B-guided* is the quarterly guide to fashionable dining, arts and shopping in Barcelona and Madrid, from news-stands and bookstores.

L'Auditori, C/de Lepant 140; **M** Marina. Spanking new, acoustically pure and architecturally sterile. Classical music concerts are held here regularly.

Centre Artesà Tradicionàrius, Travessera de Sant Antoni 6–8, Gràcia; **M** Fontana. The place for traditional Catalan music.

Centre de Cultura Contemporània de Barcelona (CCCB), C/Montalegre 5, **t** 933 06 41 00, *www.cccb.org*; **M** Catalunya. Check listings or the website for concerts.

L'Espai de Danza i Música, Travessera de Gràcia 63, **t** 934 14 31 33; **M** Diagonal. All sorts of dance perfomances take the stage here.

Gran Teatre del Liceu, Ramblas 51–9, *www.liceubarcelona.com*; **M** Liceu. Reopened in 1999, once again offers opera fans the chance to hear their favourite arias.

Mercat de les Flors, C/de Lleida 59, **t** 934 26 18 75; **M** Espanya. This especially beautiful theatre, converted from a 19th-century wholesale flower market, offers a full range of events, from two-day theatre marathons to big-name international performances.

Palau de la Música Catalana, Sant Francesc de Paula 2, **t** 932 68 10 00; **M** Urquinaona. Magnificent; where lovers of classical music will really feel at home.

Gay and Lesbian

Barcelona has a very open and thriving gay scene, the epicentre of which is the 'Gaixample' or 'Eixample Rosa', in the area framed by Paseo de Gràcia, Gran Vía de les Corts Catalanes and C/d'Arago. Here you'll find numerous gay businesses, including shops, saunas, restaurants and hairdressers. Stop by **Zeus** (C/de Riera Alta 20) to pick up a copy of the Barcelona/Sitges Gay Map (*Plano Gay*). The general gay info hotline, **t** 900 60 16 01 (6pm–10pm only). Other organizations are:

Casal Lambda, C/Ample 5, **t** 934 12 72 72, *www.lambdaweb.org*; **M** Barceloneta.

Coordinadora Gai-Lesbiana, C/Buenaventura Munoz 4, **t** 900 60 16 01; **M** Arc de Triomf.

Front d'Alliberament Gai de Catalunya, C/Verdi 88, **t** 932 17 26 69; **M** Fontana.

Where to Stay

Barcelona has fairly limited gay accommodation, so be sure to make a reservation early.

Hs Centro, C/Balmes 38, **t** 649 55 02 38, **f** 932 72 08 75; **M** Passeig de Gràcia. The proprietor, Jordi, is full of information and advice. Cash only.

****Hotel California**, C/Rauric 14, **t** 349 3 317 77 66, **f** 933 17 54 74; **M** Liceu. In the heart of Barri Gòtic, this has clean and pleasant rooms at affordable prices. A/c and TV.

P. La Nau, Rda de Sant Pere 53, **t/f** 932 45 10 13; **M** Arc de Triomf. Friendly staff and affordable rooms in the Eixample. Cash only.

Eating Out

La Diva, C/Diputacio 172, **t** 934 54 63 98; **M** Urgell. A gay restaurant which offers Mediterranean cuisine and nightly drag shows. *Open Tues–Fri 1–3.30 and 9–12, Sat–Sun 9–midnight.*

Castro, C/Casanova 85, **t** 933 23 67 84; **M** Urgell. Mediterranean/international cuisine. Very gay. *Open Sun–Fri 1–4 and 9–1.30, Sat 9–1.*

I Què?, C/Topazi 8, **t** 934 16 07 33; **M** Fontana. A favorite lesbian hang-out serving sandwiches, pizzas, salads, etc. *Open Mon–Fri 1–4 and 6–2, Sat 8pm–3am.*

La Singular, C/Francisco Giner 50, Gràcia, **t** 932 37 50 98; **M** Diagonal.Run and frequented mostly by women, with delicious pasta, seafood and tapas. *Open Mon–Fri 1–4 and 8–12, Sat 8–1.*

Bars and Clubs

Barcelona's gays and lesbians tend to share the same bars and clubs.

A few favourites are:

Aire, C/Valencia 236, **t** 934 51 84 62; **M** Urgell. Reasonably priced drinks and music from the 70s, 80s and 90s. *Open Thurs–Sat 11pm–3am.*

Arena, C/de Balmes 32; **M** Passeig de Gràcia. One of the liveliest discos of the moment.

Café Dietrich, C/Consell de Cent 255; **M** Universitat. A very elegant spot with regular live music performances.

El Cono de Tu Prima, Consell de Cent 294, **t** 934 87 77 22; **M** Universitat. In vogue at the moment with glamorous drag queens. *Open midnight–6am.*

Free Girls, C/Marià Cubí 4; **FGC** Muntaner. Bar-disco popular with a young lesbian crowd.

G Café, C/Muntaner 24; **M** Universitat. This coffee shop/bar is decorated in Gaudí-style and usually has painting or photo exhibits. *Open Mon–Fri 4pm–2.30am, Sat–Sun til 3am.*

Metro, C/Sepúlveda 185, **t** 933 23 5257; **M** Universitat. Some say this is the best gay disco in town. It has two floors, three bars and a dark room. *Open midnight–5am.*

Octopussy, C/Moll de la Fusta 4, **t** 932 21 40 31; **M** Drassanes. Very popular and trendy at the moment. *Open Fri and Sat midnight–4am.*

Punto BCN, C/Muntaner 63; **M** Universitat. A long-time favourite, with two floors.

Satanassa, C/Aribau 27; **M** Universitat. An indisputable classic and very popular.

may be closed when an exhibtion is being mounted), where Ferdinand the Catholic (never a favourite in Barcelona, after he wed Isabel and subjected Aragón's interests to Castile) narrowly escaped an assassination attempt by a disgruntled peasant. Banquets, funerals and even parliaments were held here; according to tradition, Ferdinand and Isabel received Columbus here after his first voyage in 1493. Begun in 1359 by Guillem Carbonell (architect to Pere 'the Ceremonious'), its six huge rainbow arches cross a span of 56ft, with wooden beams filling in the ceiling between; viewed from the corner of the hall, the arches appear to radiate from a single point. In the antechamber, a detached fresco shows a procession led by a king and bishop (*c.* 1300). The hall is linked to the apse of the **Capilla Palatina de Santa Agata**. Begun in 1302 by Jaume II and his queen Blanche of Anjou, it houses the lavish *Retablo del Condestable*, Jaume Huguet's masterpiece of 1466, and what is claimed to be the stone where the breasts of Santa Agatha were laid after Roman soldiers snipped them off in Sicily.

A narrow, almost hidden staircase leads out to the curious skyscraper that rises over the square: five storeys of galleries built by Antoni Carbonell in 1557 and anachronistically named the **Mirador del Rei Martí** after the popular humanist king, to hide the unpleasant truth that it was really a spytower for the hated viceroy, or Lloctinent, a position set up by Ferdinand. Just left of the Palau Reial is the **Palau del Lloctinent**, also by Carbonell, and former keeper of the Archives of the Crown of Aragón. One of the world's greatest collections of medieval documents, these were moved in 1994 and the building is now closed. Walk outside Plaça del Rei to C/de les Comtes, to peek into the fine courtyard with a magnificent coffered ceiling over the stair.

Nearby is the entrance to the **Museu Frederic Marés** (*Pla de Sant Iu 5;* ***M*** *Jaume I; open Tues and Thurs 10–5, Wed, Fri and Sat 10–7, Sun 10–3; closed Mon; adm*), occupying the part of the royal palace that King Ferdinand granted to another of his popular gifts to Barcelona, the Spanish Inquisition. Incredibly, big as it is, it contains only a fraction of the collections amassed by sculptor Frederic Marés (1893–1991), Spain's champion hoarder. His obsessive accumulations of the sublime and the ridiculous are beautifully arranged: on the ground floor, armies of *ex votos* are followed by an astonishing array of 12th–14th-century wood sculptures of sweet-faced Virgins and stylized crucifixes; on the first floor is art from the Middle Ages to the 19th century. Venture upstairs and you'll be immersed in the 16 rooms of Marés' **Museu Sentimental**, swollen with every kind of 19th-century flotsam and jetsam.

The Cathedral: La Seu

Plaça de la Seu; ***M*** *Jaume I; open Mon–Fri 8–1.30 and 4–7.30, Sat and Sun 8–1.30 and 5–7.30.*

C/de les Comtes continues around to the front of Barcelona's huge Gothic cathedral, which, with its fat apse, octagonal towers and spires, is hard to miss. It's at least the third church to stand on this site; the first was flattened in al-Mansur's raid on the city in 985; of the second, a Romanesque one built by Count Ramón Berenguer I, only two doorways remain. The earliest bit of the current model is the right transept, built in 1298 by Jaume II, and it's worth pausing by its **Portal of Sant Iu** (St Ives; leading on to C/de les Comtes); the carvings on the left of it depict St George and Barcelona's first count, Wilfred the Hairy, fighting a dragon and griffon respectively.

The **façade**, based on the 1408 plans by a French master named Carli, faces the **Plaça de la Seu**; though a wonderful backdrop to the *sardanes* danced here at noon on Sunday, it sits suspiciously on such a venerable church – perhaps because it was begun in 1882. It might not even have been finished then had the canons not feared the worst: during their moment of power in 1820, the Liberals proposed engraving the then blank wall with the Catalan Constitution and Civil Code.

The Interior

Catalan Gothic is best known for its conquest of space: although La Seu has only three aisles, the architects made it look like five. Modern lighting now dispels its mysterious, cavernous gloom, but it remains rich and atmospheric.

The first chapel on the right, the star-vaulted **sala capitular**, contains the lucky crucifix borne by Don Juan on the mast of his flagship at the Battle of Lepanto in 1571; the S-shaped twist in Christ's body came about, they say, from dodging a Turkish cannonball. Stuck in the middle of the nave, the elaborate 14th–15th-century **choir stalls** (*open Mon–Sat 9.30–1.30 and 2.30–4; adm; ticket includes lift to the roof*) were emblazoned with the arms of numerous kings in 1514, when Emperor Charles V summoned them to Barcelona as Knights of the Golden Fleece. The choir faces the elegant, low-vaulted **crypt** designed by the Mallorcan Jaume Fabre, in charge of the cathedral works from 1317 to 1339. The relics of Barcelona's co-patroness, the 4th-century virgin martyr Santa Eulàlia, lie in an alabaster sarcophagus carved with scenes of her martyrdom, attributed to Pisan sculptor Lupo de Francesco. The rest of the crypt has been curiously arranged to resemble theatre boxes. Set against the wall to the right of the altar, Ramón Berenguer I and his wife lie in painted, velvet-covered sarcophagi, while a door leads into the sacristy and the **treasury** (*not always open*). Of the chapels radiating from the ambulatory, the fourth on the right has the best art.

The Romanesque **Porta de Sant Severo** leads to a medieval oasis, the charming green garden of the **cloister**, begun in 1385. Its iron-grilled chapels were once dedicated to the patron saints of Barcelona's guilds ('Our Lady of Electricity' is still going strong) and many leading masters are buried in the floor. A lovely pavilion holds the **Fountain of Sant Jordi**, topped with St George. At Corpus Christi (which was, until the 19th century, Barcelona's most lavish holiday, when each guild competed to make the most elaborate or alarming float) flowers are wound around the fountain and a hollow egg is set to dance in the jet of water (*l'ou com balla*). No one need look far for an egg, either, as a flock of white geese natter away next to the fountain by their pond. They have been there since anyone can remember, symbolic of Santa Eulàlia's

The Moor Under the Organ

Until recently, there was a Moor's head called the *carcassa* under the cathedral's ornate 16th-century organ. Traditionally, it represented the head of Ali Baba, defeated at Lepanto, and on feast days it vomited forth sweets for the children. It may also have been a reminder of the Templars, who were a powerful force in medieval Catalunya. Count Ramón Berenguer IV the Great joined the Templars in 1131 in response to an emissary sent by the founder of the order, Hugues de Paynes (Hug de Pinós, himself probably a Catalan), whose shield bore three Moors' heads, symbolic of knowledge and understanding – hence the Baphomet, the idol the Templars were accused of worshipping. The Moor's head (often blindfolded) pops up throughout the Mediterranean in places claimed by the Catalans, notably the islands of Mallorca, Corsica and Sardinia. The Templars continued to counsel and train the kings of Aragón until Jaume II, builder of this cathedral, banned the order at the end of the 13th century, not long before the pope dissolved it on charges of heresy.

virginity or a memory of the geese that saved Rome. One chapel houses the **Cathedral Museum** (*open daily 10–1; adm*), with Bartolomé Bermejo's masterpiece, *Pietà* (1490), one of the first oil paintings in Spain, amid *retablos* and reliquaries retired from duty.

As you leave the cloister, don't miss its lovely Porta de Santa Eulàlia. This gives on to C/de Bisbe, which passes under a neo-Gothic bridge (1928) that links the 16th-century **Casa de los Canónigos** to the Generalitat. Back on Pla de la Seu,more religious art, garments, silver and ceramics have been pensioned off in the **Museu Diocesà** (*Pla de la Seu 7, www.arquebisbatbcn.es;* ***M*** *Jaume I; open Tues–Sat 10–2 and 5–8, Sun 11–2; closed Mon; adm*). On Thursdays, a **flea market** takes place just below in **Plaça Nova**. The dreary façade of the **Collegi d'Arquitectes** (1962) is enlivened by a sketchy frieze of Catalan dancers by Picasso; his only piece of public art in Barcelona.

Plaça de Sant Jaume

This square has been the heart of civic Barcelona since it served as the Roman forum, at the intersection of the *cardus maximus* and *decumanus,* and today locals come here to dance the *sardana* on Sunday evenings from 7 to 9. It was recarved out of a warren of streets in the 1840s along with C/de Ferrán, and is still something of a forum, opening up an ongoing, face to face dialogue between the Catalan government (the Generalitat) and Barcelona's City Hall (the Ajuntament). Created by Jaume I in 1249, the Generalitat was made up of representatives of the three Estates of the Catalan *corts* (Church, military, and civilian) and in 1359 it assumed fiscal responsibility for the realm, making it Spain's first real parliament since Roman times. The **Palau de la Generalitat** (*guided tours 2nd and 4th Sun of month, in English at 11am; adm free, but bring ID and arrive early to sign up*) was begun in the 15th century to give it a permanent seat. When Philip V abolished the Generalitat in 1714, the palace was occupied by the Reial Audiencia, but its original role was never forgotten: in 1931, Francesc Macià proclaimed the Catalan Republic from its balcony; it was the seat of the autonomous government until Franco, and since 1977 it has resumed its original function.

The Generalitat turns its oldest and fairest face towards C/del Bisbe Irurita, a façade built in 1416 by Marc Safont peopled by gargoyles and Catalunya's patron, St George, on the medallion over the door. In 1456, the Generalitat made St George's Day (23 April) the Festival of the Rose, when men give their love a red rose, while women offer a book. Every year, thousands queue up to see displays of roses in the courtyard.

Across Pla de Sant Jaume, the Generalitat faces the **Ajuntament** (*open Sat and Sun 10–2; bring ID*) from where the Council of a Hundred, also founded by Jaume I, ruled the city from 1272 to 1714 like an Italian Republic. The building's neoclassical **façade**, added in the 1840s, is unexciting, but the Gothic façade on C/de la Ciutat preserves some of its charm. The oldest part of the building is the 14th-century **Saló de Cent**, though it was restored in the 1880s; the **Saló de las Cròniques** is lined with golden murals by Josep Sert (1928) who went on to decorate New York's Rockefeller Center.

From Pla de Sant Jaume, narrow C/Paradí leads to the summit of Mons Tàber, marked by an ancient millstone in the pavement. Here, just inside the Gothic courtyard of the Centre Excursionista de Catalunya, are four impressive Corinthian columns and part of the podium from the 1st-century AD Roman **Temple of Augustus**.

El Call

In the Middle Ages, Barcelona's Jewish quarter (*El Call*) was just west of C/Bisbe and Pla de Sant Jaume, on modern C/del Call. In the 11th and 12th centuries this little neighbourhood was the intellectual centre of Catalunya. The first sign of trouble occurred in 1243, when Jaume I ordered that El Call be set apart from the rest of the city, and that its residents wear long, hooded cloaks with coloured bands. Much of this segregation was to protect the Jews from persecution by Reconquista fanatics; Jews expelled from other territories were made welcome here by the count-kings, to the extent that El Call incited a dangerous amount of working-class envy. In 1391, rumours that the Black Death had been brought by the Jews incited riots in the quarter that led to 300 deaths. King Joan I had the 22 instigators put to death, but could not halt the growing tide of anti-Semitism, and in 1424 the Jews were expelled from El Call, and the stones of their synagogues and cemeteries were later quarried to build the Generalitat and Lloctinent. On tiny C/de Marlet, off C/de Sant Domènec del Call, one stone remains, inscribed in Hebrew: 'Sacred foundation of Rabbi Samuel Hassareri, of everlasting life. Year 692.'

East and South of Plaça de Sant Jaume

From the north (Gothic) side of the Ajuntament, C/de Hèrcules leads to the **Plaça de Sant Just** and two palaces: **Moxió**, adorned with *esgrafiados*, and **Palamòs** (*open 3rd Sun of month 10.30–2, or by appt*). The latter, housing a Gallery of Illustrious Catalans, was the grandest private address in medieval Barcelona, built in the 13th century atop the Roman wall, with a fine Romanesque-Gothic courtyard; it's now the seat of the academy of fine arts. Here, too, is the parish church of the count-kings of Aragón, **Les Sants Just i Pastor** (*if the front door is locked, try the back*), founded according to tradition by Charlemagne's son, Louis the Pious in 801. It is the last church in Spain to preserve its ancient privilege of *Testimentos Sacramentales* bestowed by Louis himself, which gives any citizen of Barcelona the right to make a will, orally, without a notary or writ, if said before the altar of Sant Feliú.

In 1893 Joan Miró was born in a Parisian-style arcade called **Passatge de Crédit**, built in 1879 between C/de Ferrán and the 1514 Palau Centelles, on Baixade de Sant Miquel. Several old palaces on C/de Avinyó, at the end of Baixade de Sant Miquel, were converted into brothels around the turn of the last century; the ladies in one were the subject of young Pablo Picasso's 1907 *Les Demoiselles d'Avignon*, his unfinished manifesto of Cubism, a painting that was so incomprehensible even to other artists that it wasn't exposed publicly until 1937. If you walk along Avinyó, note the fine *esgrafiados* that embellish the houses at **Nos.26** and **30**.

Into La Ribera: Carrer Montcada

North of Via Laietana is La Ribera, Barcelona's maritime quarter in the Middle Ages, when the sea came in as far as the Estaciò de França. It has a decidedly funkier atmosphere than the Barri Gòtic, never really having recovered from Madrid's amputation of half of its streets in 1718 to construct the hated Ciutadella. Amid the genteel decrepitude, however, passes one of the highlights of Barcelona: Carrer Montcada, a street given in 1148 by Ramón Berenguer IV to a rich merchant named Montcada in return for services rendered. Montcada sold property lots to his buddies and they created a medieval Millionaires' Row. The presence of big money led to the founding of the *correus volants* (flying runners), the Spanish postal service, first referred to in 1166. These early Catalan pony express riders, the *Troters*, were headquartered at the northern end of C/Montcada, by the tiny Romanesque chapel of **Santa María d'en Marcús**, where they would ride in to be blessed before setting out.

In the 15th–17th centuries, the millionaires' descendants rebuilt their palaces, with walls right up to the street, making C/Montcada into a narrow gully. Today, most of the once-secret palaces are museums or galleries, thanks to an initiative taken in 1963 to restore the loveliest mansion of them all, the 15th-century **Palau Aguilar** (with a courtyard by Marc Sanfont) and the adjacent Baró de Castellet and Meca palaces to house the **Museu Picasso** (*C/Montcada 15–19; **t** 933 19 63 10, www.museupicasso.bcn.es; **M** Jaume I; open Tues–Sat 10–8, Sun and hols 10–3; closed Mon; adm*). This is the best place in Spain to see the works of a man acclaimed as the greatest artist of the 20th century. The core of the collection, donated by Picasso's secretary, Jaume Sabartés, represents the artist's early works, beginning with the drawings of an exceptionally gifted 8 year old in Málaga and his first major academic painting, *Science and Charity*, painted in 1897. This is followed by much of his Barcelona work, including a menu *à la* Toulouse-Lautrec for Els Quatre Gats (1900), where he had his first exhibition in 1901. Other works include some from his Pink Period in Paris (1904–6), some Cubist paintings (1907–20) and 58 studies of Velázquez's *Las Meninas*, painted in 1957 and donated by Picasso. Temporary exhibitions in the adjoining Palau Meca are usually good.

A few steps down at No.12 C/de Montcada, the **Museu Tèxtil i de la Indumentària** (***t** 933 10 45 16; www.museutextil.bcn.es; open Tues–Sat 10–6, Sun 10–3; closed Mon; adm, combined ticket with Museu Barbier-Mueller d'Art Precolumbi available*) is housed

Picasso and the Origins of Cubism

Born in Málaga in 1881 and relocated with his family to Barcelona in 1895, Picasso was one of the first Andalucíans to thoroughly identify with his adopted city and become an honorary Catalan. From 1895–97 he studied at the School of Fine Arts in the Llontja where his father taught, then drifted into the city's Bohemian artistic milieu headquartered at Els Quatre Gats, where his precocious talent was recognized and encouraged by Barcelona's most famous painter of the day, Ramón Casas. Even so, Picasso never had much money in Barcelona and he knew at first hand about the impoverished, outcast subjects of his first, 'Blue' Period (1901–04), painted before he took off to Paris and invented Cubism. His interest in Cézanne's studies of structure and form have long been cited as the seeds for his monumental break with the past, but in 1990 American artist Ellsworth Kelly hit on another possible inspiration behind Picasso's fragmentation and dissolution of form: the *trencadis* (broken tiles) used by Gaudí to decorate so much of his architecture. Only, chances are, Picasso never saw even the Park Güell: most of it was not for public viewing when he lived in Barcelona.

in the 16th-century Gothic Palau dels Marquesos de Lió, with a café in its attractive courtyard. Dedicated to textiles and fashion, its exhibits date back to the 3rd century and include rare embroideries from Granada, a 16th-century Tournai tapestry of the Siege of Rhodes; Baroque shoes, and classic frocks by Balenciaga.

Next door, another Gothic palace holds the **Museu Barbier-Mueller d'Art Precolumbi** (***t*** *933 10 45 16; www.bcn.es/icub; same hours as Textile museum; adm*), an exquisite collection of Precolumbian art, showcasing the incredible craftmanship of Latin American civilizations between 2000 BC and AD 1500.

Further along at No.20 is the finest Baroque palace in Barcelona: the 17th-century **Palau Dalmases**, complete with a sumptuous café dripping with velvet. Don't miss the flamboyant stair, carved with Neptune and Amphitrite racing up the waves in defiance of gravity; opposite, the **Galerie Maeght**, in the 16th-century Palau dels Cervelló, puts on excellent changing exhibitions and has a large art shop.

Santa María del Mar

M *Jaume 1; open daily 9–1.30 and 4.30–8.*

The east end of C/de Montcada runs into the Passeig Born and the apse of Santa María del Mar, the most perfect and pure expression of the Catalan Gothic anywhere. The site has long been holy: the first church here was built in the 4th century over the tomb of Santa Eulàlia. When Jaume I conquered Mallorca in 1235 he promised a temple to Mary, Star of the Sea, the patroness of his sailors, but his promise remained unfulfilled until Alfons III took Sardinia. He laid the first stone of the church in 1329 and entrusted the design to stone mason Berenguer de Montagut, who may have had technical assistance from the Mallorcan architect Jaume Fabre.

By this time the portside neighbourhood of La Ribera was firmly established as one of the medieval suburbs or *vilanovas* that grew up outside the city walls along C/Argenteria, the main road from the Barri Gòtic to the port. As Catalan maritime interests expanded, so did the population of sailors, porters, tradesmen and small merchants. Santa María was to be their church, and for 50 years all able-bodied men in the parish donated their labour to build it. In 1714 its interior was damaged during the French and Spanish bombardment; even graver, in 1936, Anarchists set it ablaze, its elaborate Baroque fittings feeding a fire that burned for ten days. Yet however wonderful the furnishings might have been, the current lack of any decoration at all only enhances its sublime beauty.

The austere exterior, startling in its simplicity, looks anything but Gothic. A great dark mass, the façade on Plaça Santa María is only embellished with a rose window; a simple relief of Christ with his hands up, like the victim of a hold-up; a pair of octagonal towers and wildflowers sprouting from the cracks in the stone. Enter (*from Psg del Born*), and what was closed and fortress-like from without opens up to a miraculous spaciousness within, early evidence of the Catalan vocation for daring architecture. A minimum of interior supports hold up the vaults: the four simple octagonal piers of the nave standing some 42ft apart, a distance unsurpassed in any other medieval building. Two lofty aisles, half the width of the nave, have only simple niches for chapels between the buttresses. The whole converges on a semicircular apse, the raised altar defined by a transcendent crescent of slender columns like a glade in a forest. At the foot of the altar, two stone reliefs depict the longshoremen who carried the stone for the church from Montjuïc. Along the church's southern flank, a low wall and the fan-shaped **Fossar de les Moreres** marks the mass tomb of citizen resisters to the Bourbon troops of Philip V in 1714.

Around Santa María del Mar: La Llotja

The neighbourhood around Santa María del Mar is undergoing a slow but steady process of gentrification. Most street names recall their medieval trade: C/Argenteria, for example, was the silversmiths' street, while C/Canvis Vells and C/Canvis Nous were the streets where money was changed on *bancos* (benches, hence 'bank'). The **Plaça del Palau**, the neoclassical **Duana Vella** (the old customs house, now occupied by the Guardia Civil) has a series of murals in the Sala de Actos. Diagonally across Pla del Palau stands **La Llotja**, or the stock exchange, the secular cathedral of Catalan mercantile imperialism, paid for by a three per cent tax on imports and exports. Vast sums were lavished on the building, which was built by Pere Arbei for King Pere III the Ceremonious in 1380. Though slapped with a neoclassical facelift in 1802, the magnificent Gothic **Sala de Contractacions** inside was left untouched, and until Barcelona's *bourse* moved to Psg de Gràcia in 1996, it was the oldest continuously operating stock exchange in Europe. Sadly, the gates are now closed and the future is uncertain.

The grand old **Estaciò de França**, just south on Av. Marquès de l'Argentera, has lost most of its train passengers to the Estació de Sants, but as one of its new roles it plays host to the annual New Year's bash. Between Santa María del Mar and the Parc de la Ciutadella, the trendy, bar-lined **Passeig del Born** (1876) was used for medieval tournaments. At its north end, another institution awaits a new role: the beautiful wholesale **Mercat del Born**, a striking iron structure with a roof of patterned tiles by Josep Fontseré, which looks set to be reincarnated as the city's central library.

Parc de la Ciutadella

Open daily, Nov–Feb 10–6; Mar, Oct 10–7; April, Sept 10–8; May–Aug 10–9.

The year 1714 is a bitter date in the annals of Barcelona. In that year, after an extraordinary eleven-month resistance, the besieged city and independent Catalunya fell to the troops of Philip V. To punish the city the Bourbon king moved its university to Cervera and demanded the evacuation (without any compensation) of much of La Ribera to construct, at Barcelona's expense, the Ciutadella, one of the most massive fortifications ever built in Europe. When the progressive Catalan General Prim took power in 1869, he gave the loathed mastodon to the city, designating 150 acres for a park and selling the rest as housing to finance the demolition of the walls.

In 1888, Barcelona's dynamic mayor Francesc de Paula Ruis i Taulet made the new park the site of a Universal Exhibition, which city historians believe was the key event that saved the city from sliding into provincial backwaters. It also served as a stage for architectural innovation: in this case, the colourful, eclectic *modernista* style.

The main entrance of the park, on Psg Lluís Companys, is dominated by a relic from the great fair: the **Arc de Triomf** by Josep Vilaseca, a peculiar piece of *mudéjar*-style ceramic brickwork topped with four crowns that manifests, if nothing else, the eternal Catalan longing to be different. Several other buildings around the Passeig would seem to share this longing: the elephantine **Palau de Justicia**, made entirely of stone from Montjuïc; the **Grupo Escolar Pere Vila**, with its ceramic reliefs, and behind it, the idiosyncratic brick and ironwork **Central Catalana d'Electricitat** of 1897.

The park itself is well used, especially at weekends, when families come to paddle in the little boats under the **Cascada**, a pile of rocks and mythological allusions by Josep Fontserè, said to have been assisted by Gaudí, then a student. Gaudí is credited with the arrangement of the boulders, as well as the ironwork at the park's second gate, on Av. Marqués de l'Argenteria. East of the lake was the fort's **Plaça d'Armes**, now a formal garden,where *El Desconsol* (*Despair*), a copy of Josep Llimona's famous Rodinesque nude of 1907, gazes into her lily pond. The square has the only surviving structures from the Ciutadella: a chapel, the Governor's Palace and the Arsenal, now the seat of the Catalan Parliament. Though there are plans to move the pictures to the Palau Nacional on Montjuïc in 2003, it currently shares space with the **Museu d'Art Modern** (*Edifici del Parlament; www.mnac.es;* **M** *Ciutadella-Vila Olímpica; open Tues–Sat 10–7, Sun 10–2.30; closed Mon; adm*), which offers a slice of modern art from 1850 to 1920. A fine introduction to Catalan *modernista* and *noucentisme* art, it features paintings and sculptures by Casas, Fortuny, Nonell, Julio González, Nogués and Rusinyol, as well as furniture, including exquisite pieces designed for Domènech's Casa Lleó Morera.

The Ciutadella also contains Barcelona's excellent, if slightly cramped, **Zoo** (*open Nov–Feb daily 10–5; Mar and Oct daily 10–6; April and Sept daily 10–7; May–Aug 9.30–7.30; adm exp*) though this too may be moved to roomier quarters within a few years. Near the zoo's aquarium stands the fountain of the **Senyoreta del paraigua**, 'The lady with the umbrella', the symbol adopted by the city from the 1888 Exhibition. Other survivors of the big fair line the park's under-the-lindens Passeig Tilers: Josep Amargós donated both the pretty **Umbráculo**, a cast-iron greenhouse for shade plants; and the iron and glass **Hivernacle**, or winter greenhouse. In between, the neo-Pompeian **Museu de Geologia** (*www.museugeologia.bcn.es; open Tues, Wed, Fri, Sat and Sun 10–2, Thurs 10–6.30; closed Mon; adm*) was Barcelona's first public museum. Best of all is the great brick **Castell dels Tres Dragons**, designed by Domènech i Montaner as the Universal Exhibition's café. This was the herald of *modernista* architecture in 1888, with its innovative use of exposed plain brick and iron, crowned with whimsical ceramic decoration. These days it's the **Museu de Zoologia** (*www.museuzoologia.bcn.es; open Tues–Wed and Fri–Sun 10–2, Thurs 10–6.30; closed Mon; adm*).

Vila Olímpica and Barceloneta

Until the late 1980s, the seafront between Barceloneta in the south and the Besos river in the north was occupied by Poblenou's dreary 19th-century industrial sprawl. Barcelona traditionally took no delight in its waterfront, and closed it off from public access. Even if you could get to a beach, the water stank.

The need to house 15,000 athletes for the 1992 Olympics, combined with the city's need for space to play, propelled the Ajuntament to undertake Barcelona's biggest urban-renewal project of the last century. The coast was cleared to create the **Parc de Mar**, opening up five kilometres of public beaches, and architects Oriol Bohigas, Josep Martorell and David Mackay were given the task of creating a **Vila Olímpica** that could be converted into housing (some 2,000 apartments) after the games. The promise to make the new housing affordable was just a promise, and the few businesses that have moved into the American-style commercial area are not exactly your neighbourhood shop. What completes the jarring soulless suburban air of the Vila Olímpica are its wide streets, prominent car parks and the big desolate spaces between the traffic set with outsize sculptures and fountains.

There's no starker contrast to the Vila Olímpica than the city's effort to build a planned neighbourhood by the sea. This is **Barceloneta**, or 'Little Barcelona', a 15-minute walk south along the Passeig Marítim. After the destruction of 61 streets and 1,262 homes in La Ribera to build the Ciutadella, a French military engineer with the delicious name of Prosper Verboom designed a neighbourhood for the displaced on this 25-acre triangle of land, following the most progressive urban-planning ideas of the 18th century. The streets were laid out in a grid, with a market in the centre square and long, narrow blocks of houses, permitting every room to have a window; as all houses were allowed only one upper floor, all had access to sunlight. Verboom's height prohibition was modified in 1837 and ignored ever since, so that most houses in Barceloneta have at least four floors, turning the streets into mini canyons. Traditionally inhabited by families of sailors and fishermen, Barceloneta is still vibrant and densely populated. If by chance it's not undergoing one of its periodic mechanical overhauls, you can sail up to Montjuïc from here on the **aerial cableway** (***t*** *934 43 08 59;* ***M*** *Barceloneta; operates from Torre de Sebastià to Montjuïc, stopping at the World Trade Centre; open mid-June–mid-Sept daily 10.30–8; Mar–mid-June and mid-Sept–mid-Oct daily 10.30–7; mid-Oct–Feb daily 10.30–5.30; €8.50 return; €4.25 one way*).

Port Vell and Along the Seafront

What may bring the Barcelonans back to Barceloneta is the redevelopment of the old port, or Port Vell, just to the south. The **Palau de Mar**, overlooking the Port Vell Marina, has been rehabilitated into restaurant space and into the **Museu d'Història de Catalunya** (*Moll de la Barceloneta;* ***M*** *Barceloneta; open Tues and Thurs–Sat 10–7, Wed 10–8, Sun and hols 10–2.30; closed Mon; adm*), designed to give an overview of Catalan history from the Palaeolithic era to the present. Up from here, the old **Moll d'Espanya** is occupied by a shopping mall and nightlife vortex, **Maremagnum**; an **IMAX cinema**, showing the usual IMAX mix of nature extravaganzas and rock concerts throughout the day; and an **Aquarium** (*www.aquariumbcn.com;* ***M*** *Drassanes or Barceloneta; open July–Aug daily 9.30am–11pm; June and Sept daily 9.30–9.30; Oct–May Mon–Fri 9.30–9, Sat–Sun 9.30–9.30; adm exp, audioguide available*). Kids can enjoy the three new interactive centres, though the vast central tank steals the show, encircled by a 225ft viewing tunnel equipped with a slow human conveyor belt and serenaded by gentle New Age music;.

A handsome wooden bridge, the **Rambla de Mar**, links the Moll d'Espanya to the foot of the Columbus monument (*see* below) and rotates to let sailing boats through; next to it, the **Moll de la Fusta** has long been a favourite seaside promenade, but its future hangs in the balance while the city considers what to make of it. The final stage of the Port Vell development is I. M. Pei's huge semicircular **World Trade Centre**, now fully open and containing all the facilities required to spearhead Barcelona's ambition to become the Mediterranean's busiest cruise and container port.

At the foot of the Moll d'Espanya begins the seaside Psg de Colom, where Cervantes lived at No.2 during his stay in Barcelona. Two blocks behind this runs the **Carrer Ample**, for several centuries the city's most aristocratic address, where Emperor Charles V, the kings of Hungary and Bohemia, and Barcelona's greatest merchants stayed and worshipped at the **Basilica de La Mercè** (***M*** *Drassanes or Barceloneta; open Mon–Sat 10–1 and 6–8.30, Sun 10–1.30 and 7–8.30*). Our Lady of Mercy joined Santa Eulàlia as co-patroness of Barcelona when she appeared in a vision to Jaume I, asking him to found an order devoted to the deliverance of Christian captives held by Barbary pirates. The first church dates from 1267, but has since been altered and rebuilt; its concave façade was transferred here from a Baroque church that was destroyed to make way for the Ajuntament's annexe. The fittings are Baroque, too, but there's a fine Gothic statue of the Virgin, carved in 1361 by Pere Moragues. These days her devotees include members of F. C. Barcelona, who sing her a hymn of thanks whenever the team wins an important match. In September (*3rd week*) all Barcelona celebrates the **Festa Major de la Mercè**, with music, dancing and daring *correfoc*.

Columbus and the Drassanes

Towering over the port in the Porta de la Pau is another souvenir of 1888, the **Monument a Colom** (Columbus Monument; *open summer daily 9–8.30; winter Mon–Fri 10–1.30 and 3.30–6.30, Sat–Sun 10–6.30; adm*), a 164ft cast-iron column made from melted cannons, topped by the admiral himself. He's been married: in honour of 1992, Catalan conceptual artist and matchmaker Antoni Miralda fixed him up with the Statue of Liberty in New York, and talked Birmingham into supplying the wedding ring; Paris made Liberty's wedding gown and Valencia sewed the world's biggest pair of blue jeans for the groom. You can ascend into the crown under his feet for the overall view in a lift. At the foot of the column you can catch a ***bus nautic*** (water bus) across Port Vell to Barceloneta or take one of the tour boats.

In a way it's ironic that Barcelona should honour the one man who led to the loss of its prestige and prosperity, as Spain turned to the riches from across the Atlantic and Seville took over as the premier port. A far more fitting memorial to the city's own past is the **Drassanes**, or royal shipyards, Columbus' neighbour on the Porta de la Pau. Enlarged in 1255 by Pere II the Great, the yards took their present form in 1388, the construction costs shared by Pere III the Ceremonious, the city, and the Corts. Given to the city by the navy in the 20th century, the Drassanes is the largest and best-preserved medieval shipyard in the world and houses the **Museu Marítim** (*Av. de les*

Drassanes; **M** *Drassanes; open daily 10–7; adm*), devoted to Catalunya's proud seafaring history. High, atmospheric vaults stow away ships' models, painted chests, figureheads and a copy of the *Llibro del Consulat del Mar*, medieval Europe's first maritime code, as well as a fascinating display of Mallorcan cartography from the Middle Ages. Recent additions include a beautiful old ship down at the docks, and the virtual reality 'Great Adventure of the Sea' (*headphones in English*).

Barcelona's Showcase Promenade: Las Ramblas

Columbus also marks the beginning of Barcelona's most famous street and one of the world's most urbane thoroughfares, Las Ramblas. *Ramla* means 'sand' in Arabic, and long ago this is what it was, the sandy bottom of a torrent that passed just outside the walls of the medieval city. In the dry season it became Barcelona's major thoroughfare, where the butchers had their stalls, where employers came in search of day-labourers, and where the gallows bore their strange fruit. By 1366 the torrent was paved over, and at the end of the 18th century, after Barceloneta had been laid out, it was decided to make the Ramblas a park lane. Trees were planted and benches installed; cast-iron streetlights, kiosks and flower stalls were added in the 19th century. In 1859 the first of the plane trees was planted and thrived so well that the Barcelonans have developed a saying, 'to grow like a tree in the Ramblas'.

Day and night the Ramblas (there are actually five connected streets) are crowded with natives and visitors from every continent. Kiosks selling newspapers in every conceivable language, cafés, hotels, burger stands, and magically tacky souvenir stands have sprouted up; Catalan Elvis impersonators, unicyclists, flamenco buskers and dozens of 'human statues' use it as a stage. If not the 'real' Barcelona, the Ramblas nevertheless have a big share of Barcelona's soul. And, like the rest of post-Olympic Barcelona, it has been tidied up, to the detriment of all the seedy sexy shops that once dominated the lowest *rambla*, **La Rambla de Santa Monica** (now they're squirrelled away in the side streets). From the 15th to 18th century the area was a major producer of artillery, most notably of a colossal 35,420lb cannon named 'Santa Eulàlia' cast in 1463, which blew up into smithereens when fired for the first time. Charles V in his endless warfare showered so much business on the 12 foundries here that they were called his 'twelve apostles'. The foundries have been supplanted by a wax museum, the **Museu de Cera** (*4–6 Rambla de Santa Monica;* **M** *Drassanes; open winter Mon–Fri 10–1.30 and 4–7.30, Sat–Sun 11–2 and 4.30–8.30; summer daily 10–10; adm*), where Nixon, Franco and Pinocchio keep company with the British Royal Family.

The next *rambla*, **Rambla dels Caputxins**, defines the heart of Barcelona's old theatre district. The first wooden playhouse was built in 1579 by the Hospital de la Santa Creu, after Philip II granted it a monopoly on dramatic spectacles to raise revenue. Today the site is occupied by the recently refurbished **Teatre Principal** (1850s), designed by Francesc Daniel Molina. In the **Plaça del Teatre** stands a monument to Serafi Pitarra, the 'founder of Catalan theatre', which you can learn all about in the **Theatrical Museum** (*C/Nou de la Rambla 3;* **M** *Drassanes or Liceu; open Mon–Sat 10.15–1* *and 4.15–7; guided tours only, in groups of no more than 30, so arrive early; tours every 15mins; adm*) in the nearby **Palau Güell**. The real reason to visit is the building itself: this was Gaudí's first major project for his patron, the financier Eusebi Güell, completed in 1888 to coincide with the Universal Exhibition.

Although badly damaged by Anarchists in the Civil War, much of the extraordinarily rare and precious materials Gaudí used in the rather morose Hispano-Moorish-medievalish interior remain intact. Here and there you can spot other signs of future Gaudí greatness: in the powerfully atmospheric crypt of a cellar; in the superb screen of parabolic arches by the *mirador*; in the three-storey-high parabolic cupola over the main salon, forming a honeycombed beehive pierced with silvery light. The upper floors are still under restoration, but a steep staircase leads out on to the rippling roof. The beehive dome is contained in a spire with a row of parabolic windows, topped by a lightning rod and a bat; these keep company with a forest of chimney and ventilator sculptures, each different and covered in Gaudí's signature *trencadis*.

At the head of the Rambla dels Caputxins, on the edge of the theatre district, stood an institution that Barcelona was especially proud of: the 4,000-seat **Gran Teatre del Liceu** (***M** Liceu; open for visits 9.45am–11am, last adm 10.15; information office open Mon–Fri 2–8.30*), rebuilt after a fire in 1861 as one of Europe's largest and most sumptuous auditoria, with five huge, semicircular balconies. For decades Spain's only opera house, presenting a regular season of grand opera, the Liceu often featured such home-grown virtuosi as Montserrat Caballé and Josep Carrers (José Carreras). In 1994, disaster struck during last-minute work on a stage set, when it burned to the ground again. The campaign to construct a clone began at once and, by late 1999 the prima donnas were again tickling the ears of Barcelona's opera mavens.

Pla Boqueria, with its colourful mosaic by Miró, marks the centre of the Ramblas. Here at No.82, a bank now occupies the **Casa Bruno Quadros** (1896), a former umbrella-maker's, studded with bright oriental parasols and defended by a swirling dragon holding a brolly designed by Josep Vilaseca. Opposite, another *modernista* shop, the **Antiga Casa Figueras** (1902), still sells luscious cakes. There are two worthy detours south of Pla Boqueria, into the once piquant **Barri Xinès** or 'Chinatown'. The first, down C/de Sant Pau, leads to the 12th-century Romanesque **Sant Pau del Camp** ('St Paul's in the Field'; ***M** Paral.lel; open Wed–Mon 11.30–1 and 6–7.30, Tues 11.30–12.30*). The façade is decorated with blind arcading and strikingly archaic reliefs of the hand of God, the Evangelists, and funny masks; most charming of all is the tiny cloister with its paired columns and triple-lobed Moorish arches and garden.

The second detour, just down C/de l'Hospital, leads to the **Antic Hospital de la Creu**, founded in 1024 and relocated in 1926 to Domènech i Montaner's *modernista* masterpiece near the Sagrada Família (*see* p.140), leaving behind a mostly 15th-century complex. The two huge Gothic arches on either side of the courtyard are the entrance to the Library of Catalunya, with a million volumes. Just inside the former **Casa de Convalecencia**, the vestibule is richly adorned with magnificent *azulejos* (1682) by Llorenç Passoles; others can be seen on the stair leading to the Gothic chapel, now a gallery called **La Capella** (*open Tues–Sat 12–2 and 4–8, Sun 11–2; adm free*), showcasing the work of young artists. Across the lane is the 18th-century Surgery College, now the

Real Academia de Cirugía y Medicina, with an elliptical anatomical amphitheatre retaining the original marble dissection table that revolves so students could all have a good peek at the guts. The neglected cloister with its orange trees has some lively carvings to show if you don't mind the smell of urine. Across Pla Boqueria, C/Cardenal Casañas leads into the **Barri del Pi** (named after a pine tree), another of the medieval *vilanovas* that grew up outside the Roman walls. It separates the Ramblas from the Barri Gòtic and has its spiritual centre in Plaça del Pi, where **Santa María del Pi** extols the virtues of Catalan Gothic, brooding like a cyclops with its huge rose window.

Beyond Pla Boqueria the next *rambla*, **Rambla de Sant Josep**, is the most perfumed, lined with kiosks selling flowers and birds and miniature rabbits. On the left, a large *modernista* neo-Gothic arch beckons you into the lively century-old Mercat de Sant Josep, better known as **La Boqueria** (*open Mon–Sat 8am–8.30pm*), founded in 1830 and still the place to find the greatest choice of produce in Barcelona. Just up from the market, the ivory-coloured neoclassical **Palau de la Virreina** (*99 Rambla de Sant Josep;* ***M*** *Liceu; open Tues–Sat 10–8.30, Sun 10–2.30; call* ***t*** *933 01 77 75 to see the Catalan national coin collection*) was built in 1778 for the Viceroy of Peru with loot he skimmed off the fabulous silver mines of Potosí. He died soon after, leaving it to his widow, the Virreina (hence its name), and it has been converted into an exhibition space.

The next *rambla*, the **Rambla dels Estudis**, was named after L'Estudi General, or University, that once stood here, founded by Martí the Humane and suppressed by Philip V; nowadays the promenade is full of the whistles and chirps of its permanent bird market. Monuments on this segment include the 18th-century **Església de Betlem**, its once Baroque interior blasted away in the Civil War; opposite, the arcaded **Palau de Moja**, from the same century, now houses the Generalitat's department of culture on the Ramblas. Further up, a right on to C/Canuda leads to the **Plaça Vila de Madrid**, with 2nd–4th-century AD **Roman tombs** that once lined the road out of the city; you can see how much the ground level has risen over the centuries. On the left, C/del Bonsuccès will take you to the glowing new **Museu d'Art Contemporani de Barcelona** (**MACBA**; *1 Plaça dels Àngels, www.macba.es,* ***M*** *Universitat; open winter Mon, Wed, Thurs, Fri 11–7.30, Sat 10–8, Sun 10–3; summer Mon, Wed, Fri 11–8, Thurs 11–7.30, Sat 10–8, Sun 10–3; adm*), designed by American architect Richard Meier in 1995. A pure white, light-filled space, its great glass front and ramps overlook the roofs and laundry of the old Raval quarter, while the is art crushed into second place at the back. Vibrant and varied nonetheless, the core collection includes such lights as Antoni Tàpies, Calder, Dubuffet, Barceló, Klee, Oldenburg, Raschenberg, and Christian Boltanski – don't miss his sinister bank vault-like *Réserve des Suisses Morts* (1991). Next door, a former orphanage has been turned into the **Centre de Cultura Contemporània de Barcelona** (**CCCB**; *C/Montalegre 5, www.cccb.org,* ***M*** *Universitat; open summer Tues–Sat 11–8, Sun 11–3; winter Tues, Thurs and Fri 11–2 and 4–8, Wed and Sat 11–8, Sun 11–7; adm*), hosting imaginative temporary exhibitions and supporting local projects.

The last little segment of the Ramblas, the **Rambla de les Canaletes**, is named after a magical fountain dispensed beneath a pretty four-headed streetlight that promises that all who drink of it will stay in or return to Barcelona.

Around the Plaça de Catalunya and the Palau de la Música

This vast, rather jumbly square is the hub of human and pigeon life in Barcelona, dividing the medieval city and the 19th-century extension, or Eixample; nearly all the city buses, metro and FGC lines converge here, under banks crowned with neon signs and the El Corte Inglés department store, a cross between a ferry boat and a radiator. In the centre are two fountains, a giant upside-down stair on a pedestal, and an older, wistful sculpture by Barcelona's own Josep Clará called *The Goddess*.

Tucked like a pearl behind the *plaça*, the simple Romanesque church, monastery and double-decker Gothic cloister of **Santa Anna** (*C/de Santa Anna;* ***M*** *Catalunya; open daily 9–1 and 6.30–8.30, hols 10–2*) hosted the Corts held under Ferdinand the Catholic – the last parliament before Aragón and Catalunya were tacked on to Castile. East of here, off Av. Portal de l'Angel, in a *modernista* fantasy of a house by Puig i Cadafalch, is **Els Quatre Gats** (The Four Cats; *C/Montsió 3;* ***M*** *Urquinaona or Catalunya;* ***t*** *933 02 41 40*), Barcelona's legendary bohemian-intellectual meeting place. Founded in 1897 by four artists (Rusinyol, Casas, Pere Romeu and Maurice Utrillo's father Miquel), it published its own art review and put on avant-garde puppet shows, recitals by young composers and exhibitions, including Picasso's first. Six years later, when everybody who was anybody had passed through, the original closed, to be replaced by the Cercle de Sant Lluc, a pious Catholic club that counted Gaudí among its members. Now, though, there's a new Quatre Gats, re-created with much of the original décor.

For *modernista* architecture in its most delightful extreme, continue down C/Montsió, take a left on to Vía Laietana and then right on to C/Mes Alt Sant Pere, where you will discover Lluís Domènech i Montaner's 1908 **Palau de la Música Catalana** (*C/de Sant Francesc de Paula 2,* ***t*** *932 95 72 00;* ***M*** *Catalunya or Urquinaona; if you can't book a concert ticket, you can book a tour; open daily 10–3.30; visits by guided tour only, departing every 30 mins in English, Spanish and Catalan, and lasting 50 mins, beginning with a tedious 20-min video; adm*). There's an old joke: one Catalan starts a business, two start a corporation, and three start a choral society. Josep Clavé was one of the founders of the Orfeò Català, which paid for the Palau de la Música; these days it also serves as Barcelona's principal concert hall, in spite of its famously bad acoustics. Undulating, polychromatic and adorned with floral and musical motifs in tiles and mosaics, it's almost too ripe and rich in these narrow streets, like a bouquet stuffed into a cupboard. The interior is, if anything, more colourful, an exuberant epiphany of stained glass and ceramics, with a hemicyclical stage set composed of half-tile, half-3D ceramic musical maidens before a background of *trencadis*.

The Eixample

In the 18th and early 19th century, the Ciutadella and city walls built by the Bourbon king Philip V after the city's defiant revolt in 1714 were a constant, humiliating reminder of Barcelona's subjection to Madrid. As the population grew and the industrial revolution took its first baby steps, the city became increasingly claustrophobic in its confines. Barcelona endlessly petitioned the government in reactionary Madrid to remove them, and finally succeeded in August 1854, during a brief interlude of liberalism. As soon as word reached Barcelona, a wild celebration filled the streets as every man, woman and child grabbed a tool and started hacking away at walls. The Bourbon wall was made of tougher stuff than the Berlin wall: it took ten years to dismantle, and was so despised that not a block of it was left in place.

Now that it had room to grow, the city sponsored a competition for the plan of the new extension, or **Eixample**. The winning plan (imposed by Madrid – Barcelona's Ajuntament had chosen another) was that of an engineer named Ildefons Cerdà, who designed a modular grid with distinct chamfered corners at the intersections to allow the new steam trams to turn more easily. But, unlike most grid plans, Cerdà's idea wasn't to create lots to buy and sell as easily as possible. He had Utopian visions: his abstract plan would eliminate social classes – there was no reason why one block should be better than another – and he planned markets, parks and social services to be distributed at equidistant points. Few city plans have been more hated, their intentions so thoroughly ignored by developers. With the 'Pla Cerdà' Barcelona quintupled in size over the next 50 years. Height and density restrictions soon went by the wayside; the trees and patio gardens were destroyed. Only one of Cerdà's parks came into being (near the Sants station); his vision of the **Plaça de les Glòries Catalanes** (where the Eixample's three big boulevards, the Diagonal, the Meridiana and Gran Vía de les Corts Catalanes meet) as the throbbing centre of Barcelona life has been sabotaged by its conversion into a giant elevated roundabout, in the presence of Spain's largest shopping mall, while recent architectural additions include Rafael Moneo's **Auditori** and the **Teatre Nacional de Catalunya** by Ricardo Bofill. In spite of Cerdà's egalitarian intentions, social snobbery won out and, just as Paris has its Right and Left Banks, Barcelona has its Right and Left Eixample, divided by the delightful linden-lined **Rambla de Catalunya**. The Right Eixample is the more prestigious: here, to make up for the enforced equality of the Pla Cerdà, *modernista* architects created visual fireworks to flaunt the status of their wealthy clients. If the Barri Gòtic is Europe's largest medieval neighbourhood, the Eixample holds its greatest trove of Art Nouveau buildings. Over the past decade the Ajuntament has sponsored a massive programme to restore, polish and preserve this unique legacy; in some cases, even Cerdà's gardens have finally come into being, planted in the heart of the blocks.

The Passeig de Gràcia and the Fairest of Discords

The greatest concentration of *modernista* masterpieces is along the Eixample's most elegant boulevard, the Passeig de Gràcia, the old road from the Barri Gòtic to the once separate town of Gràcia. The beautiful street lamps arching halfway over the street from white *trencadi* bases at once set the boulevard apart. If you love architecture, though, take the first right from the Psg de Gràcia to C/de Casp, where at No.48 stands the **Casa Calvet** (1898), Gaudí's first apartment building – the ironwork detail, the two crosses, and the decorative elements presage his future masterpieces on the Passeig de Gràcia. The most dazzling stretch of it, between C/Consell de Cent and C/d'Aragó, is known as the **Mansana de la Discòrdia** – a pun on *mansana*, which means both 'apple' and 'block'; here every passer-by can play the role of the Trojan

Paris and award the prize to the fairest of the three *modernista* beauties. The first, at No.35, is the **Casa Lleó Morera** (1905), Domènech i Montaner's most lavish residential building, decorated with sculpture by Eusebi Arnau. As the ground floor was destined to house a photographer's studio, Arnau covered it with nymphs and reliefs relating to electricity and cameras, all sacrificed in 1943 in the interest of larger shop windows; the original cupola and interior furnishings were removed as well (three nymphs, holding a camera, a gramophone and a lightbulb, survive on the second floor).

Three doors down at No.41 stands Puig i Cadafalch's **Casa Amatller**. In 1898 Amatller, Barcelona's Willy Wonka of Catalan chocolate, hired Puig to give an existing apartment building the Gothic treatment. Puig's Gothic, however, is like no one else's: the façade, decorated in discreet *sgraffito*, culminates in a remarkable stepped gable richly aglitter with blue, pink and cream tiles. Don't miss the sculptural details by Eusebi Arnau, including Catalunya's patron St George battling the dragon, and step inside to the **Institut Amatller d'Art Hispànic** (*open for tours Thurs at 11 and 12, by appt only,* ***t*** *932 16 01 75; library open Mon–Fri 10–1.30; closed July and Aug*), where you can glimpse some of Puig's original furnishings.

Next door, the **Casa Batlló** (*No. 43*) was a similarly nondescript residential Eixample building when textile magnate Josep Batlló commissioned Gaudí to give it a facelift in 1904. Being a Catalan nationalist like every other *modernista* architect, Gaudí transformed its flat façade into an allegory of St George and the dragon, a rippling, magical skin of different shades of blue ceramics and *trencadis*. His collaborator Josep Jujol i Gilbert topped it with an equally sublime coloured roof: the dragon's scaly back. The characteristic Gaudí pinnacle with its bulb dome and cross is St George's lance, placed to one side to complement the symmetry of the Casa Amatller; the *trencadi*-covered chimneys, invisible from the ground, are the dragon's multi-spiked tail. You can step into the vestibule (*Mon–Fri*) to look at the magnificent blue ceramic light-well, but to see the stunning first-floor apartment, you'll have to rent it for an hour or two.

Around the corner from the Mansana de la Discordia, the **Fundació Antoni Tàpies** (*C/Aragó 255;* ***M*** *Passeig de Gràcia; open Tues–Sun 11–8; closed Mon exc on hols; adm*), is headquartered in Domènech's building for his brother's publishing company, Editorial Montaner i Simón (1880–85). It's an early example of his love for good, bare Catalan brick and iron, a prototype of *modernisme*. The *Núvol i Cadira*, hovering over the building like a giant steel-wool pad, demonstrates Tàpies' love of everyday materials. Born in Barcelona and educated at law school, Tàpies (1923–94) turned to art during the Second World War, painting in a Surrealist vein before turning to abstract works. His imaginative use of mixed media – from scraps of paper, rags and *objets trouvés*, to furniture and musical instruments – led him to be considered as one of the most influential Spanish artists of the latter half of the 20th century. In 1984 he set up his foundation for the study of contemporary and non-Western art; today, it displays a selection of Tàpies' art upstairs and changing exhibitions of other people's below.

Further up Passeig de Gràcia: La Pedrera

Casa Batlló created such a sensation that some even richer people immediately hired Gaudí to outdo himself a few blocks up the Passeig de Gràcia. Here he was given

Genius and Crank

Antoni Gaudí i Cornet (1852–1926) was one of the most innovative architects of any time, and his major works such as La Pedrera have been listed in Unesco's catalogue of World Heritage properties. Although Gaudí was regarded as an eccentric or even a hippies' architect in the 1960s, you don't have to be in Barcelona long to realize that his reputation has since been polished and used to fuel an industry of its own: you can take an all-Gaudí tour, purchase models of his benches in Parc Güell, or even build your own little Casa Batlló from a paper kit. Although classed as a *modernista*, Gaudí's creation of new forms and textures and his vision of decoration as being as integral to the structure as its walls or roof went far beyond anything built by his colleagues. No architect ever studied nature more intently; in his buildings, stone became organic, sensuous, dripping; iron was wrought into whiplash ribbons, trailing leaves and spider webs; the old Muslim art of covering surfaces with broken tiles (*trencadis* in Catalan) was given a new vibrant, abstract meaning, reaching a kind of epiphany in the Parc Güell. Gaudí ingeniously reinvented the almost impossible parabolic arch, last seen with the Hittites: he would create hanging models made of chains, suspend carefully measured weights from them, take photos from every angle and turn the photos upside down. Much of the mathematic work he and his colleagues had to do in those pre-computer days is mindboggling. He also had the luck to draw on a highly skilled craft base to give his imagination substance.

So it tends to come as a surprise to learn that Gaudí, whose very name in Catalan means 'delight', was the last man you'd want to invite over for dinner (to begin with, he was probably the only Catalan vegan who ever lived). Obsessive, morbidly pious, a nationalistic egomaniac, he regarded La Pedrera purely as a pedestal for a 40ft-high statue of the Virgin Mary and a pair of angels, an idea his client prudently vetoed after the 1909 Setmana Trájica when Barcelona was still smoking from another of its periodic bouts of church burnings; the kind of wealthy industrialists who hired Gaudí made their bundles by keeping the working people of Barcelona so downtrodden that anarchism seemed to be their only hope. Gaudí didn't get it. La Pedrera was his last secular building (1910), before he devoted the rest of his life trying to expiate the church-torching sins of his fellow citizens by building the Sagrada Família.

a virgin chamfered corner of the Eixample, and the result, the **Casa Milà**, was just what the Milàs ordered: the most extraordinary, singular apartment building ever, nicknamed *La Pedrera*, 'the stone quarry'. The five-storey stone façade undulates around the bevelled corners of the block like a cliff sculpted by waves of wind, pierced by windows that look as if they have been eroded into the stone, underlined by kelp-inspired balconies of forged iron spilling over the edges. This sea cliff of stone rises to a white, foamy crest of a **roof**, topped a garden of reddish chimneys grouped like bouquets of visored knights and four globular stair exits iced in white *trencadis*. The roof itself is supported by a great wavy tunnel of Gaudí's catenary parabolic arches. The interior is nearly as striking as the façade, with its two irregular circular patios open to the sky, enclosed in winding ramps.

On the fourth floor a *modernista* apartment, **El Pis de la Pedrera** (*open daily 10–8; adm free; guided visits Mon–Fri at 6pm, Sat, Sun at 11am; July–Sept Fri and Sat has La Pedrera by Night, with drinks and music 9pm–midnight;* **t** *934 84 59 95*) has been recreated, full of the then latest gadgets; the **Espai Gaudí** offers a thorough overview of the man's work through models, drawings, photos and videos.

Around La Pedrera: Other Modernista Highlights

Just beyond La Pedrera, Av. Diagonal slices across the waffle of the Eixample. If in the Mansana de la Discòrdia you gave the prize to Puig i Cadafalch, two of his principal works flaunt themselves just to the right. His neo-Gothic-Plateresque Palau Barón de-Quadras (1904) is now the **Museu de la Música** (*Av. Diagonal 373;* **M** *Diagonal; open winter Tues and Thurs–Sun 10–2, Wed 10–8; summer Tues–Sun 10–2; closed Mon; adm*), with a fascinating collection of antique and exotic instruments from the 16th century onwards, including one of Adophe Sax's original saxophones and a fine collection of guitars. At Nos. 416–20, Puig's massive neo-Gothic apartment block, the **Casa de les Punxes** (1903–5), or 'House of Spikes', bristles with the pointiest witch's-hat roofs ever, as needly spires rise out of its brick gables. Here, too, at No.442 is the **Casa Comalat** (1911) designed by one of Gaudí's followers, Salvador Valer, with an undulating rear façade and a magnificent entrance hall of tile and stained glass.

If you awarded your apple to Domènech i Montaner, follow C/Mallorca (running to the right off Psg de Gràcia), where in 1893 he added a ceramic façade to the **Casa Montaner** (*C/de Mallorca;* **M** *Diagonal; open Sat 10–1, call* **t** *934 87 22 33 to be certain*) now the seat of the Delegació del Govern a Catalunya, Madrid's representatives in the region. At No.291, *a modernista* furniture showroom now occupies Domènech's **Casa Thomas** (1898), a neo-Gothic apartment house with decorative ceramic appliqués.

The Sagrada Família

Entrance from C/de Sardenya; **M** *Sagrada Família; open April–Aug daily 9–8; Mar and Sept–Oct daily 9–7; Nov–Feb daily 9–6; adm.*

George Orwell, writing of the church burnings during the Civil War in his *Homage to Catalonia*, wondered why there was one that the mobs always spared, a peculiar one with spires shaped like bottles looming high over the Right Eixample. These 350ft bottles, of course, belonged to Gaudí's Sagrada Família. Slightly smaller than St Peter's in Rome, occupying an entire block of the Cerdà plan, the Templo Expiatorio de la Sagrada Família is surely the most compelling, controversial and most unfinished building site in the world, today the symbol of Barcelona and of the scale of the city's extraordinary ambition.

The temple was begun in 1882, the brainchild of a bookdealer named Josep M Bocabella Verdaguer, fervent follower of reactionary Pope Pius IX and founder of a society dedicated to St Joseph, devoted to expiating the sins of *modernisme*. He originally hired Francesc del Villar, who planned a neo-Gothic church, but only got as far as the crypt before disagreements with Bocabella led to his replacement by Gaudí in

1883, when Gaudí was only 31. He finished the crypt and then continued to work on and off on the project for the next 43 years, which grew grander with each plan. In his last 15 years he accepted no other commissions, and when money ran low, he sold everything he owned for the project and moved into a hut on the construction site. He spent his free time soliciting funds, and lived on a diet of bread, water and prayer.

Gaudí intended the Sagrada Família to be 'an immense palace of Christian memory' and wanted every possible aspect of Catholic doctrine to be expressed in some nook or cranny of the temple. There were to be three façades, dedicated to the Birth, the Passion and the main one, to Glory; each of these would have four towers, symbolizing the twelve Apostles. Four higher towers would be dedicated to the Evangelists and, between them, a truly colossal 575ft tower would symbolize the Saviour, with a large tower to the Virgin on the side. Gaudí started on the **Birth Façade** and finished one tower, before absent-mindedly wandering in front of a streetcar in 1926. He was buried in the crypt chapel. His followers attempted to have him canonized; by 1935, they had completed the façade according to his models. Orwell was wrong when he wrote that the Anarchists never damaged the Sagrada Família: in 1936 they broke into the workshops and set fire to every plan and model they found; then, adding insult to injury, they set about breaking into the tombs of Bocabella and Gaudí in the crypt.

And so the temple stood until 1954, when the Joseph society raised enough money to continue the project in the manner of Gaudí, instructing architects to guess the master's intent from a few surviving drawings. Since 1987, architect Jordi Bonet and sculptor Josep Subirachs have been in charge. Their work has offended purists, who believe the temple is best left as it was when Gaudí died, as a memorial to his unique genius; they also point out that Gaudí never even followed his own models, but was ever changing and revising his plans as he went along. The Josephines, however, insist that Gaudí wished the Sagrada Família to be like the cathedrals of the Middle Ages, constructed over generations. Subirachs completed the **Passion Façade** in 1998, but there is something depressing about the result. Where the Birth façade has Gaudí's unmistakable textured, organic style, like some primordial growth, Subirachs' is sinister and kitsch, as purposefully brutal as its subject matter, decorated with robotic sculptures and a magic square based on the number 33. He is currently putting on the finishing touches: a great bronze door carved with letters from the Gospel, four huge apostles and a 25ft metal Christ. For a small fee you can take the **lift** (*open 10–5.45*) up the Passion Towers, for a vertiginous ramble high over the city.

The **interior** is still a building site. The nave, Gaudí's would-be 'forest of stone', was completed in 1999, above which an awesome crane awaits its part in the grand scheme. Bonet is now concentrating on the apse, due for completion by 2010, and the Josephines hope to finish the whole by the centenary of Gaudí's death, in 2026.

The **Museu de la Sagrada Família** is housed in the crypt, with photos, diagrams, plaster models, bits of sculpture, and an astonishing catenary model, made of chains and weighted sacks, used by Gaudí to build the Crypt Güell.

The Avinguda Gaudí, lined with cafés, leads from the Sagrada Família through a neighbourhood called Camp de l'Arpa to another gargantuan *modernista* work, this time one that is both complete and useful. Domènech i Montaner died before finishing his **Hospital de la Santa Creu i Sant Pau** (*C/de Sant Antoni María Claret;* ***M*** *Hospital de Sant Pau; you can visit the lobby and wander around (but not in) the pavilions*), but his son finished the job for him in 1930. Covering nine blocks of the Eixample, it's a lovely place to visit even if you're perfectly well, conceived as a garden city of 26 mosaic-encrusted pavilions, topped with tiled roofs.

South of the Sagrada Família, the brick *modernista*-Moorish **Plaça de Toros Monumental** (*Gran Vía de los Corts Catalanes 749;* ***M*** *Monumental; open April–Sept daily 10.30–2 and 4–7; adm*) dates from 1911, with three towers supporting huge yellow, white and blue ceramic dinosaur eggs. Its **Museu Taurí** keeps a collection of famous bulls' heads and memorabilia of the great bullfighter Manolete.

Montjuïc

Montjuïc is lovely for walking, but watch out for learner drivers. In summer, a free ***bus*** *runs from Pla d'Espanya to the Poble Espanyol; every ½hr, bus No.61 from* ***M*** *Espanya loops from the Palau Nacional past the Poble Espanyol, Olympic stadium and Fundació Miró to Pla Dante, where the* ***telefèric de Montjuïc*** *continues up to the castle. You can also take the* ***funicular*** *from* ***M*** *Paral.lel ; for times,* *see p.105.* *The* ***cable car*** *from Barceloneta to Miramar is not currently working, but a* ***tourist train*** *(April–Sept daily 10am–11pm) plies between Pla d'Espanya and Miramar.*

The southern end of Barcelona is closed off by the 705ft slope of Montjuïc, Barcelona's grandstand and showcase. Its peculiar name is derived either from 'Mons Jovis' – the mountain of Jove – or from the 'mountain of Jews' for the large Jewish cemetery discovered there. For most of Barcelona's history it was reserved for defence, but in 1914, the entire northern slope was beautifully landscaped by Jean-Claude Forestier and local architect Nicolas Rubió i Tuduri. The driving force, of course, was a show, although politics and economics kept intruding, and it wasn't until 1929 that the International Exhibition was under way. It bequeathed a permanent fair to the city and provided homes for its collections of medieval art and archaeology. Then, in 1992, the Exhibition's stadium became the centrepiece of the Olympic ring.

Plaça d'Espanya and Around

The show begins in the round Plaça d'Espanya, marking the end of the Left Eixample and the wide boulevard of the **Parel.lel**, cutting down to the sea. This street has had a number of official names in its career, but has been known simply as the 'Paral.lel' ever since 1794, when it was discovered to lie exactly on the 41° 44' parallel – fascinating to the Barcelonans, whose city otherwise refuses to square with the compass. During the first half of this century, the Paral.lel was known as 'the Montmartre of Barcelona' for its music halls, several of which have survived. One edge of the circular *plaça* is occupied by the city's smaller, older bullring, the Moorish-style **Les Arenes**.

The main entrance to Montjuïc is guarded by a pair of tall **Venetian campaniles**, framing the grand view of the main exhibition palaces; various trade fairs occupy the buildings throughout the year. In between, the **Font Mágica** (*4 May–4 Oct Thurs–Sun and eves before hols, shows every half-hour 9.30pm–11.30pm, ending at midnight; 4 Oct–4 May Fri–Sat 7pm–8.30pm, shows every half-hour*), created by engineer Carlos Buigas for the 1929 exhibition, performs a dazzling aquatic ballet of colour and light while blue searchlights radiate a peacock's tail of beams from the Palau Nacional.

To the right of the fountain, the Ajuntament has reconstructed (1986) the elegant **Pavelló Barcelona** (*Av. Marqués de Comillas, www.miesbcn.com;* **M** *Espanya; open Nov–Mar daily 10–6.30; April–Oct daily 10–8; adm*), designed by Bauhaus architect Mies van der Rohe ('I would rather be good than original') for Germany's exhibit in the 1929 fair; the key exhibit is Mies' *Barcelona Chair*, denizen of a million waiting rooms.

The Palau Nacional: Museu Nacional d'Art de Catalunya (MNAC)

www.mnac.es; **M** *Espanya; open Tues–Sat 10–7, Sun 10–2.30; adm.*

From the fountains, a never-ending stair (and outdoor escalators that crank up on approach) ascend to the Palau Nacional, home of the remarkable **Museu Nacional d'Art de Catalunya**. It contains the world's foremost collection of Romanesque murals, rescued in the 1920s from decaying chapels in the Pyrenees; strikingly bold, expressive paintings, directly translated from Byzantine art and illuminations, with sharply delineated, brightly coloured forms and hieratic attitudes. The divine figures stare out hypnotically with riveting dark eyes, red circled cheeks, stylized stringy hair and weird elongated hands that look like flippers. In the most primitive, the artist of the 11th-century San Miquel de Marmellar could hardly draw a face. The four finest are all from the 12th century: Santa María d'Aneu; Santa María de Taüll, with an unforgettable, weird scene of David beheading a Goliath with a sausage body; Sant Joan de Boí, with jugglers and the *Stoning of St Stephen*; and Sant Climent de Taüll, with its famous *Christ in Majesty*, one of the most commanding, direct images in medieval art. The striking crucifix called the *Majestat Batlló* portrays Christ, not in the exquisite agony favoured in the rest of Spain, but dressed like a king in a beautiful tunic, open-eyed and serene, symbolizing the triumph over death. The Catalan gift for surrealism is expressed in the comic martyrdoms of the 12th-century *Durro Altar Frontal*.

At the end of the Romanesque section are secular murals of a griffon from the palatine room of San Pedro de Arlanzer near Burgos, and the ceiling of the chapterhouse of Sigena in Aragón (1200), damaged by fire in 1936 but still superb, its Old and New Testament figures inspired by English miniatures and Norman Sicilian mosaics.

Catalan Gothic art is equally well represented, with 13th-century murals of the Siege of Mallorca, beautiful works by master Jaume Huguet, and the refined *retablo* of the *Virgin of the Councillors* (1445) by Lluis Dalmau. When, in 2003, the Museu d'Art Modern is relocated here, the museum will offer a complete feast of old and new Catalan art.

Around the Palau Nacional

A short walk just west of the Palau Nacional, you'll find the **Botanical Gardens of Montjuïc** (*open winter Mon–Sat 10–3; summer Mon–Sat 10–5*), the **Mirador del**

Llobregat (one of several Montjuïc belvederes, this one with Josep Llimona's statue of a weary St George) and another relic of the 1929 fair, the **Poble Espanyol** (*Av. Marqués de Comillas, www.poble-espanyol.com;* **M** *Espanyol;* ***t*** *933 25 78 66; open July and Aug Mon 9–8, Tues–Thurs 9–2, Fri and Sat 9–4, Sun 9–midnight; Sept–June Mon 9–8, Tues–Sat 9–2, Sun 9–midnight; adm, free adm with a reservation at a nightclub or big restaurant, 50% reduction with Bus Turístic ticket, see p.105*). Conceived as an anthology of Spanish architecture with the slogan 'Get to Know Spain in an Hour', here the replicas of famous buildings across the country were cunningly arranged with Disneyland deftness; souvenir and craft shops occupy every other building, while some show screenings of the film *Barcelona Experience* (*hourly 10.30–8*).

Montjuïc's other attractions lie east of the Palau Nacional. Just behind it are the formal gardens of the Exposition's **Palauet Albéniz** (*Psg de Santa Madrona; adm by written request only*), named after the Catalan composer and official Barcelona residence of the Spanish King and Queen. Just downhill from here, the **Museu d'Etnològic** (*Psg de Santa Madrona;* **M** *Poble Sec; open Wed and Fri–Sun 10–2, Tues and Thurs 10–7; closed Mon; adm*) has a fascinating collection from Morocco, Japan, Australia, Africa and particularly Latin America: Amazonian shrunken heads, skeleton dolls from Mexico, a Peruvian head deformer, and more. Below this, steps lead down to the oldest gardens of Montjuïc, **La Rosaleda**, with its Font del Gat ('cat fountain') and the **Teatre Grec**, carved from an old quarry in 1929 and used for the summer Greek theatre festival. Just across from here, in the 1929 Graphic Arts Palace, the **Museu Arqueològic** (*Psg de Santa Madrona;* **M** *Poble Sec; open Tues–Sat 9.30–7, Sun 10–2.30; closed Mon; adm, free Sun*) is a 'prequel' to the Palau Nacional, covering Palaeolithic to Visigothic Catalunya. It contains finds from the ancient Greek colony Empúries, Iberian vases and Roman mosaics of chariot races, as well as a very interesting Balearic collection featuring megalithic models and Carthaginian sculpture from Ibiza.

Further up, off Av. de l'Estadi, the **Anella Olímpica** holds the Olympic swimming pool, the **Piscines Bernat Picornell** (*bring your passport and some money if you want to swim*) and the **Estadi Olímpic**, originally built for the 1929 fair. Barcelona made a bid for the 1936 games here, but lost out to Hitler's Berlin; in defiance it decided to hold a non-fascist 'People's Olympics', an event spoiled by another fascist named Franco, whose revolt began the Civil War the day before the games were to open. The interior was rebuilt to hold 70,000 for the 1992 games, preserving the 1929 façade and its bronzes by Pau Gargallo. The gate is often open so you can look around and visit the **Galeria Olímpica** (*open July–Sept Mon–Sat 10–2 and 4–8, Sun 10–2; June Mon–Sat 10–2 and 4–7, Sun 10–2; April–May Mon–Sat 10–2 and 4–6, Sun 10–2; Oct–Mar Mon–Fri 10–1 and 4–6, Sun 10–2; adm*), with videos of the opening and closing ceremonies. The adjacent covered arena, the **Palau Sant Jordi**, designed by Japanese architect Arata Isozaki, is one of the most beautiful in Europe and is used for sports and concerts alike. Tucked on the hill nearby is the **Institut Nacional d'Educzio Fisica de Catalunya**, designed by Barcelona's own Ricardo Bofill. The elegant white needle nearby, death to any passing Zeppelin, is the **Torre de Telefònica**, a telecommunications tower.

Fundació Joan Miró to the Castell Montjuïc

Av. de l'Estadi continues to the **Fundació Joan Miró** (*Av. de l'Estadi, www.bcn.fjmiro.es;* **M** *Paral.lel then take Funicular;* **t** *933 29 19 08; open Tues, Wed, Fri and Sat 11–7 (July–Sept 10–8), Thurs 10–9.30, Sun and hols 10–2.30; closed Mon exc hols; adm*), in a beautiful white building bathed in natural light, designed in 1972 by Miró's friend Josep Lluís Sert, a student of Le Corbusier (and enlarged in 1986 by Sert's collaborator, Jaume Freixa). A native of Barcelona, Miró (1893–1983) moved to Paris in 1919 where he soon joined the Surrealist movement, only to go a step beyond by evolving his own playful, personal language to express the dream reality of the creative unconscious. Central to all the works is the tension between abstraction and representation, reflecting the duality of character that Miró considered fundamental to the Catalan identity. Most of the works are the output of Miró's final two decades, but he also conceived the Fundació as a forum for experimentation and study, and it holds wide-ranging special exhibitions of contemporary art as well as a permanent collection of works made by artists in homage of Miró. The core, of course, is an excellent sampling of the artist's own paintings, sculptures, textile works and drawings made between 1917 and the 1970s. They're not all bright and spontaneous; most strikingly the lithographs of the *Barcelona Series*, inspired by the horrors of the Civil War.

East of the Fundació Miró, the **Jardins Mossèn Jacint Verdaguer** are especially pretty in the spring. A sculpture in honour of the *sardana*, the Catalan national dance, stands opposite the old fun park, earmarked to be replaced in 2004 with a new bucolic 'macropark' for the Forum of Cultures, while overhead the cable car swoops up to the **Castell de Montjuïc**.

The first real castle on this site was thrown up in 30 days during the Catalan Rebellion in 1640, when the defenders won a stirring victory over the Castilian forces of Philip IV. The rest of its history is singularly unhappy. Rebuilt in 1759, it spent years honing an expertise in torturing political prisoners; in 1909 the Anarchist founder of Barcelona's secular Modern Schools, Francesc Ferrer, was executed here following the 'Tragic Week' church burnings – even though Ferrer wasn't even in Barcelona at the time – raising a storm of protest throughout Europe. A decade later in the infamous La Canadiense electrical strike (Spain's worst and bloodiest, putting the lights out in Barcelona, causing severe food shortages, and shutting down 70 per cent of its industry), 3,000 workers were imprisoned in the castle. In October 1940, the President of the Generalitat, Lluís Companys, was captured by the Gestapo in France and handed over to Franco, who had him secretly taken to the castle and shot; a stone marks the spot. Finally, in 1960 the military ceded the castle to the city, which today uses this haunted ground for its **Museu Militar** (*open Mar–Oct 9.30–7.30; Nov–Mar 9.30–4.30; adm*), with an intriguing collection of models, maps, weapons, lead soldiers and armour acquired by insatiable hoarder, Frederic Marés (*see* p.123).

Below, near the cable-car station at **Miramar**, you can enjoy an especially fine view of the city. Next to the bar there, incongruously overlooking the bustling docks, are the **Jardins de Mossèn Costa i Llobera** (*Ctra de Miramare*), with their superb, if rather neglected, succulent collection: a Manhattan of towering cacti interspersed with exotic specimens that look as if they have dropped in from another planet.

Into the Hills: Around the Edge of Barcelona

On the map, the ragged edges of the Eixample's grid mark its contact with older, once independent towns or hills that defy its modular lines. One of the ex-towns, Gràcia, is worth a visit for itself; other suburbs attracted moneyed Barcelona in the early 20th century, leaving some fine works by Gaudí to mark its passing, notably the sublime Park Guëll. Other sites are of more specialized interest: **Horta**, for instance, on the far northwest edge of Barcelona in the Collserola foothills, has its **Parc del Laberint** (*Psg del Vall de Hebrón;* ***M*** *Montbau, then a 10-min walk; open Nov–Feb Tues–Sun 10–6; Mar and Oct Tues–Sun 10–7; April and Sept Tues–Sun 10–8; May–Aug Tues–Sun 10–9; closed Mon; only 750 admitted at a time; adm, adm free Wed and Sun*), a park belonging to the Marqués de Alfarràs, who in 1799 hired Italian architect Domenico Bagutti to lay out the formal gardens, lake, canals, pavilions and a cypress **maze**. These days access to the park is via a footbridge by the Olympic **Velódrom**, set in its own park with a 'sculpture-poem' by Joan Brossa and a reconstruction of Josep Sert's **Pavilion of the Spanish Republic**, built for the 1937 Paris Exposition Universal as a cry of defiance in the midst of the Civil War: the original housed Picasso's *Guernica*, Julio González's *Montserrat*, Miró's lost *El Segador* and Calder's *Mercury Fountain*.

Park Güell

'Toto, I don't think we're in Kansas anymore.'

Dorothy, in *The Wizard of Oz*

M *Lesseps, then walk 400yds up Travessera de Dalt and turn left up steep C/Llarrard; bus No.24 from Pla de Catalunya; open Nov–Feb daily 10–6; Mar and Oct daily 10–7; April and Sept daily 10–8; May–Aug daily 10–9.*

It is a characteristic paradox of Spain for it to contain within its borders both our century's greatest monument to Death – Franco's Valle de los Caídos – and its greatest evocation of the infinite variety and magic of life – Gaudí's Park Güell, located south of Horta on one of Barcelona's great balconies, 'Bald Mountain', Mont Pelat. The park owes its existence to tycoon Eusebi Güell, who bought two farms here in 1902 to lay out an exclusive English garden suburb (hence the 'k' in Park). To attract buyers, he gave his pet architect free reign to create a grand entrance, a central market area for residents and terraced drives. As a housing development it was a flop, so Güell came to live here himself, and after his death his family donated the park to the city.

In the midst of the dull, not-so-hoity-toity *urbanización* that actually was built on Bald Mountain, the Park Güell glows like an enchanted mirage. The entrance is flanked by two fairy-tale **pavilions** as bright as candy, crowned by sloping roofs of swirling coloured mosaics, cupolas, a magic mushroom and Gaudí's signature steeple with its double cross. The grand stair swoops around the most jovial **salamander** imaginable, clinging to the fountain and covered with brightly coloured *trencadis*. On top of the stair, the remarkable cavernous **Sala Hipóstila** opens out onto Gaudí's covered market, known as the **Hall of a Hundred Columns**, with its thick forest of hollow Doric columns (there are, in fact, only 86). The shallow vaults of the ceiling are covered with white *trencadis* and beautiful ceramic medallions by Jujol. The scalloped roof of the hall is rimmed with a snaking ceramic collage – predating collages – that also serves as the back of fantastic **serpentine bench** on the terrace above. Designed mostly by Jujol, immense care went into the apparently random patterns of colour, words, and simple and abstract designs, creating new delights with each turn and change of light. Then there are Gaudí's extraordinary nubby **porticoes**, sloping in and out of the hillside, made of stone found on the site and fitted together to form sinuous passageways with curling walls and fanciful planters. No two columns are alike; one resembles Carmen Miranda holding a pile of rocks on her head instead of fruit salad.

Before moving to his hut by the Sagrada Família, Gaudí lived for 20 years in a house by the park's C/del Carmel entrance. Designed by his associate Francesc Berenguer, it is now the **Torre Rosa** or **Casa-Museu Gaudí** (*open Mar–Sept daily 10–7; Nov–Feb daily 10–6; adm*) and contains plans and examples of the wonderful organic furniture that Gaudí designed for his houses.

Up from the Park Güell, bus No.25 continues to one of the city's newer urban spaces, the **Parc de la Creueta del Coll**, with a popular palm-rimmed pool and beach as its centrepiece, and sculptor Chillida's giant gentle claw, the *Elogi de l'aigua* ('praise water') suspended over the water.

Gràcia

***M** Fontana or Diagonal; **FGC** Gràcia; **bus** No.22 or 24 from Pla de Catalunya.*

Gràcia, the most distinctive of all the towns absorbed by the growing city, was a vortex for liberal and progressive ideas throughout the 19th century: Anarchists, workers, feminists, vegetarians, Protestants and ardent Republicans flourished here, formed societies and movements, and published an astounding number of periodicals (one in Esperanto). Today Gràcia still has a laid-back neighbourhood atmosphere, a nice contrast to the Barcelona of big art and monuments. **Plaça Rius i Taulet** is its spiritual heart, dominated by a 125ft belltower adorned with symbols of the zodiac, while nearby **Plaça del Sol** is the centre of Gràcia's nightlife. Not far from the Fontana metro station is Gaudí's first house, the **Casa Vicens** (*C/de les Carolines 18–24; closed to visitors*), built 1883–5. Islamic in inspiration, its façade is adorned with brickwork and checkerboard patterns of green and white tiles (the owner was a tile merchant), and has a delightful iron gate and fence of date-palm fronds.

Tibidabo

***FGC** Av. del Tibidabo, then **Tramvia** Blau to Pla Dr Andreu, then **Funicular**; **Tibibus**: July and Aug only, every half-hour from Pla de Catalunya from 11.30am.*

For an incomparable view over Barcelona, ascend the highest peak of the Collserola, the 1,804ft Tibidabo, just west of the city. Its name, peculiar even by Catalan standards, comes from the Gospel of St Matthew, who quotes the devil, '*Haec omnia tibi dabo si cadens adoraberis me*' ('All this I will give to you if you will fall down and worship me'). Purists might claim the incident took place in the Sinai, but a Catalan would counter 'What's so tempting about a rocky desert?' The view from here, taking in Barcelona, Montserrat, the Pyrenees and Mallorca, is a pretty seductive alternative.

The best time to go is in the late afternoon on a clear day, as dusk falls and the lights begin to twinkle in the great city below. On the summit stands Enric Sagnier's spiky, neo-Mormon expiatory temple of **Sagrat Cor** (*open daily 10–7*), restaurants, a hotel and the **Parc d'Attracciones** (*open Tues–Fri 11–7, Sat and Sun 11–9; adm approx. €15 to ride everything*) offering one of the most panoramic Ferris-wheel rides imaginable. Admission includes the **Museu d'Autòmats del Tibidabo**, with wooden fortune-tellers, mechanical bands and other carnival gizmos from the 19th century onwards. Just south, another summit of the Collserola is occupied by Norman Foster's slender and dynamic 800ft **Torre de Collserola** (***FGC** Peu del Funicular, then **Funicular** de Vallvidrera and **bus** No.211; **bus** No.211 (or summer tourist train) from Parc d'Attracciones; open summer Sat and Sun 11–7, Wed–Fri 11–2.30 and 3.30–7; winter Sat and Sun 11–7; adm*), a high-tech telecommunications tower built for the Olympics that offers giddy views down on Tibidabo itself. The **Museu de la Ciència** (*C/Tedor Roviralta 55; **FGC** Av. del Tibidabo, then **Tramvia** Blau; open Tues–Sun 10–8; adm*) has enough hands-on science exhibits to keep most kids entertained for at least a couple of hours.

Sarrià and Pedralbes

West of Gràcia, things get more exclusive. The schizophrenic suburb of **Sarrià** has a new part full of smart homes with doormen, but the old part is little changed; the main street, C/Major de Sarrià, connects up small squares with a lazy village atmosphere. The **Col.legi de les Teresianes** (*C/de Ganduxer 85–105; **FGC** Les Tres Torres; open Sept–June Sat 11–1 by appt only*) is a private school built by Gaudí in 1890. Although constrained by finances and the need to build quickly and functionally, he endowed the building with a distinctive upper corridor of rhythmic parabolic arches, and defined the corners with his favourite cross-crowned steeples. Sarrià boasts many a home of stately proportions, but no one's castle can better the **Torre Bellesguard** (*C/Bellesguard 46*), built at the foot of the Collserola over a summer residence belonging to King Martí the Humane. Inspired by the historical connotations, Gaudí restored the medieval walls and set a tall, neo-Gothic villa (1900–5) on the site.

To the south, another fashionable residential area, **Pedralbes**, the 'white stones', begins west of Av. Diagonal; here, the **Palau de Pedralbes** (*Av. Diagonal 686; **M** Palau Reial*), was a rather nice present to the city from the Güell family. Alfonso XIII occupied it briefly, and it became the headquarters of the Republican government towards the end of the Civil War; from its window, in 1938, President Azaña joined all Barcelona in bidding farewell to the International Brigades as they marched down the Diagonal away from a hopeless cause. One wing of the palace houses the beautiful if fragile **Museu de Cerámica** (*open Tues–Sun 10–3; closed Mon; adm, joint ticket with Museu de les Arts Decoratives available*) with a collection garnered from the famous ceramic centres of the Crown of Aragón – Paterna, Teruel, Manises, Barcelona – as well as 13th-century Arab-Catalan Mallorca and ceramics by Picasso and Miró. The **Museu de les Arts Decoratives** is located in the opposite wing, containing tapestries, furniture, and handicrafts from the Middle Ages to the present, and culminating in an exhibition that traces the evolution of Spanish industrial design. The surrounding park is shaded by ancient trees; behind, on Psg Manuel Girona, is a fence and gate guarded by Gaudí's *Pedrables Dragon* (1884). His **Pabeliones Finca Güell** (*Av. de Pedralbes 15; school open Mon–Fri 9–2*), is more extensive: an exotic, Hindu-inspired building now occupied by the Catedra Gaudí, part of the city's architecture school.

At the top of Av. de Pedralbes, a cobbled lane leads up to the **Col.leció Thyssen-Bornemisza**, housed in the renovated dormitory of the Gothic **Monestir de Pedralbes** (*Baixada del Monestir 9; **bus** No.22 from Pla de Catalunya; **FGC** Reina Elisenda, then a 15-min walk; open Tues–Sun 10–2; closed Mon; adm*). Although Madrid received the bulk of the Baron's collection, his Catalan wife made sure that 72 of his paintings settled in Barcelona. These include works by early Italian masters such as Lorenzo Daddi, Lorenzo Monaco and Fra Angelico, whose sublime, ephemeral *Madonna of Humility* steals the show. There are smaller works by Lotto, Titian, Tintoretto, Veronese and a fairy-tale *Stoning of St Stephen* by Dosso Dossi, and later works by Giambattista and Giandomenico Tiepolo, Guardi and Canaletto; there's also an excellent portrait by Velázquez, *Mariana de Austria*, with her Habsburg face and a foxy *Santa Marina* by Zurbarán, and paintings by Rubens and Lucas Cranach (a *St George*, for Catalunya).

For a bit more money, your ticket can include a tour of the convent itself, founded by Elisenda, the fourth wife of Jaume II, in 1326. A rare time capsule of 14th-century Catalan Gothic, it was built quickly and has scarcely been altered. The three-storey cloister with its slender columns, garden and fountains is serene and lovely, around which lie the Poor Clares' tiny austere prayer cells and the small, irregular **Capilla de Sant Miquel**. This houses the finest Gothic fresco cycle in Catalunya, Ferrer Bassa's *Seven Joys of the Virgin* and the *Passion* (1346). Elsewhere you can visit the kitchen, refectory, stables and storeroom, where an intricate series of 3D dioramas on the life of Christ by Joan Marí has been installed. The single-naved church contains stained glass by Mestre Gil and the alabaster tomb of Elisenda, sculpted in 1364.

Barça and The Cause

Barça of course means FC Barcelona, the city's beloved and wealthy football club, magnificently headquartered in Europe's largest stadium at Camp Nou (*Av. de Aristides Maillol; M Collblanc*), south of the Diagonal and the Zona Universitaria. You've probably seen their blue and burgundy jerseys, caps and banners for sale in every kiosk and souvenir stand in the city and, if you're a supporter, getting a ticket for one of the 120,000 seats for a match was probably one of your first concerns.

If you don't succeed, you can always take some comfort in the excellent Museu del Futbol Club Barcelona (*entrance gate 9; open Tues–Sat 10–6.30, Sun 10–2; closed Mon; adm*). Barça are popular not only because they're consistently great (they performed the rare trick of winning the three European cups in 1992) but because, back in the Franco years, they offered the best alternative to the invincible machine of Real Madrid, a club pumped full of money by the stodgy old dictator until it became the best in the world. Supporting Barça became an act of protest against the regime; for Catalans, forbidden even to speak their own language, it was one of the few outlets available to express any kind of national unity.

Inland from Barcelona: Sant Cugat del Vallés, Terrassa and Montserrat

Within striking distance of Barcelona there are superb Romanesque and Visigothic churches, and the magnificent monastery of Montserrat, 'the Catalan Miracle'.

Sant Cugat and Terrassa (Tarrasa)

Northwest of Barcelona, over the Collserola mountains, **Sant Cugat del Vallés** (the Roman *Castrum Octavianum*), grew up around the Visigothic **Abbey de Sant Cugat** (*open June–Sept Tues–Sat 10–1 and 3.30–5.30; Oct–May Tues–Sat 10–1; adm*). According to legend founded either by Charlemagne or his son Louis the Pious, the Gothic church that now stands is as austere as Barcelona's Sant Pi, with a great rose window and Lombard Romanesque tower. It's the late 12th-century cloister that makes the trip worthwhile, a Romanesque masterpiece, with 144 carved capitals depicting scenes from the New and Old Testaments by the monk Arnau Cadell; one scene shows him at work. Another Catalan masterpiece, the *Retablo of all the Saints* by Pere Serra (1395), is in the small museum in the chapterhouse, portraying the Virgin and Child in the centre of an angelic sextet, surrounded by most of the saints on the calendar.

Industrial **Terrassa**, 33 kilometres from Barcelona, is Catalunya's third-largest city and one of Spain's first textile manufacturers. Woollen cloth was the mainstay of the Catalans' medieval trading empire, and early examples from Terrassa and the rest of the world are displayed in the **Museu Textil** (*C/Salmerón 25, www.cdmt.es; open Tues, Wed and Fri 9–6, Thurs 9–9, Sat and Sun 10–2; closed Mon and hols; adm*), one of the most important collections of its kind in the world. Across the street is the **Museu Cartuja de Vallparadís** (*open Tues–Sat 10–1.30 and 4–7, Sun 11–2; closed Mon and hols*), a 12th-century castle converted to a Carthusian monastery in 1344, housing a municipal museum with sculptures, ceramics and 19th-century paintings.

Best of all is a rare and picturesque ensemble of three Visigothic-Romanesque churches in the **Parque de Vallparadís** near the Cartuja. Back when Terrassa was the bishopric of Egara in the 6th century, it was common for the functions of an episcopal church to be divided between separate buildings. **Sant Pere**, remodelled in the 12th century in the Lombard style, has a Visigothic triple-lobed apse and 10th-century stone *retablo* and murals. Square **Sant Miquel**, reconstructed in the 9th century, has a seven-sided apse and a 6th-century baptistry in its centre, with a dome supported by Roman and Visigothic columns; the murals are from the 9th century.

The main church, **Santa María**, rebuilt in 1112 in the form of a Latin cross, is topped by an octagonal lantern and dome and incorporates the Visigothic apse with a horseshoe arch. It has excellent Gothic *retablos* by Huguet and 9th–12th-century frescoes; note especially the one in the apse of the murder of St Thomas of Canterbury (1170), painted only a few years after the fact.

Even then you haven't exhausted all of Terrassa's charms. An excellent alabaster *Burial of Christ* (1540) by Italian-trained Martí Diez de Liatzasolois is housed in a special chapel of the church of **L'Esperit Sant**. A magnificent 18th-century mansion,

Getting Around

Sant Cugat and Terrassa are most easily reached on **FGC trains** from the station under Barcelona's Plaça Catalunya; there are trains leaving at least once an hour (*journey time 30 mins*) to Sant Cugat, and to Terrassa (*journey time 1 hr*).

From Barcelona, there's a daily Juliá **bus** to Montserrat (departures at 9am, return 7pm, **t** 934 90 40 00; tickets available from most travel agents) leaving from Ronda Universitat 5. Alternatively, take an **FGC train** (line R5) from the station under the Plaça d'Espanya, with daily departures every hour starting at 8.36am with the last train out at 3.36. Get off at the station Aeri de Montserrat, where you link up with the thrilling ***teleferic*** (cable car) to the monastery.

You can choose from two all-inclusive tickets: one called the *TransMontserrat*, which includes metro, train, cable car, and Sant Joan funicular; and one called the *Tot Montserrat*, which includes metro, train, cable car and Sant Joan funicular, but also entrance to the museum and lunch at the self-service café. Trains return to Barcelona hourly 11.35–6.35.

For more information, call the **FGV** on **t** 932 05 15 15, *www.fgc.catalunya.net*.

Tourist Information

Sant Cugat del Vallés: Pla de Barcelona 17, **t** 935 89 22 88.

Terrassa: Raval de Montserrat 14, **t** 937 39 70 19, *www.terrassa.org, turisme@terrassa.org*.

Montserrat: Plaça de la Creu, **t** 938 77 77 77, *www.gencat.mediamb/pn/espais*.

Where to Stay and Eat

Montserrat ✉ 08691

To get a feel for Montserrat, stay overnight, but be prepared: it can get quite cold even in summer. The monks operate two hotels:

*****Abat Cisneros**, **t** 938 35 02 01 (*expensive–moderate*). A honeymooners' special. Prices depend on whether you want breakfast, full or half board.

****Hs El Monestir**, **t** 938 35 02 01 (*moderate*). Cheaper, with simpler rooms (*currently closed for renovation but expected to reopen early 2002*). *Open April to Oct*.

There's also a **campsite** near the Sant Joan funicular, **t** 938 35 02 51.

Food is mediocre and very overpriced, so you may prefer to bring a picnic. The **café** by the Sant Joan funicular (*open summer only*) is marginally better than the self-service café.

the **Casa Museu Alegre de Sagrera** (*Font Vella 29; open Tues–Sat 10–1 and 4–7, Sun 11–2; adm*) retains many of its original furnishings and a collection of Chinese art. A smattering of *modernista* industrial buildings add graceful notes to the newer parts of the city: on the Rambla d'Egara is one of the best, the former Vapor Aymerich, Amat i Jover factory (1908) by municipal architect Lluís Muncunill. This has been made into the **Museu de la Ciència i de la Tècnica de Catalunya** (*www.museu.mnactec.com; open Tues–Fri 10–7, Sat and Sun 10–2; July and Aug Tues–Sun 10–2 only; adm*), dedicated to the history of Catalunya's industrial revolution. Another fine building by Muncunill, the white **Masia Freixa** (1907) with an undulating roof and Gaudiesque parabolic arches, is in the Parc Municipal de Sant Jordi. The tourist office offer several themed guided tours around the city – there's a *modernista* tour and another devoted to the city's remarkable chimneys, including a climb up the tallest chimney in the world.

Montserrat, the 'Dream Turned Mountain'

Strange, mystical Montserrat, the spiritual heart of Catalunya and symbol of Catalan nationalism, looms 40 kilometres northwest of Barcelona up the River Llobregat. Its name, meaning 'serrated mountain', seems apt enough; the isolated, fantastical 10-kilometre massif made of jagged, pudding stone pinnacles rising precipitously over deep gorges, domes and shallow terraces, are all so different from the surrounding countryside that it seemed as if heaven itself had dropped it there to prove all things are possible. It has often been compared to an immense shipwreck.

The mountain's history begins in the Tertiary period, when powerful sea currents swept an immense pile of rubble here, which over the eons mixed with softer muck and hardened into a mass of stone. Miocene geological upheavals ten million years ago caused the sea around the mass to subside, leaving a mountain to be sculpted by the wind and rain into a hedgehog of phallic peaks with names like Potato, Bishop's Belly, Salamander, and a hundred others. Its human history is just as fantastical: St Peter supposedly came here to hide an image of the Virgin carved by St Luke in a cave; in another grotto, the good knight Parsifal discovered the Holy Grail – a legend used by Wagner for his opera. In 880, not long after Christians regained the region, the statue of the Virgin (hidden, it seems, by someone, if not St Peter, before the advance of the Moors) was discovered on Montserrat and, as is so often the case, it stubbornly refused to budge beyond a certain spot. Count Wilfred the Hairy of Barcelona built a chapel to house it, and in 976 this was given to the Benedictines of Ripoll, who added the monastery. In the Middle Ages only Compostela attracted more pilgrims in Spain; a visit here was essential before any major undertaking; Ignatio Loiola kept a vigil before the altar, consecrating his sword to the Virgin prior to founding the Jesuits in 1522. Independent and incredibly wealthy, Montserrat was favoured by Charles V, and his son Philip II rebuilt the church. During the Peninsular War, Catalan guerrillas fortified it as a base, and in reprisal the French looted and sacked the monastery (1811).

As the Catalan Renaixença gathered steam, Montserrat became its symbol. In 1918, the first Bible in Catalan was printed here, and Verdaguer, Gaudí and Pau Casals were all fervent devotees of the Virgin. Under Franco, Montserrat was the only church permitted to celebrate Mass in Catalan, and couples flocked here to be married in their own language. Even today Montserrat evokes the same image for Spaniards as Niagara Falls does for Americans; it's a traditional honeymoon destination, to receive the blessing of the *Moreneta* ('the little brown one'), as the Virgin is affectionately called, before undertaking the supreme adventure of marriage. It has also become a favourite destination for day-tripper crowds off the Costa Brava, not to mention mountain climbers and potholers. A disastrous fire in 1986 led in 1989 to the creation of the Montserrat Natural Park to restore and protect the mountain.

The monastery and the church can hardly compete with the fabulous surroundings. Only one side of the Gothic cloister remains intact, and Philip's basilica lost most of its sumptuous furnishings to the French in 1811, although newer gifts fill nearly every corner of the church. The enthroned Virgin of Montserrat presides over the high altar; the statue dates from the 12th century and is believed to be a copy, coloured black to imitate the original idol. Pilgrims still come to worship her in droves on 27 April and 8 September. The boys' choir or **Escolanía**, founded in the 13th century – the oldest music school in Europe – still performs a *virrolei* and *salve* daily at 1pm and 6.45pm, except in July. The **Museu de Montserrat** (*open Mon–Fri 10–6 (summer until 7), Sat, Sun and hols 9.30–6.30; adm*) has two sections of gifts donated by the faithful. On the main square by the cloister there's a selection of Old Masters, including an El Greco and a Caravaggio, and archaeological finds; meanwhile a modern section houses 19th-century paintings, especially by Catalans of the Renaixença movement.

Best of all, though, are the walks around the mountain, to its ruined hermitages and caves. An easy walk called **Los Degotalls** takes in a wonderful view of the Pyrenees. A funicular descends from Pla Santa Creu (*10–1 and 3.20–7, every 20 mins*) to the **Santa Cova**, where a 17th-century chapel marks the exact finding place of the *Moreneta*; another (*10–7, every 20 mins*) will take you up to the **Hermitage of Sant Joan**, from where you can take a spectacular walk in just over an hour up to the **Hermitage of Sant Jeroni** – traditionally the one given to the youngest and spryest hermit.

From the hermitage a short path rises to the highest peak in the range (4,110ft), offering a bird's eye view of the holy mountain itself, across to the Pyrenees, and over the sea to Mallorca if the weather's clear. Before leaving Montserrat, try a glass of the monks' *aromas de Montserrat* – a liqueur distilled from the mountain's herbs.

South of Barcelona: Gaudí's Crypt, Castelldefels and Sitges

When Barcelonans want to sprawl on a beach they usually head south; Sitges is very much a petal of the Fiery Rose of Anarchism that fluttered down to the sea. On the way you can visit another unforgettable Gaudí masterpiece , in the Colonia Güell.

The Colonia Güell Crypt and Castelldefels

Labour and class disputes in Barcelona led industrial magnate Eusebi Güell to consider a little adventure in paternalism in 1890. Located in the country at **Santa Coloma de Cervelló**, the **Colonia Güell** was planned as a pseudo worker's co-operative (Güell was still boss) around a cotton goods mill, with houses, a store, a school and other buildings for the workers designed by Gaudí's assistants, Francesc Berenguer and Joan Rubió Bellver. The chapel on the estate, however, was too small, and in 1898 Güell asked Gaudí to design a larger church. The sketches for this look like a cross between Coney Island and the Emerald City of Oz, but once Eusebi Güell died in 1918, funds for the church dried up, and only the **crypt** (*closed indefinitely for restoration*) was completed. Yet of all Gaudí's works, this magical primordial avant-garde grotto is the most innovative – a marvel of virtuosity and engineering. It has no right angles, no straight lines – the pillars bend at weird expressionist angles. If you've been to the museum of the Sagrada Família, you've seen the copy of Gaudí's complex dangling web of chains and weights that he photographed and reversed to help work out the incredibly difficult problems of stress and loads, inventing a form known as the hyperbolic paraboloid, tackled by modern architects with the aid of sophisticated computers. Gaudí had only the thunder and lightning of his brainstorms, but he also had something else modern architects don't have: Catalan bricklayers. There is no steel reinforcing anything, anywhere: the whole thing is made of rough-hewn stone and brick, primitive textures brightened with stained glass and *trencadi* collages. Robert Hughes' description of Gaudí's architecture as 'womb with a view' fits it to a T.

Getting Around

For the Colonia Güell, Oliveras **buses** from Pla Espanya will take you as far as the Ciutat Cooperativa; the nearest **train** station (FCG) is Molí Nou; by car, take the A2 to the Cinturó Litoral exit for Sant Boi de Llobregat and drive up the Llobregat river to Santa Coloma. Catalunya en Miniatura is easiest reached by car (just off Autopista A2, exit 3) or the FGC train from the Plaça Espanya to Sant Vicenç dels Horts, followed by a 1½km walk. Trains from Barcelona's Estació de Sants depart every 20 mins for Castelldefels (the Castelldefels-Platja station is a minute from the beach) and Sitges (30 mins from Barcelona).

Tourist Information

Castelldefels: Pla de l'Església, 1, **t** 936 64 23 61, *ajuntament@castelldefels.org*.

Sitges: Sínia Morera, **t** 938 94 42 51, *infor@sitgstur.com, www.sitges.org*.

Festivals

Sitges: Corpus Christi. Stunning carpets of flowers deck the streets of town; Carnival, *Spring*. The new Sitges hosts the most outrageous carnival in Spain; Theatre of the Vanguard, *June*. The international festival is held here each year.

Where to Stay

Sitges ✉ 08870

Sitges isn't for the staid nor the economy-minded, nor for those without a reservation. Note that things quieten down considerably in the off season, when many hotels close down, so be sure to call in advance.

Expensive

****Terramar**, Psg Marítim 80, **t** 938 94 00 50, **f** 938 94 56 04, *hotelterramar@hotelterramar.com, www.hotelterramar*. The biggest, best positioned hotel on the beach: resembling a badly decorated wedding cake, but ultra comfortable and modern, with tennis, golf, a pool and a garden with a play area.

****Gran Sitges**, Av. Port d'Aiguadolç, **t** 938 11 08 11, **f** 938 94 90 34. New and huge, with every amenity conceivable, including indoor and outdoor pools.

Moderate

***La Santa María**, Psg de la Ribera 52, **t** 938 94 09 99, **f** 938 94 78 71. Delightful, seafront

Nearby, in Torrelles de Llobregat, **Catalunya en Miniatura** (*www.catalunyaminiatura.com; open winter daily 10–6; summer daily 10–7; adm exp*) is your chance to see the best monuments of Catalunya from the perspective of a Gulliver. The highways to the south meet the coast 20 kilometres south of Barcelona at **Castelldefels**, with its huge, popular stretch of sand; beyond this lies **Garraf**, with a smaller beach and fishing port.

Sitges

Wedged between the Garraf massif and a lovely long crescent of sand, **Sitges** has been Barcelona's favourite resort ever since the *modernistas* flocked here at the turn of the century, led by painter Santiago Rusinyol (1861–1931). Rusinyol's love of jokes anticipated the arch-prankster Dalí and in his delightful summerhouse, **Cau Ferrat** (*C/Fonollar 25; open summer Tues–Fri 10–2 and 5–9; winter Tues–Fri 10–1.30 and 3–6.30; adm*), set in the old fishing village on the seaside promontory, he sponsored his Festes Modernistes from 1892 to 1899, with theatre, exhibitions, concerts and events, such as a performance by an impostor of the famous Art Nouveau American dancer Loïe Fuller – but no one was the wiser. Cau Ferrat is now a museum, with two paintings by El Greco (put into place during one of Rusinyol's parties), a superb collection of iron-work from the 10th to the 20th centuries gathered together in surreal ways, and hotel with bright, prettily furnished rooms and a little sun terrace overflowing with geraniums. Downstairs are two enormously popular **restaurants** serving local seafood. Book well in advance.

★★**Hotel Romàntic**, Sant Isidre 33, **t** 938 94 83 75, **f** 938 94 81 67. Three atmospheric 19th-century villas which are particularly popular with gay couples: close to the beach, with a romantic garden. All rooms are beautifully furnished with antiques.

★★**El Xalet**, Isla de Cuba 33–5, **t** 938 11 00 70, **f** 938 94 55 79. Small hotel near the station in one of the prettiest *modernista* houses in Sitges; book well in advance.

★★**Madison Bahia**, Parelladas 27, **t** 938 94 00 12, **f** 938 94 00 12. Recently spruced up and very comfortable, this is conveniently close to the beach and the town centre of Parelladas.

Inexpensive–Cheap

Parellades, C/de la Parellades 11, **t** 938 94 08 01. Simple, friendly *pensión* with a small terrace and large rooms – a popular budget choice.

Internacional, C/Sant Francesc 52, **t** 938 94 26 90, **f** 938 94 73 31. One of the few hostelries that stays open all year. A little bit out of town, but large rooms and friendly owners make up for the slight inconvenience.

Eating Out

You can get just about anything in cosmopolitan Sitges but, as it is a place where liquid diets dominate, you shouldn't expect to find anything especially refined.

Mare Nostrum, Psg de la Ribera 60, **t** 938 94 33 93 (*expensive*). Long established and popular serving a variety of imaginatively prepared fish and crustaceans (try the fresh cod steamed in *cava*). There's a decent wine list and a pretty seaside backdrop, as well as a good *menú* (*inexpensive*). *Closed Wed.*

El Velero, Psg de la Ribera 38, **t** 938 94 20 51 (*expensive*). On a rock overlooking the sea: good fresh seafood and an excellent *menú degustación* (*inexpensive*). *Closed Sun eve.*

Picnic, Pso Marítimo s/n, **t** 938 11 00 40 (*moderate*). Excellent seafood right on the seafront, accompanied by an extensive wine list featuring lots of regional wines and *cavas* – try the wonderful *fideuada* with cuttlefish and prawns.

La Masía, Psg Vilanova 164, Port de Aguadolç, **t** 938 94 10 76 (*moderate*). The most authentic Catalan food in Sitges.

Los Vikingos, Marqués de Montroig 79, **t** 938 94 96 87 (*inexpensive*). Covering all price ranges and a perennial favourite: fish, burgers, well-cooked chicken and steaks.

drawings and paintings by Rusinyol, Casas, Miquel Utrillo and their contemporaries. Adjacent, the **Museu Maricel** (*open Tues–Fri 9.30–2 and 4–6, Sat 9.30–2 and 4–8, Sun 9.30–2; adm*), a hospital restored by Utrillo for American millionaire Charles Deering, is adorned with Gothic windows and door, and contains an eclectic collection of medieval to modern art, including a mural of the First World War by Josep María Sert. Another museum, the **Museu Romántico** (*C/Sant Gaudenci 1; open 15 June–15 Oct Tues–Fri 9.30–2 and 5–9; 16 Oct–14 June Tues–Fri 9.30–2 and 4–6, Sat 9.30–7, Sun 9.30–3; adm*) in the centre of town, conjures up the elegance of the 19th century and its love of gadgets – not to be missed by music-box fans. There's also a huge doll collection with over 400 from around the world, dating back to the 17th century.

The extravagance of Rusinyol and his friends set the stage for Sitges' role as Barcelona's seaside cockpit of crazy good times, and as one of the biggest gay resorts on the Med. In the summer it seems that half of Europe's yuppies have washed up here, and the hotels built to accommodate them have changed the town forever. Yet Sitges retains two of its old traditions: an antique car rally to Barcelona on the first Sunday in March, and its Corpus Christi celebrations, when the streets come ablaze with flowers. It also has nude beaches to the south, the first for straights and the second for gays called the Playas del Muerto – 'the beaches of the dead'.

The Costa Brava

The Costa Brava ('Rugged Coast') officially begins at Blanes and winds its serpentine way up to the French border. The 72 kilometres between Barcelona and Blanes has been dubbed the **Costa del Maresme**, which, although it lacks the scenic grandeur of its famous neighbour, has some fine beaches, especially at **Arenys de Mar** and **Calella de la Costa**, though the real holiday madness lies farther north.

Getting Around

By Train

Blanes is most easily reached by train: regular local ones depart every 30 mins from Barcelona-Sants and Barcelona Arc de Triomf stations. The train station is 2km outside town, but buses meet most trains coming in.

By Bus

From Blanes, buses make the 8km trip to Lloret; you can also take a SARFA bus, **t** 932 65 11 58, Blanes is regularly linked to Girona (and Girona airport) by bus from the Plaça Catalunya, with Barcelona Bus, **t** 972 35 04 87. Another SARFA bus from Barcelona passes through Tossa del Mar and the other coastal villages as far as Palafrugell and Begur. From Girona there are several buses a day from the bus station to Lloret and the coast; SARFA buses from Girona depart from the Plaça de Canalejas 4.

The best way to reach the more remote places is the 'Lancha Litoral', the **sea bus** that meanders up the coast from Lloret to Port Bou. It's slow, but it stops nearly everywhere and takes in some lovely scenery without the hassle of traffic or bus schedules.

Tourist Information

Blanes: Pla Catalunya 21, **t** 972 33 03 48.
Lloret de Mar: Pla de la Vila 1, **t** 972 36 47 35.
Tossa de Mar: Av. Pelegrí 25, **t** 972 34 01 08.
Sant Feliu de Guíxols: Pla del Monestir 54, **t** 972 82 00 51.
Palamós: Psg de Mar 22, **t** 972 60 05 50.
Palafrugell: C/Carrilet 2, **t** 972 30 02 28.

Where to Stay and Eat

Not only does the Costa Brava have hundreds of hotels, but it has more camping sites per square foot than anywhere in Spain. Most of the hotels in the big resort towns are block-booked by February, but if you come in May or September you should find a room. Otherwise, reserve as early as possible. Most places are open May–September. If you are stuck for a room, contact *hotelscb@reservashoteles.net*, *www.reservashoteles.net*, **t** 972 60 00 34, an umbrella organization which covers hotels in all categories.

Blanes ✉ 17300

★★★**Beverley Park**, C/Mercè Rodereda s/n, **t** 972 35 24 26, **f** 972 33 01 10, *beverley@grn.es*, *www.beverleypark.com* (*moderate*). Big, modern, family hotel in the new part of town with a playground for children; also a pool and garden.

★**Hotel Rosa**, San Pedro Martin 42, **t** 972 33 04 80 (*inexpensive*). Reasonable, modern choice, with modest rooms and a pool.

★**Hs Soteras**, Pla Estrella de Mar 9, **t** 972 33 03 78 (*cheap*). The cheapest option in Blanes; set just a couple of blocks back from the sea.

Those fortunate enough to have visited the Costa Brava in the 1950s invariably have fits when they contemplate what speculator-man has wrought on the 'Spanish Riviera'. For her part, Mother Nature was lavish, tipsy even, as she sculpted out one scenic cove after another beneath pine-crowned cliffs, tucking lovely sandy beaches among strange boulder formations and rocky wind-sculptures, where 40 years ago fishermen berthed their boats. The Costa Brava is within reasonable driving distance of most of western Europe, which has fallen for it in a big way. To keep up with burgeoning demand, accelerated by scores of package holiday companies, hotels have been tossed up on the shore in a tidal wave of concrete that shows few signs of abating – just try to get a room in season without a reservation. After the Costa del Sol, the Costa Brava is Spain's most visited shore, but virtually all of its trade is shoe-horned into a much briefer season (mid-June–mid-Sept). If you're just passing through in the summer, consider staying in Girona or Figueres just off the coast, where accommodation is easier to find and bus connections to the beaches frequent.

Can Flores II, Esplanada del Port, **t** 972 33 16 33 (*inexpensive*). One of the most popular choices in town; big, brightly lit seafood restaurant overlooking the old port.

Can Tarranc, Ctra Blanes a Toderà s/n, **t** 937 64 20 37 (*moderate*). Perhaps the best places to eat in Blanes; very traditional Catalan dishes served up in a pretty 18th-century farmhouse about three km outside Blanes.

Lloret de Mar ✉ 17310

********Santa Marta****, Platja de Santa Cristina, **t** 972 36 49 04, **f** 972 36 92 80, *hstamarta@grn.es* (*luxury*). One of Lloret's handful of luxury hotels, on the seafront with a pool, beautiful garden, tennis courts and very good **restaurant**. *Closed 15 Dec–1 Feb.*

******Vila del Mar**, C/de la Vila 55, **t** 972 34 92 92, **f** 972 37 11 68, *hovil@grn.es* (*expensive–moderate*). Smaller than most of the monoliths around here; each room is named after a boat built in Lloret and the rooms are equipped with the latest technology. There's a pool as well as a good Mediterranean **restaurant**. *Closed Dec–Feb.*

***Residencia Reina Isabel**, C/Venècia 12, **t** 972 36 41 21, **f** 972 36 99 78 (*inexpensive*). Near the main beach and staying open all year round: rooms with slightly more character than most.

***P. Roca y Mar**, C/Venècia 51, **t** 972 37 04 03, **f** 972 37 04 03 (*inexpensive–cheap*). Another decent bet; no restaurant though. Prices drop out of season.

Lloret has a number of mediocre *hostales*, none of which stand out in any way. Some typical examples are listed below:

***El Ciervo**, Av. Mistral 8, **t** 972 36 52 33. In the centre, this has rooms with bath.

***Cotano**,C/Areny 18, **t** 972 36 48 90. Also in the centre; a dozen basic rooms with bath.

El Trull, Ronda Europa s/n at Cala Canyelles, 2km from Lloret, **t** 972 36 49 28 (*expensive*). Excellent, ultra-fresh seafood in a pretty garden setting; there's a very cheap *menú del día* (*inexpensive*), or you can splash out on the *menú degustación* (*expensive*).

Dafen (Casino Lloret de Mar), Av. Vila de Blanes 32, **t** 972 366 454. Dine in style at the casino restaurant – if you haven't gambled away your holiday spending money.

Mas Vell, San Roc 3, near the bullring, **t** 972 36 82 20 (*moderate*). Rustic atmosphere: good value seafood *al fresco*.

Tossa de Mar ✉ 17320

****Diana**, Plaça d'Espanya 6, **t** 972 34 11 16 (*expensive*). Delightfully old-fashioned villa with a pretty courtyard backing onto the seaside promenade. Inside there's an original Gaudí fireplace, Art Nouveau frescoes and plenty of light from the glass roof. Reserve well in advance. *Closed mid-Nov–Mar.*

*****Mar Menuda**, Av. Mar Menuda s/n **t** 972 34 10 00, **f** 972 34 00 87 (*expensive–moderate*). Right on the beachfront, with a pool, tennis and even a diving school.

Blanes to Pals: Beautiful but Overcrowded Beaches

Semi-industrial and an important fishing port, **Blanes** is where it all begins from Barcelona's point of view, with one of the coast's longest beaches and most popular camping areas. It sits at the foot of a hill, crowned by the ruins of the castle, and has a pretty botanical garden, **Mar i Murtra**, on the way to its most picturesque cove, Sant Francesc. Most visitors, however, descend on **Lloret de Mar**, the jam-packed, half looney fun-house of the Costa Brava, boasting an even longer beach and the coast's greatest concentration of hotels, all brimful of packaged people, most of whom come to drink something a mite stronger than 'Tea just like your Mum makes it' as one Lloret café proclaims. By now it must be Spain's most famous sign, and one that sums up Lloret precisely.

****Hotel Capri**, Psg del Mar 17, **t** 972 34 03 58, **f** 972 34 15 52 (*moderate*). Perfect location on the seafront with a pleasant terrace. *Closed Nov–April.*

****Hotel Neptuno**, C/La Guardia 52, **t** 972 34 01 43, **f** 972 34 19 33 (*moderate–inexpensive*). Reasonable, family hotel with a swimming pool for kids, a garden and not too much of a walk to the beach.

Moré, C/Sant Elm 9, **t** 972 34 03 39 (*cheap*). Ten little rooms at a very cheap price.

Victor, Av. La Palma 17, **t** 972 34 24 31 (*moderate*). Delicious, old-fashioned Catalan dishes – don't miss the fried prawns, or the typical local soup, *caldereta de pescadores* (*menú del día inexpensive*).

Bahía, Psg del Mar 19, **t** 972 34 03 22 (*moderate*). The place for good seafood and *sopa de mero* (grouper).

Es Molí, C/Tarull 5, **t** 972 34 14 14. Well-rounded menu with outdoor dining in summer months and a fireplace in the winter.

La Tortuga, San Raimon de Penyafort 11. Bar with live jazz in the summer, as well as cocktails, rumba and salsa most nights.

La Platja d'Aro-S'Agaro ✉ 17000

*******Hotel de la Gavina**, Pla de la Rosaleda s/n, **t** 972 32 11 00, **f** 972 32 15 73, *gavina@iponet.es* (*luxury*). Sumptuous whitewashed villa on the beach, with antique-decorated rooms, lush gardens, solarium, gym, tennis, and an 18-hole golf course nearby. The restaurant (*expensive*) is one of the finest in Catalunya, with a terrace on which to enjoy its *menú del día*. *Closed 13 Oct–Easter.*

****Planamar**, Paseo del Mar 82, **t** 972 81 71 77, **f** 972 82 56 62 (*inexpensive–moderate*). Central, beachfront hotel; a good base if you are interested in watersports. Pool and gym.

****La Marina**, C/Ciutat de Palol 2, **t** 972 81 71 82 (*inexpensive*). Decent *pensión* with surprisingly good facilties, including a pool.

Palafrugell and Llafranc ✉ 17200

Prices tend to be a little bit lower here. Palafrugell's coves, Calella and Llafranc and Tamaríu, each have a plenty of hotels.

*******Mas de Torrent**, Alfueras de Torrent s/n, Torrent, **t** 972 303 292, **f** 972 303 292, *mtorrent@intercom.es* (*luxury*). Stunning hotel set in an 18th-century country house four km from Pals, with individually styled rooms in the house itself, 20 secluded bungalows and a pool set in extensive gardens; lottery-winners might plump for a suite with private pool and Jacuzzi.

*****Llevant**, Francesc de Blanes 5, **t** 972 30 03 66, **f** 972 30 03 45 (*expensive–moderate*). This elegant hotel was established in the 1930s. It's small and smart, with a good **restaurant** – try for the rooms with terraces at the front with panoramic views.

*****Hotel Hostalillo**, C/Bellavista 22, Tamaríu, **t** 972 62 02 28, **f** 972 62 01 84 (*expensive –moderate*). White, modern hotel set on the cliffs above the beach, with a lovely, geranium-filled sun terrace. *Open June–Sept.*

North of Lloret, **Tossa de Mar** is one of the prettiest towns on the Costa Brava. Its **Vila Vella** – a maze of alleys, stone and whitewashed houses, embraced by a 12th-century crenellated wall and towers – is a National Historical Monument. Besides the three village beaches, intimate pine and cork-shaded coves are within easy reach. The next town north, **Sant Feliu de Guíxols**, once a major cork exporter, now prides itself on its pretty Passeig Marítim and its 11th-century **Porta Ferrada**, a Mozarabic remnant of a long-vanished monastery. You can see a fine panorama of the nearby coast from the **Hermitage of Sant Elm**, and there's a good beach at Sant Pol, some two and a half kilometres away. Inland, at **Romanyà de la Selva**, stands one of Catalunya's most impressive megaliths, the **Cova d'en Daina**. Brash and modern, the **Platja d'Aro-S'Agaro** has little to recommend it beyond its fine beach, but **Palamós** fares better in charm, with its fishing fleet and excellent sailing facilities; its Platja de la Fosca beach is safe for the smallest child. Farther north, **Palafrugell**, the most attractive of the villages, has managed to preserve some of its delight, despite the *urbanizaciones* that

★★★**Hotel Sant Roc**, Pla Atlàntic 2, Calella de Palafrugell, **t** 972 614 250, **f** 972 61 40 68 (*moderate*). Pleasantly 'lived-in', family-run hotel surrounded by gardens and a terrace with fine views of the bay. This is popular with return visitors, so do to book ahead. Prices jump in August. *Closed Nov–Mar.*

★★★**Hotel Els Pins**, C/Verge del Carme 34–6, Platja d'Aro (*moderate–inexpensive*). Family-run modern hotel with a small pool and terrace, just 25m from the beach. Prices are very reasonable in July, but leap in August.

★★**Sol d'Or**, C/Riera 18, Tamariu, **t** 972 30 04 24 (*inexpensive*). Simple, seaside hotel at a good price. *Open all year.*

★**Hs Plancton**, C/Codina 16, Calella de Palafrugell, **t** 972 61 50 81 (*cheap*). Small and basic – but good value.

★**Fonda L'Estrella**, C/de les Quatre Cases 13, near Plaça Nova, **t/f** 972 30 00 05 (*cheap*). The nicest budget choice in Palafrugell: modest rooms around a quiet courtyard.

Several of the smarter hotels – particularly the Mas de Torrent, and the Llevant (*see* above) have excellent, if pricey, **restaurants**. There are some good, less expensive places to try the celebrated cuisine of the Empurdà, too.

Terramar, Pso Cipsela 1, Llafranc, **t** 972 30 02 00 (*moderate*). Right on the seafront, serving excellent local dishes such as *arròs a la cassola*, the rice speciality of Palafrugell.

La Xicra, C/Estret 17, **t** 972 30 56 30 (*moderate*). Creative, regional cuisine with the emphasis on seafood.

Hs Cypsele, C/Ample 30, Palafrugell, **t** 972 30 01 92 (*moderate*). Good Catalan fare.

La Casona, Paratge la Sauleda 4, Palafrugell, **t** 972 30 36 61 (*moderate*). Good food at moderate prices; try the *arròs negre*.

Begur ✉ 17225 and Aiguablava ✉ 17000

★★★★**Parador Costa Brava**, **t** 972 62 21 62, **f** 972 62 21 66, *www.aiguablava@parador.es* (*luxury*). Near Begur: modern and magnificently located on the cliffs surrounded by pine trees, with one of the finest views on the entire coast (also enjoyable from the bar – which non-residents can enjoy too). With a pool and beach just below. *Open all year.*

★★★★**Hotel Aigua Blava**, Playa de Fornells, Aiguablava, **t** 972 62 20 58, **f** 972 62 21 12, *hotelaiguablava@aiguablava.com*, *www.aiguablava.com* (*expensive*). Pretty 'holiday village' set in a charming villa on different levels, with every imaginable convenience, including a pool, tennis, and volleyball. The **restaurant** (*expensive*) – with local specialities and especially good fish – is excellent.

★★**Rosa**, C/Forga i Puig 6, Begur, **t** 972 62 30 15, *hotelrosa@hotmail.com* (*moderate*). Pretty, friendly hotel in the centre. A stone-vaulted **restaurant** offers a good *menú*, and staff are happy to arrange cycle hire and give ideas for walks around town. *Closed Nov–Mar.*

Mas Comangou, C/Ramon Lluc 1, Begur, **t** 972 62 32 10. Charming eaterie situated in a 19th-century stone villa on the outskirts of town.

have sprung up on the surrounding hills. The village also provides a good base for a number of beaches and lovely coves, as well as the fishing villages of **Calella de Palafrugell**, **Llafranc** and **Tamaríu**, the latter enveloped in fragrant pine-woods. In Llafranc, walk up to the lighthouse for the scenic view over the bay; in the abandoned hermitage perched on the cliff, toss a coin in the bowl behind the door-grille and make a wish. Palafrugell is also convenient for visiting **La Bisbal**, a medieval town with a market on Fridays and a ceramics centre. La Bisbal's Romanesque castle belonged to the Bishop of Girona, and it claims to have Catalunya's finest *sardana* dance band, the 'Cobla Principal'. A bevy of medieval hamlets surround La Bisbal, the oldest of which is **Ullastret**, former Iberian settlement and Greek colony, complete with a set of Cyclopean walls. A small **museum** (*open summer Tues–Sun 10–8; winter Tues–Sun 10–2 and 4–6; adm*) in a 14th-century hermitage houses finds dug up by Ullastret's farmers near the excavated site. More recent walls, from the Middle Ages, completely surround nearby **Peratallada**.

Up on its hill, **Pals** is another attractive, if perhaps over-preserved, medieval ensemble which (with a pine-shaded golf course for the Barcelona yuppies who have bought their second homes here) has its own beach, framed by a great tree-topped chunk of rock. Near here, **Begur** is known for the intense azure of its coves, especially **Aiguafreda** and **Aiguablava**.

Torroella de Montgrí to Figueres

Ancient Greeks and Spain's First Romanesque Church

The coastal road veers inland from Pals to the castle-crowned **Torroella de Montgrí**, its rambling lanes lined with medieval and Renaissance buildings. A major port in the Middle Ages, it now lies some five kilometres inland. Its resort satellite, **L'Estartit**, is a haven for underwater enthusiasts, who can pester the sea creatures around the tiny offshore **Islas Medes**. From here the road turns inland again, by way of **Verges**, where on Holy Thursday night adults and children don skeleton costumes and cardboard skulls to perform the 'Dança de la Mort', their Hallowe'en caperings a reminder of the Black Death of the 14th century.

L'Escala, on the south shore of the Gulf of Roses, lies two kilometres from ancient **Empúries**, founded by the Greeks from Marseilles some time around 600 BC. Later an important Roman port, it was captured by Scipio in the second Punic War, and inhabited until the 9th century when it was looted and burned by Norman pirates (*open June–21 Sept daily 10–8; 22 Sept–May Tues–Sun 10–8; adm*). The modern town dates from the 16th century when it was repopulated by fishermen and is famous nowadays for its anchovies. Empúries is as pleasant to visit for its site as for the visible remains. Closest to shore stood the Greek colony, with its market, streets, cisterns and temples. Further back, in the partially excavated Roman town, two grand villas have been discovered with fine mosaics, along with an amphitheatre. A small **museum** on the site (*adm included in the ticket*), with models and an audiovisual exhibit, explains how it may have looked.

Roses, another Greek foundation on the north end of the gulf, has nice long beaches and modern development spread along them. Far more intimate and scenic (and conscious of the fact) is **Cadaqués**, refuge of artists and writers; Salvador Dalí lived in nearby Port Lligat. His lovely whitewashed **house** (*www.salvador-dali.org,* ***t*** *972 25 10 15; open 14 Mar–14 June and 16 Sept–6 June Tues–Sun 10.30–6; 15 June–15 Sept 10.30–9; adm*), overlooking the tranquil, island-studded bay, is open for guided tours, but visitor numbers are severely restricted so it's worth booking in advance. It was obviously designed as a private house – there aren't even any guest rooms – and is surprisingly restrained. There are some kooky features, like the mirror placed so that Dalí could watch the sunrise without getting out of bed, or the massive, jewellery-covered polar bear at the entrance. Only the public areas (notably the swimming pool watched over by the Michelin Man) get the full Surrealist treatment. More than the other resorts on the Costa Brava, Cadaqués has preserved the atmosphere that began to attract people in the first place, primarily because it's hard to reach by public transport, and if you're driving there's no place to park. The jewel-like beaches of Cadaqués are also too small to hold a coachload of tourists comfortably. Still, people come, especially for the International Painting and Music Festivals in July and August. Cadaqués lies at the tip of Cape Creus, where the Pyrenees meet the sea; the area is now a **Natural Park**, the stones and trees buffeted into strange shapes by the wind. At this geographical crossroads and ancient holy place, the 9th-century Catalans founded one of their most important monasteries, **Sant Pere de Rodes** (*open Oct–May Tues–Sun 10.30–1.30 and 3–5; June–Sept Tues–Sun 10–7; adm*), 'the cradle of the

Getting Around

All **trains** from Barcelona to France stop in Figueres, which is the centre of the **bus** network to the upper Costa Brava (though there are connections from Girona five times daily to L'Estartit and L'Escala). SARFA buses (**t** 932 65 11 58/932 65 12 09) run regularly from Figueres to Roses and Cadaqués. Barcelona Bus (**t** 932 32 04 59) runs regular services from Barcelona to Figueras, and SARFA run direct buses from Barcelona to Roses and Cadaqués. Port Bou and Llançà are most easily reached by trains to France. The **seabus** Lancha Litoral also serves the coast.

Tourist Information

L'Estartit: Psg Marítim 47, **t** 972 75 89 10.
L'Escala: Pla de Les Escoles 1, **t** 972 77 06 03.
Roses: Av. Rhode 101, **t** 972 25 73 71.
Cadaqués: C/Cotxe 2, **t** 972 25 83 15.
Figueres: Pla del Sol, **t** 972 50 31 55.

Festivals

Cadaqués: International Painting and Music Festivals, *July and Aug*.

Where to Stay and Eat

L'Estartit ✉ 17258

*****Panorama**, Av. de Grecia 5, **t** 972 75 80 92, **f** 972 75 71 19 (*moderate; cheap out of season*). Good place to bring the whole family without breaking the bank: nicely located on the beach, with a pool and garden. *Open all year.*

***Hotel les Illes**, C/Illes 55, **t** 972 75 12 39, **f** 972 75 00 86 (*moderate–inexpensive*). Modern hotel just minutes from the port; particularly geared towards divers who are visiting the Illes Medes.

L'Escala ✉ 17130

*****Nieves-Mar**, Psg Marítim 8, **t** 972 77 03 00, **f** 972 10 36 05 (*expensive–moderate*). This has tennis, children's activities, and a seawater pool in modern surroundings. Rooms have recently been renovated. *Closed Nov–Mar.*

****El Roser**, Pla l'Església 7, **t** 972 77 02 19, **f** 972 77 34 98, *rosaescala@teleline.es*, *www.elroser.com* (*moderate*). Charming, old-fashioned hotel with a good, popular **restaurant**.

Roses ✉ 17840

******Almadraba Park**, Platja de Almadraba, **t** 972 25 65 50, **f** 972 25 67 50 (*luxury; expensive out of season*). The chicest and sleekest hotel on the upper coast. Plush, air-conditioned rooms, with amenities including a fine, award-winning **restaurant** (open to non-residents), heated pool, sauna and tennis courts. *Open all year.*

****Marítim**, Platja Salatar, **t** 972 25 63 90, **f** 972 25 63 90 (*expensive–moderate*). Pleasant, contemporary hotel on the seafront with typical rooms and two pools (including one for the children).

*****Nautilus**, Platja Salatar, **t** 972 25 62 62, **f** 972 25 48 75, *NauHot@Terra.es* (*moderate; inexpensive in Aug*). A surprisingly good bargain; right on the beach front with good facilities including a pool.

***Puig Rom**, Pla Levant 1, **t** 972 25 41 33 (*cheap*). The cheapest place in town and good value for the central location: adequate rooms (without bath).

Romanesque' built over the ruins of a Roman temple of Venus Pirenaica. According to legend, when Rome was threatened by an invasion of infidels, Pope Boniface IV decided to send some of the Church's holiest relics, including the head of St Peter, out of the city for safe-keeping. The relics were brought to Cape Creus and hidden in a grotto in the Sierra de Rodes. However, when the emissaries who undertook the task returned to Rome, the threat had passed, and they were sent back to Spain to retrieve the precious relics – only to discover that the grotto had vanished. The monastery was then constructed on the site, dedicated to St Peter. What survives dates from 1022, a magically picturesque fortress-like ruin that is slowly undergoing restoration.

Hacienda El Bulli, Cala Montjol, 6km from Roses, **t** 972 15 04 57 (*expensive*). One of Spain's finest restaurants: on a promontory over a lovely bay (diners can tether their yachts below while eating). One-off recipes prepared by a perfectionist chef whose menu varies according to season (*menú degustación expensive*). *Closed Mon and Tues in April, May and June; closed Oct–Mar.*

Cadaqués ✉ 17488

The tourist office have a list of families in the town who rent rooms, if you prefer not to stay in one of the rather over-priced hotels.

★★★**Llane Petit**, Dr Bartoneus 37, **t** 972 25 80 50, **f** 972 25 87 78 (*expensive*). Smallish, modern and very comfortable hotel with a garden, on the beach of the same name.

★★**Port Lligat**, Platja de Port Lligat, **t** 972 25 81 62, *portlligat@intercom.es* (*moderate*). Long established, right next to Dalí's house, with fine views over the bay and a children's playground and pool. *Open all year.*

★**Hs Ubaldo**, C/Unió 13, **t** 972 25 81 25 (*moderate*). A less expensive alternative in the heart of Cadaqués – though surprisingly pricey for the simple rooms. *Open all year.*

★**P. Vehi**, C/Església 5, **t** 972 25 84 70 (*cheap*). The most inexpensive place to stay; four little rooms all without baths.

La Galiota, C/Narcis Monturiol 9, **t** 972 25 81 87 (*moderate*). The most fashionable restaurant in Cadaqués, with good seafood and soufflés. Crowded in the summer, so book ahead.

Casa Anita, C/Miguel Roset, **t** 972 25 84 71 (*inexpensive*). A long-established, famly-run café-restaurant with doodles by Picasso and Dalí. Delicious freshly fried sardines.

Cap de Creus, Cap de Creus, **t** 972 19 90 05 (*inexpensive*). Set in the heart of the Natural Park of Cap de Creus, just 100m from the lighthouse, it's worth booking ahead to get tables with stunning views. There's a very eclectic menu – which even includes a vindaloo among the local rice dishes.

Don Quijote, Av. Caridad Seriñana 6, **t** 972 25 81 41 (*inexpensive*). Just outside Cadaqués, with a nice atmosphere and set menu with typical Spanish dishes (*moderate*).

Figueres ✉ 17600

★★★**Hotel Durán**, C/Lasauca 5, **t** 972 50 12 50, **f** 972 50 26 09, *duran@hotelduran.com*, *www.hotelduran.com* (*moderate*). In the centre of town, right on the Rambla, with cosy pleasant rooms and one of the best and oldest **restaurants** (*expensive*) in Catalunya; people drive in from miles around to enjoy the excellently priced dishes such as *zarzuela con langosta* (fish stew with lobster) served up in this huge and bustling dining room. *Open all year.*

★★★**Hotel Empordà**, Ctra N11, Km763, **t** 972 50 05 62 (*expensive*). Modern, though with slightly dated décor, this hotel is three km north of Figueres; the **restaurant** has been described as 'a cathedral to Empurdan cuisine' and is one of the finest in Catalunya, acclaimed for its imaginative adaptations of regional specialities to the contemporary palate. Game dishes are a speciality, as are mint salads and *taps de Cadaqués* – an incendiary rum cake (*menú del día moderate; menú degustación expensive*).

★**España**, La Junquera 26, **t** 972 50 08 69 (*inexpensive*). A modest *pensión* with perfectly adequate doubles.

★**La Vinya**, Pla. Indústria 7, **t** 972 50 00 49 (*cheap*). Bare-bones double rooms to match the prices.

Life is Art is Life

It's a shame that the old megalomaniac didn't live forever, because Dalí was one of the funniest characters Spain ever produced. Gifted with an impeccable academic technique, he became the most famous of all the Surrealists while still in his 20s, when he painted his first, haunting 'hand-painted dream photographs' as he called them, of melting watches and human bodies fitted with sets of spilling drawers. Dalí loved the camera, and was one of the first artists to get involved with the cinema, in his 1929–30 collaborations with Luis Buñuel (*Un Chien Andalou* and *L'Age d'Or*) – surrealist films that caused riots when they were premiered in Paris. During the Civil War he offered to go to Barcelona and run a Department for the Irrational Organization of Daily Life (only to be told: thanks anyway, it already exists).

If traditional Surrealists drew their inspiration from the irrational well of the unconscious, Dalí claimed his came from 'critical paranoia' – a carefully cultivated delusion, a conscious suspension of rational thought, a way of art and a way of life. Dalí, with his alert moustache-antennae tuned into the outrageous, did it with the deadpan humour of a Buster Keaton. The serious art world considered him a publicity-mongering buffoon, who produced little of value after the 30s, and who broke nearly every taboo; he claimed to support Franco (although he lived in the USA in 1940–55), he painted religious kitsch (all the while arguing that Jesus Christ was made of cheese) and signed his name to anything, which in his reclusive, suffering old age in Figueres was exploited by art dealers. This museum is his vindication.

The views from the monastery over the coast are stunning. To get there, drive or make the stiff walk up from **Llançà**, which along with **El Port de la Selva** and **Port Bou** are clustered near the border of France, in a region called Alto (High) Ampurdán. One of the high things about it is the wind, the Tramontana, which rages through here, mainly in the winter. If it kicks up while you're around, Port Bou has one of the more protected beaches.

Figueres: to Dilly-Dalí, Catalan Style

Figueres is the capital of Alto Ampurdán, transport hub for the northern Costa Brava, and a wind sock; in the spirit of the ancient Greeks who called their terrible Furies the Eumenides ('the kind ones'), the town has erected a statue of a woman about to be blown away and called it the **Monument to the Tramontana**. It's near to Pujada Castell and Figueres' star attraction, nothing less than the 'the spiritual centre of Europe' as its creator proclaimed: everyone else calls it the **Museu Dalí** (*www.salvador-dali.org; open July–Sept daily 9–7.45; Oct–June daily 10.30–5.45; adm exp*). Salvador Dalí, born in Figueres in 1904, created this dream museum in 1974 in a merrily crazy reconstruction of his home town's old municipal theatre. The result is the most visited museum in Spain, after the Prado, with a catalogue intended to misinform, as the artist planned. Inside, expect the outrageous: the former stage has a set by Dalí, accompanied by a full orchestra of mannequins; a coin-fed Cadillac waters its snail-covered occupants. Dalí himself, who died here in 1989, is entombed nearby, his mortal coils the final exhibit.

Girona (Gerona)

Between the Costa Brava and the highest Pyrenees, the heart of the province of Girona is surprisingly untouristified, despite the hordes that descend on the Costa Brava and the ski resorts of the Pyrenees, bypassing its oasis of rolling green hills and occasional geological oddities. Yet it is tourism, more than anything, that has brought the province its new status as the wealthiest in all Spain.

Spread over a tumble of hills at the confluence of the Onyar and Ter rivers, the capital **Girona** (ancient *Gerunda*) is one of Catalunya's most atmospheric little cities. Its position has brought it a history tormented with sieges, most famously in 1809, when the city's inhabitants withstood 35,000 French troops for seven months, giving up only when their supplies were exhausted. Few of its embattled walls remain; like so many cities in Spain, Girona has burst its buttons in the last few decades.

The Old Town

Fortunately, Girona's **Old Town** (Barri Vell) has been lovingly neglected. Its dim, narrow streets and passages, its steep stairs, little plazas, archways, and solid stone buildings offer any number of elegant perspectives. In recent years, in an attempt to keep the Old Town from falling too deeply asleep, the town approved the placement of various departments of the University of Catalonia within its quarters, adding a bit of student verve to the area. Across the Onyar from the old town is Girona's Eixample, a miniature version of Barcelona's, complete with a handful of minor *modernista* buildings designed by poet Rafael Masó (see the **Casa Teixidor** and **Farinera Teixidor** in C/de Santa Eugénia). Cross between the two on the **Pont de les Peixateries Velles** for the much-photographed view of the colourfully painted houses built up directly over the river.

The main street of medieval Girona, the **Carrer de la Força**, follows the Roman Via Augusta, the road of conquest. Narrow and winding, it seems to have changed little since the day when Girona's famous Jewish quarter, **El Call**, was defined by its southernmost reaches, around the steep alleys of Sant Llorenç and Cúndaro. Like the *calls* of Barcelona and Tarragona, the quarter came under the direct authority of the king, enjoying total autonomy from the municipal council, the *Jurats* – a situation designed to exacerbate tension, for the kings not only regarded the Jewish communities as a national resource and favoured them at the expense of others, but made use of these enclaves to meddle in city affairs. But before the decline into the 15th century, when the Jurats, egged on by a fanatical clergy and jealous debtors, managed to isolate the *Call* into a ghetto with one sole entrance, Girona's Jews had founded an important school of Jewish mysticism, the Cabalistas de Girona. The most celebrated member, Moses Ben Nahman, or Nahmanides, was born in Girona in 1194 and helped diffuse Cabalistic studies throughout Europe. The old school of the Cabala has been opened as the **Centra Bonastruc Ça Porta** (***t*** *972 21 67 61; open May–Oct Mon–Sat 10–8 (winter until 6), hols 10–2; adm*) on Sant Llorenç, and just as the Muslims are building a new mosque in Granada, there are plans to refound the school. Newly opened (2001) is the **Museo de los Judeos en Catalunya** (*open May–Oct Mon–Sat 10–8 (Nov–April until 6),*

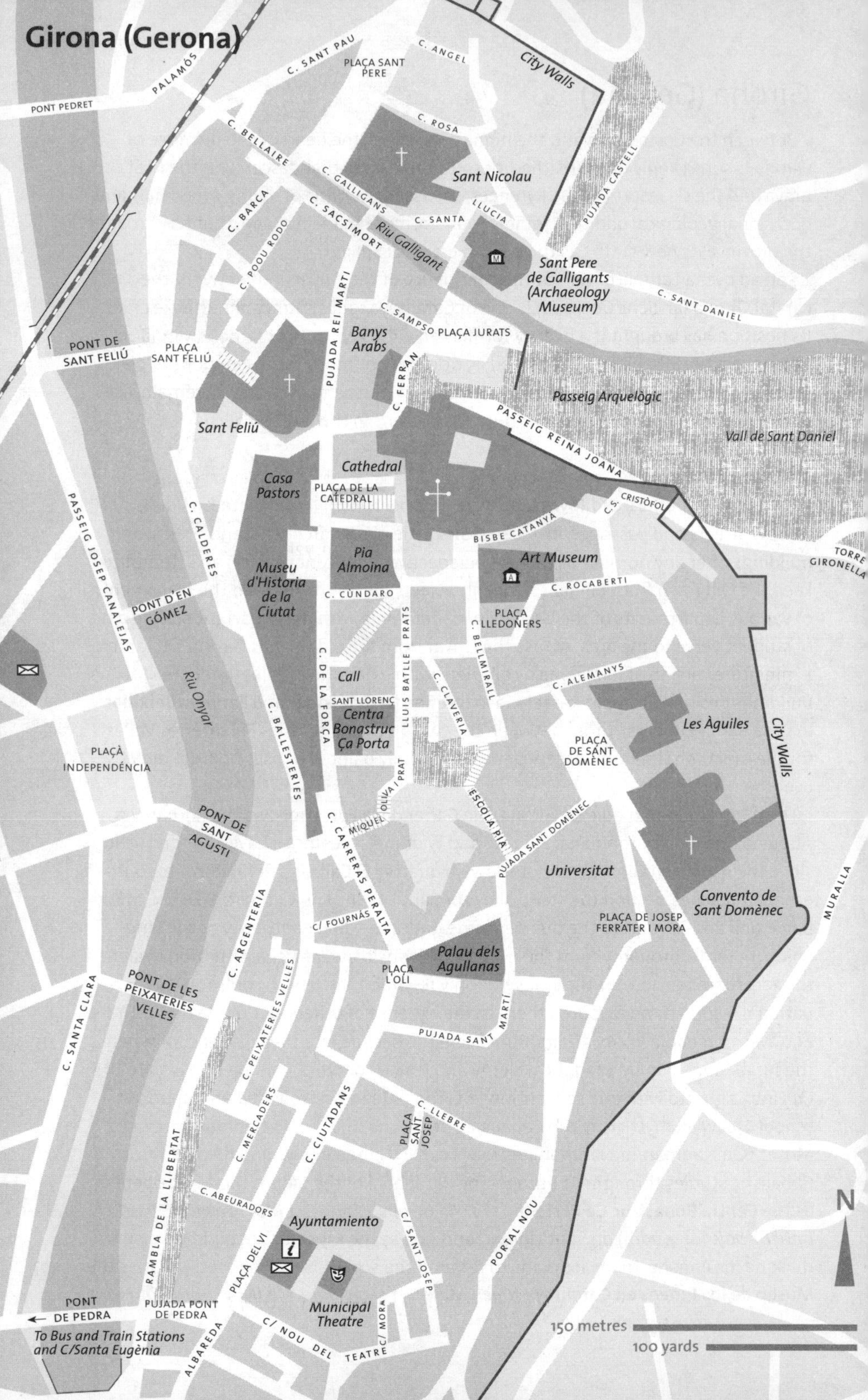
Girona (Gerona)
City Walls
C. Sant Pau
Plaça Sant Pere
C. Angel
Palamós
Pont Pedret
C. Rosa
C. Bellaire
Sant Nicolau
C. Galligans
Pujada Castell
C. Barca
C. Sacsimort
C. Santa Llucia
Riu Galligant
C. Poou Rodo
Sant Pere de Galligants (Archaeology Museum)
C. Sant Daniel
Pujada Rei Marti
C. Sampso
Plaça Jurats
Banys Arabs
Pont de Sant Feliú
Plaça Sant Feliú
C. Ferran
Passeig Arquelògic
Sant Feliú
Passeig Reina Joana
Vall de Sant Daniel
Casa Pastors
Cathedral
Plaça de la Catedral
C.S. Cristòfol
Passeig Josep Canalejas
C. Calderes
Bisbe Catanya
Torre Gironella
Pia Almoina
Art Museum
Museu d'Historia de la Ciutat
C. Rocaberti
C. Cùndaro
Pont d'en Gómez
Plaça Lledoners
Lluis Batlle i Prats
C. Bellmirall
C. de la Força
C. Claveria
Call
C. Alemanys
Riu Onyar
Sant Llorenç
Centra Bonastruc Ça Porta
Les Àguiles
C. Ballesteries
Plaça de Sant Domènec
City Walls
Plaça Independéncia
Olivа i Prat
Escola Pia
Miquel
Pont de Sant Agusti
C. Carreras Peralta
Pujada Sant Domènec
Universitat
Muralla
C. Argenteria
Convento de Sant Domènec
C/ Fornás
Plaça de Josep Ferrater i Mora
Palau dels Agullanas
Plaça l'Oli
Pont de les Peixateries Velles
C. Peixateries Velles
C. Santa Clara
Pujada Sant Martí
C. Mercaders
C. Ciutadans
C. Llebre
Plaça Sant Josep
Rambla de la Llibertat
C. Abeuradors
Ayuntamiento
C/ Sant Josep
Portal Nou
Plaça del Vi
Municipal Theatre
Pont de Pedra
Pujada Pont de Pedra
C/ Mora
To Bus and Train Stations and C/Santa Eugènia
C/ Nou del Teatre
Albareda
150 metres
100 yards
N

Sun and hols 10–3; adm), which charts the development of the Jewish community from the first mention of the Call in 898 until the expulsion of the Jews from Spain in 1492. Charts and documents describe the tense relationship between Christians and Jews, which resulted in the Call being sealed off and its inhabitants forced to wear identifying clothing, periodically blowing up into full scale attacks. There's a section dedicated to Nahmanides (*see* above), as well as an important collection of Jewish funerary stones.

Carrer de la Força continues past the **Museu d'Historia de la Ciutat** (*open Tues–Sat 10–2 and 5–7, Sun and hols 10–2; adm*) set in a charming 18th-century building with changing exhibits on the subject of cities, to **Plaça de la Catedral**, framed by the 18th-century **Casa Pastors** (law courts) and the stately Gothic **Pia Almoina**. From here a monumental stair leads up to the cathedral and its lofty **Torre de Carlomagno**.

The Cathedral

Open Tues–Sat 10–2 and 4–7.

One of the masterpieces of Catalunya, Girona's cathedral surpasses the grandeur of the stair with the widest single nave in all Christendom: 72ft across. Originally planned as a typical three-aisled nave, work began early in the 14th century. A century later the master architect Guillem Bofill (ancestor of Ricardo Bofill, Catalunya's current architectural innovator) suggested an aesthetic and money-saving improvement: to add a single great nave to the already completed apse. His proposal was so radical that all the leading architects of Catalunya were summoned to a council to solicit their opinions as to whether or not such a cathedral would stand. The majority said no, but Girona let Bofill do it anyway.

Inside there are plenty of fine details, but it's the colossal Gothic vault, supported by its interior buttresses, that steals the show. The stained glass is recent, the heads of all the saints reduced to simple black ovals – a haunting effect. The *retablo* over the high altar is a 14th-century masterpiece of silverwork, surmounted by an equally remarkable silver-plated canopy, or baldachin. A ticket will get you into a small but exceptional **museum** (*open summer daily 10–2 and 4–7; winter Mon–Fri 10–2 and 4–6; adm*), featuring the unique Tapestry of Creation, an 11th-century view of Genesis, with the Creator surrounded by sea monsters, the four wind-bags, the seasons, and Eve popping out of Adam's side. Then there's *Código del Beatus*, an illuminated commentary on the Apocalypse from the year 974, with richly coloured Mozarabic miniatures. The ticket also admits you to the trapezoidal Romanesque **cloister**, with exquisitely carved capitals, including one of a giant rabbit menacing a man.

More medieval delights await in the **Museu d'Art** (*open Tues–Sat 10–7 (winter until 6), Sun 10–2; closed Mon; adm*) next to the cathedral in the old Episcopal Palace. Among the exhibits there's a beam from 1200, carved with funny-faced monks lined up like a chorus line, a beautiful 15th-century catalogue of martyrs and a *Calvary* by Mestre Bartomeu (13th century), portraying a serenely smiling Christ with a face like Shiva, ready to dance off the Cross. Upstairs, there are rooms of 19th- and 20th-century Catalan paintings, with a selection by the masters of Olot (*see* p.171).

Getting Around

By Air

Girona's airport (**t** 972 18 66 00) receives international flights (including the 'no-frills' airline, **Buzz**, *www.buzz-away.com*), and lots of charters, but has no public transport linking it to the city itself. A **taxi** will cost about €12–15.

By Bus and Train

Girona's **bus** (**t** 972 21 23 19) and **train** stations (**t** 972 20 70 93) are side by side on Pla d'Espanya in the Eixample; all trains between France and Barcelona stop here. Buses from Barcelona with TEISA (**t** 972 20 48 68) run to Banyoles, Olot, and Besalú, with more regular services from Girona.

Tourist Information

Girona: Rambla de la Llibertat 1, **t** 972 22 65 75, *www.girona-net.com*; there's also a branch in the train station.

Where to Stay

Girona ✉ 17000

****Melià Confort Girona**, Ctra de Barcelona 112, **t** 972 40 05 00, **f** 972 24 32 33 (*luxury*). Part of a luxury chain: attracting Spanish businessmen and choosy tourists.

****Carlemany**, Pla Miquel Santaló 1, **t** 972 21 12 12, **f** 972 21 49 94, *carlemany@grn.es*, *www.carlemany.es* (*expensive*). Just a few minutes from the Barri Vell in the heart of the city, this is geared towards business travellers and offers immaculate rooms and service. The **restaurant** (*inexpensive menú del día*) is excellent.

***Costabella**, Av. de França 61, **t** 972 20 25 24, **f** 972 20 12 03 (*moderate*). Functional, modern hotel with pool to the north of the city.

** **Hotel Peninsular**, C/Nou 3, **t** 972 20 38 00, **f** 972 21 04 92 (*inexpensive*). This hotel has been newly renovated, with bright, attractive rooms and a good location just five minutes from the centre – there are wonderful views from the roof.

P. Bellmirall, C/Bellmirall 3, **t** 972 20 40 09 (*inexpensive*) A pleasant, diminutive charmer in the old town, near the cathedral, with the best breakfasts in Girona. *Open all year.*

*Condal**, C/Joan Maragall 10, **t** 972 20 44 62 (*inexpensive*). In the new part of town near the train station, with comfortable, modern rooms.

*P. Viladomat**, C/Ciutadans 5, **t** 972 20 31 76 (*inexpensive*). Popular, good-value hostel.

*Margarit**, C/Ultònia 1, **t** 972 20 10 66 (*cheap*). A decent option for a short stay: some of its simple rooms come with bath.

Albergue Juvenil, C/Ciutadans 9, **t** 972 21 80 03 (*inexpensive*). Girona's youth hostel has a perfect location in the old town, and plenty of modern facilities, including a laundry.

Eating Out

Celler de Can Roca, Ctra Taialà 40, **t** 972 22 21 57 (*expensive*). One of the local favourites: the rather grim exterior belies one of the finest restaurants in the region, run by three charming brothers. It's worth trying the *velouté de crustáceos*, a silky fish soup. *Closed Sun and Mon.*

La Penyora, C/Nou del Teatre 3, **t** 972 21 89 48 (*expensive–moderate*). As recommended by the locals: a first-class meal will verge on *expensive*, or you could go for the budget *menú del día* (*inexpensive*). It's a good bet for vegetarians, too. *Closed Sun eve and Tues.*

Albereda, Albereda 9, **t** 972 22 60 02 (*expensive–moderate*). In the basement of Girona's casino: tastefully furnished and serving beautifully prepared food, especially *bacalao* and delicious carpaccios, at reasonable prices. *Closed Mon eve.*

Cipresaia,C/General Fournas 2, **t** 972 22 24 49 (*moderate*). Near the Museu d'Art, with an elegant interior and muted atmosphere.

El Pou del Call, C/de la Força 14, **t** 972 22 37 74 (*moderate*). Another much loved local haunt serving reasonably priced Catalan dishes.

Casa Marieta, Pla Independència 5, **t** 972 20 10 16 (*inexpensive*). Across the Onyar from the cathedral: generous helpings and hearty fare such as *botifarra amb mengetes* (pork sausage with white beans).

Portal de Sobreportas

Back down the 90 steps to the Plaça de la Catedral, turn left and pass through the **Portal de Sobreportas** and its two round towers. The huge stones of their bases predated the Romans, and there's a niche hollowed out on top for a statue of 'Our Lady of Good Death' invoked by the unfortunates led through the gate on their way to execution.

To the left stands Girona's most important temple, the 13th-century **Sant Feliú** at the head of its own flight of stairs. It has a curious spire, amputated by lightning, and is believed to have been built over an early Christian cemetery, where the city's patron saint Narcís suffered martyrdom. Inside the church are two Roman and six Palaeochristian sarcophagi with fine carvings. Turning right after the Portal de Sobreportas, a door in a plain wall leads to the 13th-century **Banys Arabs** (*open April–Sept Tues–Sat 10–7, Sun 10–2; Oct–Mar Tues–Sun 10–2; closed Mon; adm*), a 13th-century version of ancient Roman *hammams*, built by Morisco craftsmen and illuminated within by an elegant eight-sided oculus on white columns.

Down the Pujada del Rei Marti and across the Galligans river stand two attractive 12th-century works: tiny **Sant Nicolau** with its three apses, and the former **Monestir de Sant Pere Galligants**, now the **Archaeology Museum** (*open summer Tues–Sat 10.30–1.30 and 4–7, Sun 10–2; winter Tues–Sat 10–2 and 4–6, Sun 10–2; closed Mon; adm*), with an extensive collection of medieval Jewish headstones and a cloister that makes an interesting comparison with the cathedral's. From here the **Passeig Arqueològic** (*open daily 10–8*) offers a garden-like stroll along the walls, with fine views over the pretty Vall de Sant Daniel from the ruins of the Roman **Torre Gironella**. Once through the Portal de Sant Cristòfol you can return to the cathedral or take C/dels Alemanys to the Plaça de Sant Domènec, with Girona's best-preserved ancient walls and all that remains of the city's old university, the Renaissance **Les Àguiles**, adorned with two eagles. Down the steps from this square is the beautiful **Palau dels Agullanas**, with its low arch spanning the junction of two stairs. From here, C/Ciutadans returns to the Plaça del Vi, with the 19th-century **Municipal Theatre**, where two Catalan *gegants* (giants) stand vigil in the courtyard, waiting for a holiday, when they're allowed to sally forth and menace the children.

Around Girona: Banyoles, Olot and Besalú

Banyoles

No one thinks of lakes when they think of Spain, but there's a pretty one just north of Girona in the Garrotxa mountains called Banyoles. For years, it slumbered peacefully under state protection until it became the site for the rowing events during the 1992 Olympics, and developments sprang up along its shores. Banyoles town has a 13th-century porticoed square, and a copy of a Neanderthal jawbone found here in its **Regional Archaeological Museum** (*open July and Aug Tues–Sat 11–1.30 and 4–8, Sun 10.30–2; Sept–June Tues–Sat 10.30–1.30 and 4–6.30, Sun 10.30–2; closed Mon; adm*), housed in the Gothic Pía Almoina. The mouldering Benedictine **Monastir de Sant Esteve**, originally founded in 812 and the core of the ancient town, is rarely open but, if it is, you can admire the beautiful 15th-century *retablo* by Joan Antigo. On the other side of the lake, the tiny village of **Porqueres** has a gem of a Romanesque church, **Santa María** (1182), and prehistoric cave paintings in nearby **Serinyà** (*ask in Girona about opening hours*). Buses take half an hour to make the trip from Girona.

Tourist Information

Banyoles: Pso Indústria 25, **t** 972 57 55 73.
Olot: Bisbe Lorenzana 15, **t** 972 26 01 41, *impc@olot.org*.
Besalú: Pla de la Llibertat 1, **t** 972 59 12 40, *besalu@ddgi.es*.

Where to Stay and Eat

Banyoles ✉ 17000

★★★★**Mirallac**, Pso Darder 50, **t** 972 571 045, **f** 972 580 887, *hrmirallac@terra.es* (*moderate; expensive June–Aug*). Lake views and large, airy rooms make this small hotel a good base to enjoy the watersports or hiking trails in the area. It's surprisingly inexpensive considering the facilities on offer, which include a pool.

★★**Hs L'Ast**, Psg Dalmau 63, **t** 972 57 04 14 (*moderate*). Near the lake, with a pool and adequate **restaurant**.

★**Can Xabanet**, C/Carmen 27, **t** 972 57 02 52 (*inexpensive*). Near the lake as well: less expensive but equally pleasant with good meals in the **restaurant**.

★**Fonda Comas**, C/Canal 19, **t** 972 57 01 27 (*inexpensive–cheap*). Down-to-earth little *pensión* in town with a decent **restaurant** serving a filling daily menu.

Ramiò, C/Sant Esteve 34, **t** 972 57 37 09 (*cheap*). This cheapest offering has just four small rooms.

Quatre Estacions, Pso de la Farga s/n, **t** 972 57 33 00 (*moderate*). The best place to eat in town; traditional cuisine based on whatever is in season. Try the mouthwatering seafood *croquetas* and finish up with a local liqueur.

Olot and Besalú ✉ 17800

★★★**Borell**, Nònit Escubos 8, Olot, **t** 972 26 92 75, **f** 972 26 67 03, *borell@agtat.es, www.agtat.es* (*moderate*). Good, small hotel in the centre of Olot.

★★★**Perla d'Olot**, Av. Santa Coloma 97, Olot, **t** 972 26 23 26, **f** 972 27 07 74, *hperla@agtat.es, www.agtat.es* (*moderate*). Friendly, very reasonable, modern hotel with gardens and a children's play area.

★★★**Hotel Cal Sastre**, C/Cases Noves 1, Santa Pau, **t** 972 68 00 49, **f** 972 68 04 81, *sastre@aftot.es* (*moderate*). Delightful, small hotel in the centre of the historic town of Santa Pau; each room is individually decorated with antiques, including beautifully hand-painted bedsteads. There's a charming **restaurant**, well known for its preparation of *fesol* (local green beans). You can even get them in dessert if you choose the *menú degustación*.

Stop, C/Sant Pere Màrtir 29, Olot, **t** 972 26 10 48 (*cheap*). For those on a tighter budget.

Les Cols, Ctra de la Canya, Mas Les Cols, Olot, **t** 972 26 92 09 (*moderate*). Market-fresh, imaginative local cuisine – one of the most reputed restaurants in the area. *Closed Sun and Mon eves*.

★**Siqués**, Av. President Companys 6–8, Besalú, **t** 972 59 01 10, **f** 972 59 01 10 (*inexpensive*). Old-fashioned, traditional stone guesthouse at the entrance to the town with a pool and a popular local **restaurant** serving classic local dishes.

★**Fonda Vanència**, C/Major 6, **t** 972 59 12 57 (*cheap*). The cheapest place to stay, though rather spartan.

★**Marià**, Pla Llibertat 4, **t** 972 59 01 06 (*inexpensive*). Pleasant little *pensión* overlooking the attractive central square.

Mas Salvanera, Mas Salvanera s/n, Beuda, **t** 972 59 09 75, **f** 972 59 08 63, *salvanera@interbook.net, www.salvanera.com* (*moderate*). Utterly charming 17th-century stone farmhouse set into the hillside about 8km from Besalú, which has just eight pretty rooms and a pool.

Olot

Between Banyoles and Olot there's an odd landscape known as the Garrotxa, pitted by 40 extinct volcanoes and endowed with a diaphanous light. The largest crater, **Santa Margarida**, is 1,148ft across and lush with greenery, while another, **Sant Pau**, is barren and lunar. The beautiful beechgrove near Santa Margarida, **La Fageda dén Jordà**, is a great place for a picnic. The unique scenery inspired innumerable Catalan landscape painters, many centred in **Olot**, on the River Fluvià, which has been the centre of a small art colony since the founding of the School of Fine Arts in 1783. The **Museu Comarcal** (*open Wed–Sat and Mon 11–2 and 4–7, Sun 11–2; closed Tues*) in Olot's neoclassical Hospici features work by the 19th-century Olot school, whose painters took the rural scenes of Millet as their starting point. A stroll through town reveals sculpture by Josep Clarà and Miquel Blay and the ornate 1915 *modernista* **Casa de Solá Morales** by Domènech i Montaner. From Olot, take the C150 for the startling view of **Castellfollit de la Roca**, perched atop a basalt escarpment 194ft over the Fluvià. The surrounding area has been designated the **Parc Natural de la Zona Volcanica**, with some very lovely walks through beech forests and across the craters of long-extinct volcanoes; there's a delightful walk to the humble, medieval town of **Santa Pau**. You can get information (and sit through a roller-coaster audiovisual account of a medieval volcano) at the park office in the **Casal dels Volcans** (*Av. Santa Coloma s/n, **t** 972 26 00 40*), at the entrance to the town.

Besalú

On down the Fluvià (14km north of Banyoles) is one of Catalunya's purest, most uncommercialized medieval ensembles, Besalú. For one brief, shining hour, after its reconquest by Louis le Deboinair in 800, it ruled an independent county before being absorbed by the House of Barcelona in 1020. From the main road, you can see the old 12th-century **fortified bridge**, built at an unusual angle, with a tower at the bend, and eight arches of irregular shape and size.

On the far side of the bridge, where the Jewish **Call** once stood, there's a Romanesque **Mikwah** (a ritual bathhouse connected to a synagogue), the only one ever found in Spain, and one of only three in Europe. Besalú has two 12th-century churches: **Sant Pere**, decorated by a pair of stone lions obviously carved from hearsay rather than an authentic model, and **Sant Vicenç**, its entrance prettily decorated with floral motifs. A domestic building of the period, **Casa Cornellà** (*open for hourly tours July–Sept Mon–Sat*) has been restored and furnished with antique tools and household items.

The Catalan Pyrenees

When the Bourbon Philip V ascended to the Spanish throne, his grandfather Louis XIV haughtily declared (according to Voltaire): 'Il n'y a plus de Pyrenées!' History, of course, proved him sadly deluded, though these great mountains have, of late, suffered a good deal of mental erosion as Spain takes its place as an equal partner in

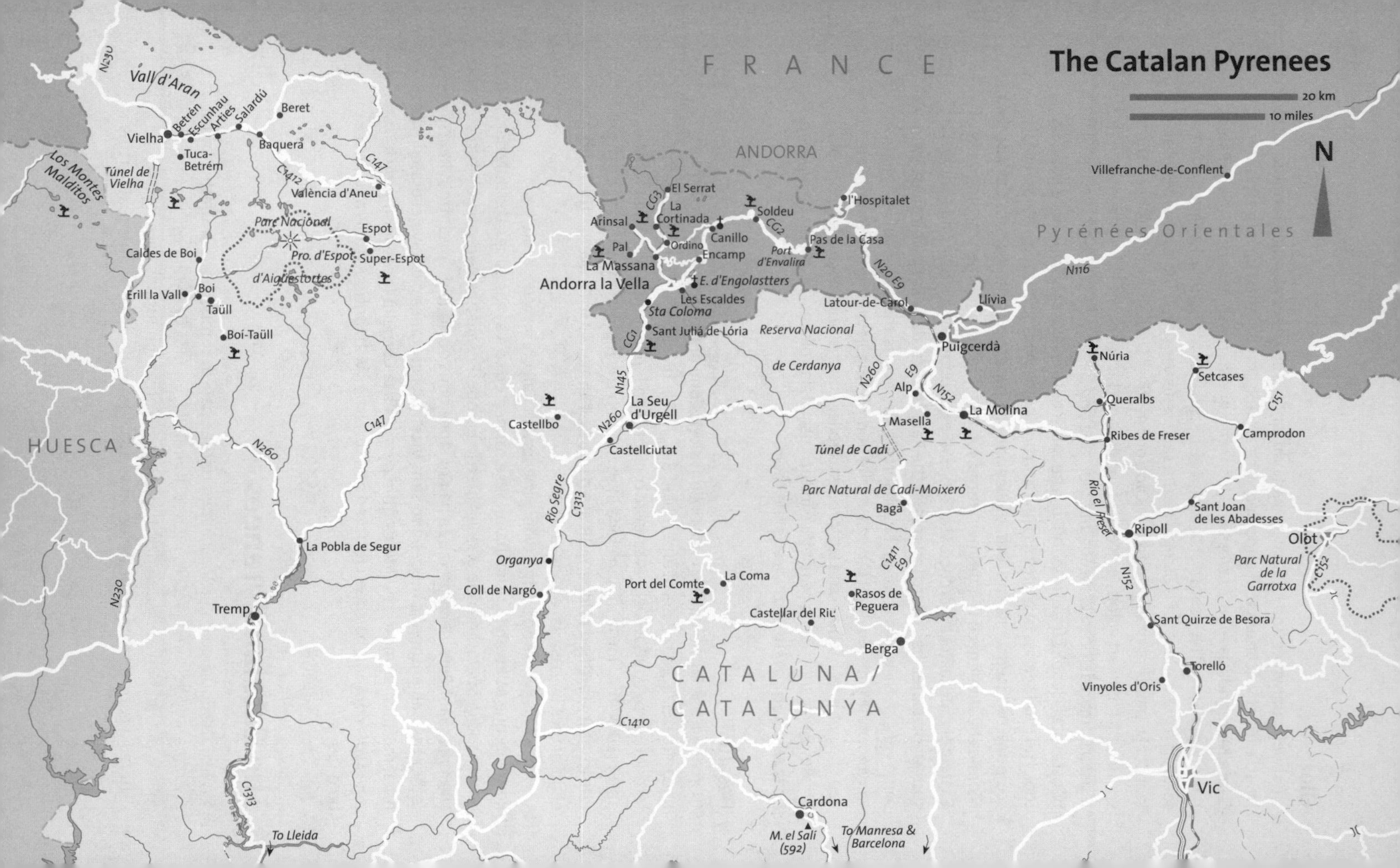

The Catalan Pyrenees
20 km
10 miles
N
FRANCE
ANDORRA
Pyrénées Orientales
HUESCA
CATALUNA/
CATALUNYA
Vall d'Aran
Vielha
Betrén
Escunhau
Arties
Salardú
Beret
Baquera
Tuca-Betrém
Túnel de Vielha
Los Montes Malditos
C1412
C147
València d'Aneu
Parc Nacional
Espot
Super-Espot
Pro. d'Espot
d'Aigüestortes
Caldes de Boi
Erill la Vall
Boi
Taüll
Boí-Taüll
N230
N260
La Pobla de Segur
Tremp
C1313
To Lleida
El Serrat
La Cortinada
Arinsal
Pal
Ordino
La Massana
Canillo
Soldeu
CG1
CG2
CG3
Encamp
Port d'Envalira
Pas de la Casa
l'Hospitalet
Andorra la Vella
E. d'Engolastters
Les Escaldes
Sta Coloma
Sant Juliá de Lória
N20 E9
Latour-de-Carol
Llívia
N116
Villefranche-de-Conflent
Reserva Nacional
de Cerdanya
Puigcerdà
N145
La Seu d'Urgell
Castellbo
Castellciutat
Río Segre
Organya
Coll de Nargó
Port del Comte
La Coma
Castellar del Riu
Rasos de Peguera
Berga
C1411 E9
C1410
Cardona
M. el Sali (592)
To Manresa & Barcelona
E9
Alp
N152
La Molina
Masella
Túnel de Cadí
Parc Natural de Cadí-Moixeró
Bagà
Núria
Queralbs
Ribes de Freser
Río el Freser
Setcases
C151
Camprodon
Sant Joan de les Abadesses
Ripoll
Olot
C152
Parc Natural de la Garrotxa
Sant Quirze de Besora
Torelló
Vinyoles d'Oris
Vic

Europe. For the Catalans and Basques, who live on both sides of the Pyrenees, the mountains have never been all that high, and when Madrid made things hot, it was customary to slip over the border to visit one's French cousin. Yet the difference between the French and Spanish Pyrenees is striking. The former are rugged and often forbidding and even at the beginning of May there can be a blinding whiteout of snow while, to the south, green valleys bask in the sun and the mountains are gentler and more benign.

Spain divides its Pyrenees into three sectors: the Catalan, the Aragonese, and the Navarrese. Of the three, the Catalan Pyrenees have the easiest access and are the most visited, although innumerable tiny villages remain tucked away in the mountain folds on the banks of sparkling streams. Because of their remoteness, smugglers were spiriting away the masterpieces of their tiny Romanesque chapels as late as the 1920s – a practice halted by their removal to Barcelona's Museu Nacional d'Art de Catalunya. Some of Spain's best ski resorts are in Catalunya, as is the lovely national park, Aigüestortes.

Vic and Cardona

Vic, set on a vast plain in the foothills of the Pyrenees, is an ancient town that served as the capital of the Ausetani Iberians and has been mildly important ever since; among its sights are the **cella** of a 2nd-century Roman temple, the picturesque **Plaça del Mercadal**, where markets have been held every Tuesday and Saturday since the 10th century, and a collection of Baroque houses and churches. In 1781 Vic saw fit to knock down its Romanesque **cathedral** and replace it with a neoclassical pile. To make up for the loss, the bishop hired Josep María Sert to cover the interior with remarkable and massive **golden murals** – a job the artist had to do again after the cathedral was set on fire in 1930. What you see here occupied him until his death in 1945, and in their evocation of the triumph of injustice to Christ and Catalunya on the west wall (including the burning of the cathedral with his first paintings), they resemble a modern man's Sistine Chapel. Here, too, are two 15th-century works which managed to escape restoration and the flames: an alabaster ***retablo*** and **tomb**, both by the same sculptor. Vic also preserves a major collection of medieval art in the **Museu Episcopal** (*currently closed while new premises are being built, which are expected to open some time in Spring 2002*), which includes beautiful works by Jaume Huguet, Pedro Serra, Ferrer Bassa, Jaume Ferrer, Lluís Borrassà and Ramón de Mur and a famous stylized, wooden *Descent from the Cross* from Erill la Vall. If you're driving, head out along the Manresa road for an extraordinary view of Montserrat. The Osona region around Vic is full of stunning countryside, dotted with picture-postcard villages like **Rupit** (to be avoided at all costs at weekends) and perfect for hiking and balloon rides; the tourist office in Vic has maps and trail information.

Cardona, to the west, is midway between Barcelona and Andorra. Spaniards know it as the Capital of Salt for the unearthly **Salí** nearby, a mountain of pure salt over 260ft high and five kilometres around the perimeter. On a hill high over the town itself is the attractive ensemble of a **medieval castle** of the powerful Dukes of Cardona (now a *parador*) and the Romanesque church of **Sant Vicenç**.

Getting Around

Vic, Ripoll, Ribes de Freser and Puigcerdà are linked to Barcelona by RENFE **trains** eight times a day. Cardona is most easily reached by train from Barcelona to Manresa and then bus; Sant Joan is connected by **buses** running from Olot to Ripoll. The hour-long **rack railway** ride from Ribes to Núria runs five times daily, connecting with the train from Barcelona.

Tourist Information

Vic: C/de la Ciutat 4, **t** 938 86 20 91, *turisme@ajvic.es*, *www.ajvic.es*, *www.impevic.es*.

Cardona: Av. Rastrillo s/n, **t** 938 69 27 98.

Ripoll: Pla de l'Abat Oliba 9, **t** 972 70 23 51, *otripoll@ddgi.es*.

Sant Joan de les Abadesses: Rambla Comte Guifré 5, **t** 972 72 05 99.

Puigcerdà: C/Querol 1 (in the Ajuntament), **t** 972 88 05 42.

Skiing

The six ski installations east of Andorra are among Spain's most sophisticated and among the easiest to reach by public transport. Check the excellent **website** *www.acem-cat.com* for complete information on all the facilities, snow reports, news and a calendar of events.

Vallter 2000, in Setcases near the French border, has 12 pistes, a slalom course, seven lifts and night illumination on some pistes: for information and to book accommodation call **t** 972 13 60 57, *www.valleter2000.com*. There are five *hostales* in Setcases and four in nearby Camprodón.

Núria has 10 pistes – a couple over 4km long – and two teleskis. Besides the hotel at Núria (*see* p.175) there are many down in Ribes: for information and to book accommodation call **t** 972 73 20 20, *www.valldenuria.com*.

La Molina, near Plandas (south of Puigcerdà), has 31 pistes (including three black and 13 red), a 5km cross-country course, five jump ramps and 20 lifts. There are 11 places to stay on site, for information and to book accommodation, call **t** 972 89 20 31, *www.lamolina.com*. The resort is now marketed together with nearby Masella as Alp2500.

Masella, the other half of Alp2500, is also south and accessible from Puigcerdà, in Alp. It is one of Spain's best, with a wide variety of pistes (37 including 6 black and 15 red). There are five hotels on site: for information, **t** 972 14 40 00; to book accommodation, **t** 972 14 42 01, *www.masella.com*.

Rasos de Peguera, Barcelona's favourite resort – 125km from the big city – is further south, near Berga in Castellar del Riu-Montmajor. It has 14 pistes, two cross-country trails (5 and 10km) and five lifts. This is a small resort with no difficult runs, making it good for families, first-time skiers and one-day skiers as road access is good. There are nine hotels in Berga; **t** 938 21 05 84, *www.ajberga.es*.

Port del Comte is at La Coma, near Coll de Nargo, with 34 pistes in excellent condition (five black and 14 red), a slalom and four artificial slopes, two with grass for summer skiing. There are two hotels on site; **t** 973 49 23 01, *www.portdelcomte.com*.

Where to Stay and Eat

Vic (Vich) ✉ 08500

★★★★**Parador de Vic-Sau**, **t** 938 12 23 23, **f** 938 12 23 68, *vic@parador.es* (*expensive*). Some 14km from Vic on C/de Roda de Tera: charming idealization of a Catalan *masia*, or country house, in a pine grove and overlooking a reservoir, with a pool, and a good **restaurant**.

★★**Ausa**, Pla Major 4, **t** 938 85 53 11 (*inexpensive*). Overlooking Vic's central square – a feast for the eyes and ears on market days.

Jordi Parramón, Cardona 7, **t** 938 86 38 15 (*expensive*). In an attractive old town house around the corner from the Roman temple and much praised for its fresh and creative cuisine. *Closed Sun eve and Mon.*

La Taula, Pla Don Miquel de Clariana 4, **t** 938 86 32 29 (*moderate*). Classic, old-fashioned restaurant in the heart of Vic serving traditional local dishes.

Rectoria d'Oris, on the Torelló–St Quieze de Besora road, Km83, Oris, **t** 938 29 02 30 (*moderate*). Converted old rectory; one of the best places to try the regional dishes made with fresh produce from the surrounding plain; prices are reasonable for the quality of the cuisine, and there's an exellent *menú*.

Cardona ✉ 08261

★★★★**Parador Nacional Duques de Cardona**, **t** 938 69 12 75, **f** 938 69 16 36, *cardona@parador.es* (*expensive*). Set in a stunning location high over the town, in part of the castle founded in 789 by Louis the Pious. The Romanesque courtyard and chapel are a museum, and the charming **restaurant** offers well-prepared Catalan specialities. The rooms themselves are furnished with Catalan antiques.

Ripoll ✉ 17500

★★★**Solana de Ter**, about 2km outside town on the Barcelona road, **t** 972 70 10 62, **f** 972 71 43 43, *hotelsolanadeter@cambrescat.es*, *www.solanadeter.com* (*moderate*). A resort unto itself with rooms, a campsite, tennis courts, a pool and children's playground in a pleasant park-like setting. Includes a very decent **restaurant** (*moderate*) featuring Catalan cuisine.

★★**P. Monasterio**, Pla Gran 4, **t** 972 70 41 33 (*inexpensive*). In the centre of town: not quite for those in habit, but close.

★**Fonda Xesc**, Pla del Roser 1 , Gombrén, **t** 972 73 04 04 (*inexpensive*). Friendly, stone-built, old-fashioned *fonda* in a tranquil village 15km west of Ripoll; it's well worth visiting for the excellent **restaurant** (*moderate*), particularly during mushroom season.

★★ **Hs del Ripollès**, Pla Nova 11, *ramontu@intercom.es*, **t** 972 70 02 15, **f** 972 70 00 27 (*moderate*). Decent, although slightly over-priced, *hostal* with a lively **pizzeria** and café-bar downstairs.

Bar El Punt, Pla Civica 10, **t** 972 70 29 84 (*inexpensive*). Sandwiches, tapas and very tasty crêpes out on the terrace.

Up at **Núria**, camping is permitted in a small area behind the sanctuary; there's also a youth hostel and one hotel; for more information, check *www.valldenuria.com*.

★★★**Vall de Núria**, Estación de Montaña Vell de Nuria, **t** 972 73 20 00, **f** 972 73 20 01, *hotel@valldenuria.com* (*expensive–moderate*). Set in the grim-looking sanctuary, but with nicely furnished rooms and a decent **restaurant** (*moderate*) serving mountain meals.

Pic de l'Àliga, **t** 972 73 20 48 (*cheap*). The youth hostel enjoys a spectactular setting right at the top of the ski-centre's cable car.

Sant Joan de les Abadesses ✉ 03000

Sant Joan offers only two places to stay, but the area has several places dedicated to Turismo Rural, to rent rooms or an apartment.

★**Can Janpere**, C/Mestre Andreu 3, **t** 972 72 00 77 (*moderate–inexpensive*). The most comfortable place, with en suite rooms and a decent **restaurant** with good-value *menús*.

Mas Janpere, Esteve Dorca i María Navarro, **t** 972 72 03 66 (*moderate*). A converted 18th-century farmhouse with newly decorated, comfortable rooms and apartments about 2km outside Sant Joan.

El Reixac, 2½km outside Sant Joan, **t** 972 72 03 73 (*moderate*). Pretty, rustically furnished apartments for between two and six people in a delightful 14th-century farmhouse, with very friendly and helpful owners.

★**Hs Nati**, C/Pere Rovira 3, **t** 972 72 01 14 (*cheap*). Basic *hostal* in the new part of town; it also has a **café-bar** with cheap daily *menús*.

Puigcerdà ✉ 17520

★★★★**Torre del Remei**, Camí Reial s/n, **t** 972 14 01 82, **f** 972 14 04 49, *remei@gro.servicom.es*, *www.relaischateaux.fr/torremei* (*luxury*). For a real treat, head for this stunning, lemony *modernista* palace, four km outside town in Bolvir de Cerdanya. With extensive gardens, a pool, a large, elegant terrace and plenty of activities including golf, hiking and skiing close by. The **restaurant**, easily the finest in the region, serves refined Cerdanyan cuisine; the *menú degustación* has a heady price, but the setting alone is worth every euro.

★★★**Chalet del Golf**, Ctra Puigcerdà-Seu de Urgell, Devesa del Golf, on the Seu d'Urgell road just out of town, **t** 972 88 09 62, **f** 972 88 09 66 (*expensive*). Cosy golf hotel with a pool, tennis, pretty gardens and the links.

★★**Hotel Del Prado**, Ctra de Llivía s/n, **t** 972 88 04 00, **f** 972 14 11 58 (*moderate*). Delightful, chalet-style hotel with a pool, and an excellent **restaurant**.

★★★**Avet Blau**, Pla Santa María 14, **t** 972 88 25 52 (*moderate*). Small and charming; just six rooms, so book in advance.

★**Internacional**, C/La Baronia s/n, **t** 972 88 01 58 (*cheap*). One of the many inexpensive *hostales*: mid-sized and well priced.

Casa Clemente, Av. Dr. Piguillem 6, **t** 972 88 11 66 (*moderate*). Huge, satisfying meals.

Ripoll and Sant Joan

One Romanesque masterpiece the smugglers couldn't cart off is in the Benedictine monastery in the otherwise dreary town of Ripoll, to the north of Vic. Founded by Count Wilfred the Hairy in 888, **Santa María de Ripoll** (*open daily 8–1 and 3–8*) held a prominent position in early medieval Catalunya and was one of the great diffusers of Arab learning to the West, its vast library full of translations of classical texts. When the monastery at Montserrat was founded, it seemed natural to give it to the Benedictines of Ripoll. The church was begun in the 12th century, suffered a devastating fire in 1835 and was rebuilt. Surviving intact, however, is the great **west portal**, now carefully shielded behind glass, the most mature expression of Catalan Romanesque sculpture, a 'Stone Bible' that encompasses nearly the whole Book, with the zodiac and some monsters thrown in for good measure. The north wing of the two-storeyed **cloister** (*open daily 10–1 and 3–7; adm*) survived as well, with its elaborate capitals. Next to the monastery, in the 14th-century **Sant Pere**, the **Museu Pirineos** (*open Tues–Sun 9.30–6 (July–Sept until 7); closed Mon; adm*) contains many of the firearms manufactured in Ripoll beginning in the 16th century, arms that were prized throughout Europe.

Just east of Ripoll, **Sant Joan de les Abadesses** on the River Ter is a medieval town named after the **Colegiata** (*open Mar–June and Sept–Oct daily 10–2 and 4–7; July–Aug daily 10–7; Nov–Mar Mon–Fri 10–2, Sat and Sun 10–2 and 4–6; adm*) also founded by Wilfred the Hairy, in 887, and likewise gloriously embellished in the 12th century. Architects from Aquitaine exerted a strong influence over Catalan builders, nowhere more so than on Sant Joan. In one of the chapels stands the church's most curious treasure, a wooden 15th-century *Deposition* nicknamed 'Las Brujas' – the witches – for the weirdness of its figures. More traditional is the lovely 14th-century alabaster **Retablo de Santa María la Blanca** and a fine Gothic cloister. In the small **monastery museum** (*included in entrance ticket price*) there is a collection of religious art dating back to the 11th century including richly decorated gold and silverware, sculptures and paintings. Also in town, the dilapidated 12th-century **Sant Pol** is worth a look for its carved tympanum. The recently restored pretty **bridge** over the trout-filled Ter dates from 1140.

Núria, Llivia and Puigcerdà

Up the river Freser from Ripoll the small spa **Ribes de Freser** is the departure point for an extraordinary vertiginous journey by private rack-and-pinion railway (*cremallera*) to the attractive stone village of **Queralbs** and beyond to **Núria** (4,166ft), a lofty bowl-shaped valley and sanctuary. Like Montserrat, Núria is a favourite name given to Catalan girls. The 11th-century cult image in the grim sanctuary, **La Mare de Deu de Núria**, has recently been proclaimed the official Patroness of Winter Sport. Fittingly, Núria has a ski station, while the valley provides lovely walks that skirt the edges of precipitous chasms. The high plain to the west, the **Cerdanya**, was divided between Spain and France by the Treaty of the Pyrenees in 1659, bestowing on France all the villages of Upper Cerdanya – but not the towns. Hence the anomaly of **Llivia**, an islet of Spanish territory located three kilometres into France. Ancient *Julia Libyca*, a main town on the Roman highway *Strata Ceretana*, Llivia was the capital of the Cerdanya, but now is visited primarily for curiosity's sake (a neutral road links it to the Cerdanya's current capital, Puigcerdà) and to visit its **pharmacy**, said to be the oldest in Europe – dating from 1415 – and now part of the **municipal museum** (*open April–Sept Tues–Sat 10–1 and 3–7, Sun and hols 10–2; Oct–Mar Tues–Sat 10–1 and 3–6, Sun and hols 10–2; adm*). Nearly every town in Spain has a palatial pharmacy with fancy woodwork, painted ceilings and antique jars – and this is the mother of them all. The medicines are stored not in cabinets, but ornate shrines, veritable *retablos* of drugs. Llivia also claims a heavily fortified **church** (*open daily June–Sept 10–1 and 3–7; Oct–May Tues–Sun 10–1 and 3–6*) from the 1400s, now used as the venue for a summer music festival.

Puigcerdà, opposite Llivia, is a typical frontier town except in the winter season when the skiers pile in; it's also the capital of Spanish ice hockey. There's a pretty lake with swans and paddle boats for hire, and the 13th-century parish church of **Sant Domènec**, its walls decorated with medieval frescoes of unholy brutes dealing the saint a splitting headache.

Some 32 kilometres south of Puigcerdà, on the upper end of the new **Tunnel of Cadí** (Spain's longest) is the tiny town of **Bagà**, one of the cradles of Catalan nationalism. Near the centre stands a statue of the knight Calcerán de Pinos, who was rescued from a Moorish prison in Almería by the miraculous intervention of the silver Byzantine cross reputedly brought over from the First Crusade and now kept in the 14th-century church of **Sant Esteban**. This is one of the access points for the beautiful, craggy **Natural Park of the Cadí-Moixeró**, with some serious trekking for experienced walkers; the Park information office in Bagà has maps and other information.

Andorra

The little **Principat de les Valles de Andorra**, as it is officially known, is an independent historical oddity in the style of Grand Fenwick and the Marx Brothers' Fredonia: a Catalan-speaking island of mountains measuring 468 square kilometres that has managed to steer clear of the French and Spanish since its foundation by Charlemagne. Its name is apparently a legacy of the Moors, derived from the Arabic *Al-gandûra* – 'the wanton woman' – though unfortunately the story behind the name has been forgotten. Andorra has two 'co-princes', the President of France (as the heir of the Count of Foix) and the Bishop of La Seu d'Urgell in Catalunya. According to an agreement spelled out in 1278, in odd-numbered years the French co-prince is sent 1,920 francs in tribute, while in even-numbered years the Spanish co-prince receives 900 pesetas, 12 chickens, six hams and 12 cheeses. Napoleon thought it was quaint and left it alone, he said, as a living museum of feudalism; how they are dealing with the advent of the euro remains to be seen.

Being Catalan, the Andorrans were always most adamant about preserving their local privileges, which they did through the **Consell de la Terra**, founded in 1419, one of Europe's oldest continuous parliaments. The citizens also claim to be the only people in the world who have avoided warfare for 800 years (surely a claim for 'small is beautiful'), though there was a close call in 1934, when a White Russian count proclaimed himself King Boris I of Andorra and declared war on the bishop at Seu – a war the bishop ended after two weeks by sending four Guardias Civils, who escorted King Boris to Barcelona and thence out of Spain.

Until the 1940s Andorra remained isolated from the world, relying on dairy farming, tobacco growing, printing stamps for collectors, and more than a little smuggling. This peaceful Ruritania began to change with the Spanish Civil War, with an influx of refugees and a new popular sport called 'downhill skiing'. And then came the great revelation: why bother smuggling when you can get the consumer to come to you? For many Andorrans, it was simply too much of a good thing: their traditional society, already swamped by emigrants (32,000 Spaniards, 4,000 French; only 12,000 native Andorrans), all but disappeared under a wave of over 6 million visitors a year, most of whom were only passing through to purchase duty-free petrol, electronics, booze and American smokes, imported tax-free by Philip Morris and Reynolds, who ran the native tobacco-growers out of business. In 1993, Andorra even gave up feudalism and voted for a constitution – although the co-princes still get their cash and cheese.

Getting There

By air: There's a small airport near La Seu d'Urgell, 23km from Andorra la Vella, especially used by ski charters. The weather, however, is unpredictable, and there are plans for regular helicopter services from Toulouse.

By train and bus: SNCF **trains** on the Toulouse–Perpignan–Barcelona line (**t** 05 62 15 18 09/03 76 82 11 38) get as close as L'Hospitalet, with bus connections the rest of the way. Other **buses** to Andorra depart from Toulouse every morning (**t** 05 62 15 18 09/03 76 82 11 38) and also from Ax-les-Thermes. From Perpignan you can catch the Villefranche train at 7.58am, which links up with the narrow-gauge **Petit Train Jaune** ('little yellow train') which passes through some awesome mountain scenery on its way to La-Tour-de-Carol, where a Pujol Huguet bus meets it at 1.35pm to go to Andorra, through the Port d'Envalira, which at 7,895ft is the highest pass in the Pyrenees range.

Tourist Information

Andorra la Vella: C/Dr Vilanova, **t** (376) 82 02 14, **f** (376) 82 58 23, *www.turisme.ad* (*open summer 9–1 and 3–7, winter 10–1 and 3–7, Sun and hols 10–1 only*).

Andorra Delegation Tourist Office: 63 Westover Rd, London SW18, **t** (020) 8874 4806.

The Syndicat d'Initiative sells a **map** of Andorra's campsites and mountain refuges (*refugios* and *cabanas*). Two hiking **trails** (*sentiers de grande randonnée*) pass through Andorra: GR 7 and GR 75.

Currency and shopping regulations

Although **Catalan** is the official language of Andorra, **French** and **Spanish** are well understood, particularly as you near their respective borders. As in the rest of Europe, francs and pesetas have now given way to the **euro**. **Cards** are widely accepted. Andorra's recent agreement with the EU on **customs allowances** has considerably increased the permitted value of goods bought in Andorra and taken back across into EU countries; check *www.turisme.ad/angles/compres.htm* for a simple table of allowances.

Entrance formalities are a breeze, though there are checks at both the French and Spanish customs and you may well find that you're stopped twice.

Telephones

If you want to dial an Andorran number from abroad, dial 00, wait for the tone, and then dial the prefix **t** 376 and the number.

Skiing

Andorra has abundant snow from Dec to April, combined with clear, sunny skies; a skier's heaven, with six major installations. See *www.skiandorra.ad*.

High season, when everywhere is extra busy, includes the following religious holidays: 4–10 Dec (4–12 in Ordino), 23–7 Jan, 3 Feb–4 Mar, 12–16 April and weekends.

Pas de la Casa-Grau Roig (6,724–8,528ft), just within the border with France, **t** 80 10 60, **f** 80 10 70. The oldest (1952), with 55 pistes, 33 ski lifts, 360 snow cannons, a slalom, and several slopes for beginners as well as the advanced, night skiing (floodlit, on the Font Negre run), two medical centres; 31 lifts, six cafés and restaurants and 40 hotels.

Ordino Arcalís (6,363–8,528ft), 17km from town; 4km from El Serrat, **t** 85 01 21, **f** 85 04 40. Served by half-hourly buses from Andorra la Vella. Perhaps the most dramatically beautiful and the best place to ski, with 27 pistes and 14 lifts, a medical centre, and cafés, restaurants and hotels in Ordino itself.

Soldeu-El Tartar (5,609–8,397ft), near Canillo, **t** 85 11 51, **f** 85 13 37, for piste condition **t** 84 81 51. The biggest and most popular complex (850ha), with 88km of slopes including 52 runs (some for children), 29 lifts, 380 snow cannons, a 2km cross-country course, a surf park, a new snowboard school and snowpark, three medical centres, four cafés and restaurants, 25 hotels and five self-catering apartment blocks. (Soldeu and Pas de la Casa have also joined forces but as they are from two different parishes the join is not as complete as Arinsal-Pal).

Arinsal-Pal, **t** 83 62 36, **f** 83 59 04. The Arinsal and Pal resorts linked up in the 2000/2001 winter season for the first time. They have joint services and share lift connections, and you can get a combined pass. There's a snow park for snowboarders, 28km of runs, monoskiing, big foot, alpine, heliskiing, 78 snow cannons and 60 instructors.

La Rabassa (6,724ft), near Sant Julià de Lòria, **t** 84 34 52, **f** 84 34 52. A cross-country skiing station featuring 15km of pistes through meadows and forests, separate pistes for snowmobiles, 2.6km of runs, 17 snow cannons, 13 lifts, a children's snow park with snow slides, sleds and the like, a sports centre with pool, gym, sauna, etc. and horse-riding and guided ecology tours. There are rooms and a café and restaurant at the refuge, which is approached by a good road.

Note that Andorra's high altitude and even terrain make it especially good for ski trekking, or *ski randonnée*; overnight accommodation is available in refuges around its rim.

Other Sports

There are a number of sports complexes and facilities all over Andorra, providing an almost inescapable lure towards holiday-fitness.

Andorra la Vella

Andorra Sports Complex, **t** 86 12 22, **f** 86 45 64. This is used for indoor sporting events and has a shiny multipurpose court with stands for 5,000 people.

Mercure health centre, Ctra la Roda, **t** 87 36 02, **f** 87 36 52, *mercureandorra@riberpueg.ad*,

Outside the summer and peak ski seasons, however, Andorra slows down considerably; even in the summer a stout pair of walking shoes and a reasonable amount of energy can take you far away from the congestion, high-rise hotels and discos to some breathtaking scenery: a storybook land of green meadows and azure lakes; minute hamlets clustered below Romanesque churches, with stone houses drying tobacco on their south walls; mountains towering in grandeur overhead: and the silence broken only by the tinkling of cowbells.

Andorra la Vella

Andorra la Vella ('Europe's Highest Capital') and the former villages of **Les Escaldes-Engordany** have melded into a vast arena of conspicuous consuming. Worth a visit, *www.andorraeskviagratis.com*. Part of the Mercure hotel, but open to non-residents, this offers saunas, a pool, gym, solarium, mini golf, Jacuzzi and, most usefully, pre-ski warm-ups and après-ski relaxation.

Serradells swimming pool, Ctra de la Comella, **t** 86 43 93, **f** 86 77 99. There are indoor and outdoor pools (including an Olympic-size one), a learning pool, gym, sauna, tennis courts, squash court and a snack bar. *Open all year Mon–Fri 7–10.45, Sat and Sun 10–8.*

Canillo

Palau de Gel, Ctra General, **t** 80 08 40, **f** 80 08 41, *www.palaudegel@andorra.ad*. A giant skating-rink: there is a 25m swimming pool, gym, sauna, games room and more, plus lessons for ice-hockey and normal/'artistic' skating. There's even accommodation, but that's aimed at teams and pros.

Encamp

Encamp Sports Centre, **t** 83 28 30, **f** 83 20 04. Has the usual facilities (squash, tennis, pools, gym etc.), plus some surprises, such as a library, exhibition hall, table tennis, billiards, martial arts and a dance hall.

La Massana

Sports Centre, in nearby Anyos, **t** 83 64 63, **f** 83 82 80. Includes a shooting gallery, solarium, massage rooms, sunbeds, Jacuzzis, Turkish baths and saunas as well as pools, squash and tennis courts. *Open 8am–11pm.*

A few kilometres north in L'Aldosa, the **sports complex**, **t** 83 72 75, **f** 83 63 24, has indoor and outdoor facilities along with saunas, Jacuzzis and a vertical sunbed. *Open 10am–10pm.*

Sant Julià de Lòria

La Rabassa Shooting Range, **t** 84 37 47, **f** 84 36 73. A new outfit with six semiautomatic posts, Olympic and universal pits, an armoured gun room and a first-aid room.

Escaldes-Engordany

Caldea, near the centre of town at Parc de la Mola 10, **t** 80 09 99, **f** 86 56 56. The largest spa centre in southern Europe: perfect for après-ski. A modern, mirrored, pyramidal structure with thermal water (60°C), air baths, indoor and outdoor Jacuzzis, hydro-massage and many, many more watery things, all in luxurious aquatic surroundings. You'll need to book the inexpensive treatments. There's also a shopping centre, restaurant and bars.

Ordino

Sports Centre, Non Vial, **t** 73 70 70, **f** 83 92 25. This has a pool, saunas and hammam. *Open Mon–Fri 9am–10pm, Sat 10–10, Sun and hols 10–8.*

Where to Stay

Andorra ✉ 61699

Andorra now has some 300 hotels, the vast majority of them spanking new. Contact The Association of Hoteliers, *www.uha.ad*, who can help you find somewhere.

Luxury

★★★★**Roc Blanc**, Pla de Co-Prínceps 5, Escaldes, **t** 87 14 00, **f** 86 02 44. In terms of glamour,

however, is the old stone **Casa de la Vall**, (*C/de la Valle, **t** (376) 82 91 29, **f** (376) 86 98 63; free guided tours by appointment Mon–Sat 9–1 and 3–7, Sun 10–2; Nov–May closed Sun; note that it is closed to visitors when sessions are underway*), the seat of the Counsell de la Terra since 1580. It's home to the famous **Cabinet of the Seven Keys**, containing Andorra's most precious documents and accessible only when representatives from each of the country's seven parishes are present. A **folklore museum** (*not open to the public*) has been installed on the top floor. You can visit the main hall and the kitchen. The latter is where the parish meetings used to take place; the councillors would walk long distances in the cold to come here, and then would warm up by the stove and eat at the table there, discussing parish business. There is also a dovecote, a fountain, ornamental gardens and a monument by Pujol.

this takes the cake, with a five-storey atrium lobby and a glass elevator, sauna and a thermal spa with a number of treatment programmes. The hotel's two **restaurants**, El Pi and El Entrecôt (*expensive*) feature a very good selection of French, Spanish and Catalan dishes.

****__Andorra Park__, C/de les Canals 24, Andorra la Vella, **t** 82 09 79, **f** 82 09 83. A charming palace set in a park with a beautiful rock-cut pool, croquet lawn, driving range and tennis court. Its **restaurant** (*expensive*) is one of the best in Andorra, with fresh pasta dishes and excellent Spanish and Chilean wines.

Expensive

*****__Plaza__, María Pla 19, Andorra la Vella, **t** 86 44 44, **f** 87 94 45. Ultra-contemporary, elegant and classy, if right in the centre of the hubbub. The La Cucula **restaurant** has a decent set menu (*moderate*).

Holiday Inn, Prat de la Creu 88, **t** 87 44 44, **f** 87 44 45. The newest in town. Well equipped, with two **restaurants** and a cafeteria.

Moderate

***__Pitiusa__, C/d'Emprivat 4, Andorra la Vella, **t** 86 18 16, **f** 86 19 88. This is modern and quiet, on the edge of town.

***__Xalet Sasplugas__, C/La Creu Grossa 15, Andorra la Vella, **t** 82 03 11, **f** 82 86 98. An even quieter and more traditional option.

Inexpensive–Cheap

__Marfany__, Av. Carlemany 99, Escaldes, **t 82 59 57. Long-established and comfortable, though only some rooms have baths; the rest have showers.

Hs del Sol, Pla Guillemó, Andorra la Vella, **t** 82 37 01 (*cheap*). One of numerous cheaper alternatives outside the capital hub and especially convenient for skiers.

Eating Out

Andorra La Vella

Molí dels Fanals, C/Dr Vilanova 9, **t** 82 13 81 (*expensive*). Best known for its Andorran mountain cuisine such as onion soup, pig's trotters and mushroom dishes; in an old mill with a garden terrace (*menus moderate–inexpensive*). *Closed Sun eve and Mon.*

La Bohême, Av. Meritxell 1, 3rd floor, **t** 82 67 16 (*moderate*). The better restaurants in Andorra tend to be French; this one serves fine fish and fowl dishes.

Versailles, Cap. del Carrer 1, **t** 82 13 31 (*moderate*). Roast boar, apple pie and traditional French food. *Closed Sun and Mon lunch, 15 June–15 July.*

Elsewhere in Andorra

La Borda de l'Avi, on the Arinsal road, **t** 83 51 54 (*menus expensive–moderate*). Andorran favourites roasted over a wood fire, as well as fresh fish, foie gras, *magret* or snails.

Topic, on the main road in Ordino, **t** 73 61 02 (*moderate–inexpensive*). Serves some 60 varieties of Belgian beer and a selection of fondues alongside a traditional menu.

La Guingueta, on the Rabassa road, Sant Julià de Lòria, **t** 84 29 45 (*expensive–moderate*). A rustic French restaurant offering dishes such as roast dove with foie gras and charcoal-grilled sea bass with cured ham.

Around Andorra

Andorra is famous for its Romanesque churches and belltowers: a 40-minute walk south of Andorra la Vella will take you to the best one, the 11th-century **Santa Coloma**, with a unique, round belltower and Visigothic arches. A winding road from Escaldes (or the *telecabina* from Encamp to the north) ascends to the isolated 11th-century **Chapel of Sant Miquel d'Engolasters**. Its fine frescoes have been replaced by copies (the originals can be seen in the Museu Nacional d'Art de Catalunya in Barcelona, *see* p.143), and its three-storey *campanile* totally dwarfs the church. Beyond the chapel lies a forest and the pretty **Lago d'Engolasters** ('lake swallow-stars') where, according to tradition, all the stars in the universe will one day fall. It's a good place for walking or fishing.

Exploring the hidden corners of old Andorra can be difficult if you're not walking or don't have a car to zigzag up the narrow mountain roads. Buses ply the two main roads through Andorra every couple of hours towards El Serrat, and more frequently towards Soldeu. **La Cortinada**, en route to Soldeu, makes for a good tranquil base, with only one very reasonably priced hotel, excellent scenery, and some of Andorra's oldest houses. In a 1967 restoration of its parish church, **Sant Martí**, some of the original Romanesque frescoes were uncovered. **El Serrat** is more touristy but worth a visit in the summer for the gorgeous panorama of snow-clad peaks from the **Abarstar de Arcalís** (via the ski resort). Another branch of the road from El Serrat leads to the three stunning mountain lakes of **Tristaina** in Andorra's loveliest and least developed northwestern corner, also the site of its finest ski resort, **Ordino-Arcalis**. In Ordino town is the **Areny-Plandolit Museum** (*visits by appointment, **t** (376) 83 69 08; open Tues–Sat 9.30–1.30 and 3–6.30, Sun 10–2; closed Mon*), the ancestral home of a long-line of local nobility, arranged over three floors; the oldest part of the building dates from 1613.

Another destination reached by bus (on the Soldeu road) is **Meritxell**, the holy shrine of Andorra. Here stands an old Romanesque church, in ruins since a devastating fire in 1972, and next to it a new sanctuary housing a copy of the 11th-century *Virgen de Meritxell*, designed in 1976 by Barcelona's overrated superstar architect Ricardo Bofill. The Andorrans have their doubts about this gruesome hybrid of their traditional architecture with the modern, which may explain why the principality decided a few years ago against going ahead with a Bofill-designed ski resort near Andorra la Vella. The lovely 12th-century church of **Sant Joan de Caselles** is located on a hillside on the north edge of **Canillo** (the big village in these parts), its interior adorned with a Gothic *retablo*, a painted wooden ceiling, and Romanesque paintings; the belltower has fine mullioned windows in the Lombard style.

La Seu d'Urgell

La Seu d'Urgell, nine kilometres south of Andorra and a good base for visiting the principality, is named after its **cathedral** (Seu), founded in the 8th century (*open summer Mon–Sat 10–1 and 4–7, Sun 10–1; winter Mon–Fri 12–1 and 4–6, Sat and Sun 11–1; adm, combined ticket available including entrance to Museo Diocesano*, see *below*). Rebuilt in 1184 in the Lombard Romanesque style, it has a fine cloister, minus one gallery. The **Diocesan Museum**'s prize exhibit is an illuminated copy of Beatus de Liébana's 10th-century *Apocalypse* (*open summer Mon–Sat 10–1 and 4–7, Sun 10–1; winter Mon–Fri 12–1 and 4–6, Sat and Sun 11–1; adm*). The rest of Seu isn't much, though the arcaded, cobbled streets of the old quarter make for pleasant strolling. The walk up to the ruins of the old castle in the little village of Castellciutat, just one kilometre west of the city, gives lovely views of the Segre valley. There's some lovely scenery to the south through the **Garganta de Organyà**, a narrow, 1,968ft walled gorge formed by the river Segre, now dammed up to form a long lake.

Tourist Information

Vielha: C/Sarriulera, **t** 973 64 01 10.

Where to Stay and Eat

La Seu d'Urgell ✉ 25000

*****Parador Nacional de la Seu d'Urgell**, C/Sant Domènec 6, **t** 973 35 20 00, **f** 973 35 23 09, *seo@parador.es* (*expensive*). Situated in what's left of the old quarter: built around a Renaissance cloister filled with plants, this has a heated pool, modern and comfortable rooms with a/c, and a worthy **restaurant**.

******El Castell**, Ctra N-620, Km224, in Castellciutat, just outside town on the road to Lleida, **t** 973 35 07 04, **f** 973 35 15 74, *elcastell@relaischateaux.fr*, *www.relais-chateaux.fr* (*luxury*). An elegant modern building of wood and stone next to the ruins of the old castle at the entrance to the town, with a pool, sumptuously decorated rooms and Seu's best **restaurant** (*expensive*), where you can try such delights as lobster tails in puff pastry and simple grilled meat dishes. Book well in advance.

Andría, Psg Brudieu 24, **t** 973 35 03 00/973 35 14 25, *hotelandria@tecnomatic.net* (*moderate*). Small and central; comfortable rooms with bath. The traditional **restaurant** is excellent, and offers a *menú del día* (*inexpensive*) and a *menú degustación* (*moderate*). *Restaurant closed Mon.*

****Nice**, Av. Pau Claris 4–6, **t** 973 35 21 00, **f** 973 35 12 21, *nice@svt.es*, *www.hotelnice.es* (*moderate*). Functional but pleasant hotel with helpful staff.

***Hotel La Glorieta**, C/Afores s/n, **t** 972 35 10 45, **f** 973 35 42 61 (*moderate*). Set on the road up to Castellciutat, with views over the Segre Valley and a pool.

***Habitaciones Europa**, Av. Valira 5, **t** 973 35 18 56 (*cheap*). Don't be misled by the lack-lustre name: bed down cheaply in one of 10 good, clean rooms.

West of Andorra

Parc Nacional de Aigüestortes and the Vall de Boí

For beautiful mountain scenery without the tax-free merchandise, head west to the heart of the Pyrenees and the **Parc Nacional de Aigüestortes i Estany de Sant Maurici**, created in 1955 and encompassing 230 square kilometres of forests, meadows, lakes and jagged snow-capped peaks, including the pristine **Sierra dels Encantats** ('the enchanted mountains') and the lofty Comoloformo, at 10,000ft, the highest mountain in the park. For jigsaw puzzle scenery, few places in the Pyrenees can match the **Lake of Sant Maurici**, completely encircled by trees and mountains. There are several well-marked trails of varying difficulty; especially pretty and none too difficult is the hike from Espot to the refuge in the Encantats, with views over the lake. **Espot** with its hotels is the major gateway into the park; an information booth at the entrance has information on trails, campsites (permits required), refuges and half- and full-day jeep excursions into the park. The **Vall de Boí**, west of the park, is lovely and secluded, dotted with remote villages whose 12th-century Romanesque churches provided the masterpieces in Barcelona's Museu Nacional d'Art de Catalunya (*see* p.143). Recently the exteriors of these slate-roofed churches and their stout square *campaniles* with storeys of mullioned windows (a style imported from Lombardy) have been restored, with replicas of their frescoes. Four of the best are within walking distance of Boí: **Sant Joan de Boí**, **Santa Eulàlia** with a six-storey tower in **Erill-la-Vall**, the curious **Santa María de Taüll** with its leaning tower, and best of all **Sant Climent de Taüll** with its six-storey belltower and the most beautiful fresco copies (the originals are in

MNAC, in Barcelona) The western entrance to Aigüestortes park is through the spa town of **Caldes de Boí**, the most developed village in the quiet valley.

The Vall d'Aran

North of the park and the Vall de Boí, the western and eastern Pyrenean massifs join in a rugged embrace, enfolding the verdant 48-kilometre-long **Vall d'Aran**. Almost inaccessible, it was first linked by road with the outside world in 1924, an aesthetic

Getting Around

The nearest **RENFE** station is in La Pobla de Segur, linked three times daily with the provincial capital of Lleida, but this region is better covered by **bus**. From Pobla there are two buses to the Vall d'Aran; it's usually best to take one of the several direct buses from Lleida to Espot and the Vall d'Aran. Two direct buses to the Vall d'Aran from Barcelona leave at 6.30am and 7.30am from the main Estació de Nord terminal (10 hrs) with the Alsina Graells bus company (**t** 932 65 68 66); the second service is via Espot. Transport into the Vall de Boí is plagued with uncertainties; it's best if you can drive.

Tourist Information

Vielha: C/Sarriulera 6, **t** 973 64 01 10.

Skiing

Check the excellent **website** *www.acem-cat.com* for complete information on all the facilities available, snow reports, news and a calendar of events.

Baqueira-Beret, a clutch of ugly ski apartments just above Vielha, is one of Spain's most modern installations. It overlooks the Vall d'Aran and boasts 53 pistes (four black and 20 red), 19 lifts, two slalom courses, and a helicopter service to the peaks for new thrills. There are five hotels on the site; for info call **t** 973 63 90 10; to book accommodation call **t** 973 36 90 00, or in Barcelona, **t** 933 18 27 76, *www.baqueira.es*.

Tuca-Betran, also easily accessible from Vielha, offers a wide diversity of pistes (18 altogether, six very difficult), served by nine lifts. There is one four-star hotel at the station; **t** 973 64 08 55. Also nearby is **Tuca Malh Blanc**, **t** 973 64 10 50.

Super Espot, near Aigüestortes National Park, offers 32 pistes (five black and 11 red), nine lifts, and modest lodgings in the town of Espot; for info and to book accommodation **t** 934 14 19 26, *www.espotesqui.es*.

Sant Joan de L'Erm, 20km west of La Seu d'Urgell at Montferrer Castellbo, concentrates on cross-country (Nordic) skiing with some very pretty courses; **t** 973 29 80 15.

Boí–Taüll, overlooking the Boí valley, with 41 slopes (including eight black and 19 red) and a range of accommodation in all price categories. For info and to book accommodation, call **t** 902 40 66 40, *www.boitaullresort.es*.

Where to Stay and Eat

Espot ✉ 25597

****Roya**, Sant Maurici 1, **t** 973 62 40 40 (*inexpensive*). Modest, in a scenic location with a good, reasonable **restaurant**. *Open all year*.

***Saurat**, C/Sant Martí s/n, **t** 973 62 41 62, **f** 973 62 40 37, *h.saurat@jazzfree.com* (*moderate*). The most expensive and best equipped of the village's hotels.

***La Palmira**, C/Marineta s/n, **t** 973 62 40 72 (*inexpensive*). The economy choice, with just seven small rooms.

There are several **campsites** along the river at the entrance to the village; the best is the **Sol i Neu**, **t** 973 62 40 01, which has a pool.

Boí ✉ 25528

***Beneria**, Pla Treio, **t** 973 69 60 36, **f** 973 69 61 91 (*inexpensive*). Fairly pleasant, with basic rooms and one of Boí's few **restaurants**, with simple but filling meals. *Open all year*.

***Hs Pascual**, Pont de Boí, **t** 973 69 60 14 (*inexpensive; cheap in summer*). By the bridge tragedy that has brought it thousands of massive electric pylons. For most of its history the valley was in practice independent, like Andorra, until Napoleon annexed it to France; it became officially part of Spain a few years later. Some of the older inhabitants still speak *Aranés*, a dialect not of Catalan, but of Gascon.

The valley's rubble houses are also unique, with their stepped gables, dormers, slate roofs, and carved wooden balconies. Many of them may be seen in **Vielha**, principal village of the upper valley (or Mijaran), all gathered in the shadow of its giant

below the village, this is the best budget option. There's a warm welcome, and the **restaurant** serves decent food. *Open all year*.

★★★★**Balneario Manantial**, Caldes de Boí, **t** 973 69 62 10, **f** 973 69 62 20 (*expensive*). An imposing spa centre, with a dramatic location and every imaginable treatment.

★★**Caldas**, Caldes de Boí, **t** 973 69 62 30, **f** 973 69 90 58 (*inexpensive*). Huge, 17th-century stone hospital converted into a pleasant hotel with spacious rooms for those 'taking the waters'. *Closed 1 Oct–24 June*.

La Cabana, Ctra de Taüll s/n, **t** 973 69 62 13 (*inexpensive*). Succulent grilled meats and local mountain dishes.

Taüll ✉ 25528

★★**P. la Coma**, C/Únic s/n, **t** 973 69 60 25 (*inexpensive*). Attractive, welcoming little pension at the entrance to the village with a good **restaurant** offering game and other regional specialities; it's very popular with locals.

★★**El Xalet de Taüll**, C/El Como 5 (*moderate*). An attractive hotel of wood and stone, perfectly located in the heart of the old village.

★★★**Boí-Taüll Resort**, Pla de l'Ermita s/n, **t** 973 69 60 00. Modern, three-storey chalet-style development at the heart of ski station, with plenty of sports facilites including a pool.

El Caliu, C/Feixanes 11, **t** 973 69 62 12 (*moderate*). Rustic, typical mountain restaurant serving delicious traditional dishes and home-made desserts. *Closed Tues in winter*.

Vielha ✉ 25530

★★★**Parador de Valle de Arán**, Ctra de Túnel s/n, on N230 tunnel road, **t** 973 64 01 00, **f** 973 64 11 00, *vielha@parador.es* (*expensive*). The building, modern and eccentric with a panoramic circular sitting room, is prettily located on a wooded slope; it has a pool and a good **restaurant** with Aranese specialities.

★★★**Fonfreda**, Pso Libertad 18, **t** 973 64 04 86, **f** 973 64 24 42 (*moderate*). Central, family-run hotel with superb mountain views and welcoming staff.

★★**Delavall**, Eth Pas d'Arro 40, **t** 973 64 02 00 (*moderate*). Near the centre of town: well priced for the good facilities which include a pool. *Open all year*.

★★**Casa Vicenta**, C/Reiau 7, **t** 973 64 08 19 (*inexpensive*). Charming little *pensión*; rooms without bath are *cheap*.

★**De Miguel**, Pla San Antoni, **t** 973 64 00 63 (*cheap*). Ten simple rooms without baths.

★**Busquets**, C/Major 9, **t** 973 54 02 38. Tiny four-room lodging house.

Vielha has a selection of **restaurants**, none of which are truly exceptional:

Era Mola, C/Marrec 4, **t** 973 64 24 19 (*moderate*). Romantic, cosy little restaurant, serving highly praised Aranese specialities; try the delicious wild mushrooms in season. *Closed 1 May–15 July and 25 Sept–1 Dec*.

Casa Turnay, Pza Major, Escanyau, **t** 973 64 02 92 (*moderate*). In the village of Escanyau is one of the Vall d'Aran's best restaurants: hearty Aranese dishes and a good-value *menú del día* (*inexpensive*). *Closed May–July*.

Salardú ✉ 25598

★★★★**Parador Don Gaspar de Portolá**, Ctra de Baqueira, Arties, **t** 973 64 08 01, **f** 973 64 10 01 (*expensive*). In Artíes (near Salardú): one of the more charming corners of the Vall d'Aran and close to the skiing at Baqueira-Beret.

★★★**Valartiés II**, C/Major 3, Artíes, **t** 973 64 43 64, **f** 973 64 21 74, *valarties@aranweb*, *www.aranweb.com* (*moderate*). Extremely pleasant and especially cosy in the winter, with its fireplaces and very fine **restaurant**, the **Casa Irene**, **t** 973 64 09 00, featuring dishes such as duck with truffles. *Closed second fortnight in Oct and Nov*.

Romanesque-Gothic church and its octagonal tower. The inside is worth a look, especially for its dashing, 12th-century *Christ de Mijaran* that originally belonged to the once mighty monastery of Mitg-Arán. Of the monastery only a chapel remains, across the new-born river Garona, which swells into the great Garonne and flows into the Atlantic at Bordeaux. A mysterious monolith near the chapel suggests the site has long been sacred. Near the town are two ski stations (*see* p.184), including the swanky, enormous **Vaquèira-Beret** (***t*** *973 64 44 55*), a favourite with the Spanish royal family.

Besides trails and ski slopes, the Vall d'Aran has a several other traditional villages and beautiful Romanesque churches, such pretty **Salardú** and rustic **València d'Aneu**.

Into the Flatlands: West of Barcelona to Lleida

Cervera and Bellpuig

In the Middle Ages Lleida was famous for its university but, like Barcelona's, it was closed by a vengeful Philip V, who combined the two institutions to create a third, Bourbon university in between the two at **Cervera**. This lasted until 1841, when the university returned to Barcelona, leaving behind a monumental university ghost town, now partly used as a cultural centre. Besides the strange forlorn buildings, there are three churches worth a visit: **Sant Domènech** for its cloister, the Romanesque **Santa María** with fine Catalan artwork, and the mysterious round **Sant Pere le Gros** (1079), thought to have served as a funerary chapel/pilgrim initiatory temple. The environs of Cervera are dotted with seldom-visited medieval hamlets, like **Biosca**, **Olujas** and, an hour's walk from Olujas, **Montfalcó Murrallat**, with a baker's dozen houses encompassed by a vast wall and a ruined Moorish castle.

Bellpuig's parish church has the marvellous Italian Renaissance tomb of Ramón Folch de Cardona, Viceroy of Sicily, by Giovanni di Nola. Ramón's armoured effigy rests its head on a helmet, while the sarcophagus is decorated with a robust pagan scene.

Lleida (Lérida)

Lleida (Lérida in Castilian), lies along the river Segre in the midst of Catalunya's most extensive plain. Its Celtic founders called it *Illizurda*, and against the Carthaginians they fought one of many battles that scar the city's history. During one war – the Spanish Succession – the defenders saw fit to turn the magnficent cathedral, **La Seu Vella**, into a barracks, leaving the town to build itself a new, far less imposing edifice.

La Seu Vella (*open Tues–Sat 10–1.30 and 4–7.30 (winter until 5.30), Sun 9.30–1.30; adm*) is mightily positioned, within the walls of the Moorish-built fortress, **La Zuda**. Begun with Templar assistance in 1203, it is a prime example of the Transitional style from Romanesque to Gothic, with a colossal octagonal tower and a 14th-century Mozarabic portal to the south called *dels Fillols*, 'of the Children'. Major restoration work revealed a lovely Romanesque-Gothic **cloister** of exceptional grace, its 12 arches woven with stone tracery resembling snowflakes; no two are alike. Its unusual position, in front of the church, recalls the patio of the mosque that once stood here; in the nave, note the lingering Moorish influence in the carved capitals.

The rest of Lleida isn't much. On C/Major you'll find the dull 18th-century **cathedral**, part of which displays a collection of works by local contemporary artists. Just across the street is the **Hospital de Santa María** (1512) built around an elegant 15th-century patio which now houses a dull **Museo Arqueològic** (*open Tues–Sat 12–2 and 6–9; closed Sun and Mon; adm free*) and, just off C/Major, there's the 13th-century **Paheria**, with a museum of local history; it conserves a rare 11th-century Catalan codex of laws, *Les Constitucions* (*open Mon–Fri 10–2 and 6–8; closed Sat and Sun*). Just to the south-west is the **Castel de Gardeny** (*not open to visitors*), seat of the first territory granted the Knights Templar in Spain (1149), with a Romanesque chapel of Santa María.

Getting Around

By Train

Lleida, Bellpuig, and Cervera are linked by most trains between Barcelona and Madrid. The RENFE station in Lleida is on Av. Francesca Macià and Rambla Ferran.

By Bus

Buses from the Pyrenees usually terminate in Lleida; the bus station is on the Av. de Blondel, which is handy for the town centre.

Tourist Information

Lleida: Regional Office, Av. Madrid 36, **t** 973 27 09 09, **f** 973 27 09 49, *oit@lleida.mailcat.net*, *www.turismedelleida.com*;
City Office, C/Major 31, **t** 902 25 00 50.

Where to Stay

Expensive–Moderate

*****Condes de Urgel**, Av. de Barcelona 21, **t** 973 20 23 00, **f** 973 20 24 04, *atsa@100mbps.es* (*expensive*). Four-star splendour at three-star prices, with an equally splendid **restaurant**, **El Sauce** (*moderate*).

*****NH Hotel Pirineos**, Gran Psg de Ronda 63, **t** 973 27 31 99, **f** 973 26 20 43 (*expensive; often moderate at weekends*). Modern, extremely comfortable (though rather impersonal) hotel on the edge of the town.

****Hotel Ramón Berenguer IV**, Pla Ramón Berenguer IV 3, **t** 973 23 73 45, **f** 973 23 95 41. Large, well-equipped modern hotel near the centre of Lleida: with pleasant rooms at very reasonable prices.

****Hotel Principal**, Pla de la Paeria 7, **t** 973 23 08 00, **f** 973 23 08 03, *principa@teleline.es* (*moderate*). Another large, modern hotel with good facilities and a handy location just off Pla Sant Joan.

Inexpensive–Cheap

***Goya**, Alcalde Costa 9, **t** 973 26 67 88 (*inexpensive*). Reasonable one-star hotel with 17 well-priced rooms.

****Santiago**, Alcalde Costa 15, **t** 973 26 97 95 (*inexpensive*). Small *pensión* with slightly poky rooms; all en suite.

***Caribe**, Anselm Clavé 20, **t** 973 24 35 84 (*cheap*). A decent cheapie offering rooms with or without showers; it's also handy for the train station.

Eating Out

Forn del Nastasi, C/Salmerón 10, **t** 973 23 45 10. One of Catalunya's best restaurants, with an extensive menu including very good seafood, charcoal grills, and house specialities (*menú del día inexpensive*). *Closed Sun eve, Mon and first fortnight in Aug.*

Sheyton, Av. Prat de la Riba 39, **t** 973 23 81 97 (*moderate*). Elegant, classic restaurant with delicious local dishes; exceptional desserts.

La Huerta, Av. Tortosa 9, **t** 973 24 24 13 (*moderate*). Next to the market just below La Seu Vella, this popular spot specializes in provincial dishes using local ingredients.

Xalet Suis, C/Rovira Roure 9, **t** 973 23 55 67 (*inexpensive*). Popular for its great fondues; as well as the classics, you can try a seafood fondue, or one of chocolate and fruit.

Casa Lluís, Pla de Ramón Berenguer IV 8, **t** 973 24 00 26 (*inexpensive*). A friendly budget choice. *Closed Sun eve and Mon.*

Getting Around

By Train

Tarragona is linked frequently to Barcelona and València by rail, and to Zaragoza, Madrid and Lleida several times a day. The RENFE station is just below the Balcó del Mediterrani.

By Bus

The bus terminal is at Rambla Nova 40. Buses depart from the vicinity of the Pla Ponent, near the Municipal Forum. For the Aqueduct, take the El Salvador bus (every 20 mins from Prat de La Riba). Nearly any bus going up the coast will let you off at Tamarit Castle and beach.

Tourist Information

Tarragona: Provincial Office: C/de Fortuny 4, **t** 977 23 34 15;
Municipal Office: C/Mayor 39, **t** 977 24 50 64, *turisme@tinet.fut.es*.

There are summer booths in Portal del Roser, Pla Imperial Tarraco, and Psg de Sant Antoni.

Where to Stay

Tarragona ✉ 43000

Tarragona's hotels fill up quickly in the summer, so book or start searching early in the day – or make a day trip from Barcelona.

Expensive

******Imperial Tarraco**, Psg Les Palmeres s/n, **t** 977 23 30 40, **f** 977 21 65 66, *imperial@tinet* (*discounts off-season; moderate at weekends*). Tarragona's finest, modern but beautifully sited on the cliff and handy for the old town; amenities include a pool.

******Ciutat de Tarragona**, Pla Imperial Tarraco 5, **t** 977 25 09 99, **f** 977 25 06 99, *hotelgn@sbgrup.copm*, *www.sbhotels.es* (*moderate at weekends*). Modern, comfortable hotel geared towards business people.

Moderate

*****Astari**, Vía Augusta 95, **t** 977 23 69 00, **f** 977 23 69 11, *astari@tinet.fut.es*. Near the sea, in typical resort style; rooms have balconies, and there's a pool, tennis and a garden.

*****Lauria**, Rambla Nova 20, **t** 977 23 67 12, **f** 977 23 67 00, *info@hlauria.es*, *hlauria.es* (*moderate*). Charming, classic hotel with a pool right in the centre of town at very reasonable prices, particularly out of season.

Inexpensive–Cheap

Some of the cheapest *fondas* and *hostales* are on Pla de la Font or Rambla Vella.

***Residencia España**, Rambla Nova 49, **t** 977 23 27 07, **f** 977 23 20 79 (*inexpensive*). Nice, modern rooms on the favourite promenade.

****Forum** Pla de la Font 37, **t** 977 23 17 18 (*cheap*). Pleasant *pensión*, offering decent rooms (without en suite facilities) on an attractive square just inside the old town.

Tarragona

Tarragona, 'the Balcony of the Mediterranean', is one of Spain's oldest cities and one of the best situated, a mighty rampart of a town nearly 200ft above the sea. The Iberians fortified it so well that many of the later Roman and medieval buildings, as if shedding old skins, rise from bases of their huge, rough-hewn blocks. The Romans were quite fond of Tarraco, as they called it, and lavished on it the entire province of Tarraconensis, or Hispania Citerior. Over the years, they made it the most elegant city on the Iberian peninsula; the poets Martial and Pliny praised its superb climate, fertile fields and delicious wines. Augustus relaxed here after his 26 BC campaign in the north of Spain. By the 2nd century AD it had 30,000 inhabitants.

Legend has it that St Paul preached in Tarragona. The Visigoths made it one of Spain's leading bishoprics in the 5th century; St Hermenegild, a Visigoth prince who converted to Catholicism, led the city in a revolt against the Arian heresies of his father King Leovigild, who had him martyred. Under Moorish rule, Tarragona is said to

★**P. Marsal**, Pla de la Font 26, **t** 977 22 40 69 (*cheap*). The best value *pensión* in the neighbourhood, with bright rooms, the nicest of which overlook the square.

★**El Callejón**, Vía Augusta 213, **t** 977 23 63 80 (*cheap*). One of several well-priced but very basic *hostales* along this street.

P. Mar i Flor, C/Gral. Contreras 29, **t** 977 23 82 31 (*cheap*). This is near the train station, with large, modern rooms and friendly service.

Eating Out

Sol Ric, Vía Augusta 227, **t** 977 23 20 32 (*expensive*). One of the best-known places in town, a 20-min walk from the Rambla Nova. It specializes in both simple and elaborate seafood; try the spicy *romesco* sauce (a mix of peppers, almonds, garlic and Priorato). The wine list is comprehensive and you can dine outside in summer. *Closed Sun eve and Mon.*

Merlot, Cavallers 6, **t** 977 22 06 52 (*expensive*). Very charming restaurant in a *modernista* town house, and serving an imaginative blend of French and Mediterranean cuisine.

Les Voltes, C/Trinquet Vell 12, **t** 977 23 06 51 (*moderate*). Dine under the arches of the Roman circus on *Romescalda*, seafood served in a piquant sauce.

El Trull, Ctra Barcelona Km1 168.5, **t** 977 20 79 12 (*moderate*). Just out of town on the road to Barcelona; set in an old converted mill, serving delicious traditional Catalan cuisine.

Les Coques, C/Baixada del Patriarca 2, **t** 977 22 83 00 (*moderate*). An attractive and long-established restaurant, very close to the cathedral; Catalan specialities include rabbit *à la Català. Closed Sun.*

Barquet, C/Gasómetro 16, **t** 977 24 00 23 (*moderate*). This is a good seafood restaurant near the Roman Theatre offering very well-priced set menus and a discerning wine list. *Closed Sun and Mon eve.*

Bufet el Tiberi, C/Martí d'Rdenya 5, **t** 977 23 54 03 (*inexpensive*). Pleasant, popular neighbourhood local serving hefty portions of traditional favourites.

Leman, Rambla Nova 27, **t** 977 23 42 23 (*inexpensive*). A café and patisserie serving delicious ice creams, as well as tempting fresh pastries.

For the freshest fish, spend an evening in the **tapas bars** in the port area of El Serallo. The most expensive places line the main Muelle Pescadores, but the streets tucked behind it are packed with more reasonable options.

Club Nàutic, C/Serallo s/n, **t** 977 24 00 68 (*moderate*). One of the better known and more inspired restaurants of the district, with imaginatively cooked seafood.

Cal Brut, C/Sant Pere 14, **t** 977 21 04 05 (*inexpensive*). Two streets back from the port, this atmospheric restaurant has been serving up excellent seafood since 1914.

Cal Martí, C/Sant Pere 12, **t** 977 21 23 84 (*inexpensive*). Another good seafood option.

have been almost entirely Jewish; when it was retaken by Ramón Berenguer IV, the new cathedral was built by Jewish architects. After peaking in the 14th century, the city declined into a backwater. The modern city has spread far beyond the hilltop walled enclosure, owing its revival to the popularity of wine and the Costa Daurada.

Upper Tarragona

As in Barcelona, Tarragona's main promenades are called the Ramblas: the Old (*vella*) and the New (*nova*). The **Rambla Nova**, decorated with *modernista* buildings, divides old Tarragona from the new and begins at the **Balcó del Mediterrani**, its famous 320ft-high balcony overlooking Tarragona's beautiful beach. Looking the other way is a statue of King Pere III's great admiral-privateer Roger of Llauria, who conquered Sicily for the crown of Aragón. Below the Balcó are the ruins of the **Roman Amphitheatre** and, in the ruined 12th-century **Santa María del Miracle**, traces of a 6th-century Visigothic church built to commemorate Fructuosus, Augurius and Eulogius, who were martyred here on a pyre. Continuing up and around the Balcó, the

Pla del Rei and the 1st-century BC **Praetorium** (*open June–Sept Tues–Sat 10–8; Oct–May Tues–Sat 10–5.30; Sun all year 10–3; closed Mon; adm*) are up to the left. Popularly called the Castle of Pilate – like Sevilla, Tarragona likes to claim Pontius Pilate – the Praetorium was really the one-time residence of Augustus and Hadrian, and later the Kings of Aragón. The French destroyed much of it, but left the tower; this has been opened as the **Museu de la Romanitat**, devoted to the urban evolution of the city; a glass lift shoots to the top for spectacular views. Underground passages lead into the spectacularly restored remains of the **Roman Circus**, visible from the Rambla Vella. Next to the Praetorium, the large and immaculately presented **Museu Arqueològic** (*open June–Sept Tues–Sat 10–8, Sun and hols 10–2; Oct–May Tues–Sat 10–1.30 and 4–7; adm*) has an especially fine array of Roman mosaics, including a famous Medusa, a terracotta mask that looks like the Roman Kilroy, an erotic oil lamp and more.

What remains of Tarragona's **Jewish quarter** is near the museum, in the narrow arched lanes around Pla Angels, where the synagogue once stood. Beyond this is the Pla del Forum and the remains of the tremendous Roman **Provincial Forum**. This gives on to the 14th-century arcaded **C/Merceria**; where it meets C/Major, the fine, 17th-century **Casa Consistorial** has been restored as a museum and information office.

The Cathedral

Open Mar–June Mon–Sat 10–1 and 4–7; July–mid-Oct Mon–Sat 10–7; mid-Oct–Nov Mon–Sat 10–12.30 and 3–6; Nov–Mar Mon–Sat 10–2; closed Sun; adm, entrance through cloister, exc. for services.

A stairway from C/Major ascends to Tarragona's cathedral, a masterpiece of the Transitional style, begun in the 12th century and completed in the 15th. The principal façade presents a mastodontic aspect, compensated by a magnificent rose window and fine 13th-century statues of saints, bishops and martyrs. The enormous **cloister** is decorated with 12th-century sculpture that alone makes the trip to Tarragona worthwhile. Moorish influences are evident in the geometric panels that fill the spaces below the arches; on the west side there's even a niche resembling a *mihrab* dated 960. The scenes over the door are especially robust and, among the fanciful capitals, don't miss the one just to the right as you enter, depicting two scenes from the medieval fable of the clever cat who feigns death to outsmart the cautious mice hiding in the rafters. The jubilant mice descend to put puss on a bier for the funeral, only to face an unexpected feline resurrection. The highlight of the **Museu Diocesano** (*open Mon–Sat 1–7; adm included in entrance ticket*) off the cloister is a 15th-century tapestry of medieval life, *La Bona Vida*. More than the other great Catalan cathedrals, Tarragona has preserved its mystical gloom – which makes it difficult to see the magnificent marble *Retablo de Santa Tecla* in the Capilla Mayor, a 1430 work by Pere Johan honouring Tarragona's patron saint, a convert of St Paul. Near the predella the details become increasingly minute and include tiny spiders and butterflies, as fine as filigree. There's a 16th-century organ, and the 14th-century **Chapel of Santa María de los Sastres** (of the tailors), a humble profession in the Middle Ages, but wealthy enough here to have endowed the cathedral's finest chapel.

To the Passeig Arqueològic

From C/Major, turn left on to aristocratic C/Cavallers. At No.14, the Gothic **Casa Castellarnau** (*open June–Sept Tues–Sat 9–9; Oct–May Tues–Sat 10–1.30 and 4–6.30; Sun all year 10–2; closed Mon; adm*) has been restored and opened as a museum; the courtyard and stair are especially fine. Near the end of C/Cavallers is the picturesque **Plaça del Pallol**, where Gothic buildings were built over ruins of the huge Provincial Forum. In the walls, the **Portal del Roser** is one of six megalithic gates; note the double axes and Iberian letters (ancient masons' marks?) carved into the Cyclopean blocks. Beyond the gate begins the **Passeig Arqueològic** (*open Oct–May Tues–Sat 10–1.30 and 4.30–6.30, Sun 10–2; June–Sept Tues–Sat 9–9, Sun 10–2; closed Mon; adm*), the other star attraction of Tarragona, where through a manicured garden you can get the best view of the walls – rugged Iberian blocks at their base, tidy Roman stone added by the Scipios on top, surrounded by walls put up by the English during the War of the Spanish Succession. The best part is near the **Minerva Tower**, where a bronze statue of Augustus, donated by the Italians in 1936, looks on authoritatively.

Lower Tarragona

Near the Rambla Vella (at the end of Vía de L'Imperi Romà) the **Plaça de la Font** occupies much of the ancient circus; in the houses on surrounding streets big pieces of it are embedded in the walls. On the other side of the Rambla Nova (*take C/Canyelles down to Lleida*) are the columns and foundations of Roman Tarraco's smaller, porticoed **Municipal Forum** (*open Oct–Mar Tues–Sat 10–1.30 and 3.30–5.30, Sun 10–2; April–May Tues–Sat 10–1.30 and 3.30–6.30, Sun 10–3; June–Sept Tues–Sat 9–9, Sun 10–2; closed Mon; adm*), where city business was transacted. Further down, on the banks of the River Francoli (from the Rambla Nova take Av. Ramón i Cajal) a huge **Roman-Palaeo-Christian Necropolis** was unearthed during the construction of a tobacco factory. Used between the 3rd and 5th centuries, the necropolis is the richest yet discovered in Spain, producing numerous funerary monuments and mosaics, from the pagan Romans to the Visigoths. Two interesting crypts remain in situ, while the best artefacts are in the adjacent **Palaeo-Christian Museum** (*open June–Sept Mon–Sat 10–1 and 4.30–8, Sun 10–2; Oct–May Mon–Sat 10–1.30 and 3–5.30, Sun 10–2; adm*). Note the strange Lions' Sarcophagus, an 4th-century ivory doll, and the mosaic of Optimus.

Tarragona also has one of the finest beaches of the Costa Daurada, the **Platja del Miracle**, and another good one that's usually less crowded at **Arabassada**, about one and a half kilometres to the north. Tarragona's lively fishermen's quarter, **El Serrallo**, a 20-minute walk from the Rambla Nova, is the place to go for good seafood and tapas.

The Roman Environs of Tarragona

Spain's finest Palaeo-Christian monument is six kilometres from Tarragona, just beyond Constanti in a vineyard in Centcelles: the **Mausoleo Romano de Centcelles** (*open June–Sept Tues–Sat 10–1.30 and 4–7.30, Sun 10–2; Oct–May 10–1.30 and 3–5.30*). In the 4th century, a substantial Roman villa was converted into a basilica dedicated to St Bartholomew. Also north of Tarragona, just off the road to Valls in the village of

El Salvador, are the remains of a two-tiered 123m-high Roman aqueduct, **Les Ferreres**, a graceful golden beauty that supplied the ancient city with water from the Gayà River.

Up the coast along the ancient **Vía Augusta** are three other Roman monuments. At six kilometres stands the impressive 30ft **Torre de los Escipiones**, thought to be a funerary monument to the two famous Scipio brothers, Publius and Gnaeus, who died fighting the Carthaginians in 212 BC; the figures in relief represent military deities. At eight kilometres a monolith marks the centre of the Roman stone quarry, the **Cántara del Médol**. At 20 kilometres the **Arco de Barà**, a triumphal arch, spans the ancient road, erected for some forgotten victory in the 2nd century.

Tarragona Province: Wine *à la Modernista*

One of the liveliest towns in the province is **Reus**, which is especially rich in beautiful *modernista* buildings, thanks to the mayor who invited Domènech i Montaner to build several structures in town. His 1901 **Casa Navàs** in Pla del Mercadal has a façade by Gaudí's cousin and a beautifully preserved interior lavish with floral motifs. In the outskirts he also built, as a prelude to his great Hospital de Sant Pau in Barcelona, Reus' **Institut Pere Mata** (1897–1912), richly decorated with blue and white ceramics.

The *Cava* of Penedés

Tarragona province encompasses three of Spain's finest wine-growing areas: Tarragones, El Priorat, and Penedés. Penedés is famed for its white wines and *cavas* (Spanish champagnes); **Sant Sandurí de Noia** is the Jerez of *cava*, packed with *bodegas* full of the bubbly and sprinkled with *modernista* buildings. Two of these, the 1920s **Caves Freixenet** (*C/Joan Sala 2, **t** 938 91 70 00*) and **Caves Codorniu** (*Av. Codorniu, **t** 938 18 32 32*), welcome visitors who just drop in. The Codorniu cellars, said to be the world's largest producer of sparkling wines, are in a superb *modernista* cathedral of parabolic arches by Puig i Cadafalch (1896–1906) built over a labyrinthine 16 kilometres of cellars. Another important town in the region, **Vilafranca de Penedés**, also has numerous *modernista* works. It is the home base of Spain's greatest winemaking family, the Torres, and has a wine museum, the **Museu del Vi** – just one of six specialized museums in Pla Jaume I, housed in a 12th-century palace; the tour includes a wine tasting and you get to keep the glass as a souvenir (*all six open Oct–May 10–2 and 4–7, Sun 10–2; June–Sept Tues–Sat 9–9; closed Mon; adm*); others include art, geology, ornithology and archaeology. Items in the last come from the Ibero-Roman-medieval ruins of **Olèrdola**, only a short walk from Vilafranca.

El Priorat

El Priorat is red-wine country, producing some of the world's most potent vintages – up to 24 per cent proof. These formidable vineyards were first cultivated by the monks at the Carthusian priory Scala Dei, in the heart of the region. It never recovered after the dissolution of the monasteries in 1831 and has been gracefully falling apart ever since. **Falset**, the modern capital of El Priorat, has, like so many of the region's villages, a lovely *bodega* done in the *modernista* style by a disciple of Gaudí, César Martinell

(1888–1973). Other *bodegas* by Martinell, all worth a visit both for their architecture and their wine, include those at **Rocafort de Queralt** (with an interior reminiscent of the Sagrada Família), at **Sarral**, at **Barbara de la Conca** and **Montblanc** (*see* p.195). Two of the finest are across the Ebro in the Terra Alta district: the **Cooperative Agricola**, a fascinating play of parabolic brick arches and vaults, in **Gandesa**, and in clifftop **El Pinell de Brai**, Martinell's masterpiece **Celler del Sindicat Agricola** (1922) adorned with an *azulejo* frieze of the grape harvest and drunken hunters by jovial Xavier Nogués. Another *modernista*, Pere Domènech, built the *bodega* in **L'Espluga de Francolí**.

Poblet

From medieval L'Espluga de Francolí, it's a lovely 40-minute walk to the famous Cistercian **Monastery of Santa María de Poblet**, founded by Ramón Berenguer IV in 1151 to commemorate the end of the Reconquista in Catalunya. For centuries, Poblet was the principality's most powerful and privileged monastery. Openly dissipated and corrupt in later years, it was so despised that when the monks were suspected of harbouring Carlist sympathies in 1835, the locals found an excuse to avenge centuries

Getting Around

By Train

The six trains a day between Lleida and Tarragona/Barcelona stop at L'Espluga de Francolí, Montblanc and Valls; another train, three times a day, goes to Falset and Móra la Nova (for Miravet, Gandesa and El Pinell), on the route between Tarragona and Zaragoza.

By Bus

There are three buses a day running between Lleida and Tarragona which stop at Poblet. Other destinations are served by provincial buses out of Tarragona; the tourist office has timetables.

Tourist Information

Reus: Pla Llibertad s/n, **t** 977 34 59 43.
Vilafranca del Penedés:C/Cort 14, **t** 938 92 03 58.
L'Espluga de Francolí: Pla de la Iglesia 9, **t** 977 87 12 20.
Montblanc: Moralla de Santa Tecla, **t** 977 86 12 32.
Valls: Pla del Blat 1, **t** 977 60 10 50.

Festivals

Valls: Midsummer Festival, *June*. A good time to see the famous Valls *castellers* in action; Firagost, *early Aug*. Local farmers offer their best produce and flowers to Mother Earth.

Where to Stay and Eat

Reus ✉ 43400

★★★**Hotel Gaudí**, C/Arabal Robuster 49, **t** 977 34 55 45 (*moderate*). Centrally located and newly refubished with large, modern rooms.

La Glorieta del Castell, Pla del Castell, **t** 977 34 08 26 (*moderate*). Reus' most celebrated restaurant, spread over three floors with rustic decoration. Typical Catalan cuisine and an excellent *menú del día* (*inexpensive*).

Vilafranca de Penedés ✉ 43400

★★★**Hotel Domo**, C/Francesc Maciá 4, **t** 938 17 24 26, **f** 938 17 08 53 (*moderate*). Right in the centre of town, this agreeable hotel has all kinds of extras including Jacuzzi and sauna for a very modest price.

Cal Ton, C/Casal 8, **t** 938 90 37 41 (*moderate*). Fine, local cuisine paired with an exellent wine list (of course) and good service.

Montblanc ✉ 43400 and L'Espluga de Francolí ✉ 43400

Most visitors to this area base themselves in Tarragona, but for a tranquil night away from the coast Montblanc can be very pleasant.

★★**Hotel Coll de Lilla**, Ctra Nacional 240, Montblanc, **t** 977 86 09 07, **f** 977 86 04 23 (*expensive*). On the road to Lilla: a scenic hotel with 12 pretty rooms, all with a/c, TV and bath. With a good **restaurant** specializing in game dishes and, from Dec–March, *calçotada* (the traditional dish of chargrilled *calçots*, a kind of onion, and lamb).

★**Ducal**, C/Francesc Macià 11, Montblanc, **t** 977 86 00 25 (*moderate*). Cosy rooms with bath.

★★**Del Senglar**, Pla Montserrat Canals, L'Espluga de Francolí, **t** 977 87 01 21, **f** 977 87 01 27, *hostaldesenglar@net-way.net*, *www .hostalsenglar@worldonline.es* (*moderate*). The pick of the *hostales*, prettily decorated with timber and pottery, with a leafy garden and decent **restaurant**. On Saturdays in August there's a barbecue. *Open all year*.

★★**Masia del Cadet**, Les Masies de Poblet, L'Espluga de Francolí, **t** 977 87 08 69, **f** 977 87 04 96. A beautifully renovated 15th-century farmhouse, with a good **restaurant** and very friendly owners.

★**Hs dels Àngels**, Plaça Angels, **t** 977 86 01 73 (*inexpensive*). Amiable and good value; in the centre of town.

Fonda Nacional, Av. Catalunya 8, Falset, **t** 977 83 01 57 (*inexpensive*). Excellent value, with a decent **restaurant**; all of the rooms have shared bathrooms.

Apart from the hotel **restaurants** mentioned above, these are worth trying for a meal:

El Cairat, C/Nou 3, **t** 977 83 04 81 (*inexpensive*). Wonderful home cooking – including home-made pasta – which uses all the fresh local ingredients. Friendly, welcoming owners.

El Molí de Mallol, Muralla Santa Anna 2, Montblanc, **t** 977 86 05 91 (*inexpensive*). Lovely old watermill, serving delicious local specialities accompanied by local wines.

of maltreatment. In their fury they wrenched apart the buildings and fed its famous library to the flames. The ruins of Poblet stood overgrown with wild flowers until the 1940s, when a band of Italian Cistercians reclaimed the monastery and restored it beautifully. They offer guided tours (*daily 10–12.30 and 3–6; adm*). Within the castle-like walls you can see the huge **wine cellar**; an evocative cloister in late Romanesque style; the fine Gothic **Chapterhouse**; the **Dormitory**; the **Refectory** and **Kitchen**. Poblet was 'Catalunya's Escorial' for its many **tombs of the kings of Aragón**, wonderfully restored by sculptor Frederic Marés (*see* p.123). Among those interred in the great church are Alfonso I el Batallador (d. 1134) and Jaume I 'the Conqueror' (d. 1276).

Montblanc

Near Poblet and L'Espluga de Francolí, Montblanc is an enchanting medieval village with well-preserved 14th-century walls and a river spanned by a Gothic bridge. At the main gate a map points out the sites; the best are the Catalan Gothic parish church **Santa María**, with a Plateresque façade, and the Romanesque **Sant Miquel**; between the two stood Montblanc's Jewish quarter. Like Tarragona itself, its province had a majority Jewish and Morisco population in the early Middle Ages.

South on Montblanc's C/Major, just outside the town walls, stands the ruined **Convent of Sant Francesc**, with a large 14th-century church that until recently was used as a winemaker's warehouse. Yet this monastery produced one of Catalunya's medieval geniuses, Ansèlm Turmeda (1352–1425), who as a young friar left his Order, moved to Tunis, and converted to Islam with a new name: Abdallah at-Tarjuman al-Mayurqí – 'the Mallorcan interpreter'. Like Catalunya's greatest mystic, Ramon Llull, Turmeda was a native of Mallorca and, like Llull, was greatly attracted by the Islamic and Sufic thought that lingered in Spain with the Moriscos. Turmeda took Llull's 'heresies' a step further by actually converting, but his books commanded such respect (among them, *La Tuhfa* in Arabic, *The Dispute with an Ass* in Catalan, and a book of moral parables called *El Fransèlm*, long-used as a text in Catalan schools) that the Church refrained from condemning him, and instead tried hard to earn propaganda points by luring him back to the fold. It failed, and Abdallah died a good Muslim and was buried in a holy tomb in Tunis, where he is worshipped as a Sufi saint.

Prades

Between Poblet and Scala Dei is Prades, another fine, walled medieval town in the mountains. In the centre, in the pretty, arcaded **Plaça Major**, stands the unusual spherical **Fountain of Prades** (if it gives a *frisson* of *déjà vu*, you've seen a copy in Barcelona's Poble Espanyol). The source of the fountain is unknown, but it has never in known memory run dry. **Siurana de Prades**, on the road to Cornudell, is even more romantic, with its Arab castle perched atop a cliff known as 'the Balcony of El Priorat', ancient stone-built houses, and a primitive Romanesque chapel down by the river gorge. The castle was the Moors' last stronghold in Catalunya, where they held out until 1153. A third important monastery in the province is nearby: **Santes Creus**, anciently walled and of elegant proportions. Like Poblet it was founded by Ramón Berenguer IV, in 1158, devastated in 1835, and has been carefully restored since.

Particularly lovely is the **church**, completed in 1221 and containing the tombs of all the notables not buried in Poblet, including Pere III (d. 1285).

Valls

Valls is famous through Catalunya for the daring and skill of its *castellers* (human towers), and its club, the Xiquets de Valls, is so good that the town erected a monument, depicting the *castellers* all piled up on top of each other (*see* 'Festivals', p.194). The most interesting streets in Valls belong to its **Call**, the Jewish quarter, still reached via its medieval arch and still well preserved; also worth a look are the Gothic **Sant Joan Baptista** and the **Chapel des Roser**, with a 17th-century portrayal in *azulejos* of the Battle of Lepanto. In the village of **Vistabella**, in the agricultural region of La Secuita between Valls and Tarragona, Gaudí's colleague Josep M. Jujol designed an eccentric little *modernista* church, **El Sagrat Cor** (1918–23), its roof spiked with a needle-sharp belltower.

The Templar Castle of Miravet

Across the Ebro from Móra la Nova stands Miravet, site of one of Spain's most remarkable Templar castles, one of the many gifts to the Order from Ramón Berenguer IV. One of their tasks was to safeguard the region's Moriscos, who enjoyed nearly total religious and economic freedom in return for their rents and taxes. The castle is located on a 1,010ft precipice over the river, and may be reached by a narrow path beginning at C/Blanc. In the deathly silence that hangs over the place you can explore the Templars' Romanesque chapel, with a spiral stair to the tower, the dormitory and refectory, and large vaulted rooms believed to have served as *bodegas* and granaries – although, curiously, no one has ever found a trace of a chimney or kitchen. The upper patio is called the Patio de la Sang ('of the blood' – here the last Templars of Miravet were beheaded after resisting the order to disband in 1308). There are wonderful views over the Ebro and the village below.

The Costa Daurada

Spain's 'Golden Coast' stretches from Barcelona to the southern tip of Tarragona province and, while its beaches are often long and even gold-coloured, they lack that most elusive quality in people and resorts: charm. The surrounding scenery tends to be featureless, the *urbanizaciones* are ugly or sleepy, or both, and unless you have young children who require nothing more than good castle-building sand, shallow sea, and their peers for a perfect holiday (most of the visitors are Spanish and French families) you may want to limit yourself to a nod from the train window.

Cunit to the Ebro Delta

For the record, from north to south, **Sitges** (*see* p.154) is by far the most interesting and exciting resort of the Costa Daurada. Nearby **Cunit** is staider and boasts an exceptionally long, seldom-crowded beach. A few miles inland, **El Vendrell**, like Valls famed

Getting Around

Cunit, Calafell, Torredembarra, L'Ametlla de Mar, Tamarit, Salou, Cambrils and Tortosa are served by three **trains** a day between Valencia and Barcelona; the larger stations see considerably more action. Sant Carles de la Ràpita is linked by **bus** with Tortosa almost every hour.

Tourist Information

Calafell: Sant Pere 29–31, **t** 977 69 29 81, **f** 977 69 29 81, *tur.calafell@altanet.org*, *www.mediateca@altanet.org*.

Cambrils: Pla Creu de la Missió, **t** 977 36 11 59.

Salou: Pla Jaume I, **t** 977 35 01 02, **f** 977 38 07 47.

Torredembarra: Av. Pompeu Fabra 3, **t** 977 64 45 80.

El Vendrell: Dr Robert 33, **t** 977 66 02 92, **f** 977 66 59 24.

Tortosa: Pla del Bimil-lenari, **t** 977 51 08 22, *ag.tortosa@altanet.org*, *www.altanet.org/tortosa*.

Sant Carles de la Rápita: Pla Carles III 13, **t** 977 74 01 00, **f** 977 74 43 87.

Where to Stay and Eat

Many of the hotels on the Costa Daurada close from October to May.

Calafell ✉ 43820

★★**Canadá**, C/Mossèn Jaume Soler 44, **t** 977 69 15 00, **f** 977 69 12 55 (*moderate; lower out of season*). Pleasant family hotel with a pool, playground and reasonable **restaurant**. *Open all year*.

★★★**Kursaal**, Av. San Juan de Dios 119, **t** 977 69 23 00, **f** 977 69 27 55 (*moderate*). Modern, beachfront hotel with a good **restaurant** run by a kindly family. *Closed 15 Oct–5 April*.

★**Salomé**, C/Narcís Monturiol 19, **t** 977 69 01 00 (*inexpensive*). Good value, pleasant hotel with a busy bar.

Da Giorgio, C/Ángel Guiméra 4, **t** 977 69 11 39 (*moderate–inexpensive*). One of the best Italian restaurants in Catalunya; excellent value for the fine quality and imaginative cuisine it serves. Leave room so as to finish up with their ice cream made with fresh mascarpone and strawberries.

Torredembarra ✉ 43830

★★★**Morros**, C/Pérez Galdós 15, **t** 977 64 02 25, **f** 977 64 18 64 (*moderate*). A modern beach hotel in traditional style. *Open Mar–Sept*.

Morros, C/Rafael de Campalans, **t** 977 64 00 61 (*moderate*). Fine seafood restaurant on the beach, with a good wine selection (*menú inexpensive, menú degustación expensive*). *Closed Sun eve and Mon exc. in summer.*

Salou and Cambrils ✉ 43840

★★★**Caspel**, C/Alfonso V 9, Salou, **t** 977 38 02 07, **f** 977 35 01 75, *caspel@costa-dourada.com*, *www.caspel-dourada.com* (*moderate*). One of the best-value hotels on the Costa Daurada; central and not far from the beach, the excellent facilities include a pool.

★★★**Hs Rovira**, Av. Diputació 6, Cambrils, **t** 977 36 09 00, **f** 977 36 09 44. A decent beachside choice, with a pool and a good seafood **restaurant**. *Open all year*.

Casa Gatell, Psg Miramar 26, Cambrils, **t** 977 36 00 57 (*expensive*). One of the great seafood restaurants run by the Gatell dynasty of chefs. It has a wonderful terrace on the port; splash out on the *menú*. *Closed Sun eve*.

Can Bosch, Rambla Jaume I 19, **t** 977 36 00 19 (*moderate*). Excellent seafood restaurant in a central and elegant location; there's a good (*moderate*) *menú*, too.

Tortosa ✉ 43500

★★★★**Castillo de la Zuda**, **t** 977 44 44 50, **f** 977 44 44 58, *tortosa@parador.es* (*expensive*). This exquisite *parador*, set in the great Templar citadel, is why most people visit Tortosa at all. Extensive renovation in 2000 has added even more comforts. With sterling views and a **restaurant** specializing in Catalan dishes.

Sant Carles de la Rápita ✉ 43540

★**Juanito Platja**, Pso Marítimo s/n, **t** 977 74 04 62, **f** 977 74 27 57 (*inexpensive*). Delightful, simple beach hotel run by a friendly family.

Can Pons, Av. Constitución 35–7, **t** 977 74 05 51 (*moderate*). Great seafood in a nautical setting; the *menú del día* is very reasonable, and the *menú degustación* very fine.

Casa Ramón, C/Pou de les Figueretes 7, **t** 977 74 14 58 (*inexpensive*). Reasonably priced seafood and an excellent wine list.

for its *castellers*, was the birthplace of the great cellist and composer Pau Casals, a Catalan nationalist, whose opposition to Franco forbade him from ever seeing his beloved home after the Civil War. In 1979 his remains were brought from Puerto Rico and interred in El Vendrell's cemetery. A bequest from the maestro turned his family home in **Sant Salvador** on the sea into the **Casals Museum**, devoted to his life, works, and memorabilia, and an auditorium has been constructed next door.

Near Sant Salvador there's the vast beach of **Coma-ruga** and **Calafell**, a modest resort with a blank-walled castle as landmark. A ruined castle gave **Torredembarra** its name, and it has one of the coast's best – if busiest – beaches. Another lovingly restored 11th-century castle, containing a fine museum of antiques, stands right next to the beach at **Tamarit**. South of Tarragona sprawls the Costa Daurada's Miami Beach-style resorts, **Salou** and **Cambrils**; the next resortlet south took a shortcut, simply dubbing itself **Miami Beach**. Beyond Platja Miami it's desolate, literally, until the fishing village-cum-resort of **L'Ametlla de Mar**, though if developers have their way the desolation won't last much longer. The Catalan challenge to Euro Disney, **Port Aventura** (***t*** *902 20 22 20, www.portaventura.es*), is a 115ha theme park near Salou that even has its own train station.

Beyond stretches the **Ebro delta** (Ebre in Catalan), which one writer described as 'a strange amphibious landscape in the sea itself'. Malarial and abandoned until the early 20th century, the delta is divided into rice paddies and dotted with *barracas*, farmhouses with thatched roofs, recalling the farmers' Valencian homeland. The deserted beaches have a certain wild charm, scattered with driftwood like old bones. A major wetland and natural park, it is fun for bird-watchers, but otherwise a fitting anticlimax to the 746km of the Ebro, which, as great rivers go, is a bit of a bore, from the days when the Greeks knew it as the Iberus and the people on its banks as Iberes. Bird-watchers should visit the park information office at the entrance to the village of **Deltelebre**, with a small aquarium (***t*** *977 48 96 79*) displaying local flora and fauna.

Tortosa

Tortosa is the principle city here, and with much of the surrounding farmland in its municipal boundaries, claims to be Spain's second-largest city. No one seems to like it much. The Catalans regard it as somehow peculiar, and the natives call themselves Tortosans rather than Catalans. The Battle of the Ebro, the last Republican offensive in the Civil War, took place here, and Tortosa suffered considerable damage. A monument commemorating the battle, which cost 35,000 lives, was erected by the river.

If fate brings you to Tortosa, there are two sights worth your time. The **Cathedral** has a charming Gothic interior with fine chapels, especially that of the city's patroness, **Nostra Senyora de la Santa Cinta**. The citadel, **La Zuda**, was a Templar stronghold in the 12th century, when Tortosa's Moors, Jews and Christians lived in exemplary harmony. The **Eixample**, the new part of town, is thick with *modernista* buildings.

On the southern tip of the delta, **Sant Carles de la Rápita** is the last resort on the Costa Daurada, splendidly located on Europe's largest natural harbour, **Los Alfaques**. The good Bourbon Charles III wanted to take advantage of nature's gift and make this a great seaport but, like so many of his fine plans, it was buried with him.

València and the Levante

09

València and the Levante

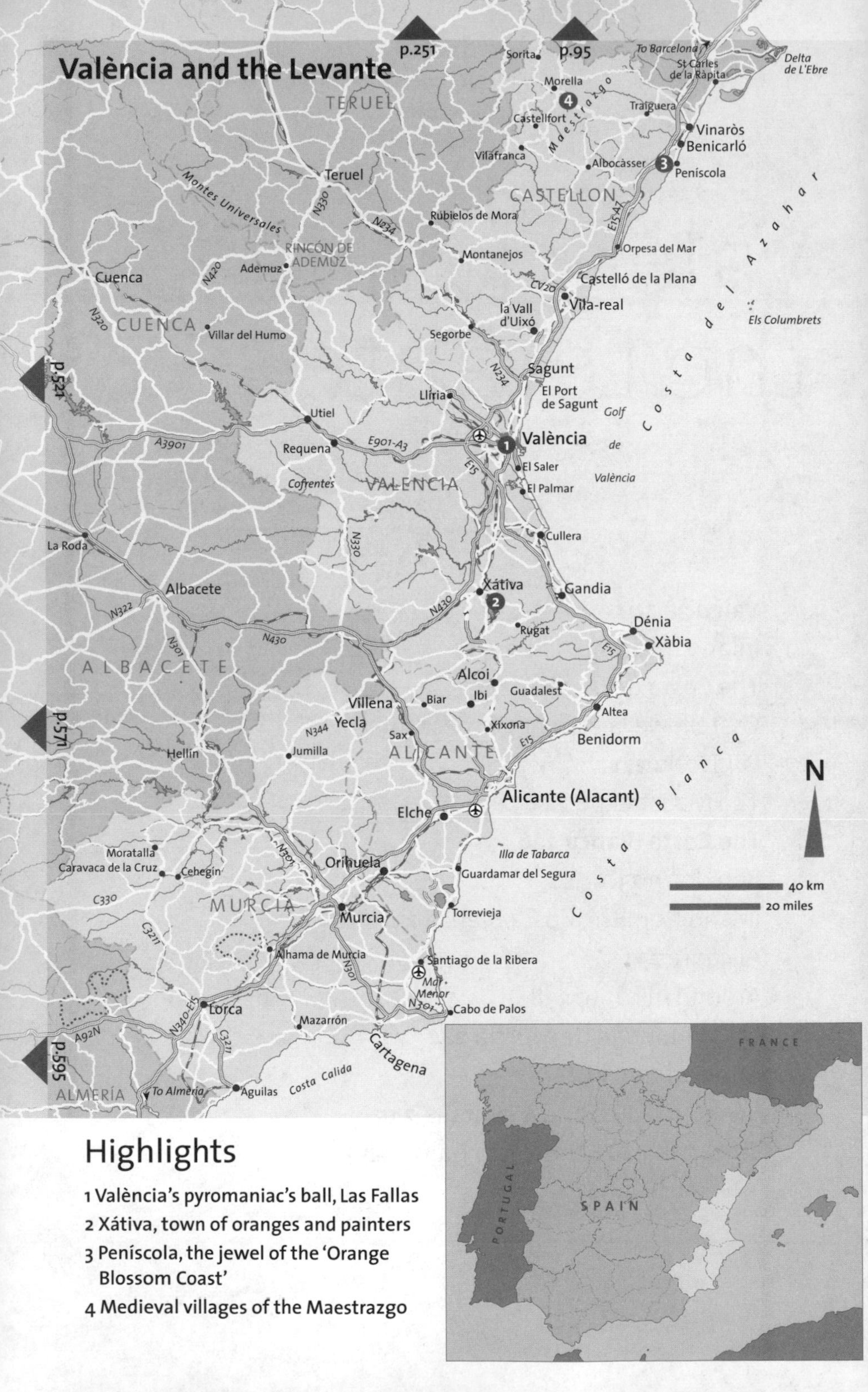

Highlights

1 València's pyromaniac's ball, Las Fallas
2 Xàtiva, town of oranges and painters
3 Peníscola, the jewel of the 'Orange Blossom Coast'
4 Medieval villages of the Maestrazgo

The modern autonomous region called *Comunitat Valenciano* covers what was once the third kingdom of the Crown of Aragón, reconquered for the Christians by Jaime I in the 13th century. It was a valuable asset, for the seemingly interminable Huerta de València is Spain's single most fertile garden plot, irrigated since Roman times by the waters of the Turia. The Levante, or 'East', as this region is commonly known, has the highest rural density in Europe, with over 800 inhabitants per square kilometre, and their capital, València, is Spain's third city and one of its most prosperous. This is the land of oranges and rice, and the home of the national dish, *paella*, which tastes better here than anywhere else. It is also the home of Costa del Azahar, with its string of modern resorts, and the Costa Blanca, which has entered the big league with the Costas Brava and Sol.

Most of the Christians who settled the new kingdom of València were Catalan and, like the Catalans, the Valencians have their Generalitat and a long Republican tradition. Over the centuries, their language has evolved into a new creature, *valenciano*, which in the fierce parochialism of post-Franco Spain is flaunted as an entirely different tongue. There's hardly a signpost that hasn't had the Castilian names wiped out and replaced by the Valencian equivalent, or merely splattered by paint bombs to express discord.

But for many it is València's light that best defines the region, a clear, diaphanous light called *La Clara* that illuminates the characteristic blue-tiled steeples and cupolas, and casts a spell over the Albufera, the great lagoon and rice paddy south of the city, where changing patterns of light and colour are worthy of a Monet.

València

València, after decades in the doldrums, is blossoming into one of the most stylish cities on the Mediterranean. She eyed neighbouring Barcelona's flamboyant makeover in the early 1990s, took careful notes, and has begun her own dramatic project of urban renewal designed to put València firmly on the international map. As with Barcelona, the new watchword is 'Design' and the centrepiece of the new development is the futuristic City of Arts and Sciences created by celebrity architect Santiago Calatrava, a huge, gleaming sculptural complex housing a state-of-the-art science museum, a theatre, a planetarium and Europe's largest aquarium.

For the moment, the city's attractions don't immediately leap out at the visitor, and those who arrive with visions of orange blossoms dancing in their heads will be disappointed once they leave the RENFE station (one of Spain's loveliest, a confection of ceramic oranges, tiles, and glittering mosaics of orange goddesses), for the first impression is of a bustling metropolis, where grand bridges span a nonexistent river and two magnificent gates stand shorn of the stupendous walls destroyed to let the city expand drably in all directions. A trip through the old quarter is, however, usually enough to dispel any initial misgivings and, if you linger a little longer, you'll begin to feel the charged atmosphere. There is an intensity in València, a feeling suggesting that if a revolution in Spain were to erupt, it would begin here.

History

As Mediterranean cities go, València is a newcomer, founded in 138 BC specifically to settle a band of defeated legionaries from Lusitania, who called it *Valentia Edetanorum*. It prospered under the Moors, who irrigated the fertile Huerta with an elaborate system of canals and made the local ceramics industry famous. When the Almoravids took the city from the Moorish king of València in 1092 the latter allied himself with El Cid, who captured 'Bright València' in 1094 and ruled the city as a personal fief until his death five years later. Its permanent Reconquest had to wait until 1238, a joint Aragonese-Catalan venture under Jaime I. Most of the Moors stayed on to work in agriculture and, by the 17th century, they constituted a third of the kingdom's population. Their happy idyll ended when Ottoman ships threatened the coast and the archbishop of València, Juan de Ribera, conjured up fears of a Morisco-Turkish conspiracy. Madrid in its paranoia believed everything it heard, and in 1609 the Moors had to go. València, which until then had been one of Spain's most prosperous cities, thriving on the silks and crops produced by the Moors, suffered a near-total economic collapse. Worse came when València, like Catalunya, picked the wrong side in the War of the Spanish Succession.

In the 1860s and 1870s, València took a leading role in the Republican movement; at the same time, in a progressive mood, it tore down its great 14th-century walls as a public works project to give jobs to the needy. During the Civil War it served as the Republicans' capital after the government had fled from Madrid, a period remembered by plaques throughout the city. València was also the birthplace of novelist Vicente Blasco Ibáñez (1867–1928), author of *Four Horsemen of the Apocalypse* and fine descriptive tales from the Huerta, like *La Barraca* and *Entre Naranjos*.

The Cathedral

Looking at a map, it's easy to trace the line of the walls that once embraced old València and find the heart of town, the **Plaza de la Reina** (Pza Zaragoza). Here the **Cathedral** (*open daily 7.30–1 and 4.30–8.15*) was built over the Great Mosque in 1262, and given for a partner the sturdy, octagonal, minaret-like tower called the **Miguelete** or **El Micalet** in *valenciano* (*open daily 10.30–12.30 and 4.30–7; adm*), completed by Pere Balanguer in 1429. If the thought of climbing 200 steps up a narrow spiral staircase doesn't dismay you, the top of the Micalet offers lovely views over València's gleaming ceramic domes and the Huerta. There are 13 bells in El Micalet, the largest weighing over five tons and dedicated on Michaelmas – hence the tower's name. The Cathedral has suffered a number of changes over the years: the main Baroque portal on the Plaza de la Reina is stale toast compared to the Romanesque **Portal de Palau** and the Gothic **Puerta de los Apóstoles** (1354), facing Pza de la Virgen and adorned with sculpture and a star of David (locally called the Salomó) in the rose window. If you happen to pass by the Puerta de los Apóstoles on a Thursday at noon, you'll see a crowd gathered around eight seated men in black shirts. They are València's famous **Tribunal de las Aguas** (Water Jury), where all disputes related to the Huerta's irrigation water are settled. The eight-member Tribunal has been elected every two years, ever since it was founded in 960, in the reign of Caliph Abderrahman III of Córdoba.

The proceedings are conducted entirely in *valenciano* and no record is made of them in writing, nor is there any appeal if a user is fined. Even the fine is traditional: not in euros, but in the medieval currency, *lliures valencianes*. The water laws of València are so fair they were copied by the rest of Spain and Spanish America in the 19th century.

The **interior** of the cathedral has been restored (since 1939) to reveal as much of its Gothic structure as possible. Best of all is the elegant, 14th-century lantern, where two storeys of alabaster windows radiate a soft light over the crossing. The Sala Capitular is now a **museum** (*open Mon–Sat 10–1 and 4.30–7; closed Sun; adm*), where you can see a Virgin by Correggio and a macabre painting by Goya that foreshadows his 'Black Paintings' in the Prado; three grinning demons whisper into the ear of a graphically depicted corpse, while St Francis Borgia wards them off with a crucifix. The museum contains a lovely gold and coloured enamel Pax Tablet by Benvenuto Cellini and, as a climax, nothing less than the alleged chalice used in the Last Supper, one of several possible Holy Grails floating around Europe.

According to legend, St Peter took the chalice to Rome, where it became a keepsake of the popes. In the 3rd century, when Pope Sixtus II was about to be martyred during Valerian's persecutions, he entrusted it to his disciple Lawrence, who sent it for safe keeping to Huesca in Aragón. When the Moors invaded, the chalice was hidden in the mountains, where the monastery of San Juan de la Peña (*see* **Aragón**, p.273) was built to house the now bejewelled relic. In 1399 King Martín persuaded the monks to hand it over, and it ended up here for safekeeping.

Great as this relic is, the faithful of València put greater trust in the heavenly power of intervention of 'Our Lady of the Forsaken' who resides next door in the round **Basilica de Nuestra Señora de los Desamparados** (*currently under restoration*). In the 14th century, a band of pilgrims appeared at the door of a charitable brotherhood and requested four days' food and lodging in a locked room without windows. Four days later, when the door was unlocked, the pilgrims had vanished, leaving behind the statue. Adorned with a radiant diamond crown and surrounded by a thousand flickering candles, this Virgin made by angels is València's patron saint.

The **Plaça del Almoina** (*open Tues–Thurs 10–1 and 5–8, Fri and Sat 10–1 and 5–11, Sun and hols 10–2; adm free*), just behind the cathedral, has been dug up to reveal remnants of old Roman baths, the forum, bits of the Via Augusta and the site where San Vicente is supposed to have been martyred. An audiovisual show gives a brief introduction and then you can pick your way across the ruins on wooden bridges.

The Generalitat and the Gates

Across lovely Pza de la Virgen stands the **Generalitat of the Kingdom of València** (*open by appointment only,* ***t*** *963 86 34 61, visits Mon–Fri 9–2, English-speaking guides can be arranged*) of 1510, once again serving its original function as the seat of the Comunitat's council. The exterior is plain, but within are two chambers with wonderful *artesonado* ceilings, the **Salón Dorado** and the especially lovely **Salón de Cortes** with its *azulejos* and frescoes of 1592 representing a meeting of the assembly.

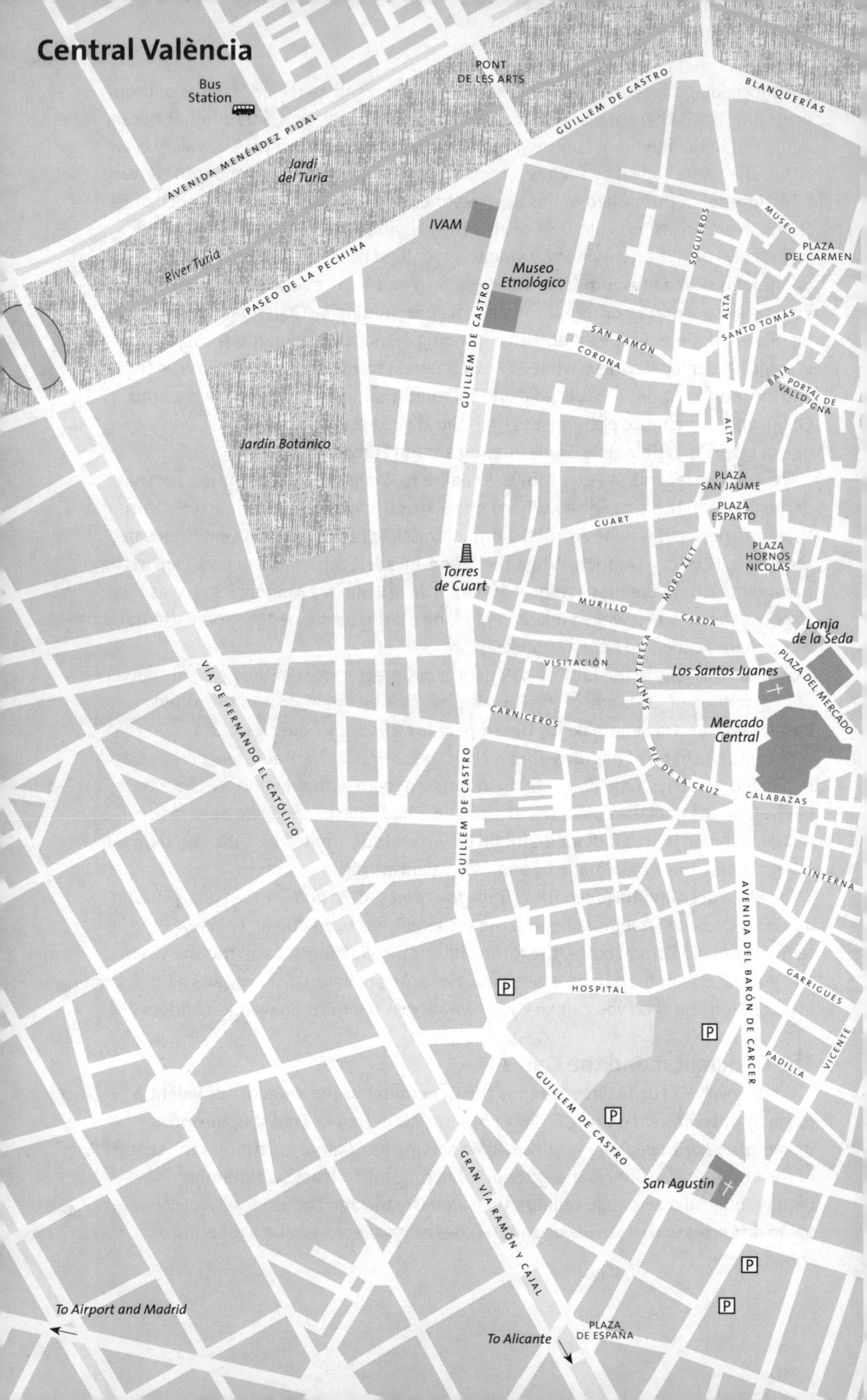
Central València
Bus Station
PONT DE LES ARTS
AVENIDA MENÉNDEZ PIDAL
GUILLEM DE CASTRO
BLANQUERÍAS
Jardí del Turia
River Turia
IVAM
PASEO DE LA PECHINA
Museo Etnológico
SOGUEROS
MUSEO
PLAZA DEL CARMEN
ALTA
SANTO TOMÁS
SAN RAMÓN
CORONA
BAJA
PORTAL DE VALLDIGNA
Jardín Botánico
PLAZA SAN JAUME
PLAZA ESPARTO
CUART
PLAZA HORNOS NICOLAS
Torres de Cuart
MORO ZEIT
MURILLO
CARDA
Lonja de la Seda
VISITACIÓN
SANTA TERESA
Los Santos Juanes
PLAZA DEL MERCADO
VÍA DE FERNANDO EL CATÓLICO
CARNICEROS
Mercado Central
PIE DE LA CRUZ
CALABAZAS
LINTERNA
AVENIDA DEL BARÓN DE CARCER
GARRIGUES
HOSPITAL
PADILLA
VICENTE
San Agustín
GRAN VÍA RAMÓN Y CAJAL
To Airport and Madrid
To Alicante
PLAZA DE ESPAÑA

Tram Station
300 metres
200 yards
N
PUENTE DE SERRANO
Torres de Serranos
PUENTE DE LOS FFCC ECONÓMICOS
Jardines del Real
Museo de Bellas Artes
CONDE DE TRENOR
PUENTE TRINIDAD
To Sagunto
NAQUERA
SERRANOS
NAVELLOS
SALVADOR
PINTOR LÓPEZ
Jardí del Turia
CONDE ALMODÓVAR
BOIX
PLAZA MANISES
TRINITARIOS
CABALLEROS
PLAZA DE LA VIRGEN
Basilica de Nuestra Señora de los Desamparados
Generalitat of Valencia
PLAZA ALMOINA
PUENTE DEL REAL
Catedral
PALAU
El Miculet
CORREJERÍA
Santo Domingo
Arzobispado
River Turia
Tower of Santa Catalina
PLAZA DE LA REÍNA
PLAZA DE TETUÁN
PASEO DE LA CIUDADELA
PLAZA DOCTOR COLLADO
PLAZA SANTA CATALINA
MAR
PLAZA REDONDA
MARQUÉS DE DOS AGUAS
San Martín
GENERAL PALANCA
LA PAZ
AV. MARÍA CRISTINA
Corpus Christi
PUENTE DE CALATRAVA
National Ceramics Museum
Colegio del Patriarca
GLORIETA
POETA
PLAZA ALFONSO EL MAGNANIMO
PLAZA PORTA DE LA MAR
PLAZA PICADERO DOS AGUAS
PLAZA COLÉGIO DEL PATRIARCA
University
SALVA
AV. NAVARRO REVERTER
Palace of Justice
BARCELONINA
PLAZA RODRIGO BOTET
QUEROL
El Corte Inglés
COLÓN
PLAZA AYUNTAMIENTO
LAS BARCAS
DON JUAN DE AUSTRIA
To Ciudad de las Artes y las Ciencias and El Saler
Ayuntamiento and Museu Historico Municipal
CORREOS
ROGER DE LAURIA
AVENIDA MARQUÉS DE SOTELO
RIBERA
PASSEIG DE RUZAFA
COLÓN
XÁTIVA
Train Station
Plaza de Toros
GRAN VÍA MARQUÉS DEL TURIA
CONDE ALTEA

Getting There

By Air

There are regular flights between València and Madrid, Ibiza, Mallorca and the Canary Islands. The airport is eight km west of town in Manises, **t** 963 70 95 00. Iberia's office is at C/de la Paz 14, **t** 963 52 05 00. British Airways can be found at Pza Rodrigo Botet 6, **t** 963 51 22 84. Bus No.15 leaves València's bus station hourly for the airport, though on Sundays this service doesn't run: get a bus to Manises and take a taxi from there.

By Sea

València's port is five km out from town and has frequent connections with Mallorca, Minorca and Ibiza, and the Canaries. For ferry information call the *estación marítima* on **t** 963 67 07 04. Trasmediterránea's office is at Av. Manuel Soto Ingeniero 15, **t** 963 67 39 72. Bus Nos.19 or 4 go directly to the port from Pza del Ayuntamiento.

By Train

The RENFE station is only a couple of blocks from the Pza del Ayuntamiento, **t** 963 52 02 02. There are eight trains a day from Madrid, via Cuenca or Albacete; three connections with Zaragoza, five to Alicante, and eight to Barcelona and Castelló. There are also trains nearly every hour to Xátiva.

A fast, efficient, local train service (FGV) links València to the villages of the Huerta. There are connections to Lliria, Buñol, Paterna and Villanueva de Castelló, from the underground station in Plaza de España.

By Bus

València's bus station is across the river Turia at Av. de Menéndez Pidal 3, **t** 963 49 72 22 or **t** 963 49 12 50; catch bus No.8 from across the street for Pza del Ayuntamiento. There are connections from here to most of the major cities of Spain, as well as to the resorts along the coasts to the north and south, and there's a Eurolines bus direct to London. Autocares V. Edo go from València to Castelló, Tarragona and Andorra once a day. In the summer there are buses to El Salér from the Plaza Porta del Mar every half-hour.

Tourist Information

València: at Estacion del Norte, C/Jativa 24, **t** 963 52 85 73;
Provincial Office, C/de la Paz, **t** 963 94 22 22;
Municipal Office, Pza del Ayuntamiento, **t** 963 94 04 17; *touristinfo.aytovalencia@tourisme.m400.gva.es*, *www.comunitat-valència.com*, *www.landofvalencia.com*.

The British Institute: C/General Sanmartín 7, **t** 963 51 88 18.

Hospital: Av. Cid, **t** 963 79 16 00.

Main Post Office, Pza del Ayuntamiento 24, **t** 963 51 67 50 (*open Mon–Sat 9am–9pm and Sun am*).

A weekly **stamp and coin market** is held in the Lonja de la Seda (*Sun mornings*), and a **flea market** (*liveliest on Sun*) stretches from Pza de Santa Catalina to Pza Redonda.

Festivals

Las Fallas, *Mar*. Come March, València's smouldering character ignites in what must be the world's greatest pyromaniac's ball, where hundreds of satirical floats, painstakingly built in the various streets and quarters of the city, are burnt in a saturnalia of gunpowder and fireworks.

Mediterranean Film Festival, *Oct*. You can find details of the annual celebration of film in València's listings guides (*see* p.209).

Where to Stay

València ✉ 46000

In Town

It's no longer easy to find a room in València, particularly during Las Fallas, and it's worth booking ahead rather than just showing up. Prices have risen dramatically with the city's new-found cachet, but you can still find good deals at weekends. Most of the better hotels are found clustered in and around the Pza del Ayuntamiento; otherwise there are some good budget rooms amid the narrow, dimly lit streets of the older part of town and around the train station (there's a string of cheapie flophouses right in front of the station).

Luxury–Expensive

******Astoria Palace**, Pza Rodrigo Botet 5, **t** 963 98 10 00, **f** 963 98 10 10, *www.hotel-astoria-palace.com*. Located in a quiet square off the Ayuntamiento, this has luxurious interiors, a gym, Jacuzzi and smooth service, as you might expect from a palace. The **restaurant** is good too.

******Reina Victoria**, C/Barcas 6, **t** 963 52 04 87, **f** 963 52 04 87, *www.husa.es*, *hreinavictoria valencia@husa.es*. In an attractive Victorian building just off Pza del Ayuntamiento, this is the elegant *grande dame* of the city's hostelries. Air-conditioned rooms are a godsend in the summer.

*****Hotel Inglés**, Marqués de Dos Aguas 6, **t** 963 51 64 26, **f** 963 94 02 51. Owned by the Melia chain, this perfectly located hotel is set in a frilly mansion right opposite the Baroque ceramics museum. It has plenty of style and old-fashioned atmosphere; at night the street is very quiet.

Moderate

*****Excelsior**,C/Barcelonina 5, **t** 963 51 46 12, **f** 963 52 34 78, *cataloni@hoteles-catalonia.es*, *www.hoteles-catalonia.es* (*expensive–moderate*). A gleaming new hotel just off Pza Ayuntamiento: well-equipped modern rooms make this great value.

*****Hotel Ad Hoc**, C/Boix 4, **t** 963 91 91 40, **f** 963 91 36 67, *adhoc@nexo.net* (rates can creep up to *expensive* in high season). Perhaps the nicest place to stay in the city, the chic little Ad Hoc is set in a converted 19th-century town house with brick walls and beamed ceilings. The charming hotel **restaurant** offers a very well-priced *menú del día* (*inexpensive*) at lunchtimes.

*****Hs Mediterráneo**, Av. Barón de Cárcer 45, **t/f** 963 51 01 42. This one is bland but conveniently located: it's small, friendly, and cool in the summer.

****P. Palacios**, C/Daoíz y Velarde 6, **t** 963 62 96 89. Located in the newer part of the city, which makes it a bit of a trek to the main sights, but the facilities are good for the price and the nearby Av. de Blasco Ibañez has plenty of restaurants and cafés.

*****Hs Londres**, C/Barcelonina 1, **t** 963 51 22 44, **f** 963 52 15 08. A good central location, friendly staff and comfortable rooms at a very reasonable price (it's worth asking about weekend discounts).

***Hotel Europa**, C/Ribera 4, **t** 963 52 00 00, **f** 963 52 03 51. A good-value hotel situated between the town hall and the train station, offering clean and attractive rooms which have large bathrooms.

Inexpensive–Cheap

****Hs Bisbal**, C/Pié de la Cruz 9, **t** 963 91 70 84. Next to the market; noisy during the day but quiet at night, and the owners speak English. Rooms are a bit austere.

****Hs Florida**, C/Padilla 4, **t** 963 51 12 84, **f** 963 51 12 84. A block west of the Ayuntamiento: this middle-range *hostal* has comfortable rooms, decent services and air conditioning.

****Hs Continental**, C/Correos 8, **t** 963 51 09 26, **f** 963 51 09 26. Well located, friendly and comfortable, with light, airy rooms.

***Hospederia del Pilar**, C/Mercado 19, **t** 963 91 66 00. Clean, friendly and pleasant: in the heart of the old town, with a lobby resembling an elementary-school classroom.

***Hs El Rincón**, C/Cardá 11, **t** 963 91 60 83. Almost opposite the Pilar and marginally cheaper. The large rooms have well-scrubbed stone floors and comfortable beds, and there's a resident ginger cat.

P. París at C/Salva 12, **t** 963 52 67 66. A reasonable option if the other hostels are full up. Rooms are spotless but very basic and lit with harsh fluorescent strip lighting.

Out of Town

******Parador El Saler**, Playa del Saler, **t** 961 61 11 86, **f** 961 62 7016 (*expensive*). Situated among the sand dunes and pine forests of the Dehesa near Saler. Contemporary, air-conditioned and next to a fine 18-hole golf course and pool, with plush rooms.

****Patilla**, C/Pinares 10, **t** 961 83 03 82 (*moderate*). Modern, functional hotel surrounded by palms and close to Saler beach: small, with TVs in each room. *Open all year*.

****Hs La Pepica**, Pso de Neptuno 2, **t** 963 71 41 11, **f** 963 71 42 00 (*inexpensive*). Sea views and light-filled rooms make this good value. There's an excellent seafood restaurant downstairs; it used to be Hemingway's favourite when it was just a shack on the beach, but now it has large premises and is always packed with local families.

Hs Tres Cepas, 22 Av. de Neptuno, **t** 963 71 51 11 (*cheap*). Here you'll find decent, clean budget rooms.

Eating Out

Any city that boasts such a fine array of international restaurants, from Persian to Mongolian, deserves to be taken seriously. Valencians are rightly proud of their **rice dishes**, which range from the famous *paella* to other lesser-known dishes such as *arros a la banda* and *arros en fesols i naps*. Another Valencian favourite are the baby eels (*angulas*) from the Albufera, which figure on many menus. Remember too that many of València's restaurants close for the month of August, as in most Spanish cities.

Expensive

La Hacienda, Av. Navarro Reverter 12, **t** 963 34 06 44. Highly acclaimed and one of the most elegant restaurants in València, with specialities like truffle soup and Grand Marnier soufflé. The only downside is that the atmosphere can be a little stuffy. *Closed Sun and Aug.*

Joaquín Schmidt, C/Visitación 7, **t** 963 40 17 10. There is no *à la carte* option at this distinctive, charmingly decorated restaurant; you select instead from one of the set menus (*expensive*), each of which features highly creative, seasonal cuisine. *Closed Sun and Mon lunchtimes.*

San Nicolas, Pza Horno de San Nicolás 8, **t** 963 91 59 84. A refined seafood restaurant on a pretty square; take your pick from an astonishing variety of local fish and then decide how you'd like to see it cooked. *Closed Sun eve and Mon.*

Seu-Xerea, C/Conde de Almodóvar 4, **t** 963 92 40 00. Here, innovative Mediterranean cuisine takes on some influence from the Far East in a fashionable and pleasantly relaxed setting; the lunchtime *menú del día* (*inexpensive*) is excellent value.

Moderate

El Ángel Azul, C/Conde Altea 33, **t** 963 74 56 56, *angelazul@interbook.net*. Chef Bernd Knöller cooks up some of the most imaginative cuisine in the city at this delightful restaurant which also features an exceptional selection of wines. The desserts are exquisite. (Prices at top of this category.) *Closed Sun, Mon and Aug.*

El Romeral, Gran Vía Marqués del Turia 62, **t** 963 95 15 17. One of the oldest restaurants in the city: on the big boulevard south of Pza Puerta de la Mar and specializing in Valencian cuisine. *Closed Mon and Aug.*

Chicote, Av. de Neptuno 34, **t** 963 71 61 51. On Levante beach: excellent seafood and inspiring rice dishes: try the *arros a banda*, rice cooked in fish stock (meal with wine *inexpensive*). *Closed Mon and 15 Nov–15 Dec.*

Casa Carmina, C/Embarcadero 4, El Saler, **t** 961 83 02 54. Universally acknowledged to be one of the best when it comes to Valencian rice dishes;it doesn't look much from the outside but is always packed with local families. The *arroz caldoso a marinera*, a soupier version of *paella*, made with langoustines, clams and squid, is excellent.

Can Bermell, C/Santo Tomás 18, **t** 963 91 02 88. A good, traditional restaurant; the favourite of an odd mixture of politicians and arty types, serving hearty regional dishes made with the freshest local ingredients.

Inexpensive

For good tapas and cheap lunchtime fixed-price menus, try the stalls around the market.

La Carme, C/Sogueros 8, **t** 963 92 21 46. Delicious, imaginative local dishes at very reasonable prices in this prettily decorated, family-run restaurant.

Setabis, Pza Dr Collado 9 near the Zona de la Lonja, **t** 963 91 62 92 (*cheap*). Archetypal little Spanish restaurant, popular for its bargain *menú del día*, with superb *paella*.

La Utielana, Pza Picadero Dos Aguas 3, **t** 963 52 94 14. A low-key little restaurant with an excellent, cheap and satisfying *menu del día*.

La Lluna, C/San Ramón 23, **t** 963 92 21 46. Lovely little vegetarian restaurant in the heart of the Barrio del Carmen: with imaginative veggie dishes. *Closed Aug.*

Mey Mey, C/Historiador Diago 19, **t** 963 84 07 47 (*cheap*). Popular Chinese, with an excellent reputation. *Closed Aug.*

La Barbacoa del Carme, Pza del Carme 6, **t** 963 92 24 48. Popular, rowdy grillhouse where your meat is grilled at the table; it's worth booking in advance. The fixed price menu is good value.

Tapas Bars

Serranos, C/Blanquerías 5, by the Torres de Serrano, **t** 96 391 70 61 (*cheap*). Good, cheap, and authentic, with a bustling interior full of young Valencians enjoying the efficient service and tucking into a wide range of perfect tapas.

Café-Bar Pilar, C/Moro Zeit 13, off Plaza del Esparto, **t** 96 391 04 97 (*cheap*). Also in the Barrio del Carmen: the place for steaming mussels (called *clóchinas*) and snails since 1918 (patrons chuck the shells into buckets lurking underneath the bar).

Damy, Mistral 7 (*cheap*). Inexpensive and serving good-value tapas and *bocadillos*. *Closed Mon*.

Bar Manoli, C/Luis Oliag 6 (*cheap*). Tapas and good, cheap *paella*.

Naturalia, C/del Mar 12, (*cheap*). Juice bar serving *agua de València* (the traditional regional cocktail of champagne, vodka and orange juice) and other fresh fruit cocktails, with or without alcohol; crêpes provide stomach lining. *Open till around 2am*.

Entertainment and Nightlife

Culture and bars are gradually reclaiming the alleys of the old town; the city could help them along a bit by adding a few watts to the street lights. That doesn't deter the Valencians from their fun, however: they have been in the grip of *bacalao* fever for a few years now. That's not an unhealthy obsession with a dried fish: *bacalao* is also the Spanish name for the techno music which has ruled the east coast and the island of Ibiza since the late 1980s. València has a serious clubbing reputation throughout Spain, no mean feat in a land so good at staying up all night.

The **Barrio del Carmen** is very lively at night with the smarter and more expensive bars edging up to Pza del Esparto and noisier local haunts starting on C/Alta, around Pza San Jaume. Among the current favourites are **Bab Al Hanax**, C/Caballeros 36, and the **Carmen Sui Generis Club** next door at C/Caballeros 38 – this street is packed with bars, clubs and small, arty restaurants. Here the street life itself can keep you entertained all night as various local characters shimmer through the Barrio. Watch out for Blancita, a tiny and ancient lady who's always dressed in white with a variety of objects pinned to her chest, including her false teeth. She roams the streets, attracting small change while her reputation grows out beyond the Barrio. Currently, the area around the new university is the place to be seen, with plenty of lively bars along the **Av. Blasco Ibáñez** and in the streets which splinter off it. There are some good clubs here too – try **Acción** at Av. Blasco Ibáñez 111, or the posey **Warhol** next door. The younger, wilder crowd head for the disco bars and restaurants of the **Plaza Xuquer** and **Plaza Honduras**, whilst the more sedate swingers congregate around the **Gran Vía Marqués del Turia** and the **Av. Jacinto Benavente**. In the summer, the bars of Malvarrosa beach groove all night: among them is the barn-like **Vivir sin Dormir** on Av. de Neptuno. There are also some huge outdoor nightclubs sheltering the young and beautiful of València; don't even bother to arrive before 3am. If you can get out to the suburb of Alboraya, the favourite disco of the moment is **Arena**, C/Emilio Baró, also used as a band venue.

Cinema and Events Listings

Original-language **films** (referred to as V.O. in listings guides) can be seen at **Filmoteca Cinema**, Pza del Ayuntamiento. There's also an annual **Mediterranean film festival** (*Oct*).

For **listings**, it's worth checking out the free *Hello València* magazine available from the tourist office, but much more comprehensive is the *Cartelera Turia* which you can buy at any newspaper kiosk for about €1.20. Other listings guides include *Qué y Dondé* and the more upmarket *València Seminal*, both available from news-stands.

From here C/Serranos leads to the **Torres de Serranos** (*currently closed for restoration*), the massive survival of the 14th-century walls. From the river the gate looks solid and imposing; from the rear it looks like a stage prop, hollowed out with platforms and stairs. This is where the beginning of the Fallas (*see* 'Nights of Fire', p.213) is announced by the Queen of the fiesta. The gate that formerly stood to the east along the river next to a Templar church (now a Guardia Civil barracks) was the famous Gate of El Cid, through which El Cid's corpse, decked out in warlike array and propped up on his faithful horse Babieca, led the attack on the Moorish besiegers who had taken courage from rumours of his death – in the film *El Cid*, this was Charlton Heston's best scene. A second muscular souvenir of València's walls, the **Torres de Cuart** (1460), stands west of the Generalitat. After a spell as an infamous women's prison, it has become an innocuous little museum dedicated to locksmiths.

To the north of the Torres de Cuart is **IVAM**, València's museum of contemporary art, which is displayed over two premises. The glassy **new building** on C/Guillem de Castro (*open Tues–Sun 10–10; closed Mon; adm, adm free on Sun*) holds an exceptional permanent exhibition of the works of Julio González, the Barcelona-born sculptor who worked with Picasso during the 1930s. The centre also houses important temporary exhibitions of national and international contemporary artists; recent shows have included a major retrospective of the works of Willem de Kooning. A few streets away, on C/Museu, the **Centre del Carme** (*open Tues–Sat 10–14.15 and 4–7.30, Sun and hols 10–7.30; closed Mon; adm free*) holds a collection of local crafts, a changing exhibition of 19th-century paintings and sculpture in its attractive Gothic cloister, and an interesting selection of the works of young local artists chosen by IVAM.

Plaza del Mercado

This square, where old València held its *corridas* and *autos-da-fé*, is an exceptionally fine ensemble, although during market hours, when it's jammed with triple-parked lorries, it goes unnoticed. Befitting an agricultural queen, València's **Municipal Market** is the city's true royal palace, Spain's largest and most beautiful market, a confection of iron and glass, topped with a parrot-and-swordfish weathervane. Inside, the astounding cornucopia of the *huerta* is on display; sometimes you find oranges weighing up to 3kg apiece.

Opposite the market stands another cathedral of commerce, the 15th-century Flamboyant Gothic **Lonja de la Seda** or silk exchange (*open Tues–Fri 9.15–2 and 5.30–9, Sun 9–1.30; closed Mon and Sat*). Twisted, rope-like columns support the ogival arches in the main hall, where a Latin inscription along the walls reads 'I am a famous building that took fifteen years to build' and exhorts the merits of honest trade; on Sunday mornings, a stamp and coin market is held here. A spiral staircase ascends to the **Salón del Consulado del Mar** or maritime law courts, topped by a magnificent *artesonado* ceiling. Across from the Lonja stands the plaza's third monument, **Los Santos Juanes**, a medieval church with a Plateresque façade.

Behind the Lonja peers the second of València's monumental towers, the 17th-century hexagonal **Tower of Santa Catalina**. Next to it in the Pza de Santa Catalina, two famous **Horchaterías** will sell you a glass of Valencian tiger milk, *Horchata de* *chufa*, made from ground almonds from the Huerta. A **flea market**, liveliest on Sundays, extends from here into the curious, enclosed **Plaza Redonda** – a kind of residential bullring, popularly known as El Clot ('the hole').

National Ceramics Museum

From here, Calle de La Paz passes the Baroque **S. Martín**, its gutted interior another victim of the Civil War. An alley in front of it leads to the 18th-century **Palacio del Marqués de Dos Aguas**, an outlandish Baroque wedding cake with frilly icing piped around every window and an amazing alabaster portal designed by Hipólito Ravira, who died a lunatic shortly after its completion. It now houses the **National Ceramics Museum** (*open Tues–Sat 10–2 and 4–8, Sun and hols 10–2; closed Mon; adm*) which has an exceptionally rich collection of *azulejos*, many with humorous or whimsical scenes (one portrays a giant mosquito chasing a dog). The 'popular' 18th- and 19th-century ceramics from Manises on the third floor are strangely reminiscent of Picasso, whose works are concentrated in their own room. The oldest plates and bowls come from Paterna, decorated with green motifs from the 13th and 14th centuries, and blue up to the 15th. There's a beautiful all-tiled Valencian kitchen and three lovely 18th-century carriages, a collection of ex-libris designs from the 1920s, and on the top floor the zany Gallery of Humorists, which fascinates even if you don't get the jokes.

Plaza del Ayuntamiento and the Plaza del Patriarca

The heart of modern València is the large, triangular **Plaza del Ayuntamiento**, its bustling life tempered by the sweet scent of flowers from numerous stalls, and cooled with a huge, floodlit fountain. This is where the great pyre which marks the climax of the Fallas takes place, and fireworks whizz from here throughout the festivities (*see* 'Nights of Fire', p.213). The Ayuntamiento houses the **Museu Historico Municipal** (*open Mon–Fri 8.30–2.30; adm free*) with a collection of beautifully illuminated manuscripts, a sword belonging to Jaume I, and an 18th-century map of València before the walls and towers came down.

Two blocks northeast, the Plaza del Patriarca was named after the **Colegio del Patriarca** (*open daily 11–1.30; adm*) founded by Bishop Juan de Ribera, the archenemy of the Moriscos. There is a small but choice collection of paintings, including three El Grecos and Ribaltas, a Hugo Van der Goes and a book of miniatures once belonging to Philip the Handsome, with a scene of 15th-century golfers. Next to it is the 1830 building of the 15th-century **University**, whose library contains a copy of probably the first book printed in Spain, *Les Trobes en Lahors de la Verge Marie*, from 1474.

Adjacent to the Patriarca, the 16th-century church of **Corpus Christi** is decorated with *azulejos* and offers some genuine Spanish Catholic hocus-pocus during its Friday morning service. As the priests chant the *Miserere*, the painting over the altar – *The Last Supper*, by Ribalta – sinks away, to be replaced by a series of four curtains that are parted at the climactic moment to reveal a starkly illuminated crucifix of the 1400s.

From here walk down C/de La Paz to the Glorieta and turn left for the grand church of **Santo Domingo** (*call to arrange an appointment,* **t** *961 96 30 00, ext. 3038*). Some tough customers have called its cloister home, beginning with St Vicente Ferrer, perhaps Spain's most ferocious religious bigot and, recently, General Milans del Bosch, mastermind of the abortive coup in February 1981, who called out the tanks in València in support of his stooge Tejero, as the latter shot up the Cortes in Madrid. Although the cloister remains a barracks, you can see the porch designed by Philip II (who was no great shakes as an architect) and the Gothic **Capilla de los Reyes**, with the elegant 16th-century tombs of Rodrigo Mendoza and his wife.

Across the Turia

From Santo Domingo stretches València's most attractive bridge, the **Puente del Real**, which once spanned the unpredictable Turia. This river either trickled or flooded once it reached València (after being 'bled' by the canals of the *huerta*) and so often inundated the city that in 1957 València lost its patience and dug it a new channel. Now the dry river bed holds gardens, children's playparks (including the excellent **Parque Infantil Gulliver** with a huge statue-cum-giant slide of the fallen giant), football pitches, and leafy walks.

Across the Puente del Real it's a short stroll to the newly extended **Museo de Bellas Artes** (*open Tues–Fri 9–2.15 and 4–7.30, Sat, Sun and hols 9–2; closed Mon; adm free*), with its striking blue-tiled dome. It's the biggest Fine Arts museum in Spain after the Prado, with a smattering of good works among the forgettable – there's a self-portrait by Velázquez, paintings by Ribalta, Pinturicchio (*Our Lady of Feveís*), El Greco (*St John the Baptist*), a triptych by Hieronymus Bosch (*The Mocking of Christ* – the original centrepiece is in the Escorial), an excellent selection of medieval Valencian art, and the only painting attributed with certitude to València's 15th-century Rodrigo de Osona. The upper floors are haunted by some astoundingly lurid Spanish Impressionism. Next to the museum you can recover from it all among the roses in the **Jardines del Real** (*open daily 6am–10pm*), which hosts free concerts during the music festival in July, and perhaps visit its rather cramped zoo (*open daily 10–9; adm*).

Knowing your *Ninots*

To get a hint of what you are missing if you aren't in València between 13 and 19 March, catch bus No.13 from Pza del Ayuntamiento to the **Fallas Museum** (*Pza Monteolivete 4, open Tues–Sat 9.15–2 and 5.30–9, Sun and hols 9.15–2; adm*) where you can see the champion *ninots* of past years as well as plenty of photos and pictures of the festivities. If you're hankering to have a go at making a *fallas* figure yourself, take bus No.27 from behind the Ayuntamiento to visit the **Museo del Artista Fallero** (*open Mon–Sat 10–2 and 4–7, Sat 10–2; closed Sun; adm*) and find out exactly how the figures are made.

La Ciudad de las Artes y Las Ciencias (The City of Arts and Sciences)

The new celebrities of the 21st century seem to be chefs and architects; chief among the latter is Santiago Calatrava whose soaring, minimalist bridges are sought after by every city looking for some designer cred. He's given his home town no less than three, two of which are connected to the stunning new **City of Arts and Sciences** which sprawls in what was once a gaping hole between the city and the sea (*take bus*

Nights of Fire

Throughout the world, the spring equinox is a popular time to light bonfires to welcome the new season, but no one does it with more enthusiasm than the *valencianos*. The holiday began to take its present form in the 18th century, when as a rite of spring local carpenters and artisans would ceremoniously burn the wooden poles that had supported the lamps they needed in the winter. Because 18 March is also the feast of St Joseph, the patron of carpenters, the rite took on a festive air, and the *valencianos* began to dress up the old poles as satirical effigies called *ninots*. Neighbourhood competions for the best effigy soon developed, and residents joined in, contributing money towards the *ninots*, hoping theirs would be bigger and more humorous than the *ninot* from the next plaza.

In the festival's present form, the *ninots* are merely small scale models for the *fallas* or 'torches' themselves – huge papier-mâché tableaux, some several stories high and redolent with satires that spare no one and need no translation. Fat women, politicians, naked girls and bug-eyed tourists are peppered throughout; slick TV announcers tempt with trays of sausages and coffins. You can spend the week as the *Valencianos* do, strolling though the city to see the *fallas*, or their *ninots* all on display in La Lonja, where the best are given prizes. *Barracas* (typical Valencian houses with thatched roofs) are set up throughout the city, dispensing doughnuts and chocolate to the passing throng. Every day at 2pm in Plaza del Ayuntamiento an ear-splitting string of fireworks, *Las Mascaletas*, is set off. In the afternoon the first bullfights of the Spanish calendar take place, and every night there are more fireworks. On the 18th, a huge offering of flowers takes place in the Plaza de la Virgen, the blooms forming a massive skirt for the statue of the Virgin made by angels.

The 19th is the long-awaited *Nit de Foc*, the Night of Fire. The prize-winning *falla* is brought to the Plaza del Ayuntamiento, and all are strung with firecrackers. Around midnight, in a prearranged order, the *fallas* and *ninots* are ignited one after another in a tremendous city-wide holocaust, or *cremá*. The prizewinners are burned last, ending up with a huge pyre in Plaza del Ayuntamiento that goes up while hundreds of tons of fireworks blast and scream and thunder overhead. Of all the months of work and millions of pesetas that went into Las Fallas, only the first prize *ninot*, the *Ninot Indulat*, is spared the flames of the *cremá* and installed in the 'Pantheon-hospice' of the museum (*see* 'Knowing your *Ninots*', facing page).

No.95 from near the Torres de Serranos). The centrepiece of the City is a massive new opera house, due for completion in late 2002, which looks like a brilliant white spaceship; the main auditorium will eventually seat 1,800 people, and there will be an outdoor theatre with room for 2,500. Just beyond it lies the **Hemisfèric** (*open Mon–Thurs 10–8.30, Fri–Sun 11–10.15; adm, booking line* **t** *902 10 00 31, combined ticket with Museu de les Ciències available*), a gigantic glassy eyeball reflected in still, pale pools crisscrossed with walkways, which has quickly become one of Spain's top tourist attractions; you'll need to book tickets in advance to be sure of getting in. Inside, there's an immensely popular planetarium, IMAX cinema and an audiovisual show called the 'laserium', all featuring the very latest technology.

The **Museu de les Ciències Príncipe Felipe** (*open Mon–Thurs 10–8, Fri–Sun 10–9; adm, temporary exhibitions are extra*) looks like the massive skeleton of a beached whale; inside, it's like stepping into a futuristic space station, with a long glassy lobby staffed by aqua-suited, smiling hostesses. The imaginative exhibits are highly interactive and enormously popular with kids of all ages; the sports section is the most popular – test your reflexes, suppleness, and speed against a dozen machines – but there are also some excellent exhibits on everything from electricty and lasers to whales and the human body. In the Espai dels Xiquets little kids (ages 3–6) get to don hard hats and climb into miniature plastic cranes and bulldozers to construct new cities. On the top floor, models and plans devoted to the entire complex will give you an idea of what's in store when it is finally completed. There's also a pleasant café overlooking the gardens and an excellent gift shop selling all kinds of souvenirs and designer household goods.

Opposite the science museum is the **Umbracle**, a long, palm-lined walk shaded by a rib cage of curving white girders; beyond this lies the site of the future **Oceanogràfic**, which, when it finally opens in 2002–2003, will be Europe's largest aquarium. The huge underwater city will incorporate enormous glass-walled tunnels, sound and light shows and recreated coastlines from the around the world, set to become home to sharks, whales, turtles, walruses and dozens of other aquatic creatures.

València's Beaches and the Albufera

València has two municipal beaches, **Levante** and **Malvarrosa** (*bus Nos.19 or 4 from Pza del Ayuntamiento*) but they are as polluted as they are convenient. Levante, however, is the place to go for fresh seafood; the Av. de Neptuno alone has some 27 restaurants.

Further south and far more pleasant and cleaner are the beaches at **Pinedo** and **El Saler**. El Saler is the best base for visiting the **Albufera** (*hourly buses go from Pza Porta del Mar to El Salér; you can hire boats from the little dock behind El Saler beach; prices vary, so shop around*), Spain's largest freshwater lagoon, separated from the sea by **La Dehesa**, a narrow sandbar shaded with pine groves. The lagoon, an important wetland which attracts thousands of migratory birds, was designated a natural park in an attempt to stave off the encroaching development and pollution which threatened to tip the balance of its delicate ecosystem. There are several villages that make good bases if you want to explore the wetlands (*the park information office is in Racó de l'Olla, **t** 961 62 73 45*), the prettiest of which is **El Palmar**, renowned for its local rice and seafood dishes. During the local festival (4 Aug), an image of Christ on the cross is taken out by boat into the middle of the lagoon, where hymns are sung. **El Perelló** is not as attractive, but the seafood restaurants along the shore have an excellent reputation. September is a good time to come, when the Albufera's emerald green rice paddies turn to gold. Wildfowl (and duck hunters) flock here from September to March, and the waters are plied by scores of eel fishermen, some in their stately old-fashioned sailing boats. The Albufera is most dramatic at dusk, when the soft colours change by the second.

Inland from València

The endless, flat plains north of the city have become home to huge ceramics factories, belching fire and dust out across the orchards. Monasteries and Roman ruins poke their heads above the smoke and charging motorways, and there's a sprinkling of sleepy, fortress-topped villages further east which offer some respite from the brash coastal resorts.

Northwest of València: Monasteries, Roman Ruins and Spas

The fields of the **Alboraia** stretch north of Malvarrosa beach, where the strange *chufa* fruit is harvested for the creamy local drink, *horchata*. The next large town is **El Puig**, sprawling around the massive **Real Monasterio de El Puig de Santa Maria** (*open Tues–Sun 10–1 and 4–7, Mon 10–1; adm*), established by order of Jaume I after an image of the Virgin Mary (which had been hidden in a bell and buried by monks fearful of the Moorish invasion) was miraculously discovered in the 13th century. The statue was crowned Queen of the Lands of València and the shrine is still one of València's most popular pilgrimage spots. The Romanesque façade of the original church is all that remains, and most of the rest of the building was raised between the 16th and 18th centuries. It now houses a **Museum of Graphic Arts and Printing** (*opening hours as above*), within which you can peer through a magnifying glass at the smallest book in the world. There are several medieval illuminated texts, a 16th-century copy of the Gothenburg bible and, on the upper floor, a selection of local ceramics recently recovered from the sea bed.

In 219 BC Hannibal initiated the Second Punic War by taking the Greek city and Roman ally of **Sagunt** (24km north of València), which proved no easy task: after an eight-month siege, the defenders, unable to hold out any longer, made a huge bonfire where they burnt their belongings, their wives and children and themselves. Historical hindsight suggests Hannibal ought to have taken the hint and driven his

Tourist Information

Sagunt: Pza del Cronista Chabret s/n, **t** 962 66 22 13.

El Port de Sagunt: Pso Maritime s/n, El Port de Sagunt, **t** 966 69 60 52 (*open summer only*).

Segorbe: C/Marcelino Blanco 3, **t/f** 964 71 32 54.

Requena: C/Garcia Montes s/n, **t** 962 30 38 51.

Festivals

Chiva: Fiesta, *mid-Aug*. Bullfights are a key part of the local festivities.

Buñol: La Tomatina, *last Wed of Aug*. A huge, boisterous tomato fight, which has been going on since the 1940s and now attracts thousands of people from all over the world.

Getting Around

By Train

RENFE trains run every half-hour between València and Castelló, stopping at El Puig and Sagunt. From Sagunt, the Teruel–Zaragoza line serves the northwest, including Segorbe. Trains also run west from València to Buñol, with less regular ones continuing to Requena.

By Bus

Infrequent bus services run from València bus station to Buñol and Requena, but the bus stops are more central than the train stations in each of these towns. There are regular buses to El Puig and Sagunt from València, and you can catch a bus from Segorbe to Montanejos. From Castelló bus station, there are direct buses to Montanejos and Sagunt.

Where to Stay and Eat

Sagunt ✉ 46500

****Hotel La Pinada**, Ctra Nacional Sagunt–Burgos Km3, **t** 962 66 08 50, *www.serbit.com.lapinada* (*inexpensive*). A modern roadside hotel with a pool and decent rooms 3km outside the city on the way to Teruel.

****P. California**, C/Buenavista 35, **t** 962 67 07 01 (*inexpensive*). A comfortable, friendly little *pensión*, this has good facilities and at a decent price.

elephants back home. Although Rome took Sagunt back from Carthage quite easily five years later, the town never recovered its former importance, even though the Moors added the great walls of the citadel over the Roman foundations, and the Spaniards added a giant steel mill. In 1902 the composer Joaquín Rodrigo was born here.

The modern town is sprinked with traces of ancient Sagunt – some of the arcades in the **Plaza Mayor** are supported by its columns. Some medieval houses remain in the Judería where, according to Sephardic tradition, the first Jews settled in Spain in 100 BC. Calle del Castillo leads up to the **Roman Theatre**, a 2nd-century creation where spectators had fine views over the sea. Recent US$6m improvements by the Generalitat – the addition of an 82ft stage and new limestone seats – have caused a vast international controversy. The idea was to make it a venue for opera and other performances, but all the locals hate it and have sued to have the improvements undone. Next to it is a modest **Archaeology Museum** and the road up to the drawbridge of the huge, rambling **citadel** (*open Tues–Sat 10–2 and 4–7, Sun 10–2; closed Mon; adm free*), its half-mile of walls draped over the ancient acropolis. You can pick out the foundations of Roman temples and French buildings from the Peninsular War and ruins left by every king of the mountain in between. The views over the deep green *huerta* are excellent. A bus from Sagunt heads down to its beach, which isn't bad if you don't mind looking at the steel mill.

L'Armeler, Subida al Castillo 44, **t** 962 664 382 (*moderate*). This enjoys a charming setting in an old town house just beneath the castle; the cuisine is a mixture of Mediterranean and local dishes. There's also a good-value *menú del día*, which is very popular with local workers.

Segorbe ✉ 12400

★★★**Maria de Luna**, Av. Comunidad Valenciana 2, **t** 964 71 13 13, **f** 964 71 12 13, *mariadeluna@retemail.es* (*moderate*). Modern, functional new development which is surprisingly inexpensive, particularly at weekends, and has a decent **restaurant** (*menú del día inexpensive*) popular with locals.

Requena ✉ 46340

★**Hotel Avenida**, C/San Agustín 10, **t** 962 30 04 80 (*inexpensive–cheap*). Furnished simply, a reasonable hotel in the heart of the city.

Mesón de la Villa, Pza de Albornoz 13, **t** 962 30 12 75 (*moderate–inexpensive*). Eat under the arches of the old palace of the inquisition; there's an excellent, well-priced *menu del día* and the restaurant is attractively set overlooking the main square of the old city. The 12th-century wine cellar is well worth a visit. Good tapas, too.

Mesón del Vino, Av. del Arrabal 11, **t** 962 30 00 01 (*moderate–inexpensive*). On a leafy avenue, this is a neighbourhood stalwart, covered in pictures of footballers and bullfighters. There's a good selection of regional dishes made with fresh local produce. You can tuck into tapas at the bar if you don't fancy a full meal.

Montanejos ✉ 12448

★★**Rosaleda de Mijares**, Ctra Tales 28, **t** 964 13 10 79 (*moderate*). Montanejos has four main *hostales*; this is the pick of them, prettily located near the small spa and very popular.

★★**Hotel Xauen**, Av. Fuente Banos 26, **t** 964 13 11 51, **f** 964 13 13 75, *xauen@hotelxauen.com* (*inexpensive*). This makes a good alternative if the Rosaleda is full.

Buñol

El Litro, Pza del Pueblo 5. Try this friendly place, which does a sturdy *menú del día* at a very good price, and is named after one of the town's two celebrated musical groups.

Some 30 kilometres northwest of Sagunt is **Segorbe**, tucked away in a peaceful valley between two sierras, with a stretch of crumbling medieval walls and towers and an attractive muddle of dilapidated tiled houses coiled around the **Cathedral**. The pretty cloister dates back to the 12th century, but most of the current building is banal Baroque. The little **cathedral museum** (*open daily 11–1; adm*) houses a collection of religious art, including paintings by Donatello and Ribalta. Just outside the town is the unusual **Fuente de los 50 Caños**, a long wall studded with 50 spouting fountains, each marked with the name and coat-of-arms of Spain's provinces. The town's tranquility is shattered in early September when horsemen come galloping through the packed streets chasing bulls in a hair-raising ceremony known as the 'Entrada de Toros y Caballos', which dates back to the 16th century.

North of Segorbe, the River Millars passes through a deep, forested ravine before irrigating the plain around Castelló. It's especially lovely around **Montanejos**, where you can paddle about in the clear, shallow water under the cliffs. So reputed are the waters here (for treating digestive disorders and poor circulation) that a spa and treatment centre have been set up.

Back near the coast, about 30 kilometres north of Sagunt, at **Vall D'Uixo** you can take a journey to the centre of the earth at the **Cuevas de San José**, where boats sail through crystal clear subterranean waters under an impressive display of stalactites. The caves have encouraged a cheesy development of snack bars, picnic areas and swimming pools and there are concerts and dance shows in summer (*for more information, call* ***t*** *964 69 05 76*).

West to Requena

The industrial sprawl around València peters out the higher you travel into the eastern sierras. **Chiva** is an attractive country town surrounded by vineyards with a Baroque church and a surprisingly big reputation for bullfighting, which is a characteristic of its local festival. The tiny town of **Buñol** is squeezed into a crevice between two peaks, one of which is dominated by the imposing ruins of a Moorish castle, which now houses a small **archaeological museum**. Steps meander down to the old town, a delightful maze of steep, narrow passages flanked with brilliantly whitewashed houses. At the bottom is the blue-tiled dome of the Iglesia de San Pedro, where there are a string of resolutely old-fashioned cafés and bars. Time seems to have stood still in this little village; it's not unusual to see old women dressed in traditional black garb complete with headscarf, and the town hall chalks up funeral details on a blackboard just outside the entrance. Buñol is best known for its annual fiesta, ***La Tomatina*** (*see* 'Festivals', p.216). The hills around the town have been scarred by mining in places, but there are still plenty of delightful hiking trails (including part of the GR7), which lead to mountain springs and waterfalls. To the southwest is the **Reserva Nacional de Caza de la Muela de Cortes**, a beautiful, wooded natural park which, though disfigured on its eastern flank by a mammoth hydroelectric station, still has some stunning countryside around the lakeside village of **Cofrentes**.

West of Buñol, **Requena** is a pleasant, quiet town with an ancient hub called the *Barrio de la Villa*, a string of delightful whitewashed squares linked by narrow streets filled with flowers. A 10th-century Moorish tower announces the entrance to the old town, up a stone slope which opens out into the **Plaza del Castillo**, where houses are clamped against the ancient walls. Beyond it lies the 15th-century Gothic church of **El Salvador**, and next to it is the **Plaza de la Villa**, the medieval administrative hub, where the town hall and the palace of the Inquisition stood. Also here are the **Cuevas** (*entrance by guided tour only: Tues–Fri at 12.15 and 1.15; Sat, Sun and hols every 30 mins 10–1.30 and 4.30–7; adm*), underground tunnels linking grain and wine stores and wine. Calle de Santa María leads to the largest and most imposing of Requena's churches, the 14th-century **Iglesia de Santa María**, with a Baroque interior. Few tourists make it this far – although Requena lives in hope – and the cool mountain air fanning the quiet streets make it a very pleasant day trip during the summer heat.

The Costa del Azahar

The 'Orange Blossom Coast', as the shore of Castelló and València provinces has been dubbed, is true to its name, lined through most of its length with orange groves; Castelló itself has a *huerta* as rich as València's, and so flat the *valencianos* call it La Plana, the plain. While there are long stretches of sand, few of the beaches here are anything to write home about. Pockets of villas and flats occupy the better stretches, but there are fewer hotels than you'd imagine.

Castelló de la Plana to Orpesa

Between Sagunt and Castelló there's little to see. **Borriana** is one of Spain's major orange ports; if you're driving through, stop to see the portal of the 16th-century parish church, flanked by two curious bears. Inland, **Villareal de los Infantes** is a busy citrus centre, founded as a neat grid in 1272 by Jaume I. Best among the beaches here are **Playa de Nules** and **Playa de Xilxes**, a little north of Almenara.

Castelló is not one of Spain's prettier provincial capitals, but it has a fine series of sandy beaches stretching from **Playa del Serrallo** (with a golf course) north towards **Benicàssim**. In town, the **Provincial Museum of Fine Arts** (*C/Caballeros; open Mon–Sat 10–8, Sun and hols 10–2; adm*) has fine paintings by Ribalta, Ribera and Sorolla, and good modern ceramics from the region. In the **Convento de las Capuchinas** (*C/Nuñez de Arce 11; open daily 4–8; adm free*) there are 10 saints attributed to Zurbarán (or copies of lost works by the master). The Gothic cathedral, flattened in the Civil War, has been rebuilt stone by stone. The town has a very lively nightlife, with scores of *bacalao* discos on the outskirts.

Benicàssim was an exclusive seaside resort at the turn of the century, but the handful of *modernista* villas have been swallowed up by major developments and giant hotel complexes; it now hosts a massive rave festival each year (*see* 'Festivals', p.220). A few kilometres inland is the Carmelite monastery at **Desierto de las Palmas**, where the sisters still brew a heady, herby liqueur that you can try at their wine-making museum (*call in advance*, **t** *964 30 09 62*). If sun, sea and sand is beginning to

Getting There and Around

By Train

RENFE has frequent services up the coast from València and down from Tarragona; there are stations at Borriana, Vila-real, Castelló, Benicàssim, Orpesa, Alcalá de Xivert, Benicarló and Vinaròs. Note that many train stations (including Benicarló, which is the nearest stop for Peníscola and Vinaròs) are set outside the town, which can make it more convenient to use the buses.

By Bus

There are two buses a day from València's bus station and from Castelló to Montanejos. Peníscola, Benicarló, and Vinaròs are linked by a municipal bus every hour; there are also three direct buses between Castelló, Benicarló and Vinaròs on weekdays (six in the summer), departing from C/Trinidad 166. On Sundays the only direct bus linking Castelló to Peníscola leaves from the same place. Three other buses link Castelló and València in a 1½hr express service.

Municipal buses leave Castelló's Pza Hernán Cortés for the beaches from Grao de Castelló to Benicàssim every 15 mins in the summer. Regular buses for the port (El Grao) depart from Pza Borrull.

Tourist Information

Castelló: Pza María Agustina 5, **t** 964 22 10 00, **f** 964 22 77 03. A particularly helpful office.
Peníscola: Pso Marítimo, **t** 964 48 02 08.
Benicàssim: C/Medico Segarra 4, **t** 964 30 09 62, **f** 964 30 01 39, *benicassim@gva.es*, *www.gva.es/benicassim*.
Vinarós: Pso de Colón s/n, **t** 964 45 33 34, **f** 964 45 56 25.

Festivals

Benicàssim: Rave festival, *June*.
Castelló: Magdalena, *23 Mar*. Nine days of dancing, fireworks and processions. At the heart of it all is the Romería de les Canyes, the religious procession up to the pretty little sanctuary of Santa María Magdalena, perched on a hilltop about five km out of town.

Where to Stay and Eat

Borriana ✉ 12530

El Morro, C/Dona Puerto s/n, **t** 964 58 60 33 (*expensive*). Right on the port, and the local favourite for rice and excellent seafood, though on the pricey side. *Closed Sun*.

pall, the Carmelites also run retreats and meditation courses. There are stunning views from the countryside around the monastery, although sadly much of the surrounding forest was burned down in the early 1990s.

Inland from Castelló and Benicàssim is a string of attractive, fortified towns; **Onda**, in the middle of a green plain, is surmounted by the '300-Tower Castle' and has a twisting old quarter dotted with reminders of its former occupants, the Templars and the Moors. There's another castle in lofty **Villafamés**, and a 15th-century palace has been converted to house the popular **Museo de Arte Contemporáneo** (*open summer Mon–Fri 11–1 and 5–8, Sat and Sun 11–2 and 5–8; winter Mon–Fri 11–1 and 4–6, Sat and Sun 11–2 and 4–7; adm*) with an eclectic selection of 20th-century works including some pieces by Miró. Further north, near the small town of **Cabanes**, a Roman arch stands alone in the middle of the plain, a relic of the Via Augusta.

The province of Castelló has something else other Spanish provinces don't: a collection of tiny volcanic islets, the **Els Columbrets**, 43 kilometres out to sea. Although not much more than rocks themselves, they are very popular with bird-watchers and underwater fishermen: excursion boats leave from **Orpesa**, the next town and beach north of Benicàssim, another former fishing village that has succumbed to the siren call of tourism.

Castelló ✉ 12000

Castelló's accommodation is generally of a good standard with bargains to be had in all price categories. You can choose to stay in the town itself or down by the port and beaches. Note that several hotels offer excellent rates at weekends.

★★★★**Intur**, C/Herrero 20, **t** 964 22 50 00, **f** 964 23 26 06, (*expensive; moderate at weekends*). Modern and posh, with a gym for the health-conscious.

★★★**Hotel del Golf**, on the Grao's Playa del Pinar, **t** 964 28 01 80, **f** 964 28 27 36 (*expensive*). Besides golf it offers tennis, a pool, and air-conditioned rooms in contemporary surroundings.

★★**Hotel Doña Lola**, C/Lucena 3, **t** 964 21 40 11, **f** 964 25 22 35 (*moderate*). A small, very comfortable, offering, with great service and a good **restaurant**.

★**Hs Los Herreros**, Av. Del Puerto 28, **t** 964 28 42 64, **f** 964 28 27 36 (*inexpensive–cheap*). Basic rooms painted in an institutional pale green; still, it's not expensive and it's well located just a couple of blocks from the port. It has a busy bar and **restaurant** downstairs.

Casino Antiguo, Puerta del Sol 1, **t** 964 22 28 64 (*moderate*). In a private club with a public dining room, classic Valencian rice dishes and good seafood.

Peñalen, C/Fola 11, **t** 964 23 41 31 (*moderate*). Superbly prepared food, popular with locals. *Closed Sun and 15 Aug–15 Sept.*

Rafael, C/Churruca 28, **t** 964 28 21 85 (*expensive*). Charming restaurant right off the fisherman's docks in El Grao; excellent seafood. *Closed Sun and last fortnight in Sept.*

Casa Teresa, C/Lope de Vega 4, **t** 964 20 15 20 (*cheap*). Unfussy and deeply authentic: specialities include game. *Closed Sun.*

Tasca del Puerto, Av. del Puerto 13, **t** 964 23 60 18 (*moderate*). Delicious rice, including a tasty *arroz negro*.

When it's time for **tapas**, head to the bustling streets around Plaza Santa Clara, especially Calle Barraca and Calle Isaac Peral, where you'll come across dozens of *tascas*, all offering an excellent range of tapas at good prices.

Benicàssim ✉ 12560

In Benicàssim you will get slightly less value for your money...

★★★★**Intur Bonaire**, Av. Gimeno Tomás 3, **t** 964 39 24 80, **f** 964 39 56 01, *bonair@intur.com*, *www.intur.com* (*expensive*). Right on the beach and a good bet: with tennis, golf, and pool facilities. There's another Intur hotel on the same street:

North of Orpesa the road is forced away from the coast by the rugged Sierra de Irta, dotted with castles and towers. The finest of these, **Alcalá de Xivert**, is an enormous ruin that once belonged to the Templars.

Peníscola

The belle of the Costa del Azahar, Peníscola has been called Spain's Mont St Michel for its location on a rugged promontory anchored to the mainland by a sandy isthmus. Intensive (and intensely ugly) tourist development along the isthmus keeps Peníscola from looking as strikingly isolated as it once did; still, the heavily fortified medieval town, with its cobbled streets and castle, is one of the prettiest scenes to grace a Spanish postcard. The Phoenicians, its first settlers, called it Tyriche, because it reminded them of Tyre; the Romans regarded it in the 3rd century BC as the boundary between their colonies and those of Carthage. Hamilcar Barca used the town as his headquarters, and here his son Hannibal, chafing under Roman constraints, resolved to make war on the upstart young empire. Jaume I won Peníscola from the Moors and handed it to the Templars, who built the castle. When the Order was dissolved,

***Intur Azor, Av. Gimeno Tomás 1, t 964 39 20 00, f 964 39 23 79. Similar facilities at a slightly lower price.

**Hotel Eco Avenida, Av. Castellon 2, t 964 30 00 47, f 964 30 00 79 (*inexpensive*). A little further up from the beach: a pleasant haven with a pool.

Villa del Mar, Pso Marítimo Pilar Coloma 2/4, **t** 964 30 28 52 (*inexpensive*). The best beach-front restaurant: lots of seafood.

Plaza, C/Cristóbal Colón 3, **t** 964 30 00 72 (*moderate*). The best restaurant in town, featuring delicious rice dishes.

Desierto de las Palmas, Pola Desierto Palmas s/n, **t** 964 30 09 47 (*cheap*). Up in the hills behind the town, overlooking palm groves and aromatic shrubs and trees tended by monks from the nearby 17th-century Carmelite monastery of the same name. With panoramic views across the coast; well worth the excursion.

Orpesa del Mar ✉ 12594

For more reasonable prices, stay at Orpesa.

***El Cid, Las Playetas, Km83, t 964 30 07 00, f 964 30 07 00 (*moderate*). Small but good beach hotel in a pretty location with pool, tennis and a garden. *Open April–end Sept.*

**Hs Orpesa Sol, Av. Madrid 11, t 964 31 01 50, (*inexpensive*). Another good option near the beach: rooms have garden views and are clean and comfortable. *Open April–end Sept.*

***Hotel Neptuono Playa, Pso La Concha 1, t 964 31 00 40, f 964 31 00 75 (*moderate*). A large, modern hotel overlooking the beach, with mountain views from the rooms at the back.

Toni, C/Delegado Varela 2, Cabanes (*inexpensive*). About 10km outside Orpesa, this old-fashioned bar draws in crowds from throughout the region for its excellent range of tapas.

Torre del Rey, Pso Marítimo 27, **t** 964 31 02 22 (*inexpensive–cheap*). Unassuming, seafront restaurant with decent rice and fish dishes, as well as cheap snacks.

Peníscola ✉ 12598

****HsR del Mar, Av. Papa Luna 18, t 964 48 06 00, f 964 48 13 63, *hostemar@dragoment.es*, *www.hostemar.com* (*expensive–moderate*). The best on the promenade with a private pool, medieval banquets, music and dancing. *Open all year.*

**La Cabaña, Av. Primo de Rivera 29, t/f 964 48 00 17, *www.hotel-lacabana.com* (*moderate*). On the beachfront, with fine views of the promontory (and many hotel neighbours, all more or less the same). *Closed 10 Dec–28 Feb.*

the town passed to the Knights of Montesa, who inherited all the Templars' possessions in the Kingdom of València. They never spread outside València and, according to most historians, quietly went about practising the same heresies and rituals that had condemned their predecessors.

The Knights of Montesa sheltered and protected Peníscola's best-loved historical personage, Papa Luna, the last of the anti-Popes of Avignon, who reigned under the name Benedict XIII. Born in Aragón, Pedro de Luna (1338–1423) seems to have been a formidable character. After having been chased from Avignon by French troops and condemned for heresy, he spent the rest of his life issuing anathemata and excommunicated everyone who wronged him, refusing even in his 90s to renounce his title of Benedict XIII. His obstinacy gave rise to the modern Spanish idiom, *mantenerse uno en sus trece*, 'to maintain one's thirteen' or, as we would say, 'he stuck to his guns'. One of the gates into Peníscola still bears his coat-of-arms.

The **Templar's Castle** (*open summer daily 10–2.30 and 4–9.30; winter daily 9.30–1 and 3.15–6; adm*), where Papa Luna resided, has been vigorously restored and contains the few relics left by his stay in its fine Gothic halls. One of his papal bulls issued here confirmed the 1411 foundation of St Andrew's University in Scotland. The façade of the 18th-century church near the castle is adorned with curious military symbols. Beware

★**Hs del Duc**, C/Fulladosa 10, **t** 964 48 07 68 (*inexpensive*). Located in an old mansion in the centre of town: the best cheap hotel on Peníscola's promontory. *Open April–Sept.*

There are many **restaurants** all over Peníscola, covering all price ranges:

Casa Jaime, Av. Papa Luna 5, **t** 964 48 00 30 (*expensive–moderate*). Smallish, family-run seafood restaurant with a terrace out on the promenade; the food is excellent and includes a variety of rice dishes.

Casa Severino, Urb. Las Atalayas, **t** 964 48 07 03 (*moderate*). Serving the provincial speciality, *paella marinara*, with dining on the terrace overlooking the sea. *Closed Wed in winter.*

Benicarló ✉ 12580

★★★**Parador de Benicarló**, Av. Papa Luna 3, **t** 964 47 01 00, **f** 964 47 09 34, *benicarlo@parador.es* (*expensive*). The best place to stay and eat in town: a modern establishment with pool, gardens, air-conditioned rooms and a restaurant featuring the freshest of seafood and authentic Valencian specialities – including Benicarló artichokes.

★★**Hotel Marynton**, Pso Marítimo 5, **t** 964 46 50 30, **f** 964 46 07 20 (*inexpensive*). Modest hotel which is much cheaper, and not far from the beach.

★**Hs Belmonte**, Pio XII 3, **t** 964 47 12 39 (*cheap*). Benicarló's best budget accommodation.

El Cortijo, Av. Méndez Núñez 85, **t** 964 47 50 38 (*expensive–moderate*). Air-conditioned, and serving a diverse range of fresh seafood: try the excellent langoustines. *Closed Sun eve, Mon and first fortnight in July.*

Vinaróz/Vinaròs ✉ 12500

★★**Hotel Miramar**, Pso Blasco Ibáñez 12, **t/f** 964 45 14 00 (*inexpensive*). Modest, agreeable family-run hotel on the seafront with a decent **restaurant**, *La Cuina*.

El Faro de Vinaros, Zona Portuaria s/n, **t** 964 45 63 62, *restaurantefaro@latinmail.com*, *www.el-faro-com* (*expensive*). A great place to splash out; two young brothers have transformed the former lighthouse that overlooks the port, and introduced a very creative, Mediterranean menu (try the moussaka with fresh tuna) accompanied by a fine wine list and delicious desserts.

Casa Pocho, C/San Gregorio 49, **t** 964 45 10 95 (*moderate*). Chirpy nautical décor and well-priced seafood. Friendly and welcoming. *Closed Sun eve and Mon.*

El Langostino de Oro, C/San Francisco 3, **t** 964 45 12 04 (*expensive*). Smart and decidedly elegant. *Closed Mon and last fortnight in Sept.*

that in July and August, elbow room in Peníscola is at a premium, the streets made narrower still by wall-to-wall souvenir stands, in the midst of which restaurants claim their own bit of pavement to set up tables. From a distance, however, it is always enchanting, especially at night when the walls and castle are bathed in golden light.

Benicarló, Peníscola's mainland connection, has a Baroque church, with a Valencian dome frosted by blue *azulejos* and a tower. **Vinaròs** nearby, an unassuming little tourist town, with nice beaches, is a small but important fishing port, famed for its sturgeon and lobsters; its Baroque church has an equally colourful portal.

The Maestrazgo (El Maestrat)

Inland from Peníscola is a region called the Maestrazgo, which translates as 'the jurisdiction of a grand master of a military order'; and of Grand Masters you can take your pick between the Templars, the Knights of Montesa, or the Knights of St John, all of whom dwelt here. It's a rugged, picturesque place, especially in its upper reaches (*see* **Aragón**, p.264). The Lower Maestrazgo, while not as wild or remote, has a number of fascinating medieval villages.

In the middle ages, the Maestrazgo was often the front line in the battle between the Moors and the Christians; the villages, set amid rugged hills and sudden outcrops of pinkish rock, were heavily fortified and surrounded by sanctuaries which still draw surprising crowds to their traditional *romerías*, pilgrimages which also give the locals a chance to show off and put on a fiesta.

The first village inland is the ceramic-making town of **Traiguera** (17km from Vinaròs), dominated by a Renaissance church with a small museum of religious bits and bobs. Just outside is one of the most visited sanctuaries in the region, **La Mare de Déu de la Font de la Salut**, a 15th-century church, hospital and palace that is still the focus of

Tourist Information

Morella: Pza San Miguel 3, **t** 964 17 30 32, **f** 964 17 30 32.

Sant Mateu: C/Historiador Betí 6, **t** 964 41 66 58, **f** 964 41 61 29.

Getting There

Two buses a day from Castelló and Vinaròs go to Morella, which is itself a terminus for buses that go once or twice a day to the villages of the Maestrazgo. Buses from Castelló pass through them all as well; get timetables from the tourist office. Be warned that the bus times (they leave at the crack of dawn and in the late afternoon) mean that it's not easy to go for a day trip without your own transport and you should think about spending the night.

Festivals

The villages of the Maestrazgo celebrate various saints throughout August, their fiestas usually being spread over a long weekend and involving minor bull-running during the day and much jollity in the evenings.

Morella: Sexennial, *every six years* (the last one was in 2000). One of the most celebrated in Spain, this is an exuberant nine-day fiesta commemorating the miracle of the Virgin of Vallivana; it involves a series of processions with 'giants' and 'fatheads' (huge papier-mâché characters), traditional dancing and fireworks. The streets are decorated with huge crêpe paper collages, the secret of their subjects jealously guarded as each street vies to create the best.

Where to Stay and Eat

Morella ✉ 12300

Morella is the only town in the Maestrazgo well prepared for visitors, though the majority of the villages mentioned above have rooms above bars, or modest *hostales*. Castelló's tourist office can provide you with a list.

***__Cardenal Ram__, Cuesta Suñer 1, **t** 964 17 30 85, **f** 964 17 32 18 (*moderate*). The best place to stay in Morella: located in a restored 15th-century palace, like a budget *parador*, with fine rooms near the centre.

***__Hotel Rey Don Jaime__, C/Juan Giner 6, **t/f** 964 16 09 11, **f** 964 16 09 88 (*moderate*). New and beautifully furnished, this is very comfortable, with superb mountain views.

*__Hs La Muralla__, C/Muralla 12, **t** 964 16 02 43 (*inexpensive–cheap*). Clean, old-fashioned, friendly and very cheerful.

***__Palau dels Osset__, Pza Major 16, **t** 964 17 75 24, **f** 964 17 75 56 (*expensive*). Some 10km outside Morella: a delightful 16th-century restored palace set in the tiny medieval village of Forcall.

Mesón del Pastor, Cuesta Jovani 5, **t** 964 16 02 49 (*cheap*). An even better restaurant than the Cardenal Ram's, featuring the local cuisine of the mountains: lots of pork and lamb with curds and honey (*cuajada y miel*) for dessert. *Closed Wed.*

Casa Roque, Cuesta San Juan 1, **t** 964 16 03 36 (*moderate*). This charming traditional restaurant serves delicious specialities from the Maestrazgo – don't miss out on the local truffles.

Vinatea, C/Blasco Alagón, **t** 964 16 07 44 (*inexpensive*). Traditional home-style cooking – and great tapas.

dozens of pilgrimages; Cervantes and several Spanish kings have made the trek in the past. To the south of the N232 is the sleepy village of **Catí**, with a winding medieval core, and another little sanctuary, **Mare de Déu de l'Avellà** perched high on a 2,952ft-pinnacle and accessed through a tunnel in the rock. Back on the N232, the sanctuary of **Nuestra Señora de Vallivana** houses the miniature statue which was credited with saving the lives of the Morellan townspeople when plague hit them at the end of the 17th century (*see* below).

Easily the most striking town in the Maestrazgo is **Morella**, surrounded by medieval walls studded with watchtowers and surmounted by a steep, isolated rock and a mighty castle. Of the four gates leading into the city, the 14th-century **Puerta de San Miguel** is the most impressive. Of the churches, the Gothic **Basilica de Santa María la Mayor** (*open daily 12–2 and 4–6*) of 1330, with its carved portals and stained glass, is not only the finest in town, but perhaps of the whole *país valenciano*. Inside, a magnificently carved marble spiral staircase ascends to the raised *coro*, where the balustrade has a frieze of the Last Judgement. The small **museum** stars a *Madonna* by the serene Italian painter Sassoferrato and a 15th-century Valencian *Descent from the Cross*. The steep streets of Morella are lined with tall, whitewashed houses with wooden balconies. Just below the castle is a **Franciscan monastery** with a museum in its fine 13th-century **cloister**, and a bizarre, macabre 15th-century fresco of the Dance of Death. From here you can take a path up to the castle itself, with magnificent views; to the north look for the **Gothic aqueduct**, built in the 14th century when Roman techniques were a dim memory. Morella's most famous fiesta is the **Sexennial** (*see* 'Festivals', opposite), which began as a testament of gratitude to the Virgin of Vallivana who miraculously saved the town from the plague which tore through the region in 1672. In desperation, the tiny figure of the Virgin was brought from her sanctuary and as soon as she arrived in the narrow streets of Morella, plague victims were leaping up from their beds and proclaiming their complete recovery.

From Morella, a dry, dusty plain stretches to Mirambel in the Teruel area (*see* p.264), with a scattering of villages guarded by castles and fortresses. **Forcall** is known for its gastronomy and craft traditions, and just to the north is **Zorita del Maestrazgo**, prettily set near the River Bergantes and the site of yet another of the area's remarkable sanctuaries. West of Forcall, across a medieval bridge, is **Todolella**, with a glowering, squat castle, well known for its rousing traditional dances, the *Danzas Guerreras*.

Two other scenic medieval towns, formerly Templar possessions, are **Castellfort** and **Ares del Maestre**. The latter is built around a would-be-soufflé of a rock, 4,323ft high, near some excellent palaeolithic art in the **Cova Remigia**. The cave lies just along the road to another pretty village, **Villafranca del Cid**, which like several other places in the Maestrazgo recalls in its name El Cid's frequent raids in the region. **Benasal** is an atmospheric little spa town, with a maze of twisting medieval streets and Gothic palaces nudging up the hillside.

Sant Mateu was once the most important town of the Maestrazgo; the Order of the Knights of Montesa which was largely responsible for the heavy fortifications in the Maestrazgo were based here, and traces of the town's former glory can be found in the Gothic palaces around Pza Mayor and in the 13th-century **Iglesia Arciprestal**. From

Sant Mateu, a minor road heads 22 kilometres south to **Albocácer**, a Templar town with a ruined castle; near this, just off the road from San Mateo is a **Calvario**, an outdoor version of the Stations of the Cross or symbolic journey along the Via Dolorosa. A typical one has a chapel atop a hill, reached by a winding path marked by intermittent shrines. The Maestrazgo is famous for its Calvarios, but Albocácer's is exceptional: a virtual maze of low, whitewashed, stone walls. Another one in maze form may be seen in the **Cuevas de Vinromá** just to the southeast. While the rest of Europe underwent the pangs of the Second World War, Spaniards were reading about the chapel atop the Cuevas de Vinromá's Calvario, where the Nationalists manufactured a miracle: several appearances of the Virgin, no less, who mouthed the philosophy of José Antonio Primo de Rivera and declared that Heaven, in league with Hitler, would soon clear the earth of the Marxist-Jewish menace that threatened it with extinction. In the euphoria of post-Civil War victory, there were plans to make the village the Lourdes of Spain, but when the Vatican remained silent on the matter and the war took its course, the miracles quickly dried up. Nowadays the only 'sight' in the old village is its prehistoric cave paintings.

South of València: The Costa Blanca

The 'White Coast' of Spain started out as a refuge from the intensity of the Costa Brava, where pioneering Germans, followed by the British and French, could have an inexpensive if unexciting holiday. Not as beautiful as the Costa Brava, nor as physically monotonous as the Costa del Sol, the Costa Blanca is no longer inexpensive, and every year more sports activities and nightclubs join hands with a growing number of hotels and apartment blocks – especially in the Babylon of Benidorm.

The Costa Blanca officially begins at Dénia; en route there are great rice plantations and minor beaches with the notable exception of the busy resort of **Cullera**, which is populated by energetic Spanish families and has a nice beach. Next is **Gandía**, set back a couple of miles from the sea. The town once belonged to the Borgia dukes, a more polite branch of the family than the band who caused so much trouble in Italy; in the 15th century they settled down in the fine Renaissance **Palace of the Dukes** (*entrance is by guided tour only (in Spanish, though there's a leaflet in English); open summer Mon–Fri 11–12 and 6–7, Sat 11–12; winter Mon–Fri 11–12 and 5–6; closed Sun; adm*). The fourth duke of Gandía, Francisco Borgia, renounced the worldly vanities his family was famous for and became a Jesuit and saint. The Jesuits bought the palace at the end of the 19th century, and it now houses a Jesuit school. Inside is a glittering collection of Manises ceramics and *azulejos*, although sadly the ancient Arab dyes are no longer possible to replicate as the plants from which they are derived have died out. Gandía was a small fishing village before mass tourism hit, and you can still pick up ultra-fresh fish at the Lonja (fish market) down at the Grao (port). There are regular buses between the town and the port from outside the train station. The long, sandy beaches are densely lined with anonymous apartment blocks, but the souvenir shops and restaurants are very popular with Spanish families and Valencian day-trippers

which give them a cheerful buzz in summer. **Oliva**, eight kilometres away, is a little quieter and less developed. Again, the town is set back from the coast but there are regular bus connections to the beaches which stretch almost as far as Dénia.

Just within Alicante province, Dénia is squeezed between Mount Montgó and the sea. The Greeks built a temple of Artemis here, and the town is named for her Roman alias Diana. Only the ruined **castle** over the town evokes Dénia's pre-tourist history, but the town with all its colourfully painted villas is one of the quieter and prettier on the Costa Blanca. The beaches are broad and sandy and it's a good base for hiking in the scrubby, wild **Natural Park of Montgó**; a stiff three-hour tramp will get you to the summit of Montgó for fine views.

Boats ply between the coves of Dénia and **Xàbia** (Jávea), an attractive former fishing village nestled beneath the villa-covered capes of San Antonio and San Martín. It has

Getting Around

By Train

There are at least 15 local trains daily between València and Gandía, the terminus of the coast line. The València–Alicante train, however, goes inland, through Xátiva; another branch from València terminates in Alcoi via Xátiva (three a day).

The Costa Blanca is also well served by its own **narrow-gauge line** (FGV) out of Alicante (15 a day, once an hour), with stations at Dénia, Teulada, Calp, Altea, Benidorm and the beaches north of Alicante. **FGV information**: Dénia, **t** 965 78 04 45; Benidorm, **t** 965 85 18 95; Alicante, **t** 965 26 27 31, *www.fgv.es*.

By Bus

There are frequent RENFE buses between València and Alicante, some direct on the *autopista*, others stopping at the resorts along the Costa Blanca. Several buses a day link Dénia with Xàbia, connecting with the train.

By Sea

Dénia is also a port with ferry links on the Flebasa line to Ibiza; for information, **t** 965 78 40 11 in Dénia or freephone **t** 900 177 177. PITRA also operate ferries, for information, call **t** 966 42 31 20. Both offices are on the harbour front.

Tourist Information

Gandía: Av. Marqués de Campo, **t** 962 87 77 88.

Dénia: Pza Oculista Buigues 9, **t** 966 42 23 67, *tourist.info@denia.net, www.denia.net*.

Xàbia: Pza Almirante Basterreche 24, **t** 965 79 07 36.

Calp: Av. Ejércitos Españoles 66, **t** 965 83 69 20.

Altea: C/Sant Pere 9, **t** 965 84 41 14, *tourist info.altea@turisme.m400.gva.es, www.altea digital.com*.

Festivals

Xàbia: Fogueres de Sant Joan, *24 June*. The summer solstice coincides with the festival of Saint John, and the townsfolk climb up high to celebrate by the fortress with bonfires and fireworks.

Where to Stay and Eat

Gandía ✉ 46700

In Gandía, swanky hotels are on the beach; modest, inexpensive ones in the town:

★★★★**Bayren I**, Pso de Neptuno 62, **t** 962 84 03 00, **f** 962 84 06 53, *recepcion@hoteles-bayren.com, www.hotelesbayren.com* (*expensive*). Of the swanky category, with a pleasant pool, dancing in the evening and a perfect seaside location.

★★★**Bayren II**, C/Mallorca 19, **t** 962 84 07 00 *recepcion@hotelesbayren.com, www.hoteles-bayren.com*. Bayren I's slightly cheaper sister.

★★★**Riviera**, Pso de Neptune 28, **t** 962 84 00 66, **f** 962 84 00 62, *hotelriviera@jazzfree.com* (*moderate–inexpensive*). A cheaper, family-run hotel overlooking the seafront. *Closed end Oct–mid-Mar.*

★★**La Casa Vieja**· C/Horno 2, Rugat (14km from Gandía), **t/f** 962 81 40 13, *lacasavieja@xpress.es* (*moderate*). A truly delightful choice, in a tiny village inland. There are just five rooms and one suite set in this attractive little 17th-century farmhouse, but the welcome is very friendly and the views of the surrounding orange groves are glorious.

Most of the **restaurants** are on the beach.

L'Ullal, C/Benicanena 12, **t** 962 87 73 82 (*expensive–moderate*). Probably the best food in town; this is a charming, attractively decorated restaurant serving imaginative Mediterranean dishes. *Closed Sun.*

La Gamba, on the Ctra Nazaret-Oliva s/n, **t** 962 84 13 10 (*moderate*). With a garden terrace and delicious seafood. *Closed Mon and Nov.*

Xàbia (Jávea) ✉ 03730

★★★★★**Villa Mediterranea**, **t** 965 79 52 33, **f** 965 79 45 81, *hotelvillamed@ctv.es, www.hotelvil-amed.es* (*luxury*). The most exclusive choice in town, with just 10 luxuriously appointed rooms and two suites in a stunning white Mediterranean-style villa with magnificent views – as far as Ibiza on a good day. An elegant terrace overlooks the huge pool.

★★★★**Parador de Xàbia (Costa Blanca)**, Playa del Arenal, **t** 965 79 02 00, **f** 965 79 03 08, (*expensive*). Well situated, with pool, a/c and a palm-filled garden, and a first-class **restaurant** emphasizing dishes of the Levante.

★★**Hotel Miramar**, Pza Almirante Bastarreche 12, **t** 965 79 01 00, **f** 965 79 01 00 (*moderate*). An attractive hotel near the seafront, with pretty, pine-decorated rooms and friendly staff. Go for the rooms with sea views.

★★**Hs Xàbia**, Pío X 5, **t** 965 79 54 61, *www.javea .net* (*inexpensive*). Small, friendly and central.

★**Hs La Favorita**, C/Magallanes 4, **t** 965 79 04 77 (*cheap*). The best budget choice.

Azorín, Toni Llido, **t** 965 79 44 95 (*inexpensive*). At the centre of the action near the port: huge plates of shellfish for a very nice price.

Tasca Tonis, C/Mayor 4, **t** 966 46 18 51 (*inexpensive*). A down-to-earth neighbourhood restaurant, always filled with locals enjoying the local dishes at very reasonable prices.

Olé, C/Bonaventura 9, **t** 966 46 23 76. In an old mansion, serving delicious tapas and a very decent selection of wines.

Calp (Calpe) ✉ 03710

Calp has numerous multi-complex, variously starred hotels. For a better bargain try:

★★**Venta La Chata**, Ctra Alicante-València Km172, **t** 965 83 03 08, **f** 965 83 03 08 (*moderate*). An attractive 18th-century villa four kilometres from the beach, with pretty views of the mountains and the sea.

★**Hs El Parque**, C/Portalet, **t** 965 83 07 70 (*cheap*). Simple but clean, and in the centre.

Los Zapatos, C/Santa María 7, **t** 965 83 15 07 (*expensive–moderate*). Good local specialities with an Arabic twist; excellent selection of regional wines.

La Cambra, C/Delfin s/n, **t** 965 83 06 05 (*moderate*). Basque meets Mediterranean in this delightful restaurant.

Bora Bora, Av. del Puerto, **t** 965 83 31 77 (*cheap*). Incredible variety of pancakes.

Altea ✉ 03590

★★★**Cap Negret**, Ctra València, **t** 965 84 12 00 (*expensive*). Luxury on the beach, with numerous facilities including a pool.

★★**Hotel Altaya**, C/Sant Pere 28, **t** 965 84 08 00 (*moderate–inexpensive*). Also on the beach: pleasant and very comfortable, helpful and friendly service; rooms with sea views.

★**Hotel San Miguel**, C/La Mar 65, **t** 965 84 04 00 (*inexpensive*). Delightful, pristine little hotel overlooking the seafront.

For the cheapest options try the budget *hostales* behind the main square.

Monte Molar, outside Altea on Ctra València, **t** 965 84 15 81 (*expensive*). For gourmets only: delicate, imaginative dishes – snails and wild rice, duck in bilberry sauce – served on a terrace overlooking the sea.

Raco de Toni, La Mar 127, **t** 965 84 17 63 (*expensive–moderate*). Excels in rice and fish dishes.

Sant Pere 24, C/Sant Pere 24, **t** 965 84 49 72 (*moderate*). Cool and pleasant, specializing in splendid rice dishes: like *arroz de langosta*.

Bella Altea, C/Concepción 16, **t** 965 84 08 84 (*moderate*). Small, rustic and very welcoming restaurant serving international cuisine.

The best area for atmospheric open-air dining is around Pza de la Inglesia.

La Capella, C/San Pablo 1, **t** 966 68 04 84 (*cheap*). One of the best of the tapas bars.

Dénia ✉ 03700

★★★**Hotel Rosa**, C/Marinas 197, **t** 965 78 15 73, **f** 966 42 47 74 (*moderate*). Pleasant, seaside, family-orientated resort, with pools for the adults and children, a playground, tennis and a **restaurant**.

★**Hs Noguera**, Marinas Pda Estaño, **t** 966 47 41 07 (*inexpensive*). Nice enough rooms on Marinas beach, and a good bargain.

Most of Dénia's **restaurants** can be found on Playa Les Rotes, but the town's cuisine has got the best reputation of the Costa Blanca:

El Poblet, Ctra Las Marinas Km2, El Poblet 43, **t** 965 78 41 79 (*expensive*). One of the very best restaurants in the area with a renowned chef; the prawns from Dénia are considered to be among the best in the world. *Closed Mon exc. in July and Aug.*

Gavila, C/Marqués de Campo 55, **t** 965 78 10 66 (*expensive*). Among the best rice and other local delicacies to be found. *Closed Sun eve.*

L'Olleta, Av. d'Alacant 19, **t** 966 42 09 52 (*expensive–moderate*). Another good spot to push the boat out; thoughtful, Mediterranean cuisine. *Closed Sun.*

El Trampoli, Playa Les Rotes **t** 965 78 12 96 (*moderate*). With a delicious menu of Valencian rice and seafood.

Pizzeria Ticino, C/Bellavista 4, **t** 965 78 91 03 (*inexpensive*). Good, cheap and cheerful pizza and pasta joint.

preserved more of its old character, and is well endowed with scenic marine grottos and dramatic coves. The shallow horseshoe shaped beach at the centre is the most popular, lined with plenty of bars and restaurants, but there are dozens of attractive little bays, guarded by the battered remnants of medieval watchtowers, which are well worth exploring in themselves. The Cape of San Antonio has been declared a marine reserve in order to prevent further development and the diving is excellent. The old town is a twisting maze of steep streets lined with whitewashed houses and topped with a Gothic church-cum-fortress, which is the best place to be to enjoy the Fogueres de Sant Joan (*see* 'Festivals', p.228) to best effect.

Next are the fairly quiet beaches of Moraira, part of the little inland town of Teulada, then the not-so-quiet but excellent sands of **Calp** (Calpe). The Greeks called Gibraltar 'Calpe' and this Calp, too, has it own mighty Rock, the **Peñon de Ifach**, swept by body-scarred beaches on either side and bored through with a tunnel to let you mount to the summit – 761ft over the sea below. Again, encroaching development led to the rock's nomination as a natural reserve only weeks before the bulldozers moved in; the climb takes about two hours and leaves from the Natural Park information office. It's a lively town, with plenty of nightlife – and has become so popular with Germans that the town now even celebrates Oktoberfest.

Altea is quieter, located on a natural balcony over the sea; its stony beach isn't as good as those of Calp but it does form a series of coves, including a nudist beach. The others are popular with families. Altea is one of the most charming spots on the Costa Blanca; artists discovered it in the 1960s and 1970s and its steep, stepped streets are packed with craft shops and artisans studios. It might have embraced tourism, but it hasn't abandoned its own sleepy charm. The old church, right at the summit of the village, has a fine blue-tiled Valencian dome, and is surrounded with plenty of excellent bars and restaurants.

Benidorm

The undisputed giant on the Costa Blanca, Benidorm has become synonymous with high rises and package tourism. The six-and-a-half-kilometre-long, generously wide sandy beach has something to do with it, and the ensemble of skyscrapers huddled together in a dense forest is awesome in a Manhattanish way; certainly it has a verve most other costa resorts lack – as well as more discotheques and Las Vegas-type shows. It's new star attraction is the mammoth theme park Terra Mítica, one of the biggest on the Mediterranean.

Behind Benidorm (you can perhaps see it best from the *autopista*) there is a peculiar mountain with a neat, square notch taken out of it – a notch shaped exactly like the islet off the coast. An old Spanish legend recounts that a giant once lived near Benidorm, and that after years of loneliness, he finally found a lady-love. She fell ill, explaining to the giant that she would die that day at the moment the sun went down. In despair, the giant watched the sun sink down behind the mountain; then, at

Tourist Information

Benidorm: Av. Martínez Alejos 16, **t** 965 85 32 24.
Guadalest: Av. Alicante, **t** 965 88 52 98.

Festivals

Alcoi: St George's Day, *23 April*. A re-enactment of the Battle of Christians and Moors is staged in remembrance of St George's personal appearance at the battle in 1276.

Sports and Activities

Off Shore

There are **watersports** of all kinds, especially at Benidorm, where waterskiing facilities, boat rentals, sailing and diving are all on offer. Windsurfing is popular all along the coast. **Yachtsmen** should obtain from the tourist offices the detailed folder on *Instalaciones Náuticas* on the Costa; another big folder, *Deporte y Cultura*, details every possible activity on the coast, from deep-sea diving to choral societies. There are **cruises** to look at the offshore islands in boats or half-submerged submarines with glass bottoms (**t** 965 85 00 52) and to Calp, leaving from the port at 9.30am.

On Shore

When you've had enough of the beach, the Costa Blanca will entertain you in other ways. Nearly every town has its **tennis** courts; Altea, Benisa (near Calp), Xàbia and Torrevieja (south of Alicante) have **golf** courses as well. The **Go-Kart** craze has really caught on in Spain, and there are circuits everywhere.

The modern **Casino Costa Blanca** is between Benidorm and Vila Joiosa; all along the coastal road from Alicante you'll see **shopping centres** with big car parks (open and abandoned), scruffy putting courses and bowling alleys.

Attractions

Terra Mítica, off the A7, just outside Bendorm *www.terramiticapark.com*. This giant theme park is the biggest crowd puller; it even has its own station on the FGV line, and FGV train travel is free if you buy your entrance pass at the station.

Aqualandia, **t** 965 86 40 06 (*under 3s get in free, adm for adults, concessions for kids; a bus leaves every half-hour from Pza Triangular*). A marine park, with lots more fun for the kids.

Safari Park Vergel, near Pego (by Dénia), **t** 965 75 02 85. For those with cars only; the lions and tigers run about freely; there's also a dolphin show and many children's activities. *Open all year*.

Benidorm also has a permanent **fun fair** just off the access route to the *autopista*.

Where to Stay

Benidorm ✉ 03500

There are so many hotels in **Benidorm**, and so many of them so similar and so booked up with packagers in the summer, that it's hard to tell them apart. Off-season you can get excellent rates. Don't bother to turn up in August without a booking.

the last minute, he wrenched out a piece of the summit and hurled it into the sea to give his beloved another minute of life. True or not, geologists have at least confirmed that the islet and the mountain are indeed made out of the same kind of rock.

La Vila Joiosa (Villajoyosa) is the last big resort before Alicante, but despite the pretty white nucleus of its old town it manages to have the least character. There are a couple of quieter coves beyond the packed main beaches, and those with a sweet tooth can indulge themselves at **Valor**, the best known of the local traditional chocolate-makers; besides their pretty *modernista*-style chocolate shop, their factory also houses a **Museum of Chocolate**.

Moderate

★★★**Los Alamos** Av. Gerona, **t** 965 85 02 12. In the heart of Benidorm near the beach, with a pool and garden.

★★**Hotel Don José**, Ctra Del Alt, **t** 965 85 50 50. Further back from the seafront, but attractive and good value. *Open Mar–Oct.*

★★**Hotel Los Ángelés**, C/Los Ángeles 3, **t/f** 966 80 74 33. Very nice, friendly little hotel down a narrow, shabby street in the old city.

Moderate–Inexpensive

★★**Hotel Mayor**· C/Mayor 16, **t** 965 85 18 19. Renovated rooms in an old hotel which even has its own pool.

★**Hs Nacional**, C/Verano 9, **t** 965 85 04 32. Not too stylish, but centrally located and with its own pool: *Open April–Oct.*

Budget accommodation tends to be clustered near the centre, away from the sea.

There is no accommodation in **Guadalest** but it is possible to find a very basic room in nearby **Collosa d'en Sarrià** at this *hostal*:

Hs Avenida, Ctra Alicante Km9, **t** 965 88 00 53 (*inexpensive*).

Eating Out

Expensive

Tiffany's, Av. del Mediterráneo 51, **t** 965 85 44 68. The poshest place in Benidorm for dining out, serving high-class international cuisine . *Closed 7 Jan–7 Feb.*

I Fratelli, Av. Dr Orts Llorca 21, **t** 965 85 39 79. As expensive as it is delicious: Art Deco-style décor and an interesting menu, throwing in a few regional dishes as well as fine Italian.

Moderate

La Caserola, Av. Bruselas 7, **t** 965 85 17 19. Serves international cuisine; it has a good atmosphere, with superb terrace dining in the summer.

La Palmera, Casa Paca Nadal, Av. De Severo Ochoa s/n, **t** 965 85 32 82. Good seafood and local rice dishes. *Closed July and Aug.*

L'Albufera, C/Girona 3, **t** 965 86 56 61 (*moderate–inexpensive*). There's an excellent range of tapas in the busy bar, as well as a restaurant serving all manner of rice dishes, including its famous namesake, the *valenciano* rice dish *l'albufera*.

Entertainment and Nightlife

Benidorm counts its pubs, nightclubs, and discotheques by the score; there are close to a 100 discos alone. Most are international in flavour and stay packed all night, disgorging their crowds only when the need for a fried egg breakfast grows too strong. Otherwise you can generally choose any form of entertainment that catches your fancy: from English to German and Scandinavian pubs, American-style bars, nightclubs in which to be serenaded by Spanish guitar and establishments in which to let loose with your own version of bath-time favourites aided by a karaoke machine. Perhaps to compensate for all this, Benidorm has taken to sponsoring a Festival of Spanish Song. The FGV runs trains between all the major disco/pub zones outside of the city centre all night during the summer.

Inland from the Costa Blanca

Inland from Benidorm, it's 27 kilometres to the very pretty medieval village of **Guadalest** with its much-ruined castle perched high atop a pinnacle. To capture it, Jaume I wrote that he had to attach wings to his soldiers' armour; the modern visitor can climb up through a tunnel. The village is the most visited place in Spain after the Prado, but if you can block out the swarming crowds, it is still a magical sight. The views from the remnants of the old Moorish fortress are breathtaking, stretching across the valley and far out to sea. Below the fortress is the **Casa Típica** (*open 10–7; adm*), which contains a rather dull collection of tools and accounts of rural life set in a charmingly renovated 18th-century house and nearby is the pretty white **Church of**

the Assumption. Not far from the nearby town of Callosa d'en Sarrià are the **Fuentes del Algar**, a string of waterfalls and natural pools hidden in the wooded mountains.

Alcoi (Alcoy), further west, is an industrial town which sprang up in the 19th-century. On St George's Day it hosts one of the most celebrated commemorations of the Battle of Christians and Moors in all of Spain (*see* 'Festivals', p.231), which dates back so long it has a museum dedicated to it, as well as local costumes, armour and so forth at the **Casal de Sant Jordi** (*open Tues– Sat 11–1 and 5–7.30, Sun and hols 10.30–2; closed Mon; adm*).

Xátiva (Játiva)

Xátiva is an hour's trip south from València, across the *huerta* and past many a dilapidated but stylish orange warehouse. Located on a pair of vine- and cypress-clad hills in the midst of these fertile flatlands, Xátiva is one of the most scenic of *valenciano* villages, best known for the three natives it exported to Italy: Ribera, known as Lo Spagnoletto in Naples for his short stature, and the two Borgia Popes, Calixtus III and Alexander VI, both born here when the family relocated from Borja in Aragón. Xátiva (its Moorish name) was such a headache to Philip V that when he finally captured it in 1707 he burned much of it and renamed it San Felipe after himself, so as to remind the inhabitants who was boss. He is remembered today in the **Museum of the Almundi**, where his portrait hangs, upside down. Suspended alongside him are a few paintings by Ribera (1591–1652) and a diverse selection of works received from the Prado. The Museum also exhibits a wide-ranging collection of archaeological finds, including many Islamic remains. All are housed within the 16th-century **Almundìn** (*open Tues–Sat 10–2; closed Mon and Sun*), the granary on C/de la Corretgeria.

In the historic centre, **Plaza del Seo** is dominated by a Renaissance **Colegiata** that is even bigger than València's cathedral, with several fine marbles and donations from the Borgias. Across the square from the church is Xátiva's prettiest building, the **Municipal Hospital**, its Plateresque façade serenaded by a charming angelic chamber orchestra over the door. The road up to the castles passes **San Félix**, the town's Visigothic cathedral, remodelled in the 13th century; it has a fine set of 15th-century paintings from València, recycled Roman columns and a stoup made from a marble capital. The **castle** (*open Tues–Sun 10–2 and 4.30–8*) that crowned Xátiva dates from the 15th century but was mostly demolished by Philip V. From the ramparts you can see across the *huerta* to València and the sea.

Alicante (Alacant)

Alicante is the air gateway to the Costa Blanca, and many of the two million people who fly in here decide to go no further. Unlike the other resorts on the coast, Alicante is a real Spanish city, with an air of its own along its seaside promenades and narrow back streets. It never tires of letting you know that, year after year, it has the warmest and sunniest winters in all Europe. And in January or February, buying a charter flight can be cheaper than the heating bills you would pay staying at home.

The Castle, Cathedral and Around

Alicante was the mightiest citadel of the Kingdom of València, and judging by the powerful **Castillo de Santa Bárbara** (*castle open Tues–Sat 10–2 and 5–8, Sun 10–3; closed Mon; access by lift from Pso de Gomis, behind the tourist office on Playa de El Postiguet; runs summer daily 7.30–12 and 5.30–8.30; winter daily 7.30–12.45 and 5.30–8.30*) that crowns the city, it still is. An English garrison spent most of Spain's wars here; Philip V blew both castle and troops up in 1707, but it was later restored, and is fun to explore, both for itself and for the stunning views it commands. The castle now contains the sculpture collection of the Fundació Eduardo Capo, one of the largest collections of contemporary Spanish sculpture in the world, attractively set in galleries within the castle and along the attractive gardens and paths which wind across the summit of the hill.

Below the castle is Alicante's lively and jovial old quarter, **Santa Cruz**, encompassing the 1662 **Catedral San Nicolás de Bari** (*open daily 7.30–12.30 and 5.30–8*), a strong,

Getting There and Around

By Air

Alicante's *El Altet* airport is 10km from the city, **t** 966 91 91 00, *www.aena.es*. Besides charters from northern Europe and the British 'no-frills' airline Go (**t** (in Spain) 901 33 35 00, *www.go-fly.com*), it handles a large number of regular domestic flights from Madrid, Sevilla, Barcelona, Palma, Ibiza, Las Palmas, Tenerife, Bilbao and Vitoria. Iberia's office is at Av. Federico Soto 9, **t** 965 20 60 00. Airport buses, No.CS, leave from C/Portugal, by the bus station, every hour on the hour (7am–10pm). Taxis are available outside Arrivals (about €12).

By Train

RENFE's station is on Av. Salamanca, **t** 965 92 02 02; ticket office, Explanada de España 1, **t** 965 21 98 67. There are frequent connections to Murcia (*see* p.244), València (*see* p.206) and Madrid. For trips up the coast, take the narrow-gauge railway, '**El Trenet**' (*see* p.228).

By Bus

Alicante's bus station is at the corner of C/Portugal and C/Italia, **t** 965 13 07 00. There are frequent connections all along the Costa Blanca; also to Granada, Almería, Barcelona, Jaén, Málaga, Sevilla, Madrid and València. There are also international buses to various European destinations, including London via Eurolines (*see* p.206).

Bus No.C1's route continues past the FEVE station to the Platja de Sant Joan and Platja de Muchavista, and takes in most of Alicante's discotheques as well. It runs approximately every 15mins and on summer weekends, all night. For information on local buses, call **t** 965 14 09 36, *www.subus.es*.

There are buses down the coast from Alicante; connections between Torrevieja and points south are also very frequent from Murcia (*see* below).

By Tram

A new tramline hugs the bay and links the beaches of Platja de El Postiguet and Platja del Albufereta (on the southern side of the Cabo de las Huertas cape). It departs from the Platja del Postiguet near Pla Puerta del Mar and stops at the FGV station.

By Sea

Trasmediterránea operate **ferries** to Ibiza, Explanada de España 2, **t** 965 14 25 51, **f** 965 20 45 26.

Tourist Information

Alicante: Municipal Office: Pza Ayuntamiento 1, **t** 965 14 92 80, *turismo@alicanteturismo.com*, *www.alicanteturismo.com*; Provincial Office: Explanada de España 2, **t** 965 20 00 00; at bus station: C/Portugal 17, **t** 965 92 98 02;

well-proportioned church, covered with red graffiti. The interior has been restored since its destruction in the Civil War, but remains dour and unwelcoming. Republican passions burned white-hot in Alicante: the founder and patron saint of the Falange, José Antonio Primo de Rivera, was imprisoned in a local convent and hurriedly executed when the locals feared the Republican government might order him freed. At the end of the war, some 15,000 Republicans waited on the docks in vain for the Republican Navy to rescue them from Nationalist reprisals. Several hundred, it is said, committed suicide. Behind the cathedral, on C/San Agustín, is the **Museu de Belenes** (*open summer Tues–Fri and Sat am 10–2 and 5–8; winter Tues–Fri and Sat am 10–2 and 4.30–7.30; closed Sat pm, Sun and Mon*), a nativity museum with a dizzying collection of Christmas figures (some for sale) from Spain and around the world, including a winsome red set from Japan.

The **Ayuntamiento** (*C/R. Altamira; open for visits Mon–Fri 8–3*) has an elegant Baroque façade and is near the **Museum of 20th-century Art** (also known as the

other branches: Rambla de Méndez Nuñes 23; at Platja de El Postiguet; and at Platja de Sant Joan (*the latter is open summer only*).
Hospital, C/San Juan, **t** 965 90 83 00.
Post Office, Pza Gabriel Miró.
Telephone Office, Av. Constitución 10 (there's another one in the bus station).

Shopping

The best streets for shopping stem from the main drag, especially **Avenida Maisonnave** and **Calle Gerona**; the latter is also home to **Croissanterie Chantal**, which serves delicious home-made cakes and fresh fruit juices. For local specialities like the delicious *túrron*, or the local date liqueur from Elche, try **El Túnel**, C/Sant Lorenç 34, or **Toní y María**, C/San Nicolas 10. For fresh produce, head straight for the delightful Art Deco-ish **Mercado Central** on Av. Alfonso X el Sabio.

Where to Stay

Alicante ✉ 03000

You will find hotels in every price range spread throughout the town, but the most popular are those near the Explanada. The cheapest places are around Santa María church, which is a great location if you want to have the nightlife of the Barrio de Santa Cruz on your doorstep.

Luxury

*******Sidi San Juan**, C/La Doblada s/n, Cabo de la Huerta, **t** 965 16 13 00, **f** 965 16 33 46, *sidisanjuan@ctv.es*, *www.hotelessidi.es*. Big, modern, exclusive hotel with all the luxuries imaginable – as well as views over Alicante's favourite beach.

Expensive

******Meliá Alicante**, Platja de El Postiguet s/n, **t** 965 20 50 00, **f** 965 20 47 56, *melia.alicante@solmelia.es*. A big chain hotel set in a huge, modern, self-contained complex overlooking the beach, complete with **restaurants** and shops. Rooms have amazing views and private terraces.

******Hotel Mediterránea Plaza**, Pza del Ayuntamiento 6, **t** 965 15 61 85, **f** 965 15 39 36, *medplaza@teleline.es*. A smart and well-equipped hotel in a renovated old building, with grand views over the Baroque Town Hall and a good, central location. The rooms on the upper floors are the sunniest and have the best views.

Moderate

*****NH Hotel Cristal**, C/López Torregrosa 9, **t** 965 14 36 59, *nhcristal@nh-hoteles.es*, *www.nh-hoteles.es*. Set a few blocks from the Explanada, this features an eye-catching crystal façade to match its name. All rooms are attractive – if a little small – and come with bath and a/c.

Museu de la Asegurada), just off pedestrian C/Mayor. It's housed in an elegant 17th-century former granary – the oldest civic building in the city – and displays works by Picasso, Braque, Gris, Miró and others (*open summer Tues–Sat 10–2 and 5–9 (winter afternoons 4–8), Sun and hols 10.30–2.30*). The museum overlooks the tiny, attractive **Plaza de Sant María**, named for the florid Baroque **Church de Santa María** (*open daily 7.30–12.30 and 5.30–8; visitors are requested to make a small donation towards the restoration of the church*) which looms over it. Begun in the 13th–14th centuries, the church features an extraordinary golden Plateresque altar, with a resplendent Virgin peeking from a heavily gilded cave. There's more Baroque architecture at the **Palacio Maisonnave** (*C/Labradores 9; open Mon–Fri 9–2, Sat 9–1; closed Sun*), an 18th-century aristocratic mansion which now houses the municipal archives, built on the remains of the Roman necropolis.

The city's latest attraction is the **MARQ**, a brand-new, state-of-the-art **archaeology museum** (*open Tues–Sat 10–2 and 4–8, Sun and hols 10–2; adm*) located behind the

****Hs Galicia**, C/Arquitecto Morell 1, **t** 965 22 50 93. More reasonably priced; two blocks from the bus station, in a modern building.

Inexpensive–Cheap

****Montecarlo**, C/San Francisco 20, **t** 965 20 67 22. A good budget *hostal*, close to the town centre and near the beach.

***Hotel Marítimo**, C/Valdés 13, **t** 965 21 99 85. A simple, well-priced hotel just a block back from the Explanada, with large, airy rooms and friendly staff.

***P. Les Monges**, First Floor, C/Monjas 2, **t** 965 21 50 46. A truly special place: behind the Ayuntamiento and charmingly run with prettily decorated rooms – ochre walls and wicker furniture – lots of eccentric art, and satellite TV, music, a/c and parking. Some rooms (*moderate*) even have Jacuzzi and sauna for a bit extra.

***P. Versalles**, C/Villavieja 3, **t** 965 21 45 93. Fantastic bargain for anyone on a tight budget: a handful of large rooms are arranged around a jasmine-scented, vine-canopied courtyard, set with tables and a TV in the evenings. Shared bathrooms and kitchen; very mellow atmosphere.

Eating Out

Expensive

Delfín, Explanada de España 12, **t** 965 21 49 11. Alicante's best restaurant: delicious Alicantino versions of Valencian rice dishes, innovative international dishes and excellent seafood, all served with fine sea views.

Dársena, Pso del Puerto, just off the Explanada, **t** 965 20 75 89. In an even more scenic location with a bright and shiny interior, wonderful sea views, this is a favourite with Alacantinos. The speciality is rice dishes; there are more than a hundred varieties to choose from.

Nou Manoulin, C/Villegas 3, **t** 965 20 03 68. Housed in old brick wine cellars close to the ancient centre of town: the delicious local delicacies and cosy traditional atmosphere mean booking is essential. If you can't squeeze in, try the excellent tapas at the crowded bar.

Piripiri, C/Oscar Espla 30, **t** 965 22 79 40. Elegant eaterie serving good regional dishes. Try the *fideos*: a northern Alicante speciality using vermicelli noodles instead of rice, but save room for the delicious *mousse de Jijona túrron*. There's another popular tapas bar here, too.

Moderate

La Goleta, Explanada de España 6, **t** 965 20 03 38. With a sea view from the terrace: specializing in seafood rice dishes and mixed grills. They also offer good-value (*inexpensive*) set menus.

O'Pote Galego, Pza Santísima Faz 6, **t** 965 20 80 84. Just off an attractive square, the Galician specialities here are a must: lovely castle of Santa Barbara on Pza Doctor Gómex Ulla. It's very engaging, with finds from prehistory up to the Middle Ages, all given a bit of 21st-century pep with plenty of audiovisuals and buttons to push.

For a delightful evening stroll, head up the steep streets of the old quarter towards the tiny **Ermita de Sant Roque**, with its revered painting of the Gipsy Christ above the altar, and carry on up through narrow, stepped passages overflowing with flowers in bright blue ceramic pots to the 18th-century **Ermita de Santa Cruz**, which has spell-binding views across the rooftops and out to sea.

Alicante's Beaches

Most visitors, when they're not lounging on Alicante's fine beaches, are strolling down the shady **Explanada de España** with its flamboyant mosaics. The **Platja de El Postiguet**, at the end of the Explanada, can get very, very crowded (and none too clean) in the summer, and sometimes it seems just as many people take the bus or

grills and *merluza a la gallega*. There's also a good-value *menú del día*.

Bar Luis, C/Pedro Sebastián 7, **t** 965 21 14 46. Cool and elegant with a distinguished wine cellar and a Spanish orientated international menu full of unusual dishes created with real flair. Try the lasagne with spinach, prawns and salmon, or excellent tapas. *Closed Sun.*

Restaurante Alebrije, Pza Gabriel Miró 11, **t** 965 21 68 14. A swanky and sophisticated new restaurant with minimalist décor and a fashionable clientele. The menu offers contemporary Mediterranean cuisine.

Inexpensive

Regina, Av. Niza 19, **t** 965 26 41 39. One of Alicante's great bargains: good tapas, *paella* and seafood.

Mesón Labradores, C/Labradores 19. Good tapas, and typically Alicantan with *azulejo* walls crammed with pictures and ceramics. If it's full, try its smaller branch around the corner on C/San Pasuel 3. *Closed Mon.*

Restaurante Mixte Vegetariano, Pza Santa María. Cosy, friendly, mainly veggie restaurant with a perfect setting opposite the old church of Santa María.

Rincón de António, Patronato de Santa Cruz, just above Pza del Carmen. In the old Santa Cruz quarter, tourist-free and a favourite with the locals. No menu, but the friendly owner will be only too happy to give you a good selection.

Entertainment and Nightlife

Bodega Las Garrafas, squeezed between the modern convenience cafés, at C/Major 33. Tiny and very unusual *bodega*, filled with all things ancient: a cash till on the counter and an eccentric collection of oil lamps, cow bells and even a British police helmet hanging from the ceiling. The walls are covered with pictures of the owner with famous visitors over the last 40 years: Hemingway and Dalí are there.

The area around Pza del Carmen and below San Cristóbal, known as **El Barrio**, comes alive with bars after 1am. Every street here is crammed with bars, pubs and clubs. One of the strangest is **Celestial**, C/de San Pascual s/n, stuffed with fabulously kitsch décor and religious knick-knacks. Around Pza de Quizano and C/Carmen, you'll find **Agustito**, **Yatevale**, **Armstrong** and **Pisamorena** – along with hundreds of others. At the corner of C/Labradores and C/San Isidro is the small, hip **Austin** bar, with tables out on the street. If jazz is more your speed, try **Armstrong's**, C/Carmen 3, with live acts at weekends. Just behind the Explanada, C/San Fernando has plenty of lively bars, mainly popular with a teenage crowd, as well as the big disco **Bugatti**.

In the summer the place to be is the **Sant Joan** beach, which is overrun with all-night bars and discos. The FGV train runs all night as far as Altea.

train six and a half kilometres north to bigger and cleaner **Platja de Sant Joan**, on the other side of the jutting cape (the Cabo de las Huertas). The little coves at the end of the Cape are favourites with nudists, although the big beach, **Playa de Albufereta** (*a tram runs between here and the city beach of El Postiguet, see above*), which swoops around the southern side of the cape, is more family-oriented. The FGV train up the coast passes some **quiet coves** such as the small beach near Amerador station. It's possible to explore on the ride: just keep your eyes peeled and be prepared to jump off quickly when a nice beach catches your fancy.

Between Alicante and the Platja de Sant Joan, you can visit the **Monasterio de La Santa Faz** (*open 9–12 and 4.30–sunset; take the bus No.C-3 from Pza del Mar*), built to enshrine the supposed handkerchief that Santa Veronica loaned to Christ as he carried the Cross – although for authenticity it has to compete with a similar handkerchief in the Vatican.

A secondary road off the coast leads (24km from Alicante) to Busot and the **Cava dels Canalobres** (*open 1 Oct–20 June daily 11–5.50; 21 June–31 Sept daily 10.30–7.50; for information call **t** 965 69 92 50*), with stalactites and strange formations, where concerts are held occasionally in the summer.

Around Alicante

Xixona (Jijona) and Villena

In Alicante you may have noticed shops stacked to the ceiling with *turrón*, a nougat sweet made of local almonds and honey. Nearly all of it comes from **Xixona**, on the main road to Alcoi (try the 1880 *Crema de Jijona*), where a **Turrón Museum** will show you how it's made. The town lies below the Puerta de la Carrasqueta, a breathtaking mountain pass offering incredible views out across the valleys and the Natural Park of the Font Roja where there are some good walking and mountain-biking trails. Otherwise, this is a busy region: nearby **Ibi** makes most of Spain's toys. One company claims to be the world's largest producer of dolls' eyeballs; you can see some of them, along with a collection of historic playthings, at the **Museu Valenciano del Juguete** (***t** 966 55 02 26*), set in a pretty 18th-century mansion.

The plain west of Ibi is studded with rocky outcrops topped with ruins of medieval **castles**, with villages creeping up the flanks and tiny churches standing isolated in lush fields and orchards. Despite the ugly rash of modern buildings thrown up around them, some of these villages have retained their sleepy medieval cores; the peaceful village of **Biar** is overlooked by a 12th-century Arabic fortress, and **Sax**, a picturesque cluster of tiled roofs, huddles beneath a squat fortress with crenellated walls clamped to the peak. The most striking castle of the area looms over **Villena**; its huge, square-towered citadel dates from the 15th century, as do many of the old noble houses. Villena's Gothic church of **Santiago** is decorated with fluted columns and strange motifs, while the **Ayuntamiento** (1707) has a gracious courtyard and an **archaeology museum**. Unlike many dusty provincial collections, this one is worth a detour for the

Treasure of Villena: a hoard of solid gold bracelets, tiaras, bowls and rings discovered near the town in 1963. The pieces have been dated back to the Bronze Age (1000 BC) and were made by the ancestors of the Iberians.

Elche (Elx)

Elche, 20 kilometres west of Alicante, makes two claims on the world's attention. First, Spain's most famous piece of ancient art, *La Dama de Elche*, was unearthed here, now in Madrid's archaeology museum (*see* **Madrid**, p.509). Secondly, it has the only date-palm grove in Europe. The Moors planted the first palms, and now the trees – some 200,000 of them – nearly surround Elche. Although they produce a crop of dates (no other palms in Europe do), they are economically more valuable for their fronds, which are tied up to bleach a pale yellow and then shipped throughout Spain for Palm Sunday. Often you'll see one tied to a balcony, not because the owner has forgotten to take it down after Easter, but because the fronds are widely believed to ward off lightning. The palms are best seen in the **Huerto del Cura** (*C/Federico García Sanchis; open daily 9–9; www.huertadelcura*) just east of town, where you can pay your respects to the unusual, seven-branched Imperial Palm, thought to be around 150 years old. It's an immaculate little city, with a few scattered monuments between the pristine apartment blocks; the tourist office produces a leaflet describing a circular walk which covers most of them.

The Lady of Elche bust was discovered in 1897 in **La Alcudia** south of town. Since then further excavations have revealed nine successive civilizations, documented by a small **museum** on the site (*Ctra Dolores, 2km from town; open April–Sept Tues–Sat 10–2 and 4–8, Sun 10–2; Oct–Mar Tues–Sat 10–5, Sun 10–2; adm*). The blue-domed **Basílica de Santa María** has an elaborate 17th-century Baroque façade; ask to climb the tower for the view across the palm plantations. If you miss Elche's famous mystery play (*see* 'Festivals', p.240), the little **Museu de la Festa** (*C/Major de la Villa; open winter Tues–Sat 10–1 and 4.30–8.30; summer Tues–Sat 10–1 and 5–9; closed Mon; adm*), which is the starting point for the ceremony, gives an audiovisual taste of the performance year-round. Just behind the Basílica are the **Arabic baths**, which were converted into a convent in the 14th century (*open April–Sept Tues–Sat 10–1.30 and 4.30–8; Mar–Oct Tues–Sat 10–5; closed Sun and Mon; adm free*). Just north of the cathedral, in a restored 15th-century palace on the edge of the municipal park, another **archaeology museum** (*open Tues–Sun 10–1 and 4–8; closed Mon*) contains a copy of La Dama de Elche, along with finds from prehistoric, Phoenician and Roman times. There's also a Greek headless torso of Venus. On Plaza de Arrabal a small **Museum of Contemporary Art** (*open Tues–Sun 10–1 and 5–8; closed Mon*) contains paintings, sculptures and ceramics by modern Valencian artists. The stolid Gothic **Ajuntament** (Town Hall) has been in use since 1445, and just off the square in front of it is the charming **Calendura Tower**, with two mechanical figures which have been chiming the hours since the 18th century.

Orihuela, also on the road to Murcia, is an oasis; a prosperous town set in its own very fertile *huerta*. Los Reyes Catolicas held court here in 1488, and it remained an important city long after; there are plenty of grand reminders of its illustrious past

Getting Around

By Bus

The helpful **information office** in the bus station can help you get to grips with the confusing number of different bus companies.

MOLLA buses go from Alicante to Elche every half-hour from 7am to 9pm (Mon–Fri) and hourly from 8am to 9pm (weekends).

BAILE buses connect Alicante with Santa Pola hourly, on weekdays from 7.30am to 9pm, on weekends from 9am to 9pm.

COSTA AZUL buses go south from Santa Pola from 7am to 8pm every 2 hrs.

Tourist Information

Elche: Pza del Parc, **t** 965 45 27 47.
Orihuela: Francisco Díez 25, **t** 965 30 27 47.
Santa Pola: Pza Diputación 6, **t** 966 69 22 76.
Torrevieja: Pza Ruiz Capdepont, **t** 965 71 59 36.

Festivals

Elche: Misteri d'Elx, *mid-Aug*. A medieval mystery play still takes place each year in Elche's Basílica; the only mystery play in the world to have survived the ban decreed by the Council of Trent in the 17th century.

Where to Stay and Eat

Elche ✉ 03200

★★★★**Huerto del Cura**, Porta de la Morera 14, **t** 965 61 00 11, **f** 965 42 19 10 (*expensive; weekends moderate*). An associate *parador*, with bungalows scattered around the palm grove, as well as a pool, tennis courts and an very good range of other sports facilities; all rooms have a/c and private bars (*see* below for **restaurant**).

★★★**Hotel Mileno**, Prolongación Curtidores s/n, **t** 966 61 34 01, **f** 966 61 20 60 (*moderate*). A smart, modern choice with excellent facilities including a pool, set in amongst palm groves and close to the Huerta del Cura.

★★**HsR Candilejas**, C/Dr Ferrán 19, **t** 965 46 65 12, **f** 965 46 66 52 (*inexpensive*). Within easy walking distance of the Parque Municipal and palm groves: simple but clean; fine for an overnight stay.

Elche can also claim three clean and relatively unspoilt **beaches** on the outskirts of town, where it is possible to find good cheap accommodation.

Hs Maruja, at La Marina, **t** 965 41 91 26 (*cheap*). Basic but clean and well situated at the water's edge. *Open Mar–Sept only*.

scattered among the narrow streets of the old town, including the idiosyncratic **Cathedral** (*open Mon–Fri 10–1.30 and 5–7.30, Sat 10–1.30; closed Sun; adm to museum*). Finished in 1355, its interior is a fantasy of spiralling pillars and corkscrew-rib vaulting; the **cathedral museum** has a Velázquez and other masters in its fine collection. The delightful cloister which adjoins it belongs to the destroyed Convent of La Merced and was moved here in 1942. Perhaps the town's most over-the-top monument is the **Church of Santa Domingo** (*open Tues–Sat 9.30–1.30 and 5–8, Sun and hols 10–2; adm free*), which became a university in 1569. It has two large cloisters; a subdued Renaissance one with gardens, and a frilly Baroque one which was added in the 18th century. The old refectory contains some of the finest examples of *azulejo* tiling in València, but the *pièce de résistance* is the church itself, a dizzying swirl of sublimely kitsch cherubs and gilt which cover every inch of the walls and roof. A little further out of town, well beyond the university, is **El Palmeral**, Orihuela's own palm grove, one of the largest in Spain. Back in town, the Gothic **Church of Sant Justa y Rufina** (*open Mon–Fri 10–1.30 and 5–7.30, Sat 10–1.30; closed Sun; small donation requested*) prickles with gargoyles, including a small fleet taking wing from the square belltower, built in the 14th century. There's another fine example of Catalan Gothic in the little **church of Santiago** (*open Mon–Fri 10–1.30 and 5–7.30, Sat 10–1.30; closed Sun; small donation

Els Capellans, Porta de la Morera 14, **t** 966 61 00 11, **f** 965 42 19 10 (*expensive*). The restaurant of the *parador* can claim to be one of the town's finest, with views over the palms; some of the desserts are made with the local dates.

Restaurante Parque Municipal, Psg de l'Estació s/n, **t** 965 45 34 15 (*moderate*). Specializing in rice dishes under the palms in the city's central park; there's even a terrace with tables scattered around a fake bust of *La Dama de Elche*.

Mesón E1 Granaino, across the river at Josep María Buch 40, **t** 965 46 01 47 (*moderate*). Decked out in traditional style and serving varied *paellas*, *cocidos* and the local speciality, *tarta de almendra*. *Closed Sun*.

Orihuela ✉ 03100

★★**Hs Rey Teodomiro**, Av. Teodomiro 10, **t** 966 74 33 48 (*moderate–inexpensive*). The only choice in the town itself: it's set in a bland, modern building not too far from the station, but the management is kindly, and the rooms are spacious, attractively decorated and well equipped.

★★★**Montepiedra**, right on Orihuela's beach at Dehesa de Campoamor, **t** 965 32 03 00 (*moderate*). Set in gardens, with a large, pretty pool and spacious rooms.

Santa Pola ✉ 03130

★★**Hotel Casa del Gobernador**, on Isla de Tabarca, **t** 965 96 08 86, **f** 965 11 42 60. This is the only hotel on the island; perfect for divers or bird-watchers who want an early start, or anyone who wants to cut off from the hubbub of the coast for a while.

★★**Hotel Patilla**, C/Elche 29, **t** 965 41 10 15, **f** 965 41 52 95 (*hotel and restaurant moderate*). A well-located, decent hotel with a remarkably good **restaurant** all kitted out like the interior of a ship.

★**Hs Michel**, C/Felipe II, **t** 965 41 18 42 (*moderate–inexpensive*). Reasonably well-priced *hostal* just 400m from the beach.

Batiste, Playa de Poniente, **t** 965 41 14 85 (*moderate*). The best spot for seafood.

Palomar, Playa de Levante s/n, **t** 965 41 32 00 (*moderate*). With a magnificent terrace right on the seafront and good local specialities; there's also a well-priced *menú del día*.

Torrevieja ✉ 03180

★★**La Cibeles**, Av. Dr. Marañón 26, **t** 965 71 00 12 (*moderate*). A pleasant beach *hostal* situated on the coast.

★**Hotel Juan Carlos**, C/Apolo 87, **t** 965 71 69 69, **f** 965 70 70 94 (*moderate*). This offers large, light rooms with a/c – which can block out the traffic noise.

requested) just opposite the tourist office. Orihuela also has a host of smaller museums, including two dedicated to the town's biggest festivals: the **Museu de Semana Santa** (*open Mon–Fri 10–1 and 5–7, Sat 10–1; closed Sun; small donation requested*), with pictures and costumes from the Holy Week processions; and the **Museu de la Reconquista** (*open Mon–Fri 11–1 and 5–7; closed Sat and Sun; small donation requested*), with exhibits dedicated to the battles between the Moors and the Christians which are enacted annually in the middle of July. The former home of local poet **Miguel Hernandez** (*open Tues–Sat 10–2 and 5–7, Sun and hols 10–2; closed Mon; adm free*) has been opened as a small museum; it displays a selection of his personal possessions set in a characteristic late 19th-century house with a corral for goats and a small orchard. If you want to see one of the grander mansions of the era to find out how the other half lived, visit the **Palacio de Rubalcava** (*open Tues–Fri 10–2 and 5–8, Sun and hols 10–2; closed Mon and Sat; adm free*). Apart from housing the tourist office, there is some magnificent tiling, as well as fine examples of furniture, pottery, sculpture and paintings dating back three centuries. If you get the chance, visit the **Teatro Circo**, a fanciful, circular theatre from the late 19th century, designed for circuses as well as regular theatrical performances, which has been prettily restored.

South of Alicante

The landscapes south of Alicante are mostly flat and not especially attractive, though in February the blossoming almonds provide a pretty lace edging. The resorts to the south are also less exciting. **Santa Pola**, the largest, has good beaches and a landmark, fortified **Isla de Tabarca**, which you can visit on an excursion boat. The island is surrounded by an underwater marine reserve, and arranges diving expeditions. The old Governor's residence has been converted into the only hotel on the island (*see* p.241). Behind Santa Pola, the salt flats have been converted into a nature reserve, with flamingos and other birds (*guided tours are available; check with the information office*). **Guardamar del Segura** is more scenic than Santa Pola with its palms and pines; **Torrevieja** has been blighted with scores of modern hotels. Still, the rocky bay at the centre of the town has been turned into an amazing swimming pool, and there's a long, lively street market which draws big crowds for the evening *paseo*. To the south there are some tranquil beaches, as yet not too developed, belonging to Orihuela. Known collectively as **Las Playas de Orihuela**, the best and easiest to get to are the Playa La Zenia and the Playa Cabo Roig.

La Comunidad de Murcia

In the division into autonomous regions of post-Franco Spain, no one wanted Murcia, so it became its own little region. In opinion polls, with questions like 'who would you like your daughter to marry?' the Murcians always come out at the very bottom. They don't really deserve it; they just happen to have been the first emigrants looking for work in Barcelona at the turn of the century. On the other hand the Moors, who gave it its name, *Musiyah*, loved it well and farmed its *huerta*; most Muslim scholars would say that Ibn Al-Arabi of Murcia (1165–1240), mystic and poet of love, was the greatest Spaniard that ever lived.

Murcia Town

Whatever other Spaniards may think, Murcia is a congenial little city. The streets of the old quarter follow the twists and turns of the ancient Moorish town, dotted with a rich collection of Renaissance and Baroque churches, many converted from former Mosques. The **Cathedral** (*currently undergoing major restoration, so that large sections of it are closed; due to reopen mid-2002*), not far from the river, is easy to find by its unusual **tower** (*ask the museum custodian to open the door if you'd like to climb up*), built by four different architects between 1521 and 1792. The cathedral itself has a fine Baroque façade and Gothic portals on either side. The interior, in a mixture of styles, is notable for its 15th-century **Vélez Chapel**, an exuberant Plateresque national monument. An urn on the main altar contains an odd relic: the innards of Alfonso the Wise. In the Cathedral **museum** (*open daily 9–1 and 4–8*) a Roman sarcophagus relief of the muses shares space with a collection of religious artefacts.

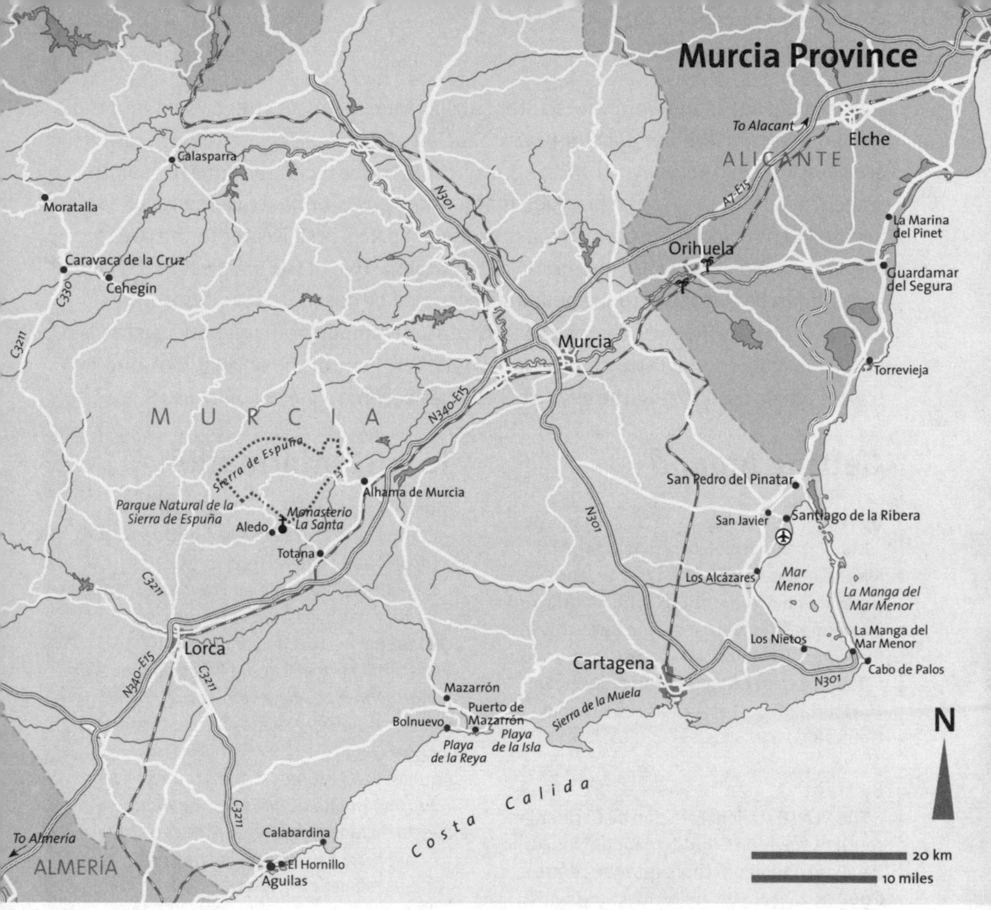

From the cathedral head up the pedestrian C/de Trapería, where, at the first block, stands the **Casino** (*also undergoing major restoration, but it's still possible to sit in one of the salons, and ladies shouldn't miss the chance to visit the loos which are covered with a sea of primping nymphs*), which manages to combine exuberantly a dozen eclectic styles: there's a Moorish vestibule, an English-style reading room and, most extravagant of all, a florid Louis XV ballroom, dripping with monstrous, glittering chandeliers and frescoes. Just off the C/de Trapería is the **Teatro Romeu**, on a large, pleasant square. The 19th-century theatre has already been incinerated twice – and a local legend predicts a third fire because this temple of frivolity was built on a monastic graveyard. Further north is Murcia's **archaeology museum** (*Pso Alfonso X 5; open Mon–Fri 9–2 and 4–8, Sat 10–1.30; closed Sun; adm free*), which houses a good collection of Iberian artefacts and Roman sculptures and coins.

Not far from here is the 17th-century **convent** which now houses Murcia's **university**, but has retained it's pretty double-decker cloister. This is one of the most animated neighbourhoods, with dozens of tapas bars and terrace cafés. Just to the southeast is the **Museo de Bellas Artes** (*Obispo Frutos 12; open summer Mon–Fri 9–2, Sat 11–2; winter Mon–Fri 9–2 and 5–7.30, Sat 11–2; closed Sun; adm*), with a collection of paintings dating from the 15th century, including a *St Jerome* by Ribera.

On the far side of the Gran Vía Escultor Salzillo, Murcia's main street, you'll find the **Salzillo Museum** (*Pza San Agustín 3; open Sept–June Tues–Sun 9.30–1 and 4–7, closed Mon; July and Aug daily 9.30–1 and 4–7*), dedicated to the works of Murcian sculptor Francisco Salzillo (1707–83) who made many of the *pasos*, or floats, used in Murcia's Semana Santa processions, which make it one of Spain's best. Nearer to the river are the adjoining plazas of Las Flores and Santa Catalina, two of the prettiest in the city, surrounded by elegant Baroque buildings occupied by dozens of bars, restaurants and cafés. Just by the river, there's the 13th-century **Almudí** (granary) now used as a municipal gallery, and a stretch of Moorish walls and one of the ancient look-out towers which used to ring the city – this too has become a gallery of local art.

Getting Around

By Air

Murcia's airport is located near the Mar Menor in San Javier, **t** 968 17 20 20, and there are daily connections with Madrid and Barcelona. The low-cost airline Buzz now also flies direct to Murcia, **t** (UK) 0870 240 7070, **t** (Spain) 917 49 66 33, *www.buzzaway.com*. The Iberia office is at Av. Alfonso el Sabio, **t** 968 28 50 93.

By Train

The **RENFE** station (Estación de Carmen) is south of town, on C/Industria (bus Nos.9 and 11 will take you from there into the centre); **t** 968 25 21 54. There are connections with Águilas, Alicante, Lorca, Cartagena, València, Albacete, Madrid and Barcelona. A **narrow-gauge train** links Cartagena with Los Nietos (near Cabo de Palos and its beaches) once every 1½hrs, and this service is complemented by hourly FEVE buses between Cartagena and Cabo de Palos.

By Bus

Murcia's central bus station is in the west of town on Pza de Casanova, **t** 968 29 22 11 (you can get some good tapas in the station bar). There are buses going throughout the day to Orihuela, Caravaca, Lorca, Cartagena, Águilas and Mazarrón (and from here, frequent connections to Puerto de Mazarrón); there are less frequent buses towards the Mar Menor: San Pedro, Los Alcázares, Cabo de Palos and La Manga del Mar Menor. Also connections with Granada, Sevilla, Almería, Mojácar, Barcelona, Málaga and Torrevieja.

Tourist Information

Murcia: Regional Office, Palacio González Campuzano, Plaza Romea, **t** 968 27 76 76 (*open Mon–Fri 10–2 only*); City Office, Plano de San Francisco 8, **t** 968 35 87 20, *www.ayto-murcia.es/turismo*.

Cartagena: Puertas de San José, Pza Bastarreche, **t** 968 50 64 83, *cartagena@marmenor.net*, *www.ayto-cartagena.es*.

Lorca, Palacio de Guevara, C/Lope Gisbert 12, **t** 968 46 61 57.

Águilas: Pza Antonio Cortijo, **t** 968 49 32 85, *turismo@aiguilas.org*, *www.aguilas.org*.

Puerto de Mazarrón: Av. Dr Meca 20 (Edif. Bahía Mar), **t** 968 59 44 26, *mazarron.turismo@serconet.com*, *www.serconet.com/mazarron*.

Moratalla: in the Ayuntamiento, C/Constitución 22, **t** 968 73 02 58.

Los Alcázares (Mar Menor): C/Fuster 63, **t** 968 17 13 61.

La Manga del Mar Menor: Urb. Castillo del Mar, San Javier, **t** 968 14 18 12.

San Pedro del Pinatar: Parque de los Reyes de España, **t** 968 18 23 01.

Festivals

Murcia: Semana Santa, *Easter*. The city's Holy Week processions have earned a reputation for being some of the finest in Spain.

Caravaca: Caballos del Vino, *3 May*. Here, the commemoration of the Battle of the Moors and Christians takes on a different spin from those in other towns in the region, after Caravaca's Knights opted for wine over water (*see* p.248).

Opposite is the **Véronicas market**, piled high with glistening fresh local produce; Murcian vegetables are acknowleged to be the finest in Spain, and this is also the place to find the famous fresh prawns from the Mar Menor (*see* below).

Inland to Lorca and Moratalla

The main highway south to Andalucía blasts through the vast, dusty plain south of Murcia, skimming past a ragbag collection of small towns and the scrubby slopes of distant mountains. **Alhama de Murcia**, about 35 kilometres southwest of Murcia, is

Where to Stay and Eat

Murcia ✉ 30000

★★★★**Hotel Conde de Floridablanca**, Corbalán 7, **t** 968 21 46 26, **f** 968 21 32 15, *cataloni@hoteles-catalonia.es*, *www.hoteles-catalonia.es* (*expensive–moderate*). Delightful, air-conditioned Baroque palace in the old town.

★★★★**NH Rincón de Pepe**, Pza Apóstoles 34, **t** 968 21 22 39, **f** 968 22 17 44 (*expensive*). More modern, and also with a/c (a definite plus when the torrid *leveche* wind blows in the summer): perhaps the most comfortable rooms. It has a **restaurant** (*see* below).

★★★★**Arco de San Juan**, Pza de Ceballos 10, **t** 968 21 04 55, **f** 968 22 08 09, *reservas@arcosanjuan.com*, *www.arcosanjuan.com*. Modern, elegant and comfortable.

★★★**Hispano II**, C/Radio Murcia 3, **t** 968 21 61 52, **f** 968 216 859, *hotel@hotelhispano.com*, *www.hispano.com*. Comfortable rooms with a/c at reasonable prices. Its cheaper, scruffier sister around the corner (**P. Hispano I**, C/Trapería 8, ***t*** as above) is only worth it if you're on a budget. The main hotel **restaurant** (*moderate*) is a favourite with Murcians.

★★★**Pacoche Murcia**, Cartagena 30, **t** 968 21 33 85 (*moderate*). Centrally located with its own garage, this is functional but quiet.

★★**La Huertanica**, C/Infantes 3–5, **t** 968 21 76 68, **f** 968 21 25 04 (*moderate*). Another central, if bland option; the top rooms have amazing views.

★★**P. Segura**, Pza Camachos 19, **t** 968 21 12 81 (*cheap*). Over Murcia's old bridge: comfortable, basic rooms.

★**Hs Pacoche**, C/González Cebrián 9, **t** 968 21 76 05 (*cheap*). Ageing, but the price is right.

★**P. Perro Azul**, C/Simon Garcia 19, **t** 968 22 17 00. You can't miss 'the blue dog': it's painted bright cobalt blue. Decent, comfortable rooms, a good bar downstairs and a good, central location for partying in the bars around Pza las Flores. There's a laid-back, mellow bar downstairs, with reggae accompanying the tapas.

The **hotel restaurants** of the **Rincón de Pepe** (*expensive*), **Hispano** (*moderate*) and **Arco de San Juan** (*expensive*) all enjoy excellent reputations; Rincón de Pepe's is undoubtedly the finest in town (*see above for phone numbers*).

Los Apóstoles, Pza Apóstoles 1, **t** 968 21 77 79 (*moderate*). Touristy but decent. Traditional local cuisine, with the menu changing daily and pretty brick décor. *Closed Aug.*

Paco Pepe, C/Madre de Dios 15, **t** 968 21 92 76 (*moderate*). Solid Murcian dishes at this very popular little local restaurant, which does a good *menú del día* (*inexpensive*).

Bocatta's Todo 100, C/Platería 44 (*cheap*). Small square with a kiosk, run by nice people and with a friendly atmosphere; very cheap fuel sandwiches.

Alegría, Pza San Antolín 4, **t** 968 29 09 10. Health-food shop near the bus station – gorgeous wholemeal seed bread.

There are several good areas In Murcia for **tapas**: try around the cathedral, where there are several traditional establishments. Perhaps the best is the very stylish, elegant **La Muralla** bar at the hotel Rincón de Pepe, which has incorporated a stretch of the Moorish walls. Also good, and a bit more down to earth, are the bars around Pza de las Flores. There are several lively, younger tapas bars – and plain old drinking bars – around the huddled at the foot of the **Sierra de Espuña**, a Natural Park, which is Murcia's rainiest corner and consequently startlingly green and lush after the pale aridity of the plain. The park is home to deer, wild boars, black vulture and golden eagles, and there are some truly breathtaking views from the serene peaks. Alhama de Murcia has a winning, if shabby, medieval core, and a crumbling castle, and is a good base if you want to go walking in the hills. Also on the fringes of the Park is tiny **Aledo**, another ancient Moorish town, with the remnants of the Arabic walls and tower, and the rosy 15th-century church of Santa Maria la Real. The larger, nearby town of **Totana** is surrounded by hills pocked with strange stone domes, which were used to collect snow before the spring thaw. It's long been a centre for ceramic production, and is

university. Perhaps unexpectedly, Murcia has got a lively gay scene; check out the **Maricoco** bar (C/Vitorio), where you'll get plenty of pointers as to where to head afterwards.

Lorca ✉ 30800

★★★★**Hotel Alameda**, C/Musso Valiente 8, **t** 968 40 66 00 (*moderate*). Much nicer than seems likely from the outside, and so well located that it might make the price (very reasonable for the facilities) worthwhile.

★**P. del Carmen**, Rincón de los Valientes 3, **t** 968 46 64 59 (*inexpensive*). Centrally located, with clean rooms and very friendly staff.

★**Hotel Félix**· Av. Fuerzas Armadas 146, **t** 968 46 76 54 (*cheap*). Not very central but the cheapest place to stay in town. It's recently been renovated and all rooms have TV.

Casa Roberto, C/Musso Valient, **t** 968 44 16 17 (*inexpensive*). Good regional cuisine served up in modern surroundings.

Barcas Casa Cándido, C/Santo Domingo 13, **t** 968 44 16 17 (*inexpensive*). Has an excellent daily menu and typical Murcian rustic décor.

Cartagena ✉ 30200

★★**Los Habaneros**, San Diego 60, **t** 968 50 52 50 (*moderate*). At the entrance to the old city, this has air-conditioned rooms and a decent **restaurant** serving local dishes (*menú del día inexpensive; menu dégustacion verging on expensive*).

★★**Hotel Cartagenera**, C/Jara 3, beside Pza Tres Reyes, **t** 968 50 25 00 (*moderate*). Slightly cheaper and more central, if rather bland.

La Tartana, Puerta de Murcia 14, **t** 968 50 00 11, **f** 968 52 21 31 (*inexpensive*). There are good local dishes at the restaurant, and delicious tapas at the bar.

Mazarrón ✉ 30800

★★**Hotel Guillermo II**, C/Carmen 7, **t** 968 59 04 36 (*moderate–inexpensive*). Good service, pleasant rooms and a decent **restaurant**.

★★★**Hotel Bahia**, Playa de la Reya s/n, **t** 968 59 40 00, **f** 968 15 40 23, *hotelbahia@ctv.es* (*moderate*). Good for holidays, near the sea.

★★★**Hotel La Cumbre**, Urb La Cumbre, **t** 968 59 58 61, **f** 968 59 44 50 (*moderate*). Has wonderful sea views, large well-equipped rooms, and a huge pool.

Miramar, Playa de la Isla, **t** 968 59 40 08 (*moderate*). Near the port and serving good-value shellfish platters; good tapas, too.

Virgen del Mar, Pso de la Sal, **t** 968 59 50 57 (*moderate*). One of the better restaurants; great views and good for rice and seafood.

El Puerto, Pza del Mar, **t** 968 59 48 05 (*moderate*). Another firm favourite for fish, at the entrance to the fishermen's port.

Águilas ✉ 30880

★★★**Carlos III**, C/Rey Carlos III 22, **t** 968 41 16 50, *correo@hotelcarlosiii.com* (*moderate*). Small, prettily located near the sea with clean '70s-style rooms bursting with facilities and popular with Spanish families. *Open all year.*

★★**Hotel Sur**, Torre de Cope 24, Calabardina (9km from Águilas), **t** 968 41 94 66, **f** 968 41 94 66 (*moderate*). A small, charming Mediterranean-style villa on the promontory with eight rooms and beautiful sea views.

★★**P. Cruz del Sur**, Constitución 38, **t** 968 41 01 71 (*inexpensive–cheap*). Newly done-up, near the beach and extremely good value.

Ruano, Urb. La Kabyla 9, **t** 968 41 96 09 (*moderate*). Good seafood. Try the *tortilla de marisco Ruano*, which is huge and bursting with seafood. The *menú* is good value.

well known for its wine jars, the massive *tinajas*. Seven kilometres out of town is the humble little sanctuary of **La Santa**, still a pilgrimage site.

Lorca, the prettiest town in Murcia, was an outpost against the Moors of Granada and a small artistic centre. There are still more than 500 artisans practising in Lorca; the **Centro de Artesania**, next door to the tourist office, is well worth a visit and has an excellent selection of local crafts and modern design on offer. The tourist office itself is housed in the elegant **Palacio de los Guevara**, better known as the House of Columns for its twisting Baroque doorway. The heart of the town is the elegant **Plaza Espanya**, overlooked by the monumental **Colegiata de San Patricio** (*open Mon–Fri 11–1 and 4.30–6.30, Sat and Sun 11–1; adm free*) with its sumptuous Baroque façade. Nearby

Las Brisas, Explanada de Muelle 14, **t** 968 41 00 27 (*moderate*). Good seafood and regional dishes like *fideuá*, views out to sea and delicious home-made desserts.

Moratalla ✉ 30440

*****Hotel Barceló Cenajo**, Embalse del Cenajo, **t** 968 72 10 11, **f** 968 72 06 45, *elcenajo@barcelo.com*, *www.barcelo.com* (*expensive–moderate*). Just outside the town, but well signposted, this is an elegant, romantic hotel with palatial rooms and all the trimmings, including three pools. Prices at weekends can be extraordinarily good value.

***Hospedería Rural La Tejera**, Ctra de la Puerta Km2, **t** 968 70 62 61, **f** 968 73 07 08 (*moderate*). One of several new hotels dedicated to Turismo Rural, which have been springing up in the region recently. This one is rustically decorated and has a pool.

***P. Reyes**, C/Tomas el Cura, **t** 968 73 03 77 (*cheap*). Above a popular local bar of the same name, with pleasant rooms (all with bath) including a five-bed family room, all at an exceptionally cheap price.

Caravaca de la Cruz ✉ 30440

*****Hotel Central**, Gran Via 18, **t** 968 70 70 55 (*moderate*). Aimed at business travellers, this is slightly impersonal but the rooms are good value, and the **restaurant** is decent.

****P. Victoria**, C/Maria Girón 1, **t** 968 70 86 24 (*moderate–inexpensive*). A simple, central *pensión*; rooms with or without bath.

***Hospedería Molino de Argos**, Camino Viejo de Archivel, **t** (*mobile*) 606 30 14 09. Set in a converted mill 10km outside Caravaca, this is a charming spot to while away a few days in the peace and quiet.

Alhama de Murcia ✉ 30840, Aledo ✉ 30840 and Totana ✉ 30850

These towns are the main access points for the Sierra de Espuna.

***Hs Tánger**, Av. Ginés Campos 2, Alhama de Murcia, **t** 968 63 06 99 (*inexpensive*). The handiest option if you want to explore the Natural Park of the Sierra de Espuña.

****Hotel el Pinito Oro**, Urb Montysol, **t/f** 968 48 45 90 (*moderate*). Just outside Aledo: reasonable rooms with fantastic views across the mountains and a pool. Decent mountain-style fare in the **restaurant**.

**** Hotel Plaza**, Pza de la Constitución 5, Totana, **t** 968 42 31 12 (*moderate*). Attractive rooms with all mod cons, in the town centre.

Mar Menor ✉ 30380

******Cavanna**, Gran Vía de la Manga, **t** 968 56 36 00, **f** 968 56 44 31 (*expensive–moderate*). Excellent facilities including a pool, tennis and children's activities between the two seas. Rooms have a/c. *Open May–Sept.*

****Hotel Corzo**, Av. Aviacion 8, Los Alcazares, **t** 968 57 51 31 (*moderate*). A smart option; decent rooms and close to the beach.

****Hotel Los Narejos**, Av. de la Constitución, Los Alcazares, **t** 968 57 56 34 (*inexpensive*). Very reasonably priced, though without very much charm.

There are many **restaurants** around here, enough to suit all budgets, and lots which have terraces on the seafront.

Miramar, Pso del Puerto 14, Cabo de Palos, **t** 968 58 30 33 (*moderate*). Excellent seafood is served alongside great sea views and a wide range of local rice-based specialities; the *menú del día* (*inexpensive*) is also very good value.

is the **Ayuntamiento**, topped with elaborate allegories of Charity and Justice, and just across from it is the old granary, the **Posito**, which now houses the municipal archives. Calle Santo Domingo holds another string of glowering Baroque edifices, including the **Convento de Santa Domingo**, which also houses a collection of objects from religious processions, and the Casa de los Morenos has a musty **archaeological museum** (*open Tues–Fri afternoons only; closed Sat–Mon; adm free*), with local finds from the Bronze Age and Iberian settlements. A lone Roman column, located just off buzzing Pza Vicente, marks the distance between Lorca and Cartagena on the old Roman *Via Herculea*. Lorca is famed for its *Semana Santa* celebrations which are particularly lively on Good Friday, with a sumptuous show of the triumph of Christianity. The ancient walls of the **castle** begin their snaking climb from close to the little church of Santa María: the original Moorish fortress was crushed by Alfonso X, who had it rebuilt and renamed the main tower the Torre Alfonsina. Its twin, the **Torre del Expelón**, still bears some traces of its Moorish decoration, but they are only open on 23 November, the day when the castle was conquered by Alfonso's troops. It's a long, sweaty climb uphill,but the views over the straggling *barrio antiguo* dotted with medieval churches are lovely.

Caravaca, further north and more out of the way, sits under a hill crowned with the striking **Real Alcázar–Santuario de la Vera Cruz** (*open Tues–Sun for guided visits in Castellano only at 11, 12, 1, 4.30, 5.30 and 6.30; closed Mon; adm*). In 1231 (13 years before Caravaca was reconquered by the Christians), the Moorish lord asked a priest he had imprisoned to perform a mass so that he could see what it was like. The priest reluctantly agreed, and was gathering together all the necessary items when he realized he had no cross. He was about to call it all off when two angels brought one in through the window. The sanctuary, with its pink marble Baroque façade, was built in the 17th century to house this relic, but it was stolen during the Civil War and never found (though the Vatican sent a copy containing a sliver of the True Cross). The event is recalled every year on 3 May, when the Cross is taken in a procession to a small Baroque temple at the bottom of the town and 'bathed'. There is a small **museum** (*open Mon–Sat 8–2 and 4.30–8.30, Sun 10–2 and 4.30–8.30; adm*) of religious art next to the church. After the Reconquista, Caravaca was donated to the Templars who are vividly remembered in the village's fiesta of the Moors and Christians; this festival is celebrated all over the region, but Caravaca has a special spin on it. According to another old legend, the Knights Templars broke out of the beseiged castle in a desperate search for water; unable to find any, they stocked up on wine instead and headed back to party – or drown their sorrows. The mad dash is commemorated annually with the Caballos del Vino, eleborately cloaked horsemen who are charged with taking the local wine to the temple for a special blessing.

Just to the east of Caravaca is **Cehegín**, another steep village wound around the gentle mound of a hill surrounded by vines and fruit orchards. It was once the site of the Roman town of Begastri, and it's possible to pick your way among the ruins if you contact the local archaeology museum (*call* **t** *670 58 72 71*). To the north is **Calasparra**, encircled by rugged mountains, with a dilapidated Roman aqueduct and the remnants of an Arab fortress.

The ancient, sleepy village of **Moratalla** vies with Lorca for the title of prettiest Murcian town (and doesn't have a motorway skimming past it, either). Set on a high plateau, and seemingly indifferent to tourism, this old town is nonetheless well preserved and welcoming. The lush surrounding landscape is a sight for sore eyes after the monotonous aridity of the Murcian plains. The steep streets wind towards a crumbling Arabic fortress and the impressive edifice of the 16th-century **Church of the Asunción**, where most of the locals gather to gossip on moonlit nights.

Cartagena and the Costa Cálida

Cartagena was the major city of the Carthaginians in Spain, who honoured it by naming it after their own capital. It prospered by dint of its gold and silver mines, and it was a major blow to Hannibal when Scipio Africanus besieged and captured it. It next made history when Francis Drake raided the port and snatched its guns in 1585. When the message of the First Internationale reached Spain, it was eagerly received here; revolts by radicals in Cartagena and Alcoi in 1873 led to the downfall of Spain's first Republican Government. The Civil War inflicted more damage; nor does the presence of a major naval base improve its appearance.

Cartagena's port is dominated by its **Arsenal** (1782) and decorated with an early (1888) submarine, Isaac Peral's big white torpedo called the *Cartagena*. The old town is clustered around the woebegone, ruined 13th-century cathedral, where a path twists uphill to give a wonderful bird's-eye view of the remarkable **Roman theatre**, considered one of the finest in the whole of Spain. From here you can climb further to admire the views from the **Castillo de la Concepción**, which was built during the 13th century with stones recycled from the amphitheatre. The town is thickly studded with Roman ruins: walls, doorways and stretches of old Roman roads appear in the most unlikely places, and what the medieval builders left of the amphitheatre has been discovered beneath the shabby bullring. Behind the port, the **Calle Mayor** is the place to stroll during the evening *paseo*; it's dotted with florid *modernista* buildings, like the pink-domed **Ayuntamiento**, and the **Casino**, a popular place to stop for a drink. A hiking path, about 12 kilometres long, leads up over the cliffs of the Sierra de la Muela for dizzying views down into tranquil coves.

Murcia is anxious to get a piece of the tourist action which has proved so profitable for neighbouring València and has named its rocky coast the **Costa Cálida** (the 'Warm Coast') in an attempt to makes itself more attractive to the tourists. The biggest area of development straddles the unusual **Mar Menor**, a warm, shallow and salty lagoon, covering 170 square kilometres, and dotted with islets. It's separated from the sea by a narrow, beach-lined strip of land called **La Manga** ('the sleeve') where the worst excesses of Murcia's holiday development has taken place. Along La Manga you can choose between the calm, warm beaches on the Mar Menor, or the cooler beaches along the Mediterranean. Moorish kings would come to the Mar Menor for their ritual 'nine baths'; today some of the ancient pools are still used in **San Pedro del Pinatar** for rheumatism therapy. The next resort along is **Santiago de la Ribera**, a bit more upmarket, with a popular sailing and watersports club. Because of its warmth the Mar Menor is also used as a great prawn nursery, where Spain's favourite snacks may be harvested right up to the beginning of winter. These resorts are all very popular with the Spanish.

The dusty road to the west lumbers past huge, ghostly greenhouses packed with tomatoes, still one of the region's biggest industries, and one of the few crops to thrive in the Murcian desert heat. There isn't much in **Mazarrón**, the next large town, but its seaside satellite, **Puerto de Mazarrón**, seven kilometres away, is an agreeable, matter-of-fact tourist town full of Spanish holiday homes and plenty of long beaches. From here the coast gets wilder and more difficult to access unless you have your own transport, and the beaches correspondingly less crowded; you can still catch a bus along the coast to **Bolnuevo**, though, for a swim near the **Enchanted City**, an area of strange, wind-eroded rocks and pinnacles.

Ruined watchtowers from the 16th century guard the coast to **Águilas**, the last resort before Andalucía. The Tartessians were the first to found a city here, on a promontory overlooking two bays, but Barbary pirates caused its abandonment until 1765 when Carlos III and the Count of Aranda laid out a new, modern town. English mining interests in Águilas shipped away iron ore but left behind the game of football, which the locals claim (as do the Bilbaínos) they played before anyone else in Spain. The old town is dominated by a 15th-century castle-fortress, and there's a jaunty striped lighthouse at its feet, which is still in operation after more than a century and a half. But it's the beaches that draw the punters to Águilas; the coast is pocked with a series of delightful coves and peaceful beaches. One of the loveliest and most secluded is **Playa Amarilla**, between Mazarrón and Águilas, but the **Plaza Hornillo** nearby has a handy string of bars and restaurants and is well served by buses from Águilas in summer.

Aragón

10

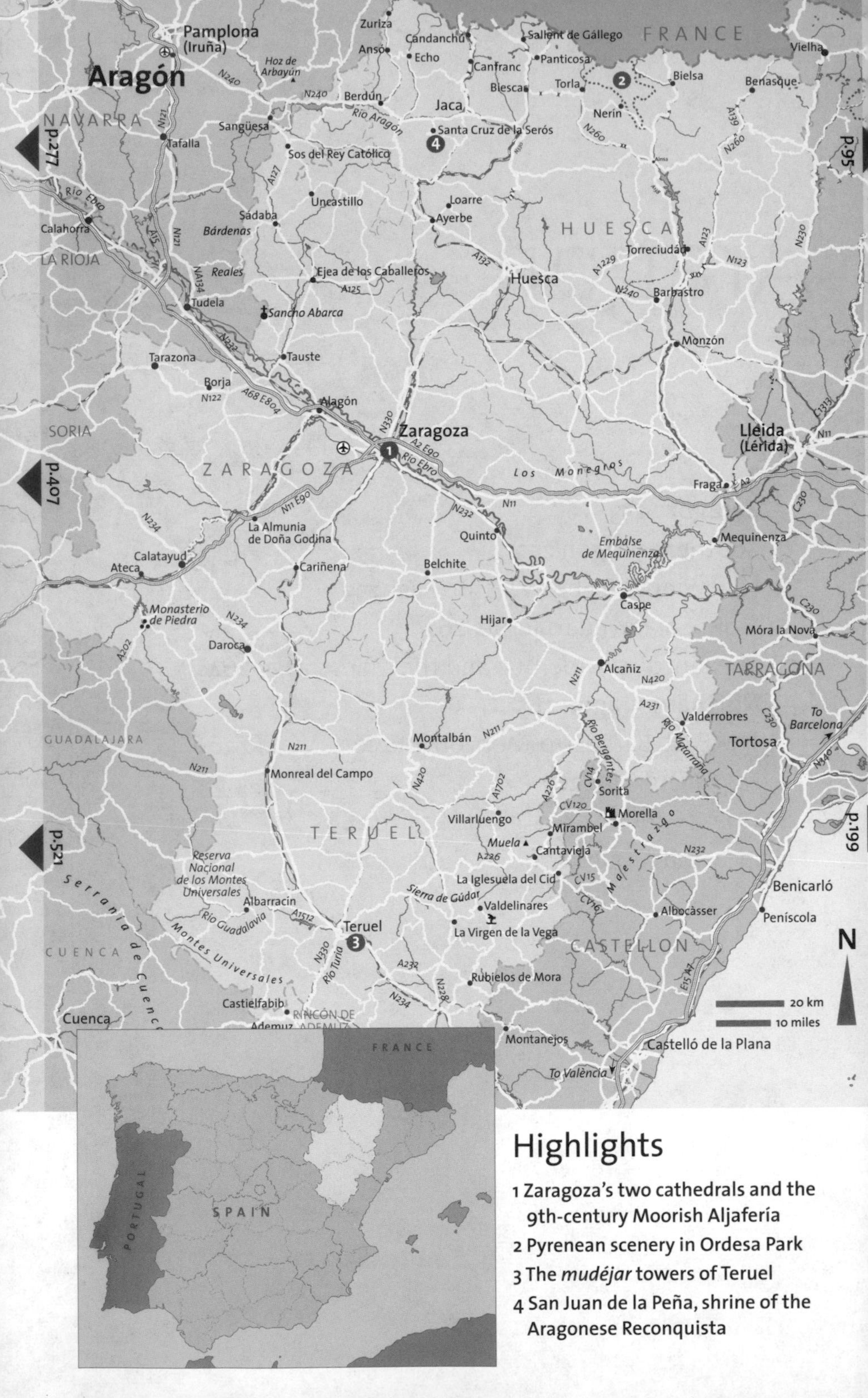

p.277
p.95
p.407
p.521
p.199

Highlights

1 Zaragoza's two cathedrals and the 9th-century Moorish Aljafería
2 Pyrenean scenery in Ordesa Park
3 The *mudéjar* towers of Teruel
4 San Juan de la Peña, shrine of the Aragonese Reconquista

Most people travelling between Madrid and Barcelona see only the bleak plain of the Ebro out of the window and have little desire to see any more. Yet Aragón's finest features lie off the beaten highway, in the seldom-explored mountains of the south and in the Pyrenees of the north, here at their highest and most majestic, offering almost endless hiking and skiing possibilities. Another attraction is Aragón's villages, some of Spain's most medieval and remote, often set against unforgettable scenery. Although an Aragonese nationalist was elected to the *Cortes* for the first time only in 1986, the region has historically been a kind of buffer-state between the Catalans and the Basques and their respective aspirations for independence. In the old days, the Aragonese, those most stubborn of Spaniards, boasting the oldest and some of the most liberal *fueros* or privileges, were not so tractable: Philip II had to put down a major revolt. Union with the Catalans in 1137 brought the Crown of Aragón a Mediterranean empire and international renown.

At Aragonese fiestas, you're likely to see some brisk hoofing in the *jota*, a traditional dance; not one of Spain's more elegant ballets, but without doubt one of the most energetic. In the Pyrenean valleys, sword dances are still performed. The region also produces considerable quantities of wine; of these, Carineña is perhaps the best, and served in many restaurants, alongside hearty mountain cuisine and game dishes, or rather more refined fare if the glint of Aragón's Michelin stars catches your eye.

Zaragoza

Zaragoza, the capital of Aragón, is centrally located and, if not the most charming of cities, it has seduced the Aragonese, who have emptied the countryside to move here. It can get bitter in the winter and too warm in the middle of summer; still, it's the best base for visiting Aragón.

A Real Pillar of the Church

Don Quixote made it within sight of Zaragoza but refused to enter (because another author's false Don Quixote had been there already!). Even so, he enjoyed one of the best sights the city can offer: the view of its great towers and domes from the distance. Close up, Zaragoza reveals itself to be a busy city of over half a million people; over 70 per cent of all Aragonese call it home. Located on the Ebro, in the midst of a fertile *huerta*, it has been prominent ever since the Romans, who gave it its name: Caesar Augusta.

One peculiarity of Zaragoza is that it has two cathedrals, forcing the bishop to shuttle back and forth every six months. Newer and decidedly larger, the 17th-century **Basílica de Nuestra Señora del Pilar** (*open daily 5.45am–9.30pm*) rises from the banks of the Ebro on the spot where, according to legend, the Virgin appeared on a pillar to St James (Santiago) and required a church to be built. From a distance it looks as if she got an Imperial Ottoman mosque instead, complete with four 'minarets' and a hierarchy of 11 domes. There's nothing else like it anywhere in Spain. The interior manages to be both vast and overdone. Goya had a hand in painting the domes, most

Zaragoza
150 metres
100 yards
N
River Ebro
Puente de la Almozara
Avenida la Almozara
Plaza Europa
Echegaray
Santa Lucía
Plaza de Santo Domingo
Predicadores
Teatro del Mercado
Casta Álvarez
Palacio la Aljafería
Aljafería
Paseo María Agustín
Mayoral
San Pablo
Basilio Boggiero
San Pablo
Plaza San Pablo
San Pablo
Plaza de Portillo
Avenida da Madrid
Conde de Aranda
Avenida
Plaza Corona
Audiencia
To Madrid and Logroño
Plaza de Toros
Viajes Viaca Bus Station
Ramón Pignatelli
Plaza José María Forqué
Plaza Miguel Salamero
Train Station (Estacíon el Portillo)
Paseo María Agustín
Dr Fleming
Avenida Cesar Augusto
Plaza Miguel Salamero
Manuel Escoriaza y Fabro
Vincent Berdusán
José Anselmo Clavé
Oscense Bus Station
Agreda Automóvil
Hernán Cortes
Bilbao
Paseo Pamplona
Plaza de Aragón
Tarragona
Paseo Teruel
Glorieta de los Zagríes
Plaza de Basilio Paraiso
Patio de la Infanta
Cortés de Aragón
Avenida Pintor
Avenida de Valencia
Gran Vía
Paseo de las Damas
Paseo de Sagasta
Corona de Aragón
Cortés de Aragón
Av. Fernando el Católico
Félix Latassa
To Valencia and Teruel

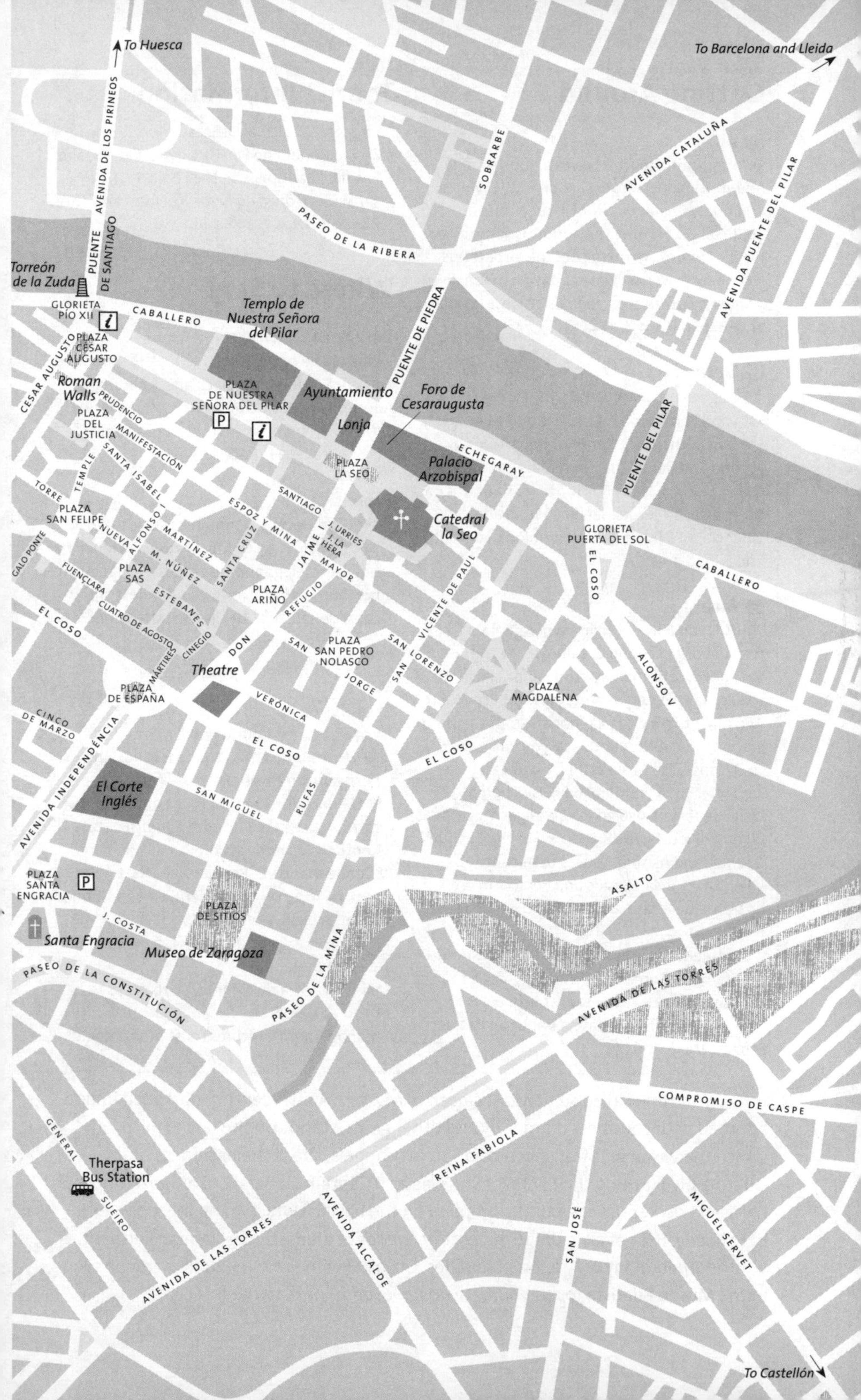
To Huesca
To Barcelona and Lleida
AVENIDA DE LOS PIRINEOS
SOBRARBE
AVENIDA CATALUÑA
AVENIDA PUENTE DEL PILAR
PASEO DE LA RIBERA
PUENTE DE SANTIAGO
Torreón de la Zuda
GLORIETA PÍO XII
CABALLERO
Templo de Nuestra Señora del Pilar
PUENTE DE PIEDRA
PLAZA CÉSAR AUGUSTO
CESAR AUGUSTO
Roman Walls
PRUDENCIO
PLAZA DE NUESTRA SEÑORA DEL PILAR
Ayuntamiento
Foro de Cesaraugusta
Lonja
PUENTE DEL PILAR
PLAZA DEL JUSTICIA
MANIFESTACIÓN
ECHEGARAY
PLAZA LA SEO
Palacio Arzobispal
TEMPLE
SANTA ISABEL
TORRE
PLAZA SAN FELIPE
SANTIAGO
ESPOZ Y MINA
Catedral la Seo
J. URRIES
J. LA HERA
GLORIETA PUERTA DEL SOL
NUEVA
ALFONSO I
MARTÍNEZ
JAIME I
SANTA CRUZ
GALO PONTE
MAYOR
EL COSO
CABALLERO
M. NÚÑEZ
PLAZA SAS
FUENÇLARA
VICENTE DE PAUL
PLAZA ARIÑO
ESTEBANES
REFUGIO
CUATRO DE AGOSTO
EL COSO
CINEGIO
SAN
PLAZA SAN PEDRO NOLASCO
SAN LORENZO
ALONSO V
DON
SAN
Theatre
MARTIRES
JORGE
PLAZA MAGDALENA
PLAZA DE ESPAÑA
VERÓNICA
CINCO DE MARZO
EL COSO
EL COSO
AVENIDA INDEPENDENCIA
El Corte Inglés
SAN MIGUEL
RUFAS
ASALTO
PLAZA SANTA ENGRACIA
PLAZA DE SITIOS
J. COSTA
Santa Engracia
Museo de Zaragoza
PASEO DE LA MINA
PASEO DE LA CONSTITUCIÓN
AVENIDA DE LAS TORRES
COMPROMISO DE CASPE
GENERAL SUEIRO
Therpasa Bus Station
REINA FABIOLA
AVENIDA ALCALDE
SAN JOSÉ
MIGUEL SERVET
AVENIDA DE LAS TORRES
To Castellón

Getting Around

By Air

Zaragoza's airport receives a number of ski-oriented charters from London in the winter, and domestic flights from most points in Spain all year round. The airport is some 20km west of town, **t** 976 71 23 00; the **airport bus** (Ebrobus) leaves six times a day from Pza de Aragón, **t** 976 34 38 21. **Iberia**'s office is located at C/Bilbao 11, **t** 976 21 34 18.

By Train

Zaragoza has a modern train station, the Estación Portillo, on Av. Clavé, **t** 976 24 02 02. From here there are frequent departures to Madrid and Barcelona. There's also one each day to Huesca, Jaca and France (to Canfranc); three a day to Teruel, San Sebastián and València; and five a day to Pamplona, Logroño and Bilbao.

By Bus

Buses can leave from anywhere. Points to the east of town, and Catalunya, Madrid, Valladolid, Extremadura, Soria and Galicia are the domain of Agreda Automóvil, at Pso M. Agustín 7, **t** 976 22 93 43 (not far from the train station); for Huesca and Jaca, you will need La Oscense, Pso M. Agustín 7, **t** 976 43 45 10. For Soria, Borja and Tarazona, use Therpasa, Gral Sueiro 22, **t** 976 30 00 45; Viajes Viaca, at Pignatelli 120, **t** 976 28 31 00, go to the Basque Country and Asturias. Buses to Alicante, València, Murcia, Burgos and Benidorm are operated by Tezasa, at Juan Pablo Bonet 13, **t** 976 27 61 79.

Continental routes are operated by (among others) Julia, Hernán Cortés 6, **t** 976 23 87 73. For others, check at the tourist office.

Local buses, TUZSA, have a booth on Pza de España, **t** 976 22 64 71.

Tourist Information

Zaragoza: Municipal Offices at Torréon de la Zuda, Glorieta de Pio XII, **t** 976 20 12 00; and Pza del Pilar, opposite the Lonja, **t** 976 39 35 37/91 (*both open daily 10–8*); Huescan Office, Pza de Sas, **t** 976 29 84 38.

Where to Stay

Zaragoza ✉ 50000

One of the prime places to look for a room in Zaragoza is down the back alleys between Alfonso I and Don Jaime, particularly on C/Méndez Núñez and the streets around it, the area called El Tubo.

Expensive

******Gran Hotel**, C/Joaquín Costa 5, **t** 976 22 19 01, **f** 976 23 67 13. After extensive renovations, this elegant *grande dame* can reclaim her laurels as one of the city's finest: air-conditioned, beautifully furnished doubles (cheaper at weekends).

Moderate

****Las Torres**, Pza del Pilar 11, **t** 976 39 42 50, **f** 976 39 42 54. Comfortable rooms with views straight across to the basilica; the best value in this bracket.

*****El Príncipe**, C/Santiago 12, **t** 976 29 41 01, **f** 976 29 90 47, *www.hotel-elprincipe.com*. Centrally located just off Pza del Pilar.

****Conde Blanco**, C/Predicadores 84, **t** 976 44 14 11, **f** 976 28 03 39. Modern, air-conditioned rooms a block from the Ebro.

Inexpensive

****Hs Plaza**, Pza del Pilar 14, **t** 976 29 48 30, **f** 976 39 94 06. The friendly, Basque management captures most of this end of

notably the one called *Saint Mary, Queen of Martyrs*. A 14th-century, darkened image, adorned with countless diamonds and other gems, stands on the jasper pillar, on which the Virgin was transported to Spain by angels; she is the patroness of the Guardia Civil (during the Civil War she was also Captain General of Zaragoza, and defused two Republican bombs dropped on the basilica which hang like trophies in her chapel). Best of all is the 16th-century *reredos* of alabaster by Damián Forment, who adorned many of Aragón's churches; Goya's sketches for the domes can be seen in the **Museo Pilarista** (*open daily 9–2 and 4–6; adm*) next to the basilica.

the tourist trade with their variously shaded pastel rooms; many have panoramic views over the plaza.

Hs Santiago, C/Santiago 3–5, **t** 976 39 45 50. Not such good value as the **Plaza**, but this lemon-coloured *hostal* becomes cheaper the longer you stay.

Cheap

Fonda la Peña, C/Cinegio 3, **t** 976 29 90 89. These clean, airy doubles (with shared bath) are a good budget bet. The ***comedor*** (*inexpensive*) serves hearty meals, too.

Eating Out

Aragonese cuisine is substantial and simple, with lots of beans, potatoes, eggs, lamb and codfish. That said, Zaragoza offers some tasty and varied eateries.

Bodega de Chema, Latassa 34, **t** 976 55 50 14 (*expensive*). *Cabrito asado* (roast kid) is one of many great Aragonese dishes served at this classic *bodega*; it's also a fine spot to try Aragón wine; book ahead.

Moderate

La Matilde, Casta Alvarez 10, **t** 976 44 10 08. Classic French dishes. *Closed Sun*.

La Casa del Ventero, Pso 18 de Julio 24, in Villanueva de Gállego, **t** 976 18 51 87. This village 14km north of the city has one of the best restaurants in the province: French cooking with a number of tasty Aragonese dishes as well. *Closed Sun and Mon*.

Casa Emilio, Av. Madrid 5, **t** 976 43 58 39. Further from the old centre but excellent value: be sure to try the delicious fresh fish.

El Corte Inglés, the main branch of the department store at the southern end of Av. de la Independencia. The top floor boasts a good restaurant, popular with the Aragonese.

Inexpensive

La Zanahoria, C/Tarragona 8, near the train station, **t** 976 35 87 94. Small, mellow and friendly vegetarian restaurant serving good-value, delicious dishes: try the blue cheese soufflé or a vegetable curry.

Tapas Bars

The inhabitants of Zaragoza claim that their tapas bars can give Madrid and Sevilla a run for their money. Many are scattered around El Coso, in the heart of the city (particularly the narrow alleys around C/Estebanes, C/Martires and C/Cinegio). The following stand out:

Arranque, C/Jordan de Urriés. Stuffed with good vibes, music and tapas galore.

Bodegas Almau, C/Estebanes 10, **t** 976 29 98 34. Not technically a tapas bar at all but well worth a tipple or two; the same family has run low-key Almau for five generations, with the mustard walls lined with barrels of local wines; there are, of course, also tapas to soak them up.

Casa Juanico, C/Sta Cruz 21. Located just off C/Santiago, this is a small, traditional place with a green frontage.

Cervecería Marpy, Pza Santa Marta. Just south of La Seo is the king of tapas, where the friendly waiters sport vivid *torero* kits and the multiplicity of meat and seafood tapas are displayed at the bar. You can in fact not only eat your fill but a proper meal here.

Tasquilla de Pedro, C/Cinegio 3, **t** 976 39 06 58. Tapas aficionados should head for the hoards of tapas piled on the counter here, in the heart of El Tubo.

Los Victorinos, C/Lahera 4. Its diminutive dimensions can't contain this bar's overflowing character: don't let the bulls' heads on the walls put you off some great tapas.

Chipen, on the corner of C/Alfonso I with C/Prudencio. Come to get good fresh bread.

At the far end of Pza del Pilar stands the old cathedral, **La Seo** (*open summer Tues–Fri 10–2 and 4–7, Sat 10–1 and 4–7, Sun 10–12 and 4–7 (winter afternoons 4–6); closed Mon; adm*), in a crazy quilt of styles, with a *mudéjar* wall of brick and tile on the outside, but within, a lovely alabaster *retablo* from the 15th-century and charming capitals carved with children. The nearby **Tapestry Museum** (*open summer Tues–Sat 10–2 and 4–7 (winter afternoons 4–6), Sun 10–2; closed Mon; adm*) displays 15–18th-century French and Flemish works. On Pza del Pilar, a third monument, the Renaissance Exchange or **Lonja** (*open if an exhibition is on, Tues–Sat 10–2 and 5–9, Sun 10–2; closed Mon*) stands between the cathedrals; step in to see its hall of tall Ionic columns, where Aragón's grain dealers used to meet. Outside in the plaza, modern grain dealers sell their seeds to pilgrims, who over the centuries have helped create Spain's plumpest pigeons. The plaza itself is a strange medley of shapes and styles: from La Seo to the translucent pink entrance to the Museo del Foro de Cesaraugusta; from the Basilica to the shiny Rubiks cube of a tourist office; the entire array is beautifully illuminated at night.

Downtown Zaragoza

On the far side of the plaza, across from La Seo, one of the municipal tourist offices is shoe-horned into the **Zuda tower**, a vestige of the medieval walls, adjacent to fragments of the wall of Caesar Augusta that once bristled with 200 towers. From here, walk up Av. C. Augusto to C/San Pablo and **San Pablo** church, topped by the most beautiful of Zaragoza's many towers, a 13th-century *mudéjar* work; inside there's a wooden *retablo* by Damián Forment. Av. C. Augusto continues up to the main thoroughfare, El Coso; near the corner, the **Audiencia**, guarded by two fierce giants bearing clubs, is crowned with a tympanum portraying the Triumph of Caesar. This was the ancestral home of the Luna family, which produced not only Viceroys, but an anti-Pope (*see* Peníscola, p.221) and an operatic villain (*see* below).

Continue down El Coso, past the **Plaza España** and **Paseo Independencia**, the heart of city life, to C/Rufas. This will take you to the **Plaza de Los Sitios** (of the Sieges) commemorating Zaragoza's heroic resistance to Napoleon's troops in 1808. In 1908 the city held a Hispano-French centenary fair, for which the monument and an exhibition palace, now the **Museum of Zaragoza** (*open Tues–Sat 10–2 and 5–8, Sun 10–2; closed Mon*), were erected. The ground floor is devoted to archaeological exhibits, including bronze tablets in Iberian and Latin, while upstairs the best of the paintings are by Goya, who was a native of Fuendetodos, 50 kilometres south of Zaragoza.

Back towards the Pso Independencia via C/Costa, the church of **Santa Engracia** was founded by Ferdinand and Isabel, whose images kneel over the door; in the crypt, two 4th-century Palaeo-Christian sarcophagi are said to contain the remains of scores of local martyrs, who must be wedged in like sardines in a can. From Santa Engracia, cross large Pza Aragón and Pza Paraíso for Zaragoza's version of Barcelona's Passeig de Gràcia, the **Paseo Sagasta**, where you'll find out what local *modernistas* were up to; No.11, the **Casa Juncosa** by Ricardo Magdalena (1906), is the best Art Nouveau work in the city. Near Pza Paraíso, the Caja de Ahorros de Zaragoza bank houses the reconstructed 14th-century **Patio de la Infanta**, an elegant Renaissance work adorned with medallions portraying the kings of Spain, that originally formed part of the palace of Gabriel Zaporta, one of Charles V's biggest financiers.

The Aljafería

Open summer Sat–Wed 10–2 and Fri–Wed 4.30–8, Sun 10–2; winter Sat–Wed 10–2 and Fri–Wed 4–6.30, Sun 10–2; closed Thurs; adm.

Zaragoza's prime attraction, the **Aljafería** is a short walk from the train station (or a ride on the No.23 bus from the Basílica del Pilar or Pza Aragón). This palace, begun as a defensive work in the 9th century, later served as a residence of the local

Berber-Moorish dynasty and after the Reconquista, of the Aragonese kings. Until 1706, it was the seat of the Aragonese Inquisition, an institution set up by the Catholic kings and regarded by the Aragonese as an underhand attempt by the Castilians to sidestep the special privileges (*fueros*) of Aragón. To prove their point, the Zaragozans murdered the first Inquisitor in the cathedral. Destroyed and misused for centuries since, restoration work on the Aljafería has been ongoing since the 1940s.

Walk around the huge walls to the entrance by the tiny jewel-like **Mosque**, itself the best piece of Moorish architecture outside Andalucía. The oldest part of the Aljafería, the Moorish **Torre del Trovador**, provided the set for Antonio García Gutiérrez's play, *El Trovador* (1830), and Verdi's opera, *Il Trovatore* (1853), within which Manrico was imprisoned by the nasty Conde de Luna. The Gothic additions – notably the stair and throne room with their *artesonado* ceilings – were added by Ferdinand and Isabel.

Southern Aragón

Southern Aragón is a case of the blind man and the elephant: your opinion of it will depend entirely on which corners of it you come to first. The landscape is a jumble of awful, barren plateaux, patches of scrubland and green, fertile valleys, scattered with appealing medieval villages as soon as you're vaguely off the beaten track. There are, unfortunately, more of the former, and this region is, now as always, one of Spain's poorest. More serious battles of the Civil War were fought here than anywhere else in the country, which hasn't helped. **Belchite**, once an important town and now a ghostly ruin, was a victim of bitter house-to-house fighting in the 1938 Ebro offensive. The ruins include a Romanesque church and some fine old buildings, and the government has left them standing as a reminder.

Following the Ebro: West to East

Not a few towns in Spain (we could mention Barcelona) seem to have been dropped into place from outer space. **Tarazona**, with its startling *mudéjar* towers hanging over the cliffs, is certainly one of them. Most of these towers are in the older quarter of town, gracing the churches of **La Magdalena**, **La Concepción** and **San Miguel**. Tarazona is famous for its 16th-century **Ayuntamiento**, with reliefs of the capture of Granada across the façade; another landmark is the old, arcaded **bullring**, its arches bricked up and turned into apartments. Tarazona's **Cathedral** is odd, too, sporting a dome like La Seo's in Zaragoza, a tower like La Giralda's in Sevilla, mixed in with several other styles.

On the way to Zaragoza, the road and railway line pass **Borja**, in the middle of a big wine-growing region. The peculiar crag you see with chimneys sticking out of it is explained as the ruins of **Borja castle**, the ancestral home of that celebrated family of schemers and connoisseurs of poison, the Borgias, who played petty-noble hoodlums in Aragón before they hit the big time in Renaissance Italy.

The Zaragoza–València road passes through mostly nondescript towns. **Caspe** can show a **Roman mausoleum** in its town square, relocated from lands flooded by the

Getting Around

If you're relying on public transport, expect frustrations. This is a sparsely populated region, and the buses and trains are both infrequent and slow.

By Train

There are about four trains daily; you can get to either Zaragoza or València from Teruel, with no really interesting stops in between; in Teruel, **t** 902 24 02 02.

By Bus

The bus station in Teruel is on Ronda 18 Julio; the most frequent destination is Zaragoza, **t** 978 60 10 14, but there will be a daily bus to Cuenca and to Barcelona, **t** 978 60 20 04, as well as Madrid, **t** 978 60 34 50, and to most of the provincial towns. In the Maestrazgo, the service is informal; it's no place to hurry.

Tourist Information

Teruel: C/Tomás Nogués 1, just off C/Ramón y Cajal (the main street), **t** 978 60 22 79 (*open daily 10–2 and 4–8*).

Festivals

Albarracín: Fiesta, *Sept*. Crowds flock in and a really festive atmosphere develops, with the plaza converted into a bullring and the narrow, cobbled streets scattered with sand.

Cantavieja: *4th Sun of May* and *3rd Sun of Sept*. Cantavieja's fiestas see its medieval streets lined with market stalls selling everything you could possibly want, from huge nylon panties to hammers.

Skiing

Valdelinares, on the Sierra de Gúdar near to Teruel, is the only ski resort in southern Aragón. There are eight pistes and a slalom course and two *hostales* in the resort, as well as others scattered around in the surrounding villages, **t** 978 78 80 08, *www.valdelinares.com*.

Where to Stay and Eat

Southern Aragón sees few tourists, but you can find modest accommodation in all the towns and villages mentioned in this section.

Alcañiz ✉ 44600

★★★**Parador La Concordia**, Castillo de los Calatravos, **t** 978 83 04 00, **f** 978 83 03 66 (*expensive*). One of the most beautiful *paradores* in the country, set in the Castillo de los Calatravos. It offers doubles with a/c and has been newly renovated.

★★**Guadalope**, Pza España 8, **t** 978 83 07 50, **f** 978 83 32 33 (*inexpensive*). Tastefully kitted out rooms with vistas over the *ayuntamiento* and church. Its **restaurant** is open to all, but it cheaper for hotel guests.

Meseguer, Av. Maestrazgo 9, **t** 978 83 10 02, **f** 978 83 01 41 (*inexpensive*). On the edge of town: ordinary from the outside but with comfortable air-conditioned rooms and the best **restaurant** (*inexpensive*) in the area, specializing in fish dishes and local game.

Valderrobres ✉ 44580

★**Hs Querol**, Av. Hispanidad 14, **t/f** 978 85 01 92 (*inexpensive*). Nineteen reasonably priced rooms and a very inexpensive *menú*.

Ateca ✉ 50210

★★★**Monasterio de Piedra**, C/Monasterio de Piedra, in the hamlet of Nuévalos, near Ateca, **t** 976 84 90 11, **f** 976 84 90 54, *www.sta.es/monastpiedra* (*moderate*). It's worth going out of your way to spend a night at this converted monastery: first-rate accommodation, with a pool, tennis courts, and a good **restaurant** (*inexpensive*).

Daroca ✉ 50360

★★★**Posada del Almudi**, Grajera 7, **t** 976 80 06 06, **f** 976 80 11 41, *www.staragon.com/posadadelalmudi* (*inexpensive*). Exquisitely restored 16th–17th-century palace; very reasonable rates, with an excellent **restaurant** serving wonderful desserts and a cheap *menú del día*.

★★**HsR Agiria**, Ctra Sagunto-Burgos, **t** 976 80 07 31 (*cheap*). A cheaper option, but rather less atmospheric.

Albarracín ✉ 44100

Albarracín is becoming a small resort, as its charming streets and mountain views begin to attract ever more visitors. Beware, however, that there's little chance of finding rooms in fiesta time (Sept; *see* above) unless you book well in advance.

★★★**Albarracín**, C/Azagra, **t** 978 71 00 11, **f** 978 71 00 36 (*moderate*). In a restored old building at the lower end of the old town, this is the best quality (and priciest) option.

★★**Caserón de la Fuente**, Carrerahuertos, **t** 978 71 03 30 (*moderate*). Just below the main road heading out of town, this restored old house has a tranquil setting.

★★**Doña Blanca**, Llano del Arrabat 10, **t** 978 71 00 01 (*inexpensive*). Fairly central, with comfortable rooms and balconies.

Hs Olimpia, C/San Antonio 9, **t** 978 71 00 83 (*inexpensive*). Cheaper but newly refurbished rooms under friendly management, at the bottom of the old town.

El Rincón del Chorro, C/del Chorro 15, **t** 978 71 01 12 (*moderate*). All rough walls and hanging hams; the portions are huge and there's a good vegetable and soup section: try the *pisto*: vegetables baked with eggs.

Teruel ✉ 44000

Be warned that accommodation may be thin on the ground during the annual bikers' rally (around 15 Sept).

★★★**Parador de Teruel**, Apt 67, **t** 978 60 18 00, **f** 978 60 86 12, *Teruel@parador.es* (*expensive*). This one is nothing new, and its location outside the city means it's a bit inconvenient, if tranquil.

★★★**Reina Cristina**, Pso del Övalo 1, near San Salvador tower, **t** 978 60 68 60, **f** 978 60 53 63 (*expensive*). In a comfortable spot, though a little bit pricier, with decent, modern rooms.

★★★**La Parada del Compte**, Antigua Estación de Ferrocarril, Torre del Compte, **t** 978 76 90 72, **f** 978 76 90 74 (*expensive*). For a quirkier character out of town, try this converted village railway station (*moderate menú*).

★★★**Oriente**, Av. Sagunto 5, **t** 978 60 15 50 (*moderate*). This is situated just over the other side of the viaduct, and consequently better value.

Hs Alcazaba, C/Joaquín Costa 34, **t** 978 61 07 61 (*inexpensive*). More modest lodgings close to the plaza, with a friendly bar below.

Hs Aragon, C/Santa María 4, **t** 978 60 13 87 (*cheap*). Around the corner in a quiet, yet very central location.

To help ward off the effects of its cold winters, typical **Teruel cuisine** relies heavily on soups and stews, all washed down with strong, wholesome wines. The area is also known for its cured hams, which you'll see dangling from most food-shop and *bodega* ceilings. Teruel itself is not really noted for outstanding restaurants, but there's better than average fare at the following:

Torre del Salvador, C/Salvador 20, **t** 978 60 52 63 (*moderate*). Just along the road from its namesake.

La Menta, Bartolomé Esteban 10 (*moderate*). Popular with locals, this is a tasty place to sample Aragonese specialities.

Reina Cristina (*see* above). The hotel's restaurant (*inexpensive*) provides a carefully presented and good-value *menú*, piped music aside.

La Parilla, San Esteban 2, **t** 978 60 59 23 (*inexpensive*). A characterful carnivorous tavern with a welcoming hearth.

Portal del Carmen, C/Glorieta 2, Rubielos de Mora, **t** 978 80 41 53 (*expensive*). Set in a 17th-century Carmelite convent, an hour's drive southeast of Teruel on the C232.

Cantavieja ✉ 44140

★★**Balfagón Alto Maestrazgo**, Av. del Maestrazgo 20, **t/f** 964 18 50 76, *www.maestrazgo.arrakis.es/balfa.htm* (*inexpensive*). Clean, good-value rooms. The popular **restaurant** has a daily *menú* with Maestrazgan specialities.

Pensión Julián, García Valiño 6, **t** 964 18 50 05 (*cheap*). Simple, cheap and friendly setup in an old house in the centre, with a hearty ***comedor***.

Anywhere else, especially in the Maestrazgo, you'll likely find only the sparest of *fondas* or rooms over a bar. In any season but summer remember to ask if there's heating, since this province is known to have the worst climate in Spain.

big Mequinenza reservoir, which turns the Ebro into an impressive lake for some 48 kilometres. Most of **Mequinenza** was drowned,too, but it now has a finer lakeside location than ever before, and a well-preserved medieval **castle**. **Alcañiz**, to the south, is a big town, with a *parador* installed in the 12th-century **castle** that once belonged to the Order of Calatrava. The 16th-century Ayuntamiento, Lonja buildings and the church on the Plaza Mayor are the only sights, dwarfing the square; but it's a pleasant enough place to sit and have a drink under the arches. If you're heading towards the coast, tiny **Valderrobres** is worth a detour for its improbably grand **Santa María la Mayor** (12th century) and her beautiful rose window, along with a **castle** of the kings of Aragón, a Renaissance **Ayuntamiento**, and a pretty main street along the river.

From Calatayud to Teruel

Sooner or later you'll pass through **Calatayud**, an important road and railway junction, but it's a dour and shabby place and there's little reason to stay. Calatayud (from the Arabic 'castle of Job') specializes in octagonal *mudéjar* church steeples; **Santa María La Mayor** has the best, set above an ornate Plateresque-*mudéjar* façade. Close by, on the Sigüenza road, **Ateca** has a converted mosque for its main church, **Santa María**, with a later *mudéjar* tower much like those in Teruel. There's a detour to the south to the **Piedra Monastery**, a 13th-century Cistercian house. Most of it is a hotel now, but the surroundings, with plenty of trees and a 150ft **waterfall** along the Río Piedra, must surely be the garden spot of all southern Aragón.

South from Calatayud, **Daroca**'s pride is its **walls**, with 114 towers in varying states of decay. The gates are well preserved and impressive. Charles V built them; Daroca was a thriving town in his time, as evidenced by several fine *mudéjar* **churches**, a lovely fountain called the **Fuente de Veinte Caños** ('20 spouts') outside the walls, and a one-kilometre **tunnel** dug under a mountain to carry off flood waters – a very unusual fit of public works for 16th-century Spain. The tunnel was not an entirely original idea, as a curious history details tunnels being dug around Daroca throughout the 8th, 9th and 10th centuries. They were designed to carry water from the mountainside to the early Yemeni settlers, who were the original tribal founders of the town. A later quirk of Darocan history evolved from a miracle that took place during the ousting of the Arabs on 23 February 1239. Legend tells how a local priest was in the midst of celebrating a mass for the soldiers who were to fight for Christian virtue, when the Arabic foe made a surprise attack. The priest hastily hid six consecrated hosts intended for the army captains, in a shroud. But the battle was bitter and bloodthirsty, and when the shroud was unfolded, all the hosts had turned to blood. The Santísimo Misterio de Daroca became widely known, and almost two centuries later King Ferdinand and Elisabeth I decorated the shroud with a golden frame, said to have been made from the first gold brought from the Americas.

About 20 kilometres before Teruel, a sideroad follows the Río Turia valley into the Montes Universales. At the centre of this bare and rocky district is a town that is an attraction in itself: **Albarracín** is a national monument, one of the least changed in all

Spain. Its oldest streets are fairy-tale medieval, riddled with narrow, cobbled lanes and half-timbered houses in flaking shades of Savoy red, their projecting balconies leaning out over the thoroughfares at precarious angles. Albarracín has an unusually long circuit of walls, not because the town was ever bigger than it is now, but to protect it from attacks from the dominating hillsides. As befits a fairy-tale town, Albarracín has a number of legends attached to it, one of which concerns the **Torre de Doña Blanca** that perches above the town. It's said that the ghost of a beautiful, enchanted princess appears here every full moon at midnight, dressed in white, to bathe in the river Guadalaviar. She had fallen in love with a young Jewish man, but it was a forbidden love, and she dutifully expired from wistful longing in her tower.

Teruel

As a provincial capital, Teruel looms large on the Spanish map, but it's small and a little woebegone up close. Already a poor backwater, Teruel suffered as much as any Spanish city in the Civil War. In the freezing winter of 1937 (Teruel is famous for these), the Republicans fought their way up the steep slopes and seized the town; two weeks later, the Nationalists did the same thing and got it back. Since then a little prosperity has seeped in. The reason for visiting is to see the best *mudéjar* churches in Spain: four of them, with tall, glorious towers of delicately patterned brick and tiles. Teruel retained a large Moorish population after the 12th-century Reconquest, and it was Moorish craftsmen who gave the city its pride and its symbol.

Heartbreak in Old Teruel

The fourth *mudéjar* tower is **San Pedro**, and below it a little chapel has been built to house the remains of **Los Amantes de Teruel** (*open Mon–Sat 10–2 and 5–7.30, Sun 10.30–2 and 5–7.30; adm*). The star-crossed lovers of the tale were Diego de Marcilla and Isabel de Segura; he had six years to go out and win his fortune; when, on the appointed day, Diego failed to appear, Isabel's impatient father married her off. Of course, he had made his fortune, but was then captured by the Moors and held in València by Queen Zulima, who told Isabel he was dead. On his release, he was recaptured by bandits in the pay of Zulima. Though he escaped, he arrived in Teruel a day late, and the lovers were left no option but to expire in each other's arms. The same tale is told in Boccaccio's *Decameron*, except that his lovers are named Girolamo and Salvastra; scholars never tire of speculating whether Teruel's lovers were Boccaccio's source, or if some local light simply invented them. There can't be fewer than 100 versions of this folk-tale motif floating around Europe, so take your pick. Nowadays, you can join sympathetic honeymooners in visiting this shrine of sorrow. The lovers' effigies are beautifully sculpted, holding hands between the sarcophagi and, should you so wish, you can peek at the mummified remains. Spanish children, apparently unmoved by the trials of true romance, summarize the tale in a nursery rhyme:

Los Amantes de Teruel,
Tonta ella y tonto él.
(The famous lovers of Teruel – she was crazy and him as well.)

If you come by train, you'll get an immediate introduction to Teruel *mudéjar* in the form of the **Escalinata**, built in the 1920s, a long, elegant (though poorly maintained) stairway leading up from the station to the town. At the top, the most elaborate of the *mudéjar* towers stands just a block to the left: that of **El Salvador** (*open daily 11–2 and 5–8; adm*), built right over the street with a narrow arch to let people pass. Like minarets, the towers of Teruel are always separate from their churches. **San Martín**, the next tower, also has an arch underneath; it's a few blocks north on Pza Perez Prado (*open summer 11–2 and 5–9; otherwise as El Salvador; adm*). The tower of the **Cathedral** (*open daily 11–2 and 4–8; times may vary on Sun and festivals; adm*) pales by comparison, but it does have a unique, *mudéjar*-style brick dome to compensate. Teruel really is an unlikely honeymoon destination, but besides its *mudéjar* towers it offers a few things to see. The **Provincial Museum** (*Pza Fray Anselmo Polanco s/n,* ***t*** *978 60 01 50; open Tues–Fri 10–2 and 4–7, Sat and Sun 10–2; closed Mon*) is an interesting diversion, housed on four floors of the recently restored 16th-century palace of the provincial Casa de Comunidad. The **Fountain of the Torico**, a bull with a star between its horns, is the symbol of the city, set in the quiet **Plaza Mayor**. Everything changes when the annual **motorbike rally** comes to town and the plaza literally reverberates. A primeval bikers' ritual takes place there, consisting of individual bikers trying to create the maximum noise and fumes possible on that two legged beast; it's a weird cacophony greeted with applause from the cyclists and dismay by the locals. The plaza also displays some of Teruel's ventures into modernism, having two appealing Art Nouveau houses. From Pza Mayor, it's a short walk to the northern end of town and **Los Arcos**, a 16th-century aqueduct you can walk across, the work of the same French engineer who dug the tunnel at Daroca. There are no stories about the peculiar, eight-sided tower called the **Castillo de Amberes** nearby; nobody seems to know who built it, or why. Behind it, near the bus station, the streets around Pza Judería provide the most incongruous sight in Teruel on Saturday nights, when all southern Aragón's fast crowd congregates at the scores of hole-in-the-wall bars.

The Rincón de Ademuz and the Maestrazgo

Quite a few of Teruel's bikers speed in from these two pockets of quiet villages, where by day you're more likely to see shepherds with their flocks. If you're aiming for Madrid or Cuenca, you'll pass through the **Rincón de Ademuz**, a spot of land that was independent through much of the Middle Ages, and now survives as an island of València province within Aragón. The villages, such as Ademuz and Castielfabib, are among the least modern in Spain, and the countryside in the valley of the Río Turia is lovely.

In the **Maestrazgo**, between Teruel and València, the scenery is wilder and the villages a little more colourful, with pointed arches overhanging the streets and Moorish *ajimez* windows. **La Iglesuela del Cid** is perhaps most characteristic, but tiny **Mirambel** is prettier, a sudden apparition of a perfect walled village materializing around a bend in the road. The town has recently won a national prize for the restoration of its modest monuments, including the old, half-timbered gatehouses and elegant belltower. Mirambel is reached through vertigo-inducing **Cantavieja**, a Templar foundation that was a Carlist stronghold during both of their rebellions. Cantavieja preserves an imposing 16th-century church and Ayuntamiento hemming in a rough but beautiful plaza. It's a quiet enough place unless you happen to arrive on one of the two fiestas (*see* 'Festivals', p.260) when thousands descend from the hills. If you have a car you can enjoy the view from **Muela Monchen,** a famous *mirador* outside the town.

Northern Aragón

Besides ski slopes, Northern Aragón's prime attractions are its unspoilt medieval villages and mountain scenery. Public transport to nearly all points is possible but often time-consuming; the service is good but infrequent. Don't come with a tight schedule or a plane to catch within a couple of days – unless you have a car.

The East: Barbastro, Monzón and Torreciudad

One of Aragón's more remote corners, this is a good place to see the difference irrigation has made to the land. **Los Monegros** (just to the south of Monzón) provides the 'before' picture: a wasteland as dry and barren as anyone could wish. **Barbastro** is the largest town in the desolation and famous for Somontano wines, which are explained in a state of the art ***museo del vino*** above the tourist office; it is also possible to visit surrounding *bodegas* (*ask at the tourist office for details*). Barbastro's 16th-century **Cathedral** (*open summer 10–1.30 and 4.30–7.30; winter 9–1 and 6–8*) has a polychrome alabaster *retablo* by Damián Forment. Also ask at the tourist office about the fantastic diaporama at the adjacent **Centro de Interpretación**, after which no doubt you'll wish to visit the scenic Sierra de Guara (not to mention the majestic 20 blocks of pink granite near Abiego, placed there by German sculptor, Ulrich Rükriem). Buses from here (*departing at 2pm*) travel 13 kilometres to **Alquézar**, one of

Getting Around

By Train

Monzón is on the railway line between Lleida and Zaragoza (three a day).

By Bus

Barbastro and Monzón are both on the Huesca–Lleida bus route (three times a day).

Tourist Information

Barbastro: Av. de la Merced 64, **t** 974 30 83 50, **f** 974 30 83 51, *turismo@barbastro-ayto.es* (*open Sept–June Tues–Sat 10–2 and 4.30–8; closed Mon; July and Aug daily 10–2 and 4.30–8*).

Monzón: Pza Aragón, **t** 974 40 48 54.

Torreciudad: Santuario de Torreciudad, **t** 974 30 40 25.

Where to Stay and Eat

Barbastro ✉ 22300

****Hs Clemente**, C/Corona de Aragón 5, **t** 974 31 01 86, **f** 974 30 83 81, *clemente.3066@cajarural.com* (*moderate*). New, bright rooms with classy bathrooms.

***Hs Pirineos**, C/General Ricardos 13, **t/f** 974 31 00 00, *www.barbastro.com/pirineos* (*inexpensive*). Relaxed and peaceful atmosphere; good service, too.

***Hs Palafox**, C/Corona de Aragón 20, **t** 974 31 24 61 (*inexpensive*). A bit cheaper than the Pirineos but nothing special, although the rooms are perfectly clean.

***Hs Roxi**, C/Corona de Aragón 21, **t** 974 31 10 64 (*inexpensive*). Not as good as the Palafox but conveniently close if it's full.

El Pueyo, 3km out of town, on the road to Huesca, **t** 974 31 50 79 (*moderate*). In the restored ancient monastery of Santuario de El Pueyo near a pretty 14th century church. The food is almost as good as the spectacular views over the Pyrenees and Natural Park of the Sierras de Guara.

Cenador de San Julián, Av. de la Merced 64, **t** 974 31 12 05 (*inexpensive*). A swish *menú* in the same complex as the tourist office.

Flor, C/Goya (*inexpensive*). A really good-value *menú* is served here, just over the bridge from the centre.

Pirineos (*see* above) (*inexpensive*). Hearty, home-made food can be had in the *hostal*'s dining room.

Monzón ✉ 22400

****Vianetto**, Av. de Lérida 25, **t** 974 40 19 00, **f** 974 40 45 40, *www.monzon.net/vianetto* (*inexpensive*). This hotel also has one of the town's best **restaurants**; with the godsend of air conditioning.

****Hs Bellomonte**, Bellomonte 1, **t** 974 40 20 44 (*cheap*). Small, very comfortable *hostal* with a decent **restaurant** (*inexpensive*).

Aragón's most picturesque villages, crowned by a well-preserved 12th-century castle and large **Colegiata** (16th century).

Monzón, the other large town of the region, was a very important Templar enclave. It came their way as part of a deal: when the King of Aragón, Alfonso el Batallador, died without an heir in 1131, the Aragonese nobles were shocked upon reading his will to discover that he had bequeathed the kingdom to the Sepulchre of the Lord in Jerusalem and its guardians, the Knights Templar. The nobles quickly talked Alfonso's brother, Ramiro the Monk (Ramiro II) into taking the Crown. He dutifully married, sired a daughter, married her off at the age of two to Count Ramón Berenguer IV of Barcelona and returned to his monastery. Ramón Berenguer could now add 'King of Aragón' to his titles, and he generously compensated the slighted Templars with Monzón and many other properties. Ramón Berenguer's descendant, Jaume I the Conqueror, was educated here in the ruined **castle** that still dominates the town.

Near Graus, on the banks of a lake, **Torreciudad** has had a shrine of the Virgin since the 12th century. One of its most fervent devotees was Escrivá de Balaguer (d. 1975), an Aragonese priest who in 1928 founded the Opus Dei – a shadowy organization of ultra-conservative Catholic technocrats that ran most of Spain in the later Franco years. It has since spread to some 80 countries around the world, with the blessing of John Paul II, who beatifed Escrivá in 1992. Some of Opus Dei's rites, like flagellation, are downright medieval; and yet their main concerns are education (they run a university in Pamplona) and getting their members or sympathizers into the upper echelons of business and government – the organization came close to taking over Spain in the 1970s, and Mexico in the 1950s.

Las Cinco Villas

Lying west of Zaragoza, the region of Las Cinco Villas was named after five villages promoted to the status of towns by Philip V in gratitude for their help during the War of the Spanish Succession. The five (Tauste, Ejea de los Caballeros, Sádaba, Uncastillo and Sos del Rey Católico) all offer picturesque ensembles of old buildings and a quiet kind of atmosphere.

Tauste, closest to Zaragoza, boasts a fine *mudéjar* church of the 13th century, the convent of **Las Clarisas** and, a few kilometres away over the mountains, the sanctuary of **Sancho Abarca**. Among its fine 16th-century houses, **Ejea de los Caballeros** has a fortified Romanesque church, **San Salvador** (1222) with a stork-topped tower, more befitting a castle than a church, and beautiful Romanesque sculpture on one of the two fonts. The first Aragonese Parliament is said to have been formed in the church of **Santa María**. In **Sádaba**, there's a 16th-century church in Aragonese-Gothic style and a large, square 13th-century castle just outside town, outwardly in good condition, but a wreck inside.

The last two of the Cinco Villas, nearer the Pyrenees, are the most rewarding. **Uncastillo** seems entirely medieval, its houses adorned with proud escutcheons on steep streets crowded beneath the great ruined castle. Arcaded **Plaza del Campo** is

Getting Around

Las Cinco Villas are served from Zaragoza (Autobuses Cinco Villas, Av. de Navarra 81, **t** 976 33 33 71 and Sangüesa, Estación del Portillo in Zaragoza). Sos del Rey Católico is easiest to reach, via any Pamplona–Zaragoza bus; buses from Zaragoza station will take you right there four times a day.

Tourist Information

Ejea de los Caballeros: Pza de la Magdalena, **t** 976 66 11 00, **f** 976 66 38 16, *www.aytoejea.es*.

Sos del Rey Católico: Pza de la Villa 1, **t** 948 88 80 65, *www.territoriomuseo.com* (*open Sept–May daily 10–2 and 4–8; June–Aug daily 10–2 and 5–9*).

Where to Stay and Eat

Ejea de los Caballeros ✉ 22100

★★Hs Cuatro Esquinas, Salvador 4, **t** 976 66 10 03 (*inexpensive*). Tucked away behind the church, with a bustling little **restaurant**.

Sos del Rey Católico ✉ 50680

★★★Parador Ferdinand de Aragón, C/Arq Sainz de Vicuña 1 (signposted from all over the village), **t** 948 88 80 11, **f** 948 88 81 00, *sos@parador.es* (*expensive*). Modern rooms in a traditional stone and wood-beamed building. Friendly, cosy atmosphere and a relatively good **restaurant** (*menú moderate*).

Fonda Fernandina, Pza del Mesón, **t** 948 88 81 20 (*cheap*). The budget traveller's dream come true: in an old mansion with a huge foyer, grand ceiling and sweeping staircase; comfortable, vividly painted rooms, and a low-key **restaurant** (*moderate–inexpensive*) serving tasty food (and excellent home-made cheesecake) under the beady eye of a boar's head.

Las Coronas, C/Pons Sorolla 2, **t** 948 88 83 48 (*inexpensive*). An inviting restaurant on the Pza de la Villa with a huge hearth for spit roasts and tables and chairs under the arches outside. It also has Turismo Rural rooms (*cheap*). The tourist office has details of further Turismo Rural options.

Vinacua, Pza del Mesón, **t** 948 88 80 71 (*inexpensive*). The local hangout, with some affordable *menús*.

the centre, near the most interesting of Uncastillo's numerous churches, Romanesque **Santa María la Mayor**, with a fine carved façade and a battlemented Gothic tower. There are remains of a Roman spa by the hot springs at **Los Bañoles**.

Sos added 'del Rey Católico' to its name in 1924, honouring Ferdinand, who was a baby here. It is the most visited town of the five and the most beautiful; a wander through its old streets reveals a snapshot of its history, from the Romanesque and Gothic windows of its houses, to the sweeping view from the esplanade near the castle church. Like Uncastillo it has a number of noble mansions, most importantly, the **Palacio de Sada**, birthplace of Ferdinand and now a museum, housing artworks and historical odds and ends related to the king. Go inside Romanesque **San Esteban** to see the gorgeous 14th-century frescoes in its crypt, painted by a husband and wife duo (but the steep spiral stairs down are definitely not for tall statures!).

Huesca and the Castillo de Loarre

Huesca, the provincial capital of northern Aragón, is unlovely but prosperous; it sits in the middle of its own fertile *hoya* (irrigated farmland), and is within easy striking distance of some of the loveliest scenery in Spain, from the central Pyrenees to many green, forested valleys dotted with blue glacial lakes. Spaniards associate Huesca with the *Leyenda de la Campana* ('Legend of the Bell'), illustrated by a painting in the

Getting Around

By Train

Huesca is most easily reached by train from Zaragoza (for bus connections, *see* 'Zaragoza', p.256). The train station is on C/Zaragoza (information, **t** 974 24 21 59).

By Bus

Huesca's bus station is on Av. del Parque 3 (information, **t** 974 21 07 00). To get to the Castillo de Loarre, catch the bus to Ayerbe and get off at Loarre, then walk 6½km. There are only three connections a day so plan in advance (or stay over in Loarre or Ayerbe).

Tourist Information

Huesca: Pza de la Catedral, **t** 974 29 21 70, **f** 974 29 21 54, *turismo.aytohuesca@aragob.es* (*open daily in summer 9–8; in winter 9–2 and 4–8*). Housed in a modern mixture of marble and metal.

Where to Stay

Huesca ✉ 22000

*****Pedro I de Aragón**, Av. del Parque 34, **t** 974 22 03 00, **f** 974 22 00 94 (*expensive*). The smartest place to stay in Huesca: marble-floored rooms are fully equipped with a/c and TV, and the hotel pool is an added enticement (should you need one) in the summer months.

*****Sancho Abarca**, Pza de Lizana 3, **t** 974 22 06 50, **f** 974 22 51 69 (*moderate*). This little member of the Husa chain, near the old centre, provides plushly draped rooms.

***Hs Lizana 1** and ****Hs Lizana 2**, Pza Lizana 6 and 8, **t** 974 22 07 76, **f** 974 23 14 55, *www.airtel.net/profesionales/lizana2* (*inexpensive*). Friendly family management presides over a range of rooms, from those in the cheaper Lizana 1 to the ones in Lizana 2, its smarter sister; there's also a garage available.

Casa Paco, on the corner of C/Ricafort and C/Aínsa, and the adjacent **Augusto**, **t** 974 22 00 79 (*cheap*). Both places are owned by the team at Casa Paco, providing cheaper, central rooms.

Eating Out

Huesca is renowned for its gastronomic superiority in Aragón, boasting two Michelin-starred restaurants. Local specialities include *pollo al chilindrón* (chicken in a sauce of onion, garlic, pepper and tomato), *ternasco* (lamb roasted with garlic and potatoes) and *salmorrejo* (eggs with pork cutlets). The local wine comes from the area east of Huesca, called Somontano, and is noted mostly for Alcañón, a light, fruity white, as well as some highly palatable reds.

Las Torres, C/Maria Auxiliadora 3, **t** 974 22 82 13 (*expensive*). One of the places endowed with a star and serving some of the best food in Huesca town: imaginatively prepared Aragonese and international dishes.

Lillas Pastia, Pza de Navarra 4, **t** 974 21 16 91 (*expensive*). Succumb to the eight-course *menú* or a selection *a la carta*, served in a wing of the old casino, garbed in an outrageous mix of décors; an indulgent place to dine in style.

Venta del Sotón, on the Ctra Tarragona–San Sebastián, Km226, in Esquedas (28km north of Huesca on the A132), **t** 974 27 02 41 (*expensive*). A converted country house restaurant: excellent *chorizos y longanizas a la brasa*, Aragonese baby kid with artichokes, *pollo al chilindrón* and salted beef dishes.

Flor de Huesca, Porches de Galicia 4, **t** 974 24 03 40 (*inexpensive*). A tasty four-course *menú* is served here, near Pza de Navarra.

El Bodegón, C/Pedro IV 4, **t** 974 23 16 81 (*inexpensive*). Recently opened and trying hard to please, its *menú* offers a good-value, recommended meal.

La Campana, Coso Alto 78, **t** 974 22 95 00 (*inexpensive*). Sombre looking but serving superlative *cabritillo asado en horno de leña* – baby kid baked in a traditional wood oven. The *menú del día* is good value.

Hervi, Santa Paciencia 2, **t** 974 24 03 33 (*inexpensive*). A busy, friendly bar/restaurant in the centre of town, with excellent tapas and a decent *menú*.

Granja Anita, Pza de Navarra 5. One of those oh-so-tempting breakfast venues, with a dangerous array of delectable pastries on display, not to mention the obligatory *chocolate con churros*.

Ayuntamiento (*open Mon–Fri 9–2 and 4–8*): faced with rebellious nobles, Ramiro II ('the Monk'; *see* above) summoned them to his palace to ask their advice on a bell he meant to cast, so big that it would be heard throughout all Aragón. As the nobles filed in, one by one, the monkish king had their heads cut off. Ramiro II's admirers claim it's all a load of rubbish, but you can visit the actual **Sala de la Campana** underneath the **museum** in Pza de la Universidad (*open Mon–Sat 10–2 and 5–8, Sun 10–2*), in a building that began its life as a Moorish *alcazar*, and served for many years as the palace of the kings of Aragón, then in 1354 as a university. Exhibits range from the prehistoric to medieval Aragonese painting.

Ramiro II and his brother Alfonso el Batallador are buried in Huesca's oldest church, the 12th-century **San Pedro el Viejo** (C/Cuatro Reyes; *open Mon–Sat 10–1.30 and 4–7.30; closed Sun*); the cloister's capitals have some fine carvings of monsters. The lovely late-Gothic **Cathedral** has a landmark octagonal tower, and a west portal topped by an unusual *mudéjar* gallery; within is another of Damián Forment's great alabaster *retablos*. The **cathedral museum** (***museum** open winter Mon–Fri 10.30–1.30 and 4–7, Sat 10.30–1.30, closed Sun; summer open until 7.30 in the evenings; adm;* ***cathedral** open daily 8–1.30 and 4–7*) holds mainly primitive art from the region. It's also well worth poking your head through the beautifully carved walnut doors of the **casino** on Pza de Navarra; founded in 1904, it has been restored to its former glory after a stint as a military hospital during and after the Civil War, with a pale green decorated stairwell climbing gracefully up to the Red and Blue Rooms. It remains full of all its gambling accessories, though it's more of an elderlies' club now.

Huesca is the base for visiting Aragón's showpiece **Castillo de Loarre** (*open July and Aug daily 10–8; 2 Mar–1 Oct* (*exc July–Aug*) *Tues–Sun 10–1.30 and 4–7, closed Mon; 2 Oct–1 Mar Wed–Sun 11–2.30, closed Mon and Tues*), an 11th-century military masterpiece on a rocky eminence overlooking the great plain of Aragón, a 30-minute car ride away. The castle, built by Sancho Ramírez, the great king of Navarre, so perfectly fits into its surroundings that it approaches environmental art. It has been lovingly restored and is exciting to explore; outstanding are its three great towers – La Vigía, el Homenaje, and la Reina – and its gem of a Romanesque **chapel**. If you pass through nearby **Ayerbe**, stop to see the **Gothic palace** of the local Marqués.

Jaca and Around

The attractive, bustling little town of Jaca, only 30 kilometres from France, is the only real town in Aragón's Pyrenees and is nearly everyone's point of departure for the mountains to the north and east (which are far more rugged and less exploited than Catalunya's Pyrenees) and for the secluded valleys and villages to the west. If you're heading north to France at the end of your Spanish trip, it's your last chance to pick up some Spanish wine and that *paella* pan you've been meaning to buy all along.

Jaca was a point of departure even in the Middle Ages: for Santiago de Compostela. Pilgrims taking the Aragonese road would cross the mountains near Canfranc, then the next day make for Jaca before turning west. Even earlier, Jaca served as the first capital of Aragón when in 760 it was regained from the Moors. In 795, when the Moors tried to take it back, the women defended it so fiercely they never tried again, an event commemorated each May by a mock battle between groups of local ladies. French influence crossed the border with the pilgrims and, in Jaca, Spain's very first Romanesque church, the **Cathedral** (*open daily 7.30–2 and 4–8.30*), was constructed at the beginning of the 11th century. Although meddled with over the years it's still impressive; note the finely carved capitals, and the silver shrine of Santa Orosia, Jaca's patron saint, who was martyred by the Moors for refusing to renounce her faith. The row of cafés under the arches alongside the cathedral are a good place to contemplate its satisfying squatness. The **Diocesan Museum** (*open Tues–Sun 11–2 and 4–7; closed Mon*) in the cloister is especially worthwhile, featuring many Romanesque frescoes garnered from abandoned chapels in the Pyrenees. Jaca's other principal monument, the pentagonal **Ciudadela** (*open daily 11–12 and 6–8; earlier afternoon hours out of summer*), was begun by Philip II after the Aragón revolt – one of the numerable headaches faced by His Majesty the Bureaucrat. Take a stroll along the ramparts of the Camino Monte Pago for fine views of the River Aragón, or walk down to the handsome medieval **Puente de San Miguel** on the pilgrims' road, one kilometre from town. Before setting out on excursions, check in at Jaca's tourist office, a goldmine of information on the Pyrenees; it can also sell you a good hiking map.

East of Jaca: Ordesa National Park

In the misty dawn of Aragón this was the county of Sobrarbe. Much of its heart is now part of the **Parque Nacional de Ordesa**, created in 1918. One of Spain's most beautiful, the park is crowned by the **Tres Sorores**, 'the three sisters': three mountains over 10,102ft high. In the late spring, hundreds of waterfalls cascade towards the Río Arazus in the valley, and in summer edelweiss adorn the slopes. There are trails through the poplar groves for strollers and 984ft cliffs for alpinists; the most beautiful is the six- to seven-hour **Soasso Circle** route which skirts along the Río Arazus and then up the valley for some spectacular scenery over the gorge, climaxing in the **Mirador Calcitarruego**. Anyone in reasonable shape can make it, but you should wear hiking boots and take something for lunch. Provisions are obtainable in **Torla**, a small stone village at the entrance of the park, with plenty of accommodation as well. Just north of Torla, on the other side of a pretty gorge, the narrow **Garganta de Escalar**, lies the now rather decrepit spa resort of **Balneario de Panticosa**, with mineral springs providing cures for dodgy tummies, bad backs and respiratory problems.

South of the park, **Aínsa** was the capital of the ancient kingdom of Sobrarbe and is the loveliest town in the region. The Sobrarbe claims to be the least populated area of Europe, aided by the numerous actual and proposed reservoirs which have wiped out whole villages. Aínsa's old walled centre is crisscrossed with medieval streets, and an elegant **Plaza Mayor** overlooks the new quarters below, now interspersed with an ample supply of restaurants, hotels, discothèques and boutiques. Its austere, Romanesque church holds one of the hugest fonts imaginable and rests on a pleasingly vaulted crypt. In the castle a small **Ecomuseo** (*open 1 July–15 Sept 10.30–2 and*

Getting Around

By Train

Jaca is best reached by train from Zaragoza (for bus connections, *see* 'Zaragoza'). The train station (information, **t** 974 36 13 32) is at the northern end of C/Juan XXIII; a local bus makes connections from here to the centre of town.

By Bus

In Jaca the bus station is more convenient than the train station, on Av. Jacetania behind the cathedral (information, **t** 974 35 50 60). From Jaca there's a daily bus to Ansó and Hecho, and two buses daily to Pamplona and Zaragoza via Huesca and Biescas, 30km from Torla and the Ordesa Park. A daily bus from Sabiñánigo (between Huesca and Jaca) links Biescas, Torla and Aínsa (**t** 974 48 00 45). You may just want to rent a car and save yourself the hassle (although be warned that vehicle access into the heart of the park is restricted in high season).

Benasque may be reached from Monzón (with its train station, **t** 974 40 12 44); buses are more frequent during the ski season: the bus station is on Av. Lérida (**t** 974 40 06 32). Jaca runs a fairly good shuttle service to the resorts in the winter.

Tourist Information

Jaca: Av. Regimiento de Galicia 2, **t** 974 36 00 98, **f** 974 35 51 65, *consultas@aytojaca.es* (*open 9–2 and 4.30–8*).

Ordesa National Park: In summer, there's an information office at the Park entrance in **Bielsa**: Pza Mayor, **t** 974 50 11 27; also in **Torla**: C/Fatas s/n, **t** 974 48 61 52; and in **Aínsa**: at the crossroads in the new town, **t** 974 50 07 67, *ainsa@pirineo.com* (*open Tues–Sat 10–2 and 4–8, Sun 10–2*).

Festivals

Aínsa: Morisma, *Sun preceding 14 Sept, every other year*. The Morisma is re-enacted biennially to mark the reconquest of Aínsa in 724 by King Garci Ximeno.

Fungal Festival, *7 Oct*. Believe it or not, this is equally famous.

Sports and Activities

Opportunities for hiking, climbing and a host of other activities abound in **Ordesa National Park** (*see* p.271). From **Nerín**, a 4x4 bus sets off twice daily on a four-hour trip to *miradors* at 7,216ft, with spectacular views. If you'd prefer to do the hiking yourself, the bus leaves at 7am, dropping you off at 8am at the top *mirador* and picking you up 10 hours later.

Skiing

Northern Aragón offers Spain's most varied and challenging skiing, and facilities are mostly up to date and relatively reasonable in comparison with Europe; a bit out of the way, they are also likely to be less crowded.

5–8.30) has been set up, with exhibitions of fossils and Pyrenean fauna. Aínsa is the perfect base for excursions into the mountains, to remote villages and dolmens.

If you'd prefer to be a bit further away from it all, head for **Nerín**, beautifully situated in the Parque Nacional; turn off at Escalona and follow the lovely Cañón de Añisclo; Nerín is signposted most of the way. It has an unobtrusive Romanesque church and the shell of a 12th-century hermitage, and fewer inhabitants than were recorded in 1488. From here, you can catch a ride up into the Pyrenean peaks for the fantastic views from some lofty *miradors* (*see* 'Sports and Activities', above). **Bielsa**, near the French border, is the departure point for the 15-kilometre hike along the **Valle de Pineta**, Ordesa's 'twin' valley, on the banks of the Río Cinca. A pre-Romanesque hermitage, a lake and glacier and magnificent views (and fewer fellow-hikers) are some of the highlights. Farther east, the mountains become so formidable that the

Package deals are available in Madrid, Barcelona, Zaragoza and from travel agents anywhere in Aragón. All have equipment for hire.

Cerler, near Benasque, has very modern facilities including five restaurants, two discos and five bars, and 38 pistes on the highest slopes the Pyrenees can offer. There are two hotels and a *hostal* at the resort (and 10 hotels and four *hostales* in Benasque), an ice palace and a wide range of other activities; **t** 974 55 10 12, *www.cerler.com*.

Benasque also has **La Maladeta**, a series of downhill runs and cross-country trails, but you have to make your own way up there.

Astún, near Jaca and the Canfranc rail station, has 45 pistes (12 are difficult, three very difficult), two slalom courses (one giant), one hotel and oodles of apartments for hire, and easy transport from Jaca; **t** 974 37 30 34, *www.astun.com*.

Candanchú, Astún's older sister on the other side of Canfranc, offers 55 pistes, as well as cross-country skiing, four hotels and four *albergues* at the station and bars, cafés and discos; there's easy transport from Jaca; **t** 974 37 31 92, *www.candanchú.com*.

El Formigal, near Sallent de Gállego, has 53 very open pistes without obstacles (one is 7km long), served by one *telecabina* and 22 other lifts. There's a slalom course, lots of recreational facilities and four hotels at the station; **t** 974 49 00 00, *www.formigal.com*.

Panticosa, also near Sallent de Gállego (Sabiñánigo, between Jaca and Huesca, is the closest train station – 40km distant), has 38 pistes, a slalom course and eight hotels and numerous bars and restaurants at the station; **t** 974 48 72 48, *www.panticosa-loslagos.com*.

Where to Stay and Eat

Jaca ✉ 22700

★★**Conde Aznar**, Pso de la Constitución 3, **t** 974 36 10 50, **f** 974 36 07 97, (*moderate–inexpensive*). This is traditionally comfortable, with a garden and good **restaurant** (*see* below).

★★**La Paz**, C/Mayor 41, **t** 974 36 07 00, **f** 974 36 04 00 (*moderate*). Modern and comfortable with an outrageous glass-domed **restaurant**.

★**Hs París**, Pza de San Pedro 5, **t** 974 36 10 20, *www.jaca.com/hostalparis* (*cheap*). By far the most atmospheric of the cheaper options, with polished, antique, red pine floors throughout and large, airy rooms.

★**Hs Somport**, Echegaray 11, **t** 974 36 34 10 (*cheap*). Just off C/Mayor; this one is a bit less characterful.

The tourist office can provide a list of ***casas particulares*** (rooms in private houses).

For your last **meal** on Spanish soil before hitting the French border, there are a few places in Jaca worth a visit:

La Cocina Aragonesa, C/Cervantes 2, **t** 974 36 10 50 (*expensive*). Conde Aznar's well-regarded restaurant, offering a posh atmosphere and some wonderful food. *Closed Thurs*.

Mesón Serrabio, C/Obispo 3, **t** 974 36 24 18 (*inexpensive*). Excellent regional cuisine, with an inexpensive *menù del dìa*; a particularly inviting place when the weather turns sour.

Spaniards call them **Los Montes Malditos** (the 'cursed mountains'). The tallest of the Pyrenees are here: **Aneto** (11,165ft) and its sister peak, **Maladeta** (10,850ft). **Benasque** is the base for visiting them, for summer climbs and hikes, or winter skiing. The village itself, of stone houses with slate roofs, is hemmed in by the mountains and remains wonderfully picturesque and tranquil.

West of Jaca

In 724, the nobles of Sobrarbe gathered at the remote chapel of **San Juan de la Peña** and solemnly vowed to rid Aragón of the Moorish invaders, and ever since then the old monastery has been the chief shrine of the Aragonese Reconquista. According to legend, the chalice of the Last Supper (now in València) was hidden here for centuries. The whole valley has a positively supernatural feel when the clouds hang low over

Mesón El Rancho Grande, C/del Arco 2, **t** 974 36 01 72 (*inexpensive*). A very charming, low-ceilinged, 'olde worlde' place to linger over your meal.

El Viejo Rancho, C/Bellido 11, **t** 974 36 10 52 (*inexpensive*). Around the corner and confusingly similarly named, another welcoming eaterie housed in an old stone building.

El Arco, C/San Nicolas 4, **t** 974 34 80 87 (*inexpensive*). Worth a visit even for the most dedicated carnivore, this cheaper, family-run restaurant serves delicious, inventive vegetarian cuisine.

Jaca is also good for **tapas**:

La Nicolasa, Escuelas Pias 3, **t** 974 35 54 12 (*inexpensive*). A superb range, from prawns to country pies, served under half-timbers.

Torla ✉ 22376

In Torla, by Ordesa Park, there are magnificent mountain views:

Villa de Torla, Falás 5, **t** 974 48 61 56, **f** 974 48 63 65 (*moderate*). With wholesome rooms and a pool. *Open all year*.

*__Ballarín__, Capuvita 11, **t** 974 48 61 55 (*inexpensive*). Simple, comfortable rooms.

Casa Borruel, **t** 974 48 60 67 (*cheap*). A friendly *casa rural* in the centre, offering more of the atmospheric and traditional. For more *casas rurales*, ask at the Turismo Rural office or at the tourist office on the main square.

Balneario de Panticosa ✉ 22661

***__Gran Hotel__, Ctra Balneario, **t** 974 48 71 61 (*moderate–inexpensive*). Good facilities: a pool, tennis and sauna, and very comfortable rooms (cheaper with shared bath).

Aínsa ✉ 22330

As with many such towns, there's really no need to subject yourself to new Aínsa when you can stay reasonably up in the old centre.

__Posada Real__, Pza Mayor 6, **t 974 50 09 77, **f** 974 50 09 53 (*expensive–moderate*). Fancy four-posters with soaring views out to Monte Perdido and a truly plush suite on top, with a mosaic bathroom. All enquiries at Bodegón de Mallacán (on the plaza); the same owner runs the huge, dark **Casa del Marqués** (a luxurious Turismo Rural abode), an old stone house off the Plaza that sleeps up to 15 and has a large terrace.

***__Casa de San Martín__, C/Unica 1, San Martín de la Solana, **t/f** 974 50 31 05, *samartin@encomix.es* (*expensive*). A beautifully sited, small hotel in a property previously owned by the omnipresent local monastery, north-west of Aínsa.

Hotel Sánchez, Av. del Sobrarbe 10, **t** 974 50 00 14, **f** 974 50 07 75 (*inexpensive*). A clean and comfortable new-town option, with balconies, a/c, a pool and half board.

Casa El Hospital, C/Santa Cruz 3, **t** 974 50 07 50 (*inexpensive*). An attractive *casa rural* by the church in the old town, with smallish but delightful rooms furnished with local rustic pieces; some quads and a studio, all with a/c and heating. Enquire at the shop underneath or knock on the big door opposite.

Casa Damaso, C/Portal Bajo 9, **t** 974 50 01 69, *www.staragon.com/casadamaso* (*inexpensive*). A modern apartment for four people in one of the old-town, old stone houses; it has a spacious feel, vistas and even a washing machine.

the freshly scented pines, and the trees' autumnal golden hues are worth a trip in themselves. Parking for the old monastery is a little over a kilometre uphill from the site, amongst pine woods with picnic tables. It's a pleasure of a 10-minute walk down (*take the path through the woods marked off to the left, around 100m past the new monastery*) or await the regular shuttle bus. For more information about the local landscape and walks in it, visit the **Casa Forestal** (opposite the new monastery). The **old monastery** (*open 1 June–31 Aug daily 10–2.30 and 3.30–8; 16 Mar–31 May and 1 Sept–15 Oct daily 10–2 and 4–7; 16 Oct–15 Mar Tues–Sun 11–2 and 4–5.30 but closed Mon; adm*), under an overhanging cliff, is on two levels. The crypt is actually the original 9th-century Mozarabic chapel, with jewel-coloured frescoes interrupted by stalactites, and intricate decorations on the inside of the side apses. Next door are the old and distinctly damp dormitories. Upstairs the 12th-century Romanesque **church** is

Bodegón de Mallacán, Pza Mayor 6, **t** 974 50 09 77 (*moderate*). An upmarket, pricey *menú* in an intimate setting, specializing in game and local *setas* (mushrooms).

Callizo, Pza Mayor, **t** 974 50 03 85 (*inexpensive*). This has an impressive *menú*, imaginatively and professionally presented.

Fez, C/Mayor, **t** 974 50 08 99 (*inexpensive*). A cheaper old-town *menú*.

L'Alfil Tapas, C/Travesera, **t** 974 50 02 99 (*inexpensive*). A cheap and cheerful tapas option, with large portions.

Nerín ✉ 22375

Palazio, **t** 974 48 90 02, **f** 974 48 90 26 (*expensive–inexpensive*). A carefully planned hotel with amazing views down the valley; every room has an Internet connection and there's a colour scheme for each floor, peaking in orange under the wooden eaves; if you're on for a splurge, go for the top-floor suite, with its enormous bed and hydromassaging bath. The owners are a mine of information on walks and mountain sports; and the hotel **restaurant** can supply a simple and filling *menú* (*inexpensive*).

Añisclo Albergue, **t** 974 48 90 10, **f** 974 48 90 08 (*cheap*). If you're after a cheaper stay, this offers basic bunk-bedded rooms for four to eight, with half and full board available.

Bielsa ✉ 22350

******Parador de Monte Perdido**, Valle de Pineta, **t** 974 50 10 11, **f** 974 50 11 88, *bielsa@parador.es* (*expensive*). A modern hotel with 24 rooms and a **restaurant** (*moderate*) serving mountain specialities.

Benasque ✉ 22440

***Hotel El Puente II**, San Pedro, Ctra Francia, **t** 974 55 12 11, **f** 974 55 16 84 (*moderate*). Offers a posh ambiance and mountain views.

****Araguells**, Av. de los Tilos 1, **t** 974 55 16 19, **f** 974 55 16 64 (*inexpensive*). A well-equipped, central alternative.

There are decent **restaurants** attached to Benasque's smart hotels, as well as more informal *comedores* at the various bars.

Filly, opposite the Red Cross station on the road leading up to the peak (*cheap*). A nice café serving good tapas, light meals and a delicious selection of filled croissants.

Valle del Hecho ✉ 22720

Casa Blasquico, Pza de la Fuente 1, **t** 974 37 50 07 (*inexpensive*). Identified as *pensión*, but with five attractive rooms and a small **restaurant** (*moderate*) with a nationwide reputation: the imaginative menu is a surefire treat. Book ahead for rooms and food.

***Hs De la Val**, Cruz Alta 1, **t** 974 37 50 28, **f** 974 37 52 51 (*inexpensive*). Offers decent and affordable rooms.

Valle de Ansó ✉ 22700

In Ansó choice is limited; two of the best are:

****Hs Estanés**, Pso Chapitel 9, **t** 974 37 01 46 (*inexpensive*). Charming and old, with a garden. Good-value and very popular little fish **restaurant** (*inexpensive*).

Posada Magoria, next to the Estanés, **t** 974 37 00 49 (*inexpensive*). All low ceilings and wooden beams; very much a traditional house, and comfortable to boot, with good home-made, home-grown vegetarian meals.

perfect in its simplicity and flanked by kings and nobility. Outside it are the **tombs** of Ramiro I and Pedro I of Aragón, as well as the pantheon of the Aragonese and Navarran nobles, with delicately carved caryatides; in the 18th century Charles III had many of the earlier rulers reinterred here with neoclassical fittings that clash completely with the unadorned church. Off the other side stands a florid Gothic concoction abounding in ivy and snails (both symbols of death). The 12th-century **cloister** – or rather the half of the cloister that has survived – is the main reason for coming, magnificently and fancifully carved by the Maestro de San Juan de la Peña. Particularly satisfying is the naïve depiction of Adam and Eve and their inevitable expulsion from Eden; Adam's face is a caricature of fear. Joseph's dream is equally enchanting: he lies, clad in his nightcap, on a polka-dotted pillow, while a butterfly-like angel descends. Note also the unusual portrayal of the Last Supper. The hamlet of

Santa Cruz de la Serós, eight kilometres downhill, had an auxiliary convent, its surviving 11th-century church of **Santa María** (*same opening hours as the monastery*) modelled on Jaca's cathedral. At the crossroads is the smaller, 9th-century church of **San Caprasio**.

Berdún was a day's journey for the pilgrim from Jaca. The beauty of the area, and its abundant and unusual plant and bird life, inspired an English artist, John Boucher, to found a field studies centre for painters, bird-watchers, botanists and architects, amateurs and professionals alike.

This is the region of **Old Aragón**, and there are two secluded valleys here which have seen little change since the Middle Ages. The eastern one, the **Valle del Hecho**, was the birthplace of Alfonso el Batallador and still preserves its ancient Aragonese dialect; the principal village, **Hecho**, couldn't be more charming or better sited. In July and August, Hecho and the surrounding hills turn into a contemporary sculpture garden as part of the 'Simposio de Escultura y Pintura Moderna'. It has spawned an open-air gallery of sculpture, set west of the village and affording great views over the valley. There's an **ethnological museum** (*open daily 11–2 and 6–9; adm*) near the village church. An easy walk away is the hamlet of **Siresa**, where a number of lovely hikes begin. Alfonso el Batallador was educated here in the monastery of the ancient church of **San Pedro de Siresa**.

In the **Valle de Ansó** the old villagers speak yet another near-vanished dialect, and it's one of the few places in Spain where you may catch sight of a woman in her traditional costume any day of the week. Some of Ansó's houses are adorned with inexplicable symbols; thought to be a memory of the valley's once-sizeable population of *agotes*, the mysterious pariahs of the Pyrenees, believed to be the descendants of Visigoths, Moors, Cathar heretics or, most commonly and erroneously, lepers. They lived on both sides of the Pyrenees under apartheid laws of segregation until the late 18th century and have since vanished without a trace. Ansó is a bit more conscious of its own whitewashed charms than Hecho and its **Museo Etnológico** (*open daily 10.30–1.30 and 4–8; adm*) of odds and ends may be visited in the old church on the Plaza de San Pedro. Ansó is also a good base for hiking, particularly for exploring the beautiful **Valle de Zuriza**, 13 kilometres north.

The Basque Lands, Navarra and La Rioja

11

The Basque Lands, Navarra and La Rioja

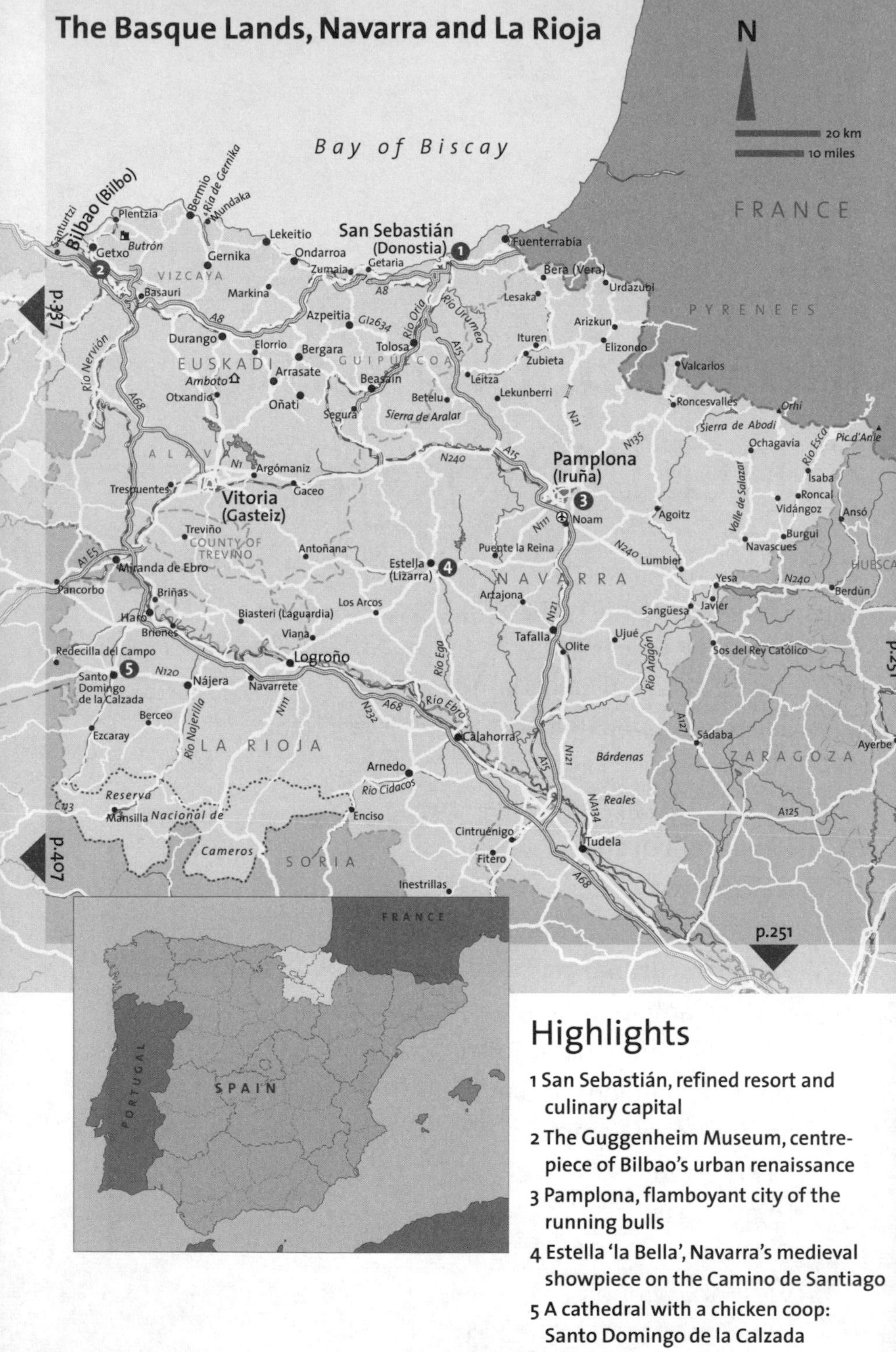

p.337
p.407
p.251
p.251

Highlights

1 San Sebastián, refined resort and culinary capital

2 The Guggenheim Museum, centrepiece of Bilbao's urban renaissance

3 Pamplona, flamboyant city of the running bulls

4 Estella 'la Bella', Navarra's medieval showpiece on the Camino de Santiago

5 A cathedral with a chicken coop: Santo Domingo de la Calzada

The Basque Lands (Euskadi)

The Basque Lands, known in the Basque language as Euskadi ('collection of Basques'), comprise, according to the autonomy agreement of 1981, the three provinces of Vizcaya, Guipúzcoa and Álava. To the Basques themselves, however, Euskadi encompasses all lands inhabited by Basques: the 'Seven Provinces' that include Labourd, Haute-Navarre and the Soule in France and the northern part of Navarra. When it isn't raining, Euskadi is one of the most charming corners of Spain: rural for the most part, lush and green, crisscrossed by a network of streams that meander every which way through steep, narrow valleys in their search for the sea. Great stone country houses resembling Swiss chalets dot the hillsides and riverbanks – though the next valley over may have a grotty little town gathered about a mill. Spain's industrial revolution began in Euskadi, and even today the three Basque provinces are among the most industrialized and wealthy in the country. But in most of Euskadi, industry and finance seem remote. Basque nationalism, on the other hand, is ever present; every bridge, underpass, and pelota court has been painted with the Basque flag and slogans of the notorious ETA ('Euskadi Ta Askatsuna', 'Freedom for Basques'), the small but violent minority that has given this ancient people a bad press.

An Introduction to the Basques

Nomansland, the territory of the Basques, in a region called Cornucopia, where the vines are tied up with sausages. And in those parts there was a mountain made entirely of grated Parmesan cheese on whose slopes there were people who spent their whole time making macaroni and ravioli.

The Decameron, VIII

Wild stories like Boccaccio's have often been told about the Basques and their inscrutable ways, but the conclusions reached by many scholars from many different fields are almost as hard to believe. It seems likely that the Basques are no less than the aborigines of Europe, the descendants of Cro-Magnon hunter-gatherers and painters, having survived in their secluded valleys during the great Indo-European migrations of peoples from the east thousands of years ago. Tests have shown that the Basques have the world's highest incidence of Rh negative blood, characteristic of the indigenous prehistoric European race. There are also slight but telling physical differences between the Basques and their neighbours: not only are they bigger and stronger, but the distinct shape of their skulls is matched only by those of their ancestors, buried under dolmens in 2000 BC.

History

The Basques have no written records, and in other people's histories they always seem to be causing trouble. The Romans conquered but did not tame them, and respected them as soothsayers. Visigoths, Moors and early Christian kingdoms managed even less control over them. Medieval clerics railed against them for fleecing and harassing pilgrims. Political organization into towns and Christianity came late to the Basques, and when they did agree to recognize the suzerainty of Castilla it was on terms that retained their *fueros* (privileges) and ancient laws, one of which stated that every king, upon being crowned, should come to Gernika and swear under the sacred oak tree to uphold their laws.

The Basques (except those in Navarra) lost their *fueros* in retaliation for their support of Fernando VII's reactionary brother Don Carlos in the Carlist wars (1876). Around the same time Euskadi began to industrialize, and while many prospered, the majority of workers, seeing their traditional society threatened on all sides, flocked to the newly raised banner of Basque Nationalism. When the Republican government offered the Basques autonomy in exchange for their support in the 1930s, they jumped at the chance, despite reservations about the government's secularism (the Basques have always been among Spain's most fervent and conservative Catholics). When the Civil War broke out, they remained loyal to the Republic, and even the priests fought side by side with the 'reds'. To break their spirit, the German Condor Legion practised the world's first saturation bombing of a civilian target, at Gernika. Franco later singled out the Basques for reprisals of all kinds, outlawing their language and running the region as a police state, so that even the thousands of Castilians who immigrated to Euskadi to work in the factories felt oppressed enough to sympathize with Basque Nationalist goals. Since Franco, the democratic government has done much to right past grievances in Euskadi: the Basques were the first to gain autonomy, their own police and their own independent TV station. The region is bilingual: Basque is taught in the primary schools, and amnesty was granted to any member of the ETA who renounced violence. But terrorism continues unabated, and it will take many years before the ETA lose their support or, as Mao put it, 'pond for the fish to swim in'. Still, the great majority of Basques vote their aspirations through the PNV (Partido Nacional Vasco) rather than the political wing of the ETA, Herri Batasuna, and on the whole they are progressive, veering left on most issues (strongly anti-nuclear and anti-NATO). After all that, the Basques are an extremely friendly people, and they will make sure you enjoy your stay in their beloved Euskadi.

Basque Culture

Basques have always played an important role in Spanish affairs, far out of proportion to their numbers. They were great sailors and explorers, shipbuilders and whalers, *conquistadores* and pirates, and nowadays they run most of Spain's banks. Basque whalers are said to have landed in the Americas before Columbus; it was Basque sailors who helped the English conquer Wales, built the Spanish Armada, fought in the American revolution and founded a number of Spanish colonies including the Philippines and the city of Buenos Aires. The conquistador Lope de Aguirre (so well portrayed by Klaus Kinski in Herzog's film *Aguirre, the Wrath of God*) and Pedro de Ursua were Basques; the Basque captain Sebastián Elcano became the first man to sail around the world. Two of Spain's most influential saints, St Ignatius de Loyola and St Francis Xavier, were also Basque.

The Basque Lands (Euskadi)

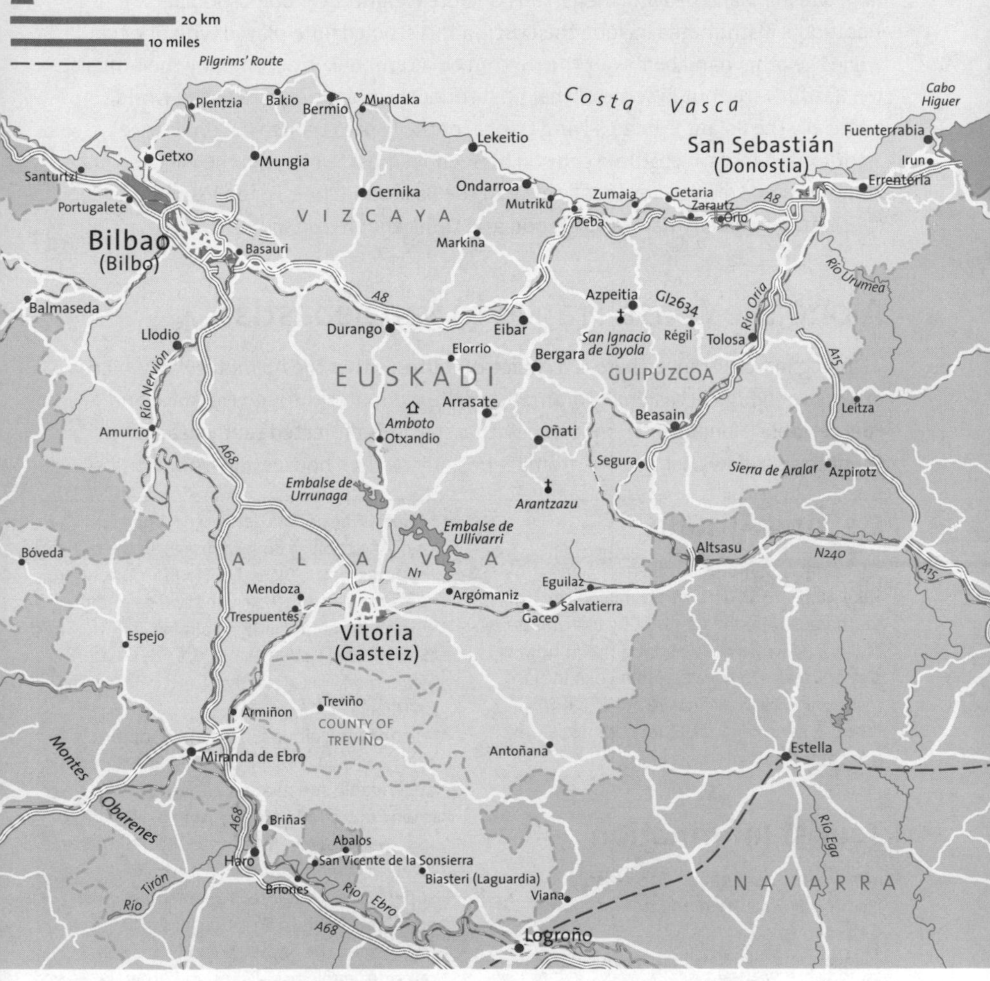

Traditional Basque culture is full of stories built up around the region's countless dolmens, erected as houses by the 'gentiles', or *jentillak*, friendly giants who lived side by side with the Basques. If the rest of Spain used to tell tales about the magical Moors and their hidden treasures, the Basques, who had little contact with the Moors, did the same with their gentiles. The *jentillak* are said to have taught the Basques some special skills, like cultivation, but one day, when strange omens appeared in the sky, they all disappeared under a dolmen, saying 'Kixmi (Jesus Christ) is born, our time is over.' They've never been seen again, although in some villages especially strong, tall people are said to be descended from them. Strength, endurance, agility and competitiveness are the traditional Basque virtues in work, dancing and especially sports. The Basques invented *pelota* (*jaï alaï*), to combine two Basque loves, agility and gambling – although originally *pelota* seems to have been a sacred sport, played against the church wall. Less sacred but widespread are log-splitting, wrestling and heaving mega-kilo concrete weights over one's shoulders. Traditional instruments include the *txistu*, a three-holed flute played with one hand while the other hand beats out the rhythm on a tambour. To accompany their music the Basques step out in some of the most furiously athletic dances in the world, especially the Bolant Dantza (Flying Dance) or the Espata Dantza (Sword Dance). Traditional dances in costume can still be seen on most Sundays in the village square, and traditional recipes are equally alive in the Basque kitchen. For an insight into their considerable culinary flair, *see* the **Food and Drink** chapter, pp.61–70.

Along the Coast: France to San Sebastián

Driving in from France, there is a choice of routes: either the A8 motorway, which is expensive though occasionally dramatic, or the old routes through Hendaye and **Fuenterrabía** (Hondarribia), endowed with a spacious protected sandy beach. Fuenterrabía glows with colour: from its brightly painted houses and its balconies

Getting Around

It's only 20 minutes by bus from San Sebastián to Irún or Fuenterrabía on the frontier; connections are frequent by bus and train and not a few people watching their budgets stay in Irún (or in France) rather than in the more pricey capital. If you're not in a hurry, take the narrow-gauge **El Topo** for a leisurely ride through some fine scenery.

Tourist Information

Irún: Puente de Santiago, Barrio de Behobia s/n, **t** 943 62 26 27; in the train station, **t** 943 61 67 08.

Fuenterrabía (Hondarribia): Javier Ugarte 6, **t** 943 64 54 58.

Where to Stay and Eat

Fuenterrabía ✉ 20280

There is little choice in the moderate and inexpensive ranges (rooms are a better bargain over the border in Hendaye, but Fuenterrabía makes for a more pleasant stay).

★★★**Parador de Hondarribia**, Pza de Armas 14, **t** 943 64 55 00, **f** 943 64 21 53, *pilardemiguel@parador.es* (*luxury*). Prettily situated in the castle that housed so many kings and dukes on French business over the centuries.

★★★**Hotel Obispo**, Pza del Obispo, **t** 943 64 54 00, **f** 943 64 23 86 (*expensive*). In the old residence of the Bishop of Hondarribia, with sumptuously refitted rooms and splendid views. Internet facilities available.

★★**San Nicolás**, Pza de Armas 6, **t** 943 64 42 78 (*moderate*). Has attractive, functional rooms on the plaza.

★★**Hs Alvarez Quintero**, C/Alvarez Quintero 7, **t** 943 64 22 99 (*cheap*). One of a few *hostales*; dependable and relatively good value.

Ramon Roteta, Villa Ainara, Irún 1, **t** 943 64 16 93 (*expensive*). Offers gracious dining in a lovely villa with a garden; grand cuisine and superb desserts. *Closed Sun eve and Thurs.*

Arraunlauri, Pso Butrón 3, **t** 943 64 15 81 (*moderate*). The best bet next to the sea, offering simple fish dishes and other scrumptious seafood.

Irún ✉ 20300

★★★**Alcazar**, Av. Iparralde 11, **t** 943 62 09 00, **f** 943 62 27 97 (*expensive*). At the top of the price range.

★★**Lizaso**, C/Aduana 5–7, **t** 943 61 16 00 (*inexpensive*). Possibly the best deal in Irún, with decent rooms.

Romantxo, Pza de Urdanibia, **t** 943 62 09 71 (*moderate*). Has good home cooking.

Larretxipi, Larretxipi 5, **t** 943 63 26 59. Pricier than some of its neighbours, but the fish is excellent.

loaded with flowers, to its fishing fleet, which has not balked at confronting France in the EU's battles over fishing rights. The town has had its share of sieges – you can still see the ancient walls and a castle of Charles V, now a *parador*. In the evening, head out towards the lighthouse on Cabo Higuer for views of the sunset over the bay.

Irún, the grim border stop of endless waits, is further up the Bidasoa valley, with only plenty of cheap accommodation to recommend it. You can flee the bustling coast for the serene **Valley of Oyarzun** inland, one of Euskadi's rural beauty spots, dotted with the pretty villages of **Oyarzun**, **Lesaka** and **Vera de Bidasoa**.

If you're driving you can take the coastal road from Fuenterrabía along Monte Jáizkibel for its superb views over the Bay of Biscay, the French coast and the Pyrenees. Just east of San Sebastián, the long ribbon town of **Pasajes de San Juan** (Pasai Donibane) lines the east bank of an estuary, with more picturesque old houses. Victor Hugo lived in one for a while, and the Marquis de Lafayette lodged in another before sailing off to aid Britain's American colonists in their revolution. Philip built part of the Invincible Armada here, although now all such business affairs are handled by San Juan's ugly stepsister across the estuary, **Pasajes de San Pedro**.

San Sebastián (Donostia)

Long before there were any *costas*, wealthy Spaniards spent their summers bathing at San Sebastián, following in the footsteps of Queen Regent María Christina who made San Sebastián all the rage in 1886. It's been a classy place to go ever since, a lovely, relaxed, Belle Epoque resort in a spectacular setting, built around one of the peninsula's most enchanting bays, the oyster-shaped Bahía de la Concha, sheltered by a wooded islet, the Isla de Santa Clara, and by Monte Urgull, the hump-backed sentinel at the easternmost tip of the bay.

Playa de la Concha and the Comb of the Winds

Sheltered within the bay is the magnificent golden crescent of the **Playa de La Concha**, San Sebastián's largest beach; at its western end is a promontory topped by the mock-Tudor **Palace of Miramar of María Cristina**, now used for receptions and special exhibitions. A tunnel under the Miramar leads to the **Playa de Ondarreta**, a traditional society retreat. Ondarreta itself meets a dead end at seaside Monte Igueldo, crowned by a **Parque de Atracciones** (*attainable by funicular or by road*), which has spectacular views. Back on the shore, near the base of the funicular, stands one of the most talked-about monuments of modern Spanish sculpture, Eduardo Chillida's **Peine de los Vientos**, the 'Comb of the Winds'; the sculptor's house is on the cliffs above. Nearly all the city behind these beaches dates from the 19th century; San Sebastián is an ancient place, but it has been burnt to the ground 12 times in its history, lastly by Wellington's drunken soldiers, who celebrated their conquest of the town with the accustomed murder and mayhem. Nowadays, the river **Urumea**, lined with promenades, divides the 19th-century part of town from the lively newer quarter of **Gros**, with its own, rather less sheltered, beach.

N
150 metres
100 yards
Monte Igueldo
Parque de Atracciones
Funicular
Peine de los Vientos
Isla de Santa Clara
Aquarium
Playa de Ondarreta
Bahía de la Concha
PASEO DE IGUELDO
AVENIDA DE SATRUSTEGUI
INFANTA CRISTINA
AVENI DA DE ZUMALACARREGUI
CALLE MATIA
Palace of Miramar
PASEO DE HERIZ
Playa de la Concha
PASEO DE LA CONCHA
ALTO DE MIRACONCHA
PASEO DEL DUQUE DE BAENA
CUESTE DE ALDAPETA
CAMINO VIEJO DE ALDAPETA
To Palacio Aiete

San Sebastián (Donostia)

Mar Cantábrico
British Cemetery
Monte Urgull
Castillo de la Mota
Paseo Nuevo
Museum of San Telmo
Museo Naval
Santa María del Coro
Plaza de la Trinidad
Calle 31 de Agosto
San Vicente
Paseo de Salamanca
La Parte Vieja
Mari
Puerto
Calle Mayor
San Jerónimo
Plaza de la Constitución
Iñigo
Pescadería
Fermín Calbetón
Aldamar
El Muelle
Puente de Zurriola
Playa de Gros
Playa de Zurriola
Palacio de Congresos Kursaal y Auditorio
Avenida de la Zurriola
Alameda del Boulevard
Paseo República Argentina
Ayuntamiento
Parque de Alderdi Eder
Peña Florida
Plaza de Gipuzkoa
Calle Okendo
Calle Andía
Paseo de Colón
Calle de Zabaleta
Calle de San Francisco
C Nueva
Secundino Esnaola
Gros
Calle Miramar
Centro Romántico
Puente de Santa Catalina
Plaza de Euskadi
Calle Miracruz
Avenida de la Libertad
Plaza de Cervantes
Calle Loiola
Calle de San Marcial
Etxaide
Paseo de la Concha
Plaza de Zaragoza
Zubieta
Fuenterrabía
Paseo de los Fueros
Paseo de Francia
Mercado de la Brecha
Paseo del Duque de Mandas
Calle de San Martín
Catedral de Buen Pastor
Puente de María Cristina
Estación del Norte
Calle de San Bartolomé
Calle de Easo
Calle de Urbaneta
Calle Urdaneta
Calle Reyes Católicos
Calle de Prim
Paseo del Árbol de Guernica
Río Urumea
Plaza Easo
Calle Moraza
Estación de Amara
To Bus Station
Parque de Cristina Enea
Río Urumea

Getting Around

By Air

San Sebastián's airport to the east, near Fuenterrabía, **t** 943 65 88 00, has connections to Madrid and Barcelona. The bus to the airport, Fuenterrabía and Irún departs from Pza Guipuzkoa, **t** 943 64 13 02, every 12 mins – note that this is really the bus for Fuenterrabía, and lets you off across the road from the airport.

By Train

RENFE trains depart from the Av. de Francia, in Gros, from Estación del Norte, **t** 943 28 30 89. There are frequent connections with Irún and Hendaye, Paris, Burgos and Madrid; less frequent trains to Barcelona, Pamplona, Salamanca, Vitoria, Zaragoza and León. Good Talgo trains whizz all the way to Madrid, Málaga, Córdoba, Algeciras, València, Alicante, Oviedo and Gijón. Topo trains, **t** 943 47 08 15, and Eusko Trenbideak-Ferrocariles Vascos (Feve-Eusko Tren), **t** 943 45 01 31, depart from the Estación de Amara. Topo run to Hendaye via Oyarzun, whilst EuskoTren leave for Bilbao, stopping everywhere on the way.

By Bus

A bewildering number of small bus companies leave from the station on Pza de Pio XII on the southern end of town, a block from the river. The ticket office is nearby on C/Sancho el Sabio 33, though some lines have their offices on Pso de Vizcaya. There are five buses daily to Oviedo, seven to Burgos and five to Galicia. Within Euskadi buses depart every half-hour to Bilbao and Vitoria and up to ten times a day to Pamplona. There are 19 bus lines in San Sebastián itself (**t** 943 28 71 00); No.16 goes to Igueldo and the **funicular** (*summer daily 10–10, every 15 mins*).

By Bike

Cycling is a great way to explore San Sebastián, especially along the 12-km seafront promenade; you can get from one end of the city to the other without having to cross a road. Bikes can be hired from Pso de la Zurrida 22, **t** 943 27 92 60.

By Boat

Motor boats make excursions out to the Isla de Santa Clara every half-hour from the port, where you can also rent a rowing boat if you want to do it yourself.

Tourist Information

San Sebastián: Municipal Office: on the river, C/Reina Regente, **t** 943 48 11 66.

Basque Government: Pso de los Fueros 1, **t** 943 42 62 82.

Post Office: C/Urdareta, behind the cathedral.

Internet Access: try Easonet Comunicaciones, C/Usandizaga 2; and Net Line, C/Urdareta 8.

Tours: There are **walking tours** every Thurs, Fri and Sat in July and Aug with **Guitour**, **t** 943 43 09 09; a guided **tour bus** departs from in front of the tourist office every hour, picking up and dropping off at all the major sights, **t** 696 42 98 47.

Where to Stay

San Sebastián ✉ 20000

San Sebastián is not the place for bargains; many of the cheaper *hostales* and *fondas* are packed with university students all year. As a rule, the further back you are from the sea, the less expensive the accommodation will be.

Luxury–Expensive

★★★★★**María Cristina**, Oquendo 1, **t** 943 42 49 00, **f** 943 42 39 14 (*luxury*). Offering a touch of Belle Epoque elegance, this old *grande dame* is one of Spain's best hotels; it looks on to the Río Urumea's promenade.

★★★★**Hotel Londres y Inglaterra**, Zubieta 2 (on La Concha beach), **t** 943 44 07 70, **f** 943 44 04 91, *h.londres@paisvasco.com* (*luxury*). This boasts splendid views, first-class service, and plenty of charm, as well as one of the city's best **restaurants** (*moderate*).

★★★**La Galeria**, C/Infanta Cristina 1–3, **t** 943 21 60 77, **f** 943 21 12 98, *hotelgaleria@facilnet.es* (*expensive*). A couple of minutes from Playa Ondarreta on a lovely quiet street, this French-inspired turn-of-the-century *palacete* has rooms full of antiques and individuality.

Moderate

San Sebastián being the posh resort it is, you'll find most *hostales* here fall into the *moderate* category.

★★**P. Bikain**, C/Triunfo 8, **t** 943 45 43 33, **f** 943 46 80 74. Has four-star facilities at a very good price, near the beach and the *parte vieja*; spotless rooms, parking facilities, and a very helpful owner.

★★**P. Donostiarra**, C/San Martin 6, **t** 943 42 61 67, **f** 943 43 00 71. Has light, airy rooms with either a little balcony of flowers or a glassed-in *solana* full of pot plants.

Inexpensive

The best you'll find will be at the higher end of *inexpensive*, and there are a fair few both in the *parte vieja* and in the centre.

★★**Hs Eder II**, Alameda del Boulevard, **t** 943 42 64 49. A well-run place at the edge of the *parte vieja*, right in the centre.

★**P. Easo**, C/San Bartolomé 24, **t** 943 45 39 12. A good bargain choice.

Camping de Igueldo, Paseo Orkelaga, **t** 943 21 45 02. The best camping option, up on Monte Igueldo, though quite expensive.

La Sirena, **t** 943 31 02 68, *udala-youthhostel@donostia.org*. A youth hostel at the end of Ondarrena beach, at the foot of the road up Monte Igueldo; the cheapest place in town.

Eating Out

As eating is the municipal obsession, it's not surprising that the city can claim three of Spain's most renowned restaurants – award-winning cathedrals of Basque cuisine. For something cheaper, try following the crowds through the tapas bars of the *parte vieja*.

Expensive

Arzak, Alto de Miracruz 21, **t** 943 27 84 65. A constantly changing menu of delights (the *menú de degustación* makes for one of the finest splurges in northern Spain). *Closed Sun eve and Mon.*

Akelare, in Barrio de Igueldo, **t** 943 21 20 52. Combines exquisite meals with a beautiful setting and views over the sea. *Closed Sun eve and Mon.*

Nicolasa, Aldamar 4, **t** 943 42 17 62. The third culinary shrine, founded in 1912, specializes in classic Basque cookery and offers plenty of choice. *Closed Sun eve and Mon.*

Rekondo, Pso de Igueldo 57, **t** 943 21 29 07. A superb and elegant choice, specializing in grilled fish and meat and boasting a huge wine cellar.

Moderate

Urepel, Pso de Salamanca 3, **t** 943 42 40 40. This is notable for serving fine Basque food at reasonable prices.

Inexpensive

Casa Tiburcío, C/Fermin Calbeton, **t** 943 42 31 30. A popular choice in the *parte vieja* offering an unusually varied *menú* and an excellent choice of tapas treats.

Makrobiotika, C/Intxaurrondo Kalea 52. San Sebastián's best vegetarian restaurant, serving a variety of cereal-based dishes. Take bus No.13 or 24 from the centre as it's a bit of a trek.

Ttun Ttun Taberna, C/San Jeronimo 25, **t** 943 42 68 82. This unassuming tavern is an enclave of Basquedom, serving a wonderful soul-satisfying *menú*.

Bar Tamboril, C/Pescaderia 2, **t** 943 42 35 07. Offers tasty *pintxos*.

Entertainment and Nightlife

Serious party action is centred around the Parte Vieja; you'll find late-night bars and clubs around the end of Ondarreta beach.

Akerbeltz, C/Mari. A tiny bar with a popularity that far exceeds its size, so everyone just congregates outside to enjoy the view of the bay with their beer.

Be Bop, Pso de Salamanca. There are a few bars in the area with live music; this one's a jazz haunt.

Café Remember Rock, C/Republica Argentina s/n. A regular venue for live rock shows.

Etxekalte, C/Mari 1. Almost always packed to the brim, with dance music split between two floors.

La Parte Vieja and Monte Urgull

Most of the action takes place beneath Monte Urgull in the narrow streets of La Parte Vieja, or old town. From **La Concha** beach, its entrance is guarded by a beautiful square, the **Parque de Alderdi Eder**, and the enormous 19th-century **Ayuntamiento**, formerly the casino. What remains of the city's fishing fleet may be seen in the harbour behind the Ayuntamiento, an area rimmed by souvenir shops, pricey tourist restaurants and a pair of salty museums: the recently refurbished **Museo Naval** (*open summer Tues–Sat 10–1.30 and 5–8.30, Sun 11–2; winter 10–1.30 and 4–7.30, Sun 11–2*) and at the far end of the port, the **Aquarium** (*open July–Sept 10–10; Oct–June 10–8; adm*).

From here you can stroll along the outer edge of **Monte Urgull** on the Paseo Nuevo, a splendid walk between turf and surf. In the late afternoon, when the light is best, head up one of the paths to the summit of the rock where the half-ruined **Castillo de Santa Cruz de la Mota** (16th century) and an ungainly, kitsch statue of Christ (from the Franco era) keep an eye on the holiday-makers on La Concha beach below.

The centre of La Parte Vieja is the arcaded **Plaza de la Constitución**; within a few blocks of this stand San Sebastián's three best monuments: the hyper-ornate façade of **Santa María del Coro** (18th century) on Vía Coro, the fine Gothic church of **San Vicente** on San Vicente and, nearby, the old Dominican **monastery**, now the fascinating **Museum of San Telmo** (*open Tues–Sat 10.30–1.30 and 4–8, Sun 10–2; summer 10.30–1.30 and 5–8.30, Sun 10–2; adm*). The monastery's church is adorned with golden murals by the Catalan artist Josep Sert (1930) on the history of the Basque people. Old Basque tombstones, with round heads adorned with geometric patterns, are lined up in the cloister; upstairs you'll find three El Grecos, two bear skeletons, Basque charms and amulets, Basque sports paraphernalia, the interior of a Basque cottage and more.

The main attraction of La Parte Vieja is its countless bars, where the evening crowds hasten to devour delectable seafood tapas. Eating is the city's greatest preoccupation, and a fun excursion is to gather some good food and row it out to **Isla de Santa Clara** (*in summer a regular ferry leaves from El Muelle, the dock behind the Ayuntamiento; boats run 10–8*) for a picnic.

San Sebastián to Bilbao: the Costa Vasca

West to Leiketio

The first town west of San Sebastián is **Zarautz**, first put on the map in the Middle Ages thanks to whaling and shipbuilding, and later popularized in a more leisurely fashion when more summering royalty – this time Belgium's King Baudouin and Queen Fabiola – inaugurated its international reputation. Zarautz's shipbuilders built the *Vitoria*, the first ship to circumnavigate the globe, while the next fishing town to the east, **Getaria**, produced the man who captained it, Juan Sebastían Elcano (*see* facing page): approaching from the east, you'll see a massive stone monument in his honour. From the coastal road, you wouldn't think there was much to it, but pass through the old town gate and you will find one of the loveliest villages of Euskadi, hugging the steep slope down to the sheltered harbour. Besides its charm it offers

The First Man to Sail Around the World

In the great age of discovery, no Spanish or Portuguese captain worth his salt would set out without a Basque pilot, the heirs of centuries of experience in whaling boats. Columbus took a Basque pilot, and Elcano was second in command to Portuguese navigator Ferdinand Magellan; it is possible that the Basques may actually have found the American coast in medieval times, and kept the knowledge a closely guarded secret. In 1519, Magellan suggested he might find a quick route to the Indies by sailing southwest around the newly discovered continent of America to the Molucca islands, then cutting back to Spain around the Cape of Good Hope. Charles V backed Magellan's attempt; he gave him five ships, which in August set forth from Sevilla, though one turned back before attempting the Straits that took Magellan's name (October 1520). If he felt dismayed by the breadth of the Atlantic, Magellan must have been appalled at the extent of the Pacific. Even worse, by the time his little fleet made it to what is now the Philippines, in 1521, a civil war had just broken out, which through tragic accident numbered Magellan among its victims. Elcano took over the helm and reached the Molucca islands, before sailing halfway around the world to Sevilla in the only surviving ship. He arrived in October 1522, the holds stuffed to the brim with spices. In spite of his singular feat, Elcano was destined to remain forever in Magellan's shadow – except in the eyes of his fellow Getarianos. As well as a monument, they erected a statue of Elcano just outside the old town gate, and stage a historical re-enactment of his homecoming every four years.

two little beaches, Euskadi's finest *txakoli* wine and the fine early 15th-century church of **San Salvador**, with the *ex voto* of a ship and an unusual altar. From the port, with its brightly painted boats and seafood restaurants, a path leads up to **El Ratón** (Mouse Island), lovely and natural with flitting birds and fine views.

West of Getaria the N634 rises dramatically over the sea before descending to **Zumaya**, a pleasant town set at the mouth of the River Urola. The town's chief attraction, the **Museo Zuloaga** (*open Jan–Sept Sun only 10–2; adm*), is just before town, a villa set in a small park of ancient trees. This was the home of the Basque painter Ignacio Zuloaga (1870–1945), and it holds El Grecos, Goyas, Moraleses, two saints by Zurbarán and medieval statues and *retablos*. Below stretches the pine-rimmed beach of **Playa Zuloaga** and another beach to the west at **San Telmo**, a dramatic swathe of sand under sheer red cliffs, known for its pounding surf.

On the border with Vizcaya province, **Ondárroa** is a pretty fishing port, but most people press on to **Lekeitio** (Lequeitio) with its better beaches, or **Carraspio**, an elegant old port that catches more fish than tourists.

A Detour Inland: Gernika

The ancient, sacred city of the Basques is mostly rebuilt now, and most of the inhabitants are too young to remember the horror that occurred one market day in 1937. But beyond its beautiful setting in the Mundaka valley, and the oak tree by the 19th-century Basque parliament building (*Las Casas Juntas*), there's not much to see. The oak is the **Tree of Gernika**, the seedling of a more ancient one, under which the kings of Castile would swear to uphold Basque *fueros* and ancient laws. Remnants of its 300-year-old trunk can be seen under a nearby pavilion, to serve as a potent symbol of freedom and hope, and not only for the Basques; Gernika shocked the world because it was the first time modern technology was used as a tool of terror.

About five kilometres east of Gernika, the **Cueva de Santimamiñe** (*guided tours Mon–Fri at 10, 11.15, 12.30, 4.30 and 5.30. Only 15 people allowed in at a time; get there early*) has Euskadi's best Palaeolithic art. A path leads from the cave into the **Forest of Oma**, where local artist Agustín Ibarrola has fused art with nature by painting luminous multicoloured bands on the trees, to achieve an array of perspective tricks.

Along the Coast to Bilbao

Just north of Gernika the Río Oka becomes a broad flat estuary (Ría de Gernika) with the pretty beaches of **Laida** and **Laga** near its mouth and more on the western shore at **Pedernales** and **Mundaka**. Continuing round the lake, **Bermeo** is Euskadi's largest fishing port, a colourful town that makes few concessions to tourism. Further towards Bilbao, near **Bakio**, the hermitage-topped islet of **San Juan de Gaztelugatxa** is

Getting Around

The coast is served by frequent buses from San Sebastián and Bilbao; the narrow-gauge Eusko Trenbideak line stops four or five times a day at Zarautz, Zumaya, Deva and Durango on the way to Bilbao; another branch runs out of Bilbao via Gernika and Mundaka.

Tourist Information

Zarautz: Nafarroa Kalea, **t** 943 83 09 90.
Getaria: Parque Aldamar 2, **t** 943 14 09 57. *Open summer only.*
Zumaya: Pza Zuloaga, **t** 943 14 33 96. *Open summer only.*
Lekeitio: Independentzia Enparantza, **t** 946 84 40 17. *Open in summer only.*
Bermeo: C/Askatsun Bidea 2, **t** 946 17 91 54.
Gernika: C/Artekale 8, **t** 946 25 58 92.
Oñati: Foru Enparatza 11, **t** 943 78 34 53.

There are weekly **markets** in **Gernika** (*Mon*), **Bermeo** (*Tues*) and **Tolosa** (*Sat*).

Where to Stay and Eat

Zarautz ✉ 20800

Zarautz can be as pricey as San Sebastián.

★★★★**Karlos Arguiñano**, Mendilauta 13, **t** 943 13 00 00, **f** 943 13 34 50 (*luxury*). A formidably expensive modern hotel, but its **restaurant** is one of the best along this bit of coast, with sophisticated seafood in a warm, welcoming atmosphere. *Closed Sun eve and Mon.*

P. Txiki-Polit, Musika Plaza s/n, **t** 943 83 53 57, **f** 943 83 37 31 (*inexpensive*). The best budget option; an unusual circular 1950s building with decent rooms and a very popular **restaurant**; the *menú del día* is a great deal.

Camping Talai-Mendi, Monte Talai-Mendi, **t** 943 83 00 42 (*inexpensive*). A quiet campsite near the beach.

Aiten-Etxe, Elkano 3, **t** 943 83 25 02 (*expensive*). If not the most elegant, this does offer fine, uncomplicated seafood accompanied by magnificent views along Zarautz's main beach. *Closed Sun eve and Tues.*

Getaria ✉ 20808

P. Guetariano, C/Herrerieta 3, **t** 943 14 05 67 (*inexpensive*). A cheerful house at the main crossroads; friendly, with magazines in the lounge and comfortable en suite rooms.

★★**Hs San Prudencio**, **t** 943 14 04 11 (*cheap*). Bargain lodgings (for the area) by the beach; rooms are without bath.

Kaia Kaipe, Gral. Arnao 10 (upstairs), **t** 943 14 05 00 (*expensive*). With good Basque seafood and views, this is one of many restaurants crowding the harbour where you can drink the local *txakolí* wine.

Elkano, Herrerieta 2, **t** 943 14 06 14 (*expensive*). Boasts the best grilled fish on the harbour.

linked to the mainland by a bridge, with magnificent views along the cliffs. In the old days it supported a castle; the best one remaining in the vicinity is the 11th-century **Castillo de Butrón** (*open daily 10.30–8; adm*), rebuilt in fairy-tale style in the 19th century and located in the wooded hills (take the C/6313 west of **Gatika**).

Inland from San Sebastián

The main road from San Sebastian takes you to **Tolosa**, a riverside town tainted with the aroma of paper mills and famous for sweets. Just south of here the twisting GI2634 branches westwards into the mountains, passing **Régil**, with its beautiful views, and continuing to the ancient village of **Azpeitia** and nearby **Sanctuary of St Ignatius**, where in 1491 Ignatius was born, the last of 13 children of a noble family, and founder of those intellectual stormtroopers of Christ, the Jesuits. The house, built by the saint's grandfather after a four-year exile among the Moors, is a fortress-like *mudéjar* structure redesigned as a museum. Next to this stands Carlo Fontana's **Basílica**, one of the outstanding Baroque works in all Spain. Begun in 1689, it took nearly 50 years to complete and no expense was spared. The ornate church rotunda,

Zumaya ✉ 20808

Some of the bars in the main square have *inexpensive* rooms, and cheaper food can be found on C/Erribera.

★★★**Zelai**, Itzurun s/n, **t** 943 86 51 00, **f** 943 86 51 78 (*expensive–moderate*). Has comfortable rooms in a new building on the cliffs. There's a good **restaurant**, and a thalassotherapy pool for natural healing.

Agroturismo Jesuskoa, in Zumaya's Barrio de Oikina, **t** 943 86 17 39 (*inexpensive*). Has horses to rent and six rooms in a restored farmhouse just outside town; on weekends most of Zumaya comes out to sit under the trees and eat good grilled fish meals.

Asador Bedua, Barrio Bedina, **t** 943 86 05 51 (*moderate*). Serves excellent grilled surf and turf in a friendly atmosphere.

Lekeitio ✉ 48280

★★★**Emperatriz Zita**, C/Santa Elena Etorbidea s/n, **t** 946 84 26 55, **f** 946 24 35 00 (*moderate*). A modern palace of a place built over the ruins of the home of the last Austro-Hungarian empress.

Mesón Arropain, Ctra Marquina Ispaster, **t** 946 84 03 13 (*expensive*). A friendly restaurant 5km from Lekeitio; serves excellent fish smothered with bubbling *salsas*, washed down with good *txakoli*.

Zapirain, Igualdegui 3, **t** 946 84 02 55 (*moderate*). Serves abundant fish dinners.

Gernika ✉ 48300

★★**Gernika**, Carlos Gangoiti 17, **t** 946 25 03 50 (*moderate*). One of two only two simple options in town.

Lezika, near Santimamiñe caves (*moderate*). A fine restaurant in an 18th-century Basque chalet set in a charming woody grove.

Mundaka ✉ 48360

★★**Atalaya**, Itxaropen Kalea 1, **t** 946 17 70 00, **f** 946 87 68 99 (*moderate*). One of the loveliest hotels in the region, right on the river in one of those glorious Basque buildings of a century ago with glass galleries all around. It has small but lavishly appointed rooms with minibars.

Asador Zaldua, Sabino Arana 10, **t** 945 87 08 71 (*moderate*). Offers a wonderful array of fresh fish and succulent steaks, grilled to perfection. *Lunch only Nov–June.*

Oñati ✉ 20400

You couldn't find a nicer spot to stay in this part of Guipúzcoa.

★**Etxe Aundi**, Torre Auzo 10, **t** 943 78 19 56, **f** 943 78 32 90, *cu37993@cempresard* (*inexpensive*). Has all the comforts and a good **restaurant** in a lovely old building.

Txopekua, Barrio Uribarri, **t** 943 78 05 71 (*inexpensive*). A good restaurant in a Basque homestead on the road to Aránzazu.

topped by a 211ft-high dome, is flanked by a broad expanse of monastery buildings forming a vast, striking façade, rendered characteristically Spanish by interspersing sections of exuberant décor amid stretches that are plainly austere. Any ornament here, though, pales in comparison to the dome's interior, which, designed by a group that included Joaquín de Churriguerra, suitably defines the *churrigueresque*.

Southwest of Tolosa on the N1, beyond the mountain village of **Segura**, is **Oñati**, the capital of the Pretender Don Carlos in the Carlist wars. This was one of the few towns in Euskadi to be ruled by a noble, and it retained a sort of independence until 1845. For many years the town had the only Basque **university**, founded in 1540; its building has a beautiful Plateresque façade and a plain but distinguished arcaded courtyard. Oñati is known also for its well-preserved medieval palaces, one of which saw the birth of *conquistador* Lope de Aguirre. The parish church of **San Miguel** (15th century) contains a number of treasures, including the alabaster tomb of the university's founder, Bishop Zuázola de Ávila, attributed to Diego de Siloé, and an attractive Plateresque cloister. Other noteworthy buildings include the **Ayuntamiento** and the Franciscan **Convento de Bidaurreta**, but perhaps its greatest charm is the town's setting in a rich, rolling valley, dominated in the distance by the bluish pointed peaks of Mount Amboto and Udalaitz. A scenic road from Oñati climbs in nine kilometres to the **sanctuary of Aránzazu**. Here, in 1469, a shepherd found an icon of the Virgin by a thorn bush and a cow bell. The church that houses it has been rebuilt innumerable times, lastly in 1950. A curious temple of Basque modernism in a lonely and rugged setting, its two towers, covered with a distinctive skin of pyramidal concrete nubs, create a waffle-iron effect.

Vitoria (Gasteiz)

Vitoria has style. It also has the air of a little Ruritanian capital – because it is one. The seat of the inland province of Álava and, since 1980, the capital of Euskadi, Vitoria has grown to be one of Spain's modern industrial centres, a phenomenon that has so far done little harm to one of the most surprisingly urbane cities in the nation. Although Wellington soundly defeated the forces of Joseph Bonaparte here in 1813, Vitoria's name has nothing to do with victory, but recalls the height (*Beturia* in Basque) on which the city was built. In the Middle Ages this was a hot border region between the kingdoms of Navarra and Castile. The Navarrese King Alfonso VI founded a fortress and town here in 1181, but the Castilians managed to snatch it away soon after. Like everything else in medieval Castile, Vitoria boomed, and extended itself logically in concentric rings of streets. Hard hit by the wars and plagues of the 1300s, Vitoria stagnated for centuries, and began its recovery only with the industrial boom of the 1890s. It has preserved itself beautifully throughout, probably an important factor in getting itself named capital of the Basque autonomous government, the Eusko Jaurlaritza, in 1981. It is also the home of the University of the Basque Country, established by the government shortly after it took power and now the world's leading centre for the study of the Basque language and its history.

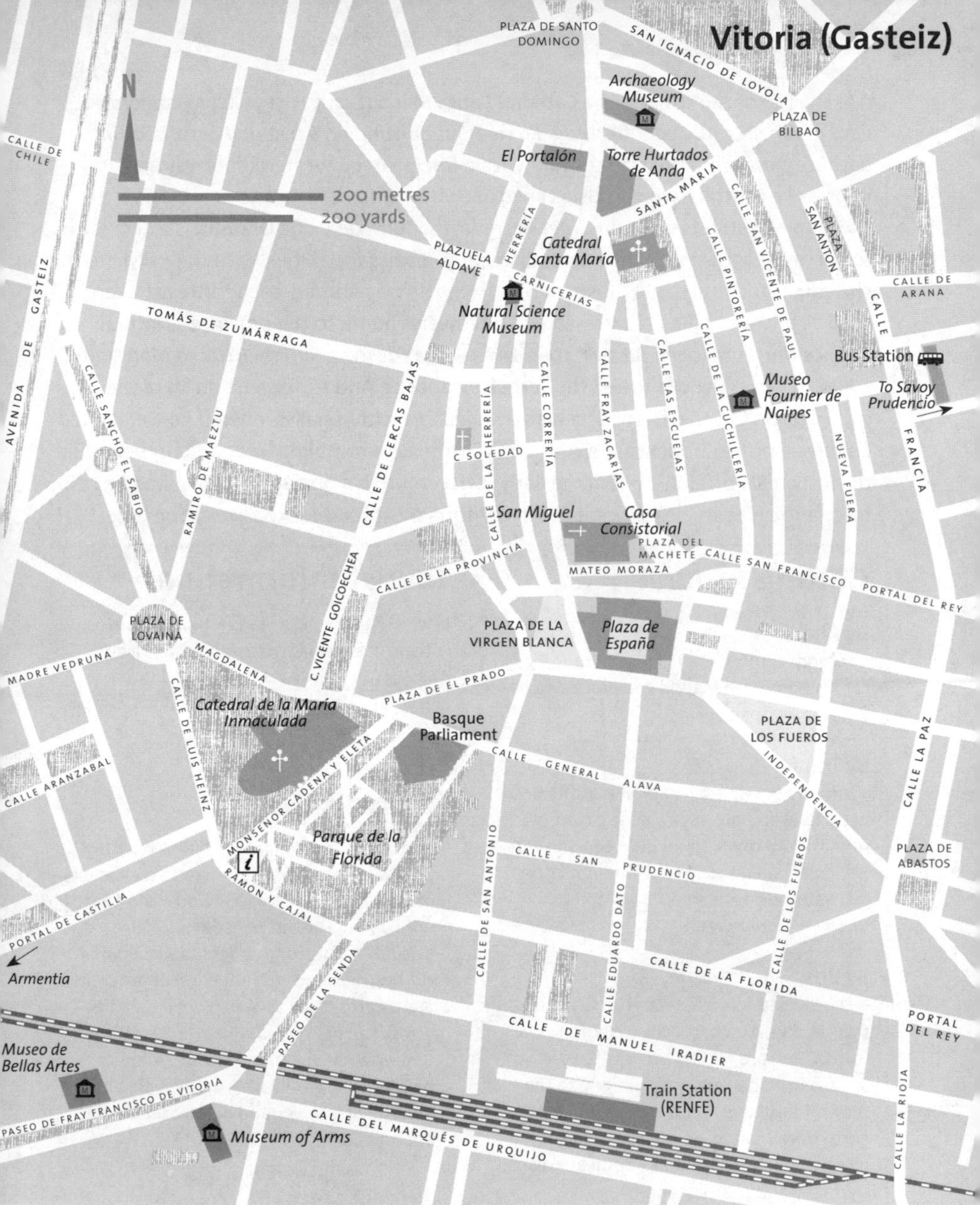

La Casco Vieja

The old city, with its core of concentric streets, begins with **Plaza de la Virgen Blanca**, a delightful example of asymmetrical medieval town design and the hub of Vitoria's big party (*see* 'Festivals', p.294); it takes its name from the statue over the door of **San Miguel**, the 14th-century church that turns a lovely portico towards the top of the square. Behind the church is C/Fray Zacarías, the high-status street for palaces, as evidenced by two 16th-century Plateresque beauties, the **Palacio Episcopal** and the **Palacio Escoriaza-Esquivel**; the latter has a refined courtyard with a marble loggia.

At the top of the street is the **Catedral Santa María** (**t** *945 25 51 35, www.catedralvitoria.com; free guided tours Mon–Fri 11–2, Sat, Sun and hols 11–2 and 5–10; book in advance*), also from the 14th century, with a finely carved western doorway and impressive central nave, the aisles lined with the tombs of Vitoria's notables.

A couple of streets west, on C/del Herrería, the **Torre de Doña Otxanta** is a defensive tower of the 15th–16th centuries. Italian early Renaissance cities, with their skylines of skyscraper-fortresses, set a fashion that found its way abroad; such fortresses were used as private castles. Now restored, the tower is home to the province's **Natural Science Museum** (*open Tues–Fri 10–2 and 4–6.30, Sat 10–2, Sun 11–2; closed Mon; adm*).

Another conspicuous tower, the **Torre Hurtados de Anda**, lurks just north of the cathedral on C/Correría: this is a blank-walled fort with a half-timbered house planted on top – a proper urban castle. Also on C/Correría is a rambling brick and timber structure called **El Portalón**. Built in the early 16th century, it's one of the oldest buildings in town and gives an idea of what most of Vitoria must have looked like at the time.

Getting Around

By Air

Foronda airport, 9km west of Vitoria, has connections with Madrid and Barcelona (**t** 945 16 35 00).

By Train

Vitoria's stylish train station is at the head of C/Eduardo Dato, (**t** 945 23 02 02) six blocks from the old town. Trains between San Sebastián and Madrid pass through Vitoria, and Salvatierra is a stop along RENFE's Vitoria–Pamplona run.

By Bus

The bus station is at C/Los Herran 50, **t** 945 25 84 00, a short walk east of the old town. There are regular services to San Sebastián, Bilbao and Logroño, and to the provincial villages. Being on the main route north from Madrid, you can get a bus to nearly anywhere from here: Bordeaux, Paris, Germany and even London.

Otherwise you'll have **hitchhike.** Generally the more remote the area, the more likely you are to get a ride – friendly locals will often stop and ask you if you want a lift.

By Car

Though small, Vitoria can be a puzzle if you are driving. Most of the centre is a closed-off pedestrian zone, and parking is hard to find.

Tourist Information

Vitoria: Parque de la Florida, **t** 945 13 13 21.

There is a weekly **market** held in Pza de Abastos (*Thurs*); also a **flea market** in Pza Nueva (*Sun*), and a **clothes market** in C/Arana (*Wed* and *Thurs*).

Festivals

Fiesta de la Virgen Blanca, *4 Aug*. A typically berserk six-day Basque blowout, with plenty of *cava*, high-powered fireworks and parties until dawn. The festival begins when *Celedón*, a dummy in a beret and workman's clothes, descends from the top of the cathedral as gracefully as Mary Poppins, gliding across the plaza on a wire attached to his umbrella. On the morning of 10 August, he glides magically back up the wire and into the bell tower, and it's all over for another year.

Where to Stay

Vitoria ✉ 01000

Expensive

****__Hotel Ciudad de Vitoria__, Portal de Castilla 8, **t** 945 14 11 00, **f** 945 14 36 16. Has more character than most, with friendly staff and an indoor garden; good discounts are available at weekends and in summer.

Across the street at No. 116, the **Archaeology Museum** (*open Tues–Fri 10–2 and 4–6.30, Sat 10–2, Sun 11–2; closed Mon; adm*) contains Roman finds and Basque discoidal tombstones, as well as fascinating medieval finds like the strange *Relief of Marquinez*. There are over 100 artificial caves in the province of Álava, and exhibits recount the story of the religious hermits who occupied many of them a thousand years ago.

The House of Cards

Palaces are fewer in the eastern quarter of old Vitoria; the houses here tend to be plainer, though older, especially those in the former medieval Jewish ghetto that covered much of this area. On C/Cuchillería, in the Plateresque Palacio Bendaña, Spain's biggest manufacturer of playing cards (an old Vitoria speciality) has opened the **Museo Fournier del Naipes** (*open Tues–Fri 10–2 and 4–6.30, Sat 10–2, Sun 11–2; closed Mon*). The collection includes plenty of Tarot decks; originally there was no difference between cards for fortune-telling and those for playing games.

******General Álava***, Av. Gastéiz 79, **t** 945 22 22 00, **f** 945 24 83 95. Best value among several large hotels in the new part of town, with modern, comfortable rooms and TV.

Moderate

*****Almoneda**, C/Florida 7, **t** 945 15 40 84, **f** 945 15 46 86, *information@hotelalmoneda.com*. This recently renovated little hotel has simple, tasteful rooms and a pleasant lounge full of eclectic antiques.

Inexpensive

Vitoria offers a wide range of *inexpensive* choices, mostly catering for businessmen.

****Dato 28**, C/Dato 28 (near the rail station), **t** 945 14 72 30, **f** 945 23 23 20. Convenient, modern and imaginatively furnished; and a good bargain.

***Achuri**, C/Rioja 11, **t** 945 25 58 00, **f** 945 26 40 74. Reasonable and well equipped.

Cheap

P. Álava, C/Florida 25, **t** 945 23 35 88. This *pensión* is run by a fantastically welcoming old couple, with light and breezy rooms; situated between the train station and the Casco Viejo.

Eating Out

Most of the good bars and restaurants are in the old town.

El Portalón, Correría 151, **t** 945 14 27 55 (*expensive*). Especially good, ranging over three floors of a 16th-century building, with traditional Basque food.

Casablanca 3, C/Dato 38 (*inexpensive*). An unassuming exterior belies the tasty offerings inside; creamy pumpkin soup, and tender roast duck.

Dolomiti, C/Ramón y Cajal, **t** 945 23 34 26 (*inexpensive*). The best and most popular pizzeria in town, run by a former cycling champ named Galdós; it also serves up Italian dinners.

Nightlife

Vitoria has its share of nightlife, mostly in the Casco Vieja, though C/Dato, near the station, can also be noisy after hours. Some of the clubs, a few on C/San Prudencio stay open until 6 or 7am.

Cerveceria Gambrinus, C/Florida 15. A popular place to begin the evening, with a beer and some *pintxos*.

Café Caruso, C/Enrique de Eguren 9. A coffee house hosting occasional concerts and exhibitions.

El Elefante Blanco, Plaza San Antón. Currently the most popular disco.

Salsumba, C/Tomás de Zumárraga. The place for salsa.

Gaztetxe, C/Fray Zacarías. For alternative music of all sorts (though mostly rock).

The New Cathedral and the Museum of Fine Arts

The tourist office shares the pretty **Parque de la Florida**, Vitoria's monumental centre, with the stern, no-nonsense **Basque Parliament** building (*call* **t** *945 24 78 00 if you want to sit in the gallery and watch them deliberate*) and the remarkable 'new cathedral', the **Catedral de la María Inmaculada**. Here, the Basques, who don't like anything frumpy but do like the Middle Ages, got together in 1907 to build a totally 'medieval' building, by medieval methods. Most of it is already finished, though there is enough decorative work left to do inside to last them another century or two. The style seems to be part-English Gothic, part-Viollet-le-Duc, and the most endearing feature is the rows of comical modillions around the cornices – lots of satirical and monster faces, including caricatures of the architects and masons.

Vitoria is a city of unexpected delights; one example, completing the park's monumental ensemble, is one of the most resplendent Art Deco petrol stations in Europe, just behind the cathedral. Another, a few blocks southeast on C/Eduardo Dato, is the fantastical **RENFE station**, done in a kind of Hollywood Moorish style with brightly coloured tiles. The city has just finished constructing a new embellishment, **Plaza de los Fueros**, designed and decorated by Eduardo Chillida. It's a strange space – part-Roman amphitheatre, part-basketball court – that the locals haven't quite worked out how best to use; it seems to get most use after the bars have closed. At one end, an untitled Chillida sculpture is enclosed within angular walls.

Parque de la Florida, laid out in 1855, retains much of the Romantic spirit of its times, with grand promenades, hidden bowers and overlooks. It was the centre of the city's fashionable district, and a shady walkway from the southern end of the park, the Paseo de la Senda, takes you to the elegant **Paseo de Fray Francisco de Vitoria**, lined with the Hispano-Victorian mansions of the old industrialists. One of these houses, now the **Museo de Bellas Artes** (*open Tues–Fri 10–2 and 4–6.30, Sat 10–2, Sun 11–2; closed Mon; adm*), features a well-displayed collection ranging from early paintings to Picasso and Miró, with a handful of Spanish masters in between, all in a beautifully restored space with original features such as a Tiffany-style stained-glass skylight.

Some of the finest works are of the type museums here call *Escuela Hispano-flamenca*, paintings from the early 16th century, when the influence from the Low Countries was strong. One of the finest works, a triptych of the Passion by the 'Master of the Legend of Santa Godelina', shows the same sort of conscious stylization as an Uccello; the longer you look at it, the stranger it seems. Medieval, painted, carved wood figures are well represented, and there are no fewer than three paintings by Ribera, including a *Crucifixion*. As in all Basque museums, Basque painters are more than well represented. Here you'll find some surprises, such as a great early 20th-century landscapist named Fernando de Anarica, or his contemporary Ramon Zubiaurre, whose *Autoridades de mi Aldea* shares the not-quite-naïve sensibility of Rousseau or Grant Wood. The façade of a 13th-century hermitage has been reconstructed in the museum's garden. Back along the Paseo at No.3, the **Museum of Arms** (*open Tues–Fri 10–2 and 4–6.30, Sat 10–2, Sun 11–2; closed Mon; adm*) houses suits of armour, medieval weapons, and dioramas and displays on Wellington's victory at the Battle of Vitoria.

Around Vitoria

There aren't a lot of sights in the vicinity, but to the west of Vitoria you can visit Roman ruins, including a long, 13-arched bridge at **Trespuentes**, near the remains of a pre-Roman town, the **oppidum of Iruña** (*open summer Tues–Fri 11–2 and 4–8, Sat 11–3, Sun 11–2; winter Tues–Sat 11–3, Sun 10–3; closed Mon; adm*).

To the east of Vitoria, the miniscule village of **Gaceo** (on the N1) offers nothing less than one of the finest ensembles of Gothic fresco painting anywhere in Europe. These are in the simple church of **San Martín de Tours** (*the address of the keyholder is posted on the church door*); covered in plaster, they were not rediscovered until 1966.

Research places these works sometime between about 1325 and 1450. The style is slightly archaic, and though Byzantine and Romanesque influences are present, they are distinctive enough for scholars to speculate about an obscure 'Basque-Navarrese' school of artists. Thanks to the plaster most of the paintings are well preserved though oddly enough many of the faces have vanished. The figures around the Trinity on the apse seem to be arranged to represent the commemoration of All Saints' Day: various scenes of *Los Bienaventurados*, the Blessed – apostles, martyrs, confessors, virgins and more, all arranged neatly by category. The choir vault too is entirely covered in frescoes, stock images of the Life of Christ divided by charming borders of *trompe l'œil* designs and fantasy architecture. At the bottom right is something no medieval mural picture-book could be without: the souls of the damned getting variously swallowed up in the mouth of hell or cooked in a big pot.

South of Vitoria there's not of sightseeing to be done, but some of the best Rioja vines come from a region known as **La Rioja Alavesa**, along the Ebro river. The key wine town here is walled, medieval **Laguardia** (Biasteri) where you can learn all about local wines and their production at **La Casa del Vino**, and visit *bodegas*.

Between Vitoria and Bilbao

Along the coast, the narrow twisting roads will take you nearly a day. The more common route west is the A8 motorway, with its exorbitant tolls, and the slower, parallel N634, both of which cut inland near Deba and follow some of the more somnolescent landscapes of Euskadi. On the BI632, **Elorrio** is an attractive village of grand palaces and impressive little squares, adorned with a set of unique crucifixes from the 15th–16th centuries. From the centre it's a lovely walk out to the hermitage of **San Adrián de Argiñeta**, where you can see the 9th- and 10th-century tombs of Argiñeta, carved out of rock, some adorned with pinwheel-like stars.

Six kilometres further lies **Durango**, the biggest town in the area. To the south, the Duranguesado massif juts abruptly out of rolling green hills, creating Vizcaya's most dramatic mountain scenery and harbouring the **Parque Natural Urkiola**; to the north is the minute village of **Bolívar**, home town of the family of the great Liberator of South America, Simón de Bolívar. His Art Deco monument dwarfs the village square, while near the old parish **church of Santo Tomás** you can see the 'cattle trial yards' and the huge weights hauled by oxen at festivals. **Markina** (Marquina), further north, is

Getting Around

Durango and Elorrio are both served by **BizkaiBus** from Pso del Arenal in Bilbao, and **EuskoTren** services between Bilbao and San Sebastián call at Durango.

Tourist Information

Durango: C/Bruno Maurizio Zabala 2, **t** 946 03 00 30.

Where to Stay and Eat

This isn't tourist country, but you should be able to find simple accommodation anywhere near the A8.

Durango ✉ **48200**

*****Hotel Kurutziaga**, C/Kurutziaga 52, **t** 946 20 08 64, **f** 946 20 14 09 (*expensive*). An 18th-century mansion converted into a modern business hotel, with a restaurant.

****Hs Juego de Bolos**, San Agustinalde 2, **t** 946 81 10 99 (*inexpensive–cheap*). Durango's simple *hostal*.

Josu Mendizabal, C/San Antonio, in Berriz, **t** 946 22 50 70. Don't count on Durango for a meal. Just outside town is this very popular restaurant with plenty of fresh seafood.

Markina ✉ **48200**

****Vega**, Abesúa 2, **t** 946 16 60 15 (*moderate*). A nice, central spot for a good night's sleep.

Niko, San Agustín 4, **t** 946 16 89 59 (*cheap*). Good cooking on a bargain *menú*.

nicknamed the 'University of Pelota'; its historic *frontón* has produced champions who have made their mark around the world. On the right bank of the Río Artibay stands the uncanny, hexagonal church of **San Miguel de Arretxinaga**, built around an altar constructed by the giant *jentillak* (or, some say, fallen from heaven) that consists of three massive rocks sheltering a statue of St Michael.

Bilbao (Bilbo)

If you were to say only a decade ago that Bilbao was destined to become an international art Mecca, the select few who had ever visited the place would have laughed in your face. Bilbao meant rusty old steel mills and shipping. Travellers who weren't there on business didn't linger, unless they got lost in the maddening traffic system. Getting lost, however, would have allowed more people to appreciate Bilbao's uncommon setting, tucked in the lush green folds of Euskadi's coastal mountains, the grimy city filling up every possible pocket for miles along the Nervión, a notorious industrial by-product of a river, adopting the colour of chocolate milk or robin's-egg blue, depending on the day. The name is Bilbo in Basque, just like the hobbit, but its inhabitants lovingly call it the *Botxo*, the Basque word for hole or orifice.

The orifice was originally a scattering of fishing hamlets huddled on the left bank of a deep *ría*, where the hills offered some protection from the Normans and other pirates. In 1300, when the coast was clear of such dangers, the lord of Vizcaya, Diego López de Haro, founded a new town on the right bank of the Ría de Bilbao. It quickly developed into the Basques' leading port and Spain's main link to northern Europe, exporting Castile's wool to Flanders and the swords Shakespeare called *bilbos*. In 1511 the merchants formed a council to govern their affairs, the Consulado de Bilbao, an institution that survived and thrived until 1829.

The 19th century had various tricks in store: the indignity of a French sacking in 1808 and sieges by the Carlists in both of their wars; Bilbao was the 'martyr city' of the

Liberal cause. But the 19th century also made Bilbao into a great industrial dynamo. Blessed with its fabled iron mountain, nearby forests, cheap hydraulic power and excellent port, Bilbao got a double dose of the Industrial Revolution. Steel mills, shipbuilding and other industries sprang up, quickly followed by banks and insurance companies and all the other accoutrements of capitalism. Workers from across the country poured into gritty tenements, and smoke clogged the air. It became the fourth city of Spain, and still is; it looks like Spain's Pittsburgh, and back at the turn of the century it was just as full of worker misery and exploitation. Social activism combined with Basque nationalism created a sturdy anti-fascist cocktail; during the Civil War, Bilbao was besieged again and Franco punished it crushingly. Then, in the late 1950s, Bilbao was whipped forward to become once more the industrial powerhouse of Spain, but on an artificial life-support system that was unplugged in the new Spain of the EU. The iron mines gave out. In the 1980s, unemployment soared from six per cent to 20 per cent.

Something had to be done to save the Botxo from becoming a real hole, and the Basques found the political will to do it. Thanks to banking, insurance and such less obviously dirty business, the economy was doing pretty well in spite of all the lay-offs, and this has allowed the city to embark on an ambitious redevelopment programme, reclaiming vast areas of the centre formerly devoted to heavy industry. The rusting machinery has been removed and the once-seedy dock area gentrified. The hugely popular Guggenheim Museum, which opened in October 1997, has by itself significantly boosted the city's prestige, attracting almost four million visitors to date. Other new projects include cleaning up the Nervíon (it even has a few fish now), a concert hall and convention centre (completed in 1998), and a library, a park, a hotel, offices and residential buildings all to be built on the site of the old shipyards. A 'passenger interchange', which will put local and international bus and train services under one enormous roof, is planned, and the metro, with sleek, modern stations designed by Sir Norman Foster, was completed in 1995. The airport got an elegant new terminal designed by Santiago Calatrava in December 2000, and the port is being given a boost as part of a vast harbour expansion project. New industries are being enticed here, too: the European Software Institute has based its headquarters in the 370-acre technology park in nearby Zamudio. Bilbao is shaping up to become one of the cities of Europe's future; come back in a few years and see.

The Casco Viejo

The Casco Viejo, centre of the city from the 15th–19th centuries, is a snug little region on the east bank of the Nervión; tucked away from the centre, it remains the city's heart. The Puente del Arenal leaves you in **Plaza de Arriaga**, known as *El Arenal* for the sand flats that stood here. Befitting Basque tradition, its monuments are both musical: the opera house, or **Teatro Arriaga**, and a glorious Art Nouveau pavilion in steel and glass that holds Sunday concerts. Adjacent is the arcaded **Plaza Nueva**, now a bit down-at-heel, but in its day the symbol of Bilbao's growth and prosperity.

Philosopher Miguel de Unamuno was born on nearby C/La Ronda, not far from the **Museo Vasco** (*La Cruz 4; open Tues–Sat 10.30–1.30 and 4–7, Sun 10.30–1.30; closed Mon;*

Universidad de Deusto
PLAZA SAN PÍO X
AVENIDA DE MADARIAGA
AVENIDA DE LAS UNIVERSIDADES
Ría de Bilbao
SAN PEDRO DE DUESTO
ABANDOIBARRA
Museo Guggenheim
Palacio Euskalduna de Congresos y de la Música
ALAMEDA DE MAZARREDO
PLAZA DEL MUSEO
Parque de Doña Casilda de Iturrizar
Museo de Bellas Artes
PLAZA DEL SAGRADO CORAZÓN
PLAZA PEDRO BASTERRECHEA
Campo de San Mamés
GRAN VÍA DE DON DIEGO LÓPEZ DE HARO
ABANDO
PLAZA DE FEDERICO MOYÚA
INDAUTXU
PLAZA DE INDAUTXU
Termibus
AMETZOLA
Convento de Capuchinos
Museo Taurino
Plaza de Toros Vista Alegre
Park Ametzola
ZABALA

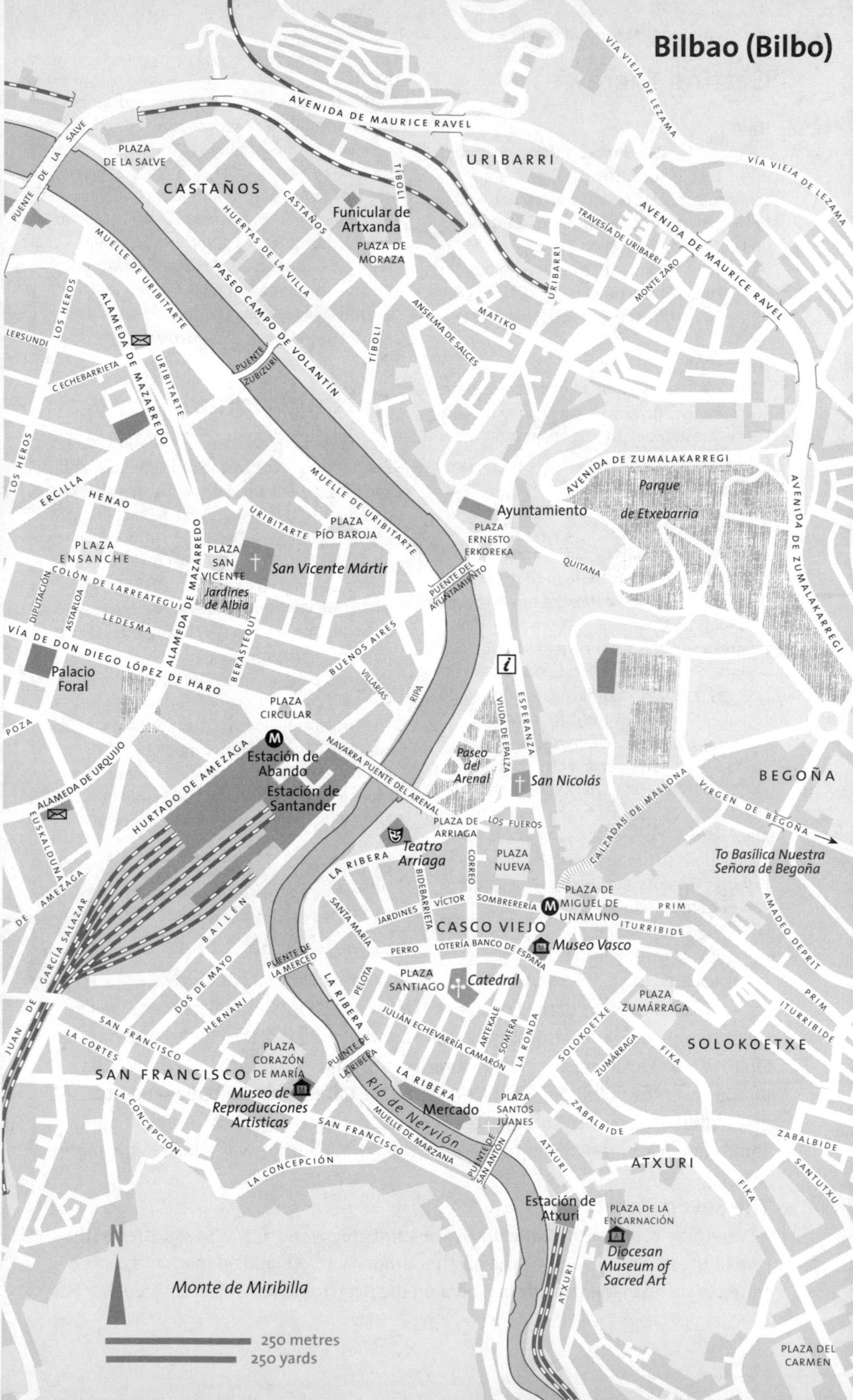

Bilbao (Bilbo)
Avenida de Maurice Ravel
Uribarri
Castaños
Plaza de la Salve
Puente de la Salve
Funicular de Artxanda
Plaza de Moraza
Tíboli
Travesía de Uribarri
Monte Zaro
Matiko
Anselma de Salces
Huertas de la Villa
Paseo Campo de Volantín
Muelle de Uribitarte
Puente Zubizuri
Alameda de Mazarredo
Uribitarte
Los Heros
Lersundi
C Echebarrieta
Ercilla
Henao
Avenida de Zumalakarregi
Parque de Etxebarria
Ayuntamiento
Plaza Ernesto Erkoreka
Quitana
Plaza Pío Baroja
Plaza Ensanche
Plaza San Vicente
San Vicente Mártir
Jardines de Albia
Colón de Larreategui
Ledesma
Diputación
Astarloa
Berastegui
Puente del Ayuntamiento
Buenos Aires
Villarías
Ripa
Vía de Don Diego López de Haro
Palacio Foral
Plaza Circular
Poza
Estación de Abando
Estación de Santander
Navarra
Puente del Arenal
Hurtado de Amezaga
Alameda de Urquijo
Euskalduna
Amezaga
Juan de García Salazar
Viuda de Epalza
Esperanza
Paseo del Arenal
San Nicolás
Calzadas de Mallona
Virgen de Begoña
Begoña
To Basílica Nuestra Señora de Begoña
Plaza de Arriaga
Los Fueros
Teatro Arriaga
La Ribera
Plaza Nueva
Correo
Bidebarrieta
Sombrerería
Víctor
Jardines
Santa María
Plaza de Miguel de Unamuno
Prim
Iturribide
Amadeo Deprit
Casco Viejo
Perro
Lotería
Banco de España
Museo Vasco
Bailén
Dos de Mayo
Puente de la Merced
Pelota
Plaza Santiago
Catedral
Plaza Zumárraga
Julián Echevarría
Camarón
Artekale
Somera
La Ronda
Solokoetxe
Zumárraga
Fika
Hernani
San Francisco
La Cortes
Plaza Corazón de María
Museo de Reproducciones Artisticas
Puente de la Ribera
Río de Nervión
Mercado
Plaza Santos Juanes
Zabalbide
Muelle de Marzana
Puente de San Antón
La Concepción
Atxuri
Santutxu
Estación de Atxuri
Plaza de la Encarnación
Diocesan Museum of Sacred Art
Monte de Miribilla
N
250 metres
250 yards
Plaza del Carmen
Vía Vieja de Lezama

Getting There

By Air

Bilbao's Sondika airport is the busiest in northwest Spain, with daily flights from London, Brussels, Frankfurt and Milan, and to most airports in Spain, including Santiago and Vigo (for information, **t** 944 53 23 06). The airport is 10km north of the centre; a bus service (No.A-3247) runs roughly every 45 mins to the airport from C/Sendeja, **t** 944 75 82 00.

By Ferry

The P&O Portsmouth–Bilbao ferry operates twice weekly, arriving in Santurzi, 13km from the centre of town. There's an information and bookings office in the centre (C/Cosme Echevarrieta 1, **t** 944 23 44 77).

By Train

Bilbao has several train lines and about a dozen stations, non-suburban commuters need only be aware of three of them. The main RENFE station, with connections to France, Madrid and Galicia is known as Estación de Abando, Pza Circular (**t** 902 24 02 02). Next to Abando at Bailén 2, but facing the river with a colourful tile front, is the Estación de la Concordia, where scenic, narrow-gauge FEVE trains serve Santander and Oviedo (**t** 944 23 22 66). The little Estación Atxuri, at Atxuri 6 in the Casco Viejo, is used by the Basque regional line, Eusko Trenbideak (**t** 944 33 95 00) for connections to San Sebastián by way of Durango, Zarautz and Zumaya. A separate line serves Gernika, Mundaka and Bermeo.

By Bus

All inter-urban bus lines arrive and depart from Termibus, a newly constructed terminal near San Mamés stadium in the Ensanche, C/Guturby 1, **t** 944 39 52 05. There are hourly services to San Sebastián, Vitoria and Santander, and several buses a day to Madrid, Pamplona, Barcelona, Galicia and Castilla-León. BizkaiBus serves destinations within Vizcaya, including Durango, Gernika and the coastal villages from a separate terminal on Pso del Arenal, near the Casco Viejo.

Getting Around

Bilbao's complex topography makes it a beast to negotiate by car; miss one turn, and you may have to circle around 40km (no exaggeration!), only to end up in a field of orange barrels called Asua Crossroads from which few have ever returned. If you ever make it to the centre, parking will prove equally frustrating; you'll find city-run garages at Pza Nueva, Instituto Correos, Pza del Ensanche and Pza de Indautxu. If the car you parked in the street vanishes, call the Grúa Municipal (towing), **t** 944 20 50 98.

Nearly all of Bilbao's attractions are within walking distance in the centre; the efficient city bus line (Bilbobus) and Metro will take you there if you're elsewhere. For a **radio taxi**, call **t** 944 16 23 00, **t** 944 44 88 88.

By Metro

The metro consists of a single line, and is the easiest way to get to the beaches at Getxo

adm). Located in an old Jesuit cloister, it displays a scale-model of Vizcaya, a reconstruction of the rooms of the Consulate, the old merchants' organization, as well as tools, ship-models and Basque gravestones. In the middle of the cloister is the ancient Idolo de Mikeldi, the museum's treasure; like a primitive depiction of the cow that jumped over the moon. Behind the museum, the **Catedral de Santiago** sends its graceful spire up over the old quarter. Begun in the 1200s, most of the elegant grey stone church is 14th–15th-century Gothic, though the façade was added in the 1880s.

The Seven Streets

Everything south of the Cathedral is the calm grey world of the 'Seven Streets', the core of the original village. All the neighbourhood's colour and animation is concentrated in the 1929 **Mercado de la Ribera** on the riverfront, the largest covered market and Plentzia; there are stations in the Casco Viejo, Abando (for long-distance trains), Pza Moyua (closest to the Guggenheim), Indautxu and San Mamés (for Termibus). Fares vary depending on the distance travelled; tickets valid for 10 rides offer a small saving. Services run every five minutes within the centre, and every 20 minutes to Plentzia, **t** 944 25 40 25.

By Tram

The first line of a new tram system is expected to be complete within the next year or so, filling the last gap in inner Bilbao's public transport network. The line runs alongside the Nervión, connecting Estación Atxuri with San Mamés via Abando, the Guggenheim and Abandoibarra.

By Taxi

To continue around the coast from Plentzia, without your own car, you'll need to take a taxi to Mungia from where buses go to Bermeo.

Tourist Information

Bilbao: Main Office, Pso del Arenal 1, **t** 944 79 57 60;
also at Abandoibarra 2, by the Guggenheim;
also at the airport: **t** 944 53 23 06.
Post Office: Alameda de Urquijo 19.
Telephones: Buenos Aires 10 and Barroeta Aldamar 7; both in the Ensanche near the rail station.
Internet Access: Net House, C/Villarias 6; or Web Press, C/Barraincue near the Guggenheim.

Tours: **walking tours** of the Casco Viejo leave from the tourist office (Pso del Arenal) every Tues, Thurs and Sat at 10.30am (€3 approx.; pay half-hour prior to departure);
Bilbao Bus Tours (**t** 944 15 36 06): make a circuit from the Guggenheim to the Funicular de Artxanda; buses leave every two hours from 10am to 6pm (€6 approx.).

Shopping

The Siete Calles are a good place to start, particularly **C/Bidebarrieta** and **C/Correo**, with plenty of upmarket clothing and shoe shops, and tacky souvenir places knocking out ceramic 'Puppys'. For something funkier try **C/Somera**, where youthful fashions dominate and subversive 'grow shops' line the street. The trendiest boutiques are concentrated in the **Ensanche**, mostly south of the Gran Vía around Pla Indautxu; **C/Ercilla** is a good place to start hunting.

Where to Stay

Bilbao ✉ 48000

The 'Guggenheim Effect' has filled Bilbao's hotels with the kind of educated, culture-seeking tourist other cities dream of, so book in advance.

Luxury

Catering mainly for businessmen, these hotels often offer big discounts at weekends. The ones below are central and popular:

in Spain. Nearby, the **Diocesan Museum of Sacred Art** (*open Tues–Sat 10.30–1.30 and 4–7, Sun 10.30–1.30*) displays over eight centuries' worth of religious art and finery; vestments of gold brocade, glittering silverware and numerous sculptures and paintings by Basque artists.

The 'Seven Streets' being hemmed in by cliffs, Bilbao's centre migrated over the bridge as the city grew, while garden suburbs grew up on the cliffs. Behind the church of **San Nicolás**, an elevator ascends to the upper town, from where it's a short walk to the Viscayans' holy shrine, the **Basílica de Begoña** with its unusual spire stuck on an early 16th-century church. Inside a venerated statue of the Virgin holds court with some huge paintings by the slapdash Neapolitan Luca Giordano, probably the most popular painter of his day. There are fine views of the old town below.

★★★★★**Lopez de Haro**, Obispo Orueta 2, **t** 944 23 55 00, **f** 944 23 45 00, *www.hotellopezde-haro.com*.

★★★★**NH Villa de Bilbao**, Gran Vía 87, **t** 944 41 60 00, **f** 944 41 62 59, *www.nh-hoteles.es*.

★★★★**Hotel Indautxu**, Pza Bombero Etxaniz, **t** 944 21 11 98. Has all the necessary comforts in a good quiet location; the house **restaurant** Etxaniz (*expensive*), does delicious things with fish and lobster. *Restaurant closed Sun and early Aug.*

Expensive

★★★**Conde Duque**, C/Campo Volantin 22, **t** 944 45 60 00, **f** 944 45 60 66, *www.hotelconde-duque.com*. Over the river from the Guggenheim, with near-*moderate* prices.

Moderate

★★**Hotel Iturrienea Ostatua**, C/Santa Maria 14, **t** 944 16 15 00, **f** 944 15 89 29. Definitely the choice option in the Casco Viejo; great care and attention have gone in to equipping the rooms with a mix of antique and new furniture, while hosts of flowering plants trail from the balconies.

★★**Hotel Ripa**, C/Ripa 3, **t** 944 23 96 77. On the riverfront just opposite the Casco Viejo, with nice recently renovated rooms.

Inexpensive

Most of these are found in the Casco Viejo.

★★**Hs Arana**, C/Bidebarrieta 2, **t** 944 15 64 11. Has comfortable, modern rooms.

★★**Roquefer**, Lotería 2, **t** 944 15 07 55. In an old building with high ceilings, and nice showers down the hall.

Cheap

★★**Don Claudio**, C/Hermógenes Rojo 10, **t** 944 90 50 17. A good bet, although away from the centre.

P. Martinez, C/Villarias 8, **t** 944 23 91 78. A good, clean cheapie in the centre.

Eating Out

This city may not get as wild about cuisine as San Sebastián, but eating is still a pleasure. For the purest Basque cuisine, look for the strangest names.

Expensive

Zortziko, Alameda de Mazzarredo 17 (near Pza de España), **t** 944 23 97 43. The city's finest restaurant, where the quirky décor and fine service prepare you for innovative and immaculately presented treats from the kitchen: green almond soup and *estofado* of wild pigeon, washed down with fine Rioja wines. *Closed Sun and first fortnight in Sept.*

Bermeo, C/Ercilla 37, **t** 944 70 57 00. Traditional and sumptuous; if it's on the menu, try the special Basque *cocochas*: 'cheek and throat' of hake in a garlic and parsley sauce. *Closed Sat lunch, Sun eve and first fortnight in Aug.*

Goizeko-Kabi, C/Particular de Estraunza 4–6, **t** 944 42 11 29. Has the right-sounding name and, indeed, excellent cooking to match.

GVictor, Plaza Nueva 2, **t** 944 15 16 78. Has been around for over 40 years, to build up its enviable reputation as one of the Casco Viejo's best restaurants; the *bodega* boasts over 1,500 different wines. *Closed Sun and Aug.*

The Ensanche

Nobody in the 19th century had a sharper sense of urban design than the Spaniards, and wherever a town had money to do something big, the results were impressive. Bilbao in its boom years had to face exponential population growth, and its mayors chose to plan for it; in the 1870s they annexed the '**Anteiglesia de Abando**', an area of farmland across the river and commissioned a trio of planners, Severino de Achúcarro, Pablo de Alzola and Ernest Hoffmeyer, to lay out what came to be known as the **Ensanche** ('extension'). They came up with a simple-looking but really rather ingenious plan, with diagonal boulevards dividing up the broad loop of the river like orange segments. The Ensanche begins across from El Arenal; just over the bridge from the old town, a statue of Bilbao's founder, Diego López de Haro, looks benignly over the massive banks and circling traffic in the **Plaza Circular**. This has become the business

Expensive–Moderate

Guggenheim, Guggenheim Museum Bilbao, **t** 944 23 93 33 (*expensive–moderate*). Full of light, organic lines, and furniture designed by Frank Gehry; the food is a snapshot of some of the best of Basque cooking.

La Granja, Plaza de España (*moderate*). An attractive old place right on the plaza.

Inexpensive

Amboto, C/Jardines. A seafood place off Pza Arriaga that specializes in *merluza* (hake) in a delicious crab sauce.

Metro Moyúa, Gran Vía 40, **t** 944 24 92 73. Offers a good *menú* of *nouvelle* (Basque) *cuisine*.

Guggen, Alameda de Rekalde 5. Perhaps the best of those cashing in on their proximity to the Guggenheim, with a solid *menú*.

Vegetariano, C/Urquijo 33, **t** 944 44 55 98. Has great value *menús* of innovative vegetable-based dishes. *Open Mon–Fri lunch only*.

Café Boulevard, Arenal 3. First opened in 1871, providing cultured society with a meeting place before the opera, and revamped 50 years later, the café retains its elegant Art Deco interior.

Within Bilbao there are three main **tapas** areas to head for where you can stave off those hunger pangs.

Saibigain, C/Barrencalle Barrena 16. Curing hocks of ham dangle above a lovely, tiled wooden bar.

Victor Montes, Pza Nueva. Boasts a vast array of delectable *pinxtos*, and plenty of *crianzas* and *reservas* to wash them down. The arcaded central Pza Nueva has numerous great old *taperías*, with tables outside and elegant dining rooms for full-blown meals.

Café Iruña, Jardines de Albia. Across in the Ensanche the later-evening crowd gather in the streets around C/Ledesma, centred around this legendary and beautiful *mudéjar*-style café.

Nightlife

One cultural form of which the city is particularly enamoured is **opera**, hosting regular performances throughout the year. Fans of Bertolt Brecht and Kurt Weill will be disappointed to learn that 'Bill's Ballhaus in Bilbao' was only a figment of their imagination. Less highbrow culture is generally limited to weekends, in the streets of the Casco Viejo.

C/Barrenkale is a busy place with a number of clubs, while C/Somera has friendly and funky bars, very popular with the Basque Nationalist community; in the Ensanche, there are more bars on C/Pérez Galdós and C/Licenciado Poza.

Teatro Arriaga, Pza de Arriaga 1, **t** 944 16 33 33. Regular operatic performances take place here, alongside theatre and comedy.

Palacio de la Música y de Congresos Euskalduna, Abandoibarra 4, **t** 944 03 50 00. This puts on opera, plays and musicals, and sometimes big-name foreign acts.

The Cotton Club, C/Gregorio de la Revilla 25. Stages occasional live jazz and blues.

Distrito 9, C/Ajuriagerra. The big techno club in town.

district, with the big grey skyscraper of the Banco Bilbao Vizcaya, built in the 1960s, to remind us who is the leading force in the city's destiny today. The RENFE station occupies one corner of the square; behind it, on the riverfront, is one of the city's industrial-age landmarks: the Bilbao–Santander **rail station**, a charming Art Nouveau work with a wrought iron and tile façade, designed by Severino de Achúcarro. The vast desolation of tracks and sidings behind these stations is about to be reclaimed as the centrepiece of Bilbao's facelift: the **Intermodal**, a huge commercial project to be built on air right over the tracks. A brand new station under an elliptical glass dome is also envisaged. South of the stations, **Plaza Zabálburu** marks the beginning of Bilbao's less salubrious quarters. On the cusp lie the Vista Alegre **bullring** and the **Museo Taurino** (*open Mon–Fri 10.30–1 and 4–6; adm*), with mementoes from over 250 years of bull-fighting history, including a magnificent embroidered cape by Goya.

From Pza de España, the **Gran Vía de Don Diego López de Haro**, the main boulevard of the Ensanche, extends westwards. A block to the north, the façade of the El Corte Inglés department store is one vast high relief mural evoking the industry and history of Bilbao. The centre of the Ensanche scheme is Pza de Federico Moyúa, or **La Elíptica**. Here, the Hotel Carlton, still one of the city's posh establishments, served as the seat of the Basque government under the Republic and during the Civil War. From La Elíptica, C/Elcano takes you to the **Museo de Bellas Artes** (*open Tues–Sat 10.30–1.30 and 4–7.30, Sun 10–2; adm*), on the edge of the beautiful Parque de Doña Casilda Iturriza. Its worthy collection ranges from Flemish paintings (Metsys' *The Money Changers* is one of the best) to Spanish masters such as Velázquez, El Greco, Zurbarán and Goya, as well as modern art by Picasso, Gauguin, Léger and Mary Cassatt, and 19th- and 20th-century Basques. Overflow from the Guggenheim has brought in more visitors, and the museum is currently being enlarged to accommodate them. The park itself is an agreeable place, with carefully labelled exotic trees, a lagoon, and a new light-and-colour bauble called the 'Cybernetic Fountain'.

Since the 1980s, major developments have taken place along the Nervión, and the evenings see the Bilbaínos stream in to stroll along its banks in a new riverfront park. Halfway along, the billowing, glass-floored **Zubi Zuri** ('white bridge') sails over the river, from where a funicular glides up to the hilltop park on **Monte Artxanda** (*runs every 15mins, 7.15–11; adm*), with its several restaurants and extensive views.

The Guggenheim Museum

Av. Abandoibarra 2, 48001; ***t*** *944 35 90 80 (groups* ***t*** *944 35 90 23) www.guggenheim-bilbao.es; open Tues–Sun 10–8 (last adm 30 mins before closing); adm. Long queues (up to an hour) are frequent, especially at weekends. You can wander round independently or pick up a free audioguide with information on the key works.* ***Free guided tours*** *(in English) take place several times daily; you can register up to 30mins ahead (at the information desk in the main lobby).*

Downstream from Zubi Zuri a 60ft tower of steel and golden limestone heralds the presence of Frank O. Gehry's **Museo Guggenheim**. This titanium clipper ship occupies the **Abandoibarra flats**, until 1987 home to Bilbao's biggest shipyard; it fits in perfectly, at once utterly futuristic and yet in keeping with the city's industrial past.

The museum's innovative design attracts universal curiosity: most visitors spend as much time wandering around the exterior as they do looking at the artwork inside, Depending on the angle from which you see it, ships' hulls, truncated fish bodies, and palm trees all protrude from the bulging mass, the juxtaposition of natural forms and 21st-century technology suggesting a new genre of 'bio-architecture'.

The interior spaces are no less remarkable, with galleries radiating out from a 150ft-high atrium of white light and swooping curves, a sculptural work of art in its own right and Frank Gehry's contribution to the Guggenheim legend. Outside the atrium, the Nervión is incorporated into the museum's design by way of an ingenious raised walkway, rising and curving and creating a union between river and water garden.

The Collection

After Gehry's architectural fireworks, the collection itself has a hard act to follow; whether or not it succeeds will depend on when you go. Thanks to its links with major galleries worldwide, the Guggenheim has excellent access to the masterworks of 20th-century art, yet the shifting nature of the exhibits means there's no guarantee what will be on show and it's worth calling ahead to avoid disappointment.

If the **permanent collection** is up, look out for a good selection of European avant-garde art: there's a pivotal Miró, a selection of Kandinskys, some Modiglianis and scattered works by Picasso and Klee. Underpinning these is a distinguished collection of Abstract Expressionism, with works by Robert Motherwell, Pollock and De Kooning; the polychromatic chaos is balanced by a tranquil Rothko and Yves Klein's *Large Blue Anthropometry* (1960). A patchy collection of Pop Art includes a subdued Lichtenstein, and there are some fine pieces by Schnabel, Dubuffet and Basquiat, and a moving monographic exhibition devoted to Anselm Kiefer.

Elsewhere, there's a small collection of works by Basque and Spanish artists – sculptures by Chillida and Cristina Iglesias, and textural paintings by Tàpies – which the museum's directors have pledged to augment with future purchases.

The Guggenheim Effect

The Guggenheim's success has spawned ambitious restoration projects throughout Bilbao, most notably alongside the museum on the **Abandoibarra flats**, where an immense new development is set to sprout up under the direction of Mexican architect Cesár Pelli. An extensive park area is also planned, completing the 'green corridor' between Parque de Doña Casilda Iturriza and Pso del Arenal.

Navarra

Europe's traditional front door to Spain, Navarra is also a good introduction to the Spanish plurals, the 'Spains' combining a sizeable, often nationalistic Basque minority up in the misty western Pyrenees and a conservative, non-Basque Navarrese majority tending the sunny gardens of the Ebro valley flatlands to the south. The combination hasn't always been comfortable, and only now that much of the population has abandoned the countryside have tensions between the two groups loosened up. Much of this 'loosening up' is concentrated in Pamplona, the capital both groups share, packed into an ecstatic week-long bacchanalia of inebriated recklessness, bull running and partying known as 'Los Sanfermines' (*see* pp.318–19).

Navarra: A Potted History

To understand the standoffish, James Dean role Navarra traditionally plays, you need a bit of Spanish history, which is full of the phrase 'except Navarra'. Even in Spain, 'the nation of nations', the region has stood apart ever since 605, when the Franks tried to harness it as part of the Duchy of Vasconia, a huge untenable territory that extended from the Garonne to the Ebro. Charlemagne himself came down in

778, either to discipline the unruly duchy or to force it to join his fight against the Moors, and after razing the walls of Pamplona he went stumping back to France – except for his rear guard, which the furious Basques of Pamplona ambushed in 778 at the pass of Roncesvalles ('Valley of the Thorntrees').

Charlemagne taught the Navarrese that owing nothing to nobody was the way to go, and within a few years of his passing they created the independent kingdom of Navarra. Its most talented king, Sancho III 'the Great' (1004–34), firmly established the *camino francés* through Navarra and controlled much of French Basque country and Galicia, and pocketed Castile and León after the death of its last count, setting up his son Ferdinand I as the first to take the title of 'King of the Spains'. The centre was too precocious to hold, and by the time of Sancho IV (1054–76) Navarra was once again a fierce rival of Castile, but avoided entanglements – marital or martial – by playing the French card. 'The Flea between Two Monkeys', as it became known, was ruled by three different French dynasties between 1234 and 1512, when Ferdinand the Catholic slyly demanded that Navarra let his armies march through to France. His demand, as he anticipated, was refused and he used the refusal as an excuse to grab Navarra south of the Pyrenees. France was left with only Basse Navarre, a thimble-sized realm but one that gave her a long line of kings, with the accession of Henri IV (1589–1610). Ferdinand kept the Navarrese happy by maintaining their *fueros*, which in practice gave the region an independence enjoyed by no other in Spain; it was ruled by a

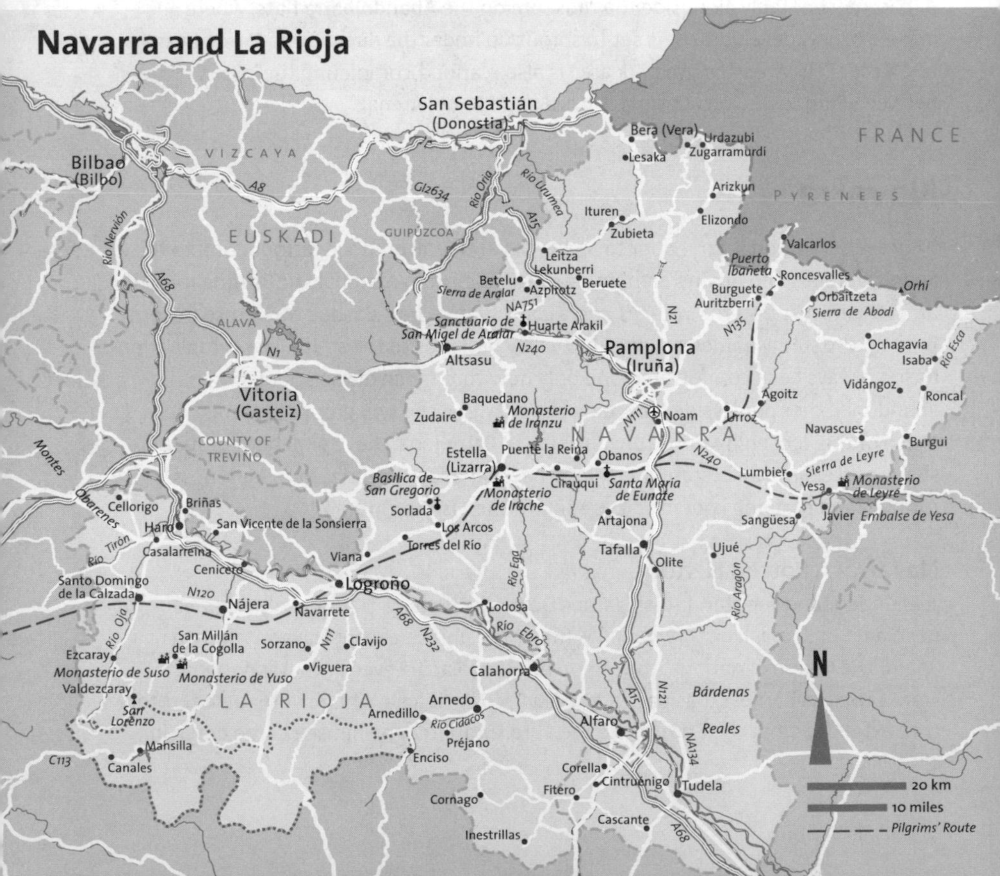

viceroy, minted its own coins and had its own government. Napoleonic and Liberal attempts to do away with the *fueros* in the cause of central unity turned the Navarrese into fierce reactionaries and the most ardent of Carlists (supporters of the pretender, Charles III). In the 1930s Navarra rejected the Republic's offer of autonomy; instead, the Navarrese Carlist *requetés*, in their distinctive red berets, became some of Franco's best troops, fighting for their old privileges and Catholicism – just as the Basques were, only on the Republican side. Franco rewarded Navarra by leaving the *fueros* intact, making it the only autonomous region in Spain until his death.

Approaches from France: Down the Valleys of the Pyrenees

The Navarrese Pyrenees don't win altitude records, but they're green, wooded and shot through with legends, many lingering in the mists around Roncesvalles, for centuries the pass most favoured by French pilgrims. Much of Navarra's Basque population is concentrated in the three valleys of Roncal, Salazar and Baztán where seemingly every house in every hamlet is emblazoned with a coat of arms – for the Basques have traditionally considered themselves all equal and therefore all noble.

The Eastern Valleys: Valle del Roncal and Valle de Salazar

Like many Pyrenean valleys, the Roncal was so remote for centuries that the central authorities were content to let it run its own show. Time has changed a few things: timber logged on its thickly forested slopes now travels by truck instead of careering down the Esca River, and the valley's renowned sheep's cheese, *queso de Roncal*, is now made in a factory (but according to farm traditions). Mist often envelops Isaba, the Valle del Roncal's biggest town, gathered under its fortress church of San Cipriano (1540). Every 13 July since 1375, at stone frontier marker no.262, the mayor of Isaba and his colleagues don traditional costume, march up to meet their counterparts from the Valle de Baretous in France and ask them three times for the 'Tribute of the Three Cows', in exchange for the right to graze their herds in the Valle del Roncal in August – something both sides used to kill for before the annual tribute was agreed on. Isaba provides an excellent base for exploring the magnificent mountain scenery: hike up the region's highest peaks, Pic d'Anie (8,200ft) and Mesa de los Tres Reyes (7,900ft), or make the most beautiful walk of all, into the Parque Natural Pirenáico to the *refugio de Belagua*, set in a stunning glacial amphitheatre.

Roncal is a pretty village surrounded by pine forests. The great, amiable Basque tenor Julián Gayarre (1844–90) was born here and lies buried in a suitably high operatic tomb just outside town; the **Casa-Museo Julián Gayarre** (*open Tues–Sun 10–1.30 and 5–7 (winter afternoons 4–6); closed Mon; adm*) contains costumes and photos from his glory days.

The sparsely populated **Valle de Salazar** is much less visited but just as lovely, abubble with trout streams, beech forests and old white stone Basque chalet-like *caserónes*. **Ochagavía** is another good base for walks.

Getting Around

By Bus

There are no trains here; and in most cases the buses from Pamplona go only once a day. La Roncalesa (**t** 948 30 02 57) serves the Valle del Roncal, as does La Tafallesa (**t** 948 22 28 86), the latter stopping at Yesa, near the lake, and 4km from the monastery of Leyre (*see* below). Río Irati buses (**t** 948 22 14 70) go to the Valles de Salazar and Aezkoa; there's one bus daily to Ochagavía, and one to Orbaizeta. Roncesvalles is served by La Montañesa (**t** 948 21 15 84); you can go as far as Burguete and then walk 3km. La Baztanesa (**t** 948 22 67 12) serves the Valle de Baztán.

Tourist Information

Roncal: **t** 948 47 52 56.
Ochagavía: **t** 948 89 06 41.
Roncesvalles: Antiguo Molino, **t** 948 76 03 01.

Where to Stay and Eat

Navarra as a whole has made efforts to improve cheaper accommodation. Traditional houses have been restored as *casas rurales*, or B&Bs: contact the Pamplona tourist office for their *Guía de Alojamientos de Turismo Rural*. A central office, **t** 948 22 93 28, will book beds for pilgrims on the Camino de Santiago.

Valle del Roncal ✉ 31680

★★★**Isaba**, Ctra Roncal s/n, in Isaba, **t** 948 89 30 00, **f** 948 89 30 30, *hotelisaba@ctv.es* (*moderate*). Luxurious, this is the most modern in the valley, with a sauna and gym.

★**Hs Lola**, Mendigatxa 17, **t** 948 89 30 12, *www.hotelesruralesnavarra.es* (*inexpensive*). A *hostal* providing good rooms, along with a decent **restaurant**.

★**Hotel Ezkaurre**, **t** 948 89 33 03, **f** 948 89 33 02 (*inexpensive*). Tucked down a back street, this classic mountain *hostal* has comfortable rooms and a cosy sitting room, complete with fireplace and stunning views.

Venta de Juan Pito, Puerta de Belagua (at the mountain refuge), **t** 948 89 30 80 (*inexpensive*). Fill up on local dishes such as *migas pastor* (fried bread) and Roncal cheese. *Open July–Sept; rest of year weekends only*.

In **Roncal** itself you can choose between:

★**Hs Zaltua**, Castillo 23, **t** 948 47 50 08 (*moderate–inexpensive*).

P. Begoña, C/Castillo 118, **t** 948 47 50 56 (*inexpensive*).

Ochagavía ✉ 31680

Most of the accommodation in the Salazar valley is in *casas rurales*.

Casa Ballent, **t** 948 89 03 73 (*inexpensive*). One of the best, with cosy bedrooms, a welcoming owner and views from the terrace over the Pyrenees and the communal vegetable patch.

To the north, a road leads into the vast beech and ancient yew **Forest of Irati**, the largest primeval forest in Spain, with majestic **Mt Orhi** (6,618ft) as a backdrop. One of the richest wildlife habitats in the Pyrenees, it is the haunt of red squirrels, deer and wild boar, as well as that of the ghost of Jeanne d'Albret, queen of Navarra and mother of Henri IV, a nasty, diehard, Protestant fanatic. Poisoned in 1572, Jeanne tours her old domain on windy nights with an escort of Basque *lamias* or nymphs, with whom she would never have been caught dead while still alive.

To the south is the spectacular **Hoz de Arbayún** (*see* p.322), home to Spain's largest colonies of rare griffon vultures (*buitres*).

Roncesvalles (Orreaga)

Of all the Pyrenean passes, introverted Roncesvalles was the most renowned in the Middle Ages. French pilgrims would mumble verses from the *Chanson de Roland* as they paid their respects to the sites associated with Charlemagne and his nephew Roland, then say their first prayer to another gallant knight, Santiago. From

*Hs Ori-Alde, t 948 89 00 27 (*cheap*). This 12-room place features Basque cooking in its kitchen. *Open July–Oct.*

**Hs Salazar, C/Mayor s/n, in Oronz, t 948 89 00 53, f 948 89 03 70 (*inexpensive*). Just south of Ochagavía, this has a pool and pretty views.

Auñamendi, Pza Guarpide 1, **t** 948 89 01 89, *auniamendi@jet.es* (*moderate*). Some of the smaller rooms are *inexpensive*; serves trout with ham and a good asparagus and prawn pudding.

Roncesvalles ✉ 31650

If you have no luck at any of the places below, try one of several *casas rurales* in the vicinity. The erstwhile pilgrim stops of Burguete (Auritz) and Espinal (Auritzberri) are also still good places to stay.

Hs La Posada, t 948 76 02 25 (*inexpensive*). If you want to stay in comfort there are 18 spacious rooms in the *Colegiata*, with a fine **restaurant located in the medieval inn that formerly served the pilgrims.

*Hs Casa Sabina, t 948 76 00 12 (*moderate*). Next to the monastery entrance, with six pleasant rooms and tasty Navarrese cuisine.

**Hs Loizu, 3km away, in Burguete, t 948 76 00 08, f 948 79 04 44, *hloizu@cmn.navarra .net* (*moderate*). A good choice, with plenty of atmosphere for its reasonable rates.

**Hs Burguete, t 948 76 00 05 (*inexpensive*). Whenever Hemingway decamped to the Pyrenees he stayed here; despite its fading elegance, this antique-bedecked old place is still a great choice for slumming it in style.

Urdazubi/Urdax ✉ 31711

Hs Irigoienea, C/Salvador, **t** 948 59 92 67, **f** 948 59 92 43, *hoirigoienea@jet.es* (*inexpensive*). A charming place to spend a few nights.

Menta, on the Dantxarina road, **t** 948 59 90 20 (*moderate*). Out on the terrace, you can feast on a superb mix of Navarrese and French dishes, with game in season; there's a good wine list. *Closed Mon eve and Tues.*

Elizondo ✉ 31700

***Baztán, on the main road, t 948 58 00 50, f 948 45 23 23, *hotelbaztan@biaipe.net* (*moderate*). Modern with panoramic views, a pool and a garden. *Closed Dec–Mar.*

**Hs Saskaitz, M. Azphilikueta 10, t 948 58 06 15, f 948 58 09 92, *hotelelizondo@biaipe.net* (*moderate*). A cosy enough place in the centre of town.

Casa Galarza, C/Santiago 1, **t** 948 58 01 01 (*inexpensive*). Tthis haven of traditional Baztanian cuisine and cheese serves *txuri-tabeltz*, a stew of lamb's tripe for which Elizondo is famous. *Closed Tues.*

Casa Rural Urruska, 10km away in Barrio de Bearzún, **t** 948 45 21 06 (*inexpensive*). Simple but solid home cooking attracts hungry clients from all down the valley, while live-stock baa and moo on the ground floor.

Roncesvalles' Colegiata it's 781km to Compostela, a distance the fittest pilgrims could cover in 20 days. The Colegiata had a sad, has-been look back in the 1970s, when the medieval floods of pilgrims had dried to a trickle of eccentrics. No one predicted that in the 1990s the number of pilgrims who stopped to have their documents stamped would grow by the thousands.

Up the Colegiata

The pilgrims' routes from France converged at the busy frontier town of **Valcarlos**, where Charlemagne was camping when he heard Roland's horn Oliphant warning of danger. Charlemagne was too far away to rescue his rear guard, but they were all dead anyway; Roland puffed so hard on his horn that he blew his brains out. From here the road winds up through lush greenery to the town of Roncesvalles, where the 12th-century church of **Sancti Spiritus** (the 'Silo de Charlemagne') is said to have been originally built as Roland's tomb. Set back from the road, its **Colegiata** is a French-style Gothic church consecrated in 1219. The front caved in under the snow in 1600 (hence the zinc roof) and was replaced by a **cloister**, with access to a 14th-century chapter-house housing the tomb of Sancho the Strong. The stained glass (1960) shows a scene from the 1212 battle of Las Navas de Tolosa, when Sancho led the Navarrese to their greatest victory over the Moors. The chains in the chapel are among those that bound 10,000 slaves around the emir's tent. The **museum** (*open Easter–Oct 10.30–1.30 and 4–6; Nov–Easter 10–2 and 4–7; adm*) is fascinating, containing such treasures as the emerald that fell from the Emir's turban when giant King Sancho burst into his tent at Las Navas de Tolosa, an 11th-century *pyx*, or golden box, used to hold the Host, and a reliquary called 'Charlemagne's chessboard' (*c.* 1350) for its 32 little cases, each designed to hold a saintly tidbit. Among the paintings are an excellent 15th-century Flemish triptych and a *Holy Family* by Morales.

An easy and beautiful path from the monastery leads up to the **Puerto Ibañeta** (3,150ft) where the Basques dropped boulders on the Franks.

Western Valleys: Valle de Baztán and Valle de Bidasoa

Frequent rains off the Atlantic make the valleys west of Roncesvalles so lush that they're called the 'Switzerland of Navarra'. Both are dotted with unspoiled villages, streams and quietly beautiful scenery that wasn't always so quiet.

In the early 17th century, the **Valle de Baztán** played host to a legendary colony of witches who held their black sabbaths (*akelarres*) in the vast **Cuevas de Zugarramurdi** (*open daily 9–7; adm*), carved out of the mountain by the *Infernuko Erreka* (Hell's Stream). In 1609, the Logroño inquisition tortured 13 to death and ignited six others at an *auto-da-fé*. On the summer solstice the locals still gather in the caves for feasting and dancing. The lovely stalactite-studded **Cuevas de Urdax** (*guided tours roughly every 20 mins in summer*) are just to the south at Urdazubi/Urdax.

Elizondo, the chief village in the Baztán valley, has an informal tourist office (*C/Jaime Urrutia, **t** 948 58 12 79*) where you can pick up a map that pinpoints the historic houses. Further south a road turns east to France by way of the spectacular **Izpegui pass** (*summer only*).

Navarra's westernmost Pyrenean valley, the **Valle de Bidasoa**, embraces streams filled with salmon and trout and, more prosaically, the main San Sebastián–Pamplona road. Local buses serve charming old Basque villages such as **Vera** (**Bera**) **de Bidasoa**, only a couple miles from the French frontier, where the former home of the anarchistic Basque novelist Pío Baroja (1872–1956; author of *Memorias de un hombre de acción*) is now an **ethnographic museum** (***t*** *948 63 00 20 for an appointment*). **Lesaka**, equally pretty, claims one of the best-preserved fortified feudal houses in Navarra.

To the south, thousands of acres of oak, beech and chestnut forest comprise the **Parque Natural del Señoro de Bértiz** (*garden open Mon 4–6, Tues–Fri 10–2 and 4–6, Sat and Sun 10–2 and 4–7*). West of here, **Zubieta** and **Ituren** are famous for a spring carnival ritual that might have been invented by Dr Seuss: men called the *joaldunak* dress up in striped dunce's caps and lacey smocks, and tie a pair of *polunpak* (giant bells) to their backs using an intricate network of laces. Thus arrayed, the *joaldunak* make a *zanpantzar*, a group of 20 or so who march from village to village, their *polunpak* smacking and jangling as they walk.

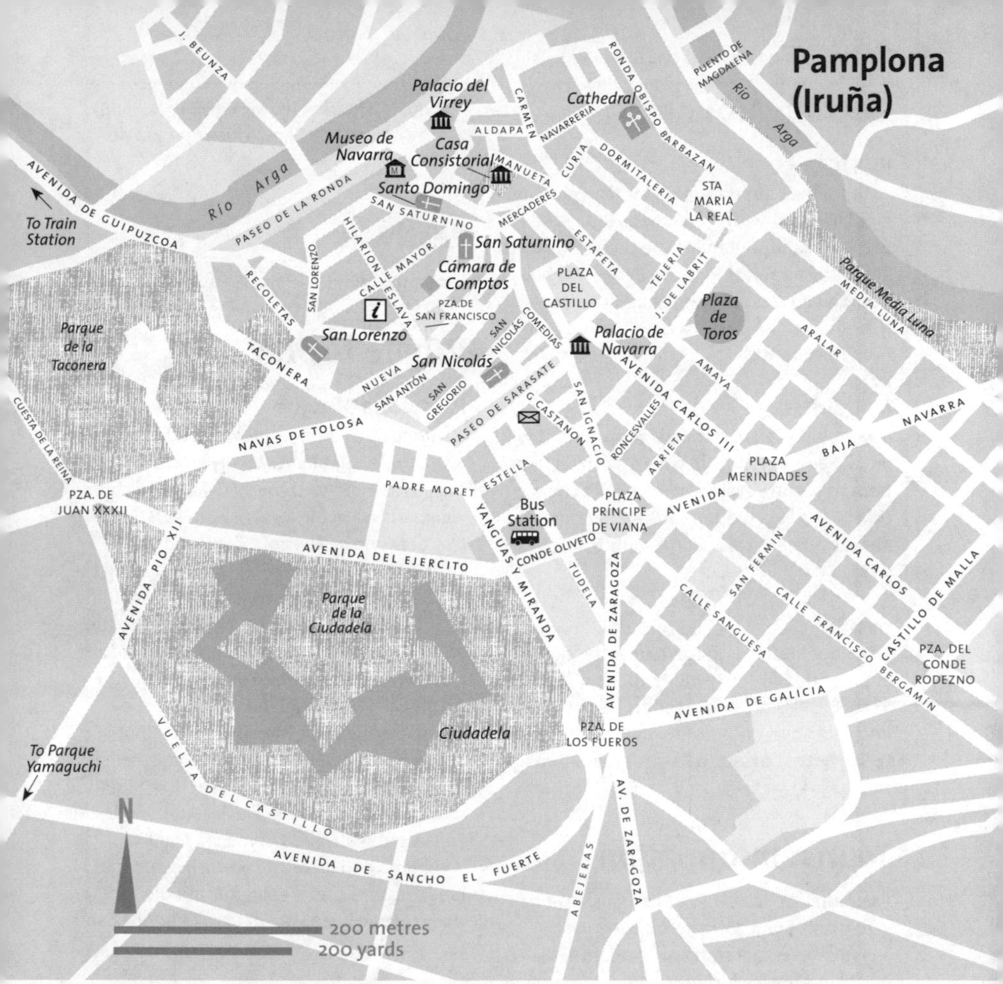

Pamplona (Iruña)

Whether you call it Pamplona, the town founded by Pompey in 75 BC, or by its older name Iruña, which means simply 'the city' in Basque, the capital of autonomous Navarra sits on a strategic 1,400ft mound on the beautiful fertile plain, its existence as inevitable as its nickname, the 'Gateway of Spain'. For a few years in the 730s, the Arabs used it in reverse, as the gateway to France, until their dreams of Europe were hammered at Poitiers. Over the next decades the Vascones regained control of Pamplona, clobbered Charlemagne after he burnt their walls, and set up their own king. In 918 the Moors came back and razed Pamplona to the ground again. To encourage rebuilding, Sancho III the Great invited his subjects in French Navarre to come and start trading in what became the two new districts of Pamplona, San Cernín and San Nicolás. The fact that the three districts of the city were practically independent and had their own privileges led to violent rivalry, so much so that in 1521 the French Navarrese unsuccessfully besieged Pamplona in an effort to regain San Cernín and San Nicolás. Wounded while fighting for Castile was a certain Captain

Getting Around

By Air

Pamplona's airport is 9km south of the city, **t** 948 16 87 00, with connections to Madrid, Barcelona and Santander. The cheapest way to get to the airport is to take a Beriainesa bus from the bus station (every half-hour) to Noaín, which drops you a few hundred metres from the airport.

By Train

Pamplona's train station is 2km out of town on Av. San Jorge. Bus No.9 makes connections from the centre every 10mins, **t** 948 13 02 02; tickets and information can also be had at the railway office in town at C/Estella 8, **t** 948 22 72 82.

By Bus

The bus station is in town, near the citadel, at C/Conde Oliveto 8; information **t** 948 22 38 54. Besides provincial connections, there are six buses to Vitoria, four to Bilbao, seven to San Sebastián, six to Zaragoza, and two to Huesca and Jaca.

Tourist Information

Pamplona: C/Eslava 1, Pza San Fransisco, **t** 948 20 65 40, **f** 948 20 70 34, *oit.pamplona@cfnavarra.es*; the staff here operate a booking service for *casas rurales* throughout Navarra, **t** 948 20 65 41, **f** 948 20 70 34, *central.reservas@cfnavarra.es*.

Post Office: just off Pso de Sarasate.

Internet Access: try IturNet, C/Iturrama 1, though it's an inconveniently long hike away in the new part of town.

There is a **market** (*every morning exc. Sun*) at the Mercado de Santo Domingo, Pza de los Burgos.

Festivals

Los Sanfermines, *see* pp.318–19.

Where to Stay

Pamplona ✉ 31300

During San Fermín, hotel prices double and often triple, supplemented by scores of over-priced rooms in *casas particulares*, advertised weeks ahead in the local newspapers, *Navarra Hoy* or *Diario de Navarra*. If you end up sleeping outside, any of the gardens along the walls or river are preferable to the noisy, filthy, vomit-filled citadel. Keep a close eye on your belongings (petty criminals, go into overdrive along with everyone else during the fiesta) and check in what you don't need at the *consigna* in Pza San Fransisco by the tourist office; everyone else does too, so get there early. Two free **campsites** are set up along the road to France, but don't leave anything there you might really miss. If you stay outside Pamplona and drive into town, beware that breaking into cars is epidemic but discerning: thieves have been known to take Tampax and toothbrushes but leave everything else.

Luxury

******Iruña Palace Los Tres Reyes**, Jardines de la Taconera, **t** 948 22 66 00, **f** 948 22 29 30, *www.hotel3reyes.com*. Just a short walk from the old town, the palace pampers its guests with every possible convenience including an indoor, heated pool and tennis courts.

Íñigo López de Recalde, who convalesced in Pamplona, got religion in a militant way and founded the Jesuits.

Pamplona seems to have been naturally conducive to that sort of thing, with a reputation for being crazily austere, brooding and puritanical. For anyone who knows the city only for throwing the wildest party in Europe, this comes as a shock of *desfase* or maladjustment, a word that means (and gleefully celebrates) the unresolved contradictions that coexist in post-Franco Spain. Stern Catholicism is part of the city's fabric. 'From the top to the bottom of Pamplonese society, I have found the whole place poisoned by clerical alkaloid,' grumbled Basque philosopher Unamuno. 'It oozed out

Expensive

★★★**Maisonnave**, C/Nueva 20 (next to Pza San Francisco), **t** 948 22 26 00, **f** 948 22 01 66. Offers comfort and prestige and a peaceful garden at the back.

★★★**NH El Toro**, at Berrioplano (5km from Pamplona on the Guipúzcoa road), **t** 948 30 22 11, **f** 948 30 20 85. Has quiet rooms in a traditional-style mansion, overlooking a statue group of the *encierro*.

Moderate

★★★**Europa**, C/Espoz y Mina 11 (just off Pza Castillo), **t** 948 22 18 00, *heuropa@cmn.navarra.net*. One of Pamplona's prettiest choices with its flower-bedecked balconies, some of which overlook the *encierro* action in Estafeta; the **restaurant**, one of the city's finest, is run by the same management as the Alhambra (*see* below).

★★★**Yoldi**, Av. San Ignacio 11, **t** 948 22 48 00, **f** 948 21 20 45, *www.webs.navarra.net/hyoldi*. Has long been the favourite of *toreros* and *aficionados* in general.

★★**Eslava**, Pza Virgen de la O, **t** 948 22 22 70, **f** 948 22 51 57. Small, quiet, cosy, and run by a friendly family, with views over the walls of Pamplona.

★**La Perla**, Pza Castillo, **t** 948 22 77 06, **f** 948 21 15 19. Hemingway always stayed at this, Pamplona's oldest hotel – at least, as long as room 217 was available; the others, recently renovated, still have their high ceilings and plaster mouldings from 1880.

Inexpensive

★**Hs Bearán**, San Nicolás 25, **t** 948 22 34 28, **f** 948 22 34 28. One of the few decent *hostales* you are likely to find; all doubles with bath.

★★**Hs Navarra**, C/ Tudela 9, **t** 948 22 51 64, **f** 948 22 34 26. Miraculously revived by a lick of paint and flowering plants on the balconies; it's convenient for early morning buses and five minutes walk from the *casco viejo*; all rooms with bath.

P. Lambertini, C/Mercaderes 17, **t** 948 21 03 03 (*inexpensive–cheap*). Has a comfy living room stuffed with books and knick-knacks, and balconies overlooking the route of the *encierro*. Ask for one of the lovely rooms at the back, which boast extensive views across the Cuenca de Pamplona.

Cheap

The cheaper *hostales* and *fondas* are mostly on C/San Gregorio and C/San Nicolás.

Casa Santa Cecilia, C/Navarrería 17, **t** 948 22 22 30. Located in an 18th-century palace, and providing one of the nicest cheap sleeps under lofty ceilings in huge rooms.

Otano, San Nicolás 5, **t** 948 22 50 95. A long-term favourite for its nice rooms with baths, and a good (*inexpensive*) **restaurant-bar**.

Excaba, **t** 948 33 03 15. The nearest campsite, 7km to the north.

Eating Out

Expensive

Josetxo, Pza Príncipe de Viana 1, **t** 948 22 20 97. A gourmet institution in Pamplona for 40 years. Try to book one of the small Belle Epoque dining rooms upstairs, and choose such delicacies as *ajo arriero con langosta* (seafood casserole with lobster) or the chef's prize *solomillo a la broche con salsa de trufa* (steak fillet on a spit with truffle sauce). *Closed Sun and Aug*.

of every corner...one drop in the eye is enough to infect you forever.' In the 1950s, the secretive Opus Dei, Christianity's ultra-conservative fifth column, chose Pamplona to build their Universidad de Navarra. In the 1960s the city's new tennis club still built separate swimming pools for men and women. Forty years later, a new Pamplona prides itself on setting up Spain's first shelter for battered women, the first city workshops for training disadvantaged youth and the first urban rubbish-recycling program. 'Pamplona is a city that gives much more than it promises', said Victor Hugo. It certainly will if you come the second week of July for the Sanfermines, but expect it to take your money, your watch, your sleep and a lifetime supply of adrenalin as well.

Hartza, C/Juan de Labrit 19, **t** 948 22 45 68. Famous for *bonito encebollado* (tuna with onions), hake dishes and good home-made desserts. *Closed Sun eve, Mon and mid-July–early Aug.*

Alhambra, C/Bergamín 7, **t** 948 24 50 07. Look out for more imaginative dishes at this fashionable place: potatoes stuffed with truffles and scampi and home-made desserts; there is also a good *menú degustación* (*moderate*). *Closed Sun and mid-July–early Aug.*

Rodero, C/E.Arrieta 3, **t** 948 22 80 35. Delicious dishes based on Navarrese, Basque and French-style recipes are prepared with the finest seasonal ingredients at this family-run restaurant. *Closed Sun and Aug.*

Europa, C/Espoz y Mina 11, **t** 948 22 18 00. Indulges diners with refined service and classic Navarrese meat and game dishes; try the stewed breast and thigh of pigeon, smothered in rich gravy. *Closed Sun.*

Moderate

Sarasate, **t** 948 33 08 20. On weekends half of Pamplona drives 11km out towards Irún to dine on the imaginative dishes served at this traditional *caserío* with a fireplace for winter dining and a terrace in the summer. *Closed Sun eve and Mon.*

Chalet de Izu, Avda Baja Navarra 47, **t** 948 22 60 93. Near Parque Media Luna, with plenty of swish atmosphere and good *menús.*

Asador Olaverri, C/Santa Marta 4, **t** 948 23 50 63. Great for a big grilled meat and wine feast. *Closed Sun eve and mid-July–mid-Aug.*

Baserri, C/San Nicolás 32, **t** 948 22 20 21 (*moderate*). Hard to beat for *cocina en miniatura*; its fine creations repeatedly walk away with top honours at Pamplona's annual Concurso de Pinchos. You can try a selection of them, and delicacies such as fresh rocket and smoked cod salad, on the excellent *menú especial.*

Casa Sixto, C/Estafeta 81, **t** 948 22 51 27. Well known for its succulent home-cooked game dishes. *Closed Wed and Oct.*

Inexpensive

La Campana, C/Campana 12, **t** 948 22 00 08. The chef prides himself on his unusual recipes, such as chicken in champagne.

Casa Paco, C/Lindatxikía (behind San Nicolás church), **t** 948 22 51 05. A favourite for lunch since the 1920s.

Sarasate, C/San Nicolás 19, **t** 948 22 57 27. For the best vegetarian meals in Pamplona. *Closed Sun and eves, exc. Fri and Sat.*

Cafés and Bars

As well as elegant cafés, Pamplona has some 700 bars, or one for every 280 inhabitants, many of whom seem to be in them day and night. Favourite late-night bar-crawling zones in the Casco Viejo are C/San Nicolás and San Gregorio, San Lorenzo and Jarauta, and Navarrería, the latter still popular with the Basques and alternative Pamplonese.

Café Iruña, Plaza del Castillo. You can tuck into *inexpensive* light meals until 2.30am at this famous 1888 *modernista* place.

Mesón del Caballo Blanco, near the cathedral in Redín. An atmospheric stone house with a terrace; a delightful place to linger; in winter sandwiches are served around the fire.

Roch, C/Comedias. Small, lively and usually packed at the start of *la marcha*, thanks in part to their superb *fritos de pimiento* tapas.

El Cordovilla, in the Casco Viejo. A bar that claims to make the biggest *pinchos morunos* (kebabs) in the world.

A Walk through the Casco Viejo

Pamplona was squeezed in a tight girdle of walls until the early 1900s, when the city spread in all directions and accumulated around 185,000 inhabitants in the process. But for all its 20th-century flab, the vital organs in the historic Casco Viejo remain intact, beginning with the city's heart, **Plaza del Castillo**, shaded by the knitted boughs of plane trees, circled by too many cars and framed by arcades sheltering stylish cafés. Off the southwest corner extends the **Paseo de Sarasate**, populated by stone kings and queens and the overwrought **Monumento a los Fueros**, erected by popular subscription after Madrid tried to mess with Navarra's privileges back in 1893.

Off the east end of Pza del Castillo, the narrow streets jammed with shops and bars were once the Judería, where Pamplona's Jews, 'a gentle and reasonable race' according to the King of Navarra, lived unmolested until Navarra was gobbled up by Ferdinand and Isabel's Castile. Behind these, tucked up near the ramparts, the gracious 14th–15th-century Gothic **Cathedral** hides behind a dull-witted, neoclassical façade, slapped on in the 18th century by a misguided do-gooder; a shame because the original front, according to travellers' descriptions, was as lusty as the one at Cervatos (*see* **Cantabria**, p.348). When completed, it was the second-largest cathedral in Spain after León's, and suitable shelter for the beautiful alabaster tombs of the cathedral's sponsors, big-nosed Charles III 'the Noble' and his big-nosed queen Leonora de Trastámara, sculpted in the 15th century by Jean de Lomme of Tournai. The kings of Navarra were crowned before the Romanesque *Virgen del Sagrario* on the high altar. The delicacy of the Gothic **cloister** (1280–1472) approaches gossamer in stone and reaches a climax of decorative bravura in the justly named **Puerta Preciosa** (1325), carved with a superb *Dormition of the Virgin*. Off the cloister, the **Museo Diocesano** (*open Mon–Fri 10–1.30 and 4–7, Sat 10–1.30; closed Sun; adm*) occupies the refectory and kitchen where pilgrims once dined and contains two remarkable reliquaries: the 1258 *Relicario del Santo Sepulcro* and the 1401 *Relicario del Lignum Crucis*, adorned with precious stones.

The narrow lanes around the cathedral belong to the **Navarrería**, the original Basque quarter, populated in the Middle Ages by cathedral builders and farmers who tilled the bishop's lands. Here on the promontory you'll find the most impressive segment surviving of the **walls** built by Philip II, with so great a reputation for impregnability that no one tried to challenge them until the French tried to hole up here against Wellington. Just west, the 13th-century **Palacio del Virrey** started out as the royal palace and now houses the local military government.

Continuing past the attractive **Portal de Zumalacárregui** (16th-century, but renamed after the Carlist hero), the **Museo de Navarra** (*open Tues–Sat 10–2 and 5–7, Sun 11–2; closed Mon; adm*) occupies a huge 16th-century hospital and contains everything from Roman mosaics to an 11th-century ivory coffret from Leyre and a fine portrait by Goya. Just below the museum, wooden barricades remind you that this is the beginning of the *encierro*; the bulls leave their corral near Pza Santo Domingo and head up C/Mercaderes and C/Estafeta. Follow their route and you'll come to Pza Consistorial and the colourful, Baroque **Casa Consistorial**, topped with jaunty allegorical figures. Pamplona's nobles built their finest escutcheoned palaces just off this square, along C/Zapatería and C/Mayor. Nearby in C/Ansoleaza, the well-preserved Gothic **Cámara de los Comptos Reales** (*open Mon–Fri 9–2*), the kings' mint in the 12th century, has a magnificent porch opening on to a vault and patio with some original decorations.

The *francos*, invited to Pamplona by Sancho the Great, lived just to the south in their two rival quarters named after, and defended by, 13th-century churches that doubled as fortresses. These are **San Saturnino** in C/San Saturnino and **San Nicolás** in lively, bar-lined C/San Nicolás; a plaque by the former marks the site where the first Pamplonans were converted by San Saturnino. Further west, **San Lorenzo** is best known for its chapel dedicated to San Fermín, built by the city in 1717, where his bust

Pamplona's Annual Meltdown: Los Sanfermines

Before Hemingway there was Fermín, son of a Roman senator and first bishop of Pamplona. His family had been converted by San Saturnino (or Cernín) of Toulouse, who was martyred in the 3rd century AD by being dragged around town by a bull. Fermín, for his part, travelled as a missionary to the Gauls and was beheaded in Amiens for his trouble. Some time between then and 1324, when Pamplona held its first fiesta, Fermín decided to take bullfighters under his saintly cape; by 1591 his festival had found its current dates and form. Although it's the running of the bulls that has made Los Sanfermines world-famous, this insanely dangerous activity is only a tiny portion of the nine days of nonstop revelling when 'Pamplona becomes the world capital of happiness', a state of hyper-bliss fuelled by three million litres of alcohol. Each year.

There is some order to the madness. The Sanfermines officially open at noon on 6 July, when thousands of Navarrese in their festival attire (white shirts and white trousers or skirts, red sashes and red bandanas) gather in front of the town hall to hold their bandanas aloft as a rocket called *El Chupinazo* is fired off the balcony and a city councillor cries in Spanish and Basque: 'People of Pamplona! Long live San Fermín!' The city explodes with a mighty roar, while popping tens of thousands of champagne corks (and smashing the bottles on the pavement, usually causing the first casualties).

In the afternoon the giants and big heads (*gigantes y cabezudos*) – as essential to the fiesta as the bulls – leave their 'home' in the bus station. The eight 13ft plaster giants supported by dancers date from 1860 and represent kings and queens, whirling and swirling the minuet, their sweeping skirts flowing in the air. They are accompanied by the *cabezudos* and *kilikis*, big-headed figures in tricorn hats, with names like Napoleon and Patata, who wallop children on the head with foam rubber balls tied to bats. This is also the prerogative of the *zaldikos*, the colourfully dressed men wearing cardboard horses around their waists; all are accompanied by dancers, *txistularis* (Basque flutes) and *gaiteros*.

At four o'clock a massive scrum, the *Riau Riau*, begins when members of the Corporación de San Fermín dressed in all their finery try to proceed 400m down C/Mayor to the chapel of San Fermín at San Lorenzo's for vespers, but everyone else tries to prevent them in a gung-ho defiance of authority, to the extent that it's often late at night before the Corporación achieves its goal. The mayor of Pamplona has tried for several years to ban the chaotic *Riau Riau*, but it seems to be unbannable. After a first night of carousing and dancing in the streets, the dawn of 7 July and every following day is welcomed with the *dianas*, a city-wide wake-up call performed on screeching pipes.

Traditionally the *encierro* started at 7am (so that festivities kicked off on the seventh hour of the seventh day of the seventh month), though nowadays the bulls begin their daily charge at 8am. If you want a good place to watch, wedge yourself into a spot along the route – Cuesta de San Domingo, Mercaderes and Estafeta – at least an hour earlier. Before running, the locals sing a hymn to Fermín and arm themselves with a rolled-up newspaper to distract the bull's attention, since the animals – 1,200lbs of muscle and fury – charge at the nearest moving object, ideally at a flung newspaper instead of a falling runner. A rocket goes up as the first bull leaves the corral; a second rocket means that all are released; and a third signals that all have made it to the bullring – on a good run the whole *encierro* lasts only three minutes. The most dangerous moments are when the runners and bulls have to squeeze into the runway of the bullring, or when a bull gets loose from his fellows and panics. People (and not all of them tourists) get trampled and gored every year; if you run you can hedge your bets by running on weekdays, when it's less crowded, and by avoiding the *toros* of the Salvador Guardiola ranch, holders of the most blood-stained record.

The spirit of abandon is so infectious that, even if you come determined not to run, you may find yourself joining in on a self-destructive spur of the moment. Women do defy the authorities and run, although the police try to pull them out. During the *encierro* the lower seats of the bullring are free (again, arrive early), except on Sunday; from here you can watch the bulls and runners pile in and, afterwards, more fun and games as heifers with padded horns are released on the crowd in the ring. The traditional breakfast is huge (bull stews, lamb's sweetbreads, ham and eggs in tomato sauce, washed down with gallons of chilled rosé and *pacharán*).

The bullfights themselves take place daily at 6.30 in the evening – tickets sell out with the speed of lightning and are usually only available from scalpers. The *sombra* seats are for serious *aficionados*, while members of the 16 *peñas* (clubs devoted to making noise and in general being as obnoxious as possible) fill up the *sol* seats and create a parallel fiesta if the action in the ring isn't up to scratch or create pandemonium if it is. Afternoons also see other bull sports that are bloodless (for the bull, at any rate): the dodging, swerving *concurso de recortadores* or leaping *corrida vasca-landesa*.

Between the bullfights there are concerts, *jotas* and Basque dances, processions of the relics of San Fermín and other religious services, parades and activities for young children and senior citizens. At night fireworks burst over the citadel and the *toro de fuego* or 'fire bull' carried by a runner and spitting fireworks chases children down the route of the *encierro*. Then there's the midnight *El Estruendo de Irún*, led by an enormous drum called the *bomba*, in which hundreds of people – just about anyone who can lay their hands on anything that makes a sound – gather and let loose in an ear-bashing sonic disorder.

At midnight on 14 July Pamplona winds down to an exhausted, nostalgic finale, a ceremony known as the *Pobre de mí*; everyone gathers in front of the town hall (or in the Plaza del Castillo for the livelier, unofficial ceremony), with a candle and sings 'Poor me, poor me, another San Fermín has come to an end'. As the clock strikes twelve everyone removes their red scarves and agrees, like Hemingway, that it was 'a damned fine show' and promises to do better and worse next year. Diehards party on until 8am the next day, and perform one last feat, the *encierro de la villavesa*: the bulls all being dead, they run along in front of a bus instead.

reliquary quietly resides 51 weeks of the year, presiding over weddings; so many Pamplonese want to be married under his protective eye that there's a two-year waiting list.

Pamplona is well endowed with parks: good for naps during the fiesta. The oldest, the French-style **Parque de la Taconera**, closes out the west end of the Casco Viejo and has one of the city's nicest cafés, the **Vienés**, in a charming old kiosk. Just south, the star-shaped **Ciudadela**, built on the orders of Philip II, is now a green park inside and outside the steep walls. The prettiest garden, **Parque Media Luna**, lines the river east of the city and has a path ending at the medieval bridge used by the pilgrims. The park in front of the **Plaza de Toros** – the third largest in the world – was renamed Paseo Hemingway and has a grizzled bust of the writer whose *The Sun Also Rises* (1926) made Pamplona a household word.

East of Pamplona: Sangüesa, Javier and Leyre

Pilgrims from Mediterranean lands would cross the Pyrenees at Somport in Aragón and enter Navarra at Sangüesa, home of one of the very best Romanesque churches and one of the craziest palaces in all Spain, but these days, if the wind's wrong, the pong of the nearby papermill hurries visitors along; note that if you go by bus from Pamplona (*La Veloz Sangüesina*, **t** *948 22 69 95*) there are only three a day and you'll be stuck with the stink longer than you might like. If you're driving, there's enough interest in the area to make a day's excursion.

Sangüesa

Sangüesa was a direct product of the pilgrimage, purposely moved from its original hilltop location in the 11th century to the spot where the road crosses the River Aragón. In 1122 Alfonso el Batallador, king of neighbouring Aragón, sent down a colony of *francos* to augment Sangüesa's population, and ten years after that ordered the Knights of St John to build a church well worth stopping for: **Santa María la Real**. This possesses one of the most intriguing and extraordinary portals on the whole *Camino*, so strange that some believe that its symbols were sculpted by *agotes* or by a brotherhood of artists on to something deeper than orthodox Catholicism; even the damned are laughing in the *Last Judgement* on the tympanum, presided over by a Christ in Majesty with a secret smile. Below, the elongated figures on the jambs show stylistic similarities to Chartres cathedral, although again the subjects are unusual: on the left the three Marys (the Virgin, Mary Magdalene and Mary Solomé, mother of St James); on the right Peter, Paul and Judas, hanged, with the inscription *Judas Mercator*. The upper half of the portal is by another hand altogether, crossed by two tiers of Apostles of near-Egyptian rigidity and another Christ in Majesty surrounded by symbols of the four Evangelists. If the church is open, ask the sacristan to show you the capitals in the apse, hidden behind the Flemish Renaissance *retablo*; the well in the corner is also a rare feature for a church. Walk around to see the beautiful carved corbels on the apse and the octagonal tower.

Sangüesa's arcaded Rua Mayor is lined with palaces, including the **Casa Consistorial**; behind this is the austere 12th-century, twin-towered **Palacio del Príncipe de Viana**. The 12th-century church of **Santiago**, with a battlemented tower and carved capitals, conserves a large statue of St James, discovered under the floor in 1965. The slightly later, Gothic **San Salvador** has a pentagonal tower and a huge porch over a carved portal; its Plateresque choir stalls come from Leyre. Around the corner in C/Alfonso el Batallador, the brick **Palacio Vallesantoro** catches the eye with its corkscrew Baroque portal and the widest, most extraordinary wooden eaves in Spain, carved with a phantasmagorical menagerie that makes the creatures on Santa María look tame.

Javier and Leyre

Sangüesa is the base for visiting two of Navarra's holy sites. **Javier**, 13 kilometres away, is topped by a picturesque if over-restored battlemented **castle** (*open 9–1 and 4–7; adm*), the birthplace in 1506 of St Francisco de Javier (Xavier), Jesuit apostle of the Indies and Japan. Though the castle is now a Jesuit college, you can take the tour and learn a lot both about St Francis, and castles; this one dates back to the 11th century, was wrecked in 1516, and restored after 1952. Perhaps most fascinating is the fresco *Dance of Death*, a grim reminder of the grip of the Black Death.

Just north of Javier, the Río Aragón has been dammed to form the vast **Yesa Reservoir**. A road from Yesa leads up to the **Monasterio de San Salvador de Leyre** (*open daily 10.15–2 and 3.30–7; adm*), founded in the 8th century and reoccupied in 1950 by the Benedictines, who began a restoration programme that unfortunately obscures much of the older building. Visits begin in the 11th-century pre-Romanesque **crypt**, where the church appears to be sinking into the ground; the columns are runty stubs weighed down by heavy block capitals that stand at about chest level. The church above, harmonious, light and austere, provides the perfect setting for the Benedictines' beautiful Gregorian matins and vespers. The bones of the first 10 kings of Navarra lie in a simple wooden casket. The west portal, the **Porta Speciosa**, is finely carved with saints and monsters. A 10-minute walk upwards affords a magnificent

Tourist Information

Sangüesa: **t** 948 87 14 11.
Javier: **t** 948 88 03 42.

Where to Stay and Eat

Sangüesa ✉ 31430

****Yamaguchi**, on the road to Javier, **t** 948 87 01 27, *yamaguchi@interbook.net* (*inexpensive*). A cosy place offering a pool and a pleasant **restaurant**.

Mediavilla, C/Alfonso El Batallador, **t** 948 87 02 12 (*moderate*). A Basque *asador* serving delicious charcoal-grilled fish and meat with excellent local wine. *Closed Mon.*

Javier and Leyre ✉ 31411

******Hotel Señorio de Monjardín**, Ctra de Leyre s/n, **t** 948 88 41 88, **f** 948 88 42 00 (*expensive*). A brand new hotel 3km from Leyre on the N240 with some luxurious suites and a **restaurant** featuring Navarrese cuisine and seasonal game dishes.

*****Xavier**, **t** 948 88 40 06, **f** 948 88 40 78 (*moderate*). An antique place to stay and eat next to the castle.

****Hospedería de Leyre**, **t** 948 88 41 00, **f** 948 88 41 37, *info@monasterio-de-leyre.com* (*moderate*). This charming former pilgrims' hostel is the perfect antidote to stress; its **restaurant** specializes in traditional Navarrese cuisine. *Open Mar–Nov.*

view of the artificial lake and Navarrese countryside from the **Fountain of San Virila**, named after Leyre's 8th-century abbot. Virila came here to pray for a peek into infinity; he visited so frequently that he was granted his wish. To the abbot, the vision was a brief, but sublime moment, but when he went down to tell his monks about it he found that all had changed: his eternal second had lasted 300 years.

Nature is a main attraction in eastern Navarra. The Sierra de Leyre divides the Roncal and Salazar valleys (*see* pp.309–11), but there are two splendid gorges close at hand. The **Foz de Lumbier** has a pleasant riverside trail for walking or cycling, and is a breeding site for griffon vultures and the rare, red-beaked variety of chough. Even more spectacular, the 1,000ft, sheer-sided, limestone **Hoz de Arbayún** runs for six kilometres further north along the Rio Salazar, with more griffon and a few Egyptian vultures; both gorges are accessible from Lumbier.

South of Pamplona to Tudela

The green valleys of the Pyrenees are a distant memory south of Pamplona; here the skies are bright and clear, the land arid and toasted golden brown after the last winter rains, except for the green vineyard swathes of La Ribera, cradle of Navarra's finest, freshest rosés.

Tafalla and Olite

In the 17th century, a Dutchman named E. Cock described Tafalla and Olite as the 'flowers of Navarra'. Old **Tafalla** has wilted a bit over the centuries, but it still has an impressive Pza Mayor and claims one of the finest and biggest *retablos* in the north: a masterpiece by Basque artist Juan de Ancheta tucked away in the austere church of **Santa María**. West of Tafalla, **Artajona** has the air of an abandoned stage set: majestic medieval walls with startlingly intact crenellated towers defend little more than the 13th-century fortress church of **San Saturnino**. Its tympanum shows the saint exorcizing a woman, watched by Juana de Navarra and Philip the Fair of France, while the lintel depicts Saturnino's martyrdom with the bull. The walls, redone in the 1300s, were first built between 1085 and 1103 by the Templars and canons of Saint-Sernin (San Saturnino) of Toulouse, at a time when the Counts of Toulouse were among the chief players in Europe, leading the First Crusade and fighting side by side with El Cid.

Olite, south of Tafalla, is dwarfed by its huge **Castle of Charles III** (*open Mon–Sat 10–2 and 4–7; closed Sun; adm*), built for the king of Navarra in 1407, with *mudéjar* décor inside. Hanging gardens were suspended from the great arches of the terraces, and there was a *leonera* (lion pit), and a very busy set of dungeons; the Navarrese royal families led messy, frustrated lives. The Gothic chapel, **Santa María la Real** (*open 9.30–12 and 5–8*) has a gorgeous 13th-century façade, while the Romanesque church of **San Pedro** (*same hours*) has a portal adorned with two stone eagles, one symbolizing force and the other gentleness.

East of Tafalla and Olite lies the striking medieval village of **Ujué**, set on a hill corrugated with terraces, where a shepherd, directed by a dove, found the statue of the

Getting Around

By Train

Most trains between Pamplona and the main junction of Altsasu stop at Huarte-Arakil; trains linking Pamplona and Zaragoza call at Tafalla, Olite and Tudela. Conda (**t** 948 22 10 26) stops at Tafalla, Olite and Tudela on the way to Zaragoza.

Tourist Information

Olite: **t** 948 74 17 03.
Tudela: Plaza Vieja 1, **t** 948 84 80 58.

There are regular **markets** in **Tafalla** on Pza Navarra (*Fri*); in **Olite** in Pso del Portal (*Wed*); in **Fitero** in Pza San Raimundo (*Tues* and *Fri*).

Festivals

Tafalla: Pilgrimage, *1st Sun after St Mark's day* (*25 April*). Every year since 1043, Tafalla's Black Virgin has been the object of a solemn pilgrimage that departs from Tafalla at 2am.
Olite: Festival of Navarra, *summer*.

Where to Stay and Eat

Tafalla ✉ 31300

★★Hs Tafalla, on the Zaragoza road, **t** 948 70 03 00, **f** 948 70 30 52 (*inexpensive*). Has nice rooms and food, especially those involving asparagus, lamb and hake. *Closed Fri.*

Tubal, Plaza de Navarra 2, **t** 948 70 08 52 (*expensive–moderate*). The chef Atxen Jiménez draws in diners from Pamplona and beyond with her delicious variations on classic Navarrese themes – *menestra de verduras* and innovations such as crêpes filled with celery in almond sauce. *Closed Sun eve, Mon and late Aug.*

Olite ✉ 31390

★★★Parador Príncipe de Viana, **t** 948 74 00 00, **f** 948 74 02 01 (*expensive*). Next to the castle of Charles III in the converted 13th-century Castillo de los Teobaldos. A garden, a/c and beautiful furnishings make castle-dwelling a delight, as do delicious Navarrese gourmet treats in the dining room.

★★Hotel Merindad de Olite, Rúa de la Juderia 11, **t/f** 948 74 07 35 (*moderate*). Offers pleasant rooms decorated in a quirky faux-medieval style.

★★Casa Zanito, Rúa Mayor 16, **t** 948 74 00 02, *zanito@cmn.navarra.net* (*inexpensive*). Offers simple, cheerful rooms and excellent meals, based on market availability, rounded off with good home-made desserts.

Gambarte, Rúa del Seco 13, **t** 948 74 01 39 (*inexpensive*). A pleasant place serving the most reasonably priced food in town. *Closed last fortnight in Sept.*

Ujué ✉ 31390

Accommodation in this area is restricted to *casas rurales*.

Casa El Chofer 1, **t** 948 73 90 11. Come here for good *cheap* rooms with private bath.

Mesón las Torres, **t** 948 73 81 05 (*moderate*). This has long been *the* place to dine, with Navarrese taste sensations and Ujué's special candied almonds.

Tudela ✉ 31500

★★Hs Remigio, C/Gaztambide 4, **t** 948 82 08 50, **f** 948 82 41 23 (*moderate*). Because there is nowhere to stay in the old town, and prices are high elsewhere, this is likely to be your best bet.

Casa Ignacio, C/Cortaderos 11, **t** 948 82 10 21 (*moderate*). Tudela is the chief producer of the ingredients of Navarra's *menestra de verduras*: delicious asparagus, artichokes, peas, celery and lettuces. Book a table here to taste them at their freshest. *Closed Tues and 15 Aug–15 Sept.*

La Estrella, C/Carnicerías 14, **t** 948 41 11 21 (*inexpensive*). Serves up platefuls of good home cooking based around garden vegetables. *Closed 16–30 Sept.*

Cintruénigo ✉ 31592

Maher, C/La Ribera 19, **t** 948 81 11 50 (*expensive–moderate*). The most seductive reason to stop in the village is to dine at what could well be the best restaurant in all of Navarra. Delicious regional specialities are served laced with an imaginative *nouvelle cuisine* touch: there's a traditional *menú* (near the bottom of the *moderate range*), or for a splurge opt for a *menú degustación*.

black Virgin now kept in the 13th-century Romanesque-Gothic church of **Santa María** (*see* 'Festivals', p.323). The doorway has finely carved scenes of the Last Supper and the Magi and the altar preserves the heart of King Charles II of Navarra.

Tudela

Founded by the Moors, Tudela, the second city of Navarra and capital of La Ribera region, was the last town in Navarra to submit to Ferdinand the Catholic, and it did so most unwillingly. Before the big bigot, Tudela had always made a point of welcoming Jews, Moors and heretics expelled from Castile or persecuted by the Inquisition, and it was no accident that its tolerant environment nurtured three of Spain's top medieval writers: Benjamin of Tudela, the great traveller and chronicler (1127–73); the poet Judah Ha-Levi of the same period; and doctor Miguel Servet (1511–53), one of the first to write on the circulation of the blood.

Don't be disheartened by Tudela's protective coating of gritty sprawl, but head straight for its picturesque, labyrinthine Moorish-Jewish kernel, around the elegant, 17th-century **Plaza de los Fueros**; the decorations on the façades recall its use as a bull ring in the 18th and 19th centuries. The Gothic **Cathedral** (*open daily 9–1 and 4–7; closed Sun afternoon and Mon; adm*) was built over the Great Mosque in the 12th century and topped with a pretty 17th-century tower. The north and south portals have capitals with New Testament scenes, while the west portal, the Portada del Juicio Final, is devoted to the Last Judgement, depicted in 114 scenes in eight bands. The Flamboyant Gothic choir is delightfully carved with geometric flora, fauna and fantasy motifs. Under the main chair, the figures of two crows pick out the eyes of a man – symbolizing the dean who commissioned the work but refused to pay the sculptors the agreed price. The main altar has a beautiful Hispano-Flemish *retablo* painted by Pedro Díaz de Oviedo while, in the chapel of Santa Ana, there is a cupola that approaches Baroque orgasm. The 13th-century cloister, with twin and triple columns, has capitals on the life of Jesus and other New Testament stories.

Just east of Tudela is a striking desert region straight out of the American Far West. Known as the **Bárdenas Reales**, here erosion has sculpted steep tabletops, weird wrinkled hills and rocks balanced on pyramids. The best way to see it is from the GR13 walking path, crossing its northern extent from the Hermitage of the Virgen del Yugo.

West of Pamplona: Aralar and San Miguel in Excelsis

Navarra's magic mountain, **Aralar**, is a favourite spot for a picnic or a hike, gracefully wooded with beech, rowan, and hawthorn groves. It has been sacred to the Basques since Neolithic times, when they erected 30 dolmens and menhirs around Putxerri, the biggest concentration of Neolithic monuments in all Spain. A panoramic road climbs over Aralar between Huarte-Arakil and Lekunberri, and at the top is Navarra's holy of holies, the **Sanctuary of San Miguel in Excelsis** (*open 9–2 and 4 to sunset*), where St Michael, heeding a plea for help, humbled a dragon into submission

Tourist Information

Lekunberri: Plazaola 21, **t** 948 50 72 04.

Where to Stay and Eat

****Hs Ayestarán II**, C/Aralar 22, Lekunberri, **t** 948 50 41 27 (*inexpensive*). This fosters a pleasant old-fashioned atmosphere, offering tennis, children's recreational facilities, a pool and garden; *menús* feature home-cooked stews, stuffed peppers and codfish with almonds.

San Miguel de Aralar, t 948 56 10 66. The pilgrims' hostel is rugged and comfortable enough, but isn't famous for its food.

***Hs Basa Kabl, t** 948 51 01 25, *basakabi@jet.es* (*inexpensive*). Here you can sleep and eat reasonably right in the centre of Leitza.

Asador Betelu, t 948 51 30 26. West of Leitza, between Betelu and Azpirotz, attracting hordes of hungry diners. *Closed Thurs eve.*

Taverna Oilade, in Leitza (*inexpensive*). Functions as the town beanery, bar, mess hall and gambling den; good fish soup and other filling dishes.

(*see* box, below). In art Michael is often shown with a spear, not slaying so much as *transfixing* dragons to the earth: these hills are sources of underground water. The Sierra de Aralar is so karstic as to be practically hollow, and under the sanctuary is an immense subterranean river that makes moaning dragonish sounds, feeding an icy lake under a domed cavern.

The gloomy stone chapel, built by the Count of Goñi, was consecrated in 1098, but has had an empty air ever since French Basques plundered it in 1797, when they knocked off St Michael's head (or so say apologists who find the crystal head too weird). You can see the chains worn by Teodosio de Goñi as penance and an enamelled Byzantine *retablo*; the only comparable work in Europe is the great altarpiece in St Mark's in Venice. Tentatively dated 1028, it was probably stolen in Constantinople by a Crusader and sold to Sancho the Great, who donated it to the chapel.

The Knight, the Dragon and the Archangel

In the 9th century, Count Teodosio de Goñi went off to fight the Saracens with his Visigothic overlord King Witiza. He was returning home when he met a hermit (the devil in disguise) who warned him that his wife was unfaithful. Seething with rage, the knight stormed into his castle, saw two forms lying in his bed and without hesitation slew them both. When he ran out he met his wife returning from Mass; she told him, to his horror, that she had given his own aged parents the bed. Horrified, Teodosio went to Rome to ask the pope what penance he could possibly do. After three nights the pope had a dream that Teodosio should wear heavy chains in solitude until God showed his forgiveness by breaking them. Binding himself in chains, Teodosio went up to the top of Mt Aralar and lived for years as a hermit. One day, he was sitting next to a cave when a scaly green dragon emerged, smoke billowing from its nostrils. Teodosio implored the aid of St Michael, who magically appeared, sword in hand, and spoke to the dragon in perfect Basque: '*Nor Jaunggoitkoa bezaka*?' ('Who is stronger than God?'). The dragon slunk back into its cave, and the archangel struck off the knight's chains, leaving behind a statue of himself: an angelic figure with a large cross on its head and an empty glass case where the face ought to be.

Every year the figure goes on a fertility-blessing tour through a hundred Navarra villages; on Corpus Christi pilgrims visit the chapel to pay their respects.

Southwest of Pamplona: the Camino de Santiago

Few places in Europe can boast such a concentration of medieval curiosities as this stretch of the road, where the mystic syncretism of the Jews, Templars, pagans and pilgrims was expressed in monuments with secret messages that still tease and mystify today.

From Pamplona to Estella

A turn off the N111 (about 15 kilometres from Pamplona) leads to the old village of **Obanos**, and one and a half kilometres beyond to a lonely field and **Santa María de Eunate** (*open Tues–Sun 10–1 and 4.30–7; closed Mon*), a striking 12th-century church

Getting Around

By Bus

La Estellesa buses (**t** 948 21 32 25) stop at Puente le Reina and Estella from Pamplona en route to Logroño five times a day.

Tourist Information

Puente la Reina: **t** 948 34 08 45.
Estella: San Nicolás 1, **t** 948 55 63 11.
Los Arcos: **t** 948 44 10 04.
Viana: **t** 948 44 63 02.

Where to Stay and Eat

Puente la Reina ✉ 31100

****Mesón del Peregrino**, on the Pamplona road, **t** 948 34 00 75, **f** 948 34 11 90 (*moderate*). This stone and timber place isn't as old as it looks, but it still offers cosy, air-conditioned rooms and a pool, and serves excellent meals with a French gourmet touch. *Closed Sun eve and Mon.*

***Hs Puente**, in the centre, **t** 948 34 01 46 (*inexpensive*). Has some cheaper rooms without bath.

Fonda Lorca, in the main plaza (*cheap*). The cheapest option of all.

Estella (Lizarra) ✉ 31200

*****Irache**, in Ayegui (3km away on the Logroño road), **t** 948 55 11 50, **f** 948 55 47 54, *hotelirache@tsai.es* (*moderate*). The largest and most comfortable hotel, set in a 1970s *urbanización*, offering a/c and a pool.

***Hs Cristina**, C/Baja Navarra 1, **t** 948 55 07 72 (*inexpensive*). A simple place managed by a kindly woman.

Fonda Izarra, C/Caldería, **t** 948 55 06 78 (*cheap*). The doubles here are the cheapest in Estella.

La Cepa, Pza Fueros 8, **t** 948 55 00 32 (*moderate*). Specializes in Basque and Navarrese cuisine (*menú degustación moderate*). *Closed all day Wed and most eves exc. Fri and Sat.*

La Navarra, Gustavo de Maeztú 16, **t** 948 55 00 40 (*expensive–moderate*). Another good bet, perhaps more for its medieval atmosphere than its food, which though good, is a bit pricey. *Closed Sun eve and Mon.*

Los Arcos ✉ 31210

****Hotel Monaco**, Pza del Coso 22, **t** 948 64 00 00 (*moderate*). One of the pair of choices in town.

****Hs Ezequiel**, La Serna 14, **t** 948 64 02 96 (*moderate*). Slightly dearer, though pilgrims get a 10 per cent discount.

Viana ✉ 31230

La Granja, Navarro Villoslada 19, **t** 948 64 50 78 (*moderate–inexpensive*). The cooking is average, but this also provides rooms with bath and it is in the centre.

Borgia, Serapio Urra, **t** 948 64 57 81 (*expensive–moderate*). Avant-garde décor forms the setting for Aurora Cariñanos' temple of personal, imaginative cuisine, where you can dine delectably on dishes such as *pochas con caracoles al tomillo* (fresh haricot beans with snails and thyme), accompanied by an excellent cellar. *Closed Sun eve and Aug.*

built by the Templars. This one was purposely made irregular, and is surrounded by a unique 33-arched octagonal cloister – hence its name 'Eunate' (the Hundred Doors). Many knights were buried here, and it's likely that its peculiar structure had deep significance in the Templars' initiatory rites. There are only a few carved capitals – some little monsters, and pomegranates – on the portal, which oddly faces north. During its restoration, scallop shells were discovered along with the tombs; the church served as a mortuary chapel for pilgrims. The lack of a central keystone supporting the eight ribs inside hints that Arab architects were involved; the Romanesque Virgin by the alabaster window is a copy of the one stolen in 1974.

The *camino francés* from Roncesvalles and the *camino aragonés* converged at the 11th-century bridge in **Puente la Reina**, which hasn't changed much the days when pilgrims marched down the sombre Rúa Mayo, passing through the arch of another Templar foundation, **El Crucifijo**, a church with two naves. The smaller one was added to house a powerful 14th-century German crucifix left by a pilgrim, where Christ is nailed not to a cross but to a Y-shaped tree.

Estella (Lizarra): Town of the Star

Estella, known as Estella la Bella for its beauty, was a much anticipated pilgrimage stop. It owes its foundation in 1090 to a convenient miracle: nightly showers of shooting stars that always fell on the same place on a hill intrigued some shepherds, who investigated and found a cave sheltering a statue of the Virgin. The spot is marked by the **Basílica de Nuestra Señora de Puy**, and the Virgin is still there, but the old basilica was replaced in 1951 with a concrete and glass star-shaped church. South of the arcaded main square, Pza de Santiago, the 12th-century parish church of **San Miguel** sits on a craggy rock atop its original set of steps. March straight up them for the magnificent portal, where Christ in majesty holds pride of place among angels, Evangelists and the Elders of the Apocalypse.

Near San Miguel, Estella's medieval bridge crosses over to the 12th-century **San Sepolcro,** with a fascinating façade added in 1328. The tympanum has an animated Last Supper, Crucifixion, Resurrection and what looks to be the harrowing of hell; statues of the apostles flank the door; one apparently holder of a stack of pancakes. The piquant centre of old Estella is lined with with churches and palaces along Calle de la Rúa ('street of the street'), most notably the Plateresque brick **Casa Fray Diego**, now the Casa de Cultura. Off to the left the 12th-century synagogue has been converted into **Santa María de Jus del Castillo**, where the apse is decorated with a rich assortment of Romanesque modillions. The church is dwarfed by the adjacent 13th-century monastery of **Santo Domingo**, now a retirement home.

Further up, stairs lead up from **Plaza de San Martín** to the 12th-century **San Pedro de la Rúa** (*open summer 10.30–1.30, and at 4.30, 5.30 and 6.30; adm*), defended by a skyscraper bell tower. The Moorish-inspired foiled arch of the portal is crowned by a relief of St James in a boat with stars, blessed by a giant hand emerging from the water. Inside, the church has a unique column made of three interlaced 'serpents' and the black Virgin de la O, and in the Baroque chapel to the left, St Andrew's shoulder blade; the story goes that the Bishop of Patras took it with him for good luck while making the pilgrimage in 1270. Luck failed him in Estella, where he died and was buried in San Pedro's cloister, along with his relic. The apostle's shoulder blade wasn't going to have any of this, and made itself known by emitting a curious light over the tomb. Of the cloister, only two galleries survive, but the capitals are especially good.

Opposite San Pedro is the 12th-century **Palacio de los Reyes de Navarra**, one of the best-preserved civic buildings from the period. One capital bears the oldest known depiction of Roland fighting the giant Ferragut; another shows a scene of devils and animal musicians. Inside, the **Museo Gustavo de Maeztú** (*open Tues–Sat 11–1 and 5–7, Sun 11–1; closed Mon; adm*) displays works by Estella's best-known painter (1887–1947).

Estella is an important producer of DO Navarra wine, and the most interesting *bodega* is the **Benedictine Monasterio de Irache**, two kilometres west at **Ayegui** (*open Mon–Fri 10–2 and 5–7, Sat and Sun 9–2 and 4–7; closed Mon and Tues eve*). First recorded in 958, it later received a generous endowment from Sancho the Great, who helped finance one of the very first pilgrims' hospitals here. It has an austerely beautiful Romanesque church under a Renaissance dome: the original north door is decorated with hunting scenes, while the sumptuous Plateresque cloister features grotesque and religious capitals. The small **wine museum** preserves Irache's 1,000-year-old custom of offering free drinks to pilgrims.

From Estella to Logroño

After Estella, the pilgrims walked to **Los Arcos**, tucked off the N111, where the 16th-century church, **Santa María** has a cathedral-size Gothic cloister, carved choir stalls and frantic Baroque *retablos*. West of Los Arcos, **Torres del Río** has a striking octagonal church, **Santo Sepolcro**, built by the Knights of the Holy Sepulchre; like Santa María Eunate, it may have been a mortuary chapel for pilgrims. Just outside La Rioja, **Viana** fits a lot of monumentality into a small space, including some splendid mansions, the elegant 17th-century **Casa Consistorial**, crowned with a huge escutcheon, and also the 13th–14th-century church of **Santa María**, hidden by a magnificent concave Renaissance façade, with a coffered ceiling designed and carved by Juan de Goyaz (1549). The Gothic interior is airy and lovely, culminating in an intricate Baroque *retablo*. A marker in front of the church signals the last resting place of Cesare Borgia (1475–1507). When Julius II, archenemy of the Borgias, was elected pope in late 1503, Cesare's conquests in Italy were lost and he fled to Aragón, the cradle of the Borgias, only to be imprisoned by Ferdinand the Catholic. Navarra proved to be his only refuge, and he died here in Viana, fighting Castilian rebels.

La Rioja

La Rioja, the smallest autonomous region in Spain (5,000 sq km), is celebrated far out of proportion to its size for its distinctive red wine edged with vanilla (*see* **Food and Drink**, pp.65–7). The banks of the Ebro are frilly with vineyards and pinstriped with rows of garden vegetables on the plains of Rioja Baja around Calahorra. In the Sierra de la Demanda in the southwest, the mountains are high enough to ski down; while in the gullies of Rioja Baja, dinosaurs once made the earth tremble, or at least left their curious tracks in a prehistoric bog, which petrified for posterity. Later, in the 11th century, Riojans began the history of Castilian Spanish as a written and poetic language and contributed to the invention of Santiago, with a first sighting of the battling Son of Thunder at Calvijo and miracles and saints along its stretch of the pilgrimage road.

Logroño

Half of all the 250,000 Riojans live in Logroño, their shiny, up-to-date capital. It began under the Visigoths as *Gronio*, the 'ford', but really bloomed only with the advent of the pilgrimage, when a stone bridge was built over the Ebro by San Juan de Ortega. Unfortunately, in its haste to become a modern agricultural market, the medieval part of town has run to seed.

A Walk Around Logroño

Logroño is a big long sausage of a town, but the interesting bits are concentrated in a small area near the Ebro. Barely an arch survives of San Juan's first bridge, which was replaced in the 1800s by the **Puente de Hierro**, or iron bridge. Just off this the pilgrims would pass in front of the 16th-century fountain and lofty Gothic **Santiago**, the oldest church in town. This was rebuilt in 1500, with a single nave a startling 53ft wide and still standing, in spite of the fact that its architect had no confidence in his handiwork and left town as soon as it was completed. It has a Renaissance *retablo*, and at the front a mighty 18th-century statue of Santiago Matamoros ('St James Moor-killer') who rides a steed with *cojones* as big as beach balls.

The skyline of Logroño is stabbed by church towers, including two slender 18th-century Churrigueresque towers by Martín de Beratúa that frame the magnificent Baroque façade of the cathedral, **Santa María de la Redonda** (*open 8–11 and 6–8*) in Pza del Mercado, a front that belies the Gothic-inspired gloom inside; the rotundity of its name (the first Romanesque church was octagonal) is recalled in an exuberant round Rococo altar. Near here, in a high-security strong box, is the *Tabla de Calvario*, supposedly painted by Michelangelo for his friend and muse Vittoria Colonna. Logroño's most distinctive landmark is its nubby pyramidal 'Needle', the 149ft 13th-century spire atop the lantern of **Santa María de Palacio**, in C/Marqués de San Nicolás, a church said to have been founded by no less than Emperor Constantine. If it's open, pop in to see the Renaissance choir stalls, the 13th-century *Nuestra Señora de la Antigua*, and what remains of the Gothic cloister. Another tower, brick 11th-century *mudéjar* this time, looks over **San Bartolomé** with a ruggedly carved, time-blackened 14th-century Gothic façade; the smooth white interior, recently restored, has lovely shallow choir vaults.

The 17th-century Palacio del General Espartero in Pza San Agustín now holds the **Museo Provincial de La Rioja** (*open 10–2 and 4–9, Sun and hols 11.30–2, closed Mon;*

Getting Around

By Train

Several trains each day link Haro, Logroño, and Calahorra on the Bilbao–Zaragoza route. The RENFE station is located at C/Calvo Sotelo 9, **t** 941 25 85 55. Information and bookings can also be obtained at Pza de Europa, **t** 941 24 02 02.

By Bus

Several buses a day run to Burgos (via the towns on the pilgrims' route), Zaragoza, Vitoria, Pamplona and Rioja's villages. In Logroño the bus station is at Av. de España 1, **t** 941 24 35 72, and the train station (with a left luggage office) is nearby in Pza de Europa, **t** 941 23 59 83.

Tourist Information

Logroño: Kiosco del Espolón, **t** 941 26 06 65.

There is a twice weekly **market** (*Tues and Fri 8–2*) where you can get hold of country produce and products held at Mercado del Campo, Marqués de la Enseñada 52.

Where to Stay

Logroño ✉ 26000

Logroño has a surprising number of spanking new hotels.

******Carlton Rioja**, Gran Vía del Rey Juan Carlos I 5, **t** 941 24 21 00, **f** 941 24 35 02 (*expensive*). An antique place tasting of old-world charm.

*****Ciudad de Logroño**, Menéndez Pelayo 7, **t** 941 25 02 44, **f** 941 25 43 90, *hotels@pretur.es* (*expensive*). This is central, modern and comfortable, with views looking out over a park.

*****Hotel Murrieta**, Marqués de Murrieta 1, **t** 941 22 41 50, **f** 941 22 32 13, *hotels@pretur.es* (*moderate*). Central and welcoming.

*****Hs Marqués de Vallejo**, Marqués de Vallejo 8, **t** 941 24 83 33, **f** 941 24 02 88 (*moderate*). A handsome place near the cathedral, recently restored and offering reasonable half-board rates.

****Hs la Numantina**, C/Sagasta 4, **t** 941 25 14 11 (*inexpensive*). A slightly cheaper alternative close by.

Residencia Daniel, C/Juan 21, **t** 941 25 29 48 (*inexpensive*). Spotless rooms set amid the bustle of the *casco viejo*.

Eating Out

For **tapas**, try C/Laurel and C/San Juan.

El Cachetero, C/Laurel 3, **t** 941 22 84 63 (*expensive*). A popular choice for four generations, Logroño's best restaurant serves mouth-watering *menestras* and local delicacies such as pigs' trotters stuffed with mushrooms, capers and paté; book in advance as it fills up fast. *Closed Sun and Wed eve and 1–15 Aug.*

El Rincon del Vino, Marqués de San Nicolás 136, **t** 941 20 53 92 (*expensive–moderate*). As well as a vast selection of the promised *vino*, they have a fine *asador* serving delicacies like sirloin steak with wild mushroom stuffing.

Las Cubanas, C/San Agustín 17, **t** 941 22 00 50 (*moderate*). Join the locals for a delicious *menestra*; the place owes its popularity to excellent, good-value regional cuisine, and its friendly atmosphere. *Closed Sun and mid-July–1 Aug.*

Zubillaga, C/San Agustín 3, **t** 941 22 00 76. Serves up succulent roast meats and fish, along with treats like leek and *gambas pastel*. *Closed Tues eve, Wed and 5–20 Nov.*

adm), full of art gathered from disappeared churches (14th-century painting from San Millán and *San Francisco with Brother Lion* by El Greco), Flemish coffers and academic 19th-century paintings from the Prado's storerooms. There are a number of wine cellars in the area, including **Bodegas Marqués de Murrieta** at Ygay (*Ctra de Zaragoza Km403*, ***t** 941 25 81 00*), founded in 1872 and famous for its 35–40-year-old *Gran Reservas* .

Calahorra and La Rioja Baja

Down the Ebro, east of Logroño, La Rioja Baja is flat, fertile, well watered and endowed with a sunny Mediterranean climate. Olive oil and wine are the mainstays of the economy, with the kind of peppers the Spanish devour by the kilo coming in a close third. Few tourists pass through, and those who do are mostly dinosaur fanciers.

Calahorra

Calahorra owes its quiet contented look to its rich *vega* planted with orchards and vegetables, and has been inhabited for so long (since Palaeolithic times) that St Jerome speculated that it was founded by Tubal, grandson of Noah. In 187 BC the town was grabbed by Rome, then, in a dispute between Pompey and Sertorius in AD 72, it held out against Pompey until all the defenders died of starvation, a fanaticism that gave rise to the expression 'Calagurritan hungers'. The Romans rebuilt it, and Calahorra returned the favour by giving Rome Marcus Fabius Quintilian (42–118), its first salaried professor of rhetoric.

Although an episcopal see since the 5th century, Calahorra's **Cathedral** has been fussed with frequently. Behind a fruity, floral neoclassical façade pasted on in 1700,

Tourist Information

Calahorra: Angek Olivan 8, **t** 941 14 63 98.
Arnedo: Carrera 1, **t** 941 38 39 88.

There are regular **markets** in **Calahorra** on Pza del Raso (*Thurs*); in **Alfaro** (*Fri*); in **Cervera de Río Alhama** (*Fri*); and also in **Arnedo** (*Mon* and *Tues*).

Where to Stay and Eat

Calahorra ✉ 26500

★★★**Parador Marco Fabio Quintiliano**, Parque Era Alta s/n, **t** 941 13 03 58, **f** 941 13 51 39, *calahorra@parador.es* (*expensive*). Near the scanty Roman ruins of Calagurris, with good views, comfortable rooms and a/c; it has a good **restaurant** serving regional and international cuisine.

★★**Chef Nino**, C/Padre Lucas 2, **t** 941 13 35 16 (*inexpensive*). New, central and air conditioned; the restaurant serves an excellent Basque-Riojan *menú*.

La Taberna de la Cuarta Esquina, Cuatro Esquinas 16, **t** 941 13 43 55 (*moderate*). Calahorra's best-known restaurant is justly renowned for its well-prepared fish, game and vegetable dishes and reasonably priced wines. *Closed Tues and 6–31 July*.

Arnedo ✉ 26580

★★★**Victoria**, Pso de la Constitución 97, **t** 941 38 01 00 (*expensive*). Recent and comfortable, offering good value with a pool and tennis court. Situated just out of the centre.

★★**Virrey**, Pso de la Constitución 27, **t** 941 38 01 50, **f** 941 38 30 17 (*moderate*). A welcoming place closer to the centre; one of the few hotels in the *comunidad* with facilities for the disabled.

Picabea, C/Virrey Lezana 1, **t** 941 38 13 58 (*inexpensive*). Serves good seafood and Arnedo's famous almond-filled pastries, or *fardelejos*. *Closed Sun and Mon eve*.

Sopitas, C/Carrera 4, **t** 941 38 02 66 (*inexpensive*). A long-established place serving traditional favourites in an old *bodega*. *Closed Sun*.

Enciso ✉ 26580

Posada de Santa Rita, Ctra de Soria 7, **t** 941 39 60 71 (*inexpensive*). Set in a little red 19th-century house, this is a cosy place to stay, with a small library devoted to dinosaurs.

La Fábrica, Ctra de Soria 10, **t** 941 39 60 51 (*inexpensive*). Offers delicious meals based on game, served in an atmospheric old flour mill. *Open daily in summer; otherwise Sat, Sun and hols only*.

the nave with graceful star vaulting is a product of 1485 and the furnishings are equally eclectic. The Plateresque cloister houses the **Museo Diocesano** (*open Sun and hols 12–2*) with a 12th-century Bible and 15th-century Custodia called *El Ciprés*, made of gold and silver, donated by Henri IV. Near the cathedral, the church of **Santiago** and its *retablo* of St James is considered the finest neoclassical work in La Rioja. The church of **San Andrés** has a Gothic portal illustrating the triumph over paganism and the arch **Arco del Planillo** is the only gateway surviving from the Roman walls of Calagurris; other Roman bits are further along Camino Bellavista.

Tracking La Rioja's Dinosaurs

La Rioja Baja has 5,000 footprints – Europe's largest concentration of dinosaur tracks, or ichnites – dating back 120 million years to when La Rioja was lush, warm and wet and the denizens of the Cretaceous (post-Jurassic) stomped through the marshes. Somehow, the conditions for preserving their prints were particularly good: a different kind of mud filled in the tracks, preserving the impression after the mud was turned to stone. The best places to find them are in **Préjano** just east of Arnedillo and the Los Cayos gully at **Cornago**. **Enciso** has the largest number, especially at the Valdecevillo bed; it also houses the **Centro Paleontogólico** (*open winter Mon–Sat 11–2 and 3–6, Sun 11–2; summer daily 11–2 and 5–8; adm*), a collection of bones and other prehistoric relics. Other sites include **Igea** and the Peñaportillo gully in **Munilla**.

Along the Pilgrim Route: West of Logroño

Beyond Logroño, the segment of the Camino de Santiago that crosses La Rioja is short but choice and full of interest, even though only a fraction of the monuments a 12th-century pilgrim would have known remain intact. A nearly obligatory detour remains: the famous pair of monasteries at San Millán de la Cogolla.

Navarrete and Nájera

Eleven kilometres west of Logroño, **Navarrete** makes ceramics and rosé wine, and merits a stop for its medieval gate to the hospital of San Juan de Arce, doing duty as the entrance to the cemetery. It has lively capitals, picturing St Michael, a pair of picnicking pilgrims, and Roland grappling with the giant Ferragut. The 16th-century church of the **Asunción**, sometimes attributed to Juan de Herrera, has an elaborate Churrigueresque *retablo* and a triptych by Rembrandt's student Adrian Ysenbrandt.

Arabic **Nájera** has an illustrious pedigree. After the Moors flattened Pamplona in 918, the kings of Navarra chose to live in Nájera, mainly to keep an eye on the upstart kingdom of Castile. In 1052, one of them, son of Sancho the Great García III was hunting on the banks of the Najerilla when he saw a dove fly past. He sent his falcon after it and followed the birds through the trees into a cave, from which a bright light emanated; inside he found the dove and falcon cooing side by side and a statue of the Virgin and Child, a jar of fresh lilies, a lamp and a bell. To celebrate the miracle, García founded the church, which was rebuilt in the 15th century as the monastery of **Santa**

Tourist Information

Nájera: C/Garran 8, **t** 941 36 00 41.
San Millán: **t** 941 37 32 59.
Santo Domingo: C/Mayir 72, **t** 941 34 12 30.

Where to Stay and Eat

Nájera ✉ 26300

★★★★**Hostería Monasterio de San Millán**, **t** 941 37 32 77, **f** 941 37 32 66, *hosteria@sanmillan.com* (*expensive*). This is in the monastery itself, with a good **restaurant**.

★★**San Fernando**, Pso San Julián 1, **t** 941 36 37 00, **f** 941 36 33 99 (*inexpensive*). On the Najerilla river and centrally located.

P. El Moro, C/Mártires 21, **t** 941 36 00 52 (*inexpensive*). Situated in the old town, this is the cheapest option.

El Mono, C/Mayor 43, **t** 941 36 30 28 (*moderate*). Nájera's favourite for monkfish stuffed with lobster.

Los Parrales, C/Mayor, **t** 941 36 37 35 (*moderate*). A few doors down, this family-run place is another fine choice, and has a summer terrace.

★★**Monasterio de Valvanera**, to the south (*see below*), **t** 941 37 70 44 (*inexpensive*). Offers a chance to stay with the monks in their atmospheric hill-top retreat, and wake up in clean mountain air to a spectacular view of the Sierra de la Demanda. The monks serve good meals (*inexpensive*), and a nip or two of their herbal liqueur is more than enough to guarantee a good night's sleep.

Santo Domingo ✉ 26250

★★★★**Parador de Santo Domingo de la Calzada**, Pza del Santo 3, **t** 941 34 03 00, **f** 941 34 03 25, *santodomingo@parador.es* (*expensive*). Grim on the outside but lovely within, this hotel occupies the pilgrim's *hostal* built by Santo Domingo; the restaurant serves a delicious *menú* (*moderate*).

★★**Hospederia Cistercisense**, C/Pinar 2, **t** 941 34 07 00 (*inexpensive*). A pleasant guesthouse run by Cistercian nuns.

El Rincón de Emilio, Pza de Bonifacio Gil 7, **t** 941 34 09 90 (*inexpensive*). A well-known restaurant specializing in regional cuisine.

El Peregrino, Avda Calahorra 19, **t** 941 34 02 02 (*inexpensive*). Local dishes are served in a garden for similar prices. *Closed Mon*.

Ezcaray ✉ 26280

★★★**Echaurren**, Héroes del Alcázar, **t** 941 35 40 47, **f** 941 42 71 33 (*moderate*). Since the beginning of the 20th century, this has been the place to sleep and eat; recently it has been renovated. *Closed Nov*. It's usually essential to book a table at the hotel's **restaurant**, known far and wide for its stylish food and fair prices (*menú inexpensive*).

★★**Iguareña**, C/Lamberto Felipe Muñoz 14, **t/f** 941 35 41 44 (*inexpensive*). A good, quiet second choice, with a Basque **restaurant** attached (*moderate*).

María la Real (*tours 9.30–11.30 and 4–7.30; adm*). A beautiful Flamboyant Gothic door, the **Portal of Charles V**, leads into the serene Gothic-Plateresque **Claustro de los Caballeros**, with 24 arches half-veiled by intricate sculpted screens carved to imitate lace: no two are alike. The solemn 15th-century **church** has an enormous *retablo* holding the miraculous 11th-century statue of the Virgin. Originally she wore a large ruby, but this was pinched by Pedro the Cruel in 1367 to pay the Black Prince for whipping the French army of his brother Enrique de Trastámara. The ruby now glows on the State Crown of England, but it cost the Black Prince his life – from a Spanish fever.

At the entrance of the holy cave are 16th-century tombs of the 10th–12th-century dynasties of Pamplona and Nájera, among them the original sarcophagus of Sancho III's 21-year-old wife Blanca, beautifully carved with a Christ in Majesty, the Massacre of the Innocents and the death of the queen. Up the spiral stair is the remarkable Isabelline Gothic choir (1493–95), featuring the armoured King García; painted kings and queens create a charming *trompe l'œil* effect.

San Millán de la Cogolla: Yuso and Suso

From Nájera it's a 17-kilometre detour south into the Sierra de la Demanda and **San Millán de la Cogolla**, a village that grew up around two monasteries, Yuso ('the lower') and Suso ('the upper'). San Millán (473–574) spent much of his 101 years living in the caves on the hill and in the 7th century his followers built the first monastery at **Suso** (*open 10.30–1.15 and 4–7.15*), signposted up a two-kilometre narrow road. Carved out of a hill, the shadowy little church has a cloister where Gonzalo de Berceo, the first poet to write in Spanish, loved to sit. The church was heavily damaged by al-Mansur in the Reconquista and rebuilt with Romanesque and Visigothic arches.

The 11th-century tomb, with its recumbent alabaster effigy of San Millán, has been empty since 1053, when King García III decided to load Millán's relics on to a cart and take them to Nájera. However, once they reached the bottom of the hill, the oxen refused to budge another inch; García built a new, more splendid, monastery on the very spot. Called **Yuso** (*rather long guided tours by the monks; open Tues–Sun 10.30–1.30 and 4–6.30; closed Mon*), it is known as the 'Escorial of La Rioja' after it was rebuilt on a grand scale in the 16th century. The monastery is proudest of its anonymous 10th-century monk, who, while writing a commentary in the margins of the *Emilian 60 Codex*, lapsed for 43 words into the vernacular – the first known use of Castilian. It's engraved on stone in the **Salón de Reyes**.

The Renaissance **church** has weighty ogival vaulting and a 16th-century *retablo* on the life of San Millan; the small **museum** contains the reliquary chests of San Millán and San Felices de Bilibio, commissioned in 1063 and covered with ivory plates.

Santo Domingo de la Calzada and Its Chickens

As they made their way across La Rioja, pilgrims looked forward to **Santo Domingo de la Calzada**, a delightful walled village that owes its name and existence to the first road saint, Domingo (1019–1109) who devoted his life to building bridges and generally making the pilgrims' way easier, making him the patron saint of engineers and public works (hence *de la Calzada*, 'of the causeway'). His church, now the **Cathedral of La Rioja** (*open daily 10–2 and 3.30–7*) was founded on land donated in 1098 by King Alfonso VI. Reconstruction began in 1158 and took centuries to finish:the neoclassical façade is matched by a 243ft tower, built by Martín de Beratúa in 1762.

The Gothic interior is simple but lavishly decorated, but what everyone remembers best are the rooster and hen, cackling in their own late-Gothic henhouse. Their presence recalls the miracle that took place in Santo Domingo's *hostal*: a handsome 18-year-old German pilgrim named Hugonell, travelling with his parents, refused the advances of the maid, who avenged herself by planting a silver goblet on him and accusing him of theft. Hugonell was summarily hanged by the judge while his parents sadly went on to Compostela. On the way back, they passed the gallows and were amazed to find their son still alive and glad to see them, telling them it was a miracle of Santo Domingo. They hurried to the judge and told him; the judge, about to dig into a pair of roast fowl, laughed and said their son was as alive as the birds on his table, upon which both came to life and flew away. Since then, a white hen and a cock have been kept in the church, and are replaced every month.

The church and chapels are filled with beautiful art, including the magnificent tomb of Santo Domingo, designed by Felipe de Vigarni (1517–29)and the huge Plateresque *retablo* (1540), the last and best work of Damián Forment. The Gothic-*mudéjar* cloister is now used as a **museum** (*open Mon–Sat 11–7*).

Wine Towns in Rioja Alta

To the north along the Ebro lies the Rioja Alta, a lush region of abrupt natural features rising above rolling hills, carpeted with vineyards and roads lined with brash spanking new wine *bodegas* that speak of La Rioja's rising reputation, and just might lose their sharp kitsch edge over the next 200 years.

Haro

At the confluence of the Ebro and Tirón, Haro is a working wine town built around a large arcaded square. Its chief monuments are a handful of noble houses, the attractive **Casa Consistorial** (1775) and the 16th-century church of **Santo Tomás** up in

Tourist Information

Haro: Plaza Hermanos F. Rodríguez, **t** 941 30 33 66.

There are regular **markets** (*Tues* and *Sat*) held on Arco de Santa Bárbara.

Festivals

Batalla del Vino, *29 July*. The people of Haro have decided that the fiesta of San Felice is an appropriate excuse to have a good time. Everyone dresses in white and, after the Mass, fortified with *zurracapote* (Rioja *sangría*, made with red wine, citrus fruit and cinnamon) and armed with every conceivable squirter and sprayer, opposing groups douse one another with 100,000 litres of wine. This Dionysian free-for-all takes place 3km from Haro at the **Peña de Bilibio**, below the pass of the Conchas de Haro.

Where to Stay and Eat

Haro ✉ 26200

★★★★**Los Agustinos**, C/ San Agustín 2, **t** 941 31 13 08, **f** 941 30 31 48 (*expensive*). Superbly restored, occupying a former Augustinian monastery that later served as a prison: note the graffiti carved into the columns of the garden cloister. Rooms are quiet, equipped with a/c and satellite TV.

★★★**Iturrimurri**, Ctra. N. 124 Km41, **t** 941 31 12 13, **f** 941 31 17 21 (*expensive*). Along the highway, overlooking Haro, this modern hotel is plain, comfortable and has a pool.

★**Hs Aragón**, La Vega 9, **t** 941 31 00 04 (*cheap*). Basic, but your only bet for a cheap sleep.

Terete, C/ Lucrecia Arana 17, **t** 941 31 00 23 (*moderate*). Fills the centre of Haro with the divine aroma of its roast lamb, among a huge choice of other dishes; good (*inexpensive*) *menú*. *Closed Sun eve, Mon and Oct.*

Beethoven I and II, C/ Santo Tomás 3–5 and Pza de la Iglesia 8, **t** 941 31 11 81 (*moderate*). Traditional mushroom, fish and vegetable dishes are the prizes at these two good dining rooms.

Briñas ✉ 26200

★★★**Hospederia Señorio de Briñas**, C/Travesia Real 3, **t** 940 30 42 24, *hsbrinas@arrakis.es* (*expensive*). Has some unique split-level rooms in a carefully-restored mini palace, tastefully decorated with antiques.

★**El Portal de La Rioja**, Ctra. De la Victoria 42, **t** 941 31 14 80. As well as *inexpensive* rooms with bath, there is an excellent **restaurant** serving chops grilled on vine cuttings (*chuletas al sarmiento*), a craft shop and a **wine museum** with century-old bottles.

Bodega Browsing

Haro is the growing and marketing centre for the wines of Rioja Alta, with a clutch of *bodegas* near the train station. While most of these welcome visitors, they usually require advance notice. An exception is Bodegas Bilbaínas, (*C/Estación 3, t 941 31 01 47*), with a pretty façade in *azulejos*, usually open mornings and late afternoons. Along Costa del Vino, you'll find the celebrated cellars of the CUNE, or CVNE (*t 941 31 06 50*), home of a fine bubbly; Chilean-owned López de Heredia (*t 941 31 01 27*), makers of one of the best Riojas, Viña Tondonia; and the vast, French-founded Rioja Alta (*Av. Vizcaya, t 941 31 03 46*), with 25,000 barrels. The even larger Federico Paternina (*t 941 31 05 50*), founded in 1896 by the Plaza de Toros, houses four million bottles, and welcomes visitors daily except for Monday. Another, Martínez Lacuesta Hnos (*C/Ventilla 71, t 941 31 00 50*), is in the old gas company that became obsolete back in 1891, when Haro became the first city in Spain to have public electric street lighting – hence the slogan '*Ya se ven las luces, ya estamos en Haro*'. Among the shops, Selección Vinos de Rioja (*Pza Paz 5, t 941 30 30 17*) offers tastings and a wide variety of different Riojas.

Pza Iglesia, bearing a handsome, recently restored, Plateresque façade with sculpture and reliefs in several registers, paid for by the Condestables de Castilla.

Since 1892, Haro's **Estación Enológica** (*C/Bretón de los Herreros 4, just behind the bus station*), has tested new wine-making techniques and varieties; its **Wine Museum** (*open Mon–Sat 10–2 and 4–8, Sun 10–2*) offers detailed explanations of the latest high-tech processes used in La Rioja. For a far less serious initiation, come on 29 July when **San Felices** is celebrated with a Batalla del Vino (*see* 'Festivals', p.335). This Dionysian free-for-all takes place 3km from Haro at the Peña de Bilibio, below the striking rock formation and pass of the Conchas de Haro, 'the Shells of Haro', where Felices, a hermit-follower of San Millán, lived in a cave. Archaeologists have recently discovered a 10th-century church and the ruins of a Roman town, Castrum Bilibium, or Haro la Vieja, just under the rocks.

Cantabria, Asturias and Galicia

12

Highlights

1 Santillana del Mar and the Palaeolithic caves of Altamira
2 The spectacular Picos de Europa
3 Pre-Romanesque churches outside Oviedo
4 Pilgrimage's end: Santiago de Compostela
5 A Coruña, the 'Crystal City' of glass balconies

Beyond the Basques, the rest of 'Green Spain' divides into two little regions and a big one. Rustic Cantabria, Spain's dairy land, and hard-working, cider-fuelled Asturias face each other across the fantasy landscapes of the Picos de Europa. And if you needed any more proof of Spain's diversity, off in the northwest corner there is Galicia, a dour Celtic land of rugged granite coasts, hidden beaches and memorable seafood; here you'll find Spain's *finis terra*, and the end of the pilgrim's way at Santiago de Compostela.

Cantabria, Asturias and Galicia

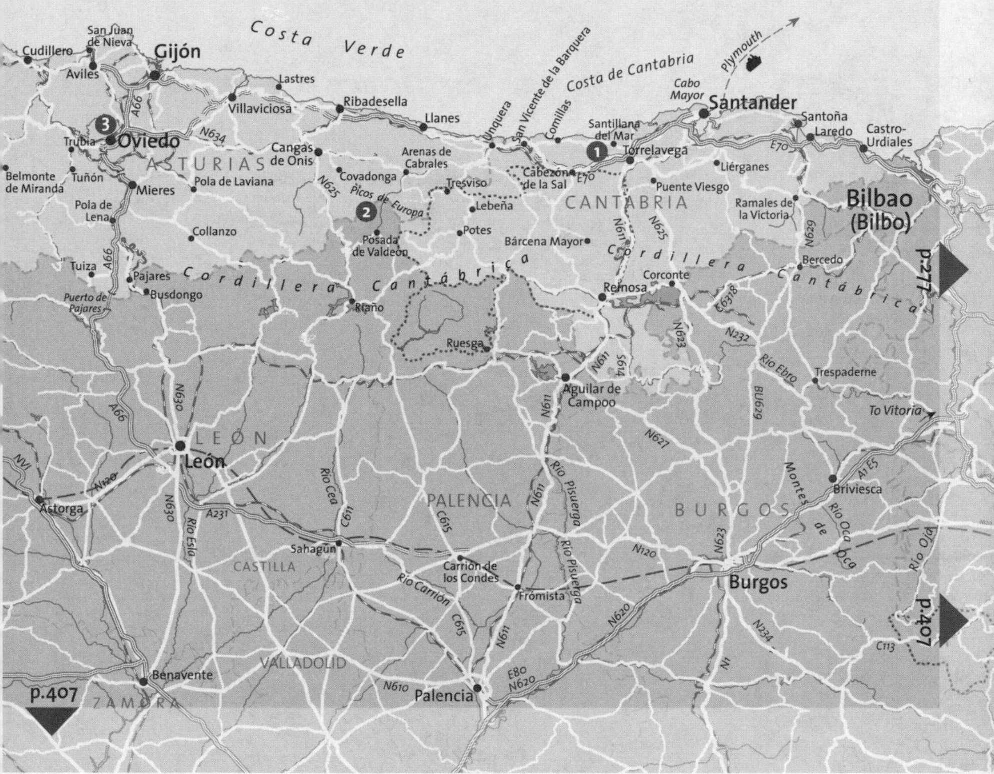

Cantabria

Spain's steep, emerald-green dairy land, Cantabria is wedged between the extraordinary Picos de Europa, the Cordillera Cantábrica and a coastline of scenic beaches. Santander, the capital and only large city, is a major summer resort and, while there are a handful of other tourist spots (Laredo, Comillas, and the medieval Santillana del Mar), much of Cantabria is serenely rural, claiming to have the highest density of cows in Europe. The majority of the bovine population lives indoors, and in the evening the most common Cantabrian sight is the farmer, often wearing wooden clogs, driving home an ox-cart laden with grass. On rainy winter evenings in the more remote areas they gather to hear the strains of the rabel, a three-stringed instrument from the Moors, made only of wood cut by the light of a full moon.

Like La Rioja, Cantabria historically considered itself part of greater Castile. When the government was dividing up Spain into autonomous regions, the devolutionists feared that if La Rioja and Cantabria were added to the new region of Castilla y León, they would feel insignificant and liable to be lured by the wily Basques into joining Euskadi. A provision in the constitution allows Cantabria and La Rioja to change their minds and join Castilla y León if they care to, but so far autonomy suits them just fine.

Cantabria

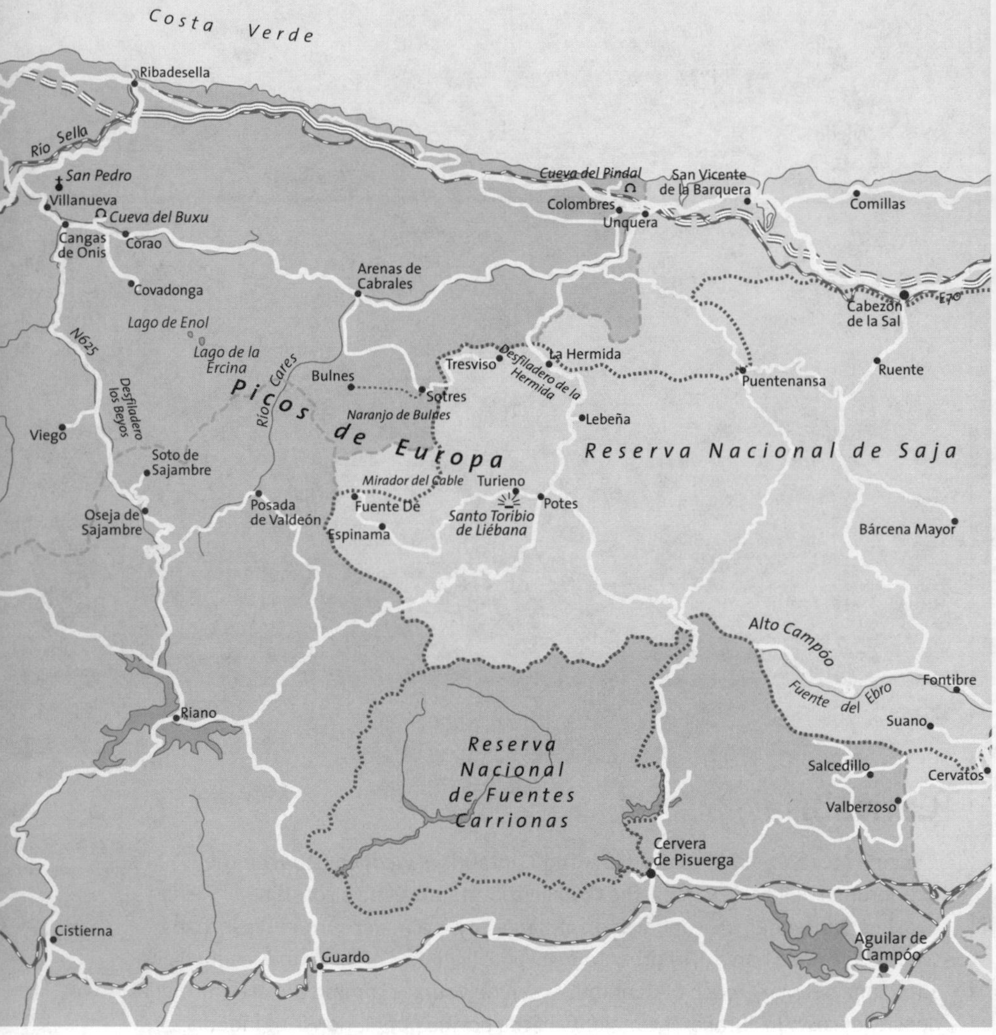

Bilbao to Santander: the Costa Esmeralda

If this eastern stretch of coast is all you see of Cantabria, you may think what you have read about rural serenity is pure fiction. This seems to be the busiest coast in all northern Spain in summer or at weekends, when half of Bilbao is out here looking for a bit of beach; they all seem to end up on the endless sweep of sand at Laredo.

Castro Urdiales and Laredo

Just an hour west of Bilbao, Castro Urdiales is one of Cantabria's most scenic fishing ports, endowed with a beach and seafood restaurants that draw hordes of *bilbaínos*. It

was a Templar stronghold in the Middle Ages, and Templar touches can still be seen in the frieze around the top of the church of **Santa María de la Asunción**, a magnificent Gothic temple with massive buttresses and pinnacles. Inside there's a 13th-century sculpture, the *Virgen Blanca,* and a series of Gothic woodcarvings. You can also see the *Santa Cruz*, or 'holy cross', the Christian standard at the battle of Las Navas de Tolosa (1212). Over the striking Roman/medieval bridge, most of the walls of Castro's pentagonal **Templar castle** have survived, now sheltering a lighthouse. Castro Urdiales' beach is at the other end of town, but the best is eight kilometres west at **Islares**, a magnificent strand of sand interspersed with shallow lagoons.

Getting Around

By Train

The two daily FEVE trains between Santander and Bilbao stop near Laredo; Pza de las Estaciones s/n, **t** 942 21 16 87.

By Bus

Several Turytrans buses a day run along the coast between Santander and Bilbao; from Santander they depart from Pza de las Estaciones s/n, **t** 942 21 19 95.

Tourist Information

Castro Urdiales: Av. De la Constitución 1, **t** 942 87 15 12.
Laredo: Alameda de Miramar s/n, **t** 942 61 10 96.
Santoña: C/Santander 5, **t** 942 66 00 66.
Noja: Pza de la Villa 1, **t** 942 63 15 16.

There are **markets** in **Castro Urdiales** (*Thurs*); and in **Laredo** at the Mercado Municipal (*Mon–Sat*).

Where to Stay and Eat

Castro Urdiales ✉ 39700

Castro is a more interesting place to stay than Laredo, though inexpensive places are hard to find (ask at a bar). Most of the bars are concentrated along C/de la Rúa and the Pso Marítimo.

******Las Rocas***, Av. de la Playa s/n, **t** 942 86 04 00, **f** 942 86 13 82 (*expensive*). A luxurious and tranquil place; the plum choice near the beaches.

*****Miramar**, Av. de la Playa 1, **t** 942 86 02 04, **f** 942 87 09 42 (*expensive*). A stylish hotel with attentive service and excellent views of the cathedral from its second-floor **restaurant**; also near the beach.

***El Cordobés**, C/Ardigales 11, **t** 942 86 00 89 (*moderate*). An old-fashioned establishment prettily located in the Mediavilla.

***Hs Alberto**, Av. de la República Argentina 2 (near the town park), **t** 942 86 27 57 (*cheap*). This offers cheerful bathless doubles.

Mesón El Marinero, La Correría 23 (in Casa de los Chelines, by the fishing port), **t** 942 86 00 05 (*moderate*). The place to go for heaped plates of delicious, fresh seafood at reasonable prices; and you can feast for less on a wide selection of tapas at the bar.

El Segoviano, La Correría 19, **t** 942 86 18 59 (*expensive*). Castro's second culinary shrine. Make your way here for roast suckling pig or a seafood grill.

Islares ✉ 39798

****Hs Arenillas**, **t** 942 86 07 66 (*moderate*). A quiet and pleasant *hostal* near the beach.

Camping Playa Arenillas. A large and comfortable campsite, also by the beach.

Laredo ✉ 39770

Hotels in Laredo are small and fairly pricey, and reservations are essential in the summer.

*****Miramar**, Alto de Laredo s/n, **t** 942 61 03 67, **f** 942 61 16 92 (*moderate*; *expensive in high season*). Modern, with huge windows to take in the huge sea views.

*****Risco**, C/La Arenosa 2, **t** 942 60 50 30, **f** 942 60 50 55 (*expensive*). Commodious rooms with views over the protected bay and beach; the **restaurant** (*moderate*) is generally rated as Laredo's top seafood palace, featuring elaborate creations such as a *capricho* of lobster, chicken breasts and figs.

****Montecristo**, C/Calvo Sotelo 2, **t** 942 60 57 00 (*moderate*). One of the better beach hotels in town. *Open mid-April–mid-Sept.*

Squash, Av. Reina Victoria s/n (near Playa de Salvé), **t** 942 60 40 69 (*moderate*; *expensive in season*). Nothing to do with the game, but instead offers modern hotel rooms near the beach and furnished apartments for five.

***Hs Salomón**, C/Menéndez Pelayo 11, **t** 942 60 50 81 (*moderate*). With immaculate rooms and wooden floors, this is the best deal in the centre.

El Rincón del Puerto (*moderate–inexpensive*). A few long tables under an awning next to a grill at the far end of Laredo's fishing port, where you can feast on fresh sardines, prawns, striped tuna, paella, fish soup and other delicacies.

Playa, Av. de la Victoria, **t** 942 61 22 03 (*inexpensive*). Another good place to go for simple seafood.

Asador Orio, Av. José Antonio 10, **t** 942 60 70 93 (*inexpensive*). Good-value meals.

Cantabria's biggest resort, **Laredo**, has little in common with its namesake on the Río Grande. This Laredo does have an old town, hidden somewhere among the *urbanizaciones*, but you'll remember it mostly as a somewhat brash and totally modern holiday playground and for its pride and joy, **Playa de Salvé**, a sheltered, three-mile-long crescent of sand. Not really glossy or chic, Laredo especially attracts families, who cover its splendid beach and fill the scores of cafés, bars, and discothèques in the Puebla Vieja over the harbour. This medieval part of town was walled in by Alfonso VIII of Castile to safeguard the region from pirates; its 13th-century church **Santa María de la Asunción** has five naves (rare for the period) and curiously carved capitals.

West of Laredo the parade of beaches continues: **Santoña** is another fishing-port resort and home town of Juan de la Cosa (b. 1460), the cartographer who accompanied Columbus on his second voyage to America (1493). Another lovely area, **Noja**, has a further stretch of fine, sandy beaches and a considerable villa and apartment *urbanización* along the shore. The rest of the way to Santander there are plenty of unexploited beaches particularly around Cape Ajo and to the west of it.

Santander

The capital of Cantabria, Santander has a lot in common with San Sebastián – a large city beautifully situated on a protected bay, popularized by royalty as a summer resort. Again, after the First World War, it was *the* fashionable place to go for *madrileños*, especially with the founding of an international summer university, offering holiday-makers highbrow culture to complement its wide beaches. Still, despite this and its widely acclaimed International Music Festival in August, Santander lacks the excitement and *joie de vivre* of San Sebastián. The Santander of the festivals shows a bright and modern face to the world, but the real atmosphere of the place is still best represented by the pigeon-spattered statue of Franco in the centre and the grey streets still named after Nationalist hoodlums of the Civil War.

The Cathedral and Museums

In the centre, Santander's much-altered and rebuilt **Cathedral** is interesting mostly for its early Gothic crypt; this now forms the separate church of **Santísimo Cristo**, where a glass floor has been installed over the remains of a Roman building. The **Museo de Prehistoria y Arqueología** on C/Juan de la Cosa (*open Tues–Sat 10–1 and 4–7, Sun 11–2; closed Mon; adm*), has exhibits devoted to Cantabria's prehistoric cave-dwellers, including tools and reproductions of their art. The best parts of old Santander lie to the north, across the main Av. Calvo Sotelo. Near the Ayuntamiento, the **Museo de Bellas Artes** (*Mon–Fri 10.30–1 and 5.30–8, Sat 10.30–1; closed Sun; adm*) has, besides a contemporary art collection of dubious merit, a Zurbarán and several Goyas, including a portrait of Ferdinand VII. Nearby, the **Casa Museo de Menéndez Pelayo** (*open weekdays only 9.30–11.30; guided tours every half-hour*) has an extensive collection of books donated to the city by the scholar himself. Standing behind the Ayuntamiento, the iron and glass market is the most colourful sight in Santander, especially the pride of the town: the glorious fish market.

Getting There

By Air

Santander's airport is 7km away at Maliaño (no buses), with daily connections to Madrid and Barcelona. Iberia, Pso de Pereda 18, **t** 942 22 97 00; Aviaco, at the airport, **t** 942 25 10 07.

By Ferry

From Santander, Brittany Ferries sail to Plymouth twice-weekly (mid-Mar–mid-Nov). For information, call **t** 942 36 06 11, or visit the ticket office at the Estación Marítima.

By Train

The train stations are both on Pza de las Estaciones. RENFE, **t** 942 28 02 02, has connections with Madrid, Palencia, Reinosa, Segovia and Valladolid. The narrow-gauge FEVE, **t** 942 21 16 87, has trains to Bilbao, Oviedo, Unquera and Torrelavega; unfortunately they miss out the coastline towns east of Santander, which are served instead by buses.

By Bus

The central bus station is conveniently opposite the train stations on Navas de Tolosa, **t** 942 21 19 95. Connections include: Continental Auto to Burgos, Madrid and Ontaneda-Vejores; Turytrans to nearly all the coastal towns and resorts, and to Bilbao, Zarauz, San Sebastián, Llanes, Oviedo, Gijón, Vitoria and Pamplona; Intercar to Galicia, Asturias and Euskadi; Fernández to León and Autocares de Cantabria to Logroño. The main line up to the Picos de Europa is Palomera, with runs to Potes and Fuente Dé. Within Santander itself there are frequent buses and trolleys (Nos.1, 2 and 7) that run from the centre to El Sardinero 20 minutes away.

By Boat

Lanchas Reginas runs a service to the beaches across the bay, with departures every 15 minutes from 10.30am to 8.30pm from the Muelle de Ferrys, two blocks from the cathedral. They also offer tours of the bay and excursions around the Río Cubas.

By Taxi

For a **radio taxi** call **t** 942 33 33 33, or **t** 942 36 91 91.

Tourist Information

Santander: Regional Office: Pza. de Velarde 5, **t** 942 31 07 08, **f** 942 31 32 48; Municipal Office: Jardines de Pereda, **t** 942 21 61 20; branches at the centre of the beach strip, **t** 942 74 04 14, and in the bus station.

Post Office: on the corner of Av. Alfonso XIII and C/Calvo Sotelo.

Public Telephones: C/Hernán Cortés 37.

Internet Access: InSisTel, C/Méndez Nuñez 8.

There are **markets** in Pza de la Esperanza (*Tues, Wed, Fri* and *Sat* for ***food****; Mon* and *Thurs* for **clothes**); and in Pza de México (*Mon, Wed, Fri* and *Sat* for **food***; Tues* and *Fri* for **clothes**).

Festivals

Festival Internacional de Santander, *Aug*. Since 1951 this has showcased an extraordinary variety of music and dance from around the world. Along with all the big-league culture, popular Spanish and Latin American song, dance, magic shows and fireworks take place nightly at the Auditorium and the Finca Altamira. For information contact the **Oficina del Festival**, Palacio de Festivales de Cantabria, C/Gamazo s/n, 39004 Santander, **t** 942 21 05 08/942 21 03 45/942 31 48 19 /942 31 48 53, **f** 942 31 47 67. **Tickets** are on sale in advance from the ticket booth at the Palacio de Festivales, from any branch of the Caja Cantabria bank, or from the special Festival booth in the Jardines de Pereda, near the library, **t** 942 31 33 42 (*open 11–2 and 5–8*).

Shopping

C/San Francisco and other streets in the vicinity make a pleasant stroll. The pedestrian-only streets, **C/Arrabal** and **C/del Medio**, have some good clothing boutiques, as well as local arts and crafts galleries.

Where to Stay

Santander ✉ 39000

July, August and September are the busy (and expensive) months here, when the music festival and International University are in full swing. Prices are high, though there are plenty of *casas particulares* to preserve your budget. Hang around the bus and train stations and someone will probably lead you to one.

Luxury

Santander's most elegant places to stay are all on the back side of town by the beaches.

★★★★★**Hotel Real**, Pso de Pérez Galdós 28, **t** 942 27 25 50, **f** 942 27 45 73, *www.realsantander .husa.es*. A lovely *modernista* hotel near Playa de la Magdalena offering marvellous bay views, fine rooms and a fine garden.

★★★★**Rhin**, Av. Reina Victoria, **t** 942 27 43 00, **f** 942 27 86 53, *www.gruporhin.com*. Enjoys a smart location facing the beaches.

Expensive

★★★**Hotel Sardinero**, Pza de Italia 1, **t** 942 27 11 00, **f** 942 27 16 98. This is popular and conveniently near the beaches of Sardinero and the casino.

★★★★**Castelar**, C/Castelar 25, **t** 942 22 52 00, *www.grupocastelar.com*. A recent addition to the smart ranks, with sea views.

Moderate

★★**Paris**, Av. de los Hoteles 6, **t** 942 27 23 50, **f** 942 27 17 44. The best choice in this range, with palatial, elegantly-furnished rooms in a rambling old queen of a building.

★★**Méjico**, Calderón de la Barca 3, **t** 942 21 24 50. Central, pleasant and recently remodelled.

Inexpensive

The cheaper hotels have gained a certain notoriety for being either dreary or rip-offs. If the quoted price seems ridiculously high, find out what it includes: a common sting is to include a 'secret' breakfast for which you will be charged whether or not you ever find out about it. An official room-only price list should be posted somewhere near the front door.

★★**Hs La Mexicana**, C/Juan de Herrera 3, **t** 942 22 23 50. Large, good-value and central, with friendly management and comfortable rooms (*cheap* out of season).

★**P. La Porticada**, C/Mendez Nuñez 6, **t** 942 22 75 17. Sparkling rooms with balconies set in a building that speaks of vanished glory. Rates are cheaper with shared bathroom.

Cheap

★**Hs Gran Antilla**, C/Isabel II 8, **t** 942 21 31 00. Well worn, but a good deal for this town.

Camping Bellavista, **t** 942 27 48 43. Located by the Cabo Mayor lighthouse.

Eating Out

Santander is hardly known for its cuisine, but the seafood is always good, and the traditional place to get it is the rather piquant Barrio Pesquero, just behind the train stations. Around the beaches, restaurants tend to be more elaborate in every way.

Moderate

Bodega del Riojano, Río de la Pila 5 (north of the Jardines de Pereda), **t** 942 21 67 50. One of Santander's typical *bodegas* in the old quarter, offering healthy servings of tapas. *Closed Sun eve.*

La Casona, C/Cuesta 6 (near Ayuntamiento), **t** 942 21 26 88. An old favourite that over five decades has accumulated a collection of over a hundred paintings; the seafood and grilled meats are the specialities.

Iris, Castelar 5, **t** 942 21 52 25. One of numerous eateries in the Puerto Chico, with sumptuous displays of seafood.

Zacarías, C/Hernán Cortés 38, **t** 942 21 06 88. A total '*mar y montaña*' Cantabrian culinary experience, including excellent cheeses.

Casa José, C/Mocejón 2. One of the best in the *barrio* with a good (*inexpensive*) *menú*.

La Sardina, C/Dr Fleming 3, in El Sardinero, **t** 942 27 10 35 (*expensive*). A fashionable place in a very pretty setting, offering imaginative renderings of traditional dishes.

Nightlife

Nightlife is concentrated in two places. In the old town, the vast number of bars and clubs around **C/de la Pila** and **Pza de Cañadío** are where you're most likely to find live music and a raucous good time. Somewhat more staid entertainment can be had around **El Sardinero**; the Pza de Italia attracts the older set, while overdressed youth in search of fun head for the numerous bars and discothèques in C/Panamá.

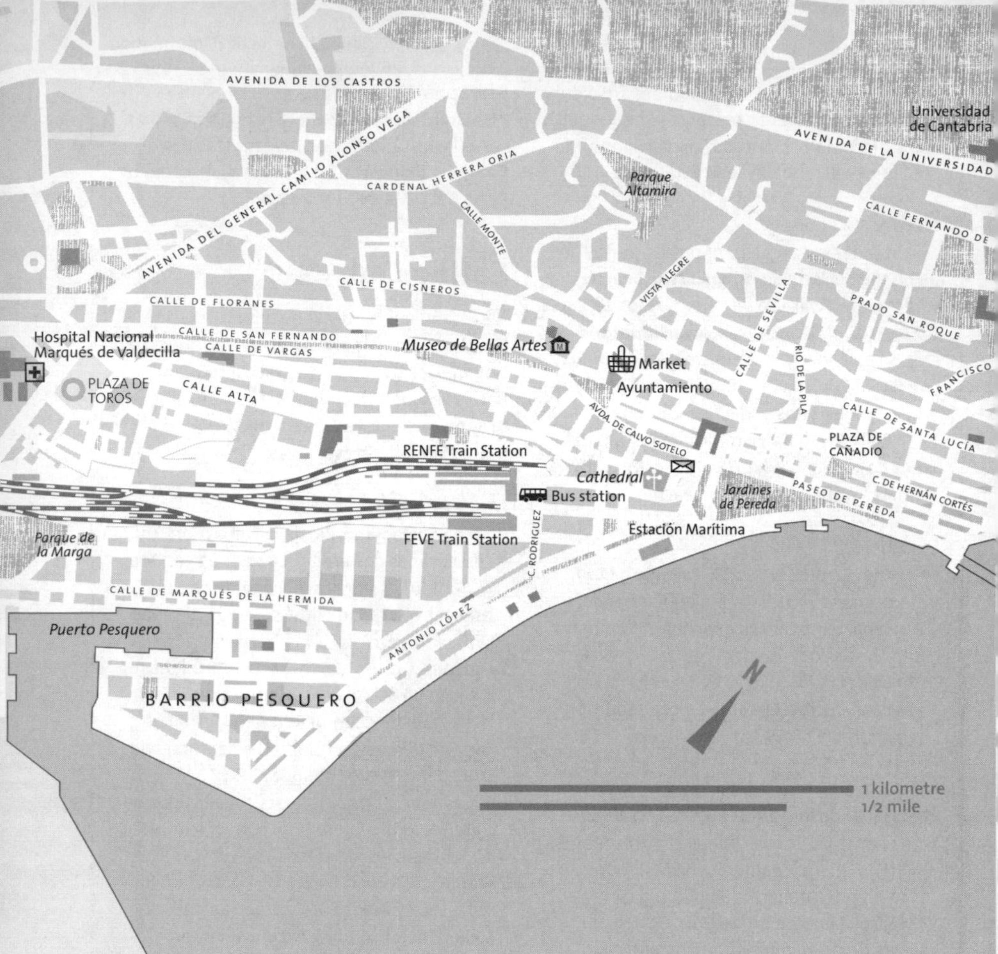

El Sardinero

The 1941 fire destroyed most of Santander's character but it spared the suburb of **El Sardinero**, with its fine twin beaches, imaginatively named **Primera** (First) and **Segunda** (Second), backed by the enormous Belle Epoque casino, recently refurbished in an effort to revive some of the city's lost panache. El Sardinero is separated from the working end of the city by the beautiful **Peninsula de la Magdalena**, a city park fringed by two more splendid beaches, the **Playa de la Magdalena** and the **Playa del Promontorio**. The Tudor-style **Palacio de la Magdalena** sitting at the end of the peninsula was a gift from the city to Alfonso XIII; when the king accepted it, Santander's return to fashion as a summer resort was guaranteed. Today the building forms part of the university.

Besides the beaches in the city, there are several miles of golden dunes across the bay at **Somo**, **El Puntal** and **Pedrena**, linked every 15 minutes by boat from the centre of town; **Playa las Atenas** nearby is a naturist beach. Just west of Santander at Liencres, there is another fine and very popular beach, **Valdearenas**, a huge expanse of sand bordered by pine woods.

South of Santander: the Heart of Cantabria

South of the capital the land gradually rises to the **Montañas de Santander**, a pretty, hilly region that supports only a handful of villages. There are plenty of wide open spaces along these high roads of the old County of Castile, but few attractions besides the solitude: caves of prehistoric art, untouched forests, the source of the Ebro and one of the sexiest churches in Europe.

The Caves of Puente Viesgo and Saja National Reserve

If you haven't made an appointment in advance to see the caves of Altamira, you can at least get into Cantabria's second most spectacular set of prehistoric grottoes at **Puente Viesgo**. Of five caves, only one is open to the public: the **Cueva de Castillo** (*open Tues–Sun 9–12 and 3.30–6.30; closed Mon; adm, adm free for EU passport holders; children under 12 strictly not admitted*). Decorated with graceful line drawings of stags, horses and other animals, this ensemble is believed to predate the even more eloquent art at Altamira.

Getting Around

Reinosa's bus station, at the south end of town, is served from Santander by García, **t** 942 75 40 67, and Alsa, **t** 942 75 40 67; Ansa goes to Bilbao (summer only, **t** 942 75 28 13). Donato, **t** 942 12 20 47, links Reinosa to Espinilla and La Lomba in the Alto Campóo.

Tourist Information

Torrelavega: Ruíz Tagle 6, **t** 942 89 29 82.
Reinosa: Av. Puente Carlos III, **t** 942 75 52 15.

There is a weekly **market** in Reinosa (*Mon*).

Where to Stay and Eat

Puente Arce ✉ 39478

One of the best restaurants in the whole of Cantabria can be found at this village, situated 12km inland from Santander on the road to Torrelavega:

El Molino, Barrio Monsignor 18, **t** 942 57 50 55, **f** 942 57 52 54 (*expensive*). In an old mill on the river, with valuable oil paintings hanging on the walls, excellent fish (an *ensalada cantabrica* with seafood and lots of ginger), a large selection of wines and a truly monumental gastronomic *menú* (*moderate*). *Closed Sun eve and Mon, exc. in summer.*

Puente Viesgo ✉ 39478

*****Gran Hotel Puente Viesgo**, Blvd de la Iglesia, **t** 942 59 80 61, **f** 942 59 82 61 (*expensive*). If you have come to see the caves, you can stop at this sumptuous modern establishment connected to a spa that's good for rheumatism and neurological troubles; it has a pool, sauna and all the amenities.

****Pensión Carrion**, at neighbouring Alceda, **t** 942 59 40 16 (*cheap*). A more realistic alternative.

Mesón El Cazador, Ctra General s/n, **t** 942 59 42 50 (*moderate*). A good country restaurant in San Vicente de Toranzo, south of Puente Viesgo; offers boar, pheasant and other game dishes.

Reinosa ✉ 39200

*****Vejo**, Av. Cantabria 83 (in the newer part of town), **t** 942 75 17 00, **f** 942 75 47 63, *hvejo@ceoecant.es* (*moderate*). The most comfortable option, with a garden, bar and good **restaurant**.

****San Cristóbal**, 16 de Agosto 1, **t** 942 75 17 68 (*inexpensive*). More economical, with simple, bathless rooms.

***La Casona**, in Nestares, **t** 942 75 17 88 (*inexpensive*). This old inn on the Reinosa–Cabezón de la Sal highway is a scenic place to stay if you're driving.

Reinosa, on the rail line, is the main hub in this part of the Cantabrian mountains, with most of the area's hotels and restaurants. Northwest of here, in Fontibre, is the source of northern Spain's longest river, the **Ebro**. The most beautiful part of the region lies to the west, in the virgin valleys of the **Saja National Reserve**, where beech, oak and birch forests follow the courses of clear streams. The region's most important ski installation, **Alto Campóo**, lies to the west in the village of Hermandad Campóo de Suso (***t*** *942 77 92 22 to check on snow conditions*).

A Trinity of Romanesque Churches

South of Reinosa you'll find good Romanesque churches – in **Bolmir** and more significantly in **Retortillo**. The most extraordinary of all, however, is further south in **Cervatos**: the singular 12th-century **Colegiata**, at the top of a newly cobbled lane. It has a tympanum with an oriental design, a frieze of lions and, carved on to the corbels and capitals in the apse, unabashedly erotic figures that a respectable guidebook hesitates to describe.

The Coast West of Santander

This lush seaside stretch has been spared any Laredo toadstools, and what tourist development there is remains fairly discreet. When the summer hordes have left and the little roads are yours alone, it is haunting in a fairy-like way. Even in the rain.

Santillana del Mar

The tour buses disgorge their hundreds daily upon this tiny village (which despite the 'del Mar' is not on the sea), and in summer it can be a ghastly tourist inferno, with no place to put your car for a mile around. If you come at all, do it out of season, or spend the night after the day-trippers have all gone.

Santillana is at once an evocative medieval town of grand palaces and a country village of dairy farmers, whose pastures lie on the hills just beyond the mellowed stone and half-timbered houses that line its one street. The village is famous as the birthplace of Spain's favourite fictional rogue, Gil Blas, and home of the real Marqués de Santillana, Íñigo López de Mendoza, the Spanish Sir Philip Sidney, a warrior, poet and courtly lover whose house still stands on C/del Cantón. It owes its name,

Getting Around

By Train

FEVE trains from Santander go as far as Torrelavega, with frequent bus connections to Santillana. Another FEVE station is 3km from San Vicente.

By Bus

Suances, Santillana, Comillas and San Vicente are linked around six times daily to Santander by La Cantábrica de Comillas or SA Continental buses from Santander.

Tourist Information

Santillana del Mar: Pza de Ramon Pelayo s/n, **t** 942 81 82 51.

Comillas: Aldea 6, **t** 942 72 07 68.

San Vicente de la Barquera: Av. Generalísimo 20, **t** 942 71 07 97.

There are weekly **markets** in Suances (*Tues*); Comillas (*Thurs*) and San Vicente (*Sat*).

Where to Stay and Eat

Santillana ✉ 39330

Ask at the tourist office for a list of *casas particulares*, though many are in the newer suburbs en route to Altamira; or else, head for C/Los Hornos or Av. Le Dorat, which have plenty of rooms.

★★★**Parador Gil Blas**, Pza Pelayo 11, **t** 942 81 80 00, **f** 942 81 83 91, *santillana@parador.es* (*expensive*). Wonderfully atmospheric with medieval rooms and an elegant dining room; reserve well ahead in season, and request a room on the first or second floor.

★★★**Hotel Altamira**, C/Cantón 1, **t** 942 81 80 25 (*expensive–moderate*). A good second choice in another palace nearby, with a patio and garden; its elegant dining room serves big plates of roast meats (and some seafood); it's possibly the best **restaurant** in town.

Solar de Hidalgos, C/Santo Domingo 5, **t** 942 81 83 87, **f** 942 81 83 87 (*expensive–moderate*). Treads a fine line between ancient elegance and modern comfort, in yet another palace.

La Casa del Organista, C/Los Hornos 4, **t** 942 84 03 52, *organist@arrakis.es* (*moderate*). Has gorgeous wood-panelled rooms and sloping ceilings, in a refurbished medieval mansion overlooking fields on the edge of town.

El Canton, C/Canton 3, **t** 942 84 02 74 (*inexpensive*). A lovely, welcoming *posada*, with the cheapest rooms with bath in the old quarter.

Camping Santillana, **t** 942 81 82 50. Just north of the village, this is one of the pricier campsites in this area, but it has all the amenities, including a pool and tennis courts.

however, to St Juliana, an Anatolian martyr under Diocletian whose remains have lain here since the 6th century. She is honoured with the **Colegiata**, a 12th-century masterpiece with a fine weather-beaten façade, rebuilt in the 1700s with bits and pieces of the Romanesque original tacked on. Inside, the impressive altar is made of silver from Mexico – plenty of the *hidalgos'* younger sons went off to America to make their fortune, and many of the family mansions in the village are *casas de indianos*. There is a beautiful **cloister** (*open 10–1 and 4–6; adm*), with capitals carved with biblical and hunting scenes. The ticket to the cloister will also get you into the **Museo Diocesano** (*across town near the car park; open 10–1 and 4–6*) in the 17th-century Convento de Regina Coeli, displaying an exceptional collection of ecclesiastical artefacts from all over Cantabria, all perfectly restored by the nuns. On the eloquent Plaza Ramón Pelayo stand a **museum** devoted to the region's seafaring past, the **Ayuntamiento** and the **Palacio de Barreda-Bracho**, now the Parador Gil Blas.

The Caves of Altamira

From Santillana you can walk up to Altamira in 20 minutes, though don't expect to get in unless you've written three years in advance (to the **Centro de Investigación de**

Los Blasones, Pza de la Gándara 8, **t** 942 81 80 70 (*inexpensive*). Here you can feast on local and mountain specialities: from *fabada* to grilled *langostinos* (crawfish).

Otherwise, **tapas** and reasonably priced meals can be had in the **bar** nearest the Colegiata.

Comillas ✉ 39520

Ask at the tourist office for a list of *casas particulares*.

*****Casa del Castro**, San Jerónimo, **t** 942 72 00 36, **f** 942 72 00 61 (*expensive–moderate*). Right in the centre in a fine old building with a pretty garden and comfortable rooms.

****Hs Esmeralda**, C/Antonio López 7, **t** 942 72 00 97 (*moderate*). Closer to the beach.

***Fuente Real**, C/Sobrellano 19, **t** 942 72 01 55 (*cheap*). A basic alternative.

El Capricho de Gaudí, Barrio de Sobrellano, **t** 942 72 03 65 (*expensive*). Comillas is the only place where you can dine in a building designed by Gaudí. The interior, if not entirely as he planned it, has been beautifully restored. The food, too, is a work of art, mostly seafood with a *nouvelle cuisine* touch; the *menú* (*moderate*) is a bargain. Call ahead as it's usually booked solid in season.

Gurea, C/Ignacio Fernandez de Castro 11, **t** 942 72 24 46 (*moderate*). A good alternative, serving excellent and unusual Basque dishes like *merluza* in crayfish sauce.

Fuente Real, **t** 942 72 21 59 (*inexpensive*). Just outside the grounds of El Capricho, with its ancient sign and décor of *azulejo* tiles, this cheerful seafood haunt has been a favourite for over a century.

San Vicente de la Barquera ✉ 39540

*****Miramar**, Pso de la Barquera 20, **t/f** 942 71 00 75. Modern, and with great views of the bay and the rising Picos de Europa to admire from its **restaurant**.

****Luzón**, Ctra Santander–Oviedo, **t** 942 71 00 50 (*moderate*). A solid, square stone inn smack in the centre of town facing the tidal basin.

***La Paz**, C/del Mercado 28, **t** 942 71 01 80 (*inexpensive*). Has recently been remodelled and offers stylish, if bathless, rooms.

Camping El Rosal, **t** 942 71 01 65. Conveniently close to the beaches, on the main road just outside San Vicente.

Boga-Boga, Pza José Antonio, **t** 942 71 01 35 (*expensive*). Expect more seafood at this place, where the award-winning chef turns out Cantabrian recipes you've never imagined: red peppers stuffed with *langostinos*, for instance. Definitely worth a try.

Maruja, Av. Generalísimo s/n, **t** 942 71 00 77 (*moderate*). For a less serious seafood attack, you can do well here.

Altamira, Santillana del Mar, Santander) and are one of the 20 chosen ones permitted the 15-minute glimpse at one of the sublime masterpieces of Upper Palaeolithic art. Still, an extraordinary number of people show up at the caves to pay homage to the genius of the artists of *c.* 12000 BC, who covered the undulating ceiling with stunningly exuberant, vividly coloured paintings of bison, horses, boars and stags. Only at Lascaux (France) will you find such masterful technique; the movement and strength in the coiled, startled and galloping bisons, the attentive deer and frisking horses are simply awesome. As they say, 'This is the infancy of art, not an art of infancy.'

The story of the discovery of Altamira, however, is a parable of perceptions. As at Lascaux, an ancient landslide sealed the entrance of the caves and tunnels (and more or less vacuum-packed the paintings) until it was rediscovered by a hunter and his dog in 1868. In 1875, Don Marcelino de Sautuola, an amateur prehistorian, was intrigued by the black drawings on the walls in the outer rooms, and over the years explored them, in 1879 taking his nine-year-old daughter María along. The child wandered a little deeper into the caves, and lifted her eyes to the superb polychrome paintings. Although no one had ever seen the like, the Marquis at once recognized the ceiling for what it was: a ravishing work of genius from the Stone Age. With dismay, de Sautola found he was utterly ridiculed; the scholars simply refused to believe that people who used stone axes were capable of painting. Only after his death did the discovery of a dozen painted caves in the Vézère valley in the Dordogne lead to a change of mind.

Although the 'white disease' caused by the moisture in the breath of visitors has restricted admission to the caves, since 2001 it's possible to do the next best thing: visit an exact replica, constructed in a new museum building at enormous expense by the Cantabrian government. There's a small stalactite cave to explore, too, which is prettily lit to emphasize nature's wonders as compensation for the inaccessibility of the more fragile works of man. A fascinating **museum** (*open Mon–Sat 9.30–2.30; closed Sun; adm*) installed on the site means you can also view a video and photos.

Comillas, with a Little *Modernista* Madness

Definitely *the* place to be on this stretch of the coast, the seaside resort of Comillas offers a bit of Catalan quirkiness in a gorgeous setting, framed by two endearing beaches: the **Playa Comillas** and the longer **Playa de Oyambre**. Comillas' old town, with its rough cobbled streets and arcaded mansions, has long been a quiet watering hole for the Madrid and Barcelona aristocracy; the latter brought along their favourite architects in the 19th century to add a *modernista* flair (*see* box, p.352).

Their peculiar legacies are up on the hills to the west of the village centre. There you will see Gaudí's **El Capricho**, recently restored and pressed into service as a restaurant. If not one of the architect's more ambitious works, it is a delightful house, with an eccentric, perfectly non-functional tower, half-lighthouse and half-minaret.

Next to El Capricho you can have a peek into a vanished lifestyle at the **summer palace of the Marqués de Comillas** (*open summer daily 10–1.30 and 4–6.30; closed Mon and Tues in winter; adm*), newly restored after years of sitting empty. Designed by another Catalan, Gaudí's friend Joan Martorell, this ponderous palace in a quirky

The Instant Marquis

The Spain of the Industrial Revolution is a little-known land, but it certainly produced some marvels, and some incredible robber-baron careers. Antonio López was a local boy who went abroad and made a fortune in shipping and slaves, then came back home and purchased the title of Marquis of Comillas. The new Marquis' son married the daughter of Joan Güell, who had also started in Cuba and ended up as Spain's biggest textile magnate. Like Cosimo de' Medici in old Florence, this robber baron had a talented aesthete to succeed him, whose sponsorship of Gaudí sparked the golden age of *modernista* architecture in Catalunya. It was the Güell connection that brought Gaudí to Cantabria, where he helped with the López family palace in 1878 and came back to build El Capricho in 1883. The centre of López interests was Barcelona, where they ran factories, banks and the Transatlántica shipping line (which later fell into the grasp of the greatest of all Spanish robber barons, Juan March, and still runs most of the Spanish island ferries). The López family lived on the Ramblas in Barcelona, but they spent their summers here, bringing with them their Catalan friends and making Comillas a genteel upper-class resort. López's castle-like mansion, on the hill overlooking the town, was one of the most spectacular private homes in its day, and the heart of the glittering social season Comillas knew at the turn of the century.

modernista neo-Gothic style is protected by an imitation castle wall with oubliettes. The Marquis' **chapel** adds the perfect touch of discreet surrealism to the ensemble; the interior holds furnishings by Gaudí and marble sepulchres of the Marquis' family.

The third member of the trio stands on the opposite hill, across the main road through Comillas, but it commands the views for miles around. Construction of the **Universidad Pontificia** began in 1883, with a plan by Martorell and some financial help from Antonio López. The sumptuous main building (*open daily 9–3; adm*) contains decorations by a third major figure of Catalan modernism, Lluis Domènech i Montaner, who also created the wonderfully florid **Monument to Antonio López**.

The next resort to the west, **San Vicente de la Barquera**, is still as much a fishing port as a holiday retreat, though it's hugely popular with *madrileños* in summer. Marvellously sited on a hill in the last elbow-bend of the marshy Río Escudo, it is linked by a causeway to the eastern coast, near the town beach.

The Picos de Europa

They are not the highest mountains in Spain, or even in the Cantabrian–Pyrenean *cordillera*, but the Picos de Europa have a certain cachet. So many peaks, packed closely together in a small area, make a memorable landmark for Spain's northern coast. No one knows where the name came from, though it may have been that these mountains, visible far out to sea, were the first sight of the continent for Atlantic sailors. To the Asturians they are known as the Urrieles.

Thank Asturian ecologists for their efforts in keeping Spain's most beautiful mountains enchanting and unspoiled: what development there is (ski resorts, hotels) is mostly in western Cantabria and Northern Léon. The Picos are divided by rivers into three tremendous massifs: **Andara**, mostly in Cantabria; **Urrieles**, in the middle; and **Cornión**, to the west. The highest peak, Torre de Cerredo, stands 8,606ft – not all that much as mountains go. But for sheer beauty and rugged grandeur, for the contrast of tiny rural villages in fertile green valleys against a backdrop of sheer, twisted stone peaks crested with snow the year round, the Picos de Europa are hard to beat.

The range seems to have been dropped from heaven, especially for hikers (*see* 'Sports and Activities', p.354); there are trails for Sunday walkers and sheer cliffs for serious alpinists, not to mention a wonderful array of birds and wildlife.

Potes and the Valley of Liébana

The eastern mountains of the Picos are the most visited and most accessible. The main entrance from the coast begins at **Unquera** (a FEVE stop on the coast to the west of San Vicente); from here, the N621 climbs up through the **Desfiladero de La Hermida** into the idyllic little valley around the village of **Lebeña**, with its parish church – the 10th-century Mozarabic **Santa María** – signposted south of the village on the N62. **Potes**, the capital of the Valley of Liébana, is the metropolis of the Picos, where you can garner information, catch buses, change travellers' cheques and stock up on supplies. For all its tourist traffic Potes is still a gracious town, with stone arcades to shelter the cafés on the main street and a warren of medieval lanes behind. There are also a number of jeep excursions on offer. The main monument in Potes itself is the 15th-century **Torre del Infantado**, a massive, square defensive-residential work in the centre of town.

One of the most popular excursions from Potes is the four-kilometre trip up to the **Monasterio de Santo Toribio de Liébana**. Don't miss it, because this is the only place in Cantabria where a visit will earn you an indulgence – time off from purgatory. It is a

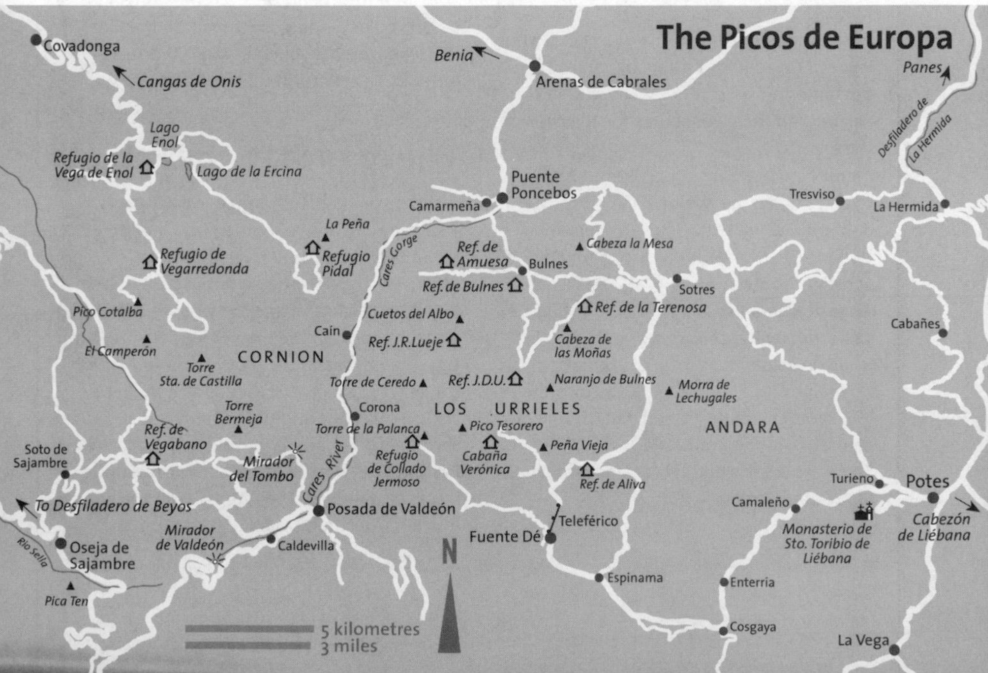

Getting Around

By Bus

Palomera buses, **t** 942 88 06 11, serve Potes up to four times daily from Santander, via Unquera, San Vicente and Torrelavega. There are two buses (one in winter) daily between Santander and León that stop at Potes and Lebeña. From Potes there are three buses from the central square to Fuente Dé and the *teleférico*. A summer-only service runs from Cangas to Posada de Valdeón; Posada is also served by daily buses from León. Beyond the main villages the only transport is provided by **taxi**; in Posada (for Land Rovers to Caín) **t** 987 74 26 09.

By Jeep

Jeeps make the link between the upper station of the *teleférico* to the *refugio de Aliva* if you're not up to the walk. Arenas de Cabrales is the main hub in the northern Picos, with Land Rover services to Poncebos and Sotres and daily buses to Cangas de Onis and Panes. **4WD taxis** can be hired in Sotres for journeys deeper into the mountains, **t** 985 94 50 24.

Tourist Information

Unquera: (Val de San Vicente) Residencial Tina Mayor, **t** 942 71 72 82.

Potes: C/Independencia s/n, **t** 942 73 07 87 (for more detailed information and maps try Bustamente's on central Pza Capitán Palacios, an excellent source for all books on the area).

Turieno: National Park Office, Urb. La Molina, **t** 942 73 05 55. The National Park runs free daily guided walks during summer in the Liébana valley and Cabrales, covering a variety of routes.

Arenas de Cabrales: Ctra General, **t** 985 84 52 84, *turismo@cabrales.org*.

Posada de Valdeón: Travesía Los Llanos, **t** 987 74 05 49. Free guided walks into the hills around Posada are run daily in summer courtesy of the National Park.

There are weekly **markets** in **Unquera** (*Tues*) and in **Potes** (*Mon*).

Sports and Activities

Hiking

Hiking in the high Picos is practical only from the end of May to October, but even then you may get a soaking. Low-level walks can be done at any time of year.

Hiking boots are universally recommended because of patches of loose shale on the trails and slopes.Bring warm clothes, a lightweight plastic poncho, a sleeping bag and food for any nights in the refuges, and binoculars to take in the wonderful array of wildlife.

If you're going for an extended holiday, get the detailed **maps** published by the Federación Española de Montañismo, usually available at Potes, the main base for visiting the mountains. The **guide** *Picos de Europa* by Robin Collomb (West Col, Reading) is a great help, with up-to-date detailed information on guides, itineraries and mountain *refugios* (free overnight shelters). This is available from:

Federación Asturiana de Montañismo, C/Melquiades Álvarez 16, Oviedo, **t** 985 21 10 99.

Federación Cántabra de Montaña, C/Rubio 2, Santander, **t** 942 37 33 78.

Delegación Leonesa de Montaña, Pso de la Facultad 3, León, **t** 987 25 00 52.

Horse Riding and Cycling

A stable in Turieno, next to Potes, offers several guided **riding excursions** in the Picos. If you want to do it yourself, Viajes Wences and other firms in Potes rent **mountain bikes**.

Where to Stay and Eat

There's no need to rough it. Nearly every village has at least one *casa particular* or *fonda* or a place to camp, and you can purchase supplies or dine out in a traditional restaurant. Every village has its specialities, and the shops on the main street of Potes are treasure houses of the mountains' finest; you can purchase local cheeses and charcuterie, honey in various original flavours and *orujo*, the Cantabrian firewater sold in dangerous-looking little bottles all over town. It's made from the pulp of grapes stems after the wine harvest, like French *marc* or Italian *grappa*.

Potes ✉ 39570

★★**Picos de Valdecoro**, C/Roscabao, **t** 942 73 00 25, **f** 942 73 03 15 (*moderate*). At the top of the list.

★★**Infantado**, on the Fuente Dé road, **t** 942 73 09 39, **f** 942 73 05 78 (*moderate*). Modern, stone-built and one of the best here.

★★**Picos de Europa**, C/San Roque 6, **t** 942 73 00 05, **f** 942 73 20 60. A small place run by a friendly, knowledgeable fellow whose son prepares excellent meals in the **restaurant**, having studied with the culinary master Juan Mari Arzak.

★**Casa Cayo**, C/Cántabra 6, **t** 942 73 01 50 (*inexpensive*). A modernized mountain hotel, with simple but comfortable rooms overlooking the river and a very popular *comedor* downstairs.

Posada de Bistruey, La Vega (9km south of Potes), **t** 942 73 60 95 (*inexpensive*). If Potes is too hectic, head for this peaceful roadside *posada*, run by a friendly family who provide a hearty breakfast, free sweets, and spotless rooms with bath at bargain prices.

★★**Hs La Serna**, C/La Serna 9, **t** 942 73 09 24 (*cheap*). The only budget choice to have rooms with bath.

Camping El Molino, La Vega, **t** 942 73 04 89 (*inexpensive*). Offers a pleasant setting.

El Fogon de Cus, C/Capitán Palacios, **t** 942 73 00 60 (*moderate*). Has the best name in town for local dishes and Basque cooking.

Paco Wences, C/Roscabao s/n, **t** 942 73 00 25 (*inexpensive*). A good place to try the local *cocido liebaniego*, a hearty stew made of *garbanzo* beans, *chorizo*, black pudding and anything else to hand.

Fuente Dé ✉ 39588

★★★**Parador Río Deva**, **t** 942 73 66 51, **f** 942 73 66 54 (*expensive–moderate*). Since 1965, this magnificently sited hotel has been a part of the Picos experience. A modern building at the end of the *teleférico*, many of its rooms have grand views; the hotel organizes jeep excursions up into the peaks, and its **restaurant** specializes in mountain and Castilian dishes, with an *inexpensive menú*.

★★★**Hotel del Oso**, **t** 942 73 30 18 (*moderate*). You could do just as well, immersed in equally stunning mountain scenery, at this modern place owned by the Rivas family.

★★**Del Oso Pardo**, 10km east at Cosgaya, **t** 942 73 04 18, **f** 942 73 01 36 (*moderate*). This is a beautiful stone original, also owned by the Rivas family. A bonus is the superb mountain cuisine: try the trout and cheesecake (*tarta de queso*) or the *menú*.

Espinama ✉ 39500

Refugio de Aliva, about 7½km up from Espinama, **t** 942 73 09 99 (*inexpensive*). Has a **restaurant** and 24 rooms available on a first-come, first-served basis. Ring in advance; a Land Rover from Espinama will take you up. *Open 15 June–30 Sept.*

For other *refugios* in the Picos, ask at the Potes tourist office.

Arenas de Cabrales ✉ 33554

★★★**Picos de Europa**, Ctra General, **t** 985 84 64 91, **f** 985 84 65 45 (*expensive*). The poshest choice in town, with smart rooms, a pool, and a good **restaurant**.

Casa Cipriano, at Sotres, **t** 985 94 50 24 (*cheap*). Run by Cipriano López, the mountaineering mogul of Sotres, this simple *pensión* is the place to go for information on outdoor activities; the staff can arrange Land Rover taxis and climbing guides. Good hearty stews and *raciones* are served in the bar.

Albergue Bulnes, at Bulnes, **t** 985 84 59 43 (*cheap*). The only places to stay in Bulnes are in *casas rurales* or hostels; this one has good clean dormitory accommodation, a fairly basic ***comedor***, and can offer advice on the best hiking trails in the area.

Posada de Valdeón ✉ 24915

Posada has several *casas particulares* and some fine *fondas*.

★★**Hs Campo**, Ctra. Cordiñanes, **t** 987 74 05 02 (*inexpensive*). Has good-value modern rooms with bath, and wonderful views from the terrace. The **cafeteria** serves decent stews and *fabadas*.

P. Begoña, C/de los Llanos 2, **t** 987 74 05 16 (*cheap*). The authentic mountain experience: small, spartan rooms with goatskins on the floor, terrific meals, a warm welcome, and rock-bottom prices.

Camping El Cares, Santa Marina de Valdeón, **t** 987 74 26 76. Has 400 pitches and plenty of facilities, including horses for hire.

long-established pilgrimage site, allegedly the home of the world's largest chunk of the True Cross. In its earliest days the monastery was ruled by the Abbot Beato de Liébana, whose *Commentaries on the Apocalypse* were popular in Spain throughout the Middle Ages. In the cloister here you can see a full set of copies of one of them: mad and brilliant pictorial prophecies from an age when people were convinced the world would soon be meeting its end.

From Fuente Dé to Arenas de Cabrales

The classic excursion from Potes is to take the bus west up to the stunning old village of **Espinama** and, one and a half kilometres beyond, to **Fuente Dé**. Here you can catch the *teleférico* for an awesome, vertigo-inducing ride 2,568ft up the sheer cliff to the **mirador del Cable** (*the teleférico runs July–Sept daily 9–8; adm; in peak season, arrive very early or you'll get stuck waiting, maybe for hours*). Once at the top, walk four kilometres up to the **Refugio de Aliva**, a popular modern version of the old mountain refuge; a path from here leads back down to Espinama. The most important village in the area is **Arenas de Cabrales**, connected by Land Rover with Poncebos and Sotres and renowned for its stinking mountain cheese – 'never matured in manure, never contains worms', the tourist literature boasts.

The Divine Gorge

Between Caín and Poncebos, the **Cares Gorge** (better known as the 'Garganta Divina') extends north to south across the Picos. It is a spectacular 12-kilometre walk over sheer drops down to the Río Cares, made relatively easy by a footpath sculpted into the mountainside. The classic approach is from **Caín** in the south, itself linked to Posada de Valdeón by a regular four-wheel-drive service. Walking south from **Poncebos** isn't much more strenuous, but you risk either staying in Caín, which has limited lodgings, or walking the nine kilometres further south to sleep in Posada. Chief village of the high Valley of Valdeón, Posada is a serenely magnificent place to rest up in; here tiny farming villages and their rustic granaries, or *hórreos*, look like mere toys under these lofty peaks.

Asturias

The Principality of Asturias is the Spanish Wales, a rugged country of mines, majestic mountains and a romantically beautiful coastline. The proudest date in Asturian history is 718, when a band of Visigoths, led by the legendary Pelayo, defeated the Moors in the misty mountain glen of Covadonga, setting off the Reconquista and founding the first Christian kingdom in Muslim Iberia. Their beautiful churches are Asturias's chief artistic patrimony; the language they spoke, el Bable, or 'Babel', survives only as a dialect against Castilian, its direct descendant.

In later years, Asturias fell into an obscurity that lasted centuries. The discovery of iron ore and coal in the 19th century rapidly transformed its traditional agricultural economy into a mining one with radical tendencies. These brought about the second great date in Asturian history: an epic miners' revolt in October 1934.

The modern autonomous region of Asturias is in its way one of the most progressive in Spain. One of the last areas to be touched by tourism, it is fighting to maintain its integrity and environment against big developers who would exploit the magnificent Picos de Europa and the coast; instead, Asturias would have you stay in a rural village, to learn something of its culture and architecture.

Asturian Picos de Europa: Cangas and Covadonga

The salmon-filled Río Sella defines the west edge of the western Massif de Cornión, which in its northernmost reaches forms part of Covadonga National Park. Most easily reached from Ribadesella on the Asturian coast, or through the stunning narrow gorge **Desfiladero de los Beyos** (N625) from León and Riaño, the region lacks

Getting Around

By Bus and Taxi

ALSA buses, **t** 902 42 22 42, serve Cangas de Onis several times daily from Oviedo and Llanes, and twice a day from León; connections to Covadonga and Arenas de Cabrales are provided by **EASA**, **t** 985 84 81 33. **Taxis** can be hired in San Juan de Beleño on **t** 985 84 30 17.

Tourist Information

Cangas de Onís: Jardines del Ayuntamiento, **t** 985 84 80 05. National Park information at Casa Dago, **t** 985 84 86 14.

Free **guided walks** into the mountains leave daily from the car park at Lago de la Ercina.

Internet Access: Ingapublic, C/El Censo 15.

There is a **market** (*Sun*) in Cangas de Onís.

Where to Stay and Eat

Cangas de Onís ✉ 33550

Cangas has pricey hotels and a score of *hostales* (*inexpensive*; *cheap* out of season).

*******Monasterio de San Pedro de Villanueva**, in Villanueva (2km from Cangas), **t** 985 84 94 02, **f** 985 84 95 20, *cangas@parador.es* (*expensive*). Behind the carved capitals at its door, this 12th-century monastery has been converted into one of the most luxurious of *paradors*, with palatial guest quarters. The views are superb, as is the **restaurant**'s traditional Asturian cuisine.

***Plaza**, La Plaza 7, **t** 985 84 83 08 (*inexpensive*). Small, friendly, and well located in town.

Los Arcos, Av. Covadonga 17, **t** 985 84 92 77 (*moderate*). This place has established an enviable reputation for game dishes such as partridge with broad beans; don't miss out on their wonderful home-made desserts.

Casa Juan, Av. de Covadonga 20, **t** 985 84 80 12 (*moderate*). *Fabada* and other Asturian dishes are served at this place, established in 1943. *Closed Tues and Wed eves and June.*

Sidrería Polesu, C/Angel Tárano s/n (*cheap*). A traditional *chigre*, full of locals, with good *raciones* of local meats and cheeses.

Covadonga ✉ 33589

Accommodation here is scarce. A number of bars and restaurants hang out *camas* signs along the main road.

*****Hotel Pelayo**, **t** 985 84 60 61, **f** 985 84 60 54 (*expensive in season, otherwise moderate*). Basic and a bit overpriced.

***Peñalba**, in La Riera (3km from Covadonga), **t/f** 985 84 61 00 (*inexpensive*). A newly converted 16th-century house with just a few rooms, away from the tourist bustle.

La Cabaña, on the road to Covadonga, **t** 985 84 82 84 (*moderate*). An old stone house in traditional Asturian style, serving winter warmers such as *cabrito asado* (roast kid), together with seafood dishes. *Closed Thurs.*

Hospedería del Peregrino, 200m below the sanctuary in Covadonga, **t** 985 84 60 47 (*moderate*). Has a well-deserved name for its *fabada*, seafood and mountain dishes which include freshly caught salmon.

Asturias

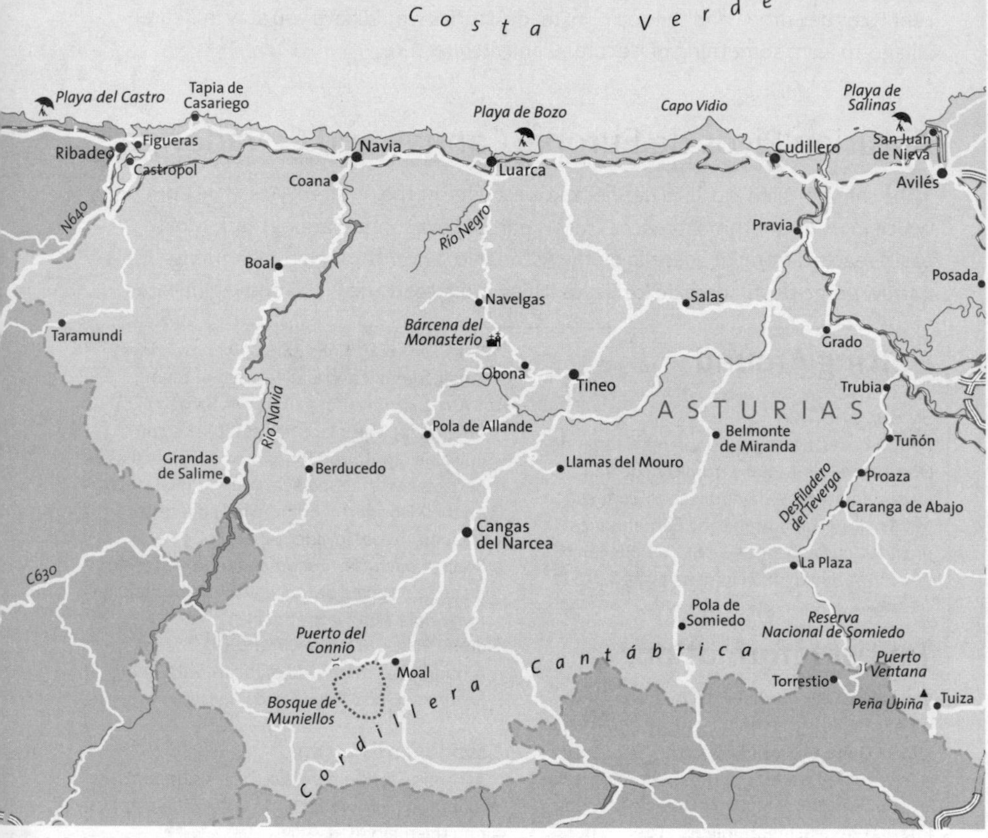

the high drama of the mountains further east, but is nonetheless green and tranquil, and for Spaniards constitutes a pilgrimage.

Cangas de Onís claims to be the first capital of Christian Spain, where the Asturian kings set up shop right after their victory at nearby Covadonga. The most beautiful things here are the high **medieval bridge** (erroneously called 'Roman'), and the **Capilla de Santa Cruz** (*open June–Sept Wed–Sun 10–1 and 3–6.30; closed Mon and Tues; Oct–May open Sat and Sun 9–1 and 3–6.30; closed Mon–Fri; get the key at the Ayuntamiento, and they might also let you have the key for the cave of Buxu*), where the kings worshipped. It was built over a dolmen, and according to legend its founder was Favila, the successor of Pelayo. The original building may really be as early as the 5th century, though it was completely rebuilt in the 15th.

East of Cangas, in Cardes, the **Cave of Buxu** (*open April–Sept Wed–Sun 10–12.30 and 4–6.30; Oct–Mar Wed–Sun 9–1 and 3–5; closed Mon and Tues; max. 25 visitors per day; adm, adm free Wed*) contains rare paintings from the Solutrian era (20–15000 BC).

From here it's 10 kilometres to **Covadonga**, dominated by an enormous 19th-century **basilica**. Here Pelayo, supposedly the son-in-law of Roderick, the last Visigothic king, and 300 followers managed to ambush a small Moorish expedition and defeat them, according to legend. Next to the basilica is the **cave** where Pelayo fought with his back to the wall and now rests in peace in a sarcophagus next to his wife.

The Asturian 'Costa Verde': East to West

Although the Picos attract mountaineers and hikers from all over the world, the very attractive coast of Asturias sees relatively few foreigners. There are over 50 sandy beaches, most of them on unmarked roads just off the main coastal N632; some have spectacular locations, and a few can offer relative peace and quiet even in the middle of August.

Llanes to Villaviciosa

This eastern section of the coast is well endowed with beaches and quiet coves, especially around **Llanes**, an agreeably funky old town that becomes loaded with *madrileños* in the summer. To the east, near Vidiago and the Playa de France, there's a peculiar Bronze Age monument called **Peña-Tú** or the 'Cabeza del Gentil' (the gentile's head). Even older are the cave drawings in the **Cueva del Pindal** (*open Wed–Sun 9.30–1 and 3–5.30; closed Mon and Tues; adm; guided tours in Spanish, although guide speaks English*) near Colombres, featuring the only known painting of a mammoth in Spain.

Ribadesella, at the mouth of the meandering Río Sella, makes an excellent base for forays along the coast or into the western Picos. Split in two by the river and bridge, with a picture-postcard backdrop of mountains, Ribadesella has a handful of old streets, a long protected beach, and plenty of chances for hiking, pony trekking,

Getting Around

By Train and Bus

FEVE trains along the coast take in much of the marvellous scenery. Two trains a day run between Santander and Oviedo, with stops at Unquera, Colombres, the beaches at Nueva and Villaharmes and Ribadesella; a further three a day go from Oviedo to Llanes. To continue west up the coast from Ribadesella you'll have to take a Gijón-bound bus. FEVE has frequent connections between Gijón and Avilés, and west to Cudillero, Luarca, Soto de Luiña and Ortigueiro. ALSA buses link all these towns with Oviedo as well, while RENFE links Gijón with Oviedo, Madrid, Barcelona and the rest of the peninsula.

By Car

Turning the old N632 along the coast into a reasonable route has been the biggest road project in this part of the country for some years. Most of it is already finished, and getting around in your own car is not a problem.

Tourist Information

Llanes: Alfonso IX, La Torre **t** 985 40 01 64.
Ribadesella: El Muelle, **t** 985 86 00 38 (*summer only*).
Villaviciosa: Parque Vallina, **t** 985 89 17 59 (*summer only*).

There are weekly **markets** in **Llanes** (*Tues*); and in **Ribadesella** and **Villaviciosa** (*Wed*).

Where to Stay and Eat

Llanes ✉ 33500

Expensive–Moderate

*****La Posada del Rey**, C/Mayor 11, **t/f** 985 40 13 32. One of the nicest hotels in the old quarter, its stylish modern rooms occupying a converted 16th-century town house.

Moderate

*****Montemar**, C/Jenaro Riestra, **t** 985 40 01 00, **f** 985 40 26 81. On the beach, with modern, comfortable rooms with TV.

*****Don Paco**, Parque Posada Herrera, **t** 985 40 01 50. In Llanes itself, you can stay in this 17th-century palace; it's quiet, with a garden, and the main hall of the mansion is now an elegant **restaurant**, serving mostly seafood.

Inexpensive

***Hs Migal**, in Cué, **t** 985 40 12 01. Both Llanes and the villages near the beaches have plenty of inexpensive *hostales*, such as this good-value place in the pretty village of Cué.

***P. La Guia**, Pza de Parres Sobrino, **t** 985 40 25 77. The decent rooms in this lovely old building have a decidedly bohemian air.

El Pescador, C/Manuel Cué s/n, **t** 985 40 22 64 (*moderate*). Serves wonderfully unusual seafood dishes (try the sea urchin omelette), with vibrant décor and music to match.

Casa Moran, at Puente Nuevo (on the Posada–Robadella road), **t** 985 40 74 85 (*moderate*). In season there are some wonderful instant restaurants, nothing more than a shelter and a few tables, where canoeing and fishing. The beaches lie just across the Sella to the west of town. Just outside town are the stalactitic **Tito Bustillo Caves** (*open April–mid-Sept Tues–Sun 10–1 and 3.30–5.15; closed Mon, also closed Sun July and Aug; adm*), where some 15–20,000 years ago the residents painted the walls with stylish animals and humans, worth a visit even though their sienna, purple and black tones have faded.

Farther west, into what is officially known as the 'Costa Verde', you'll find quiet beaches in the tiny hamlets of **Caravia** (Baja and Alta) and, near **Colunga**: **La Isla**, **La Griega** and **Lastres**. Equally renowned for its clams and *sidra*, Lastres's stack of red-tile-roofed houses and noble mansions overlooks one of Asturias' most picturesque fishing harbours.

Apple orchards line the coast around **Villaviciosa**, the cider capital of Asturias, set at the mouth of a deep *ría*; nearby are two beaches: a long stretch at **Rodiles**, and across

you can get anything finned at bargain rates. A few kilometres outside Llanes, this popular place features the likes of *fabada asturiana* and roast lamb. *Closed Tues.*

Mirentxu, on the harbour in Llanes (*inexpensive*). A bit classier than many, this restaurant does the seafood Basque-style.

Ribadesella ✉ 33560

Ribadesella has more accommodation than most villages around the coast.

★★★★**Gran Hotel del Sella**, La Playa, **t** 985 86 01 50, **f** 985 85 74 49 (*expensive–moderate*). A posh beachside hotel with a/c, a pool, tennis courts and garden; a bit of Costa del Sol luxury on the Atlantic. *Open April–Sept.*

★★★**Ribadesella Playa Hotel**, C/Ricardo Congas 3, **t** 985 86 03 69, **f** 985 86 02 02 (*moderate*). A grand residence from the turn of last century, this has a lovely waterfront location and rooms with all the modern luxuries.

★★**Hs Suave**, C/La Bolena 13, **t** 985 86 03 69 (*inexpensive*). A good bet for cheaper accommodation within the old quarter.

Bohemia, Gran Vía, **t** 985 86 11 50 (*moderate*). Possibly the best restaurant here, offering plenty of seafood but also dishes such as *entrecôte* with *cabales* cheese.

Sidrería Corroceu, facing the harbour. A noisy. convivial spot for tapas and cider.

Lastres ✉ 33330

This growing resort can still be the best bet for a peaceful few days. There are also *casas particulares* and rooms over bars.

★★**Hotel Eutimo**, C/San Antonio s/n, **t/f** 985 85 00 12 (*moderate*). This lovely old house, run by a chatty old lady, has individually decorated rooms with views over the sea.

Casa Eutimo, C/San Antonio s/n, **t** 985 85 00 12 (*moderate*). Something of a tradition round these parts, serving a marvellous *sopa de marisco* and other seafood delights.

Villaviciosa ✉ 33300

Away from the beaches, this is still and agreeable place to stay.

La Casona de Amandi, at Amandi, **t** 985 89 01 30 (*expensive*). A *casa de indiano* built by a returned emigrant to the Americas, this is now a thoroughly charming eight-room hotel in a lovely formal garden, decorated with antiques.

★★★**Casa España**, Pza Carlos I, **t** 985 89 20 30, **f** 985 89 26 82 (*moderate*). Occupies a *casa de indiano* in the monumental centre of town, with cheerful yellow décor in the rooms and a pleasant café on the plaza.

★★**Hs El Congreso**, Generalísimo 25, **t** 985 89 11 80, **f** 985 89 19 07 (*moderate–inexpensive*). Has views over the verdant Parque Vallina from the balconies of its modern rooms; the **restaurant** (*moderate*) serves some of Villaviciosa's tastiest seafood.

Sol, C/Sol, **t** 985 89 11 30. Here plenty of soul is provided by the ancient proprietor, a former guitarist, who stands at his bar and plays (and can talk about) 1930s jazz records all day; very nice rooms at bargain rates.

Sidrería La Oliva, C/Eloisa Fernandez 6 (*cheap*). A friendly and atmospheric *sidrería*, full of locals knocking back bottles of cider and filling up on a variety of satisfying *raciones*.

the *ría*, at **Tazones**, a picturesque fishing village on a little cove. One kilometre south of town, signposted off the O121, the Romanesque **San Juan de Amandi** is noted for its beautiful sculpture: graceful geometric patterns on the portal and the usual vigorous but mystifying scenes on the capitals.

Gijón and Avilés

With some 250,000 people, Gijón (*Xixon* in Asturian dialect) is the largest city in Asturias, a salty, slightly gritty port with few sights but plenty of personality and excellent long beaches. A major industrial centre, it had to be almost totally rebuilt after the Nationalists devastated it in the Civil War.

Getting Around

By Air

There is an airport 15km west of Avilés near the town of Piedras Blancas, **t** 985 12 75 00; daily flights to Madrid, Barcelona and Malaga, and three weekly flights direct to London with Iberia. ALSA buses link the airport with Gijón, Avilés and Oviedo.

By Train and Bus

Frequent FEVE trains to Avilés and Cudillero, **t** 985 34 24 15, and hourly RENFE services to Oviedo **t** 985 35 11 61, leave from the new Estación de Langreo in the centre; long-distance RENFE trains to León and Madrid set off from a separate station a couple of blocks away on Av. Juan Carlos 1, **t** 985 17 02 02. The bus station, a monstrous Art Deco affair, is on C/Llanes 5, with services to Oviedo, into the mountains of Asturias, and along the coast as far as San Sebastián and Galicia.

By Car

Finding a place to park can be a problem in the centre. If your hotel doesn't have parking, there is a convenient garage under Pza 6 de Agosto. For a **taxi**, **t** 985 14 11 11.

Tourist Information

Gijón: Regional Office, C/Marqués de San Esteban 1, **t** 985 34 60 46;
municipal information is available from InfoGijón, C/Maternidad 2 **t** 985 34 55 61, who also have a series of booths scattered along the beaches and waterfront; they organize free daily **walking tours** in summer.
Post Office: Pza 6 de Agosto, Gijón.
Internet Access: Ciberia, C/Begoña 4, Gijón, is conveniently central; while Cafeteria San Siro, Av. Rendueles 16, is a more authentic cybercafé at the end of Playa San Lorenzo.

Avilés: Ruiz Gómez 21, **t** 985 54 43 25.

There is a daily **market** in Gijón at La Camocha, C/La Camocha s/n, and a **flea market** (*Sun mornings*) in the car park of Estadio El Moliñón, out in Gijón's eastern suburbs. There is a weekly market in **Avilés** (*Mon*).

Sports and Activities

Diving and Golf

Contact the **Divers' Federation** in Gijón (**t** 985 13 01 45). There are two **golf courses** in the region: at Gijón (**t** 985 33 31 91) and Siero (**t** 985 41 70 84).

Where to Stay

Gijón ✉ 33200

****__Parador Molino Viejo__, in Parque Isabel La Católica, **t** 985 37 05 11, **f** 985 37 02 33, *gijon@parador.es* (*luxury*). The best rooms in town, with all the usual facilities (except a pool, but the beach is a 10-minute walk) and serves Asturian suppers in its **restaurant**.

***__La Casona de Jovellanos__, Pza Jovellanos s/n, **t** 985 34 12 64, **f** 985 35 61 51, *www.hotelesasturianos.com* (*moderate*). Offers plenty of history alongside its modern comforts: built to house the great reformer's Asturian Institute of Navigation and Mineralogy,

There's little to see in Cimadevilla, but you can visit the home of the city's most famous reformer, the 16th-century **Museo Casa Natal Jovellanos** (*Tues–Sat 10–1 and 5–8, Sun 11–2; closed Mon; adm free*). Though everyone comes for the *Retablo del Mar* by local woodcarver Sebastian Miranda, the museum has assembled a cross section of 19th- and 20th-century Asturian painting and a selection of smooth curvilinear sculptures by José María Navascués, as well as the obligatory personal effects.

The centre of town occupies the isthmus leading to the newer quarters; there you will find the enclosed and arcaded **Plaza Mayor**, surrounded with cafés and restaurants. Behind it are the recently discovered **Termas Romanas** (*open July–Aug Tues–Sat 11–1.30 and 5–9, Sun 11–2; Sept–June Tues–Sat 10–1 and 5–7, Sun 11–2; closed Mon; adm,*

renovation work turned up remains of Cimadevilla's original Roman walls, which can now be seen in the fancy **restaurant**. Next door is one of the city's most popular *chigres*, a good place to start off the evening's festivities.

****Castilla**, C/Corrida 50, **t** 985 34 62 00, **f** 985 34 63 64, *www.hotelesasturianos.com* (*inexpensive*). Has smart modern rooms with bath on the classiest street in Gijón; very good out-of-season rates.

***Hs Narcea**, **t** 985 39 32 87 (*cheap*). The cheapest *hostal* in Gijón, offering basic, bathless rooms.

Eating Out

Gijon

Expensive

La Pondala, Av. Dionisio Cifuentes 27 (in the suburb of Somió), **t** 985 36 11 60. On the go for nearly a hundred years, this specializes in rice and seafood dishes: try the *arroz con almejas* and the delicious *merluza rellena de mariscos* (hake filled with shellfish) or more straightforward dishes such as roast beef with potatoes, washed down with some vintage wines. You have a choice of three smart dining rooms and, in summer, dining on the garden terrace. *Closed Thurs.*

Las Delicias, Barrio Fuejo (by the Evaristo Valle museum), **t** 985 36 02 27. Also in Somió you'll find this long-established, upmarket eaterie, which pairs surf and turf – *lubina al horno* (sea-bass from the oven), *medallones de solomillo, escalopines de ternera a la sidra* – with very good service. *Closed Tues.*

Casa Gerardo, Ctra Nacional in Prendes (8km from Gijón), **t** 985 88 77 97. Breathes new life into traditional Asturian cooking, with innovations like *rodaballo en aceite de canela* (turbot in cinnamon oil) accompanied by tomato marmalade, happily sharing a menu with old favourites like *fabada*. *Closed Mon, and lunch on Fri and Sat.*

Moderate

Santo Remedio, Pza de los Remedios 1, **t** 985 35 91 49. Perhaps the only vegetarian option in all Asturias.

Torremar, C/Ezcurdia 120 (one block back from the beach), **t** 985 33 01 73. Offerings include seafood and Asturian dishes such as *fabes con almejas* (broad beans with clams).

Inexpensive

Sidrería Plaza Mayor, C/Recoletas. One of several convivial places around the plaza; good for a less ambitious dinner.

La Iglesiona, C/Begoña 34, **t** 985 35 42 31. Does an excellent *menú del día*, as well as delicious *menestras* and *raciones*.

Avilés ✉ 33400

This unlikely destination also has a few good restaurants.

San Félix, Av. de los Telares 48, **t** 985 56 51 46 (*expensive–moderate*). An old *sidrería* that is now a restaurant in the classic Spanish style, serving sumptuous seafood (sea bass in champagne, no less).

Café Colón, C/de la Muralla. At least stop for a drink at this the town's gathering spot, where Avilés' history is spelled out in modern murals.

adm free Tues), part of a 2nd-century baths complex notable for its under-floor hypocaustal central heating. Award-winning computer animations explain how the baths worked. This is the start of the main beach, the **Playa de San Lorenzo**. In the new town, the **Museo Etnográfico** (*open Tues–Sat 10–2 and 5–9, Sun 11–2 and 5–9; closed Mon; adm, adm free Tues*) will impart all the secrets of *sidra*-making.

Avilés, to the west, is another industrial town with a disheartening sprawl, but a well-preserved historic centre worth exploring. Just north of Avilés, an old lighthouse guards the *ría*, at **San Juan de Nieva**, and a long, gorgeous beach at **Salinas**.

Oviedo

The ancient and modern capital of Asturias, Oviedo is a working town, with a fine cathedral, a university almost 400 years old, and two of Europe's most exquisite pre-Romanesque churches. Founded by Fruela I in 757 as a fortress guarding the key road over the mountains to the coast, Oviedo served as capital of Christian Spain until the

Getting Around

By Train

All trains now leave from the station at the head of C/Uria in the centre of town. RENFE, **t** 902 24 02 02, has hourly connections to Gijón and less frequent links to León , Barcelona, Burgos, Zaragoza, Pamplona, and to Madrid, Valladolid and Palencia. FEVE trains, **t** 902 10 08 18, run east to Santander and Bilbao, and west along the coast to Ferrol.

By Bus

A new Estación de Autobuses is under construction next to the train station. In the meantime, all buses leave from a cunningly disguised underground terminal on Pza Primo de Rivera, at the end of C/de Fray Ceferino near the train station, reached through a rather dowdy shopping arcade. ALSA, the biggest company, **t** 902 42 22 42, serves destinations throughout Asturias and Northern Spain, as well as Madrid, Sevilla, Barcelona, Valladolid and Valencia; international buses go as far as Paris, Geneva, Zürich and Brussels.

By Car

Parking can be a pain in Oviedo, as can getting around in general. Almost all of the old centre is closed to traffic; as a last resort there is a parking garage underneath the Campo de San Francisco.

Tourist Information

Oviedo: Pza de Alfonso II, El Casto 6, by the cathedral, **t** 985 21 33 85.

Post Office: C/Alonso Quintanilla.

Internet Access: Laser, C/San Francisco 9.

There is a weekly **market** (*Thurs*), and a **flea market** (*Sun*), both in Pza del Fontan.

Where to Stay

Oviedo ✉ 33000

Luxury–Expensive

*******Hotel de la Reconquista**, C/Gil de Jaz 16, **t** 985 24 11 00, **f** 985 24 11 66. A couple of blocks from the Parque de San Francisco, this lovely 17th-century palace has been converted into a plush hotel of the highest order; all rooms have satellite TV and a/c.

Gran Hotel España, C/Jovellanos 2, **t** 985 22 05 96, **f** 985 22 21 40. Elegant and conveniently situated downtown.

*****La Gruta**, Alto de Buenavista (at the west end of town), **t** 985 23 24 50, **f** 985 25 31 41. This snazzy, immaculate hotel offers the best views in town for half as much.

Moderate

La Ovetense, C/San Juan 6, **t** 985 22 08 40. In the centre near the cathedral, this is one of the best options in this category.

Asturian kings conquered León in 1002. The city suffered terribly in the insurrection of 1934 and during the Civil War. It used to earn a living from the surrounding mines, but today Oviedo has the look of a place where people stamp papers for a living.

The Cathedral

The middle of Oviedo (*take C/Uría from the station*) is occupied by the tranquil, shady **Campo de San Francisco**, a typically lavish Spanish city park. From here C/San Francisco leads to the oldest part of the city, and the asymmetrical **Cathedral**, an attractive Gothic temple from the 14th century; its lovely tower with its delicate stone latticework is Oviedo's landmark. In the Capilla Mayor look for an enormous florid 16th-century *retablo* of the life of Christ sculpted by Giralte of Brussels. Best of all, a door in the right transept leads to the original church of Alfonso el Casto, now known as the **Cámara Santa** (*open Mon–Fri 10–1 and 4–8, Sat 10–1 and 4–6.30; closed Sun; adm, adm free Thurs*), strange and semi-barbaric, with fine carvings of the Apostles on the capitals of the outer chamber and disembodied heads on the walls. The upper

****Santa Clara**, C/Santa Clara 1, **t** 985 22 27 27, **f** 985 22 87 37. Also central, this is modern and well-equipped offering good discount rates at weekends.

Inexpensive–Cheap

***Hs Belmonte**, C/Uría 3, **t** 985 24 10 20. A family-run place, one of the best of several inexpensive *hostales* that cluster on and around C/Uría, near the RENFE station.

****Hs Arcos**, C/Magdalena 32 (just off Pza Mayor), **t** 985 21 47 73. It might be nicer to stay in the old centre, notably at this place, where there are some rooms with bath.

P. Riesgo, C/Nueve de Mayo 16, **t** 985 21 89 45. Has cheap and cheerful rooms with shower, on a pedestrianized street near the centre.

Eating Out

Casa Fermín, San Francisco 8 (near the park), **t** 985 21 64 52 (*expensive*). This remains the oldest and the best restaurant, offering classic Asturian cuisine and seasonal Spanish regional dishes in a refined atmosphere (*menú inexpensive*). *Closed Sun.*

La Mar del Medio, C/Mon 18, **t** 985 22 55 75 (*expensive–moderate*). Has excellent fish and seafood in a suitably nautical ambience; arrive early as it fills up quickly at lunch times, or pop in and try the tasty *pintxos*. *Closed Sun eve and Mon.*

El Raitán, **t** 985 21 42 18 (*moderate*). Specializes in grilled meats; a dozen different kinds, on the special **evening** *menú de carnes*.

El Cabroncin, Ctra Paredes 1 (in Lugones, 2km from Oviedo), **t** 985 26 63 80 (*moderate*). For something a bit different, drive out to this charmingly rustic *comedor*, and try the inventive interpretations of traditional Asturian cooking: kidney beans with rabbit cutlets and slivers of *calamari*, followed by truly decadent chocolate ravioli smothered in orange cream.

Villaviciosa, C/Gascona, **t** 985 20 44 12 (*Inexpensive*). Hearty Asturian stews and good *fabadas* bubble away at all the *sidrerias* around C/Gascona. This is one good recommendation.

Entertainment and Nightlife

Oviedo is the centre of Asturian rock, and you can see what the local groups are getting up to in the desperate-looking clubs all along **C/Rosal**, one street south of the Campo de San Francisco. Otherwise, the action is on the nearby streets in the old town, with more clubs and bars for the younger set: Pza Riego, Pza del Fontan, C/Canóniga and C/Ildefonso Martínez. The best places for a simple drink are the informal bars around Fontan.

chamber, the Capilla de San Miguel, was built by Alfonso el Casto in 802 to house the relics of Visigothic Toledo rescued after its capture by the Moors, and largely rebuilt in the 12th century. Today it contains the cathedral's precious treasures: the *Cruz de la Victoria*, supposedly borne by Pelayo at Covadonga, and pictured today on Asturias' coat-of-arms; the *Cruz de los Angeles* (808), a golden cross embedded with huge rubies and carved gems, reputedly made by the angels themselves and donated by Alfonso II; and a silver-plated reliquary chest of 1073. The cathedral is also famous for its relics: a phial of the Virgin Mary's milk and one of Judas' 30 pieces of silver.

The Asturian Pre-Romanesque Churches

Oviedo has the finest of Asturias' post-Visigothic pre-Romanesque churches. Enjoying the patronage of its kings, this little capital can claim the beginnings of medieval architecture, a sophisticated art that seems to have come out of nowhere at a time when most of Christian Europe was still scratching its carrot rows with a short stick. The major influence clearly comes from North Africa or the Middle East, via Christian refugees from those newly Islamized countries. Hints of later Byzantine elements feature in the details, but this is all – Byzantium was 1,700 miles away. Even with these influences, much in these provocative prototypes that never made it to the assembly line is original and beautiful. In 1985 UNESCO declared them the best architecture produced in 9th-century Christian Europe.

The oldest of these churches, **San Julián de los Prados** (*northeast of the centre up C/de Martínez Vigil*) was built by Alfonso el Casto, but more interesting are those built by his successor, Ramiro I. **Santa María de Naranco** and **San Miguel de Lillo** (*open Tues–Sat 9.30–1 and 3–7, Sun and Mon 9.30–1; adm, adm free Mon*) can be found halfway up the Cuesta de Naranco, a hill overlooking the town (*facing the RENFE station, turn left to the sign at the bridge over the tracks and continue 3km; city bus No.6 makes cameo appearances, starting from C/Gil de Jaz*). Incredibly, the perfectly proportioned Santa María is believed to have been part of the king's summer palace. Built of a fair golden stone, it is an enchanting building supported by unusual flat buttresses and flanked by two porches. The lower level is believed to have served as a waiting chamber; the upper, with a rough-hewn altar on the porch, was the main hall. Inside are blind arches of subtly decreasing height, topped by round medallions.

Up the road, San Miguel is a more traditional cruciform church, although of stunted proportions after an ancient amputation removed two-thirds of the original length. Its round windows are adorned with beautiful stone traceries, and what the guides claim to be a circus scene is carved on the door jamb.

The Asturian Hinterland and Cantabrian Mountains

The principality, beyond the coast and the Picos, is *terra incognita* for most foreigners – a hilly, wooded land of small mining towns and agricultural villages, criss-crossed with walking paths. Much of it is protected, especially in the national hunting

Getting Around

By Train

The RENFE train between Oviedo and León stops at Pajares and Pola de Lena.

By Bus

All the main towns in southern Asturias can be reached by bus. ALSA buses from Oviedo, Pza Primo de Rivera, **t** 985 28 12 20, go to Salas, Puerto de Somiedo, Cangas del Narcea, Tineo and Pola de Allande. Empresa Fernández, Aniceto Sala, Oviedo, **t** 985 23 83 90, has buses to Mieres, Pola de Lena and Turón; there are also a six or so daily buses down the west coast to Cudillero and Luarca, as well as from Gijón. Alcotán, C/Padre Suárez 27, Oviedo, **t** 985 21 76 17, has buses to Pola de Laviana.

By Car

If you're driving in the snow, it's essential to call ahead for road conditions, **t** 985 25 46 11. For car hire, shop around the main companies in Oviedo, along C/Ventura Rodríguez.

Tourist Information

Salas: Pza de la Campa, **t** 985 83 09 88.
Tuñón: **t** 985 76 15 34.
Pola de Somiedo: Centro de Recepción e Interpretación del Parque, **t** 985 76 37 58.
Tineo: C/Mayor, **t** 985 80 01 87.
Cangas del Narcea: C/P. L. Alvarez 17 (in the bus station), **t** 985 81 14 98.

There are **markets** in **Mieres** (*Sun*); in **Grado** (*Wed* and *Sun*); in **Pola de Somiedo** (*Tues*); in **Tineo** (*Thurs*) and in **Cangas del Narcea** (*Sat*).

Skiing

Valgrande Pajares, 3km from the Busdongo train station, offers 15 slopes from the very difficult to the very easy, 10 lifts and two chairlifts, **t** 985 49 61 23.
San Isidro, near Puebla de Lillo (León province), offers three very difficult runs in the Cebolledo circuit, as well as five of average difficulty and four easy ones; there's a chair-lift and seven ski lifts, **t** 985 73 50 66. There are a couple of hotels at Puebla de Lillo, but no public transport.
Lietariegos Pass, San Emiliano, is a ski installation on the slopes of Peña Ubiña.
Maraña, near Riaño; also on Peña Ubiña.

Where to Stay and Eat

Puerto de Pajares ✉ 33693

Albergue Toribión de Llanos, in Brañillín, **t** 985 95 70 40 (*cheap–inexpensive*). Provides dormitories and some double rooms; you can step straight out of the hotel and on to the ski lifts.

preserves that cover the northern slopes of the Cordillera Cantábrica. The coast is excellent – rugged cliffs, few tourists, plenty of shellfish and beaches everywhere. Public transport is limited throughout the area, and you'd do well to rent a car – and pack a big lunch – before setting out. Be sure to pick up one of the large, detailed maps at the tourist office in Oviedo.

Around Oviedo: Miners' Valleys and More Churches

Southeast of Oviedo, the AS244 passes **Pola de Laviana**, a typical Asturian copper-mining town on its way to Reres National Reserve and the beautiful mountain pass, **Puerto de Tarna**. The next pass to the west, **Puerto San Isidro**, has a major ski installation (both passes can be reached by bus from Pueblo de Lillo in León province).

Directly south of Oviedo, along the train route and highway to León, the views become increasingly magnificent as you ascend to the dramatic **Puerto de Pajares**, another ski spot on the border with Léon. The landmark in this part of the Cantabrian mountains is the jagged-peaked 7,855ft **Peña Ubiña**, which sturdy walkers can tackle

Puerto de Pajares, **t 985 95 70 36 (*cheap*). A little further from the slopes; it has fairly basic rooms with bath and central heating.

La Rectoral de Tuiza, in Tuiza de Arriba, **t** 985 45 14 20 (*expensive*). Families and walkers tackling the heights of Peña Ubiña can set up base in a complete *casa rural* with space for up to five, in a beautiful setting high up in the mountains.

Mieres ✉ 33600

Hs Villa de Mieres, C/Teodoro Cuesta 33 (off the Oviedo–León road), **t** 985 46 70 04 (*cheap*). Offers good home cooking in modern, smart surroundings.

Casa Villa, C/Aller, **t** 985 46 00 33 (*moderate*). Serves a broad variety of Asturian favourites.

Salas ✉ 33600

Salas is a convenient stopover on the N634, with a few inexpensive *hostales* over bars. There are basic camp sites within the Somiedo Park at Valle de Lago and Saliencia.

Castillo de Valdés, Pza Campa, **t** 985 83 22 22, **f** 985 83 22 99 (*inexpensive*). A restored 16th-century palace; its adjoining **restaurant** is the local dining hot spot. Servings include imaginative Asturian dishes, and locally fished salmon.

Pola de Somiedo ✉ 33840

Casa Miño, C/Rafael Rey Lopez, **t** 985 76 37 30, **f** 985 76 37 50 (*moderate*). The most comfortable choice in these parts, with nicely furnished spacious rooms and central heating – important at these altitudes.

Mierel, C/Fernando Alvarez, **t** 985 76 39 93 (*inexpensive*). Small but perfectly formed, with individually decorated rooms and three apartments for longer stays. The **restaurant** serves hearty mountain meals and wicked *fabadas*.

Casa Cobrana, in Valle del Lago, **t** 985 76 37 48 (*cheap*). Offers simple, peaceful comfort and good meals, at the head of the beautiful trail to Lago del Valle.

Cangas del Narcea ✉ 33800

Cangas has the widest range of choices in this region.

*Peña Grande**, out on the main road, **t** 985 81 23 92 (*inexpensive*). One of the best places to stay, with a **restaurant**.

*Hotel La Pista**, Vega de Rengos (20km south), **t** 985 91 10 04 (*inexpensive*). Near the entrance to Bosque de Muniellos, this has four good-value rooms with wooden floors and pitched ceilings, a **restaurant** (*inexpensive*) and an extremely welcoming owner.

Tineo ✉ 33870

Don Miguel, El Viso, **t** 985 80 03 25 (*cheap*). A *hostal* with a handful of rooms.

Hs Casa Sole, on the main road, **t** 985 80 60 44 (*cheap*). The least expensive, offering pleasant rooms with or without bath.

in around four or five hours from **Tuiza de Arriba** (*to reach Tuiza, take the side road from the highway at Campomanes*). From Pajares, you can make the much shorter climb up the 5,580ft **Pico de los Celleros**.

Up to the *Cordillera*, and Somiedo National Park

Southwest of Oviedo, the Cantabrian mountains harbour the wild **Parque Natural de Somiedo**, the wildlife stronghold of the Cordillera. While bears and wolves roam amid dense beech and oak forests, wallcreepers and even lammergeyers circle the vertical crags stretching up to towering, 7,000ft-high peaks.

One approach is by way of **Trubia**, a village known mostly for its enormous armament works. Ten kilometres south of Trubia on the road to the park you can stop at **Tuñón** for another one of Asturia's churches, **San Adrián**, built by Alfonso III (866–910). Inside are some of the oldest frescoes anywhere in Spain, traces of sun symbols over the altar and zigzag motifs taken straight from the Grand Mosque of Córdoba. The lady in the tobacco shop opposite has the key, but the only guide is the unusually friendly bat that lives in the choir.

The Dress Rehearsal

The event of the 20th century in Asturias was the epic miners' revolt of 1934, a full-scale battle that eerily prefigured the Spanish Civil War. Because of the large numbers of workers in mining and industry, Asturias was politically the odd man out, an island of belligerent Marxists in the middle of the arch-conservative northwest. Mining and metalworking go way back in Asturias, but really took off at the beginning of the 20th century, when *indianos* forced home by Spain's loss of Cuba and the Philippines began to invest their money here. In the First World War, Spanish neutrality made for a boom in the mining areas, one which collapsed in the 1920s, leaving Asturias with the angriest proletariat in Spain.

Along with the Basques and Catalans, Asturians were strong supporters of the Republic when it appeared in 1931 but, for many of their leaders, the new regime was only a stepping stone to Socialism. The depression increased popular discontent, but what really set the workers boiling was the radical right-wing national government elected in 1934. Under Prime Minister Gil Robles, it began dismantling all the reforms of its leftist predecessors and openly postured for the restoration of the monarchy. On 4 October 1934 the trade unions declared a general strike in Asturias in protest. Barcelona and Madrid also rose up but failed to follow through, leaving the Asturians on their own and in a fighting mood. The main centres of the revolt were Mieres, Sama and Oviedo, but it was the munitions works at Trubia, near Somiedo, that turned the strike into a war. The workers occupied it and seized some 30,000 rifles inside. Soon there was a 30,000-man 'Red Army', and a revolutionary committee was formed to govern the province.

The government sent in a dependable general named Mola, leading a force made up mainly of Moroccan troops – northern Morocco was still a Spanish protectorate. The Moors were mercenaries who had fought against their own people, but they were fiercely loyal to their commander, a certain Francisco Franco. Franco, a Galician married to an Asturian woman, felt right at home. He had already led troops, using the Spanish Foreign Legion, to crush a general strike in Asturias in 1917. The Legion was also present in 1934. An outfit not much like the romantic French version, this one was now led by a fascist psychopath named Millan Astray, famous for his missing arm and eye-patch. As for the Moors, some of them must have enjoyed the irony of a Spanish commander, an heir to Pelayo, bringing them to a place where they hadn't set foot for a thousand years. The government had to make its point, and the revolt was crushed quickly and with the utmost ferocity. Many of the mining towns were thoroughly wrecked, and the troops slaughtered nearly 1,300 Asturians in reprisals after the surrender on 19 October. A year and a half later, after new elections brought the leftist Popular Front to power, the coup that began the Civil War started with the same cast of characters: General Mola, who was to be the new dictator, but who died in an air crash at the start; the Foreign Legion; and the inevitable Francisco Franco, whose Moroccans won him the title of *caudillo* (leader). The best-equipped and trained forces in Spain, they used their practice in Asturias to get the jump on the disorganized government and citizens' militias, and gained control of much of Spain within a month, an advantage that helped assure the Nationalists' final victory.

Further south, the villages of **Proaza** and **Caranga** are separated by a pretty gorge, the **Desfiladero del Teverga**, beyond which the road cuts south through a magnificent forest to the Puerto Ventana, perhaps the least-used Asturian mountain pass. Just the other side, from the Leonese village of **Torrestio**, you can hike in three hours into the heart of Somiedo and its mysterious lakes.

A second approach to Somiedo is via the N634, the main road west from Oviedo. This will take you through the fat village of **Grado**, where everybody comes on Wednesday and Sunday for the markets, and **Salas**, with its medieval monuments and palaces. From Salas you can head south and follow the valley of the Pigüeña towards Somiedo. Many *vaqueros* still live in the vicinity – some of their conical-roofed *pallozas* (huts), along with several Celtic *castros* (hill forts) lie further up towards **Pola de Somiedo**, the chief town in the district.

West of Oviedo: Ancient Pottery and Primeval Forests

Back on the main route west from Oviedo, after Salas the next village is **Tineo**, a great trout-fishing area crossed by a branch of the Santiago pilgrimage route. Further south, a dirt road leads up to the tiny borough of **Llamas del Mouro**, where potters, isolated from the rest of the world, still create the shiny black ceramics made by their Celto-Iberian ancestors. The pieces are fired in the ancient style, in circular ovens buried in the earth. Only the family of Jesús Rodríguez Garrido continues to make and fire pottery; they sell it too.

Cangas del Narcea, the largest town in southwest Asturias, is modern and has little to waylay you; head instead further south to **Pico de la Masa** (near Puerto del Connio) for the view over the magnificent 5,000ha **Bosque de Muniellos** (*only 20 people a day are allowed into the forest; make sure you write in advance to the* ***Agencia de Medio Ambiente del Principado de Asturias****, 1 Pza General Ordóñez, Oviedo 33007*), one of Europe's last and most extensive forests of primeval oak and beech. A strictly protected wildlife preserve, it is the last refuge of the rare urogallo, a kind of capercaillie with red eyebrows. The trail through the forest begins at **Tablizas**, a short hike from Moal. The whole hike takes about five-and-a-half hours and will leave you mourning for ancient times, when (they say) a squirrel could cross the whole of Iberia without ever touching the ground. East of Muniellos lies the **Reserva Nacional de Degaña**, another lovely, wooded area with meadows and small glacial lakes, which in Roman times was mined for its gold.

Asturias' Western Coast

The Asturian coast west of Avilés could well be the best chance in this book for a peaceful and agreeable seaside holiday. The shoreline itself does not seem dramatic until you see it close up: wild cliffs of jumbled, glittering metamorphic rock, mixed in with long stretches of beach where you can easily find uncrowded spots even on August weekends. Cudillero and Luarca happen to be two of the most delightful seaside villages on earth, and there are plenty of isolated beaches between them.

Tourist Information

Cudillero: Pza de San Pedro, **t** 985 59 01 18 (*summer only*).

Luarca: Olavarrieta 27, **t** 985 64 00 83 (*summer only*).

Navia: Pza del Ayuntamiento, **t** 985 63 00 94 (*summer only*).

Castropol: Los Callejones, **t** 985 63 51 13 (*summer only*).

There are **markets** in **Cudillero** and **Navia** (*Fri*), and in **Tapia de Casariego** (*Mon* and *Fri*).

Where to Stay and Eat

Cudillero ✉ 33150

Moderate

★★**Azpiazu**, Playa de Aguilar, **t** 985 58 32 10, **f** 985 58 36 85. The best-known hotel on Playa de Aguilar; it specializes in seafood, and has a terrace where you can tuck into shellfish soup and cider-marinated dishes.

★★**La Casona de Pio**, C/Río Frío 3, **t** 985 59 15 12. Sympathetically designed to fit into the old port, this modern establishment provides style and comfort, right in the centre.

★**La Lupa**, in San Juan de la Piñera (2km east of the village), **t** 985 59 09 73. Perhaps the best place to sleep in this village is at this old inn.

Inexpensive

P. Alver, C/Garcia de la Concha 8, **t** 985 59 00 05. Colourful paintings adorn the breezy rooms in this welcoming, central *pensión*.

P. El Camarote, C/Garcia de la Concha 4, **t** 985 59 12 02. Has impressively large rooms with bath, and is run by a friendly family.

For dinner, head for the seafront, where numerous **restaurants** line the tiny harbour.

Casa Marino, **t** 985 59 01 86 (*moderate*). In a lovely setting with a view of the sea and mountains, Concha de Artedo has one of the many pretty beaches in the area (off the coastal road west of Cudillero). Look out for this place, which serves top-class seafood, and a memorable *zarzuela de mariscos y pescados* (shellfish and fish casserole).

El Remo. A less expensive place, also on the harbour, that does a good *paella*.

Luarca ✉ 33700

★★★**Gayoso**, Pso Gómez, **t** 985 64 00 54 (*expensive*). Bright, central and airy, this is Luarca's one swanky hotel.

★★**Casa Consuelo**, at Otur (6km west of town on the N634), **t** 985 47 07 67 (*inexpensive*). One of the best **hotel-restaurants** in the area, where the food served in the large dining rooms attracts people from miles around with classic Asturian *fabada* and cider, and a good-value *menú*.

★**Hs Oria**, C/Crucero, **t** 985 64 03 85 (*inexpensive*). This offers clean rooms with bath.

Los Cantiles, at Villar, **t** 985 64 09 38 (*inexpensive*). The closest camp site, on the cliffs above Luarca.

La Mesón del Mar (*moderate*). As in Cudillero, for dinner you need look no further than the harbour; nearly every restaurant has outside tables to enjoy the view. This one at the far end offers a wonderful seafood *menú gastronómico* with a bit of everything in the day's catch; well worth the price.

La Dársena (*inexpensive*). The least expensive spot on the harbour (no tables outside), and a good one.

Figueras del Mar ✉ 33793

★★★**Palacete Peñalba**, El Cotarelo, **t** 985 63 61 25, **f** 985 63 62 47 (*moderate*). At the farthest western limit of Asturias, near Castropol, you'll find the region's loveliest hotel. Set in a glorious Art Nouveau mansion designed by a follower of Gaudí, it is a listed monument, and retains its gardens and many of its original furnishings; all rooms have TV and minibar.

Cudillero and Luarca

The first resort west of Avilés, **Cudillero** was for many years well protected from the tourist hordes by its geography; the only way into this fishing village was along its narrow, cobbled main street, which snakes down almost vertically for around three kilometres. The hordes can now sweep down to Cudillero on a smooth new road, straight into the impossibly picturesque little harbour at the bottom of the cliffs. Still there are few hotels, and except for the summer days when it fills up with *madrileño* day-trippers, Cudillero would be a perfect place to hide away for a few days. If you have your own car you can find plenty of good beaches nearby, especially the broad **Playa de la Cueva** (visible from a high viaduct on the coast highway, though in fact it is many miles away).

Luarca, with its sheltered harbour at the mouth of the Río Negro, is a little more tourist-orientated, but it is still in every respect the most satisfactory place for a holiday on Spain's northern coast. The village was an important place in medieval times, first as a whaling port and then from trade with the Americas. The best way to see it is to follow the first signposted road in from the east – a back road that will take you to the cemetery, high on a cliff with a stunning view over the village below. Luarca is still an important fishing port, mostly for tuna, and the harbourfront ensemble makes a pretty photograph. Old Luarca stretches inland from there, with some stately palaces from the 17th and 18th centuries, and some old quarters with narrow alleys climbing up the steep hills.

There is a fairly acceptable beach right in the centre of Luarca, but for something special head for **Playa del Barayo**, a beautiful natural area to the west.

Southwest of **Navia** at **Coaña** you can visit the extensive remains of another Celtic *castro* – foundations of stone walls, paved streets and the circular foundations of houses. The similarity between these and the *vaquero* huts led some to believe that the *vaqueros* were a lost Celtic tribe. Near the main road, there's a monolith carved with the star symbol so widespread in northern Spain. The Asturian coast ends with **Castropol**, another attractive fishing port sheltered on the broad Ría de Ribadeo.

Galicia

If Asturias is Spain's Wales, then Galicia is in many ways its Ireland, for many years so far removed from the mainstream of Spanish life that it might as well have been an island. Here the Celtic invaders of 1000 BC found their cosiest niche, in the same kind of rain-swept, green land facing the setting sun that their brethren had settled farther north in Brittany and Cornwall. The Moors left no mark in Galicia, having been expelled in the 8th century by the kings of Asturias – who promptly turned their attention to the richer spoils of the south.

While the rest of the north expanded into the newly won lands of the Reconquista, the Galicians, or *gallegos*, were hemmed in by Portugal and forced to turn inwards, dividing their land into ever smaller holdings with every generation. Famines were common and, as soon as the New World was discovered, they emigrated in droves. Even today Galicia is one of the poorest regions in Spain, yet few places have such a lasting charm. The coastline is pierced by a dozen estuaries, or *rías*, wild and scenic in the north, and in the south, sheltering serene beaches and tiny coves, perfect for the smuggling that has long been a mainstay of the economy. Rivers in deep, narrow valleys with fantasy names – the Éo, the Ulla, the Lor, the Sil and Jallas – spill down wild mountains on their way to the sea. Bright green gardens cover every inch of cultivable land, although a third of the acreage is wasted by the granite walls each Gallego has erected around his plot. Each farm, however small, has a sturdy, self-sufficient air, with its cow and conical hayrack, its trellis of vines (producing excellent white wines similar to Portugal's 'green' wines) and compact rows of turnips, peppers, maize, cabbage, peas and Spain's finest potatoes. Many cottages have granaries (*hórreos*), monumental pieces of granite set up on pillars to protect the grain from rodents and wet, with window-like vents to permit air to circulate, topped by a gabled roof with crosses. Early travellers mistook them for hermitages.

Because of the endless division of land, much of Galicia is covered higgledy-piggledy with farms and houses in some 31,000 'villages' (most with populations of 100–200), sprinkled here and there with the showy bungalows of the *americanos* who made their fortunes in Argentina. Many older houses have balconies closed in by glass 'crystal galleries', adorned with elaborate white mullions. Also distinctly *gallego* are

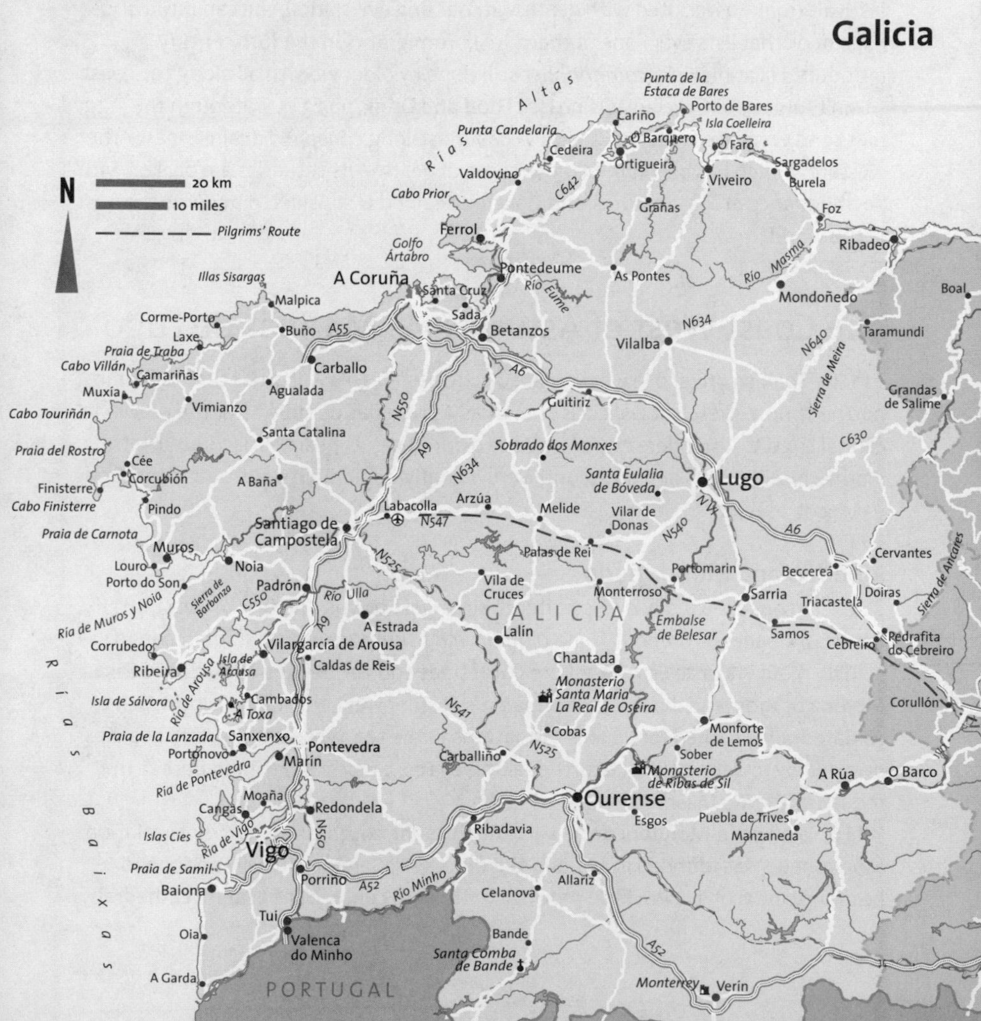

the sculpted granite crosses seen at crossroads. Some apparently guided pilgrims, or marked out the high roads, or fulfilled vows, or perhaps even served the same geomantic organization as Neolithic menhirs and dolmens, only carved into acceptable Christian forms. In the Rías Baixas, and along the rivers leading into them, you'll see the stately manor country villas the Gallegos call *pazos*, from the Roman *palatio*.

Galicia's language, Gallego, is chock-full of x's (pronounced 'sh') and closely related to Portuguese, and spoken by a greater percentage of the population than Basque or Catalan are in their respective regions. Even García Lorca penned verses in Gallego, inspired by the language of Alfonso the Wise's masterpiece, the *Cantigas de Santa María* and the evocative poetry of Rosalía de Castro (1837–85, especially her *Cantares Gallegos*). Rosalía was a key figure in the Rexurdimento (Literary Renaissance), inspired by the Catalans and, similarly, a forerunner of Spain's nationalist movements.

Culturally, Galicia has always looked to its ancient roots. The national instrument, the gaita, is very similar to Breton or Irish bagpipes, and Gallegos like nothing better than to give it a good blow at festivals. Celtic influences are also strong in Galicia's festivals (many associated with death, witches and evil spirits); you can buy a 400-page book that lists every one of them. Irish immigrants in the 16th century introduced lace-making (*camarinhas*), still done by older women all along the coast.

Don't forget the Galician cuisine (*see* **Food and Drink**, pp.63–5). Although the jagged rocks and windswept seas of Galicia's coast have long conspired against man – the western stretch has been dubbed the 'coast of death' – its estuaries are packed with an abundance of sea creatures, and Galician seafood is considered by some the best in the world.

The Coast West of Asturias: As Mariñas de Lugo

In the Spanish drive to leave no coast unchristened, this wild Atlantic-thundered northernmost stretch of Galicia is known as As Mariñas de Lugo after the provincial capital Lugo. It surrenders every so often to admit sandy beaches decorated with storm-chiselled cliffs and rocks; until very recently, deplorable slow roads conspired to keep it a secret.

Ribadeo and Mondoñedo

Galician *rías* are usually named after their largest towns. The first *ría* west of Asturias, **Ribadeo**, is named after a piquant old fishing town that staggers up to a dusty main **Praza de España**, where palm trees and the delightfully eclectic **Casa Morena** of 1905 lend it a lost Californian air. Further west, the long, sandy beach of **As Catedrais** is named for its rock formations in the sea, while other pretty beaches dwarfed by towering cliffs lie further along by **Foz**, a workaday fishing port at the mouth of the Rio Masma.

If Foz is no prize, **Mondoñedo**, 18 kilometres to the south, offers some consolation. Mondoñedo was founded in 1117, and the diocese of San Martín de Mondoñedo became capital of its own little province in the 15th century. The granite **cathedral**

Getting Around

Besides **buses** from Lugo, Gijón and A Coruña, the **FEVE** train from Gijón or Oviedo makes several trips each day along the coast to Ferrol, stopping at Ribadeo, Foz, Burela, Viveiro, Covas, O Barqueiro and Ortigueira.

Tourist Information

Ribadeo: Pza de España, **t** 982 12 86 89.
Viveiro: Av. Ramón Canosa, **t** 982 56 08 79.

There are **markets** in **Mondoñedo** (*Thurs* and *Sun*); in **Foz** (*Tues*); in **Viveiro** (*Mon*, *Thurs* and *Sat*); and **Cedeira** has a fish market (*daily*), and a market for other food (*Wed* and *Sat*).

Where to Stay and Eat

Ribadeo ✉ 27700

*****Parador de Ribadeo**, C/Amador Fernández, **t** 982 12 88 25, **f** 982 12 83 46, *ribadeo@parador.es* (*expensive*). If short on atmosphere, this is comfortable and homey, and has fine views over the harbour, set in a scenic, quiet spot overlooking the *ría*;the **restaurant** features the day's catch.

***Hs Ros Mary**, C/San Francisco 3, **t/f** 982 12 86 78 (*inexpensive*). Run by a very friendly old gentleman; has pleasant if uninspiring rooms just off Pza de España.

Huerta de Obe, Ctra Santa Cruz, **t** 982 12 87 15 (*moderate*). The beaches west towards Foz are well supplied with campsites, but if you prefer a *casa de campo*, this comfortable place provides many services, and a pool.

Oxardín, C/Reinante 20, **t** 982 11 02 22 (*moderate*). Book a table here to feast on baked oysters or turbot with razor-shell clams (*longueirós*). *Closed Mon in winter.*

Mondoñedo ✉ 27740

***Montero II**, C/Candido Martínez 8 (across from the cathedral), **t** 982 52 10 41 (*inexpensive*). For character, opt for this recently restored place decorated with antiques.

Avoltiña, Ctra Lorenzana (*inexpensive*). Here you can have a simple yet satisfying dinner.

Viveiro ✉ 27850

Most places offer big discounts off season.

El Pazo da Trave, in Galdo, **t** 982 59 81 63, **f** 982 59 80 40 (*expensive–moderate*). A luxurious old stately home in the countryside with an excellent **restaurant**, serving marine exotica such as *cebiche de bonito*.

****Las Sirenas**, **t** 982 56 02 00, **f** 982 55 12 67 (*moderate*). Among a clutch of hotels along Covas beach; smart, with rooms, flats and studios sleeping up to four. *Open year round.*

***Hospedaje Garcia**, Praza Maior, **t** 982 56 06 76 (*cheap*). Has one self-contained apartment and a few bathless but spotless rooms, most with balconies overlooking the square.

O Muro, C/Pardo de Cela 28, **t** 982 56 08 23 (*moderate*). Just inside the walls, serving up steaming plates of *pulpo*.

was begun in 1219 and when the time came to slap on a Baroque façade, it was done with surgical discretion, preserving the Romanesque portal and Gothic rose window in harmonious blind arches. The interior is still late Romanesque and decorated with some remarkable 14th-century frescoes of the Massacre of the Innocents; there's also a wonderful organ with trumpets (1710) and a painted Gothic statue known as the Virgen Inglesa, which was brought over from St Paul's in London for safekeeping during the Reformation. On the pretty Alameda, the Baroque church **Os Remedios** is decorated with grand Churrigueresque *retablos*, and lots of candles, too, for it's said the remedies in its name are usually granted.

Las Rías Altas: West of Foz to Viveiro, O Barqueiro and Ortigueira

To the west, beyond the ceramic town of **Sargadelos**, the Rías Altas (Upper Estuaries) begin in earnest, offering some of the best wild and windy coastal scenery in Iberia. Fragrant eucalyptus groves dot the coast around **Viveiro**, the choice place to stay in the Rías Altas, sheltered by its partly ruined medieval walls from the ravages of the Atlantic, automobiles, and time itself. In the 18th century it imported linen from the Baltic in exchange for Galician agricultural goods but these days its outer fishing port **Celeiro**, on the opposite side of the estuary, deals mostly in sardines. Three medieval gates survive, along with the fancy **Puerta de Carlos V** (1548) on Av. Galicia, erected to curry favour with Charles V. Inside, the narrow lanes and pretty **Praza de Pastor Díaz** are paved in granite and lined with medieval houses sucking in light through their *solanas*, while the austere but pure 12th-century Romanesque **Santa María del Campo** provides a town centrepiece. Viveiro has some ravishing beaches: the sand plain of **Covas** sweeping out to a treetop rock 'castle', **O Faro** facing the ocean, and **Xilloi** and **Ares** near Celeiro, where legend has it an ancient city sank into the sea for refusing to hear the preaching of St James.

The next estuary west, the **Ría do Barqueiro**, provides a magnificent setting for the little hamlet of **Vicendo** and its pretty azalea gardens, the wide beach at **Arealonga** and, over the *ría*, for **O Barqueiro**, a picture-postcard amphitheatre of white, slate-roofed houses cupped around a bijou lobster port, in a landscape of piney fjords. A road leads down the *ría* to the tiny fishing hamlet and fabulous curling sandy beach of **Bares**, marked by a lighthouse and blocks of walls from the days when it served as a port for Phoenician ships en route to the tin mines of Cornwall.

On the east bank of the **Ría de Santa María de Ortigueira**, **Ortiguera** is a peaceful, unremarkable town with white sandy beaches that never get too crowded, while on the west bank the long toes of the Sierra de Capelada extend to Cape Ortegal, where the fishing village of **Cariño** is the last to look over the Cantabrian sea.

Cliffs, Lizards and Cedeira

West of Cariño the road takes in spectacular views of the 2,008ft cliffs of the **Garita de Herbeira** en route to the village and tiny sanctuary of **San Andrés de Teixido**, perched on savage, wave-battered cliffs. Wild horses roam the meadows and woodlands here, and pilgrims flow in year round for, as the saying goes, '*A San Andrés de Teixido, que no vai vivo vai morto*' ('If you don't go while alive, you'll go dead') – reincarnated as a lizard or toad, creatures which are never harmed in the village. On 8 September, the dead are given a formal invitation to the festival, when colourful, archaic dough figures are baked to be consumed before Mass, and pilgrims who over the past year had a close brush with the Grim Reaper are carried to the church in coffins. A corniche road continues to the lovely town of **Cedeira**, which marks a series of stunning beaches, dunes and and lagoons that stretch all the way to Ferrol.

The Galician Interior: the Road to Santiago

Pilgrims who made it as far as Villafranca del Bierzo (*see* p.441) had to gird their loins for one last trial: the Puerto Pedrafita in the Sierra de Ancares. This is Galicia at its wildest, driest and bleakest, deceptively carpeted with blooms in the spring, but the haunt of werewolves and witches when the sun goes down – a zone apart, bound in dreams and legends. The regional government, the Xunta de Galicia, has recently restored the atmospheric old *camino francés* and placed yellow scallop-shell markers every 500m. The *camino* itself rarely coincides with the highways, making this last leg of the journey especially pleasant for walkers.

O Cebreiro, Os Ancares, and the Pilgrim's Road

After Villafranca, the *camino* (and the road), ascends relentlessly to the 3,609ft pass at **Pedrafita**. Here, in 1809, Sir John Moore's troops – fleeing to A Coruña, with Marshal Soult's terrible army in hot pursuit – nearly rebelled. Discipline had already vanished in Villafranca, where the soldiers had sacked, raped and looted the homes of their Spanish allies; at Pedrafita and at **O Cebreiro**, another 650ft up and a famous brunt of blizzards, hundreds of men froze to death. Such was their haste that the soldiers threw thousands of pounds in gold – the army's pay – over the cliff, along with hundreds of horses, while all the women and children were abandoned in the icy wilderness. It was one of the blackest pages in the history of the British army, and a near miracle that Moore was able to restore order and continue to the coast.

Today O Cebreiro has a huge car park to allow everyone to enjoy the tremendous views (in good weather) and have a look at the village's Celtic *pallozas*, oval stone huts topped with conical straw roofs. A cluster of four now houses the **Museo de Artes y Costumbres Populares** (*usually open 12–2 and 5–7*). Pilgrims never failed to pay their respects in the squat slate church of **Santa María del Cebreiro**, where one of the greatest miracles of the road took place: in the late 13th century, an old priest, tired of celebrating Mass for just one shepherd in the winter, was grumbling away during the Transfiguration when he and his parishioner were astonished to see the host transformed into flesh and the wine into blood. The chalice is displayed in the right aisle; next to it are the miraculous paten and a silver reliquary for the blood and flesh donated by celebrity pilgrims Ferdinand V and Isabel I in 1489.

O Cebreiro and the mighty mountains to the north form part of the **Reserva Nacional de Os Ancares**, part refuge of the rare capercaillie (especially around Degrada) and part hunting reserve of roebuck and boar. **Becerreá**, on the Lugo road, is the main base for excursions into Os Ancares. From O Cebreiro, the *camino* ascends vertiginously to **O Poio** pass (4,387ft), but from here it's all downhill through mountain meadows, chestnut groves and tiny hamlets. During the construction of the cathedral at Compostela, every pilgrim would pick up a chunk of limestone in the quarries outside Triacastela, and carry it 100km to the kilns to be melted into mortar.

At San Xil, the *camino* splits and one branch passes down the Ouribio valley to the huge Benedictine **Abadía de San Xulián** (*open 10.30–1 and 4.30–7*) at Samos. Founded in 655, abandoned with the arrival of the Moors but rebuilt a few years later, the abbey had a famous library in the Middle Ages. The tiny slate chapel of San Salvador is from the 9th century, but the medieval monastery burned down in the 16th century and its replacement in 1951, leading to the reconstruction of the two cloisters, one late Gothic and the other, larger, very strict and buttoned-down Spanish Baroque. In the centre flows the lovely Fountain of the Nereids, said to be the work of Velázquez.

Getting Around

By Bus

Lugo's bus station, Pza de Constitución, **t** 982 22 39 85, serves the towns in this section; buses from Lugo to León pass through Becerreá and Pedrafita.

By Train

Lugo and the junction at Monforte de Lemos are linked by train to León, A Coruña, Ourense and Vigo, with Talgos to Zaragoza, Barcelona, Bilbao and Irún. Lugo's station is on Pza Conde de Fontao, **t** 982 22 21 41. There's a RENFE office at Pza Maior 27, **t** 982 22 55 03.

Tourist Information

Lugo: Pza Maior 27, **t** 982 23 13 61.

Post Office: Rúa San Pedro 5.

Internet Access: Cybercafés (*cibers* in Galicia) congregate around Rúa Vilalba, just outside the walls.

Where to Stay and Eat

O Cebreiro and Os Ancares ✉ 27600

****Hs San Giraldo de Aurillac**, near the *pallozas*, **t** 982 36 71 25 (*inexpensive*). Now a *mesón*, offering authentically medieval rooms in a Benedictine convent founded by monks from St Géraud d'Aurillac in France in the 11th century.

****Hs Piornedo**, in Cervantes, **t** 982 16 15 87 (*inexpensive*). A stone building with reasonable rooms and lovely mountain views.

You will find other places to stay in **Becerreá**, which has some basic *hostales*, as well as a few of bars that serve decent meals.

Sarriá ✉ 27600

*****Alfonso IX**, Peregrino 29, **t** 982 53 00 05, **f** 982 53 12 61 (*moderate*). Sarriá has plenty of choices; this one also has a good **restaurant**.

****Hs Londres**, Calvo Sotelo 13, **t** 982 53 24 56, **f** 982 53 30 06 (*inexpensive*). Has doubles with baths for less.

Casa Nova de Rente, Barbadelo, **t** 982 18 78 54. Offers comfortable rooms in a countryside environment for a good price.

Lugo ✉ 27000

******Gran Hotel Lugo**, Av. Ramón Ferreiro 21, **t** 982 22 41 52, **f** 982 24 16 60 (*expensive*). At the top of the scale, offering a pool, piano bar, a/c, a good seafood **restaurant** (Os Marisqueiros) and a pizzeria.

*****Méndez Núñez**, Reina 1, **t** 982 23 07 11, **f** 982 22 97 38 (*moderate*). Within the walls, with modern rooms.

***España**, Rúa Vilalba 2, **t** 982 23 15 40 (*inexpensive*). Has good-value, functional rooms with views over to the cathedral.

Although Lugo boasts of quirky delicacies such as pancakes with pig's blood, it also has good seafood restaurants:

Alberto, Rúa da Cruz, **t** 982 22 85 72 (*moderate*). One of the best, offering classic and modern Galician dishes. *Closed Sun*.

Restaurante La Barra, Rúa Pracer 4, **t** 982 25 29 20 (*moderate*). Serves mouthwatering meat and fish in an Art Deco-meets-Starbucks ambience.

Campos, Rúa Nova 4, **t** 982 22 97 43 (*inexpensive*). Has traditional Gallego suckling-pig, octopus and seasonal game dishes.

Pulperia Palmira, Pza Comandante Manso 17 (*cheap*). An ultra-basic but very friendly *comedor*; share a table, and feast on mountains of fresh octopus at bargain prices.

Vilalba ✉ 27400

*****Parador Condes de Vilalba**, Valeriano Valdesuso, **t** 982 51 00 11, **f** 982 51 00 90, *vilalba@parador.es* (*expensive*). This crenellated fortress bestows on its visitors feudal fancies – the windows in the 10ft-thick walls were made to shoot arrows at attackers far below. Book early to nab one of its six rooms, all centrally heated, and equipped with modern necessities like TVs and minibars. The **restaurant** in the cellar offers baronial dining on free-range capons, fresh Galician produce and wine. *Closed Dec*.

*****Villamartín**, Av. Tierra Llana, **t** 982 51 12 15, **f** 982 51 11 35 (*inexpensive*). This is modern, functional and half the price of the *parador*.

Castroverde ✉ 49110

Pazo de Vilabade, **t** 982 31 30 00, **f** 982 31 20 63 (*expensive*). One of the nicest Galician *pazos*, furnished with antiques and a lovely garden.

The two branches of the *camino* meet in **Sarriá**. In its quietly aloof medieval core there's a ruined castle, the little Romanesque church of San Salvador and a pilgrims' hostel in the **Convento de los Mercedarios**. Ten kilometres west, the villagers of **Portomarín** supply Galicia with excellent *aguardiente*: firewater that they not only distil, but drain during the nightly *marcha*.

And the Last Leg of the *Camino*

At **Vilar de Donas**, 'Ladyville' (just off the pilgrim's road 15 kilometres west of Portomarín), the 13th-century granite church of **San Salvador** has a ruined Gothic cloister and a pretty Romanesque-Gothic portal; inside the granite walls are emerald green from the damp, while the rounded apse is embellished with 15th-century paintings. The altar stone is carved with the miracle at O Cebreiro, with Jesus emerging out of the chalice; the 15th-century baldachin in the transept is one of the few to survive intact in Galicia. San Salvador was once the seat of the Knights of Santiago in Galicia; on the tombs, crossed swords are visible, the symbol of the order.

If it weren't for the proximity of Santiago itself, the last two days' march along the *camino* would be disappointing, especially for the modern pilgrim. The old road passes over a medieval bridge at **Furelos**, before arriving in **Melide**, with its endearing Praza do Convento and ancient roadside cross, marking the geographic centre of Galicia. Further west, **Arzúa** was the pilgrims' traditional last overnight stop, some 30 kilometres short of their goal. Finally, three kilometres from Compostela, they would reach the now desolate **Monte del Gozo** or Mountjoy (Km717 along the *autopista*), affording the long-awaited sight of the towers of Santiago. The first member of each pilgrimage band to sight the cathedral towers was called the 'King', a proud title that was passed down as a surname. These days Santiago's sprawl and traffic conspire to make the last few kilometres a hellish welcome to a heavenly goal.

Detours off the Camino

Lugo may be the capital of Spain's poorest province, but it happily dozes away in cosy retirement on the banks of the Minho after a career of some consequence. Its Celtic name *lug* means either the sun god or sacred forest, and when the Romans took it over in the 2nd century AD, they renamed it Lucus Augusti, made it the capital of their province of Gallaecia and endowed it with a remarkable, dark, slate corset of walls, the best-preserved ancient fortifications in Spain, just over two kilometres long and 28ft high and interspersed with 85 rounded towers. For all that, it was grabbed by the Suevi in the 5th century, the Visigoths in 585, and the Moors in the 8th century.

Four ancient gates pierce the dark fastness. Pilgrims would enter the southern gate to visit Lugo's **cathedral**, built in 1177 and encased in a Baroque skin that offers a modest prelude to the great façade at Santiago de Compostela. Inside are fittings from every century: a Romanesque chapel and another from 1735, lavish and Baroque in the shape of a rounded Greek cross, dedicated to the Virgen de los Ojos Grandes, 'Our Lady of the Big Eyes', designed by Fernando de las Casas, master of the Obradoiro façade at Compostela. Glass protects a walnut *coro* carved with a proto-Art Nouveau flair by Francisco Moure (1590–1621); his detailed scenes include an anatomy lesson.

Next to the cathedral, elegant Praza Santa María holds the handsome 17th-century **Bishop's Palace**, built in the style of a typical Gallego *pazo*. Just west, **Praza do Campo** was the Roman forum; Lugo's medieval neighbourhood, **La Tinería**, extends here around Rúa Cruz and Rúanova. Rúa da Raiña heads north to big and busy **Praza de Santo Domingo** with two Gothic churches: 14th-century **Santo Domingo** and 16th-century, *mudéjar*-influenced **San Francisco**. The delicate cloister and refectory now house an interesting **Provincial Museum** (*open Sept–June 10.30–2 and 4.30–8.30, Sun 11–2; July and Aug 10–1 and 4–7, Sat 10.30–2 and 4.30–8; closed Sun*) containing Celtic and Roman finds. Lugo's beauty spots are along the Río Minho; in the **Parque Rosalía de Castro**, just outside the Santiago gate.

West of Lugo: Santa Eulalia de Bóveda, and a Mystery

Some 16 kilometres southwest of Lugo (*take the Ourense road for four kilometres, then bear right towards Friol and follow the signs*) is the extraordinary 4th-century subterranean chapel of **Santa Eulalia de Bóveda** (*open for guided tours in Spanish, Oct–May Tues–Sat 11–2 and 3.30–5; June–Sept Tues–Sat 11–2 and 3.30–7.30, Sun and hols 11–2; closed Mon*), built over a Celtic temple as a Roman nymphaeum, and later as a mausoleum. Discovered in 1962, steps lead down to what must have been an antechamber of some kind. A horseshoe arch with mysterious reliefs leads into a vaulted room with a shallow pool in the centre (perhaps used for immersion baptisms by the early Christians), decorated with colourful, winsome murals of birds and trees, variously dated 4th or 8th century. The columns by the pool were found nearby and re-erected around the rim; under the pavement, an efficient drainage system kept the water clear. According to the guide, the only known building similar to Santa Eulalia is in the Ukraine, and just as mysterious.

Another rewarding detour is northwest to the evocative ruins of **Sobrado dos Monxes** (*open 10.15–1.15 and 4.15–6.15*), Galicia's greatest monastery, founded by the Cistercians in 1142. Although the original building hasn't survived, a fresh handful of monks have been doing what they can to preserve the massive Baroque church, the lovely if rotting choir stalls, and the monumental, ogival kitchen; also intact are the 13th-century chapel, a sacristy (1571) by Juan de Herrera, a 12th-century chapterhouse, and three 17th- and 18th-century cloisters, wreathed in lichens and wild flowers.

Heresy, Galician Style

According to popular belief, the right wall of Santa Eulalia once contained the tomb of Galicia's first 'saint', Prisciliano, whose doctrines, a syncretism of old Celtic and Christian beliefs, attracted many followers in Galicia and León but upset the Church. For one thing, Prisciliano believed works of the spirit obliterated sexual differences, and that monks and nuns should live together. His followers walked barefoot to stay in contact with the earth's forces, were vegetarians, did a bit of sun-worshipping on the side and retreated to hermitages in the holy mountains of the Celts. The counsel of Zaragoza (380) interdicted him and, when that had no effect, the bishop of Triers had him beheaded five years later – making Prisciliano one of the first holy men to be martyred by the Church instead of by Romans.

Santiago de Compostela

The original European tourist destination, Santiago de Compostela (pop. 90,000) still comes up with the goods. Not only does it boast a great cathedral where pilgrims are promised 50 per cent off their time in Purgatory, but the moss-stained Baroque city is pure granite magic, a rich grey palette of a hundred moods crowned with curlicues. The university keeps the ancient streets full of life year round and fuels the raw *urbanización* that engulfs the perimeters.

Expect rain; this city, the 'Urinal of Spain', never fails to remind you that showers are good for granite, fostering the elegant patina on its monuments and the micro-gardens that sprout out of the stone.

History

The story goes that in the year 813, a bright star led Pelayo, a hermit shepherd to the forgotten tomb of St James the Greater, the legendary Apostle of Spain. The place was named Compostela, a corruption of the Latin *Campus stellae* 'Field of the star'. Of course apostles don't compost like everyone else, and the remains of James were just what Christian Spain required at the dawn of the Reconquista. Local bishop Theodomir confirmed the relics' authenticity and built a chapel; in 829 Alfonso II the Chaste of Asturias built a much larger chapel over the tomb. So many pilgrims began to arrive that an even larger church was needed and supplied by Alfonso III the Great in 896. This in turn fell to al-Mansur and his Moorish armies when they swept through in 997; al-Mansur took the bells as a souvenir for the Great Mosque at Córdoba, but left the Apostle's tomb alone, awed by the piety of a single monk, who fearlessly knelt there and prayed during the battle.

Sometime in these early days James the humble fisherman was given a new posthumous role as Santiago Matamoros, the hero of the entirely apocryphal Battle of Clavijo of 844. This legend was 'confirmed' in a 12th-century document known as the *Privilegio de los Votos de Santiago*, purporting to be by Ramiro I of Asturias, the grateful victor of Clavijo, vowing a tax in perpetuity to the saint's church in Compostela (a tax that was annulled only in 1834).

In 1075, the new tax paid for the present cathedral. By 1104, Compostela was made an archbishopric; in 1189, Alexander III decreed it a Holy City, on a par with Jerusalem and Rome. In 1236, Ferdinand III the Saint brought back Santiago's bells from the Great Mosque. In 1589, with Drake ravaging the coast, Santiago was tucked away for safekeeping but, in a fit of amnesia, no one could remember where. Still, the pilgrims came, and only in the 19th century did a cathedral workman stumble across the most important relics in Spain (1879). How to make sure they were genuine? An authenticated apostolic bone chip from Pistoia was sent over and fitted the notch in the skull like a hand in a glove.

Santiago de Compostela was also named a European City of Culture for the year 2000. Along with the generous funding for a wide range of cultural events, the city has gained some significant public works, including a communications port designed by Norman Foster, and a generous park by the architect J. P. Kleihues.

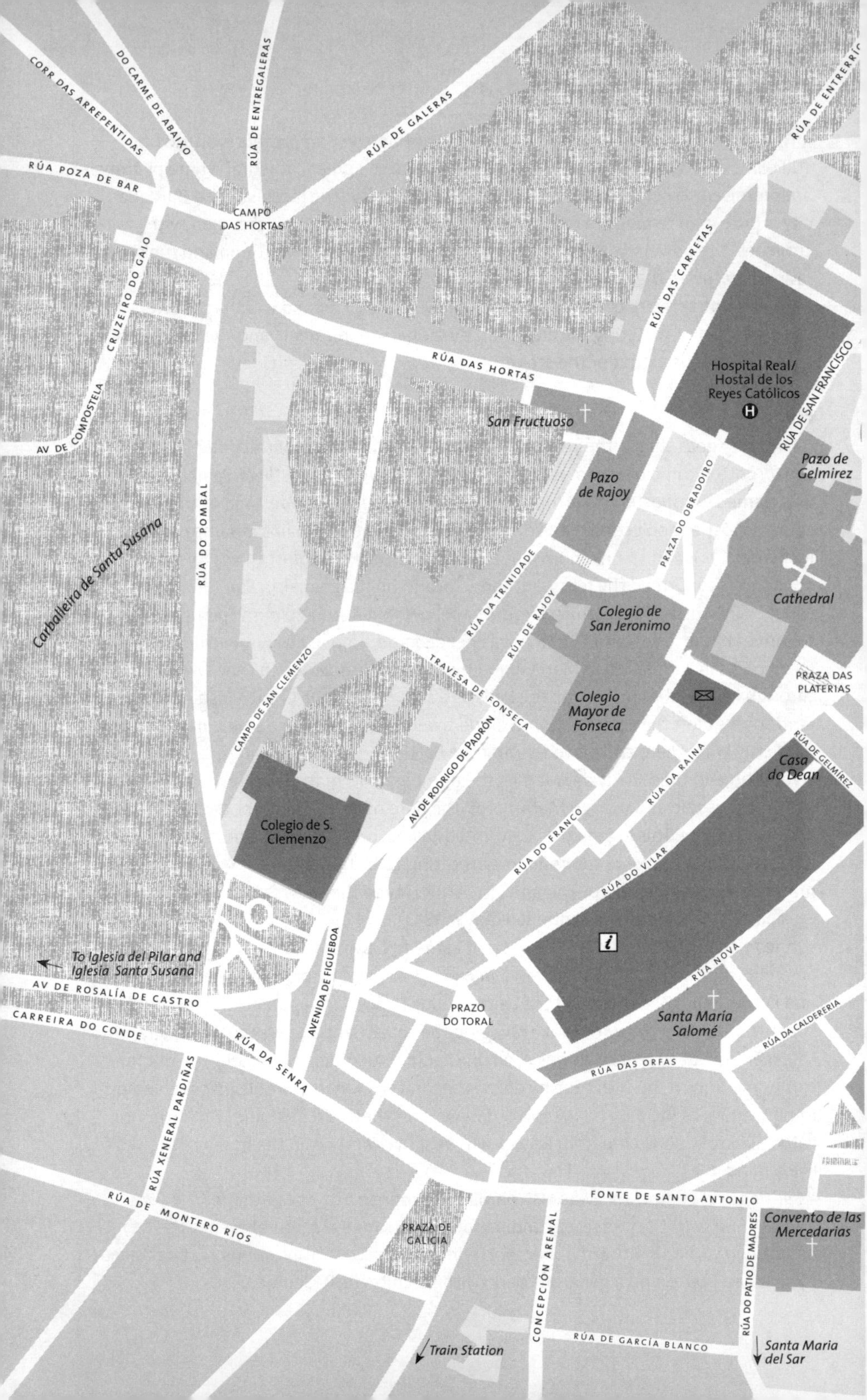
Corr das Arrepentidas
Do Carme de Abaixo
Rúa de Entregaleras
Rúa de Galeras
Rúa de Entrerríos
Rúa Poza de Bar
Campo das Hortas
Cruzeiro do Gaio
Rúa das Carretas
Rúa das Hortas
Hospital Real/ Hostal de los Reyes Católicos
Rúa de San Francisco
Av de Compostela
San Fructuoso
Pazo de Rajoy
Praza do Obradoiro
Pazo de Gelmirez
Rúa do Pombal
Carballeira de Santa Susana
Rúa da Trinidade
Rúa de Rajoy
Colegio de San Jeronimo
Cathedral
Campo de San Clemenzo
Travesa de Fonseca
Praza das Platerias
Colegio Mayor de Fonseca
Av de Rodrigo de Padrón
Rúa da Raina
Rúa de Gelmírez
Casa do Dean
Colegio de S. Clemenzo
Rúa do Franco
Rúa do Vilar
Avenida de Figueboa
To Iglesia del Pilar and Iglesia Santa Susana
Rúa Nova
Av de Rosalía de Castro
Prazo do Toral
Santa María Salomé
Carreira do Conde
Rúa da Senra
Rúa da Caldereria
Rúa das Orfas
Rúa Xeneral Pardiñas
Fonte de Santo Antonio
Rúa de Montero Ríos
Convento de las Mercedarias
Praza de Galicia
Concepción Arenal
Rúa do Patio de Madres
Rúa de García Blanco
Train Station
Santa Maria del Sar

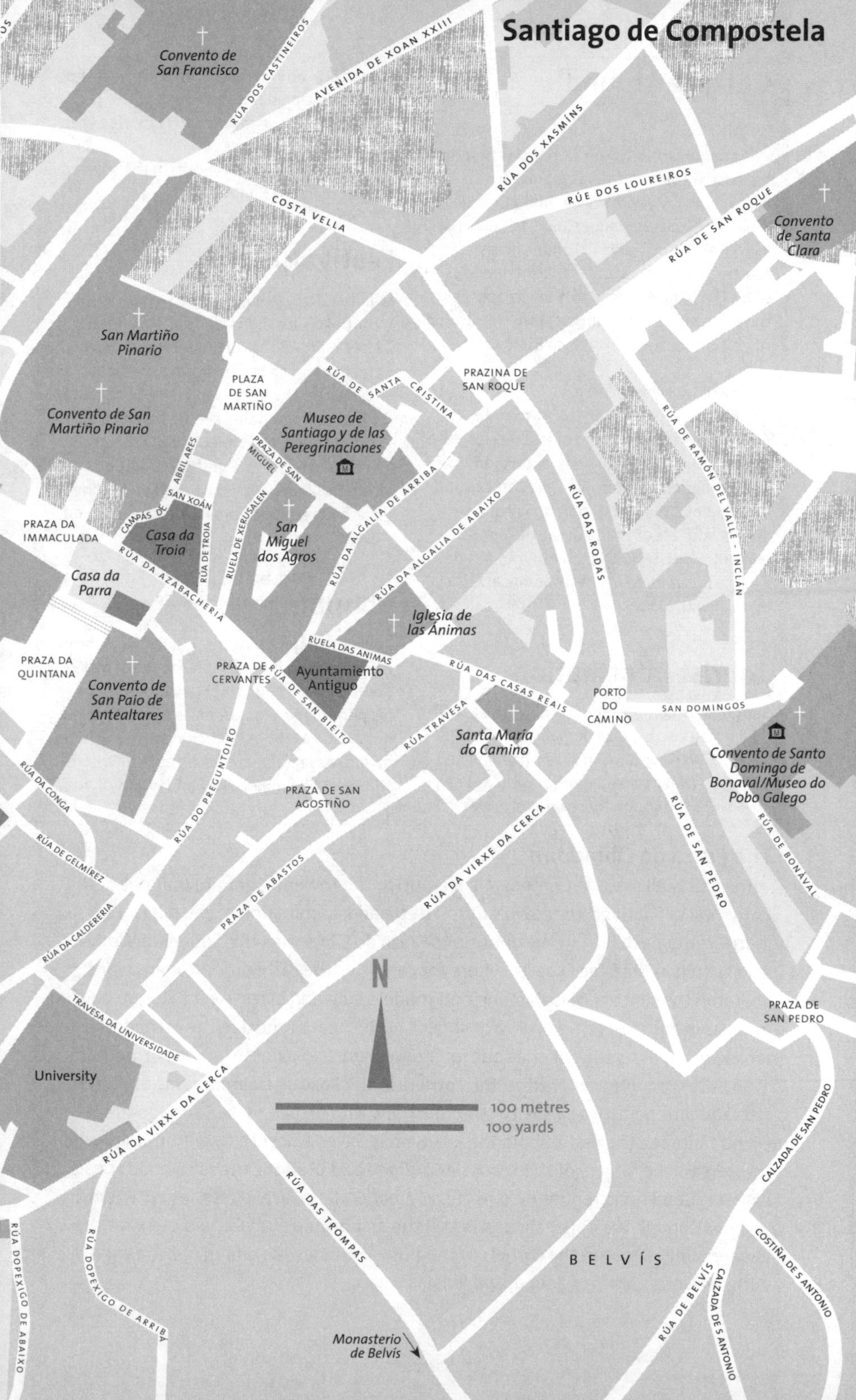
Santiago de Compostela
Convento de San Francisco
Rúa dos Castiñeiros
Avenida de Xoan XXIII
Rúa dos Xasmíns
Rúe dos Loureiros
Costa Vella
Rúa de San Roque
Convento de Santa Clara
San Martiño Pinario
Convento de San Martiño Pinario
Plaza de San Martiño
Rúa de Santa Cristina
Prazina de San Roque
Museo de Santiago y de las Peregrinaciones
Praza de San Miguel
Rúa de Ramón del Valle - Inclán
Abril Ares
San Xoán
Campas de
Praza da Immaculada
Casa da Troia
Rúa de Troia
Ruela de Xerusalen
San Miguel dos Agros
Rúa da Algalia de Arriba
Rúa da Algalia de Abaixo
Rúa das Rodas
Casa da Parra
Rúa da Azabacheria
Iglesia de las Ánimas
Praza da Quintana
Convento de San Paio de Antealtares
Praza de Cervantes
Ruela das Animas
Ayuntamiento Antiguo
Rúa de San Bieito
Rúa das Casas Reais
Porto do Camino
San Domingos
Rúa Travesa
Santa María do Camino
Convento de Santo Domingo de Bonaval/Museo do Pobo Galego
Rúa do Preguntoiro
Praza de San Agostiño
Rúa da Conga
Rúa de Gelmírez
Rúa da Virxe da Cerca
Rúa de San Pedro
Rúa de Bonaval
Praza de Abastos
Rúa da Caldereria
N
Travesa da Universidade
University
Praza de San Pedro
100 metres
100 yards
Calzada de San Pedro
Rúa das Trompas
Rúa Dopexigo de Abaixo
Rúa Dopexigo de Arriba
Belvís
Costiña de S Antonio
Rúa de Belvís
Calzada de S Antonio
Monasterio de Belvís

Getting Around

By Air

Santiago's airport, **t** 981 54 75 00, is 11km to the east at Labacolla. It has regular flights to Barcelona, Madrid, Sevilla, Santa Cruz de Tenerife, Bilbao, Santander and San Sebastián, as well as direct flights to London, Paris, Amsterdam, Geneva and Frankfurt. Iberia's office is at Gral Pardiñas 36, **t** 981 57 20 24; there are buses to the airport from the station run by Empresa Freire, **t** 981 58 81 11.

By Train

Santiago's train station is a 10-minute walk from the centre at the end of Rúa do Hórreo, **t** 981 52 02 02, with daily connections to Madrid, Ourense, A Coruña, Vigo, Zamora and other points. The bus station is way out on San Cayetano, **t** 981 58 77 00, at the opposite end of town; city bus No.10 links it to Pza de Galicia. **Buses** go to nearly all points in Galicia, especially the Rías Altas.

Tourist Information

Santiago de Compostela: Rúa de Vilar 43, **t** 981 58 40 81; also in Praza de Galicia, **t** 981 58 44 00. **Walking tours** in Spanish (*daily*) and English (*three times a week in summer*) can be booked through these offices.

Post Office: on Travesía de Fonseca, near the Praza do Obradoiro.

Internet Access: a good central *ciber* is Cyber Nova 50, C/Nova 50.

There is a **market** (*Mon–Sat*) in the covered market in Pza de San Félix.

Festivals

St James' Day, *25 July*. On years when Santiago's feast day lands on a Sunday, a **Holy Year** (Año Xacobeo) is proclaimed and the city launches into a year's worth of festivities. The next such year will be 2004, when visitors should keep an eye out for music, dance and street activities that celebrate all things *gallego*; both traditional and contemporary. A special Santiago hotline has been set up to provide information on events: **t** 981 54 19 99.

Shopping

The use of **jet** (hard, black, polished lignite) is said to be in memory of a local coal-worker, Contolay, who helped St Francis of Assisi on his pilgrimage. Two jet-makers are still in business. Have a look at **Regueira** (at Azabachería 9) and **Mayer** (at Platerías 6), both of whom still specialize in jewellery and works of art.

The Praza do Obradoiro

Irresistibly all roads in Compostela lead up to the towering granite magnet of the Cathedral of Santiago, the town's *raison d'être* and culmination of the pilgrim's journey. Approach it from the enormous Praza do Obradoiro, the 'Square of Works', also known as Praza de España, where for centuries the cathedral's stonemasons liberated the soul of Galicia's stone and made it sing and blaze like a Baroque bonfire. In the rain and mists, at morning or sunset or the heat of the day, the cathedral façade changes its tune; it cries out for a new Monet to paint its moods or, perhaps even better, a composer. Next to the cathedral, the **Pazo de Gelmírez** was built in the 12th and 13th centuries by the two archbishops who helped make Santiago great: Diego Gelmírez, the first to hold the job, who received a licence to mint money when he oversaw the forgery of the *Votos de Santiago* and used the funds to build the cathedral, and Arias, reputedly 'one of the great ecclesiastical pirates of 13th-century Spain'. Although the upper section is still the archbishop's palace, you can visit the lower medieval rooms; the corbels in the huge Romanesque dining hall are carved with delicious scenes of a medieval feast.

Where to Stay

Santiago ✉ 15780

Finding a place to stay at any price is easy in the city that has received visitors for 1,100 years; even on 25 July you may be met at the station by landladies luring you to their *hostales* for around €12 a head.

Luxury–Expensive

*******Hs Los Reyes Católicos**, Pza del Obradoiro, **t** 981 58 22 00, **f** 981 56 30 94, *santiago@parador.es*. Poor pilgrims used to stay in this magnificent 15th-century building, but since 1954 it has been reserved for visitors with well-padded wallets, the luxurious *ne plus ultra* of Spanish *hostales*. Furnished with antiques, art and fountains, most rooms look on to four shady patios; some are simple, while the bridal suites have been enjoyed by VIPs from Franco on up. Probably the priciest *parador* in Spain.

*******Araguaney**, Alfredo Brañas 5, **t** 981 59 59 00, **f** 981 59 02 87. The trendiest place to stay, modern, central, and offering every conceivable service, except perhaps easy parking – a headache in the *casco viejo*.

*****Virxe da Cerca**, Rúa Virxe da Cerca 27, **t** 981 56 93 50, **f** 981 58 69 25, *www.galinor.es/pousadasdecompostela*. Offers stylish serenity and beautiful gardens in an 18th-century Jesuit residence. Staying in the new but sympathetically conceived extension is slightly cheaper.

Moderate

*****Hogar San Francisco**, Campillo de San Francisco 3, **t** 981 57 24 63, **f** 981 57 19 16. For a cheerful Catholic atmosphere near the centre, get a room at this former Franciscan Missionary College.

****Costa Vella**, Rúa Porta da Pena 17, **t** 981 56 95 30, **f** 981 56 95 31. A beautiful and peaceful place to stay, located on a traffic-free street above the Convento de San Francisco. It's worth paying a little extra to get one of the sunny rooms that look out majestically across the city, and the views from the shower are surely amongst the best in Spain. Remains of Santiago's old walls can be seen in the lovely garden.

Casa Grande de Cornide, in Calo-Teo (off the Padron road), **t** 981 80 55 99, **f** 981 80 57 51. Run by a friendly duo in a lovely setting with a pool.

Inexpensive

****Hs Suso**, Rúa del Vilar 65, **t** 981 58 66 11. On Santiago's prettiest street, this pilgrims' favourite is run by a jovial fellow who knows everything and is probably responsible for the tasty tapas in the bar downstairs.

Continuing around the square, the Plateresque **Hospital Real** (1501–09) was constructed for poor pilgrims by Ferdinand and Isabel with the booty from taking Granada in 1492. Built by Enrique de Egas, its façade concentrates its embellishments in a few key spots, especially in the crowded triumphal Gothic-Renaissance altarpiece of a doorway. A Christian's Who's Who from Adam and Eve onwards fills the chiselled niches. The building, a hospital until 1953, has been converted into a *parador*. The enormous 18th-century **Pazo de Rajoy**, designed as a seminary and now the town hall, is pure Parisian neoclassicism, by French architect Charles Lemaur. Next, the 16th-century **Colegio de San Jerónimo** was founded as a university. Classes were held just behind in the **Colegio Mayor de Fonseca**, built by Juan de Álava (1546) around a lovely, peaceful cloister with a beautiful *mudéjar* ceiling, still a favourite place for weary scholars to enjoy a breath of fresh air.

The Cathedral of Santiago

And back to that Baroque firecracker, the Obradoiro façade of the cathedral where the two towers shoot like huge flames to heaven. On the right, the Tower of the Bells

★**Hs La Estela**, Raxoi 1 (by the cathedral), **t** 981 58 27 96. Friendly and charming, with a lovely patina of age.

★**Avenida**, Fonte de San Antonio 4, **t** 981 57 00 51, **f** 981 56 58 17. Characterful for the price, this offers immense rooms with polished wooden floors in a restored 18th-century house.

Cheap

★★**Hs Mapoula**, Entremurallas 10, **t** 981 58 01 24. Situated just inside the *casco viejo*, this has pleasantly airy rooms with bath; some look out over the main pilgrimage route.

Hospedaje Mera, Rúa Porta da Pena 15, **t** 981 58 38 67. On the opposite side of the old quarter, this peaceful *pensión* offers well-priced rooms with or without bath; those with private terraces enjoy wonderful views across the city.

Eating Out

Eating in Santiago is a bound to be a pleasure; the competition is keen and the food has to be good to succeed. Rúa del Hórreo has the biggest concentration of restaurants: displaying one window of tempting seafood after another.

Expensive

Toñi Vicente, Rúa Rosalia de Castro 24, **t** 981 59 41 00. A new star has emerged in Santiago's culinary cosmos – Toñi Vicente's breathtakingly original take on Gallego cuisine has picked up awards and accolades from all quarters. Try the *lubina braseada en fondo de buey* (grilled sea bass on a bed of crab), a thoughtful combination of rich flavours and delicate herbs, or the delicious mango ravioli. *Closed end July–early Aug*.

Anexo Vilas, Av. de Villagarcía 21 (on the outskirts), **t** 981 59 83 87. The informal tapas bar serves delicious seafood and *empanadas*, while the dining room upstairs produces uncomplicated, fresh food and shows Gallegan cuisine at its very best. For pudding, try the Postre Xacobeo, followed by a local *digestif* made from apples or peaches (*menu moderate*). *Closed Mon*.

Don Gaiferos, Rúa Nova 23, **t** 981 58 38 94. For tradition mixed with international, seasonal dishes, try this beautiful vaulted dining room. *Closed Sun*.

Roberto, San Xulián de Sales, **t** 981 51 17 69. For a special treat, drive out 8km to Vedra in the Valle de Ulla, where Roberto prepares some of the most delicious, imaginative dishes in all Galicia in a lovely country villa. *Closed Sat and Sun eve*.

was built by José Peña de Toro in the 1600s, while the left-hand one was added by Fernando Casas y Novoa in the 1750s, when he tackled the main façade. A lively triple-ramp stair leads up to a pair of doors, arranged to form a cross in stonework; stacked above are two calm windows in a shallow arch like the eye of a hurricane just before the front peaks in a flickering crest of granite fire. At the foot of the steps is a door that leads into the delightful **crypt of Master Mateo** or 'Catedral Vieja' (*open Mon–Sat 11–1.30 and 4.30–6.30, Sun 10–1.30 and 4–7; adm, keep your ticket for the treasury, cloister and museum*), built by the great master builder to distribute the weight of his Romanesque façade, but so elaborately, with ancient columns, capitals, and fine sculpture under the vaults that people used to think this was the first cathedral.

Inside the Cathedral: the Pórtico de la Gloria

Perhaps the most startling surprise for many visitors awaits just within the busy Baroque doors up the staircase, where the original 12th-century façade of the cathedral survives intact. This is the sublime **Pórtico de la Gloria**, nothing less than the greatest single piece of Romanesque sculpture, anywhere. Sculpted in warm brown

Moderate

Vilas, Rosalía de Castro 88, **t** 981 59 10 00. Another worthy bastion of Gallego cuisine in a turn-of-the-century house. *Closed Sun*.

Alameda, Porta Faixera 15, **t** 981 58 47 96. Has been serving up hearty Galician fare for more than 30 years – all types of *empanadas*, some filling stews and dishes hot from the oven, and local wines.

Inexpensive

Pampín, Puente Espino (at Calo-Teo on the Padrón road), **t** 981 80 31 70. For a feast of fresh seafood that won't break the bank.

O Cabaliño do Demo, Rúa Aller Ulloa, **t** 981 58 81 46. A relaxing little vegetarian haunt with a wide range of wholefood goodies, including some reasonable Mexican and Eastern dishes. The bar downstairs can provide details on Santiago's gay scene.

Casa Manolo, Rúa Travesa 27. Try to squeeze in to this permanently packed little restaurant, where a colossal €5 *menú* drags in the crowds every lunch time and evening.

Bars and Nightlife

Santiago's lively bars offer a wonderful way to eat and drink a rainy night away. The area around Rúa Franco is the focal point of the evening *marcha*.

El Franco, Rúa Franco 28. A typical place for a first *aperitivo*.

Mesón do Pulpo, Vista Alegre 30. Has *raciones* of octopus with peppers and paprika.

Bodeguilla de San Roque, San Roque 13 (near Santa Clara). Serves good wine with platefuls of delicious breast-shaped *tetilla* cheese and ham.

La Borriquita de Belém, San Paio. For a jazz accompaniment to your drinks, try this place, not far from the cathedral.

Metate, Colexón de San Paio. Chocoholics shouldn't miss out on the hot chocolate and chocolate cocktails served at this former chocolate factory.

Derby, Huérfanos 29. The prettiest café in town; unchanged since the 1920s.

Café Jacobus, Rúa Azevacheria 5. Claims the widest selection of exotic coffees, infusions, and sinful chocolate concoctions; one of the few places in the old quarter that's busy after midnight.

When you can't eat or drink any more, you can dance it off:

Casting, in Hotel Aranguaney. The discothèque for Santiago's beautiful people.

Ruta 66, C/Perez Constanti. A popular place with plenty of action.

Ultramarinos, at the entrance of the Puerta del Camino. An ultra-modern hang-out for the young and trendy.

granite between 1168 and 1188 by Master Mateo (dated and signed on the lintel of the central arch) its three doorways are dedicated to the Triumph of the Apocalypse, full of movement, life and rhythm; if the end of the world is like this, you want to be there. Nearly all the 200 or so figures are smiling or laughing, beginning with St James himself on the central pillar, carved with the tree of Jesse, showing the genealogy of Christ from Adam to the Virgin Mary.

Above St James in the central arch, Christ in Majesty appears 'like jasper and carnelian' according to the text in Revelations, raising both hands in blessing, surrounded by the four Evangelists, Apostles, angels and an ogival rainbow of musicians: the 24 Elders of the Apocalypse (plus a few stand-ins), each with a different instrument on his lap. On the two side pillars apostles and prophets chat pleasantly together; Chinese monsters grimace on the lowest frieze. The door on the right is dedicated to heaven and hell, mostly, and depicts children suffering the torments of the damned with their parents – on the surface a powerful psychological trick to make parents toe the line – while the scenes above the left door are even more elusive. After drinking in this most eloquent draught of medieval happiness, pilgrims would line up behind the central pillar before the curly-haired figure of Master Mateo, who is humbly kneeling to offer the cathedral to God; his nickname, '*O Santo dos Croques*', 'Saint Bump-on-the-Head', comes from the millions who have bowed their heads to touch Mateo's in the hope that some of his genius would rub off.

The **Romanesque interior** of the cathedral is essentially as Master Mateo left it, a long, majestic, barrel-vaulted nave lined with galleries. The huge, silver high altar glimmers in the penumbra, visible since the 1940s when the enclosed Baroque choir was removed. Of the chapels along the nave the most important is the first on the right, the 16th-century **reliquary chapel** and Royal Pantheon, with medieval tombs of Galicia's royal family, and reliquaries containing bits of the True Cross and the head of St James the Lesser, who was occasionally purposefully confused with James the Greater for propaganda ends. Next on the right is the **Treasury**, aglitter with the silver hammer used to pound open the Holy Door in Holy Years, silver scallop shells, a score of other showy religious trappings and a celebrated 16th-century monstrance.

When you get right up to it, the glow-in-the-dark 17th-century **high altar**, lavishly coated with Mexican silver, turns out to be a pointless piece of tomfoolery, its cast of knick-knack characters borrowed from a giant's Christmas tree. Just over the altar itself sits a stiff idol, a 12th-century statue of Santiago, the patron saint of Spain. The thing to do is climb the narrow stairway positioned behind the altar, kiss the statue's robe and receive a holy card (for the certificate of indulgence, the *compostellana*, pilgrims should apply with their documents to the *Oficina arzobispal*, in the back of the cathedral).

To the side of the high altar, look out for the ropes and pulleys suspended from the octagonal dome, from which, on high feast days, the **Botafumeiro**, the world's largest censer, is suspended and swung with terrifying force across the entire length of the transept in a comet-like arc of perfumed smoke and sparks. Weighing in at 54kg, the Botafumeiro is a smaller brass version of the original silver model made in 1602 and pilfered by Napoleon's troops: it takes eight men, the *tiraboleiros*, to swing it on a system invented in the Middle Ages. Don't miss it if you're in town on a holy day, and try not to think about the time when Catherine of Aragón attended Mass and the Botafumeiro broke loose and flew out of the window. The ten chapels radiating like petals from the ambulatory are all worth a look, especially the Romanesque **Capilla de San Salvador**, where pilgrims received Communion. Off the north transept, a doorway topped with a 13th-century relief of the Magi leads into the Romanesque **Capilla de la Corticela**. Off the south transept, a 16th-century Gothic-vaulted **cloister** big enough for a football match holds the **Cathedral Museum** and **Library**.

The highlight is a faithful but incomplete restoration of Master Mateo's granite *coro*, torn down in a spring-clean of the late 16th century, but the computer-designed facsimiles can't match the delicacy of the few original pieces that have survived. Elsewhere in the museum there is an illuminated 12th-century *Codex Calixtinus*, while the library houses the Botafumeiro when it's not in use. The **Sala Capitular** contains the cathedral's impressive collection of tapestries, and there are pretty views from the upper rooms across the Praza do Obradoiro.

Around the Cathedral

Although low key after the Obradoiro façade, the cathedral's other entrances each deserve a look. Circumnavigating the Pazo de Gelmírez, you'll come first to the split-level **Praza das Platerías**, named after the silversmiths whose shops once filled the arcades. The double **Puerta de las Platerías** is the only one to remain essentially unchanged from the Romanesque cathedral. Locals use the doors as a short cut across town, as in the Middle Ages, when cathedrals were covered public squares as much as religious shrines. From here you can gaze up the Cathedral's highest tower, the ornament-laden 260ft **Berenguel** designed by Galician humanist Domingo de Andrade in the 1710s to hold the town clock. The *praza*'s geometric Baroque **chapter-house** and the **fountain of the horse** were both designed by Fernández Sarela.

Continuing past the bulk of the Berenguel is the enclosed Praza da Quintana; the upper level is named 'of the living' and the lower 'of the dead', recalling the Roman cemetery that once occupied the spot. Alongside the square runs the stern, unforgiving façade of the **Convento de San Paio de Antelares**, 'Pelayo before the Altars', containing a **Museo de Arte Sacro** (*entrance at rear, open summer only Mon–Fri 10–1 and 4–7, Sat 4–7; closed Sun; adm*), where a celebrity Virgin holds the Child in one hand and thumps a devil with the other. In the lower square is the **Puerta Santa**, opened only during a Holy Year (*see* 'Festivals', p.384). The doorway of 1611 consists of 24 compartments, each pigeonholing a carved figure from the Romanesque choir.

The Gallop to the Scallop

The very first thing a medieval pilgrim did upon arriving in the city was stop in the Barrio de los Conchieros, buy a scallop, eat it (this is where French pilgrims learned to make *coquilles St Jacques*, after all) and stick the shell on the turned-up brim of his or her hat, as visible proof that they had made it at last; strict laws forbade the selling of scallops anywhere else along the *camino*. By the 16th century, the real shell was replaced by a fancy souvenir replica, either in silver or in jet.

The scallop, that tasty bivalve that thrives in the *rías* of Galicia, has been associated with the Santiago pilgrimage since the early Middle Ages. In Compostela, as usual, they can explain it with a miracle: a young Gallego, on the eve of his wedding, was spirited into the sea by his wayward horse and believed drowned, although in truth the horse was running along the waves to meet the stone boat bringing the body of St James to Galicia. When the bridegroom returned, escorting the boat, his body was covered with an armour of milk-white shells, so amazing the locals that they converted at once to the new faith. Its Spanish name, *venera*, calls up associations with the vagina and Venus, the goddess of love, who was born of the sea foam and surfed ashore on a giant scallop shell. For pilgrims, the shell also symbolized the end of the journey, the resurrection and unity in the world – the sea from which it came, the earth in its stony hardness, and the sun in its radiant lines. It's hard to think of another symbol so polyvalent, embracing sex, death, dinner and spiritual wholeness – not to mention a multinational company peddling the Super or Unleaded souls of the dead dinosaurs that fuel the way.

Another attraction in Praza de la Azabachería was the chance for destitute pilgrims to hang their rags on an iron cross and pick up new clothes from the Benedictines at **San Martín Pinario**, founded in 912 as the special protector of the Apostle's tomb. Inside, the vast Claustro de la Portería with its elegant fountain was completed by Casas' Casas y Novoa, while just beyond is an extraordinary, floating 17th-century staircase with Aztec decorations. Beyond, the huge barrel-vaulted church is the stage for Casas y Novoa's *retablo mayor*, a feverish blast of intricate gilded detail, a nightmarish vision of total paradise marked by the merciless destiny of the unbelieving Moors stage left and right. Casas y Novoa was also responsible for the almost as frantic Capilla del Socorro on the right side of the nave. The stately, colonnaded 18th-century church façade facing Pza San Martín grows like an altarpiece above a sunken Baroque staircase, designed by a Dominican named Manuel de los Mártires, all granite ribbons squirming below the level of the pavement, like nothing else in Spain.

Elsewhere in Santiago

Santiago is a delight to wander in, its narrow streets and intimate squares paved with granite flagstones, lined with old buildings, their walls tinged with green and gold by moss and lichen. The founders of the two great mendicant orders of the 13th century both made pilgrimages and personally founded monasteries. In 1214, St Francis founded the **Convento de San Francisco**, while St Dominic founded the rather larger **Convento de Santo Domingo de Bonaval** in 1220. The Baroque façade hides a handsome Gothic church from the 1300s and the chapel of the Pantheon of Illustrious Gallegos, last resting place of poet Rosalía de Castro and the caricaturist Castelao (died 1950), the Goya of the Civil War. The convent and cloister house the **Museo do Pobo Galego** (*Mon–Sat 10–1 and 4–7, Sun 11–2; adm*) with a good ethnographic collection and a memorable triple spiral staircase, a stunning architectural *tour de force* by Domingo de Andrade.

Back to the Rías: the Golfo Ártabro

Two of Galicia's most important ports, Ferrol and A Coruña, occupy either end of the 20-kilometre Golfo Ártabro, savagely bitten out of the northwest coast. Either dawdle west along the Rías Altas (*see* pp.375–6), or race up the A9 motorway from Santiago.

Ferrol and Betanzos

Plump on the big fat Ría de Betanzos, swollen by four rivers, the salty city of Ferrol was named after its lighthouse (*faro*). Gently, slowly, the port city has dropped the article 'El' from the front of its name and the 'del Caudillo' stuck on the back in honour of Francisco Franco, born here in 1892, son of a naval supply officer who grew up to be the youngest general in Spanish history before his career as dictator. Ferrol has a pretty enough medieval core, a planned 18th-century quarter and a modern quarter that looks like a SimCity computer game. The best thing to do is just wander among the pretty houses with 'crystal galleries' and the casino and gardens.

Getting Around

By Air

A Coruña's airport is 9km away at Alvedro, **t** 981 18 72 00, with connections to Madrid, Barcelona and Sevilla. There's an airport bus into town.

By Boat

Three boats daily ply the *ría* between Ferrol and A Coruña, arriving right next to Coruña's tourist office; from the same spot, summer-only launches go to Playa de Santa Cristina.

By Train

Ferrol and A Coruña are linked by RENFE with Pontedeume and the main junction at Betanzos, Santiago, Ferrol, Lugo, Vigo, Padrón and Villagarcía de Arousa. In A Coruña the station San Cristóbal is a bit out of the way on Av. Joaquín Planelles, **t** 981 15 02 02 – best to take bus No.1 from the nearby bus station to the historic centre. There's also a RENFE travel office on Fontán 3, **t** 981 22 19 48. In Ferrol, RENFE and FEVE share the same station, **t** 981 37 13 04 and **t** 981 37 04 01.

By Bus

A Coruña's bus station is on Caballeros near the RENFE station, **t** 981 23 96 44, with connections to the Costa da Morte and all major points in Galicia; Alsa provide services to Madrid, Leon, and the Basque country.
El Rápido buses serve Betanzos and Monfero. Ferrol's buses depart around the corner from the train station, **t** 981 32 47 51 and go to Betanzos, Viveiro, Foz, Ribadeo and Lugo.

Tourist Information

Ferrol: Magdalena 12, **t** 981 31 11 79.
Pontedeume: Av. Saavedra Meneses 2, **t** 981 43 02 70.
A Coruña: Regional Office, Dársena de la Marina, **t** 981 22 18 22;
municipal information and the Coruña Card (combined adm to the city's attractions) are available in Jardines de Méndez Núñez, **t** 981 21 61 61, *www.turismocoruna.com*.
Post Office: Alcalde Manuel Casas s/n, by the Marina, A Coruña.
Internet Access: Net Print Center, Pza María Pita 4, is the most central of the city's *cibers*.

There are regular **markets** in **Pontedeume** (*Sat*); in **Betanzos** (*Tues*, *Thurs* and *Sat*); and in **A Coruña** (*Mon–Fri*) in Mercado San Agustín.

Where to Stay and Eat

Ferrol ✉ 15400

★★★**Parador do Ferrol**, Almirante Fernández Martín, **t** 981 35 67 20, **f** 981 35 67 20, *ferrol@parador.es* (*expensive*). Franco saw to it that his home town got a *parador*; its ageing, nautically decorated rooms have handsome views over the *ría*.

★★★**Hotel Suizo**, Dolores 17, **t** 981 30 04 00, **f** 981 30 03 06 (*moderate*). Located in a modernist building and has a pleasant café.

Casa Tomás, **t** 981 38 02 40 (*moderate*). Along the waterfront at Neda, a 10-minute drive out towards Ortigueira, this is a favourite with specialities straight from the *ría*: *jurelos en escabeche* (fresh sardines in oil, garlic, basil and wine vinegar) and grilled crayfish (*menu moderate*). *Closed Sun eve and Mon.*

Borona, Dolores 52, **t** 981 35 50 99. It's not much to look at, but it does serve delicious *nouvelle cuisine*. *Closed Sun.*

There are cheaper rooms are on Pardo Bajo.

★★**Hs Almendra**, Almendra 4, **t** 981 35 81 90 (*inexpensive*). A good choice.

Pataquiña, Dolores 35, **t** 981 35 23 11 (*cheap*). Offers heaps well-prepared Gallego specialities; try *salsa Pataquiña*, a mixture of shrimp and crab cooked in brandy and garlic.

Rising steeply over the head of yet another small estuary, lovely **Betanzos** is a far more ancient place, a Celtic village that grew into the Roman port of Brigantium Flavium. It thrived into the 18th century, when the Mandeo and Mendo rivers washed in so much silt that they stole Betanzos' seacoast. Progress stopped, leaving a time capsule: houses and mansions of all sizes with wrought-iron balconies, or *solanas*, line the narrow lanes that wind up the hill from the harbour's medieval gates. Life

Betanzos ✉ 15300

*Hs Barreiros, Argentina 6, t 981 77 22 59 (*cheap*). The best bargain, with simple rooms and a good cheap **restaurant**.

Casanova, Pza García Hermanos 15, **t** 981 77 06 03 (*moderate*). In a rustically romantic setting; serves up tasty salmon and lamprey dishes for the bold.

A Coruña ✉ 15000

A Coruña fills up in summer, so arrive early or book ahead. The bar zone around Rúa Franja and Pza María Pita keeps going well into dawn when the fishing fleet pulls in and everyone goes to watch the auctioning of the catch.

****Finisterre, Pso del Parrote 20, **t** 981 20 54 00, **f** 981 20 84 62 (*expensive*). The best-located and most luxurious hotel in A Coruña, overlooking the sea, with pools, tennis courts, a nursery, playground and even a casino.

***Riazor, Av. Pedro Barrié de la Maza 29, **t** 981 25 34 00, **f** 981 25 34 04 (*expensive*). A pleasant, less costly alternative with a fine beachside location and modern rooms.

***Ciudad de La Coruña, Polígono Adormideras, **t** 981 21 11 00, **f** 981 22 46 10, (*expensive*). Near the Torre de Hércules, with frequent buses into the centre; has modern rooms, all with sea views.

Hs Mar del Plata, Pso de Ronda 58, **t 981 25 79 62 (*moderate*). Has fairly pleasant rooms with bath.

*Hs El Parador, Olmos 15, **t** 981 22 21 21 (*moderate*). Well kept, and among the cheaper central places.

Hs Alborán, Ruego de Agua 14, **t 981 22 65 79, **f** 981 22 25 62, *www.meiganet.com/hostalalboran* (*inexpensive–cheap*). Run by a comically bickering old couple; has pleasant rooms that are perhaps not as distinguished as they look from outside.

*Hs Las Rias, San Andrés 141, **t** 981 22 68 79 (*inexpensive*). Good and friendly, offering all the necessary facilities in unusually spacious rooms.

*Hs Palacio, Pza de Galicia 2, **t** 981 12 23 38 (*cheap*). Clean and welcoming, with very low rates.

When it comes to **eating out**, seafood rules menus in A Coruña, and there's no shortage of spots in which to enjoy it.

Coral, Callejón de la Estacada 9 (near the port), **t** 981 22 31 99 (*expensive*). This is one of the best seafood places; exceptional, delicately prepared shellfish is served in a classy setting (*menú moderate*). *Closed Sun exc. in summer.*

A La Brasa, Juan Flórez 38, **t** 981 27 07 27 (*expensive*). As its name implies, specializes in meat and fish sizzling from the grill; work up an appetite and order the *punta trasera de ternera a la parrilla*, a whopper of succulent steak with baked potatoes.

Casa Pardo, Novoa Santos 15, **t** 981 28 00 21 (*expensive, menú moderate*). Another good and long-established place to eat seafood, famous for melt-in-your-mouth monkfish. *Closed Sun.*

La Marina, Av. de la Marina 14, **t** 981 22 39 14 (*moderate*). A popular place offering fish and solid traditional dishes. *Closed Sun eve, Mon and June.*

Casa Jesusa, Rúa Franja 8, **t** 981 22 19 00 (*moderate*). Probably the best of a gauntlet of *marisquerías* on this street, dishing out giant platters heavily laden with seafood at slightly lower prices than its competitors. *Closed Mon.*

Mesón Laporte, Rúa Franja 23 (*inexpensive*). A tiny and authentic old *pulperia*, where *mamá* and *papá* dish out excellent tapas and *raciones* at bargain prices.

O Vexetariano, Puerta de Aires 3, **t** 981 21 38 26 (*inexpensive*). Comes up with the ovolactarian goods, featuring an excellent and varied menu of international dishes, washed down with organic wines.

revolves around the charming, monumental **Praza de García Hermanos**. Most of the surrounding buildings are from the 18th century, including a neoclassical palace now used as the National Archives of Galicia; this runs a small but interesting historical **Museo de las Mariñas** (*open daily 5–8, Sat 11–1*). The three attractive churches are just off the square: the 14th-century **Santa María del Azogue**; 15th-century **Santiago**; and Gothic **San Francisco**, inspired by the basilica at Assisi.

Rather than take the NVI directly to A Coruña, follow the Ría de Betanzos up to the local resort of **Sada** to see **La Terraza**, the finest *modernista* building in Galicia, designed by López Hernández, made of glass and giant music stands. The road to A Coruña passes the **Pazo de Meirás**, residence of Countess Emilia Pardo Bazán (*see* below), and later Franco, whose descendants still own it.

A Coruña

Occupying the length of the Ría da Coruña and the southwest fringe of the Golfo Ártabro, A Coruña is the liveliest city in Galicia, a big (pop. 230,000), exuberant, commercial capital with character to spare. Sprawling over a peninsula and attached to the mainland by a thin neck of land, it has beautiful windswept beaches facing the Atlantic and a magnificent sheltered harbour in the estuary that has made its fortune and paid for all of its hypnotic wall of windowed balconies or *solanas* that gave A Coruña its nickname 'Crystal City'.

A Coruña's relationship with Britain goes back to its first settlers, Phoenician merchants who imported tin from Cornwall. The Romans called it Ardobicum Corunium, and tenuously associated it with Hercules, who reputedly had a hand in building the lighthouse. The Suevians and the Moors took turns running the show until 1002; in the Middle Ages, English pilgrims to Santiago often landed here, among them Chaucer's Wife of Bath and his patron John of Gaunt, who came in 1386, though unsuccessfully, to claim the Spanish throne for his wife, daughter of Pedro the Cruel.

In the 'Groyne'

The classic view of A Coruña is of its harbour along Av. de la Marina, lined with a solid wall of crystal galleries set in white balconies, a window cleaner's vision of hell. It is magical to sail into, just as Drake fearlessly did in 1589, swooping down in the night with 30 ships to rub salt in Philip's wounds. Only a young girl named María Pita stood in the way, not only raising the alarm to save the city but somehow swiping Drake's flag in the process. In gratitude A Coruña gave her name to its biggest, busiest square, **Praza María Pita**, where the older part of A Coruña – what old British seadogs called 'the Groyne' – begins. Galicia's greatest novelist, Countess Emilia Pardo Bazán, was born in 1851 near the harbour at Rúa Tabernas 13; the mansion now houses the **Royal Gallego Academy** and a small **museum** (*open Mon–Sat 10–12*) dedicated to her. The **Colegiata de Santa María del Campo**, begun in the 1210s and finished in the 1400s, stands at the top of the square. Its sculptors were star-struck: star decorations run along the roof and on the west façade; the triple portal has a carving of the Three Magi. Over the north door two angels stand by as someone seems to fall out of the sky with star symbols, or perhaps Ezekiel's wheel of fire, whirling up in the cosmos. Inside are some fine Romanesque tombs, polychrome statues and just to the left of the altar, another star, carved on a capital. Just down from here, the little Plazuela de Santa Bárbara is A Coruña's most charming, site of the **Convento de Santa Barbara** (1613), where cloistered Poor Clares live behind the carved portal.

Santo Domingo stands on the edge of the evocative **Jardín de San Carlos**, set in the walls of the old fortress of San Carlos. It contains the granite tomb of Sir John Moore,

Philip II and the Invincible Armada

The pious Philip II had more than one bone to pick with Queen Elizabeth's England in the 1580s: Elizabeth had recently invented the Bloody Mary by lopping off the head of Mary Queen of Scots, Philip's favourite candidate for the English throne, and England was helping the Protestants of the Netherlands in their revolt against Spain; Spanish trade routes were threatened but, worst of all, Elizabeth had confirmed the country's Protestant orientation. To solve all of his problems and force England back into the Catholic fold, Philip decided to build up the biggest fleet of warships in Spanish history, and coordinate this invincible armada with an invasion of England by his army in the Netherlands. Finally, on 22 July 1588, an Armada of 130 enormous galleons, manned by 10,000 sailors and 19,000 soldiers, set sail from A Coruña. They were intercepted by Lord Howard, giving rise to a week of sea battles, but it was only when Howard sent fireships that the Spaniards were panicked into breaking up their formation. They met defeat at Gravelines soon after, and were forced home around Scotland to suffer greater indignity in the thrall of appalling storms; by the time the Invincible Armada limped back to Spain, only 76 half-wrecked galleons pulled into port, minus 15,000 soldiers.

who in 1809 led the routed, dispirited British army across Galicia with the French on his tail. At Elviña, just before A Coruña, he sent most of his troops ahead to board ships for home, just as Marshal Soult launched into a vicious attack; Moore managed to stall the French long enough for 15,000 of his men to embark under Soult's nose, an operation that has been called a precursor to Dunkirk.

Just opposite, A Coruña's busy military history is remembered in the **Museo Militar** (*open 10–2*) in the old church of San Francisco. From here, bus No.3 will take you out two kilometres to the northernmost tip of the peninsula and the 431ft **Torre de Hércules** (*open Mon–Fri 10–2 and 4–6; closed Sat afternoon and Sun*), A Coruña's proudest symbol. Built in the 2nd century AD in the time of Trajan, it's the oldest continuous working Roman lighthouse, but with an external skin from 1791. Bring a pep pill: it's 242 steps to the top for the splendid view of the city and ocean.

On the other side of the isthmus lie A Coruña's beaches, **Praias de Ríazor** and **Orzán**. Quieter (except in August), cleaner and prettier strands are outside the city at **Santa Cristina**, **Bastiagueiro**, **Santa Cruz**, **Mera** and **Lorbe** (the farthest, 16 kilometres away).

West of A Coruña: A Costa da Morte

Before tourism invented the Costa del Sol and the Costa Blanca, the Galicians dubbed this region down to Finisterre the 'Coast of Death' in homage to its numerous drownings, shipwrecks and ancient Celtic memories; from the end of the earth, from the end of the Milky Way, Celtic warriors would sail out to their reward in the seven-towered castle of Arianhrod. The scenery within this wild land of the setting sun is romantic, the waves are dramatic, and the beaches pale and inviting; only the water is icy cold.

Ría de Corme e Laxe

Heading west of A Coruña and Carballo, **Buño** is Galicia's traditional pottery town *par excellence*. The road north of Buño ends up at **Malpica**, where the granite cliffs first relax their vigilance. Appropriately enough, the Costa da Morte has some fine dolmens, or Neolithic tombs, beginning with Malpica's **Pedra de Arca**; there are more inland on the road to Bayo. The nearest swimming is to the southwest, at the sheltered **Praia de Niñons**, passing by way of the romantic, ivy-shrouded castle known as the **Torres de Mens**, next to a tiny Romanesque chapel decorated with erotic figures.

To the west lie two picturesque fishing villages, **Corme Porto** and, across the estuary, **Laxe**, which has a white beach, safe even for children; still more remote is the enormous **Praia de Traba**, south along the coast.

Ría de Camariñas

After some very rugged coast, the rocks relent to admit another *ría* shared by the remote fishing hamlets of **Camariñas** and **Muxía**, both renowned for intricate bobbin lace. From little, white and increasingly trendy Camariñas you can walk five kilometres to **Cabo Villán** and its lighthouse, a savage piece of torn coast which makes you feel small and far removed from civilization, but for the experimental windmills set up to harness the winds that whip the cape. **Muxía** has always been a bit more important, as the proud escutcheons on the houses testify. It is also the holy city of

Getting Around

A Coruña and Santiago are the main bases for transport to the Costa da Morte, but **buses** are not all that frequent; if you intend to visit more than one destination in a day, study bus schedules before setting out. Carballo, 35km southwest of A Coruña, is the main bus junction for the coastal villages.

Where to Stay and Eat

The gastronomic prize of the the Death Coast is its barnacles, or *percebes*, which cost a small fortune; the people who gather them from the shore get washed away so often that it is impossible for them to buy insurance.

Malpica ✉ 15113

★★**Hs J. B.**, by the beach, **t** 981 72 19 66 (*inexpensive*). Comfortable and open all year.

★**Hs As Garzas**, in Barizo, **t** 981 72 17 65. Has a **restaurant** and a fine location.

San Francisco (*inexpensive*). Good for reasonable fresh seafood.

Camariñas ✉ 15123

★**Hs Triñares II**, Area da Vila, **t** 981 73 61 08 (*inexpensive*). A handful of rooms with bath.

★**Hs La Marina**, M. Freijó 4, **t** 981 73 60 30 (*cheap*). Of the *hostales*, this one is nearest the sea with the best views and **restaurant**.

Corcubión ✉ 15100

★★★**El Hórreo**, Sta Isabel, **t** 981 74 55 00, **f** 981 74 55 63 (*moderate*). Beautifully located near the sea, this is the largest, most pretentious hotel on the Costa da Morte; it has a pool and garden.

Casa Leston, Ctra Finisterre (at Sardiñeiro), **t** 981 74 73 54 (*moderate*). Can't be beaten for fresh fish and simple good food.

Finisterre ✉ 15155

★**Finisterre**, Federico Ávila 8, **t** 981 74 00 00, **f** 981 74 00 54 (*inexpensive*). The largest and nicest place at the end of the world.

Don Percebe, Ctra Faro, **t** 981 74 05 12. Try this place for bountiful seafood.

Los Tres Golpes, C/Huertas 9, **t** 981 74 00 47. Serves excellent shellfish, featuring the freshest of fresh lobster.

the Costa da Morte, with its seaside sanctuary of **Nostra Señora de la Barca**, where the Virgin Mary herself is said to have sailed in a ship of stone when Santiago was preaching in these parts (it wasn't her only Spanish holiday: she made a similar appearance riding a stone pillar in Zaragoza). Parts of the Virgin's own magic boat may be seen around the church, including the hull, the Pedra de Abalar, which moves whenever it is stepped upon by a person completely free of sin.

Ría de Corcubión and the End of the World

Further south, a byroad off the C552 leads up to the lighthouse at **Cabo Touriñán**, while another branch leads to the huge (and hugely exposed) beach, the **Praia do Rostro**, before continuing south to the little industrial port of **Cée** and **Corcubión**. Here white beaches are sprinkled under the pines, among them **Praia Sardiñeiro** with a few bars and restaurants.

Beyond lies the traditional westernmost point of Europe, the granite houses of **Finisterre** (or Fisterra) huddled like barnacles on the rocks around the church of the miracle-working **Christ of the Golden Beard**, who came out of the sea. Two kilometres beyond is Cabo Finisterre with its lighthouse, the world's end, where Roman legions and pilgrims from Santiago came to gaze at the sun sinking into the limitless horizon. For the best overviews, take the road up to **Vista Monte do Facho**.

From Cée, the C550 follows the coast to **Ezaro**, a wild, picturesque place where the massive granite boulders on 1,968ft Mount Pindo, 'the Celtic Olympus', have mysterious engravings and ruins of ancient shrines. South, the dune-backed beach of **Carnota** is the longest in Galicia, but prone to drownings: even strong swimmers should be wary.

Into the Rías Baixas

The Lower Estuaries, or Rías Baixas/Bajas, almost at once have tamer, greener scenery than their wild cousins to the north; here the ocean is predictably warm enough to maintain a regular holiday trade. These less exposed, less continuously 'flushed' *rías* can, however, get a bit dirty if you swim in the innermost coves.

The Ría de Muros e Noia

Under Monte Costiños on the north edge of the *ría*, **Muros** is a fine, old-fashioned, granite Gallego town, with narrow, arcaded lanes, a palatial market, and a fountain with a stone turtle, all stacked under its Gothic parish church. There's a good beach at **Louro**, 'the golden', 1.6km from Muros on the tip of the cape.

Noia (Noya) is full of legends, beginning with its name, after Noah, whose dove is said to have found the olive branch here, anchored on the holy Celtic mountain of Barbanza. This local Mt Ararat is adorned with numerous dolmens and in Noia itself you can visit the mysterious cemetery next to the Gothic **Santa María a Nova** (1327) where guildsmen between the 10th and 16th centuries left headstones carved with symbols far more pagan than Christian.

Getting Around

RENFE **trains** between A Coruña and Vigo pass through Padrón and Vilagarcía. There are hourly **buses** (7am–9pm) from Santiago to Noia, from where connections can be made to Porto do Son and beyond. From Vilagarcía buses leave for Isla de Arousa.

Tourist Information

Vilagarcía de Arousa: Av. Juan Carlos I, 37, **t** 986 51 01 44.

Cambados: Rúa Novedades.

O Grove: In the port, **t** 986 73 14 15.

There are **markets** in **Noia** (*Thurs*); in **Rúa do Mercado** (*Sun*); in **Vilagarcía** (*Tues* and *Sat*); and in **Cambados** (*Thurs*).

Festivals

Cambados: Wine Festival, *1st Sun of Aug*. Annual celebration of Albariño, hosted in the lovely gardens of the *parador*.

Where to Stay and Eat

Muros ✉ 15250 and Noia ✉ 15250

★★**Hs La Muradana**, Av. de la Marina 107, **t** 981 82 68 85 (*inexpensive*). A good place to eat and sleep.

★★**Hs Ceboleiro**, Av. Galicia 15, **t** 981 82 44 97. A friendly place, with the best **restaurant** (*inexpensive*).

Padrón ✉ 15900

★★★**Escala**, Pazos, **t** 981 81 13 12, **f** 981 81 15 50 (*moderate*). The fanciest place in Padrón.

★★**Hs Casa Cuco**, Av. de Compostela, **t** 981 81 05 11 (*inexpensive*). Of all the places to stay, this has the best name going, providing rooms with or without bath.

La Casa Grande de Cornide, in Cornide, **t** 981 80 55 99, **f** 981 80 57 51. A *pazo-hosteria* from the 18th century with suites, a library and a museum.

Chef Rivera, Enlace Parque 7, **t** 981 81 04 13 (*moderate*). The culinary star of Padrón, this is your chance to dine on José Rivera Casal's superb, seasonal dishes (if you're not squeamish, the lamprey *empanada* is exquisite) and a mix of traditional Gallego and international cuisine.

Casa Ramallo, in Rois, **t** 981 81 12 10. Don't miss this favourite restaurant of Spanish novelist and Nobel Prize-winner, Camilo José Cela.

Vilagarcía de Arousa ✉ 15900

Prices here are over the odds.

★★★★**Pazo O Rial**, O Rial 1, Ctra Vilagarcía-Cambados, **t** 986 50 70 11, **f** 986 50 16 76 (*moderate*). Set in a pine wood, this 17th-century place is sweet and quiet and near the sea, with a pool and satellite TV.

Often windy beaches and lagoons dot the coast of the *ría* south from Noia to the sculpted dunes of Corrubedo. From **Oleiros** you can drive up to a pair of miradors (1,633ft) for great views, or visit the exceptional dolmen, **Axeitos**: an enormous rock measuring nearly 16 square metres, supported by eight smaller ones.

Ría de Arousa to Pádron

The Ría de Arousa is touristically the most developed of all Galicia's estuaries. The first town you come to, **Santa Uxia** (or Eugenia) **de Ribeira**, combines tourism with its status as Spain's top coastal and underwater fishing port. At the head of the estuary, at the mouth of the blood-sucking lamprey-rich River Ulla, **Padrón** is the raggle-taggle capital of Galicia's favourite vegetable *tapa*, midget green *pimientas de Padrón*.

Padrón has plenty of legendary baggage to accompany its peppers: it is ancient *Iria Flavia*, the port where Santiago's disciples sailed with their precious cargo, anchoring their stone boat to a stone 'memorial pillar' (*pedrón*), now displayed under the altar in the 17th-century church of **Santiago**. The stone boat was met by a pagan queen, Lupa,

★Hs 82, Pza de la Constitución 13, **t/f** 986 50 62 22 (*inexpensive*). Small but more than pleasant; and there are several others like it along the waterfront.

Chocolate, in Villajuán (Vilaxoán, 2km away), **t** 986 50 11 99 (*expensive*). Splurge at Galicia's most famous restaurant, where divine grilled fish or tender Texas-sized steaks are prepared by a flamboyant owner, accompanied by famously bad service. There are also 18 attractive **rooms** (*inexpensive*).

Loliña, Alameda 1 in Carril, **t** 986 50 12 81 (*moderate*). The day's catch gets the home-cooked treatment, served in a sun-baked courtyard. *Closed Sun eve, Mon and Nov.*

Cambados ✉ 36630

★★★Parador de Cambados Albariño, Pso de Cervantes, **t** 986 54 22 50, **f** 986 54 20 68, *cambadosalbarino@parador.es* (*expensive*). Occupies an old country *pazo* (manor house) with a beautiful garden and a **restaurant** featuring seafood.

★El Duende, Ourense 10, **t** 986 54 30 75, **f** 986 54 29 00 (*inexpensive–cheap*). Offers a nice, cheaper alternative by the sea.

O Arco, Real 14, **t** 986 54 23 12 (*cheap*). Remains the classic place to dine, with a good *menú*.

O Grove/A Toxa ✉ 36980

★★★★★Gran Hotel La Toja, Isla A Toxa, **t** 986 73 00 25, **f** 986 73 00 26 (*luxury*). In high season, for high rates, you can enjoy golf, tennis, a spa, a heated pool, while rubbing shoulders with the likes of Julio Iglesias, all of it in a park setting.

★★★★Louxo, **t/f** 986 73 02 00 (*expensive*). Bask here in almost as much luxury for just over half as much.

★★★Mar Atlántico, Pedras Negras San Vicente do Mar, **t** 986 73 80 61, **f** 986 73 82 99 (*moderate*). On the other side of town; similarly well equipped, with tennis courts.

★★La Lanzada, Playa de la Lanzada , **t** 986 74 32 32, **f** 986 74 48 61 (*inexpensive*). Has lovely views over the ocean from its breezy rooms.

★Hs Isolino, Av. Castelao 30, **t** 986 73 02 36 (*inexpensive*). One of the best deals in town, offering good-value, modern rooms at the heart of O Grove's night-time scene.

O Crisol, Rúa Hospitál 10, **t** 986 73 00 99 (*expensive*). A long-time favourite for its excellent seafood and fine service.

Beira Mar, Av. Beiramar 30, **t** 986 73 07 41 (*expensive*). Serves delicious oysters plucked straight from the *ría*, in elegantly modern surroundings.

Caldas de Reis ✉ 36650

★★Acuña, Herrería 2, **t** 986 54 00 10, **f** 986 51 00 10 (*moderate*). Attached to the spa, it has not refurbished its charming *modernista* air, with *solanas* overhanging the river.

Casa Loureiro, Cardín 26, in Saiar, **t** 981 53 52 38 (*inexpensive*). This provides five nice rooms in a farmhouse.

who mockingly gave the Christians two wild bulls to transport the coffin. When yoked the bulls turned into peaceful oxen. Astonished, Lupa converted at once and was baptized by Saint James, who popped out of his coffin in the ox cart to do the job.

Vilagarcía to Isla A Toxa

The big town on the south bank is **Vilagarcía de Arousa**, the glossy base for Galicia's drug-smuggling barons; the woodsy, sand-fringed **Isla de Arousa** is reputedly the key drop-off point for Colombian cocaine in Europe. All this nefarious underworld activity seems far away in **Cambados**, an atmospheric, noble town with plenty of old family crests. It's also the capital of Albariño, the dry, fruity white wine that is ideal with heaving plates of *mariscos*. From Cambados, the C550 circles down to the resort of **O Grove**, linked by a bridge to **Isla A Toxa**), a sand-rimmed islet that first became famous when a donkey left for dead was miraculously restored after a few days. Now adorned with a casino and golf course, A Toxa is designed for people with bags of money, leaving O Grove for those who don't, but who know how to have a good time.

The Ría de Pontevedra

Although nothing in the southern Rías Baixas is as touristy as the Ría de Arousa, the Ría de Pontevedra fills up in the summer. The scenery is domesticated and pretty, while most of the beaches are extremely safe. Pontevedra, the provincial capital, is a handsome confection of granite, the best urban architecture in Galicia after Santiago.

The end of the Salnés peninsula dividing the Arousa and Pontevedra estuaries is occupied by the tremendous sweep of the **Praia da Lanzada**, one of Galicia's finest beaches. Nearby **Portonovo** and its neighbour **Sanxenxo** are jumping little resorts, with beaches like sugar and a chamber-of-commerce claim that they get more sun than the rest of Galicia. Roads from Sanxenxo or Combarro go up to the abandoned medieval **Monasterio de Armenteira**, where the Virgin favoured a monk named Ero: one morning, while listening to the song of a bird, he was granted a look into eternity. To him the ecstasy lasted but a few minutes, but upon returning to the monastery he found that centuries had passed (a similar story crops up in Navarra, *see* pp.321–2.)The rose window on the main façade of the church is believed to have been a mandala for meditation, the carved archivaults around the door are *mudéjar*, and the guardian will show you the unusual octagonal cupola inspired by Islamic architecture. Look for the peculiar masons' marks left on the walls.

Getting Around

By Train and Bus

In Pontevedra the RENFE station, **t** 986 85 13 13, and bus station, **t** 986 85 24 08, are next to each other, but a long walk along Alféreces Provisionales; buses C1 and C2 can take you into town, except on Sundays. Frequent buses serve the main *ría* villages.

By Boat

Up to eight ferries a day run from Portonovo and Sanxenxo to the Isla de Ons, from July to mid-September. Three boats make the longer journey out from Marin.

Tourist Information

Sanxenxo: Av. Generalísimo, **t** 986 72 02 85.

Pontevedra: Main office at General Mola, **t** 986 85 08 14;
municipal booths are in the Alameda and the Jardínes de Castro Sampedro.
Walking tours (only in Spanish) are available during July, Aug and Sept.
Post Office: on Oliva, down the road from the Capilla de la Peregrina.
Internet Access: at Santa Clara 2, just outside the *casco viejo*.

There is a **market** in **Pontevedra** (*Mon–Sat*) in the Mercado by the river.

Festivals

Pontevedra: Feast of the Virgen La Peregrina, *Aug*. Celebrated with folk dances and a procession of hundreds of revellers, while the 18- to 30-year-olds have been known to wreak havoc by indulging in an all-out red wine war.

Where to Stay and Eat

Sanxenxo/Sangenjo ✉ 36000

There are scores of places, but just try to get one in the summer without a reservation.

★★★**Rotilio**, Av. do Porto 7, **t** 986 72 02 00, **f** 986 72 41 88 (*expensive*). Some of the best are along Praia de Silgar, such as this modern fashionable place (with a superb seafood **restaurant**).

★★**Hs Minso**, Av. do Porto 1, **t** 986 72 01 50, **f** 986 69 09 32 (*expensive*). Welcoming, and recently renovated.

Pontevedra

Pontevedra is the perfect genteel granite Gallego town. Its streets are shaded with arcades, its squares marked with stone crosses. Ancient tradition states that it was first called *Helenes*, founded by Teucer (Teucro), who fought at Troy. *Teucro* means 'Trojan' in Castilian, and there is, in fact, a Teucro who fits the bill, a son of Scamander, who is recorded as leading a band of Cretans to western Spain to found a colony.

It's also significant that Teucro named the city after Helen, the sister of the twins Castor and Pollux, the favourite gods of Roman warriors. The cult of the warrior twins inspired the soldiers of the Reconquista in the apocryphal tradition that St James was the twin brother of Jesus. If this weren't enough, Pontevedra (along with Mallorca, Barcelona and Corsica) also claims to be the birthplace of Columbus; there's a statue to him at the west end of the Alameda looking towards the distant Americas.

Pontevedra's promising mythological progress was stymied back in the Middle Ages, when the Río Lérez silted up the port. By the time of Columbus, all the marine business had moved south to Vigo, leaving a compact, endearing and exceptionally vibrant **Zona Monumental**, its showcases all within a stone's throw of the Praza da Peregrina. Here you'll find the twin-towered 18th-century **Virgen La Peregrina** church, built in the shape of a scallop, to house a statue of the city's patroness. Behind the

*****Panadeira**, Praia da Panadeira, **t** 986 72 37 28 (*moderate*). A friendly little establishment in a pretty spot.

Pontevedra ✉ 36000

********Galicia Palace**, Av. de Vigo 3, **t** 986 86 44 11, **f** 986 86 10 26 (*expensive*). Central and comfortable but not that luxurious, although it does have a garage.

******Parador de Pontevedra**, Barón 19, **t** 986 85 58 00, **f** 986 85 21 95, *pontevedra@parador.es* (*expensive*). Prices are only a smidgeon higher here, and you get the chance to sleep in a Gallego *pazo* from the 11th century, with a magnificent stone staircase and a garden.

******Virgen del Camino**, Virgen del Camino, **t** 986 85 59 04, **f** 986 85 09 00 (*moderate*). Comfortable and with a garden.

*****Comercio**, A. González Besada 3, **t** 986 85 12 17, **f** 986 85 99 91 (*inexpensive*). Adequate and central, with a better than average restaurant.

*****Hs Rúas**, Sarmiento 17, **t** 986 84 64 16, **f** 986 84 64 11 (*inexpensive*). Pleasantly located in the Zona Monumental, has good rooms with bath, some with balconies overlooking the pretty Praza da Verdura.

Casa Maruja, Av. Santa María 12, **t** 986 85 49 01. Right on the edge of the *casco viejo*, and probably the best budget deal in town.

Monasterio de Poio, 2km from Pontevedra, **t** 986 77 00 00. The Mercedarian monks up here run a cheap guesthouse.

Casa Solla, at San Salvador de Poio (2km out of town), **t** 986 85 26 78 (*expensive*). Pontevedra has one of the leading restaurants in Galicia; famed for its devotion to traditional recipes, the freshest seafood and meat, matched by excellent service. *Closed Thurs and Sun eve.*

Doña Antonia, Soportales de la Ferrería 4 (on the first floor), **t** 986 84 72 74 (*expensive*). Has a reputation for imaginative dishes – duck breasts, baked honeyed lamb and seafood salads; also a delicious chocolate *tarta de trufa* with coffee cream. *Closed Sun.*

Casa Román, Av. Augusto García Sánchez (south of the centre), **t** 986 84 35 60 (*moderate menú*). Prides itself on its select shellfish. *Closed Sun eve.*

La Navarra, Princesa 13. Pontevedra has plenty of opportunities to eat economically in the bars in the Zona Monumental: this one serves a range of wines and snacks.

A. Picota, Rúa de la Peregrina 4. Serves tasty *charcuterie* and cheese.

Virgen, there's a lovely 16th-century fountain in a small garden and the 13th- and 14th-century church of **San Francisco** with some good tombs. Across the street, C/Pasantería descends from Pza da Ferrería to Pontevedra's most perfect square, the **Praza da Leña**, with granite porticoes and an ancient cross as its centrepiece. On one side two houses have joined to form the **Museo Provincial** (*open 10–1.30 and 4.30–8, Sun 11–1; closed Mon*), with a collection of jet figures, Celtic gold work, and art, including works by the Gallego caricaturist Alfonso Castelao.

If Pontevedra has a drawback it tends to be olfactory, a strong pong which wafts in when the wind's up from the massive paper mill to the south, which usually puts people off from exploring further. Persevere. Near **Mogor** are some of the most important petroglyphs in Spain, a labyrinth and spirals carved by the Celts. Another 15 kilometres further south along the C550s, **Bueu**, a sleepy fishing village with two *hostales*, makes a great base from which to explore the surrounding beaches. The sands continue down to the tip of the cape, **Hio**, site of Galicia's most elaborate stone crucifix, sculpted out of a single block of granite in the 19th century by José Cerviño of Pontevedra, with a Descent from the Cross and souls in Purgatory.

The Ría de Vigo

The Ría de Vigo is the economic star of Galicia's estuaries, widening to form the sheltered inlet of **San Simón**, site of one of Europe's largest oyster beds. At the mouth of the estuary, the enchanting **Cíes islets** (*now a national park; the only place to stay there is a campsite; call* **t** *986 43 83 58 to see if there's a place and buy a voucher with your boat ticket*) protect the port from tempests off the Atlantic. Linked by a lick of sand that forms a sheltered lagoon of calm, crystal water, the islands offer a perfect lazy day out on the beach. Their shelter enables mussel farmers to moor their wooden platforms or *bateas* safely in the estuary, where the molluscs incubate on ropes suspended in the water. Vigo itself has grown to be the largest city in Galicia (pop. 250,000).

Vigo

Nothing less than Spain's premier fishing port, Vigo occupies a privileged hillside spot that attracted both ancient Phoenician and Greek seamen. Its name comes from the Roman *Vicus Spacorum*, but the city claims that its true founder was an early 12th-century troubador, Martín Codax. In 1702, the English surprised a joint Spanish and French treasure fleet just returned from the New World and captured some of the ships but 11 were sunk or run aground near the tiny islets by the suspension bridge; some sources say the silver had already been unloaded, but they haven't stopped treasure-seekers from looking. For all that, there's not much to 'see' in Vigo beyond the fine views towards the sea, although the old part of town hugging the fishing port, the **Barrio del Berbés**, is thick with atmosphere and rough, cobbled streets. As in A Coruña, there's a very lively fish auction by the waterside at the crack of dawn.

Getting Around

By Air

Vigo's airport is 8km from town, with connections to major Spanish cities and Lisbon, **t** 986 26 82 00.

By Bus andTrain

This sector of the coast is well served by buses, and there are several trains daily between Pontevedra and Vigo and beyond. The train station is at the top of Rúa Alfonso XIII, a 15-minute walk uphill from the port, **t** 986 43 11 14. Frequent buses (to Tui, A Garda, Baiona, Pontevedra, O Grove, Vilagarcía, Santiago and A Coruña) depart from the bus station near Pza de España, a few blocks beyond the train station; for information, **t** 986 37 34 11. Bus R4 runs along Rúa Príncipe in the centre to the bus station.

By Boat

Weekdays from 6am–10pm and Sundays from 9am–10.30pm, ferries (taking foot passengers only) sail every half-hour to Cangas, every hour to Moaña and up to 10 times daily from mid-June to mid-Sept to the **Islas Cíes** from Vigo's Estación Marítima near El Berbés (Naveira Mar de Ons, **t** 986 22 52 72). For the Cíes, buy your ticket to the islands as early in the day as possible. This way you'll be free to choose the time of your return boat – the latest sailings fill up first. The islands are also accessible from Cangas and Baiona in summer.

Tourist Information

Cangas: Rúa Real, **t** 986 30 50 00.

Vigo: Las Avenidas, by the port, **t** 986 43 05 77.

Post Office: Reconquista 2, off Praza de Compostela.

Internet Access: República de Argentina 24; and also at Euris, Ventura Misa 14 (in Baiona Academia).

Tui: Ponte Tripes, **t** 986 60 17 89.

There are regular **markets** in **Cangas** (*Fri*); in **Baiona** (*Mon*); and in **Tui** there is a weekly market (*Thurs*) featuring both Gallego and Portuguese produce.

Where to Stay and Eat

Vigo ✉ 36200

★★★★**Gran Hotel Samil**, Apartado 472 (5km south on the Praia de Samil), **t** 986 24 00 00, **f** 986 24 19 00 (*expensive*). A good place to luxuriate beside the beach; extensive facilities include a pool and tennis courts.

★★★★**Bahía de Vigo**, Canovas del Castillo 24, **t** 986 22 67 00, **f** 986 43 74 87 (*expensive*). Has great views of the port and the *ría*; its **restaurant**, claimed to be the biggest *marisquería* in Spain, serves up colossal *parrilladas* of grilled seafood.

★★★**Ensenada**, Alfonso XIII 7, **t** 986 44 79 00, **f** 986 44 74 14 (*moderate*). Modern and in the centre with fine views across the bay.

★★**Hs Puerta del Sol**, Puerta del Sol 14, **t** 986 22 23 64 (*inexpensive*). Pleasant and well looked after, in a solid old stone building with glassed-in balconies.

★★**Hs La Nueva Colegiata**, Praza da Iglesia 2, **t** 986 22 09 52 (*cheap*). Still sparkles after its recent paint job; all rooms have bath, and double glazing to counter the wake-the-dead tolling of the bells across the plaza. C/Carral is a good area for cheap sleeps.

Eating out is an excellent reason for staying in Vigo. To every kind of seafood and shellfish add the delicacies from the River Minho: salmon, lamprey and baby eels, *anguillas*, the latter two favourite stuffings for *empanadas*.

Síbaris, Av. García Barbón 122, **t** 986 22 15 26 (*expensive*). Gets kudos for its first quality land and sea cuisine in an upmarket, intimate setting. *Closed Sun*.

El Castillo, Monte del Castro, **t** 986 42 12 99 (*moderate*). Dine here with a superb view; exquisitely grilled fish and meat are the specialities. *Closed Sun eve and Mon*.

El Mosquito, Pza da Pedra 4 (near the port), **t** 986 22 44 11 (*moderate*). For seafood or roast leg of lamb, the long-established people's choice in Vigo is a classic place with a familiar atmosphere.

José Luis, Av. Florida (out by the stadium; take a taxi), **t** 986 29 95 22 (*moderate*). Come here for something different; serves excellent mushroom, game and Basque dishes and a good list of Riojas to wash them down. *Closed Sun*.

Bodegón Centro, in Manuel Núñez. When you get sick of fish try the delicious hams and cheeses served here.

Gal Gala, Rúa Pracer 4, **t** 986 22 14 17 (*inexpensive*). Vigo's only vegetarian restaurant, interestingly located on its only red-light street. *Closed Sun eve and Mon*.

There's normally plenty going on in the streets immediately surrounding the old port. Regular open-air **concerts** are held in the summer in the Parque Quiñones de Léon; from classical music to big-name rock artists.

Varadero, Rúa Montero Rios. The liveliest of a range of bars along this pedestrianized street, just back from the water, with a disco. There's a less frenetic scene on Rúa Churruca near the RENFE station, a series of bars playing every conceivable music genre.

Café Concierto Joker, Rúa Carral 3. For something a bit more interactive, this place has a regular programme of live blues, jazz and swing bands, and a large dance floor.

Baiona ✉ 36300

****Parador Conde de Gondomar**, Monte Real, **t** 986 35 50 00, **f** 986 35 50 76 (*expensive*). Galicia's finest, housed in a modern reconstruction of a typical Galician *pazo* within the medieval walls of Monterreal, in a lovely park; it offers a pool, tennis, children's recreation, and a short walk to the beach.

Pazo de Mendoza, Elduayen 1, **t** 986 38 50 14, **f** 986 38 98 88 (*moderate*). Age will impart character to the rooms at this newly restored *casona* from the 18th century; in the meantime, guests can comfort themselves in the sensational **restaurant**, Baiona's finest, where the best of Gallego traditions and ingredients are combined with the finest elements of *nouvelle* sensibility. The monumental *menú degustación* (*expensive*) offers such delights as cuttlefish brochette in *Albariño tempura*.

*Hs Mesón del Burgo**, Barrio del Burgo, **t** 986 35 60 18 (*moderate*). One of a wide range of moderate options in Baiona.

Hs Tres Carabelas, Ventura Misa 67, **t** 986 35 54 41, **f** 986 35 59 21 (*inexpensive*). A fine old inn on a narrow cobbled lane right in the middle of town, with prices at the top end of this category.

Pedro Madruga, Ramón y Cajal 1, **t** 986 35 73 67 (*expensive*). Renowned as one of Baiona's finest *marisquerias*; its ample selection of (mostly live) crustaceous goodies decorates an outside counter, and provides pre-dinner entertainment for the crowds, who are invariably waiting for a table; remember to book in advance.

O Moscón, Alférez Barreiro 2, **t** 986 35 50 08 (*moderate*). Known for its fine lobster (*bogavante*).

A Garda ✉ 01300

Convento de San Benito, Pza de San Benito, **t** 986 61 11 66, **f** 986 61 15 17 (*moderate*). Set in a renovated 16th-century monastery with a lovely garden in the cloister; its restaurant, called Os Remos, serves a delicious lobster and rice dish.

*Pazo Santa Tecla**, **t** 986 61 00 02 (*moderate*). Alternatively, you could stay near the top of Monte Tecla in this delightful place with views in every direction. *Open June–Sept*.

El Gran Sol, Malteses 32 (*inexpensive*). Good fish soups and seafood wait at this friendly family-run *taberna*. *Closed Sun*.

Tui ✉ 36700

***Parador San Telmo**, Av. Portugal, **t** 986 60 03 09, **f** 986 60 21 63 (*expensive*). Overlooking the Minho, set in a large reproduction of a typical Gallego *pazo* 1km below town, with a garden, tennis and a pool; all very refined.

***Colón Tuy**, Colón 11, **t** 986 60 02 23, **f** 986 60 03 27 (*moderate*). Offers similar facilities for less.

*Hs San Telmo 91**, Av. de la Concordia 88, **t** 986 60 30 11 (*inexpensive*). Otherwise try here; all rooms with bath.

O Cabalo Furado, Pza Generalísimo, **t** 986 60 12 15 (*moderate*). Offers good home cooking. *Closed Sun*.

Abadía do Pelouro Aixeto, at Caldelas de Tui, **t** 986 62 90 24 (*expensive*). For something special, look into this restaurant in Caldelas de Tui (12km from Tui), where two delightful apartments are also available.

Mesón Taqueyui, Pza Generalísimo (*cheap*). Counters the marine obsession with *raciones* of ham and *queso de tetilla*.

South of Vigo to the Ría de Baiona

Vigo's main beaches, white **Praia de Canido** and **Praia Samil**, are just west and often crowded, but the main lure is **Baiona** (Bayona), one of Galicia's choice resorts. The coast is embellished with little beaches of soft sand, namely **Ladeira**, **Santa María** and the magnificent crescent of **Praia América**.

To the south, **A Garda** has a clutch of nouveau-riche *americanos'* bungalows, though people have lived there for much longer: the excavated Celtic *castro* on Monte Santa Tecla, a 40-minute walk up from the village, is one of the most important fortified hill settlements in Spain; it was inhabited from the 7th century BC up to Roman times.

The nearest beach is at **Camposancos**, three kilometres away, overlooking the wide Río Minho, Galicia's prettiest river and the frontier between Spain and Portugal.

Tui

One of the seven ancient capitals of Galicia, Tui is picturesquely piled upon its acropolis; like Pontevedra, it claims to have been founded by wandering Greeks after the Trojan War. It was the capital of the Visigoth King Witiza in 700, and has seen many battles and border skirmishes with Portugal. Tui's granite lanes and houses are crowned by the military profile of the **Catedral de Santa María** with its powerful walls and keep; which did double duty as Tui's castle until the 13th century. There is a fine Romanesque porch and a portal from 1225, carved with the Adoration of the Magi by French-trained sculptors, one of the first and finest Gothic works in Galicia. The interior contains the relics of San Telmo, otherwise known as Pedro González of Astorga (confessor of King Saint Ferdinand of Castile), who died while working among the seafolk of Galicia in 1246. He is the patron saint of Spanish sailors, who confused his name with their first patron St Elmo (or Erasmus), who sends sailors his lucky fire to light upon their masts. His tomb oozes a vinegary gunk much prized as a cure-all.

In half an hour you can walk from the centre of Tui to the lovely Portuguese walled town of **Valença do Minho**, crossing an iron bridge built by Gustave Eiffel.

Up the Minho to Ourense

Galicia's least known and only landlocked province is an introspective place, with more valleys, they say, than towns, descending from the great tableland of Castile to form the frayed coastline of *rías*. The province is famous for wine, hot springs, and Spain's walking sarcophagus, Julio Iglesias.

From Tui to Ribadavia

Both the train and road follow the wooded banks of the Minho, offering one more chance to cross into Portugal on the ferry from Salvaterra do Minho to the delightful city of **Monção**. To the east, the river takes on a wide and elegiac quality, around the beginning of the wine-growing region of Ribeiro. Ribeiro's charming 15th-century capital, **Ribadavia**, has the best-preserved Jewish *barrio* in Galicia, a web of narrow lanes around the church of Santiago. Ribadavia has a beautiful **Praza Mayor** and some interesting Romanesque churches: **San Juan** has a 13th-century *cruceiro*, while the **Convento de Santo Domingo** has a fine Gothic church and a simple cloister. You can learn about the local wines at the **Museo del Ribeiro** (*open 10–1 and 5–8*) or visit the ruined **Castillo de los Condes de Ribadavia**.

South of Ribadavia, the village of **Celanova** has a venerable Benedictine monastery of **San Salvador** (*ask for the key to the cloister*), with a gargantuan *retablo* of 1697 and the choir is a masterpiece of Gothic carving. East of Celanova (and south of Ourense on the N525) the medieval town of **Allariz** is a monument in itself and site of two more Romanesque churches: **Santiago**,with an unusual round apse; and **San Esteban**.

Ourense (Orense)

Continuing up the Río Minho, Ourense puts its best face forward, greeting visitors with a graceful **Ponte Romano**. The biggest stone bridge in Spain, it was built by the Romans and rebuilt on the ancient piers in the 13th century by Ourense's bishop. It is still used, to put it mildly: traffic is Ourense's day-in day-out nightmare.

If you can find a place to park, or don't mind walking a mile in from the bus or train stations, you can see what first attracted the Romans: the steaming hot springs, *Aquae Urentes*, known by the Visigoths and Suevi as Warm Sea (hence *Ourense*). The main source, **Las Burgas**, still steams out of the neoclassical fountain at a constant, nearly boiling temperature midway down Rúa do Progreso.

Up from here, the arcaded **Praza Maior** is Ourense's historic core and hub of its social life. The old episcopal palace houses the **Museo Arqueológico Provincial** (*open daily 9.30–2.30; closed Mon*), with finds spanning from the Neolithic era to the Bronze Age. In the corner of Praza Maior, the **Cathedral** was begun in the 12th century and is entered through the **Pórtico del Paraíso**, a 13th-century reproduction of Santiago's Pórtico de la Gloria. The high altar contains the reliquary of St Martin of Tours, while the florid Baroque chapel houses Ourense's oddest attraction, the Santísimo Cristo, boasting real hair and a wood and fabric body; according to legend it was made by Nicodemus and floated ashore near Finisterre. The **Museo Catedralicio** (*open 11.30–1 and 4.30–7*) off the 12th-century cloister has one of Galicia's first printed books and the 'Treasure of San Rosendo': rare 10th-century chesspieces carved out of rock crystal.

Around Ourense

From Ourense, take the N525 north to the monumental Cistercian monastery of **Oseira** (*open daily 9.30–12.30 and 3.30–5*), founded in 1137 by four hermits. The façade has a gigantic Churrigueresque doorway and the odd crest of two bones with the tree of knowledge; the massive church dates from the 12th century.

The most majestic scenery in these parts begins just east of Ourense, heading up the Minho along the N120, where the cliffs over the river rise ever steeper. At **San Esteban**, dominated by its Romanesque **Monasterio de Ribas de Sil** (and its three atmospheric cloisters) the Sil flows into the Minho, and along the latter are wild gorges to walk along. The nearly as dramatic C536 east of Ourense goes up to **Esgos**,

Getting Around

By Train

Ourense is the main hub here, with trains to Santiago, Lugo, A Coruña, Vigo, Ribadavia, León and elsewhere. RENFE's Estación Empalme is across the river, **t** 988 21 02 02; tickets also on sale at Rúa do Paseo 15, **t** 988 21 46 04.

By Bus

The bus station is 1km from the centre on the Vigo road, **t** 988 21 60 27, with frequent services to Vigo and all major points in Galicia.

Tourist Information

Ribadavia: Praza Mayor, **t** 988 47 12 75.
Ourense: Curros Enríquez 1, **t** 988 37 20 20.
Verín: Casa del Esculo, **t** 988 41 16 14.

There are **markets** in **Ourense** (*7th* and *17th* of month); in **Allariz** (*1st* and *15th* of month); in **Ribadavia** (*10th* and *25th* of month); and in **Verín** (*Wed* and *Fri*).

Where to Stay and Eat

Ribadavia ✉ 32000

★★**Hs Pza**, Pza Maior, **t** 988 47 05 76 (*inexpensive*). Well restored and well run, right in the heart of the old quarter; its **restaurant** is one of the better choices in town.

Hospedaje Vista Alegre, Av. Rodriguez de la Fuente 14, **t** 988 47 12 86. Offers decent and very cheap bathless rooms, and serves a good-value *menú*.

Ourense ✉ 32000

★★★★**Gran Hotel San Martín**, Curros Enríquez 1, **t** 988 37 18 11, **f** 988 37 21 38 (*expensive*). Recently completely renovated with large rooms with a/c, in the old part of town.

★★★**Auriense**, at O Cumial Xeixalbo, **t** 988 23 49 00, **f** 988 24 50 01 (*moderate*). If you've got a car, this new hotel is a few minutes from the centre and offers a pool and tennis in a quiet setting.

★**Hs San Miguel II**, San Miguel 14, **t** 988 23 92 03 (*cheap*). A basic, central option, handy for the **restaurant** next door.

San Miguel, San Miguel 12, **t** 988 22 07 95 (*expensive–moderate*). Next door to Hs San Miguel is one of Ourense's best restaurants, specializing in seafood fresh from the coast, accompanied by Galicia's finest wines, served in the traditional *taza*. *Closed Tues.*

Martín Fierro, Sáenz Díez 17, **t** 988 37 20 26 (*expensive*). Choose one of three dining rooms and tuck in to the surf or turf delicacies from the grill, or try the tasty pilgrims' menu (*moderate*). *Closed Sun.*

Carroceira, San Miguel 10, **t** 988 22 05 66. Has a simple, good *inexpensive* menu. *Closed Mon.*

Queixo, Pan e Viño, Pza Flórez. For tapas stick around the cathedral; this place has good hams and farm cheeses.

Puebla de Trives ✉ 32600

★★★**Pazo Casa Grande**, Marqués de Trives, **t/f** 988 33 20 66 (*inexpensive*). Set in a lovely 18th-century building with seven atmospheric rooms that share a private chapel.

★★**Queixa**, Manzaneda (ski resort), **t** 988 30 97 47, **f** 988 31 08 75 (*moderate doubles, and about €90 for a bungalow for six*). Offers a heated pool, tennis, children's activities and more. Book ahead.

Verín ✉ 32600

★★★**Parador de Verín**, 4km outside Verín, **t** 988 41 00 75, **f** 988 41 20 17, *verin@parador.es* (*expensive*). Located next to the 13th-century castle, with lovely views across the valley below; eat in its **restaurant**, which has seafood among other Gallego treats.

then continues to rise higher and higher to **Puebla de Trives**, where the ski resort of **Manzaneda** (*call* ***t*** *988 31 08 75 to see if there's any snow*) has 10 pistes of all degrees of difficulty, served by a chairlift and three other ski lifts.

If you're heading southwest from Ourense towards Bragança or Zamora, you may want to stop in the old walled town of **Verín**, capital of the wine-growing Monterrey valley. Don't pass up the chance to try a bottle of Verín red – as long as you aren't driving anywhere. This high-octane Galician wine can pack 14 per cent alcohol.

Old Castile and León

13

Old Castile and León

Highlights

1 Lacy Gothic spires of Burgos Cathedral
2 Haunted landscapes and Dark-Age monasteries of El Bierzo
3 León's perfect French Gothic cathedral, covered in storks' nests
4 Salamanca: Spain's gracious medieval university city
5 The weirdest Spanish castle, at Coca

Old Castile and León encompasses two ancient kingdoms of Spain and the *meseta* – a flat, semi-arid table-top 2,295–3,280ft above sea level, where the climate, summed up in an old Castilian proverb, is nine months of winter and three months of hell. It looks like no other place in Europe: endless rolling dun-coloured plains, spotted with scrub and wrinkled mountains, but few trees; during the mindless free-for-all of the Reconquista nearly all of the forests were axed. Depending on your mood you may find the *meseta* romantic and picturesque, or brooding and eerie, but you will never forget it. From this unlikely land, however, came the culture, language and people

who would dominate in their day not only the nations of Iberia, but a good part of two continents. Even today Burgos, seat of the first counts of Castile, is the headquarters of all that is pure Castilian and *castizo*, down to the proper lisping pronunciation of the name of Castile's hero, El Cid, or 'El Theed'.

In early times Castile not only resembled America's Far West, but played the same kind of frontier role twice in European history. After the Romans whipped the native Iberians, retired legionaries were given land to raise wheat. The Visigoths followed in their tracks, but the Moors found little to like and conquered Old Castile without settling it. The Christian kingdoms to the north erected a string of border fortifications that gave the region its name Castile ('land of castles') sometime around 800. In 882 the first part of Castile was reconquered by Alfonso III of Asturias; two years later, Diego Porcelos founded Burgos and became the first of Castile's counts. According to the medieval *Romance de Fernán González*, the Good Count Fernán González obtained Castile's independence from Asturias–León in the 10th century by selling the king of Asturias a horse and goshawk. The king, lacking any handy cash, promised Fernán González he'd pay him double the price for every day that he didn't pay. The king forgot his promise, and by the time Fernán reminded him, the sum was so vast that all the king could do was give him Castile.

Fernán González formed his fledging state politically into seven counties: the Antiguas Merindades de Castilla. Unlike the feudal Christian kingdoms to the north, Castile was settled by free men or *hidalgos*, who owned their farms and bore responsibility for defending them. The difficulties in repopulating the empty land were eased by the development of the *camino de Santiago*, especially after Castile was 'tamed' by the reconquest of Toledo by Alfonso VI and El Cid in 1085. It set off a medieval boom: settlers moved in and towns sprouted along the length of the road. Most have been collecting dust since Charles V sucked them dry in the 16th century.

Northern Castile and León

The northern reaches of Castilla y León are its oldest, encompassing some of the most striking, weird and unknown landscapes in Spain. Here lie the rich monasteries, ancient churches and great Gothic cathedrals of Burgos and León and, in between, picturesque little towns that are sometimes little changed since medieval pilgrims wended their way to Compostela.

Approaches to Burgos

This section covers the approaches to Burgos from the east and north, whether you're coming in slowly along the pilgrims' road from La Rioja, quickly on the *autopista* from Bilbao, or through the magnificent mountain scenery of the Cantabrian range from Santander.

The pilgrimage road follows the N120 from Santo Domingo de la Calzada (*see* pp.334–5) and enters Castile at medieval **Redecilla del Campo**. Traditionally, the border

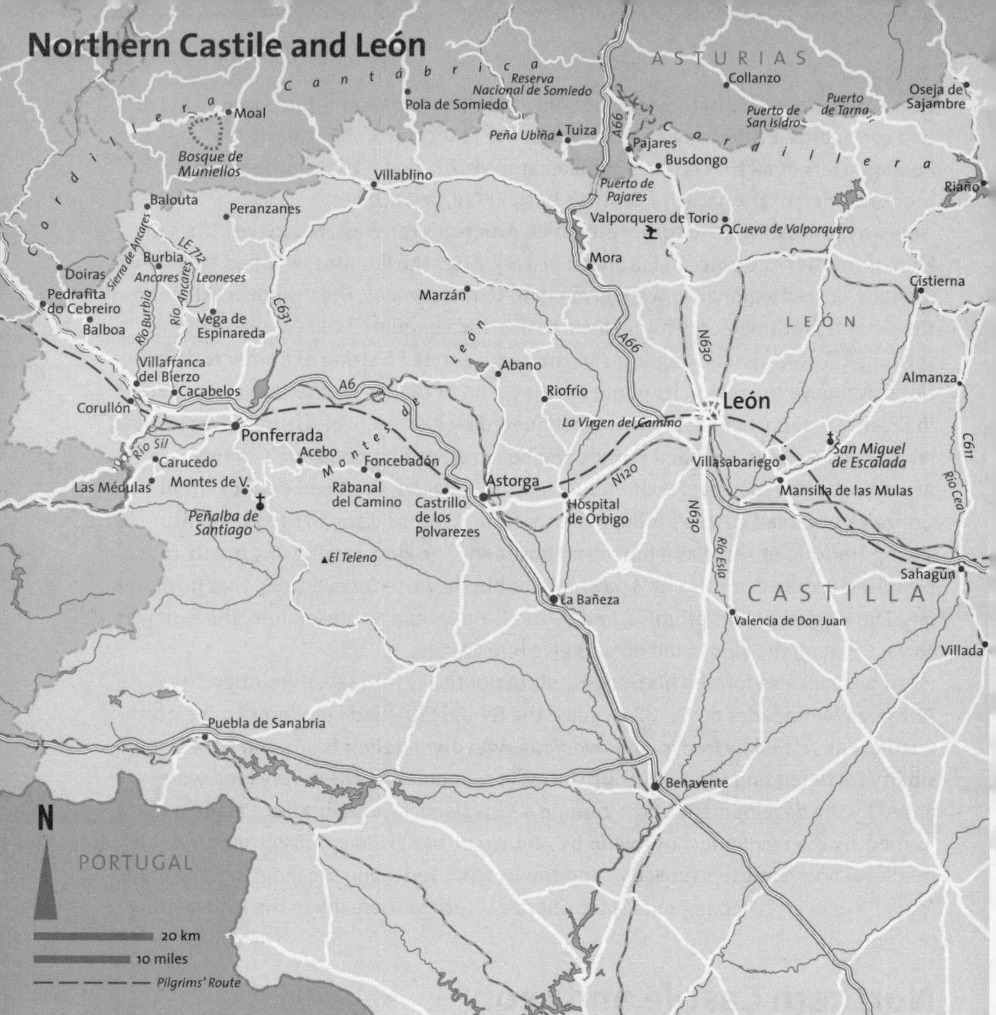

is marked by the deeply forested **Montes de Oca**. At their foot, a walking path from Villafranca climbs up the pine-forested slopes, emerging at **San Juan de Ortega**. The church is named after one of the builder-saints and the original apse (1142) proves his skill as an architect: an elegant design of slender round columns and three receding arches around alabaster windows. Inside, San Juan is buried in a magnificent tomb, with an effigy and delightful cartoon-like scenes from his life carved in the base.

The Bilbao–Madrid motorway A1 runs into Castile near **Miranda de Ebro**, a major town where glass balconies hang over the river, while the Ebro itself sculpted the stunning **Hoces del Sobrón** gorge, through the nearby **Montes Obarenes**. The road, the *autopista*, and the train funnel dramatically through the pass at **Pancorbo**, for V. S. Pritchett 'a place of horror, for the rock crowds in, comes down in precipitous, yellow shafts, and at the top has been tortured into frightening animal shapes by the climate'. Between Pancorbo and Burgos, **Briviesca**'s octagonal church, **Santa Clara** (1565), has star vaulting and a florid, carved *retablo mayor*.

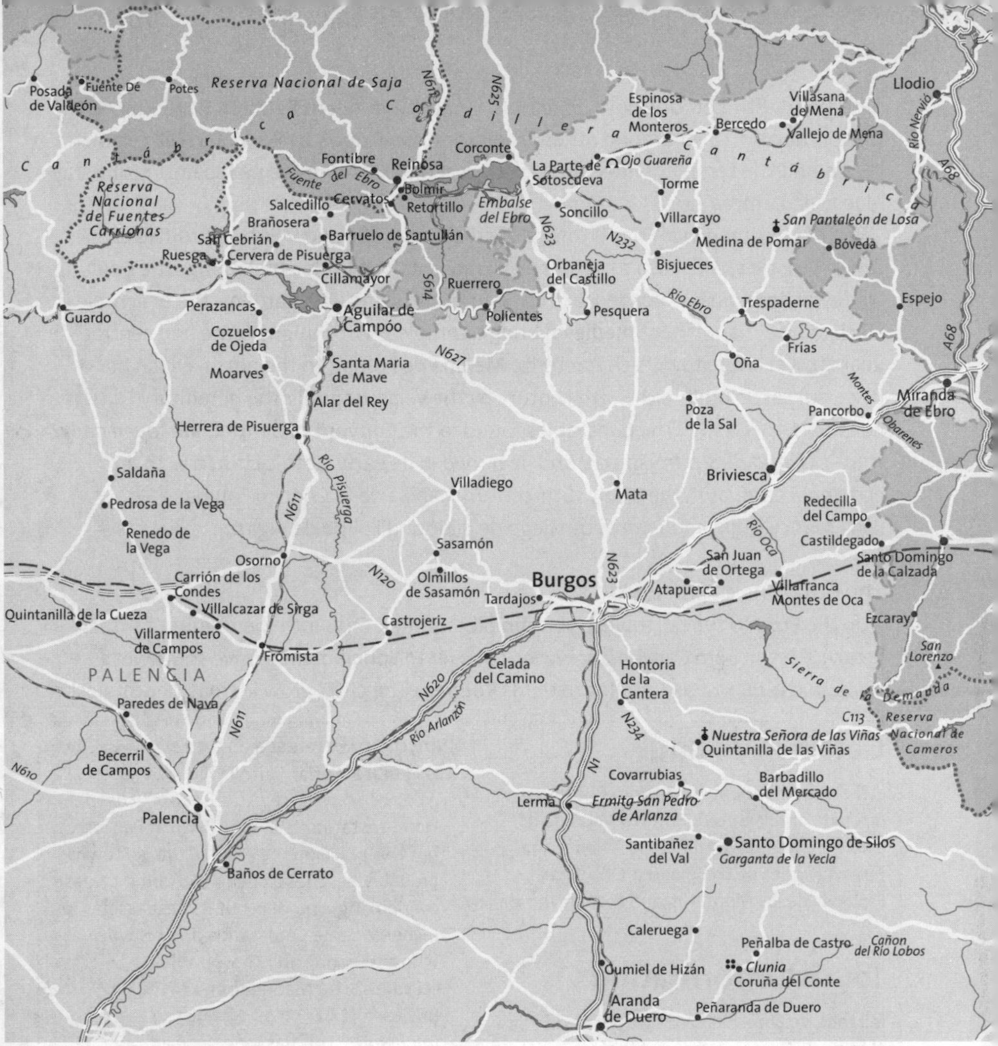

Northeast Approaches

This bulge of the map in northeast Burgos province, the cradle of Old Castile, is full of curiosities and remarkable scenery. Medieval **Oña**, north of Briviesca had one of the first castles of Castile and was granted its *fueros* in 950 by Fernán González. In 1033, Sancho the Great of Navarra, heir of Castile, ordered the old royal stronghold replaced by the Benedictine **Monasterio de San Salvador** to serve as a royal pantheon. Rebuilt in 1640, the monastery is now used as a psychiatric hospital. However, the town offers guided tours of its **church** (*open 10–2 and 4–6; adm*). The entrance is through the 15th-century Pórtico de los Reyes, carved with figures of kings; beyond is the oldest Romanesque façade in Castile (1072), with Flemish-Gothic paintings just inside, and a *mudéjar* door. Although the walls of the long, narrow church date from the 11th century, the interior was redone in the 15th by Fernando Díaz. His starry dome measures 4,306 sq ft and is the second largest in Spain after Tarragona; below, flanking the ultra-florid 18th-century Baroque *retablo*, is the magnificent **Panteón Real**. Sancho the Great is here (d. 1035), among others, their tombs arranged by Fernando Díaz into charming little temples with elaborate tracery and Hispano-Flemish paintings by Fray Alonso de Zamora.

East of Oña, medieval **Frías** is one of Castile's most striking villages: a ruined 12th-century castle spirals up a rocky outcrop known as 'the Molar' high above the hanging whitewashed houses, arcaded lanes and intimate vegetable gardens; the ensemble is reached by a magnificent **medieval bridge**, complete with mighty gate and central guard tower. More towers characterize **Medina de Pomar**, to the north, which has a powerful castle built in the 14th century by the Velasco family, the hereditary Constables of Castile. The Constables founded the **Convent of Santa Clara** (*open daily 11.30–1.30 and 6–8; adm*) in 1313, and lie buried in its early Gothic church with an octagonal star-vault; the lovely 16th-century Capilla de la Concepción has a Renaissance grille and *retablo* by Diego de Siloé and Felipe de Vigarni.

The Canyons of the Ebro

Up the Ebro to the northwest, you can pick up the C6318 into the mountains (*see below*). For the Ebro Canyons, however, cut over to **Soncillo**, then drive southwest through the Puerta de Carrales towards Ruerrero. The cliffs grow increasingly majestic

Getting Around

There are frequent **buses** from Burgos to Belorado and less frequently to Miranda de Ebro, a major **railway** junction. At least one bus a day goes up to Briviesca, Oña, Frías, Espinosa de los Monteros, and Poza de la Sal.

Tourist Information

Miranda de Ebro: Río Ebro 33, **t** 947 33 04 71.
Medina de Pomar: Condestable 16, **t** 947 14 72 28.
Villarcayo: Santa Marina 10, **t** 947 13 04 57.

There is are weekly **markets** in **Oña** (*Fri*); in **Medina de Pomar** (*Thurs*); and in **Espinosa de los Monteros** (*Tues*).

Where to Stay and Eat

Villafranca Montes de Oca ✉ 09240

El Pájaro, Ctra Logroño–Burgos, **t** 947 58 20 29 (*cheap*). Probably your best bet for a simple room and a meal along this stretch of the pilgrims' route.

Hospital de la Reina. A restored hospital for pilgrims, inaugurated by Queen Sofia.

Pancorbo/Briviesca ✉ 09240

Casa Rural El Ferial, San Nicolás 59, **t** 947 35 42 02 or **t** 947 35 42 76 (after 9pm) (*cheap*). Hotel-restaurants line the road at Pancorbo, but this place on the edge of the old town is probably best; it's a cheap bed and breakfast overlooking a garden, but its best asset is its owner, Vicente Cardiñanos, and his wife, who are wonderfully hospitable.

****El Valles**, Ctra Madrid–Irún Km280 (in Briviesca), **t** 947 59 00 25, **f** 947 59 24 84 (*moderate*). This has long been a favourite stopover for its quiet rooms and good filling food for the road.

El Concejo, Pza Mayor 14, **t** 947 59 16 86 (*expensive–moderate*). Prettily set in a 15th-century mansion in town, and serving a tasty leek and prawn *pastel* in cheese sauce and imaginative desserts; good wine list. *Closed Mon.*

Medina de Pomar ✉ 09500

*****Las Merindades**, Pza Juan de Salazar, **t** 947 19 08 22 (*moderate*). Located in a pretty, historical building with the village's best, moderately priced **restaurant** downstairs; try the *solomillo a los ajos tostados* (sirloin with toasted garlic).

and fantastical as you drive towards **Orbaneja del Castillo**: vultures and eagles circle high over the ruddy canyon walls, sculpted by aeons of wind and rain to form soaring bridges, castle walls, haunted towers or snaggle-toothed caves. From Orbaneja the road curls up to the N623, the main Santander–Burgos highway.

The Far Northeast Corner: in the Cordillera Cantábrica

Near Soncillo the C6318 leads into the secret corner of Burgos province; from the north, the N629 from Laredo will take you straight there. Here, near the cave complex of **Ojo Guareña** (*not open to visitors*) by **Quintanilla-Sotoscueva**, are the **Hermitages of SS. Bernabé** and **Tirso** (*open Tues–Sun 11–1.15 and 5–7.15; closed Mon*), set on a panoramic esplanade with their façades built into the cliffs; inside are 17th- and 18th-century paintings and wax *ex votos*. The C6318 continues east to medieval **Espinosa de los Monteros**, with its 14th-century **Castillo de los Condestables** on the far bank of the river Trueba, and the Constable's Baroque palace. Venture further east and you'll be rewarded with three Romanesque churches: **San Miguel** at Bercedo, with a good portal and animal carvings; the 12th-century Templar **Santa María** at Siones, with an elegant double archway in the apse, strange and beautiful capitals, a 12th-century statue of the Virgin and a Visigothic baptismal font; and **San Lorenzo** at Vallejo de Mena, with a gallery of arcades along the south façade and a handsome apse.

Burgos

First it must be said that Burgos is genteel and quite pleasant; its river, the Arlanzón, so filled with frogs in spring and early summer that they drown out the traffic with their croaking; the chief promenade, the Paseo del Espolón, is one of Spain's prettiest, adorned with amazing topiary hedges. Burgos contains one of the greatest collections of Gothic art and monuments in southern Europe. Yet throughout much of its history, Burgos' role has been that of a stern military camp, from the day of El Cid Campeador to Franco el Caudillo who, during the Civil War, made Burgos his temporary capital; the city where, it was said, 'the very stones are Nationalist'. Here, in 1970, Franco held the infamous Burgos trials, in which 16 Basque separatists (two of them priests) were tried in a kangaroo court. Six were sentenced to death, though outraged world opinion convinced Franco to commute the sentences.

The Kingdom of Castile was born in Burgos, and it is fitting that the city itself began as a castle erected on the Moorish frontier in 884. In 926 it took its first step away from Leonese rule, electing its own judges; in 950, one of the judges' successors, Fernán González, declared his independence as Count of Castile. His descendant, Ferdinand I, elevated the title to king and married the heiress of León. Burgos remained sole capital of Castile until 1087, when Alfonso VI moved to Toledo (perhaps to put some distance between himself and the overbearing Cid). The frontier was moving south and this city that had done so much to create the ethos of Spain now found itself something of a backwater. But Burgos has always remained true to the cause and remains the most aristocratic, pious, polite and reactionary city in Spain.

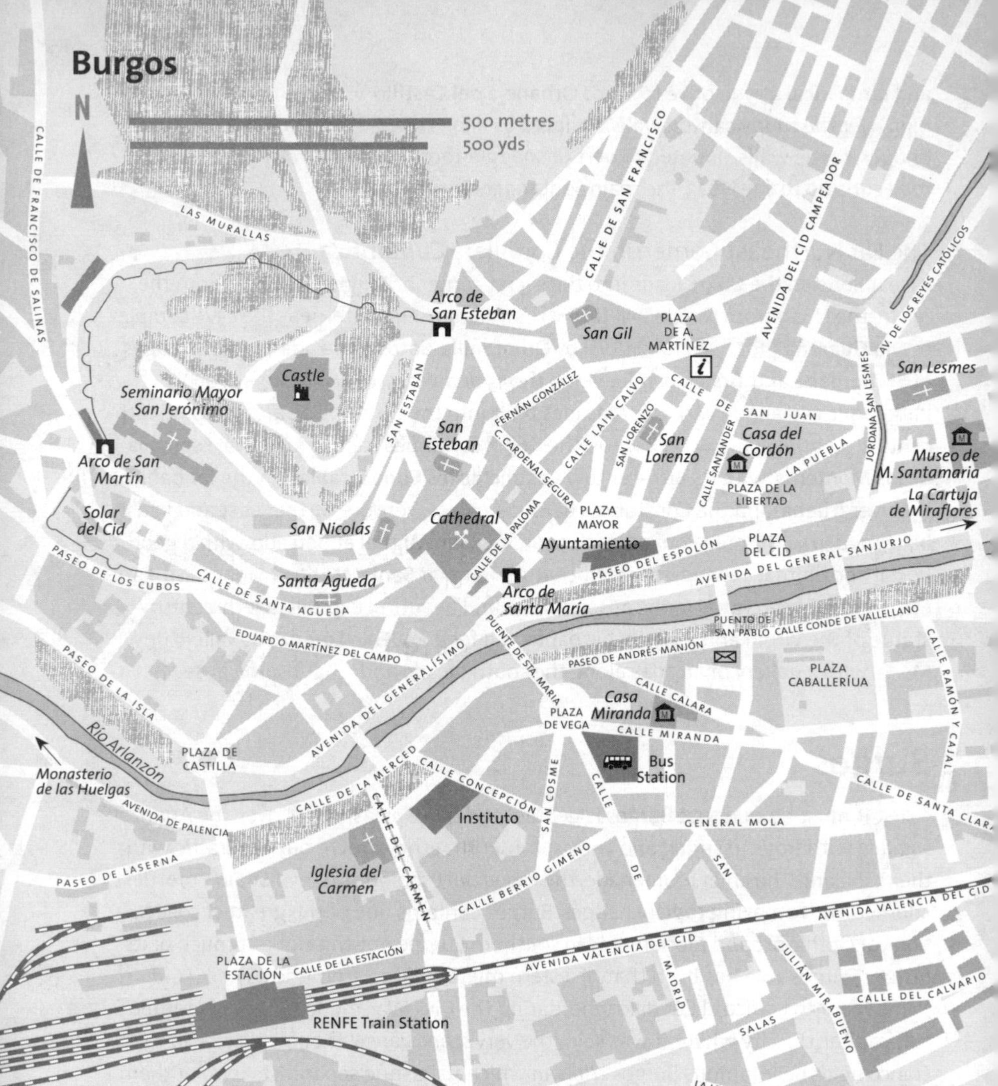

Arco de Santa María

Burgos' glistening white, fairy-tale front door, the **Arco de Santa María**, was originally part of the medieval walls, but after the Comunero revolt it was embellished to appease Charles V; triumphal arches like this were a Renaissance conceit (the first one was made at Naples for a Spanish king), and they were especially favoured by the vainglorious and ambitious Charles. The Emperor himself is portrayed in a Burgos pantheon that includes its first judges, King Fernán González, and El Cid. You'll be well acquainted with the designer of the arch before you leave Burgos; Francisco de Colonia and Juan de Vallejo, along with Francisco's father Juan, are responsible for the great openwork spires of the cathedral, looming just behind the arch.

The Cathedral

Along with León and Toledo, Burgos has one of Spain's greatest Gothic cathedrals, one of the most diaphanous churches ever built: half of stone, half of light and air. In 1221, in honour of his marriage to Beatrice of Swabia, Ferdinand III and the English bishop Maurice laid the first cornerstone. On the north side, a stair leads up to the **Puerta del Sarmental**, its 13th-century tympanum depicting Christ and the four Evangelists (sitting studiously at their desk, writing the Gospels). The first portal to be finished, the south-side **Puerta Alta de la Coronería** (1257) is the most interesting, with its Apostles, Almighty, and a peculiar row of mere mortals, the Blessed and the Damned, in between. Around the corner of the transept, the **Puerta de la Pellejería** is part of the original 13th-century work. From up here you can get a good view of the forest of spires, especially on the lantern, adorned with scores of figures. Note how the windows in the bell towers were made so wide that from most points of view you can actually see through the towers. Three generations of the Colonia family devoted themselves to moulding the soft grey stone of Burgos into these virtuoso lace towers and spires. Colonia is Cologne, in Germany; Hans of Cologne began the works in the

Getting There

By Train

RENFE is on Av. Conde Guadalhorce, across the river from the cathedral, **t** 947 20 35 60; tickets are also available from the office at Moneda 21, **t** 947 20 91 31. Burgos is on the main Irún–Madrid rail line (connections to Pamplona, Vitoria, Bilbao, Valladolid, etc.), with less frequent links to Zaragoza, Palencia, León and La Coruña; also to Salamanca, Barcelona, Málaga, Madrid, Córdoba and Vigo on Talgos.

By Bus

The bus terminal is on C/Miranda, across the river from the Arco de Sta María, **t** 947 26 55 65. There are buses to León (one daily), Santander (three daily), Madrid (seven daily), Soria, Bilbao, San Sebastián and Vitoria (four or more daily), and the provincial villages. Even if there may be only one bus a day to villages not on a main route, such as Frías, they're often conveniently timed for a day trip.

Tourist Information

Burgos: Pza Alonso Martínez 7, **t** 947 20 31 25.
Post Office: Pza Conde de Castro.
Internet Access: there's expensive access at Ciber Café Cabaret, C/La Puebla 21 (*open afternoons only*).

Where to Stay

Burgos ✉ 09000

Luxury–Expensive

*******Landa Palace**, just outside Burgos on the Madrid road, **t** 947 20 63 43, **f** 947 26 46 76 (*luxury*). A member of the prestigious Relais et Châteaux group, providing a memorable stay in an over-the-top pseudo-medieval tower furnished with antiques, an indoor atrium and pool, and beautiful rooms (they may be in a castle, but they have mod cons El Cid would think were sorcery). A meal in the Landa's equally palatial **restaurant**, the region's finest, will set you back some €*35–40*.

******Hotel Husa Puerta de Burgos**, Vitoria 69, **t** 947 24 10 00, **f** 947 24 07 07 (*expensive*). An option in the centre of Burgos.

*****Del Cid**, Pza Santa María 8, **t** 947 20 87 15, **f** 947 26 94 60 (*expensive*). Magnificently located opposite the cathedral, with well-equipped modern doubles, garage space and a secret connecting tunnel with their excellent restaurant next door.

Moderate–Inexpensive

****Norte y Londres**, Pza Alonso Martínez 10, **t** 947 26 41 25, **f** 947 27 73 75 (*moderate*). Charmingly old-fashioned; a whiff of charm and elegance in the middle of town.

late 1400s, and his son Simón and grandson Francisco carried on the job, followed by Juan de Vallejo, who built the Plateresque crossing tower. At night these hundreds of pinnacles pattern out the sky, illuminated along with the Arco de Santo María for a dazzling *tour de force*.

The **west façade**, with its delicate stone tracery and over-the-top gallery of statues of Spanish kings, incorporates two Stars of David, an unintentional reminder that more than one of Burgos' bishops hailed from a Jewish family before 1492, as did the city's greatest sculptors, Diego and Gil de Siloé, the masters of Isabelline Gothic. Their work inside makes up one of the cathedral's main attractions. Tragically, the three portals of the west façade were destroyed in the name of improvement, in the 18th century, and replaced with pallid substitutes.

Along with the cathedral of Santiago, this is one of the two great treasure-houses of Spain, loaded with the masterworks and superb detail from the tiniest carving in the choir stalls to its beautiful star-vaulted domes. The enclosed **choir** is almost entirely shut off from the rest of the church. You can peer through the grille work to see the magnificent gold-trimmed star vault of Juan de Vallejo's **lantern**, under the central

*****Cordón**, La Puebla 6, **t** 947 26 50 00 (*moderate*). Another lovely old building with glass balconies; has rooms bordering on *expensive*.

****Hs Hilton**, Vitoria 165, **t** 947 22 51 16. For fun, you can stay up the road at the Hilton (not related to the chain.

Cheap

****Hs Manjon**, Conde Jordana 1–7, **t** 947 20 86 89. Has good *cheap* rooms close to the river; most have private bath.

***Hs Hidalgo**, **t** 947 20 34 81. Right off the Pza Mayor, this well-kept and old-fashioned *hostal* is on a street that is (at least at night) relatively quiet.

P. 196, Av. Vitoria 196, **t** 947 22 94 74. This new *pensión* has spotless rooms with bath at bargain rates, though it's a bit of a trek from the centre; take the bus marked Gamonal from Av. Arlanzon.

Residencia Juvenil Gil de Siloé, Av. General Vigón, **t** 947 22 03 62. The youth hostel.

Eating Out

Casa Ojeda, Vitoria 5, **t** 947 20 90 52 (*expensive*). The most popular place in town, with the best tapas in its bar and good local cuisine in its dining room; try the partridge and wild mushroom salad.

Mesón del Cid, Pza Santa María 8, **t** 947 20 59 71 (*moderate menu*). For a medieval atmosphere in a 15th-century building facing the cathedral, and delicious roast sucking-lamb, this is the place to go. The dining rooms are on various levels throughout the building, which once held one of Spain's first printing presses.

Asador de Aranda, Llana de Afuera s/n (at the back end of the Cathedral), **t** 947 26 81 41 (*moderate*). Serves classic *burgales* dishes like *cochinillo asado* (roast suckling-pig), without the price-hike of being on the plaza.

Gaona, Virgen de la Paloma 41 (near the cathedral), **t** 947 20 40 32 (*moderate*). Has Basque cooking in a glassed-in terrace; peppers stuffed with cod is a treat.

Corral de los Infantes, just inside the Arco de Santa María (*inexpensive*). Offers Castilian specialities like *olla podrida* and 'medieval lentils'; outdoor dining in the summer.

Mesón el Cardinal, Huerta del Rey (just north of the cathedral) (*inexpensive*). Has a wide array of fancy *bocadillos*, *tortillas* and seafood tapas.

Casa Olonso, Pza Santo Domingo de Guzmán 10, near the statue of El Cid (*inexpensive*). Offers a decent *menú*: *paella*, *merluza*, stuffed pork chops or Castilian snails.

Gaia, C/San Francisco 31. A grungy and subversive vegetarian restaurant with a budget *menú del dia*.

tower, which Philip II declared could not have been built by men, but only by angels. Four stately round piers support a profusion of intricate carved decoration; a Spanish twist on Renaissance styles, married harmoniously into a Gothic building. Under its majestic beauty a simple slab marks the **tomb of El Cid and Ximena**, his wife, their bones relocated here with great pomp in 1921. The other tomb in the *coro* belongs to Bishop Maurice, topped by his enamelled copper effigy; try to get in to see the magnificent carving on the wood and inlaid stalls: unabashed pagan figures on the seats, New Testament scenes above. They were done by Felipe de Vigarni, who also sculpted the dramatic scene on the ambulatory behind the main altar.

De Vigarni also carved the tomb of Don Gonzalo de Lerma in the 16th-century **Capilla de la Presentación**, to the right of the choir. To the left, the **Chapel of Santa Ana** has a wonderfully ornate polychromed altar by Gil de Siloé. One of Diego de Siloé's masterpieces, the diamond-shaped, drippingly Plateresque **Golden Stair** (1523), forms the most strikingly original feature of the interior, the perfectly proportioned solution to the Puerta Alta, 30ft above the floor of the cathedral.

Buffalo Jesus and the Fly-Catcher

The two features that impress, though, are just inside the west door. First, to the right as you enter, is the glass-doored **Capilla del Santo Cristo**, where ladies gather to worship one of the strangest cult idols of any religion: the 13th-century **Cristo de Burgos**, a figure made of buffalo hide, real hair and fingernails, in a green frock and warm to the touch. The head and arms can move, like a doll; these were probably somehow manipulated to impress the faithful, back in the age of miracles.

Nearly as famous is the 15th-century mechanical clock across the nave near the roof, the **Papamoscas** ('fly-catcher'), a grinning devil who pops out of a hole in the wall to strike the hour. The most spectacular chapel, the octagonal **Capilla del Condestable**, was built by Simón de Colonia for Pedro Hernández de Velasco in 1482–94. The tomb faces the elaborate altar by Vigarni and Diego de Siloé. The constable clutches his sword even after death; his lady's little dog sleeps at her feet. Velasco was Constable during the conquest of Granada, whose Moorish craftsmen inspired the geometric star-vaulting. The chapel has its own sacristy, a treasure chest full of trinkets and a wonderfully voluptuous auburn-haired *Magdalen* by Giampetrino, a pupil of Leonardo da Vinci. This being Burgos, she's usually locked up (*ask the man in the souvenir shop to open the door*).

The nearby **Sacristía Mayor** is adorned with one of the cathedral's lighter scenes, a Baroque bubble bath of a heaven. Off the cloister, the **Museo Diocesano** (*open daily 9.30–1 and 4–7; adm*) contains El Cid's marriage agreement and the leather-bound coffer he filled with sand, then passed off as gold as security to two Jewish money-lenders, who made him a sizeable loan.

Around the Cathedral

Just northwest of the cathedral on C/Fernán González, **San Nicolás de Bari** contains an incredible wall-sized alabaster *retablo* by Francisco de Colonia (1505), depicting 36 scenes from the Bible and more angels than could dance on a head of a pin.

The city's **castle** was blown up by the French in 1813 – an explosion that shattered most of the cathedral's stained glass – and little remains to be seen up here besides the fine view of the city. In Pza Alonso Martínez, you'll notice a grim little building called the **Capitanería**, guarded by military police and adorned with commemorative plaques. This was the Nationalist capital during the Civil War; here Franco assumed total power among the rebels and directed his campaigns in the north. C/Santander is Burgos' main shopping street; at its head is the **Casa del Cordón**, named after the rope (really a Franciscan monk's belt) carved over the door in honour of St Francis. This palace was built by the Condestable de Velasco in 1485. Ferdinand and Isabel received Columbus here after his second voyage, and 18 years later, an ageing Ferdinand sent Ponce de León off to discover the Fountain of Youth.

Nearby, the attractive, arcaded **Plaza Mayor** has recently been refurbished and pedestrianized, although the shady **Paseo del Espolón** along the riverfront is the city's real centre; at the far end, a mighty equestrian **statue of El Cid** seems ready to fly off its base and attack any enemy crossing **San Pablo Bridge**. The bridge itself is embellished with stone figures of El Cid's wife, his companions and a Moorish king. Across the bridge the **Casa Miranda** (1545) houses the **Museo de Burgos** (*open Tues–Fri 10–2 and 4–7.30, Sat 10–2 and 4.45–8.15, Sun 10–2; adm*) with an archaeological collection.

Monasterio de Las Huelgas

*Open Tues–Sat 10.30–1.15 and 3.30–5.45, Sun 10.30–2.15; closed Mon; adm, adm free Wed. Daily **guided tours** (in Spanish).*

On the outskirts of Burgos lie two of Spain's richest monasteries, both well worth a visit. A 20-minute walk to the west will take you to the Cistercian convent of **Las Huelgas**, founded by Alfonso VIII in 1187 at the behest of his wife Eleanor, (back then *Las Huelgas Reales*, the monastery's true name, meant 'the royal repose'). The abbess of Las Huelgas enjoyed more power and influence than any other woman in Spain except the queen herself, until her powers were revoked in the 19th century. In 1219 San Ferdinand III started the custom of Castilian kings going to Las Huelgas to be knighted into the Order of Santiago – not by any inferior, mind you, but by Santiago himself; in the cloister you can see the statue of the saint, his moveable arm holding out a sword made especially for the purpose. The tours take you through the English-Gothic church, which also serves as a pantheon of Castilian kings and royal ladies. The French desecrated the tombs, though the one they missed, that of Alfonso X's son Ferdinand de la Cerda, produced such a fine collection of goods as to form the nucleus of Las Huelgas' **Museo de Ricas Telas**, a fascinating collection of fabrics and medieval dress, showing considerable Eastern influence.

These are not the only Moorish touches in Las Huelgas: note the geometric tomb of the Infanta Doña Blanca, the peacock and stars in the *mudéjar* **cloister**, and the **Capilla de Santiago**. The grandest chamber, the **Sala Capitular**, contains a trophy from Alfonso VIII's great Battle of Las Navas de Tolosa – the silk flap of the Moorish commander's tent – and Don Juan's banner from Lepanto, which he gave to his daughter Ana, abbess of Las Huelgas. Some 43 nuns still live at Las Huelgas, painting porcelain and baking cookies.

La Cartuja de Miraflores

Open Mon–Sat 10.15–3 and 4–6, Sun 11.20–12.30, 1–3 and 4–6; adm free.

Burgos' second great monastery is a half-hour's walk to the east, through a park of shady trees. Miraflores was founded by Juan II in 1441 and is still used as a monastery, so you can see only the church, built by the Colonia family; yet this alone contains more great art than many a cathedral. Here Isabel the Catholic commissioned the great Gil de Siloé to sculpt the **tomb of Juan II and Isabel of Portugal** as a memorial to her parents, and four years' work saw him create the most elaborately detailed tomb of all time. It looks as if Siloé used a needle rather than a chisel to sew the alabaster robes of the effigies: Juan is pensive, his wife reading a book. Isabel owed her succession to the her brother's death, and as a posthumous thank you had Siloé carve his memorial too. The tomb of the Infante Don Alfonso shows the young prince (1453–68) at prayer among a playful menagerie of animals, putti and birds entwined in vines. Siloé also did most of the gilt *retablo* of the high altar, said to be made with gold that Columbus presented to the Catholic kings at the Casa de Cordón.

Other works of art include a painting of the Annunciation by Pedro Berruguete and the carvings on the lay brothers' choir (the middle section of the Carthusian church's traditional three divisions – the monks' choir is in the front, the general public in the back). In the side chapel there's a wooden polychrome **statue of St Bruno** carved by the Portuguese Manuel Pereira, so lifelike 'it would speak if it weren't a Carthusian monk' as the *burgaleses* like to say.

Southeast of Burgos

The most popular corner for a day out from Burgos is the mountainous region to the southeast, on or off the N234 towards Soria, where it's hard to tell where one sierra begins and another ends. Covarrubias and Santo Domingo de Silos are firmly marked on the tourist map, but you'll need a car to take in the prizes just off the beaten track such as San Quirce or the Visigothic church of Quintanilla de las Viñas.

A Scatological Abbey and a Visigothic Beauty

Interior open only the first Tues of each month 9.30–6.

The **Abadía de San Quirce** is not easy to find; signposts guide you from **Hontoria de la Cantera**. Founded by Count Fernán González after his defeat of the Saracens on this spot in 929, the church conserves its original structure, with a fortified tower in the centre; the west door has 11 modillions showing the Creator, Adam and Eve, Cain and Abel and, in between, earthy reliefs of men squatting and defecating, with inscriptions reading *io cago* and *mal cago* (bluntly, 'I shit', and 'I shit badly'); one thinks of the anarchical defecating figure, the *caganer*, that accompanies every Catalan Christmas crib. Other reliefs decorate the north door and modillions supporting the charming bubble of an apse, unusually illuminated by two round bull's-eye windows and a regular Romanesque window, which was probably originally a bull's eye as well;

Getting Around

Transport here is mostly nonexistent. There are several **buses** daily from Burgos to Aranda de Duero, and in general one a day to Santo Domingo de Silos, Caleruega, Lerma, and Covarrubias, but that's about it.

Tourist Information

Covarrubias: **t** 947 40 63 11.

Santo Domingo de Silos: in the Ayuntamiento, **t** 947 39 00 70.

Lerma: C/Audiencia 6, **t** 947 17 01 43. Offers guided tours of the town (*Tues–Sun 11–2 and 4–7*).

Aranda de Duero: C/de la Sal, **t** 947 51 04 76.

Where to Stay and Eat

Covarrubias ✉ 09346

******Arlanza**, Pza Mayor 11, **t** 947 40 64 41, **f** 947 40 63 59 (*moderate*). Occupies a handsome old mansion in the centre of town; its **restaurant** serves medieval banquets of trout and roast lamb every Saturday night with music and ancient Castilian dances; book ahead.

Casa Galin, Pza Doña Urraca, **t** 947 40 65 52 (*inexpensive*). Another fine old house, where people come from miles around to tuck into an authentic *olla podrida* and other mainstays for ridiculously low prices. *Closed Tues in winter.*

Torreón de Doña Urraca, Pza Doña Sancha, **t** 947 40 31 08 (*moderate*). Has a delightful terrace. *Open only in summer.*

Santo Domingo de Silos ✉ 09610

******Tres Coronas**, Pza Mayor 6, **t** 947 39 00 47, **f** 947 39 00 65 (*moderate*). Located in a charming 17th-century house, with 16 intimate rooms. It's **restaurant**, Casa Emeterio (*menú moderate*), features Castilian cuisine.

****Arco de San Juan**, Pradera de San Juan 1, **t/f** 947 39 00 74 (*moderate*). Near the famous cloister, this is a quiet place with a delightful garden.

Mesón Asador, C/Principal, **t** 947 39 00 53. Family-run with *inexpensive* rooms and dinner included.

Padre Hospedería, **t** 947 39 00 68. Men 'in need of spiritual exercise' can eat and sleep for a song (well, almost) in the monastery; call in advance.

Aranda de Duero ✉ 09400

Aranda gets plenty of business travellers and concentrates its functional hotels near the highway; most have cheap weekend rates. There are two special places to eat, however.

******Los Bronces**, Ctra Madrid–Irún Km160, **t** 947 50 08 50 (*moderate*). A functional hotel near the Burgos exit.

******Tres Condes**, Av. Castilla 66, **t** 947 50 24 00, **f** 947 50 24 04 (*moderate*). Typical of the area; practical, like Los Bronces.

Mesón de la Villa, Pza Mayor 3, **t** 947 50 10 25 (*expensive*). Serves some of the best food in the area, including poultry and garden vegetables raised on the owner's farm, and accompanied by the finest bottles of Rioja (*around €30*). *Closed Mon.*

Rafael Corrales, Carrequemada 2, **t** 947 50 02 77. An *asador* that opened in 1902, serving baby lamb baked in a wood oven, washed down with Ribera del Duero. *Closed Thurs.*

inside the capitals are carved with the legend of San Quirce and a naked woman who suckles serpents, with lions on either side.

Further south on the N234 is **Quintanilla de las Viñas**, where four kilometres up under the steel-toned Montes de Lara and the ruins of the Castilla de Lara, the gold-stoned Visigothic **Nuestra Señora de las Viñas** (*open Wed–Sun 9.30–2 and 4–7 (winter 10–5); closed Mon, Tues and the last weekend of each month; if no one's there, try the guardian's house, marked Turismo, 1km south*) drinks up the sun. This is nothing less than the last Visigothic basilica in Spain, dated 7th century or just before the invasion of the Moors. Made of large blocks incised with Christian graffiti, only the square apse and part of the transept have survived the past 1,300 years. The exterior of the former is beautifully girdled with friezes of animals, birds and plants, and what are believed to be the monograms of the founders. Inside, on the triumphal arch, there's another bird frieze and a rare example of Visigothic syncretism: angels with rocket wings, Byzantine in style or perhaps even more akin to the winged figures on Roman tombs, holding up portraits identifying Christ with the moon (a bearded figure, with a crescent moon LVNA on his head like horns) and the Virgin (or Church) with the sun SOL. Blocks in the apse show heavily coiffed, symmetrical but inexplicable 'astral' figures, sculpted by another artist who had trouble getting the arms and hands on right.

Fernán González Country

South of Quintanilla de las Viñas, the Arlanza river runs east–west through a valley known in the 10th century as the Valley of Towers, the frontier of old Castile, pushed this far south by 'the Good Count' Fernán González.

Medieval **Covarrubias** is Old Castile's half-timbered showcase of porticoed squares and lanes, guarded by the only surviving 10th-century Mozarab tower in the Valley of Towers, the **Torreón de Doña Urraca**. The ex-Colegiata, **San Cosme y San Damián** (*open Wed–Mon 10.30–2 and 4–7; closed Tues; adm*) was rebuilt in 1474 as the pantheon for the Infantes de Covarrubias; in 1848, the remains of Fernán González and his wife were transferred from San Pedro de Arlanza and placed next to the altar in a 4th-century Roman sarcophagus. The 17th-century organ, one of the most beautiful in Spain, still works, although you'll have to attend Mass to hear it.

South of Covarrubias, the star attraction in these parts is **Santo Domingo de Silos** (*open Tues–Sat 10–1 and 4.30–6, Sun, Mon and hols 4.30–6; adm*), a Benedictine monastery founded in 954 by Fernán González and ruled in the next century by the abbot who gave it its name. Rebuilt after al-Mansur burned it to the ground, the monastery was re-founded in the 19th century by French Benedictines, who have made it famous for **Gregorian chant** (*sung at 9am Mon–Sat and noon on Sun, and at 7pm*). They inherited the most beautiful Romanesque **cloister** in Spain, superbly elegant, double-decked and ivory coloured, built around an ancient cypress tree. The lower section dates from between the late 11th and early 12th centuries and has fascinating capitals on twin columns carved by a sculptor versed in motifs of the Córdoba caliphate. On the corners of the cloister, eight large reliefs on the life of Jesus are in a similar style; one shows the only known representation of Christ dressed in pilgrim's garb. Off the cloister is a **museum** with Mozarabic illuminations and the Romanesque tympanum from the first church, among other things. After all this, the **church**, rebuilt in the neoclassical style in the 18th century, seems dull.

A mere two and a half kilometres from Santo Domingo towards Caleruega lies the spectacular **Desfiladero de la Yecla**, a narrow gorge, full of vultures, hawks and buzzards that has been fitted with wooden walkways.

Way Down South in Burgos Province

The N1 south of Burgos to Madrid passes through **Lerma**, another town on the Arlanza river, founded by the son of Fernán González in 978. It owes its impressive appearance to the Duke of Lerma (Francisco Gómez de Sandoval y Rojas), who ruled

Spain between 1598 and 1618 for Philip III. It was the duke's idea to expel the *moriscos*, and devote a part of the proceeds from their expropriated property into making Lerma a unique monumental complex, with at least six monasteries and a four-towered **Palacio Ducal** (*currently undergoing restoration*). This is linked by a flying walkway to the **Colegiata de San Pedro**, bearing the duke's crest over the door.

Much further south, **Gumiel de Hizán** marks the northern limits of DO Ribera del Duero, the largest and finest wine region in Castile, producing a variety of reds. You can try them in one of the old *bodegas* in **Aranda de Duero**; Vega Sicilia is the most illustrious name. East of Aranda, picturesque **Peñaranda de Duero** is built around the sprawling castle of its medieval lords, who in the safer 16th century decided to move down into the Plaza Mayor. A Plateresque portal marks their **Palacio de los Zúñiga y Avellaneda** (*open Tues–Sun 11–1 and 3–5; closed Mon*), built around an elegant two-storey patio; rooms are adorned with superb *artesonado* ceilings and plasterwork.

North of Peñaranda, the isolated 11th-century **Ermita del Santo Cristo** (*open summer Tues–Sun 10–2 and 5–8; winter Tues–Sun 10–2 and 3–6; closed Mon*) is made from stones cannibalized from the Roman city of **Clunia**, just north, near Peñalba de Castro, where the guardian lives. Founded under the reign of Augustus, it counted 30,000 inhabitants at its peak. Clunia was abandoned with the fall of Rome, leaving the forum, a theatre, baths, temples, and houses with mosaics.

Along the Pilgrim Route: Burgos to Carrión de los Condes

If the medieval pilgrim survived the storms, cut-throats and wolves at Roncesvalles, the Navarrese who exposed themselves when excited, and the dupers and fleshpots of Burgos, they then had to face the flattest, hottest and most monotonous landscape in Europe. The idea is that with nothing to look at one becomes introspective and meditative, receptive to enlightenment. Off the highways, 20th-century intrusions are rare; hamlets of humble adobe houses, church towers crowned with storks and huge dovecotes evoke the Middle Ages as powerfully as any cathedral.

From Burgos to the Puente de Fitero

After Burgos, the pilgrim's path goes straight to Castrojeriz, leaving the N120 in **Tardajos**. Like many towns along this road, **Sasamón**, 33 kilometres west of the capital, takes pride in its churches, particularly that of **Santa María la Real**, with an exact 12th-century copy of the Sarmental door on Burgos cathedral. The main road, however, heads south of Tardajos to pass through the haunting, ravaged remains of the 14th-century **Monasterio de San Antón**, its once magnificent vaults hanging miraculously in the void. Westward is the medieval castle and village of **Castrojeriz**. Beyond that, the ruthless horizons of the *meseta* come into their own. The last hill for miles, the windswept **Alto de Mostelares** (2,950ft), looks over the Pisuerga river, which is spanned by the **Puente de Fitero**, a handsome bridge with 11 arches crafted in the 11th century by pilgrimage-promoter Alfonso IV.

Frómista

Frómista has been a key pilgrims' stop since the days of the *Codex Calixtinus* for its 'perfect Romanesque church', golden **San Martín** (*open summer 10–2 and 4.30–8; winter 10–2 and 3–6.30*), founded in 1035 by the widow of Sancho the Great. Restored

Getting Around

By Bus

Daily buses run from Burgos to Aguilar de Campóo and Cervera de Pisuerga, to Palencia, Frómista, Sahagún, Saldaña and Carríon (on the Burgos–León route), to Sasamón and Grijalba.

By Train

Frómista and Aguilar can also be reached by train on the line that runs between Palencia and Santander.

Tourist Information

Frómista: Pza del Tui 11, **t** 979 81 01 13. *Open summer only*.

Aguilar de Campóo: Pza de España 30, **t** 979 12 20 24.

Cervera de Pisuerga: **t** 979 87 04 50

Where to Stay and Eat

Castrojeriz ✉ 34440

★★**Méson de Castrojeriz**, Cordón 1, **t** 947 37 74 00 (*inexpensive*). Offers a handful of rooms in an old mill (and a new annex), a peaceful setting. In the dining room you'll be served up simple favourites like trout stuffed with ham (*moderate*).

Frómista ✉ 34440

HsR de Los Palmeros, Pza San Telmo, **t** 979 81 00 67 (*expensive*). This began as a *hostal* for pilgrims, although the medieval has been seasoned with several styles since; furnished with antiques, its 10 rooms are complemented by a fine **restaurant** (*moderate*) with an *artesonado* ceiling. *Closed Tues in winter*.

★**Hs San Telmo**, Martín Veña 8, **t** 979 81 01 02 (*moderate*). A good second choice if the Hostería de los Palmeros is full.

Fonda Marisa, **t** 979 81 00 23. Costs even less and cooks up good, cheap *menús*.

Villalcázar de Sirga ✉ 34440

There's nowhere to stay except at the pilgrims' shelter behind the town hall.

Mesón Villasirga, Pza Mayor, **t** 979 88 80 22 (*moderate*). A popular and very charming old *posada*; it features baked suckling-pig with almonds along with other Castilian favourites. Book at weekends. *Open daily May–Oct; otherwise Fri, Sat and Sun only*.

Aguilar de Campóo ✉ 34800

★★★**Valentin**, Av. Generalísimo 21, **t** 979 12 21 25, *www.ocioteca.com/valentin* (*moderate*). A scenic mountain hotel in an elegant old building with a garden and good **restaurant**.

★★**Villa de Aguilar**, Alférez Provisional, **t** 979 12 22 25 (*inexpensive*). For those on a tighter budget; all rooms with bath.

★★**HsR El Convento**, in Santa María de Mave (12km from Aguilar), **t** 979 12 36 11 (*inexpensive*). A serene place occupying a lovingly restored Benedictine monastery, the perfect place to spend a night if you're travelling the Romanesque route.

Cortés, El Puente 39, **t** 979 12 30 55. Simple and satisfying food awaits here: there are inexpensive menus, or you can splurge on the *caldereta de pescados y mariscos* (a huge seafood stew for two).

Cervera de Pisuerga ✉ 34840

★★★**Parador Fuentes Carrionas**, Ctra de Resoba, **t** 979 87 00 75, **f** 979 87 01 05, *cervera@paradors.es* (*expensive*). On the edge of the Picos near man-made lakes and newborn rivers, this is a plush headquarters for nature lovers, with a good **restaurant**.

Gasolina, by Pza Mayor, **t** 979 87 07 13 (*inexpensive*). Come here for a meat orgy; they will fill you up with offerings from their oven and grill.

Uko, Ukaldo Merino 15. This place has made a name across Spain for its puff pastries.

in 1893 by the arch-restorer of France, Viollet-le-Duc, San Martín is now a national monument stripped of all its trappings. Two slender round turrets buttress the west door, beyond which the proportions of the three-aisled, three-apsed, barrel-vaulted interior, crowned by an octagonal tower, satisfy the soul. But just as noteworthy is the extraordinary amount of sculpted detail inside and out, on the modillions and capitals; the original 11th-century carvings are superb and easy to distinguish from the fond fancies of the restorers, who based their work on medieval sarcophagi and marked their work with an R. The whole is a tantalizing book of hundreds of medieval symbols and occult messages; a pair of binoculars comes in handy and a crick in the neck is probably unavoidable.

Beyond Frómista, the tawny little villages of Palencia merge into the tawny earth. **Villalcázar de Sirga** was once a thriving town and key Templar possession. The Knights, at the start of the 13th century, built the enormous church of **Santa María la Blanca** (*if it is closed, find the sacristan who lives around the corner on the street left of the church*), with what must be the tallest porch in Spain sheltering a richly decorated double portal. Pilgrims would make a beeline to the **Capilla de Santiago** and its miraculous Virgin, who looks a little worse for wear, but modern visitors tend to head for the beautifully carved **tombs** sculpted by Antón Pérez de Carrión of the Infante Don Felipe (the son of Ferdinand III the Saint) and his second wife, Leonor Ruiz de Castro, shown curiously gagged. Here too is the tomb of a Knight Templar, with his hawk and sleeping lion: a rare burial, as most Templars were buried face down in the earth without a casket. The magnificent *retablo mayor* was painted by the school of Berruguete.

North of Frómista: the Románico Palentino

If you've the time, you could wander into the northern part of Palencia province, into the foothills of the Cantabrian mountains, known as the Románico Palentino for its rare collection of some 200 mostly untouched Romanesque churches (the greatest concentration in Europe). It seems that masons brought in to build churches along the *camino* came up here to build churches in the new villages, founded to repopulate the region. Aguilar de Campóo makes the best base, though you really need a car, patience, and that most elusive of objects: a good map of Spain (try to find the *Nuevo Atlas de España*).

Northwest of Alar del Rey (on the Santander–Palencia N611) are two of the finest Romanesque works in the region. **San Andrés de Arroyo** (*open summer 9.30–1.15 and 4.15–7.15; winter 9.30–noon and 3.15–6.15*) is a Bernardine convent founded in 1190 with an interesting little museum; the entrance to the chapterhouse is beautiful and the cloister has extraordinary twin columns and capitals, decorated with interlacings and exotic flora. The second church, golden-stone **Moarves de Ojeda**, has a superb portal, with a Christ in a mandorla, four Evangelists and 12 Apostles; the capitals are crowded with people and inside there's a 13th-century baptismal font.

Alternatively, if you stick to the N611, north of Alar del Rey, you'll find **Santa María de Mave**. The monastery, founded in 1208, has a fine portal, an octagonal lantern and

Renaissance murals in one of its three apses; it has now been converted into a charming hotel (*see* p.423).

Aguilar de Campóo and Around

Set in the green mountain valley of the Río Pisuerga and next to a large man-made lake, Aguilar de Campóo is a picturesque town of cookie bakers and decidedly leaning, medieval houses adorned with big, bold coats-of-arms. The Aguilar (eagle) of its name refers to its rocky limestone outcrop, its eagle's nest, crowned by a ruined, five-towered **castle** built in the 11th century. At the foot of the castle, the **Hermitage of Santa Cecilia** (*get the key in the casa rectoral*) was founded in 1041, and has exceptional capitals: one shows the Massacre of the Innocents, by 11th-century knights in fishscale armour. On the arcaded Pza de España, the Gothic **Colegiata de San Miguel** has the Renaissance mausoleum of the Marquesses of Aguilar and a **museum** (*open 10–1 and 5–8*) full of tombs and sculptures.

The road directly north of Aguilar takes in more Romanesque charmers at **Matalbienga**, **Cillamayor** and **Revilla de Santullán**, where the church has a handsome portal showing 15 figures sitting at desks, and other sculptures that verge on the pornographic. Further along there are 12th-century examples at **Brañosera** and **San Cebrián de Muda**.

West of Aguilar towards the mountains, **Cervera de Pisuerga** was once an important frontier settlement, but has retired to its meadows and old family manors. Its recently restored 16th-century Gothic church, **Santa María del Castillo**, built on the medieval citadel, has a fine Hispano-Flemish *retablo* by Felipe de Vigarni and a beautiful *Adoration of the Magi* by Juan de Flandres.

Along the Carrión River

West of Frómista, into the *campos góticos*, the Visigothic plains, the pilgrims' route continues to Carrión de los Condes, which also occupies one of Old Castile's chief north–south arteries. Palencia and environs were more important in Roman and Visigothic times than now; among the things to see are two Roman villas and the oldest dated church in Spain.

Back on the Pilgrim Track: Carrión de los Condes to Palencia

West of Villalcázar de Sirga, Carrión de los Condes is named after the River Carrión and not for putrefying nobility, although admittedly, the Counts of Carrión were truly rotten: after marrying El Cid's two daughters purely for their glittering dowries, they beat their wives, tied them up and left them for dead. Outraged, El Cid gathered up a posse and killed the Counts, who are now buried in the Renaissance cloister of **San Zoilo**, a Benedictine monastery founded in 1047, when the Emir of Córdoba sent the 4th-century relics of Zoilo to the Count of Carrión. It looks its best on Friday nights, when the monastery hosts medieval dinners complete with troubadours (to book, call ***t*** *979 88 00 50*). Over the 16th-century bridge from San Zoilo, the heart of

Carrión has two worn 12th-century Romanesque churches that preserve interesting portals. **Santiago**, in Pza Mayor, has a Christ in Majesty and apostles and representatives of 22 medieval guilds, including soldiers bashing each other, and contortionists. **Santa María del Camino** has a capital on the portal depicting the Tribute of 100 Maidens sent yearly by Castilians to the Moors; other figures are of Samson fighting the lion and women riding beasts. The interior is out of kilter, although whether it was done so intentionally is hard to fathom; it could just be falling over. Lastly, the **Convent of Santa Clara** has just opened a small **museum** (*open Tues–Sun 10.30–12.30 and 4–6*), with religious art and a 17th-century organ.

To the south of Carrión lies **Paredes de Nava**, the birthplace of painter Pedro Berruguete (d. 1504) who worked in Urbino and introduced the Renaissance style to Spain as court painter to Ferdinand and Isabel, and his son Alonso (d. 1561), a pupil of Michelangelo, who brought Mannerism back with him and served as court painter to

Getting Around

By Train

Palencia is easy to leave: there are frequent trains to Burgos, Valladolid, Ávila, Madrid and Santander (via Frómista and Aguilar de Campóo); trains to León call at Paredes de Nava. The RENFE station is at Jardinillos, **t** 979 74 30 19.

By Bus

Carrión de los Condes is connected by bus with Frómista and Palencia; there are at least two buses a day. The bus station is close to the train station, on Av. Dr Simón Nieto, **t** 979 74 32 22.

Tourist Information

Palencia: Mayor 105, **t** 979 74 00 68.
Carrión de los Condes: Pza Santa María. *Open summer only.*

Where to Stay and Eat

Carrión de los Condes ✉ 34120

San Zoilo, **t** 979 88 00 50, **f** 979 88 10 90 (*moderate*). This monastery provides good rooms and a **restaurant**.

Estrella del Bajo Carrión, Ctra Palencia-Riaño (south of Carrión in Villoldo), **t** 979 82 70 05, **f** 979 82 72 69 (*moderate*). A comfortable and modern family residence with a garden; good meals (*moderate*).

Hs La Corte, Santa María, 34, **t** 979 88 01 38 (*inexpensive*). Rooms are available along with a decent **restaurant**.

El Resbalón, C/Marqués de Santillana, **t** 979 88 00 11 (*cheap*). Rooms and a **restaurant** which serves filling *menús* (*inexpensive*) including wine and dessert.

Palencia ✉ 34000

***Rey Sancho de Castilla**, Av. Ponce de León, **t** 979 72 53 00, **f** 979 71 03 34 (*expensive*). Has recently been restored and offers a number of diversions – swimming, tennis, TV, bingo – and activities for children.

***Castilla La Vieja**, Av. Casado del Alisal 26, **t** 979 74 90 44, **f** 979 74 75 77 (*expensive*). For the same price and facilities (though no pool), this is another sound choice with a good **restaurant**.

Monclús, Menéndez Pelayo 3, **t** 979 74 43 00 (*moderate*). Comfortable and good value.

Lorenzo, Casado del Alisal 10, **t** 979 74 35 45 (*moderate*). *Mama* 'La Gorda' cooks up the best and most traditional food in town; among her specialities is *pisto*: creamed tomatoes, peppers and onions. *Closed Sun.*

Casa Damian, Ignacio Martínez de Azcoitia 9, **t** 979 74 46 28 (*moderate*). Serves up steaming bowls of Castilian *menestra de verduras*, its speciality, and other regional dishes. *Closed Mon.*

Ecuador-Casa Matías, Martín Calleja 19. For something cheaper, come here to eat hams, sausages and wines.

Taberna Pza Mayor. Serves *raciones* of *gambas* and other nice things.

Charles V. A few of the Berruguetes' paintings, including a *retablo mayor*, remain in **Santa Eulalia**, with its delicious belltower. The adjacent **museum** (*open Mon–Sat 11–1 and 4–6, mornings only on Sun*) has an impressive collection of works by other masters of the Renaissance, including Gil de Siloé and Juan de Flandres.

Palencia

Palencia is one of the bigger wallflowers in the garden of Spain's provincial capitals; in 1185 Alfonso VIII made it the site of Spain's first university (though in 1239 it was removed to Salamanca). Part of the blame for Palencia's failure to thrive rests squarely on the shoulders of Charles V who, after sucking the city dry to pay for the bribes he needed to be elected as Holy Roman Emperor, rubbed out the city's prospects and privileges in revenge for its leading role in the Comunero revolt.

The one thing they couldn't take away is its Gothic **cathedral**, nicknamed La Bella Desconocida ('the Unknown Beauty'), in Pza San Antolín (*open 10.30–1 and 4–6; adm to crypt and museum*). The exterior is austerely plain except for two portals; Juan de Flandres' Renaissance *retablo mayor* is the prize in an interior that has remained more or less unchanged – a lack of Baroque curlicues and rolling eyeballs is a tell-tale sign of decline in a Spanish town. The oldest part of the crypt (673) is the only known surviving example of a Visigothic martyrium, built by King Wamba before he was shuttled off to a monastery. Among the highlights in the **museum** is the early *San Sebastián* by El Greco and a Virgin and Child by Pedro Berruguete. Don't miss the clock in the transept, where a lion and knight strike the hours with gusto.

Ten kilometres south of Palencia in the village of **Baños de Cerrato** (two kilometres from Venta de Baños), the Visigothic King Recesvinto (*see* National Archaeology Museum, **Madrid**, pp.509–10) founded the sturdy church of **San Juan de Baños** back in 661 (*open Tues–Sun 9–1 and 5–7; closed Mon; Patricio, the guardian, lives just opposite*), the purest surviving example of Visigothic architecture. Fretwork windows and a carved doorway (and a belfry, added by the restorers) relieve the simple stone exterior. Inside, the nave is divided by rows of horseshoe arches, and the capitals, doorways and the apse are discreetly decorated with finely carved eight-pointed crosses (*croix pattées*), scallop shells, solar spirals and palms. Recesvinto's rather complex dedicatory inscription survives intact on the triumphal arch, framed by modillions decorated with diving eagles. In its use of robust architectural volumes and the concentration of intricate detail in a few places, San Juan has been called the first Spanish church.

North of Carrión de los Condes: A Roman Villa

From Carrión de los Condes, the C615 follows the River Carrión up beyond Renedo de la Vega towards **Lobera**, where a sign points the way to **Pedrosa de la Vega**. Here, in 1968, the 3rd–4th-century Roman **Villa of Olmeda** (*open winter 10–1.30 and 4–6; summer 10–1.30 and 5–8; closed Mon*) was discovered, with its perfectly preserved polychrome mosaic floors, including geometric designs and mythological scenes. Nearby, the **church of San Pedro** in the medieval village of **Saldaña** houses finds from the ongoing excavations.

Along the Pilgrims' Road to León

The *camino de Santiago* continues its flat way towards León. Framed by the Cordillera Cantábrica to the north and the lower, softer Montes de León to the west, the province was a refuge for Mozarabs from Andalucía in the first days of the Reconquista, and the remnants of their monasteries are among the finest monuments along the whole road.

Sahagún and its Mudéjar Bricks

During the 12th century, when it was the seventh official stop of the *Codex Calixtinus*, Sahagún had a population of 12,000 and artificially concentrated so much wealth in the middle of nowhere that it earned the nickname 'the Las Vegas of the Middle Ages'. Today a mere 3,000 souls attempt to fill the Plaza Mayor, darkened old porticoes and forlorn, chewed-up houses.

Sahagún's rise and fall went hand in hand with that of Spain's most powerful Benedictine abbey, **San Benito**. The seeds of its glory were sown in the 11th century when Sancho III of Castile snatched León, the inheritance of his brother Alfonso, and locked Alfonso up in the abbey. But Alfonso made a secret pact with the abbot of San Benito, who helped him escape and take refuge with the Moors in Toledo.

In 1072 Sancho was assassinated and Alfonso was crowned king of Castile and León. Like Henry VIII, Alfonso VI married his way through six wives; those from Aquitaine and Burgundy put him into contact with Cluny, the great promoter of the Santiago pilgrimage. Never forgetting the help he received at Sahagún, the king refounded San Benito in 1080 under the new Cluniac reforms, poured money into the abbey and founded a huge pilgrims' hospital. In its heyday San Benito even minted its own coins; in 1534 its theological school had the status of a university.

Getting Around

Sahagún is linked by **trains** between Palencia and León and less frequently by **buses** between León and Carrión de los Condes.

Tourist Information

Valencia de Don Juan: Av. Carlos Pinilla, t 987 75 07 01. *Open summer only*.

Where to Stay and Eat

Sahagún ✉ 24320

*Hs Alfonso VI**, C/Antonio Nicolás 6, **t** 987 78 11 44 (*inexpensive*). A relatively smart choice.

★**Hs Hospedería Benedictina**, Santa Cruz, **t** 987 78 00 78 (*inexpensive*). Has sparkling rooms with bath.

★**Hospedería Monástica, t** 987 78 01 50 (*cheap*). In summer, the Benedictine nuns at San Pedro de las Dueñas run this serendipitous place, offering tasty, inexpensive meals to the public at weekends.

Fonda Asturiana, t 987 78 00 73 (*cheap*). A colourful place with good, inexpensive food.

Valencia de Don Juan ✉ 24200

★★**Villegas II**, C/Palacio 17, **t** 987 75 01 61 (*moderate*). An intimate family hotel with a little garden pool, overlooked by the five pretty rooms in the centre of town.

★★**Hs El Palacio**, C/Palacio 3, **t** 987 75 04 74 (*moderate–inexpensive*). Nearby is this charming inn, decorated with antiques and a document saying that King Philip III once slept here. Run by Asturians, it also has an excellent *sidrería* and good home cooking. *Closed Oct–May*.

Philip II brought San Benito low by moving the school to Navarra's Monasterio de Irache in 1596 and constraining the abbey to pay nearly all of its rents to the crown. In the 18th century two fires finished off what remained, leaving only a 17th-century portal at the west end of town and the adjacent ruins of the 12th-century Gothic **Capilla de San Mancio**. Smaller bits of San Benito are in the **museum** (*open in summer 10–1 and 4.15–6.30; closed in winter*) in the Monasterio Santa Cruz.

What Sahagún never had was a ready supply of building stone, which led the craftsmen who immigrated here from the Moorish lands to develop an architecture in brick, a medium that permitted new decorative patterns and delicacy. The first example, **San Tirso** (*open Tues–Sat 10.30–1.30 and 4–6, Sun 10–1.30; closed Mon*) was built near the monastery in the first decade of the 12th century, with its squat, tapering skyscraper tower rising out of three round apses; **San Lorenzo** is just a little later and more obviously Moorish in design, but its interior was redone in the 18th century (the chapel has Renaissance reliefs by Juan de Juni); both churches have porticoes for the town's once-famous markets.

San Miguel de Escalada

Open summer Tues–Sat 10–2 and 5–8, Sun 10–3; winter Tues–Sat 10–2 and 4–6, Sun 10–3; closed Mon.

This region was the new frontier back in the early days of the Reconquista, when the kings of Oviedo had just added León to their title. Among the first pioneers on the scene were Abad Adefonso and his companions, refugees from Córdoba, who in 913 founded the beautiful church of **San Miguel de Escalada** (just before Mansilla, take the road 8km northeast). A lovely portico of horseshoe arches, an *ajímez* window and a heavy 11th-century tower mark the exterior, while the interior (*should be reopening after major restoration*) is proof in golden limestone that the Cordovans never forgot the classic symmetrical Roman basilica form and its proportions. Delicate horseshoe arches divide the three aisles, and separate the transept and triple apse from the main body of the basilica (like the Byzantines, the Mozarab liturgy called for a screen between the holy precinct and the parishioners). The capitals have simple palmette designs; luxuriant floral and geometric reliefs with lions and peacocks eating grapes decorate the chancels and friezes; over the door you can just make out the highly elaborate dedicatory inscription. The ceiling, a later *mudéjar* addition, bears the arms of León and Castile.

León

León tuvo veintecuatro reyes
antes que Castilla leyes
(León had 24 kings before Castile even had laws)

Radiant under the famous spires of its cathedral, León is a singularly happy city of clean boulevards shaded by horse-chestnut trees: one of the few places in Spain to

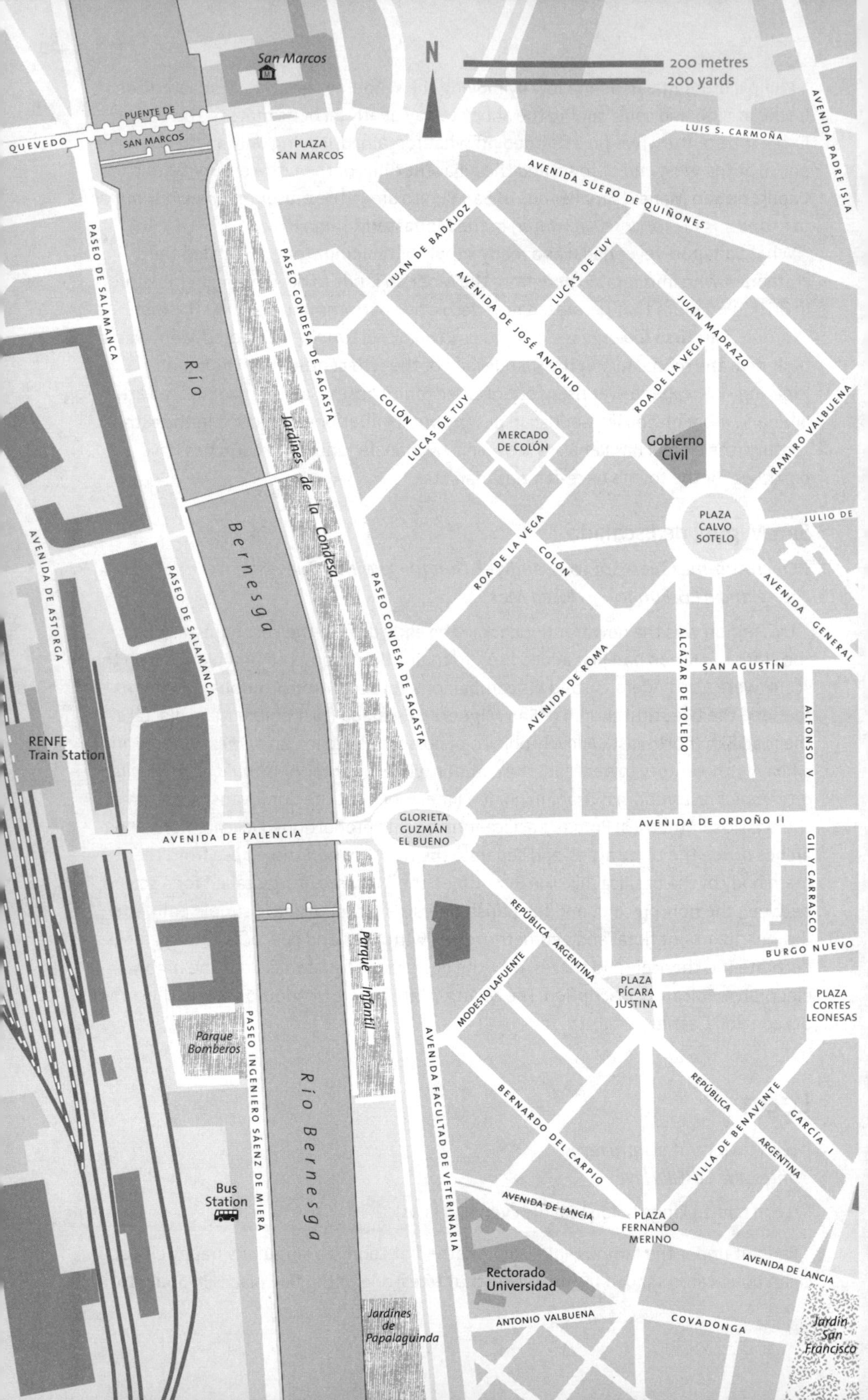

San Marcos
N
200 metres
200 yards
PUENTE DE
SAN MARCOS
QUEVEDO
PLAZA
SAN MARCOS
LUIS S. CARMOÑA
AVENIDA PADRE ISLA
AVENIDA SUERO DE QUIÑONES
PASEO DE SALAMANCA
PASEO CONDESA DE SAGASTA
JUAN DE BADÁJOZ
AVENIDA DE JOSÉ ANTONIO
LUCAS DE TUY
JUAN MADRAZO
ROA DE LA VEGA
Río
Bernesga
Jardines de la Condesa
COLÓN
LUCAS DE TUY
MERCADO
DE COLÓN
Gobierno
Civil
RAMIRO VALBUENA
PLAZA
CALVO
SOTELO
JULIO DE
AVENIDA DE ASTORGA
ROA DE LA VEGA
COLÓN
AVENIDA GENERAL
PASEO DE SALAMANCA
AVENIDA DE ROMA
ALCÁZAR DE TOLEDO
SAN AGUSTÍN
ALFONSO V
RENFE
Train Station
GLORIETA
GUZMÁN
EL BUENO
AVENIDA DE ORDOÑO II
AVENIDA DE PALENCIA
GIL Y CARRASCO
REPÚBLICA ARGENTINA
BURGO NUEVO
Parque Infantil
MODESTO LAFUENTE
PLAZA
PÍCARA
JUSTINA
PLAZA
CORTES
LEONESAS
Parque
Bomberos
PASEO INGENIERO SÁENZ DE MIERA
Río Bernesga
AVENIDA FACULTAD DE VETERINARIA
BERNARDO DEL CARPIO
REPÚBLICA ARGENTINA
VILLA DE BENAVENTE
GARCÍA I
Bus
Station
AVENIDA DE LANCIA
PLAZA
FERNANDO
MERINO
AVENIDA DE LANCIA
Rectorado
Universidad
ANTONIO VALBUENA
COVADONGA
Jardines
de
Papalaguinda
Jardín
San
Francisco

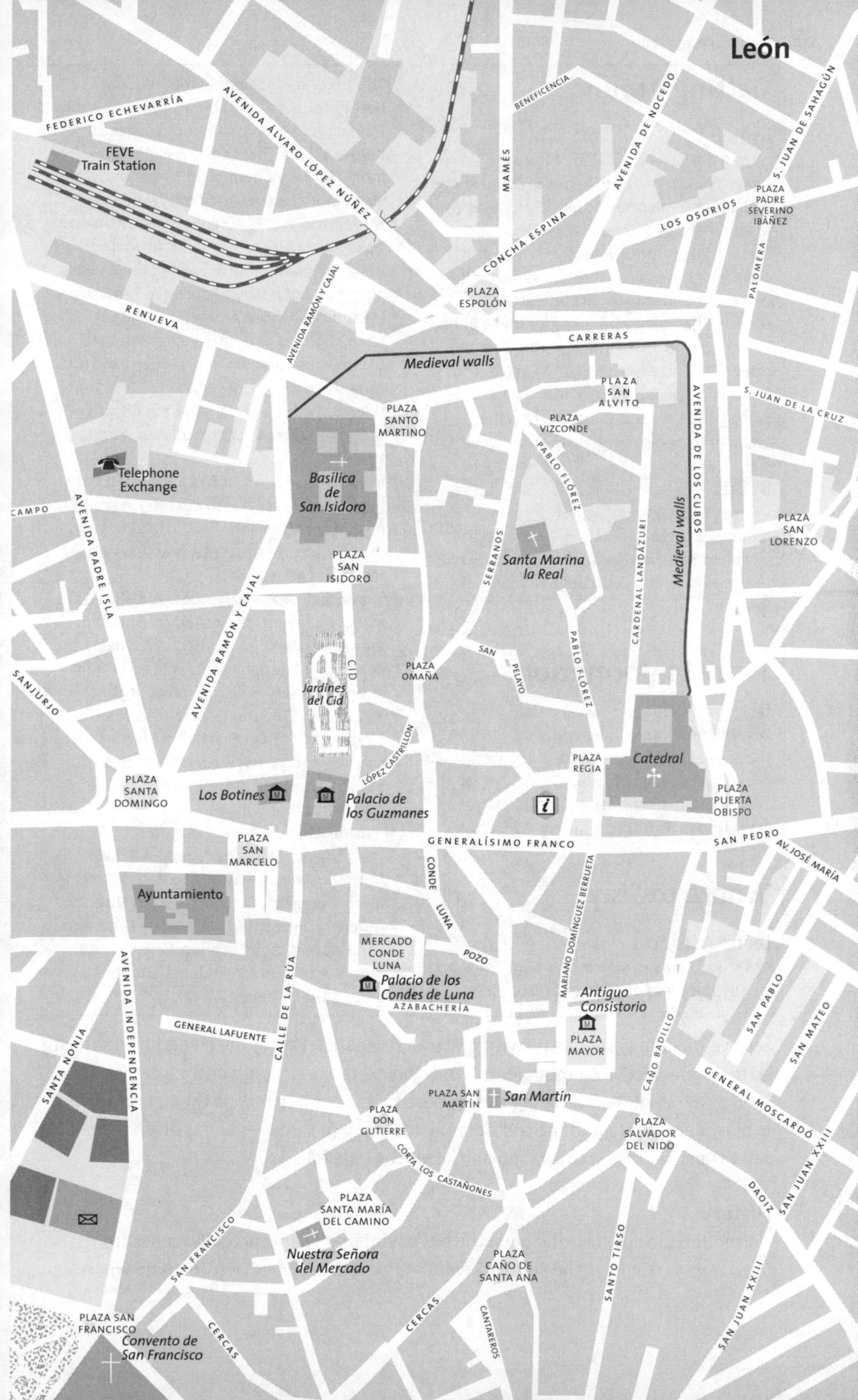
León
Federico Echevarría
FEVE Train Station
Avenida Álvaro López Núñez
Beneficencia
Mamés
Avenida de Nocedo
S. Juan de Sahagún
Plaza Padre Severino Ibáñez
Los Osorios
Concha Espina
Palomera
Plaza Espolón
Renueva
Avenida Ramón y Cajal
Carreras
Medieval walls
Plaza San Alvito
Plaza Santo Martino
Plaza Vizconde
S. Juan de la Cruz
Pablo Flórez
Telephone Exchange
Basílica de San Isidoro
Campo
Avenida Padre Isla
Avenida de los Cubos
Medieval walls
Plaza San Lorenzo
Cardenal Landázuri
Serranos
Santa Marina la Real
Plaza San Isidoro
Sanjurjo
Avenida Ramón y Cajal
Cid
Jardines del Cid
Plaza Omaña
San Pelayo
Pablo Flórez
López Castrillón
Plaza Regia
Catedral
Plaza Santa Domingo
Los Botines
Palacio de los Guzmanes
Plaza Puerta Obispo
Plaza San Marcelo
Generalísimo Franco
San Pedro
Av. José María
Conde Luna
Ayuntamiento
Mariano Domínguez Berrueta
Pozo
Mercado Conde Luna
Palacio de los Condes de Luna
Azabachería
Antiguo Consistorio
Avenida Independencia
General Lafuente
Calle de la Rúa
Plaza Mayor
San Pablo
San Mateo
Caño Badillo
Santa Nonia
Plaza San Martín
San Martín
General Moscardó
Plaza Don Gutierre
Plaza Salvador del Nido
Corta los Castañones
Daoiz
San Juan XXIII
Plaza Santa María del Camino
San Francisco
Nuestra Señora del Mercado
Plaza Caño de Santa Ana
Santo Tirso
San Juan XXIII
Plaza San Francisco
Convento de San Francisco
Cercas
Cercas
Cantareros

Getting Around

By Train

The RENFE station is at Av. Astorga 11, **t** 987 27 02 02. There are frequent connections with Burgos, Palencia, Medina del Campo, Madrid, Astorga, Ponferrada, Ourense and Lugo; regular trains depart for Oviedo and Gijón nine times a day through some magnificent mountain scenery and at least 500 tunnels. The Transcantábrico journey to Bilbao begins early in the morning at the FEVE station, Av. Padre Isla 48, **t** 987 23 31 98, stops for lunch at Mataporquera near the Picos de Europa and arrives at Bilbao early in the evening, stopping everywhere in-between.

By Bus

Buses, **t** 987 21 10 00, depart from the terminal south of the RENFE station, on Pso Ingeniero Sáenz de Miera, for the villages in the province and Oviedo, Burgos, Santander, Salamanca and Madrid.

Tourist Information

León: Pza de Regla 4, **t** 987 23 70 82.
Post Office: Av. de la Independencia
Telephones and Internet Access: Locutório Telefónico, C/de la Rua 6.

There is a **market** (*Sat*), but works in Pza Mayor mean its future location is uncertain.

Where to Stay

León ✉ 24000

*****Parador San Marcos**, Pza San Marcos 7, **t** 987 23 73 00, **f** 987 23 34 58 (*luxury*). This luxurious *parador* is not only Spain's best hotel, but a veritable antiques museum – even the bedrooms are furnished with unique pieces. There are less expensive rooms in the modern building behind, with views over the river and pretty gardens.

****Alfonso V**, C/Padre Isla 1, **t** 987 22 09 00, **f** 987 22 12 44 (*expensive*). This attractively designed place is the newest hotel; it's well equipped but nearly as pricey as San Marcos.

***Quindós**, Av. José Antonio 24, **t** 987 23 62 00, **f** 987 24 22 01 (*moderate*). Situated in the new part of town, very modern and arty; comes with excellent service.

Riosol, Av. de Palencia 3, **t** 987 21 68 50, **f** 987 21 69 97 (*expensive*). Large, pleasant and by the river.

***Paris**, C/Ancha 18, **t** 987 23 86 00, **f** 987 27 15 72, *hparis@lesein.es* (*moderate*). A brand new hotel with all the usaual facilities and friendly service; situated a few steps away from the Cathedral.

Hs Boccalino, Pza San Isidoro 9, **t** 987 20 30 60, **f** 987 22 78 78 (*moderate*). Sunny rooms in a peaceful location overlooking the Real Basílica de San Isidoro; the **restaurant** downstairs serves decent Italian meals.

*Hs Gúzman El Bueno**, C/López Castrillon 6, **t/f** 987 23 64 12. One of the best *inexpensive* choices in León – well-polished rooms with bath in a restored old house, around the corner from Los Botínes.

*Pensión Avenida**, Av. de Palencia 4, **t** 987 22 37 63 (*cheap*). On a busy street in a building from the 1920s – may be one of the nicest in town. Decent clean rooms. Ask for Nisa.

Residencia Universitaria Miguel de Unamuno, San Pelayo 15, **t** 987 23 30 10. Offers *cheap* rooms with bath for students; situated behind the cathedral.

achieve modern *urbanización* with grace and elegance. Part of the credit for this must go to its hyperactive Ayuntamiento, which blankets the city with posters depicting itself as a friendly lion, advising the Leonese to ride the bus, recycle their glass and not to blaspheme in front of the children. The founding of a university has given the old city a transfusion of young blood and keeps the bars full.

History

Although the lion has long been the city's symbol, its name actually comes from *Legio Septima Gemina*, the Roman Seventh Legion, established here in AD 68 when

Eating Out

León is famous for sweetbreads and black puddings (*morcilla*), game dishes and garlic soup with trout.

In the Barrio Húmedo, Pza San Martín is the bopping headquarters not only for bar hopping and tapas tasting but also for inexpensive restaurants.

Adonios, C/Santa Nonia 16, **t** 987 20 67 68 (*expensive*). Elegantly decorated in hacienda style, León's finest restaurant serves fish, fish, and more fish – more varieties than a Basque port could muster, prepared in every way imaginable. Traditional favourites like *merluza en salsa verde* are cooked to perfection, or you can try exotica like swordfish *a la brasa*.

Bitacora, C/García I 8, **t** 987 21 27 58 (*moderate*). The focus here is also seafood, with jaunty nautical décor to match. The *berengenas rellenas de marisco* (aubergines stuffed with shellfish) comes recommended, or splash out on scallops served with caviar. *Closed Sun.*

Casa Pozo, Pza San Marcelo 15 (near the Ayuntamiento), **t** 987 22 30 39. Specializes in both trout and salmon and prime fresh ingredients (*moderate menu*). *Closed Sun eve and 1–15 July.*

El Faisán Dorado, Cantareros 2, **t** 987 25 66 09 (*expensive–moderate*). Has a good name for excellent game and lobster dishes, and friendly service; good wine list too. *Closed Sun eve and Mon.*

Bodega Regia, Gral. Mola 5, **t** 987 21 31 73 (*moderate menu*). Specializes in simple, traditional dishes at reasonable prices. *Closed Sun and Feb.*

El Nuevo Racimo de Oro, Pza San Martin 8, **t** 987 25 41 00 (*inexpensive*). Seek out this 12th-century building where good Leonese cuisine is served to hungry crowds; there's a decent bar as well and plenty of atmosphere. *Closed Sun in summer and Wed rest of the year.*

Mesón Leonés del Racimo de Oro, Caño Badillo 2, **t** 987 25 75 75. The same management also runs this less expensive place, which specializes in regional dishes like roasts and Serrano ham; the tables overlook the patio and the *bodega* dates back to the 12th century.

Zalacain, C/de la Rúa 24, **t** 987 21 08 21 (*inexpensive menú especial*). An excellent and unusually smart vegetarian restaurant, with options for uncompromising carnivores. Both can be sampled on the superb *menú especial*.

Sorrento, Lancia 14, **t** 987 20 21 01. Why not try the excellent *cecina* ('cow ham', the local speciality).

La Poveda, Ramiro Valbuena 9, **t** 987 22 71 55. Track this place down for home cooking at the best price (*inexpensive menú*).

La Competencia, just off Pza San Martín. Most of the bars in the Barrio Húmedo give away free tapas with drinks, each specializing in a different delight: the pizza here is good.

El Rincon del Gaucho, just off Pza San Martín. The *patatas bravas* at this bar is worth stopping off for.

Camilo de Blas, Generalísimo 13. If you're in the mood for indulgence, don't miss this place, León's most venerable pastry shrine.

Viuda de Pedro Peréz, Pozo 13. Try one of their ultra-refined cakes.

Galba built a fort to guard the plain and the Roman road from Zaragoza. Reconquered from the Moors in the 850s by Ordoño I of Asturias (850–66), León changed hands several times more before King Ordoño II (914–24) moved his capital here. Even then, factionalism in the royal family left the city weak and prey to Moorish re-reconquests until 1002.

After this last Moorish hurrah, León, rebuilt and refortified, reconquered Castile. But just as León eclipsed Asturias, Castile – first a county, then a separate kingdom – eclipsed León. In 1252, under Ferdinand III the Saint, the union of the two kingdoms was finalized. Castile never looked back, but for León the marriage spelt nothing but decline: the nobles went off to the court in Burgos and the people left to settle the new frontiers gained by the Reconquista.

Into this vacuum of power and influence stepped the Church: the pilgrims' road became the chief source of income. Medieval pilgrims eagerly looked forward to León, with its Hilton of a *hostal*, where they could catch their breath for the last leg of their journey. Broken and crushed during the Comunero revolt against Charles V, León sank into oblivion until the invention of the railway made its mines viable once again. These in turn declined, leaving León its share of modern autonomy atavists who, remembering the good old days of the 10th and 11th centuries, preach '*León sin Castilla*' ('León without Castile'). As yet their movement has little support – it's too much like a mother rejecting her own child.

The Cathedral

The Spaniards call this the most splendid articulation of French Gothic in Spain, 'La Pulchra Leonina' ('Belle of León'), a cathedral so remarkable that it would stand out even in France for its superb and daring walls of stained glass. A like amount of glass caused Beauvais, its closest rival in window-acreage, to collapse, a disaster León has so far managed to avert by increasing support to the walls: expect some scaffolding.

The original church was twice destroyed before 1204, when Alfonso IX began a new church of warm golden stone in unheard-of dimensions, modelled on the soaring Gothic cathedrals of Chartres and Reims. His successor, Ferdinand III, worried by the expense, tried to limit its size, but the Leonese responded by putting up their own money for the construction and by the 15th century it was more or less completed.

Outstanding 13th-century sculptures decorate the north, south, and especially the **west portal** with its three finely carved tympana – the one in the centre illustrates a lively Last Judgement, the devils boiling the sinners beneath a triumphant Christ. The exterior, however, pales before the soaring spectacle of the **interior**, stripped in the 19th century of all its Baroque frosting, leaving it bare and breathtaking, especially when the late-afternoon sun streams in to ignite the richest and most vivid **stained glass** imaginable, 1,800 square metres of it, all glowing reds and golds, greens and violets. The oldest glass, in the chapels around the apse and the great rose window of the 12 Apostles in the front, dates from the 13th century; the latest is from the 19th, and made entirely by Spanish artists.

If you can draw your eyes from the walls of glass, note the **choir** in the centre of the nave, set behind an ornate triumphal arch of a façade and embellished with 15th-century alabaster carvings by Juan de Badajoz the elder; its midsection of glass was added fairly recently so you can see straight through to the altar, swimming in reflections of the windows. The *retablo mayor* contains an excellent Renaissance painting of Christ's Burial by Nicolás Francés. The chapels in the ambulatory house beautiful Gothic tombs, and there's an altar to Nuestra Señora del Dado, at which a disgruntled gambler allegedly once flung his dice, hitting the Christ Child on the nose and making it bleed. Through the Plateresque Puerta del Dado, the **cathedral museum and cloister** (*open Mon–Fri 9.30–2 and 4–7, Sat 9.30–1.30; closed Sun; adm; if the doors are locked, wait for the harried woman with the big keys*) has a big collection of Romanesque

Virgin Marys; also a *Crucifixion* by Juan de Juni and a Mozarabic Bible. The cloister itself was damaged in the 14th century and reworked with classical motifs by Juan de Badajoz the elder.

Around the Cathedral: the Barrio Húmedo

Alongside the cathedral run León's **walls**, built by Alfonso XI in 1324 over the Roman and early medieval fortifications; nearly half of the original 80 bastions remain intact. To the east extend the narrow lanes of the old town, known as the **Barrio Húmedo**, 'the humid quarter'. The elegant **Old Consistorio** (1677) presides in the **Plaza Mayor**; the adjacent **Plaza de San Martín** is the most humid corner of the humid quarter.

From the cathedral, busy C/Generalísimo Franco (the old Roman *decumanus*) leads up to Pza de Botines and Pza San Marcelo, where all of sudden you come upon León's version of Sleeping Beauty's castle, **Los Botines** ('the spats'). Antoni Gaudí's most conventional work, it was built in 1891 – 'in a moment of doubt', according to one of his biographers – as a private residence, with pointy turrets, typically swirling ironwork and a statue of St George (patron of Gaudí's native Catalunya) overhanging the door; judging by the grin on the dragon's face, the saint is scratching him in just the right spot. Two fine Renaissance palaces share the plazas: the arcaded **Ayuntamiento** and the **Palacio de los Guzmanes** (now the provincial Diputación), with a sumptuous façade designed by Rodrigo de Hontañón in 1559.

San Isidoro and the Panteón de los Reyes

If León's cathedral is one of the best in Spain, the city can claim a similar pedestal for the Romanesque frescoes in its **Real Basílica de San Isidoro**. Founded in the 9th century, razed to the ground by al-Mansur, it was rebuilt by Ferdinand I, the first to unify León and Castile in 1037 and the first to call himself 'King of the Spains'. In 1063 León bagged the relics of St Isidoro of Sevilla, that 6th-century, encyclopedia-writing Visigothic doctor of the Church whose bones, upon hearing of the Reconquista, asked to be transferred to Christian territory. These chattering bones must have driven the Moors in Sevilla crazy, since they packed them off to León; the basilica was at once rededicated to him, enlarged and given its belltower. Once here, the gentle Isidoro was conscripted into Reconquista duty; you can see him over the side door, on horseback in his bishop's gear, whacking the Moor with John Wayne gusto.

The façade has two entrances; the church is entered through the right-hand 11th-century **Puerta del Perdón**, topped by a tympanum sculpted with the Descent from the Cross, the Three Marys and the Ascension. This is the first Door of Pardon along the *camino de Santiago*; if a pilgrim were too ill or weak to carry on, he or she could touch the door and receive the same indulgence granted to someone who made it to Compostela. The barrel-vaulted interior, desecrated by Soult's French army in the Peninsular War, is a disappointment; of the 12th-century original only the transept capitals and chapel remain.

The more ornate **Puerta del Cordero**, its tympanum carved with the Sacrifice of Isaac, leads into the original narthex of the church, the **Panteón de los Reyes** (*open summer Tues–Sat 9–2 and 3–8, Sun 9–2; winter Tues–Sat 10–1.30 and 4–6.30, Sun 9–2;*

closed Mon; adm, adm free Thurs pm), founded by Ferdinand I. Its two small groin-vaulted chambers are supported by elaborately carved capitals (Daniel in the Lions' Den and the Resurrection of Lazarus), and decorated with extraordinary, vivid frescoes from the 12th century, among the best-preserved Romanesque paintings anywhere to exist in their original setting. Stylistically similar to the 5th-century frescoes and mosaics in Santa Costanza (which all the pilgrims on their way to Rome would have visited), Christ Pantocrator and the Evangelists, with human bodies and animal heads, reign over scenes of the shepherds, the Flight to Egypt, the Last Supper, the Tears of St Peter, the Seven Cities and Seven Lamps of the Apocalypse. Best of all, there's an allegory of the months, beginning with two-headed Janus, Roman god of the door, who looks both backward and ahead at the 'hinge' of the old and new years.

Although the French desecrated the tombs and burned the library, they missed the treasures in the Pantheon's **museum** (*same hours as Pantéon*): St Isidoro's original silver reliquary, the chalice of Doña Urraca, and lovely Mozarab caskets covered with ivories and enamels. The library, rebuilt in the 16th century by Juan de Badajoz, has an illuminated Bible of 960 that somehow escaped the French firebugs.

The Hospital de San Marcos and the Archaeology Museum

León's third great monument lies at the end of the garden along the riverside Paseo Condesa de Sagasta. The **Hospital de San Marcos** was built in 1173 as headquarters for the Order of the Knights of Santiago, charged with the pilgrims' protection; at their hospital the weary, blistered pilgrim could prepare for the rigours ahead. In 1514, when the powerful knights were more devoted to their own status, they set about rebuilding their headquarters thanks to an enormous donation by Ferdinand the Catholic: a payoff for electing him as Grand Master and surrendering their semi-autonomy to the Crown. Over the 16th to 18th centuries the monastery was given its superb 330ft Plateresque façade; its frieze of busts, niches, scallop shells, pinnacles, and lacy reliefs culminating in the portal topped by Santiago Matamoros and the arms of Charles V, who inherited the title of Grand Master from Ferdinand. Used after 1837 as a barracks, the building was purchased by the government in 1961 and converted into Spain's most beautiful luxury hotel. Non-guests can partake at the bar, and visit the upper choir of the adjacent church of **San Marcos** with its cockleshell façade. The chapterhouse and sacristy by Juan de Badajoz the younger contain the **Provincial Archaeology Museum** (*open Tues–Sat 10–2 and 4–6, Sun 10–1.30; closed Mon*), with a small but prize collection.

North of León

Northern León province encompasses the southern slopes of the Cordillera Cantábrica and the Picos de Europa and one of Spain's best caves, the **Cueva de Valporquero** (*open 10–2 and 4–7; adm; bring shoes with good grips and a jacket*), 46 kilometres from León through the spectacular gorges of the Torio river. The caves have no prehistoric art, but four kilometres of colourful galleries with little lakes, esplanades, a stalactite 'cemetery', and a chamber of wonders. Another beauty spot is the **Puerto de Pajares** (4,525ft), the lofty pass in the Cordillera Cantábrica used since antiquity as the main gate between León and Oviedo. The Leonese gateway to the Picos de Europa is **Riaño**, from where you can visit the **Valle de Valdeón** and **Valle de Sajambre** (*see* The Picos de Europa, **Cantabria**, p.352).

West of León

Two distinct regions fill the area between León and Galicia: between Astorga and Ponferrada is **La Maragatería**, the homeland of the Maragatos, one of Spain's marginal peoples, and west of Ponferrada is **El Bierzo**, a unique mountainous region, with some of the province's prettiest wooded valleys, distorted and eroded by mining and a favourite abode for contemplative 10th-century hermits.

Along the Pilgrimage Road to Hospital de Órbigo

On the N120, not far from the industrial sprawl west of León, is, for better or worse, the only modern chapel along the *camino de Santiago*: **La Virgen del Camino**, a concrete box built in 1961 by Brother Coello de Portugal which houses a much-venerated 16th-century statue of the Virgin, set in a Baroque *retablo*; the stained-glass workshop at Chartres produced the ugly windows and Catalan sculptor Subirachs contributed the weird emaciated bronze figures that cover the front.

Astorga, Gaudí and the Maragatos

Astúrica Augusta was an important administrative centre for the Romans, close to the mines and a main station along their celebrated *Vía de la Plata*, the 'silver road' that ran down to Zamora and Sevilla and across to Galicia, to transport the gold of the Bierzo, the silver of Galicia and the copper of Asturias. Like León, Astorga had its own bishopric by the 3rd century; like León it remained important in the Middle Ages because of the pilgrimage. It has genteelly declined ever since, helped along by a bit of pillaging and sacking in the Peninsular War.

The best way to approach Astorga is to circle the centre, still belted by half of its robust Roman-medieval **walls**, and enter on the northwest side of town, where the Cathedral and Bishop's Palace looming over the walls make a startling impression. Begun in 1451, the **Catedral de Santa María** took until the 18th century to complete, with too many cooks along the way; even the colour of the towers doesn't match. The façade was inspired by the cathedral in León, except that here the ornamentation on the façade is floridly Baroque: intricate garlands, columns and reliefs of the Descent from the Cross, the Adulterous Woman, and the Expulsion of the Merchants from the Temple. All the interest of the interior is concentrated in the *retablo mayor*, in marble high relief, by Gaspar Becerra (1520–70), an Andalucían who studied with Michelangelo. Off the neglected cloister, the **Museo Diocesano** (*open daily 10–2 and 4–8; adm*) houses some fine medieval pieces, including a 10th-century casket of gold and silver that belonged to Alfonso III, a figure of Santo Toribio by Gaspar Becerra and a 12th-century painted tomb.

Getting Around

RENFE links Astorga and Ponferrada with León, Lugo and beyond, four times a day – although note that for Astorga the station is a long hike – while **buses** go to the centre. Astorga is the point of departure of buses for La Maragatería; Ponferrada for El Bierzo; and León for the villages in the south. The Cueva de Valporquero is accessible only by **car**, although there are often excursions organized from León.

ALSA has frequent **buses** to Cacabelos and Villafranca del Bierzo from León and Ponferrada; a less regular service calls in at Villafranca on the way to Galicia. To continue into Los Ancares from here you'll need to have transport, hitch, or take a **taxi**; Jesus Taxi in Villafranca have 4WD vehicles for forays into the mountains **t** 987 54 03 05.

Tourist Information

Astorga: Glorieta Eduardo de Castro 5, **t** 987 61 82 22.

Internet Access: at Cybercentro, C/Puerta Obispo 9 (*open 11–2 and 5–11*).

Ponferrada: Gil y Carrasco 4, **t** 987 42 42 36.

Villafranca del Bierzo: Av. Diaz Ovelar, **t** 987 54 00 28.

There is a **market** in **Astorga** (*Tues*), and in **Ponferrada** (*Wed* and *Sat*).

Where to Stay and Eat

Astorga ✉ 24700

★★★**Hotel Gaudí**, Pza Eduardo de Castro 6, **t** 987 61 56 54, **f** 987 61 50 40 (*expensive*). By far the finest place to stay, not far from the cathedral; its good, moderately priced **restaurant** features several Maragato dishes and fish.

★★**Hs Gallego**, Av. Ponferrada 78, **t** 987 61 54 50 (*inexpensive*). Has the cheapest rooms with bath, in a new building just out of town.

★★**Hs La Peseta**, Pza San Bartolomé 3, **t** 987 61 72 75 (*moderate*). Central, this claims to be the best **restaurant** in Astorga; sample the generous wines of El Bierzo with heaped plates of *pulpo a la Gallega* (octopus) or conger eel. *Closed Sun eve, exc. Aug.*

Ponferrada ✉ 24400

★★★★**Del Temple**, Av. de Portugal 2, **t** 987 41 00 58, **f** 987 42 35 25 (*expensive*). The largest and best-endowed hotel, set in a pseudo-Templar castle; it can be noisy though.

★★★**Bérgidum**, Av. de la Plata 2, **t** 987 40 15 12 (*expensive–moderate*). A friendly place offering contemporary comforts.

La Fonda, Pza Ayuntamiento, **t** 987 42 57 94 (*moderate–inexpensive*). Uses local ingredients to create some interesting dishes (try the *gambas* with bacon). *Closed Sun eve.*

Las Cuadras, Tras la Cava 2, **t** 987 41 93 73 (*inexpensive*). Serves tasty tapas and excellent fish, right by the castle walls.

Villafranca del Bierzo ✉ 24500

★**Hs Casa Méndez**, Espíritu Santo,1, **t** 987 54 24 08 (*inexpensive*). Family-run with good home cooking and decent rooms with bath.

★**Hospederia Convento San Nicolás El Real**, C/Travesía San Nicolás 4, **t** 987 54 24 75, **f** 987 54 04 83, *info@estancias.com* (*inexpensive*). Occupies the old convent and pilgrims' *hostal*; the guest areas have modernized, but original frescoes and paintings remain in the halls. Out in the cloister a **restaurant** serves food with a religious theme – 'Archbishop's Salad', and steak in 'pilgrim sauce'.

La Escalinata, Pza de Prim 4, **t** 987 54 07 06 (*moderate*). Friendly, with bright modish décor and a menu of ever-changing delights, in a lovely location near the castle.

Astorga seemed like a dusty, declining nowhere to Juan Bautista Grau y Vallespinós when he arrived as its new bishop. In 1887, hoping to give his see a dynamic jump-start into the 20th century, he commissioned the most imaginative architect he knew, his friend Antoni Gaudí of Barcelona, to build him a new **Palacio Episcopal**. The rest of Astorga had deep reservations about the *modernista* fairy-tale castle; once the bishop died in 1893, the public's hostility burst so violently that Gaudí quit and refused to return to Astorga. Without his input, this pale asymmetrical castle (completed only in 1963) lacks the extraordinary detail and colour that characterize Gaudí's works in Barcelona. Instead of a bishop, the palace now houses the **Museo de los Caminos** (*open daily 11–2 and 3.30–6.30; adm*), a collection of pilgrimage paraphernalia along with some equally glowering examples of contemporary provincial art. For a hint of Gaudí's intentions, don't miss the atmospheric throne room with its discreet stained glass.

West of Astorga: Villages of the Maragatería

The mostly ruined villages of the Maragatería have been in decline ever since the railway took over the Maragatos' ancestral occupation, but **Castrillo de los Polvazares** (6km from Astorga, just off the *camino de Santiago*) has been restored to the verge of

Maragato Mysteries

Before leaving, look at the top of the cathedral apse, decorated with the figure of a Maragato named Pero Mato, who fought with Santiago at the legendary battle of Clavijo in 844. Astorga is the 'capital' of the Maragatos, who have lived here and in the villages to the west for as long as anyone can remember. Until the 19th century, they were muleteers and carriers, transporting nearly all the goods between Castile and Galicia, a line of work forced on them by their stubborn, almost uncultivatable land; their name has been traced back to the Latin *mercator*, or merchant. Grave and dry in manner, their honesty and industry were proverbial and no one hesitated to trust them with huge sums of money. Until recently they still wore their ancient costumes: huge slouched hats, very broad-bottomed breeches called *zaraguelles* (from the Arabic word for kilts) and red garters for the men; for the women, a crescent-shaped cap covered with a mantle and heavy earrings. They kept very much to themselves, marrying only other Maragatos; and twice a year, at Corpus Christi and the Ascension, all would gather in Astorga, and at exactly 2pm would begin a dance called El Canizo and finish at exactly 3; if any non-Maragatos attempted to join in, the dance would stop immediately.

Who were the Maragatos? Common beliefs that they were Celts, Visigoths or Berbers who came over in the 8th century and managed to hold on to this enclave after converting to Christianity have been called into question by Dr Julio Carro, who in the late 1950s discovered a Punic necropolis near the village of Santa Colomba de Somoza west of Astorga – hardly where you'd expect to find one, because the Phoenicians were sailors and León isn't exactly on the coast. Among the finds were figurines nearly identical to those found at Punic sites in Ibiza and dressed in a style very similar to the Maragatos. Carro's conclusion, based on his discoveries and on Maragato cultural traditions, was that they were descended from Phoenicians and Iberians enslaved by the Romans to work the gold mines of El Bierzo. The Maragatos themselves agree, and to thank Carro for discovering their true origins, they put up a stone plaque to him in the village of Quintanilla de Somoza. These days the Maragato traditions and insularity have practically vanished, but you can still try one of their famous cakes (*mantecadas*) in any Astorga pastry shop.

being twee, with old stone houses now mostly holiday homes, a score of roadside crosses and a main cobbled street built wide for mule trains.

Further west, pilgrims tackled the wild Montes de León, climbing up to the (4,935ft) **Foncebadón** pass. At the top stands the spindly **Iron Cross**, planted by a pilgrim untold years ago. Later pilgrims have added, one by one, the mound of slate stones at its foot, just as the Celts 'gave' stones to roadside shrines to placate the dangers ahead.

El Bierzo

In the old days the Romans dug for gold in these hills; the modern Leonese extract the iron and cobalt. El Bierzo has bleak mining towns, lovely mountain scenery and tobacco fields, charming villages that time forgot, and ancient hermitages. Its isolation and warm climate attracted so many anchorites early on that it was known as the Thebaid of Spain. Beyond the Iron Cross the pilgrims' road descends into the fertile valleys of El Bierzo by way of **Acebo**.

Ponferrada

Both the easy N-VI and the dramatic, lonely (but well-signed) pilgrims' track over the Montes de León lead to Ponferrada. It is the largest town of El Bierzo, and sums up the region's split personality, part of it mine-blackened and slag-heaped, the other half medievally pretty. It owes its name to a long-gone bridge with iron balustrades, erected over the Río Sil by the local 11th-century pontifex, Bishop Osmundo.

On the east bank of the Sil stands Ponferrada's proudest monument, the 12th-century **Castillo de los Templarios** (*open Tues–Sat 10.30–2 and 5–7, Sun mornings only; closed Mon; adm*), its triple ramparts built to defend the pilgrims from the Moors; its fairy-tale gate and towers were added later, in 1340. In 1811 the French went out of their way to vandalize it, resulting in heavy restoration. Here and there you can see Templar crosses and *taus* carved on the walls. While building the castle, the Templars discovered a statue of the Virgin in the heart of a holm oak tree, now enshrined in the **Basilica de Nuestra Señora de la Encina** (1577), with a good *retablo mayor*.

Into the Valley of Silence

South of Ponferrada, the Oza river winds through the beautiful **Valle del Silencio** where, between the 7th and 10th centuries, hermits took up their abode under the dramatic white flanks of Monte Aquiana. The jewel of El Bierzo is the little Mozarabic church of **Peñalba de Santiago** (*open Tues–Sat 10.30–1.30 and 4–7, Sun 10.30–1.30; closed Mon*), in a spectacular setting at the head of the valley, beyond the village of Montes (*take the left turning over the river, and leave your car at the entrance to the medieval hamlet*). Founded by Saint Genadio and dedicated in 913, its perfect proportions are reminiscent of palaeochristian basilicas in Africa, as is its shape: rectangular with three cupolas and two apses rather oddly facing one another. The rough stone and slate exterior doesn't prepare you for the refinement and fine craftsmanship inside, beginning with a pretty double-arched portal crowned by horseshoe arches.

Las Médulas

Twenty kilometres southwest of Ponferrada is **Carucedo**, the point of departure for an unusual journey through an ancient ecological disaster, **Las Médulas**. In the 1st century AD, the Romans noted the soft red soil was sprinkled with gold and minium (or red lead, used for painting), but to extract it meant sifting through thousands of tons of earth. Labour was no problem: some 60,000 slaves were brought in to dig a complex network of galleries, wells, dams and canals – one over 40 kilometres long – to erode the soil. Whole hills collapsed in the process, and new ones of left-over tailings were piled up by the slaves, leaving behind a landscape like a row of jagged red spinal cords – or medullas. From the village of Las Médulas, four kilometres from Carucedo, you can stroll (*bring sturdy shoes*) past the ancient canals, galleries, rock needles and surreal caves – a natural disaster perhaps, but a strangely beautiful one.

Northwest of Ponferrada: the Ancares Leoneses

North of Ponferrada, a lonely road heads north to Vega de Espinareda and the beautiful, densely forested, mountainous **Ancares Leoneses**, now under the jurisdiction of the National Park. The park not only protects a number of endangered species – a few brown bears, Iberian wolves, roe deer and capercaillie – but also a dying way of life in its 27 remote mountain hamlets, with their traditional architecture and *pallozas*, straw-topped round stone huts first built by the Celts. The best examples are along the tiny roads up the Ancares river valley.

West of Ponferrada: The Valle del Bierzo

Cacabelos, 12 kilometres west of Ponferrada, was another important stop on the *camino*, although these days it's best known for cultivating the vines of DO El Bierzo and its church of Las Angustía. The *Codex Calixtinus*' 10th stop on the *camino*, **Villafranca del Bierzo**, is one of the most attractive small towns along the whole road, embraced on all sides by mountains, built at the confluence of the Burbia and Valcarce rivers. As its name suggests, the town was founded by the French in the 11th century and in its heyday it had eight monasteries and six pilgrims' hospitals; today it makes wine and lodges visitors to the region.

On the hill where pilgrims entered Villafranca is the well-preserved 16th-century **Castillo de los Marqueses de Villafranca** and the 12th-century **Santiago**, a simple Romanesque church but an important one, with the second Puerta del Perdón along the road. Pilgrims too weary or ill to continue had only to touch the door to achieve the same indulgences as they would at Compostela. All of the church's eroded decoration is concentrated around the Puerta del Perdón; you can see three kings on horseback, a Crucifixion and Christ in Majesty. The pilgrims would descend from the church and castle to walk along wide, atmospheric **Calle del Agua**, 'Water Street', often a real street of water, so frequently has the Burbia flooded it. The Pza Mayor was set higher up away from danger, and near this you'll find the church of **San Francisco**, all that remains of a monastery founded by St Francis himself during his pilgrimage. It has a magnificent 15th-century *mudéjar artesonado* ceiling, much of which has been recently restored. Down on the banks of the Burbia, **La Colegiata de Santa María** (*open Tues–Sun 10–2 and 4–8; closed Mon*) was rebuilt in 1544 to designs by Rodrigo Gil de Hontañón. Construction continued into the 18th century, when the money ran out, leaving the nave cut short. However, the part-Gothic and part-Renaissance interior is uncommonly grand; note the chapel of the Trinity and a reliquary by Juan de Juni.

Southern Castile and León

Here, a feast of architectural ornament in Valladolid and Salamanca gives way to sparse, monotonous plains, liberally sprinkled with decorative, crumbling castles as reminders of the region's once-thriving trade career. Further south, beyond the hubs of the provincial capitals, the villages become ever more remote and minute as you head into the *sierras* towards Extremadura.

Zamora

Zamora is a fine old city on the banks of the Río Duero, boasting a golden necklace of small Romanesque churches and a jewel of a cathedral. Despite these treasures, it's off the main tourist route – even in June it's very likely that you'll have it to yourself.

Needless to say, this wasn't always the case. Zamora 'the well-walled', under the great shepherd-chieftain and escaped Roman slave Viriato, was a nightmare for the Romans. In 1072, the siege of Zamora was a nightmare for El Cid, who at the time served as a standard-bearer to Sancho II of Castile. Sancho was besieging his sister Urraca, whom El Cid refused to fight as she was his foster sister; finally Sancho was treacherously murdered and succeeded by his brother Alfonso VI. The city joined the Comunero revolt under Antonio de Acuña, the last battling bishop, who had seized his bishopric in Zamora by force. When the Comuneros collapsed, he was thrown out – only to acquire a private army, capture Toledo and proclaim himself archbishop.

When Franco faced dissenting priests, he built a prison in Zamora to contain them all – more were imprisoned here, it is said, than in all of the Warsaw Pact countries.

The Churches

The dusty Plaza Viriato, with a dramatic statue of Viriato and a battering ram called 'The Roman Terror', is the core of old Zamora; the town's many churches circle the plaza like the numbers on a clock. All are lovely, if not spectacular, and among those to aim for is **Santa María la Nueva** behind the old hospital (the Diputación Provincial), with its unusual 8th-century capitals in the Byzantine style and **Museo de la Semana Santa** (*open Mon–Sat 10–2 and 5–8, Sun 10–2; adm*) where the Virgins and Jesuses of the *pasos* hang out 51 weeks of the year. If the hospital is at 'noon' on the plaza, at one o'clock you have **Santiago de Burgos**; at three o'clock **San Andrés** with a fine interior and *artesonado* ceiling; at six o'clock **Santa María de la Orta**, built by the Templars, with a *mudéjar* arcaded cornice.

Calle Ramos Carrion (at nine o'clock) leads towards the cathedral, passing by way of the 1160 **La Magdalena** with its pretty rose window and sculpted portal to

Getting Around

By Train

Zamora's Plateresque train station lies at the bottom of the hill on C/Tres Cruces; several regular trains and Talgos link Zamora to Madrid and Ávila daily, **t** 980 52 11 10 for information.

By Bus

From the bus terminal (two blocks north near the bullring) about 20 buses a day depart hourly for Salamanca and less frequently to Toro, Valladolid, Madrid and Barcelona; there are four a day to Benavente, and two to Fermosella; **t** 980 52 12 81 for information.

Tourist Information

Zamora: Santa Clara 20, **t** 980 53 18 45, **f** 980 53 38 13 (*open Mon–Fri 10–2 and 5–9, Sat and Sun 10–2 and 5–8*).

Where to Stay

Zamora ✉ 49000

★★★★**Parador Condes de Alba de Aliste**, Pza de Viriato 1, **t** 980 51 44 97, **f** 980 53 00 63 (*expensive*). One of the most atmospheric and elegant in all Spain, located in the 15th-century ducal palace, with a lovely courtyard; public rooms are furnished with antiques and coats of armour and even the bedrooms have a pleasant old feel, not to mention the marvellous marble bathrooms; there's a pool the *parador* shares with the public and a **restaurant** (*moderate*) serving the finest of local cuisine; worth every euro.

★★★**HsR Real de Zamora**, Cuesta de Pizarro 7, **t/f** 980 53 45 45, *hostzamora@wanadoo.es* (*moderate*). Less grandly atmospheric, but with the odd chance of a ghost or two, you can stay in a 16th-century palace of the Inquisition where Pizarro once slept: now a comfortable hotel near the Puente de Piedra (all rooms have satellite TV and minibars) but the *menú* and breakfast are poor value.

★★**Dos Infantas**, Cortinas de San Miguel 3, **t** 980 50 98 98, **f** 980 53 35 48 (*expensive–moderate*). Recently renovated with a very stylish, modern entrance and bar, as well as comfortable, quiet rooms.

★**HsR La Reina**, C/La Reina 1, **t** 980 53 39 39 (*inexpensive*). A friendly *hostal* on Pza Mayor; clean rooms with TV.

There are also a whole clutch of *hostales* in a modern building at Benavente 2.

Eating Out

Paris, on the east side of town at Av. Portugal 14, **t** 980 51 43 25 (*moderate*) has a delightful inner garden and some of the best food in Zamora, with a wine list to match.

Pizarro, in the aforementioned Hosteria Real (*inexpensive*). A lovely, atmospheric place to dine, especially in the courtyard on a summer's night, with a fountain built into the rockface splashing away; on Saturday nights there's usually live classical music. However, the *menú*, though hearty, is somewhat overpriced.

España, Ramón Alvarez 3, **t** 980 53 17 31, (*inexpensive*). Just off Pza Mayor, this is an elegant place where you can eat well for less; there's a cheap *menú* and simple *a la carta* food.

Boriles, Pza Viriato, **t** 980 53 37 52 (*inexpensive*). A small, unassuming café forming part of the Diputación Provincial building. Various *terrazas* on Pza Mayor are ideal for watching Zamoran life drift by.

San Ildefonso, with photogenic arches, buttresses and a Flemish triptych, brought over by Charles V.

The Plaza Mayor is more of a terraced café affair, graced by the **Iglesia de San Juan** which boasts two soaring arches stretching the length of the nave inside. The **Iglesia de San Cipriano**, on the street of the same name, is also worth a visit for its simply lit, wonderfully pure interior; a ladder leads up to a little gallery and the Romanesque side apses have delightful, naïve carvings on the capitals.

The Cathedral

At the far west end of Zamora stands the Cathedral, crowned by its striking fish-scale Byzantine dome, and corner turrets. Inside are some fine ironwork grilles and wonderful carved choir stalls – pious images on the backs, and indecorous scenes hidden away below, vignettes of amorous nuns and monks that were censored for years. The **museum** off the cloister (*open Mon–Sat 11–2 and 4–7; closed Sun; adm*) contains an enviable treasure: the magnificent **Black Tapestries**, made in Flanders in the 15th century. The 'black' refers to the sheer density of stitches and detail put into the scenes of the Trojan War, the battles of Hannibal, and the Parable of the Vine, where everyone swans about in elegant Renaissance finery.

The broad remit of the **Museo de Zamora** (*open Tues–Sat 10–2 and 4–8, Sun 10–2; adm, adm free Sat and Sun*) is beautifully laid out in Pza de Santa Lucìa, a sensitive architectural mix of old and new and a generous use of woods. The church on **Plaza de San Esteban**, on the other side of Pza Mayor, holds the modern sculpture of Baltasar Lobo (*open Tues–Sat 12–2 and 7–9, Sun 12–2; closed Mon*).

Around Zamora

Zamora divides itself as a province between the **Tierra del Pan** (bread land) north of the Duero and **Tierra del Vino** (wine land) south of the river, which sums it up quite well. The wheat-growing Tierra del Pan has the most to see: northwest near Galicia, there's the pretty glacial lake, **Lago de Sanabria**, 3,280ft above sea level and the centrepiece of Spain's newest national park. **Puebla de Sanabria** is the main town, located on a cliff over the river Tera, dominated by a well-preserved 15th-century castle; in the parish church, note the four curious slate figures in 11th-century dress. **Benavente**, an ancient city on a promontory between the Esla and Orbigo, had one of Spain's most elaborate *alcázars*, built in the 15th century; unfortunately only the **Torre de Caracol** ('snail tower') survived the fire set by Napoleon's troops and now houses a *parador*. There are a couple of interesting 12th-century churches: **San Juan del Mercado** contains an unusual image of the Virgin holding a Templar cross in a wheel, while **Santa María de Azoque** has a more orthodox Annunciation tableau.

Where to Stay and Eat

Puebla de Sanabria ✉ 49300

There are quite a few places to stay, where holiday-makers come to swim in the lake and fish in the streams of the park. For information on ***casas rurales***, **t** 989 62 03 85.

*****Parador**, Ctra del Lago 18, **t** 980 62 00 01, **f** 980 62 03 51 (*expensive*). Near to the town, modern, with fine views and, as usual, a good **restaurant**.

****Hs La Trucha**, Padre Vicente Salgado 10, **t** 980 62 00 60 (*inexpensive*). All the rooms here have bath; and the ***comedor*** has a reasonable set *menú* (*inexpensive*).

***Hs Galicia**, Animas 22, **t** 980 62 01 06 (*cheap*). Seven no-frills beds and a cheap **restaurant**.

Benavente ✉ 49600

******Parador Rey Fernando II de León**, Pso Ramón y Cajal, **t** 980 63 03 00, **f** 980 63 47 93 (*expensive*). Elegantly furnished in the Torre del Caracol, with an *artesonado* ceiling from another demolished monument.

****Hs Avenida**, Av. Gral. Primo de Rivera 17, **t** 980 63 10 31 (*inexpensive*). This is comfortable enough. *Open all year.*

***Hs Paraíso**, Obispo Regueras 64, **t** 980 63 33 81 (*cheap*). Ten adequate rooms with showers down the hall.

Near the Portuguese frontier (*take the N122 towards Alcañices, and turn off towards the village of El Campillo*) the 8th-century **San Pedro de la Nave** stands isolated in a field, a late Visigothic masterpiece transported stone by stone from the banks of the Elsa when it was dammed in 1931. Built of rosy limestone in the form of a Greek cross, with a tower-lantern rising out of the crossing, its exterior is decorated with a frieze of vines and birds. The imposing interior is embellished with some of the finest and last Visigothic sculpture: more friezes with faces, solar symbols and birds, and superb carved trapezoidal capitals carved with powerfully modelled figures of the apostles, of the sacrifice of Isaac, interrupted by a big hand from stage left, and of Daniel in the lions' den, or rather in the lions' lake, according to the Latin inscription above (LAQVM LEONVM); the prophet stands ankle deep in water, lapped at happily by two big cats.

South of the Duero in the Tierra del Vino the most important town is **Fermosella** on the Portuguese border, the last refuge of Bishop Acuña's Comuneros. The imposing Gothic parish church contains a collection of Romanesque and Gothic statues.

Salamanca

Spain's great medieval university town, Salamanca is one of the country's charmers, a dream city of golden stone, embroidered into a thousand tiny Plateresque details and later put into Baroque curling irons by the prolific Churriguera family. Although the university was ranked in the Middle Ages as one of Europe's finest, it began to decline in the strict clericalism and intolerance initiated by Philip II; Francoism, being virulently anti-intellectual, almost dealt it a death blow, although the glamour of Salamanca's name continued to lend it status. But there's nothing like thousands of students to keep a town awake, and their lively presence complements the serene magnificence of Salamanca's monuments.

Plaza Mayor

Despite its prominent place in Spanish history, Salamanca is not big, and you can walk nearly everywhere from the **Plaza Mayor**. This urban heart of gold was built at the beginning of the 18th century, a happy collaboration by Alberto Churriguera and Andrés García de Quiñones, members of Salamanca's two great Baroque dynasties. Like most of Salamanca's monuments, the plaza is made of *piedra de Villamayor*: a fine grained sandstone that is pale, moist, and easy to handle when freshly quarried, but when left in the sun hardens and darkens to a deep, golden-brown patina. The plaza is Salamanca's stage and general meeting-place, and in the evening the whole city relaxes in the cafés, on occasion entertained by the *Tunas*, the bands of student minstrels in Renaissance costume. It doubles as a hall of fame, with busts of national greats – and schmucks like Franco – carved on medallions around the arcades.

South of the plaza, Rúa Mayor passes another local landmark, the 16th-century **Casa de las Conchas** ('House of the Shells'), which now houses the Provincial Tourist Office. Built by Dr Talavera Maldonada, a member of Ferdinand and Isabel's royal council and a Knight of Santiago, he covered the whole surface with the scallop-shells of

St James, giving the house a wonderful nubby texture; shells are even incorporated in the iron grilles over the windows. The great, domed **La Clerecía** (1750), nearby, belonged to a Jesuit seminary, and nowadays to the Universidad Pontificia.

The Cathedrals

***New**: open daily 9–2 and 4–8; **Old**: open daily 10–1.30 and 4–7.30; adm.*

Rúa Mayor continues down to Pza de Anaya and Salamanca's two cathedrals, built side by side. From the outside, at least, the much larger **New Cathedral** dominates. One of Gothic's last hurrahs, it is adorned with pinnacles, cosmic Plateresque details (even an elephant makes an appearance) and a belltower modelled after the one in Toledo. It was completed in 1560 as a symbol of Salamanca's aspirations and prestige – just as the terror and intolerance of the times were undermining both. **Inside**, the New Cathedral is lofty and elegant. Among its chapels near the main altar is the talisman *Christ of the Battles* – a simple Romanesque image carried by El Cid and invoked before his battles, surrounded by some of the frothiest Baroque imaginable. Underneath lies the tomb of Bishop Jerónimo, El Cid's chaplain and founder of the old cathedral. Another chapel is crowded with wooden sculptures of every conceivable saint; in its window is the inevitable Spanish *memento mori*: Death.

Dwarfed in comparison, the Romanesque **Old Cathedral** makes itself known from the outside by its **Torre del Gallo**, an unusual silvery 'fish-scale' Byzantine dome, flanked by turrets and topped by a rooster. Built in 1160, its magnificent Romanesque interior remained unsurpassed by the New Cathedral. Brightly lit by the windows at the base of the dome, the rich colours of Nicolás Florentino's ***retablo mayor*** are wonderfully vivid, its 53 paintings crowned by an awesome vision of the Last Judgement. Paintings on the side walls depict various miracles – including one that occurred during the building of this very cathedral, when a stone block fell on the head of a mason, inflicting only a headache (judging by his expression). The block itself hangs from one of the columns, which themselves have beautiful capitals. In the back of the church a door leads to the **Capilla de San Martín**, with late 13th-century frescoes of saints and another Apocalypse. The chapels off the former cloister (modernized to death in the 18th century) are especially interesting. The first, the **Capilla de Talavera**, has unique star-vaulting, the tattered standard of the Comuneros – a rare memento of the great revolt – and the privilege, bestowed when the chapel was built in the 12th century, of celebrating Mass according to the Mozarabic rite (*see* Toledo Cathedral, pp.566–8). The **Capilla de Santa Barbara** (1340) has at its centre the tomb of Bishop Lucero – he of the well-worn feet, polished by countless anxious candidates for Doctorate degrees. It was customary to pass the night before the examination in the chair before the altar, feet propped up on the bishop's in a vigil of study. The examiners would come to the chapel in the morning and grill the student, who, if successful, would leave in a triumphal procession, attend a bullfight and, mixing the bull's blood with olive oil, inscribe his name on the cathedral or university building for posterity. The **Capilla de Los Anayas** has another bishop's tomb, enclosed by an ornate *verja* (iron grille); against the wall is a beautifully crafted 14th-century organ with *mudéjar* designs, believed to be the oldest in Europe. The **chapterhouse** contains a **museum** featuring paintings by Fernando Gallego (a native of Salamanca).

The University

Open Mon–Sat 9.30–1.30 and 4–7, Sun 10–1; adm.
Casa-Museo Unamuno open Oct–June Tues–Fri 9.30–1.30 and 4–6, Sat and Sun 10–1.30; July–Sept mornings only; closed Mon; adm.

A block from the cathedral is the **Patio de las Escuelas**, with a statue of the mystic and poet Fray Luis de León, Salamanca's most famous professor. This is the main entrance to the university, founded as the Escuelas Salamantinas in 1218 by Alfonso IX of León. From that moment its growth was prodigious; with the union of León and Castile it incorporated the fledging university of Palencia; in 1254 Alfonso the Wise endowed it with a law school and professorships; the following year Pope Alexander ranked it in the same category as Oxford, Paris and Bologna. At its peak it enrolled 10,000 students in 25 colleges and boasted one of Europe's best faculties of astronomy – consulted by Columbus before his famous voyage – as well as the first woman professor, Beatriz de Galindo (1457–1535), who taught Queen Isabel her Latin. One of Spain's most prominent thinkers of the 20th century, the Basque Miguel Unamuno, taught classics here and served as rector into the Civil War.

During the Peninsular War the French demolished 20 of the colleges, but fortunately spared the **University** and its unsurpassed Plateresque façade; in a low medallion over the door are smug portraits of Ferdinand and 'Elisabetha' and the elegant Greek inscription: 'From the Kings to the University; from the University to the Kings'. Inside the old lecture rooms are placed around a two-storey cloister, linked by a gorgeously carved **Renaissance stair**, where giant insects frolic with bishops popping out of pots. On the ground floor the **Lecture Hall of Fray Luis de León** has been perfectly preserved since the day in 1573 when the professor, in the middle of a lecture, was carted off by the Inquisition. For five years he languished in a dire prison cell; upon his release, he returned here and without further ado, calmly resumed his

Getting Around

By Train

The train station is a 20-minute walk north of the centre via Pza de España, in Pza de la Libertad, **t** 923 12 02 02; there are trains to Ávila and Madrid, Ciudad Rodrigo and into Portugal; others go up through Valladolid and Burgos to Irún, or to Zaragoza and Barcelona.

By Bus

The bus station is a 15-minute walk from Pza Mayor on Av. de Filiberto Villalobos 73–85, **t** 923 23 67 17; there are at least 13 buses daily to Zamora (fewer at weekends), two to León, five to Valladolid, five to Cáceres and express buses almost hourly 6am–9.30pm to Madrid. Two or three buses daily go to Galicia, the Basque Lands, Barcelona and Cádiz; four to Asturias and Ávila, and five to Sevilla. Many go to Ciudad Rodrigo and surrounding villages.

Tourist Information

Salamanca: Provincial Office: Casa de las Conchas, Rúa Mayor s/n, **t** 923 26 85 71, **f** 923 29 60 07 (*open Mon–Fri 9–2 and 5–7, Sat and Sun 10–2 and 4–7*).

Municipal Office: Pza Mayor 4, **t** 923 21 83 42 (*open daily 9–2 and 4.30–6.30*).

Where to Stay

Salamanca ✉ 37000

Expensive

★★★★**Parador de Salamanca**, Teso de la Feria 2, **t** 923 26 87 00, **f** 923 21 54 38. Just across the Roman bridge with a fine view of the city's enchanting skyline. One of Spain's newest *paradores*, it offers a pool, garden and a/c.

★★★★**Palacio de Castellanos**, C/San Pablo 58, **t** 923 26 18 18, **f** 923 26 18 19. In the centre, in a late 15th-century palace, with a lovely patio and plush, modern and pricey rooms.

★★★★**Gran Hotel**, Pza Poeta Iglesias 3, **t/f** 923 21 35 00. A good central choice furnished with elegant rooms.

★★★★**Plaza del Ángel**, Pza del Ángel 5–7, **t** 923 21 75 18, **f** 923 21 96 97, *www.hotelplazadelangel.com*. A fine new contender, with very stylish rooms and swish bathrooms.

lecture with 'As we were saying yesterday...'. In the same room, Unamuno, who at first had given Franco some much-needed intellectual backing, claiming the Nationalist rising was 'necessary to save Western Civilization', had his famous confrontation with the lunatic Falangist Millán Astray. Chairing a Columbus Day commemoration in 1936, Unamuno listened to a string of speeches in praise of Franco, then stood up and denounced both sides. Astray went berserk, bellowing 'Death to the intellectuals' while his bodyguards drew arms. Franco's wife saved Unamuno from the Falangist fury, though he was dismissed from his post as rector and died in disgust two months later. He is remembered in the **Casa-Museo Unamuno** by the door.

Your ticket will also get you into the **Escuelas Menores** ('the Lesser Schools' – ie. for non-aristocrats), equally endowed with a fine cloister; one room contains Ferdinand Gallego's *Sky of Salamanca*, a beautiful scene of the zodiac salvaged after the Lisbon earthquake in 1755. Next to it, the **Museo de Bellas Artes** (*open Tues–Sat 10–2 and 4.30–8, Sun 9.30–2.30; closed Mon; adm*) contains an eclectic collection and *artesonado* ceilings. The most interesting piece, an anthropomorphic menhir from the 10th century BC, is in the foyer, while in the courtyard are *verracos* and *cerdos* (swine), Celtiberian gravestones similar to the ones found around Ávila. From here you can walk down to the Río Tormes, spanned by a beautiful 400m **Roman bridge**, and guarded by a headless *cerdo*. The brick Romanesque-*mudéjar* church of **Santiago**, with its three elegant apses, sits on the city side of the bridge.

Moderate

★★**Amefa**, Pozo Amarillo 18–20, **t** 923 21 81 89, **f** 923 26 02 00. A luxurious charmer in the centre of town.

★★★**Las Torres**, Pza Mayor 26, **t** 923 21 21 00, **f** 923 21 21 01. About as central as you get, but this has seen better days. Some rooms have balconies over the plaza.

Inexpensive

★★**Emperatriz I**, C/Compañía 44, **t** 923 21 92 00, **f** 923 21 92 01. This is housed in an old stone building on a central, pedestrianized side street. They also offer an economical *menú* and a garage.

★**Hs Tormes**, Rúa Mayor 20, **t/f** 923 21 96 83. Stands out by dint of its great location, between Pza Mayor and University; the rooms are clean and pleasant, and you can eat cheaply in its small **restaurant**.

Cheap

There are scores of inexpensive *fondas* and *pensiones*, of which the following are excellent examples:

P. Lisboa, Meléndez 1, **t** 923 21 43 33.

P. Marina, Doctrinos 4, **t** 923 21 65 69.

Eating Out

Chez Victor, Espoz y Mina 26, **t** 923 21 31 23 (*expensive*). Just off Pza Mayor, this is one of Spain's best French restaurants, with imaginative, creative cuisine, especially duck and game dishes. Top it all off with the 20-year-old port. *Closed Mon, Sun eve, and Aug*.

Le Sablon, Espoz y Mina 20, **t** 923 26 29 52 (*moderate*). Has an excellent reputation for its equally French-influenced cuisine and elegant desserts. *Closed July*.

La Montaraza, José Jáuregui 9, **t** 923 26 00 21 (*moderate*). A traditional Salamanca favourite that serves up a heaving board of tapas, or meals with oven-baked soup, cod, and cheese cake. *Closed Mon and Aug*.

Rio de la Plata, Pza Peso 1, **t** 923 21 90 05 (*inexpensive*). Arrive early if you want a table at this little restaurant with excellent *turbot a la plancha*. *Closed Mon and July*.

Roma, C/Ventura Ruiz Aguilera 10, near the Pza Mayor, **t** 923 21 72 67 (*inexpensive*). Thanks to the student population, you can easily eat for less in spots like this with meals around the €6 mark; there are many other places like it.

Convento de Las Dueñas and Convento de Santa Clara

Behind the cathedral, at the head of the Gran Vía, the **Convento de Las Dueñas** (*open daily 10.30–1 and 4.30–7; adm*) was founded in 1419 for the Dominican Mothers. In the 16th century, an unusual five-sided **cloister** (*open daily 10–2 and 4–7*) was added, its upper gallery adorned with capitals carved by some kind of Plateresque Edvard Munch, depicting disturbing, nightmarish, twisted torsos, skulls and hundreds of shrieking faces of the damned. Across from Las Dueñas stands another Plateresque masterpiece, the **Convento de San Esteban** (*open Mon–Fri 9–1.30 and 4–8, Sun 9.30–1.30 and 4–8; closed Sat; adm*) with a filigree façade as delicate as that of the University; inside it has a tranquil cloister, and a huge wedding cake of a *retablo* by José Churriguera. The frescoes near the upper choir are unintentionally funny, depicting rows of martyred saints, all holding their heads like a queue of bewildered waiters. Behind this is another Romanesque church, **Santo Tomás de Canterbury**, the first in the world dedicated to St Thomas, erected just three years after his martyrdom by English residents of Salamanca. On the other side of this is the newest star in Salamanca's art constellation, the 13th-century **Convento de Santa Clara** (*open Sept–June Mon–Fri 9.30–1.40 and 4–6.40, Sat and Sun 9–2.40; closed Mon and Tues in July and Aug; adm*) – a beautiful set of 13th–18th-century frescoes were found under coats of whitewash, and a superb polychrome 14th-century ceiling found behind a false one in the church, and another one, from the Renaissance, in the cloister.

Elsewhere in Salamanca

West of Pza Mayor, the triangular **Plaza de Agustinas** is one of the city's scenic corners, framed by the **Convento de Las Agustinas** (containing the well-known Immaculada by Ribera) and the ornate 16th-century **Palace of Monterrey**. A block down is the **Casa de las Muertes** ('House of the Dead'), named after the skulls incorporated in the Plateresque façade. Unamuno died in the house next door, at No.4, and his neo-Rodinesque statue broods across the square. The church of the **Convento de Santa Ursula** (*open daily 11–1 and 4.30–6; adm*) just to the north of the square houses a magnificent tomb of Archbishop Alonso Fonesca by Diego de Siloé. Two towers from great aristocratic solars survive as landmarks east of Pza Mayor: the **Torre del Aire** (Tower of Air) with its elaborate windows, and the **Torre del Clavero** (Tower of El Clavero) with a picturesque crown of turrets. As you stroll through the city, look for the brass door-knockers shaped like a hand: the Mano de Salamanca, a memory of the Islamic charm, the 'Hand of Fatima'. Well worth a visit, if only to behold the jewel-like edifice, is the **Museo de Art Decó y Art Nouveau** (*open Tues–Fri 11–2 and 5–9, Sat and Sun 11–9; closed Mon; adm*), housed in Casa Lis by the Old Cathedral.

Around Salamanca

The province of Salamanca for the most part resembles a northern extension of Extremadura. Much of the land is devoted to raising fighting bulls, who roam about in vast fields dotted with holm oaks. Spain's most remote villages are located in

Getting Around

There is only one train a day from Salamanca to Ciudad Rodrigo, and it leaves town at an ungodly 5am; otherwise you'll have to rely on buses from Salamanca to Ciudad Rodrigo, Alba de Tormes, Ledesma, Béjar and the villages of the Sierra. Connections exist, if not particularly often. Remember, life is a journey, not a destination.

Tourist Information

Ciudad Rodrigo: Pza de Amayuelas 5, by the Old Cathedral; **t** 923 46 05 61 (*open Mon–Fri 9–2 and 5–7, Sat and Sun 10–2 and 6–8*). For information on the town, *try www.ciudadrodrigo.net*.

Internet Access: Academia Bravo, Pza Mayor 17, offers remarkably good-value Internet access.

Béjar: Pso Cervantes 6, **t** 923 40 30 05.

Where to Stay and Eat

Ledesma ✉ 37000

*****Balneario de Ledesma**, **t** 923 57 02 50 (*moderate*). Ledesma's only hotel, belonging to a large, fairly modern spa. *Open mid-Mar–Nov*.

Ciudad Rodrigo ✉ 37500

******Parador Enrique II**, Pza Castillo 1, **t** 923 46 01 50, **f** 923 46 04 04, *ciudadrodrigo@parador.es* (*expensive*). This ivy coated hotel has recently been renovated; intimate and charmingly furnished, it enjoys lovely views (try to get Room 10 with a round dome) and runs the best **restaurant** in town (*moderate*); try the city's speciality, stuffed shoulder of lamb (*paletilla de cordero rellena*).

*****Conde Rodrigo**, Pza San Salvador 9, **t** 923 46 14 08 (*inexpensive*). By the cathedral in a lovely old palace, this is the town's other atmospheric option.

Hs Arcos, Pza Mayor 17, **t** 923 46 06 64/923 48 07 49 (*inexpensive*). Newly done, immaculate rooms overlooking the plaza (individual occupancy thankfully half-price).

P. Parìs, C/Toro 10, **t** 923 48 23 49 (*cheap*). A good cheapie in a little street off Pza Mayor.

La Artesa, Pza Mayor (*inexpensive*). Has a good-value *menú*, tasty tapas and cheap breakfasts.

El Sanatorio, Pza Mayor (*inexpensive*). Unfortunately named, but an old favourite for no frills tapas and a hearty *menú*, replete with *torero* mementoes.

Hong Kong, Ctra de Salamanca 10, **t** 923 48 13 67 (*inexpensive*). If you're *hasta las narices* with Spanish dishes, try this remarkably

Salamanca's sierra – some of them, it is said, had not even heard of God until the 20th century.

Northwest of Salamanca, there's some very green, un-Castilian scenery and even a couple of beaches along the Río Tormes. The river wends all the way to **Ledesma** at the tip of the **Embalse de Almendra**, a vast reservoir close the confluence of the Tormes with the Duero. Ledesma is an attractive walled town with a pretty Plaza Mayor, a couple of medieval churches and a Roman bridge. Upriver, the **Arribes del Duero** is a region of steep, 300m-walled canyons, lakes and rugged hills. The village of **Saucelle** also makes a pretty goal, in the centre of a large almond-growing area.

Ciudad Rodrigo

On the Portuguese frontier, Ciudad Rodrigo was captured from the Moors in the early 12th century and named after Count Rodrigo González Girón, who led its resettlement. A magnificent set of walls added in 1190 remains almost intact; Spaniards are fond of aerial views of the city, enclosed in its perfect multi-pointed star. During the Peninsular War, Wellington took it from its French occupiers after a bitter, 11-day good-value Chinese restaurant, with a gaudy pavilion bar and tasty doughnut-like bread.

Alba de Tormes ✉ 37800

★★**Alameda**, Av. Juan Pablo II, **t** 923 30 00 31 (*inexpensive*). You can get a fine, air-conditioned double here in this quiet corner of town; it also has a very reasonable **restaurant**.

Villages of the Sierra

The villages of the Sierra are mostly unspoiled, but hardly undiscovered, and if you'd like to stay over in summer, make a reservation.

Béjar

★★★**Colón**, Colón 42, **t/f** 923 40 06 50 (*moderate*). The Sierra's best hotel, with a bar, garden and **restaurant**.

★**Comercio**, Puerta de Ávila 5, **t** 923 40 02 19 (*inexpensive*). A cheaper, welcoming choice.

La Alberca

★★★**Las Batuecas**, Av. de las Batuecas 6, **t** 923 41 51 88, **f** 923 41 50 55 (*moderate*). A fine place amid chestnuts and cherry trees with a good **restaurant**, on the edge of the old town.

★★**Paris**, C/San Antonio 2, **t** 923 41 51 31 (*inexpensive*). A comfortable place on the main road with 22 rooms.

Hs La Balsá, C/La Balsada 4, **t** 923 41 53 37 (*cheap*). Rooms with bath, TV and telephone in an old house just off Pza Mayor.

You'll pass no shortage of half-timbered restaurants as you wind your way through the village to the plaza.

Candelario

★★**Hs Cristi**, Pza Béjar 1, **t** 923 41 32 12, **f** 923 41 31 19 (*inexpensive–cheap*). A good-value bet; rooms with shared bath considerably cheaper.

★**Hs El Pasaje**, Las Eras s/n, **t** 923 41 32 10 (*inexpensive*). Similarly priced, with 12 comfortable rooms. *Open all year*.

Miranda del Castañar and San Martín del Castañar

★**Hs Condado de Miranda**, Paraje la Perdiza, Miranda del Castañar, **t** 923 43 20 26 (*inexpensive*). All rooms have bath, and there's an affordable *menú*.

There are also a handful of ***casas rurales*** in Miranda del Castañar; **t** 923 26 85 71 for more information.

La Posada de San Martín, C/Larga 1, San Martín del Castañar, **t** 923 43 70 36 (*moderate*). A new restaurant with rooms in the centre, with good meat dishes and desserts. *Open Holy Week–Oct*.

siege, earning himself the Spanish title of Duque de Ciudad Rodrigo from the grateful King Ferdinand VII. Since then much of the damage inflicted by British guns has been restored, although the breach in the walls near the Cathedral has been preserved as a reminder. This side of the elegant Gothic **Cathedral** (*open daily 10–1 and 4–7; often longer in summer*), built soon after the conquest by Count Rodrigo, took a licking. Its other portals are still in good nick; note especially the 12 figures from the Old Testament over the south door, and the beautiful Portico del Perdón on the main façade. Inside, under the complex vaults of the nave, the **choir stalls** are the work of the fertile imagination and delicate chisel of Rodrigo Alemán (who is also credited with the naughty choir in Zamora, *see* p.444), and there are more imaginative carvings from the 14th and 16th centuries in the **cloister** (*closes half an hour before the cathedral*), added in 1325. Ciudad Rodrigo has a charming, 17th-century **Plaza Mayor** with an unusual **Ayuntamiento** (***galería*** *open Mon–Fri 9–2*) that seems more Latin American than Spanish, perhaps not too surprisingly as many of the city's Renaissance palaces were built by men who had made their fortunes with the *conquistadores*. One of the highlights of the city is the walk around the **medieval walls** (nearly 2½km) and the wonderful views from the **castle of Enrique II** (now the *parador*). When it becomes unbearably hot, locals migrate down to the river below: the perfect spot for a cool swim. Next door to the castle, great works are underway to renovate the Palacio de los Águilas, whidh is due to open in 2002 as a national sculpture museum.

South of Salamanca

Between Salamanca and Ávila, set in a pretty *vega*, pottery-making **Alba de Tormes** has a history bound up with the proud Dukes of Alba and Santa Teresa, who in 1571 founded the **Convento de las Carmelitas** with the Duke's support. She returned to the convent to die, and her remains (or at least her heart and arm) are venerated in the church; a beautiful relief over its door depicts the Annunciation, with the Angel Gabriel carrying a caduceus like the god Mercury. Of the Dukes' castle, only the **Homage Tower** remains. When the Grand Duke was in residence, Lope de Vega's plays were often premiered here before being performed in Madrid; some of its 16th-century frescoes have been restored.

In the rugged **Sierra de Béjar** and the **Sierra de la Peña de Francia** in the southern extreme of the province, tiny villages were secluded for centuries. They are wonderfully atmospheric places, their narrow medieval streets lined with leaning, half-timbered houses, refreshingly cool in the summer when par-boiled Spaniards ascend, seeking relief from the plains of Extremadura and Castile. Most beautiful and most visited is **La Alberca**, a gem of a village (and now a national monument) in a magnificent setting. With its profusion of geraniums and petunias, it's almost alpine, and although the Plaza Mayor has been prettified, it remains very quaint. The parish church has a unique pulpit of coloured granite, and if you're lucky you'll run into one of the village's celebrations, when the women don the most ornate costumes in Spain. When they're not dressing up, they're stitching gorgeous, primitively exuberant embroideries. Some two kilometres south of La Alberca, the road rises to **El Portillo** pass, marking the beginning of the magnificent **Valle de Las Batuecas**, a Natural Park with needle-like peaks and its own lush microclimate; it's a fine spot for a picnic. The road winds dramatically down to the bottom of the valley with breathtaking vistas en route, where the river banks around the **Monasterio de los Carmelitos** (early 1600s) bear prehistoric rock paintings amid the outlandish formations. Turn off at the sign for the monastery and follow the signposted walk to the paintings; although they're barely visible, the walk is beautiful, following the river, with natural pools, figs and blackberries in season. North of La Alberca, an equally winding road ascends the conical **Peña de Francia** (6,174ft), a favourite goal of walkers, where a Gothic church houses an image of a Virgin discovered by a French pilgrim; the views are again stupendous and in the summer there's a restaurant/bar. Other beautiful old villages of the Sierra are **El Cabaco**, 10 kilometres from La Alberca, **Mirador de Extremadura** and **Candelario**, four kilometres from the major town of **Béjar**, which itself boasts some fine streets and the Palacio de los Duques, with a lovely Renaissance patio. If the above seem too cosmopolitan, try **Miranda del Castañar**, 37 kilometres from Béjar, or the even smaller **San Martín del Castañar**; alternatively, you can always head south into **Las Hurdes** (*see* **Castilla La Nueva**, pp.574–6).

Valladolid

Valladolid, sovereign of infirmity
The priest's early death, the maggot's Compostela.

Such was the opinion of Guillem de la Gonagal, the 16th-century 'François Villon of Extremadura', said to have died in a brothel here in 1546. The judgement seems harsh for a city that has experienced so much of Spain's history and culture. Philip II was born in Valladolid, and Columbus died here in 1506, impoverished and almost forgotten. Valladolid was twice capital of Spain, and Cervantes wrote the first part of *Don Quixote* in a little house on C/del Rastro. More recently it was nicknamed Fachadolid, for being the heart of Spanish facism. Valladolid has attractions that almost make it worth a short stay, but to see them you'll have to pay a price. For all its history, Valladolid is a stupefyingly ugly city, and probably always has been. Lately it has enjoyed considerable industrial growth, becoming the largest city of Old Castile. Many writers have blamed it for destroying much of its older quarters in the process, but this is one city where you may want to cheer on the wrecking crews. The new developments are neither better nor worse than elsewhere in Spain, but the old, an amorphous blot of shabby alleys and ghastly misbegotten churches, will not be the memory of Spain you would wish to take home with you. Nobody in Valladolid seems unhappy to see it go. But if you want to see San Pablo church and the Colegio San Gregorio, two of the most unusual architectural fantasies in all Spain, steel yourself and plunge in. Valladolid hosts a film festival every November, the country's second biggest after San Sebastián.

Getting Around

By Train

Lots of trains serve Valladolid, with regular daily connections to all the cities of Old Castile and León (except Soria and Segovia) as well as Galicia and the northern coast. Trains go about every half-hour to Madrid, some via Ávila. In this region, there may be quicker connections than you see up on the boards at the station. It is worth asking at the information desk or the ticket counter; all trains pass through the big junction at Medina del Campo, and by changing there you may reach your destination faster. In Valladolid the station is on the southern edge of town, on Pso de Campo Grande (**t** 983 20 02 02).

By Bus

The bus station is a 10-minute walk west of the train station, at Puente Colgante 2, under a highway overpass, **t** 983 23 63 08, with connections to the same places, as well as Soria, Barcelona and provincial towns such as Toro, Tordesillas and Arevalo.

Tourist Information

Valladolid: On the other side of the Campo Grande from the train station, at C/Santiago 19, **t** 983 35 18 01 (*open daily 9–2 and 5–7*).

Festivals

Film Festival, *Nov*. The great cinema fest, second only to San Sebastián.

Where to Stay

Valladolid ✉ 47000

*****Olid Meliá**, Pza de San Miguel 10, two blocks from San Pablo, **t** 983 35 72 00, **f** 983 33 68 28 (*expensive*). If you must stay in

The City

Most people's introduction to Valladolid will seem innocuous enough; both the bus and train stations are near the **Campo Grande**, a large park on the eastern edge of town. From here, follow the pedestrian C/de Santiago to the city centre and the huge **Pza Mayor** lined with Savoy-red buildings and café terraces, with most of the restaurants and cheap hotels on or around it. In the 16th century the plaza earned renown for spectacular *autos-da-fé*, a practice inaugurated by Philip II in 1559 after a secret community of religious freethinkers was discovered in the town. Heading west down San Francisco Ferrari, you'll come to the **Cathedral** (*open Tues–Sat 10–1.30 and 4.30–7, Sun 10–2; closed Mon; adm for its museum*). It was begun in 1580 as one of the first works of Juan de Herrera, and in the 1720s Alberto Churriguera was given a chance to try and complete it. This combination of Spain's apostle of austerity and its most exuberant Baroque master explains the mess you see; plenty of hacks have monkeyed with it since, but quite understandably the city has given up; the cathedral will never be finished and fair-sized shrubs are already growing out of the cornices. Just behind it is a small 14th-century Gothic jewel, **Santa María la Antigua**.

San Pablo and San Gregorio

It is hard to explain the presence of these two buildings in Valladolid (they are next to each other on Pza de San Pablo, just down C/de las Angustias from the cathedral) – their façades are as eccentric as Toledo Cathedral's Transparente, and completely unlike anything else in Spain. Both façades are huge curtains of sculpture, woven with fantastical forms and ornate decoration, completely disregarding the norms of

Valladolid, perhaps indulge in the best hotel, which was recently renovated.

****Imperial**, Peso 4, **t** 983 33 03 00, **f** 983 33 08 13 (*moderate*). For full-on marble and chandeliers, this is the place.

****El Nogal**, Conde Ansúrez 10, **t** 983 34 02 33, **f** 983 35 49 65 (*moderate*). A smart, small hotel with hydromassaging showers and a reasonably priced **restaurant**.

***Enara**, Pza de España 5, **t** 983 30 02 11, **f** 983 30 03 11 (*inexpensive*). Well-worn rooms in an old house on a rather noisy square.

P. Dani and **Dos Rosas**, C/Perú 11, **t** 983 30 02 49 and **t** 983 20 74 39 respectively (*cheap*). Here clean rooms with shared bath are managed by sisters on different floors of an old, central house.

Eating Out

Mesón Panero, Marina Escobar 1, **t** 983 30 70 19 (*moderate*). Near Cervantes' house, this excellent, subterranean restaurant prides itself on game dishes in season, Valladolid codfish stew and tasty *patatas a la importancia* (potatoes fried in batter with garlic). *Closed Sun.*

El Figón de Recoletos, Acera de Recoletos 3, **t** 983 39 60 43 (*moderate*). Typically Castilian, serving the city's finest roast lamb (*lechazo asado*) from the woodburning oven. *Closed Sun and mid-July–mid-Aug.*

El Caballo de Troya, C/Correos 1, **t** 983 33 93 55, **f** 983 33 81 57 (*inexpensive*). Attractively set in a patio-endowed 16th-century inn near Pza Mayor, this complex comprises **Santi** restaurant (with a *moderate–inexpensive menú* and tasty stews) and the cheaper but cosy **Mesón Taberna**, with a palatial hearth.

The **Plaza Mayor** is a good bet for breakfast (with some cafés open from 6.30):

Café Continental. Serves good value continental breakfasts with outsized croissants.

Lion d'Or. Adds a touch of elegance.

religious architecture. **San Pablo**, where Philip II was baptized, had its façade added in 1601. The big coat-of-arms also displayed on it is that of the Duke of Lerma, who picked up the bill. Its great lions and dozens of saints and angels seem like figures of some mechanical clock, ready to come alive at the stroke of the hour. The Castilian Cortes often met here, and the interior is full of tombs of Spanish notables, but there hasn't been much to see inside since the thorough looting undertaken by the French in 1809. Napoleon could have overseen the job himself; he made the **Capitanía General** across the square his headquarters on his visit to Spain.

San Pablo's anonymous sculptors were undoubtedly inspired by the earlier (1496) Isabelline Gothic **Colegio de San Gregorio**, very similar in conception. Its architect, Mattias Carpontera, is said to have committed suicide just before the façade was completed. At its centre a pomegranate tree, commemorating the conquest of Granada, springs from a fountain of cherubs. Ragged men with clubs called *maceros* guard the doors, a curious fashion copied in other churches, such as Ávila cathedral.

Museo Nacional de Escultura

Inside, the Colegio San Gregorio has been restored to house this large collection (*open Tues–Sat 10–2 and 4–6, Sun 10–2; closed Mon; adm*). The name is a little misleading; it's all religious sculptures, taken from churches in Valladolid and elsewhere in Castile. Very little is of any merit – Alonso Berruguete's statues from an enormous *retablo* in the first three rooms, the anonymous 1463 **Retablo de San Jerónimo** and some 15th-century choir stalls up on the second floor by Diego de Siloé. The rest, room after room of gaping Virgins and blood-splattered Christs, will either make you queasy or make you laugh. A French immigrant, Juan de Juni (*c*. 1540) is the master of this, and his *El Entierro de Cristo* is rivalled only by Gregorio Fernández's *Cristo Yacente* in the expression of anguish and depiction of wounds. The school's restored chapel has a lovely statue of *Death* himself; in the cloister, restorers of the 1880s tried to clear the air with some silly, fanciful **gargoyles**, which are more fun than anything in the museum.

Other Museums

Both Cervantes' and Columbus' houses have been turned into museums: the **Casa de Cervantes** (*C/del Rastro; open Tues–Sat 9.30–3.30, Sun 10–3; closed Mon; adm*) and **Casa de Colón** (*C/Colón, open Tues–Sat 10–2 and 4–6, Sun 10–2; closed Mon; adm*). Better than these, the old **Philippines Convent** behind the Campo Grande has a **Museo Oriental** (*open Mon–Sat 4–7, Sun 10–2; adm*), displaying works acquired over centuries of missionary work in the Far East. Nine rooms are filled with paintings and porcelain from China, and three more with folk art of the Philippines and elsewhere.

Around Valladolid

In the heartland of Castile you would expect castles, and these are, sure enough, the major attraction of the flat, monotonous country around Valladolid. Few ever served any military purpose, other than intimidating the populace and defending the

Where to Stay and Eat

★★★**Parador Nacional**, on highway 620, Tordesillas, **t** 983 77 00 51, **f** 983 77 10 13 (*expensive*). In a modern building in the pines, with a good **restaurant** (*moderate*).

★★★**El Montico**, on the same highway, towards Salamanca, **t** 983 79 50 00, **f** 983 79 50 08 (*expensive*). In a restored farmhouse, with a pool, tennis courts, and a charming but pricey **restaurant**.

★**Los Toreros**, Av. Valladolid 26, **t** 983 77 19 00, **f** 983 77 19 54 (*inexpensive*). A comfortable place near the old town, with a **restaurant**.

El Torreón, Dimas Rodríguez 11, **t** 983 77 01 23 (*moderate*). The best place to dine in Tordesillas; it does all the Castile basics under a repro 15th-century ceiling from Santa Clara.

Good value **eateries** and **tapas bars** border Pza Mayor:

Café Bar El Escudo, Pza Mayor 9. Full of local produce, with a good selection of tapas, *raciones* and grilled food until 10pm.

There are a few hotels and *pensiónes* each in Medina del Campo, Toro and Simancas. **Medina del Campo** also has a pair of good **restaurants**:

Monaco, Pza España 26, **t** 983 80 10 20 (*inexpensive*). Superbly set on the piazza, serving simple dishes and an excellent, cheap *menú*.

Continental, Pza Hispanidad 15, **t** 983 80 10 14 (*inexpensive*). This has been in business for over 50 years, thanks to good home cooking.

nobility during the civil wars. That they survived while so much else has been lost is a key to Castile's history. In the 15th century this was indeed the heartland, a region of new towns whose prosperity was based on the *Mesta*, that peculiar half-corporation, half-co-operative that kept all Europe supplied with prized merino wool. The Habsburgs destroyed the region's economy for ever, and towns like Toro and Tordesillas, that had figured so prominently in the chronicles of Ferdinand and Isabel, never fulfilled their early promise.

Medina del Campo stands as a symbol of so much that went wrong. Once one of the greatest trade fair towns of the continent, merchants from as far as Germany and England made the annual trip here over the Pyrenees to expedite the trade in wool, Vizcaya iron and Toledo silk. Medina's fairs inaugurated the use of letters of exchange among merchants – the beginning of modern banking – and the city's financiers arranged the exchequers of all Castile's kings up to Charles V. The Habsburg bankruptcies put an end to all this, and Medina dwindled to an insignificant village in just over a century. Spain's biggest sheep market is still held here, but there's little to see of the old Medina; Charles V's army razed it to the ground. **La Mota Castle** (*open Mon–Sat 11–2 and 4–6, Sun 11–2*) survives, east of town; Queen Isabel often stayed here, and in the town itself is a small palace where she died in 1504.

Madrigal and Toro

Some 30km south, **Madrigal de las Altas Torres** makes a fine sight, its crumbling 14th-century walls rising above the plain. There's little left inside them, but you can visit Isabel's birthplace here at the Convento de las Angustias (she wasn't born in a nunnery; the building incorporates an old palace belonging to Isabel's family). **Toro**, north of Medina on the Zamora–Valladolid road, has a site almost as picturesque, on red cliffs above the Duero; it has grown old more gracefully than Madrigal. Toro's landmark is a remarkable 12th-century Romanesque Colegiata, with a broad 16-sided Byzantine *cimborio* over the crossing, similar only to those in Zamora and Salamanca.

The Colegiata's west front, the Pórtico de la Gloria, is one of the best works of Spanish Romanesque sculpture. The Battle of Toro, fought during the civil war that followed the death of Enrique IV, inaugurated Spain's Golden Age by making Ferdinand and Isabel undisputed masters of the country. Ferdinand's army did not really defeat the partisans of Juana la Beltraneja; the battle was a draw, but Juana's Portuguese supporters gave up and went home, ensuring Isabel's hold on the throne of Castile.

Tordesillas

Like Toro, Tordesillas was once a thriving town, its name synonymous with the Pope Alexander Borgia's 1494 Treaty of Tordesillas that divided the discoveries in the New World between Spain and Portugal. Its better days are recalled in its lovely arcaded **Plaza Mayor** (unfortunately used as a car park); in **San Antolín**, with a Plateresque tomb and a magnificent *retablo* by Juan de Juni, and a fine little museum of sculpture (*open Mar–Nov Tues–Sun 10.30–1.30 and 4.30–6.30; closed Mon; otherwise* ***t*** *983 77 09 80; adm*); most of all in the **Convent of Santa Clara** (*open 1 April–30 Sept Tues–Sat 10–1 and 3.30–6.30; 1 Oct–31 Mar Tues–Sat 10.30–1.30 and 3.30–5.30, Sun (all year) 10.30–1.30 and 3.30–5.30; closed Mon; adm, adm free on Wed*), the last abode of Isabel's daughter,

The Comunero Revolt

At the end of the Middle Ages, Europe was opening up and looking for new horizons, and no economy was better prepared to discover a New World than Castile's. A new urban society had appeared, based around the great trade fairs of Medina del Campo, Badajoz, Sevilla and Cádiz, and on some of Europe's biggest, most advanced manufactures: cloth, metalwork and leather, not to mention Castile soap. Art and culture were thriving, and in this period Spain was on the verge of attaining a prominence in Europe that it had never before known.

The conquest of Granada in 1492 brought a real change in Spanish society. Suddenly there was plenty of other people's land to be grabbed, and the grandees of the north used gangster methods against the Muslims and each other to get it. They soon found that such methods worked equally well against the mercantile towns back home and launched into an orgy of assaults against city rights and riches. Nobles used legal trickery to snatch vast areas of land from the towns, then proclaimed new tolls everywhere, nothing more than protection rackets in the countryside they controlled. To gain a slice from the profits of trade, they resorted to daylight robbery and kidnapping of merchants and town officials, with a veneer of legality provided by the nobles' ancient rights to hold courts of law.

Ferdinand and Isabel did little to stop any of this, and the situation worsened under the ineffectual regencies that followed Ferdinand's death in 1516. Spain had lost control of its destiny; its strings were pulled from Flanders by the ministers of the heir, Charles V. Charles himself, only 16, cared for nothing but hunting, but the men who manipulated him saw Spain as a cash cow, and they milked it as much as possible to finance Habsburg ambitions of universal monarchy. Now the towns had two gangs after what was left of their wealth. The situation was becoming serious;

Queen Juana the Mad. Her son, Charles V, kept her locked up here for 46 years under guard: intent on keeping Castile for himself, he allowed Juana no visitors to confirm or deny the rumours that she was sane. Parts of Santa Clara were begun as a palace by Alfonso XI in 1340; his son, Pedro the Cruel, converted it into a convent. The **Patio de San Pedro** and the **Capilla Mayor** offer some of the most lavish *mudéjar* work in Castile, with colourful *azulejos*, lattice-work façades and a remarkable *artesonado* ceiling. North of Tordesillas and Mota del Marquéz, **San Cebrián de Mazote** has an early 10th-century Mozarabic church, with three aisles divided by horseshoe arches with superb carved capitals and a painted ceiling. Nearby **Torrelobatón** has a fine medieval castle, and near Zaratán (20km west of Valladolid) the church of **Santa María de Wamba** preserves its original Mozarabic arches.

As for castles, there are fine ones at **Fuensaldaña**, **Simancas** (this one has housed the state archives of Spain since the time of Charles V) and **Cuéllar**, a village famous for its annual *encierro*, or 'bull-running'. **Coca Castle** may be the strangest in Spain, a 14th-century stronghold of notorious local tyrants, the Fonseca family. A veritable flight of *mudéjar* fancy, with unique fluted turrets, it looks as if it were built more for decoration than defence.

the depredations of the Habsburgs caused a national financial collapse in 1519. In Castile, the area that suffered the most, rebellion was in the air.

What came to be called the Comunero Revolt (for the *comunes*, or free towns) started on 30 May 1520, with a revolt of the wool workers in Segovia. They lynched Rodrigo de Tordesillas, delegate to the Cortes, and chased all royal officials out of town. The Spanish army being busy annoying the French, the way was clear for the revolt to spread; by July Salamanca, Toro and Toledo had joined, and a *junta* was formed in Ávila. On 20 August, the government tried to seize a store of rebel weapons at Medina del Campo but the local minutemen beat them back, a victory that inspired most of the other Castilian towns to join. Tordesillas was taken, and became the rebel capital.

The *junta* had great hopes for mad Juana, the rightful queen and mother of Charles. Though sympathetic to the rebels, she refused to sign a declaration deposing Charles. This was the turning point. Now the private armies of the nobles felt free to go on the warpath once more against the towns. They recaptured Tordesillas for Charles in December, and the end came when the returned royal army met the rebel army at Villalar on 23 April 1521. Though numerically superior, the rebels lost for lack of cavalry; their leader, Juan de Padilla, was captured and killed in the aftermath. The king, whose position was still uncertain, turned his most conciliatory face to the rebels. The survivors were pardoned in 1522, and Charles even decreed a number of the reforms the Comuneros had demanded. But with the end of the revolt, the rape of Castile's towns and business became a *fait accompli*. Had the Comuneros won, Spain might well have developed the same kind of progressive economy and society as England and France, and avoided the terrible decline of the coming centuries; its history, and the world's, would have been very different.

From Valladolid to Soria

Coca Castle has a worthy competitor at **Peñafiel** (*open summer Tues–Sun 11.30–2.30 and 4.30–8.30; winter Tues–Sun 12–2 and 4.30–7.30; closed Mon; adm*), on a narrow ridge overlooking the Duero. This ship-shape (literally) white castle, built in 1466 to follow the crest of its difficult site, is 700ft long and only 79ft wide, giving it the appearance of a stage set. Wander through the old village streets by the Plaza del Coso, which gets to play bullring at fiesta time.

The road to Soria generally follows the Duero, and the countryside becomes considerably greener and prettier in the neighbourhood of **El Burgo de Osma**. This town, important until the 1700s, has shrunk into one of the truly beautiful villages of Castile, with bits of its old walls crumbling beneath the trees, and fields and gardens encroaching on its very centre. It also has an exceptional little **Cathedral** (*open summer Tues–Sun 10–1.30 and 4–7; winter Tues–Sun 10.30–1 and 4.30–6.30; closed Mon*) with a beautiful 13th-century Gothic façade; the tower, Burgo de Osma's landmark, is a Baroque addition, and there are some arches of the original Romanesque church and a harrowing *Cruxifixion* within, among a hotchpotch of different styles. Its founder, San Pedro de Osma, is entombed inside in a 13th-century sarcophagus covered with lively and colourful medieval scenes. The **museum** contains a major collection of illuminated manuscripts, especially the *Beato*, a 1065 codex of commentaries on the Apocalypse. Burgo de Osma is not the original town here; its predecessor, Osma (or *Uxama*) was a Roman city, but has now declined to a tiny

Festivals

Peñafiel: Fiesta, *15 Aug*. The Plaza is transformed into a bullring for the occasion.

Where to Stay and Eat

El Burgo de Osma ✉ 42300

★★★**Il Virrey**, C/Mayor 4, **t** 975 34 13 11, **f** 975 34 08 55 (*moderate*). Offers the luxury of a four-star hotel and a pork-orientated **restaurant**.

★**Virrey Palafox**, Universidad 7, **t** 975 34 02 22, **f** 975 34 08 55 (*inexpensive*). Family-run with a **restaurant** (*inexpensive*), renowned for Castile's classics.

★★**P. Casa Agapito**, C/Universidad 1, **t** 975 34 02 12 (*cheap*). A real bargain.

Berlanga de Duero ✉ 42360

Posada de los Leones, C/Los Leones, **t** 975 34 31 55, *www.berlangadeduero.es* (*inexpensive*). Right in the old centre, this *marqués*' town house was abandoned after the Civil War and recently converted; with 12 rooms, a pretty patio and an (*inexpensive*) *menú*.

Medinaceli and Santa María de Huerta ✉ 42240

★★**HsR La Cerámica**, C/Santa Isabel 2, Medinaceli, **t/f** 975 32 63 81, *www.3dgraf.com/laCeramica* (*cheap*). A beautifully restored *casa rural* in the old centre, with a yellow and terracotta **restaurant** and good half-board deals.

Hs El Mirador, Campo San Nicolás, Medinaceli, **t/f** 975 32 64 54 (*cheap*). A friendly place on the edge of the old village, with soaring views over the surrounding countryside. Decent **restaurant** (*inexpensive menú*).

P. Santa María, Marqués de Cerralbo, Santa María, **t** 975 32 72 18 (*cheap*). Has eight modest rooms. You can also stay in the **monastery** itself: for details, **t** 975 32 70 02.

Restaurante Arco Romano, C/Barranco 2, Medinaceli, **t** 975 32 61 30 (*inexpensive*). Small, family-run and traditional restaurant in the shadow of the arch.

hamlet just a short distance away. Both are overlooked by a ruined **castle** on Roman foundations. Just over 14 kilometres north of town, wild and rugged scenery skirts the **Canyon of the Río Lobos**; here, just outside Varo, the church of **San Juan de Otero** (now called San Bartolemé) was built in the 12th century by the Templars. In this isolated spot the Templars could afford to express some of their heretical doctrines in the design. One of the windows is in the form of an inverted pentangle, and there are other unusual geometric forms and patterns inside.

From Burgo de Osma, it's a short jump to Soria (on the way, stop at **Calatañazor**, a perfect medieval Castilian time capsule). But, better still, consider a detour through the fascinating and little visited country to the southeast, in the valley of the Duero.

The Upper Duero

The landscape, if you're not alert to it, may pass you by, but you'll find it sticks in your memory after you go. Most of Soria province is like this: unusual, intense shades of green and gold, wrinkled hills ploughed into subtle patterns of furrows, bare mountains topped with crumbling castles. The towns and villages, little changed since the Middle Ages, come in the same gold and brown as the hills. Most are genteel and decaying, ready, it seems, to seep back at any moment into the land that gave them birth.

Heading south from Burgo de Osma, you meet the Duero under the walls of **Gormaz Castle**, a huge, half-ruined, barbaric-looking pile built by the Moors in the 10th century. The walls are half a mile around, and worth the climb for the fine Moorish gateway and the view. From Gormaz, a long detour to the south will take you to **Termancia** (*same hours as Numancia,* see *p.464**; adm*) in a small patch of mountains called the Sierra de Pela, near the village of Tiermes. This was an important Celtiberian town, and though unexcavated it's an exceedingly strange site, with tunnels and stairs and caves dug out of the bare rock. Scanty ruins of the Roman Termancia that succeeded it can be seen below.

The next town up the river from Gormaz, **Berlanga de Duero**, has a squat, round-towered castle, arcaded streets and medieval gates, and the fine, plain, early Gothic **Colegiata**. Friar Romas de Berlanga, the town's favourite son, is buried here. He was a 16th-century Bishop of Panama, who changed the course of history by introducing bananas into the New World from Africa. Best of all, eight kilometres south in **Casillas de Berlanga**, you can visit a Mozarabic jewel, the 10th-century **Ermita de San Baudelio de Berlanga** (*open April, May, Sept and Oct Wed–Sat 10–2 and 4–7, Sun 10–2; June–Aug Wed–Sat 10–2 and 5–9, Sun 10–2; July and Aug Mon–Sat 10–2 and 5–9, Sun 10–2; Nov–Mar Wed–Sat 10–2 and 3.30–6, Sun 10–2; closed Mon and Tues exc. in July and Aug; adm*), a grey stone cube in an austere landscape, built as an outpost on the frontiers of New Castile. Since antiquity, the cube has represented the element earth; inside, the central palm pillar, radiating horseshoe arches, supports the celestial sphere. A mini-mosque of horseshoe arches, symbolizing the dark forest of the soul, leads to Baudelio's holy cave; the chapel on top, being suspended between heaven and earth, was the ideal place for a holy man to live and pray. Most extraordinary of all, hidden away just under the roof and above the top of the central palm pillar, is an enchanting kiosk, just big enough for one person, symbolic of paradise and accessible only by ladder – Jacob's ladder. Frescoes of animals and hunting scenes decorate the walls, but the best ones have been spirited away to the Prado in Madrid.

Almazán, a growing town of some 6,000 people, second-largest in the province, has managed to keep nearly all its medieval walls and gates, as well as the 12th-century church of **San Miguel**, with a Moorish dome of interlaced arches. The nearby village of **Morón de Almazán** has a lovely plaza surrounded by a Renaissance church and palaces. South from Almazán, you meet the main Madrid–Barcelona road and rail line at **Medinaceli**; three kilometres from the new town, its beautiful core survives defiantly on a hill and is very much in the process of being spruced up and sold off, with escutcheoned palaces and a Roman **triumphal arch**, the only triple one in Spain. Some 30 kilometres east, **Santa María de Huerta**'s Cistercian monastery was founded in 1162 by Alfonso VII, shut down in 1853 and repopulated by the order in 1927. It is like a small museum of Gothic architecture and sculpture, with a fine chapel and beautifully vaulted century refectory (*open Tues–Sun 9–1 and 3–7; closed Mon; adm*).

Soria

It may be one of Spain's smallest provincial capitals, but Soria will seem like a metropolis after the bitsy villages of the rest of the province. It is a town of distinction, full of early medieval monuments and beautifully set among forested hills overlooking the Duero.

Around the Centre of Soria

Soria's centre, connecting the old town with the new, is the **Plaza Ramón y Cajal**. The plaza faces a big park lined with white benches, the **Alameda de Cervantes**, with perhaps Spain's only public tree-house, and the **Museo Numantino** (*open 1 June–30 Sept Tues–Sat (Mon–Sat in July and Aug) 9–2 and 5–9, Sun 9–2; 1 Oct–31 May Tues–Sat 9–8.30, Sun 9–2; Sept–June closed Mon; adm*) with finds from the ancient city of Numancia (*see* below). Soria's two finest medieval churches stand at the northern and southern edges of the old town: **San Juan de Rabarera** (*opens half an hour before each service*) on C/Caballeros (*c.* 1200), with an unusual apse, in transition from Romanesque to Gothic, and **Santo Domingo** (*temporarily closed for works*) on C/La Aduana Vieja (*c.* 1160), with a spectacular carved tympanum over the west portal, displaying hundreds of figures of saints and angels. The main shopping stretch and Pza Mayor are pleasantly pedestrianized making a stroll through the town a rare car-free treat; behind Pza Mayor, C/Real traverses the old town on its way to the Duero, passing two 13th-century churches: the ruined **San Nicolás** and **San Pedro** (*open 1 July–31 Aug Mon 11–1 and 5–7, Tues–Sat 10–1.30 and 4.30–8, Sun 9–1 and 4.30–7; 1 Sept–30 June Tues–Sat 10–1 and 4.30–5.30, Sun 9–1 and 4.30–7, closed Mon; adm*), the latter with a beautiful Romanesque cloister.

Getting Around

By Train

Soria's only train service runs twice a day to Madrid; it's easy to reach Zaragoza or Bilbao, though, with a change at Castejon del Ebro. You'll have to take a cab to the station, outside Soria; there's no bus. RENFE information: **t** 975 21 10 95.

By Bus

The city has a new bus station, on the western edge of town, **t** 975 22 51 60, with a few daily runs to Logroño, Pamplona, Zaragoza, Barcelona, Burgos, Valladolid, Salamanca and Madrid. There are also services to Burgo de Osma, Almazán and, less regularly, to the smaller villages of the province. There are two daily direct buses from Burgo de Osma to Madrid.

Tourist Information

Soria: Pza Ramón y Cajal, **t** 975 21 20 52 (*open Mon–Fri 9–2 and 5–7, Sat and Sun 10–2 and 5–8*). Ask about **guided tours** of the town and surrounding area.

Where to Stay and Eat

★★★**Parador Antonio Machado**, Parque del Castillo, **t** 975 21 34 45, **f** 975 21 28 49 (*expensive*). Named after the *modernista* poet who lived in Soria, this heads the list of the city's hotels, a modern but comfortable place among the ruins of the old castle.

★★★**Husa Alfonso VIII**, Alfonso VIII 10, **t** 975 22 62 11, **f** 975 21 36 65 (*moderate*). Spacious modern rooms in a smart outfit, with bizarre artwork; centrally located.

★★**HsR Solar de Tejada**, C/Claustrilla 1, **t** 975 23 00 54, *solartejada@wanadoo.es* (*moderate*). By far the most creative place to rest your bones in the centre, this ex-lingerie shop has been originally converted, with swirling metal bedframes (spot Mount Ararat) and some beautiful blue mosaic bathrooms; with a range of rocking horses in the living room.

★★★**Leonor**, Pso del Mirón, **t** 975 22 02 50, **f** 975 22 99 53 (*moderate*). Named after Machado's wife, who died tragically after only two years of marriage; quiet, with fine views across the town to Antonio's *parador*.

★★**Viena**, C/García Solier 5, **t** 975 22 21 09 (*inexpensive*). Adequate but anonymous rooms near the Alameda; cheaper with shared bath.

Fonda Ferial, Pza del Salvador 6, **t** 975 22 12 44 (*cheap*). A slightly shabby but traditional *fonda*, right in the centre by Pza Ramón y Cajal.

Mesón Castellano, Pza Mayor 2, **t** 975 21 30 45 (*inexpensive*). A traditional, ham-lined place with a good name for its excellent local cuisine.

Capri, C/San Benito 8, **t** 975 22 12 84 (*inexpensive*). This place serves better-than-average cheap meals.

Valonsadero, Monte Valonsadero, **t** 975 18 00 06 (*moderate*). The *domingueros* (Sunday drivers) make for this delicious restaurant, surrounded by greenery outside town.

Soria is famous for its banks and bars; for tapas and *cañas* (beer) in the latter, head towards Pzas Mayor, San Clemente, or Ramón Benito Aceña.

Círculo de la Amistad de Soria, on pedestrianized C/El Collado. For a bit of pomp and a comfy sofa, try this place, where elderlies gather under candelabra.

San Juan de Duero

Soria's riverfront, strung between two hills (one has a monastery, the other a *parador* and a ruined castle), is an attraction in itself: a lovely, peaceful spot with groves of poplars, an island, and a weir on the lazy Duero. You can rent canoes from the bar next to the old stone bridge, or cross to the other side and see **San Juan de Duero** (*both* ***church*** *and* ***museum*** *open Nov–Mar Tues–Sat 10–2 and 3.30–6, Sun 10–2; April, May, Sept and Oct Tues–Sat 10–2 and 4–7, Sun 10–2; June–Aug Tues–Sat 10–2 and*

5–9, Sun 10–2; Sept–June closed Mon; adm), founded by the Knights of St John around 1200. The arcade of its ruined **cloister**, standing strangely alone in a field, is unlike any other in Spain: half of it Gothic, the remainder intertwined pointed arches that look from a distance like spiral loops. The church next to the cloister is still in good shape, with vivid scenes of the Massacre of the Innocents on its capitals. A small **museum** has been installed. Medieval Soria was an important Jewish city, and many of the artefacts – headstones and sarcophagi, mostly – are reminders. Take a walk down the avenue of poplars on the eastern bank of the river, and you'll pass two other old monuments: the 13th-century **San Polo** church, a Templar foundation built right over the road (*a private home and closed to the public*) and, further on, the octagonal **Hermitage of San Saturio** (*open summer daily 10–2 and 5–8; slightly more restricted hours otherwise*), romantically set into a cliff over the river. It isn't surprising that these sites should be out of the ordinary. As the Templars would have known, this corner of the Duero must have been a holy site since remotest antiquity. Forget the made-up story of a San Saturio, hermit and patron of Soria – and don't even bother guessing who San Polo might have been. It was common early Christian practice to appropriate ancient deities and turn them into saints, so, for Saturio and Polo, simply read Saturn and Apollo.

Numancia

Open Nov–Mar Tues–Sat 10–2 and 3.30–6, Sun and hols 10–2; April, May, Sept and Oct Tues–Sat 10–2 and 4–7, Sun 10–2; June–Aug Tues–Sat 10–2 and 5–9; Sun and hols open 10–2; closed Mon (exc. in July and Aug); adm.

In this ancient city, 19 years of the Iberian Arevaco tribe's struggle against the Romans culminated in one of the famous events of antiquity. A year-long Roman siege in 132 BC seemed on the verge of success when the people of Numancia chose not to accept the inevitable. Instead they set fire to their town with themselves in it, a grand gesture of heroic defiance that Spanish poets and politicians haven't yet tired of talking about. There's little to see on the site (*six kilometres north of Soria in the direction of Logroño; to go by bus ask at the Soria tourist office*); a few straight streets and foundations from the later, Roman town on a hillside overlooking the modern village of **Garray**, and traces of the four miles of walls. In northern Soria province, you can trace the source of the Duero into a landscape of grey mountains and pine forests. **Vinuesa**, off the Burgos road, is a beautiful, untouched village on route to the sequestered Laguna Negra ('black lagoon') and the Sierra de la Hormaza.

Madrid

14

To Parque del Oeste, MONCLOA & Museo de America
ARGÜELLES
MALASAÑA
C. DE ALBERTO AGUILERA
CALLE DE FUENCARRAL
P. DEL PINTOR ROSALES
CALLE DE LA PRINCESA
PLAZA DOS DE MAYO
C. DE LA PALMA
CALLE SAN BERNARDO
C. ESPIRITU SANTO
Casa de Campo
C. L. FERNANDA
V. RODRIGUEZ
CALLE DE AMANIEL
Templo de Debod
Museo Cerralbo
PLAZA DE ESPAÑA
C. DEL PEZ
MADERA
PLAZA DE S. ILDEFONSO
To Ermita de San Antonio de la Florida
C. DE LA LUNA
BARCO
Príncipe Pío Railway Station
San Antonio de los Alemanes
PASEO DE LA FLORIDA
Río Manzanares
CUESTA S. VICENTE
Convento de la Encarnación
PLAZA DE SANTO DOMINGO
GRAN VIA
Jardines Sabatini
C. BOLA
Real Monaterio de las Descalzas Realas
CALLE CARMEN
C. PRECIADOS
C. MONTERA
PLAZA DE ORIENTE
Palacio Real
Teatro Real
Campo del Moro
BAILEN
C. DEL ARENAL
PUERTA DEL SOL
CALLE MAYOR
PLAZA MAYOR
Casa de la Panaderia
Casa de la Villa
Torre de los Lujanes
C. DE LA PASA
Mercado de San Miguel
Palacio de Santa Cruz
C. DE LA CRUZ
Catedral de Nuestra Señora de la Almudena
CALLE
PASEO DE LA VIRGEN DEL PUERTO
PUENTE DE SEGOVIA
CALLE DE SEGOVIA
CALLE ATOCHA
CONCEP. JERONIMA
Colegiata de San Isidro
PLAZA DE LA PAJA
C. COLEGIATA
PLAZA TIRSO DE MOLINA
San Andrés
REDONDILLA
CAVA BAJA
CAVA ALTA
CABEZA
PLAZA DEL HUMILLADERO
DUQUE DE ALBA
CALVARIO
LAVAPIES
CALLE JUAN DUQUE
C. SAN FRANCISCO
CALLE TOLEDO
ENCOMIENDA
HUMILLADERO
RIBERA DE CURTIDORES
C. MESON DE PAREDES
GRAN VIA DE SAN FRANCISCO
Basílica de San Francisco El Grande
El Rastro
EMBAJADORES
PASEO DE LOS MELANCOLICOS
CALLE DE AMPARO
C. DE EMBAJADORES
C. CARNERO
RONDA SEGOVIA
CALLE DE MIRA EL SOL
PUERTA DE TOLEDO
N
RONDA DE TOLEDO
500 metres
500 yards

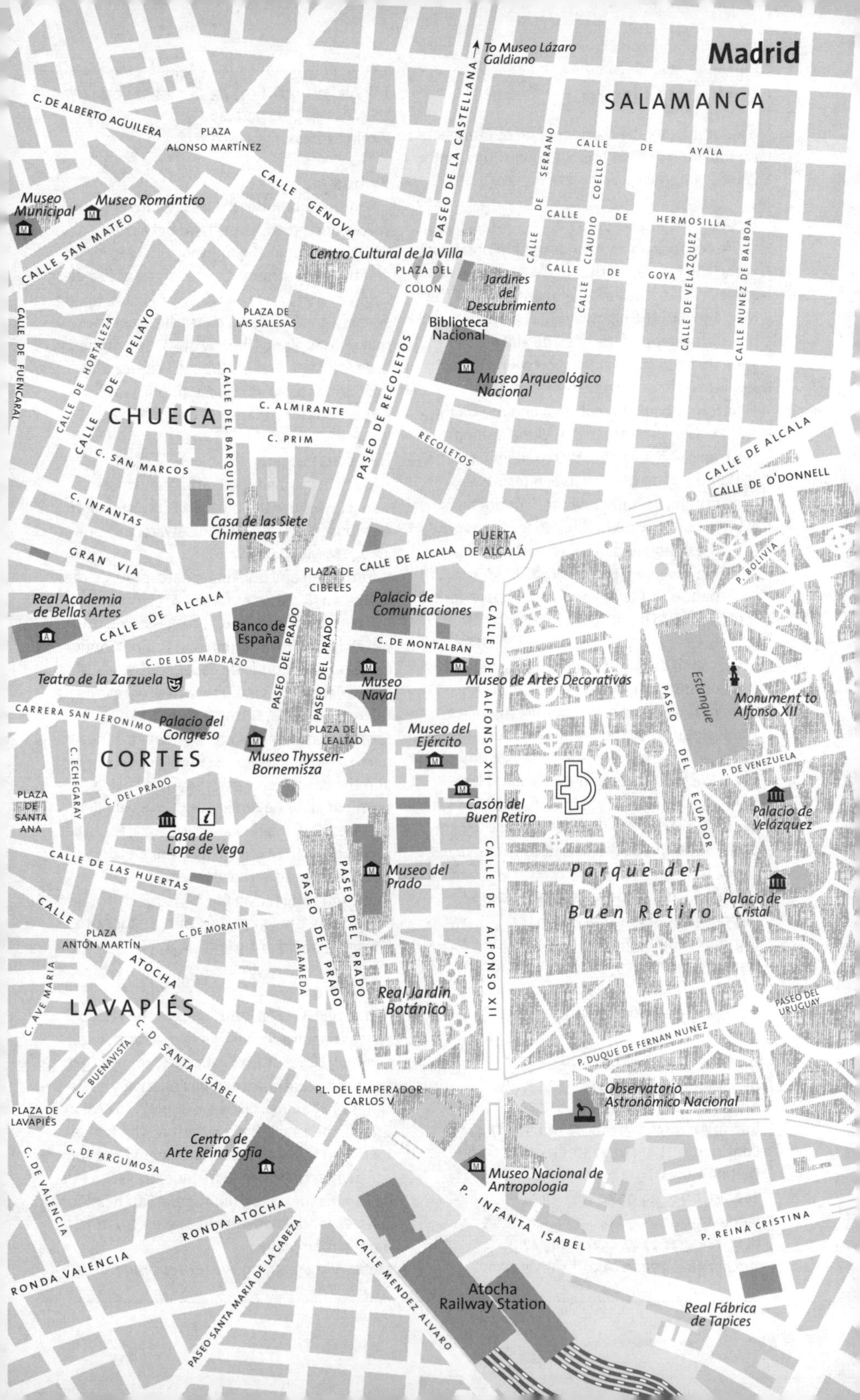

Madrid

To Museo Lázaro Galdiano

SALAMANCA

C. DE ALBERTO AGUILERA

PLAZA ALONSO MARTÍNEZ

CALLE GENOVA

PASEO DE LA CASTELLANA

CALLE DE SERRANO

CALLE DE AYALA

CALLE CLAUDIO COELLO

CALLE DE HERMOSILLA

CALLE DE GOYA

CALLE DE VELAZQUEZ

CALLE NUNEZ DE BALBOA

Museo Municipal

Museo Romántico

CALLE SAN MATEO

Centro Cultural de la Villa

PLAZA DEL COLON

Jardines del Descubrimiento

Biblioteca Nacional

Museo Arqueológico Nacional

CALLE DE FUENCARRAL

CALLE DE HORTALEZA

CALLE DE PELAYO

PLAZA DE LAS SALESAS

CALLE DEL BARQUILLO

PASEO DE RECOLETOS

CHUECA

C. ALMIRANTE

C. PRIM

RECOLETOS

C. SAN MARCOS

C. INFANTAS

Casa de las Siete Chimeneas

CALLE DE ALCALA

CALLE DE O'DONNELL

GRAN VIA

PLAZA DE CIBELES

CALLE DE ALCALA

PUERTA DE ALCALÁ

P. BOLIVIA

Real Academia de Bellas Artes

CALLE DE ALCALA

Banco de España

PASEO DEL PRADO

Palacio de Comunicaciones

CALLE DE ALFONSO XII

C. DE MONTALBAN

C. DE LOS MADRAZO

Teatro de la Zarzuela

Museo Naval

Museo de Artes Decorativas

Estanque

Monument to Alfonso XII

CARRERA SAN JERONIMO

Palacio del Congreso

PLAZA DE LA LEALTAD

Museo del Ejército

PASEO DEL ECUADOR

CORTES

Museo Thyssen-Bornemisza

P. DE VENEZUELA

C. ECHEGARAY

C. DEL PRADO

Casón del Buen Retiro

Palacio de Velázquez

PLAZA DE SANTA ANA

Casa de Lope de Vega

CALLE DE LAS HUERTAS

Museo del Prado

Parque del Buen Retiro

Palacio de Cristal

CALLE ATOCHA

PLAZA ANTÓN MARTÍN

C. DE MORATIN

ALAMEDA

Real Jardín Botánico

PASEO DEL URUGUAY

LAVAPIÉS

C. AVE MARIA

C. D SANTA ISABEL

P. DUQUE DE FERNAN NUNEZ

C. BUENAVISTA

PL. DEL EMPERADOR CARLOS V

Observatorio Astronómico Nacional

PLAZA DE LAVAPIÉS

Centro de Arte Reina Sofía

C. DE ARGUMOSA

C. DE VALENCIA

Museo Nacional de Antropologia

P. INFANTA ISABEL

RONDA ATOCHA

P. REINA CRISTINA

RONDA VALENCIA

PASEO SANTA MARIA DE LA CABEZA

CALLE MENDEZ ALVARO

Atocha Railway Station

Real Fábrica de Tapices

Getting There

Madrid is smaller than most great European capitals, and getting into and out of the centre is surprisingly easy and convenient.

By Air

The **Aeropuerto de Barajas** is 15km northeast of the city centre, off the N11/A2 highway to Barcelona (Ctra de Barcelona) and also off the M40 and A10, the highways that come in from the northern tip of the city. The airport has gone through some expansion over the past few years. There are now three terminals – **T1** (international), **T2** (national and regional) and **T3** (Iberia shuttle to Barcelona and Air Nostrum) – so if you have to connect expect a slight hike (5–10 mins between terminals).

In T1 there are both BBVA and American Express **currency exchange offices** (rates are usually exactly the same), as well as a **cash machine** covering Servired, Visa, Plus, Cirrus, Eurocheque and Telebanco banking networks. Terminal 1 also has a **post office** (*open Mon–Fri 8.30am–8.30pm, Sat 8am–1pm*); a **RENFE office** (*open daily 8am–9pm*); a **pharmacy**; a free **accommodation service** (*open daily 8am–midnight*); all major **car hire agencies**; and various green **tourist information** stands (*each terminal has one stand open 24 hours*). There are two **left-luggage** (*consigna*) locations, one in T1 next to Sala 2, the other in T2 near the entrance to the metro, and they are open round the clock (around €2 per day).

Useful Airport Telephone Numbers

Airport information: **t** 913 93 60 00.
Flight information: **t** 902 35 35 70.
Left luggage: **t** 913 93 60 00, ext. 32180.
Lost and Found: **t** 913 93 60 00, ext. 32400.
RENFE Office: **t** 902 24 02 02.

Airline Offices in Madrid

Air Europa: **t** 902 40 15 01, **t** 912 92 70 31.
American Airlines: **t** 913 05 81 74.
British Airways: **t** 913 05 42 12, **t** 913 87 43 00.
Continental: **t** 915 59 27 10, **t** 913 05 46 26.
Delta Airlines: **t** 913 05 82 72.
EasyJet: **t** 902 29 99 92.
Iberia: **t** 902 40 05 00.
KLM: **t** 902 22 27 47, **t** 913 05 43 47.
Lufthansa: **t** 902 22 01 01, **t** 913 05 42 42.
TAP Air Portugal: **t** 913 05 58 68, **t** 913 05 42 37.
US Airways: **t** 913 93 71 46.
Virgin Express: **t** 900 46 76 12.

By Bus

Fast, air-conditioned buses (white with yellow and green stripes) run between Barajas' national and international terminals and the underground bus terminal at Pza de Colón every 15 mins daily 4.45am–2am, taking 25 mins–1 hr dependin on traffic. The buses make stops along the way at Av. de América, C/de María de Molina, C/de Velázquez and C/de Serrano. The fare is €2.40 one way.
Airport bus information: **t** 914 06 88 43.

By Coach

Most, but not all, inter-urban and international buses use the big new **Estación Sur de Autobuses**, at C/de Méndez Alvaro, **t** 914 68 42 00 (**M** Méndez Alvaro).
Information and booking: Enatcar-SAIA, C/de Alcalá 478, 28027 Madrid, **t** 913 27 13 81.

A big exception is the Auto-Res company, which has its own terminal at Pza de Conde de Casal 6 (**M** Conde de Casal, southeast of Retiro Park, **t** 915 51 72 00) with services to Cuenca, Valencia, Extremadura, and parts of Castile. Continental Auto, C/Alenza 20 (head north from **M** Ríos Rosas) takes you to Burgos and the Basque country; they also have a terminal at Av. de América 34 for Alcalá de Henares, Guadalajara and Sigüenza. For other towns close to Madrid, check the 'Getting There' sections for those towns.
Information: Estación Sur, **t** 914 68 42 00; Auto-Res, **t** 915 51 72 00; Continental Auto, **t** 915 33 04 00 or **t** 913 56 23 07.

By Metro

The metro is fast, efficient and the cheapest way to the airport, costing €0.90 for a single (*sencillo*) ticket. It takes about 45 mins to get to the city centre, involving a relatively easy series of changes: take Line 8 (pink) to Mar de Cristal, then switch to Line 4 (brown), which takes you to the Alonso Martínez, where you can switch to Line 10 (dark blue) to get to Pza de España and Line 5 (light green) to head for Gran Vía and Sol further in. The metro runs 6am–1.30am daily.
Metro: **t** 915 52 59 09, *www.metromadrid.es*.

By Taxi

A taxi from the airport to the centre can cost you anything from €13 to €19, depending on where you are headed in the city centre.

Buying Bus and Metro Tickets

Bus and metro operate on the same ticket, with a single price for all journeys, costing about €0.90. A *bono*, which is valid for 10 trips, costs €5 and is a good investment if you're in the city for a few days. Each metro station has a staffed ticket booth, though some now sport automated ticket machines, which are relatively easy to use. There are information kiosks which sell Metrobus tickets in Pza de Cibeles, Puerta del Sol and Pza del Callao. *Estancos* (tobacconists) and news-stands also sell them.

By Train

All long distance trains now leave from just two stations: Estación de **Atocha** and Estación de **Chamartín**. Atocha, quite close to the city centre at the southern end of the Pso del Prado, handles AVE trains to and from Córdoba and Sevilla, Largo Recorrido (long distance) trains to and from Lisbon, Valencia, Andalucía and all points south, plus trains on the Regionales (short distance), and *Cercanías* (local) rail networks. **Chamartín**, just past Pza Castilla at the northern end of Pso de la Castellana, takes most of the trains to and from France, and those serving northern and central Spain, plus some local trains. There's a metro stop at both Atocha and Chamartín, but the quickest way to travel between the two is via the underground section of the main rail line, with stops at Recoletos (just northwest of the Retiro park) and Nuevos Ministerios (on the Pso de la Castellana, 2½km north of the Pza de Cibeles). Many trains to and from distant places use this line to hit both Atocha and Chamartín, and you may jump on any train that does to get from one to the other.

RENFE: C/de Alcalá 44 (**M** Sevilla). *Open Mon–Fri 9.30–8*. For buying rail tickets in Madrid. For all RENFE and AVE enquiries, call **t** 902 24 02 02. RENFE offers telephone reservations; for an extra €3, they will messenger the ticket anywhere within the capital.

Getting Around

By Metro

Opened in 1919, Madrid's metro is the third oldest in Europe and is safe, clean and well used, even at night: trains run 6am–1.30am. Its main faults are that its connections are often inconvenient and that in the summer it can be more than a bit stuffy and hot.

Study the metro map carefully before setting out. There are so many stops and lines in the centre of the city, it's easy to be tricked into taking a half-hour ride (with a change or two) for a distance that could be covered in 10 minutes on foot. For navigation, you have to know your line number, and the name of the terminus in the direction you want to travel. Stations are distinguished by a red diamond over the entrance.

Metro information: **t** 915 52 59 09.

By Bus

Only a few EMT bus lines will be of use to the visitor (*see* 'Useful Bus Lines', below) – but buses can be preferable to the metro if you want to see Madrid. Many buses go through Pza de Cibeles, Puerta del Sol and Pza del Callao. You enter at the front, pay the driver or validate your ticket, and leave by the doors in the middle. Some drivers object to large suitcases. The sequence of places served from each stop is usually clearly marked. Buses run 6am–midnight, after which there is a skeleton night service through the city, leaving from Pza de Cibeles and Puerta del Sol every half-hour until 3am, and every hour 3am–6am.

EMT information: **t** 914 06 38 10.

Useful Bus Lines

Line 1: Moncloa–Pza de España–Gran Vía–Pza de Cibeles–Puerta de Alcalá–C/de Velázquez–C/de Ortega y Gasset (Salamanca district).

Line 3: Pza de Alonso Martínez–C/de Fuencarral–Puerta del Sol–C/del Arenal–Pza de San Francisco–Puerta de Toledo.

Line 14: Pza del Conde de Casal–Atocha–Pso del Prado–Pso de Recoletos–Pso de la Castellana–Chamartín.

Line 19: C/de Serrano–C/de Alfonso XII (Parque del Retiro)–Atocha–Méndez Alvaro (Estación Sur bus terminus).

Line 27: Atocha–Pza Canovas del Castillo–Pza de Cibeles–Pza de Colón–Nuevos Ministerios–Pza de Castilla.

Line 33: Príncipe Pío–Casa de Campo (for Parque de Atracciones and Zoo-Acuario).

By *Cercanías* (Local Trains)

Run by RENFE, this is primarily useful for commuters, but also comes in handy for day trips (*see* **Around Madrid**, pp.521–70). All trains pass through the main stations of Atocha, Recoletos, Nuevos Ministerios and Chamartín.

***Cercanías* information**: t 902 24 02 02.

By Taxi

Madrid has 15,500 taxis, so finding one is rarely a problem. Local government-regulated taxis are white with a red diagonal stripe on each front door. A lit-up green light with a sign saying 'Libre' means they're free, 'Ocupado' that they're not. They are all metered but there are surcharges for luggage, for the airports and bus and railway stations, for journeys at night (11pm–6am), and for leaving the city limits. As elsewhere in Spain, taxis are cheap enough: the average ride across the city centre costs well under €3. For radio taxis, the meter is set from the spot where the driver receives the call.

Radio Taxi: **t** 914 47 51 80, **t** 914 47 32 32.

Radio Taxi Independiente: **t** 914 03 75 11, **t** 914 05 12 13.

Radio Telefono Taxi: **t** 915 47 82 00, **t** 915 47 85 00.

Tele-Taxi: **t** 913 71 21 31, **t** 913 71 37 11.

By Car

Driving in Madrid can drive you round the bend in more ways than one, whether you're stuck in endless traffic or sailing along with the flow, for, once they get into third gear, *madrileños* don't like to stop – a yellow light means accelerate, not slow down. While a car is certainly nice to have to get around on day trips out of the city, it is fairly useless for getting around Madrid because there's no place to put it once you get there. Some hotels have car parks; otherwise you may as well put your car in the nearest 24-hour underground car park (approximately €15 for 24 hours, or €1 an hour). Cars with foreign plates are especially vulnerable to thieves. Parking is regulated by ORA (Operación de Regulación del Aparcamiento) and rules are in force Mon–Fri 9am–8pm and Sat 9am–2pm. Illegally parked cars may be towed; call **t** 913 45 00 50 to find out if they've nabbed yours.

Tourist Information

The tourist offices in Madrid are pretty basic. They offer maps, some brochures on typical sightseeing, and give out a free booklet called *En Madrid*, though it's worth the extra €1.50 to buy the *Guía del Ocio*, which is much more complete. They will help with accommodation, but when the offices are busy they will direct you to the accommodation services in the train stations and airports.

General tourist office number: **t** 902 10 00 07.

Main Tourist Office: C/del Duque de Medinaceli 2, **t** 914 29 37 05, **M** Banco de España (*open Mon–Fri 9–7, Sat 9–1; closed Sun*).

Aeropuerto de Barajas: **t** 913 05 86 56 (*open Mon–Fri 8–8, Sat 9–1; closed Sun*).

Estación de Chamartín: Gate 16, **t** 913 15 99 76 (*open Mon–Fri 8–8, Sat 9–1; closed Sun*).

Mercado Puerta de Toledo: Ronda de Toledo 1, Stand 3134, **t** 913 64 18 76, **M** Puerta de Toledo, (*open Mon–Fri 9–7, Sat 9.30–1.30; closed Sun*).

City of Madrid office: Pza Mayor 3, **t** 913 66 54 77, **t** 915 88 16 36, **M** Sol (*open Mon–Fri 10–8, Sat 10–3; closed Sun*).

Main Post Office: Palacio de Comunicaciones, Pza de Cibeles, **M** Banco de España (*open Mon–Sat 8.30am–9.30pm, Sun 8.30–2*).

Telephones: Apart from numerous public booths, there are Telefónica offices at Gran Vía 28 (*open Mon–Sat 9am–midnight, Sun noon–midnight*), or at the Palacio de Comunicaciones; they are indispensable for reversed charge calls (*cobro revertido*).

Guided Tours

The *Descubre Madrid* brochure (available at the tourist office), lists the possibilities. The following organizations offer very similar hop-on, hop-off **bus tours**:

Madrid Tour: **t** 902 10 10 81, *www.citysight-seeing-spain.com*. Runs June–Aug daily 9.30am–11pm; Sept–May daily 9.30am–9pm.

Madrid Vision, **t** 913 02 03 68. Runs daily 9am–7pm, and in summer night tours are also offered.

The tourist office offers bus tours outside Madrid (€6; €4.50 concessions). For **walking tours** of the city, contact:

Patronato Municipal de Turismo, C/Mayor 69, **t** 915 88 29 06, **f** 915 88 29 30, *www.munimadrid.es* (*open Mon, Tues, Thurs and Fri 8.30am–2.30pm, Wed 8.30–2.30 and 4–6*). Reservations via Cajamadrid, **t** 902 48 84 88.

Embassies in Madrid

Canada: C/de Núñez de Balboa 35, **t** 914 23 32 50, **f** 91 423 32 51, *www.canada-es.org* (**M** Núñez de Balboa).

Ireland: C/de Claudio Coello 73, **t** 915 77 17 87, **f** 915 77 69 34 (**M** Serrano).

UK: C/de Fernando el Santo 16, **t** 917 00 82 00, **f** 917 00 82 72, *www.ukinspain.com* (**M** Alonso Martínez).

USA: C/de Serrano 75, **t** 915 87 23 03, *www.embusa.es* (**M** Rubén Darío).

Banks and Credit Cards

Banking hours: Mon–Fri 8.30am–2pm, and from October to April the same hours on Sat.

Most banks will exchange money, even if they don't have a sign saying '*cambio*'. Most international banks have major branches around C/de Alcalá or in the Salamanca district. Credit cards are accepted in most hotels, shops, and restaurants. There are ATM machines (*telebancos*) on most street corners.

American Express is at Pza de las Cortes 2, **t** 913 22 54 45 (**M** Banco de España; *open Mon–Fri 9–7.30, Sat 9–2*). Besides offering travellers' cheque services, *post restante* for card-holders, and other travel services, Amex is a reliable way to have cash sent from home.

Change Express, Cra de San Jerónimo 11, **t** 900 63 36 33 (**M** Sol), is the agent for Western Union, the fastest way to have money transferred to you in Spain.

Credit Card Helplines: American Express, **t** 915 72 03 20 (24-hour); **Diner's Club**, **t** 917 09 59 00; **MasterCard/Eurocard**, **t** 915 19 21 00; **Visa**, **t** 900 97 44 45.

Emergency Services

Call (fire, police, ambulance): **t** 112.

Lost and Found

For general lost and found, call **t** 915 88 43 46. **Objetos Perdidos**, Pza de Legazpi 7, **t** 915 88 43 44 (**M** Legazpi), is primarily for objects found on the metro or in taxis. If you've lost something on an EMT bus, go to C/de Alcántara 24, **t** 914 06 88 10 (**M** Lista).

Festivals

Madrid puts on some excellent fiestas, ranging from new artsy events to the most traditional. Among the most fun are the old-fashioned neighbourhood *verbenas*, or street festivals. The tourist office has a website at *www.munimadrid.es*, which lists events on a monthly basis, as does their bimonthly *En Madrid What's On* leaflet. Also look in the *Guía del Ocio*, which offers extensive coverage. A few of the city's most important and unusual celebrations are listed below.

Noche Vieja, *31 Dec–1 Jan*. Communal gathering in the Puerta del Sol to see the old year out. Try the custom of eating a grape on each of the 12 chimes – it brings good luck.

Carnaval, *mid–late Feb*. The week leading up to Lent is occasion for a parade, a certain amount of dressing up, gigs and parties. Uniquely *madrileño*, however, is the wacky Burial of the Sardine (*Entierro de la Sardina*), an old tradition in which a papier-mâché sardine in a coffin is paraded around the city with a jazz band on Ash Wednesday and set alight in the Pso de la Florida near the entrance to the Casa de Campo. It commemorates the time when starving *madrileños* received a long-awaited consignment of fish, only to discover that it was rotten, and the only thing to do was burn it on the spot.

Dos de Mayo, *2 May*. An official holiday celebrating Madrid's rising against Napoleon's forces in 1808. The main events take place around the Pza Dos de Mayo in Malasaña, including live bands. The Comunidad de Madrid stages other events, especially in the Jardines de las Vistillas by the Palacio Real.

San Isidro, *15 May*. Madrid's patron saint has his feast day on the 15th, but merits a whole week of festivities leading up to the big day. The bullfights at Las Ventas last an entire month, and with typical *madrileño* modesty are claimed to be the most important in the world. Everything from traditional events to flamenco shows takes place in Pza Mayor, Casa de Campo, Las Vistillas, etc.

San Antonio de la Florida, *13 June*. A *verbena* honouring Madrid's celestial matchmaker. According to tradition, any young women hoping to get hitched should deposit 13 pins in the baptismal font inside the church of San Antonio de la Florida and pray for San Antonio to do his work.

Verbena de la Paloma, *14–15 Aug*. The biggest of the lot, celebrating the Assumption of the Virgin, this takes place in the Barrio de los Austrias, from C/de Bailén to Pza Mayor. Madrileños dress up in traditional clothes, and dance the *chotis* along the colouful lantern-decked streets of old Madrid.

Festival de Otoño, *late Oct–Dec*. The autumn festival has grown to become one of the biggest music and theatre events in Madrid, with a huge variety for all tastes.

Shopping

Opening hours: usually Mon–Fri 10am to 1 or 2pm then 5 or 5.30 until 8 or 8.30pm.

Most shops also open on Saturday mornings, while some, like book and record shops, may open on Sundays. More and more larger chain stores are open during the daytime *siesta*, and Corte Inglés open the first Sunday of each month.

Books and News

Foreign newspapers are sold around the Puerta del Sol, Gran Vía, C/de Alcalá, Pza de Cibeles, and in the Salamanca district.

Booksellers, C/de José Abascal 48; **M** Ríos Rosas. The best shop for English titles.

La Casa del Libro, Gran Vía 29; **M** Gran Vía. Claims to be Spain's largest bookshop – there are several floors of it, including a so-so English-language section.

FNAC, C/de Preciados 28, **t** 915 95 62 00; **M** Callao or Sol. With floor upon floor of CDs, videos, video games, books, magazines and newspapers, and a concert ticket agency.

De Viaje, C/de Serrano 41, *www.deviaje.com*; **M** Serrano. An exhaustive collection of city guides, travel literature and maps spanning the world. Also a travel agency.

Clothes and Accessories

Madrid has not one fashion centre, but several, each with its own distinctive character. For designer labels, the streets to head for are those crisscrossing the prosperous Salamanca district, north of the Retiro: Serrano, Goya, Claudio Coello, Velázquez and Ortega y Gasset (**M** Serrano, Velázquez and Núñez de Balboa). Here are the international fashion celebrities, such as Chanel, Kenzo, Giorgio Armani and Gianni Versace (all on **C/de Ortega y Gasset**).

For affordable mainstream fashion for men and women, **C/de la Princesa** between Argüelles and Moncloa metro stations is the best hunting ground. Other cheap-and-chic stomping grounds are the streets around Preciados and Sol, with lots of off-the-rack lycra and funky denim. For more upscale, creative clothes, the streets around the Pza de las Salesas – Prim, Almirante, Conde de Xiquena, Argensola – have some good, non-chain stores, though original fashions don't come cheap. Chueca, though known for catering to gay men, has a number of funky shops selling offbeat and not terrifically expensive women's clothing, and the shoe outlets on Augusto Figueroa are not to be missed by anyone with even the most minor foot fetish. Hortaleza and Fuencarral are the avenues for alternative fashion – club clothes, sporty-funky, vintage and purely outrageous are all on these two, up from the Gran Vía.

Department Stores and Malls

ABC Serrano, C/de Serrano 61; **M** Rubén Darío. The old headquarters of the right-wing newspaper ABC, in a fanciful Neo-Mudéjar building. There's a somewhat incongruous mixture of fast-food, photo shops and clothing stores.

El Corte Inglés, C/de Preciados 3 (**M** Sol); 2 Pza Callao (**M** Callao); C/de Goya 85–7 (**M** Goya); C/de Raimundo Fernández Villaverde 79 (**M** Nuevos Ministerios); C/de la Princesa 56 (**M** Argüelles). All branches are open Mon–Sat 10am–10pm, and first Sun of every month. Everything you could possibly want under one roof: supermarket, department store, hair stylist, cafeteria, currency exchange, hardware store, travel agency, CDs and books.

Madrid 2 (La Vaguada), Av. Monforte de Lemos 36; **M** Barrio del Pilar. A gigantic shopping mall in the very north of the city, with all the chain stores that are otherwise littered about the streets of the city: Mango, Zara, Massimo Dutti, Bershka, Cortefiel.

Food and Drink

La Casa del Bacalao, C/del Marqués de Urquijo 1; **M** Argüelles. Those with a taste for salt cod can stock up at this tiny, traditional, marble-floored emporium of the stuff.

Casa Mira, Carrera de San Jerónimo 30; **M** Sol. For *turrón*, the almond nougat once made by Toledo's religious communities, you can do no better than this ancient shop which also sells all sorts of other luscious goodies.

La Leonesa, C/de Santa Isabel 1; **M** Antón Martín. One of the best places to fill up on the hearty offerings of Castilla y León, especially sausages and cheeses.

Mantequerías González, C/de León 12; **M** Antón Martín. First opened in 1931, this quaint old *mantequería* has now become a true *tienda del gourmet*, with an excellent selection of wines from all over Spain, cured and fresh cheeses, pâtés and a good variety of sausages. The freshly made *empanada gallega* (tuna with raisins) is scrumptious.

La Oleoteca, C/de Juan Ramón Jiménez 37; **M** Cuzco. Arguably the best place to buy olive oil, as well as a dazzling array of vinegars and olives.

Markets

Market shoppers should be aware that the mêlée round a busy stall is actually the *madrileño* version of an organized queue. The convention is that each new arrival calls out '*¿Quién es el último?*' ('Who's last?') in order to find out their place in the serving order. Nobody would dream of standing in line.

Mercado de Antón Martín, C/de Santa Isabel 5; **M** Antón Martín. One of the most central of the bustling *castizo* food markets, with two floors of stalls selling all manner of fresh produce. *Open daily 9–2 and 5.30–8.30.*

Mercado de las Maravillas, C/de Bravo Murillo 122; **M** Cuatro Caminos. A beautiful ('marvellous') building in a bustling neighbourhood, great for a taste of real Madrid.

El Rastro, Pza de Cascorro, C/de Ribera de Curtidores and around; **M** La Latina. Madrid's most celebrated flea market. The best time to visit is early in the morning, from autumn to spring. Once devoted solely to antiques and curios (the speciality of many of the permanent shops here), there are now stalls selling all sorts of junk: shoes, jewellery, bags; second-hand, ethnic, and new-age fashions; plants; household goods; pirate tapes; and rack after rack of sunglasses. If it's antiques and curios you're after, head for C/de Mira el Río Baja and its neighbours. You may find not only genuine antiques, but reputedly stolen goods (perhaps very recently: beware that El Rastro is renowned for its pickpockets). There are good bric-a-brac stalls in Pza del General Vara de Rey, and a more upmarket shops in the characterless Mercado Puerta de Toledo. The Pza del Campillo del Mundo Nuevo is the place for plants and old books. *Held Sun morning*.

Secondhand Book Market, Cuesta de Claudio Moyano; **M** Atocha. A street where, on fine days (and especially Sun), secondhand bookstalls offer their tempting and sometimes bizarre wares, maybe even the one title you've been searching for all these years.

Specialities and Rarities

El Caballo Cojo, C/de Segovia 7; **M** Sol or Opera. An amazing range of exquisite ceramics, handicrafts and furniture behind.

Casa Seseña, C/de Cruz 23; **M** Sol. The place to go for traditional *madrileño* velvet-lined capes, mantillas and beautifully embroidered Manila shawls.

Félix Manzanero, C/de Santa Ana 12; **M** La Latina. Señor Manzanero builds his guitars from scratch, selling them alongside his tremendous collection of antique guitars.

Maty, C/de Maestro Victoria 2 (near church of San Gínes); **M** Opera. Everything for the flamenco dancer, from castanets in different woods and sizes, and low wide-brimmed black hats, to mantillas and haircombs.

Sargadelos, C/de Zurbano 46; **M** Colón. Both genuinely Spanish and original, the porcelain produced by this co-operative is among the most distinctive anywhere, known for its deep blues and translucent whites. Modern designs are based on traditional themes.

Sports and Activities

Football

The capital has two main soccer stadia that regularly play host to 50,000-plus fans.

Estadio Santiago Bernabéu, C/de Concha Espina 1, **t** 914 57 06 79; **M** Santiago Bernabéu. Real Madrid's giant stadium.

Estadio Vicente, Calderón, Pso de la Virgen del Puerto 67, **t** 913 65 82 09; **M** Pirámides. Atlético de Madrid's ground, by the river.

Bullfighting

The San Isidro festivities see the biggest names at the Ventas bullring, while in August and September large crowds are drawn to impromptu *corridas*.

Pza de Toros de las Ventas, C/de Alcalá 237, **t** 913 56 22 00; **M** Ventas. Between March and October there are *corridas* every Sunday afternoon. Note that tickets (no credit cards) are sold only two days in advance and range from €6 for a seat in the sun (*sol*) to €72 or more for the best one in the shade (*sombra*); buy directly from the office at Las Ventas to avoid the hefty commission charges. No matter where you sit, rent a cushion.

Swimming and Sports Facilities

Madrid has a wide network public swimming pools, some of which are located within larger athletic complexes which also offer things like tennis courts, paddleball courts, football fields, etc. The best of the bunch are:

Canal de Isabel II, Av. Islas Filipinas 54, **t** 915 54 51 53; **M** Ríos Rosas. *Open daily 11am–8pm.*

Piscinas Casa de Campo, Casa de Campo; **M** Lago or Puerta del Angel. *Open mid-May to mid-September daily 10.30am–8pm.*

Polideportivo Barrio del Pilar, C/de Monforte de Lemos, **t** 913 14 79 43; **M** Barrio del Pilar or Begoña. *Open Mon–Fri 9am–8pm.*

Polideportivo de la Elipa, Acceso Parque de la Elipa, **t** 914 30 35 11, **t** 914 30 39 39; **M** La Estrella.

Golf

There are a number of golf courses in the metropolitan area, none of them cheap. The following clubs are the best equipped:

Club de Campo Villa de Madrid, Ctra de Castilla Km2, **t** 915 50 20 10; bus No.84. *Open daily 8.30am–dusk.* Thirty-six holes.

El Olivar de la Hinojosa, Av. de Dublín, **t** 917 21 18 89; **M** Campo de las Naciones. *Open Mon–Fri 8.30am–11pm, Sat, Sun and hols 8am–11pm.* One nine-hole course and one eighteen-hole course, plus a driving range.

Where to Stay

Madrid ✉ 20080

With some 50,000 hotel rooms in Madrid, there are always enough to go around. Regrettably, few are at all interesting. If it's reliability or familiarity you're looking for, there are all the world's big chains to choose from, or you could stay at any of a hundred other three-, four- or five-star hotels – all pleasant and well-staffed, and all pretty much the same. Many are along the Gran Vía and other major streets – convenient but often intolerably noisy.

At the top end of the scale, Madrid has well over a third of all the luxury hotels in Spain. You could always pamper yourself at the Ritz, but only, if money is no object. At the other extreme, finding a good, inexpensive room for the night is not a problem if you're prepared to share a bathroom; otherwise you'll be hard pressed to find a double for under €30.

The **price categories** for a double room in Madrid are different from those used in the rest of the guide. *See* **Practical A–Z**, 'Where to Stay', p.92, for price ranges.

If you haven't got the time or the inclination to find accommodation yourself, contact the following booking agency:

Brújula Agency, C/de la Princesa 1, **t** 915 59 97 05. There are branches at Atocha station (**t** 915 39 11 73) and Chamartín station (**t** 913 15 78 94), and at the airport bus terminal in Pza del Colón (**t** 915 75 96 80).

Luxury

★★★★★**Hotel Miguel Angel**, C/de Miguel Angel 29–31, **t** 914 42 00 22, **f** 914 42 53 20, *reservas .hma@oh-es.com*; **M** Gregorio Marañón. One of Madrid's plusher hotels in one of Madrid's plusher, less touristy neighbourhoods. With two **restaurants** (one, La Broche, has three

Michelin stars), a splendid summertime garden dining room, laundry service, health club (stationary bikes can be delivered to your room!), pillow menu, etc., it is high luxury. Swanky modern-style décor.

★★★★★**Hotel Orfila**, C/de Orfila 6, **t** 917 02 77 70, **t** 917 02 77 72, *inforeservas@hotelorfila.com*, *www.hotelorfila.com*; **M** Colón. The only hotel in Madrid that belongs to the Relais et Chateaux chain, the Orfila is also arguably Madrid's most beautiful hotel, a sensitively converted 19th-century *palacete*. There's an idyllic garden, tearoom and **restaurant**. The décor is restrained luxury, with antique furniture, oil paintings and delicate silk wallcoverings.

★★★★★**Hotel Palace**, Pza de las Cortes 7, **t** 913 60 80 00, **f** 913 60 81 00, *madrid@westin.com*, *www.palacemadrid.com*; **M** Banco de España. Perfectly located between the Prado and Sol, turn-of-the-20th-century architecture meets the latest facilities in one of the city's largest luxury hotels. But it's far from impersonal, and **restaurants** and bars in the stunning public areas make it a bustling, friendly place to stay or just to be. Among the facilities offered are a business centre, gym, *bodega*, hairdresser, airport shuttle.

★★★★★**Hotel Ritz**, Pza de la Lealtad 5, **t** 915 21 28 57, **f** 915 23 87 76; **M** Banco de España. Consistently rated among the best hotels worldwide. A stay at the Ritz is all about being pampered – from the renovated and sumptuous rooms, to the fabulous **restaurants** and 'place-to-be-seen' garden terrace. The hotel is close to the Prado and is just a stone's throw from the Retiro and the boutiques of Salamanca. The décor includes embroidered linen sheets, handwoven carpets and antique furniture. It has all the facilities you'd expect from a five-star hotel.

★★★★★**Hotel Santo Mauro**, C/de Zurbano 36, **t** 913 19 69 00, **f** 913 08 54 77; **M** Rubén Darío. Built as a palace late in the 19th century, the classicism of the public areas of this small-but-perfectly-formed luxury hotel contrasts with the contemporary Postmodernism of the rooms. Tucked away in a residential neighbourhood, the hotel is frequented by the rich and famous who also like their privacy. Facilities include car park, pool, garden and sauna.

★★★★★**Hotel Villa Magna**, Pso de la Castellana 22, **t** 915 87 12 34, **f** 915 75 31 58, *hotel@villamagna.es*, *madrid.hyatt.com*; **M** Rubén Darío. The Villa Magna's modern – albeit bland – surroundings are more than made up for by the quality of service and facilities on offer at this hotel away from the city centre. The establishment of choice for many visiting sports stars and celebrities, the Villa Magna is also home to one of Madrid's most famous (and justly so) **restaurants**, Le Divellec. Other facilities include a fitness centre, business centre, babysitting, car hire and limousine service.

Expensive

★★★★**Hotel NH Alcalá**, C/de Alcalá 66, **t** 914 35 10 60, **f** 914 35 11 05, *nhalcala@nh-hoteles.es*; **M** Príncipe de Vergara. Friendly staff provide a warm welcome at this popular hotel, and many longtime visitors to Madrid wouldn't dream of staying anywhere else. The courtyard garden looked on to by the quieter interior rooms is a verdant reminder of the nearby Retiro. All rooms have satellite TV. There's also a car park, currency exchange, bar and **café**.

★★★★**Hotel Castellana Intercontinental**, Pso de la Castellana 49, **t** 913 10 02 00, **f** 913 19 58 53, *madrid@interconti.com*, *www.interconti.com*; **M** Rubén Darío. Having undergone redecoration, this well-located – albeit unattractive from the outside – hotel is perhaps the best value at the top end of the scale. The best rooms overlook the interior garden, itself one of the capital's best-kept secrets, with live jazz in summer. The rooftop gym-terrace-bar offers wonderful views. Other facilities include a restaurant, baby-sitting, beauty salon and laundry.

★★★★**Hotel Emperador**, Gran Vía 53, **t** 915 47 28 00, **f** 915 47 28 17, *www.emperadorhotel.es*; **M** Callao. Home to the only remaining rooftop hotel pool in Madrid, commanding stunning views up and down the Gran Vía, the Emperador is at the very heart of the capital's traditional shopping centre. Just a short walk from Sol and Pza de España, its large, well-decorated rooms are much in demand all year round. Additional facilities include a **café**, gift shop, sauna and baby-sitting service.

★★★★**Hotel Tryp Ambassador**, Cuesta de Santo Domingo 5–7, **t** 915 41 67 00, **f** 915 59 10 40; **M** Santo Domingo. Right in the centre but tucked into a quiet street between the Palacio Real, Teatro Real and Gran Vía, this luxurious establishment is arguably the capital's best-kept secret. The attractive patio garden and glass atrium make the hotel an oasis of light and calm in the summer months. All rooms have satellite TV and minibar. Children under two stay free.

★★★★★**Hotel Villa Real**, Pza de las Cortes 10, **t** 914 20 37 67, **f** 914 20 25 47, *villareal@slh.com*, *www.slh.com/villareal*; **M** Banco de España. Although only built in 1990, the Villa Real has captured the neoclassical feel of the elegant neighbourhood. It's ideally situated for the main museums and the Puerta del Sol. It's a member of the Small Luxury Hotels of the World group. Facilities include Jacuzzis, car hire desk and airport shuttle.

Moderate

Hotel Atlántico, Gran Vía 38, **t** 915 22 64 80, **f** 915 31 02 10, *h-atlantico@mad.servicom.es*, *hotel-atlantico.com*; **M** Callao. Of the Gran Vía hotel line-up, this is one of the nicer options, an historic building with decent facilities, in the centre of everything. With currency exchange, a/c, satellite TV, **café**, and safety-deposit boxes in all rooms.

★★★★**Hotel Bauza**, C/de Goya 79, **t** 914 35 75 45, *www.hotelbauza.com*; **M** Goya. Fully refurbished in the Philippe Starck mold, this well-appointed hotel has earned itself an extra star in the process, and offers excellent value. Facilities include Internet access, laundry service, library and video games.

★★★**HSR Galiano**, C/de Alcalá Galiano 6, **t** 913 19 20 00, **f** 913 19 99 14; **M** Colón. The Spanish system of categorizing hotels makes this a *hostal*, albeit a three-star one. However, this charming former palace knocks spots off most of the city's hotels with its intimate old-world feel. It has a car park.

★★★**Hotel Inglés**, C/de Echegaray 8, **t** 914 29 65 51, **f** 914 20 24 23; **M** Sevilla or Sol. With 150 years of history under its belt, this family-run hotel lies equidistant from the shopping areas of Preciados and Carmen and the bars of Santa Ana. There's a relaxed and very comfortable atmosphere in the public areas and sunny rooms, but those giving on to Echegaray itself can be noisy at the weekend. Facilities include a car park, bar, gift shop, ticket agency, fax service, laundry, health club and room service.

★★★★**Hotel Mayorazgo**, C/de la Flor Baja 3, **t** 915 47 26 00, **f** 915 41 24 85, *mayoraz@globalnet.es*; **M** Pza de España. Offers stylish, international – if anonymous – comfort. Facilities include **café**, hairdresser, gift shop, currency exchange and car park.

★★**Hotel Paris**, C/de Alcalá 2, **t** 915 21 64 91, **f** 915 31 01 88; **M** Sol. The chandeliered hotel lobby is as packed with character as it is with china bric-a-brac, but the friendly staff soon make visitors feel right at home. Two steps away from the Puerta del Sol, the best of the wooden-floored rooms look onto the courtyard garden and keep the sound of traffic at bay. All rooms have TV and safe. There's a money exchange and laundry service.

★★**Hotel Plaza Mayor**, C/de Atocha 2, **t** 913 60 06 06, **f** 913 60 06 10, *info@h-plazamayor.com*, *www.h-plazamayor.com*; **M** Tirso de Molina or Sol. Beautifully, renovated installations in an old stone building just across the street from one of the quieter edges of the Pza Mayor. All rooms have a/c and TV. There's a **bar-restaurant** and currency exchange.

★★★**Hotel Rafael Ventas**, C/de Alcalá 269, **t** 913 26 16 20, **f** 919 26 18 19; **M** Carmen. Bright, breezy and very modern, this is near the bullring and attracts a number of *toreros*. The staff are very helpful. There's a car park, garden, swimming pool, **café** and bar.

★★★**La Residencia de El Viso**, C/de Nervión 8, **t** 915 64 03 70, **f** 915 64 19 65; **M** República Argentina. A tiny, charming hotel, in one of Madrid's poshest, lushest, most picturesque residential neighbourhoods to the north of Salamanca. A refreshing antidote to the big chains, it has only 12 rooms. Built in the 1930s, it has been well adapted. With car park, **café** and garden.

★★★**Hotel Tirol**, C/del Marqués de Urquijo 4, **t** 915 48 19 00, **f** 915 41 39 58; **M** Argüelles. Moderate.Slightly off the beaten track, and better value than many that only marginally more central. Spacious, airy rooms, clean, and close to the lovely Parque del Oeste. There's a car park, currency exchange and **café**. All rooms have a/c and satellite TV.

Inexpensive

★★Hs Americano, Puerta del Sol 11, 3° and 4°, **t** 915 22 28 22, **f** 915 22 11 92; **M** Sol. The interior is surprisingly lovely, with firm beds and a quaint salon to sit in. All rooms have TV, phone and private bath.

★Hs Don Juan, Pza de Vázquez de Mella 1, 2°, **t** 915 22 31 01, **f** 915 22 77 46; **M** Chueca or Gran Vía. Here you'll find a funky zebra-tiled floor, velvet couch and big old armoire filled with books, but light, airy rooms with shiny tile bathrooms, safety-deposit boxes, TV and a/c. Other services include luggage storage and washing and ironing. If it's full, try the other *hostales* in the same building: the Covadonga, Zamora and Vázquez de Mella.

Hs Dulcinea, C/de Cervantes 19, 2°, **t** 914 29 93 09, **f** 915 32 70 78, *donato@teleline.es*; **M** Antón Martín. Just what you expect old Madrid to be: whitewashed façade and wrought-iron balconies. All rooms have bath and TV, just like at its sister *hostal* across the street, the Corbero.

Hs Las Fuentes, C/de las Fuentes 10, 1°D, **t** 915 42 18 53, **f** 915 42 18 54, *reserva@hostallas-fuentes.com*, *www.hostallasfuentes.com*; **M** Opera. A classically *castizo* building in a classic *castizo* neighborhood, with the Pza de Oriente, the Palacio Real and the Teatro Real just a stone's throw from this quiet street. Spacious rooms with private bath, a/c and phone. There's Internet hookup and room service.

★Hs Lorenzo, C/de las Infantas 26, 3°, **t** 915 32 79 78, *hostallorenzo@wanadoo.es*; **M** Gran Vía or Banco de España. Silky bedspreads and wooden fixtures add a nice touch to this airy, sparkling-clean *hostal* between Chueca and Gran Vía, just steps away from a plethora of bars, restaurants and clubs. All rooms have bath, TV, phone and a/c, and cold drinks are available in the reception area.

★★Hs La Plata, Gran Vía 15, 4°B, **t** 915 21 17 25, **f** 915 31 97 37, *egarrido@telcom.es*; **M** Gran Vía. In a truly majestic old building on the Gran Vía, this place lives up to its grand location, though the lovingly decorated public spaces outdo the rooms, which are simple, though with high ceilings, private bath, TV, a/c and phone.

Hs Prim, C/de Prim 15, 2°, **t** 915 21 54 95, **f** 915 23 58 48; **M** Chueca. On a quiet street close to Recoletos, the Prim is ideal if you want budget lodgings in an upscale shopping neighbourhood. Funky retro leather chairs in the lounge, and all rooms have a/c and TV. With bath or without.

HSR Principado, C/de Zorrilla 7, 1° dcha, **t** 914 29 81 87, **f** 913 69 40 60, *hr.principado@wanadoo.es*; **M** Banco de España. Old-world décor in an old-world corner of the city, up the street from the splendid Teatro de la Zarzuela, the Congreso de los Diputados and the Thyssen-Bornemisza. The rooms are simple and monastic, with carved wooden headboards and severe Spanish white lace designs on the bedlinen and bath towels. All rooms have private bath and TV. It's excellent value for the neighbourhood.

★★★Hotel Reyes Católicos, C/del Angel 18, **t** 913 65 86 00, **f** 913 65 98 67, *www.reyescatolicos.com*; **M** Puerta de Toledo. Set in a very nice old neighbourhood near the Basílica de San Francisco el Grande; small, personal, and a good bargain for the services offered, which include a café, fax service and disco. All rooms have a/c, TV and safe.

★★Hotel Santander, C/de Echegaray 1, **t** 914 29 95 51, **f** 913 69 10 78; **M** Sevilla or Sol. High-ceilings, a jumble of furniture from all over and the light-filled, although sometimes noisy, exterior rooms make the Santander a firm favourite of many budget travellers. Obliging staff and a great location close to shops and bars mean it's best to call ahead and reserve. All rooms have TV, phone, a/c and safe. Additional facilities include fax, laundry and room services.

★★Hs Sil, C/de Fuencarral 95, **t** 914 48 89 72, **f** 914 47 48 29; **M** Bilbao. At the end of Fuencarral away from the Gran Vía, this family-run *hostal* is kept spick and span by the pleasant couple who run it. With private baths and a/c, the TV- and phone-equipped rooms are really good value for a stay during Madrid's sweltering summer.

★HSR Sudamericana, Pso del Prado 12, 6°izqda, **t** 914 29 25 64; **M** Banco de España. One of the friendliest and quietest lodgings in Madrid, occupying a fine old building with leafy views towards the Prado.

★★HSR La Torre, C/de Espoz y Mina 8, 3°, **t** 915 32 43 03; **M** Sol. Probably the best-value option in this area, a bright, squeaky-clean *hostal* which has large twin rooms with fabulous balconies, giving views of rooftop gardens, and, down the street to the left, the Puerta del Sol's landmark Tío Pepe advert.

★**HSR Vetusta**, C/de Huertas 3, 1°, **t** 914 29 64 04; **M** Sol. Has a balcony dripping with geraniums, and good-value rooms.

Cheap

★**Hs Almirante**, C/del Almirante 4, 2°, **t** 915 32 48 71; **M** Chueca. Slightly 1970s-style rooms (minus the TV sets, which look even older), but the place is cute, the owner nice, and for €9 a person, the price is unbeatable. Lunch and breakfast are also a steal. Book ahead.

★**Hs Corona**, C/de la Libertad 4, **t** 915 21 67 67; **M** Banco de España. Slightly run-down *hostal* on a perfectly picture-postcard Chueca street. Rooms are small but sweet, and those that look out on to the street heave at night with the neighbourhood scene. Rooms with or without bath.

★★**Hs La Perla Asturiana**, Pza de Santa Cruz 3, **t** 913 66 46 00, **f** 913 66 46 08, *perla asturiana@mundivia.es*, *www.perlaas-turiana.com*; **M** Sol. In a grand old building looking out on to Atocha and Pza de Santa Cruz to the back of the Pza Mayor. Sunny common rooms brim with the odd school group. Rooms have bath, TV and phone, and the salon has computers (Internet access).

Hs Madrazo, C/de los Madrazo 10, 1°, **t** 914 29 45 75; **M** Banco de España. In a tranquil, elegant neighbourhood, this is bare-bones, but the quality–price ratio is astounding. Rooms with or without bath. Guests have use of dining facilities and microwave.

★**Hs Río Navia**, C/de las Infantas 13, 3°izqda, **t** 915 32 30 50; **M** Gran Vía. The inside isn't quite as grand as the outside, though the swooping glass chandelier, knick-knacks and carved wooden mirrors do help. Luminous rooms, some of which look out onto the street, others onto a reasonably well-kept patio. Rooms have bathroom and TV.

Youth Hostels

Madrid is not exactly a youth hostel town. There are three official IYHF albergues and the pricing is standard throughout: €7.20 for those under 26, and €11 for those over 26. The price includes a bed in a dormitory and breakfast.

Albergue Juvenil, C/de Santa Cruz de Marcenado 28, **t** 915 47 45 32, **f** 915 48 11 96; **M** San Bernardo or Argüelles. This one tends to fill up with school groups.

Albergue Juvenil Richard Schirrmann, Casa de Campo, **t** 914 63 56 99, **f** 914 64 46 85; **M** Lago. Suffers from a slightly spooky locale in the Casa de Campo.

Albergue Juvenil San Fermín, Av. de los Fueros 36, **t** 917 92 08 97, **f** 917 92 47 24, *albergue@san-fermin.org*, *www.san-fermin.org*; **M** Legazpi; bus No.23 from Pza Mayor, or No.85, 86 or 59 from Estación de Atocha. With luggage storage, bike rental, washer, dryer, towel and sheet rental and Internet room.

Eating Out

See also **Food and Drink** chapter, p.83.

No place in Spain, except perhaps the Costa del Sol, can offer such a wide choice. Besides the country's best gourmet restaurants, you can sample the cuisine of every region of Spain and a score of other lands without straying half a mile from the Puerta del Sol. Most of the old well-known establishments are in Old Madrid and the Santa Ana and Huertas area. Surprisingly, thanks to the sizable Argentinian population in Madrid, you can get a good pizza in many places. Vegetarians are increasingly well catered for (*see* 'Vegetarian Restaurants', p.483).

Price Categories

Price categories differ slightly from those used in the rest of the guide. *See* **Practical A–Z**, 'Food and Drink', p.83 for price ranges.

Specialities

Traditional *madrileño* cuisine is a reflection of the cooking of Castile: roast meats and stews. The pinnacle of the capital's culinary arts is *cocido*: part soup, part meat and two veg. The meal, chickpeas and vegetables are cooked in broth, then removed and set aside. Added to the broth are *fideos* (long spaghetti), which is then served as the first course of a *cocido completo*. In winter, most restaurants offer a *cocido* on their Tuesday *menú del día* (Thursday is traditionally *paella* day). Even the capital's most expensive restaurants will offer their version of the dish.

Callos a la madrileña might just convince you to give tripe a go. Cooked in a rich spicy sauce based on *pimentón*, or sweet red pepper, the tripe is manageable, having been cut into bite-sized pieces.

Despite its land-locked location, Madrid ranks among the world's main consumers of seafood and fish. Oysters are readily available throughout the winter months, as are all other manner of crustacea, shipped down overnight from Galicia, along with *pulpo*, or octopus, a firm favourite in the capital's bars.

Expensive

Botín, C/de los Cuchilleros 17, **t** 913 66 42 17, **t** 913 66 30 26; **M** Sol. Hemingway called it 'the best restaurant in the world' no less. According to the Guinness Book of Records, it is the oldest restaurant in the world, founded in 1725; 19-year-old Goya worked in the evening washing dishes here, and it even features, as the plaque reads, in a scene in the classic 19th-century novel about Madrid, *Fortunata y Jacinta*, by Benito Pérez Galdós. Justly renowned for its beautiful original interior and roasts, it is one of the priciest in the area, but the quality–price ratio is unbeatable. *Open daily 1–4 and 8–midnight.*

Casa Santa Cruz, C/de la Bolsa 12, **t** 915 21 86 23, **t** 915 21 61 60; **M** Sol. Originally the parish church of Santa Cruz, this restaurant is an exquisite throwback to another age, from its stunning dining room, with its intricately carved vaulted ceiling and regal appointments, to the menu of classic Spanish cuisine, which includes things such as suckling lamb, steak in wine sauce, artichokes filled with shellfish, and other traditional dishes. Daily *menús* vary from €36 to €59. Reservations recommended. *Open daily 1–4 and 8.30–midnight.*

El Cenador del Prado, Pso del Prado 4, **t** 914 29 15 61; **M** Antón Martín or Sevilla. Delicious Mediterranean cuisine served in luxurious surroundings. *Open Mon–Fri 1.30–4 and 9.30–midnight, Sat and Sun 9.30pm–midnight; closed Aug.*

Come Prima, C/de Echegaray 27, **t** 914 20 30 42; **M** Sevilla. A giant step up from Madrid's often uninspiring Italian offerings, Come Prima imported a chef from London's famed San Lorenzo to dream up a mouthwatering menu from all over Italy: *vitello tonato*, *risotto selvatico* (wild mushroom risotto), prawn brochettes in mint sauce, as well as pasta and meat. The elegant Italian-country décor and fashionably dressed fellow diners make it a great place for a night out. Reservations recommended. *Open Tues–Sun 1.30–4 and 9–midnight, Mon 9pm–midnight.*

Le Divellec, Hotel Villa Magna, Pso de la Castellana 22, **t** 915 87 12 34; **M** Núñez de Balboa. Reservations essential. This is one of Madrid's top gourmet restaurants, with a French chef who really knows his stuff. Excellent seafood. *Menú* around €30. *Open Mon–Sat 1–4 and 8.30–midnight.*

Lhardy, Carrera de San Jerónimo 8, **t** 915 22 22 07; **M** Sol or Sevilla. A Madrid institution founded in 1839, and nearly unchanged. The dining rooms upstairs feature French and *muy castizo madrileño* cuisine. Downstairs, clients help themselves to sweet or savoury delicacies, then pay at the door. *Open Mon–Sat 1–3.30 and 8.30–11, Sun 1–3.30pm.*

El Olivo, C/de General Gallegos 1, **t** 913 59 15 35; **M** Cuzco. It took a Frenchman, Jean Pierre Vandelle, to make Spaniards appreciate the finer points of olive oil. It is Mediterranean cuisine at its best, with Jean Pierre on hand to advise. Aside from the myriad oils, it has one of the best selections of sherry in the capital. *Open Tues–Sat 1–4 and 9–midnight.*

Posada de la Villa, C/de la Cava Baja 9, **t** 913 66 18 80; **M** La Latina. *Muy auténtico*, both in the décor and in the kitchen, where a wood-fired oven produces succulent suckling pig. Although popular with tourists, the food is excellent and the building spectacular. *Open Mon–Sat 1–4 and 8–midnight, Sun 1–4pm; closed Aug.*

Robata, C/de la Reina 31, **t** 915 21 85 28; **M** Gran Vía. As Madrid boasts the third largest fish market in the world (after Tokyo and San Francisco), little wonder that there should be so many good Japanese restaurants. Robata has a sushi bar, normal tables or a Japanese salon. *Open Wed–Sun 1.30–3.45 and 8–11.*

Thai Gardens, C/de Jorge Juan 5, **t** 915 77 88 84; **M** Serrano. Palm fronds, waterfalls and exquisite East Asian décor make this one of the sexiest restaurants in Madrid, and the food is as attractive and well dressed as the beautiful-people crowd that eats here. Spring rolls and sate are standard staples, but the more exotic the dish the better: try the chicken with mint and shallots in lime sauce. Curries are delicate and flavourful. Weekday *menú moderate*. Reservations recommended. *Open Sun–Thurs 2–4 and 9–midnight, Fri and Sat 2–4 and 9–1.*

La Vendimia, Pza del Conde del Valle de Suchil 7, **t** 914 45 73 77; **M** San Bernardo. Set in one of the capital's loveliest and overlooked squares, this neoclassical celebration of all that is best about modern Basque cooking is an absolute treat. Try the *txangurro*, a type of lobster, in its many forms. *Open Mon–Sat 1–4 and 9–midnight, Sun 1–4pm.*

Viridiana, C/de Juan de Mena 14, **t** 915 23 44 78; **M** Banco de España or Retiro. Although a symbol of the economic boom of the late 1980s, Viridiana is no nouveau riche hangout. One of the best of Madrid's wine cellars, faultless service, and imaginative but classical dishes make for a memorable meal. *Open Mon–Sat 1.30–4 and 9.30–midnight; closed Aug.*

Moderate

La Ancha, C/de Zorrilla 7, **t** 914 29 81 86; **M** Banco de España. Chances are you'll be rubbing shoulders with an errant MP taking it easy after a hard day at the nearby Parliament. The formula is simple: impeccable service, the finest ingredients and wines, and dishes that know their limits, based on traditional cuisine. *Open Mon–Sat 1.30–4 and 8.30–11.30.*

La Barraca, C/de la Reina 29, **t** 915 32 71 54, *www.interocio.es/labarraca*; **M** Gran Vía. An upscale *arrocería* which continues the art of Spanish rice – *paellas*, 'black' rice and other delicacies are the speciality, but meat and fish dishes are also available. The wine list is extensive and excellent. Reservations recommended. *Open daily 1–4 and 8.30–11.30.*

Casa Ciriaco, C/Mayor 84, **t** 915 48 06 20; **M** Opera. Founded in 1917, with a beautiful old tiled bar for tapas grazing, and tasty traditional food in the restaurant. The King and Queen are said to dine here. *Open Thurs–Tues 1–4 and 8–midnight; closed Aug.*

Casa Gallega, Pza San Miguel 8, **t** 915 47 30 55; **M** Sol. Just off Pza Mayor sits this traditional Galician restaurant, which has been packing them in since 1940. The seafood is brought from Galicia and, although the terrace gets crowded in summer, it's worth booking a table and sitting back to watch the locals. *Open daily 1–4 and 8–midnight.*

Casa Hortensia, C/del Olivar 6, **t** 915 39 00 90; **M** Tirso de Molina. The emphasis is very much on the food, so don't be put off by the lack of décor. Asturian cooking at its best, with a *fabada* – bean stew – famed throughout the city, served with traditional cider poured from shoulder height by the waiters. *Open Tues–Sat 1–5 and 8.30–1.30, Sun 8.30pm–midnight.*

Casa Marta, C/de Santa Clara 10, **t** 915 48 28 25; **M** Opera. Just behind the Teatro Real, this intimate restaurant offers superb service, a relaxed atmosphere and some beautifully prepared dishes, such as *el bacalao Marta*, or *duelos y quebrantos* – a stew mentioned in *El Quijote*. Very reasonable prices. *Open Mon–Sat 1.30–4 and 9–midnight.*

Casa de Vacas, C/de Jorge Juan 12, **t** 915 77 16 07; **M** Serrano. An imposing cow's head and watercolours of bullfights greet you on the ground floor of this neighbourhood haunt, perfect for post-shopping nourishment in Salamanca. Excellent meat and grilled fish, and tasty *pinchos* if you have to wait for a table in the dining room upstairs. The *menú del día* is a very reasonable downstairs. *Open Mon–Sat 1–4 and 9–midnight, Sun 1–4pm.*

Casa de Valencia, Pso del Pintor Rosales 58, **t** 915 44 17 47; **M** Argüelles or Ventura Rodríguez. Rice rules, with more than 14 different *paellas*, and a range of *fideuá* (*paella* done with macaroni), all washed down with stunning *cavas*. *Open Tues–Sat lunch and dinner, Sun lunch; closed Aug.*

La Cocina del Desierto, C/de Barbieri 1, **t** 915 23 11 42; **M** Chueca or Gran Vía. Exquisite Northern African décor, complete with bronze chalices and handmade rugs and cushions, and excellent North African dishes, from creamy hummus to grilled *pimiento* salad, meat pies to tajines. The *menú de degustación* offers a little of everything, and is one way (€15) to deal with the inevitable indecision. Reservations recommended at weekends. *Open daily 1.30–4 and 9–11.*

Cornucopia, C/de la Flora 1, **t** 915 47 64 65; **M** Opera. Tucked away on the ground floor of a 19th-century palace can be found this gem of a restaurant. It's European cuisine with a slight American flavour, backed up by affordable but well-chosen wines. If you're packing in the meals, then there's a very reasonable midday menu. *Open Tues–Sun 1.30–4.30 and 8.30–midnight.*

Currito, Pabellón de Vizcaya, Casa de Campo, **t** 914 64 57 07; **M** Lago. In summer, this is quite simply the best open-air place to eat in Madrid. It's not bad inside either. It might seem like a long trek from the centre, but it's not that far to savour excellent roast meats and fish (or better still barbecued), along with more modern dishes, and all accompanied by fine wines. *Open Mon–Sat 1.30–4 and 8–11.30, Sun 1.30–4pm.*

Entre Suspiro y Suspiro, C/de Caños del Peral 3, **t** 915 42 06 44; **M** Opera. One of Madrid's precious few restaurants serving *haute* Mexican *cuisine*, with a truly authentic chicken in *mole* sauce, a variety of *ceviches*, and rich, filling bean soup (*crema de frijoles*). Vegetarians will not be disappointed. Reservations recommended. *Open Mon–Fri 2–4.30 and 9.30–11.30, Sat 9.30–11.30pm.*

El Espejo, Pso de Recoletos 31, **t** 913 08 23 47; **M** Banco de España. Despite its location and the elaborate (but fake) 1920s décor, El Espejo offers excellent food at affordable prices. There's a beautiful outdoor terrace overlooking the Pso de Recoletos. The daily *menú* varies according to the time of year. *Open daily 1–3 and 9–midnight; café open throughout the day.*

Extremadura, C/de Libertad 13 and 31, **t** 915 31 89 58; **M** Chueca. The name says it all. If you want a taste of this western, and still largely remote, region, then this is the place. *Migas* (breadcrumbs with bacon and grapes) and winter salads, backed up by roast goat, and finished off with home-made *orujo* (schnapps) of varying flavours – bottled snake or a lizard included. *No.13 open Tues–Sat 1.30–4 and 9–midnight, Sun 1.30–4pm; no.31 open Thurs–Mon 1.30–4 and 9–midnight, Tues 1.30–4pm.*

Restaurante Ginza, Pza de las Cortes 3, **t** 914 29 76 19; **M** Banco de España. There are more than 50 varieties of sushi at this labyrinthine Japanese restaurant. Downstairs is a sushi bar with a conveyor belt from which you can grab the sushi that grabs you – once you're done, your empty plates are used to calculate your bill. Upstairs is a simple dining room with pretty Japanese flower arrangements, thanks to the owner's connection to the local Floral Art association. *Open Tues–Sun 1.30–4 and 8.30–midnight.*

Gran Café Gijón, Pso de Recoletos 21, **t** 915 21 54 25; **M** Banco de España. A legendary haunt of Madrid's intellectuals, the Gijón has been in business since 1888; it's good for breakfast, a set lunch, or afternoon tea or coffee. *Open Sun–Fri 9am–1.30am, Sat 9am–2am.*

Lombok, C/de Augusto Figueroa 32, **t** 915 31 35 61; **M** Chueca. This sexy, minimalist restaurant's claim to fame is its owner, Jesús Vasquez, one-time host of the hilarious trashy TV show *Gente con Chispa* (People with Sparkle). The food is surprisingly good, the staff friendly and ambience downright festive, which explains its success even after Jesús was rocked by scandal and lost his TV job in 2000. The food is creative and eclectic – vegetable tempura, asparagus quiche, duck with camembert – and the desserts are decadent and delicious. *Open Mon–Fri 2–4 and 9–midnight, Sat 9pm–midnight.*

Malacatín, C/de la Ruda 5, **t** 913 65 52 41; **M** La Latina. A genuine Madrid experience, book their renowned *cocido* (€13) for lunch and ask what time to show up. *Open Mon–Sat 1–3.30pm; closed 15 July–15 Aug.*

Oh Pizza Mía!, Pza Isabel II 2, **t** 915 47 21 24; **M** Opera. Stills of Spanish movie stars cover the brick walls of this dining room, serving perfect thin-crust pizza and focaccia for pre- or post-theatre meals. The upstairs bar is a neighbourhood classic. *Open daily 1–4 and 8–1; bar-café upstairs open daily 9am–midnight for drinks and tapas.*

La Recoba, C/de la Magdalena 27, **t** 913 69 39 88; **M** Antón Martín. A legend in its time, this smoky little spot is possibly the only place in Madrid where you can eat a filling pizza at 4am. You can chomp on *empanadas* (try the meat-filled Argentinian variety), salads and crêpes to the strains of bolero, tango or whatever live music is on tap for the night. Reservations recommended at the weekend. *Open daily 9.30pm–6am.*

Ribeira do Miño, C/de Santa Brígida 1, **t** 915 21 98 54; **M** Tribunal. A classic, bustling marisquería with rushing waiters, and lobsters and fish nets on the walls. Meat and other dishes are available, but the mind-boggling *mariscadas*, a pile of every shellfish known to the Galician coastline, is the must-have meal here, served with bread and cold white wine. Takeaways are available. Reservations recommended at the weekend. *Open Tues–Sun 1–4 and 8–midnight.*

Sarrasín, C/de la Libertad 8, **t** 915 32 73 48; **M** Chueca. With its policy of a *menú*, and a limited choice of dishes based on simple but tasty ingredients, this is one of the more enjoyable and affordable of the many (mainly) gay restaurants now flourishing in Chueca. *Open Mon–Sat 1–4 and 9–midnight.*

La Taberna de la Daniela, C/de General Pardiñas 21, **t** 915 75 23 29; **M** Goya. Don't even think of just turning up. If you want to enjoy one of the best *cocido madrileños* in town (and this is all they offer, aside from sea bream in the evenings), then you'll have to book. If you can't get a table, pass by to try the tapas. *Open Mon–Thurs noon–4.30 and 8–11.30, Fri and Sat noon–4.30 and 8–1.*

Taquería del Alamillo, Pza del Alamillo, **t** 913 64 20 88; **M** La Latina. This casual Mexican spot in a hidden corner of old Madrid is a favourite among *madrileños*. Specialities include *molcajetes*: stone gourds with sizzling chicken or beef, which come with tortillas. Try the *enchiladas en salsa verde*, *quesadillas de huitlacoche* (corn grain) or classic *nachos* with guacamole. If you're lucky, dinner is topped off with a shot of tequila on the house. Reservations recommended. *Open Tues 8pm–midnight, Wed–Sun 1.30–4 and 8–midnight.*

Terraza 'El Ventorillo', C/de Bailén 14, **t** 913 66 35 70; **M** Opera. One of the most traditional *terrazas*, with good food and tapas to go with the lovely views over the cathedral and Parque de Atenas. *Open Sun–Thurs 11am–2am, Fri and Sat 11am–2.30am.*

El Tocororo, C/del Prado 3, **t** 913 69 40 00; **M** Sevilla. Here you can munch on tasty *tostones* (fried plantains), *ceviche*, *ropa vieja* (meat strips in seasoning) or chicken in *mole* sauce and other classic Cuban dishes. The surroundings are bright and friendly, with South American art on the walls and plants dangling here and there. The weekday *menú* is only €10, but the extensive à la carte menu is hard to resist. *Open Tues–Sun 1.30–4 and 8.30–midnight.*

Inexpensive

Círculo de Bellas Artes, C/del Marqués de Casa Riera 2, **t** 915 21 69 42; **M** Banco de España. Who would have guessed that in one of Madrid's grandest buildings, in a giant chandeliered salon looking out onto the confluence of the great thoroughfares of the Gran Vía and Alcalá, you could eat a quite excellent midday meal for only around €8.50? A little-known secret, and the food isn't half bad: things such as *bacalao con pisto* (cod with mixed vegetables in tomato sauce), duck carpaccio, and pork brochettes in sweet and sour sauce make it interesting. À la carte is pricier, but the site makes it worthwhile. *Open daily 1.30–4pm.*

Doner Kebap Istanbul, C/de Valencia 9, **t** 914 67 59 09; **M** Lavapiés. Turkish delights abound in this spic-and-span kebab house, and filling, tasty falafels can be had for €2–2.50. Plenty of vegetarian platters are available, but beware: the *haloumi* (bread with cyprus cheese, tomato, lettuce and savoury sauce folded in) is especially addictive. *Open Tues–Thurs 1–5 and 7–1, Fri 1–5 and 7–3, Sat 1pm–3am, Sun 1pm–1am.*

Falafel, C/de Valarde 8, **t** 914 48 55 20; **M** Tribunal. You could do worse than try the best falafel and kebab in the capital, along with Mediterranean salads and side dishes, all served by expat Israeli Giora Gilead. *Open Mon–Thurs 12.30–4 and 8–midnight, Fri and Sat 12.30–4 and 8–2, Sun 8pm–midnight.*

Fausto el Paladar, C/del Aguila 1, **t** 913 64 56 40; **M** La Latina. This casual, friendly Cuban enclave on the fringes of La Latina is a great place to sip a *mojito* and dig into a plate of *arroz a la cubana*. Weekend nights, the walls shake with live music. *Open Mon–Thurs 12.30–5 and 8.30–11, Fri and Sat 12.30–5 and 8.30–1, Sun 12.30–midnight.*

Ketutín, C/de Ricardo Ortiz 47, **t** 913 56 91 24; **M** El Carmen. Just across the M30 ring road from the bullring at Ventas, Ketutín is very much a neighbourhood restaurant. Home cooking at its best, with the emphasis on roast meats, soups and other traditional Castilian dishes. The lunchtime menu, at €9, is unbeatable. *Open Tues–Sat 1.30–4 and 9–midnight, Sun 9pm–midnight.*

Pizzeria Cervantes, C/del León 8, **t** 914 20 18 98; **M** Antón Martín. Tucked away on a cobbled street not far from the Prado, this centuries-old taberna was converted into a lively neighbourhood crêperie by a friendly bunch of Argentinian exiles. Excellent pastas and salads (loads of veggie options) plus an economical and filling *menú del día. Open Mon–Fri 11am–1am, Sat and Sun noon–2am.*

La Vega, C/de Ventura de la Vega 13, **t** 914 29 08 07; **M** Sevilla. Dating back to 1950, this has long been a favourite with students and struggling artist-types, drawn by the generous portions of home cooking. Thursday is *cocido* and not to be missed.

El Viajero, Pza de la Cebada 11, **t** 913 66 90 64; **M** La Latina. A rare rooftop dining terrace serving delicious pasta (the pumpkin ravioli in light cheesy sauce is exquisite), plus some truly succulent grilled meats. *Open Tues–Thurs 1pm–12.30am, Fri and Sat 1pm–1am, Sun 1–7pm.*

Viuda de Vacas, C/de la Cava Alta 23, **t** 913 66 58 47; **M** La Latina. This is the third generation of the Canovas family keeping Castilian cooking alive. Something of a mecca for the unpretentious foody – the restaurant has engendered many of the wine bars and restaurants which now populate this increasingly trendy area. *Open Mon–Wed, Fri and Sat 1.30–4.30 and 9–midnight, Sun 1.30–4.30pm.*

Vegetarian Restaurants

Madrid used to be a veggie's nightmare, but things have changed and the capital now boasts a wide selection of restaurants; many are excellent value. Try one of the following:

Al Natural, C/de Zorrilla 11, **t** 913 69 47 09; **M** Banco de España (*moderate*). A contradiction in terms, this is a vegetarian restaurant that serves meat dishes and – horrors! – permits smoking, but the stroganoff mushrooms, barley soup and *judías verdes con piñones* (green beans with pignoli nuts) are good enough to make up for it. There is something to satisfy anyone, from carrot purée to chicken in hazelnut sauce, and yummy pizzas. The weekday three-course *menú* is €10. *Open Mon–Sat 1–4 and 9–midnight, Sun 1–4pm.*

La Biotika, C/del Amor de Dios 3, **t** 914 29 07 80; **M** Antón Martín (*inexpensive*). Tucked away between Atocha and Huertas for over 20 years, this plant-filled wholefoods eatery has a tasty and filling *menú* for €6.60 (with vegan options), plus a shop with things like veggie croquetas and scrumptious carrot cake for takeaway. *Open daily 1.30–4.30 and 8–11.30; shop open Mon–Sat 10am–11pm, Sun and hols 1.30–4.30 and 8–11.30.*

Chez Pomme, C/de Pelayo 4, **t** 915 32 16 46; **M** Chueca or Gran Vía (*inexpensive*). A mod vegetarian spot in the heart of Chueca, with brightly painted lacquered tables and Japanese-style lanterns. The *menú del día* is a mere €6.60 and includes a salad or purée of the day, plus an inventive main meal – spinach pie, rice and beans or vegetarian *empanada. Open daily 1.30–5 and 8.30–12.30.*

El Estragón Vegetariano, Pza de la Paja 10, **t** 913 65 89 82; **M** La Latina (*moderate*). Following the square's restoration, the Pza de la Paja has seen a mushrooming of new bars and restaurants. El Estragón has some 20-odd tables distributed throughout different levels. The clientele is young, often expat, and the mood relaxed. *Open daily 1–4.30 and 8–midnight.*

La Sastrería, C/de Hortaleza 74, **t** 915 32 77 71; **M** Alonso Martínez, Chueca or Gran Vía (*inexpensive*). Dressmakers' dummies, piles of ironed shirts and an old sewing machine complete the 'tailor' theme to which this owes its name. It serves Spanish food with a creative twist, plus veggie options. At night, hot sandwiches, treats such as Black Forest gateau and tiramisu, coffees and drinks are available. Breakfasts are also served. *Open Mon–Fri 10am–2am, Sat and Sun 11am–3am.*

Tapas

Almacén de Vinos, C/de Calatrava 21, **t** 913 65 36 46; **M** La Latina. One of the most atmospheric old-fashioned bars in La Latina, with traditional tiles and equally authentic tapas, serving excellent seafood and crisp, chilled *vermut. Open daily 11–2.30 and 7–10.*

Bacco, C/de Manuel Fernández y Gonzáles 17, **t** 914 20 21 75; **M** Sevilla. With a slightly more *modernillo* décor (kooky spiral lamps) than most of the other traditional tapas bars in Huertas, Bacco serves a variety of excellent, creative tapas similar to what you find in the Basque country. Treats such as fresh tuna with *pimientos*, classic crab salad and mozzarella-and-tomato tapas come in canapé size as *pinchos*. Also on offer are *raciones* such as goat's cheese with zucchini and classic tortillas. *Open daily 7pm–2am.*

Bodegas El Mano, C/de Jesús del Valle 1, **t** 915 31 36 85; **M** Noviciado. A homey but cavernous wine bar in one of Madrid's older, lesser-known neighbourhoods. Aside from the usual tapas (*croquetas*, *chorizo* in cider, etc.), there is an excellent selection of *pinchos*, such as pungent *queso de cabrales* and the soft-but-not-creamy *torta del casar*, plus delicate *mojama* (cured tuna). *Open Mon 8pm–1am, Tues–Sat 1–4 and 8–1, Sun 1–4pm.*

Las Bravas, C/de Alvarez Gato 3, **t** 915 32 26 20; **M** Sol. The name comes from the hot sauces poured liberally on their deep-fried potato chunks. Excellent tortillas, as well as *pulpo* and *oreja* (pig's ear). The ideal stop-off point to take on tasty carbohydrates as you make your way through the bars dotted around the Santa Ana area. Nothing less than an institution. *Open daily 11–3.30 and 7.30–2.*

La Carpanta, C/del Almendro 22, **t** 913 66 57 83; **M** La Latina. Located at the epicentre of the weekend wine-and-*pinchos* scene, just off the Pza de los Humilladeros, this young, lively bar offers a truly dizzying selection of wines (over 50, all excellent) and a wide variety of *pinchos* and tapas (beef carpaccio, goat's cheese salad, wild mushrooms and *pimientos*, burgos cheese with anchovy garnish) to pick at, either on the wooden tables and stools inside, or else outside, where the crowds spill out on summer weekends. Real meals can be had in the restaurant in back, though space is tight. *Open Sun–Wed 11am–1.30am, Thurs 11am–2am, Fri and Sat 11am–3am.*

Casa Montes, C/de Lavapiés 40, **t** 915 27 00 64; **M** Lavapiés. Easily overlooked, but one of the longest-running bars in Lavapiés. Genial Don Cesar pours some excellent wines, and serves fine tapas such as *mojama* (cured tuna fish), anchovy canapés and delicate cured ham. *Open Tues–Sat noon–4 and 8–midnight, Sun noon–4pm.*

Casa Paco, Pza de Puerta Cerrada 11, **t** 913 66 31 66; **M** Sol or La Latina. One of Madrid's classic *tabernas*, intimate and covered with colourful tiles, a good stop for just a tapa or a dinner built around excellent grilled meats. Around €27–30 for the full whack. *Open Mon–Sat 1.30–4 and 8.30–midnight.*

La Casa de las Torrijas, C/de la Paz 4, **t** 915 32 14 73; **M** Sol. An atmospheric blast from the past, serving a fine selection of wines and a rarity – *torrijas*, sweet bread fritters, a bit like French toast but soaked in wine and spices and dipped in sugar before they're fried. Savoury tapas, too. *Open Mon–Sat 10–4 and 6–10.30; closed Aug.*

Cervecería Cervantes, Pza de Jesús 7, **t** 914 29 60 93; **M** Banco de España or Antón Martín. Beer steins hanging on the walls give the place a vaguely German feel, despite its eminently Spanish name and the line-up of ham legs behind the counter. There are splendid tapas, which include dainty *tostadas* of grilled mushrooms, salmon or smoked cod, the classic *pulpo gallego* and smooth, melty pâté platters. *Open Mon–Sat noon–1am, Sun noon–4pm.*

Desahogo Taberna, Pza San Miguel, **t** 915 59 08 97; **M** Opera. Some of the most imaginative tapas in the city and a very decent selection of wines to accompany them. *Open Tues–Sat noon–4 and 8.30–midnight.*

Ebla Bar, C/de Martín de los Heros 7, **t** 915 42 78 84; **M** Pza de España. Across the street from Madrid's artsier movie houses, this is a lively, friendly, though slightly cramped spot (especially when the movies let out) serving scrumptious Lebanese tapas like felafels, taboule salad and a variety of kebabs, along with a smattering of Spanish offerings. *Open daily 3pm–1.30am.*

La Moderna, Pza de Santa Ana, **t** 914 20 15 82; **M** Sevilla. Probably the best of the six or so tapas bars which line the south side of the Pza Santa Ana. Hemingway did not drink here, which means the proprietors make an effort to provide a good range of wines and imaginative tapas. *Open Sun–Thurs 11am–12.15am, Fri and Sat 11am–1.15am.*

Taberna de Antonio Sánchez, C/de Mesón de Paredes 13, **t** 915 39 78 26; **M** Tirso de Molina. One of the landmarks of Lavapiés, a friendly *taberna* founded by a bullfighter in 1830 and full of taurine memorabilia. Excellent tapas or full meals. *Open Mon–Sat noon–4 and 8–midnight, Sun noon–4pm.*

Taberna los Austrias, C/del Nuncio 17; **M** La Latina. So Spanish it hurts: dark exposed wooden beams, brick walls, tables fashioned from wooden wine barrels, and the food doesn't disappoint: grilled green peppers with cod, shrimp in Béarnaise sauce, wild mushroom canapés, baked Brie, and on and on. *Open Sun–Thurs noon–4 and 8–midnight, Fri and Sat noon–4 and 8–12.30.*

Taberna del Avapiés, C/de Lavapiés 5, **t** 915 39 26 56; **M** Antón Martín. Located in an old ecclesiastic gaol in Madrid's former Jewish neighbourhood. The staff are unusually helpful – they might even let you do some tasting before you select your drink Tapas are a cut above the usual: well-selected cheeses, and lovingly prepared fresh salads. *Open Mon–Thurs 7.30pm–1am, Fri 7.30pm–2am, Sat 1–3.30 and 7.30–2, Sun 1–4.30pm.*

Taberna los Conspiradores, C/de Moratín 33, **t** 913 69 47 41; **M** Antón Martín. A curious tiny neighbourhood bar specializing in tapas from the region of Extremadura – delicious cured and soft cheeses and hams, plus wines from all over Spain. Fun and airy despite its microscopic size. *Open Tues–Thurs 7pm–1am, Fri 7pm–2.30am, Sat and Sun 1–4 and 7–3.*

Taberna Dolores, Pza de Jesús 4, **t** 914 29 22 43; **M** Antón Martín. Tucked away behind the Palace Hotel, this relic from the 1930s owes its fame to the sublime canapés it serves, alongside a beautifully pulled *caña*. *Open Sun–Thurs 11am–1am, Fri and Sat 11am–2am.*

Tienda de Vinos, Corner of C/de Barbieri and C/de Augusto Figueroa; **M** Chueca. Not a wine store but a renowned scruffy restaurant beloved for selling every dish at the same low price – hence its more popular name, La Comunista. *Open Mon–Sat 1–4.30 and 9.30–midnight, Sun 9.30pm–midnight.*

La Torre de Oro, Pza Mayor 26, **t** 913 66 50 16; **M** Sol. A noisy, hectic Andalucían tapas bar with delicious *pescaditos fritos* (whitebait) and other delights, served by cheerful waiters. *Open daily 10am–1am.*

Cafés

Acuarela Café, C/de Gravina 10, **t** 915 22 21 43; **M** Chueca. Antique chic and a lively atmosphere at this trendy gay café. Wine, caipirinhas and aromatic teas are on offer. It's especially convienent for shoe-shoppers as it is located right near the discount stores on Augusto Figueroa. *Open daily 3pm–3am.*

Café Barbieri, C/del Ave María 45, **t** 915 27 36 58; **M** Lavapiés. A beautiful old café, yellowed with age, with huge, Baroque wall mirrors and a civilized atmosphere. Soothing by day (symphonies play in the background and there are speciality coffees and infusions to enjoy over a paper) and quietly sophisticated and sociable by night, this also offers occasional film-screenings. *Open Sun–Thurs 3pm–2am, Fri–Sat 3pm–3am.*

Casa Braulio, Av. de los Toreros 43, **t** 913 56 11 82; **M** Ventas. A must if you fancy a quick tapa before or after attending the bullfights at Ventas, which is just round the corner. Braulio has been packing them in for 60 years, lured by the home-cooking. They'll also prepare snacks to take into the ring. *Open Mon–Fri 8am–11pm, Sun noon–11pm.*

Café Comercial, Glorieta de Bilbao 7, **t** 915 21 56 55; **M** Bilbao. North of the Museo Municipal, and an institution among the locals and intelligentsia. It has cushy old leather seats for prolonged sitting and reading. *Open Sun–Thurs 7.30am–1am, Fri and Sat 7.30am–2am.*

Café Figueroa, C/de Augusto Figueroa 17, **t** 915 21 16 73; **M** Chueca. Chueca's gay crowd favour this chatty, relaxed, late 19th-century café. *Open Sun–Thurs 2.30pm–midnight, Fri and Sat 2.30pm–2.30am.*

Café Manuela, C/de San Vicente Ferrer 29, **t** 915 21 70 73; **M** Tribunal. An Art Deco café with story-telling nights and poetry recitals, and excellent drinks. *Open daily 3.30pm–3am.*

Café del Nuncio, C/de Segovia 9, **t** 913 66 08 53; **M** La Latina. A classic Madrid haunt, which spreads out onto the little plaza outside in summertime. Their yummy milkshakes and sweet almond *horchata* are great antidotes to the dehydrating effects of summer sightseeing. *Open daily 12.30pm–2.30am.*

Café Ruiz, C/de Ruiz 11, **t** 914 46 12 32; **M** San Bernardo or Bilbao. A legend among *madrileños*. The dark wood, mirrors and corduroy-upholstered banquettes are unmistakeably Spanish, as are the smoke fumes in the rooms further back. Peaceful by day, crowded and noisy at night. All the typical coffees, plus some intriguing delicacies such as the *tierra del fuego*: chocolate and vanilla ice cream with whisky, hazelnuts and hot chocolate. *Open Sun–Thurs 2pm–2am, Fri and Sat 2pm–3am.*

Embassy, Pso de la Castellana 12, **t** 915 76 48 77; **M** Serrano or Colón. Since 1931 this has been the fashionable tearoom in this diplomatic corner of Madrid, with plenty of atmosphere to go with its little sandwiches or cocktails. *Open Mon–Sat 9.30am–1am, Sun 9.30am–11pm.*

El Jardín Secreto, C/del Conde Duque 2, **t** 915 41 80 23; **M** Pza de España. An Asian paradise with rattan furniture from Indonesia, hanging lamps from the Philippines, and teas from Ceylon, India and China. Plus home-made cakes and ice creams. *Open Tues–Sun 5–11pm.*

Mallorca, C/de Serrano 6, **t** 915 77 18 59; **M** Retiro. Madrid's pastry shop and gourmet food store extraordinaire, with excellent coffee, fresh squeezed orange juice, and adorable mini sandwiches (salmon and cream cheese, cured ham), quiches, vegetable tarts and croissants at the little bar. An excellent spot for checking out the local shopaholics taking a breather in between Armani and Adolfo Domínguez. *Open daily 9.30am–10pm.*

Mendocino Café, C/de Limón 11, **t** 915 42 91 30; **M** Noviciado or Pza de España. A San Francisco café magically transported to a cobbled Spanish lane: oil paintings on the walls (for purchase), weekly poetry readings, easygoing staff and even a Sunday brunch with pancakes and maple syrup or scrambled eggs. Exhibitions and other cultural activities make this a real neighbourhood hangout for the local artsy types. *Open Mon–Thurs 9am–midnight, Fri 9am–2am, Sat noon–2am, Sun noon–midnight.*

Café de la Esquina, C/Príncipe del Anglona 1, **t** 913 66 91 13; **M** La Latina. Just up from C/de Segovia, this little café is a dream in the summertime, with outdoor tables where you can enjoy a devilish chocolate cake or another of their scrumptious sweets and a cappuccino or herbal tea. The speciality coffee is Café de la Esquina, a sweet, strong blend of tequila, curaçao, cream and coffee. Inside, there's soft lighting and softer red velvet chairs. *Open Mon–Sat 6pm–2.30am, Sun 6pm–2am.*

El Riojano, C/Mayor 10, **t** 913 66 44 82; **M** Sol. Just a few steps from Sol, this charming shrine to cream puffery is nothing less than the purveyor of fine traditional pastries to Spain's senators ever since 1885. *Open daily 10–2 and 5–9.*

Ritz, Pza de la Lealtad 5, **t** 915 21 28 57; **M** Banco de España. Pamper yourself at the city's plushest outdoor tearooms in the gardens of the Ritz. *Open for breakfast 7.30–11am, for tea 4.30–7.30pm, for drinks and snacks 7.30am–1am.*

Nightlife

In Madrid there is one bar for every 96 inhabitants, so there's always somewhere to go, from beloved ancient holes in the wall which haven't been decorated since the time of Alfonso XII, to chic boulevard cafés where the *madrileñan jeunesse dorée* discuss movies and modern art.

First-time visitors to Madrid are often surprised at just how late *madrileños* stay out. In general, people go to *tascas* or *tabernas* after work, and then move on to *bars de copas* (bars that only serve drinks) as the night wears on. Discos don't even begin to get started until 1am, which puts the 11pm dinnertime into a more logical perspective.

Most bars still play an eclectic mix of music, and few apply any sort of dress code – except for in the Salamanca area. The rule generally is to settle on an area, and then wander from bar to bar until the wee hours, ending the revelries with a hot chocolate before collapsing into bed. You'll find one close to your hotel in which to happily send an afternoon down the drain, but here are some of the most interesting and famous:

El Almendro, C/del Almendro 13; **M** La Latina. A neighbourhood legend, with old-fashioned décor and *castizo* atmosphere, although the crowd is distinctly young and cute. *Open Wed–Sun 1–4 and 7–midnight.*

El Anciano Rey de los Vinos, C/de Bailén 19; **M** Opera. With *vermut* on tap and a dizzying array of wines. An old-world atmosphere (if slightly overlit) on a shady corner across the street from the Palacio Real. *Open Thurs–Tues 10–3 and 5.30–11.*

Bar El Plaza, C/de Martín de los Heros 3; **M** Pza de España. A stark, modern bar with shiny wood floors, undulating easy chairs and a prismatic tiled bar. It's full of young professionals enjoying post-movie drinks, and if you're lucky you might catch live music or a theatre piece, which occasionally materialize (free of charge) on weekend nights. Drinks €4–6. *Open Wed–Sun 7.30pm–3.30am.*

Begin the Beguine, C/de Moratín 27; **M** Antón Martín. With a mind-boggling array of old wine and liquor bottles, this is a curious spot and perfect if you don't have much to say to your companion. Just read the walls! Wine €1–2, mixed drinks €4–5. *Open Sun–Thurs 8pm–12.30am, Fri and Sat 8pm–3.30am.*

La Boca del Lobo, C/de Echegaray 11; **M** Sevilla. An old-time cellar bar playing old-time music from the 30s up to the 60s, attracting a nice mixed crowd. *Open daily 11pm–5am.*

Café Barbieri, C/del Ave María 45; **M** Lavapiés. Virtually unchanged since 1902, and as popular as ever with both elderly *castizos* and newer arrivals. *Open Sun–Thurs 3pm–2am, Fri and Sat 3pm–3am.*

Café Belén, C/de Belén 5; **M** Chueca or Alonso Martínez. A cosy, intimate bar on a tranquil street at the northern end of Chueca. In the summer, the shutters are open and both the music and the mood are relaxing and welcoming. *Open daily 3.30pm–2.30am.*

Café Madrid, C/de Belén 7; **M** Chueca or Alonso Martínez. A lovingly decorated Art Nouveau bar with frescoes on the ceiling. A jazz theme, both in the music and the retro drinks. Alcoholic coffees are a speciality, but the best thing is the vibe – neither the music nor the booze ever pound too hard. *Open daily 6pm–3am; closed Sun in July and Aug.*

La Candela, C/del Olmo 2; **M** Antón Martín. A bare-bones bar with *trompe l'œil* wall designs, this is the place to check out Madrid's real *gitano* scene, complete with occasional impromptu flamenco if you're lucky. Things don't get going until 1am at the earliest. *Open daily 10.30pm–5.30am.*

Centro Cubano, C/de Claudio Coello 41; **M** Serrano. Serves the best *mojitos* and daiquiris in town. Not for lovers of Fidel, though. *Open daily 2–4.30 and 9–midnight.*

Cervecería Alemana, Pza Santa Ana 6; **M** Sevilla. A perfect German-Spanish beer-hall and one of Hemingway's many old watering holes. It has a fascinating display of photos and other taurine memorabilia. Still a local favourite, despite being on the tourist trail. *Open Sun, Mon, Wed and Thurs 10.30am–12.30am, Fri and Sat 10.30am–2am.*

Champañería-Librería María Pandora, Pza Gabriel Miró 1 (Las Vistillas), *www.mariapandora.com*; **M** Opera or La Latina. In the leafy area of Las Vistillas, this out-of-the-way bar is worth the hike for the atmosphere: a shelf full of old books, intimate tables with craggy candles, and *cava* cocktails as well as fruity nonalcoholic drinks (€4.50–5). A nice ending for a romantic evening, especially as it's by the park. *Open Mon–Thurs 7pm–2am, Fri and Sat 7pm–3am, Sun 4pm–2am.*

Colorado Express, C/de Martín de los Heros 4; **M** Pza de España. One of the few places in Madrid where you can get Budweiser by the bottle and snarf down excellent Mexican and South American bar snacks. Packed but good. *Open daily 6pm–2am.*

Delic, Costanilla de San Andrés 14; **M** La Latina. Frequented by the so-cool-it-hurts set and their wannabes. The crowd is as entertaining as the décor, which seems airlifted from a lounge somewhere deep in New York's Lower East Side. Insouciant-verging-on-arrogant waiting-staff – even more like the Big Apple! There's a full list of mixed drinks, coffees and the house infusion: mint tea just like they make it in Marrakesh. With outside tables on the hip Pza de la Paja, this is unmissable, even if only for the rich sociological observations to be made. *Open Sun, Tues and Wed 11am–midnight, Thurs–Sat 11am–2am.*

Flamingo, C/de la Palma 11; **M** Tribunal. A temple to Spanish hard rock, this place alternates between disco bar and live music venue, but it is undoubtedly the cornerstone of the Malasaña music scene, a stone's throw from Louie Louie and other classic spots in the neighbourhood. *Open daily 9pm–dawn.*

Los Gabrieles, C/de Echegaray 17; **M** Sevilla. A handsome, cool, ancient (19th-century) bar, lined with decorative tiles, and full of loud music and lively company. Note that prices here double after 5pm. *Open daily 2pm–2am.*

Los Gatos, C/de Jesús 2; **M** Antón Martín. A veteran bar with a relaxed local ambience and a loyal following among the torero crowd. *Open daily 11am–2am.*

El Limbo, C/de Bailén 39; **M** Opera or La Latina. A trip back to the 1970s, with kitschy décor and an eclectic, alternative scene offering cabaret, art exhibitions and anything else that takes their fancy. Good trance music at the weekend. *Open Mon–Thurs 10pm–4am, Fri and Sat 10pm–5am.*

Louie Louie, C/de la Palma 43; **M** Tribunal. An under-30s crowd is drawn to this famous bar, where you'll have to knock to get in. The walls are covered with every imaginable bit of music paraphernalia, and the music played is classic 1970s rock. Lots of motorcycle helmets here.

El Parnaso, C/de Moratín 25; **M** Antón Martín. A cavelike den filled with bronze sculptures of water nymphs, turn-of-the-century oil lamps and other vaguely Art Nouveau trinkets and decorations. Brazilian drinks are a speciality, especially the *caipirinhas* (around €4–5), and in summer the coconut, chocolate and almond *batidos* (milkshakes) are a welcome relief. *Open Sun–Thurs 8pm–12.30am, Fri and Sat 8pm–3.30am.*

Star's Café, C/del Marqués de Valdeiglesias 5; **M** Banco de España. A loungey spot during the day, but this fun, funky, gay-friendly spot comes alive at night, with techno and house music blaring from the DJ station mounted on the wall. All sorts of entertainment is on offer all week long, from art exhibitions to fashion shows. Weekend nights are total dance fever in the downstairs disco den. *Open Mon–Wed 9am–2am, Thurs 9am–3am, Fri and Sat 9am–4am.*

La Taberna de los Cien Vinos, C/del Nuncio 17; **M** La Latina. A great alternative to the equally legendary Taberna los Austrias next door, the Cien Vinos has plenty of wine and a carefully culled list of *raciones* and salads served in a quiet, calm, more elegant atmosphere than its next-door neighbour. *Open Tues–Sun 1–3.45 and 8–1.*

Taberna Maceira, C/de Jesús 7; **M** Antón Martín. A tiny bit of Galicia in Madrid, but casual and young, with brick walls and a cosy, bubbling atmosphere. Arrive early if you want to try fresh *berberechos* or other tasty tapas. *Open Tues–Sun 1–5 and 8–1.30.*

Teatríz, C/de Hermosilla 15; **M** Serrano. Now something of an institution, Teatríz's 80s designer interior still draws the Salamanca smart set. Restaurant, disco and bar all in a former theatre. *Open daily 1.30–4 and 9–1.*

El 21, C/de Toledo 21, **t** 913 66 28 59; **M** Sol or Tirso de Molina. An old city institution, with a battered marble bar and peeling bullfighting posters. During the day, the place is filled with old men nursing their drinks, but it has become a popular hangout for the younger set in the evenings and at weekends. *Open daily 11–3 and 7–11; closed Aug.*

La Vieja Estación, Av. Ciudad de Barcelona; **M** Atocha. The city's largest and wildest multi-*terraza* is set in a big chasm next to Estación de Atocha. With bars, dance floors and an Argentine restaurant spread over several layers, this is one of the best places in the city for dancing out beneath the stars. *Open May–Sept daily till 6am.*

Villa Rosa, Pza de Santa Ana 15; **M** Sevilla. A classic stop on any nocturnal Madrid itinerary, the Villa Rosa has seen everyone from Federico García Lorca to Pedro Almodóvar pass through its doors, and was featured in Almodóvar's *High Heels*. With a varied mix of entertainment, it always has something fun to offer. *Open Mon–Sat 11pm–5am.*

Viva Madrid, C/de Manuel Fernández y González 7; **M** Sevilla or Antón Martín. One of Lorca's old haunts, which retains its gorgeous tiled façade; inside there are more coloured tiles, carved wood, and caryatids, plus the obligatory free-flowing beer taps. *Open daily 1pm–2am.*

Clubs

If you're only here for a short stay and plan to do culture by day and clubbing by night, you'll need to fit a *siesta* in – things don't really start happening here until at least midnight. Many of the bars listed above also play music and have dance floors.

Arena, C/de la Princesa 11, **t** 915 59 19 43; **M** Pza de España. When it first opened this attracted gossip-magazine celebrities but has since toned down the scene, welcoming all to its nights of techno and occasional world music. *Open daily midnight–5am.*

Flamingo, C/de Mesonero Romanos 13, **t** 915 31 48 27; **M** Gran Vía. On Thursdays it's called 'Cream' and plays house, 'Ocho y Medio' Fridays are for techno pop, and Sunday nights are for the famous Shangay Tea Dance, the drag-and-anything-goes party organized by the local gay freebie magazine. *Open Wed–Sun midnight–5am.*

Joy Eslava, C/del Arenal 11, **t** 913 66 37 33; **M** Opera or Sol. The best-known and best-loved disco, with pounding music and scantily clad go-go dancers of both sexes. It attracts a varied fauna, from businessmen to drag queens. *Open daily 11.30pm–6am; adm Mon–Fri €12, Sat and Sun €15.*

Kapital, C/de Atocha 125, **t** 914 20 29 06; **M** Atocha. With seven floors of fun, including cinema, karaoke bar and chill-out areas, the idea is you don't need to go anywhere else. At this price, you'd better be sure. The rooftop bar has fantastic views. *Open Thurs–Sat midnight–6am; adm €12.*

Kathmandú, C/de Señores de Luzón 3, **t** 916 34 42 01; **M** Sol or Opera. This almost 20-year-old disco (drinks not cheap) just changes with the times. 'Metronome' Thursdays are electronica and trip hop, 'Salute!' Fridays are for funk, soul, jazz, Brazilian and disco, and Saturdays are called 'Kaleidoscope' – pure dance heaven. *Open Thurs midnight–5am, Fri and Sat midnight–6am; adm€5.*

Palacio de Gaviria, C/del Arenal 9, **t** 915 26 60 69; **M** Sol or Opera. In a former palace, the labyrinthine and ornate interior offers a range of ambiences, drawing a mixed crowd. *Open daily 10.30pm–dawn; adm €7.20.*

Sala Público, Pza de los Mostenses 11 (corner of Gran Vía 68), **t** 915 47 57 11, *www.coppelia-madrid.com*; **M** Pza de España. A relative newcomer, this two-room basement club has techno-house in one room and more ambient music in the other. Thursdays are the dark-horse night, offering a mixed bag of drum 'n' bass, hip-hop and anything else that comes to the DJ's mind. *Open Thurs–Sun midnight–6am.*

Soho, C/de Jorge Juan 50, **t** 915 77 89 73; **M** Príncipe de Vergara. An attempt to create a New York atmosphere in snooty Salamanca. Good funk and soul on the second floor. *Open Mon–Sat 8pm–2.30am.*

El Sol, C/de los Jardines 3, **t** 915 32 64 90; **M** Gran Vía. Endearingly scruffy, Sol occasionally puts on live gigs, but most of the time offers late-night funk, '70s and '80s to an eclectic crowd more interested in having a good time than in being seen. *Open Tues–Sat 11.30pm–6am.*

Entertainment

For listings information, the *Guía del Ocio* is the most complete guide, covering all aspects of entertainment and nightlife. The two main newspapers, *El País* and *El Mundo*, also have complete daily cinema listings. For foreign-language films look under the '*versión original*', '*subtitulada*' or 'VOS' heading.

Cinema

M Callao (Gran Vía) is the mecca for big-screen Hollywood-import fans, with the occasional local production drawing in the Spanish crowds. The following occasionally show films in English with Spanish subtitles.

Alphaville, C/de Martín de los Heros 14, **t** 915 59 38 36; **M** Pza de España.

Filmoteca, Cine Doré, C/de Santa Isabel 3, **t** 915 49 60 11; **M** Antón Martín.

Princesa, C/de la Princesa 3, **t** 915 41 41 00, *www.cinentradas.com*; **M** Pza de España.

Renoir Plaza de España, C/de Martín de los Heros 12, **t** 915 41 41 00; **M** Pza de España.

Live Music

Bar Café Clamores, C/de Albuquerque 14, **t** 914 45 79 38, *www.salaclamores.com*; **M** Bilbao. A daily dose of jazz starts promptly at 10pm. Smoky but fun, and with lots of twists – tango-inspired jazz, Cuban jazz and other variants have all passed through its doors. *Open Sun–Thurs 6.30pm–3am, Fri and Sat 6pm–5am.*

Café Central, Pza del Ángel 10, **t** 913 69 41 43; **M** Sol or Antón Martín. Voted among the world's best jazz venues by Wire magazine, It attracts world-class names to a genuine café setting. *Open Mon–Thurs noon–1am, Fri and Sat noon–3am; adm often €6–12.*

Café del Mercado, Puerta de Toledo, **t** 913 65 87 39; **M** Puerta de Toledo. Salsa took Madrid by storm in the early '90s. The fever has cooled off somewhat but, if you're looking to dance the night away, try this place. It's in the by now almost abandoned market at the end of C/de Toledo, but still attracts top-class bands. *Open daily 10pm–4am.*

Downtown, C/de Covarrubias 31; **M** Alonso Martínez. A must for blues fans. *Open daily 10.30pm–3am.*

Siroco, C/de San Dimas 3, **t** 915 93 30 70; **M** San Bernardo. A small temple to live music: hip-hop, acid jazz, and everything electronic. *Open Wed and Thurs 9.30pm–4am, Fri and Sat 11pm–5am.*

Suristán, C/de la Cruz 7, **t** 915 32 39 09, *www.suristan.com*; **M** Sol. The only club dedicated to world music. Spacious and relaxed, with a table area. *Open daily 10pm–5.30am.*

La Taberna Encantada, C/de Salitre 2, **t** 915 28 52 38; **M** Antón Martín. A nerve centre of the Latina-Lavapiés bar scene, this is alternative heaven: live folk, rock and world music.

Vapor Blues, C/de Doctor Esquerdó 52, **t** 915 04 21 50; **M** Sainz de Baranda. Live music Thursday through Saturday, for the over-25 blues/rock/soul set. An excellent place for good beer (many imported brands) and good music. *Open daily 11pm–4am.*

Theatre, Opera and Dance

Madrid does not have the thespian image of its rival Barcelona; nevertheless, a wide range of theatre is on offer. It fares better with dance, boasting the Ballet de la Comunidad de Madrid; there are also two national dance companies, the Compañía Nacional de Danza and the Ballet Nacional de España. As for classical music, the reopening of the Teatro Real has done much to reinvigorate the scene. Keep an eye open for posters and check the listings; some of the principle venues are listed below:

Auditorio Nacional de Música, C/del Príncipe de Vergara 146, **t** 913 37 01 40, **t** 913 37 01 39, *www.auditorionacional.mcu.es*; **M** Cruz del Rayo or Prosperidad. Home to the Orquesta Nacional de España, the *auditorio* also stages some jazz events. The concert season is Oct–June, with guest orchestras. Getting tickets can be difficult, but last-minute tickets can often be had.

Círculo de Bellas Artes, C/del Marqués de Casa Riera 2, **t** 902 42 24 42; **M** Banco de España or Sevilla. Guitar recitals, European soloists and Sufi music are just a few examples of the wildly varied music schedule.

Sala Triángulo, C/de Zurita 20, **t** 915 30 69 91; **M** Antón Martín. Perhaps the most consistently creative fringe theatre in Madrid.

Teatro Albeniz, C/de la Paz 11, **t** 915 31 83 11; **M** Sol. The Albeniz is the centrepiece of the autumn festival, and puts on a wide range of dance and music, showcasing visiting international companies, as well as domestic contemporary productions.

Teatro Calderón, C/de Atocha 18, **t** 914 29 58 90; **M** Sol or Tirso de Molina. One of Madrid's classic dramatic theatres which often hosts revivals of flamenco and other traditional Spanish music genres.

Teatro de la Comedia, C/del Príncipe 14, **t** 915 21 49 31; **M** Sevilla or Sol. The home of the Compañía Nacional de Teatro Clásico (equivalent to the Royal Shakespeare Company). You can almost always see something by Tirso de Molina, Calderón de la Barca or Lope de Vega, and some lesser-known Golden Age playwrights, though the performances can be slightly dumbed-down.

Teatro de Madrid, Av. de la Ilustracíon, **t** 917 40 52 74; **M** Barrio del Pilar. Has a line-up of Spanish and international dance companies.

Teatro Real, Pza de Oriente, **t** 915 16 06 60; **M** Opera. There's a full schedule of first-run opera in this spectacularly refurbished opera house almost 150 years old, but now with state-of-the-art acoustics. It also stages *bel canto*, symphonic works and ballets. It is home to the Compañia Nacional de Danza.

Light opera fans will want to see a ***zarzuela***, Spain's answer to Gilbert and Sullivan. The season is from June to September, though the Teatro de la Zarzuela and the Auditorio Nacional stage some winter productions.

Centro Cultural de la Villa, Pza de Colón, **t** 915 75 60 80; **M** Colon or Serrano. Often offers a big *zarzuela* line-up in the summer.

Teatro de la Zarzuela, C/de los Jovellanos 4, **t** 915 24 54 00; **M** Banco de España or Sevilla. A magnificent, mid-19th-century miniature La Scala, this offers much more than its name suggests: everything from light opera to chamber music, dance and music theatre.

Flamenco

In Madrid, the most typical way to 'do' flamenco is to go to a ***tablao***, a dinner-theatre or cabaret experience that is often pricey and unavoidably filled with foreigners like you, but somehow that's all part of the deal.

Candela, C/del Olmo 2, **t** 914 67 33 82; **M** Antón Martín. A must if you want to mingle with figures from the flamenco world. Performances usually start at 11pm.

Casa Patas, C/de Cañizares 10, **t** 913 69 04 96; **M** Antón Martín. Attracts some of the best performers, with dance a regular feature. The bar-restaurant is separate from the performing area, and famous faces from the flamenco world are often seen there.

Peña Chaquetón, C/de Canarias 39, **t** 916 71 27 77; **M** Delicias. Those looking for flamenco in its purest form should head to one of the capital's oldest, and last, *peñas*. A world away from the *tablaos*, with an almost scholarly approach on the part of the aficionados who turn up to hear some of the finest singers and guitarists in the country.

Gay and Lesbian Madrid

The gay scene is out there in every way, shape and form, centred around the neighbourhood of Chueca. For information, contact:

Colectivo de Lesbianas, Gays, Transexuales y Bisexuales de Madrid (COGAM) and **Federación Estatal de Lesbianas y Gays** (FELG), C/de Fuencarral 37, general **t** 915 22 45 17, helpline **t** 915 23 00 70, **f** 915 24 02 00, *www.cogam.org*; **M** Gran Vía. Madrid's largest, most vocal gay organization, which publishes a monthly politically orientated magazine, *Entiendes?* and offers all sorts of facilities and services. *Open daily 5–11pm.*

The best-known magazines are *Shangay* and the *Shanguide*, the hilariously hip freebie and listings guide that is omnipresent in Chueca's bars, shops and cafés. *Zero* covers more current events, while *Gesto* tries to offer the most challenging, provocative content.

Eating Out

Café Acuarela, C/de Gravina 10, **t** 915 22 21 43; **M** Chueca. Antique chic and a lively atmosphere at this trendy gay café. Has a comfy mixture of candelabra, angelic cherubs and velvet cushions. It crams in a mixed clientele and is very relaxed, but can get packed. *Open Sun–Thurs 3pm–3am, Fri and Sat 3pm–4am.*

Gula Gula, Gran Via 1, **t** 915 22 87 64; **M** Gran Vía. Booking essential (*moderate*). One of Madrid's gay crossover successes. Drag queen waitresses, loud, this is a place to see and be seen. The food is good, with a set menu, or a salad bar. *Open Mon–Thurs 12.30–4 and 8–midnight, Fri and Sat 12.30–4 and 8–2, Sun 8pm–midnight.*

Momo, C/de Augusto Figueroa 41, **t** 915 32 71 62; **M** Chueca (*moderate*). Creative cuisine and adorable waiters to entertain you. *Open daily 1–4 and 9–midnight.*

Bars and Clubs

La Lupe, C/de Torrecilla del Leal 12; **M** Sevilla. Attracts gay men and women to its coffee bar by day. In the evening it's relaxed, with good music and distinctly uncamp. *Open daily 9pm–3am.*

Ohm, Pza de Callao 4; **M** Callao. A fun dance scene for people of all stripes – gay, lesbian, straight. *Open Fri and Sat midnight–6am.*

Rick's, C/de Clavel 6; **M** Gran Vía. An institution among the gay/lesbian dance crowd. Flimsy clothes (and pumped-up bodies) is the name of the game. *Open daily 11.30pm–dawn.*

Shangay Tea Dance, Gran Vía 37, **t** 915 31 48 27; **M** Gran Vía. Without a doubt the best tea dance in Madrid. Also plays great disco music and has shows. *Open Sun 9pm–2am.*

Soho, Pza de Chueca 6; **M** Chueca. The nerve-centre of the gay neighbourhood; and the outside tables are excellent for people-watching. *Open Tues–Sun 9pm–dawn.*

Strong Center, C/de Trujillos 7, **t** 915 31 48 27; **M** Opera or Sol. If you're looking to lose yourself, head for the legendary darkroom. It's very, very large. *Open daily midnight–dawn.*

Tábata, C/de Vergara 12, **t** 915 47 97 35; **M** Opera. Recently all the rage among the gay dance crowd, despite its inconveniently un-Chueca location. *Open Wed–Sat 11.30pm–dawn.*

XXX Café, Gran Vía 16, **t** 915 32 84 15; **M** Gran Vía. Frequented more by men than women, it is an obligatory stop on the gay bar circuit. *Open Sun–Thurs 1pm–1.30am, Fri and Sat 1pm–2.30am.*

Sifting through all the books that have ever been written about Spain, opinion on this unlikely capital seems about evenly divided. Some writers are sure it's the heart and soul of the nation, but the dissent has been coming in ever since the city has been on the map; many follow Richard Ford in counselling that the less time you spend in Madrid, the better you'll like it. Like Bonn or Washington, it is an entirely artificial capital, created on the whim of the early Habsburg kings. The city has great museums, wide boulevards and a cosmopolitan air. It doesn't have a beautiful setting, or a tolerable climate, or many noteworthy churches or monuments – it's difficult to imagine a capital more impoverished architecturally.

So why stay, when places like Toledo and Segovia are just a short train-ride away? Art is one reason; not surprisingly, the city of Velázquez and Goya and connoisseur Habsburg and Bourbon kings has one of this planet's greatest hoards of paintings. Old Madrid, the area around the Plaza Mayor that has changed little since the 17th century, is another. The biggest reason for many, though, is that Madrid is better equipped than any city in Spain to give you a good time. *Madrileños* claim their city stays up later than any in Europe; there's good cause to, with an infinite variety of nightlife and attractions that may make you forget all about Velázquez and Goya.

History

Settlements have come and gone here since the Palaeolithic era, but the first permanent town seems to have been built by the Arabs, who constructed a fortress Alcázar on the site of today's Palacio Real, and a small circuit of walls that extended only as far as Pza Mayor and Pza Isabel II. Their name for it, *Mayrit*, came from the Matriz, a little stream that ran in the valley where C/de Segovia is now. Mayrit met the Reconquista in 1083, two years before Toledo; El Cid may have been around to assist Alfonso VI in its capture. The walls were extended in the 11th and 12th centuries. The new southern gate, the Puerta del Sol, gave its name to the square that later replaced it, standing at the centre of Madrid today.

One strange interlude in the city's history came in the 1380s, when King Juan I gave the city in fief to the exiled last king of Little Armenia, Leon VI. In the centuries that followed, the town's growth was steady and slow. Royal patronage came first with Enrique IV, who tacked a Renaissance façade onto the old Moorish Alcázar to make it one of his palaces, but it was Charles V who first began to spend much time here; both he and his son Philip II found the climate eased their gout. Up to that time Spain had had no real capital. The Cortes traditionally alternated its meetings in all the Castilian cities, so that none would be offended, and the necessity of an occasional royal presence in all of Spain's diverse regions made vagabonds of all the earlier kings. Philip declared Madrid the permanent capital in 1561, giving the Habsburg monarchy a strong, central, specifically Castilian capital from which to combat the separatist tendencies of the outlying regions, and at the same time creating a counterweight to the contentious older cities of Castile, most of which had supported the Comunero revolt just 40 years earlier.

Unfortunately, neither the Habsburgs nor the Bourbons went out of their way to replan or embellish their capital. Besides palaces, their only important contributions are the two great parks, the Retiro and the Casa de Campo, that define the eastern and western boundaries of the old town and help so much to make Madrid habitable. Most travellers of that era, from the 16th to 18th centuries, write of Madrid as crowded, unpleasant, even unhealthy; sanitation and other urban amenities lagged far behind other European capitals of the day. The city must have seemed a curious juxtaposition of a sophisticated royal court, with its palaces and gardens, on top of an overgrown Castilian provincial town. Nevertheless, at this time Madrid was home to Velázquez and Goya, to Calderón and Lope de Vega, as well as many other important figures of the 'Golden Age of Spain'.

Politically the city learned to speak for itself in 1808, in the famous revolt of the 'Dos de Mayo'. When Napoleon's men attempted to kidnap the Spanish royal family, a spontaneous patriotic uprising occurred; though soon suppressed by the French, it has been a golden memory for the Spanish ever since. Madrid's next chance for heroism came with the Civil War. In the early days of that conflict, four Nationalist columns, including most of Franco's Army of Africa, advanced to positions within sight of the Royal palace (General Mola mentioned a 'fifth column' of sympathizers supposedly hidden within the city: it was just propaganda, but a new phrase was born). Bitter street fighting in the western suburbs continued until March 1937. At first, the defence of the city was almost entirely in the hands of the newly formed Socialist, Communist and Anarchist militias. Their untrained fighters, many women among them, wore street clothes, held meetings to discuss tactics with the officers, and some commuted daily to the front on the Metro, or in cars commandeered from the wealthy. The Republican government soon fled to València, but as the world watched in suspense, Madrid held. '*No pasarán*' – 'they shall not pass' – was the famous slogan, coined by La Pasionara, and the city became a symbol that caught the imagination of Europe, the first community in that dark time to make a successful stand against fascism. In November 1936 the International Brigades and the first squadrons of Soviet aeroplanes began to arrive, and they helped defeat the last Nationalist attempts to encircle the city.

Before the Civil War, Madrid had grown into a bright and cosmopolitan cultural capital; its cafés and clubs frequented by the artists and writers of the 'Generation of 1898' as well as politicians and the Spanish élite. Though most of the glitter, as well as the substance, disappeared under 40 years of Franco, the city grew tremendously. The Franco government, determined to see their capital outstrip Barcelona, encouraged new industry and migration from other corners of Spain. Though the city flourished, the environmental cost was high; once lovely boulevards were flattened into urban motorways, and the outskirts of the city were disfigured by the wasteland of factories, junkyards and shantytowns you see today.

After Franco's death in 1975, however, Madrid's civic pride was allowed to resurface. As the seventies gave way to the eighties, and the traditionally puritanical and austere Spaniards woke up to the attractions and pleasures of economic success, the city found itself at the cutting edge of a social revolution. Earning (or otherwise acquiring) vast sums became a fashionable compulsion, and the popular press coined the term '*los beautiful people*' for the new jetset that filled Madrid's restaurants and *terrazas*. The early 1980s became known as the *movida*, when bars sprang up all over the city, legalized drug consumption flourished, and under a socialist government's patronage the arts underwent not so much a renaissance, as a resurrection.

Enrique Tierno Galván, who was elected Mayor of Madrid in 1979, was seen by many as the sponsor and orchestrator of the city's great cultural revival. A remarkable mayor, he dedicated himself to improving the city's quality of life; he planted thousands of trees, created new parks in the outlying districts, repaired some of the damage done by the traffic planners, and even found some water to direct through the dusty stream bed of the Manzanares. *Madrileños* called Tierno 'The Old Professor' for his habit of lecturing them on the importance of trees and greenery, and all of them, regardless of politics, mourned his death in 1986.

The Spanish economy grew faster than that of any other member country in the first five years after Spain joined the European Community, and, as property prices soared, Madrid benefitted from much needed investment. Art-fever gripped the city with the growth of ARCO, Madrid's annual contemporary art fair, the opening of the Reina Sofía modern art museum and the acquisition of the famous Thyssen-Bornemisza collection. In 1991, the right-wing Partido Popular gained control of Madrid's regional parliament and, under Mayor José María Alvarez del Manzano, one of their first priorities was to set about making final preparations for Spain's golden year of celebrations, 1992. Barcelona had won the Olympics, Seville was hosting the World Fair, and Madrid came a poor third as European Cultural Capital. As it turned out, Madrid's contribution was not particularly remarkable; many of the projects planned to mark the event, such as the Opera House, were not quite finished in time. But it was at the end of the year that the real blow came. For three years Spain's socialist government had been artificially warding off economic slump by pouring money into construction projects to furnish the nation for the celebrations. Even before the fiesta was over, recession hit hard, with all the usual trappings: high unemployment, high interest rates, and currency devaluation. Nobody appreciated this sudden downturn and, in the 1993 general election, the PSOE, their name already blackened by corruption scandals, lost control of the greater Madrid area. The PP took the helm, winning the elections in 1996, and in March 2000 they won a second term.

Madrid has now come to terms with the fact that the boom years are over; although city life has lost the hedonistic, opportunistic sparkle and easy glamour that distinguished it in the swinging 1980s, the *madrileñan* spirit is not dampened easily, and there's as much optimism as caution built into their image of the future.

Puerta del Sol

Ten streets radiate from this, the nerve centre of the city, as well as three metro lines and dozens of bus lines; however you're travelling, you're soon likely to cross the 'Gate of the Sun', and everyone agrees that it remains the centre of all things in Madrid, if not the universe. The gate from Alfonso's walls is long gone, and the plaza is chaotic, dirty and crowded, but it endears itself to the *madrileños* in a way no formal postcard plaza ever could.

Orientation

Madrid goes on and on – today it is home to 4 or 5 million people, depending how you add them up – but almost everything of major interest will be found within one mile of the Puerta del Sol between the Parque del Retiro in the east and Plaza de Oriente in the west, home of the newly opened opera house and the Palacio Real. Near the Retiro and the broad boulevard called the Paseo del Prado, you'll find the '*triángulo de arte*', Madrid's triple crown of art museums, the Prado, Thyssen, and Reina Sofía. The Puerta del Sol sits squarely in the centre, and the oldest quarter of the city, around the Plaza Mayor, is just to the west of it. Keep these landmarks in mind, and learn a few of the main streets, and you'll not get too lost – Madrid isn't nearly as complicated as it looks on the map. Because the centre, where most of the interest lies, is so compact, Madrid is easy to get about on foot, but if you've got sore feet, taxis are relatively cheap. That said, Madrid's buses and metro do come in handy to reach some of the more outlying sights.

Here, at the mouth of a shopping street (C/de Carmen), stands a sculpture of their own emblem, the **Oso y Madroño** (bear and strawberry tree). It's a small, unshowy bronze, a low-key symbol of community identity, now rather upstaged by an equestrian **statue of Charles III**. Little that is *auténtico* in Madrid ever strays far from Sol; jammed into this tight-knit district of narrow streets are scores of curious shops and family businesses that have been running for generations, while the *tascas* south of the plaza, their windows piled high with shellfish and other delicacies, are some of the oldest and best-known bars in town. In the 19th century, Sol's fashionable cafés made it the liveliest place in Madrid, a centre not only for gossip but for the revolts and demonstrations that convulsed the city. From here, you can choose to head either west to the old town and the Palacio Real, or east to the Retiro and the museums.

The Paseo del Arte: Madrid's 'Golden Triangle'

If the Prado wasn't already enough to make Madrid a major art destination, the reopening of the Reina Sofía Art Centre in 1990 and the nation's permanent acquisition of the Thyssen-Bornemisza collection in 1992 removed all doubt. Madrid is rightly proud of its 'golden triangle' of art treasures – three superb museums all within strolling distance of each other, linked by the leafy Paseo del Prado.

The three collections complement each other neatly. The **Museo del Prado** is best known for its hoard of masterpieces of Spanish painting from the 12th to the early 19th centuries, and for its rich collections of 15th–17th-century Flemish painting, as well as Italian art by the likes of Titian, Raphael and Botticelli, collected by the kings of Spain. Its annexe, the **Casón del Buen Retiro**, covers the 19th century. The **Museo Nacional Centro de Arte Reina Sofía** picks up the thread with its permanent collection of 20th-century art (including Picasso's masterwork, *Guernica*). The newcomer on the scene, the **Museo Colección Thyssen-Bornemisza**, is a remarkable gathering of European and American art spanning eight centuries. Its highlights include early

Italian paintings, 17th-century Dutch works, and paintings by 20th-century masters including Braque, Mondrian, Picasso and Warhol. Fortuitously, it manages to fill in a few of the gaps left by the Prado and the Reina Sofía, with collections of Impressionism and Post-Impressionism, German Expressionists such as Munch, Schiele and Kandinsky, and a restrained but well-informed selection of Pop Art and geometrical abstracts.

A **Paseo de Arte voucher** will allow one visit to each of the three big museums, the Prado, Reina Sofía and Thyssen, for €8; but don't even think about trying to 'do' the three in a single day unless you are likely to be satisfied with a mere snippet of each.

Museo del Prado

Pso del Prado, ***t*** *913 30 28 00,* http://museoprado.mcu.es; ***M*** *Banco de España or Atocha; wheelchair accessible; open Tues–Sat 9–7, Sun and hols 9–2; closed 1 Jan, Good Friday, 1 May and 25 Dec; adm, adm free Sat after 2.30pm, Sun, and on 18 May, 12 Oct and 6 Dec.*

Charles III intended this to be a natural history museum when it was begun in 1785, but the building crumbled forlornly until Ferdinand VII, that most hated of kings, decided to act on an idea that had been in the air for centuries. Realizing that his discerning predecessors had accumulated one of Europe's greatest hoards of art, he decided that they should be relocated under one roof, and that this roof should be that of the Prado. The collections were opened to the public in 1819, and although the building has been restored since, the collections have changed little. Spanish noble families who collected paintings are likely still to have them: the habit of donating to museums never took root here as in the rest of Europe. For the masterpieces of the Prado we can thank the practised eyes of Charles V, Philip II and Philip IV; not only did they know good painting when they saw it, but it was Philip IV who, in his will of 1665, made all the paintings Crown property and prohibited the dispersion of a single one.

There was considerable disgruntlement when in 1993 the government invested an unprecedented (though bargain) sum in acquiring the Thyssen collection while apparently neglecting the Prado's arguably more pressing needs, in particular, its space problem. The exhibition areas are only large enough to display a seventh of the

Finding Your Way Around the Prado

Expect crowds, but don't be dismayed by huge mobs at the entrances: they're likely to be tour groups counting heads, and you should be able to pass right through. The earlier you go, the fewer of these you'll have to contend with.

The main entrance is closed owing to the restoration of the façade, but there's a secondary entrance (Puerta de Murillo) at the southern end. However, the best place to begin a comprehensive visit is to enter at ground level by the Puerta de Goya at the north end of the main building, the **Edificio Villanueva**. The museum is laid out chronologically: the **ground floor** is mostly medieval and Renaissance, covering 14th–16th-century Spanish, Flemish, German and Italian works. The **first floor** covers Baroque, plus some of the Goyas. The rest of these are on the **second floor**.

vast collection, and among the 'unseen' canvases are significant works by Spanish masters. Of the 6,000 works not on display, a good 3,500 of them are on loan to museums around the world. The Prado's biggest ongoing expansion project involves an entirely new building: next door to the Claustro de los Jerónimos, a new wing has been designed for temporary exhibitions, restoration workshops and a research library, to be connected to the main building by an underground tunnel. The **Casón del Buen Retiro** (*closed until end of 2002*) is also being expanded to create more storage space. When it reopens it will house the Prado's collection of 19th-century painting as well as works from the Middle Ages. The Prado is also planning to take over the **Palacio del Buen Retiro** (*currently home to the Museo del Ejército*), though since the entire Museo del Ejército will have to be relocated to Toledo, that changeover may well stretch into 2003–4.

The Collections

14th–16th-century Spanish Art

The first ground-floor rooms, starting from the Puerta de Goya, are devoted to medieval religious works. Don't be in too much of a hurry to see Velázquez: some of the best art in the Prado is here, including some stunning 14th- and 15th-century *retablos*: *Archbishop Don Sancho de Rojas* by **Rodríguez de Toledo** and *The Life of the Virgin and St Francis* by **Nicolás Francés**. The great Córdoban master **Bartolomé Bermejo**'s *St Dominic Enthroned* stands out for sheer dramatic realism.

This rich collection of early Spanish painting continues with Renaissance-influenced works such as **Fernando Gallego**'s eerie *Cristo Bendiciendo*. **Pedro Berruguete** contributes, among much else, an *Auto-da-Fé Presided Over by St Dominic* that is almost satirical, with bored church apparatchiks dozing under a baldachin while the woebegone heretics are led off to the slaughter. *St Peter Martyr*, by the same artist, beams beatifically from beneath the meat cleaver splitting his skull.

15th–16th-century Flemish and German Art

Even before Philip II, who valued Flemish art above all others, the Low Countries' close commercial and dynastic ties ensured that some would turn up here. Today the Prado's collection of Flemish art is almost as unmissable as its Spanish collection. The works are arranged roughly chronologically, beginning with the 15th-century so-called Primitives, including paintings by **Robert Campin** and breathtakingly detailed work by **Rogier van der Weyden**. Weyden's *Descent from the Cross* (*c*. 1435) is astonishing, framed like a scene from a mystery play, in which Gothic stylization is all but forgotten in favour of the realistic visual representation of a whole spectrum of human emotions. Within the tight confines of the composition the figures just float off the surface of the panel. There are a number of endearing **Hans Memling** paintings, including an *Adoration of the Magi* triptych (1470–2).

The biggest crowds, though, will be around the works of **Hieronymous Bosch** (1450–1516, known in Spain as 'El Bosco'). His psychological fantasies, including *The Garden of Earthly Delights, The Hay Wain, The Adoration of the Magi* and the table in the centre of the room decorated with *The Seven Deadly Sins* are too familiar to need any comment. Philip II bought every one he could get his hands on, and it should not be surprising to find the most complex of all Spanish kings attracted to this dark surrealism as we are today. More works by Bosch can be seen in Philip's apartments at El Escorial. If you like Bosch, you should also get to know his countryman **Joachim Patinir**, some of whose best work can also be found in this section. Probably no other museum has such a large complement of terror to balance its own beauty; between Goya (*see* below), Bosch and the other northern painters, and the religious hacks, a trip to the Prado can seem like a long ride in a carnival funhouse. If you approach it in this way, the climax will undoubtedly be *The Triumph of Death* by **Pieter Brueghel the Elder** (1525–69), with its phalanxes of leering skeletons turned loose upon a doomed, terrified world. To Philip II, who is said to have kept a crowned skull on his night table, it must have seemed a deeply religious work. The Dutch, on the other hand, in the middle of their war of independence, would probably have been reminded of the horrors of intolerance and militant religion that were searing contemporary Europe.

German paintings are few, but choice. **Albrecht Dürer**'s rather presumptuous *Self-portrait* (1498) is an interesting study, painted at a time when self-portraits were uncommon, and composed in a style that is often compared to Leonardo da Vinci's *Mona Lisa* (a copy of which hangs in the Italian section), although it was actually painted five years earlier. Also of interest are Dürer's companion paintings of *Adam and Eve*, **Hans Baldung Grien**'s angular *Teutonic Three Graces* and sinister *Three Ages of Man and Death*, and works by **Cranach** and **Mengs**.

Italian and French Schools

In the Prado's Italian collection, there are several paintings by **Raphael** (1483–1520), all religious subjects, including the classic *Holy Family* (1518); from **Fra Angelico** (1397–1455) comes an intensely spiritual *Annunciation*; and there is an unusual trio of scenes by **Botticelli** (1444–1510) from Boccaccio's *Decameron*, *The Story of Nastagio degli Onesti*. **Andrea del Sarto**, **Mantegna**, **Antonello da Messina**, **Veronese**, **Caravaggio**, **Bassano**, **Tintoretto** and **Correggio**, among the other Italian masters, are all represented, and there are rooms full of works by **Titian** (*c.* 1490–1576). His *La Gloria* may be his biggest ever canvas, a colourful, preposterous cloud-bedecked imagining of the Holy Trinity that gently nudges the boundaries of kitsch. Charles (who is also in the picture, sometimes called his 'Apotheosis'), is said to have gazed upon this picture constantly while on his deathbed. Among the 17th- and 18th-century French works on display are paintings by Poussin and Watteau.

16th–17th-century Spanish Art

To appreciate the genius of Domenikos Theotocopoulos, or **El Greco** (1540–1614), there is no substitute for a visit to Toledo, but the Prado houses fine examples of what are sometimes called his 'vertical pictures' – Mannerist depictions of biblical figures with elongated limbs and faces – including *The Annunciation* and *The Adoration of the Shepherds*. El Greco was also a skilled portraitist and his *Nobleman with his Hand on his Chest* is particularly haunting.

17th-century Flemish and Dutch Art

Rubens (1577–1640) is well represented here, with his epic *Adoration of the Magi* dominating a whole roomful of florid biblical paintings, and his chubby *Three Graces* among other mythological subjects in an adjacent gallery. A room nearby contains his famous collaboration with **Brueghel the Younger**, the *Allegory of the Five Senses*, a complete universe of philosophy in its five enormous canvases. Rubens' works are followed by those of later Flemish masters: delicate portraits by **Anton van Dyck** (1599–1641), complex studies by **David Teniers** and, in a room of small canvases, one of the greatest works of Brueghel the Younger, the untitled 'snowy landscape'.

The Prado's small Dutch collection consists mostly of 17th-century hunting scenes, still lifes and the like, but there is one good **Rembrandt** (1606–69), a dignified portrait of a regal woman thought to be Artemisia, wife of King Mausolus.

17th–18th-century Spanish Art

By the 17th century, the religious pathology of the age becomes manifest, notably in a disturbing painting by **Francisco Ribalta** of the crucified Christ leaning down off the Cross to embrace St Bernard. Elsewhere, St Bernard comes in for more abuse, this time at the hand of **Alonso Cano**, who illustrates the old tale of the praying saint receiving a squirt of milk in his mouth from the breast of an image of the Virgin.

Other, uneven, works by Spanish Baroque masters fill a dozen galleries: José de Ribera (1591–1652), Francisco de Zurbarán (1598–1664) and Bartolomé Esteban Murillo (1618–1682) among others. **Ribera** was a follower of Caravaggio's style and he used dark colours, starkly lit, to suggest pious ascetism, pain, suffering, and earthy sensual pleasure. His paintings of mythological and religious subjects (such as *St Andrew* and *The Martyrdom of St Philip*) are shot through with sinister undercurrents; he was particularly keen on using scruffy urchins and decaying beggars as models in order to inject warts-and-all realism into his work. **Zurbarán** was a *sevillano* contemporary of Velázquez, but was totally unlike him in style. The Prado has some examples of his finely worked still lifes; these have a sacramental quality, with everyday objects laid out like devotional offerings. **Murillo** churned out plenty of sentimental tosh, some of which has found its way here, but his *Holy Family* (1650) is sweet and unaffected; a lovingly painted moment.

Velázquez

On a day when there are as many Spaniards as foreigners in the Prado, the crowds around the works of Diego de Silva y Velázquez (1599–1660) can be daunting. Many Spanish consider their countryman to be the greatest artist of all, and you may find these several rooms, the largest Velázquez collection by far, to be a convincing argument. Many of the works have recently been cleaned or restored, making the audacity of his use of light and colour stand out even more clearly.

Almost all of his best-known paintings are here: *Los Borrachos* (*The Topers*), *Las Hilanderas* (*The Tapestry Weavers*) and *The Surrender of Breda*, which the Spaniards call *Las Lanzas* (*The Lances*). His portraits of court dwarves, such as *Francisco Lezcano*, give his sitters an air of humanity and dignity generally denied them in daily life.

Also present are the royal portraits: lumpy, bewildered Philip IV, a king aware enough of his own inadequacies to let Velázquez express them on canvas, appears in various poses. Of his children, we see the six-year-old Infante Balthasar Carlos in a charming, mock-heroic pose on horseback, and again at the age of 16. It was this prince's untimely death soon after the latter portrait that gave the throne to the idiot Charles II. His sister, the doll-like Infanta Margarita, appears by herself and in the most celebrated of all Velázquez's works, *Las Meninas* (*The Maids-of-Honour*, 1656), a composition of such inexhaustible complexity and beauty that the Prado gives it pride of place. In it, not only does Velázquez capture eloquently the everyday atmosphere of the Spanish court (the little princess, her bizarre entourage and, unseen except for in a mirror in the background, her royal parents), he also turns the then-accepted artistic limits of perspective and dimensional space inside out. Velázquez painted himself in the picture, but the red cross on his tunic, the badge of the Order of Santiago, was added by King Philip's own hand, as a graceful way of informing the artist of the honour he was conferring on him.

Goya

The Goya collection is spread over the first and second floors. Like Velázquez, Francisco de Goya y Lucientes (1746–1828) held the office of court painter, but at the service of an even more useless monarch, Charles IV. Also like Velázquez, he was not inclined to flattery. Critics ever since have wondered how he got away with making his royal patron look so foolish, and the job he did on Carlos' wife, Queen Maria Luisa, is legendary. In every portrait and family scene, she comes out looking half-fairy-tale witch, half-washerwoman. Her son, later to be the reactionary King Ferdinand VII, is pictured as a teenager, and Goya makes him merely disagreeable and menacing.

Among the other famous Goyas you may compare the *Maja Desnuda* (*Nude Maja*) and the *Maja Vestida* (*Clothed Maja*), and *Los Fusilamentos del Dos de Mayo* (*The Executions of the Second of May*) and *Los Fusilamentos de Moncloa* (*The Executions of Moncloa*), the pair commemorating the uprising of 1808 and its aftermath. The latter, much the better known, shows the impassioned patriots' faces caught in the glare of a lantern, facing the firing squad of grim, almost mechanical French soldiers. Nothing like it had ever been painted before, an unforgettable image and a prophetic prelude to the era of revolutions, mass politics and total war that was just beginning, inaugurated by the French Revolution and Napoleon. The setting is Madrid's Casa de Campo, and the spires of the old town can be made out clearly in the background.

Representing his early work, Goya's remarkable *cartoons* – designs for tapestries to be made by the Real Fábrica for the king's palaces – provide a dose of joy and sweetness, their vivid colours bathed in clear Castilian sunshine. These are on the second floor at the Puerta de Murillo end of the building. Most, such as *El Quitasol* (*The Parasol*) and *La Fiesta de San Isidro* (*The Festival of San Isidro*) are idealized pastorial scenes, and the creatures inhabiting them seem less Spanish than celestial.

In stark contrast are some of the Prado's greatest treasures, its collection of Goya's *Pinturas Negras* ('Black Paintings'), late works which are separated from the others by a stairway as if it were feared they would contaminate the sunnier paintings upstairs.

All the well-known images of dark fantasy and terror are here: *Saturn Devouring One of his Sons, Duel with Cudgels, The Colussus* (*Panic*), and even a nightmarish vision of the same San Isidro festivities Goya painted so happily when he was healthy.

Casón del Buen Retiro

C/de Alfonso XII 28, ***t*** *913 30 28 00;* ***M*** *Retiro or Atocha. Closed until late 2002 or early 2003; when open, opening times as Museo del Prado.*

The Casón del Buen Retiro was originally the ballroom of the Palacio del Buen Retiro, another building the Prado is revamping to expand its exhibition space. In the past, it housed the Prado's collection of 18th- and 19th-century Spanish art, including painters such as Mario Fortuny, Joaquín Sorolla, José de Madrazo, Federico de Madrazo, Francisco Pradilla and Vicente López.

Museo Nacional Centro de Arte Reina Sofía

C/de Santa Isabel 52, ***t*** *914 67 50 62,* ***f*** *914 67 31 63, http.//.museoreina sofia.mcu.es;* ***M*** *Atocha; wheelchair accessible; open Mon and Wed–Sat 10–9, Sun 10–2.30; closed 1 Jan, 24, 25 and 26 Dec; free* ***guided tours*** *Mon and Wed at 5pm, Sat at 11am; adm, adm free Sat after 2.30pm, Sun, 18 May, 12 Oct and 6 Dec.*

With the continuing success of ARCO, Madrid's annual contemporary art fair, founded in the early 1980s, and with promising work emerging from local artists, the *madrileños*' active interest in modern art has never been at such a high. It was partly in order to satisfy this popular passion that the Spanish government set about providing their capital with a world-class 20th-century art museum, to replace the old Museo Español de Arte Contemporáneo.

Conversion of Madrid's defunct General Hospital began in 1980 and the Centro de Arte Reina Sofía was inaugurated by the queen in 1986. Cynics muttered that the timing of the opening was no more than a vote-catching ploy in this, an election year, since the building wasn't actually ready. After this abortive inauguration, it was back to the drawing board and, four years and several more millions of pesetas later, a second opening ceremony was held. The building, graced by its three landmark glass lifts (or 'crystal towers'), was by now fully equipped to house both temporary exhibitions and a permanent collection of art; all it lacked was a quorum of internationally famous paintings. It was two more years, however, before the Reina Sofía really made its début as an art centre to be reckoned with: in 1992, Spain's golden year, Picasso's *Guernica* was moved here from the Casón del Buen Retiro (*see* above). The move was a controversial one, carried out in spite of Picasso's own instructions, left with New York's Museum of Modern Art, that it should return the painting to Spain when liberty was restored there, and that it should hang in the Prado, as a gesture towards the modernization of that collection but also as the ultimate exorcism of the Civil War and Franco. His wish was granted in 1981, and millions of Spaniards made the pilgrimage to the Prado to see a part of their history denied them under 40 years of dictatorship. When the Spanish government proposed the removal of the painting to the Reina Sofía, there were bitter objections from Picasso's surviving relatives, but these were overruled in the interests of the fulfilment of a master plan: the Prado was to hold the Old Masters, the Casón del Buen Retiro the 19th-century art, and the Reina Sofía the 20th-century works, with *Guernica*, arguably the 20th century's most famous painting, taking pride of place.

The Main Collection (Second Floor)

The Reina Sofía's permanent collection contains works by every one of Spain's most celebrated 20th-century artists, which together amount to solid evidence, if any were needed, to back up the nation's claim to the title of contemporary creative superpower. Pablo Picasso, Salvador Dalí, Joan Miró, Juan Gris, Julio González, Antoni Tàpies, José Gutiérrez Solana and Antonio Saura are all represented.

The opening rooms set the scene for the avant-garde works to come; **Anglada-Camarasa**'s *Portrait of Sonia de Klamery, Countess Pradère* rubs glittering shoulders with the sombre portraits of **Ramón Casas**. The next room is devoted to **Solana**; in his *Tertulia at Café de Pombo* (1920) we are given a glimpse into that typically *madrileño* institution of the late 19th and early 20th century: the ***tertulia***, a gathering of the intelligentsia in the city's cafés; Solana includes himself in the coterie.

The curvy, colourful works of **Sonia Delaunay** and severely graceful lead sculptures of **Jacques Lipchitz** come next, along with works by other members of the early avant-garde. In the adjacent gallery, increasingly mature paintings by **Juan Gris** line the walls, while a very tiny room displays the superb fluid traceries, deconstructed busts and skin-skeletons of **Pablo Gargallo** (1881–1934), who introduced Picasso to metal sculpture and in turn was influenced by Cubism. Gargallo's arch *Mask of Greta Garbo with Lock of Hair* flicks an insouciant glance as you pass through to some early, supernatural-looking **Miró** portraits, divided from his later works by the sculptures of **Julio González** (1876–1942). One of the first to render iron as an artistic medium and to speak as much with void space as with solid material, he shares space with the delicate sculptures of the American Abstract Expressionist **David Smith**.

One room away, a hefty knot of people are usually gathered around *Guernica*, placed alone along one wall of the central gallery. Picasso's stern-faced *Woman in Blue* (1901) presides over an adjacent gallery of his early work.

Alexander Calder's (1898–1976) *Constellation* (1940), an airy wood and wire mobile of abstract spheres, floats nonchalantly in a nearby room, alongside other early Surrealist works: **Jean Arp**'s bold wood reliefs, **André Masson**'s cerebral paintings and the lyrical paintings of **Vassily Kandinsky**, founder of Abstract Expressionism.

Dalí's works are also given a room to themselves; particularly outstanding are *Girl at the Window*, *The Invisible Man* and *The Great Masturbator*. Some of his early paintings show him dabbling in the Cubist style. A product of his collaboration with Man Ray, *Portrait of Joell*a, sits in the next room along with other Surrealist works. Dalí's collaborations with the experimental film-maker **Luis Buñuel** are screened in Room 12.

Significant numbers of Spanish artists took up residence in Paris between the wars, and a selection of their output is grouped together in a gallery devoted to the various movements which evolved in Spanish art after the First World War. In an interesting

Finding Your Way Around the Reina Sofía

The paintings, sketches and sculptures occupy the second and fourth floors of the building and are grouped chronologically and according to stylistic or conceptual affinity; you'll find you have to weave about to follow the intended order of the rooms. The first part of the collection is on the second floor (Rooms 1–17) and covers the final years of the 19th century until the end of the Second World War. Later works are on the fourth floor (Rooms 18–45). Temporary exhibitions (often several at once) can be found in Espacio UNO on the ground floor and on the third floor. There is also an excellent bookshop, a decent café-restaurant, an oasis of a courtyard garden, a library, a music archive and education unit, and enough supplementary resource areas to fully justify its status as an energetic multimedia community arts centre.

juxtaposition, three works – by **José de Togores i Llach** (*Nudes on a Beach*; 1922), **Rosario Velasco** (*Adam and Eve*; 1932) and **Balbuena** (*Nude*; 1932) – each exhibit an obsessive, almost architectural interest in the smooth rendering of the human form.

The penultimate rooms are given over to the Asturian painter **Luis Fernández**, the elegant sculptures of **Alberto Sánchez** and the vivid, schematic compositions of **Benjamín Palencia**, while the final room is dedicated to sculpture. Though it focuses on **Miró**'s bronzes, other notable pieces include **Angel Ferrant**'s creations made from 'found objects', and **Ramón Marinello**'s *Figures in Front of the Sea* (1936).

Fourth Floor

Up here the museum picks up the story in the 1940s when the Spanish art scene was characterized by a desire to rebuild in the wake of the Civil War. Postwar trauma is evident in some of the earliest works, but, as the '40s gave way to the '50s, a more liberal mood of catharsis took hold. Among the works from this period are boxy sculptures by **Jorge de Oteiza**; bristling pieces by **Pablo Serrano**; and filmy compositions by **Manuel Mompó**, as well as the geometric canvases of the co-operative **Equipo 57**.

All these avant-garde theories are put into their European context in the next series of rooms. The bathos of **Francis Bacon**'s bleak figures contrasts with the monochrome minimalism of **Yves Klein**, while organic **Henry Moore** sculptures complement the three-dimensional pieces by **Lucio Fontana**. **Antonio López García** (1936–), a leading member of the Madrid Realism movement, has some meticulous urban portraits of Madrid, placed alongside life-sized figures sculpted by **Francisco López Hernández**. Nearby, the works of the Basque **Eduardo Chillida** are scooped from wood and terracotta, or wrought from iron and stone. After the ripped, rucked and daubed fabric works by **Millares** and the turbulent paintings of **Antonio Saura**, the series culminates in a room devoted to texture-obsessed **Antoni Tàpies**.

The **Equipo Crónica** group jibe at American mass culture in works such as the Pop Art painting *Painting is like Hitting* (1964), in the company of **Eduardo Arroyo**'s dark, cartoonish night paintings. But Minimalism strikes back with the bright, clear canvases of **Ellsworth Kelly**, the huge iron cubes of **Donald Judd**, and **Soto**'s staggering *Yellow and White Extension*, before **Schnabel**'s vast, lucid *Buen Retiro Ducks* series, painted as a gift to the Spanish people.

Museo Colección Thyssen-Bornemisza

*Palacio de Villahermosa, Pso del Prado 8, **t** 914 20 39 44, **f** 914 20 27 80, www.museothyssen.org; **M** Banco de España; wheelchair accessible; open Tues–Sun 10–7; adm, tickets for temporary exhibitions sold separately. If you want a break, ask for a wrist stamp ('sello') at the information desk.*

The directors of the Reina Sofía, reeling from the media response to the controversies surrounding their early policies, were glad to have the spotlight eased off them for a while in 1993, when everyone's attention switched up the road to the Palacio de Villahermosa. Thanks to the persuasiveness of his wife, Carmen 'La Tita' Cervera, Baron Hans-Heinrich Thyssen-Bornemisza had already decided on Madrid as the temporary home for the cream of his unique collection of art. In 1993, the arrangement was made permanent: the Spanish government purchased the collection for the extremely reasonable sum of 44,000 million pesetas (€264 million). Despite the recession, and the further millions required to convert the palace building to receive the collection, the acquisition seemed to represent an unmissable opportunity to boost Madrid's, and Spain's, already high profile on the international art scene.

The collection, started in the 1920s by the present baron's father, Baron Heinrich Thyssen-Bornemisza, is idiosyncratic, eclectic and fun, and offers a fascinating insight into the personal taste of two men with a magpie-like compulsion. Like a prized and precious stamp collection, the museum contains a little of everything – there's an entry on practically every page of art history, from the religious works of 13th-century Italy to the brash output of Europe and the US in the 1960s and '70s – with the Barons' particular favourites represented in larger quantities (they liked 19th-century American painting; you might not). The present Baron Thyssen is a standard bearer of art for the modern world and his is widely regarded as the world's finest private art collection after that of the British Royal Family. He has claimed that he learned all he knows about art appreciation simply by hanging his pictures up and looking at them; with an approach as honest and pragmatic as this it is wholly consistent that he decided to make it possible for the general public to share his enjoyment.

To create the gallery spaces, architect Rafael Moneo was given a shell of a building, and his finished work is bathed in a pleasant balance of natural and artificial light, with walls washed in a warm cross between salmon and terracotta.

Second Floor

The collection opens with one of its highlights, a treasure-trove of gems of **Primitive and Medieval Italian religious art**, including a hauntingly simple and lovely

Finding Your Way Around the Thyssen-Bornemisza

The chronological sequence begins on the top floor and works its way, anticlockwise, downwards, so that the modern works could benefit from being hung in the high-ceilinged ground-floor rooms. In the basement is a café and a space for temporary exhibitions.

13th-century statue of the Madonna and Child, and some 14th-century gilded panels of exquisite beauty. These are followed by **15th-century works from the Low Countries**, among them Jan van Eyck's stirring and brilliantly executed monochrome *Annunciation Diptych* (*c.* 1435–41). *Clothing the Naked* (*c.* 1470) by the Master of St Gudule offers an interesting illustration of the development of perspective techniques. The next room contains **15th-century Italian works** such as Bramantino's spooky *Resurrected Christ*, and Ercole de' Roberti's charming mythology, *The Argonauts Leaving Colchis* (*c.* 1480), a rarefied work from the Humanist court of Ferrara.

Early Renaissance portraits form another high point of the collection. There are plenty of familiar faces here, including **Holbein**'s *Henry VIII* (*c.* 1534–36), **Memling**'s *Young Man at Prayer* (*c.* 1485), **Campin**'s uncompromisingly crisp *Stout Man* (*c.* 1485) and **Messina**'s *Portrait of a Man* (*c.* 1475–76), fixing you with a direct, intelligent gaze. There is also a *Portrait of Giovanna Tornabuoni* (1488) by **Domenico Ghirlandaio**, one-time tutor to Michaelangelo, who includes a Latin inscription behind the sitter's neck: 'if art could portray character and virtue, no painting in the world would be more beautiful'. The Hispano-Flemish Juan de Flandres, contributes the exquisite, wistful *Portrait of an Infanta* (*c.* 1496), a Spanish princess minus all the usual trappings.

Rafael Moneo designed the long and windowed **Villahermosa Gallery** to recall *gallerias* in Italian palaces. Most of the works here are portraits – favoured by the first Baron Thyssen. Here another Raphael, the Raphael, painted the *Portrait of a Young Man* (*c.* 1515), believed to be Alessandro de' Medici.

Off the gallery, a row of rooms contains **16th-century paintings**. The first is dedicated to the Italians. Alongside works by Giovanni Bellini, Sebastiano del Piombo and Domenico Beccafumi is Vittore Carpaccio's delightful *Young Knight in a Landscape* (1510), remarkable for its richly detailed allegorical backdrop.

Among the **16th-century German works** in the next two rooms are five scenes of a strikingly vivid Crucifixion by Derick Baegert, from a painting cut up centuries ago. Dürer's *Jesus among the Doctors* (1506) is a brilliant, oppressively compact composition built around a central motif of two pairs of hands: the youthful ones of Jesus and the sinewy ones of one of the six suspicious-looking priests that seem to be closing in on him. From the same school is another of the Thyssen's signature works, Hans Baldung Grien's stylish, enigmatic *Portrait of a Woman* (1530).

Dutch paintings from the same century fill the next room, starring Marten van Heemskerck and the quirky Joachim Patinir, while the **great masters of 16th- and 17th-century painting** are in the following rooms: Tintoretto and El Greco are represented, while Titian's *St Jerome in the Desert* (1575) is an excellent example of his late style, painted with broad brushstrokes and a colour tonalism, radical for the age, that would reverberate down through the late works of Cézanne.

The **Baroque** collection kicks off with *St Catherine of Alexandria* (1597), an early Caravaggio, whose later style informs the works of José de Ribera and Mattia Preti. These are followed by brighter canvases by Murillo and Claude Lorraine before the collection takes a diversion into 18th-century Venice; there are views by Canaletto and Francesco Guardi, Giambattista Tiepolo's luminous *Death of Hyacinth* and Pietro Longhi's delightful *The Tickle* (1755). Rubens dominates the Flemish and Dutch

Baroque paintings, which include one of the museum's interesting juxtapositions: Matthias Stom's *Supper at Emmaus* (*c.*1633–9) and Hendrick ter Brugghen's *Esau Selling his Birthright* (*c.*1627). Both lend intense drama to climactic biblical moments by casting them in candlelight.

First Floor

A series of rooms is devoted to **17th-century Dutch paintings**, the best and most endearing of which show jolly, ribald genre scenes from peasant life, such as Frans Hals' skittish *Fisherman Playing the Violin* (*c.*1630). These are followed by **Rococo and neoclassical works**, including a Watteau and portraits by Reynolds and Gainsborough, which number among the few English paintings in Madrid. Next comes an unusual collection for a European museum: paintings by **19th-century American artists**. It's a mixed bag, from chocolate-boxy autumnal sunsets by Frederic Edwin Church, John Frederick Kensett and Jasper Francis Cropsey to an innovative still life by John Frederick Peto, *Tom's River* (1905), displaying a bold sense of composition years ahead of its time, as well as canvases by American painters who lived in Europe most of their lives, James McNeill Whistler and John Singer Sargent.

Among other **19th-century European works** are three late Goyas, including the delightful laughing *El Tio Paquete*. There is a fine, shimmery late work by Corot, and another by John Constable, *The Lock* (1824), full of silvery highlights and rich colours, a fitting prelude to the selection of **Impressionist** paintings. This is rather slim, but the **Post-Impressionists** and **Fauve** painters are better represented: a few gloriously lurid Van Goghs; a Cézanne; Degas' gauzy, snapshot-like *Swaying Dancer*; a lovely portrait by Toulouse-Lautrec and some riotously coloured works by Dufy, Derain and Vlaminck. Some of the leading exponents of **Expressionist painting** are here, among them Ernst Ludwig Kirchner (1880–1938), Max Beckmann (1884–1950) and Egon Schiele (1890–1918). The iconic early 20th-century **Blaue Reiter movement** is represented by typically symbolic horsey works by Franz Marc and August Macke.

The years of the Weimar Republic led to the final stage of **German Expressionism**, the **Neue Sachlichkeit** (New Objectivity); Otto Dix's quasi-photographic *Hugo Erfurth with a Dog* stands out, its precision in tempera a throwback to the early Renaissance. From Christian Schad there is his discomforting *Portrait of Doctor Haustein* (1928), a tense, psychologically charged work in which the doctor of the title stares out at the viewer, the distorted shadow of his mistress looming behind him.

Ground Floor

A radical change in atmosphere marks the beginning of the collection clumped together as the **Experimental Avant-gardes**. **Cubism** is represented by its three brightest stars, Georges Braque, Pablo Picasso and Juan Gris, and the spin-offs they inspired, Léger, the Delaunays, and the Czech master Frantisek Kupka. The Russian pre- and post-Revolution avant-garde are well represented, and there is plenty of space to appreciate the scale of the Mondrians and Filonov's astounding untitled canvas.

A section entitled '**The Synthesis of Modernism**' contains Chagall's delightful, dreamlike *The Rooster* (1929), and more by Picasso and Braque, plus glittering works by Ernst, Klee, Kandinsky, Léger and Miró, followed by **American Modernists**: Mark Rothko, Georgia O'Keeffe, Jackson Pollock and emigré Surrealist Arshile Gorky.

Along with a Magritte and other Surrealist works, Baron Thyssen got his hands on an excellent Dalí, his *Dream Caused by the Flight of a Bee Around a Pomegranate a Second before Awakening* (1944), but it is the very last section that contains perhaps the most striking works of all: Edward Hopper's *Hotel Room* (1931); a characteristically disturbing Francis Bacon; an unforgettable Lichtenstein (*Woman in the Bath*; 1963); a Hockney; a startling Tom Wesselmann; and one of the best works in the museum: Richard Estes' multilayered slices of New York (*Telephone Booths*; 1967).

Parque del Buen Retiro

***M** Retiro, Atocha, Menéndez Pelayo or Ibiza; wheelchair accessible.*

In the days of Philip IV, this entire area was a royal preserve, including a fortress, a palace (both long gone) and this park, begun by the Conde-Duque Olivares in 1636 for Philip. Apart from growing smaller – it once extended westwards to Pso del Prado – the Retiro has changed essentially little since, an elegant, formal garden, perfect for the decorous pageants and dalliances of the Baroque era. Among its 400-odd acres are cool fountains, a Japanese garden and a seemingly endless expanse of quiet paths among old shady trees where you can easily forget you're in the centre of a major metropolis. A favourite thing to do is rent canoes or paddleboats on the **Estanque**, the broad lagoon at the park's centre. Come on any Sunday, when all Madrid comes to relax, drink *horchata* in the cafés and watch other impromptu entertainments.

An eclectic assortment of buildings dot the Retiro and host a regular schedule of exhibitions and shows. Both the **Palacio de Velázquez** (***t** 915 73 62 45; open Mon and Wed–Sat 11–8, Sun and hols 11–6*) and the enchanting glass and iron **Palacio de Cristal** (***t** 915 74 66 14; open Mon and Wed–Sat 11–8, Sun and hols 11–6*) date from the 1890s and were designed by Ricardo Velázquez Bosco; both are now under the wing of the Reina Sofía museum and are used for temporary exhibitions. At the southern end of the park, seek out the *Angel Caído* ('Fallen Angel', 1878) by Ricardo Bellver and the **Observatorio Astronómico Nacional** (*C/de Alfonso XII 3, **t** 915 30 64 18; **M** Atocha; open Mon–Fri 9–2; adm free*), where you can star-gaze if you make an appointment.

Sandwiched between the park's southwestern corner and the Pso del Prado is the **Real Jardín Botánico** (Botanical Garden; *Pza de Murillo 2; **M** Atocha; wheelchair accessible; open June–Aug daily 10–9; Sept–May daily 10–dusk; adm; free **guided tours** in Spanish only, group tours must be arranged in advance*). This special urban oasis has been completely restored according to the original plans, and features an estimated 30,000 plants, many of them from far-flung corners of the globe.

Museums near the Prado and the Parque del Retiro

This neighbourhood has been Madrid's fashionable centre for over a century, and has therefore attracted quite a few museums. These are about all there is to interest the visitor these days for, tasteful as it is, this is one of the duller corners of the city.

Closest to the Prado, the **Museo del Ejército** (Army Museum; *C/de Méndez Núñez 1*, **t** *915 22 89 77*; **M** *Retiro or Banco de España; wheelchair accessible; open Tues–Sun 10–2; closed Mon; adm, adm free Sat*) pokes its scores of old cannons menacingly out at the surrounding apartment blocks. Like the building itself, most of the exhibits have also seen better days. You can get the army's side of the story on the Carlist, Napoleonic and Civil Wars as you browse through rooms full of shiny military bric-a-brac.

More interesting is the **Museo Naval** (Naval Museum; *Pso del Prado 5*, **t** *913 79 52 99*; **M** *Retiro or Banco de España; open Tues–Sun 10.30–1.30; closed Mon and Aug; adm free*), occupying a corner of the Ministry of Defence. Whatever relics of the Age of Exploration were not locked away in Seville's Archive of the Indies ended up here. Some of the most fascinating are the maps and charts, not simple sailors' tools, but lovely works in which art and scholarship are joined. Juan de la Cosa's *Mapa Mundi* of 1500 is the earliest Spanish map to show parts of the American coast. Much of the museum is given over to ships' models, some of which are wonderfully detailed and precise, offering real insight into the complexity and artfulness of the age of sail. Columbus' Santa Maria is one of these, and it is a reminder of the Admiral of Ocean Sea's achievement to see how small and frail his craft really were.

Just around the corner, the **Museo de Artes Decorativas** (Museum of Decorative Arts; *C/de Montalbán 12*, **t** *915 32 64 99*; **M** *Retiro or Banco de España; wheelchair accessible; open Tues–Fri 10–5, Sat, Sun and hols 10–2; closed Mon; adm, adm free Sat after 2pm and Sun*) has a comprehensive collection of furniture, costume, ceramics, and work in wood as well as textiles, gold and silver from the 15th to the 20th century – six floors of it, in fact, covering every aspect of Spanish design.

A few streets west of the Prado towards Pza Santa Ana is the **Casa-Museo de Lope de Vega** (House of Lope de Vega; *C/de Cervantes 11*, **t** *914 29 92 16*; **M** *Antón Martín or Sevilla; open Tues–Fri 9.30–2, Sat 10–1.30; closed Sun, Mon, hols and Aug; adm, adm free Sat*), where that 'phoenix of Spanish wits' spent the last 25 years of his life. The house was restored to how it might have looked according to an inventory of goods and furnishings found there upon his death; one of the rooms contains personal memorabilia. Perhaps the nicest bit is his little garden, diligently restored to its 17th-century appearance. Vega's bitter enemy, **Cervantes**, lived and died on the same street, but his house is long gone and has now been replaced with a plaque.

North of the Prado: Plaza de Cibeles to Plaza de Colón

Since the Bourbons, this has been the most self-consciously monumental corner of Madrid, spread into a grid of impossibly wide boulevards and traffic-filled plazas. Most of it is not much fun for walking, and the best approach is to pick out what you'd like to see and bus- or metro-hop between them. The Paseo del Prado meets C/de Alcalá at the **Plaza de Cibeles**, considered la *madrileñísima* (the most Madridy) of all, where streams of traffic swirl around Ventura Rodríguez' fanciful fountain of the goddess Cybele in a carriage drawn by lions. The elaborate marble pile on the southeastern side of the plaza is nothing more than the city's main post office, named the **Palacio de Comunicaciones** (***museum*** *open Mon–Fri 9–2 and 5–7, Sat 9–2; adm free*), designed by Antonio Palacios (1904). East of here, C/de Alcalá continues to Pza de la Independencia and its centrepiece, the stately, neoclassical **Puerta de Alcalá** (1778), once the actual gate on the road to Alcalá de Henares.

Madrid's great north–south artery, Pso de la Castellana, is joined to Pso del Prado by Pso de Recoletos, built in the 1830s and 1840s. Along its shady flanks are some of Madrid's most celebrated traditional cafés, among them the **Gran Café Gijón** and **El Espejo**. In the Madrid of the 19th century, architectural tastes favoured the grandiose, and there may be no better example than the **Biblioteca Nacional and Museo del Libro** (*Pso de Recoletos 20, **t** 915 80 78 00, www.bne.es; **M** Serrano or Colón; wheelchair accessible; **library** open Mon–Fri 9–7, Sat 9–2; adm free; **museum** open Tues–Sat 10–7, Sun and hols 10–2; adm free*), a florid pile built by Isabel II and nicknamed the 'Prado of Paper' for its forest-defying collection of printed works.

Museo Arqueológico Nacional (National Archaeology Museum)

*C/de Serrano 13, **t** 915 77 79 12; **M** Serrano or Retiro; wheelchair accessible; open Tues–Sat 9.30–8.30, Sun 9.30–2.30; closed hols, 1, 3 and 10 Nov, 6, 24 and 31 Dec; adm, adm free Sat after 2.30pm, Sun, 18 May, 12 Oct and 6 Dec; call in advance to see the replica of Altamira.*

This is the only comprehensive archaeology museum in the country and, if you can read a little Spanish, the explanations will provide a thorough education in the comings and goings of Spain's shadowy prehistory. Not that the museum is limited to Spain: there is also a surprisingly good collection of Greek vases, and an Egyptian room full of mummies and gaping schoolchildren, along with some very fine jewellery and engraved seals. Many of the Greek and Egyptian relics were actually found in Spain, testimony to the close trade relations ancient Iberia enjoyed with the rest of the Mediterranean world. The museum continues to be active in acquisitions; it recently added an extensive new collection of shields and coins to its holdings.

The tour begins on the **second floor** with the Palaeolithic, Neolithic, Copper, Bronze and Iron Ages in Iberia, then moves on to Northern Africa, Egypt and the near east. Among the urns and pottery shards you will find the **sarcophagus of Amenemhat**, which belonged to a Nubian priest of Ancient Egypt, along with the funerary accoutrements that accompanied him into the afterlife. The Iberians of the Bronze Age were at least up to date in metalworking, and the collection of small expressionistic bronze figurines shows a fine talent, similar in many ways to the famous bronzes from the same period found in Sardinia. Spain's entry into the literate world is chronicled in a host of inscriptions from all over the country. There are some in Iberian, a non-Indo-European language that died out completely with the advent of the Romans; not surprisingly, they haven't completely deciphered any of them. From the Roman era, there are indifferent mosaics and copies of Greek sculpture, along with larger-than-life statues of emperors. The bronze tablets from AD 176, inscribed with the laws and orations of Septimus Severus, would have been set up in public places –

a landmark in the development of political propaganda. The practice was begun by Augustus and used by several of the more energetic emperors that followed. There are also working models of a Roman catapult and ballista (a kind of giant crossbow).

On the **third floor** you will find a decent reproduction of the Altamira caves, as well as relics dating back to Roman, Visigothic and Islamic Iberia, the latter focusing on the marvellous carvings and craftsmanship of Muslim Andalucia.

A visit to this museum, however, is really a pilgrimage to the first and greatest of the great ladies of Spain, *La Dama de Elche*. Nothing we know of the history and culture of the Iberians can properly explain the presence of this beautiful 5th-century BC cult image. As a work of art she ranks among the finest sculptures of antiquity. Pre-Roman Spain was one of the backwaters of the Mediterranean and, while it would be sacrilege in Spain to suggest this lady was the work of a foreign hand, the conclusion seems inescapable. The dress and figure are reminiscent of some eastern Mediterranean image of Cybele, and the Greeks could often capture the same expression of cold majesty on the face of an Artemis, Ariadne or Persephone. Elche, where the bust was discovered, was then in the Carthaginian zone, and that meant easy access to all the Mediterranean world; an artist from anywhere could conceivably have turned up to execute the high priests' commission. Nevertheless, many experts disagree, and find in La Dama's unapproachable hauteur something distinctly Spanish. She holds court these days from a large glass case on a pedestal in the museum's main hall, returning the stares of the schoolchildren with chilly disdain. She shares the room with her less formidable cousins, the very few other Iberian goddesses that have ever been found, including the 4th-century BC Dama de Baza and the Dama de Cerra de los Santos.

Spanish early Christian art is one of the museum's surprises. The architectural sculpture and mosaics show a strong and original sense of design, and a tendency to contemplative geometry that seems almost Islamic. The Visigoths haven't much to offer outside the Treasure of Gurrazar, a collection of vigorously barbaric bejewelled crowns and crosses, all in solid glittering gold, that were found in the Visigothic capital, Toledo. King Recesvinto's crown (*c.* 650) has his name dangling from it in enamelled golden letters; to the mainly illiterate Visigoths, these must have seemed like magic symbols. A small number of Moorish and medieval Christian works complete the collection.

On the **top floor**, the modern age comes as a refreshing surprise. Though it may seem incongruous, you can admire cases of porcelain from the 17th-century kitchen of Isabel Farnese, glass vitrines filled with Counter-reformation age jewels owned by the Austrian kings and queens, and a gem-studded rifle from the Bourbon age. A lovely collection of items from the beginning of the scientific age includes periscopes, compasses, globes and an astrolabe for observing the cosmos.

Outside, near the gate, a small cave has been dug to house replicas of the Upper Palaeolithic paintings of **Altamira**, in Cantabria (*closed exc. by special arrangement*): flowing and vigorous bisons, bulls and other animals in red and black. The museum has gone to great lengths to copy the atmosphere of the real cave; the lighting is so realistically dim, you can barely make out the pictures.

Plaza del Colón

Across from the Archaeology museum, this broad crossroads overlooks the **Jardines del Descubrimiento**, planted in the 1970s and decorated with great blocks of sandstone as part of a **Monument to Columbus**, carved with reliefs and quotes from the admiral's journals; at night its billowing fountains are lit to resemble the sails of his ships. Below the gardens, underneath the 'waterfall-at-the-end-of-the-world', stands the **Centro Cultural de la Villa** (***t*** *915 75 60 80*), a municipal arts centre. Completing the ensemble is the original neo-Gothic Columbus monument, erected in 1885.

South of the Prado

In this direction, Pso del Prado passes the Jardín Botánico towards the shadowy districts around **Atocha**. Relatively recently, the entire plaza was buried under a ghastly, multilevel highway interchange *madrileños* called the 'scalextric' after the model racing car circuit. Mayor Tierno saw it dismantled just before he died. The original wrought iron and glass structure of Atocha station dates from the 1880s, and the station put in 100 years of faithful service until at last it was earmarked for a facelift. In 1992 the station reopened as a shining new temple to rail travel, complete with an indoor shopping and eating emporium. Its centrepiece is an acclimatized tropical garden, with nervous-looking goldfish swimming in pools beneath soaring palm trees and steam filtering down through ducts in the roof.

Southeast of Atocha you can visit a handicrafts workshop fit for kings. In the Palacio Real, El Escorial, and in all the other royal residences around Madrid hang works of the **Real Fábrica de Tapices** (Tapestry Factory; *C/de Fuenterrabia 2,* ***t*** *914 34 05 51;* ***M*** *Menéndez Pelayo; wheelchair accessible; open Mon–Fri 10–2; closed Aug; adm*). Ever since Philip V founded it in the 1710s as Spain's answer to Paris' Gobelins, the weavers of the Real Fábrica have served the Spanish élite's love of fine, pictorial tapestries – not only decorative, but an asset to any draughty palace during the chill Castilian winters. Its best-known productions, of course, are those woven to Goya's designs before he became court painter, the cartoons for which hang in the Prado.

Much of the work that comes to the factory in these centrally heated days involves repairing older works, requiring an impressive amount of skill, matching colours and intricate designs. You may watch the master weavers (there are 42 now, compared with 400 before the Civil War) at work on 18th-century looms any weekday morning, and those with gargantuan bank accounts can order a genuine tapestry as a souvenir.

Old Madrid

Shoehorned into a tight half-kilometre between the Puerta del Sol and the Palacio Real is a solid, enduring Castilian town, often known as 'El Madrid de las Austrias' because most of it was built under the reign of the Habsburgs, and as evocative in its own way as Segovia or Toledo. Old Madrid has changed little since Goya painted its delicate skyline of cupolas and spires. Neither menaced by modern office blocks nor done up picture-pretty for the tourists, the quarter has enjoyed the best of possible fates: to remain as it was. Traditionally home to the Spanish nobility, the recent economic boom has seen major refurbishment of its grand old *palacetes*, and it is now home to Madrid's young, beautiful-people set. It's still a living neighbourhood; loud, busy and a bit unkempt, perhaps, but still Madrid's best and cosiest refuge from the cosmopolitan noise of the rest of the city.

Plaza Mayor

Although Philip II got Juan de Herrera started on designs fit for a Pza Mayor as early as 1532, the project was only completed in 1620 for Philip III; after several fires, the plaza achieved its present form in 1811 under Juan de Villanueva. Few squares in Spain are lovelier, and none is better used. Between concerts, festivals, political rallies and the popular Sunday market peddling stamps, coins, and trinkets, something is likely to be on when you visit. If there isn't, at least someone will be strumming a guitar at the hoofs of the **equestrian statue of Philip III**, while all Madrid passes through and the tourists look on from the cafés. Subsequent kings of Spain were crowned here, and they returned to preside over fiestas, bullfights, the Inquisition's *autos-da-fé*, even archaic knightly tournaments. Kings traditionally took their places in the elegant building with twin spires on the north side of the plaza, the **Casa de la Panadería** (1590), so called after the bakery that preceded it on the site. Its façade was decorated with murals in the late 17th century, and was redecorated in 1992 by Carlos Franco in a groovy neo-hippie celebration of Madrid. Take time to look in the shop windows. Off C/de Toledo is a shop claiming to sell the biggest sizes of ladies' lingerie in the world. Its lovingly designed window may be the most unforgettable sight Madrid can offer.

Plaza de la Villa, La Latina and Lavapiés

Just a couple of hundred metres west of Pza Mayor, on C/Mayor, some of Madrid's oldest buildings can be seen around the **Plaza de la Villa**. The distinguished **Casa de la Villa** (***guided tours*** *in Spanish (for English call ahead) on Mon at 5pm; meet at Pza de la Villa 5,* ***t*** *915 88 29 06; adm free*), by Gómez de Mora, the same architect who created the Plaza Mayor, is one of Madrid's finest buildings, though his simple design of 1599 was given Baroque flourishes by those who completed it in 1696. Inside are the **council chambers**, where the elected officials of Madrid deliberate under a *trompe l'œil* Baroque ceiling by Antonio Palomino, and the enormous painting of *The Third of May* (1872) by Parmorli, as well as a copy of Goya's famous *Allegory of Madrid*, the original now in the Museo Municipal (*see* p.518).

Across the square is the 15th-century **Torre de los Lujanes**, with its tri-lobed Gothic portal, *mudéjar* arch and neighbouring palace. According to legend, it once imprisoned no less a personage than King François I of France. Near the square, at **Calle Mayor 59**, is a rare example of blooming Art Nouveau (1914), never as popular here as elsewhere in Spain. The playwright Pedro Calderón de la Barca died in 1681 in the narrow old house at **No.61**. Just a few yards west the streets around the charmingly rickety glass-and-steel **Mercado de San Miguel** (completed in 1916) make up the busiest and most colourful corner of old Madrid. To the south, Pza del Humilladero,

Pza de Cascorro, and Pza Tirso de Molina are centres of La Latina (***M** La Latina,* ***M** Tirso de Molina*), the heart of old Madrid and a run-down but pleasant place for a stroll. The stretch of C/de la Ribera de Curtidores south of Cascorro is home to Spain's best-known and longest-running outdoor market, **El Rastro** (*Pza de Cascorro and C/de la Ribera de Curtidores;* ***M** La Latina. Held Sun 9am–2pm; see* 'Shopping', p.473). Bordering the Rastro to the east is Lavapiés (***M** Lavapiés*), perhaps Madrid's most distinctively *castizo* district (*castizos* being the 'true born' children of the city, similar to London's Cockneys). The word is now used for whatever is genuinely Madrid, from stew to Goya to *zarzuela*. In July and August you can catch a *zarzuela* in **La Corrala** at C/Tribulete 12, a part-preserved example of a late 19th-century tenement block built around an open courtyard. Lavapiés is the base for many of the city's fringe theatre companies and, as such, it is colourful and characterful, if not wholly salubrious.

A Few Old Churches and a Nunnery

Amazingly, despite its four centuries as capital of Catholic Spain, Madrid hardly has a single church worth going out of your way to visit (the Capilla del Obispo is the great exception to the rule; *see* below). It didn't even have a proper cathedral until the official opening of **Catedral de Nuestra Señora de la Almudena** (*C/de Bailén,* ***t*** *915 42 22 00;* ***M** Opera; wheelchair accessible; open Mon–Sat 10–1.30 and 6–8, Sun 10–2 and 6–8.45;* ***Mass**: Mon–Sat at 10am and noon, Sun at 10.30, noon, 6 and 7*) in 1992. The Cathedral is not quite the stunning culmination of *madrileño* religious passion its builders had hoped for. It was over 100 years in the building, interspersed with political and bureaucratic delays, and the result can only be described as eclectic, with a heavy neo-Baroque dreamed up by Carlos Sidro and Francisco Chueca Goitea, who retook the reins in the 1980s. Founded on the site of the old Almudena Mosque, the most beautiful part of this bulky, ungainly building is its high ceiling of triangular panels painted with Moorish-inspired patterns in muted earthy reds, browns and greens. Overall, the Cathedral feels light and airy, but empty; the abstract stained glass adds much-needed splashes of colour.

Before 1992, Madrid had a stand-in cathedral in the shape of the huge, twin-towered **Colegiata de San Isidro** (*C/de Toledo 37–9,* ***t*** *913 69 23 10;* ***M** La Latina; open Mon–Sat 8.30–12.30 and 6.30–8.30, Sun and hols 9–2 and 5.30–8.30; adm free*), really a monastery church, built for Madrid's Jesuit community in the 1620s, with an elaborate Churrigueresque façade added later. This church was dedicated to Madrid's patron saint by Charles III, and Isidro's remains are still here. It's said that Isidro liked to pray a few streets away in the **Iglesia de San Andrés** (*Pza de San Andrés 1,* ***t*** *913 65 63 76;* ***M** La Latina; open Mon–Sat 8–1 and 5.30–8*), more typical of the blank, severe style of Madrid's older parishes. San Andrés was burnt during the Civil War, and both it and the Plaza have recently been restored.

Behind San Andrés, on Costanilla San Andrés, the splendid **Capilla del Obispo** (Bishop's Chapel; *Pza de la Paja 9; entrance around the back;* ***M** La Latina*) luckily escaped the flames of the Civil War and survives remarkably intact. Designed in the 1540s as a pantheon for the family of Don Francisco de Vargas, Councillor to Ferdinand and Isabel and their grandson Charles V, it is the finest Renaissance work in Madrid, although even at that late date the chapel's vaulting is Flamboyant Gothic. The intricate Plateresque carvings, chapel furnishings, family tombs (especially the alabaster monument of the Bishop of Plascencia, covered with delightful musical angels) and the stupendous gilded high altar soaring to the ceiling, attributed to Francisco Giralte, a pupil of Alonso Berruguete, are the finest in Madrid.

Next door, restoration continues on the façade of the lavish Baroque Capilla de San Isidro, with its heavy ornate cornice, though badly damaged in 1936, the sumptuous interior of polychrome marbles and gilding has been recently restored.

Madrid's largest church, the **Basílica de San Francisco el Grande** (*Pza de San Fransisco, **t** 913 65 38 00; **M** Puerta de Toledo or La Latina; open summer Tues–Sat 11–1 and 5–8; winter Tues–Sat 11–1 and 4–7; adm with **guided tour***) does live up to its big name, topped with a dome measuring 108ft in diameter, but there's little more to say for it, except that it has an early Goya, *San Bernardino of Siena*, in the chapel of the same saint.

North of C/Mayor, off C/Arenal, is the **Real Monasterio de las Descalzas Reales** (*Pza de las Descalzas Reales 3, **t** 915 42 00 59; **M** Sol or Opera; open Tues–Thurs and Sat 10.30–12.45 and 4–5.45, Fri 10.30–12.45, Sun and hols 11–1.30; **church** open only at Mass times, 8am and 7pm; visits by **guided tour** only, in Spanish; adm, free to EU passport-holders on Wed*), hoarding several centuries' accumulation of rich tapestries, furniture, art and holy relics, though you'll have to submit to a tour to see them. First dating from the 16th century, the convent was renovated in the late 1700s, but it remains properly austere on the outside as befitting the order founded by Santa Teresa, the shoeless Carmelites, sworn to poverty, sandal-wearing and pious observance. The two-storey **cloister**, lined with precious, tile-adorned chapels, still functions; in the 1980s the nuns won an award for creating the best new museum in Europe. The most important artworks have long since been relocated to the Museo del Prado, but a few gems remain, including works by Titian, Goya, Brueghel, Zurbarán and Rubens.

Palacio Real or Palacio de Oriente (Royal Palace)

*C/de Bailén, **t** 915 42 00 59; **M** Opera; wheelchair accessible.*
*Open April–Sept Mon–Sat 9–6, Sun and hols 9–3; Oct–Mar Mon–Sat 9.30–5, Sun and hols 9–12; closed frequently for official functions; adm (includes **Farmacia**), free to EU passport-holders on Wed.*
***Optional tours** in English and other languages for an extra €1.*

Any self-respecting Bourbon had to have one. Philip V, who commissioned the palace in 1738, had to be talked out of an even grander version by his wife, who thought 2,800 rooms would probably meet her needs. Originally this was the site of the Moorish Alcázar, converted by Henry IV into Madrid's first Royal Palace. It was here that Velázquez lived and painted for Philip IV, and many of his works are infused with the atmosphere of its old, shadowy chambers. A great fire occasioned the 18th-century replacement, very much in the style of Versailles and other contemporary palaces. The exterior is grand and elegant enough, the effect heightened by its setting on a bluff above the Manzanares. Alfonso XIII was the last king to use the Palace as a residence. Juan Carlos' tastes are more modest: he lives quite comfortably at the suburban Palacio de la Zarzuela, without any semblance of an old-style court.

The entrance to the palace is by way of the **Plaza de la Armería**, a courtyard big enough to hold the entire Pza Mayor, and the stage for the **changing of the guard** (*first Wed of each month, exc. July, Aug and Sept, at noon*), which comes complete with a military band and some impressive horsemanship, all done in early 1900s style.

Fortunately, not all 2,800 rooms are open, but even so expect a mild delirium after the first three dozen or so, each with its tapestry, portraits of bewigged sycophants, half-ton chandelier and indolent mythological deities painted on the ceiling. Some rooms do stand out in the miasma of pomp: persevere, and you will be rewarded with frescoes by Giambattista Tiepolo, Francisco Bayeu and Antonio Velázquez, violins by Stradivarius, paintings by El Greco and Goya as well as Rubens, Van der Weyden and Watteau, and many other favourites of the age.

The **Farmacia Real** (1594) is located in the first set of rooms you pass, containing many original fittings and jars. The **Armería Real** reopened in 2000 after lengthy restoration, with a stunning collection of medieval pieces, as well as those of Charles V and Philip II. Charles V had a truly Quixotic fascination with armour and his collection makes up most of what you see today.

Two formal parks make up the grounds of the Palacio Real: the **Jardines Sabatini**, which have seen better days, and the larger **Jardines del Campo del Moro** (*Pso de la Virgen del Puerto; **M** Príncipe Pío; open winter Mon–Sat 10–6, Sun and hols 9–6; summer Mon–Sat 10–8, Sun and hols 9–8*). Planted like an English park in 1842,they are a miniature version of the Versailles gardens, with lovely views up to the palace.

Ermita de San Antonio de la Florida (The Goya Pantheon)

*Pso de la Florida 5, **t** 915 42 07 22; **M** Príncipe Pío; wheelchair accessible; open Tues–Fri 10–2 and 4–8, Sat and Sun 10–2; closed hols; adm, adm free Wed and Sun.*

A pedestrian flyover through the railyards of the woebegone Estación de Príncipe Pío will take you to the narrow island between the tracks and the river, where two identical neoclassical chapels stand, both dedicated to the same St Anthony. The one you want is opposite the seated statue of the painter; the other is a replica, built when the original was made into the Goya Pantheon. Around 13 June, the replica is the focus of the week-long *verbena* dedicated to Anthony, when the *paseo* is closed off for the festivities.

The original church was designed by Philip Fontana for Charles IV, and contains one of the milestones of Spanish art. In 1798, Goya was commissioned to do a series of frescoes on the walls, ceiling and dome, and he did them in a way never seen before in any church. St Anthony, in the dome, is clearly recognizable, but that is Goya's only concession to the usual conventions of religious art. The scores of figures covering the ceiling have the same faces as the people in his celebrated cartoons, only instead of angelic *madrileños* they have become angels in fact. Every one has the quality of a portrait; the peaceful rapture expressed in their faces has at its source nothing the

Church could provide, but a particular secret perhaps known only to Goya. He painted the whole thing in 120 days; the restorers in 1996 took three times as long, but the frescoes are now more beautiful than ever. An audiovisual guide offers surprising close-ups. The artist is buried here, and the church has become his monument.

Around the Plaza de España and the Gran Vía

The Gran Vía is the Madrid of the bright lights, the main shopping and business area, replete with awkward skyscrapers, grand imperial cinemas with enormous hand-painted billboards, hamburger joints, banks – and swarming with traffic and people late into the night. Part of the excitement comes from the area's wildly eclectic array of early 20th-century architecture along C/de Alcalá and Gran Vía. North of the Gran Vía are the two flavoursome old districts of Malasaña and Chueca, once seedy and druggy but now top night-time destinations. Marking the western end of the Gran Vía is the broad **Plaza de España**, much beloved by local winos, so you may not want to linger too long. Running northwest from Pza España is the beautifully landscaped **Parque del Oeste** (*Pso del Pintor Rosales; **M** Argüelles*), complete with **La Rosaleda** at its centre, a rose garden where each spring Madrid's international rose exhibition takes root. The little park wears an unexpected ornament: a sandstone Egyptian temple of the 4th century BC. The **Templo de Debod** (*Parque de la Montana, **t** 914 09 61 65; **M** Ventura Rodriguez or Pza de España; open April–Sept Tues–Fri 10–2 and 6–8, Sat and Sun 10–2; Oct–Mar Tues–Fri 9.45–1.45 and 4.15–6.15, Sat and Sun 10–2; closed Mon and hols; adm, adm free Wed*) is nothing very elaborate, but it is genuine. In 1968, the Egyptian government sent it, block by block, as a token of appreciation for Spanish help in the relocation of monuments during the building of the Aswan dam. Amazingly, the little temple seems cheerfully at home, orientated to the same sunrise, looking over the peculiar city below. If you don't suffer from vertigo, take the ***teleférico*** from here for the views of the Casa de Campo, the Manzanares and the Palacio Real with the city beyond.

Casa de Campo

***M** Batán or Lago; **teleférico** (**t** 915 41 75 70, www.teleferico.com; wheelchair accessible) from Parque del Oeste April–Sept Mon–Fri 11–3 and 5–8.30, Sat, Sun and hols 11–3 and 4.30–9.30; Oct–Mar Sat, Sun 12–3 and 4–8; bus No.33 from **M** Príncipe Pío.*

When the Habsburgs decided to make Madrid their capital, they didn't give much thought to amenities. One of their tricks was to chop down every tree of the forests that once surrounded Madrid, sell them as firewood all over Castile, and use the money to embellish their palaces. Philip II, an avid hunter like most of his kin, soon regretted this, and he had this tract of land reforested. The Casa de Campo was the happy result: a stretch of quiet, green countryside for picnics and outings, in spite of a slightly shady reputation for illicit goings-on. During the summer, the **outdoor pool** and **boating lake** are packed with sizzling *madrileños*.

Within the park's boundaries are two more big draws: the **Parque de Atracciones** (***t*** *915 26 80 30 or* ***t*** *914 63 29 00; open winter Sun–Fri noon–11pm, Sat noon–1am; summer Sun–Thurs noon–11pm, Fri and Sat noon–3am; adm, individual adm charges for rides*), a permanent funfair offering thrills and chills on its 'Flume Ride' and roller-coasters; and the **Zoo-Acuario de Madrid** (***t*** *915 12 37 30; wheelchair accessible; open Mon–Fri 10.30–8, Sat and Sun 10.30–9.30; adm exp*), with 150 kinds of mammals and 100 kinds of birds. The star is Chulín, the first panda to be born in captivity in the West (though he's rarely visible), but the zoo also has a tropical aquarium, dolphin pool, ostrich zone and snake den.

A Spanish Match

Spain in the 17th century made itself the true homeland of the picaresque, the inspiration for the first novels, and Spaniards set the fashions and the manners for all Europe in the age of Baroque. Life was a stage, and a man wasn't a man until he'd gone out and had an adventure – even if he was the son of a king. The **Casa de las Siete Chimeneas** (*Pza del Rey;* ***M*** *Banco de España*), just north of the Gran Vía and C/de Alcalá, belonged to John Digby, Earl of Bristol, in Spain on government business, and in March of 1623 it received a very unusual lodger: none other than the 21-year-old Prince of Wales, the future Charles I. Charles had travelled to Spain incognito, with his friend the Duke of Buckingham, under the names 'John Brown and Tom Smith'. The Earl, who was keeping an eye on Charles for his father, James I, wrote home that the pair were 'sweet boys and dear virtuous knights, worthy to be put in a new *romanso*'.

The visit had a purpose: Spain and England were enjoying a rare period of peace, and there was talk of marrying Charles to the Infanta Doña María. Naturally, he wanted to have a look at her first. Riding to Spain was the easy part; getting into the court of Philip IV, who didn't much care for Protestant heretics, proved much harder. Charles first saw his Infanta when their coaches passed in a Madrid street; later, go-betweens managed to contrive a meeting during the *paseo* on the Prado – Charles would know her by the blue ribbon in her hair.

When word of this got out, Charles' presence could no longer be kept a secret. Finally the King consented to a state entrance for Charles in the biggest spectacle Madrid had to offer, a gala bullfight in the Plaza Mayor with all the court in attendance, watching from the balconies.

Charles apparently liked what he saw (according to Olivares, he devoured the Infanta with his eyes 'like a cat does a mouse'), for he tried without success to surprise her in the Casa de Campo, where she and her friends were out at dawn gathering May dew. But this is history, not a *romanso*, and politics and religion made it a match never to be. Charles stayed in Madrid for six months; he met Velázquez and Van Dyck, and went back home with presents from the royal family that included paintings by Titian and Correggio. This began Charles' own career as an art collector, and he amassed quite a remarkable collection before he lost his head. His philistine Roundhead successors had no use for such trumperies and sold them off at a ridiculous price – to the King of Spain.

North of the Puerta del Sol

The area immediately north of the Puerta del Sol is central Madrid's main middle-of-the-road shopping district, with pedestrian precincts crammed with chain stores. The broad, dignified C/de Alcalá sweeps out to the northeast, and here, housed in the former Palacio Goyeneche, is the **Real Academia de Bellas Artes de San Fernando** (*C/de Alcalá 13, **t** 915 22 14 91; **M** Sol or Sevilla; wheelchair accessible; open Tues–Fri 9–7, Sat–Mon and hols 10–2; adm, adm free Wed; free **guided tour** (Spanish only) Wed at 5pm*). The façade was stripped of all ornament in 1773, and the building has looked like Cinderella after the ball ever since.

The rooms display a fascinating selection from the last five centuries of Spanish painting; alongside the more quirky works there are some moody Riberas, fine paintings by Murillo and Sorolla, El Greco and Velázquez and some remarkable life-size monks by Zurbarán. Among the excellent Goya canvases is his famous *The Burial of the Sardine*, showing the riotous *fiestas* that mark the end of carnival (*see* 'Festivals', p.471). The national print collection (**Calcografía Nacional**) was founded in 1789 and is Spain's principal centre for the study of etchings and engravings; it has an impressive number of printing plates and tools, which get exhibited in rotation.

Inside, **temporary exhibition space** and the **Calcografía Nacional** are on the mezzanine level between the ground and first floors, and the **permanent collection** is on the first and second floors. This is displayed in vaguely chronological order, with 14th–18th-century works on the first floor and newer works upstairs, though there is some overlap. Goya is on the first floor.

Off the northern side of Gran Vía lie the neighbourhoods of Malasaña and Chueca. A jumble of crowded streets, which by day are home to locals, and by night thronged with revellers, piquant **Malasaña** still lives off its reputation as the epicentre of the *movida* years, and every other doorway seems to be a club. The town hall has cleaned the area up recently, and cleared out many of the badly parked cars, more or less pedestrianizing it. The heart of the district is the **Plaza de Dos de Mayo** (***M** Tribunal*), lined with pleasant *terrazas*, but scene of the bloody insurrection of 2 May 1808 later immortalized by Goya (*see* his works in the Prado, p.500).

East of Malasaña, **Chueca** has prospered in its role as the capital's gay district, and its bars, restaurants and fancy and quirky shops (not all of which are exclusively gay by any means) are among the hippest in the city. It's the real Madrid, and a perfect setting for the city's very good **Museo Municipal** (*C/de Fuencarral 78, **t** 915 88 86 72; **M** Tribunal; open Tues–Fri 9.30–8, Sat and Sun 10–2; closed Mon and hols; adm*). Housed in the 18th-century Hospicio de San Fernando, with an exuberant Churrigueresque portal by Pedro de Ribera, the museum has been renovated and greatly expanded in recent years. More *madrileños* come here than tourists, and you can sense their growing civic pride as you watch them scrutinizing the old maps and prints, pointing out landmarks and discussing how their city has changed. The collection is large, and you can learn as much as you care to about Madrid and its history. Spaniards love to make room-sized models of their cities, and there is a remarkable example here that accurately reproduces the Madrid of the 1830s. Here, too, you'll find Goya's *Allegory of Madrid*, its chequered history reflective of the interesting times in which he lived.

Moncloa and the Ciudad Universitaria

Miguel Primo de Rivera always liked to think of himself as a great benefactor of education, and it exasperated him that Spain's university students spent most of the 1920s out in the streets calling him names. He began this sprawling, suburban campus (***M** Ciudad Universitaria*) in 1927, partly to appease them but mostly to get them out of town. This institution, the nation's largest, began as the Complutensian University, founded by Cardinal Cisneros in Alcalá de Henares. After it moved to Madrid, it was based in the quarter north of the Gran Vía. De Rivera's new campus was unfinished when the Civil War broke out; the University found itself in the front line, a potent symbol of the nature of the war as Franco's artillery pounded the halls of knowledge to rubble. Franco later rebuilt them in a stolid, authoritarian style. Today the campus is well kept, but as dull for visitors as it must be for its students.

Near the southern end of the Ciudad Universitaria lies a Latin American treasure-trove. After being cocooned in renovation for a dozen years, the superb Art Deco **Museo de América** (*Av. de los Reyes Católicos 6, **t** 915 49 26 41; **M** Moncloa; wheelchair accessible; open Tues–Sat 10–3, Sun and hols 10–2.30; closed Mon; adm, adm free Sat after 2pm and Sun*) emerged glistening like a butterfly in 1994. In its new incarnation it is cool, elegant and beautifully designed. On display is one of Europe's largest collections of artefacts from the Aztecs, Incas, Maya and other New World cultures, many of them plundered in the time of the conquistadors, but others acquired much later by more honourable means. Among the most beautiful are **gold ornaments** from Colombia and Costa Rica, some over 1,000 years old, and ancient Peruvian and Chilean **textiles**. There is also an extremely rare post-Classic Mayan codex, the ***Códice Tro-Cortesiano***, a 112-page document in hieroglyphs, relating, among other things, news of the Spanish arrival. **Spanish engravings** depicting indigenous South Americans as fantastical giants, headless monsters or cheerful cannibals give a fascinating insight into the popular state of mind at the dawn of the Age of Exploration, and a series of 16th- to 18th-century **maps** illustrates the rapid growth of Western knowledge of this alien territory. The museum also covers aspects of contemporary Latin American culture; **film showings** highlight current social and cultural issues in the context of the past.

Salamanca Quarter and Museo Lázaro Galdiano

Paseo de Recoletos runs along the west end of the fashionable Barrio de Salamanca, laid out when the last walls were knocked down in the 1860s. Much of the cheerless waffle iron of swanky avenues bears an eerie resemblance to the neighbourhoods around New York's Park Avenue, with a scattering of old mansions wearing a certain Victorian panache, illegally parked cars with diplomatic licence plates and bored concierges walking other people's Pekineses. The main reason to come here is to shop (head for Calles Serrano, Goya, Claudio Coello, Velázquez and Ortega y Gasset), but Salamanca can boast one of Madrid's best museums, the **Museo Lázaro Galdiano**

(*C/de Serrano 122, **t** 915 61 60 84; **M** Gregorio Marañón or Núñez de Balboa; wheelchair accessible; closed for renovation until late 2002; when reopened, open Tues–Sun 10–2; closed hols, Aug, 1, 3 and 10 Nov, 6, 24 and 31 Dec; night-time tours available in the summer; adm, adm free Wed*). The founder, who died in 1948, had a better eye and deeper pockets than the other Madrid collectors whose homes have been turned into museums. Among the 37 rooms of art, he assembled one work by nearly every important Spanish painter, two visionary paintings by Hieronymous Bosch, a Rembrandt portrait and even some English paintings, including works by Gainsborough, Turner and Reynolds. There's nearly a whole room of Goyas, including two early 'Black Paintings', as well as some prints, drawings and lithographs. Galdiano's tastes were remarkably eclectic, and on the ground floor articles from the Moors, Byzantines, Persians and Celts share space with medieval armour, early clocks and two exceptional treasures: the Gran Sagrario de Limoges (*c.* 1300) and an engraved goblet made for Rudoloph II of Prague.

Peripheral Attractions

There's not much reason to leave the central area of Madrid, but a few museums in the outlying districts may catch your fancy. The **Palacio Real de El Pardo** (*Cenitra de El Pardo, **t** 913 76 15 00; **M** Moncloa then bus No.83 (30 mins) from Pso de Moret nearby every 10–15 mins; wheelchair accessible; open Mon–Sat 10.30–6, Sun and hols 9.25–1.40; closed when used by a visiting head of state; adm, adm free Wed*) built by Charles III, stands in a planted forest some 13 kilometres north of the centre. Now used to lodge visiting VIPs, it was used by Franco as his residence throughout the dictatorship, and offers a rare glimpse into how he worked, with his office left as it was when he died.

Madrid's main bullring, the **Plaza de Toros Monumental de Las Ventas** (*C/de Alcalá 237, **arena t** 913 56 22 00; **M** Ventas; 1½km walk from Pza de la Independencia; wheelchair accessible; **museum** open Tues–Fri 9.30–2.30, Sun 10–1; adm free; **box office** open Fri–Sat 10–2 and 5–8, Sun 10–bullfight*), designed by Rodríguez Ayuso, is the busiest and most prestigious in Spain. Around the back is the recently rearranged **Museo Taurino**, the largest and most complete museum of bullfighting.

Over in Chamberí, the **Museo Sorolla** (*Pso del General Martínez Campos 37, **t** 913 10 17 31; **M** Rubén Darío or Gregorio Marañón; open Tues–Sat 10–3, Sun and hols 10–2; adm, adm free Sat after 2pm, Sun, 18 May, 12 Oct and 6 Dec*) takes you back a century into the Valencian painter's home, with its refreshing Moorish garden. Joaquín Sorolla (1863–1923) was one of the most fashionable painters of his day and his house and studio remain much as he left it, offering a charming insight into the man, his times and his art.

Around Madrid

15

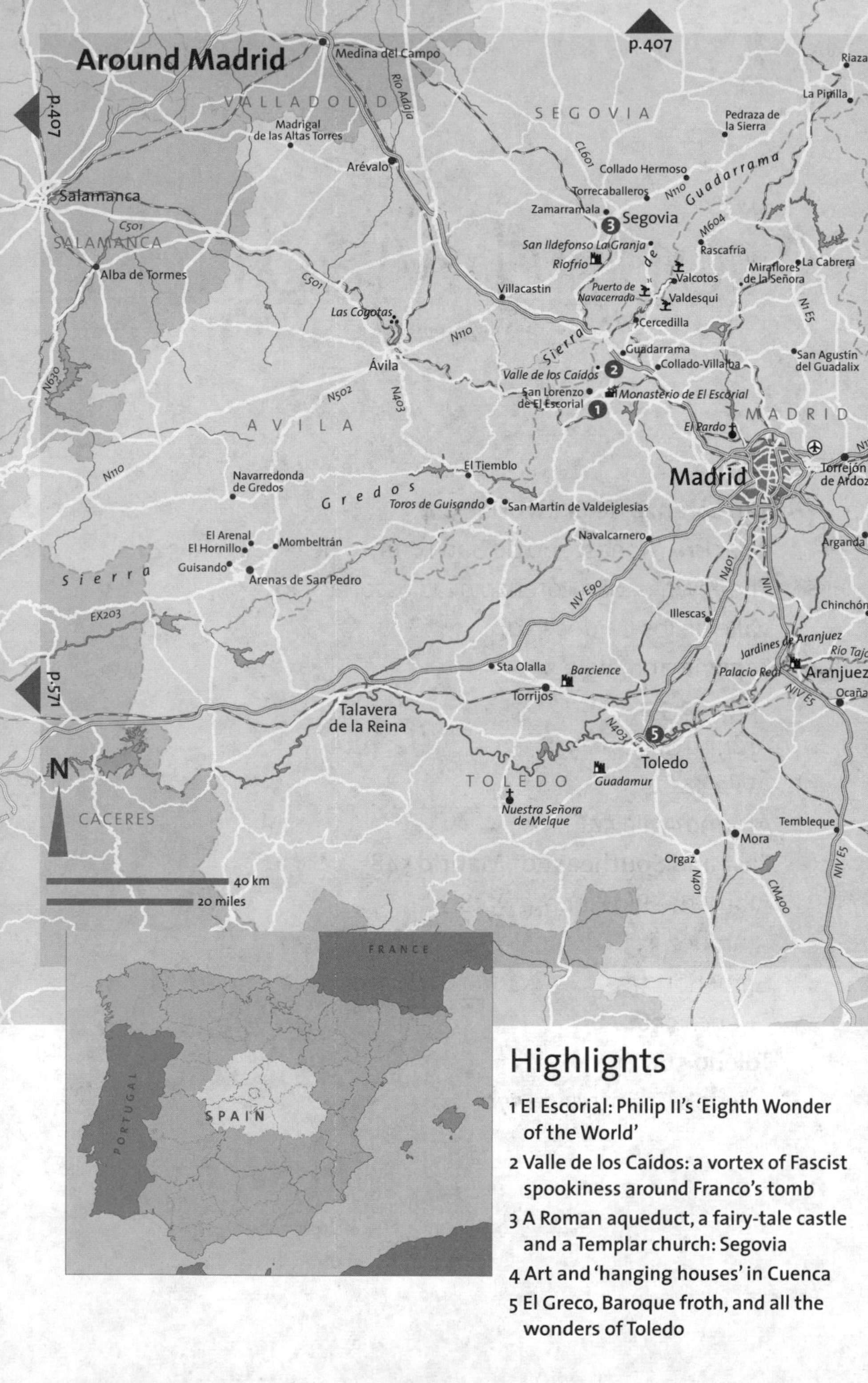

Highlights

1. El Escorial: Philip II's 'Eighth Wonder of the World'
2. Valle de los Caídos: a vortex of Fascist spookiness around Franco's tomb
3. A Roman aqueduct, a fairy-tale castle and a Templar church: Segovia
4. Art and 'hanging houses' in Cuenca
5. El Greco, Baroque froth, and all the wonders of Toledo

Beyond the caprice of Charles V and Philip II, Madrid's location made it the logical site for Spain's capital. Not only is Madrid roughly central to the country as a whole, but its growth filled a vacuum at the centre of a region containing many of the most important cities of 16th-century Spain. Philip's new capital thus had a sort of ready-made Île-de-France around it, a garland of historic and lovely towns, each with something different to offer the visitor.

Everyone goes to **Toledo**, of course, and romantically beautiful **Segovia** also comes in for its share of visitors. But Madrid also serves as a convenient base for visiting **Ávila**, resolutely medieval behind its famous walls, the distinguished old university

town of Alcalá de Henares, quiet, seldom-visited Sigüenza, the citadel of Cuenca with its cliffside houses, the royal palaces at Aranjuez, or San Lorenzo de El Escorial.

Whenever Madrid's traffic, cacophonous nightclubs, and endless museum corridors become too much, any of these towns can provide a day's diversion and a little peace and quiet. And if Madrid is just the kind of metropolis you're trying to get away from, you can always set yourself up in one of them – and make day trips to Madrid.

San Lorenzo de El Escorial

The Spaniards aren't shy; they matter-of-factly refer to Philip II's combination palace-secretariat-monastery-mausoleum as 'the eighth wonder of the world'. Any building with a façade 528ft wide, 2,673 windows, 16 patios and 15 cloisters is entitled to some consideration, but it's not so much the glass and stone of El Escorial that make it remarkable, but the neurotic will of the king who conjured it up. This is the vortex of Spain, full of magnificence and poison, a folly on an imperial scale. To the Protestants of northern Europe, hard pressed to keep Philip's armies and priests at bay, this building was a diabolic horror, the seat of evil on earth. Philip himself would have calmly disagreed (for he was always calm), explaining that what he really had in mind was the re-creation of the Temple of Solomon. Despite all the effort Philip

Getting There

By Train

Trains to El Escorial (Cercanías line C 8a, direction Ávila; 1 hr) start from Madrid-Atocha, and also stop at Madrid-Chamartín. There are usually hourly departures in the day, and more at peak times. Trains come in at the village of El Escorial and are met by local buses that make the short trip to San Lorenzo and the monastery. The alternative is a gentle 2km-walk uphill from the station, along a fragrant avenue shaded by chestnuts and pines, past the Casita del Príncipe (*see* p.529). General RENFE information: **t** 902 24 02 02; Cercanías information: **t** 915 06 61 95/915 06 61 37.

By Bus

Remember that the proper name of the town beside the monastery is San Lorenzo de El Escorial, and it appears that way in bus timetables. The bus, Nos.661 and 664, is faster than the train, and is run by Herranz, **t** 915 43 36 45 or **t** 918 90 41 22, from Bay 3 of the Intercambiador de Transportes (bus interchange) next to **M** Moncloa in Madrid, to the stop in Pza Virgen de Gracia in San Lorenzo, very near the monastery. Daily buses leave every half-hour in the morning, every hour thereafter; journey 1 hr). Herranz also goes once daily from San Lorenzo to the Valle de los Caídos, allowing enough time to see the place (journey 20 mins). Tickets are sold in a little office in a bar on C/Reina Victoria.

By Car

From Madrid take the Ctra N-VI (Ctra de La Coruña) northwest, then the M505.

Tourist Information

San Lorenzo de El Escorial: C/Floridablanca 10, **t** 918 90 15 54, near the bus station.

Festivals

As with much of the Sierra de Guadarrama, El Escorial holds its town fiestas during the first two weeks of September.

Fiesta of San Lorenzo, *10 Aug*. The town's patron saint is the pretext for much fun with processions and a fair at the entrance to the Casita de Arriba.

Anniversary of Franco's Death, *20 Nov*. Sees a motley crowd gather at Valle de los Caídos.

expended in stamping out heretical opinions in his long reign, especially brutally in the Netherlands, he seems to have entertained quite a few of his own on the sly, possibly picked up during his years spent in the Low Countries. He found geomancers to select the proper site for the millennial temple, astrologers to pick the date for laying the corner stone (23 April 1563), and hermetic philosophers to help with the numerical mysticism that is supposedly built into every proportion of the building.

An *escorial* is a slag heap – there once was some sort of mine on this site – and so the proper title of Philip's dream-house translates as the Royal Seat of the Royal Saint Lawrence of the Slag Heap. The reasons for the dedication to San Lorenzo are unclear. Supposedly Philip won a victory on the saint's day in 1557, at St Quentin in Flanders, and vowed to build him something in return; this is unlikely, as the dedication wasn't made until 10 years after El Escorial was completed. An even less probable tale has Philip's architects planning this rectangle of buildings and enclosed courtyards as an echo of the saint's gridiron attribute (San Lorenzo was roasted alive on one; he is supposed to have told the Romans: 'You can turn me over now; I'm done on this side'). While San Lorenzo is not one of the most popular saints, there's an obscure legend that he brought the Holy Grail to Spain, and this may help to explain the tangled web of esotericism behind Philip's work. Philip's original architect, Juan Bautista de Toledo, had worked on St Peter's in Rome; you may find that these two chilly, overblown

Where to Stay

El Escorial ✉ 28280

★★★★**Victoria Palace**, C/Juan de Toledo 4, **t** 918 96 98 90, **f** 918 96 98 96, *www.hotelvictoria-palace.com* (*expensive*). Recently restored to its former glory; the best rooms face south over the woodlands.

★★★**Miranda Suizo**, C/Floridablanca 18, **t** 918 90 47 11, **f** 918 90 43 58 (*expensive; cheaper Sept–July*). Recent restorations have diluted some of the former Swiss charm: but it's comfy nonetheless, with lovely views of the monastery and an authentically alpine **café** serving afternoon teas of hot chocolate and *picatostes* (fried bread soldiers dipped in sugar) to a genteel and devoted clientele.

★★★**Florida**, C/Floridablanca 12, **t** 918 90 17 21, **f** 918 90 17 15 (*moderate*). Another good option, just down from the Miranda Suizo.

★★**Hs Cristina**, C/Juan de Toledo 6, **t** 918 90 19 61, **f** 918 90 12 04 (*inexpensive*). Friendly, with a small garden and a **restaurant**.

★★**Hs Vasco**, Pza de Santiago 11, **t** 918 90 16 19 (*cheap*). Good budget choice with a decent **restaurant** (*inexpensive*); the good-value *menú* is worth considering in a town where dining isn't always cheap.

Eating Out

Beef from the Sierra de Guadarrama has been given its own denomination of origin; and if you're an avid meat eater, there's nothing finer.

Charolés, C/Florida Blanca 24, **t** 918 90 59 75 (*expensive*). Steeped in tradition, this is one of the town's best eateries: its weekly Wednesday *cocido* is a grand affair and an event in itself.

El Croché, C/San Lorenzo 6. An old-world café connected to Charolés and the perfect place to head for a mid-afternoon coffee or snack if you don't fancy tackling the full-on restaurant routine.

Fonda Génara, Pza San Lorenzo 2 (*moderate*). This is situated on the pretty Plaza de la Constitución, and has a terrific midday *menú* (*inexpensive*).

Parrilla Príncipe, Floridablanca 6, **t** 918 90 16 11 (*moderate–inexpensive*). An intimate and restful haven located inside an 18th century *palacete*, with lovely views of the monastery. It offers excellent meat and fish in a spot that, for all its elegant, English-style décor, attracts a surprisingly varied crowd. *Open Wed–Mon 1–4 and 8.30–midnight.*

symbols of the Counter-Reformation have much in common. Work commenced in 1563, but Bautista died four years later, and El Escorial was entrusted to his brilliant pupil, Juan de Herrera, who saw the task through to its completion in 1584. It kept him busy; even though Herrera had little time to spare on any other buildings, his reputation as one of the great Spanish architects was confirmed. By creating the *estilo desornamentado* (unadorned style), stripping the Renaissance building to its barest essentials, he captured perfectly the nation's mood of austere militancy. Philip was more than pleased, and as he contemplated the work in progress from the spot on the hills above El Escorial, still called *La Silla de Philip II* (King Philip's Seat), he must have dreamed just a little of the dawn of a new classic age, where Christianity and Renaissance achievement were to be combined in the spiritually perfect world empire of Spain.

If you come to El Escorial for a classic revelation, you'll have to settle for dry classicism; those who have read too much about the dark side of Philip's Spain and come expecting a monkish haunted house will be equally disappointed. As huge as it is, there's nothing gloomy or menacing about El Escorial. Its crisp lines and soft grey granite combine for an effect that is tranquil and airy both inside and out. Everything is remarkably clean, as if dust and age had been banished by royal decree; somehow El Escorial looks as bright and new as the day it was completed.

Palacio y Monasterio de San Lorenzo el Real de El Escorial

Open April–Sept Tues–Sun 10–6; Oct–Mar Tues–Sun 10–5; closed Mon and hols; adm, adm slightly extra for the 45-minute guide; adm free for EU passport holders on Wed; ***t*** *918 90 59 02/03; note that adm to Basílica only is free.*

El Escorial is managed by the Patrimonio Nacional. They sell tickets, guidebooks and souvenirs inside the north entrance. They also run guided tours, in various languages; if you want to join one, you may be asked to wait for a large enough group to gather. If you prefer, you can explore the complex independently, in any order you like (the official tour route is clearly signposted). However, without any guidance, you may miss out on a lot of intriguing details, such as the many manifestations of Philip's obsession with mystical patterns in designing and building the place. You may also find, as you make your way from room to room and up and down dim stone staircases, that you quickly lose all sense of direction, and fail to appreciate, for example, the strategic location of the royal mausolea and Philip's apartments in relation to the Basilica. (James Michener was not ashamed to admit he came here twice without realizing the mausoleum had a church, though a 139,932 sq ft basilica with a 300ft-high dome would elsewhere be hard to miss.) You can walk right in to the Basilica (*entrance is free*), through the monumental western entrance, under the statue of San Lorenzo with his gridiron, and from here, along the central axis of the complex, the symmetrical grandeur of Bautista and Herrera's plan will begin to unfold.

Palacio de los Borbones (Bourbon Palace) and Nuevos Museos (New Museums)

The official tours begin in the northeastern quarter of El Escorial, a quarter never used by Philip II, but converted by the Bourbons Charles III and Charles IV into a royal residence. These two do not seem to have had any interest in Philip's conception of El Escorial, but used it only as a sort of glorified hunting-lodge. Not surprisingly, they refurbished these rooms as a similar, though smaller version of the Bourbon Royal Palace in Madrid. The **Bourbon Apartments**, with their tapestries after works by Goya and others, have now been restored to their former splendour, and they form a pleasant contrast to the austerity of their surroundings. One of the most interesting rooms is the **Hall of the Battles** (*just reopened to the public after restoration work*), with its fresco over 200ft long representing every detail of the 1431 Battle of Higuerela, a victory of King Juan II over the Moors of Granada.

Downstairs there is an exhibition of some of the machinery and tools used to build the complex, plus architectural drawings and scale models tracing the progress of the construction work. Upstairs again, the **New Museums** occupy a long corridor along the eastern walls, with windows looking out over intricate knot gardens. Much of Philip's collection of paintings is displayed here, including fanciful works by Bosch (*The Crown of Thorns* and *The Seven Deadly Sins* among others), Patinir, Titian, Veronese, Ribera, El Greco and Dürer; later additions include a Velázquez.

Palacio de Felipe II

Such is the reputation Philip earned for himself – the evil genius of the Inquisition and all – that the little palace he tacked on to the back of El Escorial for himself comes as a genuine surprise. Few kings have chosen a more delightful abode: a few simple rooms reminiscent of the interiors from paintings of Vermeer, with white walls, Delft-blue tiles, and windows opening on to gardens and forests on all sides. These rooms suggest that Philip's famous self-inflicted isolation had less monkishness about it than the desire of a cultured, bookish monarch to ensure the necessary serenity for the execution of the royal duty he took so seriously. Philip did not like courtiers, and he didn't care to go out. Alone with his trusted secretaries, he governed the affairs of his empire meticulously, reading, rereading and annotating vast heaps of documents and reports. Aesthete and mystic, he approached politics with the soul of a clerk, and each of his long list of mistakes was decided upon with the greatest of care.

It was here that Philip received nervous, respectful ambassadors on a throne 'hardly grander than a kitchen chair'. Here, in his perfect temple, where the wisdom of Solomon was to be reborn, they brought him the news of the Armada's disaster, the national bankruptcies, the independence of the Netherlands, and all the little pinpricks in between. Here he endured the wasting disease that killed him, causing him to stink so badly that neither servants nor visitors could bear his presence. He made sure his bed was situated right above the High Altar of his Basilica, and had a spyhole cut in the bedchamber wall so that he could observe the endless Masses and bad art down below. Here, with only a crowned skull on his night table to keep him company, he awaited the reward of the virtuous.

The art and furnishings of the apartments may not necessarily be an accurate representation of Philip's tastes, but there is a copy Philip had made of Bosch's *Hay Wain*, one of his favourites, the original of which hangs in the Prado. In the throne room, be sure to see the marvellous inlaid wood **doors**, decorated with *trompe l'œil* scenes and architectural fantasies, done by an anonymous German artist of the 16th century; they are among the most beautiful things in the whole of El Escorial.

Mausoleums, Sacristy, Chapterhouse and Library

An opulent but narrow staircase leads down to the **Panteón Real**, situated beneath the Basilica's High Altar. All manner of stories have grown up around this pantheon of bad kings. Charles II, it is said, spent whole days down here, ordering the gilded marble tombs to be opened so that he might gaze on his mummified ancestors. As in the Basilica, the most expensive stone from around the Mediterranean was used in its construction; the red jasper of the pavement and pilasters is so hard it had to be cut with diamond-tipped saws. The adjacent room is called, charmingly, the **Pudrería** (the 'rotting chamber'), where Habsburg and Bourbon potentates spent 20-odd years mouldering until they became sufficiently dried out for their interments. Royal relations fill a maze of corridors beyond the Pantheon of the Kings, guarded by enormous white heralds with golden maces. Don Juan, victor of Lepanto, is the best known of them, though the tomb everyone notices is the tall, marble wedding cake that was built to hold 60 baby princes and princesses; it is now more than half-full. Don Juan, the father of the current king, Juan Carlos I, is the most recent addition, having got in – despite never having ruled and being over age – largely on the say so of his son. Beyond are the **Sacristía** (sacristy) and **Salas Capitulares** (chapterhouses), which house some of El Escorial's collections of religious art.

Another section that may be seen is the **Biblioteca** (library), measuring 180ft by 30ft and entered by a stair near El Escorial's main gate. Philip's books meant as much to him as his paintings. His librarian, Benito Arias Montano, contributed much to the esoteric conception of El Escorial, and he built Philip one of the largest collections of Latin, Greek, Hebrew and Arabic philosophical and mystical works in Europe. His agents watched over all the book-burnings of the Inquisition, saving anything that was especially interesting. That his hoard of 40,000 volumes survives almost unchanged since Philip's day is due only to the benign neglect of the generations that followed; 18th-century travellers reported that the monks watching over the collection were all illiterate. The frescoes of 1590–2 that cover the vaulted ceiling, by the Italian Pellegrino Tibaldi, are an allegory of the seven liberal arts, portraying seven of the famous philosophers and scientists of antiquity. The large globe of nested spheres in the centre of the library is Philip's orrery, used in making astronomical calculations.

Basílica and Patio de los Reyes (Patio of the Kings)

In many ways, the Basilica is the *raison d'être* of the entire complex. Three tremendous naves and four enormous pillars form the shape of the cross and sustain the sky-high cupola, in the image and likeness of St Peter's. Once inside, you will quickly become aware of the heightened atmosphere of a holy-of-holies. With very few windows, the Basilica was purposely kept dark as a contrast to the airiness of the rest of El Escorial. No church in Spain is colder inside; even in the hottest days of July the thin air seems pure distilled essence of Castile.

Just inside the entrance, in the narrow **lower choir**, note the unusual ceiling and its 'flat vaulting', an architectural trick of very shallow vaulting that creates the illusion of flatness. From here, the eye is drawn to the bright *retablo*, framed in darkness. Its paintings are by several then-fashionable Italian artists, including Pellegrino Tibaldi, who like Juan Bautista was a pupil of Michelangelo. Above these is a golden figure of Christ on the Cross, and at its foot a tiny golden skull that stands out even across the great distance; its hollow eyes seem to follow you as you pass through the Basilica. The golden figures you see are really only of gilded bronze; otherwise, they wouldn't be here. Originally the Basilica was full of real gold ornaments, and the precious stones of the Tabernacle were some of the most valuable possessions of the Spanish royal house. Napoleon's troops did a thorough job of looting El Escorial in 1808, and made off with the whole lot. Connoisseurs that they were, they left the artwork in peace. Notable are the gilded bronze ensembles to the sides of the altar, the families of Charles V and Philip II (with all three of his wives) at prayer. Beneath the high altar is the *primera piedra*, the cornerstone of El Escorial.

The eight central domes are decorated with frescoes by Lucas Jordan, and as you walk up the marble stairway to the *capilla mayor*, you can contemplate an uncharacteristically brilliantly coloured Renaissance *retablo* by Juan de Herrera. In all, there are over 40 chapels in the basilica; one that stands out is that which houses Benvenuto Cellini's stunning *Crucifixion*, a seminal piece of 16th-century Italian sculpture.

The west doors of the Basilica open onto the **Patio de los Reyes**, which is El Escorial's main courtyard. It is named after sculptures by Monegro representing six mighty Kings of Judea, which adorn the church's western façade. On the far side of the courtyard is the **west gate**, the main ceremonial entrance to El Escorial, while to the right and left are the *colegio* and the monastery, which are still in use and not open to the public. The two statues in the centre represent David and Solomon.

Beyond the Monastery

Two little country houses within walking distance of El Escorial are included in the admission ticket. The **Casita del Príncipe** and the **Casita de Arriba** (also known as the Casita del Infante), built in 1772 and 1767 respectively by Juan de Villanueva for Charles IV, are tasteful, cosy and full of pretty pictures, and worth a visit if you just can't get enough of those Bourbons or have time to kill before the bus comes. The Casita del Príncipe has neat, well-tended gardens, appropriately called Los Jardines del Príncipe, in typically Spanish style, with box hedges laid out in knot patterns, and roses and shrubs flourishing among the fruit trees in the ancient orchards. It's worth taking a field guide to European trees on the walk down to the Casita del Príncipe: the **bosquecillo** has some magnificent examples, many well over 100 years old. Fans of Romantic architecture will enjoy a walk round the **Terreros** neighbourhood which runs down behind the Victoria Palace Hotel; there are several good-value restaurants around here which cater to locals with summerhouses in the area.

San Lorenzo de El Escorial

Since the building of El Escorial, a pleasant little town has grown up by it. San Lorenzo has held on to its village atmosphere despite having an air of sophistication thrust upon it thanks to the presence of a private university and an influx of well-to-do settlers. *Madrileños*, keen to escape their city of summer-baked concrete, are drawn here not only by the palace but also by the beauty of the setting in the cool, forested foothills of the Guadarramas. San Lorenzo is a much more attractive commuter base than any of Madrid's fringe of new-town suburbs and, for urbanites, it's a popular summertime resort. The town boasts a tiny, exquisite theatre, the **Real Coliseo** (*C/Floridablanca 20, **t** 918 90 44 11*), which was founded by Charles III, just a short walk from El Escorial.

Valle de los Caídos

Death is the patron saint of Spain.
Váldez Léal

If you're one of those who came to El Escorial expecting freakishness and gloom, you needn't be disappointed yet. From the town, there's a regular bus service to Francisco Franco's own idea of building for the ages. The **Valley of the Fallen** is supposedly meant as a memorial to soldiers from both sides of the Civil War, but it was old Republicans and other political unfortunates languishing in Franco's jails who did the work in the 1950s, many of whom died whilst blasting a 860ft tunnel-like church out of the mountainside, and erecting a 410ft stone cross above. The crowds of Spaniards who come here in a holiday mood on any weekend seem to care little for history or politics; they linger at one of Spain's most outrageous souvenir stands, then take the children up the funicular railway to the base of the cross. For local colour, there'll be a few ancient widows in black who come every week, and perhaps a pair of maladjusted teenagers in Falangist blue shirts. If you're in the area around 20 November, make the trek: it's the **anniversary of the *generalísimo*'s death**, attracting a strange mixture of followers.

The **cross**, held up by faith and structural steel, is claimed to be the largest in the world. Around its base are a series of titanic sculpted figures in some lost, murky symbolism: lions, eagles and pensive giants lurch out above you. The view takes in the hills and valleys for miles around, as well as the monastery Franco built for the monks who look after the **basilica** below.

This cave-church is impressive, in the way the palace of a troll-king might be. The nave goes on and on, past giant, disconcerting Fascist angels with big swords, past dim chapels and holy images, finally ending in a plain, circular altar. José Antonio Primo de Rivera, founder of the Falangists, is buried here. His original interment in the royal crypt of El Escorial was too much even for many of Franco's supporters, and he eventually had to be moved here. Franco is here too; the company he chose for his last resting place is perhaps the last word on what kind of man he really was. **Franco's tomb** is a plain stone slab on the floor near the altar, opposite José Antonio's. The gentlemen behind you in sunglasses and Hawaiian shirts are, if you haven't guessed, plain-clothes policemen, waiting for someone to try and spit on the old Caudillo.

Segovia and Ávila

For whatever cool breezes refresh Madrid in its torrid summers, thank the **Guadarramas**, the chain of low mountains north of the city that stretches from Ávila in the west almost as far as Soria. Its highest peaks are near Madrid, and the snow on them often lasts until May or June. The Guadarramas have a near monopoly of the pretty scenery in this part of Spain; though the heights are drab and grey, the lower regions contain green patches of forest and pastureland with a bit of the same alpine ambiance found in the Pyrenees and Cantabrian chains.

Once over the crests of the Guadarramas, the traditional boundary between the two Castiles, you're back in the medieval atmosphere of Old Castile, with its Romanesque churches, flocks of sheep and lonely castles. Two of its cities, Ávila and Segovia, are within easy reach of Madrid and are candidates for convenient day trips. Segovia, though, one of the most beautiful cities of Spain, is a place where you may wish to spend more time.

Segovia

Three distinct cultures have endowed this once-prominent town with three famous monuments. The Romans left Segovia a great aqueduct, and the age of Emperor Charles V (Carlos I of Spain) contributed an equally famous cathedral. The third, Segovia's Alcázar, should be as well known. Though begun by the Moors and rebuilt in the Middle Ages, its present incarnation is pure 19th-century fantasy, a lost stage set from a Wagnerian opera. Segovia has its other monuments – a unique style of Romanesque church, and the *esgrafiado* façades of its old mansions – but the memory the visitor takes away is likely to be mostly a fond impression. The delicate skyline silhouetted on a high, narrow promontory between two green river valleys gives the city the appearance of a great ship among the rolling hills of Castile. To enter it is to climb into a lost, medieval dream-Spain of unusually quiet streets (rampaging tourists apart), where the buildings are all of one shade of warm, tan stone, making all old Segovia seem a single work of art.

When the Emperor Trajan built the aqueduct in the early 2nd century, Segovia was already a venerable city. Under Rome, and later the Visigoths and Moors, it attained little distinction, but it survived. After it fell to the Christians in the 11th century, Segovia blossomed in the cultural and economic expansion of medieval Castile. Its Romanesque churches and palaces were built on the profits of an important textile industry, and by the time of the Catholic kings it was one of Spain's leading cities.

Segovia

Convento de las Carmelitas Descalzas
La Vera Cruz
Monasterio de El Parral
Casa de la Moneda
Alcázar
San Esteban
Palacio Episcopal
San Juan de los Caballeros
La Trinidad
San Andrés
Cathedral
San Martín
Museo de Arte Contemporáneo Esteban Vicente
Casa de los Picos
Aqueduct
San Millán
Plaza de S. Justo
Plaza del Salvador
Plaza de Colmenares
Plaza de San Esteban
Plaza Mayor
Plaza del Socorro
Plaza de S. Martín
Plaza Espejos
Plaza del Seminario
Plaza de la Artillería
Plaza del Azoguejo
Plaza Sancti Spiritu
Plaza de la Reina Victoria Eugenia
Plaza del Dr Gils
Carretera de Arévalo
Carretera de Zamarramola
Cuesta de los Hoyos
C/ de S. Marcos
Calle de la Moneda
Alameda del Parral
Río Eresma
Río Clamores
Paseo de Santo Domingo de Guzmán
Paseo de San Juan de la Cruz
Puerta de Santiago
Calle del Dr Velasco
Paseo del Obispo
C/ Capuchinos Baja
Calle Capuchinos Alta
Cuesta de San Bartolomé
C/ S. Nicolás
C/ de la Trinidad
C/ S. Agustín
C/ del Taray
Calle de Velarde
Calle de Daoiz
Ronda Don Juan II
C/ Dr Cast Elo
C/ Escuderos
Calle Valdeláguila
C/ Cronista Lecea
C/ de Colón
C/ Infanta Isabel
C/ Judería Vieja
Calle de San Valentín
Paseo del Salón
C/ Juan Bravo
C. Obispo Gandasegui
Calle de Cervantes
Puente de Sancti Spiritu
Calle de San Millán
Calle de Carretas
Avenida de Fernández Ladreda
C/ Gober. Fernández Jiménez
Calle San Francisco
Calle de la Independencia
Calle de los Coches
Paseo Ezequiel González
Vía Roma
Avenida del Padre Claret
Calle de Almira
Calle de las Morenas
To Madrid
To Train Station
N
100 metres
75 yards

Like most of Europe's medieval cities that have survived intact, Segovia's present-day serenity hides a dark secret. The economic policies and foreign wars of Charles V and Philip II ruined Segovia as thoroughly as the rest of Old Castile, and it is only the four centuries of stagnation that followed that allow us to see old Segovia as it was.

Plaza Mayor and the Cathedral

Although new districts have grown out past the Roman aqueduct to the south and east, the **Plaza Mayor** (the former Plaza Franco) remains the centre of the old town, with its arcades and cafés. From here, the **Cathedral** (*t 921 46 22 05; open Mar–Oct daily 9–6.30; Nov–Feb daily 9–5.30; adm*) is just a stone's throw away. This has been called the 'last Gothic cathedral' of Spain; most of the work was done between 1525 and 1590, though parts were not completed until the 18th century. Segovia's old cathedral had been burned during the Comunero revolt, and Charles V contributed much to its replacement as an act of reconciliation. Juan Gil de Hontañón, who designed the Catedral Nueva at Salamanca, here carried the tendencies of his earlier work further. Segovia is finer in form and proportion than Salamanca, and less encumbered with ornament, expressing the national mood of austerity in grandeur in much the same way as El Escorial. The best parts of this cathedral are the semi-circular eastern end, where an exuberant ascent of pinnacles and buttresses (which surely inspired Gaudí in his Sagrada Familia) covers the chapels behind the main altar, the unique squarish belltower and an elegant dome over the choir. The latter two are Renaissance elements that fit in perfectly; in an age of architectural transition it was the greatest part of Juan Gil's accomplishment to make a harmonious combination of such diverse elements. The architect chose to be buried in the spare, well-lit interior. There's little to see inside – a comment on the hard times 16th-century Segovia had come into – and the small **museum** (*adm*) inside is almost painful to visit. See the **cloister**, though, if it's open; this is part of the original cathedral, built in the Isabelline Gothic style by Juan Guas and moved here and reassembled after it survived the fire.

Alcázar

*Pza de la Reina Victoria Eugenia, **t** 921 46 07 59, **f** 921 46 07 55.*
Open summer 10–7; winter 10–6; adm.

The **Alcázar**, jutting out on its cliffs over the confluence of the Río Eresma and the smaller Clamores, was one of the great royal residences of Castile when Segovia was at the height of its prominence. Alfonso the Wise spent much of his reign here, as did other kings of the 12th and 13th centuries. By the 19th, though, the old, forgotten castle had declined into a military school; in 1862, some young cadets set fire to it, in the hope they might be transferred to Madrid. No one, it seems, bothered to record the name of the architects who oversaw the Alcázar's restoration in the 1880s. Even worse, some writers have sniffed that the job they did is 'not authentic'. Some people find fault with these forgotten heroes of the picturesque, who saw fit to turn the Alcázar into a flight of fancy worthy of the Mad King Ludwig, with pointed turrets and curving, crenellated walks. The German tourists look puzzled, and a little

Getting There

By Train

Unless you've a hankering for slow and uncomfortable train journeys, Segovia is better reached by bus. There are nine trains every weekday and seven daily at weekends from Madrid-Atocha (Regionales line R 2, via Villalba de Guadarrama), leaving at two minutes past the even hours, plus 3.02pm. The journey takes just over 2 hrs. All trains pass through Madrid-Chamartín some 15 mins after leaving Madrid-Atocha. The journey takes you through some rugged, craggy scenery, and there are good views of the huge cross of the Valle de los Caídos as the train approaches Los Molinos. Trains back to Madrid depart Segovia at 55 past the even hours.

Segovia's station is located in the modern part of town, about 20 minutes' walk from the old city, or a short ride away by local bus.

There is also a RENFE ticket office in Segovia (*open Mon–Fri 5.30am–9.30pm, Sat and Sun 7.30am–9.30pm*); RENFE information, **t** 902 24 02 02.

By Bus

La Sepulvedana, a comfortable, modern fleet, runs 15 buses every weekday (fewer at weekends) from Pso de la Florida 11, Madrid, to Segovia's bus station on central Pso Ezequiel González. The buses are a great deal quicker than the train, taking around an hour, but cost a little more. For information, contact La Sepulvedana, Pso de la Florida 11, Madrid, **t** 915 30 48 00 (*open Mon–Sat 6am–9.30pm, Sun 8.30am–9.30pm*); Segovia: **t** 921 42 77 07, *www.lasepulvedana.com*.

Segovia also has bus connections to Ávila (*Mon–Fri twice daily, Sat and Sun once daily*), Valladolid, La Granja, and all the villages in Segovia province.

Tourist Information

Segovia: Main Tourist Office, Pza Mayor 10, **t** 921 46 03 34, **f** 921 44 27 34 (*open Mon–Fri 9–2 and 5–7, Sat and Sun 10–2 and 5–8*); even if it's closed, there's plenty of information up on the doors and windows outside;

There's also an office by the viaduct at Pza del Azoguejo 1, **t** 921 46 22 914, **f** 921 42 09 08 (*open Mon–Sat 8–8, Sun 10–8*).

Where to Stay

Segovia ✉ 40000

Expensive

★★★★**Parador Nacional**, Ctra de Valladolid, **t** 921 44 37 37, **f** 921 47 37 62. Two km out of town and only convenient if you have a car: in a plain modern building, but with fine views of the town, a pool and one of the best **restaurants** of any *parador*.

★★★**Los Linajes**, C/Doctor Velasco 9, **t** 921 46 04 75, **f** 921 46 04 79. One of the best choices in Segovia – in one of the most serenely pretty locations of any hotel in Castile: on the northern walls with a terrace overlooking the valley of the Eresma, and only a short walk from the cathedral.

★★★**Infanta Isabel**, C/Isabel la Católica 1, **t** 921 46 13 00, **f** 921 46 22 17. Small, elegant, and overlooking Pza Mayor.

★★★★**Los Arcos**, Pso de Ezequiel González 26, **t** 921 43 74 62, **f** 921 42 81 61. New and a little more expensive, lacking the character of the hotels in the old city, but with every possible modern convenience.

Moderate

★★**Las Sirenas**, C/Juan Bravo 30, **t** 921 46 26 63, **f** 921 46 26 57. Stately establishment with a/c and TV in all rooms.

disappointed to find a castle on the Rhine in Castile; still, they admit it's a very good Rhine castle. The Alcázar is *better* than authentic; the protruding fortress tower stretches an impressive 262ft, with 12 individual towers.

As if the architects had ordered them for effect, sombre ravens perch on the turrets and walls. The people of Segovia who look after the castle have joined in the fun, fitting out the interior in a fashion that would make the characters of any Sir Walter Scott novel feel quite at home. There are plenty of 14th-century cannons and armour,

Inexpensive

★★Hs El Hidalgo, C/José Canalejas 5, **t** 921 46 35 29, **f** 921 46 35 31. Good quality *hostal* in a characterful 18th-century building close to Pza Mayor; with an attractive **restaurant** and cheaper rooms nearby in **El Hidalgo 2**.

★HsR Juan Bravo, C/Juan Bravo 12, **t** 921 46 34 13. Another pleasant and central choice.

★Hs Plaza, C/Cronista Lecea 11, **t** 921 46 03 03, **f** 921 46 03 05. A perfectly reasonable alternative: small, clean and close to Pza Mayor.

Cheap

P. Ferri, C/Escuderos 10, **t** 921 46 09 57. A good budget bet near the plaza; there's no sign, but try the door at the end of the hallway.

P. Cubo, Pza Mayor 4, **t** 921 46 09 17. Spotlessly clean; the better of the Pza Mayor *hostales*, reached through a door to the right of the Herranz bookshop.

Eating Out

More than anywhere else in Castile, Segovia takes dining seriously, and the streets around Pza Mayor and the aqueduct are packed with dimly lit *típico* restaurants, each with a luxuriant display of fresh fish, furred and feathered game, bunches of thyme, rosemary and lavender, glistening heaps of offal, and, taking pride of place, a freshly butchered piglet. Here master *asadores* of reputation serve up Spain's best *cochinillo* (roast suckling pig, traditionally only 21 days old and so tender that you can cut it with the blunt edge of a plate), along with roast, milk-fed lamb and other formidably heavy Castilian specialities.

Mesón de Cándido Pza Azoguejo 5, **t** 921 45 59 11 (*expensive*). Having headed the list for 50 years or so, this is situated beside the aqueduct and has a decidedly picturesque exterior (as depicted on most of Segovia's tourist brochures). The late Señor Cándido wrote cookbooks on Castilian cuisine – and he played host to all the famous folk who have ever passed through Segovia (autographed photos on the walls, of course, to prove it). *Open daily 1–5 and 8–11.30.*

Restaurante José María, off Pza Mayor at C/Cronista Lecea 11, **t** 921 46 11 11/921 46 02 73 (*moderate*). First-rate in every department (try the breaded frogs' legs, another local treat); and relatively low prices. José María started his career as an apprentice under Cándido and is passionate about Castilian wines – the man who singlehandedly brought Segovia's excellent Ribera del Duero reds into the spotlight by serving them as his house wine now owns his own vineyard, not far from the legendary vineyards of Pesquera and Vega Sicilia.

La Cocina de Segovia, Pso Ezequiel González 26, **t** 921 43 74 62 (*moderate*). More elaborate, creative cooking.

Other renowned *asadores* hold court at:

Casa Duque, C/Cervantes 12, **t** 921 43 05 37 (*expensive*).

La Oficina, C/Cronista Lecea 10, **t** 921 46 08 04/921 46 02 83 (*moderate*).

El Bernardino, C/Cervantes 2, **t** 921 43 32 25 (*moderate*).

Restaurante Lazaró, C/Infanta Isabel, **t** 921 46 03 16 (*inexpensive*). Centrally located, with a good cheap *menú*, as well as *cochinillo*. Similar places on C/Juan Bravo and Pza de San Martín abound. Sensitive souls should lay off the *sopa castellana* (spicy garlic soup with a poached egg), especially in cheaper places, where it's greasy enough to lubricate a Mersey Tunnel. It's not bad, though.

After all that food, a short walk up to the **Plaza Mayor** wouldn't do any harm. Among the rows of cafes under its portals, **La Concha** is the best, with tables and chairs outside.

an harquebus or two, stained glass and dusty paintings of Visigothic kings. Some of the interiors survived the fire; there are fine *artesonado* ceilings in the Sala de Las Piñas and in the throne room, built by Henry IV but furnished as it might have been in the days of Ferdinand and Isabel. The **plaza** at the Alcázar's entrance, with old mortars left over from the days of the military school, was the site of Segovia's original cathedral.

Old Quarters and Romanesque Churches

Between the Cathedral and Alcázar lies the oldest district of Segovia. The *esgrafiado* work on some of the houses is a local speciality; a coat of stucco is applied, then scraped away around stencils to make decorative patterns. In a small plaza just west of the Cathedral stands the finest and most representative of the city's Romanesque churches, the 13th-century **San Esteban**, with a lively belltower in the Italian style. The arcaded porch around two sides of the church is the trademark of Segovia's late Romanesque architecture. Such porches adorned all the old churches, and most likely the old cathedral too; in the Middle Ages they were busy places, serving as the centres of business and social life the way arcaded streets and squares do in other Spanish towns. Across the plaza is the **Palacio Episcopal** (*Pza de San Esteban, **t** 921 46 09 63; open Fri–Sat 10–2 and 5–7*) or Archbishop's Palace, its plain façade enlivened only by the reliefs of a serpent-woman and other curious medieval fancies over the entrance.

Within Segovia's walls, the streets meander languidly; to meander along with them is a treat, and fortunately the old town is small enough that you will never get utterly lost. The medieval parish churches are everywhere: **San Andrés**, a solid, simple work from the 12th century on Pza Merced; the church of **La Trinidad** on Pza de Doctor Laguna (off C/de la Trinidad), with an interior restored to something like its original appearance; **San Martín** on C/Juan Bravo (with a tiny museum attached) and **San Juan de los Caballeros** on Pza de Colmenares, both smaller versions of San Esteban (though both are older) with the characteristic arcades and towers. C/Juan Bravo is named after the Segovian military leader of the Comunero revolt, who was executed after the defeat at Villalar in 1521. Segovia remembers enough of its ancient pride and liberty to keep him as a hero to this day, and his statue can be seen in the plaza. Nearby, the **Casa de los Picos** is another Segovian landmark, a 15th-century mansion with a façade like a waffle-iron, with protruding stone diamonds, a style copied in many later buildings in Spain and even one famous church in Naples.

One of Segovia's finest churches is outside the walls, near the centre of the new town on Av. de Fernández Ladreda. Built in the 12th century, **San Millán** is also the oldest, but the capitals of its arcade, charmingly sculpted with scenes from the Bible and from everyday life, have survived much more clearly than those at the other churches and this structure is thought by many to be the finest example of the Segovian Romanesque.

The Aqueduct

Nothing else remains from Roman Segóbriga, but for the city to have merited such an elaborate water supply it must have had nearly as many inhabitants in the first century AD as it does now, namely 50,000. Trajan, one of the Spanish emperors of the Roman Empire, most likely ordered its construction. Its two-storey arcade rises 97ft over busy Pza Azoguejo below, making it the tallest surviving Roman aqueduct.

The Romans, antiquity's master plumbers, did not build it there just to show off. An aqueduct's purpose is to bring water from a distant source, in this case the Río Frío, over 15 kilometres away. Over the length of it a constant downward slope must be maintained to sustain the flow, and wherever it crosses a valley such as this an arcade must be built to keep the flow level. The actual watercourse, a channel cut into the stone and lined with lead, is at the very top. What you see here is only a small part of the system; the Romans built an underground watercourse from here to the Alcázar, and from the other end you can follow the arcade, ever shallower as the ground rises, up C/Fernán García from Pza Azoguejo and right out of the city.

Note the notches cut into the rough stone on the arcade; these allowed for scaffolding to be attached to build the higher levels, and for block and tackles to hoist up the heavier stones. The Romans never cut corners; this was built to last for centuries to come, and would probably have survived unchanged had not several of the arches been destroyed in a siege by the Moors in the 11th century. Some 400 years later, Queen Isabel hired the monks of El Parral monastery to oversee the reconstruction, and when they had finished they replaced the little statue of Hercules that had stood in a niche over the centre with an image of the Virgin Mary.

A Templar Church and a Rogue's Retreat

On no account should you leave Segovia without a walk through the valley of the Eresma. Through either of the old *mudéjar* gates in the city's northern walls, the road leads down to the river through willow and poplar woods dotted with wild flowers. Following the road under the walls of the Alcázar, you cross the river and arrive at the church of **La Vera Cruz** (*Ctra de Zamarramala,* **t** *921 43 14 75; open summer Tues–Sun 10.30–1.30 and 3.30–7; winter Tues–Sun 10.30–1.30 and 3.30–6; closed Mon and Nov; adm*), one of the most interesting surviving Templar foundations, standing on a low hill in open countryside.

The church was built in 1208, and with the dissolution of the Templars in 1312 it became a regular parish church. The last few centuries have seen it abandoned, and its relic of the True Cross (*la vera cruz*), a sliver of wood, moved to the little village of Zamarramala, about one and a half kilometres away. Today the church is used by a Catholic brotherhood that grandiosely styles itself the 'Knights of St John'. Like many Templar churches, this one is round-ish, with 12 sides; at its centre is the two-storeyed chamber, the 'inner temple' where the Templar secret rites took place, as opposed to the 'outer temple' which belonged to the common Church rituals.

None of the paintings or furnishings are as old as the Templars, but a 15th-century picture of the Last Supper, with the apostles seated at a round table, is worth a look. You can climb the belltower for one of the best views of Segovia and the Alcázar, taking in the many churches and monasteries in this holy valley, now largely unused.

The closest, the 17th-century **Convento de las Carmelitas Descalzas** (*Alameda de la Fuencisla,* **t** *921 43 31 85; open June–Sept daily 10–1.30 and 4–8; Oct–May daily 10–1.30 and 4–6.30*) has the tomb of St John of the Cross – or what's left of him; like that of any Spanish saint worth his salt, his corpse was chopped up finely for holy relics.

To reach the most interesting of the monasteries, **El Parral** (**t** *921 43 12 98; open Mon–Sat 10–12.30 and 4–6, Sun 10–11.30; Gregorian chants at noon*), retrace your steps from La Vera Cruz to the river and continue up the opposite bank. On the way you'll pass the remains of the **Moneda**, or mint, where American gold and silver were turned into coins before 1730.

El Parral's founder, Juan Pacheco, Marqués de Villena, ranks among the slipperiest of all Castilian court intriguers. A protégé of the famous favourite Álvaro de Luna during the reign of Juan II, he played a role in the wars between the partisans of Isabel and Juana la Beltraneja by taking first one side, then the other, and occasionally both. He apparently chose this site because it had brought him luck; he had killed three men here in duels. In its day, El Parral was famous throughout Spain for its woods and gardens. The place is still lovely, and the long-neglected church has now been restored, holding a number of interesting tombs of famous Segovians (and some of the Marqués' illegitimate children).

A Burst of Abstraction

Pza de Bellas Artes s/n, ***t*** *921 46 20 10; open Tues–Sat 10–2 and 5–7, Sun 10–2.*

A recent, and far more contemporary addition to Segovia's landscape is the **Museo de Arte Contemporáneo Esteban Vicente**. Esteban Vicente (1903–2000), a Segovian-born member of the New York school of abstract expressionists, spent much of his life on the East End of Long Island, but left instructions in his last will and testament for his artwork to be returned to his native town. His blazing works can now be viewed in the old Palacio de Enrique IV, refreshing amid a day of sandstone and ancient history.

Around Segovia

Another Bourbon Palace: La Granja de San Ildefonso

Open summer Tues–Sat 10–6, Sun 10–2; winter Tues–Sat 10–1.30 and 3–5, Sun 10–2; closed Mon; adm, adm free for EU passport holders on Wed; gardens open summer daily 10–8; winter daily 10–6; ***t*** *921 47 00 14/20.*

La Granja ('the farm'), is one of the works of Philip V, he of the insatiable appetite for palaces. The building has a certain rococo elegance of the sort American millionaires love to copy, but its fame has always been its **gardens**. Philip originally conceived of La Granja as a scaled-down version of Versailles (his father, Louis XIV's, palace) and the gardens, laid out in the 1740s, completed the picture. There are some 70 acres of them, with remarkable fountains everywhere (26 in all) decorated with pretty pagan deities. There is only one day of the year when they all work, on 25 August, and it's worth watching them come alive.

The palace itself is furnished in 18th-century French style, with an impressive collection of tapestries and spectacular cut-glass chandeliers. You can see where they were made at the **Crystal Factory** (*La Real Fábrica de Cristales de la Granja, Pso del Pocillo 3,* ***t*** *921 47 17 12; open Tues–Sun 11–8; closed Mon; adm*) in the village of **San Ildefonso**.

La Granja is an easy excursion from Segovia, only 11 kilometres southeast of town. To get there, take a bus or follow the N601 (Carretera de la Granja) to San Ildefonso.

Ten kilometres south of Segovia, **El Palacio de Riofrío** (*same hours as La Granja*) is on a side road, off the N603. Here Isabella Farnese, Philip V's second wife, let her taste for all things Italian run riot after Philip's death. She intended to use this palace and hunting lodge as a bolt hole in the event of her being turfed out of La Granja. Work began in 1752, and Rebaglio, her architect, brought echoes of Madrid's Palacio Real to a building which would otherwise have had an overwhelmingly feminine feel, with its pink walls and pretty wooded parkland. Part of the palace is now a hunting museum.

Turning northwards off the N110 a few kilometres on, you come to **Pedraza de la Sierra**, an exceptionally beautiful walled village with a lovely medieval **castle** (*open Wed–Sun 11–2 and 4–6; closed Mon and Tues*) and a jumble of antique shops. The arcaded main square serves as the village stage at festival time and is transformed into a bullring for the villagers' September *corridas*.

If you carry on the N110 to **Riaza**, just past the town you'll see a turning south to the **Hermita Hontanares**. Along this road lie a series of villages which tell the story of the depopulation of rural Spain throughout the 1950s and 1960s all too graphically. The so-called *pueblos negros Segovianos* of El Muyo, Serracín and Becerril have begun to attract weekenders, but many of the houses, constructed of slate, are tumbling down.

Further on lie the *pueblos rojos* of El Negredo, Madriguera and Villacorta; so called because of the clay soil which blows everywhere, leaving the houses coated with a

Festivals

Pedraza: International Music Festival, *5–11 July*. Each night, some 25,000 candles illuminate the village streets during the course of the annual festival.

Where to Stay and Eat

La Granja

★★Hotel Roma, C/Guardas 2, **t** 921 47 07 52, **f** 921 47 02 78 (*moderate*). Charming hotel set close to the entrance to the palace: quieter and cheaper than Segovia; a good choice if you have a car.

Zaca, C/Embajadores 6, **t** 921 47 00 87 (*moderate*). A small eatery specializing in stews. *Open at midday only; booking essential at weekends.*

Torrecaballeros

Segovians are enthusiastic gastronomes, so much so that they're more than happy to travel a kilometre or 20 to indulge themselves in a gargantuan roast lunch at a celebrated farmhouse restaurant in one of the Guadarrama mountain villages. 10km northeast of Segovia on the N110 is the typical Castilian village of Torrecaballeros, with a handful of hotels as well as an extremely popular restaurant.

La Posada de Javier, Ctra Segovia–Soria, **t** 921 40 11 36 (*moderate*). Perfect for local specialities including *judiones de La Granja*, butter beans stewed with *chorizo* and various extremities of pork, and *cordero asado* (lamb roasted in a wood-fired oven). Not cheap, but extremely popular. Book ahead.

Collado Hermoso

★★Molino de Río Viejo, Ctra Segovia–Soria Km172, **t** 921 40 30 63, **f** 921 40 30 63 (*moderate*). Small, friendly hotel in a converted watermill: the owners run horseback excursions into the sierra and surrounding countryside.

Pedraza de la Sierra

★★★El Hotel de la Villa, C/Calzada 5, **t** 921 50 86 51, **f** 921 50 86 53 (*expensive*). One of two superb hotels in this village, set in an old building and full of character.

★★La Posada de Don Mariano, Pza Mayor 14, **t/f** 921 50 98 86 (*expensive*). Also in an old building, and also superb; excellent value.

This is another magnetic village for *segoviano* and *madrileño* foodies:

El Yantar de Pedraza, Pza Mayor, **t** 921 50 98 42 (*expensive*). Overlooking the square and serving wonderful roast lamb.

La Olma, Pza del Granado 1, **t** 921 50 99 81 (*expensive*). Even better: all the usual delicacies, brilliantly prepared.

Getting Around

The three ski resorts in the Guadarramas between Segovia and Madrid are particularly popular with *madrileños*, as they're easy day trips; take the N601, the scenic road that runs from Segovia to Collada-Villalba via San Ildefonso-La Granja; or take any train on the Madrid–Segovia line (R2 or C8b), disembark at the small resort of **Cercedilla**, and take the funicular up to Puerto de Navacerrada or Puerto de los Cotos.

Skiing

Resorts in the Sierra de Guadarrama

Puerto de Navacerrada, **t** 912 62 10 10, offers the most challenging skiing, with 16 pistes for skiers at various levels of skill, plus a slalom and a cross-country course. The resort has 12 lifts, and is at an altitude of 5,773ft; the highest pistes start at 7,288ft.

Valcotos and Valdesquí, both slightly higher than Puerto de Navacerrada, are a few kilometres up the C604 towards **Rascafría**. They're small resorts with simple facilities.

Valcotos, **t** 914 35 15 48, in the Cotos mountain pass, has the prettiest location; it has seven pistes and eight lifts.

Valdesquí, **t** 915 15 59 39, generally has the best snow, and is good for beginners; it has 23 pistes and 10 lifts.

Resorts in the Sierra de Ayllón

La Pinilla, **t** 921 55 03 04, is a resort in the middle of the Sierra de Ayllón, 10km south of the pleasant town of Riaza, which is 72 kilometres northeast of Segovia on the N110. It's a popular choice for intermediate skiers, with 16 pistes, running from 7,455ft down to 4,920ft, and 12 lifts.

Where to Stay and Eat

Puerto de Navacerrada

This is the only resort that has hotels close to the slopes.

*****Pasadoiro**, Ctra de la Granja, **t** 918 52 14 27 (*inexpensive*). Provides modest but comfortable accommodation.

Navacerrada

Downhill from Puerto de Navacerrada, this is the fashionable place to stay, with a wider choice of lodgings.

********Arcipreste de Hita**, Ctra Nacional 601, Km12, **t** 918 56 01 25, **f** 918 56 02 70 (*moderate*). Has excellent facilities, including a sports and fitness centre, and a pool.

*******La Barranca**, Ctra Monte Público, Pinar La Barranca, **t** 918 56 00 00, **f** 918 56 05 40 (*moderate*). Popular business conventions venue, also with a pool and tennis.

*****Hs Mayte**, Av. de Madrid 5, **t** 918 56 02 97 (*inexpensive*). Twelve central rooms with shared bathroom facilities.

When it comes to **eating out,** Señor Felipe has the monopoly:

Asador Felipe, C/Mayo 3, **t** 918 56 10 41 (*inexpensive*). With a summer terrace and the best beef, lamb and suckling pig in the area.

Restaurante Felipe, Av. Madrid 2, **t** 918 56 06 36 (*inexpensive*). Across the road: excellent fish; wild mushrooms in autumn and winter.

La Fonda Real, Ctra Madrid–Segovia Km53.5, **t** 918 56 03 05 (*inexpensive*). Traditional Castilian cooking: uphill towards the Puerto de Navacerrada and with fabulous views.

Rascafría

This is a good alternative if you're skiing at Valcotos or Valdesquí and have transport.

********Santa María de El Paular**, C/El Paular, **t** 918 69 10 11, **f** 918 69 10 06 (*luxury–expensive*). A little more luxurious than Los Calizos, this is in the converted wing of an ancient Benedictine monastery, replete with fitness centre and pool, and correspondingly *caro*.

******Los Calizos**, Ctra Miraflores–Rascafría Km30.5, **t/f** 918 69 11 12 (*moderate*). Probably the best value: in a charming doll's house of a building.

Riaza

This is where you'll find the nearest hotels to La Pinilla.

******Casaquemada**, C/Isidro Rodríguez 18, **t** 921 55 00 51 (*moderate*). Nine comfy rooms.

******La Trucha**, Av. Doctor Tapia 17, **t** 921 55 00 61, **f** 921 55 00 86 (*inexpensive*). Offers a pool.

*****Hs Los Robles**, C/Médico Valentín Gil 6, **t** 921 55 00 54 (*cheap*). Simple but very reasonable, this provides double rooms with basin.

fine red dust. These villages, barely inhabited, lie among some of Spain's finest holm oak forests, with the sturdy Sierra de Ayllón as a backdrop.

Ski Resorts Around Segovia

For winter visitors to Madrid suffering from a build-up of oppressive car fumes, a lungful of crisp mountain air could be the perfect antidote. There are four skiing centres near Segovia which are within easy reach of the capital. These resorts are all quite low-key, and experienced skiers looking for a challenge would find the pistes disappointing, but they have plenty to offer beginners or near-beginners. All four resorts have ski schools and equipment hire facilites and function from Christmas until early spring. For recorded information on snow conditions, call **t** 913 50 20 20.

Ávila

For two cities so close together and with so much history in common, Segovia and Ávila, 115 kilometres northwest of Madrid, could hardly appear more unalike. Chance, with a little help from the geography, has made them into stone images of complementary sides of the Spanish character. Secure on its natural hilltop fortress, Segovia had the leisure to become a city of kings and merchants, and relaxes in aesthetic surrounds, full of trees. Ávila stands more exposed, and it has always had the air of a frontier camp, coarse and austere, a city first of soldiers, and later of mystics.

Ávila's **walls** are its main attraction, the only complete circuit of fortifications to exist around any Spanish city. Though medieval, they rest on Roman foundations, and their rectangular layout is the classic form of the Roman *castrum*. This was a Roman frontier post against the Celtic tribes they had displaced from the area, and after the 8th century Ávila found itself performing the same role in the constant wars between the Moors and the Christians. Through most of the 11th century it was the front line, often changing hands, until Alfonso VI decided in 1088 to construct these walls (built 1090–9), and make the town a secure base for further Christian advance.

Except for Saint Teresa, who was a native and spent much of her career as a writer and monastic reformer behind Ávila's walls, the town has kept very quiet ever since. For a proper view of the walls, though, you'll have to cross the River Adaja, leaving town on Av. de Madrid, and on to the N501, turning right over the bridge.

San Vicente

Modern Ávila has almost completely forsaken the old walled town. The bus and train stations are out in the eastern extension, and however you arrive you are likely to approach the historic centre from this direction. Here, just where the Av. de Portugal reaches the walls, is the Romanesque **Basílica de San Vicente** (*Pza de San Vicente*, **t** *920 25 52 30; open summer Tues–Sun 10–2 and 4–8; closed Mon*), the most interesting of Ávila's churches. Parts of it are as old as the late 12th century, including the fine sculptural work on the west portal. San Vicente was another native of Ávila, who was martyred along with his sisters, SS. Sabina and Cristeta, during the

Getting There

By Train

Unlike Segovia, a train journey to Ávila is worth the effort, with spectacular scenery and a quicker ride (a little under 2 hrs from Madrid). From 6.15am to 8.30pm, trains on the Regionales line R 1 from Madrid run roughly once an hour from Atocha and more frequently from Chamartín (via Villalba de Guadarrama and El Escorial) and arrive at the station in the new town on Av. José Antonio, a 10-minute walk from the city's old walls. Most of the trains to and from Galicia, Asturias, Salamanca and even the Basque provinces and Burgos pass through here. RENFE information, Madrid: **t** 902 24 02 02; Ávila **t** 920 25 02 02.

By Bus

Buses from Madrid (taking slightly under 2 hrs) are run by Larrea (***t** 915 39 00 05*) and leave around eight times a day from Estación Sur (C/Méndez Álvaro, **M** Méndez Álvaro; ***t** 915 30 48 00*).

By Car

Hop across from the speedy A6 to the windy Ctra N-VI towards Villacastin and turn on to the N110 for Ávila.

Tourist Information

Ávila: Pza de la Catedral 4, across the square from the cathedral, **t** 920 21 13 87, **f** 920 25 37 17.

Festivals

Summer Fiestas, *17–25 July*.

Fiesta de Santa Teresa, *15 Oct*. Processions and festivities for Ávila's favourite saint.

Where to Stay

Ávila ✉ 05000

Expensive

★★★Parador Raimundo de Borgoña, C/Marqués Canales de Chozas 2, **t** 920 21 13 40, **f** 920 22 61 66. The *crème de la crème* of *paradores*; located in a stupendously well-converted Renaissance palace, with an excellent **restaurant** and beautifully decorated with antique furnishings.

★★★★Hotel Palacio de los Velada, Pza de la Catedral 10, **t** 920 25 51 00, **f** 920 25 49 00. A very classy, pricey palace by the cathedral, with blue rooms and huge bathrooms.

★★★★Gran Hotel Palacio de Valderrábanos, Pza de la Catedral 9, **t** 920 21 10 23, **f** 920 25 16 91. Yet another palace, but not such good value.

persecutions of Emperor Diocletian in 306. There's more graphic, vigorous sculpture inside, where scenes of San Vicente on the rack and suffering other tortures decorate his sarcophagus. The church, probably succeeding an earlier Visigothic structure, was built over the site of the martyrdom, and if the attendant will agree to take you down to the crypt you can see the rock where the Romans did them in. Watch out for snakes; it's said that a serpent guarded the saints' graves while Ávila was occupied by the Moors. A custom grew up whereby the people of Ávila would come down here to make bargains and swear oaths; if they lied, the serpent would come out and sting them (the only recorded victim was a bishop). Also down in the crypt is a much-venerated icon called **Nuestra Señora de la Soterana** (Our Lady of the Underground).

Los Verracos

This part of town, just east of the walls, is really as old as anything inside. A block from the walls, at Pza de los Navillos 3, just off Pza de Italia, a 16th-century ecclesiastical residence called the **Palacio de los Deanes** has been converted into Ávila's very good **Museo Provincial** (*Pza de Nalvillos 3, **t** 920 21 10 03; open Tues–Sat 10.30–2 and*

Moderate

★★HsR Bracamonte, C/Bracamonte 6, **t** 920 25 12 80, **f** 920 25 38 38. In a palatial building steeped in history, with a spectacular interior full of 18th-century tapestries; an excellent choice and good value.

Hospedería la Sinagoga, C/Reyes Católicos 22, **t** 920 35 23 21. A sensitive interweaving of the 15th-century synagogue building with stylish, modern décor; large, quiet rooms.

Inexpensive

★★★Hs El Rastro, Pza del Rastro 1, **t** 920 21 12 18, **f** 920 25 16 26. The best inexpensive choice: in the shadow of Ávila's walls, with plain-looking rooms, a garden and a popular **restaurant**, 'Mesón del Rastro' (*see* below). Book in advance, especially July and Aug.

★★Hs Bellas, C/Caballeros 19, **t** 920 21 29 10, **f** 920 35 24 49. Recently renovated, comfortable rooms in the old centre (cheaper with shared bath).

Cheap

P. Continental, Pza de la Catedral 6, **t** 920 21 15 02, **f** 920 25 16 91. An old chestnut, this large, recommended *pensión* has strangely slanting stairs and friendly management.

★Hs Jardín, C/San Segundo 38, **t** 920 21 10 74. Not quite so cheap; outside the walls but still within a stone's throw of the cathedral.

Eating Out

Ávila is full of good, solid, inexpensive restaurants. Most are near the eastern end of the walls, inside or out.

El Almacén, Ctra de Salamanca 6, **t** 920 25 44 55 (*expensive*). Outside the walls on the river: with regional favourites and cleverly conceived variations on traditional themes.

Doña Guiomar, C/Tomás Luis de Victoria 3, **t** 920 25 37 09 (*moderate*). Inventive cooking and friendly service.

La Casona, Pza Pedro Dávila 6, **t** 920 25 61 39 (*inexpensive*). Small, with the perfect *patrón* and huge portions.

Mesón del Rastro, Pza del Rastro 1, **t** 920 21 12 18 (*inexpensive*). Classic Castilian: veal, pickled trout, roast lamb and *judias de Barco* (bean casserole with *chorizo*); but a slightly institutional feel and unexciting *menú*.

Casa Patas, C/San Millán 4, **t** 920 21 31 94 (*inexpensive*). Just off Pza de Santa Teresa: good *tapas* and simple meals.

Bars

Bodeguita de San Segundo, C/San Segundo 19, **t** 920 21 42 47. An excellent, if pricey, place to tipple, accompanied by delicious *tapas*.

Deanes, Pza de Navillos 1. Popular bar near the museum with a lovely colonnaded patio; live classical music on summer weekends.

5–7.30, Sun 10.30–2; closed Mon), with a folk-costume and crafts collection, Roman artefacts and some fine local medieval pictures – displayed so you can see them much more clearly than in Ávila's dim churches.

The museum provides a good introduction to an interesting aspect of Ávila's ancient history. Ávila was a busy place when the Celts lived here, coming as close to a capital or religious centre as this determinedly non-urban people cared to have. Remains of their castles and monuments can be seen all over the countryside, as well as hundreds of unique stone grave-markers called ***verracos*** (boars), carved in the shape of boars or bulls. These continued to be erected under Roman rule, as late as AD 300, and some carry Latin inscriptions, such as 'to the gods Manes and Titillo'. A few can be seen in Pza Calvo Sotelo, just inside the **Puerta de Alcázar**, the main gate of the old town two blocks south. Outside the gate is the **Plaza de Santa Teresa**, the only really lovely corner of Ávila (although unfortunately *hors de combat* for a year or two whilst a subterranean car park is created underneath it). The church here with the lovely rose window is the Romanesque **San Pedro**, from the 13th century.

The Walls

Calle San Segundo runs along the eastern side of the fortification, towards the Puerta de Alcázar. In this section of the walls, you will see some stones with Roman inscriptions, and a good many others with a rectangular niche and a groove cut into them. These were the bases of the *verracos*, and the niches held the ashes of the departed chiefs and warriors. The Castilians dragged in dozens of them to help build their walls, approximately two and a half kilometres in length, with 88 towers, 2,500 turrets and nine gates. Though simple, the walls were up to date for the military needs of the 11th century and legends date the construction to May 1090; an engineer from Rome was called in to help with the design. The distinctive rounded towers, typical of ancient Roman fortifications, are called *cubos*, but the biggest bulge, facing C/San Segundo, comes as a surprise. It is the apse of Ávila's cathedral, built right into the walls as if to symbolize the Church Militant of old Castile, helping to man the battlements of the Reconquista.

It's a pleasant walk around the walls; on the southern and western sides they face open country, and the setting is sufficiently medieval to have been used for the

Ávila's Doctors of the Soul

The people of Ávila celebrate Santa Teresa de Ávila's memory as ostentatiously as the Corsicans do Napoleon's. Even if it were possible to escape hearing about her, you wouldn't be able to miss the *Yemas de Santa Teresa*: ubiquitous, candied egg-yolks that are sold in every shop in town, a traditional speciality of the local nuns.

Teresa Sánchez de Cepeda y Ahumada was born into a wealthy family of Jewish converts in 1515. She got religion young; at seven, after reading the *Lives of the Saints* she talked her brother into running away with her to be martyred by the Moors. An old stone cross called *Las Cuatro Postes*, just across the Adaja from the town, marks the spot where their uncle caught the children and brought them back. Teresa had to wait until she was 18 before she took her vows as a Carmelite, and she lived 22 uneventful years in her convent until she had the famous vision that set her off on her career as a mystic: an angel pierced her heart with a burning arrow during prayer, as depicted unforgettably in Bernini's statue in Rome, portraying Teresa in a state of eternal orgasm.

Usually Teresa's union with God was more down to earth. Shortly after her first mystical experience, she had a second while praying at the chapel of Nuestra Señora de la Soterana in San Vicente, which bade her reform the lax Carmelite order and return it to its original vows of poverty and simplicity. The subterranean Virgin also had her take off her shoes, and wearing sandals became symbolic of the new *descalzada* (shoeless or discalced) Carmelites. Teresa then spent much of her life on the road, founding and reforming 32 convents in Castile and Andalucía. Her first male convert was a 21-year-old theology student from Fontiveròs, near Ávila, named Juan de Yepes, who became her confessor and the spiritual director of the *descalzadas*. He can be thanked for ordering Teresa to write her autobiography, the frankest, most spontaneous, humorous and likeable account written by any saint on the calendar.

shooting of several movies. On the narrow west end, they overlook old bridges spanning the River Adaja and the 12th-century hermitage of **San Segundo** (*open daily 10–1 and 4.30–6*), yet another local saint, who supposedly converted Ávila in the 1st century. If you prefer a bird's eye view of Ávila from atop the walls, you can climb up by the cathedral.

The Cathedral

Pza de la Catedral, ***t*** *920 21 16 41; open summer daily 10.30–1 and 3.30–6; winter daily 3–5. Cathedral and museum closed 1 Jan, 6 Jan, 25 Oct and 25 Dec.*

It isn't much for one of the earliest Gothic churches in Spain, and though a king of León (Alfonso IX, 1188–1230) once lived here in sanctuary during a civil war. From the front it has no character at all, apart from the two bizarre stone wild men with clubs, added in the 18th century, who guard the portal. Ávila's cathedral, half-church and half-fortress, does however have a little stage presence. The critics like to speak of Gothic architecture at its best as an eloquent argument for the Christian faith; this

In 1578, still-shod (Calced) Carmelite timeservers, who spitefully labelled Teresa 'the roving nun', denounced both her and her confessor Juan to the Inquisition. Both were confined to Toledo, separately, and wrote to each other daily – the disappearance of their correspondence is considered one of the greatest losses in Spanish letters. For it was in Toledo that the two wrote their classical works of mysticism: Teresa's *Inner Castle* was based on her vision of a glittering castle of seven abodes, each a stage that the bride/soul must pass on the road to heaven to the ultimate union with God. The Church disapproved of her books when she died in 1582, but it saw fit to canonize her in 1622, repackaging the honest mystic into a miracle worker and an object of popular devotion whose chopped-off fingers soon became prized holy relics.

Juan – the future St John of the Cross – suffered far worse indignities. The Calced members of his Order imprisoned him for nine months, a period of forced reflection that resulted in his first poem, *En una Noche Oscura (The Dark Night of the Soul)* – a masterpiece of Spanish literature. This was ripe for misinterpretation because of its several levels of meaning, including the carnal; Juan assigned religious concepts genders and used often ambiguous erotic imagery to make potent poetic points with an extraordinary economy. He wrote fewer than 1,000 lines in his whole life, but into those fit a complete exposition of Catholic mysticism, expressed allegorically in songs of love and nature; poems that not only describe moods, but create them.

Although Juan managed to escape from prison when the Calced and Discalced Orders were officially separated, he made an obscure end in 1591, dying from abuse and starvation after years of suffering in the monastery at Úbeda, persecuted even on his deathbed by the prior, who had nuns sign affidavits against him. He and his poetry were vindicated when he was canonized in 1726 and made a Doctor of the Church in 1926, an honour St Teresa became the first woman to enjoy in 1970, putting Ávila in the record books as the only town to produce two Doctors of the Church.

church was for a people who needed no convincing. Strong and plain, it has the air of an outsized chapel for warrior knights. The men of the Reconquista adorned it richly inside as if it were their treasure-house, and they lined its walls with niches for tombs where they expected to be buried.

Some of the sculpted tombs are among the best works in the cathedral, including that of a learned 15th-century bishop named Alfonso de Madrigal (better known as El Tostado for his swarthy complexion). Very famous in Spain, the tomb has a statue of the bishop deep in his books, wearing robes carved with finely detailed scenes from the scriptures. There are reliefs in the north portal and, inside, some paintings and sculpture from quieter times when the wars of the Reconquista had passed on.

Although Ávila has been a backwater for many centuries, a wander round the walled city is revealing. Like many a city in Castile, Ávila is quietly prosperous, and a host of ironmongers, gentlemen's outfitters and corner shops testifies to an economy which has little need of tourists – although they are more than welcome. And, little by little, its weedy lots and ruins are being restored.

In her writings, Santa Teresa had little kind to say about Ávila; apparently it was not a place where reforming ideas were very welcome. Nevertheless, Ávila is happy to show off memories of her life in a number of convents about town. On the spot where she was born they built the **Convento de Santa Teresa** (*Pza de la Santa 4, **t** 920 21 10 30; open daily 9.30–1.30 and 3.30–7.30*), just inside the southern gate. Here, a squat church in the Herreran style houses a collection of relics and paintings showing imagined scenes from the saint's life. More of these can be seen at the **Monasterio de la Encarnación** (*Pso de la Encarnación, **t** 920 21 12 12; open summer Wed–Mon 9.30–1 and 4–7; winter Wed–Mon 3.30–6; closed Tues*) where she lived for 27 years, just north of the walled town, and at the **Convento de San José** on Pza de las Madres, off C/del Duque de Alba.

Around Ávila

Verraco-spotting and Arévalo

One of the best places to see a large number of the Iberian Celts' mysterious boar- and bull-shaped gravestones is about 50 kilometres south of Ávila, beyond the village of El Tiemblo on the N403, at a site called **Los Toros de Guisando**. At an assembly here in 1468, King Henry IV was forced to accept Isabel's right to the throne of Castile. Only six kilometres north of Ávila, there are more *verracos* around the scanty remains of **Las Cogotas**, an ancient Celtic fortress whose inhabitants gave the advancing Romans problems for centuries.

Heading towards Valladolid, the terrain stretches out into a high plain, patched with wide sweeps of green and yellow cereal fields. One of the more interesting villages in this part of the province is **Arévalo**, about 50 kilometres north of Ávila. The village appears little changed since the 1600s, with its walls, old churches, and bridges across the Río Adaja. There's been a cattle market here longer than anyone can remember.

Festivals

Arenas de San Pedro: Fiesta, *last week of Aug*. Sees lively celebrations that attract locals and visitors alike.

Sports and Activities

For information on the multitude of activities in the Sierra de Gredos, contact the **tourist office**, C/Triste Condesa, **t** 920 37 23 68.

Where to Stay and Eat

All the mountain villages have at least one or two modest *hostales* and restaurants. If you'd prefer Turismo Rural accommodation, **t** 902 42 41 41 for further information.

Guisando ✉ 28000

★★Hs Pepe, C/Linarejos 4, **t** 920 37 40 18 (*inexpensive*). One of the best and most comfortable *hostals* in its price bracket.

Bar El Puente, **t** 920 37 40 48. In the heart of the old village, this is where Guisandoners hang out; a welcoming atmosphere and incredibly good-value *tapas*.

Arévalo ✉ 05200

Asador Las Cubas, C/Figones 9, Arévalo, **t** 920 30 01 25 (*moderate*). An excellent restaurant offering Castilian fare.

Navarredonda de Gredos ✉ 28000

★★★El Parador de Gredos, Ctra Barraco-Béjar, 3.2km from Navarredonda de Gredos, **t** 920 34 80 48, **f** 920 34 82 05 (*expensive–moderate*). Spain's first ever *parador*: this one occupies an old stone hunting lodge set in a beautiful pine forest on the north edge of the mountains, not far from El Pico Almanzor, the range's highest peak at 8,502ft. Even better, rates are lower than those of many other *paradores*, and there is a good **restaurant**.

★Hs El Refugio de Gredos, C/Pajizo, **t** 920 34 80 47, **f** 920 34 81 14 (*inexpensive*). This makes a fine, simple retreat.

Arenas de San Pedro ✉ 28000

★HsR Los Galayos, Pza del Condestable Dávalos 2, **t** 920 37 13 79 (*inexpensive*). Should you decide to stay in Arenas, this is the principal place; meals are served in the attached **restaurant**.

★HsR El Castillo, Ctra de Candeleda 2, **t** 920 37 00 91. An uninspiring location on the main road, but near the castle.

El Bodegón, Pza Conde Dávalos 4, **t** 920 37 18 20 (*inexpensive*). The best place in town for a meal; excellent-value home cooking.

★Hs Alburquerque, Pza de la Soledad 2, in Mombeltrán, **t** 920 38 60 32 (*inexpensive*). Pleasant rooms and a **restaurant** serving good, simple meals.

Sierra de Gredos

Around Ávila, the countryside is pretty and often quite unusual: its green, rolling hills are broken by rocky outcrops that often have the appearance of ancient ruins. Further south, Ávila province is bounded by the **Sierra de Gredos**, a great, craggy adventure playground of a region, heaven for hikers, climbers, mountain bikers and watersports enthusiasts (*see* above). A good number base themselves in **Arenas de San Pedro**, which has become the '*capital de Gredos*', located a 70-kilometre drive southwest from Ávila. Set among the dark, spare mountains, it is a pretty village full of trees, with a square castle set right next to the Plaza Mayor; it's known for its finely crafted leatherwork and ceramics.

Near Arenas, strung along twisting mountain roads with staggering views, you will pass the traditional villages of **Guisando** (not to be confused with the Toros de Guisando), **El Hornillo**, **El Arenal** and **Mombeltrán**, which has a very well-preserved 14th-century castle.

East and Southeast of Madrid

Along the Río Henares

The railway line that trundles out of Madrid towards Zaragoza and Barcelona follows the course of the Río Henares all the way to its source, near the provincial border of Guadalajara and Soria. Trains passing this way stop at towns which have stood on the river for centuries, such as **Alcalá de Henares**, famous for its ancient university, and **Guadalajara**, in the heart of the Alcarria. Northeast of Guadalajara the line cuts through dazzling fields of sunflowers on the way to the graceful town of **Sigüenza**. It's a pleasant journey, through plenty of open countryside which, thanks to the river, is splashed with green even in the driest of summer months.

Alcalá de Henares

Anyone from the Arab world would recognize the name's origin straightaway – *al-qalat*, a fortress – and it was the Moors who built up this town, on the site of the abandoned Roman city of *Complutum*. In the 12th century, warrior bishops from Toledo captured it for Christianity and built it up; the long tradition of Church control may be one of the reasons Cardinal Jiménez de Cisneros founded his great Complutensian University here in 1508, an institution that almost immediately rivalled Salamanca as the foremost centre of learning in Spain.

In 16th-century Castile, it was possible for a man like Cisneros to be, on the one hand, an imperialist and a disturbingly fierce religious bigot and, on the other, a champion of the new humanist scholarship that was sweeping Europe. For a brief, brilliant period the University became one of the intellectual lights of the continent; its great achievement, indeed its main reason for being, was the creation of the Complutensian Polyglot Bible, the first authoritative scholarly edition in modern Europe, with Latin, Greek, Hebrew and Aramaic originals in parallel columns. Even today it remains the standard work for biblical scholars; in its day it created an academic revolution. Among the University's graduates in Spain's Golden Age can be counted Calderón de la Barca, Lope de Vega and Ignatius de Loyola.

Through the 17th and 18th centuries the University's degeneration was gradual but total, and by 1837 half its buildings lay in ruins, at which point the sad remnants were moved to Madrid. Some of the old colleges were used as the Communist headquarters during the Civil War.

Economic recovery in the 1970s and 1980s brought a change of fortune to Alcalá, which became one of the fastest growing cities of Spain, through industrial growth and the presence of a huge US air base nearby at Torrejón (a popular rendezvous for anti-NATO protesters from Madrid). Many of the old academic buildings were restored, and the university reopened its doors to students in 1977. Cisneros would have been delighted: the re-establishment of his university brought Alcalá's dormant intellectual and cultural interests back to the surface and made it lively once more.

Getting There

By Train

There are six or seven trains a day to Sigüenza on the Regionales line R 9b from Madrid-Chamartín; some of these stop at Madrid-Atocha, and all pass through Alcalá de Henares and Guadalajara. The journey to Sigüenza takes around 2 hrs. Alcalá and Guadalajara are also served by Cercanías trains from Madrid-Chamartín and Madrid-Atocha (line C–2), four times an hour for Alcalá and every half-hour for Guadalajara. RENFE information: **t** 902 24 02 02/915 63 02 02.

By Bus

This is one case where the train is so handy that you needn't worry about buses, unless you're based near the terminus at Av. de América 34, from which Continental Auto, **t** 917 45 63 00, runs a frequent service to all three towns. In Alcalá, the office and station are at Av. Guadalajara 5, **t** 918 88 16 42.

Tourist Information

Alcalá de Henares: Callejón Santa María 1, just off Pza Cervantes, **t** 918 89 26 94 (*open April–Oct daily 10–2 and 5–7.30 (July and Aug closed Mon); Nov–Mar daily 10–2 and 4–6.30*).

A second office is in Pza de Los Santos Niños, **t** 918 81 06 34 (*same hours*).

Guided tours run through Acalá's *casco histórico*, including the University, Cervantes' house and the Monasterio de Bernardas (*July and Aug Mon–Fri at noon, Sat, Sun and hols at noon and 5.15; Sept–June Sat, Sun and hols at noon and 4.30*).

Guadalajara: Pza de los Caídos 6, **t/f** 949 21 16 26.

Sigüenza: Pso de la Alameda s/n, **t** 949 34 70 07, **f** 949 34 70 08, *www.siguenza.com* (*open Mon–Fri 10–2.30 and 4–6.30, Sat 9.30–3 and 4–7, Sun 9–3.30*). Beautifully housed in a converted hermitage.

Festivals

Sigüenza: Romería, *2nd Sun in May*. A spectacular religious procession makes its way seven kilometres up to the sanctuary of Barbatona.

Hita: Medieval festival, *end of June*.

Where to Stay and Eat

Alcalá de Henares ✉ 28800

★★★**El Bedel**, Pza San Diego 6, **t** 918 89 37 00, **f** 918 89 37 16, *www.husa.es* (*expensive*). This is Alcalá's best-known hotel: in an excellent, central but quiet location close to Cardinal Cisneros' famous Colegio Mayor de San Ildefonso.

★★**Hs Miguel de Cervantes**, C/Imagen 12, **t** 918 83 12 77, **f** 918 83 05 02 (*moderate*). Right in the centre of town, opposite the Convento de la Imagen on a street running between C/Mayor and C/Santiago.

★★**HsR El Torero**, Puerta de Madrid 18, **t** 918 89 03 73 (*inexpensive*). In a historic building just outside the old city's western gate.

★**Hs Jacinto**, Pso de la Estación 2, **t** 918 89 14 32 (*inexpensive*). Good value: near the railway station (along with several other one-star establishments and *fondas*).

HsR del Estudiante, C/Colegios 3, **t** 918 88 03 30 (*expensive*). *Parador* restaurant in an annexe of the Colegio Mayor: so well known it attracts a regular clientele from Madrid. With a faithfully re-created 16th-century atmosphere, right down to the oil lamps and uncomfortable chairs. Serves traditional, but pricey, Castilian cuisine. *Open Mon–Sat 1–4 and 9–11.30, Sun 1–4 and 9–10.*

La Cúpola, C/Santiago 18, **t** 918 80 73 91 (*moderate*). Good quality, inspired meals served in a converted 17th-century convent, an elegant dining room with crisp service. Reservations recommended at weekends. *Open daily 12–5 and 8–11.30.*

Mesón del Paso, C/Diego de Torres 2, **t** 918 78 76 95 (*inexpensive*). A sweet neighbourhood restaurant with a wooden bar, friendly red and green curtains in the window and, best of all, a decent, inexpensive lunchtime *menú*. *Open Mon–Sat 11am–midnight, Sun and hols 12–3.*

Cafetería Rectorado, Colegio Mayor, Pza de San Diego, **t** 918 55 41 40 (*cheap*). Open at certain times to visitors to the Colegio Major, this is Alcalá's best-value eaterie, set in the historic

Patio de los Filósofos. Platefuls of standards such as *gazpacho*, salads, grilled *merluza* and chicken roasted in wine are served for next to nothing. *Open Mon–Fri 1–3pm*

Convento Clarisas de San Diego, C/Beatas 7. A must for anyone with a sweet tooth: the Santa Clara nuns make exquisite *almendras garapiñadas*: almonds, toasted in thick chewy toffee, freshly made each week. Ring the little door bell on the left and they pass you the goods, though you never see them; a revolving door keeps them cloistered and out of sight. *Open Mon–Sat 9–2 and 5–8, Sun 10–2 and 5–8.*

Guadalajara ✉ 19000

There are far more pleasant places to stay than Guadalajara within easy reach.

****Meliá Comfort Guadalajara**, Crta Nacional Km55, **t** 902 44 66 66, **f** 902 40 66 06 (*expensive*). Outside the centre, with all the Meliá mod cons.

*****Green Alcarría**, C/Toledo 39, **t** 949 25 33 00, **f** 949 25 34 07 (*moderate*). One of the best of a rather so-so bunch, on the outskirts of Guadalajara.

*España**, C/Teniente Figueroa 3, **t** 949 21 13 03, **f** 949 21 13 05 (*inexpensive*). This is better value: in a 19th-century palace in the centre.

Miguel Angel, Alfonso López de Haro 4, **t** 949 21 22 51 (*expensive*). Miguel Angelo offers creative variations on classical cuisine using the finest ingredients.

Casa Victor, C/Bardales 6, **t** 949 21 22 47 (*moderate*). Castilian favourites rule the menu here.

Other places to seek out local specialities such as *cabrito a la barreña* (spit-roast kid), garlic soup, and *bizcochos borrachos* (rum babas) are plentiful around the **Plaza Mayor** and **Plaza Bejanque**.

Sigüenza ✉ 19250

****Parador Castillo de Sigüenza**, Pza del Castillo, **t** 949 39 01 00, **f** 949 39 13 64 (*expensive*). A former Visigothic fortress and Moorish *alcázar* until the Christians stormed it in the 12th century and turned it into a bishop's palace. Now recently renovated from the ground up: a rather stark and forbidding hotel, with spartan décor and rooms arranged around the *patio de armas*.

***Hs El Doncel**, Pso de la Alameda 1, **t** 949 39 00 01, **f** 949 39 10 90, *hostaldoncel@futurnet.es* (*moderate–inexpensive*). Green and terracotta rooms with sparkling, marble bathrooms, overlooking the Alameda; its **restaurant** has an (*inexpensive*) *menú*.

***Laberinto**, C/Alameda 1, **t** 949 39 11 65 (*moderate–inexpensive*). Recently renovated, two-tone rooms.

*P. Venancio**, C/San Roque 3, **t** 949 39 03 47 (*cheap*). Adequate, old-fashioned rooms sharing a large, tiled bathroom.

Restaurante Calle Mayor, C/Mayor 21, **t** 949 39 17 48 (*moderate*). House specialities include *chipirones rellenos* (stuffed squid), *cabrito al ajo* (kid with garlic) and *cordero asado* (roast lamb).

Restaurante Medieval Segontia Asador, Portal Mayor 2, **t** 949 39 32 33 (*moderate*). Try the wonderful local lamb.

Restaurante Sánchez, C/Humilladero 18, **t** 949 39 05 45 (*inexpensive*). Small, popular and central.

Restaurante Sierra Ministra, C/Valencia 47, **t** 949 39 17 58 (*inexpensive*). Tasty dishes to be had *a la brasa*.

Otherwise, choose from the numerous cafés and bars found in and around the ancient and lovely Alameda Park.

Around Guadalajara and Sigüenza

HsR Princesa de Éboli, Convento de los Monjas de Abajo, Pastrana, **t** 915 55 72 72 (*moderate*). Simple *pensión* in a converted convent: excellent meals, and packed at weekends. *Out of season, open only Sat, Sun and hols.*

*****Hospederia Real de Pastrana**, Convento del Carmen, Pastrana, **t** 949 37 10 60 (*moderate*). In a Franciscan convent near the entrance to the town: just as good as the HsR Princesa de Éboli, and in as lovely a setting. *Open all year.*

***Hs El Torreón**, Pso María Cristina 7, Brihuega, **t** 949 28 03 00 (*inexpensive–cheap*). Good, inexpensive *pensión*.

El Tolmo, Av. de la Constitución 26, Brihuega, **t** 949 28 11 30 (*expensive–moderate*). A welcoming restaurant where they'll be delighted to let you sample the local cod concoction: *bacalao a la alcarreña*.

There are also some good, simple *pensiones* to be found in **Jadraque**.

Alcalá's centre is the leafy, pleasant **Plaza de Cervantes**, with a bandstand and springtime flower stands at one end and gossipy cafés at the other. Touching its edge is the arcaded **Calle Mayor**, Alcalá's busy, old main street, which comes alive with yet more café tables after the shops shut on summer evenings.

Colegio Mayor de San Ildefonso

*Pza de San Diego, just off Pza de Cervantes, **t** 918 85 40 00; only accessible by **guided tour** run by Promoción Turística de Alcalá (**t** 918 82 13 54); (in Spanish; groups may book ahead for English). **Tours** available in summer Mon–Fri at 11.30, 12.30, 1.30, 5.30 and 6.30, on Sat, Sun and hols at 11, 11.45, 12.30, 1.15, 2, 5, 5.45, 6.30, 7.15 and 8; in winter Mon–Fri at 11.30, 12.30, 4.30 and 5.30, on Sat, Sun and hols at 11, 11.45, 12.30, 1.15, 2, 4, 4.45, 6.15 and 7; combined ticket available including Colegio Mayor, Cervantes' Birthplace and Complutum, a series of Roman ruins just outside town (bus ride included in the price).*

The University buildings are spread all over town, but the best of them is the **Colegio Mayor**, which has a wonderful Plateresque façade by Rodrigo Gil de Hontañón (who also worked on the cathedrals of Segovia and Salamanca), adorned with the arms of Cisneros (note the swans – *cisnes*). Inside are the **Capilla Universitaria**, a Plateresque chapel, and a great hall called the **Paraninfo** with a dazzling, intricately carved wooden ceiling with a pitched, *artesonado* roof, used for graduation ceremonies and other congregational occasions. Most notably, it is where the King and Queen of Spain, every 23 April, officiate the awards ceremony of the Cervantes Prize, Spain's highest literary honour, on the anniversary of the eponymous Miguel's death. The guided tour is a fact-filled trip through three patios, the Paraninfo, and the imposing tomb of Cardinal Cisneros which lies within the Colegio Mayor – even though his earthly remains are interred in the Cathedral up the street.

Elsewhere in Town

Other noteworthy buildings are the **Colegio de la Palma** on C/de los Colegios and the **Casa de los Lizana**, with its brave stone lions, on C/Postigo. Most of the University colleges are built in a very austere, Herreran style, as are Alcalá's churches.

On C/Mayor is a small museum devoted to Alcalá's most famous son, Miguel de Cervantes. The **Museo Casa Natal de Cervantes** (*C/Imagen 2, **t** 918 89 96 54; open Tues–Fri 10.15–2 and 4–6.25, Sat and Sun 10–1.30 and 4–6.25; closed Mon*) is a lovingly kept reconstruction of the house in which the author was born. It's furnished to look like a mid-16th-century family dwelling, and in an upstairs room there is a display of rare editions of Cervantes' works and other ephemera, including a 2nd edition of *Don Quixote* from 1605, and various early translations into Dutch, German and Italian.

Modern Alcalá's only monument is on the street leading from the railway station. The **Hotel Laredo** or *Quinta de la Gloria* is an incredible brick confection of Moorish arches and turrets piled up by some forgotten madman of the 19th century. Its style is not really 'neo-*mudéjar*' as the sign says, but more honestly 'hyper-*mudéjar*'. The

Monasterio de Bernardas (***guided tours** in summer Mon–Fri at 1.45 and 6.30, Sat at 12.30, 1.30, 5, 5.45, 6.30, 7.15 and 8, Sun and hols at 1.30, 5, 5.45, 6.30, 7.15 and 8; in winter Mon–Fri at 1.45 and 5.30, Sat at 12.30, 1.30, 4, 4.45, 5.30, 6.15 and 7, Sun and hols at 1.30, 4, 4.45, 5.30, 6.15 and 7*), at the far end of C/Santiago, is a beautiful Baroque structure with a small but fine collection of Italian paintings from the 17th century, and various pieces of religious art. Right next to it is the **Ontario San Felipe Neri** (*due to reopen after restoration in 2002*), the one and only male cloister that is still up and running in Alcalá. When it is open, visitors are permitted to tour the church, the sacristy, and the museum rooms which contain religious artefacts and paintings.

Guadalajara

The next stop up the rail line from Madrid, this once great town of New Castile was almost completely wrecked during the long battles for Madrid during the Civil War, but rebuilt as a modern, industrial city. The only reason to stop is for the **Palacio de los Duques del Infantado** (*Pza de los Caídos 1, open Tues–Sat 10.15–2 and 4–7, Sun 10.15–2; closed Mon*) built by Juan Guas in 1461 for the founder of what was to become one of Spain's most powerful noble houses, the Mendozas. Among its members it counted statesmen, authors, even a Viceroy of New Spain. The palace, in the Plateresque style, has a façade and courtyard florid enough to please any duke. Most of the palace has been restored or rebuilt, and it now houses a provincial art museum.

Sigüenza

The cathedral alone is worth the trip, but what makes Sigüenza such a pleasant excursion from Madrid is its setting in the hills around the Henares. From the quiet, arcaded **Plaza Mayor** you can walk through a little gate into the marketplace on the cliffs above the valley, and from there pass directly into the forested hillsides that surround the town. Sigüenza is altogether far too cosy and charming to be in Castile.

The **cathedral** (*daily guided tours of chapels at 11, 12, 4.30 and 5.30; closed Mon; adm for chapels*) has a good deal in common with the one in Ávila; both were built at about the same time and both show the influence of French Gothic with a distinctive Castilian twist. Like Ávila's, the cathedral stands honest and foursquare: a castle with rose windows. They are very good rose windows, especially over the north portal, but the best features are inside. In the chapel of the Arce family is the **tomb of Martín Vázquez de Arce**, a young man who died in the wars with Moorish Granada in 1486. An unknown artist carved his figure in alabaster on the top of the sarcophagus, gently smiling and musing over a book. The image, as evocative of the medieval world as any passage from Tennyson, has become so well known it is referred to simply as *El Doncel de Sigüenza*. *Doncel*, in this case, means a king's page; Arce was an attendant of Ferdinand and Isabel. His crossed legs are not just an expression of nonchalance, but a convention of Spanish medieval art, used to show that the deceased had died while fighting for the faith.

To stroll through the rest of Sigüenza will require a little climbing up narrow streets to the **castle** that dominates the town. Like Guadalajara, Sigüenza suffered greatly in the Civil War. The castle, now a *parador*, and Pza Mayor have been almost completely restored, but plenty of bullet scars can still be seen on the cathedral tower. Several other Romanesque and Gothic churches, all quite plain, have also been restored, including the 12th-century San Vicente on C/del Jesús. There used to be two synagogues up by the castle too, but all that remains is the street name, *Calle de la Sinagoga* (also set out in Hebrew). Across Pza Obispo Don Bernardo from the cathedral is the **Museo Diocesano del Arte Sacro** (*open Tues–Sun 11–2 and 4–7; closed Mon; adm*), a museum with works by El Greco and Zurbarán and some early religious art.

Around Guadalajara and Sigüenza

The region east of Guadalajara known as the **Alcarria** was made famous by Spain's Nobel prize-winning writer Camilo José Cela in his rather pompous 1940s travel classic, *Viaje a la Alcarria* (1948). Set among the rugged hills is the village of **Pastrana**, capital of the region, a jumble of mossy-roofed houses watched over by its **Colegiata**, which houses a museum (*open daily 10.30–1.30 and 4.30–6.30; adm*) containing some remarkable 14th-century tapestries. Further north, both the NII highway and the Madrid–Zaragoza railway line pass the impressive, round-towered, 15th-century **Castillo de Jadraque**, built by the Dukes of Osuna. Other ancient villages around the region include **Hita**, which holds an annual medieval festival, and **Brihuega**, a fortified village with its old walls largely intact.

For those with transport, Sigüenza is the perfect starting point from which to explore the **Ruta Románico Rural**, northwest of the city, a picturesque route linking medieval villages that seem barely touched by the passing centuries. Fine examples of Romanesque architecture abound, such as the church of **San Salvador** in the village of **Carabias**, and the very beautiful **Ermita de Santa Coloma** in **Albendiego**, at the foot of the Sierra del Alto Rey. Particularly interesting are those churches that blend Romanesque styles with *mudéjar* influences, such as **San Bartolomé** in **Campisábalos**, and the parish church of **Villacadima**, its door decorated in Moorish botanical and geometric patterns. The highlight of this route is the town and castle of **Atienza**, once an important fortified stronghold, strategically located with commanding views of the valley it dominates. At the height of its influence in the 12th and 13th centuries, the town had 15 churches, five of which survive; all are Romanesque. West of Cogolludo, the little parish church of **Beleña de Sorbe** has a fine portal carved with the 12 months and a relief of Joseph fleeing Potiphar's wife.

Aranjuez: Yet Another Bourbon Palace

***Palaces** open summer Tues–Sun 10–6.15; winter Tues–Sun 10–5.15; closed Mon; adm exp, adm free for EU passport holders on Wed; **gardens** open summer Tues–Sun 8–8.30; winter Tues–Sun 8–6.30; closed Mon.*

There has been a royal residence in Aranjuez since the days of Philip II. His palace, built by Bautista and Herrera, the architects of El Escorial, burned down in the 17th century, and we can only wonder what sort of pleasure-dome those two could have created. Philip V began the replacement at the same time as he was building his palace at La Granja and it's hard to tell the two apart. Like La Granja, Aranjuez is an attempt to emulate some of the grandeur of Versailles; it isn't surprising, with Louis XIV meddling in Spain's affairs at every step, that the junior Bourbon wanted to show that he, too, was somebody. Aranjuez is a natural location for a palace; the water of the Río Tajo makes it an oasis among the brown hills, on the threshold of La Mancha. Centuries of royal attention have given the area more trees than any other corner of Castile, and even today it is famous in Spain for its strawberries and asparagus. A small town has grown up around the palace since the 16th century.

Come September, spectacular fiestas take place, based on the *motín de Aranjuez*. This celebrates the uprising of 1808, when, in the face of the French invasion, the locals rose up to overthrow the then prime minister, Godoy, who had advised Charles IV to flee to America as part of his own evil schemes to gain power. The mob attacked Godoy's palace in Aranjuez, and the king was forced to sack him and then abdicate in favour of his son. This is considered the inspiration for the uprising in Madrid which followed on 2 May of that year.

Getting There

By Train

Cercanías line C 3 trains from Madrid-Atocha run to Aranjuez twice hourly, so it is easy to get there or back. To make a special outing of it, pay the extra to take the **Tren de la Fresa** (strawberry train), a steam train that chuffs from Atocha's AVE platforms to Aranjuez and back once a day during the summer months. A local bus will take you right from Aranjuez station to the palace; if you'd rather walk, turn right out of the station, then left down the avenue. RENFE information, Madrid: **t** 902 24 02 02/902 22 88 22, *www.aranjuez.net*.

By Bus

Buses from Madrid, run by AISA, **t** 915 28 28 03/902 42 22 42, leave hourly from Estación Sur, C/Méndez Álvaro, **M** Méndez Álvaro, **t** 914 68 42 00. Buses from Madrid to Chinchón are run by La Veloz, **t** 914 09 76 02, from a stop near their office at Av. Mediterráneo 49 (**M** Conde de Casal). Departures in both directions leave hourly on the hour (Mon–Sat), and roughly every 90 mins (Sun). The journey takes 50 mins.

Tourist Information

Aranjuez: Pza de San Antonio 9, **t** 918 91 04 27.
Chinchón: Pza Mayor, **t** 918 93 53 23.

Festivals

Aranjuez: Motín de Aranjuez, *1st week Sept*. Fiestas celebrate the uprising of 1808 (*see* above), attracting big crowds, many dressed in period costume.

Chinchón: Fiesta de San Roque, *mid-Aug*. The Plaza Mayor turns bullring over the course of the celebrations, and the *madrileños* flock in for the occasion.

Where to Stay

Aranjuez ✉ 28300

Not many tourists stay in Aranjuez, as it is so close to Madrid.

*****Mercedes**, C/Ducachia 15 (Ctra de Andalucía), **t** 918 92 20 14, **f** 918 91 04 40 (*moderate*). Close to the palaces and surrounded by gardens and a pool.

Hs Castilla, Ctra de Andalucía 98, **t** 918 91 26 27, **f** 918 91 61 33 (*inexpensive*). Centrally situated *hostal*, with wheelchair access.

HsR Las Infantas, C/Infantas 6, **t** 918 91 13 41, **f** 918 91 66 43 (*inexpensive; cheap* with shared bath). A good cheaper option.

Chinchón ✉ 28370

******Parador de Chinchón**, Av. Generalísimo 1, **t** 918 94 08 36, **f** 918 94 09 08, *chinchon@parador.es* (*expensive*). Exceptional *parador*, with an atmosphere of cool serenity

As at La Granja, the prime attractions are the **gardens**, full of sculptural allegory and fountains in surprising places, shady avenues and riverside walks, even an informal garden like those that were called 'English gardens' in the 18th century. They'll guide you through the **Palacio Real**, packed full of chandeliers and mirrors, with porcelain, fancy clocks and court costume of the period. Within the gardens is another small palace, the **Casa del Labrador**, modelled on the Petit Trianon, and along the river is a **museum of boats**; Charles III built it as part of a project to make the Tajo navigable, but his successors turned it into a boathouse, and their pleasure craft are on display.

Chinchón

More than a few day-trippers make their way to Chinchón, a pretty village of faded terracotta-coloured roofs and steep streets. After the noise and bustle of Madrid, Chinchón feels rustic in the extreme. The village huddles on a hillside, exposed, and

pervading every nook of the stunningly beautiful 17th-century monastery; its lovely box-scented garden is filled with roses and fruit trees. Pretty rooms, with simple tiled floors and painted bedsteads.

****Hs La Cerca**, C/Cerca 9, **t** 918 94 13 00, **f** 918 93 50 82, *www.hotel-lacerca.com* (*moderate*). Uphill from Pza Mayor, on the way to the municipal swimming pool: this is plain, but neat and clean.

****Hs Chinchón**, C/José Antonio 12, **t** 918 93 53 98, **f** 918 94 01 08 (*inexpensive*). As close to the Plaza Mayor as you can get: welcoming and spotless; all rooms have TV and a/c; Room 1 has a spectacular view over the square and the hillsides beyond. With a baby rooftop pool, bar and **restaurant**.

Eating Out

Aranjuez

Such has been the boom in tourism over the last decade that most restaurants can't get local strawberries and asparagus; nevertheless, that's what people come here to eat. And they figure prominently on most of the town's restaurant menus. Most of them are expensive, though, and you may settle for *fresas con nata* (strawberries and cream) from one of the little stands around town, although the cream won't be real either. Many restaurants have elegant settings along the riverfront.

La Mina, Príncipe 71, **t** 918 91 11 46 (*expensive*). In the wing of an ancient palace: wonderfully fresh fish and seafood as well as wood-fired roasts.

Casa José, C/Abastros 32 (*moderate*). This makes a welcome change from the usual fare, if more expensive: inventive, international, *nouvelle*-inspired cuisine.

La Rana Verde, C/Reina 1, **t** 918 91 32 38 (*inexpensive*). On the riverfront: better to pay a little extra for one of the fish or game specialities than opt for the simple *menú*.

Chinchón

Mesón de la Virreina, Pza Mayor 28, **t** 918 94 00 15 (*inexpensive*). One of the better restaurants on the historic plaza: good for local specialities such as roast lamb and pork, *sopa castellana* or *pisto manchego* (the local ratatouille).

Restaurante La Columna, Pza Mayor, **t** 918 94 05 02 (*inexpensive*). Also on Pza Mayor: no views over the square, but an extremely pretty galleried patio inside; worth visiting for its great, reasonably priced, *menú del día*.

Mesón Cuevas del Vino, C/Benito Hortelano 13, **t** 918 94 02 85. A well-known and liked *mesón*, built in centuries-old caves, signposted up the hill from Pza Mayor.

Bar Los Huertos, C/Generalísimo 3. Bar with a large, pleasant courtyard graced with a fountain and spreading fig tree – the perfect place for a quick glass of *anís*.

winter mornings are frequently crisp with frost, while in summer nothing moves under the glare of the midday sun. This is one of the main production centres of ***anís***, the aniseed-flavoured liqueur; although it's not quite as popular here as over the border in France, the Spaniards still down their fair share of it. If you're in an acquisitive mood, the **Alcoholería de Chinchón**, on the Plaza, will satisfy your needs.

Chinchón is also famous for its picturesque, largely restored **Plaza Mayor**, which has served as a location for quite a few movies. Hemmed in by the higgledy-piggledy tiered wooden balconies of its surrounding buildings, it feels rather like Shakespeare's Globe. Fittingly, it is also the stage for bullfights during fiestas. Presiding over Pza Mayor, the church of **La Asunción** treasures an *Assumption of the Virgin* by Goya. A little **ethnological museum**, La Posada (*C/Morata 5*), displays local paraphernalia.

Cuenca

East of Aranjuez, the empty northern corner of La Mancha gradually rises into attractive, rolling countryside: the foothills of the **Serranía de Cuenca**, a low, dishevelled chain that marks the traditional boundary between New Castile and Aragón. Cuenca, one of the most unusual and dramatic fortress-cities of Spain, stands at the base of this chain. On the way, any aficionados of Roman Spain who can't make it to Tarragona or Mérida may wish to make a detour southeast of Tarancón to **Segóbriga** (***site** open during daylight; **museum** open Tues–Sat 10.30–2 and 4–7, Sun 10.30–2; closed Mon; adm*), an important city for the Iberians and Visigoths, as well as the Romans. The 3rd-century theatre, amphitheatre and some other buildings have been excavated, and there is small museum *in situ*. However, many of the pieces from the three sites surrounding Cuenca have wound up in its Museo Arqueológico.

Depending on how you enter Cuenca, you may not see the old town at all on arrival. A fair-sized modern city now fills up the Júcar valley, where medieval Cuenca once tended its market gardens. Many of the hotels and restaurants are here, but to see the real Cuenca, you'll have either a stiff climb or a short hop on the bus up from Pza de la Trinidad, near the confluence of the Júcar and the little Huécar. Old Cuenca waits on a high rock between the two valleys, a position that helps to explain the city's history. The odd sacking at the hands of Alfonso VIII and during the Napoleonic Wars aside, Cuenca has usually been quiet, guarded by its nearly impregnable setting. The cliffs are steep, particularly on the Huécar side, and the ***casas colgadas***, 'hanging houses', draped over them are the town's most prominent and picturesque feature.

On your way up to the Plaza Mayor, stop for breath by the **Torre de Mangana**, the last remnant of the town's Moorish *alcazaba*; no one is quite sure whether it was a minaret or part of the fortifications. Carry on up and you'll come to the **Plaza Mayor**, passing underneath the arches of the lovely 18th-century **Ayuntamiento**. The plaza is the hub of Cuenca's bizarre fiesta action (*see* 'Festivals', p.557), and with its smattering of bars and cafés, would be perfect but for the droning traffic and screamingly atrocious façade of the **Cathedral** (*open daily 9–2 and 4–7*). The front was rebuilt in the 1660s as someone's bright idea of what Gothic really ought to have looked like, but behind it the church reveals an austerely graceful Gothic interior of the 12th century.

Getting There

By Train

Cuenca isn't really a comfortable day trip from Madrid, unless you're undaunted by slow trains (2–3 hrs) and quirky RENFE timetables. There are four daily from Madrid-Atocha on Regionales line R 10, direction València. RENFE information, Madrid: **t** 913 28 90 20, Cuenca: **t** 969 22 07 20.

By Bus

Auto-Res, **t** 969 22 11 84, operate a bus service which departs seven times a day during the week and six times on weekends (2½ hrs) from Pza Conde de Casal 6 in Madrid (**M** Conde de Casal) to the bus station on C/Fermín Caballero in Cuenca. There's an 'express' service (2 hrs) twice daily.

Tourist Information

Cuenca: Municipal Office, Pza Mayor 1, **t** 969 23 21 19, **f** 969 23 53 56, *www.aytocuenca.org* (*open 9–9 in high season*). Up in the old town, this tends to be the most useful tourist office branch;

New Town Provincial Office, Glorieta González Palencia 2, **t** 969 17 88 00, **f** 969 17 88 43, *www.cuenca.org* (*open 8–3*). Useful if you happen to be in the new town.

Festivals

Fiesta, *21 Sept*. All hell breaks loose as wild cows are let loose in the main square.

Turbas, *Good Friday*. At 5.30am, the Turbas, or *borrachos* (drunks), take to the streets representing the Jews who condemned Christ. Many Cuencans are indignant at the notoriety these festivities have attained, with wild descriptions of a sort of legitimized Saturnalia. The procession is considered one of the most prestigious by the populace, who will pay in the region of €2,400 for the privilege of carrying a float in it.

Where to Stay

Cuenca ✉ 16000

Staying in the new town is somehow missing the point, unless you can't face the hike up to old Cuenca. The following are recommended in the old town:

****Parador de Cuenca, Pso Hoz del Huécar, **t** 969 23 23 20, **f** 969 23 25 34, *www.cuenca@parador.es* (*expensive*). Perched on a cliff across the Huécar gorge in the painstakingly restored former Convento de San Pablo, with pool, and delightfully described in its brochure as 'suspended between stone and thickets…its spiritual innocence revives the pleasure of meditation'.

The original features are worth a look, with some noble tombs, stained glass and sculpture; note the very unusual subjects portrayed on the inside of the north transept. The **treasury** contains two paintings by El Greco. Behind the cathedral, on C/Canónigos, is a small **Museo Arqueológico** (*open Tues–Sat 10–2 and 4–7, Sun 10–2; closed Mon; adm*) with finds from Segóbriga, Valeria and Roman sites around Cuenca.

Museo de Arte Abstracto Español

C/Canónigos; open Tues–Fri 11–2 and 4–6, Sat 11–2 and 4–8, Sun 11–2.30; closed Mon; adm.

Some of the most decorative of the hanging houses perched on the cliff's edge have been converted into one of Spain's most unusual museums, the Museum of Spanish Abstract Art, showing off the avant-garde in a medieval setting. Many visitors come to Cuenca expressly to see this audacious undertaking and the museum has acquired an international reputation. Only Spanish contemporary artists are represented, and while only fervent devotees of the abstract may spend much time on the paintings, anyone will enjoy the views from the old wooden balconies high above the Huécar.

★★★**Leonor de Aquitania**, C/San Pedro 60, **t** 969 23 10 00, **f** 969 23 10 04 (*moderate*). An upmarket *casa colgada* conversion, overlooking the Huécar gorge, but not costing the earth. There are marvellous views from the ***cafetería*** and also from the more expensive suites.

★★**Posada de San José**, C/Julián Romero 4, **t** 969 21 13 00, **f** 969 23 03 65, *www.posadadesanjose.com* (*moderate*). A 17th-century labyrinth of a convent, atmospherically converted with that winning mix of whitewashed walls and polished terracotta floors; some of the rooms have terraces which overlook the gorge, whilst the nuns' cells (which have shared bath) are much cheaper. There's also a good-value, home-made buffet breakfast.

★**P. Tabanqueta**, C/Trabuco 13, **t** 969 21 12 90 (*cheap*). Behind heavy wooden doors just past San Pedro church, this pension is a clean and economical old town option.

If you'd prefer to stay in the **new town**, try:

★★★**Alfonso VIII**, Parque de San Julian 3, **t** 969 21 25 12, **f** 969 23 29 16 (*expensive*). A modern, clean option.

Posada Tintes, C/de los Tintes 7, **t** 969 21 23 98, **f** 969 22 47 18 (*cheap*). Well-positioned, clean rooms; the owner manages two old buildings on the same street and a traditional, dark inn.

Eating Out

Local specialities to tickle your fancy include: *morteruelo*, made with grated pig's liver and game; *zarajos*, spirals of tripe; *ajo arriero*, a blend of garlic and cod; and *alajú*, made with honey and almonds. Round them all off with *resolí*, a heady blend of coffee, *anís* and brandy.

Good eateries in the **old town** include:

Mesón Casas Colgadas, C/Canónigos, **t** 969 22 35 09 (*moderate*). Stunningly situated in a 14th-century hanging house, with inspiring views over the Huécar gorge.

Posada de San José, *see* 'Where to Stay', above (*inexpensive*). Yet more gorge(ous) views, a terrace and reasonably priced food.

If you're in the **new town**, try:

Figón de Pedro, C/Cervantes 15, **t** 969 22 45 11 (*expensive–moderate*). The best new-town restaurant for classic Castilian cuisine, run by the same owner as Casas Colgadas, with a wide range of specialities.

Casa Marlo, C/Colón 59, **t** 969 21 38 60 (*moderate*). Fosters a welcoming atmosphere and inventive menu: partridge stew with figs or aubergine and mushroom pie.

Taverna de Pepe, C/Tintes 1, **t** 969 22 49 19 (*moderate*). In a lovely setting by the river, and specializing in seafood.

Fonda Tintes, C/Tintes 7 (*cheap*). The glory's in the price; it's fantastically good value.

The houses – several of them have been connected for the museum – are interesting in themselves, though restored in a trendy manner.

The museum, now 35 years old, is one of the many projects of the Juan March Foundation, one of the most important forces in the Spanish art world. Its founder, the late Juan March, is noteworthy himself; originally a poor boy from Mallorca, Spain's greatest robber baron made his fortune in contraband tobacco, eventually almost running the state tobacco monopoly out of business. After that he cornered the Spanish shipping business (with his Transmediterranea Line), put the entire Spanish coastguard on his payroll, stole the Barcelona streetcar service from the foreign syndicate that built it, and still found time to assist British Intelligence in two world wars. The Republic finally managed to land him in jail, but friends who visited him there reported finding March's private chef in attendance, tapestries on the cell walls, and three newly installed telephone lines. In return for the annoyance, March arranged all the financing for the Nationalist war effort in 1936. He died in 1962, from injuries received in the crash of his Cadillac, and his billions are now building hospitals around Spain and buying up abstract art.

The Hoz del Huécar

Just behind the apse of the cathedral near the abstract art museum, there is a long, narrow footbridge called the **Puente de San Pablo**. This begins one of the most beautiful walks you can take in this part of Spain, over the gorge (*hoz*) of the Huécar and then down into it, passing through pine-woods and fields along the riverbank with a view of the *casas colgadas* high above. Only from here does it become apparent just how unusual some of these are. What seemed like simple houses turn out to be the lobbies of upside-down medieval skyscrapers, hanging down as many as 12 storeys on the side of the cliff. The road along the Huécar re-enters the city at the picturesque **Calle de los Tintes**, a frontier between the old Cuenca and the new.

Excursions from Cuenca

The rough mountains of the Serranía de Cuenca are full of natural curiosities, best seen with a car and a little determination. By taking a loop of backroads north and east of the city you can visit the **Ciudad Encantada** (*open daily sunrise to sunset; adm*), near Villalba de la Sierra, a region of curious, wind-blown rock formations among pine woods. Some, like the 49ft 'big lump' are balanced precariously on narrow stems, like mushrooms; others have acquired names like the 'elephant' and the 'sea of stone'.

To the southwest, **Las Torcas** are a group of strange, conical sinkholes, formed by the action of underground streams. The truly determined may find their way to the Palaeolithic **cave paintings** near the village of **Villar del Humo**, interesting though not as well preserved as those at Altamira (*see* p.350). They are quite a way off even the back roads; ask the Cuenca tourist office if they are open, and for explicit directions.

The road east from Cuenca towards Teruel is wonderfully scenic, especially beyond the Valley of Ademuz into Aragón. The Castilian stretch is called the **Vía Pecunaria** or 'cattle road' and it is still one of Spain's more traditional and out-of-the-way corners.

The Devil's Handprint

On the opposite side of Cuenca, facing the Júcar, a road called the Ronda de Júcar leads down into the valley past a number of old churches, monasteries and shrines, a corner of Cuenca that has probably been a holy place for millennia. Past the chapel of Nuestra Señora de las Angustias, patroness of the city, there is a small sunken garden with an unusual stone cross, decorated at the base with radiant suns. Cuencan legend tells of a young wastrel, long ago, who was seduced by a mysterious lady into arranging a midnight tryst outside the walls (at Halloween!). Lost in her charms, he did not realize that he was about to become the subject of old legend until he slid his hand up her dress and saw a cloven hoof; for here, concealed in femininity, was the Devil himself. The wastrel escaped with his life only by reaching the refuge of this cross just as the fiend was about to snatch him, and you can see the mark of the Devil's hand on it today. More prosaically, you may consider the hand to be a symbol from some discreet and long forgotten heresy, perhaps a version of the Islamic 'Hand of Fatima', a common symbol in the Middle East that survives in other cities of Spain in the form of door-knockers.

Toledo

No city in Spain has seen more, or learned more, or stayed true to itself for so long through the shifting fortunes of a discouraging history. Under the rule of Madrid the usurper, though, the last 400 years have been murder for Toledo; its pride humbled, its talents and achievements dried up, this city with little political or economic function is entirely at the mercy of the tourists. It would, in fact, be a ghost town without them. It isn't Toledo's fault that it has become a museum city, but it carries out the role with considerable grace. Its monuments are well scrubbed, its streets lively and pleasant, and the city summons a smile and a welcome for even the most befuddled package tourist. No matter how you come to Toledo, you'll be glad when you finally arrive. The surrounding countryside, once all irrigated farmland or forest, is a desolate desert with a tinge of green, but Toledo has a beautiful setting on a plateau above the Río Tajo, and its little plazas and narrow streets are like an oasis in brick and stone.

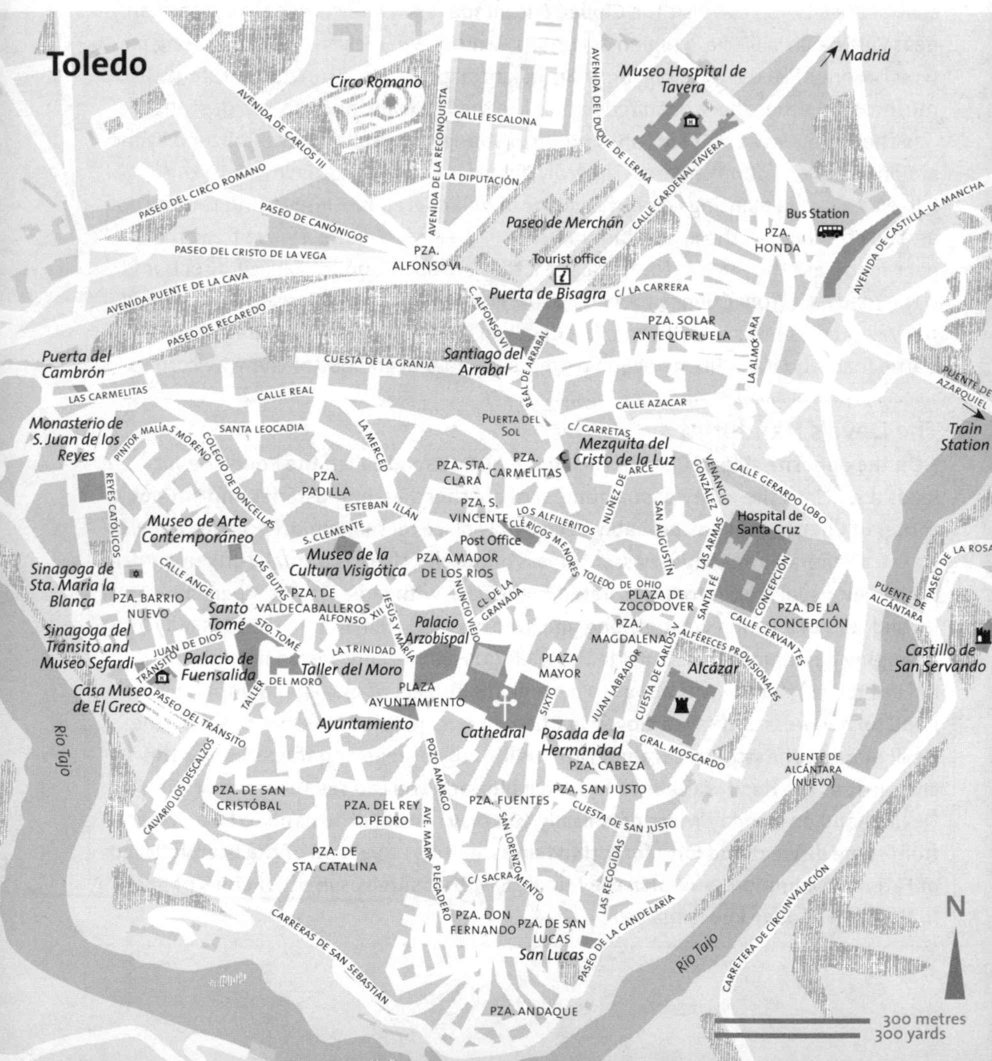

History

Toledo was a capital of sorts when the Romans found it, a centre for the local Celtiberian tribes called the Carpetani. Roman *Toletum* did not gain much distinction, but scanty remains of temples and a circus, visible off Av. de la Reconquista, indicate it must have been fairly large. The Visigoths made it their capital in the 6th century, but they weren't great builders and relatively little is left from their two centuries of rule.

In 716, Toledo fell to the Moors, giving rise to one of Toledo's many legendary tales (*see* box, p.565). Under its new masters, Toledo was to embark on a career that itself would become the stuff of legends. Here, long before the Crusades, the Christian and Islamic worlds first met in a city renowned throughout the Mediterranean for learning. A school of translators grew up in which Arab, Jewish and Christian scholars transmitted Greek and Arab science, as well as Islamic and Jewish theology and mysticism, to the lands of the north. Toledo, conveniently close to the mercury mine at Almadén, became a centre for the study of alchemy. Schools of occult philosophy and mathematics proliferated, attracting students from all over Christian Europe. One was Sylvester II, the late 10th-century Pope, who was said to have stolen a famous book of magic while he was a student in Toledo, and was accused during his papacy of consulting with a prophetic magic 'head' of gold called a 'Baphomet'. The chroniclers claimed a population for Moorish Toledo of some 200,000 people, over three times as large as it is today. Even so, it was never a centre of political power, and to the sultans and emirs of al-Andalus it meant little more than the central bastion of their defence line against the rapacious Christians of the north. In a moment of inattention they lost it to Alfonso VI and El Cid.

The conquest of the city in 1085 was never reversed, and tipped the balance of power irreparably against the Moors. For a long time, Toledo under Castilian rule continued its role as a city of tolerance and scholarship, and its Moorish and Jewish populations easily accommodated the Christian settlers introduced by the Castilian kings. Alfonso the Wise was born here, and he did much to make Toledo's learning and experience become Spain's in common. After the accession of Ferdinand and Isabel, however, disasters followed thick and fast. The church and the Inquisition were given a free hand, and soon succeeded in snuffing out Toledo's intellectual lights. The expulsion of the Jews, and later the Moors, put an end to the city's long-established culture, and the permanent establishment of the capital at Madrid put an end to the political importance Toledo had enjoyed in medieval Castile. To make matters worse, Toledo had been a focal point of the Comunero revolt, and suffered greatly after its suppression. By the 18th century the city had become an impoverished backwater, and except for the famous siege of the Alcázar during the Civil War, little has happened there since. Long ago, Toledo made its living from silk and steel. The silk industry died off with the expulsion of the Moors, and the famous Toledo blades are also just a memory, but for the cheap versions on sale for the tourists. Today, Toledo may make much of its **marzipan** (*mazapan*), but it is the visitors that keep the town going; even if *toledanos* despair when the convoys of tour buses stuff themselves through the tiny streets. Don't be discouraged: relatively few people stay the night, and after museum hours the old town becomes surprisingly tranquil.

Getting There

By Train

Toledo is off the main road and rail lines, and it's hard to get there from anywhere but Madrid. That, however, is easy enough; there are nine trains a day at one to two hourly intervals from Madrid-Atocha, most of which pass through Chamartín to Toledo's charming *mudéjar*-style station east of town (Regionales Line 9 f, journey time 60–85 mins). Any city bus will take you from the station into the centre. RENFE information, Madrid: **t** 902 24 02 02.

By Bus

There is also a convenient bus service run by Empresa Galiano Continental, **t** 915 27 29 61, with departures every half-hour from Estación Sur, C/Méndez Álvaro, **M** Méndez Álvaro **t** 915 30 48 00, Toledo **t** 925 21 58 50.

Tourist Information

Toledo: Just outside the Puerta de Bisagra (Bisagra Gate), **t** 925 22 08 43, **f** 925 25 26 48 (*open July–Sept Mon–Sat 9–7, Sun 9–3; Oct–June Mon–Fri 9–6, Sat 9–7, Sun–9–3*). If you can, stop on your way up so you won't have to make the steep trip down again.

There is a weekly **market** (*Tues*) on Pza de Zocodover.

Where to Stay

Toledo ✉ 45000

Even though most visitors don't stay overnight (it's their loss!), you may need a reservation in July and August.

Expensive

******Parador Conde de Orgaz**, Cerro del Emperador, **t** 925 22 18 50, **f** 925 22 51 66. South of the city: the *parador* is inconvenient for sightseeing (the No.7 bus connects you to the old centre), but the El Greco-esque view of the city from the terrace is superb. It has a very good **restaurant**; ideal for a picturesque, but posh, drink.

******Hotel Doménico**, Cerro del Emperador, **t** 925 20 01 01, **f** 925 28 01 03. Also overlooks the city (served by the No.7 bus): artistically decorated and surrounded by olive groves.

*****Hs del Cardenal**, Pso Recaredo 24, **t** 925 22 49 00, **f** 925 22 29 91, *www.cardenal.aser net.es*. Less expensive than the others; just outside the city walls by Puerta de Bisagra, in an old palace with a terraced garden and **restaurant**; a tranquil haven.

*****Carlos V**, C/Trastamara 1, Pza Horna Magdalena, **t** 925 22 21 00, **f** 925 22 21 05, *www.carlosV.com*. This has more good views (from the roof terrace bar and some rooms); it's elegant and correct, tucked away on a quiet street near the Alcázar and Pza Zocodover – and correspondingly pricey.

Around the Plaza de Zocodover

The name, like the *souk* of a Moroccan city, is from the Arabic for market, and this square – triangle, really – has always been the centre of Toledo. Despite bearing the brunt of Toledo's success as a tourist destination (a McDonald's now dominates one side), the square endures as a favourite place for residents to meet up and exchange gossip, and a traditional market is still held here on Tuesdays. On the long, eastern edge of the triangle, the stately building with the clock is the seat of the provincial government, rebuilt after it burned down during the Civil War. From the archway under the clock, stairs lead down to C/Cervantes and the enormous, fascinating museum contained within the 1544 **Hospital de Santa Cruz** (*Cervantes 3, **t** 925 22 10 36; open Tues–Sat 10–2 and 4–6.30, Sun 10–2; closed Mon*), a building by Enrique de Egas with a wildly decorated façade. A little bit of everything has been assembled here: archaeological finds from Toletum, paintings and tapestries, Toledo swords and daggers. The building itself is worth a visit, its long, airy halls typical of hospitals

Inexpensive

★Imperio, C/Cadenas 5, **t/f** 925 22 76 50. Modern, central and pleasant.

★P. Lumbreras, C/Juan Labrador 9, **t** 925 22 15 71. A cheaper and very central old building, in the narrow street alongside Hotel Carlos V; rooms are arranged around a tiled patio.

★★P. Santa Úrsula, C/Santa Úrsula 14, **t** 925 21 33 25. Just downhill from Pza El Salvador; relatively new, good value and very friendly.

★★Hs Nuevo Labrador, C/Labrador 10, **t** 925 22 26 20, **f** 925 22 93 99. Not the most beautiful of places, but rooms are spacious and comfortable and there's usually a vacancy.

Cheap

★Hs Santa Bárbara, Av. Santa Bárbara 8, **t/f** 925 22 02 98. Good-value *hostal* outside the old town but near the train station and connected to the sites by the No.5 bus.

Eating Out

Dining in Toledo is largely a matter of avoiding overpriced tourist troughs.

Expensive

La Lumbre, C/Real del Arrabal 3, **t** 925 22 03 73. Local cooking shares the menu with French-inspired dishes; and there's plenty for vegetarians: onion tart, leek pie and mushroom-stuffed artichokes.

Asador Adolfo, Hombre de Palo 6 and De la Granala 6 6, **t** 925 22 73 21. Considered Toledo's best restaurant and the place to go for truly flamboyant dining.

El Ábside, C/Marqués de Mendigorria 1, **t** 925 21 32 02. Equally good; the house specialities are venison and roast suckling pig.

Moderate

Hs del Cardenal, Pso Recaredo 24, **t** 925 22 08 62, **f** 925 22 29 91. Excellent hotel-restaurant: stuffed partridge is a speciality, well hung and gamey – the way Toledanos like it.

Venta de Aires, Pso Circo Romano 35, **t** 925 22 05 45. Also serves traditional Toledano fare.

La Judená, San Juan de Dios 7, **t** 925 25 65 12 on C/Reyes Católicos. In the Judería: with a menu full of traditional Castilian cuisine.

Hierbabuena, Hierbabuena 1 Cristo de la Luz 9, **t** 925 22 34 63. Light, imaginative cooking with a hint of vegetarian.

Inexpensive

Maravilla, Pza de Barrio Rey 5, **t** 925 22 23 30. Good, basic cooking: one of a small colony of inexpensive options along C/Barrio Rey.

La Abadía, Nuñez de Arce 3, **t** 925 25 11 40. Hectic but charming.

One of the prettiest places for a drink is the tiny square off C/Santo Tomé; **Cafetería Nano** sets tables out under the trees. Last but not least, try Toledo's ***mazapán***, a traditional speciality made of almond paste and sugar.

of the period, with beautiful ceilings and staircases. Spanish medicine was quite advanced in the 16th century (most physicians were Jewish and exempt from the persecutions) and the surroundings were held to be an important part of the cure. Notable among the displays are Don Juan's huge standard from his flagship at the Battle of Lepanto, paintings by El Greco, some eccentric holy scenes by the 16th-century Maestro de Sigena and a sculptural frieze from a pre-Roman Toledo house. lovely 15th-century Flemish tapestry, the *Tapiz de los Astrolabios*, shows the northern constellations in a kind of celestial garden; others detail scenes from the life of Alexander the Great.

Just around the corner of C/de la Concepción, the chapel of **San Jerónimo** is one of the best examples of Toledo's 16th-century *mudéjar* churches.

Gates of the Town and El Arrabal

North from Pza de Zocodover, the Cuesta de las Armas is the old main road to Madrid. The street descends gradually past the **Mirador** to the **Puerta del Sol**, a pretty gatehouse from the 12th century. In the 14th century, the Knights of St John rebuilt it and added the curious relief medallion, much commented on as a late example of Toledan mysticism; it shows the sun, moon and a large triangle around a scene of San Ildefonso, patron and 4th-century bishop of Toledo, receiving a chasuble woven by angels from the hands of the Virgin. According to local legend, it was presented in return for a treatise the saint wrote on the meaning of the Immaculate Conception. Further down, in the old quarter called the **Arrabal** outside the Moorish walls, is the 11th-century **Santiago del Arrabal**, another fine *mudéjar* church, a joyous excess of pointed arches and towers done in brick. In the 1480s, this was the church of San Vicente Ferrer, the anti-Semitic fire-eater whose sermons started regular riots and helped force the expulsion of the Jews. Here the modern road curves around the **Nueva Puerta de Bisagra**, more like a palace than a gate with its pointed spires and courtyard. Charles V built it, strictly for decoration, and added his enormous coat of arms in stone after the Comunero wars, to remind the Toledans who was boss.

Just outside the gate, the city's tourist office is on the edge of a park called the **Paseo de Merchán**, on the other side of which stands another 16th-century charitable institution converted into a museum, the **Museo Hospital de Tavera** (*Av. de los Duques de Lerma; open daily 10.30–1.30 and 3.30–6*), lovingly guarded by three old ladies. Cardinal Tavera was a member of the house of Mendoza, a grandee of Spain, and an adviser to Charles V. His collection, including his portrait among several works by El Greco, and the memorable *Bearded Woman* by Ribera, share space with objects and furnishings from the Cardinal's time.

The Alcázar

*Cuesta de Carlos V, **t** 925 22 16 73/925 22 30 38; open Sun 10–2 and 4–6; adm.*

Romans, Visigoths and Moors all had some sort of fortress on this spot, at the highest point of the city. The present plan of the big, square palace-fortress, the same that stands out so clearly in El Greco's famous *View of Toledo*, was constructed by Charles V, though rebuilt after destructions in the Napoleonic Wars and again in the Civil War. The second siege was a bitter one, and gave Toledo's Alcázar the curious fate of becoming the holy-of-holies for Spain's fascists and Francoists. Toledo declared for the Republic in July 1936, but a number of soldiers, civilians and Guardia Civil barred themselves inside with the idea that the coup would soon be over. Instead, what they got was a two-month ordeal, with Republican irregulars keeping them under constant fire. When the Nationalists began to exploit the brave defence for propaganda, the Republicans got serious, and finally Asturian miners succeeded in collapsing most of the fortress with dynamite charges. Still the defenders held out, under the leadership of Colonel José Moscardó, in the ruins and underground tunnels, until a relief column finally arrived in September. The courage shown by the men of the Alcázar was quite real, but Francoist Spain was never content to leave it at that. The climax of the visit here is **Colonel Moscardó's office**, where plaques in 19 languages record a telephone conversation in which the Republican commander threatened to kill Moscardó's son, whom he had captured, if the Alcázar did not surrender. With his son on the line, Moscardó intoned 'Shout *Viva España* and die like a hero!' The story is a blatant copy of that of Guzmán el Bueno in Tarifa. In this case, it's all a fake, and Moscardó's son was later found alive and well in Madrid.

The trip through the **dungeons** is interesting, with relics such as the old motorcycle that was hooked up to a mill to grind flour for the defenders, and the spot where two babies were born during the siege. The corridors are covered with plaques sent from overseas to honour the memory of the besieged soldiers, contributed by such groups as the Chilean army and an association of Croatian Nazis in exile.

Mezquita del Cristo de la Luz

From Pza de Zocodover, C/Comercio leads off towards Toledo's great cathedral; on the way, you'll notice a big street sign proclaiming C/de Toledo de Ohio, decorated with the Ohio state seal in *azulejos* (Toledans are proud of their little sister on Erie's shore, with its newspaper called the *Blade*; few of them have probably ever seen it).

King Roderick and the Tower of Hercules

Toledo is full of stories. One of the oldest speaks of a tower, built by Hercules, that stood on the edge of the city. No one knew what was in it, and it became a tradition for every Spanish king to add a new padlock to the scores that already secured the tower's thick brass door. Roderick, that scoundrel who was to be the last of the Visigoths, neglected this, and was confronted one day by two magicians in mysterious dress to remind him of his duty. Roderick's curiosity was piqued, and instead of carrying on the old custom he resolved to find out what was inside the ancient tower. The bishops and counsellors did their best to dissuade him, but in the end Roderick had the centuries' accumulation of locks prised off, one by one, and threw open the brass door. An air as chill as death issued from inside, but the king entered, alone, and climbed a narrow stair to the top of the tower. There he met the figure of a bronze warrior, larger than life, swinging a great mace back and forth and barring his entrance to the tower's inner chamber. Still undaunted, the king commanded it to stop and it obeyed. Behind it lay a chamber with walls covered in gold and precious stones, empty save for a small table bearing a small chest. This the king opened greedily, but found nothing inside but a large, folded linen scroll. Looking closer, he saw that it was covered with scenes of battle; unrolling it further, Roderick watched as the figures on it came to life, and he saw his own army go down to defeat at the hands of unknown invaders in outlandish costume. While he blinked in astonishment at the moving pictures, a thundering crash sounded from the depths of the tower; he dropped the linen scroll and hurriedly fled, escaping just in time to see an eagle soaring over Hercules' tower with a burning brand in its claws. With a scream it dropped the flame directly over it, and in scarcely more time than it took Roderick and his knights to heave a sigh, the tower burnt to the ground. Then, all at once, a great flock of birds flew up from the ashes and sped off to the four winds.

The beauty and strangeness of the old legend betray its Moorish origins: the outlandish invaders were, of course, the Moors, to whom both Toledo and Roderick fell in the year 716.

You may consider a detour here, up typically Toledan steep, narrow streets, to the church of **Cristo de la Luz**, in reality a mosque built around 980 and incorporating elements of an earlier Visigothic church. The story goes that when Alfonso VI captured the city, he and El Cid were making their triumphal entrance when the king's horse knelt down in front of the mosque and refused to move. Taking this as a portent, the king ordered the mosque searched, and a hidden niche was discovered, bricked up in the walls, containing a crucifix and a lamp that had been miraculously burning since the days of the Visigoths. The tiny mosque, one of the oldest surviving Moorish buildings in Spain, is an exceptional example of their work.

The Cathedral

*Open daily 10.30–2 and 4–6.30; **museum** open Tues–Sat 10.30–1 and 3.30–6, Sun 10.30–1; closed Mon; **t** 925 22 22 41.*

This isn't a building that may be approached directly; most of its bulk is hidden behind walls and rows of old buildings, with corners peeking out where you least expect them. The best of its portals, the **Puerta del Reloj**, is tucked away in a small courtyard where few ever see it, at the end of C/Chapinería. Circumnavigating the great building will take you all through the neighbourhood. On C/Sixto Romano, behind the apse, you'll pass an old inn called the **Posada de la Hermandad**, seat of a permanent militia-police force called the 'Holy Brotherhood' that kept the peace in medieval Castile. Coming around C/Hombre de Palo, past the cathedral cloister, you pass the entrance used today, the **Puerta del Mollete** ('muffin') where bread was once distributed to the needy.

Finally, arriving at the **Plaza Ayuntamiento** (still often referred to as the Plaza del Generalísimo) you may enjoy the final revelation of the west front. It's a little disappointing. Too many cooks have been at work, and the great rose windows are hidden behind superfluous arches, over three big portals where the sculpture is indifferent but grandiose. Before too long, the interest fades; turn your glance across the square instead, and you'll see one of Spain's most beautiful city halls, the 1618 **Ayuntamiento**, by El Greco's son, Jorge Theotocópoulos.

Don't give up on the cathedral yet; few Gothic churches in Spain can match its **interior**, which is unusually light and airy, with memorable artworks in every corner. Some 800 fine stained-glass windows from the 15th and 16th centuries dispel the gloom. Sculpture is honoured before painting, unlike most other cathedrals of Spain. Some of the best work is in the Old Testament scenes around the wall of the ***coro***, at the centre of the Cathedral (note the interesting versions of the Creation and story of Adam and Eve). The *coro*'s stalls are famous, decorated with highly detailed scenes from the conquest of Granada, done just three years after the event by Rodrigo Alemán. Behind the *coro* is the freestanding **Chapel of the Descent**, dedicated to San Ildefonso; with its golden pinnacle it seems to be some giant monstrance left in the aisle. Another oddity is the 30ft-tall painting of St Christopher on the south wall. The **Capilla Mayor**, around the main altar, also contains some fine sculpture. A famous statue on the left-hand wall is that of Martín Alhaga, a mysterious shepherd who guided Alfonso VIII's army through the mountains before its victory at Las Navas de Tolosa, then disappeared; only the king saw his face, and he directed the sculptor at his work. On the right, another statue honours the memory of Alfaqui Abu Walid. When Alfonso VI conquered Toledo, he promised this Moorish *alcalde* that the great mosque, on the site of the cathedral, would be left in peace. While he was on a campaign, however, the bishop and the King's French wife Constance conspired to tear it down; upon his return the enraged Alfonso was only dissuaded from punishing them by the entreaties of the generous Moor. Behind the altar, the beautiful *retablo* reaches almost to the vaulting.

The Transparente

Even in a cathedral where so much is unusual, this takes the cake. Early in the 18th century, someone decided that Mass here would seem even more transcendent if somehow a shaft of light could be directed over the altar. To do this a hole was chopped in the wall of the Capilla Mayor, and another in the vaulting of the ambulatory. The difficult question of how to reconcile this intrusion was given to the sculptor Narciso Tomé and his four sons, and in several years' work they transformed the ungainly openings into a Baroque spectacular, combining painting, sculpture and architecture into a cloud of saints, angels and men that grow magically out of the cathedral's stones – many of the figures are part-painted, part-sculpture fixed to the walls. The upper window becomes a kind of vortex, through which the Virgin at the top and all the rest look to be in the process of being vacuumed up to heaven. Even those who usually find Baroque extravagance a bore will raise a smile. Antoni Gaudí would have approved, and it's hard to believe he did not gain just a little of his inspiration from this eccentric masterpiece, completed in 1732. Nearby, the ratty old bit of cloth hanging from the vaulting is a Cardinal's hat; cardinals in Spain have the privilege of hanging them wherever they like before they die. It is one of several in the cathedral. Toledo's archbishop is still the Primate of Spain, and of cardinals it has known quite a few.

The Mozarabic Chapel

After the Christian conquest of Toledo, a dispute arose immediately between the city's old Christians and the officious Castilian prelates over which form of the liturgy would be used in Masses: the ancient Mozarabic form descended from the time of the Visigoths; or the modern, Church-sanctioned style of the rest of Europe. Alfonso, as any good Crusader might have done, decided on a trial by combat to decide the issue. The Mozarabic champion won, but the Churchmen weren't satisfied, and demanded a trial by fire. So they ignited some prayer books: the Roman version was blown from the flames by a sudden wind; the Mozarabic wouldn't burn at all: so Alfonso decreed that the two versions of the faith would coexist on equal footing. Though the numbers of those faithful to the Mozarabic liturgy have dwindled, their Mass is still regularly celebrated in the large chapel in the southwest corner of the cathedral, built by Cardinal Cisneros, a friend and protector of the Mozarabs. You'll be lucky to see it; this chapel, the only home of the oldest surviving Christian ritual in Western Europe, is usually locked up tight. Other sections of the cathedral are open by separate admission, from the enormous souvenir stand inside the Puerta del Mollete. The **Treasury** has little of interest, though the 10ft-high silver reliquary doesn't fail to impress. In the **Sala Capitular**, a richly decorated room with a gilt *artesonado* ceiling, you can see some unusual frescoes and portraits of all Toledo's archbishops. El Greco painted the frescoes and altarpiece of the **Sacristy**, and it contains more of his works, as well as a *Holy Family* by Van Dyck, and a gloomy representation of the arrest of Christ by Goya that makes an interesting contrast to his famous *Los Fusilamientos de Moncloa* in the Prado (Madrid).

West of the Cathedral

Here the streets become even narrower and more winding. Just three intractable blocks northwest of the cathedral, the 13th-century church of San Román has been converted into the **Museo de los Concilios y de la Cultura Visigótica** (Museum of the Councils and Visigothic Culture; *C/San Romaín s/n, **t** 925 22 78 72; open Tues–Sat 10–2 and 4–6.30, Sun 10–2; closed Mon*), the only one of its kind in Spain. 'Councils' refers to the several General Councils of the Western Church that were held in Toledo in the days of Visigothic rule, but the majority of the exhibits are Visigothic relics, jewellery and religious artworks. Some show an idiosyncratic talent, but the lesson here is that the artistic inspiration of Spain did not really change in the transition from Roman to Visigothic rule – there was simply much less of it. The building itself is much more interesting, half-Christian and half-Moorish, with naïve, original frescoes of the Last Judgement and the 12 Apostles in a garden. Painted angels and saints peer out from the ceilings and horseshoe arches. A small **Museo de Arte Contemporánea** (*C/Bulas Viejas 13; open Tues–Sat 10–2 and 4–6.30, Sun 10–2; closed Mon*) is just two blocks west of here.

The Judería

As long as the streets continue to slope downwards, you'll know you're in the right direction. The **Judería**, Toledo's Jewish quarter before 1492, occupies a narrow strip of land overlooking the Tajo in the southwestern corner of the city. El Greco too lived here, and the back streets of the Judería have a concentration of some of old Toledo's most intriguing and interesting monuments.

The church of **Santo Tomé**, on the street of the same name, is unremarkable in itself, but in a little chamber to the side, they'll show you El Greco's *El Entierro del Conde de Orgaz* (The Burial of the Count of Orgaz). The tourists come here in greater numbers than to any sight in Toledo, and more nonsense has been written about this work, perhaps, than any other Spanish painting. A miracle was recorded at this obscure count's burial in 1323: Saints Stephen and Augustine themselves came down from heaven to assist with the obsequies, and this is the scene El Greco portrays. A group of the Count's friends and descendants had petitioned Rome for his beatification, and it is perhaps in support of this that El Greco received the commission, over 200 years later. The portrayal of the burial has for a background a row of gravely serious men, each one a portrait in itself (the artist is said to have included himself, sixth from the right, and his son, the small boy in the foreground, and some commentators have claimed to find even Lope de Vega and Cervantes among the group of mourners). Above, the earthly scene is paralleled by the Count's reception into heaven.

This painting is perhaps the ultimate expression of the intense and slightly twisted spirituality of 16th-century Castile. Its heaven, packed with grim, staring faces, seems more of an inferno. Nowhere is there any sense of joy or release, or even any wonder at the miraculous apparition of the saints. It is an exaltation of the mysteries of power and death, and the longer you look at it, the more disturbing it becomes.

The **Casa-Museo de El Greco** (*Samuel Leví 3;* ***t*** *925 22 40 46, open Tues–Sat 10–2 and 4–6, Sun 10–2; closed Mon*), not far away, is where the painter lodged for most of the years he lived in Toledo. Domenico Theotocópoulos, a Cretan who had studied art in Venice, came to Spain hoping to find work at the building of El Escorial. Philip II didn't care much for him, but 'the Greek' found Spanish life and Spanish religion amenable, and spent the remainder of his life in Toledo. The city itself, as seen from across the Tajo, was one of his favourite subjects (though his most famous *View of Toledo* is now in the Metropolitan Museum of Art, New York). The best parts of the restored house are the courtyard and tiled kitchen; only a few of El Greco's paintings here are of special merit – notably a portrait of St Peter, another favourite subject.

The **Taller del Moro** or Moor's Workshop (*C/Taller del Moro,* ***t*** *925 22 71 15; open Tues–Sat 10–2 and 4–6.30, Sun 10–2; closed Mon*), just around the corner from Santo Tomé church, owes its name to the days it spent as a shop for the cathedral workmen. The building itself is an interesting work of *mudéjar* architecture; inside is a collection of the sort of things the craftsmen made. Next door is the 15th-century **Palacio de Fuensalida** (*visits possible in small private groups; contact the custodian at the palace*), which has been restored and is now the private residence of the President of Toledo.

The Synagogues

Not surprisingly, in a city where Jews played such a prominent and constructive role for so long, two of Toledo's best buildings are synagogues, saved only by good luck after centuries of neglect. The 12th-century **Sinagoga de Santa María la Blanca** (*Pza de Barrionuevo,* ***t*** *925 22 72 57; open Sat–Thurs 10–2 and 3.30–6, Fri 10–2 and 3.30–7*), so called from its days as a church, is stunning and small, a glistening white confection of horseshoe arches, elaborately carved capitals and geometric medallions that is rightly considered one of the masterpieces of *mudéjar* architecture. Just as good, though in an entirely different style, is the **Sinagoga del Tránsito** (*Pso del Tránsito,* ***t*** *925 22 36 65; open Tues–Sat 10–1.45 and 4–5.45, Sun 10–1.45; closed Mon*), built by Samuel Leví, treasurer to King Pedro I (the Cruel) before that whimsical monarch had him executed. The synagogue is much later than Santa María la Blanca, and shows the influence of the Granada Moors: the interior could be a room in the Alhambra, with its ornate ceiling and carved arabesques, except that the calligraphic inscriptions are in Hebrew instead of Arabic, and the Star of David is interspersed with the arms of Castile and León. The building now houses the **Museo Sefardí** (Sephardic Museum), assembled out of a few surviving relics from around the city. Elements of Jewish life and culture are displayed with explanatory notes, to reacquaint Spaniards with a part of their heritage they have quite forgotten.

Monasterio de San Juan de los Reyes

*San Juan de los Reyes 2, **t** 925 22 38 02; open daily 10–2 and 3.30–7.*

Before the conquest of Granada, Ferdinand and Isabel built a church here with the intention of making it their last resting place. The architect was Juan Guas, working the perpendicular elegance of Isabelline Gothic to perfection in every detail. Los Reyes Católicos wanted no doubt as to whose monument this was; their F and Y monogram, coats-of-arms, and yoke-and-arrows symbols are everywhere, even on the stained glass. The exterior of the church is famous, its western wall covered with the chains of prisoners released from the Moors during the Granada campaigns. The **cloister**, surrounding a peaceful courtyard where a lone orange tree keeps meditative company with a solitary pine, is another one of Toledo's architectural treasures, with elegant windows and vaultings on the lower level. The same merry band of 1880s restorers who worked on Valladolid's San Gregorio (*see* p.455) were let loose here, and if you go up to the second floor and gaze up from the arches you will see the hilarious collection of **gargoyles** they added: all manner of monsters, a farting monk and a frog riding a fish; see if you can find the cat.

South of the City

The **Plaza de San Juan de los Reyes Católicos**, in front of the church, has a wide prospect over the valley of the Tajo; from here you can see another of Toledo's fancy 16th-century gateways, the **Puerta del Cambrón**, and the fortified, medieval **Puente de San Martín**. The **Carretera Circunvalación**, on the other side of the Tajo, will give you more views of Toledo than El Greco ever did. On its way it passes a goodly number of country houses called *cigarrales*, the *parador*, and the 14th-century **Castillo de San Servando**, rebuilt from an older Templar foundation. Beneath the castle, the old **Puente de Alcántara**, even better than the Puente de San Martín, will take you back across the Tajo in the neighbourhood of Pza de Zocodover. For a bankside stroll around Toledo, make for the water by **El Baño de la Cava**, just west of San Juan de los Reyes.

Toledo's Countryside

It isn't pretty, and most of the attractions are castles: over 20 of them within a 48 kilometre radius of the city. **Guadamur** and **Barcience**, both west of Toledo, are two of the most interesting. Among the towns and villages, **Talavera de la Reina** is a famous pottery centre, and **Illescas** has five El Grecos in its Hospital de la Caridad. **Orgaz** and **Tembleque**, on the threshold of La Mancha, are suitably ancient and evocative; each has an interesting Plaza Mayor. At Melque, on a back road southwest of Toledo, is one of the oldest churches in Spain, the 9th-century **Santa María de Melque**.

Castilla la Nueva: Extremadura and La Mancha

16

First-year students of Spanish often think Extremadura means 'extremely hard', a translation that seems all the more probable once they find out that this was the native land of those hard men – Pizarro, Cortés, Balboa and others – who sailed to 'conquer' the New World for Spain at the expense of the Aztecs and Incas. Actually, Extremadura means 'beyond the Douro River': the territory conquered by the kings of León and held for centuries as a buffer zone between Christians and Moors.

And hard as it may seem to its natives, who have left vast tracts of countryside empty in favour of the bright lights of the city and jobs in Germany, Extremadura is not without a sweeping kind of beauty, one of rolling fields of wheat, dappled by the shadows of the evergreen holm oak, cork trees and olives. Blue mountains sunder the horizon; sleek black bulls share their pastures with storks, whose shaggy nests give a hairy toupé to church towers and castle turrets. Villages consist of low, whitewashed rows of houses, snaking over the contours of the hills, or towns filled with palaces embellished with the coats-of-arms of the nouveau riche *conquistadores*.

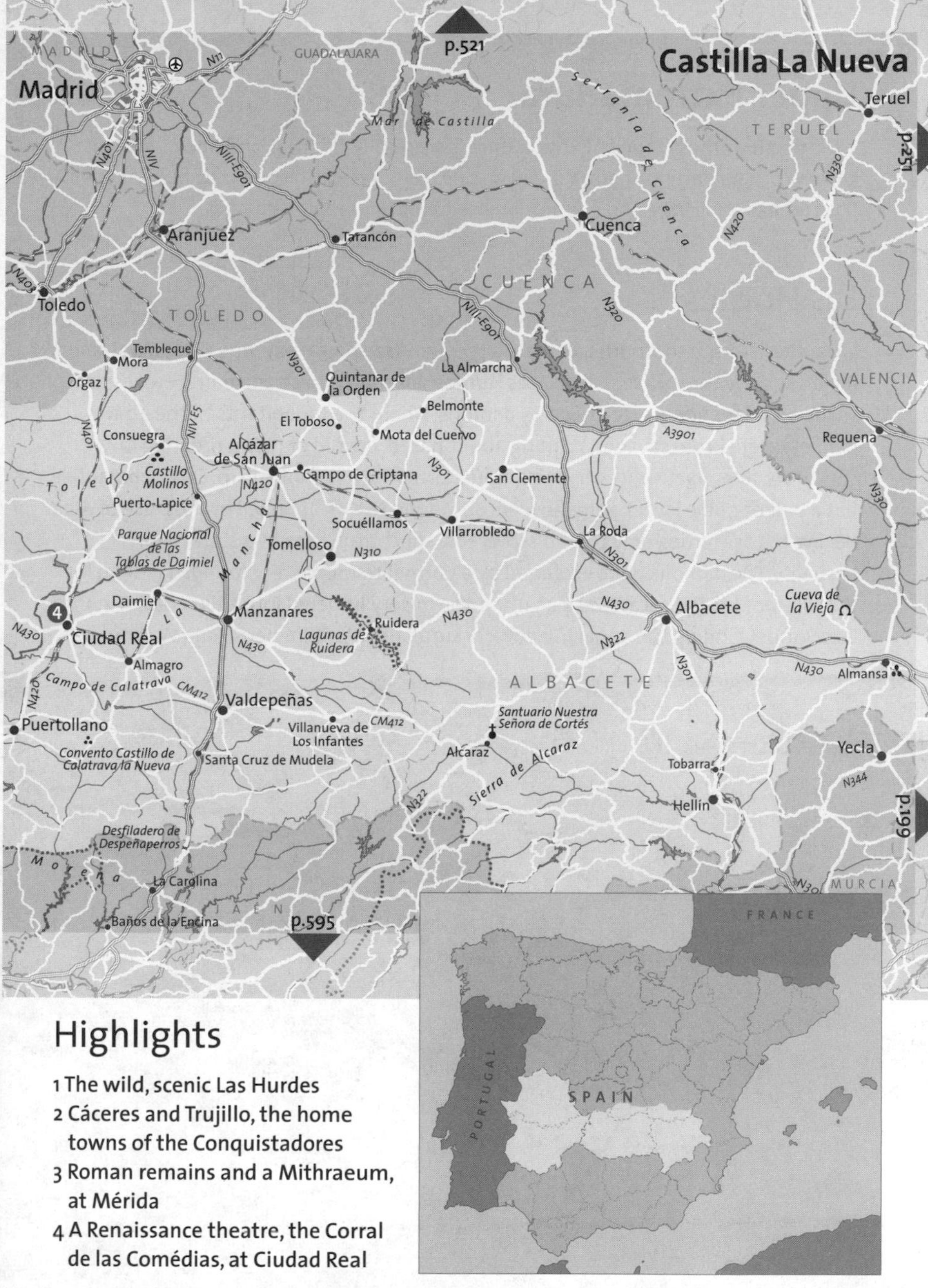

Highlights

1 The wild, scenic Las Hurdes
2 Cáceres and Trujillo, the home towns of the Conquistadores
3 Roman remains and a Mithraeum, at Mérida
4 A Renaissance theatre, the Corral de las Comédias, at Ciudad Real

The jewels of Extremadura are its cities of Cáceres, Trujillo and Zafra, the extensive Roman ruins at Mérida, the famous shrine of Guadalupe and the Monastery of Yuste, where the jaded Charles V retired from the Empire he bullied so hard to create. And lovers of scenic, out-of-the-way places can hardly do better than Las Hurdes, and the mountains and valleys to the north.

Upper Extremadura

The northernmost zone of Extremadura is scenically the best and one of the least-known corners of rural Spain, a green and peaceful retreat favoured by birds and wild boar, monks and kings, and pilgrims on the path to Guadalupe.

Las Hurdes

The sierra of the southern Salamanca province (*see* p.453) extends into an untamed region split by three valleys called **Las Hurdes**. For the Spanish the name evokes dark shadows; a legendary place ruled by demons, where the inhabitants of the 40 tiny hamlets were brute savages, running about naked, devoid of religion, eating raw chestnuts, and practising everything from polygamy to cannibalism. One popular tale has a pair of noble lovers, somehow encountering the disapproval of the Duke of Alba, fleeing to Las Hurdes, only to be discovered a short time later in a state of dire bestiality. The demons were exorcized by a Carmelite monastery founded in 1599 in the valley of **Las Batuecas** (*see* p.453), but the misery lingered into this century; in 1932 Luis Buñuel, finding the appalling poverty surreal, shot a film here, *Land Without*

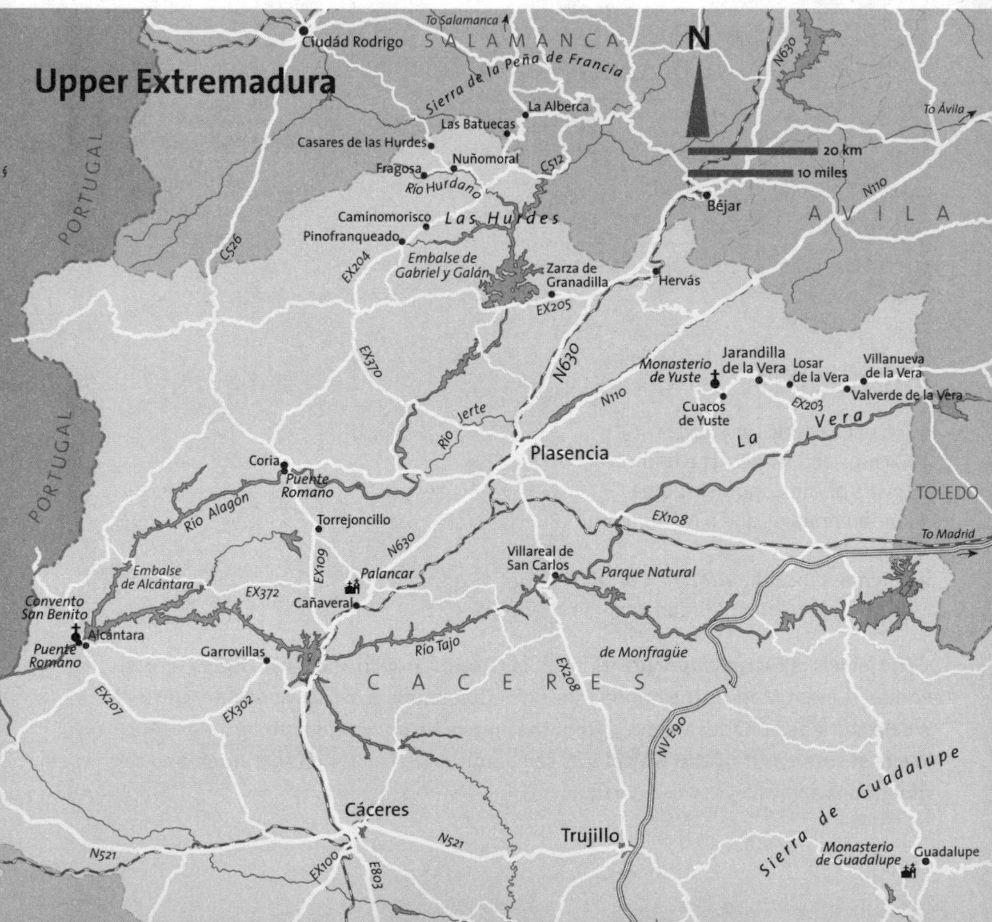

Getting Around

By Train

Cáceres is the transport hub here, with rail links to Mérida, Badajoz, Lisbon and Madrid. Plasencia has three daily connections to Madrid and Badajoz, one daily with Mérida and Cáceres. Palazuelo is the nearest station to Monfragüe National Park: 20km from its entrance at Puerta Serrana. The RENFE station in Cáceres, **t** 927 23 50 61, is on the N630 road to Sevilla a km or two from the Pza Mayor; the No.1 bus will take you there every 15 minutes: catch it at Pza Obispo Galarza or, once it's worked its way round the old town, on the corner of Av. de España and C/Primo de Rivera.

By Bus

There are several connections daily between Salamanca, Plasencia and Cáceres by bus, and three daily to Trujillo (the bus station is just off the main Madrid–Cáceres road on C/Badajoz); one daily from Cáceres and two from Trujillo to Guadalupe. There are at least five express connections between Cáceres and Madrid (taking 3–4hrs, passing through Trujillo), and two buses that pass through the city daily on the way between Badajoz and Irún. Cáceres' bus station is opposite the train station on the road to Sevilla (**t** 927 23 25 50). The No.1 bus will also take you there.

Las Hurdes: If you're driving, C512 and C515 are the main roads through the region; if you're taking the bus from Plasencia (the bus station is near the river, not far from Puente Nuevo), be prepared for some hiking; the few buses heading that way tend to go no further than either Pinofranquedo or Caminomorisco, the largest villages in the Lower Hurdes. Three buses a day go from Plasencia to Hervas, Yuste and La Vera, as well as to Coria. It's easiest to reach Alcántara and Garrovillas from Cáceres.

Tourist Information

Cáceres: Pza Mayor, **t** 927 62 50 47 (*open Mon–Fri 9–2 and 5–7 (winter 4–6); Sat and Sun 9.45–2*).

Plasencia: Pza de la Catedral 17, **t** 927 42 38 43, **f** 927 42 55 94.

Trujillo: Pza Mayor, near the steps, **t** 927 32 26 77, **f** 927 65 91 40, *www.ayto-trujillo.com* (*open daily 9.30–2 and 5–8.30 (winter 4.30–7.30); **guided tours** of the town leave the tourist office at 11.30am and variable afternoon times*).

Guadalupe: Pza Mayor, **t** 927 15 41 28.

In the summer there is also an information booth in **Pinofranqueado**.

Festivals

Villanueva: Pero-Palo Fiesta, *Shrove Tues*. It may not match Rio for size, but the essence of carnival is definitely here.

Cáceres: WOMAD, *May*. The town hosts an annual WOMAD international music festival.

Bread, that introduced the region to the rest of Spain. Over the last few decades Las Hurdes has received special attention to bring it into line with the rest of Spain: new schools, dams and roads were built and efforts made to prop up the local economy. Yet, on the outside, the villages of whitewash and slate have changed little, and wild boars trampling kitchen gardens are still a nuisance.

Exploring Las Hurdes requires a car, or a willingness to tramp through delightful scenery. The countryside is spectacular in places, decked out in a variety of greens that will be welcome if you've come from the arid south. The prettiest route is along the **Río Malvellido** in the **Altas Hurdes**, taking in picturesque villages such as **Fragosa**, **Nuñomoral** and **Casares de las Hurdes**, with wonderful panoramic views and opportunities for potholing. **El Asegur** stands out for the best traditional architecture of the region, while **La Huetre** is stuck in the biggest time warp. **El Gasco**, another of the more remote settlements, has a 160ft waterfall under the **Chorro de la Miancera**, one of the beauty spots of Las Hurdes. The village is also known for its handicrafts and

Where to Stay and Eat

This region has a glut of beautifully located *paradores* if your purse stretches that way.

Las Hurdes: Pinofranqueado ✉ 10630, Nuñomoral ✉ 10623, Riomalo/Caminomorisco ✉ 10620, Casares de las Hurdes ✉ 10618

*El Puente**, Pso de Extremadura 38, Pinofranqueado, **t** 927 67 40 28 (*cheap*). Pinofranqueado's hotel, with a pool.

P. El Hurdano, La Fuente, Nuñomoral, **t** 927 43 30 12 (*cheap*). *Hostal* with basic bathless rooms and a good **restaurant** (*inexpensive*) serving generous portions.

*Hs Riomalo**, C/Larga, Riomalo de Abajo, **t** 927 43 41 00 (*cheap*). Near Caminomorisco, this *hostal* offers 10 simple rooms (with bath) and a similarly budget *menú*.

*Hs Montesol**, Lindón 4, Casares de Las Hurdes, **t** 927 67 61 93. Eight cheap rooms.

Plasencia ✉ 22810

****Parador**, Pza San Vicente Ferrer, **t** 927 42 58 70, **f** 927 42 58 72, *plasencia@parador.es* (*expensive*). In a 15th-century convent within the town walls, this is one of the pricier *paradors*, with a posh **restaurant** (*moderate*).

*Rincón Extremeño**, C/Vidrieras 6, **t** 927 41 11 50, **f** 927 42 06 27 (*inexpensive*). A friendly and central establishment that's been going since 1930; rooms are plain but comfortable (some rather worn) and at varying prices.

*Hs La Muralla**, C/Berrozana 6, **t** 927 41 38 74 (*cheap*). Newer, cheaper rooms (with and without bath) within the walls.

Yuste ✉ 10450

****Parador**, Ctra Plasencia, Jarandilla de la Vera, **t** 927 56 01 17, **f** 927 56 00 88 (*expensive*). On the way to Yuste, stop off at this stunning castle, complete with turrets and a drawbridge, where Charles V stayed as he waited for his apartments at the monastery. The beamed **restaurant** (*moderate*) serves *cuchifrito*, a delicious kid stew.

*HsR Marbella**, Av. Soledad Vega Ortiz 113, **t** 927 56 02 18 (*cheap*). The cheapest option.

Puta Parió, C/Vicaría, Jarandilla de la Vera (*cheap*). Puta Parió means 'the whore spawned'; this bar/restaurant spawns plentiful, deliciously hearty cooking, but doesn't charge over the odds.

Losar de la Vera ✉ 04620

Hostería Fontivieja, Paraje los Mártires 11, **t/f** 927 57 01 08 (*inexpensive*). An ideal base for walking or cycling trips throughout the Valle de la Vera, with a pool.

Antigua Casa del Heno, Finca Valdepimienta, **t** 927 19 80 77 (*inexpensive*). Home cooking in an atmospheric setting with great views.

Coria ✉ 10800

*Los Kekes**, Av. Sierra de Gata 49, **t** 927 50 40 00 (*inexpensive*). A comfortable overnight stop with a reasonable **restaurant**.

musical instruments, including drums and bagpipes. Stop in **Cambroncino** to see the church that attracts such local pride, **Santa Catalina**, built entirely of slate and brick.

On the other side of the **Reservoir Gabriel y Galán** – with a sailing club and places to take a dip in the summer – you can explore castle-crowned **Granadilla**, Spain's most genial ghost town, with nearby beaches, though it's a bit of a trek from the local C513.

Going north, this road joins the N630 near **Hervás** in a pretty region of cherry orchards; the village has one of the best-preserved *aljamas* (Jewish quarters) in Spain, complete with a ruined synagogue and crooked half-timbered houses. Not surprisingly, the community owed much of its prosperity to the protection of the Templars, who aided in the conquest of Extremadura and were rewarded with large tracts of land. Worth a quick visit are the churches of Santa María de Aguas Vivas and San Juan Bautista. In the immediate countryside rambling paths lead up the mountain slopes, swathed with oaks and dotted with streams. Hervás' environs are a hunting area, principally for deer, wild boar and rabbit.

Cáceres ✉ 10000

★★★★**Meliá Cáceres**, Pza San Juan 11, **t** 927 21 58 00, **f** 927 21 40 70, *melia.cáceres@sol melia.com* (*luxury–expensive*). Occupies a magnificent *palacio* in the lovely, quiet Pza San Juan; for discreet, tasteful luxury.

★★★★**Parador de Cáceres**, C/Ancha 6, **t** 927 21 17 59, **f** 927 21 17 29 (*expensive*). Set in the Renaissance palace of El Comendador, this *parador* has an excellent **restaurant** (*menú moderate*) featuring *extremeño* dishes.

★**Iberia**, C/Pintores 2, **t** 927 24 76 34, **f** 927 24 82 00 (*moderate*). Clean, comfortable rooms in an attractive stone house by Pza Mayor.

★★**Goya**, Pza Mayor 11, **t** 927 24 99 50, **f** 927 21 37 58, *hotelgoya@inicia.es* (*inexpensive*). Good-value and modern; a/c, heating and TV.

★**P. Carretero**, Pza Mayor 22, **t** 927 24 74 82 (*cheap*). A characterful option on the square; airy, traditional rooms with shared bath.

P. Márquez, Gabriel y Galán 2, **t** 927 24 49 60 (*cheap*). Flouncy but fine doubles and triples with shared bath, just off Pza Mayor.

Atrio, Av. de España 30, **t** 927 24 29 28 (*expensive*). One of the best restaurants in Spain, serving mostly game in season (*perdiz en escabeche*); excellent *lenguado al vino*.

Torre de Sande, C/de los Condes 3, **t** 927 21 11 47 (*moderate*). A luscious setting just off Pza San Mateo in the old town; choose from a six-course *menú* or dishes *a la carta*.

Palacio de los Golfines, Adarve del Padre Rosario, **t** 927 24 24 14 (*moderate*). Another upmarket option within the walls.

El Figón de Eustaquio, Pza San Juan 12–14, **t** 927 24 81 94 (*inexpensive*). Another good restaurant for regional dishes; try the *jamón ibérico*, Extremadura's wonderful and famous ham, supposedly made from swine fed on rattlesnakes.

Chez Manou, Plazuela de las Veletas 4, **t** 927 22 76 82 (*inexpensive*). Try to get a table with a view of the old town in this atmospheric French restaurant.

El Puchero, Pza Mayor 9, **t** 927 24 54 97 (*inexpensive*). A good, cheap bet if you want to dine on the main square, although inevitably touristy: there's a very cheap (carnivorous) *menú* and some good-value *platos combinados*.

Adarve, C/San Garrido 4, **t** 927 24 48 74 (*inexpensive*). A functional, friendly café/bar, stretching from cheap breakfasts to a huge array of seafood tapas (and *raciones*) at low prices. Locals stop by for a *caña con gambas* (beer and prawns) at midday.

Chocolatería Cafetería Cáceres, Pza Mayor, **t** 927 24 97 63. An elegant location to enjoy *chocolate con churros*.

Beriberi Blues Bar, C/Donoso Cortés. A lively bar decorated with pictures of blues legends covering the bar counter and walls. Good music and a laid-back atmosphere; it's a popular student haunt.

There are plenty of places for a tipple along C/Pizarro, which is lined with bars of differing nationalities; try the Brazilian joint for a coffee or caipirinha.

Plasencia and Yuste

When Alfonso VIII of León founded this settlement, he declared '*placeat Deo et hominibus*' ('may it be pleasing to God and men'), from whence came its name Plasencia, which Alfonso hoped would attract much-needed settlers to the frontier. It does have a fine location, in a bend of the Rio Jerte, and its walls, no longer needed, have been entirely integrated into the houses. The odd silhouettes of two **Cathedrals** dominate Plasencia, twice begun and twice unfinished. The pointy Gothic bulk of the 'new' one is more interesting inside, boasting a fine *reja* (1604) and more choir stalls by the ever-inventive and ever-profane Rodrigo Alemán. The older of the two cathedrals, begun in the 13th century, has a peculiar Salamanca-Zamora-style dome over its Sala Capitular and houses an ecclesiastical **museum** (*open daily 10–12.30, Mon–Thurs and Sat also 4–5.30, Fri 5–7*). The nearby **Museo Etnográfico** (*C/Marqués de la Puebla; open summer Mon–Sat 9.30–2.30, closed Sun; winter Wed–Sat 11–2 and 5–8, Sun 11–2,*

Trujillo ✉ 10200

******Parador de Trujillo**, C/Santa Beatriz de Silva 1, **t** 927 32 13 50, **f** 927 32 13 66 (*expensive*). Situated in the 16th-century convent of Santa Clara, this has attractive, air-conditioned rooms and a serene atmosphere. The **restaurant** (*moderate menú*) serves local specialities including *cochinillo montanera* (roast suckling pig).

Hostal La Cadena**, Pza Mayor 8, **t** 927 32 14 63 (*inexpensive*). Atmospheric rooms in an old *palacio*, all with bath, a/c and TV; the beds can be lumpy, though. The lively ***comedor has a cheap *menú*.

***Hostal Nuria**, Pza Mayor 27, **t** 927 32 09 07 (*inexpensive*). Very clean rooms with bath, a/c and TV, similarly priced to La Cadena and also with a cheap *menú*.

Pensión Emilia, Pza del Campanillo 28, **t** 927 32 00 83 (*cheap*). The rooms here are basic, but the Emilia dishes up tasty home cooking in her **restaurant** (which has a budget *menú*).

Pizarro, Pza Mayor 13, **t** 927 32 02 55 (*inexpensive*). A favourite with locals and visitors alike, on the main square. Food is delicious, so arrive early to be sure of getting a table.

Mesón La Troya, Pza Mayor 10, **t** 927 32 13 64 (*inexpensive*). Adjacent to the Pizarro, this dishes up portions which defy description; the *menú* here is a bit more expensive.

Cafetería Berlin, C/Tiendas 4, **t** 927 32 26 93. Popular bar just off Pza Mayor: filled with young people and serving good tapas, including soya sausages.

Guadalupe ✉ 10140

******Parador de Guadalupe**, C/Marqués de la Romana 10, **t** 927 36 70 75, **f** 927 36 70 76 (*expensive*). Guadalupe's *parador* is in a 16th-century palace close to the church, with a lovely garden and pool, and walls embellished with reproductions by *extremeño* artists. The **restaurant** (*moderate*) features excellent regional specialities, although the *menú* is nothing spectacular.

****Hospedería del Real Monasterio**, Pza Juan Carlos I, **t** 927 36 70 00, **f** 927 36 71 77 (*moderate*). A better bet: it occupies part of the monastery housing the Virgin of Guadalupe, and offers wonderful value for almost identical accommodation and a beautifully tranquil setting arranged around a gorgeous, Gothic cloister; there's also a good, if slightly institutional **restaurant** (*inexpensive*) and big buffet breakfasts with *churros*.

Mesón El Cordero, Alfonso Onceno 27, **t** 927 36 71 31 (*inexpensive*). One worth trying for good *perdiz escabechada* and *verduras guadalupanas*. *Closed Mon.*

Alfonso XIII, Alfonso Onceno (*inexpensive*). A cheaper bet, with *menús* to match.

Atrium, Alfonso Onceno 6. A good café/bar to start and end your day: you'll find delectable pastries for breakfast, and yet more mouth-watering options for post-prandial cake.

The **Plaza Mayor** is undoubtedly a tourist trap, but it's still a scenic spot for sipping coffee if the sun is out.

closed Mon and Tues) has a collection of local costumes, crafts and farming tools . In the **Plaza Mayor**, a couple of blocks away, a funny man in green strikes the hours atop the **Ayuntamiento**; if you can get in, take a look at the *artesonado* ceiling in the main hall. Spanish tourists, on the other hand, come from far and wide to visit the **Museo de Caza** (Hunting Museum) in the 16th-century Palacio del Marqués de Mirabel on Plaza San Nicolás, with a large collection of weaponry and associated paraphernalia (*open all day in summer*).

Yuste

Plasencia is the easiest base for visiting the **Monastery of Yuste** (*open in summer Mon–Sat 9.30–12.45 and 3.30–7, Sun 9–11.45 and 3.30–6.45; in winter Mon–Sat 9.30–11.30 and 3–6, Sun 9–11.30 and 3–6; adm, adm free Thurs am*). The bus goes as far as the picturesque old village of **Cuacos**; from there it's a two-kilometre walk uphill to the monastery. After ruling a hefty percentage of the Western world for 40 years,

Charles V chose this corner of Extremadura for his final retirement, accompanied by his cat and parrot, his friend the engineer and clockmaker Torriano de Cremona and 100 servants. Whatever excesses and seeds of disaster were sown by the egomaniac during his reign, his retirement captured the popular imagination; here the world-weary emperor, discomforted by gout (you can still see his gout chair and the ramp especially constructed to give him easy access to his apartments), could fish, feed the ducks and look out over the mountains. Although Yuste was ruined after the depredations of the Peninsular War and suppression of the monasteries, Charles' apartments have been maintained as they were when he died in 1558, draped in black (but minus his cartloads of Titians and Flemish tapestries); from his deathbed he could hear Mass in the church below.

Cuacos and the pretty villages to the east in the **Valle de la Vera** are tobacco towns, and you can often see the local product hanging from the medieval arcades and carved wooden balconies. In **Jarandilla de la Vera**, the castle where Charles lived while waiting for his quarters at Yuste to be completed is now a *parador*. Other pretty villages in the valley are **Villanueva de la Vera**, with a fine plaza, and **Losar de la Vera**,

We'll Be Glad When You're Dead, You Rascal You

One of the unpleasant side-effects of the new humanistic learning of the Renaissance was the flood of self-indulgence and vanity it let loose on an unsuspecting Europe. If Man was the measure of all things, then plenty of spoiled princes were willing to follow their egos and make royal jackasses of themselves – just think of Henry VIII. It's a shame that no director has ever explored the cinematic potential of Henry's contemporary, Charles V. He would have a plot loaded with violence and intrigue, the Renaissance for a backdrop, and a villain nobody in the theatre would ever forget. To his apologists and propagandists, Charles of Habsburg represented the dream of a universal Catholic monarchy, the heir of the Romans and Charlemagne; many of his subjects preferred to see him as more of an Antichrist. Charles always tried to act more like the latter, in his decades of endless marching about Europe, disturbing the peace and bullying everybody about. Charles' latter-day appetite for food, it seems, was as great as it had once been for provinces and money, and there are hints that the real reason for his surprise abdication in 1556 was to spend more time caring for his digestion, so that he might stuff himself to the hilt while trying to avoid aggravating his gout too much. The only thing that kept him going so long at Yuste, according to one observer, was a faithful steward who would 'interpose himself between his master and an eel pie, as in other days he would have thrown himself between the Imperial Person and the point of a Moorish lance'. Besides eating, Charles' other retirement hobbies were piety and death. The monks were paid to keep up a perpetual nattering in the church adjacent to his bedroom, so that the Emperor could stare at Titian's *La Gloria* (now in the Prado, Madrid) and doze off in daydreams of sanctity; the poor brothers also had to assist in the constant rehearsals of his funeral that Charles loved to stage. Fittingly, it was at one of these, in 1558, that he caught a chill and died.

with many dilapidated 16th-century houses. The best time to visit the Valle de la Vera is in April, when the whole area is abloom with cherry blossom. Failing that, try and catch the Pero-Palo fiesta in **Villanueva de la Vera** on Shrove Tuesday (*see* 'Festivals', p.575). Nearby is **Valverde de la Vera**, with architecture even more splendid than Villanueva. The night before Good Friday sees a silent, sinister procession of *empalaos*: literally, 'beaten' penitents, each tied to a plough.

Coria and the Bridge of Alcántara

Located just north of the Río Alagón, a tributary of the Tajo, **Coria** can claim a **Roman bridge** (although water no longer flows beneath it), a lovely **castle** with a pentagonal tower, and a **Gothic cathedral** (*open daily 10–1 and 3–6.30*) with a refined interior; the treasure here is, allegedly, nothing less than the tablecloth used at the Last Supper.

At **Alcántara**, where the Alagón joins the Tajo, a dam was built creating the vast **Embalse de Alcántara**, one of several irrigation schemes of the Badajoz Plan, designed to bring the dry but fertile lands of Extremadura under cultivation. In Arabic, the word Alcántara means 'the **bridge**', a name given to the town by the Moors for the remarkable example that now spans the dry gorge below the dam. Built under Trajan in the year 105, the bridge has six lofty arches, the highest ever built by the Romans, and still makes a brave sight complete with its triumphal arch in the middle. Alcántara was the headquarters of the Order of Alcántara, founded to defend the frontier in the 12th century; you can see the tombs of the Grand Masters in the 13th-century **church**, and ruins of the knights' **castle** remain above the town. But the prettiest church in town belongs to the 16th-century **Convento de San Benito**, with a fine, recently restored Plateresque façade.

East along the reservoir lies **Garrovillas**, site of a Templar convent. Its **Plaza Mayor** is an undulating, whitewashed work of art, whilst the 15th-century church of **San Pedro** has a curious façade. Near Cañaveral, turn off for Torrejoncillo; four kilometres further on are signs to the **Convento del Palancar** (*open Thurs–Tues 9.30–1 and 4–7.30; closed Wed*), the smallest monastery in the world. Still used by Franciscan monks, the cloister is so small you can touch the facing walls with your outstretched arms.

Further east, **Monfragüe National Park** was created in 1979 to protect the unusual flora and fauna of this remote region: Iberian lynxes, boars, badgers, foxes, imperial eagles, black storks and several kinds of vulture. Although most of the park is inaccessible, many of the animals can be seen around **Villareal de San Carlos**, a village in the centre of Monfragüe, founded by Carlos III to police the notorious bandits who haunted the region. A booth in Villareal has information on trails, the best bird-watching spots and camping. The name of the park is derived from the crusading knights of the Order of Montfrag, who had their headquarters in the once-mighty, and now mighty ruined, **Castello de Monfragüe**, located at the south end of the park by the scenic **Sierra de Peñafalcón**; a statue of the Virgin brought from Palestine by the Knights is still the subject of local devotion.

Cáceres

The provincial capital, Cáceres, is the most atmospheric of Extremaduran cities. Three sides of its large, central **Plaza Mayor** face the attractive, whitewashed new town, home of the region's university; the fourth side adjoins the nearly perfectly preserved **Roman-Moorish walls** and **towers** that enclose a beautiful 16th-century city inhabited mainly by storks, swallows and bats. Much of it was built with gold from the Americas, and seemingly little has happened to it since the *conquistadores* returned to flaunt their wealth before their fellow citizens. If you come out of season, or in the dead of night, its cobbled streets seem as enchanted and timeless as Sleeping Beauty's castle. The **Torre Bujaco**, dominating Pza Mayor, is almost entirely Roman, and it's a startling experience to be in Cáceres during a fiesta, when the fireworks (and frightened storks) come careering off its roof and skim the heads of the crowd below. The gate next to it, the **Arco de Estrella**, is an 18th-century addition by one of the prolific Churrigueras. Immediately to the right looms the huge, decrepit **Casa de Toledo-Montezuma**, home of the descendants of Cortés' follower Juan Cano and his wife, the daughter of Montezuma. All of the narrow streets near here converge in the elegant **Plaza de Santa María**, with a fine Gothic church of the same name containing a beautiful 16th-century *reredos*. Among the many lovely palaces in the old town, the **Casa de los Golfines de Abajo**, just around the corner from Santa María at Cuesta de la Compañia, has the best façade, dating back even before the *conquistadores* to the 15th century. It was here that Franco declared himself Generalísimo in 1936. The lane in front of the palace descends through the **Arco Cristo**, the last Roman gate to remain substantially intact.

Cáceres' other major architectural ensemble, **Plaza de San Mateo**, was the Moorish centre of town. Tall, Gothic **San Mateo** (*open at weekends for services*) stands on the site of the old mosque; the **Casa de las Veletas** (*open Tues–Sat 9.30–2.30 and 5–8.15 (winter afternoons 4–7.15), Sun 10.15–2.30*) decorated with peculiar bright-coloured gargoyles, incorporates part of the Moorish Alcázar and its pretty cistern shaded by horseshoe arches. The building now contains the historical and ethnographic artefacts of the **Museo de Cáceres** (which extends to the Casa de los Caballos). On the same plaza, the 1477 **Casa de las Cigüeñas** ('Storks' House') is the only one in town to retain the battlements on its tower; originally there were some 30 similar towers in Cáceres, but the nobles were so prone to fighting that Isabel ordered them cut down to size. The tower still serves as a barracks and you can't get in. Nor can you enter the Gothic **Convento de San Pablo**, though in the doorway beneath the Arabic inscription you may purchase the best biscuits in town from the nuns.

If you have wheels, it would be appropriate to visit the various incarnations of cars in the eye-opening **Vostell Museum** (*open Tues–Sun 10–1.30 and 6–9; closed Mon; more restricted afternoon hours outside summer,* **t** *927 27 64 92; adm*), three kilometres from Malpartida de Cáceres in a tranquil spot by a reservoir. Founded in 1976 by Spanish-German artist Wolf Vostell, who created the 'décollage technique' and co-founded the 'fluxus' movement, the museum holds a mix of Vostell's own creations and subsequently donated works.

Trujillo

An hour east, Cáceres' quieter twin-sister, Trujillo, is nicknamed the 'Cradle of the *Conquistadores*': it's the birthplace of Francisco Pizarro (1476–1541), who, suckled by a sow, began his career here as a swineherd before he almost singlehandedly destroyed the Inca civilization, as well as that of Francisco Orellana, first European explorer of the Amazon. In the same epoch the town produced another extreme character in Diego García de Paredes (1466–1530), 'the Samson of Extremadura', a giant of a man who was the companion-in-arms of the Gran Capitán Gonzalo de Córdoba, known for holding off entire armies by himself with a sword measuring nearly two metres.

Trujillo has an especially fine **Plaza Mayor**, dominated by an equestrian **statue of Francisco Pizarro**, depicting both man and horse wearing *conquistador* helmets; if it looks familiar, you may have seen its double in Lima, Peru. Diagonally opposite across the plaza stands the grandiose **Palacio de la Conquista**, built by Hernando Pizarro. Of the five Pizarros who led the expedition to Peru, Hernando was the only legitimate son and also the cleverest; while his brothers' bloody intrigues caused their untimely deaths, Hernando stayed out of the way, married his brother Francisco's half-Inca daughter Francisca and settled here, where his descendants received the honorary title of Marqués de la Conquista. Behind this palace, the **Palacio Orellana-Pizarro** (*open Mon–Fri 10–1 and 4–6, Sat and Sun 11–2 and 4.30–7*), has an elegant Renaissance courtyard. From here, enter the old walled town through **Puerta de San Andrés** and take C/de las Palomas to **Santa María** (*open winter daily 10–2 and 4–7; summer daily 10–2 and 5–8; adm*), a fine Gothic church housing a *retablo* by the Flemish-inspired Fernando Gallego, and the tombs of numerous Pizarros and Diego García de Paredes. Further up, the restored Roman-Moorish-Castilian **castle** (*open winter daily 10–2 and 4–7; summer daily 10–2 and 5–8.30; adm*) today defends only vegetable gardens; from its height it commands views over Trujillo and its environs. The landscape is so bleak and comfortless that you can understand why the Pizarros left it all behind to sail into the unknown in search of the main chance, even if history will always condemn their cruelty and avarice, shocking even by the standards of the Age of Rapacity.

Guadalupe

One thing the *conquistadores* took to, rather than from, the New World was the cult of their Extremaduran goddess, the Virgin of Guadalupe. The little dark image, said to have been carved by St Luke, was discovered by a shepherd in the 13th century in the pretty verdant oasis of the Sierra de Guadalupe, but the statue had to wait until 1340 for a proper shrine in an Hieronymite monastery founded expressly to house her. Soon Guadalupe became a pilgrimage destination, so popular that a big city in Mexico and a Caribbean island were named after her. Deserted in the 19th century, the monastery (now Franciscan) has been reopened; its fortress-like bulk, its pinnacles, towers and domes, dominate the tiny medieval town that over the centuries has grown up around the central plaza. The setting is as superb as it is difficult to attain: Guadalupe is one of the most out-of-the-way destinations in Spain.

The most intriguing thing in the **Monastery** (*open daily 9–1 and 3.30–6.30; adm and compulsory guided tour*) is the *mudéjar* **cloister**, its two storeys of horseshoe arches enclosing Extremadura's most singular and provocative piece of architecture, the 1405 **templete**, a *mudéjar* pavilion topped by an octagonal spire consisting of three tiers of blind, gabled arches, built over a Moorish fountain. The **sacristía** is also unique: its eight Zurbaráns still hang in places designed for them in the 17th century. Few paintings are as fortunate as these, to be seen as they were meant to be seen, in a sumptuous décor far removed from the sterile walls of the museums. Various rooms of **museum** pieces are crammed full of more treasures: illuminated manuscripts and embroidered vestments, reliquaries and paintings (with three El Grecos and a Goya).

The **church** (*open daily 9–8.30*) has attractive lacy stonework over its bronze doors, all from the 15th century; inside, the **choir** houses a most enormous revolving lectern, designed to take the 40–50kg weight of the manuscripts of music, which have built-in wheels. In the gloom you can just make out the glittering Virgin of Guadalupe high above the altar; for the climactic, close-up view you must take the stairs up to the **Camarín** (*on the monastery's guided tour*), where the Virgin de las Españas turns on her gyrating enamelled throne to receive the homage of the faithful and the scrutiny of the merely curious. She is certainly old and wise, her mysterious, dark, Byzantine face peering out from her rich and gaudy jewelled attire. The enamels in the Camarín depict the glory of the Virgin before Santa Teresa and San Juan de Díos. After the Civil War two scenes were added: one depicting a Guardia Civil killed on the ramparts during 'the siege' and in the next panel, the triumphant entry of the Nationalists into Guadalupe, greeted by a friar raising his arm in a fascist salute. The scenes may have been a backhanded slap at Mexico, whose patron saint is the Virgin of Guadalupe. It was also the one country in Latin America never to recognize the Franco government.

Lower Extremadura

The beautiful bridges of Badajoz and ancient Roman Mérida span the Río Guadiana, beyond which lower Extremadura extends south through vineyards around villages that announce the proximity of Andalucía with their Moorish towers and fortresses.

Mérida

Many cities in Spain were founded by the Romans to settle their legions after the peninsula had been won. León and Zaragoza leap to mind, but in its day Mérida (founded in 23 BC as *Augusta Emerita*) outshone them all, growing to become the capital of the vast province of Lusitania and compared, with some exaggeration, to Athens. The Visigoths retained it as the capital of their western marches, but since the time of the Moors its monuments have been quarried (many of its stones going to build the Mezquita in Córdoba). Modern Mérida is only half the size of Augusta Emerita, but no place in Spain can offer more in the way of surviving monuments, scattered as they are all over the city.

Getting Around

By Train

Extremadura's train timetable is subject to constant change, so it is always best to check with the tourist office. Badajoz and Mérida are linked to Madrid four times daily and to Barcelona twice daily; Mérida has three trains daily to Cáceres and five to Badajoz. From Sevilla, one train (at 9.58am) connects Zafra on its way to Mérida and Cáceres. From Huelva there's one train to Zafra, and one to Fregenal de la Sierra. The train to Lisbon goes through Cáceres daily at the Godforsaken time of 2.59am. In all of the above cities the train stations are within easy walking distance from the centre, except Badajoz, where the station is across the river, 1½km from the centre, **t** 924 27 11 70; the No.1 bus circles the old town before heading towards the station; you can pick it up by Pza de la Libertad, amongst other places. In Mérida, **t** 924 31 81 09; in Zafra, **t** 924 55 02 15. Badajoz has a twice daily **air service** to Madrid.

By Bus

The bus tends to be more convenient, being better and quicker. Badajoz and Mérida are the hubs; there are at least five daily buses from Badajoz and Mérida to Sevilla, via Zafra, as well as connections to Córdoba; another route goes to Salamanca and points north twice a day. Buses also plough over the border to Evora and Lisbon faster than the train. Mérida has a new bus station on the other side of the river near the Puente Romano (**t** 924 37 14 04). In Badajoz buses leave from several locations, the main one being the station on C/José Rebollo López, **t** 924 25 86 61.

Tourist Information

Mérida: Next to Teatro Romano, **t** 924 31 53 53, **f** 924 31 47 14 (*open Mon–Fri 9–1.45 and 5–7.15 (winter afternoons 4–6.15), Sat and Sun 9.30–1.45*).

Badajoz: Pasaje de San Juan (just off Pza de España), **t** 924 22 49 81, **f** 924 21 02 31 (*open Mon–Fri and hols 10–2 and 5–7, Sat 10–1.30*); also Pza de la Libertad 3, **t** 924 22 27 63 (*open Mon–Fri 9–2 and 5–7*).

Zafra: Pza de España 8, **t** 924 55 10 36, *www.ayto-zafra.com* (*open Mon–Fri 9.30–2 and 5–8 (winter 5–7); Sat and Sun 10–2*).

Jerez de los Caballeros: information from the Ayuntamiento, **t** 924 73 03 84, **f** 924 75 02 04.

Festivals

Mérida: Classical Drama Festival, *July*. A celebration of drama held in the Roman theatre.

Where to Stay and Eat

Mérida ✉ 06800

★★★★**Parador Vía de la Plata**, Pza de la Constitución 3, **t** 924 31 38 00, **f** 924 31 92 08 (*expensive*). Charming *parador*, in a former convent on a quiet square in the centre of town; the **restaurant** has a *menú* and a range of *extremeño* dishes.

★★★★★**Sol Meliá**, Pza España, *www.solmelia.com* (*expensive*). The 14th-century palace on the main square is in the midst of transformation, due to open in 2002 as one of the plush Meliá chain.

★★★**Nova Roma**, C/Suárez Somonte 42, **t** 924 31 12 61, **f** 924 30 01 60, *www.novaroma.com* (*expensive–moderate*). Modern pastel rooms, and conveniently situated on a quiet, central street near the Roman theatre.

Cervantes, C/Camilo José Cela 10, **t** 924 31 49 61, **f** 924 31 13 42 (*moderate*). Spacious rooms in a modern block five minutes from Pza España, with all mod cons.

★**Hostal Nueva España**, Av. Extremadura 6, **t** 924 31 33 56, **f** 924 31 32 11 (*inexpensive*). Friendly *hostal* between the train station and Pza España, with modern doubles.

Mérida has a number of good and inexpensive **restaurants**:

Rufino, Pza Sta Clara 2, **t** 924 31 20 01 (*moderate*). The personable Rufino has presided over his bar/restaurant for more than 25 years; deservedly popular, those in the know pass up the *menú* to try local dishes *a la carta*.

Nicolás, C/Felix Valverde Lillo 13, **t** 924 31 96 10 (*inexpensive*). In a distinctive house with yellow awnings, this restaurant offers everything from *raciones* to a *menú del día*.

Museu Ibérico, C/San Juan 5 (*inexpensive*). Near Santa Eulalia, this is the locals' budget choice, with a four-course cheapie *menú*.

Casa Benito, C/San Francisco 3, **t** 924 31 55 02. Behind the creepered, bird-infested terrace lurks this *matador*'s bar, with a hearty selection of meaty tapas.

Badajoz ✉ 06000

★★★★**Barceló Zurbaran**, Pso de Castelar, **t** 924 22 37 41, **f** 924 22 01 42, *zurbaran@barcelo.com* (*expensive*). The full works, with a pool and highly regarded **restaurant** (*moderate*), Los Monjes Zurbaran.

★★★**Hotel Río**, Av. Adolfo Díaz Ambrona 13, **t** 924 27 26 00, **f** 924 27 38 74, *hotelrio@hotelrio.net* (*expensive*). Fine views, and modern, air-conditioned rooms, with a pool and excellent **restaurant**, all on the other side of the river from the old town.

★★**Cervantes**, C/Trinidad 2, **t** 924 22 37 10, **f** 924 22 29 35 (*inexpensive*). Thirty-eight quiet rooms in this characterful old house with an *azulejo* entrance, off Pza de Cervantes.

★**Hs Beatriz**, C/Abril 20, **t** 924 23 35 56 (*inexpensive*). Similarly priced and central.

★**Niza I**, C/Arco-Agüero 34–5, **t** 924 22 31 73, **f** 924 22 38 81 (*cheap*). Clean rooms with shared bath in the old town; its pricier sister, **Niza II** (from whence both are run) is not such good value.

Aldebarán, Av. de Elvas, **t** 924 27 42 61 (*moderate*). The best place to eat in town: try ravioli stuffed with minced kid and wild mushrooms, or a supremely wonderful cheese and walnut tart. *Closed Sun*.

Escuela de Restauración de Badajoz ('erb'), C/Virgen de la Soledad 6, **t** 924 22 99 97 (*moderate*). Good traditional and contemporary dishes take turns at the Chefs' school.

La Toja, C/Sánchez de la Rocha 22, **t** 924 23 74 77 (*inexpensive*). Good Gallegan cooking with a garden for outdoor dining.

Taberna La Giralda, C/Virgen de la Soledad 25B, **t** 924 23 59 11 (*inexpensive*). A new and characterful *bodega* opposite the eponymous tower, perfect for a tipple and tapas balanced on an old wine vat.

Club Taurino Extremeño, C/José Lopez Prudencio 8. This is the place for a dose of the old bullfighting spirit.

Zafra ✉ 06300

★★★★**Parador Hernán Cortés**, Pza Corazón de María 7, **t** 924 55 45 40, **f** 924 55 10 18, *zafra@parador.es* (*expensive*). A 15th-century castle, in which Hernán Cortés slept as a guest of the Dukes of Feria. The décor is Renaissance, but the comforts (pool, garden and good *extremeño* **cuisine** (*moderate*) in a magnificent setting) are 21st century and first class.

★★**Huerta Honda** on Av. López Asme 30, **t** 924 55 41 00, **f** 924 55 25 04, *www.hotelhuertahonda.com* (*expensive–moderate*). A wonderful second choice: fine rooms with lovely views of the castle, a pretty patio and tiny pool; some of the *gran clase* rooms and suites are truly outrageous, with curtained Jacuzzi baths and beautiful terracotta floors. There are two **restaurants**: the informal, blue **Mesón** (*inexpensive*), meticulously supervised by a Portuguese maître d' and deservedly popular, and the rustic red '**Barbacana**' (*moderate*).

★★**Hotel Don Quijote**, C/Huelva 3, **t** 924 55 47 71, **f** 924 55 47 82 (*inexpensive*). Friendly place with comfortable rooms. Ask for a third floor room: attic rooms with beamed, sloping ceilings and a balcony; there's a popular **restaurant** (*inexpensive*) attached.

Las Palmeras, Pza Grande 14, **t** 924 55 22 88, **f** 924 55 53 85 (*cheap*). Hiding behind the palms at the end of the lovely plaza, this hotel offers good value rooms with bath and an (*inexpensive*) *menú*.

C/Bóticas and Pza Chica are also good bets for food and drink:

La Rebotica, C/Bóticas 12, **t** 924 55 42 89 (*inexpensive*). Local specialities, like garlic soup.

Mesón Maxi, C/Bóticas 3a, **t** 924 55 28 98 (*inexpensive*). A less formal setting on the other side of the street.

La Tertulia, Pza Chica 10, **t** 924 55 35 18 (*inexpensive*). Characterful piano bar serving tapas and *raciones*.

Jerez ✉ 11400

★★★**Los Templarios**, Ctra Villanueva, **t** 924 73 16 36, **f** 924 75 03 38, *templarios5@interbook.net* (*inexpensive*). A good-value hotel, given its pool and tennis court.

★**Las Torres**, Ctra Jerez a Oliva 49, **t** 924 73 03 68 (*cheap*). Near the centre, with 12 simple rooms (cheaper with shared bath).

Mérida has a rare and magnificent front entrance: a 60-arched, one-kilometre-long **Roman bridge** spanning the Río Guadiana – the longest built in Spain and repaired by the Visigoths and Philip III. The Guadiana is a wide, shallow river with numerous islands, and the bridge, with sleek cattle grazing beneath its arches, forms a delightful rustic scene. Just to the right of the bridge is the large **Alcazaba** (*open summer daily 9.30–1.45 and 5–7.15; winter daily 9.30–1.45 and 4–6.15; a composite ticket without time limit covers entry to most monuments and is cheaper than buying individual ones*), a confusing bulwark that has served every ruler from the Romans to the Templars and Knights of Santiago; what stands now was built mainly by the Moors, using stones from the Roman theatre. Within its walls you can visit the **conventual**, or residence of the Knights of Santiago, a number of **Roman houses** with mosaics and, best of all, the ***aljibe***, or cistern (*closed for restoration but due to reopen in 2002*), its entrance adorned with lovely, carved Visigothic door-frames, from where twin corridors descend to a pool of cool water. The rest of the Alcazaba resembles a construction site.

Before tackling the rest of Roman Mérida, you can fortify yourself in one of the many cafés on nearby **Plaza de España**. The so-called **Temple of Diana** was probably a Nymphaeum before a local grandee in the 16th century used its tall Corinthian columns to frame his palace, much of which has since been cut away to reveal the impressive Roman structure. Just off Pza de España, in C/Santa Julia 1, the Palacio de Burmay houses a new **Museum of Visigothic Art** (*open Tues–Sat 10–2 and 5–7 (winter afternoons 4–6), Sun 10–2; closed Mon*) with Visigothic masonry and floral reliefs.

The Roman Museum and Theatre

Calle Romero Leal leads up to the **Museo Nacional de Arte Romano** (*same hours as Museum of Visigothic Art; adm*), housed in a grand brick building of 1986 by Rafael Mones Valles that looks as if the Romans themselves had a hand in it; it even incorporates a Roman road discovered when the foundation was dug. Roman artefacts from all over Spain are displayed on its three large floors. Among the huge mosaics, there's a curiously primitive 4th-century AD banquet scene, as well as a tall column from the Temple of Diana; busts; glass; statues; and items from Augusta Emerita's religious shrines, most interestingly a statue from the Mithraeum, which portrays the god Chronos entwined in a snake. In the basement crypt you can see the Roman road and part of the town that was inhabited by the Visigoths.

Across from the museum lies the ancient entertainment complex: the **Theatre and Amphitheatre** (*same hours as Alcazaba,* see *above*). The theatre, the best preserved in Spain, was built by Augustus' son-in-law Agrippa in 24 BC, the year after the founding of Augusta Emerita and, in forthright Roman confidence that the colony would succeed, was laboriously built in dry stone granite and designed to seat 6,000. The magnificent two-storey colonnaded **stage**, added under Hadrian in the 2nd century AD, remains intact, as do the vaulted passageways leading to the orchestra and seats in the *cavea*. The theatre is still used for a classical drama festival in July. The adjacent **amphitheatre** (1 BC) has better-preserved seats and *vomitoria*, or entrance tunnels, through which as many as 15,000 spectators could come to watch gladiators kill wild animals or each other, or sea battles when the arena was flooded. On the other side of the car park you can visit the **Casa del Anfiteatro** (*same hours as Alcazaba*), a patrician villa of the 1st century AD with a peristyle and atrium, and fine mosaics, including a beautiful one on wine-making; there's something particularly privileged about being able to walk freely over the swathes of mosaic. You can also see the pipes that fed the villa's private baths from the aqueduct. The first road left after the villa joins Av. Extremadura near the scanty remains of this, the **Acueducto de San Lázaro**, and the overgrown **Roman Circus**, where the Lusitanians watched their local hero Diocles chalk up some of his record 1,462 victories on the chariot-race circuits of the Roman Empire. In the centre you can make out where the obelisks and turning-posts once stood, as well as parts of the stands once used to seat 30,000 people.

Following Av. Extremadura back to the centre, you'll pass Mérida's best-loved shrine, the church of **Santa Eulalia** (*open Mon–Sat 10–1.45 and 5–7.15 (winter afternoons 4–6.15); included in composite ticket*), dedicated to the child martyr who, according to legend, was baked in an oven here for spitting in the eye of a pagan priest. Whatever the real story, here is as tidy an example of syncretism as you'll find in Spain, for in front of the church is a well-preserved **Temple of Mars**, which has suffered a name change to the *Hornito* (little oven) *de Santa Eulalia*, closed off by a grille, through which little girls traditionally dedicate locks of their hair to the saint. A bit further down towards the Guadiana stands the impressive triple-tiered **Acueducto de Los Milagros**, a lovely work of engineering that greets visitors who arrive by train. The **Roman bridge** next to it spans a tributary of the Guadiana.

The Mithraeum

The most beautiful art in Mérida, however, is across town next to the Plaza de Toros, in the **Mithraeum** (*same hours as Alcazaba,* see *above*). For the Roman soldiers, the cult of Mithras filled the same need as the Eleusinian Mysteries did for the ancient Greeks – the real religion, as opposed to official state rites performed in the Temples of Diana and Mars. Coincidentally (seeing as the bullring is next door) the sacrifice of bulls played an important part in Mithraic rites – rites to which the veteran legionaries of Augusta Emerita were especially devoted. Hints of frescoes remain on the walls of the underground *taurobolium* (where the bulls were killed), near a rectangular pool where the bulls' blood once flowed, now the home of turtles. In the enclosed **Casa del Mitreo** there is a brilliant-coloured mosaic floor devoted to river gods (although gone are the days when the caretaker could cheerfully moisten it with his mop to bring it to life).

Badajoz and Around

Downstream from Mérida, on the Portuguese border, sits the provincial capital of **Badajoz**, its name deriving from its Roman appellation *Pax Augusta*. Few places have been so misnamed; instead of Augustan peace Badajoz's story is essentially one of sanguinary sieges and warfare – between Moor and Moor when *Bataljoz* was an independent kingdom, then between Moor and Christian until 1229, when Alfonso IX finally captured it for good, and then, as the 'key to Portugal', between Christians of several nationalities, most terribly in 1812, when Wellington lost a third of his troops storming the French-held walls. Yet the nightmare that still haunts Badajoz is one that occurred after the siege in the Civil War, when the city was captured by foreign legionaries under Colonel Juan Yagüe, and the defenders, or any would-be refugees turned away from the Portuguese border, were corralled in the bullring and machine-gunned. Widely reported to a horrified world, this first atrocity of the Civil War tragically set the stage for countless others on both sides.

Unless you're continuing on to Portugal, there's little reason to visit Badajoz; in an effort to forget its bloodstained past, it has bulldozed most of itself and covered it over with bland *urbanizaciones*. That said, its old residential streets of low-lying pastel-coloured houses are pleasant enough to wander around and highly redolent of Latin American *pueblos*. The most elegant thing in the city is a bridge, the **Puente de Palmas**, built by Herrera in 1596, leading to a monumental gateway with round towers surviving from the old walls. **Plaza de España** is the unlovely heart of the city and home of its more-or-less **Gothic Cathedral** (*open Tues–Sun 11–1; closed Mon*), begun by Alfonso the Wise. It has pretty Plateresque windows in the tower, a finely carved Renaissance choir, and paintings in the chapels and Sala Capitular by Ribera, Badajoz native Luis ('El Divino') Morales and his fellow *extremeño* Zurbarán – although none did their best work at home. Nearby is Badajoz's 'Giralda': a bijou copy of the famous tower of Sevilla, stuck over a commercial block, while C/Gabriel Hernán leads to the **Museo Provincial de Bellas Artes** (*open summer Tues–Fri 10–2 and 6–8, Sat and Sun 10–2; winter Tues–Fri 10–2 and 4–6, Sat and Sun 10–2; closed Mon*), which contains contemporary works and a handful of paintings by Morales and Zurbarán. The biggest sight in town is the rambling Moorish **Alcazaba** (1100) overlooking both the city and the Guadiana; from its walls you can look out over the irrigated Vegas Bajas, a happy result of the 'Badajoz Plan' that has brought new growth to the city. Below the fortress stands an octagonal Almohad tower, the **Torre del Apendiz**, better known as the 'Torre Espantaperros', or 'dog-scarer'. An **Archaeology Museum** (*open Tues–Sun 10–3; closed Mon*) housing Moorish finds from Badajoz's golden days, has been lodged within the Alcazaba's walls in the Palacio de los Duques de Feria. Also worth a visit is the **Museo Extremeño e Iberoamericano de Arte Contemporáneo** or **MEIAC** (*C/del Museo 2; open Tues–Sat 10.30–1.30 and 6–9 (winter afternoons 5–8), Sun 10.30–1.30*), inaugurated in 1995 on the site of the town prison (known as the Rogues' Place). The outlandish building contains an intriguing mixture of Spanish, Portuguese and Latin American works.

Small Towns Where No One Ever Goes

From Badajoz you can take a side-trip north to the picturesque frontier town of **Alburquerque**, in the centre of a cork-producing region; its 14th-century **castle** saw plenty of action, and through its namesake in New Mexico it has gained immortal fame as the town where Bugs Bunny knew he 'shoulda made a left'. **Valencia de Alcántara** to the north is the centre of an area rich in **dolmens**, while **Olivenza**, to the south, was Portuguese until 1801, when Godoy wrote a treaty that moved the border a bit to the west. This act gained Spain its finest example of Manueline Gothic, in Olivenza's church **Santa María Magdalena** (*open daily 9–2*), decorated with graceful, spiralling pillars and an altar crowned with the genealogical tree of the Virgin. Up the hill from the church stands the **castle**, built in 1488; an *extremeño* **Ethnographic Museum** (*open Tues–Sun 11–2 and 5–8; closed Mon*) has been installed in the old Royal Bakery. Exiting through the Puerta de los Angeles you'll find the **Santa Casa de Misericordia** (*open Fri–Wed 8–1; closed Thurs*), with one chapel sumptuously decorated in early 18th-century Portuguese *azulejos*. From Mérida you can head out east along the Guadiana to tiny, whitewashed **Medellín**, the innocent birthplace of the ruthless *conquistador* Cortés and namesake of Colombia's notorious cocaine capital. After the castle, the biggest thing in town is the **monument to Cortés**; in Mexico, the land he won for Spain, such a memorial would be illegal. Southeast of here is a forbidding land known as the 'Siberia of Extremadura'. South of Mérida on the route to Zafra, **Almendralejo** is the capital of the **Tierra de Barros**: the land of clay which produces, besides ceramics, tasty wines.

Zafra

Zafra is the belle of Lower Extremadura. Known as Zafar under the Moors, it was the seat of the Dukes of Feria, the first of whom, in 1437, built the **Alcázar** with its great round towers and pyramidal merlons. Towering over the centre of town, this is Zafra's landmark and situation of one of Spain's finest *paradores* – even if you're not a guest, you can duck inside to see the marble patio attributed to Herrera, the Sala Dorada and the chapel. The nearby Plaza Mayor, with its whitewashed arcades, is split into the 18th-century **Plaza Grande** and the sweet 16th-century **Plaza Chica**, separated by an archway and with Zafra's finest streets on either side. Of its churches, the Gothic-Renaissance **Candelaria** (*open summer Thurs–Tues 10.30–1 and 6.30–8.30; winter Thurs–Tues 10.30–1 and 5.30–7.30; closed Wed*), built by the Dukes of Feria in 1546, is the most notable, containing a recently cleaned 1644 *retablo* by Zurbarán. The first duke and his wife lie in their fine alabaster tombs in the **Convento de Santa Clara** (*open summer daily 6–8; winter daily 5–7*) near Pza de España; as in Cáceres, you can purchase the nuns' excellent biscuits through the turntable at the entrance in the mornings. Here and around town, see if you can spot the duke's fig-leaf symbol, a play on his name, Figueroa. On C/Bóticas, the pretty **Casa del Ajimez** (named for its delicate *mudéjar* window) has been done up as a **Centro de Interpretación** (*open Mon–Sat 10.30–1.30; closed Sun*) on Zafra's *mudéjar* past. Alternatively, if you're feeling viticultural, **Bodegas Medino**, out along C/Cestería (*open summer Mon–Fri 10–2 and 5–8, Sat 10–2; winter Mon–Fri 10–2 and 6–8, Sat 10–2; closed Sun*), offer free wine tasting and have abundant supplies for sale.

Jerez de los Caballeros and Around

Although named after the Knights ('Caballeros' – both Templars and those of Santiago were here in the 13th century), Jerez de los Caballeros likes to point out that it's far older, having in its environs a number of megalithic monuments, especially the

Dolmen del Toriñuelo, decorated with carvings of sun symbols, five kilometres north-west of town in the *dehesa* (pasture) of La Granja. Jerez also produced its share of *conquistadores*: Balboa, discoverer of the Pacific, was born here, and Hernando de Soto, first to explore the Mississippi River, came from Barcarrota just to the north. Jerez went two better than Sevilla with its 'Giralda' towers, and their silhouettes form the city's distinctive skyline. In the heart of town, in **Plaza de España**, towers the brick **Torre de San Miguel** (1749), carved and intricately decorated. A few blocks away, the even more lavish **Torre de San Bartolomé** (1759) is embellished with polychrome *azulejos* to match the blue and gold façade of the church below. Across Pza de España stands a **Castle of the Templars** where, in 1307, the dark year of their dissolution, a number of them held out against the royal troops and were cut down in the **Torre Sangrienta** ('Bloody Tower'). The castle has recently been restored, revealing traces of the Moorish *alcazaba* that preceded it. Next to the castle, the church of **Santa María** was consecrated in 556, although the Visigothic elements have been swamped by the Baroque. Jerez's third Giralda tower, **Santa Catalina** (1772), can be seen off to the left; its church has an impressive Baroque interior.

South of Jerez is **Fregenal de la Sierra**, a pretty village in the mountains near Andalucía, full of hermitages and traditional holy places; it's the birthplace of Philip II's great librarian and reviser of the Polyglot Bible, Benito Arias Montano, who gathered the collection of heterodox books in the library at El Escorial. Also near Andalucía – and far more Andalucían and 'white' than an *extremeño* town – is **Llerena**, with a beautiful **Plaza Mayor** and its idiosyncratic church of **Nuestra Señora de Granada**, with a huge 'Giralda' tower and a façade crossed by a double-arcaded gallery.

La Mancha

We've been unfair to Nueva Castilla, chopping off its most interesting sections (Toledo, Cuenca and Sigüenza) and including them in the section around Madrid (*see* pp.521–70). What's left is the Spanish Nebraska, a moderately fertile but astoundingly empty corner of the nation, covering about 160 by 320km between the capital and Andalucía. Iberians, Romans and Moors trod these lonely plains, all no doubt wondering why they were doing so. The centuries have left this land utterly devoid of notable towns and monuments, and the lack of interest nicely complements the monotonous scenery.

It isn't so oppressive in the spring, when red carpets of poppies fill the gaps between endless fields of young wheat and budding vines, but even then you're likely to find that a quick trip through on your way to the south is more than enough.

South of Madrid: Consuegra and Lagoons

If you pass down the main road from Madrid, there are a few diversions en route. After **Tembleque**, near Toledo (*see* p.570) the first landmark is the decaying castle on the hill over **Consuegra**; one of the characteristic white conical-roofed windmills stands near it to remind you that these are the western borders of La Mancha. Near Daimiel, north of Ciudad Real, is one of the region's curiosities, the **Ojos de Guadiana**, a marshy area where the river Guadiana disappears underground, and pops back up a few miles to the west. Numerous species of migratory birds – especially various species of duck and purple herons – favour the area as a stopover, and it is included in the designated **Parque Nacional de las Tablas de Daimiel**. Sadly, though it has been a protected park since 1973, offences such as pollution of the water still persist and, in the early 1980s, the millions of gallons of water used to irrigate the huge commercial farms in this area caused the Guadiana to dry up for the first time in its history; consequently fewer waterfowl migrate through here. However, if you take the N430 or the N310 in the other direction, you will wind up in **Las Lagunas de Ruidera**, La Mancha's other surprisingly wet spot. The lagoons are formed by the serpentine meanderings of the upper Guadiana and are an ideal picnic and swimming spot for those not in a hurry to pass through La Mancha.

Ciudad Real and Almagro

Ciudad Real, capital of the province, is a small and friendly town, with various old churches but nothing show-stopping. However, if you do pause here, have a peek into the old **casino**, a smart red, pink and white *modernista* building on the corner of Pso del Prado; in the central patio hangs a candelabra worthy of taking ET home. The **Salón de Plenos of the Diputación Municipal**, nearby on Pasaje Merced and constructed in 1895, is also worth a glance. A better stop would be **Almagro**, changed little since its period of prosperity in the 16th century. Among its monuments are a lovely, arcaded **Plaza Mayor** lined with irregular green windows; a **monastery** of the Knights of Calatrava (now occupied by just three Dominican monks and in danger of closure if another one shuffles off his mortal coil); and the oldest theatre in Spain, the **Corral de Comedias** (*open Tues–Fri 10–2 and 4–7, Sat 11–2 and 4–6, Sun 11–2; closed Mon; adm*), which in summer is the centrepiece of the town's theatre festival (*see* 'Festivals', p.592); performances of recent works take place year round. This relic of the Golden Age of Spanish theatre makes an interesting comparison with its northern contemporaries – like Shakespeare's Globe, it has a row of balconies all around for the gentlemen and ladies, and a small floor in the centre for the 'pitlings' below the stage (only it's square instead of round). The **theatre museum** (*Callejón del Villar; open same hours as Corral; adm*) is just off the other side of Pza Mayor. Almost everything you see in Almagro was built by Jakob Fugger of Germany and his descendants, who started Europe's first great banking-house and at times controlled most of the continent's cloth trade. The Fuggers prospered greatly from Charles V's imperialist extravagance, and Almagro was their Spanish headquarters. They also introduced the art of making bobbin lace to this area, and beautiful designs are still worked on by the local women; if you can, buy your lace directly from them.

Towards Valdepeñas

The back road south from Almagro passes through the **Campo de Calatrava**, scene of many battles of the Reconquista. The religious knightly Order of Calatrava, right arm of the Castilian kings in these wars, was founded here, and the ruins of their headquarters at **Calatrava La Nueva**, including the rough, fortress-like church with its rose window, are evocative of that grim age of the Church Militant. An excursion into the bleak **Sierra de Alandía** to the southwest would be a novelty – this is undoubtedly the least visited part of Spain; and not without reason. Villages like Gargantiel, Cabeza

Getting Around

The region is well served by RENFE: all the southbound routes from Madrid must go through it. Madrid–Badajoz trains pass through Ciudad Real, and there are four a day that stop at Almagro. The Madrid-Sevilla AVE also stops in Ciudad Real four times a day. For train information, call **t** 926 22 02 02; the new station is 15 mins east of Pza Mayor, off Av. de Europa. Trains to Andalucía pass through Valdepeñas and the big, dull towns of Manzanares and Alcázar de San Juan, and all lines from Madrid to Murcia and Alicante stop at Albacete. For the other towns, you'll have to depend on bus services from the two provincial capitals, Ciudad Real and Albacete From Almagro there are seven buses daily to Ciudad Real and three to Madrid; call **t** 926 86 02 50.

Tourist Information

Ciudad Real: Provincial Office, Av. Alarcos 21, **t** 926 20 00 37, *infotur@cpe-cr.es* (*open Mon–Sat 10–2 and 4–7, Sun 10–2*); Municipal Office, Pza Mayor 1, **t** 926 21 10 44, *turismo@ayto-ciudadreal.es* (*open Mon–Sat 10–2 and 4–7, Sun 10–2*).

Almagro: C/Bernardas 2, **t** 926 86 07 17 (*open Tues–Sat 10–2 and 4–7, Sun 11–2*).

Albacete: C/del Tinte 2, **t** 967 58 05 22 (*open Mon–Fri 10–2 and 4–6, Sat 10–6, Sun 10–3*).

Valdepeñas: Pza de España 1, **t** 926 31 25 52, *www.ayto-valdepeñas.org*.

Festivals

Almagro: Theatre Festival, *July*. The whole month sees Almagro turned over to theatre, with a festival based on Spain's Golden Age of the 16th and 17th century; Semana Santa, *Easter*. Holy Week in Almagro makes a welcome change from the usual Ku Klux Klan lookalikes: some 300 locals get dressed up as Roman legionaries in order to perform a complicated circular manoeuvre in the plaza.

Allaraz: Romería, *4–8 Sept*. A riotous *romería* wends its way up to the Virgen de Cortes sanctuary nearby.

Where to Stay and Eat

Pisto is La Mancha's major contribution to Spanish cuisine: the classic is simply tomato and red pepper, with garlic. Most Manchegan restaurants also specialize in game dishes.

Almagro ✉ 13270

********Parador de Almagro**, Convento de San Francisco, Ronda de San Francisco 31, **t** 926 86 01 00, **f** 926 86 01 50 (*expensive*). Set in a restored 16th-century convent in the centre; one of the finer *paradores*.

La Posada de Almagro, C/Gran Maestre 5, **t/f** 926 26 12 01, *www.laposadaalmagro.com* (*moderate*). A recently and tastefully converted 16th-century inn, with simple, attractive rooms arranged around a lovely inner courtyard. The **restaurant**, lined with enormous vats, has an (*inexpensive*) *menú*.

****Hospedaría de Almagro**, Convento de la Asunción, Ejido de Calatrava, **t** 926 88 20 87, **f** 926 88 21 22 (*cheap*). Simple, clean rooms in a wing of the monastery, with a shady patio.

Mesón El Corregidor, Pza Fray Fernando Fernández de Córdoba 2, **t** 926 86 06 48 (*moderate*). Almagro's best restaurant, in an old house in the centre. *Closed Mon*.

del Buey ('ox-head') and Pueblonuevo del Terrible are more interesting on the map than in person. Much mining goes on: coal and zinc, and the famous mercury mine at **Almadén** that supplied the alchemists of Toledo. The main road is better, passing through **Valdepeñas**, Spain's biggest wine region. There are numerous *bodegas* in the town centre and off the highway (*ask at the tourist office*) and even a **Museo del Vino** for aficionados (*open Tues–Sat 10–2 and 6–8.30, Sun 12–2; closed Mon*). Much of Spain's dependable bargain brew comes from here, as well as some of its finest vintages. The highway crosses into Andalucía through the **Desfiladero de Despeñaperros**, 'hurling down the dogs', a wild rocky chute that was long a haunt of bandits.

Abrasador, C/San Agustín 18, **t** 926 88 26 56 (*inexpensive*). A new restaurant set next to the Teatro Municipal, using home-grown produce to offer typical Manchegan dishes, especially hams.

Airen, Pza Mayor 41, **t** 926 88 26 56 (*inexpensive*). A pleasant place on the plaza to *tapa*, or make a meal of it with *raciones*, the tasty pizzas (try the *pisto* topping) or the *menú*.

Daimiel ✉ 13250

****Las Tablas**, C/Virgen de Las Cruces 5, **t** 926 85 21 07 (*moderate*). A good bargain: modest, air-conditioned rooms, all with TV.

Ciudad Real ✉ 13000

******Santa Cecilia**, C/Tinte 3, **t** 926 22 85 45, **f** 924 22 86 18 (*expensive*). Extremely comfortable, with a good **restaurant**, El Real (*moderate*), featuring partridge.

******Alfonso X**, Carlos Vásquez 8, **t** 926 22 42 81, **f** 926 22 41 64 (*moderate*). A very smart, brand new hotel just off Pza Mayor; the reception is all gold and lilies (rooms are especially good value at weekends).

Miami Park, Ronda de Ciruela 34, **t** 926 22 20 43 (*moderate*). The posh sister of the **Gran Mesón** at No.32 (which is a little cheaper, though still *moderate*). *Closed Sun eve.*

For good **tapas bars** try around Pza Mayor (especially **Mesón el Ventero**, Pza Mayor 9), Pza del Pilar (including the longstanding **Casa Lucio**, C/Dulcinea del Toboso, off C/Montesa), C/Palma and around Av. Torreón (where numerous café/bars have varying musical offerings; head for **El Continental** for jazz).

Albacete ✉ 02000

*****Parador de Albacete**, Ctra N301, **t** 967 24 53 21, **f** 967 24 32 71 (*expensive*). This *parador* is slightly colourless, but perfectly comfortable, with a pool.

****Hs Albacete**, C/Carcelén 8, **t** 967 21 81 11, **f** 967 21 87 25 (*inexpensive*). A fairly decent alternative; the **restaurant** will serve you a reasonable *menú*.

Mesón Las Rejas, C/Dionisio Guardiola 9, **t** 967 22 72 42 (*inexpensive*). Specializing in typical Manchegan game. *Closed Sun in summer.*

Manzanares ✉ 13200

*****Parador de Manzanares**, on the N-IV Madrid road, **t** 926 61 04 00, **f** 926 61 09 35 (*moderate*). A nice spot with a welcome pool, though it's not as grand as some (and cheaper accordingly).

*****El Cruce**, on the N-IV, 2km from the *parador*, **t** 926 61 19 00 (*moderate*). Also has a pool and the usual mod cons, as well as a **restaurant** (*menú inexpensive*).

Campo de Criptana ✉ 13610 and El Toboso ✉ 45820

***Hs Sancho**, Pza Mayor 9, Campo de Criptana **t** 926 56 00 12 (*cheap*). Has 16 budget rooms.

Dulcinea, C/Clavileño 1, El Toboso, **t** 925 19 73 11 (*inexpensive*). Offers a fine selection of regional dishes.

Puerto Lapice ✉ 13650

Venta del Quijote, C/Molino 4, Puerto Lapice, **t** 926 57 61 10 (*moderate*). The Venta is set in an 18th-century inn in the centre of Puerto Lapice and serves splendid food. It has the most authentic atmosphere you'll find – give or take a century or two.

Alternatively, modest lodgings can be found in **Alcázar de San Juan** and at **Ruidera** near the lagoons, though most are closed from October to May.

Don Quixote's La Mancha

There's little evidence that Miguel de Cervantes ever cared to spend much time here. Certainly he would have had a big laugh at the expense of the Manchegans and literary critics who drone on about the 'poetic, essentially Spanish' landscape. Nothing could be less poetic than the bleak expanses of the region called 'the blot', and Cervantes found its empty spaces the perfect setting for a hopeless knight errant and the parable of a burnt-out, disillusioned Spain. Scholars have spent their careers tracing out the knight's imagined itinerary, and schools contend endlessly over which blank-faced, anonymous Manchegan village was the scene of the Encounter with the Windmills, the Adventures of the Inn, or Camacho's Marriage. But unless you can tell one Manchegan village from another, such scholarship may seem extravagant.

El Toboso, home of the peerless Dulcinea, and one of the very few villages Cervantes ever actually names, might be a good stopover for determined Quixotic pilgrims. Of course they'll show you Dulcinea's house, now restored and turned into a humble **museum.** By the church of San Antonio Abad the **Museo Cervantino** houses a collection of editions of *El Quijote*. Two of the nicer villages are **San Clemente** and **Campo de Criptana**, around which several much-honoured windmills can be seen, and there's a grandly exotic 15th-century castle outside **Belmonte**. **Alcaraz** nearby is a town of some distinction; with its ensemble of interesting 16th-century buildings it seems a minor version of Úbeda. It's not surprising, then, to find that Úbeda's architect, Andrés de Vandelvira, was a native and built many of them.

Albacete, the Manchegan metropolis, makes its living from artichokes and saffron from the surrounding countryside; it leads Spain in both these products, and has grown into a city of 100,000 people with dull, straight streets and little to see, other than the **museum** (*open Tues–Sat 10–2 and 4–7, Sun 9–2; closed Mon; adm*) in Parque de Abelardo Sánchez, with finds from local prehistoric sights – particularly the Alpera caves – and a collection of tiny articulated 'dolls' made from ivory and amber, discovered at the Roman necropolis of Ontur. Albacete was a ferociously Republican town during the Civil War, the training ground of the International Brigades, and few of its old churches survived.

From here you can choose between highways for València, Murcia or Alicante, the last passing a 15th-century castle above the town of **Almansa**. The surrounding area contains the **Alpera caves**, a series of archaeological sites. The best one is **La Vieja**, which has Stone Age paintings of male and female figures amid the usual hunting scenes. There are even some mysterious hand-prints. Should you want to visit, seek permission from Almansa's Ayuntamiento.

Andalucía

17

Highlights

1 Sevilla: guitars, orange blossom, *mantillas*, the whole schtick

2 The Great Mosque of Córdoba, stone labyrinth of faith

3 Spain's perfect Renaissance city: Úbeda

4 Eagles and mountain goats in the wild Sierra de Cazorla

5 Fine horses and *amontillados* in aristocratic Jerez

6 Nights in the gardens of Spain and the Moorish palace of the Alhambra in Granada

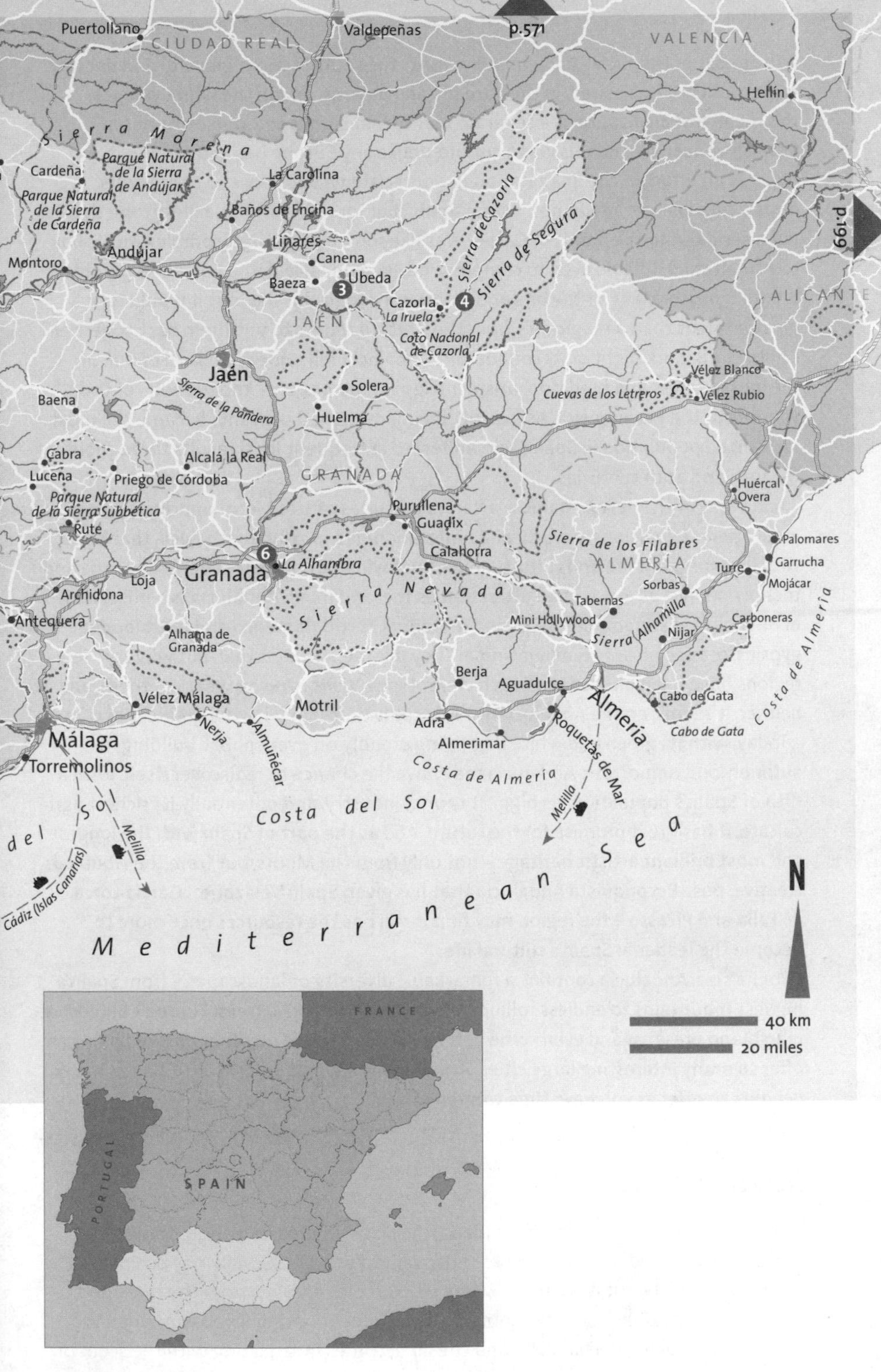

Puertollano
Valdepeñas
p.571
CIUDAD REAL
VALENCIA
Hellín
Sierra Morena
Parque Natural de la Sierra de Andújar
Cardeña
Parque Natural de la Sierra de Cardeña
La Carolina
Baños de Encina
Sierra de Cazorla
Sierra de Segura
p.199
Linares
Andújar
Montoro
Canena
Úbeda
Baeza
Cazorla
La Iruela
JAÉN
ALICANTE
Coto Nacional de Cazorla
Jaén
Solera
Vélez Blanco
Cuevas de los Letreros
Vélez Rubio
Sierra de la Pandera
Huelma
Baena
Cabra
Alcalá la Real
Lucena
Priego de Córdoba
GRANADA
Parque Natural de la Sierra Subbética
Purullena
Guadix
Huércal Overa
Rute
Sierra de los Filabres
Palomares
Calahorra
Granada
La Alhambra
ALMERÍA
Garrucha
Turre
Mojácar
Loja
Archidona
Sierra Nevada
Sorbas
Tabernas
Antequera
Mini Hollywood
Carboneras
Alhama de Granada
Sierra Alhamilla
Níjar
Costa de Almería
Berja
Aguadulce
Vélez Málaga
Motril
Almería
Cabo de Gata
Adra
Roquetas de Mar
Málaga
Nerja
Almuñécar
Almerimar
Cabo de Gata
Torremolinos
Costa de Almería
Costa del Sol
Melilla
del Sol
Cádiz (Islas Canarias)
Mediterranean Sea
N
40 km
20 miles
FRANCE
PORTUGAL
SPAIN

The ghost of Islamic al-Andalus still haunts the south; a more graceful and delicate spirit could not be desired. In the gardens and palaces, and in the white villages, this great, lost civilization is a separate reality that shines through centuries of Spanish veneer. Al-Andalus was a culture unlike any Europe has known, and it requires an effort of the imagination to appreciate its subtlety and delicacy. Its destruction was a tragedy, not just for Spain, but for the world. The ill-fortune that put al-Andalus in the hands of Castile was like someone giving a complex music box to a small child; unable even to comprehend, let alone use it, the Castilians pounded it until it broke. Many of the bits and pieces survive to this day, but it would take a greater talent than a magician's from the *Arabian Nights* to put them back together.

In the long dark night of its conquerors, Andalucía fell under the hand of one of the most useless and predatory aristocracies Europe has ever known, heirs of the warriors of the Reconquista. As a result, its impoverished peasants became the most radicalized population in Spain, as manifested in frequent local revolts throughout the 19th and 20th centuries.

And what of the new Andalucía, after its centuries of trouble, of oppression and inquisitions, expulsions, poverty and emigration? It's looking pretty well, thank you, with its exuberant life and culture, and a fun-loving population of generally sane and friendly people, as much of an attraction as the land itself. Andalucía is a minefield of unexploded stereotypes: sequined matadors, torrid flamenco and hot-blooded gypsies, orange blossoms and jasmine. They may be hard to avoid, but why try? Few regions have been blessed with such stereotypes. Visitors never weary of them, and neither, it seems, do the Andalucíans; they cultivate them with the greatest of care.

Today, with its green and white flag flying proudly on every public building, the autonomous, democratic Andalucía may have the chance to rediscover itself. With a fifth of Spain's population, its biggest tourist industry, and potentially its richest agriculture, it has great promise for the future. And as the part of Spain with the longest and most brilliant artistic heritage – not only from the Moors, but from the troubled, creative, post-Reconquista Andalucía that has given Spain Velázquez, García Lorca, de Falla and Picasso – the region may find it still has the resources once more to become the leader in Spain's cultural life.

For its size, Andalucía contains a remarkable diversity of landscapes – from Spain's highest mountains to endless rolling hills covered with olive trees, Europe's biggest marshland preserve and even some patches of desert. And no other part of Spain can offer so many interesting large cities. Andalucía is a world unto itself; it has as many delights to offer as you have time to spend.

Sevilla

Apart from in the Alhambra of Granada, the place where the lushness and sensuality of al-Andalus survives best is Andalucía's capital. Sevilla may be Spain's fourth-largest city, but it is a place where you can pick oranges from the trees, and see open countryside from the centre of town. Come in spring if you can, when the gardens are drowned in birdsong and the air becomes intoxicating with the scent of the eastern side of the country, including Barcelona, leave from Prado de San Sebastián. Information on routes and timetables is available from the tourist office, or from the information office inside the bus stations.

Getting Around

The narrow, twisting streets of old Sevilla are a delight to stroll around, and most of the main sights are bunched within walking distance of each other.

By Bus

There is a good city bus service; among the most useful lines are buses C4 and C3, which circle the perimeter of the old city, and lines C1 and C2, which make a larger circle and encompass Triana, La Cartuja, the main train station (Estación de Santa Justa) and the bus station on Pza de Armas. Night bus routes are prefaced with the letter A. The tourist office has free, comprehensive bus maps with explanations in English. On the back is a useful table called 'How to Get There'. Call **t** 900 71 01 71 for

are very helpful;

Municipal Information Centre, near Parque María Luisa, on Pso de las Delicias 9, **t** 954 23 44 65; there are also information centres at the airport, **t** 954 44 91 28, and at Santa Julia station, **t** 954 23 76 26.

Tours: Sightseeing buses and river cruises depart from the Tower of Gold. **Bus tours** are offered by Sevilla Tour, **t** 954 50 20 99, and Sevirama, **t** 954 56 06 93. **River cruises** are offered by Cruceros Turisticos Torre del Oro, **t** 954 21 13 96; Cruseros del Sur, **t** 954 56 16 72; and Buque El Patio, Pso de Colon 11, **t** 954 56 16 92.

Post Office: Av. de la Constitución 32, **t** 902 19 71 97.

Internet Access: Try In Situ, Pza Alameda de Hercules, **t** 954 90 33 94, with a café/shop; or Sevilla Internet Center, C/Almirantzago 2–10, **t** 954 50 02 75, *www.sevillacenter.com*. *Open Mon–Fri 9am–10pm, Sat and Sun 12–10pm*.

There is a big atmospheric **flea market** in the Alameda de Hércules (*Thurs and Sun*); also, in the *barrio* of La Feria, **El Jueves** (*Thurs*) is an antiques and bric-a-brac market.

Getting There

By Air

Sevilla has regular flights from Madrid and Barcelona. San Pablo airport is 12km east of the city, and the airport bus leaves from Bar Iberia on C/Almirante Lobos. Airport information is available on **t** 954 44 90 00.

By Train

Estación de Santa Justa, in Av. Kansas City in the northeast of town, is the Expo showpiece. There are several trains daily to Madrid by AVE in a staggeringly quick 2 hrs 15 mins, and a daily Talgo to Barcelona. The central RENFE office is at C/Zaragoza 29, information **t** 954 54 02 02, reservations **t** 954 22 26 93. AVE information and reservations, **t** 954 54 03 03.

By Bus

There are two bus stations in Sevilla, one at Pza de Armas, information **t** 954 90 80 40 or **t** 954 90 77 37, and one at Prado de San Sebastián, information **t** 954 41 71 11. Buses for the western side of the peninsula, including Madrid, leave from Pza de Armas. All buses for city bus information; for lost property call **t** 954 55 72 22. Buy single tickets (€0.75) on the bus; 3- or 7-day tourist passes (€6/€9 approx.) which offer unlimited travel for a set period are available at ticket offices at the Prado de San Sebastián, Pza Nueva (where there is a little 'Bono-bus' kiosk, *open 9–2 and 5–7*) and Pza Encarnación.

By Taxi

Taxis are everywhere and fairly inexpensive. Radio Taxis **t** 954 58 00 00/954 57 11 11, Tele Taxi **t** 954 62 22 22/954 62 14 61, or Radio Teléfono Giralda **t** 954 67 55 55.

By Bicycle

Bicycles can be rented at BiciBike, C/Miguel de Mañara 11B, **t/f** 954 56 38 38, just behind the main tourist office, near the Reales Alcazares.

Tourist Information

Sevilla: Permanent Tourist Office, near the cathedral at Av. de la Constitución 21, **t** 954 22 14 04, **f** 954 53 76 26 (*open Mon–Fri 9–7, Sat 10–2 and 3–7, Sun 10–2*). The staff here

Festivals

Semana Santa, *Holy Week*. Between Palm Sunday and Easter Saturday, 57 *cofradías* hoist up their *pasos* (floats) and process through the crowds along the sinuous streets from their church to the cathedral and back. It's all to music of a sonorous *marcha*, surrounded by Nazarenos and Penitents. The most important *cofradías* get top billing and process on the morning of Good Friday, the high point of the festival.

Feria, *April*. The solemnity of Semana Santa erupts in a week-long party. This medieval institution involves copious *copas* of sherry and merrymaking in ornate striped tents (*casetas*), though you need the right connections, or *enchufe*, to get into the most élite ones. Throughout the festival, the streets drip with lanterns, horses and carriages push through jubilant crowds in costume and the funfair reverberates with laughter. Festivities culminate in a spectacular firework extravaganza the following Sunday, coinciding with the opening of the bullfighting season at La Maestranza.

Feria de la Velá, *July*. In honour of Triana's patron saint, Santa Ana, the streets come alive yet again with dancing, buskers and street vendors.

Shopping

All the paraphernalia associated with Spanish fantasy, such as *mantillas*, castanets, wrought iron, gypsy dresses, Andalucían dandy suits, *azulejo* tiles and embroidery, is available in Sevilla. **C/Cuna** is the best place to find flamenco paraphernalia, and several of the convents sell jams and confectionery. **Triana** is the place to find *azulejo* tiles and all kinds of perfumed soaps.

For fashion, designer shops are on **Plaza Nueva**, and **C/O'Donnell** has a number of fashionable and more affordable boutiques. There are two branches of **El Corte Inglés**. **Vértice** is a bookshop, on Mateos Gago near the cathedral, with some English-language literature and local guidebooks, maps and history books; but if you're just after somewhere for a pleasant wander, head for the pedestrianized **C/Sierpes**.

Where to Stay

Sevilla ✉ 41000

Hotels are more expensive in Sevilla than in most of Spain so it is advisable to book ahead. High season is March and April; during Semana Santa and the April Feria you should book even for inexpensive *hostales*, preferably a year ahead. Low season is July and August and January to early March.

Luxury–Expensive

*******Alfonso XIII**, C/San Fernando 2, **t** 954 22 28 50, **f** 954 21 60 33. Built by King Alfonso for the Exposición Iberoamericana in 1929, this is the grandest hotel in Andalucía, attracting heads of state, opera stars, and tourists who want a unique experience, albeit at a price. Sevilla society still meets around its lobby fountain and somewhat dreary bar. Its **restaurant** San Fernando is good if pricey – partridge *flambé*, wheat-fed cock or Beluga caviar.

******Los Seises**, C/Segovias 6, **t** 954 22 94 95, **f** 954 22 43 34. Hidden in the maze of streets that make up the Santa Cruz Quarter, this converted 16th-century archbishop's palace contains Roman artefacts and Arabic columns and tiles which mingle with later antiques; each room is individually styled. The name is derived from *setza*, meaning sixteen, which was the number of young boys who sang and danced at the main altar of the cathedral; the tradition is still maintained on special feast days such as Corpus Christi. There is a rooftop pool here too, surrounded, bizarrely, with astroturf, and the **restaurant** is highly acclaimed.

******Hotel Taberna de Alabardero**, C/Zaragoza 20, **t** 954 56 06 37, **f** 954 56 36 66. One of Sevilla's most winning establishments; the former home of the poet J. Antonio Cavestany, who wrote a number of lyrical romantic poems about the city, the building now houses an outstanding **restaurant** and culinary school. Ten charming and intimate rooms, all with Jacuzzi as well as the usual accoutrements, are set around the light-filled central courtyard. The service is discreet and excellent, and the cuisine, as you might expect, is sublime. Prices include breakfast in the award-winning restaurant.

★★★★**Meliá Confort Macarena**, C/San Juan de Rivera 2, **t** 954 37 57 00, **f** 954 38 18 03. Situated by the Macarena walls, this is another classy establishment with a beautiful *azulejo*-tiled fountain, a pool, and far-reaching views over the city from the rooftop terrace.

★★★**Las Casas de la Judería**, Callejón de Dos Hermanos 7, **t** 954 41 51 50, **f** 954 22 21 70, *www.lascasas.zoom.es*. A row of charming and perfectly restored townhouses in the Santa Cruz Quarter, expertly run by the Medina family – well-known and very stylish *sevillano* hoteliers.

Expensive–Moderate

★★★**Hotel San Gil**, C/Parras 28, **t** 954 90 68 11, **f** 954 90 69 39. Near the Andalucían parliament is this beautiful ochre building from the turn of the last century, with a shady courtyard dotted with palm trees, fabulous mosaics and *azulejo* tiles, and lofty ceilings.

★**Hs Pza Sevilla**, C/Canalejas 2, **t** 954 21 71 49, **f** 954 21 07 73. Has a beautiful neoclassical façade by Aníbal González, architect of the 1929 Exposición, and is ideally placed near the restaurants and bars of San Eloy.

★★**Monte-Carlo**, C/Gravina 51, **t** 954 21 75 03, **f** 954 21 68 25, *hmontecarlo@arrakis.es*. Has a bright peachy façade and quiet, recently refurbished rooms. The service is friendly and helpful and they are good sources of local information.

★★**Hs Sierpes**, Corral del Rey 22, **t** 954 22 49 48, **f** 954 21 21 07. Situated in the pedestrianized shopping area, with pretty archways surrounding an interior courtyard, and spacious, airy rooms. There is also a garage and a reasonable **restaurant**.

★**Hotel Simón**, C/García de Vinuesa 19, **t** 954 22 66 60, **f** 954 56 22 41. One of the best-value options in the city, in a fine position just off the Av. de la Constitución by the cathedral, and in a restored 18th-century mansion.

Moderate–Inexpensive

★★**HsR del Laurel**, Pza de los Venerables 5, **t** 954 22 02 95, **f** 954 21 04 50, *host-laurel@eintec.es*. Overlooking a slightly touristy square, this is an engagingly quirky hotel with layered turrets and terraces that once attracted Romantic poets and novelists.

★★**Hotel Murillo**, C/Lope de Rueda 9, **t** 954 21 60 95, **f** 954 21 96 16, *murillo@nexo.es*. Old-fashioned, family-run and comfortable; the prices are very reasonable for its central location in Santa Cruz, although it can be expensive in season.

★★**Hotel Rabida**, C/Castelar 24, **t** 954 22 09 60, **f** 954 22 43 75, *hotel-rabida@sol.com*. In the quiet heart of El Arenal, with simple, well-equipped rooms set around two courtyards, one of which doubles as a salon with wicker furniture and a pretty stained-glass ceiling.

Inexpensive–Cheap

For inexpensive *hostales*, the Santa Cruz Quarter is the best place to look, particularly on the quiet side streets off C/Mateos Gago.

★**Hs Nuevo Picasso**, C/San Gregorio 1, **t/f** 954 21 08 64, *hpicasso@arrakis.es*. One of the nicest *pensiones* in this district, with a plant-filled entrance hall and a green interior courtyard hung with bric-a-brac. Rooms are spotless and attractively furnished.

★★**Hs Atenas**, C/Caballerizas 1, **t** 954 21 80 47, **f** 954 22 76 90. Quiet and very nice, in a good location between the Pza Pilatos and the cathedral. Take a cab – it's hard to find.

★**Hs Bailén**, C/Bailén 75, **t** 954 22 16 35. A delightful old building with a garden and courtyard in the Santa Cruz quarter.

★★**Hs Londres**, C/San Pedro Mártir 1, **t** 954 21 28 96, **f** 954 21 28 96. Near the Fine Arts Museum, a quiet place with pretty balconies overlooking the street.

Eating Out

Restaurants in Sevilla are more expensive than in most of Spain, but even around the cathedral and Santa Cruz there are few places that can simply be dismissed as tourist traps. Remember that the *sevillanos*, even more than most Andalucíans, enjoy bar-hopping for tapas, rather than sitting down to one meal.

Expensive

Taberna del Alabardero, C/Zaragoza 20, **t** 954 56 29 06, **f** 954 56 36 66. Northwest of La Giralda, this grand mansion is one of Sevilla's most celebrated restaurants, boasting Michelin-stars and an illustrious school for chefs. Specialities include wild-boar ragout, fresh artichokes and Jabugo ham in olive oil, and *urta* (a firm-fleshed, white fish caught locally) cooked in red wine. The staff are friendly and very knowledgeable. Head up the grand marble staircase overhung with an ornate chandelier to wood-panelled dining rooms set around the central courtyard, each with a different ambience. Its light-filled café in the central glassed-over courtyard serves an excellent set lunch and wonderful cakes and pastries in the afternoons. There is also a sumptuous tile-lined bar with an adventurous range of tapas. *Open daily all year*.

La Albahaca, Pza Santa Cruz 12, **t** 954 22 07 14. On one of Sevilla's most delightful small squares, this serves beautifully prepared classics with a Basque twist; specialities have included scorpion fish with fennel and peanuts, and mushrooms with green asparagus, but the menu is seasonal. *Closed Sun*.

Corral del Agua, Callejón del Agua 6, **t** 954 22 48 41. Well-seasoned travellers usually steer clear of cutesy wishing-wells, but the garden in which this one stands is a haven of peace and shade, perfect for a lazy lunch or an unashamedly romantic dinner. You will find it next to Washington Irving's garden.

Egaña-Oriza, C/San Fernando 41, **t** 954 22 72 54, **f** 954 41 21 06. Splendidly situated on the corner of the Jardines Alcázar, this is one of Sevilla's best-loved restaurants. Among its tempting delights are clams on the half-shell, baked *hongos* mushrooms, and a kind of *sevillano* jugged hare. *Closed Sat lunch, Sun and Aug*.

Bar España, C/San Fernando. Attached to the Egaña-Oriza, this tapas bar is chic, bright and cosmopolitan – and the Basque tapas are sensational.

Moderate

La Juderia, C/Caño y Cueto, **t** 954 41 20 52, **f** 954 41 21 06. Tucked away in the old Jewish quarter, with brick arches and terracotta tiles. There is an almost bewildering range of richly flavoured regional dishes like *cola de toro*, game in season, dozens of fish dishes and, to finish up, delicious home-made desserts. *Closed Tues and Aug*.

Marea Grande, C/Diego Angulo Iñiguez 16, **t** 954 53 80 00. Slightly out of the centre, this plush establishment is justly considered one of the city's finest seafood restaurants. *Closed end of Aug and Sun*.

Enrique Becerra, C/Gamazo 2, **t** 954 21 30 49, **f** 954 22 70 93. Enrique followed in his father's footsteps (he is the fifth generation of this family of celebrated *sevillano* restaurateurs), with this prettily tiled restaurant. The menu is based on flavoursome regional dishes accompanied by a variety of delicious breads. For dessert, try the house speciality, *pudding de naranjas Santa Paula*, made with *sevillano* marmalade from the Convent of St Paula. There is also a lively tapas bar. *Closed Sun and the last two weeks of July*.

Los Seises, C/Segovias 6, **t** 954 22 94 95, **f** 954 22 43 34. In the Hotel los Seises, deep in Santa Cruz, you'll find this restaurant with fine classic dishes served in the sumptuous surroundings of an old archbishop's palace at surprisingly reasonable prices.

Hotel Salvador Rojo, C/San Fernando 23, **t** 954 22 97 25. Near Hotel Alfonso XIII and yet virtually hidden. The décor is almost spartan, which is all the more reason to concentrate simply on the food, a selection of very creative *andaluz* dishes deftly prepared by Salvador Rojo himself.

Mesón Don Raimundo, **t** 954 22 33 55, **f** 954 21 89 51. By the cathedral, in the narrow Argote de Molina (at No.26), and set in a 17th-century convent with an eclectic décor of religious artefacts and suits of armour. A large selection of traditional *andaluz* dishes is served, based on fish, shellfish and game, to the accompaniment of fine wines from an extensive list. *Closed Sun eves*.

Ox's, C/Betis 61, **t** 954 27 95 85, **f** 954 27 84 65. A delightful *asador* (grill room) with novelties from Navarra: cod-stuffed peppers, fish and steaks grilled over charcoal for a delicious smoky piquancy. *Closed Sun eve, Mon and Aug*.

La Mandrágora, C/Albuera 11, **t** 954 22 01 84. In a country where meat and fish reign supreme, it's a nice surprise to discover La Mandrágora, a very friendly vegetarian restaurant with an excellent and wide-ranging menu; everything is home cooked – even the piquant salsas. *Closed Sun*.

Inexpensive (*see also* 'Tapas Bars', below)

Pizzeria San Marco, Meson del Moro 6–10, **t** 954 21 43 90. Run by the same family as the Restaurante San Marco (*see* above), with excellent pizzas and a wide range of pasta dishes in an old Arabic bathhouse.

Bodegón Torre del Oro, C/Santander 15, **t** 954 21 42 41, **f** 954 21 66 28. The rafters here are hung with dozens of different hams. There's a three-course set meal with wine and the *raciones* are excellent.

La Illustre Victima, C/Doctor Letamandi 35 (not far from the Pza de Alamede de Hércules). A friendly and pleasingly chaotic café, bar and restaurant with painted murals. It serves a variety of snacks, including very reasonable pasta and couscous dishes, *enchiladas* and *fajitas*, some suitable for vegetarians.

Il Garibaldi, in the Santa Cruz quarter. Has an incredible range of home-made Italian-style ice creams and frozen yogurts, as well as tiramisu and cheesecake.

Tapas Bars

Tapas bars are an intrinsic part of daily life in Sevilla, and even the smartest restaurants often have excellent tapas bars attached.

El Rinconcillo, at C/Gerona 42 (between the Church of St Pedro and the Convent of Espíritu Santo). The oldest bar in Sevilla, this is reputedly where the custom of topping a glass with a slice of sausage or a piece of bread and ham – the first tapas – began. Decorated in moody brown *azulejos*, the place dates back to 1670 and is frequented by lively *sevillano cognoscenti*, who gather to enjoy the tasty nibbles. The staff, oblivious, chalk up the bill on the bar.

Bar Manolo, on buzzing Pza de Alfalfa. The best of several tapas bars on the square. It's lively at breakfast as well as at night.

La Eslava, C/Eslava 3, **t** 954 90 65 68. A wide range of excellent tapas, including a delicious *salmorejo*, the thick *gazpacho* topped with egg and ham. The popular restaurant has a more extensive menu and can get very crowded. *Closed Sun, Mon eve and Aug*.

Infanta Sevilla, C/Arfe 36, **t** 954 22 96 89. Down towards the river, this is a very stylish bar with excellent tapas; the range is limited but the quality is outstanding. Try the *chorizo* sausage or the *bacalao*.

Entertainment and Nightlife

The Pza del Salvador fills up quickly in the evenings, so start at the **Antigua Bodeguita**, or its neighbour, **Los Soportales**. Many of the liveliest bars are around **Pza de Alfalfa**. **C/Peres Galdos** is popular with young *sevillanos*, while the vibrant Santa Cruz Quarter is favoured by more young foreigners.

Bar Berlin, C/Boteros. Loud, crammed and great fun.

Holiday, C/Jésus del Grand Poder. Come to dance until dawn, but not before 2 or 3am.

Metropol, C/La Florida. A trendy new bar, recently opened as a café by day and a *bar de copas* with a DJ by night.

If you've been longing to experience **flamenco**, Sevilla is a good place to do it. The most touristy flamenco factories are pricey; bars in Triana and other areas do it better for less. The tourist office has a notice board with up-to-date details of flamenco shows and special deals. A few venues are listed below:

El Simpecao, Pso Nuestra Senora de la O. Youthful and occasionally impromptu, this place is not too far from the real thing.

La Carbonería, C/Levies 18. The king of modern flamenco, the late El Camaron de la Isla, used to play at this bar which is still one of the best venues in the city for extemporaneous performances of all styles. Cheap food is served at the back in the main performance area. Thursday is best for flamenco.

El Tamboril, on Pza Santa Cruz. Come here for *sevillana* dancing; it's as popular with *sevillanos* as it is with tourists.

Two publications, *El Giraldillo* and *Ocio* provide listings for **music**, **theatre** and **opera**, and the tourist office is very helpful. For mainstream drama, the best-known theatre is the **Lope de Vega Theatre**, Av. María Luisa, **t** 954 59 08 53. The **Maestranza Theatre**, Pso de Cristíbal Colín, **t** 954 22 33 44, has established itself as one of the top opera houses in Europe.

See a **bullfight** in the **Maestranza** if you can, but don't just turn up! Get tickets as far ahead as possible; prices at the box office, C/Adriano 37, **t** 954 22 35 06, will be cheaper than at the little stands on C/Sierpes. The season runs April to Sept.

jasmine and a hundred other blooms. If you come in summer, you may melt: the lower valley of the Guadalquivir is one of the hottest places in Europe. The pageant of Sevilla unfolds in the shadow of La Giralda, still the loftiest tower in Spain. Its size and the ostentatious play of its arches and arabesques make it the perfect symbol for this city, full of the romance of the south and delightful excess.

At times Sevilla has been a capital, and it remains Spain's eternal city; neither past reverses nor modern industry have been able to shake it from its dreams. That its past glories should return and place it alongside Venice and Florence as one of the jewels in the crown of Europe, a true metropolis with full international recognition, is the first dream of every *sevillano*. Sevilla is still a city very much in love with itself. Even the big celebrations of Semana Santa and Feria (*see* 'Festivals', p.601) are essentially private; the *sevillanos* celebrate in their own *casitas* with friends, all the time aware that they are being observed by the general public, who can peek but may not enter, at least not without the necessary *enchufe* ('the right connection'). Sevilla is like a beautiful, flirtatious woman: she'll tempt you to her doorstep and allow you a peck on the cheek – whether you get over the threshold depends entirely on your charm.

History: from Hispalis to Isbiliya to Sevilla

One of Sevilla's distinctions is its long historical continuity. Few cities in western Europe can claim never to have suffered a dark age, but Sevilla flourished after the fall of Rome – and even after the coming of the Castilians. Roman **Hispalis** was founded on an Iberian settlement, and soon became one of the leading cities of the province of Baetica. So was **Itálica**, the now ruined city just to the northwest; it is difficult to say which was the more important. During the Roman twilight, Sevilla seems to have been a thriving town. Its first famous citizen, San Isidore, was one of the Doctors of the Church and the most learned man of the age, famous for his great *Encyclopedia* and his *Seven Books Against the Pagans*, an attempt to prove that the coming of Christianity was not the cause of Rome's fall. Sevilla was an important town under the Visigoths, and after the Moorish conquest it was second only to Córdoba as a political power and a centre of learning. For a while after the demise of the western caliphate in 1023, it became an independent kingdom, paying tribute to the kings of Castile. Sevilla suffered under the Almoravids after 1091, but enjoyed a revival under their successors, the Almohads.

The disaster came for Muslim **Isbiliya** in 1248, 18 years after the union of Castile and León. Ferdinand III's conquest of the city is not a well-documented event, but it seems that more than half the population found exile in Granada or Africa preferable to Castilian rule; their property was divided among settlers from the north. Despite the dislocation, the city survived, and found a new prosperity as Castile's window on the Mediterranean and South Atlantic trade routes (the River Guadalquivir is navigable as far as Sevilla). Everywhere in the city you will see its emblem, the word NODO (knot) with a double knot between the O and D. The word recalls the civil wars of the 1270s, when Sevilla was one of the few cities in Spain to remain loyal to Alfonso the Wise. '*No m'a dejado*' ('She has not forsaken me'), Alfonso is recorded as saying; *madeja* is another word for knot, and placed between the syllables NO and DO it makes a clever rebus, besides being a tribute to Sevilla's loyalty to medieval Castile's greatest king.

From 1503 to 1680, Sevilla enjoyed a legal monopoly of trade with the Americas, and it soon became the biggest city in Spain, with a population of over 150,000. The giddy prosperity this brought, in the years when the silver fleet ran full, contributed much to the festive, incautious atmosphere that is often revealed in Sevilla's character. Sevilla never found a way to hold on to much of the American wealth, and what little it managed to grab was soon dissipated in showy excess. It was in this period, of course, that Sevilla was perfecting its charm. Poets and composers have always favoured it. The prototypes of Bizet's Carmen rolled their cigars in the Royal Tobacco Factory, and for her male counterpart Sevilla contributed Don Juan Tenorio, who evolved through Spanish theatre in plays by Tirso de Molina and Zorrilla to become Mozart's *Don Giovanni*.

Over the 17th and 18th centuries the city stagnated, and although various industrial programmes were started up by Franco's economists in the 1950s, the city was more than ready when at last **King Juan Carlos** ushered in the return of democracy. In the late 1970s, Andalucians took advantage of revolutionary regional autonomy laws, building one of the most active regional governments in the country. In 1992, crimped and primped, Sevilla opened her doors to the world for **Expo '92**, a vainglorious display that attracted 16 million visitors.

The Cathedral and Around

La Giralda

Open Mon–Sat 11–5, Sun and hols 2–6; adm; t 954 21 49 71.

You can catch the 319ft tower of **La Giralda** peeking over the rooftops from almost anywhere in Sevilla. This great minaret, with its *ajimeces* and brickwork arabesques, was built under the **Almohads**, from 1172 to 1195, just 50 years before the Christian conquest. The surprisingly harmonious spire is a Christian addition. Whatever sort of turret originally existed was surmounted by four golden balls stacked up at the very top, designed to catch the sun and be visible to a traveller one day's ride from the city; all came down in a 13th-century earthquake. On the top of their spire, the Christians added a huge, revolving statue of Faith as a weathervane. **La Giraldillo** – the weathervane – has given its name to the tower as a whole. The climb to the top is fairly easy: instead of stairs, there are shallow ramps – wide enough for Ferdinand III to have ridden his horse up for the view after the conquest in 1248.

The Biggest Gothic Cathedral in the Whole World

Opening hours as for La Giralda; both are visited with one ticket.

For a while after the Reconquista, the Castilians who repopulated Sevilla were content to use the great Almohad mosque, built at the same time as La Giralda. But at the turn of the 1400s, it was decided to build a new cathedral so grand that 'future ages shall call us mad for attempting it'. If they were mad, they were good organizers: they got it up in slightly over a century. The architects are unknown, though there has been speculation that the original master was either French or German.

The exterior, with its great rose window and double buttresses, is as fine as any of the Gothic cathedrals of northern Spain, if you could only see it. Especially on the western front, facing the Av. de la Constitución, the buildings close in; walking around its vast bulk is like passing under a steep and ragged cliff. Some of the best original sculptural work is on the two portals flanking the main door: the **Door of Baptism** (left) and the **Door of Birth** (right), which are covered with elaborate terracotta figures sculpted by the Frenchman Lorenzo Mercadante de Bretaña and his follower Pedro Millán during the late 15th century. The ground plan of this monster, roughly 400ft by 600ft, probably covers the same area as the original mosque. On the northern side, the **Patio de los Naranjos** (Court of the Orange Trees, and planted accordingly,) preserves the outline of the mosque courtyard. The Muslim fountain survives, along with some of the walls and arches. In the left-hand corner, the Moorish 'Gate of the Lizard' has hanging from it a stuffed crocodile, said to have been a present from an Egyptian emir asking for the hand of a Spanish Infanta. Along the eastern wall is the entrance of the **Biblioteca Colombina**, a library of ancient manuscripts and an archive of the explorer's life and letters, founded by his son.

The cathedral's cavernous **interior** overpowers the faithful with its size more than its grace or beauty. The main altarpiece is the world's biggest *retablo*, almost 120ft high and entirely covered with carved figures and golden Gothic ornaments; it took 82 years to make, and takes about a minute to look at. Just behind the Large Chapel (Capilla Mayor) and the main altar, the **Royal Chapel** (Capilla Real) contains the tombs of Ferdinand the Saint, conqueror of Sevilla, and of Alfonso the Wise; Pedro the Cruel and his mistress, María de Padilla, are relegated to the crypt underneath. Above the iron grille at the entrance to the Royal Chapel, the Moor Axataf hands over the keys of the city to a triumphant Ferdinand III. The art of the various chapels around the cathedral is lost in the gloom, but there are paintings by Murillo in the Chapel of San Antonio (in the northern aisle), and a *retablo* by Zurbarán in the Chapel of San Pedro (to the left of the Royal Chapel). In the southern aisle, four stern pall-bearers on a high pedestal support the **tomb of Christopher Columbus**. The pall-bearers represent the kingdoms of Castile, León, Navarra and Aragón.

Most of the cathedral's collections are housed in a few chambers near the entrance. In the **Chapterhouse**, which has an *Immaculate Conception* by Murillo, Sevilla's bishop can sit on his throne and pontificate under the unusual acoustics of an elliptical Baroque ceiling. The adjacent **Sacristy** contains paintings by Zurbarán, Murillo, van Dyck and others, most in dire need of restoration. Spare a moment for the reliquaries. Juan de Arfe is represented here with a virtual palace, made with 900lbs of silver and complete with marble columns. Spain's most famous, and possibly most bizarre, reliquary is the **Alfonsine Tables**, filled with over 200 tiny bits of tooth and bone. They were said to have belonged to Alfonso the Wise and were made to provide extra-powerful juju for him to carry into battle.

The Archive of the Indies (Archivo de Indias)

Open Mon–Fri 10–1; closed Sat and Sun; open for research by appointment 8–3, **t** *954 21 12 34.*

In common with most of its contemporaries, parts of Sevilla's cathedral were public ground, and were used to transact all sorts of business. A 16th-century bishop put an end to this practice, but prevailed upon Philip II to construct an **Exchange** (Lonja), next to the cathedral for the merchants. Philip sent his favourite architect, Juan de Herrera, to design it. The severe, elegant façades are typically Herreran, and the stone balls and pyramids on top are practically his signature. By the 1780s, little commerce continued in Sevilla, and what was left of the American trade passed through Cádiz. Also, two foreigners had dared to publish histories of the Indies unflattering to the Spanish, so Charles III converted the building to hold the **Archive of the Indies**, the repository of all the maps and documents that the Crown had collected in the age of exploration.

The Alcázar

Open summer Tues–Sat 9.30–7, Sun and hols 9.30–5; winter Tues–Sat 9.30–5, Sun and hols 9.30–1.30; closed Mon; adm.

It's easy to be fooled into thinking this is simply a Moorish palace; parts of it could have come straight from the Alhambra (*see* pp.693–7). Most of it, however, was built by Moorish workmen for **King Pedro the Cruel** of Castile in the 1360s. The Alcázar and its king represent a fascinating cul-de-sac in Spanish history and culture, and allow the possibility that al-Andalus might have assimilated its conquerors rather than been destroyed by them.

Pedro was an interesting character. In Froissart's *Chronicle*, he is described as 'full of marveylous opinyons...rude and rebell agaynst the commandements of holy churche'. Certainly he didn't mind having his Moorish artists adorn his palace with sayings from the Koran in Kufic calligraphy. Pedro preferred Sevilla to Old Castile, and he filled his court with Moorish poets, dancers and bodyguards – the only ones he trusted. But he was not the man for the job of cultural synthesis. The evidence, in so far as it is reliable, suggests he richly deserved his honorific 'the Cruel', although to many underdog *sevillanos* he was Pedro the Just. Long before Pedro, the Alcázar was the palace of the Moorish governors. Work on the Moorish features began in 712 after the capture of Sevilla. In the 9th century it was transformed into a palace for Abd ar-Rahman II. Important additions were made under the Almohads, but almost all the decorative work was done under Pedro, some by the Granadans and the rest by Muslim artists from Toledo; it is the outstanding production of *mudéjar* art in Spain.

The Alcázar is entered by the little gate on Pza del Triunfo, on the southern side of the cathedral. The first courtyard, the **Court of León**, has beautiful arabesques, with lions amid castles for Castile and León; this was the public court, where visitors were received, corresponding to the Mexuar at the Alhambra.

Much of the best *mudéjar* work can be seen in the adjacent halls and courts; their seemingly haphazard arrangement was in fact a principle of the art, to enhance the surprise in passing from one to the next. Off the Court of León is the **Hall of Justice**, with a star-shaped coffered ceiling, where Pedro I passed the death sentence on his brother, who had had the temerity to have an affair with Pedro's wife. Behind, the secluded **Patio de Yeso** survives largely from the Almoravid palace of the 1170s, itself built on the site of a Roman *praetorium*. The **Patio de las Doncellas** (Court of the Maidens), entered through the gate of the palace façade, is named for the Christian maidens who were given as brides as peace offerings to the Moors. The courtyard leads to the **Salón de las Embajadores** (Hall of the Ambassadors), a small domed chamber which remains the finest in the Alcázar despite the jarring addition of heavily carved balconies from the time of Philip II. Another courtyard, the **Patio de las Muñecas** (Court of the Dolls), once the hub of the palace's domestic life, takes its name from two tiny faces on medallions at the base of one of the horseshoe arches; to find them should bring luck.

Spanish kings couldn't leave the Alcázar alone. Ferdinand and Isabel spoiled a corner of it for their **Casa de Contratación**, a planning centre for the colonization of the Indies, while Charles V added his own **palace**, which contains some spectacular **Flemish tapestries** showing detailed scenes of Charles' campaigns in Tunisia.

Within its walls, the Alcázar has extensive **gardens**, with reflecting pools, avenues of clipped hedges, and oranges and lemons everywhere. Near the pavilion in the lower gardens is a little **labyrinth** built for Charles V. Outside, the extensive **Jardines de Murillo** border the northern wall of the Alcázar.

From the Cathedral to the River: El Arenal

Av. de la Constitución is Sevilla's main street. Between it and the Guadalquivir is **El Arenal**, once the bustling port district. Now it is quiet and tranquil, without the distinction of the Santa Cruz Quarter, but with an earthy charm of its own. Heading down to the river, you will pass one of the surviving rampart gates, the **Postigo del Aceite** (Gate of Olive Oil), a 16th-century remodelling of an old Moorish gate.

Hospital de la Caridad

Open Mon–Sat 9–1 and 3.30–6.30, Sun 9–1; adm.

Behind a colourful façade on C/Temprado is the **Charity Hospital**, built in 1647 in the old warehouse area. The original hospital was established in the docklands Chapel of San Jorge, before its reconstruction in infinitely grander style during the 17th century. Its benefactor was a certain Miguel de Mañara, a reformed rake who has been claimed as the prototype for Tirso de Molina's Don Juan. Though it still serves as a charity home for the aged, visitors come to see the art in the hospital chapel. Unfortunately, four of a series of 12 Murillos were stolen by Napoleon, but the remaining eight still hang here, a cosy group of saints and miracles. Murillo was also responsible for the *azulejo* panels on the chapel façade. Inside are three ghoulish works of art by Juan de Valdés Leal (1622–90). A competent enough painter, he only warmed to the task with such macabre subjects as you see here. Murillo's reported judgement on these was that 'one has to hold one's nose to look at them'.

The Torre del Oro (Tower of Gold)

The **Tower of Gold**, (*t 954 22 24 19; open Tues–Fri 10–2, Sat and Sun 11–2; closed Mon and Aug; adm*) named for the gold and *azulejo* tiles that covered its exterior in the days of the Moors, was built by the Almohads in 1220. In times of trouble a chain was stretched from the tower across the Guadalquivir; in 1248 the chain was broken by an attacking fleet, the supply route with Triana was cut off and Sevilla fell. Inside, the **Museo Marítimo** (*open Tues–Sat 10–2, Sun 10–1; closed Mon*) displays models, documents, weapons and maps.

The Cathedral of Bullfighting

On the river just north of the tower, is **La Maestranza bullring**, with its blazing white and ochre arches. Perhaps the most prestigious of all *plazas de toros*, it is celebrated for its remarkable acoustics. Though begun in 1760, the Carlist Wars got in the way and it didn't get finished until 1880. You may be fortunate enough to see a *corrida* while in town (*see* 'Entertainment', p.604). Inside is the **Museo Taurino** (*t 954 22 45 77; open daily 9.30–2 and 3–6, or 9–3 when a bullfight is being held; adm*), with a small shop and all sorts of memorabilia.

Triana

Across the Guadalquivir from La Maestranza is Triana, an ancient suburb that takes its name from the Emperor Trajan. Queipo de Llano wrecked a lot of it at the beginning of the Civil War, but there are still picturesque white streets overlooking the river, and, along its banks, the charming Pso Nuestra Senora de la O hosts a colourful, cheap produce market. The neighbourhood has a reputation for being the 'cradle of flamenco', and the streets around C/Castilla and C/San Jorge are still some of the best for finding Triana ceramics; all Sevilla's *azulejo* tiles are made here.

Northwest of the Cathedral

Back across the river is the district of **San Eloy**, full of raucous bars and hotels. On C/San Pablo is **La Magdalena** (1704), flaunting an eccentric Baroque façade. Inside are two paintings by Zurbarán, and gilded reliefs by Leonardo de Figueroa.

Museo de Bellas Artes (Fine Arts Museum)

C/San Roque; open Tues 3–8, Wed–Sat 9–8, Sun 9–2, closed Mon.

This excellent collection is housed in the **Convent of Merced** (1612), expropriated for the state in 1835. It is set around three courtyards, the first of which is decorated with lustrous tiled panels from Sevilla's convents. Some fine medieval works include an especially expressive triptych by the Master of Burgos from the 13th century. **Pedro Millán**, one of the most influential sculptors of the period, is well represented, as is the Italian sculptor **Pietro Torrigiano**; his wooden St Jerome is uncannily barbaric.

Through another courtyard, the Imperial Staircase, richly decorated in Mannerist style, leads to works by the most mannered of them all, **Murillo**. More interesting are the works of **Zurbarán**, who could express spirituality without the simpering of Murillo or the hysteria of the others; the *Miracle of St Hugo* is perhaps his most acclaimed work. Occasionally he too slips up; you may enjoy the *Eternal Father* with great fat toes and a triangle on his head, or the wonderful *Apotheosis of St Thomas Aquinas*, in which the great scholastic philosopher rises as if to say 'I've got it!' Don't miss El Greco's portrait of his son Jorge, or the stark portraits by Ribera. There are also works by Jan Brueghel, Caravaggio and Mattia Preti.

North of the Cathedral: the Heart of the City

Calle Sierpes ('Serpent Street') is the heart of Sevilla's business and shopping area, a sinuous pedestrian lane lined with every sort of old shop. Just to the north stands **El Salvador**, a fine Baroque church by Leonardo de Figueroa, now picturesquely mouldering. East of here, narrow, half-timbered houses jostle for space in the old merchant district while, to the southeast, **Plaza Nueva** marks Sevilla's modern centre, embellished on one side by the elaborate Plateresque façade of the **Ayuntamiento** (1564).

La Macarena and Around

The northern end of Sevilla contains few monuments; most of its solid, working-class neighbourhoods are clustered around Baroque parish churches. The **Alameda de Hércules** runs through one of the shabbier, yet most appealing, parts of the city, with a smattering of bars and cafés. **Santa Clara** and **San Clemente** are two interesting 13th-century monasteries. The former includes one of Sevilla's best *artesonado* ceilings and a Gothic tower built by Don Fadrique, while San Clemente has a beautiful 16th-century *mudéjar* coffered ceiling and handsome frescoes by Valdés Leal. Both are set to become an interactive audiovisual museum of Sevilla's history. North of C/San Luis, the **Basilica of La Macarena** (*open daily 9–1 and 5–9; adm for museum*) is a 1940s neo-Baroque construction luridly frescoed with puffs of fluorescent angels. This is the home of the most worshipped of Sevilla's idols, a delicate Virgin with glass tears on her cheeks who steals the show in the Semana Santa parades. The adjacent **museum** (*entrance inside the chapel*) is devoted to a Barbie-wardrobe of her costumes and the elaborately carved and gilded floats which take part in the Semana Santa parades.

Santa Cruz and Beyond

If Spain envies Sevilla, Sevilla envies **Santa Cruz**, a tiny, exceptionally lovely quarter of narrow streets and whitewashed houses. It appears to be the true homeland of everything *sevillano*, with flower-bedecked courtyards and iron-bound windows, though there is something unnervingly pristine about it. Before 1492, this was the

Jewish quarter; today it's the most aristocratic corner of town. In the old days it was walled; today you may enter through the Murillo Gardens, the C/Mateos Gago behind the cathedral apse, or from **Patio de las Banderas**, a pretty square next to the Alcázar. **Santa María la Blanca** (*C/Santa María la Blanca*) was a pre-Reconquista church rebuilt in the 1660s, containing spectacular Rococo ornamentation and paintings by Murillo.

Casa de Pilatos

*Pza Pilatos, **t** 954 22 52 98; open Wed–Mon 9–7, Tues 1–5. Optional tour of the private apartments (in Spanish only).*

Amid the peaceful, eastern fringes of the old town is the House of Pilate, built by the Dukes of Medinaceli (1480–1571) and, so the story goes, modelled on the Praetorium, Pontius Pilate's official residence in Jerusalem. The **Patio Principal** is laced with 13th-century Granadan decoration, coloured tiles, and rows of Roman statues and portrait busts, which form a perfect introduction to the dukes' excellent collections of antique sculpture in the surrounding rooms. The series of delightful **gardens** and **courtyards**, cooled with trickling fountains, is ablaze with purple bougainvillea in the spring. For a voyeuristic taste of how the other half live, take the tour of the **private apartments**, furnished with 18th-century furniture, paper-thin porcelain from England and Limoges, fanciful Japanese vases and some rather humdrum paintings.

South of the Cathedral

Sevilla has a building even larger than its cathedral – twice as large, in fact, and probably better known to the outside world. Since the 1950s it has housed parts of the city's **university**, but it began life in the 1750s as the state **Fábrica de Tabacos** (Tobacco Factory). In the 19th century, it employed as many as 12,000 women to roll cigars, one of whom, of course, was Bizet's Carmen. Next to the factory, the 1929 **Hotel Alfonso XIII** (*currently under scaffolding for refurbishment*) is believed to be the only hotel ever commissioned by a reigning monarch – Alfonso literally used it as an annexe to the Alcázar when friends and relations came to stay.

María Luisa Park

For all its old-fashioned grace, Sevilla has been one of the most forward-looking and progressive cities of Spain in the 20th century. In the 1920s, while building the new port and factories that are the foundation of the city's growth today, the *sevillanos* decided to put on an exhibition. They turned the entire southern end of the city into an expanse of gardens and grand boulevards, at the centre of which is the **Parque de María Luisa**, a paradisiacal half-mile of palms and orange trees, covered with flowerbeds and dotted with hidden bowers and pavilions. Two of the largest pavilions on the **Plaza de América** have been turned into museums. The **Museo Arqueológico** (Archaeological Museum; ***t** 954 23 24 01; open Tues 3–8, Wed–Sat 9–8, Sun and hols 9–2; closed Mon and Aug*) has an excellent collection of pre-Roman jewellery and icons, and some tantalizing artefacts from mysterious Tartessos. The Romans are represented with copies of Greek sculpture and oversized statues, but also some fine glass, mosaics and finds of all sorts from Itálica and other towns. Across the plaza, in the *mudéjar* pavilion, the **Museo de Artes y Costumbres Populares** (***t*** *954 23 25 76; open Tues 3–8, Wed–Sat 9–8, Sun and hols 9–2; closed Mon*) is Andalucía's attic, with everything from ploughs and saucepans to exhibits from the city's famous fiestas.

The Plaza de España

In the 1920s at least, excess was still a way of life in Sevilla, and to call attention to the **Exposición Iberoamericana** the *sevillanos* put up a building even bigger than the Tobacco Factory. With its Baroque towers, fancy bridges, staircases and immense colonnade, Pza de España is World's Fair architecture at its grandest and most outrageous. On the colonnade, a few million of Sevilla's famous *azulejos* are devoted to maps and historical scenes from every province in Spain.

La Cartuja and Contemporary Art

The Isle of La Cartuja was part of the Expo '92 site, but it has since become seedy and run down; some of the original pavilions are now devoted to business fairs, while another bit has become the **Isla Mágica** funfair (*open Mar–Oct daily 11–11; adm exp*).

Infinitely more interesting is the partially restored Carthusian monastery of **Cartujo de Santa Maria de las Cuevas** (St Mary of the Caves*; or the Centro Andaluz de Arte Contemporaneo; open summer Tues–Sun 11–9; winter Tues–Sat 11–7; closed Mon, also Sun in winter;* ***guided visits*** *at noon and 5pm;* ***t*** *955 03 70 70*). Founded in 1399 by Gonzalo de Mena, the Archbishop of Sevilla, it grew to become a virtually self-sufficient walled city. At the peak of its affluence, it was richly endowed with masterpieces by great artists, but has since suffered numerous lootings and indignities.

Today, the atmospheric ruins of the monastery are home to the **Andalucían Centre of Contemporary Art** (*opening times as above*), the only contemporary arts centre in Andalucía. Attached to the monastery an unobtrusive, light-filled modern building is devoted to temporary exhibitions that focus on both emerging and established Andalucían and international artists, who develop projects specifically for the space. It is without doubt one of the most engaging and vibrant places to see contemporary art in Spain and it shouldn't be missed.

Around Sevilla: the Roman City of Itálica

Ctra Menda; open Tues–Sat 9–5.30, Sun 10–4; closed Mon; ***t*** *955 99 73 76.*
Local buses leave every half-hour from Pza de Armas, nr Puerto del Cachorro.

Eight kilometres north of Sevilla, towards Mérida, are the only significant Roman ruins in Andalucía. The first Roman colony in Spain, the city was founded in the 3rd century BC by Scipio Africanus as a home for his veterans. Itálica thrived in the Imperial age. Three emperors, Trajan, Hadrian and Theodosius, were born here, as were the poet Lucan and the moralist Seneca. The biggest ruins are an **amphitheatre**, with seating for 40,000, some temple remains, and a street of villa foundations.

Getting There

There are two ways to go, both of approximately equal length. The **train**, and most of the **buses**, unfortunately take the duller route through the flat lands along the Guadalquivir. The only landmark here is the Spanish-Moorish castle of Almodóvar del Río, perched romantically on a height planted with olive trees, overlooking the river. The southern route (the N-IV) also follows the Guadalquivir valley, but the scenery is a little more varied, and the road passes through two fine towns, Carmona and Écija. There are regular buses from Sevilla to these towns, from where you can easily find connecting buses for Córdoba.

Tourist Information

Carmona: Municipal Office, Alcazar de la Puerta de Sevilla s/n, **t** 954 19 09 55, **f** 954 19 00 80, *carmona@andal.es*, *www.andal.es/carmona* (*open Mon–Sat 10–6, Sun 10–3*).

Écija: Palacio de Benamaje, **t/f** 955 90 29 33 (*open summer Tues–Sun 9–2, closed Mon; winter Tues–Fri 9.30–1.30 and 4.30–6.30, Sat and Sun 9–2, closed Mon*).

Where to Stay and Eat

Carmona ✉ 39554

★★★★★**Palacio Casa Carmona**, Pza de Lasso 1, **t** 954 14 33 00, **f** 954 14 37 52 (*luxury*). Lovingly restored by Marta Medina and her artist son Felipe, this 16th-century palace is the last word in refined good taste, and a stay here will delight all the senses.

★★★★**Parador Alcázar del Rey Don Pedro**, Alcázar s/n, **t** 954 14 10 10, **f** 954 14 17 12, *carmona@parador.es* (*expensive*). Occupying a section of Cruel Pete's summer palace, the finest in Andalucía for style and comfort. It has superlative views, a garden, pool and luxurious furnishings; good value.

★★★★**Hotel Alcazar de la Reina**, Pza de Lasso 2, **t** 954 19 62 00, **f** 954 14 01 13, *www.alcazar-reina.es* (*moderate*). Set in a beautiful old house which has been tastefully restored, with a well-designed communal area and bedrooms, and one of the best **restaurants** in town, La Ferrara. Among the delicious specials served here are game, lamb and duck, all served in a lovely setting.

★**P. Comercio**, C/Torre del Oro, **t** 954 14 00 18 (*inexpensive*). One of the many *pensiones* and *hostales* in town.

From Sevilla to Córdoba

The first town along the N-IV, **Carmona** seems like a miniature Sevilla, but is probably much older. Remains of a Neolithic settlement have been found, and the Phoenician colony that replaced it prospered throughout Roman and Moorish times. Pedro the Cruel favoured it and rebuilt most of its **Alcázar**, which, with fine views over the valley, is now a national *parador*. Carmona is well worth a day's exploration. Its walls are still standing, including the grand **Puerta de Sevilla** (***t*** *954 19 09 55; open Mon–Sat 10–6, Sun 10–3; adm*). Up on the palm-decked Plaza de San Fernando stands the **Ayuntamiento**, with a Roman mosaic of Medusa in its courtyard, and next door, the **Casa Palacio des Marques de la Torres** (***t*** *954 14 01 28; open daily 11–7; adm*), the town's archaeological museum. C/Martín López leads up to the 15th-century church of **Santa María** (*open daily 9–12 and 6–9*), built on the site of an old mosque. The old quarters of town have an ensemble of fine palaces, as well as *mudéjar* and Renaissance churches. Carmona's prime attraction is the **Roman necropolis** (***t*** *954 14 08 11; open Tues–Fri 9–5, Sat and Sun 10–2; closed Mon*), a series of rock-cut tombs off Av. Jorge Bonsor. Some, like the 'Tomb of Servilia', are elaborate creations with subterranean chambers and vestibules, pillars, domed ceilings and carved reliefs.

San Fernando, Pza San Fernando, **t/f** 954 14 35 56 (*moderate*). This restaurant has the best reputation in town, although Carmona is not known for culinary excellence. *Closed Sun eve, Mon and Aug*.

Molino de la Nomera, C/Pedro, **t** 954 14 20 00. Just down from the *parador* and set in a historic 15th-century building, which can be visited separately. Offers superb food and some of the best views in town. Specializes in local meats *al horno* or *a la paradilla*.

La Cueva, Barbacan Baja 2, **t/f** 954 19 18 11 (*inexpensive*). Situated just below the city walls, this cavernous place has a heavy emphasis on pork and an extensive vegetable menu.

Écija ✉ 41400

The hotels are mostly motels on the outskirts, serving traffic on the Madrid–Cádiz highway.

★★**Hotel Platería**, C/Garcilópez 1-A, **t** 955 90 27 54 (*inexpensive*). Just off the main square with a lovely marble courtyard and helpful service; probably the best in town.

★★**Ciudad del Sol**, C/Cervantes 50, **t** 954 83 03 00, **f** 954 83 58 79 (*inexpensive*). A friendly place with air-conditioned rooms.

Fonda Santa Cruz, Romero Gordillo 8, **t** 954 83 02 22 (*moderate*). A minute's walk from the main plaza, in a back street behind the fabulously named Gasolina Bar, you will find this delightful little place with simple rooms that open out to the tiled courtyard. Try their veal, which is cooked before your eyes at the table.

Las Ninfas, in the Palacio de Benameji, **t** 955 90 45 92 (*expensive*). The setting is stylish and subtle, the food fresh and light with an emphasis on fish. You may also spot the four marble nymphs (hence the name) which once stood in Pza de España.

Bodegón del Gallego, C/A. Aparicio 3, **t** 954 83 26 18 (*moderate*). One of the best places to eat in town, serving stylish *andaluz* dishes.

Pasareli, Pasaje Virgen del Rocío, **t** 954 83 20 24 (*inexpensive*). Looks like any modern cafeteria in the heart of town, but there's a surprisingly efficient little restaurant tucked away in the corner, where you can eat well and cheaply from a large selection of meat and fish.

El Bistori, **t** 954 83 10 66. Situated back on the main plaza and specializing in food from across Spain – shellfish from Huelva, meat from Avila and *pulpo a la callega*.

Écija makes much of one of its nicknames, the 'city of towers', and tries to play down the other – the 'frying pan of Andalucía'. You may be put off by the clinical outskirts of the town and by the ill-concealed gas-holders, but Ecija is usually redeemed by its **Plaza de España**, one of the loveliest squares in Andalucía. Unfortunately, the council have taken it upon themselves to construct an underground car park beneath it, so for the moment the square lies hidden behind a 6ft-high concrete wall. Most of the town's **towers** are sumptuously ornate, rebuilt after the great earthquake of 1755 – the one that flattened Lisbon. **Santa María** has one, as does **San Juan Bautista**, gaily decorated in coloured tiles and, highest of them all, **San Gil**, within which are paintings by Alejo Fernández and Villegas Marmolejo (*all monuments open 10–1; adm free*).

Écija also has a set of Renaissance and Baroque palaces, which within Andalucía are second only to those in Úbeda; most of these showy façades can be seen on or near **Calle de los Caballeros**. Worth visiting is the **Mudéjar Palace**, dating from the 14th century, where you can find some interesting archaeological remains, some Roman mosaics and various reliefs, coins and glass. The **Peñaflor Palace** (1728) on C/de Castellar – now a five-star hotel – is one of the outstanding works of Andalucían Baroque, with a grandiose façade and a lovely patio.

Córdoba

There are a few spots around the Mediterranean where the presence of past glories becomes almost tangible, a mixture of mythic antiquity, lost power and dissipated energy that broods over a place like a ghost. It occurs in Istanbul, in Rome, or among the monuments of Egypt, and it occurs here on the banks of the Guadalquivir, at Córdoba's southern gate. Looking around, you can see reminders of three defunct empires: a Roman bridge, a triumphal arch built for Philip II and Córdoba's Great Mosque, more than a thousand years old. The first reminds us of the city's beginnings, the second of its decline; the last one scarcely seems credible, as it speaks of an age when Córdoba was one of the most brilliant metropolises of all Europe. Córdoba's growth has allowed it a chance to renovate its sparkling old quarters and monuments, and the new prosperity brought with it a contentment the city hasn't known since the Reconquista.

Everyone who visits Córdoba comes for the Great Mosque, but you should spare some time to explore the city itself. Old Córdoba is one of the largest medieval quarters of any European city, and certainly the biggest in Spain. More than Sevilla, it retains its Moorish character, a maze of whitewashed alleys opening into the loveliest patios in all Andalucía.

History

Roman *Corduba*, built on a prehistoric site, was almost from the start the leading city of interior Spain, capital of the province of Hispania Ulterior, and later of the reorganized province of Bætica. Córdoba had a reputation as the garden spot of Hispania; it gave Roman letters Lucan and both Senecas among others, testimony to its prominence as a city of learning. Córdoba became Christianized at an early date. Ironically, the True Faith got its comeuppance here in 572, when the Arian Visigoths under Leovigild captured the city from Byzantine rule. When the Arabs conquered, they found it was still an important town, and it became the capital of al-Andalus when Abd ar-Rahman established the Umayyad emirate in 756.

For 300 years, Córdoba enjoyed the position of unqualified leader of al-Andalus, a city without equal in the West as a centre of learning. If proof were needed, it would be enough to mention two 12th-century contemporaries: **Averroës**, the Muslim scientist and Aristotelian philosopher who contributed so much to the rebirth of classical learning in Europe; also **Moses Maimonides**, the Jewish philosopher whose reconciliation of faith and reason were assumed into Christianity by Thomas Aquinas. Medieval Córdoba was a great trading centre, and its luxury goods were coveted throughout western Europe. At its height, picture Córdoba as a city of bustling international markets, great palaces, schools, baths and mosques, with 28 suburbs and the first street lighting in Europe. In it, Muslims, Christians and Jews lived in harmony, at least until the coming of the fanatical Almoravids and Almohads. There's a certain decadence in the air; street riots in Córdoba were an immediate cause of the break-up of the caliphate in 1031, but here, as in Sevilla, the coming of the Reconquista was an unparalleled catastrophe.

When **Ferdinand III** 'the Saint' captured the city in 1236, most members of the population chose flight over putting themselves at the mercy of the priests, although history records that he was unusually tolerant of the Jews. It did not last. Three centuries of Castilian rule sufficed to rob Córdoba of all its glories and turn it into a depressed backwater. Only in the last hundred years has it begun to recover; today Córdoba has also become an industrial city, though you wouldn't guess it from its sympathetically restored centre. It is the third city of Andalucía, and the first and only big town since Franco's death to have elected a communist mayor and council.

La Mezquita

Open summer Mon–Sat 10–7, Sun 1.30–7; winter Mon–Sat 10–5.30, Sun 1.30–5.30; adm; ***t*** *957 47 05 12.*

La Mezquita is the local name for Abd ar-Rahman's **Great Mosque**. Mezquita means 'mosque' and even though the building has officially been a cathedral for more than 750 years, no one could ever mistake its origins. **Abd ar-Rahman I**, founder of a new state, felt it necessary to construct a great religious monument for his capital. As part of his plan, he also wished to make it a centre of pilgrimage to increase the sense of divorce from eastern Islam; Mecca was at the time held by his Abbasid enemies. The site, at the centre of the city, had originally held a Roman temple of Janus, and later a Visigothic church. Only about one-third of the mosque belongs to the original. Successive enlargements were made by Abd ar-Rahman II, al-Hakim, and al-Mansur. Expansion was easy; the mosque is a simple rectangle divided into aisles by rows of columns, and its size was increased simply by adding more aisles. The result was one of the largest of all mosques, exceeded only by the one in Mecca. After 1236, it was converted to use as a cathedral without any major changes. In the 1520s, however, the city's clerics succeeded in convincing the Royal Council to allow the construction of a choir and high altar, enclosed structures typical of Spanish cathedrals.

Most people come away from a visit to La Mezquita somewhat confused. The endless rows of columns and red-and-white striped arches are a familiar image to most visitors, but to see them in reality in this gloomy hall does not actually increase one's understanding of the work. It's worth going into some detail, for learning to see La Mezquita the way its builders did is the best key to understanding the refined world of al-Andalus.

Before entering, take a few minutes to circumnavigate this somewhat forbidding pile of bricks. Spaced around its 2,247ft of wall are the original entrances and windows, excellent examples of Moorish art, of which those on the western side are best: interlaced Visigothic horseshoe arches, floral decorations in the Roman tradition, and Islamic calligraphy and patterns, a lesson in the varied sources of this art.

The only entrance to the mosque today is the **Puerta del Perdón**, a *mudéjar* gateway added in 1377, opening on to the **Patio de los Naranjos**, the original mosque courtyard where the old Moorish fountain can still be seen amid the orange trees. Built into the wall of the courtyard, over the gate, the original minaret – said to be the model for all the others in al-Andalus – has been replaced by an ill-proportioned 16th-century

Córdoba
SANTA MARIA DE TRASIERRA
GLORIETA PRETORIO
Convento de Merced
AVENIDA DE AMÉRICA
GTA. MARGARITAS
Bus Station
RENFE Train Station
Jardines de La Agricultura
AV. CERVANTES
AV. GRAN CAPITAN
AV. RONDA TEJARES
C. JOSÉ CRUZ CONDE
AVENIDA MEDINA AZAHARA
AVENIDA REPÚBLICA ARGENTINA
PASEO DE LA VICTORIA
C. CONCEPCIÓN
C. DE GONDOMAR
PZA LAS TENDILLAS
San Nicolás
PÉRES DE CASTRO
C. DE SEVILLA
C. JESÚS MARIA
LOPE DE HOCES
C. BARROSA
CALLE DE ANTONIO MAURA
AV. GRAN
Plaza de Toros
PZA COSTA DEL SOL
Casa del Indiano
F. RUANO
C. BUEN PASTOR
B. BELMONTE
Almodovar Gate
C. ALMANZOR
PLAZA BENAVENTE
Synagogue (ruin)
Municipal Museum
PLAZA JUDÁ LEVI
AV. DOCTOR FLEMING
C. DE TORRIJOS
La Mezquita
VIA PARQUE
AVENIDA DEL AEROPUERTO
AV. CONDE DE VALLELLANO
AMADOR DE LOS RÍOS
Triunfo
Waterwheel
Alcázar de los Reyes Christianos
AVENIDA DEL ALCÁZAR
AV. CORREGIOR
Moorish Walls (ruins)
N
500 metres
500 yards

Torre de Malmuerta
AVENIDA DE LAS OLLERIAS
RONDA DEL MURRUBIAL
Moorish Walls (ruins)
CALLE DE COSTANILLAS
PLAZA COLÓN
Santa Marina
CALLE MONTERO
C. MARÍA AUXILIADORA
AVENIDA BARCELONA
San Lorenzo
Cristo de las Faroles
C. CONDE TORRES CABRERA
SANTA MARÍA DE GRACIA
C. REALEJO
C. SAN PABLO
San Andrés
C. DE ALFOSO XIII
Roman Temple (ruin)
San Pablo
C. CLAUDIO MARCELO
C. PEDRO LÓPEZ
C. GUTIÉRREZ DE LOS RÍOS
PUERTO NUEVA
CAMPO DE SAN ANTÓN
C. DE ALFONSO XII
CAMPO MADRE DE DIOS
PLAZA CORREDERA
C. AMBROSIO DE MORALES
C. MAESE LUIS
C. CARLOS RUBIO
San Pedro
Santa Victoria
National Archaeological Museum
C. DE SAN FERNANDO
Museo de Bellas Artes
PLAZA POTRO
C. DEL REV. HEREDIA
CALDEREROS
RONDA LOS MARTIRES
PASEO LA RIVERA
C. SEBASTIÁN CUEVAS
C. CORREGIDOR
RONDA ISASA
Río Guadalquivir
PUERTA DEL PUENTE
BARRIO MIRAFLORES
PUENTE ROMANO
AV. COMPOSITOR RAFAEL CASTRO
Calahorra Tower
AVENIDA DE LAS LONJAS
PZA SANTA TERESA
AVENIDA CONFEDERACIÓN
AV. DE CÁDIZ
RINCONADA

Getting Around

By Train

Córdoba is on the major Madrid–Sevilla railway line, so there are about 12 trains a day in both directions by AVE, with a journey time of 43 mins from Sevilla and 1 hr 40 mins from Madrid. There are also frequent *Talgo* services to Málaga (about 2hrs 15mins), Cádiz, València and Barcelona, and regular trains to Huelva, Algeciras and Alicante. Trains for Granada and Algeciras pass through Bobadilla Junction, and may require a change. Córdoba's station is off Av. de América, 1.6km north of La Mezquita, **t** 957 49 02 02; the ticket office is at Ronda de los Tejares 10.

By Bus

Buses for Sevilla (three plus daily), Granada, Cádiz and Málaga and most nearby towns leave from the Alsina Graells terminal on Av. Medina Azahara 29, **t** 957 23 64 74. Buses for Madrid (one daily), València (three daily) and Barcelona (two daily), leave from the Ureña office, Av. de Cervantes 22, **t** 957 47 23 52. The train is probably a better bet for Sevilla and for Málaga.

The Córdoba bus network is complicated and it's best to check with the tourist office as to times and departure points. Otherwise call the bus information line, **t** 957 40 40 40. If you want to go to Medinat az-Zahra, take bus No.01 for Villarubia or Veredón (from Republica Argentina at Azahara); it will drop you off short of the site, and you will have to walk about 2km.

Tourist Information

Córdoba: Regional Tourist Office, C/Torrijos 10 next to the Mezquita, **t** 957 47 12 35, **f** 957 49 17 78 (*open May–Nov 9.30–6; Nov–Feb 9.30–7; Mar–April 9.30–8*). Very helpful staff; Municipal Office, in the Judería on Pza Judá Levi, **t** 957 20 05 22. It's worth a visit to get a map – Córdoba has the most labyrinthine old quarter in Spain containing monuments with changeable opening times.

Tours: To arrange personal guides to the sights, call **t** 957 48 69 97, ask at the tourist office or turn up at the mosque itself.

Shopping

Córdoba is famous for its **silverwork** – try the shops in C/José Cruz Grande, where you'll get better quality than in the old quarter round the mosque. Hand-made **crafts** are made on the premises at Meryan, C/de las Flores 2, where they specialize in embossed wood and leather furniture. High-quality **leather goods** are sold at Sera, on the corner of Rondo de los Teares and Cruz Conde. The mainstream shopping areas are along C/Conde de Gondomar and C/Claudio Marcelo on either side of Pza de las Tendillas.

Where to Stay

Córdoba ✉ 14000

Near La Mezquita, of course. Even during big tourist assaults the advantages outweigh the liabilities. However, if this area is full, or if you have a car and do not care to brave the narrow streets and lack of parking, there are a few hotels worth trying in the new town and on the periphery. There's plenty of choice; the following are some of the most interesting:

Luxury

****NH Amistad Córdoba**, Pza de Maimónides 3, **t** 957 42 03 35, **f** 957 42 03 65. This was converted from an old *palacio*, though little remains to prove it, with a main entrance fronting the Pza de Maimónides, and a back entrance neatly built into the old wall of the Judería. Thoughtful management makes it a comfortable and extremely convenient place to stay and the double-room price includes an excellent breakfast buffet. Underground parking is available for a small supplement.

Expensive

***Posada de Vallina**, C/Corregidor Luis de Cerda 83, **t** 957 49 87 50, **f** 957 49 87 51. One of the nicest new hotels to have sprung up in the past year or so, directly opposite La Mezquita. An old inn dating from Roman times, there are just 15 rooms, all sparkling clean and tastefully designed, some with mosque views, others facing the patio. Attached is a good **restaurant** (*see* below).

****Lola**, C/Romero 3, **t** 957 20 03 05, **f** 957 42 20 63, *hotellola@terra.es*. Even newer, this hotel sits right in the heart of the old Jewish quarter in a lovingly restored old house with many of the original fittings and furniture, including old Bakelite phones. There are just eight rooms, each individually designed, all doubles, but varying in size. Avoid the cheaper, smaller ones and go for the suite which has a view of the tower of the Mezquita and a tiny terrace. Breakfast is served on the roof terrace or below. Parking arrangement with the El Conquistador.

******Las Adelfas**, Av. de la Arruzafa s/n, **t** 957 27 74 20, **f** 957 27 27 94. A modern hotel five minutes north of the train station, set in spacious gardens with a pool and beautiful views over Córdoba; definitely worth considering if you visit in summer, and a bargain at present for its rates in this category.

Al-Mihrab, Av. del Brillante, Km5, **t** 957 27 21 98. Situated just 5km from the centre of town, this agreeable hotel, which is a listed building, offers peace and a view of the Sierra Morena; another bargain in this category (*moderate* in low season).

Moderate

****Hotel Mezquita**, Pza Santa Catalina, 1, **t** 957 47 55 85, **f** 957 47 62 19. A recently converted 16th-century mansion sympathetically restored with many of the original paintings and sculptures, this is fantastic value for its location. The only drawback: no garage.

****Albucasis**, C/Buen Pastor 11, **t/f** 957 47 86 25. Situated in the Judería, near La Mezquita, this former silversmith's is an attractive, affordable and immaculate place with a charming flower-filled courtyard; it's one of the prettiest hotels in Córdoba. *Closed Jan–mid-Feb.*

****Hotel González**, on the edge of the Judería, **t** 957 47 98 19, **f** 957 48 61 87. Rooms contain family antiques and the arabesque patio houses a popular **restaurant**.

Inexpensive–Cheap

Hs El Triunfo, C/Corregidor Luis de Cerda 79, **t** 957 49 84 84, **f** 957 48 68 50. Right by the mosque, this is a perfectly decent no-frills option with a pleasant restaurant on its patio; at the top end of this price category.

***Hotel Los Patios**, C/Cardenal Herrero 14, **t** 957 47 83 40, **f** 957 48 69 66. Fantastic value for its location, directly opposite La Mezquita. Brand new and sparkling clean, the 24 rooms set round the hotel's patio come with TV, phone and nice bathrooms.

***Hs Seneca**, C/Conde y Luque 5 (just north of La Mezquita), **t** 957 47 32 34. A real find, with a beautiful patio full of flowers, nice rooms and sympathetic management. Not surprisingly, it's hard to get a room.

La Fuente, C/Fernando, 51, **t** 957 48 14 78, **f** 957 48 78 27. A very pleasant budget option on the way to the Pza del Potro, with rooms set round a large patio. The only drawback is that it's on a noisy road.

Plenty of other inexpensive *fondas* can be found on and around C/Rey Heredia – also known as the street with five names – so don't be thrown by all the different signs.

Hs Maestre, C/Romero Barros 16, **t/f** 957 47 53 95. Has a range of rooms from doubles to small apartments; all have private bathrooms and those in the hotel have a/c; popular with backpackers, so book ahead.

Eating Out

Don't forget that Córdoba is the heart of a wine-growing region; there are a few *bodegas* in town that appreciate visitors, including Bodega Campos, C/Colonel Cascajo; and Bodega Doña Antonia, Av. Virgen Milagrosa 5, a small restaurant serving its own wines.

Expensive

El Churrasco, C/Romero 16, **t** 957 29 08 19. Located in an old town house in the heart of the Jewish quarter, this is Córdoba's best-loved restaurant. For food and atmosphere it is perhaps the finest restaurant in southern Spain – but it's not grand; it's actually rather small, and very intimate. It specializes in grilled meats and, unless you're vegetarian, a *churrasco* is your obvious choice here. In winter outdoor heaters make it possible to dine on the patio all year round, and there's even valet parking. It also has the best cellar in Andalucía, now so large it is in a separate building along the street – ask at the restaurant if you would like to visit. *Closed Aug.*

Almudaina, Jardines de los Santos Mártires 1, **t** 957 47 43 42. Set in an attractive old house dating from the 16th century, this would be a sophisticated spot to eat, but it has sold out to coachloads of Japanese. Its menu varies from day to day, depending on market availability, and special attention is paid to local produce. Look out for *ensalada de pimientos, alcachofas a la Cordobés*, and *lomo relleno a la Pedrocheña*, which are above average. *Closed Sun June–Sept, and Sun eve Oct–May*.

Moderate

Posada de Vallina, C/Corregidor Luis de Cerda 83, **t** 957 49 87 50, **f** 957 49 87 51. Has fine service and offers *finos* and nibbles for free as aperitifs. The setting is lovely, around the hotel patio, but the food lacks subtlety. It will fill you up though: great hunks of meat or a whole partridge with a smattering of chips.

Rincón de Carmen, C/Romero 4, **t** 957 29 10 55. Family-run, noisy and full of atmosphere. The local dishes are prepared as well as at any establishment in the city, and the prices are low. It also has a very pleasant (and slightly more peaceful) café attached.

Bar Restaurante Millan, Av. Doctor Fleming 14, **t** 957 29 09 19. Close to the Alcázar, and defiantly non-touristy despite its location, this restaurant serves up a good selection of tapas as well as full meals, including house specials, *merluza al jerez* and *rape millan*, and *churrascos* and *barbacoas*.

El Somontano, Pza del Escudo, **t** 957 48 65 54, *joseansg@eremas.com*. A modern place way off the tourist trail in the new part of town, serving a fine selection of reasonably priced fare, including lamb, rabbit and venison.

Inexpensive

Córdoba is famous for its *bodegas* and there are a number dotted around the city.

El Tablón, Cardenal González 79, **t** 957 47 60 61. Just around the corner from La Mezquita, this characterful restaurant offers one of the best bargains in the city, with a choice of *menús del día* or *platos combinados*, glass of wine included.

Los Patios, C/Cardenal Herrero 18. The best of several good options on C/Cardenal Herrero, right by the Mezquita.

Bodega Guzman, C/Judios 7. Another good *bodega* worth seeking out; this one is a shrine to bullfighting with a collection of memorabilia inside.

Bodegón Rafaé, on the corner of C/Deanes and Buen Pastor. Take it or leave it, this place has true *bodega* food and atmosphere. Sausages drape from barrels, religious figurines hang next to fake bulls' heads, the radio and TV are on simultaneously; *cola de toro* with a glass of wine at one of the vinyl-topped tables will cost next to nothing.

Taberna San Miguel, Pza San Miguel 1. Better known as El Pisto, or the barrel, this is perhaps the best-known drinking hole in Córdoba. It's a big old barn of a place serving good honest tapas, with lots of little rooms and *montilla*.

Entertainment

Córdoba is the birthplace of Paco Peña – one of Spain's most famous modern flamenco maestros. Paco Peña is part of a long tradition of Córdoba flamenco and the city is a good place to catch some great players and dancers in more authentic venues than, say, Sevilla. June is the best time to visit, during the guitar festival, when flourishes and trills drift out of every other room in Córdoba's White Neighbourhood and there are several concerts every night. At other times, wait until midnight and then head for one of the secluded little flamenco bars tucked away throughout the city. These include:

Peña Flamenca Fostorito, C/Ocaña 4 (near the Pza de San Agustín).

Peña Flamenca Las Orejas Negras, Av. Carlos III 18 (in Fatima Barrio).

Tablao Cardenal, C/Torrijos 10 (strategically positioned next to the tourist office).

Though flamenco may be more authentic in Córdoba than in Sevilla, the **nightlife** is less lively. The most popular bars with locals are the street bars (*terrazas*) in **Barrio Jardín**, on the Av. de Republica end of Camino de los Sastrés. **Barrio El Brillante**, northwest of the Pza Colon is full of upper-middle class Spanish in the summer, particularly the clubs and bars around **Plaza El Tablero**.

belltower. From the courtyard, the mosque is entered through a little door, the **Puerta de las Palmas**, where they'll sell you a ticket and tell you to take off your hat.

Now here is the first surprise. The building is gloomy only because the Spanish clerics wanted it that way. Originally there was no wall separating the mosque from the courtyard, and that side of the mosque was entirely open. In the **courtyard**, trees were planted to continue the rows of columns, translating inside to outside in a remarkable *tour de force* that has rarely been equalled in architecture. To add to the effect, the entrances along the other three walls would have been open to the surrounding busy markets and streets. It isn't just a trick of architecture, but a way of relating a holy building to the life of the city around it. In Turkey they call them 'forest' mosques, and the townspeople use them like parks, places to sit and reflect or talk over everyday affairs. In medieval Christian cathedrals, where the doors were always open, it was much the same. The sacred and the secular become blurred; the latter elevated to a higher plane. In Córdoba, this principle is perfected.

In the aesthetics of this mosque, too, there is more than meets the eye. Many European writers have seen it as devoid of spirituality, a plain prayer-hall with pretty arches. To the Christian mind it is difficult to comprehend. Christian churches are modelled after the Roman basilica, a government hall, a seat of authority with a long central aisle designed to humble the suppliant as he approaches the praetor's throne (altar). Mosques are designed to free the mind from such behaviour patterns. In this one, the guiding principle is a rarefied abstraction – the same kind of abstraction that governs Islamic geometric decoration. The repetition of columns is like a meditation in stone, a mirror of Creation where unity and harmony radiate from innumerable centres. Another contrast with Christian churches can be found in the distribution of weight. The Gothic masters of the Middle Ages learned to pile stone upwards from great piers and buttresses to amazing heights, so as to build an edifice that aspires to heaven. Córdoba's architects amplified the height of their mosque only modestly by a daring invention: adding a second tier of arches on top of the first. They had to, constrained as they were by the short columns they were recycling from Roman buildings, but the result was to make an 'upside-down' building, where weight increases the higher it goes, a play of balance and equilibrium that adds much to the mosque's effect. There are about 580 of these columns, mostly from Roman ruins and Visigothic churches the Muslims pulled down; originally, legend credits La Mezquita with a thousand. Some came from as far as Constantinople, a present from the emperors. The same variety can be seen in the capitals – Roman, Visigothic, Moorish and a few mysteries.

The *Mihrab* and Later Additions

The surviving jewel of the mosque is its *mihrab*, added in the 10th century under al-Hakim II, an octagonal chamber set into the wall and covered by a beautiful dome of interlocking arches. A Byzantine emperor, Nikephoras Phokas, sent artists to help with its mosaic decoration, accompanied by a few tons of enamel chips and coloured glass cubes. Though the *mihrab* is no longer at the centre of La Mezquita, it was at the time of al-Hakim II; the aisle extending from it was the axis of the original mosque.

Looking back from the *mihrab*, you will see what was once the exterior wall, built in Abd ar-Rahman II's extension, from the year 848. Its gates are as good as those on the west façade, and better preserved. Near the *mihrab* is the **Capilla de Villaviciosa**, a Christian addition of 1377 with convoluted *mudéjar* arches that almost succeed in upstaging the Moorish work. Behind it is a small chapel, usually closed off. Luckily, you can see most of the **Capilla Real** above the barriers; its exuberant stucco and *azulejo* decoration are among the greatest works of *mudéjar* art. Built in the 14th century as a funeral chapel for Ferdinand IV and Alfonso XI of Castile, it is contemporary with the Alhambra and shows some influence of the styles developing in Granada. Far more serious intrusions are the 16th-century **Coro** (choir) and **Capilla Mayor** (high altar). Not unlovely in themselves, they would not offend anywhere but here. Fortunately, La Mezquita is so large that from many parts of it you won't even notice them. Begun in 1523, the Plateresque Coro was altered in the 18th century, with additional stucco decoration, as well as a set of Baroque choir stalls by Pedro Duque Cornejo. Between the Coro and Capilla Mayor is the **tomb of Leopold of Austria**, Bishop of Córdoba when the works were completed (and Charles V's uncle). The rest of the Christian contribution is comprised of dozens of locked, mouldering chapels lining the outer walls of the mosque. Never comfortable as a Christian building, today the cathedral seems to be hardly used, and regular Sunday masses are generally relegated to a small corner of the building.

Around La Mezquita

The tatty souvenir stands and third-rate cafés that surround La Mezquita on its busiest days unwittingly do their best to re-create the atmosphere of the Moorish *souks* that once thrived here, but walk a block in any direction and you'll enter the essential Córdoba: brilliant whitewashed lanes with glimpses into dreamily beautiful patios, each one a floral extravaganza. One of the best is **Calle de las Flores** ('street of the flowers') just a block northeast of La Mezquita, although sadly its charms are diminished by hordes of tourists.

Below La Mezquita, along the Guadalquivir, the melancholic plaza called **Puerta del Puente** marks the site of Córdoba's southern gate with a decorative **arch** put up in 1571, celebrating the reign of Philip II. Behind it, standing across from La Mezquita, is the **Archbishop's Palace**, built on the site of the original Alcázar.

The **Roman bridge** over the Guadalquivir has been patched and repaired so often that it probably isn't Roman at all any more. The stern-looking **Calahorra Tower** (***t*** *957 29 39 29; museum open daily 10.30–6*), built in 1369, once guarded the southern approaches of the bridge; now it contains a small **museum** of Córdoba's history.

Just to the west, along the river, Córdoba's **Alcázar de los Reyes Cristianos** affords a good view of La Mezquita and the town from the belvedere atop the walls. The **gardens** (*open daily 10 till dusk*) are peaceful and lovely, and the gigantic stone figures of Columbus and the Catholic Kings are impressive. If you continue walking along the Guadalquivir, you'll come to Parque Cruz Conde and the new **Córdoba zoo** (*currently being renovated; check at the tourist office for an update*).

The Judería

How lovely is Thy dwelling-place O Lord of Hosts!
My soul grows weak and longs for Thy courtyards.

Hebrew inscription on synagogue wall

As in Sevilla, Córdoba's ancient Jewish quarter has recently become a fashionable area, a nest of tiny streets between La Mezquita and Av. Dr Fleming. Part of the Moorish walls can be seen along this street, and the northern entrance of the Judería is the old **Almodóvar gate**. The streets are tricky, and it will take some effort to find C/Maimonides and the 14th-century **synagogue** (*t 957 20 29 28; open Tues–Sat 10–1.30 and 3.30–5.30, Sun 10–1.30; closed Mon*), after which you will find yourself repeatedly back at this spot, whether or not you want to be there.

The diminutive Córdoban synagogue is one of the two oldest and most interesting Jewish monuments in Spain (the other is the Tránsito in Toledo, *see* p.569). Set back from the street in a tiny courtyard, it was built in the Granadine style of the early 14th century and, according to Amador de los Rios, dates from 1315. There is an interesting plasterwork frieze of Alhambra-style arabesques and Hebrew inscriptions. The recess for the Ark (which contained the holy scrolls) is clearly visible, and the ladies' gallery still intact. Despite few obvious signs of the synagogue's original function, its atmosphere is still charged. While modern Córdoba has no active Jewish community, several *marrano* families live in the city and can trace their ancestry to the pre-expulsion age.

On Pza Maimonides is the **Museo Municipal de Arte Cordobés y Taurino** (*t 957 20 10 56; open Tues–Sat 10–2 and 4.30–6.30, Sun 9.30–2.30; closed Mon; adm*), a museum dedicated to bullfighting. Manolete and El Cordobés are the city's recent contributions to Spanish culture; here you can see a replica of Manolete's sarcophagus and the hide of Islero, the bull that did him in, along with more bullfight memorabilia than you ever thought existed.

White Neighbourhoods

From the mosque you can walk eastwards through well over a mile of twisting white alleys, a place where the best map in the world wouldn't keep you from getting lost and staying lost. Though it all looks much the same, it's never monotonous. Every little square, fountain or church stands out boldly, and forces you to look at it in a way different from how you would look at a modern city – another lesson in the Moorish aesthetic. These streets have probably changed little since 1236, but their best buildings are a series of **Gothic churches** built soon after the Reconquista. Though small and plain, most are exquisite in a quiet way. Few have any of the usual Gothic sculptural work on their façades, in order to avoid offending a people accustomed to Islam's prohibition of images. **San Lorenzo**, on C/María Auxiliadora, is perhaps the best, with a rose window designed in a common Moorish motif of interlocking circles. Have a look inside any others you find open; most have some Moorish decoration or sculptural work and many of their towers were originally minarets.

The neighbourhoods have other surprises, if you have the persistence to find them. On Pza Jerónimo Páez, a fine 16th-century palace houses the **National Archaeological Museum**, (*t 957 47 10 76; open Tues–Sat 9–8, Sun 9–3; closed Mon*), the largest in Andalucía, with Roman mosaics, a two-faced idol of Janus, and an unusual icon of the Persian *torero*-god Mithras; also some Moorish art from the age of the caliphate, Moorish-looking early Christian art, and early funeral steles with odd hieroglyphs.

East of the C/San Fernando, the wide street that bisects the old quarter, the houses are more run down than those around La Mezquita, which does not detract from their charm. The **Plaza de la Corredera** is modelled on the famous Plazas Mayores of Madrid and Salamanca, but was never completed. Continuing south, the **Museo de Bellas Artes**, (*t 957 47 33 45; open Tues–Sat 9–8, Sun 9–3*) is on the lovely Plaza del Potro; its collections include works of Valdés Leal, Ribera, Murillo and Zurbarán, two royal portraits by Goya, and works by Córdoban artists of the 15th and 16th centuries. Eastwards from here, the crooked alleys continue for almost a mile, as far as the surviving stretch of **Moorish walls** along Ronda del Marrubial.

Around Plaza de las Tendillas

The centre of Roman Corduba has, by chance, become the centre of the modern city. Córdoba is probably the slickest and most up-to-date city in Andalucía (Sevilla would beg to differ), and it shows in this busy district of crowded pavements, modern shops, cafés and wayward youth. The contrast with the old neighbourhoods is startling, but just a block off the plaza on C/Gondomar the beautiful 15th-century **Church of San Nicolás** will remind you that you're still in Córdoba.

In the other direction, well-preserved remains of a collapsed **Roman temple** have been discovered on C/Nueva. The city has been at work reassembling the walls and columns and already the front pediment is partially complete.

A few blocks north of Pza de las Tendillas, across Pza de Colón, is the Rococo **Convento de Merced** (1745), an enormous building that has recently been restored to house the provincial government and often hosts cultural exhibitions on various subjects. Don't miss it. The façade has been redone in its original painted *esgrafiado*, almost decadently colourful in pink and green, and the courtyards and grand staircases inside are incredible – more a palace than a monastery.

Medinat az-Zahra

Open Tues–Sat 10–2 and 4–6.30, Sun 10–2; closed Mon;
***t** 957 23 40 25 (check summer hours with the tourist office).*

Eight kilometres northwest of the centre of Córdoba, Caliph Abd ar-Rahman III began to build a palace in the year 936. The undertaking soon got out of hand and, with the almost infinite resources of the caliphate to play with, he and his successors turned Medinat az-Zahra ('city of the Flower', after one of Abd ar-Rahman's wives) into a city in itself, with a market, mosques, schools and gardens, a place where the last caliphs could live in isolation from the world. The scale of it is pure *Arabian Nights*.

Stories were told of its African menageries, its interior pillars and domes of crystal, and curtains of falling water for walls; another fountain was filled with flowing mercury. Such carrying-on must have aroused a good deal of resentment; in the disturbances that put an end to the caliphate, Medinat az-Zahra was sacked and razed by Berber troops in 1013. After serving as a quarry for 900 years it's surprising anything is left at all. But in 1944 the royal apartments were discovered, with enough fragments to permit the restoration of a few arches with floral decorations.

North of Córdoba

The N432 out of Córdoba leads north to the Sierra Morena, the string of hills that curtain western Andalucía from Extremadura, Castilla and La Mancha. This area is the **Valle de los Pedroches**, fertile grazing land for pigs, sheep and goats and an important hunting area for deer and wild boar. This is also healthy hiking territory, but keep yourself visible – you don't want to be mistaken for someone's supper.

A road winds 73 kilometres up to **Bélmez**, with its Moorish castle perilously perched on a rock, from which there are panoramic views over the surrounding arid countryside. **Peñarroya-Pueblonuevo** is a dull industrial town that has fallen into decline, but is useful here as a reference point.

Getting Around

Although there are **buses** that run from Córdoba up into the Sierra Morena and villages of Los Pedroches, they are infrequent and very time-consuming. To really explore, you need a **car**.

Where to Stay and Eat

North of Córdoba there's no de-luxe accommodation, but the area has a reasonably wide selection of one- and two-star hotels.

****San Francisco**, Ctra Villanueva de la Serena–Andújar, Km129, **t** 957 10 14 35 (*moderate*). A quiet place in a listed building with tennis; just 2½km from Pozoblanco.

*****Finca del Rio**, near Badajoz, **t** 924 63 66 01, **f** 924 63 67 70 (*inexpensive*). This old *cortijo* on the borders of Badajoz has been converted into a lovely hotel with all the amenities, including a pool. *Open summer only, but at a very reasonable rates.*

****Sierra de Cardeña**, C/Modesto Aguilera 29, off the main square in Cardeña, **t/f** 957 17 44 55 (*inexpensive*). Offers decent rooms and a **restaurant**.

Hs Javi, C/Córdoba 31, Bélmez, **t** 957 57 30 99, **f** 957 58 04 98 (*cheap*). An excellent value *hostal* in Bélmez which has sparkling modern rooms of hotel quality with TV, minibar and large bathrooms, set round a delightful vine-covered staircase; with parking and a pretty patio.

La Bolera, C/Padre Torrero 17, Belalcazar, **t** 957 14 63 00 (*cheap*). A basic place in Belalcázar; food is available in the numerous bars around the main square.

This area is famed throughout Andalucía for its *jamón ibérico* (locally cured ham) and suckling pig; the excellent *salchichón* from Pozoblanco; and the strong, spicy cheese made from ewes' milk. Sadly there are no outstanding restaurants around, and even indifferent ones are pretty thin on the ground. To be sure of eating really well you should head for the village tapas bars or, better still, grab some goodies from a supermarket and have a picnic on the slopes.

Bar Lucas, Pza de la Independencia, in Cardeña (*inexpensive*). A good place to eat and drink, with a very reasonably priced menu.

Gran, C/Córdoba. The best restaurant in Bélmez. *Closed Mon.*

It's well worth making the trip 40 kilometres north of Peñarroya to **Belalcázar** and one of the most extraordinary castles in Andalucía. El Castillo de Sotomayor stands just outside the village and bears down on it like some malevolent force. Set on an outcrop of rock and built on the ruins of an old Moorish fortress, work began on the castle early in the 15th century. A palace was added in the 16th century, but its dominant feature is the 150ft-high Torre del Homenaje, with wonderfully ornate carvings.

Beyond the villages of **Villanueva de Córdoba** and **Cardeña** to the east is the **Parque Natural de Sierra Cardeña**: rolling hills forested in oak, more stag-hunting grounds and ideal rambling terrain.

South of Córdoba

This is the heart of Andalucía, a vast tract of bountiful hills covered in olive groves and vines. The area is more densely populated and a bit more prosperous than most of the region's rural districts. The towns are closer together, all white, and all punctuated by the warm sandstone of their palaces and towers. It's a region few tourists enter, and the way should take you on a properly Spanish *picaresque* journey detailed with flamingos, dolmens, Rococo frippery, memorabilia of Julius Caesar, a cask of *amontillado*, a pretty fair canyon, and 139 gargoyles.

Tourist Information

Priego de Córdoba: in Casa Museo A. Zamorá, C/Rio 33, **t** 957 70 06 25 (*open Tues–Sat 10–1.30 and 5–7.30, Sun 10–1; closed Mon*).

Cabra: C/Santa Rosalia 2, **t** 957 52 01 10, *www.cabra.net* (*open Mon–Fri 10–1.30 and 6–8, Sat and Sun 10–1.30*).

Lucena: in the Castillo Moral, Pza Nueva 1, **t** 957 51 32 82 (*open Mon–Fri 9–2 and 6–9, Sat, Sun and hols 11–2 and 7–9*).

Baena: in the Casa del Tercia, Pza de la Constitución, **t** 957 67 19 46.

Montilla: in the Casa del Inca, Capitán Alonso de Vargas 3, **t** 957 65 24 62 (*open Mon–Fri 10–2, Sat and Sun 11–2*).

Festivals

Lucena: Festival de las Tres Culturas.
Jazz festival, *end of May*;
Piano Festival, *Aug*. Around the castle.

Where to Stay and Eat

Many of the villages can offer basic accommodation and food, usually in the *cheap* range. Below is a selection of some of the more unusual options.

Priego de Córdoba ✉ 14800

★★★**Villa Turistica de Priego**, 7km beyond Priego de Córdoba towards Zagrilla, **t** 957 70 35 03, **f** 957 70 35 73, *alonatur@arrakis.es* (*moderate*). Set in its own very pretty grounds with a pool and tennis courts and numerous other activities on offer.

P. Rafi, C/Isabel la Catolica 4, **t** 957 54 07 49, **f** 957 54 07 49, *hotelrafi@arrakis.es* (*cheap*). A good budget option in Priego de Córdoba itself, with mod cons like satellite TV and phone; **restaurant** attached.

Posada La Niña Margarita, in Los Villares (5km from Carcabuey on the road towards Rute), **t** 957 70 40 54 (*cheap*). A real rural retreat set in a small valley of streams and olive groves; you can rent a cottage or stay in the Posada itself. There is a **restaurant** attached.

El Alijbe, Pza Abad Palomino 7, **t** 957 70 18 56 (*moderate*). A pleasant place to eat, with a pretty terrace, good tapas and full meals.

Lucena ✉ 14900

★★★★**Santo Domingo**, C/El Agua 12, **t** 957 51 11 00, **f** 957 51 62 95 (*expensive–moderate*).

The Cordobés Subbética and La Campiña

Here in the heartland of Andalucía lies the **Parque Natural de las Sierras Subbéticas de Córdoba**, a succession of wooded hills that dip into the valleys of the rivers Zagrillo, Salado and Caicena. The landscape of oak trees, olive groves and much shrubland is home to eagles and vultures, rabbit and partridge, adders, bats and badgers; the rivers and small lakes dotted around brim with bass, perch and trout.

Priego de Córdoba is set at the foot of **La Tiñosa**, the highest mountain in the province, and has a famous ensemble of Baroque churches, monasteries and fountains; the best is the **Asunción** church (*open summer Tues–Sun 11–2 and 5.30–8; winter Tues–Sun 10.30–1.30 and 4–7; closed Mon*) with a sumptuous stucco interior and, in its Sagrario chapel (designed by Francisco Javier Pedrejas), perhaps the finest example of Baroque indulgence in all of Andalucía. Behind the church lies the prettiest part of town, **Barrio de la Villa**, a maze of tiny winding streets bedecked with pot plants and little squares. The town's other pride is the Baroque **Fuente del Rey**, set at the end of C/Río: three connecting fountain pools lined with 139 gargoyles, and a centrepiece of Neptune and Aphrodite on a horse-drawn carriage.

To the west, **Cabra** is right at the centre of Andalucía, fittingly set in a sea of olive groves and vineyards, with a sweeping view of both the Sierra Nevada and the Guadalquivir valley. Ten kilometres south of here, on the C340, is **Lucena**, one of

Part of the Husa chain and set in a former palace, this has all the four-star amenities, except a pool, at very good prices.

★★**Los Bronces**, on the Cordoba–Malaga road, **t** 957 51 62 80, **f** 957 50 09 12 (*moderate–inexpensive*). This claims to be a *pensión* but has an extraordinary range of facilities including a pool, TVs and phones, a lift and a very good **restaurant** to boot.

P. Sara, C/Cabrillana 49, **t** 957 51 61 51 (*cheap*). Perfectly good rooms, all en suite and clean, and a good pizzeria **restaurant** below.

Lucena has quite a lively **nightlife** with a number of bars, pubs and tea rooms, many of them on and around the main square. The *turismo* even supplies a *Ruta de la Tapa*, a bit like a pub crawl but with food.

Baena ✉ 14850

★★★**La Casa Grande**, Av. Cervantes 35 (Baena), **t** 957 67 19 05, **f** 957 69 21 89, *www.lacasagrande.es* (*moderate*). In a sympathetically restored old mansion, this has good-sized rooms and a fine **restaurant** attached.

★★**Iponuba**, C/Nicolás Alcalá 7 (Baena), **t** 957 67 00 75, **f** 957 69 07 02, *iponuba@interbook.es* (*moderate*). Comfortable, central and with a **café** attached.

★★**Rincón**, Llano Rincón 13 (Baena), **t** 957 67 02 23 (*cheap*). This *hostal* is the budget option; situated near the town centre.

Casa del Monte, Pza de la Constitución (in the *almacen*). Baena is limited if you want to eat out. This place is probably your best bet.

Huerta de San Rafael, Ctra Badajoz–Granada (in Luque), **t** 957 66 74 97. A real boon for this area, serving regional specialities at give-away prices.

Montilla ✉ 14550

★★★**Don Gonzalo**, Ctra Madrid–Málaga, Km447, **t** 957 65 06 58, **f** 957 65 06 66 (*moderate*). Part of the Husa chain, on the main road outside town, with gardens, pool and tennis court.

Finca Buytrón, **t** 957 65 01 52, **f** 957 65 01 52, *www.seneca-web.com* (*inexpensive*). Lies about 3km from Montilla, and dates from the 16th century. It has eight double rooms (four en suite), a large kitchen, pool, library and an open fire.

Las Camachas, Ctra Madrid–Málaga, **t** 957 65 00 44, **f** 957 65 03 32 (*expensive*). This restaurant has been awarded various medals for its cuisine: wash down tasty fish dishes with a glass or two of the local brew.

the centres of a great wine-growing region, known for making the biggest wine barrels in Andalucía. Nearby are the remains of the **Tower of Moral** (now home to the tourist office and a small archaeological museum), where Granada's last king, Boabdil el Chico, was imprisoned by Fernando in 1483.

From Cabra the A316 heads northeast to **Baena**, a town of major importance in Moorish times, now squeezing out olive oil in remarkable quantities. A clean, tightly packed town with narrow, whitewashed streets, Baena sees most of its visitors arrive for the Holy Week celebrations, when a deafening drum-rolling competition is held to see who can play the longest and the loudest; it lasts *two days*.

Twenty-two kilometres northwest from Cabra is **Aguilar de la Frontera**, and from there it's a short hop to the prince of the wine-producing towns, **Montilla**, sitting on a rise amidst endless acres of vines. Although *amontillado*, a pale dry sherry, takes its name from this town, the wine produced here is not a sherry, in that no extra alcohol is added to fortify it, unlike in Jerez. The town is refreshingly short of Baroque churches, but its *bodegas* can be visited to sample the good stuff.

From Córdoba to Úbeda

In this section of the Guadalquivir valley the river rises into the heights of the Sierra Morena; endless rolling hills covered with neat rows of olive trees and small farms make a memorable Andalucían landscape. The three large towns along the way, Andújar, Bailén and Linares, are much alike; amiable, industrial towns still painted a gleaming white.

The Gateway to Andalucía

This area is Andalucía's front door, where the roads and railways from Madrid branch off for Sevilla and Granada. Many important battles were fought nearby, including Las Navas de Tolosa near La Carolina, in 1212, which opened the way for the conquest of al-Andalus; and Bailén, in 1808, where a Spanish-English force gave Napoleon's boys a sound thrashing and built up Spanish morale for what they call their War of Independence.

The N-IV snakes along the Guadalquivir valley, and 42 kilometres east of Córdoba it brings you to the delightfully placed town of **Montoro**, sitting on a bend in the river. The facetious-looking tower that rises above the whitewashed houses belongs to the Gothic church of **San Bartolomé** in Pza de España. Also in the square is the 16th-century **Ducal Palace**, now the *ayuntamiento*, with a Plateresque façade. The beautiful 15th-century bridge that connects Montoro to its suburb, Retamar, is known as the **Puente de Las Doñadas**, a tribute to the women of the village who sacrificed their jewellery to help finance its construction. Seek out the kitsch **Casa de las Conchas** (*C/Criado 17, signposted from Pza de España*), a house and courtyard decked out in hundreds of thousands of sea shells.

Approaching **Andújar**, a further 35 kilometres down the N-IV, you'll find the countryside dominated by huge, blue sunflower-oil refineries like fallen space stations.

Tourist Information

Montoro: Pza de España 8, **t** 957 16 00 89 (*open Mon, Wed, Fri 8.30–3, Tues and Thurs 10–2 and 5–6.30, Sat 10–1; closed Sun*).

Andújar: Torre del Reloj/Pza Santa Maria s/n, **t** 953 50 02 79, *andujar_turismo@terra.es* (*open Tue–Sat 10–2 and 5–8; closed Mon and Sun*).

Festivals

Andújar: Romería, *last Sun in April*. On the Thursday, Andújarans in traditional dress layer the ground outside the Capilla del Virgen de la Cabeza with flowers. On Friday the streets fill with people parading in costume on horseback. The pilgrimage proper begins early on Saturday; pilgrims stop halfway for a giant picnic, before arriving at the sanctuary that night where an hourly mass begins. On Sunday the Virgin is brought out and paraded down the hill, where various objects – including children – are thrown at her to be blessed.

Where to Stay and Eat

Andújar ✉ 23740

*****Gran Hotel Balneario**, Calvario 101 (10km outside Andújar at Marmolejo), **t** 953 54 09 75, **f** 953 51 74 33 (*moderate*). Probably the area's best, with a pool and its own grounds.

****Don Pedro**, C/Gabriel Zamora 5, **t** 953 50 12 74, **f** 953 50 47 85 (*inexpensive*). The best place in Andújar itself, in the centre of town, with pleasant rooms and a tavern-style **restaurant** that specializes in game dishes (*moderate*). It also has a disco attached.

La Fuente, C/Vendederas, **t** 953 50 42 69, **f** 953 50 19 00 (*inexpensive*). Clean and friendly with a garage and a good **restaurant**.

Restaurante Madrid–Sevilla, Pza del Sol 4, **t** 953 50 05 94 (*expensive*). Patronized by the King and Queen of Spain, and so called for its position on the old road. It's a favourite with the hunting fraternity, as well as the royals. Fresh fish is brought in daily and game features heavily on the menu, which changes according to Sr Sotoca's mood. Choose what you want and he'll whip out to the kitchen to create it for you himself, while you choose from an extraordinary wine selection from all over the country.

Las Perolas, C/Serpiente 6, **t** 953 50 67 26 (*inexpensive*). Another great character, Ana Domínguez, runs this restaurant. She cooks up all her specials – venison, rabbit and quail – in big pots which sit steaming on the bar.

Baños de la Encina ✉ 23710

*****Hotel Baños** C/Cerro Llamada s/n, **t** 953 61 40 68 (*moderate*). The only hotel in town; neat and newly opened.

Mesón Buenos Aires, Cateyana, **t** 953 61 32 11. A reliable restaurant with good country fare, including wild boar and venison in season.

La Encina, Consultorio 3, **t** 953 61 40 98 (*inexpensive*). Has views of the castle and does a good *menú*.

Mesón del Duque, **t** 953 61 30 26 (*inexpensive*) At the top of town, opposite the Ermita Jesús del Llano; its grand name belies its simple, reasonably priced country cooking.

Andújar, Baños de la Encina and Linares all offer a few **bars** suitable for a late-night *copa* or two. There's usually a village discothèque and it's worth asking in the bars about flamenco, too.

Nothing remains of Andújar's Moorish castle, but there are a couple of surprises; the church of **Santa María**, in the plaza of the same name, has in one chapel the *Immaculate Conception* by Pacheco, Velázquez's teacher; and in another the magnificent *Christ in the Garden of Olives*, by El Greco. Thirty kilometres north of here, the **Santuario de la Virgen de la Cabeza** (*see* 'Festivals', above) is a fine spot for a picnic.

Back on the N-IV, 27 kilometres further east is the modern, unprepossessing town of **Bailén**, but don't dally here; the real treat is to be found 11 kilometres north on the N-IV at **Baños de la Encina**, where the 10th-century oval Moorish castle is one of the best preserved in all Andalucía. Dominating the town, the **castle** (*no set opening* *hours; enquire at the turismo,* **t** *953 61 41 85, for the key*) has 14 sturdy, square towers and a double-horseshoe gateway, scarcely touched by time, and from the walls you get a sweeping vista of the olive groves and distant peaks beyond Úbeda.

From Bailén the N322 heads eastward to the mining town of **Linares**, where in 1947 the great bullfighter Manolete had an off day and met his end on the horns of a bull in the ring. A further 27 kilometres will take you to Úbeda; a little more than halfway you'll pass an elegant castle at **Canena**.

Baeza

Campo de Baeza, soñaré contigo cuando no te vea
(Fields of Baeza, I will dream of you when I can no longer see you)

Antonio Machado (1875–1939)

Sometimes history offers its recompense. The 13th-century Reconquista was especially brutal here; nearly the entire population fled, many of them moving to Granada, where they settled the Albaicín. The 16th century, however, when the wool trade was booming in this corner of Andalucía, was good to Baeza, leaving it a distinguished little town of neatly clipped trees and tan stone buildings. It seems a happy place, serene as the olive groves that surround it.

The prettiest corner of the town is **Plaza del Pópulo**. It is enclosed by decorative pointed arches and Renaissance buildings, and contains a fountain with four half-effaced lions.

Heading north on the Cuesta de San Felipe, which can be reached by the steps leading off Pza del Pópulo, you pass the 15th-century **Palacio de Jabalquinto** (*open Thurs–Tues 10–2 and 4–6; closed Wed*), built by the Benavides family with an eccentric façade covered with coats-of-arms and pyramidal stone studs. Its patio (*open Mon–Fri 9–2*) boasts a beautiful two-tiered arcade around a central fountain, as well as a fine, carved Baroque staircase. Adjoining the *palacio*, the 16th-century **Antigua Universidad** was a renowned centre of learning for three hundred years, until its charter was withdrawn during the reign of Ferdinand VII. It has since been used as a school; its indoor patio, too, is open to the public (*open Thurs–Tues 10–2 and 4–6; closed Wed*). The school has found latterday fame through Antonio Machado, the *sevillano* poet who taught there (1913–19).

A right turn at the next corner leads to the 16th-century **Cathedral of Santa Iglesia** (*open winter Thurs–Tues 10.30–1 and 4–6; summer Thurs–Tues 10.30–1 and 5–7; closed Wed*) on Pza Santa María, a work of Andrés de Vandelvira. This replaced a 13th-century Gothic church (of which the chancel and portal survive), which in turn took the place of a mosque. Drop a coin in the box marked *custodia* in one of the side chapels; with a noisy dose of mechanical *duende*, a rich and ornate 18th-century silver tabernacle will be revealed. The fountain in front of the cathedral, the **Fuente de Santa María**, with a little triumphal arch at its centre (1564), is Baeza's landmark and symbol. Behind it is the Isabelline Gothic **Casas Consistoriales**, formerly the town hall, while opposite stands the 16th-century seminary of **San Felipe Neri**, its walls adorned with student graffiti – recording their names and dates in bull's blood.

The **Paseo de la Constitución**, at the bottom of the hill, is Baeza's main thoroughfare, an elegant rectangle lined with crumbling shops and bars. Two buildings are worthy of note: **La Alhóndiga**, the 16th-century, porticoed corn exchange and, almost opposite, the **Casa Consistorial**, the 18th-century town hall. Just behind the *paseo*, in Pza Cardinal Benavides, the façade of the **Ayuntamiento** (1599) is a classic example of Andalucían Plateresque. At the end of the *paseo*, the inelegant Plaza de España marks the northern boundary of historic Baeza and houses yet more bars.

Getting Around

By Train

Come to Baeza by train at your own risk. The nearest station, officially named Linares-Baeza, **t** 953 65 02 02, is far off in the open countryside, 14km away. A bus to Baeza usually meets the train, but if you turn up at night or on a Sunday you may be stranded.

By Bus

Baeza's bus station, **t** 953 74 04 68, is a little way from the centre on Av. Alcalde Puche Pardo. Baeza is a stop on the Úbeda–Córdoba bus route, with 12 a day running to Jaén (1½ hrs); eight to Granada (2 hrs); two to Cazorla and one to Málaga (4–5 hrs).

Tourist Information

Baeza: Pza del Pópulo (also known as Pza de los Leones), **t** 953 74 04 44 (*open Mon–Fri 9–2.30, Sat 10–1; closed Sun*).

Internet Access: Speed Informática, Pso de la Constitución, **t** 953 74 70 05.

Where to Stay and Eat

Baeza ✉ 23440

***Hotel Palacete Santa Ana**, C/Santa Ana Vieja 9, **t** 953 74 07 65, **f** 953 74 16 57 (*moderate*). A lavishly restored noble palace where politicians and leading *toreros* seek privacy – the closest thing you'll get to stepping back into the 18th century. There are just 14 bedrooms, reached by a marble staircase, all of them different and stuffed full of original mirrors, paintings and sculptures, but with all mod cons. There are two dining rooms, two living rooms, an indoor and outdoor patio, a *terraza* on the roof and a cellar below where *dueña* Ana Maria Rodriguez organizes private flamenco shows. The attention to detail is extraordinary and the price for such splendour a giveaway. There is also a nearby **restaurant** connected to the hotel.

***Hotel Confortel Baeza**, C/Concepción 3, **t** 953 74 81 30, **f** 953 74 25 19, *comerbaeza@ctv.es* (*moderate*). The second-best choice, behind the Iglesia del Hospital de la Purísima Concepción near Pza de España. The hotel is set in a monasterial building with rooms opening on to a peaceful arched quadrangle.

***Complejo Turistico Hacienda La Laguna**, on the Ctra Jaén–Puente del Obispo, **t** 953 12 71 72, **f** 953 12 71 74 (*moderate*). A delightful rural hotel in an old *cortijo* with lots of activities and amenities for kids and adults.

P. El Patio, C/Conde Romanones 13, **t** 953 74 02 00 (*cheap*). This Renaissance mansion arranged around a courtyard is a good budget bet.

Andrés de Vandelvira, C/San Francisco 14, **t** 953 74 43 61 (*expensive*). A restaurant inside the San Francisco convent with tables filling the arched quadrangle; for more intimacy, dine upstairs. *Closed Sun afternoons.*

La Gondola, Portales Carbonería 13, **t** 953 74 29 84 (*moderate*). Set back from the main *paseo*, with an emphasis on heavy meats and *churrascos*.

Sali, C/Cardenal Benavides 15, **t** 953 74 13 65 (*moderate*). Fish and shellfish feature with game dishes like partridge in brine; situated opposite the town hall. *Closed Wed.*

Casa Pedro, C/Cardenal Benavides, **t** 953 74 80 87 (*inexpensive*). Next door to Sali; this has a cheap *menú*.

Úbeda

Even with Baeza for an introduction, the presence of this nearly perfect little city comes as a surprise. If the 16th century did well by Baeza, it was a golden age here, leaving Úbeda a 'town built for gentlemen' as the Spanish used to say, endowed with one of the finest collections of Renaissance architecture in all of Spain. Two men can take much of the credit: Andrés de Vandelvira, an Andalucían architect who created most of Úbeda's best buildings, and Francisco de los Cobos, imperial secretary to Charles V, who paid for them. Cobos is a forgotten hero of Spanish history. While Charles was off campaigning in Germany, Cobos had the job of running Castile. By the most delicate management, he kept the kingdom afloat while meeting Charles' ever more exorbitant demands for money and men. He could postpone the inevitable disaster, but not prevent it. Like most public officials in the Spanish Age of Rapacity, though, he also managed to salt away a few hundred thousand ducats for himself, and he spent most of them embellishing his home town.

Like Baeza, Úbeda is a peaceful and happy place; it wears its Renaissance heritage gracefully, and is always glad to have visitors. Slowly, it's gearing up for them. Tourism is less of a novelty here than it was even a couple of years ago. But it's still easy to understand the Spanish expression '*irse por los cerros de Úbeda*' ('take the Úbeda hill routes'), which basically equates to getting off the subject or wasting time and arose many years ago after Úbeda gradually lost traffic to more commercial routes. Legend has it that a Christian knight fell in love with a Moorish girl and was reproached for his absence by King Ferdinand III. When questioned about his whereabouts during the battle the knight idly replied, 'Lost in those hills, sire'.

Úbeda today leaves no doubt how its local politics are going. In the **Plaza de Andalucía**, old and new districts join around an old metal statue of a fascist Civil War general named Sero glaring down from his pedestal. The townspeople have put so many bullets into it, it looks like a Swiss cheese. **The Torre de Reloj** is a 14th-century defensive tower now adorned with a clock. From here, C/Real takes you into the heart of the old town. Nearly every corner has a lovely palace or church on it. Two of the best can be seen on this street: the early 17th-century **Palacio de Condé Guadiana**, with an ornate tower and distinctive windows cut out of the corners of the building, and two blocks down, the **Palacio Vela de los Cobos** (*ask at the tourist office for opening hours*), in the same style, with a loggia on the top storey. The home of Francisco de los Cobos' nephew, another royal counsellor, was the great **Palacio de las Cadenas**, now serving as Úbeda's *ayuntamiento* and a small ceramics **museum** (*open Tues–Sat 10.30–2 and 5–7; closed Mon; adm*), at the end of C/Real. From this side it looks simple and dignified, but the main façade, facing the **Plaza Vázquez de Molina**, is a stately Renaissance creation, the work of Vandelvira.

Plaza Vázquez de Molina

This is the only place in Andalucía where you can look around and not regret the passing of the Moors, for it is one of the few truly beautiful things in this great region that was not built either by the Moors or under their influence. The Renaissance

Getting Around

Úbeda's **bus** station, C/San José, **t** 953 75 21 57, is at the western end of town, and various lines connect the city directly to Madrid, Valencia and Barcelona, at least once daily, and more frequently to Baeza, (16 daily, 20 mins), Córdoba (3 daily, 2½ hrs), Jaén (8 daily, 1½ hrs) Granada (2 daily, 2½ hrs) and Sevilla (3 daily). Cazorla and other villages in the region can easily be reached from Úbeda.

Tourist Information

Úbeda: Palacio Marques de Contadero, C/Baja del Marqués 4 (off Pza del Ayuntamiento), **t** 953 75 08 97 (*open Mon–Sat 8–3; closed Sun*).

Shopping

Traditional dark green **pottery**, fired in kilns over wood and olive stones, is Úbeda's trademark. You'll see it all over town – try to pick up some authentic pieces before they become available in Habitat. On Pza Ayuntamiento you'll find **Tito**, a class establishment that produces and fires pieces on the premises. The designs are exquisite and are packed and shipped all over the world. Otherwise, visit the potters' quarter around C/Valencia, a 15-minute stroll from the Pza Ayuntamiento.

Where to Stay and Eat

Úbeda ✉ 23400

******Parador Condestable Dávalos**, Pza de Vázquez de Molina s/n, **t** 953 75 03 45, **f** 953 75 12 59, *ubeda@parador.es* (*expensive*). In a 16th-century palace with a glassed-in courtyard, this is one of the loveliest and most popular *paradores*, and has been recently refurbished. All the beamed ceilings and fireplaces have been preserved and the **restaurant** (*moderate*) is the best in town (which isn't saying a lot), featuring local specialities. Ask to see the wine cellar.

****Palacio de la Rambla**, Pza del Marqués 1, **t** 953 75 01 96, **f** 953 75 02 67 (*expensive*). A romantic and slightly less expensive choice in the historic heart of the town, set in a magnificent ivy-clad Renaissance mansion with rooms surrounding an ivy-clad courtyard where the Marquesa de la Rambla lets out beautiful double rooms (ask for 106).

******Álvar Fáñez**, C/Juan Pasquau 5 (just off the Pza San Pedro), **t/f** 953 79 60 43 (*expensive*). Another recently converted ducal palace, with 11 tastefully decorated (albeit slightly austere) rooms, and a lovely *terraza* with views over the rooftops to the olive groves and the hills. The delightful patio looks as it did 400 years ago. There is also a **café** serving excellent tapas and a good **restaurant** in the cellar. The hotels organizes cultural and environmental excursions. Rates include breakfast.

*****María de Molina**, Pza del Ayuntamiento, s/n, **t** 953 79 53 56, **f** 953 79 36 94, *www.hotel-maria-de-molina.com* (*expensive–moderate*). Situated just behind the main square. The patio has been prettified a little too much, but the rooms have some original furniture and paintings, all with lovely bathrooms. Also has a café and very good **restaurant**: try the roasted kid leg or the deer loin.

****Sevilla**, Av. Ramón y Cajal 9, **t** 953 75 06 12 (*cheap*). You can get a clean and pleasant double with bath for very good rates here – a/c is extra.

Castillo, Av. Ramón y Cajal 20, **t** 953 75 06 12 (*cheap*). With a **café**, satellite TV and a/c.

Apart from the *parador*, there are few good **restaurants** in Úbeda.

Cuzco, Parque Vandelvira 8, **t** 953 75 34 13 (*inexpensive*). Serves local dishes and standard *andaluz* fish and meat menus. The very good-value *menú del día* includes two courses and wine.

El Gallo Rojo, Pza Torrenueva (at the top of C/Trinidad), **t** 953 75 20 38 (*inexpensive*). You'll find plenty of characters at the bar during the day, and it's a lively place to head in the evening, with excellent tapas and a restaurant.

The **bar** scene is fairly advanced in Úbeda.

Lupo, Pza de San Pedro. This bar boasts a state-of-the-art interior.

Siglo XV, C/de Muñoz García (Úbeda's liveliest street after dark). Set in a Gothic building which used to be a brothel.

buildings around the Palacio de las Cadenas make a wonderful ensemble, and the austere landscaping, old cobbles and plain six-sided fountain create the same effect of contemplative serendipity as any chamber of the Alhambra. Buildings on the plaza include the church of **Santa María de los Reales Alcázares** (*currently being restored*), a Renaissance façade on an older building with a fine Gothic cloister; the *parador*; the sedate 16th-century **Palacio del Marqués de Mancera** (*open daily 10am–11am*); and Vandelvira's **Sacra Capilla del Salvador** (*open 10.30–2 and 4.30–6; adm*), begun in 1540, the finest of Úbeda's churches, where Francisco de los Cobos is buried.

All the sculpture on the façades of Úbeda is first class, especially the west front of the Salvador. This is a monument of the time when Spain was in the mainstream of Renaissance ideas, and humanist classicism was still respectable. Mythological subjects decorate the west front and the inside of the church, while under the arch of the main door, carved panels of the ancient gods representing the five planets replace the usual Biblical scenes; Phoebus and Diana with the sun and moon; and Hercules, Aeolus, Vulcan and Neptune to represent the four elements. The **interior** (*the sacristan lives on the first door on the left of C/Francisco Cobos, on the north side of the church*) is worth a look despite a thorough sacking in 1936.

Beyond Pza Vázquez de Molina

Northeast of El Salvador, **Calle Horno Contado** has a few more fine palaces. At the top of the street, on Pza 1 de Mayo, is the 13th-century church of **San Pablo** (*open 7–9pm*), much renovated in the 16th century; inside is an elegant chapel of 1536. **San Nicolás de Bari**, further north, used to be a synagogue, though nothing now bears witness to this. On the western outskirts of town is Vandelvira's most remarkable building, the **Hospital de Santiago** (*C/Nueva; open 8–3 and 3.30–10*), which has the same plan as San Nicolás, a grid of quadrangles with a church inside. This was begun only a little earlier, in 1568, and both are supreme examples of the *estilo desornamentado*. The façade is unique, featuring quirky decoration and clean, angular lines, more like a product of the 20th century than the 16th.

Around Úbeda

If you go east out of Úbeda, you'll be entering a zone few visitors ever reach. The **Sierra de Cazorla** offers some memorable mountain scenery, especially around **Cazorla**, an undiscovered white village of narrow alleys hung at alarming angles down the hillsides. Cazorla's landmarks are a ruined Renaissance church and its castle, but there's an even better castle just east of town. **La Iruela** is a romantic ruin even by Spanish standards, with a tower on a dizzying height behind. Beyond La Iruela is the pass into the Sierra, the wild territory of hiking, hunting and fishing.

The mountain ranges of Cazorla and Segura make up one of the 10 national parks in Spain. The **Cazorla National Park** covers over half a million acres, and teems with wild boar, deer, mountain goat, buck and moufflon, while rainbow trout do their best to outwit the patient but determined anglers. The park is the source of the mighty

Tourist Information

Cazorla: Pso del Santo Cristo 17, **t** 953 71 01 02; also a Natural Park Tourist Office at C/Martinez Falero 11, **t** 953 72 01 25.

Where to Stay and Eat

Cazorla ✉ 23470

Cazorla has a surprising number of hotels, both in town and up in the mountains.

***__Parador El Adelantado__, **t** 953 72 70 75, **f** 953 72 70 77, *cazorla@parador.es* (*expensive*). Tucked about five miles inside the park, this mountain chalet has 33 rooms, a pool and a cosy log fire. It's agreeably remote, with an appealing, if slightly institutional feel. Its setting is without equal; if budget allows, this is the obvious choice as base for exploring the National Park. The **restaurant** (*moderate*) is one of the best in the area, serving lots of game dishes.

Hotel Ciudad de Cazorla, Pza de la Corredera 9, **t** 953 72 17 00, **f** 953 72 04 20 (*moderate*). The best hotel in town, with the sheer cliffs as a dramatic backdrop. Rooms are functional but undistinguished and there's a pool.

__Hotel Guadalquivir__, C/Nueva, 6, **t/f 953 72 02 68 (*inexpensive*). Twelve comfortable rooms in a good spot near the centre.

*__Don Diego__, C/Hilario Marcos 163, **t** 953 72 05 31, **f** 953 72 05 45 (*inexpensive*). A comfortable little hotel.

There are a few rural hotels near Segura:

*__Hospedería de Montaña Rio Madera__, **t/f** 953 12 62 04 (*inexpensive*). This offers all mod cons and a pool in a lovely setting.

El Mesoncillo, in La Platera (a few kilometres from Hornos), **t** 646 81 02 52. Self-catering cottages with great views, log fires and lots of chunky wooden furniture.

Guadalquivir; a hike in search of the source of Andalucía's greatest river is desperately romantic (a good map will direct you), and the area is one of Europe's richest havens for flora and fauna, with a variety of small birdlife that's hard to match.

Jaén

In the middle of the vast tracts of olive groves upon which its precarious economy depends is Jaén, the most provincial of all the Andalucían capitals. Jaén lacks the Renaissance charms of Úbeda or Baeza, but it is not quite as unattractive as many guidebooks claim; easily explored in a day along pleasant pedestrian walkways.

Jaén was the first capital of the kingdom of Granada and the old Arab quarter is well worth a visit. Its weaving, narrow lanes are at the foot of the hill, crowned by the 13th-century Moorish castle of **Santa Catalina**, built by ibn-Nasr (***t** 953 21 91 16; open Thurs–Tues 10.30–1.30; closed Wed*), and an ideal spot to take in the views of the surrounding countryside. The city's pride is its monumental **cathedral** on Pza Santa María (*open winter 8.30–1 and 4–9; summer 8.30–1 and 5–8; adm*), begun in 1548 by Andrés de Vandelvira. His work inside has suffered many changes, and the façade isn't his at all; not begun until 1667, Eufrasio López de Rojas's design was the first genuine attempt at Baroque in Andalucía, decorated with extravagant statuary by Pedro Roldán. On C/Martínez Molina, to the west, an old hospital has been restored to hold the **Museum of Arts and Popular Customs**, but the real attraction is the **Baños Arabes** (***t** 953 23 62 92; open Tues–Fri 9–8, Sat and Sun 9.30–2.30; closed Mon*), well-preserved ruins of 11th-century Moorish baths, complete with cold rooms, hot rooms and a tepidarium, discovered underneath.

Getting Around

Jaén has direct **rail** links only with Córdoba (three trains daily) and Madrid (about six). The RENFE station is on Pso de la Estación at the northern edge of town, by Pza de la Concordia. **Buses** are the best bet. The bus station is on the Av. de Madrid, near the tourist office. Buses run to Úbeda via Baeza (12 daily); Granada (14 daily); Málaga (4 daily); Córdoba (8 daily) and Almería (2 daily).

Tourist Information

Jaén: C/Maestra 13, a small street near the cathedral, **t** 953 24 26 24/953 19 04 55 (*open Mon–Fri 10–7 (summer 10–8); Sat, Sun and hols 10–1*).

Where to Stay and Eat

Jaén ✉ 23000

****Parador Castillo de Santa Catalina**, in the castle overlooking Jaén, **t** 953 23 00 00, **f** 953 23 09 30, *jaen@parador.es* (*expensive*). General de Gaulle worked on his memoirs here. The management could do with an overhaul but the views are unsurpassable.

***Infanta Cristina**, Av. de Madrid s/n, **t** 953 26 30 40, **f** 953 27 42 96, *hotelinfantacristina@swin.net* (*expensive*). The best hotel in town with big, comfortable rooms, a pool and a good **restaurant**.

***Condestable Iranzo**, Pso de la Estación 32, **t** 953 22 28 00, **f** 953 26 38 07 (*moderate*). A good hotel, with a pleasant **café** attached.

***Xauen**, Pza de Deán Maza 3 (near Pza Constitución), **t** 953 24 07 89, **f** 953 19 03 12 (*moderate–inexpensive*). Another conveniently placed major hotel.

There are a couple of acceptable budget hotels without baths; both are *cheap*.

*La Española**, Bernardo López 9, **t** 953 25 02 54.

*Carlos V**, Av. de Madrid 4, **t** 953 22 20 91.

Cafe Zeluan, Pza San Francisco. This Art Deco café is a good spot to linger over breakfast.

Casa Vicente, Arco del Consuelo, **t** 953 23 22 22 (*expensive*). Come here for a wide-ranging local specialities, mainly meat and fish, though it's somewhat gloomy. In summer, get a table out in the courtyard. *Closed Sun.*

For less formal dining, check out the numerous excellent **tapas bars** in the streets around the cathedral. What **nightlife** there is centres around the streets at the bottom end of Pso de la Estacion, bordered by C/Andalucia and the train station.

Perhaps the finest of Jaén's monasteries is that of **Santo Domingo**, in the street of the same name, with a façade by Vandelvira, while a few streets down is **Santa Clara**, the oldest. Opposite, the church of **San Bartolomé** has a fine *mudéjar* ceiling and the wonderful *Cristo de la Expiracion* by Martinez Montañes.

Huelva to Algeciras

Everyone has heard of the Costa del Sol, but there is a good deal more to Andalucía's coasts than just that narrow strip of salty Babylon – about 640 kilometres of it – from the empty spaces of Huelva to the empty spaces of Almería. The western half of this stretch is Andalucía's Atlantic coast, from Portugal to the Straits of Gibraltar; it's not all that scenic, but it has plenty of long golden beaches that haven't yet become too crowded. The piquant, sea-washed town of Cádiz is its major attraction. After Cádiz comes a glass of sherry (or two) in Jeréz de la Frontera. Here the mountains begin to close in, with their white villages. Back on the coast, there is a clutch of growing resorts including windsurf city, Tarifa; then Algeciras, a port town with the promise of a side-trip to Morocco, or to Ceuta, a tiny remnant of Spain's colonial empire in Africa.

Huelva

A Huelva una vez y nunca vuelvas.
(One trip to Huelva and you don't go back.)

This Andalucían saying does seem a little unkind, but the provincial capital is full of factories and freshly laid cement. Hit the centre, however, and small as it is it boasts an incongruously large number of fur shops and amusement arcades. The town's tourist brochure, in a unique and disarmingly modest display of candour, states that

Getting Around

By Train

The railway station, **t** 959 24 56 14, is on Av. de Italia, a five-minute walk from the centre of Huelva; there is a daily *Talgo* to Sevilla and Madrid (change at Linares for Granada and Almería), apart from regular services to Sevilla, from where there are connections to Cádiz, Jerez, Córdoba and other points in Andalucía and Barcelona; there are also regular trains to Ayamonte, on the Portuguese border.

By Bus

The Damas bus company, **t** 959 25 69 00, has its station at Av. de Portugal 9, with services to Sevilla, Granada, Cádiz and Algeciras, and other towns in the province: Ayamonte, Isla Cristina, Punta Umbria, Mazagón and Matalascañas on the coast, less often to Nerva and the mountain villages. The nearest **airport** is Sevilla.

Tourist Information

Huelva: Av. de Alemania 12, **t** 959 00 44 00, **f** 959 00 44 05 (*open Mon–Fri 9–7, Sat 10–2; closed Sun*).

Internet Access: @IberMed, C/Vasquez Lopez, Gal. Comercial, **t** 959 25 14 10 (*open 10–12*).

Where to Stay and Eat

Huelva ✉ 21000

****__Luz Huelva__, Alameda Sundheim 26, **t** 959 25 00 11, **f** 959 25 81 10 (*expensive*). Situated near the Columbus monument, with air-conditioned rooms, pool and tennis courts.

***__Tartessos__, C/Martín Alonso Pinzón 13, **t** 959 28 27 11, **f** 959 25 06 17 (*moderate*). Comfortable and central.

__Costa de la Luz__, C/Jose Maria Amo 8, **t/f 959 25 64 22 (*inexpensive*). Bang in the centre of town, a few steps from the theatre.

__San Miguel__, Santa María 6, **t 959 24 52 03 (*cheap*). Solicitous staff, offering decent rooms with bath.

Huelva's markets keep the **restaurants** well supplied with gleaming fresh seafood.

El Estero, Av. Maniz Alonso Pitizón 13, **t** 959 25 65 72, **f** 959 25 06 17 (*moderate*). Generally regarded as one of the best restaurants in town; specialities include *dorado al horno*, local pork dishes and delicious home-made puddings.

Mesón del Pozo, C/Alonso Sanchez 14, **t** 959 25 42 40 (*moderate*). Worth seeking out for its excellent pork and extensive wine list.

Agmanir, C/Arquitecto Carra, opposite C/Rabida (*inexpensive*). Serves mainly fish and seafood-based tapas and perhaps the cheapest *gambas al ajillon* in Spain.

Huelva 'has no particular historic interest'. The town was severely damaged by the earthquake of 1755, explaining the near absence of anything older than that; exceptions include the 16th-century Baroque church of **San Pedro** and the **Museo Provincial** (*Alameda Sundheim 13; open Tues–Sat 9–8, Sun 9–3; closed Mon*). The town's theatre is an Art Deco aberration, but the real curiosity is the **Barrio Reina Victoria**, a neighbourhood constructed by and for the employees of an English mining company in the 19th century. The houses sport gable ends and chimneys in true English suburban style.

Around Huelva

Cashing in on its Columbus legacy, Huelva province has published *Columbus Territory* (*free from most tourist offices in the province*), detailing an itinerary which takes in the key towns and spots associated with the great explorer, who set out on his first voyage to the New World from **Palos de la Frontera**, five kilometres southeast of Huelva. A few kilometres on lies the **Monasterio de la Rábida** (*visits by hourly guided tour only, Tues–Sun 10–1 and 4–6.15*), where Columbus planned his epic journey.

The **Muelle de las Carabelas** (*open Tues–Sun 10–7; adm*), between the monastery and the river, features full-size models of the ships that made the voyage, together with replicas of 15th-century quayside bars.

Coming from Huelva by bus to **Ayamonte**, you'll be deposited next to the pretty square behind the harbour. If you're on your way to Portugal, walk through the square and follow the signs for about 500m, where a boat (**t** *959 47 06 17*) will be waiting to

Tourist Information

La Rabida: Paraje de la Rabida, **t** 959 53 11 37.
Moguer: San Francisco s/n, **t** 959 37 23 77.
Ayamonte: Av. Ramon y Cajal s/n, 21400 Ayamonte, **t** 959 47 09 88 (*open winter Mon–Fri 9.30–1.30 and 4.30–8.30; summer Mon–Fri 10–2 and 5–9*).

Festivals

Isla Cristina: Semana Santa, *Holy Week*. The processions rival those of Sevilla.

Where to Stay and Eat

La Rábida ✉ 21810

★★★**HsR de La Rábida**, **t** 959 35 03 12 (*inexpensive*). A small, comfortable inn next to the monastery. There are only a few rooms and it is popular, so book ahead for high season.

Ayamonte ✉ 21400

★★★★**Parador de Ayamonte**, El Castillito, **t** 959 32 07 00, **f** 959 32 07 00, *ayamonte@paradoro.es* (*expensive–moderate*). Not on the beach but it has a big pool and is on the edge of the Guadiana river, with fine views over the sea and across to Portugal.

★★★**Don Diego**, C/Ramon y Cajal s/n, **t** 959 47 02 50, **f** 959 32 02 50 (*moderate*). The next best option in town, set in its own grounds.

★**Europa**, Av. de la Playa 45, **t** 959 47 12 39 (*cheap*). One of a number of cheaper options in Ayamonte.

Casino España, Pso de la Ribera (*moderate*). With its cool arches and terrace, this is a good place to try shellfish and *paella*.

Casa Luciano, C/Palma 1, **t** 959 47 10 71 (*inexpensive*). Excellent seafood and fish stews are to be had at this place, where many of the dishes are Portuguese-influenced and there's a good-value *menú del día*.

Isla Canela ✉ 21400 and Isla Cristina ✉ 21410

★★★★**Riu Canela**, Pso de los Gavilanes s/n, **t** 959 47 71 24 (*expensive*). A luxurious faux-Moorish pile with 350 rooms, pools, gardens, tennis, shops, a few steps from the beach.

★★**El Paraíso**, Playa Avenida, **t** 959 33 18 73, **f** 959 34 37 45, *hparaiso@reremail.es* (*moderate–inexpensive*). One of the choices on the beach at Isla Cristina.

Borelon, **t** 959 47 71 47, Isla Canela (*inexpensive*). A pizza-café actually on the beach.

Casa Rufino, Ctra de la Playa, **t** 959 33 08 10, **f** 959 34 34 70 (*inexpensive*). The best food in Isla Cristina is to be found here. A *menú degustación* for four people consists of eight dishes and is a relative bargain. *Lunch only, closed Wed, exc. in summer.*

Acosta, Pza del Caudillo 13, Isla Cristina, **t** 959 33 14 20 (*inexpensive*). A local favourite for fresh fish and traditional Andalucían stews. *Closed Mon in winter.*

Punta Umbría ✉ 21100

All these resorts have cheaper hotels within reasonable distance of the beaches.

★★**El Ayamontino**, Av. Andalucía, **t** 955 31 14 50, **f** 955 31 03 16 (*moderate*). This has a good **restaurant**; but a fair walk from the beach.

Ayamontino Ría, Av. de la Ria 1, **t** 955 31 14 58 (*moderate*). Sister hotel to El Ayamontino, and better located.

Hs La Playa, Av. Océano 95, **t** 955 31 01 12 (*inexpensive*). Open all year and one of the best bargains on the beach.

El Paraíso, Ctra de Huelva–Punta Umbría, Km11, **t** 959 31 27 56 (*moderate*). Locals regard this as one of the best seafood places in the area. It has two dining rooms, one beachy and informal, the other quite elegant, serving wonderfully fresh local seafood.

La Esperanza, Pza Pérez Pastor 3, **t** 959 31 10 45 (*inexpensive*). Long popular, with satisfying well-cooked dishes at reasonable prices.

take you and 40 cars across the river to the Portuguese town of **Vila Real de Santo António**. (*For cruises up the Guadiana, call* **t** *959 47 16 30*.) Just across the water are the beaches of **Isla de Canela** and **Isla del Moral**, a few kilometres from the town through a small natural park, **Marismas de Isla Cristina**.

The stretch of road between Huelva and Ayamonte has no real attraction for the tourist – orange groves interspersed with derelict buildings, scrapyards and mudflats. The peninsular of **Punta Umbría** is one of the main resorts of the area, its long sandy beaches offering all sorts of watersports.

The Sierra de Aracena

If you have a car you can comfortably explore the mountain villages in the Sierra de Aracena, less than a two-hour drive from the capital. The N435 leads you to the heart of this area, through mountainous countryside and ever-more-scenic views.

Tourist Information

Aracena: Pza San Pedro, **t** 959 12 82 06 (*open Mon–Sat 10–2.30 and 4–6.30; closed Sun*).

Jabugo: C/Carratera 9, **t** 959 12 11 32.

Festivals

Aracena: The Pilgrimage to the Sanctuary of the Virgin, *8 Sept*. The town's main **fiesta**, when brotherhoods from neighbouring villages in traditional dress ride on horseback to the top of the hill.

Almonaster la Real: Fiesta, *1st weekend in May*. Rival brotherhoods compete to create the finest crosses, and locals dress up and dance *fandangos* till dawn.

Aroche: The Pilgrimage of San Mames, *3rd weekend in Aug*. A horseback procession takes place.

Where to Stay and Eat

You'll find basic rooms and food in places like Cortegana and Aroche. The following are some of the better options.

Aracena ✉ 21200

*__Finca Buenvino__, Los Marines, Huelva, **t** 959 12 40 34, **f** 959 50 10 29 (*expensive*). A grand guesthouse up in the Sierra Morena (6km from Aracena), run by a locally well-known English family, the Chestertons. Lunch is served beside the pool; dinner is taken with the family. Book in advance.

***__Finca Valbono__, Ctra de Carboneras 1, **t** 959 12 77 11, **f** 959 12 76 79 (*moderate*). In the heart of the hills, this is a better than being in town; very friendly, sparkling clean and with a pool and **restaurant**.

__Sierra de Aracena__, Gran Vía 21, **t 959 12 61 75, **f** 959 12 62 18 (*inexpensive*). A modern place with reasonable rooms.

Restaurante Casas, C/Pozo de la Nieve 39, **t** 959 11 00 44 (*moderate–inexpensive*). At the entrance to the caves, serving Sierra pork every which way you can think of.

Almonaster la Real ✉ 21290

Casa García, Av. de San Martín 2, **t** 959 13 04 09 (*moderate*). An upmarket place with a delightful courtyard, serving various regional pork dishes and fish.

Jabugo and Galaroza ✉ 21290

__Galaroza Sierra__, Ctra Sevilla–Lisboa, Km69, Galaroza, **t 959 12 32 37, **f** 959 12 32 36 (*inexpensive–cheap*). Offers good-vaue rooms with a view in a wonderful location in the heart of the National Park.

Mesón Cinco Jotas, Ctra de San Juan del Puerto s/n (in Jabugo), **t** 959 12 10 71 (*moderate*). Here they smoke their own hams and export them to every corner of Spain, and beyond. It is now part of a chain covering all of Spain.

Just 70 kilometres from the Portuguese border, **Aracena** became part of Spain in the 13th century and fell under the control of the Knights Templar, who built the **Nuestra Señora de los Dolores**, a fine medieval church that stands in the grounds of the Moorish castle. Beneath it lies the region's major draw, the **Gruta de las Maravillas** (**t** *959 12 83 55; open 10–1.30 and 3–6; adm*) a series of natural chambers with underground lakes, which rival Nerja's for their extraordinary beauty. At El Chorro, the road forks west to **Almonaster la Real**, a pretty village with Roman origins and later Arabic influence. Its chief feature is the 10th-century mosque, but there are a number of medieval buildings and some fine examples of *mudéjar* and Gothic architecture, as well as the 14th-century church of **San Martin** and the **Puerta del Perdon**, in Manueline style. To the northwest, the road passes **Cortegana**, with its fine *mudéjar* church, on its way to **Aroche**, where white houses bask under the remains of an Almoravid fortress with 10 towers, containing a bullring. The main road back towards Huelva passes through the charming little village of **Galaroza**, and you can pause in **Jabugo** to sample what they claim is the best-tasting cured ham in all Spain.

The Coast South of Huelva

Twenty-three kilometres south of Huelva, along the coastal route, is **Mazagón**, a get-away-from-it-all family resort, surrounded by pine trees and lovely beaches. From here it's a straight shot to Torre de la Higuera, and the big hotel developments around the endless **Matalascañas Beach**, the most international of Huelva's resorts. This is

Tourist Information

Mazagón: Edificio Mancomunidad Moguer–Palos, **t** 959 37 60 44.
Matalascañas: Urbanización Playa de Matalascañas, **t** 959 43 00 86.
El Rocio: Av. de la Canaliega, **t** 959 44 26 84 (*open Mon–Fri 10–2; closed Sat and Sun*).

Festivals

El Rocío: Romería, *Pentecost*. Perhaps the oldest in Spain, when pilgrims roll in by the hundred in traditional wagons strewn with flowers. A few days of serious music and merry-making: campfires burn all night, and the atmosphere is pure electricity.

Where to Stay and Eat

Mazagón ✉ 21130

Mazagón has a number of restaurants and cafés around Av. Fuente Piña.

******Parador Cristóbal Colón**, Ctra Huelva–Matalascañas, **t** 959 53 63 00, **f** 959 53 62 28 (*expensive*). Among pine trees, looking on to Mazagón beach, this modern *parador* is the best option, with pleasant gardens, pool and air-conditioned rooms.

Matalascañas ✉ 21760

There are a number of resort hotels at Matalascañas, all packed during high season.

****El Cortijo**, Sector E–P Arcelas 15/49, **t** 959 44 87 00, **f** 959 44 83 75 (*expensive*). A pleasant alternative to the resorts, five minutes from the beach, with facilities for horse riding.

Tamarindos, Av. de las Adelfas 31, **t/f** 959 43 01 19 (*inexpensive*). Clean, near the beach and the town centre; all rooms with bath.

Da Pino, Pso Maritimo, Edit Barlovento, **t** 959 43 02 03 (*moderate*). An Italian restaurant with good food: pastas, excellent salads and steaks. *Closed Mon and Christmas*.

El Remo, Av. dos Conquistadores (*inexpensive*). A good *chiringuito* restaurant, with a *terraza*, specializing in sardines and fresh local fish.

the dead end of the coastal highway; the only place you can go is the tiny inland village of **El Rocío**, mapped only for its *romería* at Pentecost (*see* 'Festivals', p.643).

Las Marismas

Visitor centres: ***Centro de Recepción de Acebuche*** *(t 959 44 87 11), halfway between El Rocío and Matalascañas. Land Rover tours and non-guided, signposted walks leave from here.* ***La Rocina centre*** *(t 959 44 23 40, Km16), north along the A483. Signposted walk and access to the Palacio de Acebrón.*

Las Marismas, Europe's greatest marshland wildlife reserve, is another world, with a fantastically varied population of golden eagles, snowy egrets, flamingos, griffin vultures, tortoises, red deer, foxes and European lynx, boosted further in spring and autumn by hundreds of species of migratory birds.

As in the Everglades, wildlife congregates around 'islands' among the wetlands; here they're called *corrales*, built of patches of dune anchored by surrounding shrubs and stands of low pines. The threat of development from growing resorts has become Spain's top environmental concern, and the government has set aside a large slice of the area as the **Parque Nacional del Coto Doñana**. There are hides from which to observe the wildlife. Note that the 'wetlands' are largely dry in summer; whenever you come, bring mosquito repellent and watch out for quicksand.

Cádiz

If Cádiz were a village, the government would immediately declare it a national monument and put up a sign. It's a big, busy seaport, though, and tourism generally leaves it alone. It's a pity, for Cádiz (if you pronounce it any other way but 'Caddy', no one will understand you) is one of the most distinctive Spanish cities, worth spending a few days in even if there are few 'sights'. The city is a small peninsula that comes in colours – a hundred shades of off-white – bleached and faded by sun and spray into a soft patina, broken only by the golden dome of a rambling Baroque cathedral.

History

Cádiz modestly claims to be the oldest city in western Europe. It's hard to argue; the Phoenician city of **Gadir** has a documented foundation date of 1100 BC and, while other cities have traces of older settlements, it would be difficult to find another city west of Greece with a continuous urban life of at least 3,000 years. Gadir served as the port for shipping Spanish copper and tin, and was undoubtedly the base for the now-forgotten Phoenician trade routes with west Africa and England – and possibly even for explorations to America. Cádiz, however, prefers to consider Hercules its founder, and he appears on the arms of the city between his famous pillars.

Under Roman rule *Gades*, as it was called, was a favoured city, especially under Julius Caesar, who held his first public office here. Scant remains of the Roman theatre were discovered in 1980. The city remained out of the spotlight until the 16th century, when

Getting Around

By Ferry

Cádiz isn't the big passenger port it used to be, but you can still take the weekly ferries to Tenerife – Las Palmas – and Arrecife in the Canary Islands. They run a more frequently in the summer. There's also a regular ferry ride from the port to El Puerto de Santa María. Tickets: Transmediterránea office, Av. Ramón de Carranza 26, **t** 956 22 74 21/956 28 43 50.

By Train

You can go only to Jerez (20 daily, stopping at El Puerto de Santa María), Sevilla (8 daily) and Madrid directly. The station is at the landward end of the old city, near Pza San Juan de Dios, in Pza de Sevilla, **t** 956 25 43 01.

By Bus

Cádiz is served by Los Amarillos, Av. Ramón de Carranza 31 (by the port), **t** 956 28 58 52, which takes the route west to Rota and Sanlúcar de Barrameda; and also by Comes, Pza de Hispanidad 1, **t** 956 21 1763, taking the route east to Tarifa and Algeciras. City bus No.1, departing from in front of Comes, takes you from Pza de España to Cádiz's suburban beaches and to new Cádiz. Secorbus, from Pza Elio s/n, **t** 956 25 74 15, goes to Madrid.

Tourist Information

Cádiz: main office: corner of Pza de Mina and C/Calderón de la Barca 1, **t** 956 21 13 13 (*open Mon and Sat 9–2, Tues–Fri 9–7; closed Sun*); Regional Office: Pza de San Antonio 3, **t** 956 22 13 08, **f** 956 21 46 34 (*open Mon–Fri 8–3; closed Sat and Sun*).
Municipal Office: Pza de San Juan de Dios 1, **t** 956 24 10 01 (*open Sat and Sun 5–8*).

Where to Stay

Cádiz ✉ 11000

Expensive

★★★★**Atlántico**, Av. Duque de Nájera 9, **t** 956 22 69 05, **f** 956 21 45 82. Another good *parador* set in a modern building with wonderful views of the Atlantic and a large outdoor pool. The suites at the front are especially nice, and don't cost much more.

★★★★**Playa Victoria**, Glorieta Ingeniero La Cierva 4, **t** 956 27 54 11, **f** 956 26 33 00. Probably the most upmarket place in town, and the priciest, this is a huge glitzy place right on the beach, with all the facilities including a pool. However, it lacks the atmosphere of being in the old town.

Moderate–Inexpensive

★★★**Francia y París**, Pza San Francisco 2, **t** 956 22 23 49, **f** 956 22 24 31 (*moderate*). A quiet, well-run hotel near Pza Mina.

★★**P. Bahia**, Plocia 5, off Pza San Juan de Dios, **t** 956 25 90 61 (*moderate*). Has rooms with a/c and TV.

In the new part of Cádiz, there's just as much choice. The Pso Marítimo is lively, so don't feel you're missing out if you stay here. The following are similar standard hotels, both with garages and cafés attached:

★★**Regio**, Av. de Viya 11, **t** 956 27 93 31.

★★**Regioz**, Av. Andalucia 79, **t** 956 28 30 08, **f** 956 25 30 09.

Cheap

There will be no problem finding cheaper rooms. Some of the cheapest places are near the Pza San Juan de Dios in the old town. Otherwise look for the *camas* signs and take your pick. Don't hesitate to refuse anything that appears too run down.

the American trade and Spain's growth as a naval power made a major port of it once again. Sir Francis Drake visited in 1587 and, as every schoolboy used to know, 'singed the King of Spain's beard'. Later British admirals followed the custom for the next two centuries, calling every now and then for a fish supper and an afternoon's sacking and burning. The years after 1720, when Cádiz controlled the American market, shaped its present character. Its shining hour came in 1812, when the first Spanish constitution was declared here, and the city became the capital of free Spain.

★**P. Fantoni**, Flamenco 5, **t** 956 28 27 04. Full of tiles and marble with a breezy roof terrace.

P. España, Marques de Cadiz 9, **t** 956 28 55 00. Offers reasonable doubles, with bath available; right in the centre of the old town.

Eating Out

Expensive

El Faro, C/San Félix 15, **t** 956 21 10 68. Dining, of course, means more fish, and this is generally regarded as the best restaurant in the town. It is now part of a chain including Ventonillo El Chato (*see* below). You can either explore outlandish varieties of seafood unheard of in English, or more recognizable varieties, such as steamed hake with asparagus, clams with spinach, fried fish a *la Gaditana*; there is also a selection of meat dishes.

El Balandro, Alameda Apodaca 22, **t** 956 22 09 92. By the Alameda Apodaca walls, with rustic décor. The menu is a mix of seafood and Spanish specialities like *carne de Avila*.

El Candil, Javier de Burgos 19, **t** 956 22 19 71. If you feel you really can't look at another fish, try this place in the heart of town. Its garlic chicken with paprika is sensational.

Moderate

El Sardinero, Pza San Juan de Dios 4, **t** 956 28 25 05. One of the oldest restaurants in the city, with a variety of Basque and *andaluz* dishes, which you can enjoy at the outside tables.

Ventorillo del Chato, Vía Augusta Julia, Cortadura, **t** 956 25 00 25, *ventorillo delchato@raini-computer.net*. This rustic place on the road to San Fernando claims to have been around for more than 200 years and is still going strong.

Arte Serrano, Pso Marítimo 2, **t** 956 25 31 86. In newer Cádiz, along the Pso Marítimo, there's a wide choice of restaurants, nearly all with terraces or outside seating. This one specializes in meats from the Sierra, pork and game in particular.

La Montanera, C/Sacramento, **t** 956 22 06 00, and C/Reina Victoria, **t** 956 28 48 51. One of the Fogon de Mariana chain (there's an excellent one in Jerez), which offer large chunks of meat like *jamón* and *chorizo* at reasonable prices for the fish-weary.

Inexpensive

Café Bar Madrileño, Pza Mina 1, **t** 956 22 51 63. One of several good spots on Pza Mina for reasonably priced seafood restaurants; make sure you try the cheap tapas and *raciones* served here.

Nueva Ola, Pza San Juan de Dios. Specializes in *langostinos* and *dorada a la plancha*, both caught fresh from the bay.

Casa Paco, Pza San Agustin 5, **t** 956 28 54 51. Serves up excellent tapas and mighty strong Voll Damm beer, on tap in the bar; full meals are served in the delightful restaurant.

Nightlife

The town abounds with bars; the best area to find a bit of *marcha* outside summertime is around the university buildings, particularly **Pza San Francisco** and **Pza Espana** and the streets off and between them, including **C/San Francisco** and **C/Rosario**. Over the summer months the nightlife shifts to the beach area in the new part of town, particularly along the **Pso Maritimo**.

There is also a substantial gay scene in Cadiz; for information call Arcadia, a gay and lesbian collective, **t** 956 21 22 00.

The Town

The approach to Cádiz is a dismal one, through marshes and saltpans cluttered with industrial junk and modern suburbs before arriving at the **Puerta de Tierra**, entrance to the old city on the peninsula. Almost everything about warfare in the 18th-century had a certain decorum to it, and Cádiz's gates and formidable **land walls** (1757), all well preserved, are among the most aesthetically pleasing structures in town.

Neither decaying nor prettified for the tourists, the old city is great for exploring, a maze of lanes bathed in soft lamplight after dusk, when the cafés fill up with young, exuberant *gaditanos*. A walk through the myriad cobbled streets, past solid wooden doors and balconies spilling over with flowers, will take you back in history to the time when mighty Cádiz bustled as the gateway to the Americas. Keep an eye out for the little plaques, reminders of what an important role this small city has often played. In an hour or so you can walk entirely around Cádiz on the coast road, past parks like the pretty **Alameda de Apodaca**, and forts and bastions of the 18th century.

Plaza San Juan de Dios and Around

From the Puerta de Tierra, the Cuesta de las Calesas leads down to the port and railway station, then around the corner to **Plaza San Juan de Dios**, the lively, palm-shaded centre of Cádiz, with most of the restaurants and hotels on the surrounding streets. Two blocks away, the **Cathedral** exercises an ingratiating charm despite its ungainly bulk. Inside, Zurbarán's *Santa Úrsula* stands out among the paintings. The **Museo de la Catedral** (***t*** *956 25 98 12; open Tues–Fri 10–1 and 4–7, Sat and Sun 10–1; closed Mon; adm*) has a lot of ecclesiastical gold and silverware, paintings by Murillo, Zurbarán and Alejo Fernández, and an ivory crucifix by Alonso Cano.

A couple of blocks east, on the Campo del Sur, is the **Teatro Romano** (*open Tues–Sun 11–1.30; closed Mon*), a restored Roman theatre dating from the 1st century BC, backing on to a maze of streets and buildings little changed since medieval times.

Continuing westwards to **Plaza Topete**, you'll find yourself in Cádiz's almost excessively colourful **market district**. A few blocks west, the little church of **San Felipe Neri** on C/Sacramento (*open Tues–Fri 8.30–10 and 5–7; Sat, Sun and hols 9–1; closed Mon*) is an unprepossessing shrine to the beginnings of Spanish liberty. On 29 March 1812 an assembly of refugees from Napoleon's occupation of the rest of Spain gathered here and declared Spain an independent republic, guaranteeing full political and religious freedom. Though their constitution proved stillborn, it was a notable beginning for Spain's struggle towards democracy. Big marble plaques cover the façade. Inside is a beautiful *Immaculate Conception* by Murillo.

Around the corner, Cádiz's very good municipal museum, **Museo de la Cortes de Cádiz** (*C/Santa Ines,* ***t*** *956 22 17 88; open Tues–Fri 9–1 and 4–7, Sat and Sun 9–1; closed Mon and hols*), has a huge Romantic-era mural depicting the 1812 event. Its star exhibit is a 50ft **scale model of Cádiz**, made entirely of mahogany and ivory by an unknown obsessive in 1779. Among a collection of portraits of Spanish heroes is the Duke of Wellington, who in Spain carried the title of Duke of Ciudad Rodrigo. It's a short walk from here to the **Torre Tavira** (*C/Sacramento,* ***t*** *956 21 29 10; open winter 10–8; summer 10–6; adm*), with a *camera obscura* giving wonderful views over the city.

Plaza de Mina and Around

On this lovely square, in the northwestern corner of the peninsula, you'll find the tourist office and the **Museum of Fine Arts and Archaeology** (*open Wed–Sat 9–8, Tues 2.30–8, Sun 9.30–2.30; closed Mon; adm*). The archaeology section has Phoenician, Roman and Greek finds, but best are the paintings, including some Murillos and some very good portraits by Zurbarán. Moreover, while the **Oratorio de la Santa Cueva** is closed for renovation, the museum is also graced with Andalucía's only Goya frescoes.

Cádiz Province

Like those to the east, the beaches around Cádiz are popular mostly with Spaniards and are more crowded, at least in July and August. They are lovely and huge, and the towns behind them relatively unspoiled; there may be few better places in Spain to baste yourself, with plenty of opportunities for exploring *bodegas*.

Sanlúcar and Rota

Sanlúcar de Barrameda makes *manzanilla*, most ethereal of sherries, and there are a number of sherry houses that you can visit (*see* 'Sherry Houses', facing page). It is known as the port that launched Magellan on his way around the world, and

Tourist Information

Sanlúcar de Barrameda: Calzada del Ejército s/n, **t** 956 36 61 10, **f** 956 36 61 32 (*open Mon–Fri 10–2 and 5–7, Sat 10–1; closed Sun*).

Rota: C/Luna 2 (in the Palace), **t** 956 84 61 74, **f** 956 92 81 16 (*open daily 9–2 and 5–7*).

El Puerto de Santa María: C/Luna 22, **t** 956 54 24 75, **f** 956 54 22 46 (*open daily 10–2 and 6–8*).

Festivals

Rota: Feria de la Manzanilla, *end of May*. Horse riding, bullfights, traditional Andalucían dress and, of course, sherry.

Flower Festival, *15 Aug*. Sees C/Ancha covered with a carpet of faux-flowers (sawdust).

Noches de Bajo Guia, *July*. A wonderful Flamenco festival.

Feria de Tapas, *mid-Oct*. The spot to sample all Rota's wonderful gastronomic creations.

Where to Stay

It's no problem finding a place to stay in any of the coastal resorts; especially in the high season, little old ladies meet the buses to drag you off to their *hostales*. Many of the resorts around Cádiz close during the winter months.

Sanlúcar ✉ 11540 and Rota ✉ 11520

***__Los Helechos__, Pza de Madre de Dios 9, **t** 956 36 13 49/956 36 76 55, **f** 956 36 96 50 (*moderate–inexpensive*). In the old part of Sanlúcar, built around two beautiful court-yards, this is by far the most delightful hotel.

Hs La Blanca Paloma, Pza San Roque 9, Sanlúcar, **t** 953 6 36 44 (*cheap*). Unglamorous but the only place in town for tight budgets.

***__Playa de la Luz__, on the beach at Arroyo Hondo, Rota, **t** 956 81 05 00, **f** 958 1 06 06, *hpl@cdz.servicom.es* (*expensive–moderate*). A sports-orientated hotel with a lovely pool and gardens; one of a few classy modern resort hotels in Rota.

****__Duque de Najera__, C/Gravika 2, Rota, **t** 956 84 60 20, **f** 956 81 24 71, *hdm@cdz.servicom.es* (*expensive–moderate*). In the centre, with pool, satellite TV, sauna and gym.

***__Caribe__, C/Avenida de la Marika 60, Rota, **t** 956 81 07 00, **f** 956 81 00 98 (*moderate*). A slightly cheaper option in the centre, also with pool, TV and garden terrace.

P. la Española, C/Garcia Sanchez 9, Rota, **t** 956 81 00 98 (*inexpensive–cheap*). Basic but in an old mansion with a campsite in the grounds.

El Puerto de Santa María ✉ 11500

****__Hotel Monasterio San Miguel__, C/Larga 27, **t** 956 54 04 40, **f** 956 54 26 04, *monasterio@jale.com* (*luxury–expensive*). This 16th-century former monastery is the loveliest place to stay. It's marvellously soothing with tranquil cloisters, religious artefacts and a pool. The games room and the **restaurant** are particularly interesting.

****__Meliá Caballo Blanco__, Av. de Madrid 1, **t** 956 56 25 41, **f** 956 56 27 12 (*expensive–moderate*). Set in a picturesque spot, this is less pricey and also worth a try; facilities include a pool, **café** and parking.

***__Santa María__, Av. de la Bajamar s/n, **t** 956 87 32 11, **f** 956 87 36 52 (*moderate–inexpensive*). A 17th-century palace with a pool.

Columbus on his second voyage to the Indies. The town has a certain crumbling colonial charm and an exceptionally pretty main square, **Plaza de Cabildo**. Worth a visit are the church of **Nuestra Señora de la O** (*open Mon–Wed and Sat 10–1, Sun 10–12; closed Thurs*) with its fine *mudéjar* portal and 16th-century coffered ceiling, and the 19th-century **Montpensier Palace** (*open 8–2.30*), with its extensive library and paintings by Murillo, El Greco, Rubens and Goya. Although its beaches are not major-league, Sanlúcar is popular with Spanish holidaymakers for its excellent cheap seafood. The Bajo de Guía is a particularly charming fishing district, and from here you can take the boat to **Coto Doñana** for a four-hour river trip, including two stops and two guided walks. (*Two boats daily; tickets from Fabrica de Hielo, Av. Bajode Guia;* **t** *956 36 38 13; open daily 9–7.*)

*****Los Cantaros**, Curva 6, **t** 956 54 02 40, **f** 956 54 11 21, *loscantaros@rainicomputer.net* (*moderate–inexpensive*). A good central choice with parking and a **restaurant**.

P. Manolo, C/Jesus de los Milagros 18, **t** 956 85 75 25 (*inexpensive–cheap*). At the lower end of the scale; rooms all with bath.

Eating Out

Many of the restaurants here – informal cafés where you can pick out the fish that catches your fancy – are open only in summer.

Rota ✉ 11520

Casa Bigote, Bajo de Guía, **t** 956 36 26 96 (*expensive–moderate*). Famous throughout Andalucía for its delicious appetizers, classic regional dishes and seafood; the crayfish are a must, and you can try the local *manzanilla*. The tapas selection in the bar opposite is extensive and truly excellent. Get there early or you won't find a table. *Closed Sun.*

Mirador de Doñana, Bajo de Guía, **t** 956 36 42 05 (*moderate*). Another attractive and popular bar/restaurant with a panoramic view across to the bird reserve. Particularly delicious are: *cigalas* (crayfish), *angulas* (baby eels) and *nido de rapé a la Sanluqueña*, a nest of straw potato chips.

Casa Balbino, Pza Cabildo. Widely regarded as the best tapas bar in this part of town; varied tapas, all washed down by chilled *manzanilla*. It's worth waiting for a table.

La Montanera, C/Bolsa, **t** 956 36 49 83. For a change from fish try this cured ham and sausage place; part of the Fogon chain.

El Puerto de Santa María ✉ 11500

The town's speciality is *urta*, something like a sea bream. El Puerto has some deservedly popular restaurants.

Hacienda El Pinar, Viejo de Nota, **t** 956 85 42 04, **f** 956 85 23 39, *www.haciendaelpinar.com* (*expensive*). The palace belonging to the Osborne family (of sherry fame); if you call ahead, you can dine sumptuously in memorable surroundings (min. 8 people).

La Goleta, C/Babor 5, **t** 956 85 22 56 (*moderate*). The most successful restaurant, with simple but well-prepared seafood dishes, especially the fish cooked in salt, the *tosta de salmón* and the *porgy* in brandy. *Closed Mon exc. in July and Aug.*

El Faro de El Puerto, near the roundabout on Ctra de Fuenterrabia, Kmo.5, **t** 956 87 09 52, **f** 956 54 04 66 (*moderate*). The other El Faro (the original is in Cádiz), with an excellent reputation for its regional cuisine, serving some of the finest seafood in the province.

Romerijo's, at Ribera del Marisco 1, **t** 956 54 12 54 (*inexpensive*). The liveliest place, where you can eat the freshest of fish and seafood as you sit at the tables outside or enjoy a takeaway wrapped in a paper funnel. A kilogram of shellfish is enough for four people. The place is noisy and fantastic value.

Sherry Houses

Antonio Barbadillo, C/Luis Eguilaz 11, **t** 956 36 08 94. The biggest *bodega*, which makes the bulk of the *manzanilla*.

La Guita, C/Dorantes s/n, **t** 956 18 22 20. Another delicious make.

Heredoros de Argueso, C/Mar 8, **t** 956 36 01 12.

Next, on the edge of the bay of Cádiz, comes **Rota**, a flashier, slightly overbuilt resort taking advantage of the best and longest beach on the coast.

Across the bay from Cádiz lies **El Puerto de Santa María**, the traditional port of the sherry houses in Jerez, with a fair few *bodegas* of its own: Osborne, Terry and Duff Gordon among others. The town has some interesting churches, mansions of the Anglo-Spanish sherry aristocracy, and the restored, 13th-century *mudéjar* Castillo de San Marcos. The century-old bullring ranks with those of Sevilla and Ronda in prestige. It isn't a big resort, but it's typical of Cádiz province, with bright, bustling streets, excellent restaurants and some good beaches (**Puntilla** especially). **Puerto Sherry** is a modern marina, built in the late 1980s, and a pleasant place to spend a few hours.

Jerez de la Frontera

The name is synonymous with wine – the English corrupted Jerez into sherry – but besides the *finos*, *amontillados* and other varieties of that noble sauce, Jerez also ships out much of Spain's equally good brandy. Most of the big companies have their headquarters here, and they're quite accustomed to taking visitors through the *bodegas*.

Business is not as good as it was, for sherry sales are falling worldwide, but Jerez is growing. It's has an extremely attractive centre, and a few lovely buildings. Jerez's landmark is **La Colegiata**, a curious pseudo-Gothic church with a separate belltower and Baroque staircase. Works inside include a *Madonna* by Zurbarán and sculptures by Juan de Mesa. Nearby, on the central Pza de los Reyes Católicos, **San Miguel** (begun in 1482) (*open Mon–Sat 8–9, Sun 9–1*) changes the scene to Isabelline Gothic, with a florid *retablo* inside. There is a Moorish **Alcázar** at the end of C/Pérez Galdós (*open Sep–April 10–6; May–Sept 10–8; adm*), with some remains of the baths, a *camera obscura* with views over the city, an art gallery and a well-preserved mosque.

Outside town, on the road to Medina Sidonia, is the **Cartuja de la Defensión** (*open Tues, Thurs and Sat 5–6.30*), a 15th-century monastery with the best Baroque façade

Coping with a *Copa* or Two

Don't be shy. Most *bodegas* are open Mon–Fri 9–1, though not in August, or when they're busy with the *vendimia* (harvest) in September. Admission usually includes tasting sessions. However, it is worth booking ahead as numbers are restricted on guided tours. One of the most interesting *bodegas* is that belonging to González Byass, C/Manuel María González 12 (*t 956 35 70 00, www.gonzalesbyass.es*). The tour includes a visit to the old sawdust-strewn *bodega* and ends at the *degustacíon*, where the motto is, 'If you don't have a *copa* at eleven o'clock, you should have eleven at one'. You also see a video of the production process, with cellarmen demonstrating their skill at pouring sherry from distances of a metre or more into the small *copitas* (in order to aerate the wine). The following *bodegas* are also well worth a visit:

John Harvey, C/Arcos 57 (*t 956 15 10 00*). Watch out for the alligator at the tour's end.

Sandeman, C/Pizarro 10 (*t 956 31 29 95*).

Williams and Hombert, C/Paul s/n (*t 956 34 65 39*).

Getting Around

Cádiz is the base for visiting Jerez and the coasts. The Amarillo company provides regular **buses** from Cádiz to all the coastal towns, and at least five daily to Jerez. Infrequent buses connect Jerez with Rota, Sanlúcar and El Puerto. Almost all the Sevilla–Cádiz buses stop in Jerez and El Puerto, as do the trains. There are frequent connections for Arcos de la Frontera and Ronda and one bus a day to Córdoba and Granada. Jerez stations for buses and **trains** are together on the eastern edge of town, **t** 956 33 79 75. There's a regular **ferry** service from El Puerto to Cádiz – more fun than taking the bus. Parking can be hard to find if you're in a **car** but it is sometimes best to be based in Jerez in order to explore the surrounding area, to avoid the queues on the roads into Cádiz.

Tourist Information

Jerez: C/Larga 39, **t** 956 33 11 50/956 33 17 31 (*open Mon–Fri 9–2 and 4–7; closed Sat and Sun*).

Festivals

Jerez: Semana Santa, *Holy Week*. More intimate than Sevilla's, but in its way just as splendid. The nightly processions escorting the Saint and Madonna images create a city-wide pageant. Returning home at night, they are serenaded by impromptu solo voices; for the finest singers, the whole procession halts in appreciation.

Fiestas de Otoño, *Sept and Oct*. Sherry tasting and horse racing in the main square.

Where to Stay

Jerez ✉ 11400

In Jerez, there are a great many unremarkable hotels. The best two in town are close to the centre.

Expensive–Moderate

★★★★**Jerez**, Av. Alcalde Álvaro Domecq 35, **t** 956 33 06 00, **f** 956 30 50 01. Has a pool and tennis courts and is set in lovely tropical gardens, but is no bargain.

★★★★**Royal Sherry Park**, Av. Alcalde Álvaro Domecq 11, **t** 956 31 76 14, **f** 956 31 13 00. A modern place set in a park a little closer to town, with a pool and a restaurant, El Abaco.

★★★**Doña Blanca**, C/Bodegas 11, **t** 956 34 87 61, **f** 956 34 85 86. The most pleasant three-star place, refurbished, in the heart of town; clean and modern with its own parking.

Inexpensive–Cheap

★★**Serit**, Higueras 7, **t** 956 34 07 00, **f** 956 34 07 16. In the centre of town, with parking; has comfortable rooms at good rates.

★★**Virt**, Higueras 20, **t** 956 32 28 11. A middle-range bargain with air-conditioned rooms.

★**Las Palomas**, Higueras 17, **t** 956 34 37 73. Very good value.

(1667) in Andalucía, which has some sculptures by Alonso Cano. You'll need special permission to go inside, but it's worth visiting the gardens and patio.

Horses and Flamenco

While in Jerez, look out for exhibitions scheduled at the **Escuela Andaluz del Arte Ecuestre**, Av. Duque de Abrantes (***t*** *956 31 11 11*, ***f*** *956 30 99 54*). Jerez's snooty wine aristocracy takes horsemanship very seriously; they have some of the finest horses you're likely to see anywhere. The annual **Horse Fair** (*first half of May*), which can be traced back to the 13th century, is a good excuse for attending the *corrida*, drinking plenty of sherry and, of course, joining in the flamenco extravaganza. Every Thursday there is a spectacular 'horse ballet' at 12 noon, and there are regular tours between 11am and 1pm (*Mon–Wed and Fri*). Ask at the tourist office for details of any special shows; and wear something warm in the winter months – the unheated arena can get very chilly.

Eating Out

Even in a region of Spain known for the late hours it keeps, Jerez seems to go one step further. It's not at all unusual here to sit down to lunch at 3.30pm. Don't even think about dinner until after 10pm.

Expensive

El Bosque, Av. Álvaro Domecq 26, **t** 956 30 33 33/956 30 70 30. Beautifully situated in woods near the Parque de González Montoria, yet only a short distance from town; formal, elegant, well known but slightly dull. The seafood is good; try angler fish in shellfish sauce or strawberry *gazpacho*. *Closed Sun.*

Moderate

Tendido 6, Circo 10, **t** 956 34 48 35. Closer to town, by the bullring, this place has a patio with adjoining dining room, decorated on a *feria* theme, with bullfight memorabilia on the walls. You can fill up on robust helpings of traditional food. *Closed Sun.*

Gaitán, Gaitán 3, **t** 956 34 58 59. One of the favourite dining places in town. Try the Very Old Spanish Cheese (Queso Viejo de Oveja), lamb with honey and brandy of Jerez, veal sirloin in Paris coffee cream. *Closed Sun eve.*

La Mesa Redonda, Manuel de la Quintana 3, **t** 956 34 00 69. This beautifully decorated restaurant has antique furniture and paintings, giving the impression of an old aristocratic Jerez home. It has a first-class kitchen serving excellent game and seasonal specialities. Reservations essential. *Closed Sun and Aug.*

El Fogon de Mariana, C/Zaragoza, **t** 956 34 10 19. Set in a huge barn-like space complete with beams, log fire and a huge grill; the emphasis is on meat, and a lot of it – all fresh and at a very good price. They'll even throw in house wine if you order a *paradilla*.

Inexpensive

Bar Juanito. The best among a clutch of tiny tapas bars on Pescadería Vieja, in a passage off the Pza del Arenal. Try the *costillas en adobo* (marinaded grilled pork chops). It is a crush at lunchtime; arrive early in the evening (*opens at 8pm*) if you want a table.

La Taberna Marinera, **t** 956 33 44 27. One of a number of good tapas bars in Pza Rivero, just behind the Alameda Cristina.

There are many street ***bodegas*** where you can try the whole spectrum of the area's produce. Try **Alcazaba**, Medina 19, or **La Tasca**, C/Matadero s/n.

Jerez has a great **nightlife**. Around Pza Canterbury you will stumble upon a number of bars, clubs and discos. It is also justly famous for **flamenco** and here you will find the real thing; but you've got to look for it (and don't expect it to happen just because it's advertised). Here are a selection of venues, mostly situated in the gypsy quarter:

El Laga de Tio Parilla, Pza del Mercado, **t** 956 33 83 34. *Free on Thur, Fri and Sat.*

La Taberna Flamenca, Augostillo de Santiago 3.

El Rincon del Duende, C/Muro 19.

One of the most beautiful buildings in the old part of the city is the **Flamenco Centre** (*Palacio Penmartín, Pza de San Juan 1, **t** 956 32 27 11; open Mon–Fri 9.30–2; closed for two weeks during Aug*), hosting shows and activities throughout the year in an effort to promote and prolong the art.

Arcos de la Frontera and Sierra Grazalema

Starting from Jerez, **Arcos de la Frontera** is the first town you come to and one of the most spectacular, hanging on a steep rock with wonderful views over the Guadalete river valley. The narrow streets twist and turn like an oriental maze, an inheritance from its Moorish past. The older sections of town under the castle contain some ancient palaces and the Isabelline-Gothic **Santa María de la Asunción** (*open Mon–Fri*

Getting Around

Arcos de la Frontera has regular bus connections to Jerez, Cádiz and Ronda; less frequent connections to Sevilla.

Tourist Information

Arcos de la Frontera: Pza de Cabildo s/n, **t** 956 70 22 64, **f** 956 70 09 00 (*open Mon–Sat 10–2 and 5–7, Sun 10.30–12.30*).

Grazalema: Pza de España 11, **t** 956 13 22 25, **f** 956 13 20 28 (*open Tue–Sun 10–2 and 5–7; closed Mon*).

Ubrique: C/Morena de Mora 19-A, **t** 956 46 49 00, **f** 956 46 26 59 (*open Tues–Sat 10–2 and 4.30–7.30, Sun 10–2; closed Mon*).

Festivals

Arcos: Semana Santa, *Holy Week*. Fighting bulls are let loose in the streets and those who choose not to be chased by them can watch the priests in purple twist their way through incense-filled streets carrying heavy gilt images of Christ covered in flowers and lit by tall candles.

Flamenco Festival, *beginning of Aug*.

Grazalema: Romería de San Isidro Labrador, *last Sun of May*. A celebration of the sun and the earth.

Fiestas del Carmen, *3rd week of July*. Festivities culminate in the Lunes del Toro, a traditional *gralemena* festival.

Las Fiestas Mayores/Feria de Grazalema, *3rd week of Aug*.

El Virgen de los Angeles, *Sept 8*. The festival in homage to the town's patron saint.

Zahara: Romería de Arroymolinos, *June*; Fiestas de Agosto, *Aug*.

Where to Stay and Eat

Arcos ✉ 11630

***__Parador Nacional Casa del Corregidor__, Pza de Cabilda s/n, **t** 956 70 05 00, **f** 956 70 11 16, *arcos@parador.es* (*expensive*). A lovely place to stay, or simply have a coffee – there are big picture windows looking out over the plain. Book ahead.

*__Marqués de Torresoto__, Marqués de Torresoto 4, **t** 956 70 07 17, **f** 956 70 42 05 (*expensive–moderate*). Another excellent choice in an aristocratic, 17th-century mansion, wonderfully situated near the Ayuntamiento.

__El Convento__, C/Maldonado 2, **t 956 70 23 33, **f** 956 70 41 28 (*moderate*). The place to stay in the old town if the *parador* is full (which it frequently is), sharing the views but at half the price. It also has an excellent **restaurant** attached, offering typical Sierran cuisine, such as rabbit and partridge.

***__Peña de Arcos__, C/Muñoz Vazquez 42, **t** 956 70 45 32, **f** 956 70 45 07 (*moderate*). A tastefully designed building with all the amenities, but down in the new town.

Hs San Marcos, C/Marques de Torresoto 6, **t** 956 70 07 21 (*cheap*). A very good budget option in the heart of town; clean, new and with a lively café-bar.

Mesón de la Molinera, Lago de Arcos, **t** 956 70 80 02, **f** 956 70 80 07 (*expensive–moderate*). Delicious regional meat and game dishes and fabulous views of the town.

Parador de Turismo, Pza del Cabildo, **t** 956 70 05 00 (*moderate*). One of the best places to eat in town; good service but no reservations taken.

Grazalema ✉ 11610

****__Hotel Puerta de la Villa__, Pza Pequena 8, **t** 956 13 24 06, **f** 956 13 20 87, *www.grazhotel.com* (*expensive*). This recently opened hotel is the best place to stay and eat. The light, spacious rooms are furnished with outstanding views and all the mod cons. The hotel is just off the main square and is an excellent base for exploring the surrounding countryside. It also has a tiny pool, gym, sauna and the best **restaurant** in town, La Garrocha, featuring *andaluz* dishes of fresh fish, meat and vegetables, prepared in an innovative way.

La Casa de las Piedras, C/las Piedras 32, **t** 956 13 20 14 (*inexpensive*). The cheaper, functional option, just above the main square.

Elsewhere, most of the food and drink options can be found in the streets leading off Pza de España, particularly C/Agua and around Pza Andalucía.

Grazalema has a surprising number of **bars**, most of them to be found on C/Agua.

10–1 and 3.30–6.30, Sat 10–1.30; adm), with impressive 14th-century *mudéjar* wall paintings and gilt altarpieces by Andres Benitez. The 18th-century church of **San Pedro** (*open Mon–Sat 10–1 and 4–7, Sun 10–1.30; adm*), on the clifftop to the east, boasts the paintings *San Ignacio* and *La Dolorosa* by Velasquez's teacher, Pachecho. Arcos also has one of the region's most elaborate and colourful Easter parades (*see* p.653).

Further east, **Grazalema** has been famous for hand-woven blankets since Moorish times, and they are still made here on big old wooden looms. The roads leading off the plaza are especially pretty, lined with little shops and bars, and leading to Pza de los Asomaderos, a viewing area which doubles as a market on Tuesdays.

The surrounding area is the **Sierra Grazalema**, one of the most visually stunning and ecologically important parks in Spain, and makes for wonderful walks and activities such as potholing, caving, hang-gliding and horse riding. It is bounded by some of the prettiest *pueblos blancos* in Andalucía, such as **Zahara** and **Olvera**, their ruined Moorish castles sticking up bravely over the whitewashed houses. Nearby **Ubrique** hangs dramatically over the Río Majaceite; though best known for its leatherwork, it still manages to retain some of its medieval charm.

From Cádiz to Algeciras

The green, hilly countryside of this region looks much like the parts of Morocco just across the straits. The hills force the main road away from the sea, leaving a few villages with fine beaches relatively unspoilt. These make good places to take time out from your overactive holiday, though they're hard to reach unless you have a car.

The main attraction on the coastal road is **Vejer de la Frontera**, whitest of the 'white villages' of Andalucía, strangely moulded around its hilltop site like a Greek island town. The village was probably a Carthaginian citadel before becoming the Roman town of *Besipo*. Now it couldn't be more Moorish in its feel; a Moorish castle dominates the village and the 13th-century Gothic church, built over the site of a mosque, lies deep within the town's sparkling clean, narrow whitewashed streets. On the coast south of Vejer, Nelson breathed his last at Cape Trafalgar in 1805. Ten kilometres south of here is another developing resort, **Zahara de los Atunes** ('of the tunas'). This is one of the most unspoilt coastlines in southern Spain, with miles of fine sandy beach that will be all yours in spring and autumn. The town was the birthplace of Francisco Rivera, or Paquirri, the famous bullfighter. Today it is tranquil, best suited to lazing around in the company of a sundowner,but a huge new *urbanización*, Nueva Zahara, is planned just out of town on the Atlantera road, and numerous large hotels are beginning to spring up, with the whole area rechristened the 'Costa de Zahara'.

Tarifa

Tarifa, at the tip of Spain and of Europe, looks either exotic and evocative, or merely dusty and dreary, depending on the hour of the day and the mood you're in. The town is one of the top destinations in Europe for the masters of windsurfing; there's a lively bar scene and miles of beaches to choose from. Its 10th-century Moorish **castle** is the

Getting Around

By Train

Trains go to Ronda from Algeciras, and from there to all points in eastern Andalucía; there is a daily *Talgo* to Madrid and points north. The station is across from the bus station.

By Bus

Buses to Algeciras from the Comes station in Cádiz are frequent enough, but services to coastal resorts like Conil, Barbate and Zahara are less so (two per day). Algeciras' bus station is in the Hotel Octavio complex, C/San Bernardo; there are buses to La Línea (for Gibraltar) about every half-hour, and connections to the Costa del Sol.

Tourist Information

Vejer: C/Marques de Tamaron s/n, **t** 956 45 01 91, **f** 956 44 75 04 (*open Mon–Fri 9–2 and 5–9, Sat and Sun 11–2 and 6–9*).

Tarifa: northern end of Pso Alameda, outside the western wall of the old town, **t/f** 956 68 09 93 (*open summer Mon–Fri 10.30–2 and 6–8; winter Mon–Fri 10.30–2 and 5–7; closed Sat and Sun*).

Algeciras: Juan de la Cierva s/n, by the port, **t** 956 57 26 36, **f** 956 57 04 75 (*open Mon–Fri 9–2; closed Sat and Sun*).

San Roque: C/San Felipe 7, **t** 956 78 09 27 (*open Mon–Fri 9–3; closed Sat and Sun*).

Where to Stay and Eat

Vejer de la Frontera ✉ 11150

*****Convento de San Francisco**, La Plazvela s/n, **t** 956 45 10 01, **f** 956 45 10 04 (*moderate*). A delightful place; a restored former convent with tastefully designed rooms, lots of original furniture and an excellent **restaurant**, El Refectorio (*moderate*).

Zahara and Los Caños de Meca ✉ 11393

******Antonio II**, Atlanterra 1, **t** 956 43 93 46, **f** 956 43 91 35 (*expensive–moderate*). Recently built and set back from the beach, with lovely views along the coast; it has light airy rooms and a large pool area; excellent value just out of season. Its cheaper brother **Antonio** has a superb **restaurant**.

*****Portofirio**, Ctra Atlanterra 33, 200m from the beach, **t** 956 44 95 15, **f** 956 43 90 80, *porfirio@arrakis.es* (*moderate*). A delightful hotel built in Andalucian style with patios and 24 rooms arranged around a large pool and set in its own grounds. Bedrooms are with terraces and all mod cons, and there's a good, reasonably priced **restaurant**.

*****Doña Lola**, Pza Thomson 1, **t** 956 43 90 09, **f** 956 43 90 08 (*moderate*). The prettiest hotel in town, with rooms set around a patio and overlooking a large pool.

Antonio, Ctra Atlanterra, Km1, **t** 956 43 12 41 (*expensive*). Tourists flock here for high-quality fish and seafood by the beach.

Sergio, **t** 956 43 94 55 (*moderate*). Just out of the town centre, on the Atlanterra road, specializing in meat done Segovia-style, roasted pig, lamb and some seafood.

El Pirato, **t** 956 23 22 55 (*moderate*). Perfectly situated restaurant with a lovely terrace overlooking the beach and the Trafalgar.

Patio la Plazoleta, Pza Tamrín. Vegetarians won't be disappointed with the sumptuous pizza baked on the spot in Italian ovens.

Tarifa ✉ 11380

Rooms are unnecessarily expensive in the 'recently discovered' resort of Tarifa; the same is true of Conil.

site of the legend of **Guzmán el Bueno**, a Spanish knight who in 1292 was defending Tarifa against a force of Moors. Among them was the renegade Infante Don Juan, brother of King Sancho IV, who had Guzmán's young son as a prisoner, and threatened to kill him if Guzmán did not surrender. Guzmán's response was to toss him a dagger. His son was killed, but Tarifa did not fall. Fascist propaganda recycled this legend for the 1936 siege of the Alcázar in Toledo, this time with the Republicans in the villain's role.

★★**Hurricane**, Ctra N340, Km76, **t** 956 68 49 19, **f** 956 68 03 29, *www.hotelhurricane.com* (*expensive*). Further along the coast, this English-owned place is popular with windsurfers; it's unimaginably trendy but you pay for the privilege. *Closed Jan.*

★★★**Balon de España**, Ctra Cádiz–Málaga, Km77, **t** 956 68 43 26, **f** 956 68 04 72 (*moderate*). In a pretty spot by Playa de los Lances, between Tarifa and Punta Palomas to the west of town, this is one of the better options. It has two pools, a gym, tennis and horse-riding facilities. *Closed Nov–Mar.*

Hs Alameda, Pso Alameda 4 (in the old town), **t** 956 68 11 81 (*moderate–inexpensive*). One of the cheaper options in town; some of the pleasant rooms have sea views.

Mesón de Sancho, Ctra N340, Km94, **t** 956 68 49 00, **f** 956 68 47 21 (*expensive*). One of the best restaurants in the area, attached to the above-named hotel. Especially pleasing in winter with its roaring fire, it specializes in home-cooked dishes – favourites are the garlic soup, *urta* in cream sauce and *rabo de toro*. There's also a set menu (*inexpensive*), which includes wine or water.

El Pasillo, C/Guzman el Bueno 14. One of a number of atmospheric tapas bars.

Those seeking **nightlife** should wander around the old town, where the crowds congregate in the numerous bars from about 11pm, before heading down to the beachfront disco, **El Balneario**.

Algeciras ✉ 11200

★★★★**Reina Cristina**, on Pso de la Conferencia, **t** 956 60 26 22, **f** 956 60 33 23 (*expensive*). The hotel of the town's bygone elegance, scene of the Algeciras Conference of 1906, which carved up Morocco and a hotbed of spies during the Second World War. W. B. Yeats spent a winter here.

★★★**Al Mar**, Av. de la Marina 2, **t** 956 65 46 61, **f** 956 65 45 01, *al-mar@eh.etur-sa.es* (*moderate*). Right on the seafront, above the busy arcades filled with cafés and ticket offices, and looking out over the port area.

★★★**Alborán**, Álamo s/n (colonia San Miguel), **t** 956 63 28 70, **f** 956 63 23 20 (*moderate*). A wonderful building in classical Andalucían style, very atmospheric and keenly priced, with an indoor patio and porticoed terrace.

Versailles, Montero Rios 12, **t** 956 54 21 11 (*cheap*). One of a cluster of little *hostales* in the back streets behind the Av. de la Marina.

There are lots of **restaurants** in Algeciras. The streets off Pza Alta, particularly C/Alfonso XI, have a number of good ones.

Los Remos, at Villa Victoria (on the road out of San Roque to La Línea), **t** 956 69 84 12, (*expensive–moderate*). The most famous restaurant in the area, long established and Michelin-rosetted. Though in the shadow of refineries, it is surrounded by lovely gardens; red carnivores beware – it serves mostly fish.

El Copo, Trasmayo 2 (near Los Barrios), **t** 956 67 77 10 (*moderate*). A good place to splash out. The restaurant is draped with fishermen's nets and takes pride in its enormous tanks of lobsters, sea urchins, spider crabs and mussels so that any fish or seafood dishes are supremely fresh. Booking essential. *Closed Sun.*

Almazar, C/Alfonso 9, **t** 956 65 74 77 (*moderate*). One of the best restaurants in town, serving tapas at the bar and great steaks and fish in the tiny restaurant.

Asado Iruña, C/Alfonso 11, **t** 956 65 21 49 (*moderate*). Specializes in Galician dishes.

Casa Castro, Av. Blas Infante 5. One of the oldest and most atmospheric places in town to drink, founded in 1947 and covered in pictures of how the town once looked.

Algeciras

Ask at the tourist office what there is to see and you'll be told, 'Nothing. Nobody ever stays here.' Nevertheless, Algeciras has an interesting history, and an attractive setting opposite the Rock of Gibraltar if you can see through the pollution. It played a significant role in the colonization of the eastern Mediterranean, becoming an important port in the Roman era. It is still has importance as a port today, as well as being a sizeable industrial and fishing centre.

An Excursion to North Africa

The main reason for making the crossing to **Morocco** is to take a look at the limited attractions of Tangier. Unfortunately, the real treasures are all far to the south; you can't judge Morocco on Tangier and Tetuán. But even visiting an international city like Tangier is a chance to explore a fascinating society, and perhaps see a little reflection of the lost culture of al-Andalus. On the other hand, you could stop to shop at Ceuta, one of Spain's last two *presidios* on the North African coast (the other is Melilla).

Getting There

By Ferry

Algeciras's *raison d'être* is its port, and there's no trouble getting a ferry either to Ceuta (at least six boats a day, nine in summer) or to Tangier (at least two boats a day, as many as seven in summer). Ceuta is 40 mins away by ferry and Tangier is 2½ hrs away. A Jetfoil runs five times daily except Friday and Sunday. Among others, FRS Maroc, **t** 956 68 13 30, run a guided one-day tour.

There are lots of official Transmediterránea agents at the port, as well as the unofficial ticket booths along the N340. They all look extremely dodgy, though they sell legitimate tickets. You'll need your passport with you, and you are advised not to do anything foolish on these well-policed borders. There's also a summer hydrofoil service from Tarifa to Tangier and to Gibraltar.

Getting Around

If you're travelling from Ceuta, you'll have to take a **cab** or **city bus** (the one marked '*frontera*') to the border; after some cacophonous border confusion, you wait for the infrequent bus or carefully negotiate a taxi trip to **Tetuán**, 30km away. There's no train from Tetuán to Tangier, but **buses** are cheap and run regularly from the central bus station. They'll take you right to Tangier's port.

Tourist Information

Ceuta: Meulle Cañonero Dato s/n, **t** 956 50 14 10, *www.ciceuta.es*.
Tetuán: 30 Ave Mohammed V, **t** (9) 96 44 07.
Tangier: 29 Blvd Pasteur, **t** (9) 93 82 39/40.

Where to Stay and Eat

Ceuta ✉ 51001

★★★★**Parador La Muralla**, Pza de Nuestra Señora de África 15, **t** 956 51 49 40 (*expensive*). The most comfort and luxury, with a pool and gardens within the walls.

Puerta de Africa, Gran Via 2, **t** 956 51 71 91, **f** 956 51 04 30 (*moderate*). Has a heated pool.

La Kasba, General Yagüe 12, **t** 956 52 10 13 (*moderate*). The best Moroccan restaurant, with couscous, and several Spanish dishes.

Méson de Serafín, Monte Hacho, Km4, **t** 956 51 40 03. Ceuta's prettiest restaurant, with its wonderful view of Gibraltar and the coasts.

Restaurante Mar Chica, Pza Rafael Gilbert 5, **t** 956 51 72 40 (*inexpensive*). A good place to meet the locals, with decent fish dinners.

Moroccan Practicalities

Money

Wait until you get into Morocco to change money as you'll get better rates. The currency is the *dirham*, lately about 15 to the pound, 11 to the US dollar. Hotels and everything else will be almost half as expensive as in Spain.

Dealing With Dealers

This corner of Morocco, being the fullest of tourists, is also full of English-speaking hustlers. This is no exaggeration; around the bus stations and ports they're thick as flies and ten times as persistent. Entertain no offers, especially of drugs or guided tours, and do your best to ignore them. You'll also need your wits to bargain with merchants, taxi drivers and even hotel-keepers. Though you can do this firmly and gracefully, the whole process is extremely tiring. Also, crime is a problem after dark in Tetuán and Tangier.

Ceuta

Every time the Spanish make self-righteous noises about getting Gibraltar back, someone reminds them about their two colonial leftovers on the North African coast, Melilla and Ceuta. Ceuta has a mainly Spanish population; that is why it was excluded from the 1955 withdrawal from the Spanish-Moroccan protectorate. They are the stumbling block, and some way will have to be found to accommodate them before the inevitable transfer of sovereignty. Ceuta is pleasant enough, but there's little reason to go there, perhaps only to see its impressive 16th-century **walls** and moat. There's a **museum** dedicated to Spain's Foreign Legion (a band of cut-throats who became notorious during the civil war under a one-armed, one-eyed commander named José Millán Astray; their slogan: 'Long live Death'). Like Andorra at the other end of Spain, Ceuta is chiefly a big duty-free supermarket. You can easily cross into Morocco from here, though it's better to take the ferry to Tangier.

Tetuán and Tangier

Aside from its heavily polluted river and contraband appeal **Tetuán** is a decent town, full of gleaming white, Spanish colonial architecture; it has a famous market in its *medina*, a historical museum, and it's a good place to purchase Moroccan crafts. On the way into Tangier, note how the Moroccans have turned the old Plaza de Toros into flats. Once in the big square outside the port entrance, you may take your chances with the inexpensive hotels in the surrounding streets, or take a cab to fancier spots in the newer, Europeanized districts. **Tangier** may not be as romantic as you expect; some may find it more so. It is certainly exotic in parts. The wares in the *medina* are fun to look at, but the quarter itself is down-at-heel and dusty. Non-Muslims may not enter mosques in Morocco, but the old governor's palace houses two fine **museums** of archaeology and Moroccan art.

Gibraltar

At first sight it looks like a sphinx, crouching at the water's edge, her hindquarters resting in Europe, her head gazing over the sea and her forepaws stretching in front of her to form the most southerly part of our continent.

Alexandre Dumas, 1846

In under two hours, you can experience the ultimate culture shock: sailing from the smoky souks of Tangier to Algeciras, Spain, with time for *churros* and chocolate before the bus takes you off to a mysterious enclave of red phone booths, warm beer and policemen in silly hats.

The Spanish bus will really take you only as far as **La Línea** (*see* pp.667–70), a town that has built up dramatically since the reopening of the Gibraltar border in 1985, though drug crime and pickpockets are rife. Prices in Gibraltar are outrageous by Spanish standards, and if you are on a tight budget you might be best staying in La Línea – just keep an eye on your possessions.

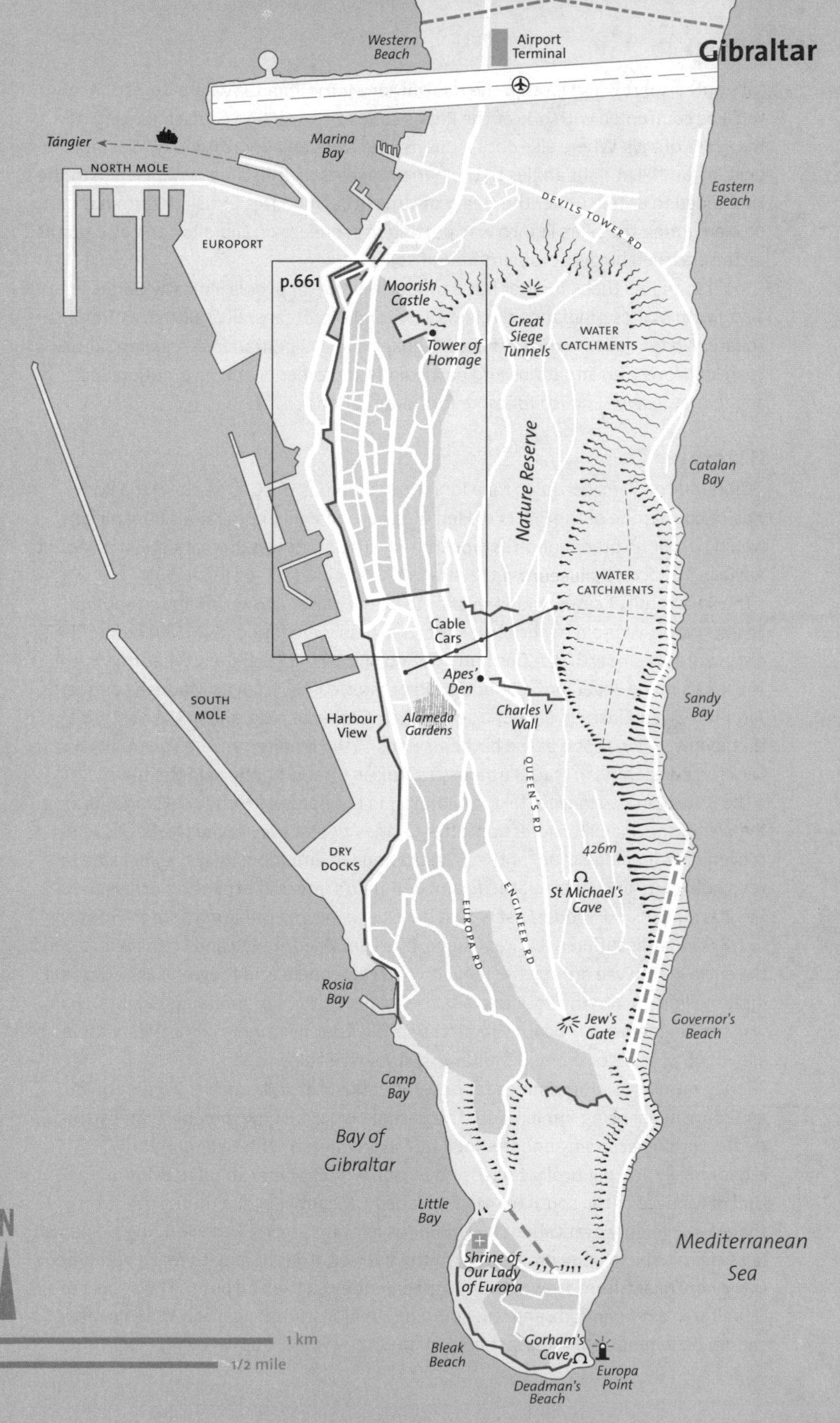
Gibraltar
Western Beach
Airport Terminal
Tángier
Marina Bay
NORTH MOLE
Eastern Beach
DEVILS TOWER RD
EUROPORT
p.661
Moorish Castle
Tower of Homage
Great Siege Tunnels
WATER CATCHMENTS
Nature Reserve
Catalan Bay
WATER CATCHMENTS
Cable Cars
Apes' Den
Charles V Wall
Sandy Bay
SOUTH MOLE
Harbour View
Alameda Gardens
QUEEN'S RD
426m
DRY DOCKS
St Michael's Cave
ENGINEER RD
EUROPA RD
Rosia Bay
Jew's Gate
Governor's Beach
Camp Bay
Bay of Gibraltar
Little Bay
Mediterranean Sea
Shrine of Our Lady of Europa
N
1 km
1/2 mile
Bleak Beach
Gorham's Cave
Europa Point
Deadman's Beach

It's only a short walk through the neutral zone into Gibraltar, where immediately you'll be confronted with one of the Rock's curiosities: you find yourself looking down the noses of 737s. Where else does a busy street cross an airport runway? The airport, built on landfill at right angles to the narrow peninsula (this area was included in the land ceded to Britain under the Treaty of Utrecht), symbolizes British determination to hold on during the years Franco was putting the squeeze on Gibraltar, and also points up the enclave's biggest problem: lack of space.

You'll soon find that Gibraltar has a unique mixture of people – mostly Genoese, along with Maltese, Indians, Spaniards, Jews and Moroccans, all as British as Trafalgar Square. While English is their official language, most Gibraltarians are bilingual, using Spanish in everyday situations and particularly in moments of high emotion and anger; they reserve English for more formal situations.

History

Gibraltar has been occupied for a long time. **Calpe**, as the Greeks knew the Rock, was, of course, one of the Pillars of Hercules, beyond which the jealous Phoenicians would permit no other nation's ships to trade. The other, less dramatic, pillar is **Mount Abyla** in Morocco, visible across the straits on clear days.

The Rock is full of caves, and can claim to be the oldest known inhabited spot in Spain; 50,000-year-old bones of Neanderthal man were found here even before their discovery at Neanderthal in Germany, but no one on the Rock knew what they were. The Rock's name, Jebel Tarik, or 'mountain of Tarik', comes from its Moorish conqueror, Tariq-ibn-Ziyad. Guzmán el Bueno seized it for Castile in 1309, and in the centuries that followed it was one of the battlegrounds of the Mediterranean. The Moors had it back for a while, and in 1540 Barbarossa's Turkish pirates briefly held the town.

The British arrived in 1704, taking Gibraltar in the name of Archduke Charles during the War of the Spanish Succession; after Charles' defeat they found the Rock such a convenient stepping-stone for their Mediterranean ambitions that they decided to keep hold of it. It was a crucial acquisition; Britain's imperial expansion across the Mediterranean and Middle East would have been inconceivable without it. From 1779 to 1783 Gibraltar suffered its Great Siege, by a combined French and Spanish force, and the enclave survived only by the tenacity of its defenders, and their presence of mind in tunnelling up into the Rock to plant their guns on the commanding heights. That was the beginning of modern Gibraltar's series of tunnels and galleries. Now there are about 34 miles of them; Gibraltar is still very well defended.

Today, numerous programmes for housing, industrial and commercial enterprise, and tourism are being implemented as part of an overall government strategy to create a strong economy underpinned by foreign investment. Geographically, economically and politically, there is no reason why Gibraltar shouldn't flourish as a kind of Monaco of the southern Mediterranean. Meanwhile, the thorny question of shared sovereignty over Gibraltar remains as relevant as ever. Renewed Anglo-Spanish talks claim to be making progress, with the two countries hoping to reach agreement in the very near future. However, any agreement must then be put to the people of Gibraltar in a referendum, and this could be a major stumbling block. When a referendum on joining Spain was last held in 1968, they voted it down by 99.6 per cent.

The Town

... a cosy smell of provincial groceries. I'd forgotten how much the atmosphere of home depended on white bread, soap, and soup-squares.

As I Walked Out One Midsummer Morning, by Laurie Lee

Despite a certain amount of bad press, Gibraltar is still much more than the replica of an English seaside town. The town itself is long and narrow, strung out along **Main Street**, home to most of the shops and pubs. The harbour is never more than a couple of blocks away, and the old gates, bastions and walls are fun to explore.

The short tunnel at **Landport Gate** will probably be your entry point if on foot. It leads to **Casemates Square**, one-time parade ground and site of public executions, and now a bustling trading centre. **King's Bastion** is now used as an electricity generating station, but probably began as an ancient Arab Gate, added to by the Spanish in 1575 and further extended in the 18th century by the British under General Boyd. It played an important defensive role at the time of the Great Siege, and it was from this spot that General Elliott commanded during the fierce fighting in 1782.

Near the centre of town, off Line Wall Road, you should spare a few minutes for the small but excellent **Gibraltar Museum** (*18–20 Bomb House Lane; open Mon–Fri 10–6, Sat 10–2; closed Sun*), which offers a painstakingly detailed room-sized model of the Rock as it was in the mid-1800s, and a thorough schooling in its complicated history. The museum is built over the remains of **Moorish baths**, with Roman and Visigothic capitals. Among its exhibits is a replica of the female skull found in Forbes Quarry in 1848, a find that predates the Neanderthal skull found in Germany by eight years.

In Library Street, the former Governor's Residence houses the **Garrison Library**, built during the Great Siege in the hope of preventing boredom in sieges to come. Nearby are the offices of *The Chronicle*, which reported Nelson's victory off Trafalgar. The **Supreme Court** looks diagonally across to the 16th-century former Franciscan

Getting There

By Air

There are at least three daily flights to London (Heathrow and Gatwick, run by British Airways in partnership with GB Airways); twice-weekly flights to Manchester and regular flights to Casablanca and Tangier. British Airways has check-in facilities at Victoria, meaning you don't see your luggage again till you arrive. Monarch Airlines also run regular flights to Gibraltar. Information: British Airways, **t** 79 300, **f** 51 562. Monarch Airlines, **t** 47 477, **f** 70 154.

By Sea

There are three ferries a week from Gibraltar to Tangier (Mon, Wed and Fri); three ferries a week from Tangier to Gibraltar (Mon, Fri and Sun). The fares are expensive, like everything else in Gibraltar. You'd be slightly better off doing it from Algeciras. Bland Line also also run a ferry service; phone for details.

Information: TourAfrica, **t** 77 666, **f** 76 754, *tourafri@gibnet.gi*. Bland Line, **t** 77 050, **f** 44 011, *jpg@gibnet.gi*.

By Bus

There is a direct **bus** service between Gibraltar and the Costa del Sol. Gibraltar's tiny buses also serve the frontier, which is only 800m from the town centre.

By Taxi

There is a **taxi tour** of the Rock, taking in all the sites and lasting about 1½ hours. The charge is about £20, plus additional costs per passenger to include compulsory admission to the Nature Reserve. It's part of a scheme by the taxi drivers' cartel and should be resisted: you can always take the cable car and walk! Gibraltar's taxis also serve the frontier. If you need to call one, contact:

Gibraltar Taxi Association, 12 Waterport, **t** 70 052, **f** 76 986, *gibtaxi@gibnynex.gi*; Gibraltar mini-cab, **t** 79 999.

By Car

If you are coming by **car** you should leave it in La Línea, as there are frequently long delays while customs check the day-trippers' stash of goodies in both directions.

Tourist Information

Gibraltar Information Bureau, Duke of Kent House, Cathedral Square, **t** 74 950, **f** 74 943, *tourism@gibraltar.gi*, *www.gibraltar.gi*.

Local information bureaux: Market Place, **t** 74 982; Gibraltar Museum, 18–20 Bomb House Lane, **t** 74 805 (*all open Mon–Fri 10–6 and Sat 10–2; closed Sun*). There are booths in the airport terminal and at Waterport coach park, **t** 47 671.

Tours: Many companies offer **guided tours** of Gibraltar and its sights; Bland Travel, Cloister Building, Irish Town, **t** 77 012, also runs a 'Trafalgar Tour' from Rosia Bay to Tarifa in Algeciras in summer.

Internet Access: Café Cyberworld, *cyber-world@gibnynex.gi*, £4.50 per hour; or General Internet Business Centre, **t** 44 227, **f** 79 992, *gibc@gibnet.gi*.

Telephones: If you are calling the Rock from elsewhere, the international calling code from Spain to Gibraltar is **t** (9567), and **t** (350).

Currency

The enclave has its own currency, the **Gibraltar pound** (tied in value to the British pound sterling) as well as its own stamps – don't be stuck with any currency when you leave, as it's hard to get rid of anywhere else, especially in Britain! These days, most shops and restaurants in Gibraltar are happy to take British, Spanish or Gibraltarian money.

Shopping

Expats residing in Spain flock across the border to pick up familiar brand-name groceries and household items at British prices; the real bargains are to be had in the top range of luxury goods. Remember that Gibraltar is VAT-free, and savings can be considerable. Here is a selection – but shop around.

Antiques: Lladro, 265 Nao/280 Jasons; 280, Lalique, Jasons.

Cashmere: Carruana, 181 Main Street (jerseys, suits and fabrics).

Cuban cigars and perfume: S. M. Seruya, 165 & 187 Main Street, and Stagnetto's, 56 Main Street.

Electronics: 140 Wingsway.

Gifts: 170 Tagore (jewellery, objets, silver); The Body Shop, 164 Main Street.

Jewellery: Sakata, 92 Main Street; The Red House, 66 Main Street; The Jewel Box, 148 Main Street, 8 Queensway Quay (cultured pearls, Cartier, Rolex, diamonds, gold).

Menswear: García, 192 Main St (Dax, Burberry, etc.).

Porcelain: Omni, 182 Main Street.

Sports and Activities

There are large populations of whales (although sightings are not so common) and dolphins within the Bay and the Straits of Gibraltar. A number of companies offer tours for dolphin viewing; the best are listed below.

For sports enthusiasts the waters are ideal for activities ranging from windsurfing to scuba-diving. In Marina Bay you can charter yachts or cabin cruisers.

Dolphin Safari, from Sheppard's Marina, **t** 71 914. A particularly good tour run by Mike Lawrence. (£25; June–Sept).

Dolphin Bay Cruises, Queensway Quay Marina, **t** 74 598, **t** 45 665, **f** 45 665, *fortuna@gibnet.gi*. Offers one and a half hours of dolphin-watching and a short spin around the Rock for £18.

Nautilus IV, based in Marina Bay, **t** 73 400, *www.dolphin.gi*. Offers tours in a semi-submersible boat, where you can ride above or watch the dolphins through an underwater viewing cabin.

Dive Chambers, Marina Bay, **t** 45 649, *www.divegib.gi*, PADI centre. Try here for diving. There are some excellent dive spots off Gibraltar and, not surprisingly, plenty of wrecks, including aircraft.

Where to Stay

Gibraltar's hotels have all undergone an extensive refurbishment programme, which has served to modernize and improve most of them; however, it has also put the prices right up.

Eliott Hotel, Governor's Parade, **t** 70 500, **f** 70 243, *eliott@gibnet.gi*, *www.gibraltar.gi/eliotthotel* (*luxury*). Offers sterile anonymity for the businessman, along with a/c, sauna, Jacuzzi, very pleasant rooftop pool and bar.

Rock Hotel, 3 Europa Road, **t** 73 000, **f** 73 513, *rockhotel@gibnynex.gi*, *www.rockhotel.gibraltar.com* (*expensive*). A resort hotel of long standing, up on the heights – about halfway up, under the cable car and near Gibraltar's casino. Considering its position and its history, this should be one of the world's great 'colonial' hotels; sadly it isn't. Visiting dignitaries and the occasional celebrity stay here, leaving their signatures on the bar menu. There's a pool, landscaped gardens and rooms with sea view and balconies, and a very pleasant **café** with views to North Africa and Spain.

★★★★**Caleta Hotel**, Sir Herbert Miles Road, on Catalan Bay, **t** 76 501, **f** 42 143, *www.caleta-hotel.com* (*expensive*). If you need a beach, this resort is very modern and recently upgraded. There are rooms with balconies, a pool, a number of good **restaurants** with reasonably priced set menus, and a bar.

Bristol, 8–10 Cathedral Square, **t** 76 800, **f** 77 613, *bristhtl@gibnet.gi* (*moderate*). In the heart of town, with a swimming pool, and TV in all rooms.

Cannon Hotel, 9 Cannon Lane (just off Main Street), **t** 51 711, **f** 51 789, *www.cannonhotel.gi* (*moderate*). You could also try this centrally located hotel with patio, bar and restaurant.

If you're on a budget, stay in La Línea if you can bear the place. Prices in Gibraltar are two to four times what they would be for comparable hotels in Spain.

Toc H Hostel, Line Wall Road (near the harbour), **t** 51 106 (*inexpensive*). The one opportunity for a cheap room in Gibraltar; they will put you up for £5pp per day. Understandably, it is usually full.

Eating Out

Sausage, beans and chips have long been the zenith of Gibraltar's culinary achievement, but food here is no longer solely restricted to authentic pub grub and fish 'n' chips. For the best restaurants on the Rock, get out of the environs of Main Street and head for

Queensway Quay, or the more established **Marina Quay**, where you will find a reasonable selection of seafood, Italian dishes and even tapas. Away from the quays, olive oil, the sun-dried tomato, or anything grilled (as opposed to fried) is almost unheard of. The least dangerous dining in the centre of town is probably Indian, where standards do rise a little. Chinese is largely inedible.

You can **drink** to your heart's content in Gibraltar (wend your way to one of its 360 or so pubs), but costs are about double the Spanish equivalent. Pubs, as in Britain, are open all day till 11pm. Wines and spirits are cheap in the supermarkets and off-licences, but no bargain in restaurants or pubs.

Expensive

Rock Hotel, 3 Europa Road, **t** 73 000, **f** 73 513, *www.rockhotel.gibraltar.com*. Arguably the most pleasant place for lunch; its colonial-style décor and discreet waiters set the scene for Gibraltar's answer to Raffles in Singapore. The steaks are flown in fresh from the UK daily.

International Casino Club, 7 Europa Road, **t** 76 666, **f** 40 843. The restaurant in the casino club is popular among the locals, and you won't find a better place for five-star service and the food is still as good; there is also often live entertainment. There's a wide range of international dishes on offer, and the terrace has great views overlooking the Bay and Algeciras – a perfect place to watch the sun go down on the Atlantic.

Moderate

El Patio, 54 Irish Town, **t** 70 822. A reasonably pleasant spot, if overpriced; it offers Basque cuisine and Mediterranean fish specialities. Fills up at lunch. *Closed Sat lunch and Sun.*

Strings, 44 Cornwalls Lane, **t** 78 800. A small, intimate restaurant, serving international dishes: smoked salmon, gravadlax, shrimp in wine sauce. *Closed Mon.*

Sax, International Commercial Centre. A piano bar/restaurant that attracts a young crowd; expect queues at weekends. The fare is mixed – English, Mexican, Italian – and the lunch menu is particularly recommended; snacks are available, and there's live music two evenings a week. *Closed Sun lunch.*

Maharaja, 5 Tuckey's Lane, **t** 75 233. One of a few Indian restaurants; this one has the simplest furnishings of the lot, and offers some of the best food. The service is efficient and friendly, and all the old Indian favourites can be found on the menu.

Da Paolo, Marina Bay, **t** 76 799. One of the most pleasant places to eat in Gib, with well-prepared fish specialities, such as fillet of John Dory in dill sauce, a particularly good Spanish wine list, a fine view and some interesting characters passing through.

The Little Mermaid, Marina Bay, **t** 77 660. A refreshing Danish addition to the culinary scene. The interior is sleek and modern, and all the usual Scandinavian specialities appear, including marinated herring, salmon and prawns; help your open sandwiches down with an Aalborg Akvazit and Tuborg chaser, instead of wine.

Waterfront Bar/Restaurant, Queensway Quay, **t** 45 666. Right on the marina, with good food at reasonable prices; try the excellent *moules marinières*, caught from within the bay in season and twice the size of anything you can get back home.

Casa Pepe, **t** 46 967. Probably Gibraltar's best tapas bar, specializing in *paella*, *jamón iberico* and fresh fish in *taberna*-style surroundings. *Closed Wed.*

Inexpensive

The Clipper, 78B Irish Town, **t** 79 791. A gastro-pub which is popular with Gibraltarians and visitors alike for its roast beef and lasagne.

The Royal Calpe, 176 Main Street, **t** 75 890. Another pub where the grub, served piping hot, is popular with everyone and authentically English.

Bull and Bush, 30 Parliament Lane, **t** 72 951. As a parting shot, drop into this patriotic pub complete with portrait of the Queen; drinks are chalked up on a slate as in days of yore. Pictures of England and English pubs cover the walls; and there are no tapas in sight, just crisps and hard-boiled eggs.

Corks, 79 Irish Town, **t** 75 566. Try this place for a change from the numerous pubs; it also serves food.

Casino, 7 Europa Road, **t** 76 666. Gibraltar's late-nightlife happens here; dress well and take lots of cash.

convent, the **Governor's Residence** today, where the changing of the guard takes place (*check with tourist office for times*).

Southport Gate, at the top of Main Street, was built in 1552, during the reign of Charles V. The wall stretching east from the gate is **Charles V's Wall**, which ends just short of the water catchments at **Philip II's Arch**. Beyond the gate you can wander through the small, shady Trafalgar Cemetery and, a few steps away, the rather more cheeful flora of the **Alameda Gardens**.

The Rock

The famous silhouette, surprisingly, does not hang over the seaward edge, but faces backwards towards La Línea. From 500 yards up, the views from the upper part of the Rock are magnificent: the Costa del Sol curves away to the east, the mountains of Morocco sit in a purple haze across the narrow straits to the south; and, way below, where the Mediterranean opens out into the wide and wild Atlantic, tiny toy-like craft plough through the waters in full sail. The Rock's entire eastern face is covered by the **water catchment system** that supplies Gibraltar's water – an engineering marvel to equal the tunnels. The upper part of the Rock has been turned into a **nature reserve** (*open Mon–Sat 9.30 to sunset; closed Sun; adm*), which can be reached by cable car (***t** 77 826, leaves every 15 mins Mon–Sat 9.30–6; adm; closed Sun*) or through the entrance at Jews' Gate, on the hairpin bend where Engineer and Queen's Roads meet.

Apart from panoramic views, admission to the reserve will get you a look at Gibraltar's best-known citizens. The **Apes' Den** is halfway up the Rock where you can see Barbary apes, a species of tail-less macaque. These gregarious monkeys are much more common on the African side of the straits and in Europe are unique to Gibraltar. There is an old saying that, as long as they're here, the British will never leave. Understandably, they're well cared for, and have been since the days of their great benefactor, Winston Churchill. The Gibraltarians are fond of them, even though (as a local guidebook solemnly notes) they 'fail to share the same respect for private property' as the rest of us.

Nearby are remains of a **Moorish wall** and, a short walk to the south, **St Michael's Cave**, a huge cavern of delicate stalactites. Lower St Michael's Cave was accidentally discovered when the caves were being converted into a military hospital during the Second World War. It contains a huge **underground lake** (*tours by appointment only; call **t** 55 606, **t** 73 527 or **t** 55 120*). It's now used for concerts and fashion shows, but do bring a waterproof hat – the roof leaks (*son-et-lumière shows can be prearranged*).

At the northern end of the Rock are the **Great Siege Tunnels** an extensive section of the original British tunnels, which were hacked and blown out of the rock during the Great Siege – the work of Sergeant Major Ince, who was rewarded for his labours with a plot of farming land and a racehorse. The Galleries have wax dummies of 18th-century British soldiers hard at work digging and blowing up Spaniards.

Gibraltar has a few beaches, but they're all on the eastern side, opposite the town, and accessible by bus. **Catalan Bay** and **Sandy Bay** are both a little built-up and crowded. **Eastern Beach** is better, though unfortunately it's next to the airport.

The Costa del Sol

At first glance, it doesn't seem the developers could have picked a more unlikely place to conjure up the Mediterranean's biggest holiday playground, for the stretch of coast between Gibraltar and Málaga is devoid of beautiful scenery. Spain's low prices are one explanation, and guaranteed sunny days another. The reason it happened here, though, is breathtakingly simple: cheap land. Forty years ago, this coast was one of the forgotten backwaters of Spain. However, after a few decades of holiday intensity, this unlikely strip is beginning to develop a personality of its own. Any hype you hear or read about the Costa is utter nonsense; on the other hand, it has become

almost fashionable to mock the Costa for its brash *turismo* exuberance, and that is uncalled for. The Costa does attract people who ask little of their holiday (or retirement) except good weather, like-minded companions, and places to play. Their presence, in such large numbers and from so many nations, has created a unique international community. It's easy to forget you're in Spain, but if you ever get homesick you can always take a break from Andalucía and have a good time by the beach.

La Línea to Malaga

The only Spanish town to border British territory, **La Línea** has something of a split personality, retaining its Spanish essence while taking in its stride a daily invasion of

Getting Around

By Bus

Two bus companies serve La Línea: Transportes Comes runs the service to Algeciras (every half-hour) and points west; and the Portillo company serves the Costa del Sol, Málaga and Madrid. Both have offices on Av. de España, just off La Línea's central square. From here it's a six-minute walk to the border with Gibraltar. The Portillo bus company has the franchise for this stretch of coast; and with the growth of tourism its service has become almost like a city bus-line, stopping every few hundred yards in the developed areas between Algeciras and Málaga, so be sure to check how long your bus will take to arrive if you're planning an intercity journey and change to an express service. There's never too long a wait in either direction. San Pedro is where the buses branch off for Ronda, an easy destination from any town on the coast. You can also go directly to Sevilla or Madrid at least once daily from the bus station in Marbella, Av. del Trapiche, **t** 952 76 44 00.

By Train

There are no trains to La Línea. The nearest railway station, eight km away at San Roque, has services to Ronda and all destinations in Andalucía. The N340 connects all the towns and villages along the coast, though at Fuengirola you can pick up a suburban train, which runs a regular service to Málaga. It stops at Torremolinos and most other points in between.

By Car

There is also the motorway, rather confusingly called the N340 or E15, but with a *peaje* or toll system. It bypasses all the towns, and is fast and usually empty.

Tourist Information

La Línea: Av. 20 de Abril, just off Pza de la Constitución (next to the bus station), **t** 956 76 99 50, **f** 956 76 72 64 (*open Tues–Fri 9–7, Sat 10–2, Mon 9–3; closed Sun*).

Casares: Town Hall, La Fuente 24, **t** 952 89 41 50.

Estepona: Av. San Lorenzo 1, **t** 952 80 20 02, **f** 952 80 09 13 (*open Mon–Fri 9–6, Sat 9–1.30; closed Sun*).

San Pedro de Alcántara: Av. Marques del Duego 69, **t** 952 78 52 52.

Sports and Activities

To discover what's on, take a quick look through the local publications – *Lookout*, a slick monthly magazine for the British on the Costa, or *The Entertainer* or *The Reporter*; a weekly English edition of Málaga's newspaper *Sur*, which appears every Friday; and various local entertainment guides.

Escuela de Arte Ecuestre, Rio Padron Alto, Ctra 340, Km159, **t** 952 80 80 77. A horse-riding school founded in 1998 and built in traditional *andaluz* style.

Estepona Golf, **t** 952 11 30 81.

Happy Divers Club, Hotel Atalaya, Ctra N340, Km168, **t** 952 88 90 00, **f** 952 80 81 66, *www.happy-divers-marbella.com*. A scuba-diving centre offering a number of courses and excursions; it also has a branch at the marina.

Where to Stay and Eat

La Línea ✉ 11300

The only reason to stay here is that it is cheaper than staying in Gibraltar. Eating out here is a lot cheaper than in Gibraltar, particularly if you want to spoil yourself on fish.

★★★**Aparthotel Rocamar**, Av. de España 170, **t** 956 17 69 23, **f** 956 17 30 19 (*moderate*). Has the most comforts.

Almadraba, Los Caireles 2, **t** 956 10 55 66 (*moderate*). Has a first-class view of the Rock and the Bay of Algeciras.

★**La Campana**, C/Carboneros 3 (just off the main plaza), **t** 956 17 30 59 (*inexpensive–cheap*). The best bargain in town, with a good little **restaurant** downstairs.

La Marina, Pso Marítimo, **t** 956 17 15 31 (*moderate*). The speciality here is a favourite of the southern coast of Spain: grilled sardines on a spit.

El Mirador, Playa Sta Barbara, **t** 956 17 08 91 (*inexpensive*). This restaurant is in an excellent position to view the Rock; it specializes in *paella*.

Estepona ✉ 29680

The main road to Estepona from Marbella has some of the finest hotels along the Costa del Sol, but be warned: this sort of splendour does not come cheap, though out of season there are good deals to be had. The town itself has a dearth of quality hotels, although there are a number of acceptable two-star places. A few good options are listed below:

★★★★★**Las Dunas Beach Hotel and Spa**, Ctra 340, Km163, **t** 952 79 43 45, **f** 952 79 48 25, *www.senda.ari.es/lasdunas* (*luxury*). One of the 'Leading Hotels of the World', and with prices to match, complete with health spa plus all the treatments, **restaurants**, bars, live music, vast pool.

★★★★★**Hotel Playabella**, Ctra 340, Km163, **t** 952 88 08 68, **f** 952 33 36 55, *www.hotelesplaya.com* (*luxury*). Without doubt the best-value luxury hotel along here; comes with several pools, its own beach, health centre, a large **restaurant** and activities for children.

★★**Dobar**, Av. de España 177, **t** 952 80 06 00 (*moderate*). Functional and the best value in terms of location, right on the seafront.

★★**Aquamarina**, Av. San Lorenzo 32, **t** 952 80 61 55, **f** 952 80 45 98, *royberhotels@costasol.net* (*moderate*). Just down from the *turismo*, recently refurbished. It has clean, spacious doubles, many with balconies, all with bath and a/c and a stone's throw from the beach.

There are plenty of inexpensive *hostales* both in the town and on the beach.

★**El Pilar**, Pza de las Flores 10, **t** 952 80 00 18 (*inexpensive*). In a pretty setting.

★**La Malagueña**, C/Raphael 1, **t** 952 80 00 11 (*inexpensive*). Next to El Pilar and offering much the same for the same price.

There are lots of **restaurants** in and around Estepona, some of them very good indeed.

Tipico Andaluz, **Bodega Sabor Andaluz** and **Sabor Roceiro**. Three restaurants grouped together at the far end of C/Caridad, all offering wonderful *embutidos* such as *jamón iberico* and *queso manchego*.

La Casa de Mi Abuela, C/Caridad 54, **t** 952 79 19 67 (*moderate*). Offers a selection of grills, including Argentinian-style *churrasco*.

El Vagabundo, Urbanización Monte Biarritz, Ctra Cádiz, Km168.5, **t** 952 88 66 98 (*moderate*). A converted outpost tower on the N340, offering a choice of international dishes, including seafood pancakes and roast duck.

Estepona has a lot to offe in the way of **nightlife**, especially at weekends. Since C/Real was pedestrianized the town centre has exploded with clubs and bars.

San Pedro de Alcántara ✉ 29670

★★**El Pueblo Andaluz**, on the coastal highway, Km172, **t** 952 78 05 97, **f** 952 78 91 04, *commercial@globales.com* (*inexpensive*). A pretty place near the beach built around an old Andalucían home with a pool, playground, **restaurant** and garden.

★★★**Cortijo Blanco**, **t** 952 78 09 00, **f** 952 78 09 16, *commercial@globales.com* (*inexpensive*). Nearby El Pueblo Andaluz, of a similar quality and run by the same management, but with parking and a nursery.

There is a wide variety of bars and **restaurants** in San Pedro itself, on the 'Ronda Road' as you leave towards the Sierras, and in Nueva Andalucía, a vast area of beautiful countryside between San Pedro and Marbella.

Méson El Coto, **t** 952 78 66 88 (*moderate*). A handsome Andalucían house offering magnificent views and a top-class kitchen specializing in delicious grills and seasonal game; situated 6km above town on the road to Ronda.

El Gamonal, Ctra Ronda–Camino La Quinta, **t** 952 78 99 21 (*moderate*). A very pretty Spanish restaurant, cosy inside, with a flowering terrace, specializing in roasts; tucked inside Nueva Andalucía near La Quinta. *Closed Wed.*

Ogilvy & Mailer, **t** 952 81 07 42 (*moderate*). On a charming site by Los Naranjos Country Club, stylish without claiming to be particularly Spanish; serves some of the finest and most innovative Mediterranean food on the coast, accompanied by Carol Mailer's carefully selected wines. A memorable evening here is surprisingly reasonable for this kind of quality. *Closed Sun.*

Activities on the Costa

There are **bullrings** in Marbella, Fuengirola, Estepona, Mijas and Benalmádena Costa, though *corridas* are infrequent and the only serious action is in Málaga. For **music**, there are concerts at the Casa de Cultura and Salon Varietés in Fuengirola and the Mijas Arts Centre, and at the Nueva Andalucía bullring near Marbella, among others; many also offer art exhibitions and guitar and dance courses. For **sports**, there are around 60 golf courses, though green fees are a little dear; tennis at many of the hotels; even snooker clubs (in Fuengirola). Of course all the **watersports** are popular; you can always make arrangements for equipment or instruction through your hotel. There are **casinos** at Benalmádena Costa and at Puerto Banús.

For kids there's a Disneyland-style **amusement park** at Benalmádena Costa called Tivoli World as well as the **Sea Life Park**. There's a small **zoo** in Fuengirola and Super Bonanza **cruise boats** for excursions between Torremolinos and Puerto Banús. **Horse riding** can be arranged at the El Castillo Salvador stables outside Fuengirola, at El Rengo (***t*** *908 75 52 75*), and at Rancho Antonio (***t*** *952 46 83 80*). The **Aquapark** in Fuengirola has slides and rides to keep the little ones amused for an afternoon. For a change, contact Viajes CHAT travel agency in Torremolinos (***t*** *952 38 71 86*), and they'll make arrangements for a **hot-air balloon ride** over the Costa, champagne included.

day-trippers and smugglers. It's a modern town with little to detain you, though staying here is an alternative to the high prices on the Rock. The *urbanizióines* begin right after the Rock and stretch eastwards to Málaga, taking in **Sotogrande**, with a few fancy villas, and **Puerto Sotogrande**, and up-and-coming marina complex. The first town of any note is unprepossessing **Manilva**. This has little save the ruins of a **Roman spa** to recommend it, but it's worth driving up from here into the Sierra Bermeja to **Casares**, a typical, white, Andalucían village perched on a hill under the ruins of its castle. Granted independence in 1796, the village has several monuments, a restored house belonging to Blas Infante's uncle, and a collection of Roman ruins.

Estepona, the first of the big resort towns east of Gibraltar, is also the quietest. Unfortunately the big developers have moved in and the town is losing its past appeal, but the old town remains a pleasant, quiet place, with narrow streets and some very pretty squares. **San Pedro de Alcántara** is a little fancier, though still pleasingly unsophisticated to look at. From here the only good road through the mountains will take you to Ronda and its surrounding villages.

Marbella

Marbella is the smartest, most expensive and complex resort in Spain. When you arrive, you might find yourself asking why – its appeal is not obvious. The place has been much maligned and, it's true, over-developed, but the old quarter is still a delight, as charming as Andalucía at its most typical, and without ever being cutesy or tripperish. Nonetheless, for the earnest tourist there is not a great deal of point in spending time in the town. You'll pay high prices without getting in on the action,

Getting Around

By Bus

Marbella is well connected by bus, with frequent Portillo services trundling into town (if you are coming from Estepona or San Pedro de Alcántara), or into the new bus station north of the centre.

By Car

The N340 connects all the towns and villages along the coast, passing just north of the centre of Marbella. There is also the motorway, rather confusingly called either the N340 or E15. It is usually fast and empty, but has a *peaje* or toll system.

Tourist Information

Marbella: Gioneta La Foutanilla, **t** 952 77 14 42 (*open winter Mon–Fri 9.30–8.30 (summer 9.30–9.30), Sat 10–2 (summer 10–4); closed Sun*).

There's also an office on Pza Los Naranjos, **t** 952 82 35 50.

Puerto Banús: Av. Principal, **t** 952 81 74 74.

Festivals

Marbella: Feria, *May*. Marbella gets into full swing; an event you're unlikely to forget.

Where to Stay

Marbella ✉ 29600

There are fewer hotels than you might imagine, as villa life is very much the form. Don't count on finding a room at any price in high season; package tours have taken over and most places are booked pretty solidly.

********Los Monteros****, Ctra Cádiz, Km187 (6km east of Marbella), **t** 952 77 17 00, **f** 952 82 58 46, *www.monteros.com* (*luxury*) One of the oldest and best-loved hotels. Its beach club is the height of restrained luxury and room prices include green fees at the hotel's own Río Real golf course.

*******Puente Romano**, Ctra Cádiz, Km178, **t** 952 82 09 00, **f** 952 77 57 66, *www.puente romano.com* (*luxury*). One of the most beautiful, if not the priciest, hotels. Its name comes from the genuine Roman bridge incorporated into its surroundings.

******Marbella Club Hotel**, Ctra de Cádiz 178, **t** 952 82 22 11, **f** 952 82 98 84, *www.marbella-club.com* (*luxury*). Alfonso Hohenlohe's jet-set retreat, which put Marbella on the map in the late 1950s, is still going strong and is Marbella's most sophisticated hotel.

******El Fuerte**, Av. El Fuerte s/n, **t** 952 86 15 00, **f** 952 82 44 11, *www.hotelelfuerte.es* (*expensive*). Next to the shopping centre, at the end of the promenade overlooking the sea.

*****Las Chapas**, Ctra Cádiz, Km192, **t** 951 05 53 00, **f** 951 05 53 33 (*expensive*). A nearly self-sufficient holiday complex with tennis, golf and watersports; situated right on the beach, 8km to the east of Marbella.

*****Don Miguel Club Med**, **t** 952 77 28 00 (*moderate*). Situated in the hills above Marbella (you won't need the address) Club Med does everything for you. It's likely to be a little regimented for some, but the food is sensational, at least in quantity. It helps if you speak French.

Surprisingly, there is a wide selection of cheaper *hostales*, most of them in the old town, around C/Peral and C/San Francisco.

****Hs Enriqueta**, Los Caballeros 18, **t** 952 82 75 52 (*inexpensive*). Particularly well placed, near the Pza Los Naranjos.

****Hotel Paco**, C/Peral 16, **t** 952 77 12 00 (*inexpensive*). An adequate two-star option.

Hs de Pilar, Mesconcillo 4, **t** 952 82 99 36 (*cheap*). British-run and popular mostly with young budget travellers.

Albergue Juvenil Marbella, Trapiche 2, **t** 952 77 14 91, **f** 952 86 32 27 (*cheap*). A youth hostel with small dormitories and some rooms.

Eating Out

There's a wealth of places to suit all tastes and pockets in and around Marbella. Some of the best options are listed below.

Expensive

HsR del Mar, Av. Cánovas del Castillo 1A, **t** 952 77 02 18. Has summer dining on the patio looking on to the pool, and cosy in winter. Specialities include duck in a sauce of *cassis* and candied figs. *Open eves only, closed Sun*.

La Camargue, Ctra Cádiz, Km178.5, **t** 952 82 40 85. Recently transformed from the Marbella Hill Club and still attracting the same select clientele. Its setting in beautiful gardens with lovely views and a flexible, interesting menu assure its continued popularity. The menu includes poached salmon with fresh basil sauce, *solomillo* with two pepper sauces, and a selection of desserts. *Open every eve in summer.*

La Meridiana, Camino de la Cruz s/n (behind the mosque), **t** 952 77 61 90. Marbella's most expensive and glamorous restaurant, offering international cuisine and designer dishes such as salad of angler fish marinated in dill, or braised veal sweetbreads with grapefruit. *Open eves only in summer.*

Francis Butler's Rustic Farmhouse, Finca Besaya, Río Verde Alto, **t** 952 86 13 86. Francis Butler is usually a charming host and the farmhouse has a magnificently tasteful Baroque interior. There's a terrace overlooking avocado trees and rooms littered with antiques with open fires in the winter. He serves international cuisine, including duck breast in mango sauce and exquisite chocolate sorbet. Booking essential (if only to ask for directions). *Open eves Wed–Sat.*

Toni Dalli, The Oasis Club, Ctra Cádiz, Km176, **t** 952 77 00 35. Housed in a Moorish mansion with a central courtyard and a magnificent view of the beach. The owner Dalli, a retired Italian opera singer, often entertains his customers personally with an aria; otherwise there's a regular lively showbiz band. Italian food is obviously the order of the day.

La Hacienda, Ctra Cádiz, Km193, Urbanización Las Chapas, **t** 952 83 12 67/952 83 11 16. Frequently described as the best restaurant on the Costa del Sol. The ingredients are super-fresh, but the service can be surly and the atmosphere strained; there's a terrace with statues and stone arches. *Closed Mon and Tues, Sept–June and 14 Nov–21 Dec.*

Club Miraflores, on the Urbanización Miraflores, Ctra Cádiz, Km199, **t** 952 83 01 02. Serves consistently good food: grilled salmon with hollandaise sauce,or baby chicken casseroled in white wine; it would be hard to imagine a more agreeable spot to spend an evening, complete with live music and dancing.

Santiago, Pso Maritímo 5, **t** 952 77 00 78. Try this long-established place for the best *paella* in Marbella – in fact some of the best Spanish cooking on the coast.

La Pesquera, on the beach at Puerto Banús. Some of the best-value seafood in the area.

Moderate

Dalli Pasta Factory, Av. Fontailla s/n, in the centre of Marbella, **t** 952 77 67 76. Toni Dalli seems to be building an empire around Marbella, and no one begrudges him his success. This one serves fresh pasta, delicious *antipasto* and a spicy *tagliolini rabiaha*. You can eat well with wine for a very reasonable price here. In Puerto Banús the Dalli brothers' Pasta and Pizza factories stand next door on C/Rivera.

Inexpensive

The tapas bars are excellent, both in the old town and in the streets behind the Alameda, such as C/Carlos Mackintosh. Plenty of inexpensive places can be found around C/Aduar. Many of the inexpensive beach restaurants that run the length of the coast, known as *chiringuitos*, are open year-round.

Casa La Vieja, C/Aduar 18, **t** 952 82 13 12. Serves up a good plate of mixed fish.

Nightlife

Most action is in **Puerto Banús**, with its late bars, discos and piano bars. The best bars in the old town are concentrated on and around the Pza de los Naranjos, and slightly off to the west at Pza de los Olivos.

Sinatra's, at the main entrance to the port. The classic hang-out of the see-and-be-seen set.

Night Café, a café by day and club by night.

Crescendo, behind Da Paolo in Puerto Banús, **t** 952 81 55 15. A very lively piano bar which slogs through each night until 5am.

In Marbella itself action can be found in the streets leading up from the Pso Maritimo and around the Puerto Deportivo.

Atrium, C/Gregorio Marañon 11. A place to investigate for early drinks; super-hip and pricey with outdoor seating and foliage.

Café del Mar, the Puente Romano's beachside bar/club. Has been in vogue for a number of years now. *Closes at 5am.*

which takes place in a score of private clubs, private villas and private yachts. Besides, few foreigners actually live in old Marbella itself, having moved out to enclaves outside the town. **Puerto Banús** is the brilliantly designed, ancient-looking (but modern) development six kilometres to the west, with a marina full of gin palaces.

Fuengirola and Around

Thirty years ago, **Fuengirola** was a typical whitewashed Spanish fishing village. It's still white, but hardly typical, and even less Spanish. The town, and its adjacent community of **Los Boliches**, may be the only place in Spain where you'll see a sign in a

Tourist Information

Fuengirola: Av. Jesús Santos Rein 6, in an old railway station, **t** 952 46 76 25 (*open daily 9.30–1.30 and 4–8, Sat am only*).

Mijas: **t** 952 48 59 00.

Benalmádena: Av. Antonio Machado 10, **t** 952 44 12 95, **f** 952 44 06 78 (*open 9–9*).

Torremolinos: Pza de la Independencia, **t** 952 37 42 31.

Where to Stay

You should come on a package tour if you find Fuengirola and Torremolinos to your taste. That's what these places are for, and you would get a better deal. If you're just passing and want to rest in anonymity by the beach, there are some possibilities.

Fuengirola ✉ 29640

★★★★★**Byblos Andaluz**, Urbanización Mijas Golf, **t** 952 46 02 50, **f** 952 58 63 27, *www.byblos/andaluz.com* (*expensive*) This haven of peace and tranquillity is only 5km from the centre of town, with every imaginable luxury and a glamorous clientele.

★★★**Florida**, Pso Marítimo, **t** 952 47 61 00, **f** 952 58 15 29, *florida@spa.es* (*moderate*). Has a pool and gardens, and though not luxurious is still a comfortable enough place.

★★**Cendrillon**, **t** 952 47 00 00 (*moderate*). Much the same as the Florida, only with tennis.

★**Yamasol**, Av. Ramon y Cajal, **t** 952 58 44 00 (*inexpensive*). Clean and functional; typical of the many inexpensive *hostales* around the centre of Fuengirola and in the suburb of Los Boliches to the north.

Torremolinos ✉ 29620

In Torremolinos and its neighbouring stretch of tourist sprawl, at Benalmádena Costa, the possibilities are endless, though these, too, will probably be packed with package tours. The following are just a few options.

There are a number of swanky four-star hotels, all offering much the same – pool, air-conditioned rooms and dull hotel food.

★★★★**Pez Espada**, Av. Salvador Allende 11, **t** 952 38 03 00 (*expensive*). Built in 1959, this was the first luxury hotel to appear in the city, and it put Torre on the map. It's fading now, but still of a high standard and in a good spot just out of the centre and near the beach.

★★★★**Alay**, Av. Alay s/n, **t** 952 44 14 40, **f** 952 44 63 80 (*expensive*). In a good location, just above the Puerto Marina, but you pay for the privilege.

Royal Al-Andalus, C/Al-Andalus 3, **t** 952 38 12 00 (*expensive*). Just off the main road and set in its own grounds, complete with huge pool and sea-facing rooms with balcony.

★★★★**Hotel Cervantes**, C/Rió Cañoles 1, **t** 952 38 40 33 (*moderate*). A few yards from all the action, this offers all the comforts you expect, with two pools, big rooms with balconies, a disco, café and a very good **restaurant**.

★★**Miami**, C/Aladino 14, in Carihuela, **t** 952 38 52 55 (*moderate*). This house was built as a holiday villa by Picasso's cousin, and is quite charming despite its shabbiness.

★★★**Sol Príncipe**, Pso Colorado 26, **t** 952 38 41 00 (*moderate*). A comfortable hotel in the Playamar area, featuring three pools and a **restaurant**.

shop-window reading '*Se habla español*'. Today the Spaniards live mostly in town; the foreigners drive in from the *urbanizaciónes* for pub-hopping or shopping. Fuengirola's outdoor **market** (*Tues*), is the best place to observe this curious community.

Unlike other resorts on the Costa, there are some things to see: the Moorish **Castillo de Sohail** above town, a **bullring**, even the brand new façade of a **Roman temple**.

Mijas

Day-trippers from Fuengirola totally overwhelm the village of Mijas, three kilometres up in the hills, but at dusk it returns to the hands of the foreign residents, who count for 90 per cent of the village's population. The coachloads pour in hoping to

Budget places are few and far between, most placed some way out of town. Some of the good bargains can be found out towards Carihuela, along Av. Carlota Alessandri.

****Sol y Miel**, Av. Blas Infante, **t** 952 44 11 14 (*inexpensive*). Your best bet, close to the main station.

Victoria, Los Naranjos 103 (opposite the bus station), **t** 952 38 10 47 (*inexpensive*). This is pleasant, conveniently placed and reasonably priced.

Hotel Guadalupe, Bajondillo, C/Peligro 15, **t/f** 952 38 19 37 (*inexpensive*). Near the beach and away from the mayhem.

Eating Out

Fuengirola

Dining in Fuengirola is an experience; you can choose from Indonesian to Belgian without going broke. There are plenty of choices along C/del Hambre and C/Moncayo.

Portofino, Edificio Perla 1, Pso Marítimo, **t** 952 47 06 43 (*expensive*). A popular Italian restaurant. *Closed Mon*.

Valparaíso, Ctra de Mijas, Km4, **t** 952 48 59 75 (*expensive*). Just outside Fuengirola, on the mountain road to Mijas; one of the most attractive and popular restaurants in the area, with bars, terrace, pool and an extensive international menu. Starters are labelled 'temptations' and women are given menus without the prices, but it's a favourite haunt. *Closed Sun exc. July–Oct*.

Café Royal, Ctra Cádiz, Km220, Benalmádena Costa, **t** 952 44 60 00, **f** 952 44 57 02 (*expensive*). In attractive surroundings at the Hotel Torrequebrada, with a fine view over coastline, serving inter-national cuisine.

Raj, C/Asturias 3, **t** 952 58 45 96 (*moderate*). An attractive Indian restaurant – a welcome addition to the already cosmopolitan culinary scene. Decorated with charming *objets d'art* brought back from India, the cuisine is from the north of the subcontinent.

Mesón El Castellano, Camino de Coín 5, **t** 952 46 27 36 (*moderate*). Serves authentic Castilian food: roast meats, especially pork and lamb, and fast, friendly service.

Casa Navarra, Ctra de Mijas (near Valparaíso), Km4, **t** 952 58 04 39 (*moderate*). Serves Navarrese cuisine, including steaks and delicious fish you choose yourself. *Closed Tues*.

Blanco, Pza de la Constitución 2, **t** 952 48 57 00 (*moderate*). A family-run restaurant in Mijas, with Basque fish specialities.

Like Carihuela in Torremolinos, where you can dine on fresh fish at a reasonable price, Los Boliches is the area to head for in Fuengirola for *chiringuitos*, no-nonsense fried fish restaurants.

Hermanos Blanco, Pso Maritimo. Typical of the *chiringuitos* in the Los Boliches area.

La Cepa, Pza Constitución, in Fuengirola (*inexpensive*). The place to come if you fancy a bit of pub grub while you observe movements on the plaza.

Torremolinos

Frutos, Ctra Cádiz, Km235, **t** 952 38 14 50 (*expensive*). A popular restaurant on the main *carretera* (next to Los Álamos petrol station), with high-quality food at reasonable prices; and the portions are generous: not a hint of *nouvelle cuisine*.

escape the coastal sprawl and find a *real* Andalucían village, which it obviously isn't, nor has it been for 30 years. Yet it's still a pretty place with a promenade offering a view out to sea, lots of pine woods, dozens of photogenic souvenir shops and 'officially licensed *burro* taxis'. The munchkin-sized **bullring** sees its fair share of action, but the town's **museum** of miniature curiosities is hard to take, even as a joke.

Torremolinos

All sources agree about Torremolinos, the 'fishing village' immortalized in James Michener's *The Drifters*. The oldest and biggest resort town on the Costa, it has

Mar de Alborán, Hotel Alay, Av. de Alay 5, Benalmádena Costa, **t** 952 44 64 27, **f** 952 44 63 80 (*moderate*). Highly recommended for excellent Basque and Andalucían cuisine, here the food, prepared by chef Alvaro Arriaga, just gets better and better. *Closed Sun and Mon*.

Casa Guaquín, C/Carmen 37, **t** 952 38 45 30 (*moderate*). The best seafood restaurants are in Carihuela, along the beach from Torremolinos, and this one is very good indeed; try such specialities of the Costa as 'fish baked in salt'.

Too Much, **t** 952 44 64 60 (*moderate*). The best of numerous reasonably priced pizzerias, with a lovely *terraza*.

El Mero, **t** 952 44 04 56 (*moderate*). An excellent seafood and shellfish restaurant in a wonderful setting overlooking the marina.

Venta los Pinos del Coto, Cañada de Ceuta s/n, Churriana, **t** 952 43 58 00 (*moderate*). Head up into the hills to this rambling, ranch-type restaurant run by a Hispano-German couple; it's a 10-minute drive. The attractive interior has stained-wood ceilings and a log fire for cold evenings. The menu is devoted to meat in large quantities. *Closed Sun eve and Mon*.

Mesón Gallego Antoxo, C/Hoxo, **t** 952 38 45 33 (*inexpensive*). Near the bus station, this is a typical Spanish restaurant with a beautiful interior and charming courtyard. There's a wide choice of fish; many dishes are cooked to Galician recipes. Wine comes in the traditional Galician ceramic jug and the drinking vessels resemble large finger bowls.

Escuela de Hostelería de Málaga, Finca La Cónsula, Churriana, **t** 952 62 24 24 (*inexpensive*). Located in an old stately home near Hemingway's house, this makes for an interesting dining experience. The hotel school's students prepare delectable lunches featuring innovative *andaluz* recipes. Booking essential.

El Vietnam del Sur, Pso del Colorado, Urbanización Playamar, Bloque 9, **t** 952 38 67 37 (*inexpensive*). Serves Vietnamese variations on Chinese cuisine – the food is delicious and affordable. *Closed Jan and Feb*.

La Chacha, Av. Palma de Mallorca (*inexpensive*). A real old-style *comedor*; you can choose from *gambas* and *pulpo* as you sit at the bar.

Nightlife

Fuengirola

Fuengirola might not rock like its cousins Torremolinos and Marbella, but it does have its fair share of bars and *discotecas*. In the centre, these are concentrated around the streets of **Pza Constitución**, and include the inevitable slew of 'authentic' Irish pubs and English bars. Off the Pso Maritimo, **C/Martinez Catena** is the place to be, with bars, discos and numerous restaurants vying for punters.

Torremolinos

The name (Torremolinos) has become a byword for hedonistic pleasure and fun, but the party is beginning to move on. There are a few discos in town, but the best action is to be found 3km down the road at Puerto Marina in **Benalmádena**. Torre is currently awash with English theme bars up and down **C/San Miguel** and **Pza de la Independencia** – take your pick, if that's your thing.

become a ghastly, hyperactive, unsightly holiday inferno. In other words, it has character. Torremolinos isn't at all interested in our opinion, or in yours either; it's doing quite well with its screaming blocks of bars, shopping centres and concrete hotels. The predominant language is English, but a dozen others can be heard in the space of a few steps. To escape, step down to one of the beach cafés, popular day and night; you might be treated to some of the local street performers sharing their talents: an *anís*-soaked troubadour mangling an aria, or a transvestite flamenco dancer whirling between the passing cars. Part of Torremolinos' character arises from its status as capital of what the newspapers like to call the 'Costa del Crime'. This is only the surface, though; the most noticeable segment of an enormous population is made up of sun-seekers from every corner of Europe. On the outskirts of Torremolinos welcome signs proclaim 'City of Tourists'.

Málaga

Much-maligned Málaga, capital not only of the Costa del Sol, but also of crime and sleaze in southern Spain, is making a determined effort to improve its reputation. In the past, a visit to the swish department store El Corte Inglés may have been the only reason a tourist considered spending any time here at all. To miss Málaga, however, means to miss the most Spanish of cities, certainly on the Costa del Sol. Whatever you may think of the place, it is alive and real. From its tattered billboards and walls splashed with political slogans to its public gardens overflowing with exotic fauna, Málaga is a jamboree bag of colours, aromas and sounds. Admittedly it cannot compete with Sevilla or Granada for sheer wealth of cultural distractions, but the *malagueños* are proud of their fun-loving metropolis. To experience a real local *juerga* (spree), treat yourself to an afternoon ramble through her many and famous tapas bars, where you will encounter more Spaniards in one afternoon than in a week in Torremolinos. Unfortunately, the old quarters of Málaga have been treated ruthlessly by town planners, and **El Perchel**, once the heart of Málaga's flamenco district, has lost a lot of its personality and charm. The essence of Málaga is within this limited area, from the elegant Av. de Andalucía to the seedy, teeming neo-Moorish market on the C/Atarazanas.

The Heart of Málaga

As the Av. de Andalucía, the main road from the west, crosses the dry rocky bed of the Guadalmedina river, it becomes the **Alameda Principal**, a majestic 19th-century boulevard. North of the Alameda is the **Plaza de la Constitución**, in the heart of the commercial centre, and the **Pasaje Chinitas**, an all-and-sundry shopping arcade. The Alameda continues into the **Pso del Parque**, a tree-lined promenade that runs along the port area, and leads to the city's **bullring**, built in 1874 with a capacity of 14,000, and very much in use today.

Just off Pso del Parque, steps lead up to the Moorish **Alcazaba**. Under the Moors, Málaga was the most important port of al-Andalus, and from contemporary

Getting Around

By Air

Málaga's often frenetic airport connects the city to Madrid, València, Almería, Sevilla, Melilla and Tangier, besides being the charter-flight gateway to the Costa. A new terminal, aptly called Pablo Ruiz Picasso, has also relieved some of the summer congestion and baggage delays. The easiest way to get into the city, or to Torremolinos or Fuengirola, is the suburban railway line (separate stops at the airport for the regular and charter terminals). These trains and local buses stop running before midnight. After that you'll have to get a taxi (about €15 to Málaga centre or Torremolinos). **Airport information**, **t** 952 04 88 04.

By Train

There are five or more daily ATVs to Madrid (4 hrs 10 mins), plus four normal trains (7½ hrs), and two trains a day to Valencia and Barcelona; direct connections also to Sevilla and Córdoba. For all other destinations in Andalucía you'll have to make a change at the almost inescapable Bobadilla Junction. The attractive little station is on C/Cuarteles. Information: C/Strachen 2, **t** 952 36 02 02.

By Bus

The main bus station is by the train station at Pso de los Tilos, to the south of the Av. de Andalucía, **t** 952 35 00 61. Connections for local destinations run every hour; for provincial destinations, generally every 1–2 hrs. Portillo, **t** 952 36 01 91, operate buses for the Costa, Sevilla, Ronda, Algeciras and the towns and villages in the interior; Bacoma, **t** 952 31 88 28, operates buses to Alora and Ronda; Los Amarillos, **t** 952 31 59 78, serves Antequera and Carratraca; Alsina Graells, **t** 952 31 04 00, serves Granada, Nerja and Almería, and also for Alicante and Barcelona.

Tourist Information

Málaga: The Costa del Sol tourist board headquarters are at Compositor Lehmberg Ruiz 3, **t** 952 28 83 54, **f** 952 28 60 42 (*open Mon–Fri 9–1.30 and 5–7; closed Sat and Sun*). Tourist offices are situated at Pasaje Chinitas 4, just north of the Alameda, **t** 952 22 94 21/952 21 34 45; at the airport, **t** 952 04 84 84, ext. 58617 (*open Mon–Sat 9–2; closed Sun*). There are booths in the bus station, **t** 952 35 00 61, and in the train station.

Melilla: Edificio Correos, Pablo Vallesca, **t** 952 68 43 05.

Where to Stay

Málaga ✉ 29000

Expensive

★★★★**Parador de Gibralfaro**, Castillo de Gibralfaro, s/n, 29016, **t** 952 22 19 02, **f** 952 22 19 04, *gibralfaro@parador.es*. In the old Moorish castle above the city with a pool; this offers the best view of Málaga, and is one of the nicest places to stay.

★★★★**Larios**, Marqués de Larios 2, **t** 952 22 22 00, **f** 952 22 24 07. Well appointed, extremely comfortable and good value.

Málaga Palacio, Av. Cortina del Muelle 1, **t** 952 22 06 98. Part of the ultra-modern AC chain, with an excellent location at the top of the Alameda, and sweeping views over the port. Try to get a room on one of the upper floors.

★★★★**NH Málaga**, Av. Río Guadiario s/n, **t** 952 07 13 23, **f** 952 39 38 62, *nhmalaga@nh/hoteles.es*. Slightly out of the centre overlooking Málaga's river. Part of an excellent chain, with all modern amenities.

Parador, Av. Cándido Lobera (in Melilla), **t** 952 68 49 40, **f** 952 68 34 86, *melilla@parador.es*. Offers panoramic views over Melilla, one of Spain's *presidios* on the African coast.

references it seems also to have been one of its most beautiful cities. Little remains of the Alcazaba, but the site has been restored to a lovely series of terraced **gardens** (*open Wed–Sun 9.30–7; closed Mon and Tues*). At the top is an **archaeological museum**, containing relics from the Phoenician necropolis found on the site and lists of Moorish architectural decoration salvaged from the ruins. There is a half-ruined **Roman theatre** on the lower slopes of the hill, and you can climb a little more to the

Moderate

★★Ánfora, C/Vallesca 8 (in Melilla), **t** 952 68 33 40. A reliable, unremarkable hotel. There are also quite a few modest *hostales* scattered around the *presidio* of Melilla.

Inexpensive

★★Alameda, Casa de Campos 3, **t** 952 22 20 99. South of here with bath available.

★Castilla, C/Córdoba 5, **t** 952 21 86 35. Along with the **Guerrero**, which is in the same building, this is a well-run establishment.

Casa Huéspedes Bolivia, Casa de Campos 24, **t** 952 21 88 26. Spotlessly clean and central. Any place near the Alameda will be decent, but avoid the dives around the train station.

Eating Out

El Compá, C/La Bolsa 7, **t** 952 22 97 06 (*expensive–moderate*). An excellent restaurant, albeit quite over-priced, specializing in fresh local fish and with a large wine selection; situated just behind the Alameda.

Méson Astorga, C/Gerona 11, **t** 952 34 68 32 (*moderate*). A really atmospheric *malagueño* restaurant that's on the up and up – a good place to enjoy a long late lunch.

Antonio Martín, out on the Pso Marítimo, right next to the sea, **t** 952 22 21 13 (*moderate*). *Malagueños* flock to the Pso Marítimo and the El Palo district east of town to fill up the many restaurants that line the beaches. This place is a favourite, with fish and rice dishes as the basis of the menu. *Closed in winter*.

Casa Pedro, Quitapenas 57, El Palo, **t** 952 29 00 13 (*moderate*). You may well be deafened by the din while you tuck into skewered sardines or Sierra-style angler fish. *Closed Mon evenings*.

La Teteria, C/San Agustin (next door to the Islamic Association of Málaga) (*inexpensive*). Málaga is also, slowly, discovering its Moorish roots, and a number of Moroccan-style restaurants have opened. This restaurant, and nearby Alcazaba, serve various couscous-based dishes, crêpes and mint tea.

El Corte Inglés, Av. de Andalucía, **t** 952 30 00 00 (*inexpensive*). If you've exhausted yourself shopping at the department store, stroll up to the top floor for a choice of three restaurants and two bars – the eat-all-you-can buffet lunch of meat and fish dishes, pastas and salads is a good bet. Also up here you'll find **El Club de Gourmets**, where you could put together some luxurious ingredients for a very special picnic.

Antigua Casa de Guardia, Alameda 18 (*inexpensive*). For sherry, shrimps and a great atmosphere come and choose a drink from one of the 20 or so barrels lining the bar with names like Pajarete 1908 and Guinda.

Bar Lo Güeno, Marín García 9. Head here for tapas – it's literally a hole in the wall serving imaginative *raciones* and a decent selection of wines.

Orellana, C/Moreno Monroy. One of the city's oldest and most classic tapas bars (they still offer a free *tapa* – or 'lid' – with your first glass of sherry).

Mesón la Aldea, C/Esparteros 5, **t** 952 22 76 89. A great tapas restaurant, with a speciality of the house you won't find anywhere else in Málaga: *carne el curry*. Try also the *flamenquin de carne*, a cheese and ham dish.

Nightlife

Málaga has a buzzing summer club scene. On a Friday or Saturday night, it's hard to move through the streets between Pza de la Constitucion and Pza de Siglo. Some of the best bars are to be found in and around **Pza de Uneibay**, **C/Granada** and in **Pza Merced**. A few bars/disco bars can also be found down by the bullring. In the summer, the action moves out to the city beaches, particularly Pedragalejo and El Palo.

Gibralfaro (*open 9–9*), the ruined Moorish castle that dominates the city (though there have been reports of robberies on the path).

Back on the Paseo, note the chunky Art Nouveau **Ayuntamiento**, one of the more unusual buildings in Málaga. On the opposite side of the Alcazaba is the **Museo de Bellas Artes**, C/San Agustín 8, in a restored 16th-century palace, much of which is given over to the works of 19th-century *malagueño* painters who made up in eccentricity what they lacked in genius. It is currently being turned into the city's Picasso museum; Picasso was a native of Málaga, though once he left it at the age of 14, he never returned. The artist's birthplace, **Casa Natal Picasso** (*Pza de la Merced, **t** 952 06 02 15; open Mon–Sat 11–2 and 5–8, Sun 11–2*), holds occasional exhibitions.

Málaga's **cathedral** (*open Mon–Sat 9–6.45; closed Sun; adm*) is a few blocks away on C/Molina Lario 5. It's an ugly, unfinished 16th-century work, immense and mouldering. Known as *La Manquita* (the one-armed lady), the only interesting feature is the faded, gaudy façade of the **sacristy**, left over from the earlier Isabelline Gothic church that once stood here.

Into the Serranía de Ronda

The Serranía de Ronda is a region of difficult topography, and it made life difficult for most would-be conquerors. A band of southern Celts gave the Romans fits in these mountains; various Christian chieftains held out for centuries against the Moors, and to return the favour the Moors kept Castile at bay here until 1485, just seven years before the conquest of Granada.

Ronda

Ronda, the only city in the Serranía, is a beautiful place, blessed with a perfect postcard shot of its lofty bridge over the steep gorge that divides the old and new towns. Because of its proximity to the Costa del Sol, it has lately become the only really tourist-ridden corner of the interior.

Don't be discouraged from a visit; the views alone are worth the trip. One of the best places from which to enjoy them is the **Alameda del Tajo**, a park on the edge of the **Mercadillo**, the new town. Next to it, Ronda has one of Spain's oldest and most picturesque bullrings, the 1785 **Plaza de Toros**, the 'cathedral of bullfighting'. It stages only about three *corridas* a year – including *La Goyesca* at the beginning of September, in traditional 18th-century costume – but it still has great prestige: the art of bullfighting was developed here.

Ronda's other landmark, the **Puente Nuevo**, was built at the second try in 1740 – the first one immediately collapsed. The bridge's two thick piers descend almost 300ft to the bottom of the narrow gorge. Crossing the bridge into the **Ciudád** (old town), a steep path heads downwards to two 18th-century palaces: the **Palacio de Salvatierra** (*tours available*), and the **Casa del Rey Moro** (*open daily 10–8; adm*). From the garden of the latter, the **Mina** – 365 steps cut out of the rock – takes you down to the bottom of the gorge.

In the old town, **Palacio de Montragon**, on Pza Montragon (*open Mon–Fri 10–7, Sat and Sun 10–3; adm*), is one of Ronda's most beautiful palaces; now housing the town museum. Just east of here is the main church, **Santa María La Mayor** (*open daily 10–8; adm*), still retaining the *mihrab* and minaret of the mosque it replaced, and the ruins of the **Alcázar**, blown up by the French.

Getting Around

By Bus

Without a car, you'll be depending on buses, run by Amarillos, **t** 952 18 70 61, or Automoviles Portillo, **t** 952 87 22 62. From Ronda you can go directly to Jerez, Cádiz, Málaga, and most of the towns on the Costa del Sol; there are also four daily buses to and from Sevilla. Ronda has connections to villages in the hinterlands – usually only once a day, so if you're day-tripping, make sure there's a return. Ronda's bus station is on Pso de Andalucía, **t/f** 952 87 22 62.

By Train

Ronda has trains, too; there are at least three a day for Algeciras and Málaga, with connections at Bobadilla Junction for Madrid and the other cities of Andalucía. Some trains stop at Gaucín and Setenil. The station is a few blocks down Pso de Andalucía, **t** 952 87 16 73.

By Car

Be warned that some streets of the Sierra towns and villages are very narrow, and difficult for a large vehicle to negotiate.

Tourist Information

Ronda: Pso de B. Infante (*open Mon–Fri 9.30–8, Sat 10–2 and 3–7, Sun 10–2 and 3–6.30*).

Sports and Activities

The Serranía offers a vast number of walking routes and plenty of rock climbing, potholing and horse riding, as well as caves, gorges, lakes and rivers. Local tourist offices will supply you with excellent walking maps of the area.

Where to Stay and Eat

Ronda ✉ 29400

Ronda has a wide choice in all ranges. There are dozens of small *hostales* and *camas* over bars – most of them quite agreeable – on all the side streets of C/Jerez in the Mercadillo. The area around Ronda has a wealth of *casa rurales*; contact **Centro de Iniciativas Turisticas**, **t** 952 87 07 39, *www.ruralandalus.es*.

********Parador de Ronda**, Pza de España, **t** 952 87 75 00, **f** 952 87 81 88, *ronda@parador.es* (*expensive*). This recently opened *parador* preserves the façade of the old town hall, but is painfully modern inside. It is the flagship of the *parador* chain; comfort and service are excellent, and the views from the duplex suites are matchless. The **restaurant** has an excellent-value menu.

******Reina Victoria**, Av. Fleming, **t** 952 87 12 40, **f** 952 87 10 75 (*expensive*). A fine, handsome old hotel with lovely views over the cliffs; the German poet Rainer Maria Rilke stayed here for a season in 1912, and wrote some of his best-known works; his room 208 is preserved as a museum. The hotel has recently been taken over by the Husa chain.

******Hotel Maestranza**, C/Virgen de la Paz 24, **t** 952 18 70 72, **f** 952 19 01 70, *reservas@hotel-maestranza.com*. This former residence of Pedro Romero, the legendary bullfighter, is one of the best options, just yards from the bullring and the heart of town, and with all the four-star comforts you would expect, including the use of a country club. It also has a good **restaurant**, Sol y Sombra.

*****Hotel San Gabriel**, C/Jose M Holgado 19, **t** 952 19 03 92, **f** 952 19 01 17, *www.ronda.net/usuar/hotelsgabriel* (*moderate*). Probably the loveliest hotel in town in terms of décor,

Around Ronda

Besides the opportunities for walks in and around the valleys under Ronda, an interesting excursion can be made to an area of curiosities 15–20 kilometres west of town. The hills around the hamlet of **Montejaque** are full of caves, two of which, the **Cueva del Gato** and **Cueva del Hundidero**, are connected, both full of stalactites and odd formations. Five kilometres south, past the village of **Benaoján**, the **Cueva de la Pileta** (*open 10–1 and 4–6; the caretaker lives in the farmhouse near the entrance,* **t** *952 16 73 43*) has some 25,000-year-old art: simple drawings of animals and magic symbols.

service, atmosphere and value. Wood panelling and old prints line the walls; individually designed bedrooms, billiards, café and a lovely, shaded patio.

Hotel Don Miguel, C/Villanueva 8, **t** 952 87 77 22, **f** 952 87 83 77 (*moderate*). Very good value for such a great spot on the cliff edge and opposite the *parador*. With excellent **restaurant** attached.

Hs Hnos Nacias, C/Pedro Romero 3, **t** 952 87 42 38 (*moderate*). Between the bullring and the main square, this has comfortable en suite rooms with a/c and heating; excellent **restaurant** attached.

There are also a number of places around Ronda – in Cortes de la Frontera, Benarraba, Genalguacil, Montejaque and Jimera de Libar.

★★★★**Sol y Sierra**, Av. Sol y Sierra 1, Cortes de la Frontera, **t** 952 15 45 23, **f** 952 15 45 18 (*expensive*). A sympathetically designed modern hotel in its own grounds with very comfortable rooms and wonderful views, a pool and an excellent **restaurant**.

★★★**Palacete de Manara**, Pza de la Constitucion 2, Montejaque, **t** 952 16 72 52, **f** 952 16 74 08, *hotelpalacete@ole.com* (*moderate*). A delightful place in a former palace with individually designed rooms, a patio and pool and an excellent **restaurant**.

Quite a few inferior tourist restaurants have been opening in conspicuous places to take advantage of day-trippers: watch out.

Tragabuches, C/Jose Aparicio 1, **t** 902 40 42 00, **f** 952 87 86 41 (*expensive*). This is a *cuatro tenedores* place, so you know you are in for a treat. The food is traditional *andaluz* combined with some unexpected flavours. The warm chocolate soufflé and ice-cream pud is out of this world. Accompanied by a superb wine list. *Closed Mon.*

Escudero, Chalet del Tajo, Pso de Blas Infante 1, **t** 952 87 13 67, **f** 952 87 45 32 (*expensive*). Under the same management, but a totally different style, serving more traditional food such as roasts and grills and with probably the best view in town, behind the bullring.

Duquesa de Parcent, C/Tenorio 12, **t** 952 19 07 63, **f** 952 87 27 16 (*expensive*). This 19th-century house has been sumptuously renovated, and features grilled pork and fish in saltcrust as the house specials.

Don Miguel, Villanueva 4, **t** 952 87 10 90 (*moderate*). Some of the best meals Ronda can offer, overlooking the gorge next to the famous bridge; they also have a bar built into the bridge itself.

Hnos Nacias, C/Pedro Romero 3, **t** 952 87 42 38 (*moderate*). An excellent-value *bodega* serving up some meaty local specialities.

Benaoján ✉ 29370

★★★**Molino del Santo**, Bulevar de la Estación, **t** 952 16 71 51, **f** 952 16 73 27, *www.andalucia.com/molino* (*moderate*). A converted water mill, close to the Pileta caves with a spring-fed pool. The kitchen serves *andaluz* cuisine. It's friendly and intimate and offers excursions each week, such as nature tours in the Grazalema National Park.

Gaucín ✉ 29400

Cortijo El Puerto del Negro, Ctra El Colmenar, **t/f** 952 15 12 39. Below the village within a 50-hectare farm, with a country-house atmosphere. Has been beautifully run by Tony and Christine Martin for seven years. With billiard room, pool, tennis, formal Andalucían garden and views of Gibraltar.

La Fructosa, C/Luis de Armiñan 67, **t** 952 15 10 72. Widely regarded as one of the best restaurants in the area. *Closed Thurs.*

The 40-kilometre 'scenic route' along the C341, which leaves Ronda to the south-west, is a breathless roller-coaster ride through the heart of the **Serranía de Ronda**. The scenery is justly famous; you'll pass by mountains and ravines sprinkled with tiny white villages nestling under crags and hair-raising mountain passes, before reaching the ancient village of **Gaucín**, with its remarkable view of Gibraltar and across to the African coast. The A366 makes a relaxing alternative route back to Málaga, all stone outcrops and dark hills, passing by way of a little-known nature reserve, the **Sierra de las Nieves**.

Antequera and Around

Known in Roman times as *Antiquaria*, it was the first of the Granadan border fortresses to fall to the Reconquista, in 1410, although subsequently it was retaken by the Moors and lost again. One of the architectural showpieces of the entire region, it has an impressive ensemble of 16th- to 18th-century buildings. The Nerja Palace houses the **Municipal Museum** (*open Tues–Fri 10–1.30 and 4–8, Sat 10–1.30, Sun 11–1.30; adm*), with many religious works including a wonderful *St Francis* by Alonso Cano. Up the Cuesta Zapateros is the 16th-century **Arco de los Gigantes**, meant as a sort of triumphal arch for the seldom-victorious Philip II; next to it, the ruins of a Moorish fortress offer views over the town to **La Peña de Enamorados** (Lovers' Rock), from which it's said a Moorish girl and her Christian lover threw themselves on realising that they were doomed to separation. East of the square, **La Iglesia del Carmen** (*open Mon–Sat 10–2 and 4–7, Sun 10–2; adm*), has one of Andalucia's finest Baroque altars.

East of Antequera

It is possible that the name of Antequera, 'old town', is related to *anta*, the local word for dolmen. Just out of town are the Neolithic monuments known as the **Cuevas de Menga**, the 'first real architecture in Spain'. Though not as impressive as the *talayots* and *taulas* of the island of Menorca, there's nothing like them elsewhere on mainland Spain. There are three, dating from anything between 4500 BC and 2500 BC. The two largest, the **Menga** and **Viera** dolmens (*open Wed–Sun 9–3.30; closed Mon and Tues*),

Getting Around

By Train

Antequera is on the rail line from Algeciras to Granada, and there are easy connections to all points from nearby Bobadilla Junction. The station is on Av. de la Estación, **t** 952 84 32 36.

By Bus

Lots of buses go to Málaga and Sevilla, less frequently to Granada and Córdoba, as well as to Olvera, Osuna and the other villages of the region. The bus station is on Av. de Garcia de Olmo, at the top of town, near the *parador*. For Antequera and the surrounding area phone Casado, **t** 952 84 19 57; for Sevilla and Granada phone Alsina Graells, **t** 952 84 13 65.

Tourist Information

Antequera: Pza San Sebastián 7, **t** 952 70 25 05 (*open 10–2 and 5–8*).

Archidona: in the Ochavada, **t** 952 71 64 79 (*open Mon–Fri 10–1.30, Sat 11–2; closed Sun*).

Festivals

Almogía: Festival of San Roque and San Sebastián, *15–18 Aug*. The town celebrates with dancing in the streets.

Carratraca: Semana Santa, *Holy Week*. 140 of the villagers perform *El Paso* in the bullring.

Where to Stay and Eat

Antequera ✉ 29200

***__Parador de Antequera__, Pso García del Olmo s/n, **t** 952 84 02 61, **f** 952 84 13 12, *antequera@parador.es* (*expensive*). A plain, modern building but with the most comforts in Antequera, including a pool; reasonably priced.

__Hotel Castilla__, C/Infante de Fernando 40, **t 952 84 32 48, **f** 952 84 30 90 (*moderate*). A new building in the heart of the old town, with a/c, bath and satellite TV.

*__Manzanito__, Pza San Sebastián, **t** 952 84 10 23 (*inexpensive*). One of the best in the town centre, with a good **restaurant** beneath.

are covered chambers about 70ft long, roughly elliptical and lined with huge, flat stones; other monoliths support the roof-like pillars. Nearby at **El Romeral**, the third of these temples (*open Wed–Sat 9–6, Tues and Sun 9–3.30*) has two chambers with domed ceilings. Originally the mound would have been about 100 yards in diameter. All three have etchings of figures and symbols around their walls.

Fifteen kilometres east of Antequera on the N342 is **Archidona**. The town overlooks acres of olive trees, but its main feature is the unique, octagonal Plaza Mayor, the **Ochavada**. Built between 1780 and 1786 by Francisco Astorga and Antonio González, it is one of the loveliest plazas in Andalucía.

South of Antequera

The sierras between Antequera and Málaga contain some of the remote villages of the region and offer some spectacular scenery: almond trees, cacti, olive groves and mountains that drop steeply away to the silver ribbon of a stream down below. Due south, towards Villanueva de Concepción, a natural park has been laid out around the rock formations at **El Torcal** (*info centre open daily 10–5; for guides call* **t** *952 60 22 79*), a tall but hikeable mountain with unusual red limestone crags. A more roundabout route south from Antequera will take you to **Alora**, where you should turn northwest towards one of Andalucía's natural wonders. **El Chorro Gorge**, in the rugged canyon of the Río Guadalhorce, has sheer walls of limestone tossed about at crazy angles. The very agile can circumnavigate it on a crumbling old concrete catwalk. It's easily reached without a car, but extremely hazardous; people regularly kill themselves.

****P. Madrona**, C/Calzada 31, **t** 952 84 00 14 (*cheap*). Clean and basic; does good *churros* and breakfasts.

Caselio de San Benito, Ctra M-C, Km108, **t** 952 11 11 03 (*expensive*). One of the finest restaurants in the area, appearing in two of Spain's top gourmet guides.

La Espuela, Pso Maria Cristina s/n, Pza de Toros, **t** 952 70 34 24 (*moderate*). The only restaurant in Spain actually inside a bullring – *rabo de toro* is usually dish of the day.

Nightlife is centred on the C/Alameda, which has a number of *bar de tapas* and pubs.

Archidona ✉ 29200

*******La Bobadilla**, Finca La Bobadilla, **t** 958 32 18 61, **f** 958 32 18 10, *www.la-bobadilla.com* (*luxury*). Turn off the road at the sign for Villanueva de Tapia, halfway to Loja. A plush but honest attempt at reconstructing the typical Andalucían *pueblo*, complete with Moorish touches, on a hilltop.

***Las Palomas**, Ctra Jerez–Granada, Km177, **t** 952 71 43 26 (*cheap*). The best bet if you are on a budget.

El Centre, C/Nueva 49, **t/f** 952 71 48 11. The best restaurant in town, just up from the square, serving tapas and regional wines.

Carratraca ✉ 29200

***El Príncipe**, C/Antonio Riobo 9, **t** 952 45 80 20 (*cheap*). The place to stay in Carratraca – in high season it is always advisable to book beforehand.

St Sa Pepe, **t** 952 45 80 49. Near the *balus*, a clean and simple place to eat. Away from the hotels, the roadside *ventas* are best for eating out.

El Chorro ✉ 29552

La Garganta, **t** 952 49 51 19, **f** 952 49 52 98. The best option if you want to stay near the gorge; offers excellent apartments with kitchen and lounge areas, great views, a rooftop pool and a good restaurant attached. Otherwise there are four self-catering cottages on a weekly let just above the town (contact Susan Mitchell on **t** 699 06 21 46 for bookings).

Getting Around

The Portillo and Alsina Graells **buses** from Málaga or Motril serve Nerja, Almuñécar and Salobreña, and connections can be made from these to the interior villages. Note that long-distance buses along the coast do not usually stop at these towns. Almuñécar's buses set off from Av. Juan Carlos I and Av. Fenecia.

Tourist Information

Torre del Mar: Av. de Andalucia 92, **t** 952 54 11 04.
Nerja: Puerto de Mar 1, **t** 952 52 15 31 (*open Mon–Fri 10–2 and 5–7, Sat 10–1; closed Sun*).
Frigiliana: Pza del Ingeniero s/n, **t** 952 53 31 26.
Salobreña: Pza de Goya s/n, **t** 958 61 03 14, *salobre@redestb.es* (*open Mon–Fri 9.30–1.30 and 4.30–7, Sat 9.30–1.30; closed Sun*).
Almuñécar: Av. de Europa, **t** 958 63 11 25, **f** 958 63 15 07 (*open Mon–Sat 10–2 and 5–9; closed Sun*).

For information about the Axarquia, call the Consorcio de Montes Alta Axarquia, **t** 952 53 78 71/952 53 78 09. Accommodation lists are available from **Almijara Travel**, Pza de Almijara 2, **t** 952 55 36 62, **f** 952 55 34 32.

Festivals

Iznate: Fiesta de la Uva Moscatel, *5 Aug*. A food and drink blowout from eight till late.
Cómpeta: Wine Fiesta, *15 Aug*. In the plaza.

Where to Stay and Eat

Comares ✉ 29195 and Cómpeta ✉ 29754

El Molino de los Abuelos, Pza 2, **t** 952 50 93 09, **f** 952 21 42 20, *www.molino-abuelos* (*moderate–inexpensive*). Possibly the best-situated hotel in the region: an old olive-pressing mill which has been beautifully converted into a small hotel. There are five rooms and an apartment, all individual, but the ones to go for are the front-facing double or the suite, which look right out across the valley. For a little extra, book the apartment – the Jacuzzi is set in an alcove with windows all round. The oil press and other bits of old machinery from the mill add to the atmosphere in the restaurant below, which serves a fine selection of reasonably priced local dishes.

*****Hotel Balcón de Cómpeta**, C/San Antonio 75, **t** 952 55 35 35, **f** 952 55 35 10, *www.hotel-competa.com* (*inexpensive*). Has reasonably priced rooms, fantastic views, a restaurant, café and pool. It also offers activities such as horse-riding, safaris, hiking and golf. For longer stays ask about the self-catering *villa turisticas*.

Nerja ✉ 29780

******Parador de Nerja**, Playa de Burriana, Almuñécar 8 (just outside town at El Tablazo), **t** 952 52 00 50, **f** 952 52 19 97, *nerja@parador.es* (*expensive*). A luxurious place; one of Nerja's two fine hotels.

The Coast East of Málaga

For some reason the tourist industry has neglected the areas east of the city. There are a few resorts strung out along the coastal highway, notably **Torre del Mar**, but they are all grim-looking places: little bits of Málaga that escaped to the beach.

Vélez-Málaga and the Axarquia

From Torre del Mar you can make a short detour inland to **Vélez-Málaga**, lying in a fertile valley at the foot of the Axarquía mountains. The old town tells of its Moorish past; the castle, **La Fortaleza**, was one of the last Moorish outposts to fall to Christian forces during the campaigns of Isabel and Ferdinand. Another detour begins on the coast east of Vélez and winds through the villages to **Cómpeta**, a truly lovely old village known principally for its sweet wines. Beyond begin the wilds of the **Reserva**

★★★★**Balcón de Europa 1**, Pso Balcón de Europa, **t** 952 52 08 00, **f** 952 52 44 90, *balconeuropa@spa.es* (*expensive–moderate*). Probably a better choice than the *parador*, though not quite as luxurious; the beautiful location on the 'balcony of Europe' in the town centre and the reasonable rates make the difference. Both hotels have lifts down to the beaches under Nerja's cliffs.

★★★**Pza Carana**, Pza Carana, **t** 952 52 40 00, **f** 952 52 40 08, *hotelplazacarana@info regocio.com* (*moderate*). Just a few minutes walk from the Balcón de Europa, with a/c and two pools.

★**Portofino**, Puerta del Mar 2, **t** 952 52 01 50 (*moderate*). A reasonable option right on the beach.

★★**Hs Marissal**, Balcón de Europa 3, **t** 952 52 01 99 (*inexpensive*). In an excellent location and good value; sea views, a/c and TV; with a **café** attached.

★**Carabeo**, C/Carabeo 34, **t** 952 52 39 41, **f** 952 52 54 44 (*inexpensive*). Done out in the style of an old English hotel, with suites and doubles; also a tapas bar and **restaurant**.

Alhambra Antonio Milon, at Chaparil (*inexpensive*). Friendly with attractive rooms and sea-facing balconies.

De Miguel, C/Pintada 2, **t** 952 52 29 96 (*expensive*). Celebrated for its international meat and fish dishes, and not least for flambéd strawberries; reservations essential. *Closed Mon and Feb.*

El Candil, **t** 952 52 07 97 (*inexpensive*). Has a good selection of Spanish dishes in a lovely setting, in a square just off the Balcón.

Almuñécar ✉ 18690

There are plenty of hotels to be found in Almuñécar along the narrow tiled streets of the old town, with cheaper ones around the Pza de la Rosa.

★★★**Hotel Helios**, Pso San Cristobal, **t** 958 63 44 59, **f** 958 63 44 69 (*moderate*). The town's smartest hotel, with a pool.

★★**Casablanca**, Pza San Cristobal 4, **f** 958 63 55 75 (*inexpensive*). A family-run pseudo-Moorish affair with rooms looking out to sea or to the castle and the sierras beyond.

Los Geranios, Pza Rosa 4a, **t** 952 63 07 24 (*moderate*). A cheerful restaurant full of geraniums and owned by a Hispano-Belgian couple; the menu is international with a Spanish bias. *Closed Sun and Nov.*

Bodega Francisco, C/Real 15, **t** 952 63 01 68 (*inexpensive*). A wonderful watering hole serving inexpensive tapas and the usual *andaluz* staples.

Salobreña ✉ 18680

★★★**Salobreña**, outside the town on the coastal highway, **t** 958 61 02 61, **f** 958 61 01 01 (*moderate*). Close to the beach with pool and garden. The **restaurant** (*moderate*) is worth trying; it does excellent barbecues in summer and the views are worth the price.

Mesón de la Villa, Pza F. Ramirez de Madrid, **t** 958 61 24 14 (*moderate–inexpensive*). The best restaurant in town, serving up local fish dishes and *rabo de toro*. *Closed Wed*. There are also a number of good *chiringuitos* along the beach during the season.

Nacional de Sierra de Tejeda (wear strong, comfy shoes to explore it). To get back to the coast, the MA137 takes you through beautiful vine-clad slopes to **Torrox** and continues to **Torrox-Costa**, an expanding resort eight kilometres from Nerja.

Alhama de Granada

For a further detour into the mountains, you can tackle the 50-kilometre drive along the C335 (becoming the C340 at Ventas) from Vélez over the Sierra to **Alhama de Granada**, balancing precariously on a rocky lip and looking down to a deep grass-banked gorge. 'Oh, for my Alhama', was the lament of Boabdil el Chico, who had to abandon this beauty spot to the Christians in 1482. Naturally, it features the remains of a Moorish **castle**; it also has a 15th-century parish church, a gift to the town from Ferdinand and Isabel. Alhama has been famous since Roman times for its spa waters; ask at the spa Hotel Balneario, to see the **Roman and Moorish baths** beneath.

Nerja

Approaching this town, the scenery becomes impressive as the mountains loom closer to the sea. Set at the base of the Sierra de Tejeda, Nerja is pleasant and quiet for a Costa resort. In Moorish times the town was a major producer of silk and sugar, an industry that fell into rapid decline after their departure. An earthquake in 1884 partially destroyed Nerja, and from then until the early 1960s it had to eke a living out of fishing and farming. Its attractions are the **Balcón de Europa**, a promenade with a fountain overlooking the sea, and a series of secluded beaches under the cliffs – the best are a good walk away on either side of the town. A few kilometres east lies the **Cueva de Nerja** (*open daily 10.30–12 and 4–6.30; adm*), one of Spain's most fabled grottoes, full of Gaudiesque formations and some Palaeolithic artworks. They were discovered in 1959 in time for the tourist boom, and have been fitted out with lights and music.

East of Nerja

The coastal road east of Nerja, bobbing in and out of the hills and cliffs, is the best part of the Costa, where avocado pears and sugar cane keep the farming community busy. **Almuñécar**, however, is a nest of dreary high-rises around a beleaguered village. Founded by the Phoenicians as *Sexi*, the only birds it's likely to attract are those heading for its **Parque Ornitológico** (*open daily 11–2 and 4–8; adm*). **Salobreña**, where the road from Granada meets the coast, is much nicer, though it may not stay that way. Dramatically slung along a steep peak overlooking the sea, the village's setting is the most stunning on the coast, and helps to insulate it from the tourist industry. The beaches, just starting to become built up, are about two kilometres away.

From here the next town is **Motril**, a large settlement set back from the sea with little to attract visitors; it's the centre of the coastal sugar-cane production, thanks to the gin family, Larios. There isn't much Costa left further east, and the only real destination choice is the spectacular mountain road that runs through the Sierra Nevada and on towards Granada.

Granada

Dale limosna mujer, que no hay en la vida nada
Como la pena de ser ciego y en Granada.

Francisco de Icaza

(Give him alms, woman, for there is nothing in life
so cruel as being blind in Granada.)

The first thing to do upon arrival is to pick up a copy of Washington Irving's *Tales of the Alhambra*. Every bookshop in town can sell you one in just about any language. It was Irving who put Granada on the map, and established the Alhambra as the necessary romantic pilgrimage of Spain. Granada, in fact, might seem a disappointment without Irving. The modern city underneath the Alhambra is a stolid, remarkably unmagical place, with little to show for the 500 years since the Catholic kings put an end to its ancient glory.

As the Moors were expelled, the Spanish Crown replaced them with Castilians and Galicians from up north, and even today *granadinos* are thought of as a bit foreign by other Andalucíans. Their Granada has never been a happy place. Particularly in the last hundred years it has been full of political troubles. At the start of the civil war the reactionaries who always controlled Granada made one of the first big massacres of Republicans. One of their victims was Federico García Lorca, the *granadino* who has come to be recognized as one of the greatest Spanish dramatists and poets since the 'Golden Age'. If Irving's fairy tales aren't to your taste, consider Lorca, for whom Granada and its sweet melancholy are recurring themes. He wrote that he remembered Granada 'as one should remember a sweetheart who has died'.

History: the Nasrid Kingdom of Qarnatah

First Iberian *Elibyrge*, then Roman *Illiberis*, the town did not make a name for itself until the era of the *taifas* in the early 11th century, when it emerged as the centre of a very minor state. In the 1230s, while the Castilians were seizing Córdoba and preparing to polish off the rest of the Almoravid states of al-Andalus, an Arab chieftain named Mohammed ibn-Yusuf ibn-Nasr established himself around Jaén. When that town fell to the Castilians in 1235, he moved his capital to the town the Moors called *Qarnatah*. Ibn Nasr (or Mohammed I, as he is generally known) and his descendants in the Nasrid dynasty enjoyed great success at first in extending their domains. By 1300 this last Moorish state of Spain extended from Gibraltar to Almería, but this accomplishment came entirely at the expense of other Moors. Mohammed and his successors were in fact vassals of the kings of Castile, and aided them in campaigns more often than they fought them.

Qarnatah at this time is said to have had a population of some 200,000 – almost as many as it has now – and both its arts and industries were strengthened by refugees from the fallen towns of al-Andalus. Thousands came from Córdoba, especially, and the Albaicín quarter was largely settled by the former inhabitants of Baeza. Although a significant Jewish population remained, there were very few Christians. In the comparatively peaceful 14th century, Granada's conservative, introspective civilization reached its height, with the last flowering of Arabic-Andaluz lyric poetry and the architecture and decorative arts of the Alhambra.

This state of affairs lasted until the coming of the Catholic kings. Isabel's religious fanaticism made the completion of the Reconquista the supreme goal of her reign; she sent Ferdinand out in 1484 to do the job, which he accomplished in eight years by a breathtakingly brilliant combination of force and diplomacy. Qarnatah at the time was suffering the usual curse of al-Andalus states – disunity founded on the egotism of princes. In this fatal feud, the main actors were Abu al-Hasan Ali (Mulay Hassan in Irving's tales), king of Qarnatah, his brother El Zagal ('the valiant') and the king's rebellious son, Abu abd-Allah, better known to posterity as Boabdil el Chico. His seizure of the throne in 1482 started a period of civil war at the worst possible time. Ferdinand was clever enough to take advantage of the divisions; he captured Boabdil twice, and

Granada
CARRETERA DE MURCIA
PLAZA HAZE GRANDE
Moorish walls (ruins)
SACROMONTE
PLAZA CRUZ DE PIEDRA
SAN LUIS
CUESTA DEL
City University
PLAZA CASTILLAS
San Salvador
CALLEJÓN DE LEBRIJA
PANADEROS
PLAZA CARNICEROS
ALBAICÍN
La Cartuja
LARGA SAN CRISTÓBAL
PLAZA SAN NICOLÁS
CUESTA ALGIBE DE TRILLO
NUEVO SAN NICOLÁS
CUESTA MARÍA DE LA MIEL
Moorish walls (ruins)
Monasterio de Santa Isabel la Real
CUESTA ALHACABA
CARDENAL PARRADO
REAL DE CARTUJA
AVENIDA DE MURCIA
TIÑA
HORNILLO DE CARTUJA
Hospital Real
AVENIDA HOSPICIO
PLAZA SAN MIGUEL BAJO
SAN JOSÉ
Puerta de Elvira
ZENETE
PULIANAS
PLAZA DEL TRIUNFO
QUIRÓS
PLAZA SAN ISIDRO
AVENIDA DE ANCHA DE CAPUCHINOS
CALLE DE ELVIRA
Jardines del Triunfo
GRAN VIA DE COLON
MADRID
DOCTOR GUIRAO GEA
SAN JUAN DE DIOS
MANO DE HIERRO
PLAZA SAN AGUSTÍN
SANTA BARBARA
SAN JERÓNIMO
AVENIDA DE LA CONSTITUCION
Basílica de San Juan de Dios
University
Bus Stand
AV. ANDALUCES
GRAN CAPITAN
MISERICORDIA
PLAZA LOBOS
San Jerónimo
Train Station
AVENIDA FUENTE NUEVA
CARRIL DEL PICÓN
PLAZA GRAN CAPITÁN
MELCHOR ALMAGRO
MARTÍNEZ ROSA
PLAZA ALBERT EINSTEIN
CALLE PEDRO ANTONIO DE ALARCÓN
CAMINO RONDA

Sacromonte Caves
Río Darro
Camino de la Silla
500 metres
500 yards
El Generalife
N
Casa del Chapiz
Chapiz
GENERALIFE
Camino Viejo
Cuesta del Rey Chico
Horno de Oro
San Juan de los Reyes
Paseo del Padre Manjón
Convento de Santa Catalina de Zafra
La Alhambra
ALHAMBRA
Casa Museo Manuel de Falla
Archaeological Museum
Antequeruela Alta
Camino Nuevo del Cementerio
Moorish Baths
Carrera del Darro
Callejón Niño del Royo
Cuesta del Caidero
Vistilla de los Angeles
San Gregorio
Santa Ana
Plaza San José
Torres Bermejas
Audiencia
Calle de Molinos
Plaza Nueva
REALEJO
Calle de Santiago
Paseo de la Bomba
Caldereria Nueva
Bus Stand
Santa Escolástica
Santo Domingo
Pavaneras
Plaza Padre Suarez
Paco Seco de Lucena
Palacio de la Madraza
Plaza San Juan de la Cruz
SAN MATIAS
Cuarto Real de Santo Domingo
Capilla Real
Calle Reyes Católicos
Corral del Carbón
San Matías
Plaza Campos
Catedral
Concepción
Paseo del Salon
Río Genil
Plaza Mariana Pineda
Plaza Pasiegas
Plaza Bib-Rambla
Alcaicería
Angel Gavinet
Pescadería
Carrera del Genil
Poeta Manuel de Góngora
Acera de Casino
Acera de Darro
Plaza Trinidad
Campo Verde
Alhóndiga
SAN ANTON
Paseo
Calle de San Anton
Bus Stand (Sierra Nevada)
San José Baja
Calle de Gracia
Calle de Recogidas
Palacio de Congresos
Obispo
Del Violon
Calle de Alhamar
Plaza de Gracia
Ermita de San Sebastián
Plaza Menorca
Calle Pedro Antonio de Alarcón
Camino Ronda
Camino Ronda

Getting Around

By Air

There are two flights daily to Madrid (*Mon–Sat*), two daily to Barcelona (*Mon–Fri*) and three flights a week to the Balearics and Canaries. The airport is 16km west of Granada, near Santa Fé. Information: **t** 958 24 52 23.

By Train

Granada has connections to Guadix and Almería (three daily), to Algeciras, Sevilla, and Córdoba by way of Bobadilla Junction, and two daily to Madrid and Barcelona; three daily to Alicante, one a day to València. The station is at the northern end of town, about a mile from the centre, on Av. de los Andaluces. Information: **t** 902 24 02 02.

By Bus

All buses leave from the the new main bus station, on the outskirts of town on the Ctra de Jaén. Information: **t** 958 18 54 80; sales **t** 902 33 04 00. Bus No.3 runs between the bus station and the city centre. The 'Alhambra' bus No.30 from the Pza Nueva will save you the trouble of climbing up to the Alhambra.

By Car

Parking is a problem, so if you plan staying overnight make sure that your hotel has parking and check whether there is a charge – it can cost as much as the accommodation in some places. Traffic police are vigilant. Fines of up to €120 are payable on the spot if you are a tourist. Ignore people at the bottom of the Alhambra trying to persuade you to park before you reach the top; there's plenty of parking by the entrance and it's a steep walk.

Tourist Information

Provincial Tourist Office, Pza Mariana Pineda 10, **t** 958 22 66 88 (*open Mon–Fri 9.30–7 and Sat 10–2; closed Sun*);

there's a smaller office inside the Corral del Carbón, C/Liberos 2, **t** 958 22 59 90 (*open Mon–Sat 9–7, Sun 10–2*);

also a branch in the Alhambra: Av. del Generalife s/n, **t** 958 22 95 75 (*open Mon–Fri 9–4, Sat 9–1; closed Sun*).

Where to Stay

Granada ✉ 18000

The city centre, around the Acera del Darro, is full of hotels, and there are lots of inexpensive *hostales* around the Gran Vía – but the less you see of these areas the better. Fortunately, you can choose from a wide range around the Alhambra and in the older parts of town if you take the time to look.

Luxury

*****__Parador Nacional San Francisco__, **t** 958 22 14 40, **f** 958 22 22 64, *granada@parador.es*. Right in the Alhambra, this is perhaps the most famous of all *paradores*, housed in a convent where Queen Isabel was originally interred. It is beautiful, very expensive (though worth it), and small; you need to book well in advance – a year would not be unreasonable.

Expensive

****__Alhambra Palace__, C/Peña Partida 2–4, **t** 958 22 14 68, **f** 958 22 64 04. An alternative choice very near the Alhambra; outrageously florid, neo-Moorish, and most rooms have terrific views over the city.

*__Hotel América__, Real de la Alhambra 53, **t** 958 22 74 71, **f** 958 22 74 70. Beside the *parador* but a third of the price, with simple, pretty rooms and a delightful garden and patio, but you'll need to book well in advance.

***__Palacio de Santa Inés__, Cuesta de Santa Inés 9, **t** 958 22 23 62, **f** 958 22 24 65, *www.lugaresdivino.com*. A 16th-century palace in the Albaícin with murals attributed to Alejandro Mayner, Rafael's disciple. Just nine rooms – some with priceless views of the Alhambra – and an art gallery.

Moderate

Casa del Aljarife, Placeta de la Cruz Verde 2, **t/f** 958 22 24 25, *most@mx3.redestb.es*. This 17th-century Moorish house with tastefully refurbished rooms is one of a few hotels in the Albaicín, and one of the most delightful places to stay, with a view of the Alhambra you won't better elsewhere. There are only three rooms so be sure to book ahead. The owners can arrange parking and will even collect you from the train station or airport.

*****Hotel Navas**, C/Navas 24, **t** 958 22 59 59, **f** 958 22 75 23. In an excellent spot offering quiet, air-conditioned rooms with a good-value **restaurant** attached.

Inexpensive

Hs Suecia, Huerta Los Angeles, **t** 958 22 50 44. A delightful budget option: clean, quiet, in its own grounds, with parking and views of the palace.

****Lisboa**, Pza del Carmen 27, **t** 958 22 14 13, **f** 958 22 14 87. Adequate if uninspiring.

Cheap

For cheap *hostales*, the first place to look is the Cuesta de Gomérez, the street leading up to the Alhambra from Pza Nueva.

Viena, **t** 958 22 18 59. One of three good Austrian-run budget options around this street; all are clean, friendly and functional.

Landázuri, Cuesta de Gomérez 24, **t** 958 22 14 06. A bit further up with a **restaurant** and a small roof terrace.

Off C/San Juan de Dios,there are dozens of small inexpensive *hostales*.

Eating Out

Granada isn't known for its cuisine. There are too many touristy places around the Pza Nueva, with very little to distinguish between them. Below are some better finds.

Expensive

Sevilla, C/Oficios 12, **t** 958 22 12 23. The best-known and best-loved restaurant in Granada, where Lorca often met fellow poets and intellectuals. Its character has been preserved and the specialities are still the local dishes of Granada and Andalucía. *Closed Sun eve*.

Ruta del Veleta, Ctra de la Sierra, Km50, **t** 958 48 61 34. Some of the finest cooking in Granada can be found here, with dishes including partridge with onion ragôut and salad of angler fish with vegetable stuffing; situated 5km away from the city towards the Sierra Nevada.

Moderate

Cunini, Pza de Pescadería 14, **t** 958 25 07 77. The *granadinos* trust dining out at this place, where the menu depends on availability. *Closed Mon*.

Mesón Antonio, Ecce Homo 6, **t** 958 22 95 99. There's no better place for agreeable dining in an intimate family-run restaurant; international meat and fish dishes are served. *Closed Sun, July and Aug*.

Mirador de Morayma, Pianista García Carrillo 2, Albaicín, **t** 958 22 82 90. In a charming 16th-century house with views over the Alhambra from the top-floor dining room; *la sopa de espárragos verdes de Huétor* (asparagus soup) is particularly good, and be sure to leave room for an *andaluz* pudding. *Closed Sun eve*.

Inexpensive

Cepillo, C/Pescadería. Everyone's favourite rock-bottom, filling menu is served up at this tiny restaurant. It's several doors away from the Cunini and is one of the few places where you can get *paella* for one – order fish or squid.

Bar Aliatar, C/San Sebastian (a small street between Pza de Bib-Rambla and C/Reyes Católicos). Try here for *bocadillos* (hot and cold sandwiches).

Tapas Bars

Granada rivals Sevilla for its tapas and has a fine tradition of serving up mini-meals for the price of a drink. Areas worth exploring are the roads off the top end of Gran Vía, particularly Calles Almireceros, Joaquin Costa, Elvira and Cetti Meriem; also try the streets off Pza del Carmen, particularly Navas; around the cathedral, Pza Bib-Rambla and C/Pescaderia are particularly good.

On the streets leading up into the Albaicin are an increasing number of Moroccan-style tea bars, or *teterías*, where you can sip mint tea in Alhambra-style décor and nibble at Moorish-inspired dishes. Try in particular Calles Calderias Vieja and Nueva and Carcel Alta.

Granada is one of the best places in Andalucía to catch **flamenco**. Though there are touristy shows in the caves of Sacromonte, there are also some more spontaneous venues, and it's well worth heading up to Sacromonte to wander around.

turned him into a tool of Castilian designs. Playing one side against the other, Fernando snatched away one Nasrid province after another with few losses.

When the unfortunate Boabdil, after renouncing his kingship in favour of the Castilians, finally changed his mind and decided to fight for the remnants of Qarnatah (by then little more than the city itself and the Sierra Nevada), Ferdinand had the excuse he needed to mount his final attack. Qarnatah was besieged and, after two years, Boabdil agreed to surrender under terms that guaranteed his people the use of their religion and customs. When the keys of the city were handed over on 2 January 1492, the Reconquista was complete.

Under a gentlemanly military governor, the Conde de Tendilla, the agreement was kept until the arrival in 1499 of Cardinal Ximénez de Cisneros, the most influential cleric in Spain and a man who made it his personal business to destroy the last vestiges of Islam and Moorish culture. The new Spanish policy – cultural genocide (*see* **History**, pp.37–8) – was as successful in the former lands of Granada as it was among those other troublesome heathens of the same period, the Indians of Central and South America. The famous revolt in Las Alpujarras (1568) was followed by a rising in the city itself, in the Albaicín. Between 1609 and 1614, the last of the Muslims were expelled, including most of those who had converted to Christianity, and their property confiscated. It is said that, even today, there are old families in Morocco who sentimentally keep the keys to their long-lost homes in Granada.

Such a history does not easily wear away, even after so many centuries. The Castilians corrupted Qarnatah to *Granada*; just by coincidence that word means 'pomegranate' in Spanish, and the pomegranate has come to be the symbol of the city. With its associations with the myth of Persephone, with the mysteries of death and loss, no symbol could be more suitable for this capital of melancholy.

A Sentimental Orientation

In spite of everything, more of the lost world of al-Andalus can be seen in Granada than even in Córdoba. Granada stands where the foothills of the Sierra Nevada meet the fertile Vega de Granada, the greenest and best stretch of farmland in Andalucía. Two of those hills extend into the city itself. One bears the **Alhambra**, the fortified palace of the Nasrid kings, and the other the **Albaicín**, the most evocative of the 'Moorish' neighbourhoods of Andalucían cities. How much you enjoy Granada will depend largely on how successful you are in ignoring the new districts, in particular three barbarically ugly streets that form the main automobile route through Granada: the **Gran Vía Colón** chopped through the centre of town in the 19th century, the **Calle Reyes Católicos**, and the **Acera del Darro**. Before these streets were built, the centre of Granada was the **Plaza Nueva**, a square that is also partly built over the Darro. The handsome building that defines its character is the **Audiencia** (1584), built by Philip II for the royal officials and judges. **Santa Ana** church, across the plaza, was built in 1537 by Diego de Siloé, one of the architects of Granada's cathedral. From this plaza the ascent to the Alhambra begins, winding up a narrow street called the **Cuesta de Gomérez**, past guitar-makers' shops and gypsies, and ending abruptly at the **Puerta de las Granadas**, a monumental gateway erected by Charles V.

The Alhambra

Open Mar–Oct daily 8.30–7.45, Tues–Sat eves 10pm–11.30pm (you can only see the Palacio Nazari at night); Nov–Feb daily 8.30–5.45, Fri and Sat eves 8pm–9.30pm; adm.

The grounds of the Alhambra begin here with a bit of the unexpected. Instead of the walls and towers, not yet even in view, there is a lovely grove of great elms called the **Alameda**, planted at the time the Duke of Wellington passed through during the Peninsular War. Take the path to the left – it's a stiff climb – and in a few minutes you'll arrive at the **Puerta de Justicía**, entrance of the Alhambra. The orange tint of the fortress walls explains the name *al-hamra* (the red), and the unusual style of the carving on the gate is the first clue that here is something very different. The two devices, a hand and a key, carved on the inner and outer arches, are famous. According to one of Irving's tales, the hand will one day reach down and grasp the key; at which time the Alhambra will fall into ruins, the earth will open, and the hidden treasures of the Moors will be revealed.

From the gate, a path leads up to a broad square. Here are the ticket booth and the **Puerta del Vino**, so called from an old Spanish custom of doling out free wine from this spot to the inhabitants of the Alhambra. To the left you'll see the walls of the **Alcazaba**, the fort at the tip of the Alhambra's narrow promontory, and to the right the huge **Palacio de Carlos V**; signs point your way to the entrance of the **Casa Real** (Royal Palace), with its splendidly decorated rooms that are the Alhambra's main attraction. Visit again after dark; seeing it under the stars is the treat of a lifetime.

The Alcazaba

Not much remains of the oldest part of the Alhambra. This citadel probably dates back to the first of the Nasrid kings. Its walls and towers are still intact, but only the foundations of the buildings that once stood within it have survived. The **Torre de la Vela** at the tip of the promontory has the best views over Granada and the *vega*. Its big bell was rung in the old days to signal the daily opening and closing of the water gates of the *vega*'s irrigation system; the Moors also used the tower as a signal post for sending messages. The Albaicín (*see* p.698), visible on the opposite hill, is a revelation; its rows of white, flat-roofed houses on the hillside, punctuated by palm trees and cypresses, provide one of Europe's most exotic urban landscapes.

Casa Real (Royal Palace)

Visits are limited to 30 mins; the desired entry time must be specified at time of ticket purchase, otherwise it will be fixed for at least 1 hr later.

Words will not do, nor will exhaustive descriptions help, to communicate the experience of this greatest treasure of al-Andalus. This is what people come to Granada to see, and it is the surest, most accessible window into the refinement and subtlety of the culture of Moorish Spain – a building that can achieve in its handful of rooms what a work like Madrid's Royal Palace cannot approach even with its 2,800.

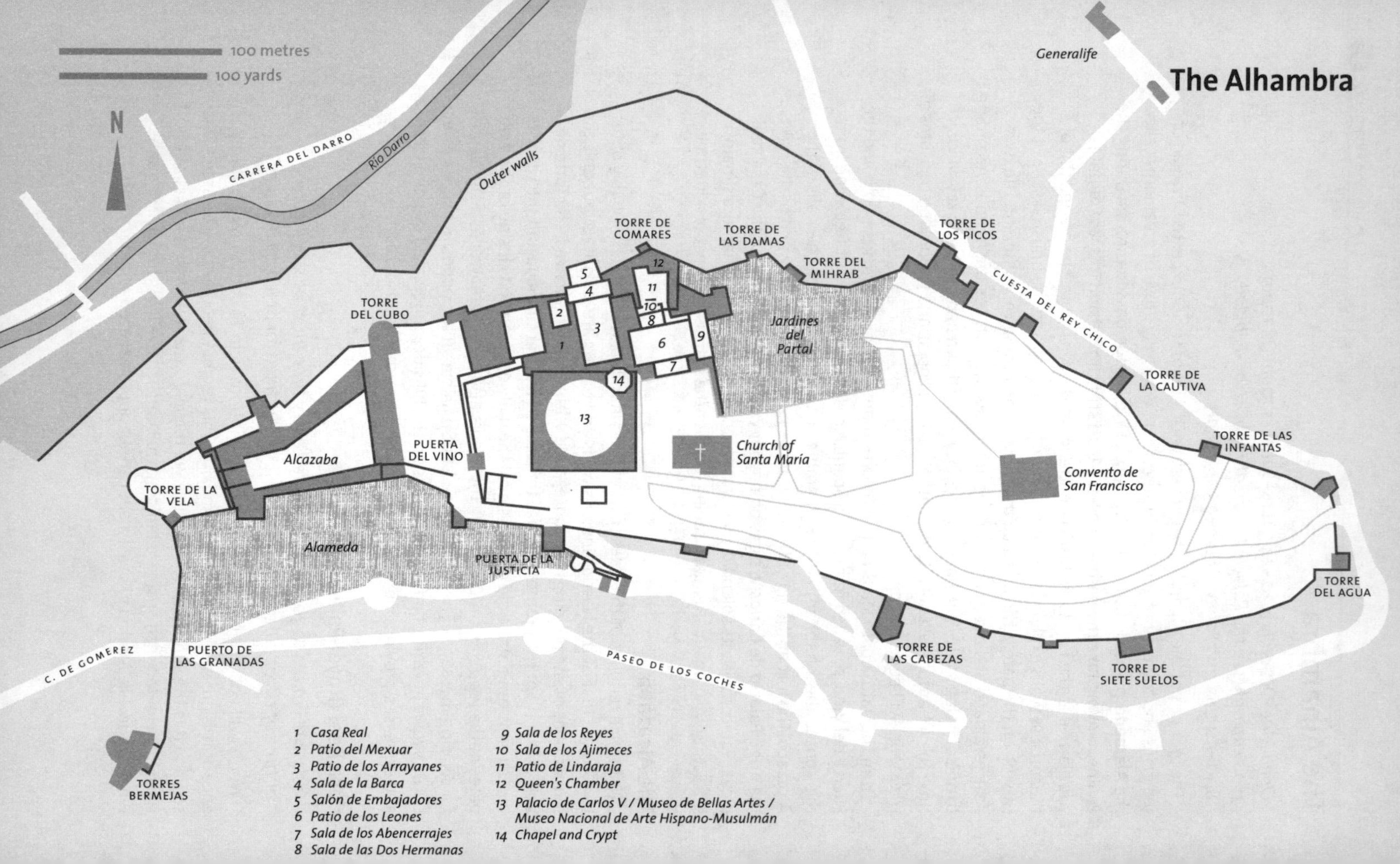
The Alhambra
100 metres
100 yards
N
Generalife
CARRERA DEL DARRO
Río Darro
Outer walls
TORRE DE COMARES
TORRE DE LAS DAMAS
TORRE DEL MIHRAB
TORRE DE LOS PICOS
CUESTA DEL REY CHICO
TORRE DE LA CAUTIVA
TORRE DE LAS INFANTAS
TORRE DEL AGUA
TORRE DEL CUBO
Jardines del Partal
Church of Santa María
Convento de San Francisco
PUERTA DEL VINO
Alcazaba
TORRE DE LA VELA
Alameda
PUERTA DE LA JUSTICIA
PUERTO DE LAS GRANADAS
C. DE GOMEREZ
PASEO DE LOS COCHES
TORRE DE LAS CABEZAS
TORRE DE SIETE SUELOS
TORRES BERMEJAS
1 Casa Real
2 Patio del Mexuar
3 Patio de los Arrayanes
4 Sala de la Barca
5 Salón de Embajadores
6 Patio de los Leones
7 Sala de los Abencerrajes
8 Sala de las Dos Hermanas
9 Sala de los Reyes
10 Sala de los Ajimeces
11 Patio de Lindaraja
12 Queen's Chamber
13 Palacio de Carlos V / Museo de Bellas Artes / Museo Nacional de Arte Hispano-Musulmán
14 Chapel and Crypt

It probably never occurs to most visitors, but one of the most unusual features of this palace is its modesty. What you see is what the Nasrid kings saw; your imagination need add only a few carpets and tapestries, some well-crafted furniture of wood inlaid with ivory, wooden screens, and big round braziers of brass for heat or incense, to make the picture complete. Most of the actual building is wood and plaster, cheap and perishable, like a World's Fair pavilion; no good Muslim monarch would offend Allah's sense of propriety by pretending that these worldly splendours were anything more than the pleasures of a moment (much of the plaster, wood, and all of the tiles, are the products of careful restorations over the last 100 years). The Alhambra, in fact, is the only substantially intact medieval Muslim palace anywhere.

Like so many old royal palaces, this one is divided into three sections: one for everyday business of the palace and government; the next, more secluded, for the state rooms and official entertainments of the kings; and the third, which few outsiders ever reached, for the private apartments of the king and his household.

The Mexuar

The small Mexuar, where the kings would hold their public audiences, survives near the present-day entrance to the palace complex. The adjacent **Patio del Mexuar**, though much restored, is one of the finest rooms of the Alhambra. Nowhere is the meditative serenity of the palace more apparent (unless you arrive when all the tour groups do) and the small fountain in the centre provides an introduction to an important element of the architecture: water. Present everywhere, in pools, fountains and channels, it is as much a part of the design as the wood, tile and stone.

Patio de los Arrayanes

If you have trouble finding your way around, remember the elaborately decorated portals never really lead anywhere; the door you want will always be tucked unobtrusively to the side; here, as in Sevilla's Alcázar, the principle is to heighten the sense of surprise. The entrance to the grand Patio de los Arrayanes (Court of the Myrtles), with its long goldfish pond and lovely arcades, was the centre of the second, state section of the palace; directly off it, you pass through the **Sala de la Barca** (Hall of the Boat), so called after its hull-shaped wooden ceiling, and into the **Salón de Embajadores** (Hall of Ambassadors), where the kings presided over all important state business. The views and the decoration are some of the Alhambra's best, with a cedarwood ceiling and plaster panels (many were originally painted) carved with floral arabesques or Arabic calligraphy. These inscriptions, some Koranic scripture (often the phrase 'Allah alone conquers', the motto of the Nasrids), some eulogies of the kings, and some poetry, recur throughout the palace. The more conspicuous are in a flowing script developed by the Granadan artists; look closely and you will see others, in the angular Kufic script, forming frames for the floral designs.

In some of the chambers off the Patio de los Arrayanes, you can peek out over the domed roofs of the baths below; opposite the Salón de Embajadores is a small entrance (*often closed*) into the dark, empty **crypt** of the Palace of Charles V, with curious echo effects.

Patio de los Leones

Another half-hidden doorway leads you into the third and most spectacular section, the king's residence, built around the Patio de los Leones (Court of the Lions). Here the plaster and stucco work is at its most ornate, the columns and arches at their most delicate, with little pretence of any structural purpose; balanced on their slender shafts, the façades of the court seem as if they hang in the air. As so often in Moorish architecture, the over-ripe arabesques of this patio conceal a subtle symbolism. The 'enclosed garden' that can stand for the attainment of truth, or paradise, or at times for the cosmos, is a recurring theme in Islamic mystical poetry. Here you may take the 12 endearingly preposterous lions who support the fountain in the centre as the months, or signs of the zodiac, and the four channels that flow out from the fountains as the four corners of the cosmos, the cardinal points or, on a different level, the four rivers of paradise.

The rooms around the patio have exquisite decorations: to the right, from the entrance, the **Sala de los Abencerrajes**, named after the legend of the noble family that Boabdil supposedly had massacred at a banquet here during the civil wars just before the fall of Granada; to the left, the **Sala de las Dos Hermanas** (Hall of the Two Sisters). Both of these have extravagant domed *muqarnas* ceilings. The latter chamber is also ornamented with a wooden window grille, another speciality of the Granadan artists; this is the only one surviving in the Alhambra. Adjacent to the Sala de las dos Hermanas is the **Sala de los Ajimeces**, so called for its doubled windows. The **Sala de los Reyes** (Hall of the Kings), opposite the court's entrance, is unique for the paintings on its ceiling, works that would not be out of place in any Christian palace of medieval Europe. The central panel may represent six of Granada's 14th-century kings; those on the side are scenes of a chivalric court. The artist is believed to have been a visiting Spanish Christian painter, possibly from Sevilla. From the Sala de las dos Hermanas, steps lead down to the **Patio de Lindaraja** (or Mirador de Daraxa), with its fountain and flowers, Washington Irving's favourite spot in the Alhambra. Originally the inner garden of the palace, it was remodelled for the royal visits of Charles V and Philip V. Irving actually lived in the **Queen's Chamber**, decorated with frescoes of Charles V's expedition to Tunis – in 1829, apartments in the Alhambra could be had for the asking! Just off this chamber, at ground-floor level, is the beautifully decorated **hammam**, the palace baths.

Follow the arrows, out of the palace and into the outer gardens, the **Jardines del Partal**, a broad expanse of rose terraces and flowing water. The northern walls of the Alhambra border the gardens, including a number of well-preserved towers: from the west, the **Torre de las Damas**, entered by a small porch, the **Torre del Mihrab**, near which is a small mosque, now a chapel; the **Torre de los Picos**; the **Torre de la Cautiva** (Tower of the Imprisoned Lady), one of the most elaborately decorated; and the **Torre de las Infantas**, one of the last projects in the Alhambra (*c.* 1400).

Palacio de Carlos V

Anywhere else this elegant Renaissance building would be an attraction in itself. Here it seems only pompous and oversized; you wonder why this emperor, with a good half of Europe to build palaces in, had to plop it down here – ruining much of the Alhambra in the process. Once Charles had smashed up the place he lost interest, and most of the palace, still unfinished today, was not built until 1616. The original architect, Pedro Machuco, had studied in Italy, and he took the opportunity to introduce into Spain the chilly, Olympian High Renaissance style of Rome. At the entrances are intricately detailed sculptural **reliefs** showing scenes from Charles' campaigns and military 'triumphs' in the antique manner: armoured torsos on sticks amidst heaps of weapons. Inside, Machuco added a classical circular courtyard. For all its Doric gravity, the patio was almost always used for bullfights and mock tournaments.

The Museums

***Museo de Bellas Artes**, open Tues 2.30–6, Wed–Sat 9–6, Sun 9–2.30; closed Mon. **Museo Nacional de Arte Hispano-Musulmán**, open Tues–Sat 9–2; closed Sun and Mon.*

On the top floor of the palace is the **Museo de Bellas Artes**, a largely forgettable collection of religious paintings from Granada churches. Downstairs, the **Museo Nacional de Arte Hispano-Musulmán** contains perhaps Spain's best collection of Moorish art, including some paintings, *azulejos*, a collection of ceramic ware with fanciful figurative decoration and lovely astronomical instruments.

Behind Charles' palace a street leads into the remnants of the town that once filled much of the space within the Alhambra's walls, now reduced to a small collection of restaurants and souvenir stands. At one end of the street, the church of **Santa María** (1581), designed by Juan de Herrera, occupies the site of the Alhambra's mosque; at the other, the first Christian building on the Alhambra, the **Convento de San Francisco** (1495) has been converted into a *parador*.

Around the Alhambra

The Generalife

Opening hours as for the Alhambra; adm inc. in Alhambra ticket.

The Generalife (*Djinat al-Arif*: high garden) was the summer palace of the Nasrid kings, built on the height the Moors called the Mountain of the Sun. Many of the visitors to the Alhambra have never heard of it, and pass up a chance to see the finest garden in Spain. To get there, it's about a five-minute walk from the Alhambra along a lovely avenue of tall cypresses. The buildings here hold few surprises if you've just come from the Alhambra. They are older than most of the Casa Real, which was begun around 1260. The gardens are built on terraces on several levels, and the views over the Alhambra and Albaicín are transcendent. The centrepiece is a long pool with many water sprays that passes through beds of roses. A lower level, with a promenade on the hill's edge, is broken up into secluded bowers by cypress bushes cut into angular shapes of walls and gateways. There's no evidence that the original Moorish gardens looked anything like this; everything has been done in the last 200 years.

Albaicín

Even more than the old quarters of Córdoba, this hillside neighbourhood of white-washed houses and tall cypresses has preserved some of the atmosphere of al-Andalus. Its difficult site and the fact that it was long the district of Granada's poor explain the lack of change, but today it looks as if it is becoming fashionable again.

From Pza Nueva, a narrow street called the **Carrera del Darro** leads up the valley of the Darro between the Alhambra and Albaicín hills; here the little stream has not been covered over, and you can get an idea of how the centre of Granada looked in the old days. On the Alhambra side, old stone bridges lead up to a few half-forgotten streets hidden among the forested slopes; here you'll see some 17th-century Spanish houses with curious painted *esgrafiado* façades. Nearby, traces of a horseshoe arch can be seen where a Moorish wall once crossed the river; in the corner of C/Baruelo there are well-preserved **Moorish baths** (*open Tues–Sat 10–2*). Even more curious is the façade of the **Casa Castril** on the Darro, a flamboyant 16th-century mansion with a portal carved with a phoenix and other odd devices. Casa Castril has been restored as Granada's **archaeological museum** (***t** 958 22 56 40; open Tues 2.30–8, Wed–Sat 9–8, Sun 9–2.30; closed Mon*) with a small collection of artefacts from the caves in Granada province, many inhabited since Palaeolithic times, and a few Iberian settlements. There is a Moorish room and, strangest of all, a collection of beautiful alabaster burial urns, made in Egypt, but found in a Phoenician-style necropolis near Almuñécar. Nothing else like them has ever been discovered in Spain, and the hieroglyphics on them are provocative in the extreme (translations given in Spanish), telling how the deceased travelled here in search of some mysterious primordial deity.

Farther up the Darro you'll have to do some climbing, but the higher you go the prettier the Albaicín is, and the better the views. Among the white houses and white walls are some of the oldest Christian churches in Granada. As in Córdoba, they are tidy and extremely plain, built to avoid alienating a recently converted population unused to religious imagery. Quite a few Moorish houses survive, and some can be seen on **C/Horno de Oro**; on C/Daralhorra, at the top of the Albaicín, are the remains of a Nasrid palace that was largely destroyed to make way for Isabel's **Convento de Santa Isabel la Real** (1501). Here, running parallel to Cuesta de la Alhacaba, is a long-surviving stretch of **Moorish wall**. There are probably a few miles of walls left, visible around the hillsides over Granada; the location of the city made a very complex set of fortifications necessary. The heart of the Albaicín is about halfway up, through **Puerta de las Pesas**, around the pretty, animated **Plaza Larga**. A few blocks away the **Mirador de San Nicolás** offers the most romantic view imaginable of the Alhambra with the snow-capped peaks of the Sierra Nevada behind it.

Sacromonte

For something completely different, you might strike out beyond the Albaicín hill to the **gypsy caves of Sacromonte**. Granada has had a substantial gypsy population for several centuries now. The most visible are those who prey on the tourists, handing out carnations with a smile and then attempting to extort huge sums out of anyone dumb enough to take one (of course, they'll tell your fortune, too). The biggest part of the community, however, still lives around Sacromonte in streets of some quite well-appointed cave homes, where they wait to lure you in for a little display of flamenco. The consensus of opinion is that the music and dancing are usually indifferent, and the gypsies' eventually successful attempts to shake out your last euro can make it an unpleasantly unforgettable affair. Nevertheless, if you care to match wits with the experts, proceed up the Cuesta del Chapiz from the Río Darro, turn right at the **Casa del Chapiz**, and keep going until some gypsy child drags you home with him. Serious flamenco fans will probably not fare better elsewhere in Granada except during the festivals, though there are some touristy flamenco nightspots – the **Reina Mora** by Mirador San Cristóbal is the best of them.

Central Granada

The old city wall swung in a broad arc from Puerta de Elvira to Puerta Real, now a small plaza full of traffic where C/Reyes Católicos meets the Acera del Darro. A few blocks north of here, in a web of narrow pedestrian streets that make up modern Granada's shopping district, is the pretty **Plaza de Bib-Rambla**, used for public gatherings and tournaments of arms in Moorish times. The narrow streets leading off to the east are known as the **Alcaicería**. This area was the Moorish silk exchange, but the buildings you see now are not original; the Alcaicería burned down in the 1840s and was rebuilt in more or less the same fashion with Moorish arches and columns.

The Cathedral

Pza de Pasiegas, ***t*** *958 22 29 59; open Mon–Sat 10.30–1.30 and 4–7, Sun 4–7.*

The best way to see Granada's **Cathedral** is to approach it from C/Marqués, just north of Pza Bib-Rambla. The unique façade, with its three tall, recessed arches, is a striking sight, designed by the painter Alonso Cano (1667). On the central arch, the big plaque bearing the words 'Ave María' commemorates the exploit of the Spanish captain who sneaked into the city one night in 1490 and nailed up this message up on the door of the great mosque this cathedral has replaced. The other conspicuous feature is the name 'José Antonio Primo de Rivera' carved on the façade. Son of the 1920s dictator, Miguel Primo de Rivera, José Antonio was the founder of the Falangist Party, which provoked may of the disorders that started the Civil War. After his capture and execution by Loyalists, his followers treated him as a sort of holy martyr, and chiselled his name on every cathedral in Spain.

The rest of the cathedral isn't up to the standard of its façade, and there is little reason to go in and explore its interior or dreary museum. As in many Spanish cathedrals, the failure of this one stems from artistic indecision. Two very talented architects were in charge: Enrique de Egas, who wanted it Gothic, like his adjacent Capilla Real, and (five years later) Diego de Siloé, who decided Renaissance would look nicer. Interior features include statues by Alonso de Mena and Alonso Cano, a *retablo* in the right aisle with paintings by Cano and Ribera, and a *St Francis* by El Greco.

Capilla Real

Gran Vía de Colón; open daily 10.30–1 and 3.30–6.30, Sun 11–1; adm.

Leaving the cathedral and turning left, you pass the outsized **sacristy**, begun in 1705 and incorporated in the cathedral façade. Turn left again at the first street, C/de los Oficios, a narrow lane paved in charming patterns of coloured pebbles; on the left, you can pay your respects to *Los Reyes Católicos*. The royal couple had already built a mausoleum in Toledo, but after the capture of Granada they decided to plant themselves here. Even in the shadow of the bulky cathedral, Enrique de Egas' **chapel** (1507) reveals itself as the outstanding work of the Isabelline Gothic style, with its delicate roofline of traceries and pinnacles. **Inside**, the Catholic Kings are buried in a pair of Carrara marble sarcophagi, elegantly carved though not necessarily flattering to either of them. The little staircase behind them leads down to the **crypt**, where you can peek in at their plain lead coffins and those of their unfortunate daughter, Juana the Mad, and her husband, Philip the Handsome, whose effigies lie next to the older couple above. Juana was Charles V's mother, and the rightful heir to the Spanish throne. There is considerable doubt as to whether she was mad at all; when Charles arrived from Flanders in 1517, he forced her to sign papers of abdication, and then locked her up in a windowless cell for the last 40 years of her life, never permitting any visitors. The interior of the chapel is sumptuously decorated. The iron *reja* by Master Bartolomé de Jaén and the *retablo* are especially fine; the latter is largely the work of a French artist, Philippe de Bourgogne. In the sacristy you can see some of Isabel's personal art collection – works by Van der Weyden, Memling, Berruguete, Botticelli (attributed), Perugino and others – as well as her crown and sceptre, her illuminated missal, some captured Moorish banners, and Ferdinand's sword.

Across Calle Reyes Católicos

Even though this part of the city centre is as old as the Albaicín, most of it was rebuilt after 1492, and its age doesn't show. The only Moorish building remaining is also the only example left in Spain of a *khan* or *caravanserai*, the type of merchants' hotel common throughout the Muslim world. The 14th-century **Corral del Carbón** was used as a coal warehouse (hence the name), but today it houses a government handicrafts outlet, and much of the building is under restoration. The neighbourhood of quiet streets and squares behind it is the best part of Spanish Granada and worth a walk if you have the time. This neighbourhood is bounded on the west by the **Acera del Darro**, the noisy heart of modern Granada, with most of the big hotels. It's a little discouraging but, just a block away, the city has adorned itself with a beautiful string of boulevards very like the Ramblas of Barcelona, wonderful for a stroll.

Northern Granada

From the little street on the north side of the cathedral, C/de la Cárcel, C/San Jerónimo skirts the edge of Granada's markets and leads you towards the old **university** district, one of the livelier spots of town. C/San Jerónimo ends at the C/del Gran

Capitán, where church of **San Juan de Dios** stands out with a Baroque façade and a big green and white tiled dome. **San Jerónimo**, a block west, is another of the oldest and largest Granada churches (1520); it contains the tomb of Gonzalo de Córdoba, the 'Gran Capitán' who won so many victories in Italy for the Catholic Kings.

Here you're not far from the **Puerta de Elvira**, in an area where old Granada fades into anonymous suburbs to the north. Climbing up towards the Albaicín, your senses will be assaulted by the gaudiest Baroque chapel in Spain, in the **Cartuja** (***t*** *958 16 19 32; open Tues–Sun 10–1 and 4–8; closed Mon*), or Carthusian monastery, on C/Real de Cartuja. Gonzalo de Córdoba endowed this charterhouse, though little of the original works remain. The 18th-century chapel and its sacristy, done in the richest marble, gold and silver, and painted plaster, fairly oozes with a froth of twisted spiral columns, rosettes and curlicues. It has often been described as a Christian attempt to upstage the Alhambra, but the inspiration more likely comes from the Aztecs, via the extravagant Mexican Baroque.

The Sierra Nevada and Las Alpujarras

From everywhere in Granada, Spain's loftiest peaks peer over the tops of buildings; from the city centre you can be scaling them in little more than an hour. Dress warmly. As the name implies, the Sierra Nevada is snowcapped nearly all year, and even in late July and August, when the road is clear and you can travel right over the mountains to the valley of Las Alpujarras (*see* 'Getting Around', p.702), it is as chilly and windy as you would expect it to be, some 10,825ft above sea level. These mountains, a geological curiosity of sorts, are just an oversized chunk of the Penibetic System, the chain that stretches from Arcos de la Frontera almost to Murcia. Their

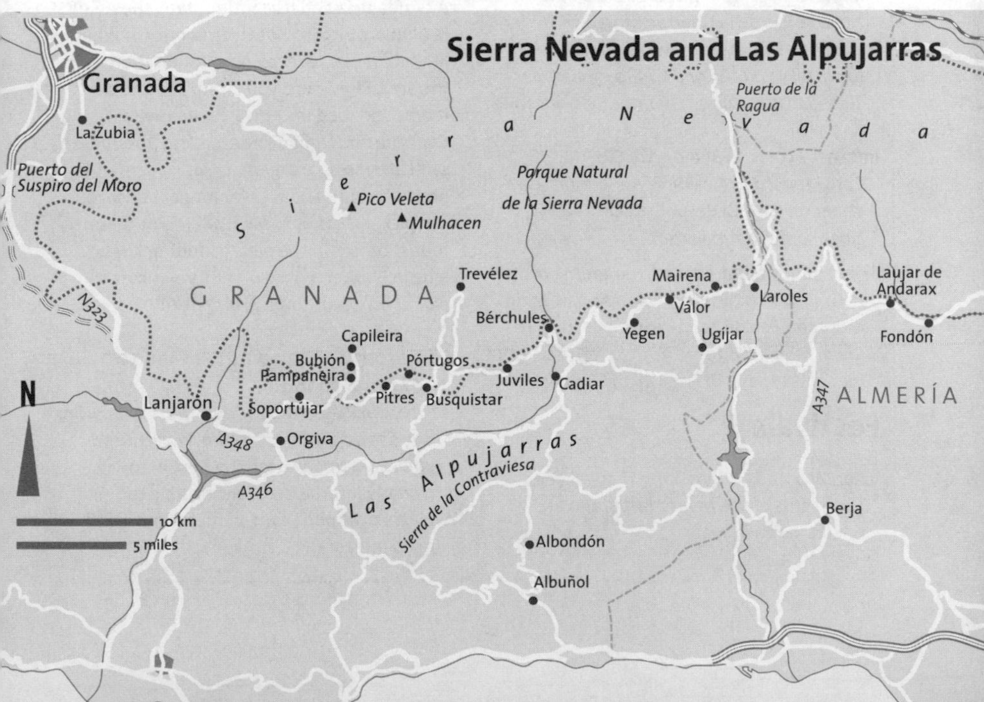

Getting Around

Las Alpujarras: a few years ago it was still possible to penetrate the white villages of Las Alpujarras by bus over the top of the Sierra Nevada. However, the high road past Mulhacén has been closed to all motorized traffic, even in high summer. If you still wish to take this incredibly scenic route you can walk, cycle, or go by horse, in the summer months.

Sierra Nevada: there are two or three buses a day from the main bus station in Granada, to the main square of the ski resort, Solynieve. Departures during the season are at 8am, 10am and 5pm, returning at 9am, 4pm and 6pm. In summer the bus leaves at 9am, returning at 5.30pm. The buses are operated by Autocares Bonal, **t** 958 27 31 00. Some 20km before you reach Veleta, you'll enter the Solynieve ski area; from here there are cable cars up to the peak itself.

Tourist Information

Lanjarón: opposite the spa, on the right as you come in from Granada: **t** 958 77 02 82 (*opening times vary*).

Pampaneira: Parque Natural de la Sierra Nevada, Pza de la Libertad s/n, **t** 958 76 31 27, **f** 958 76 33 01, *www.nevadensis.com* (*open all year Mon and Sun 10–3; summer Tues–Sat 10–2 and 4–7; winter Tues–Sat 10–2 and 3–6*).

Internet Access: In Bubión, try CiberMonfi, Café Morisco, C/Alcalde Pérez Remón 2 (a street off the Pza del Sol), **t** 958 76 30 53, *cibermonfi@hotmail.com*.

Skiing Information: contact the tourist office in Granada, or the Federación Andaluza de Montaña, Pso de Ronda 101, **t** 958 29 13 40 (*open Mon–Fri 8.30–10.30*). Call **t** 958 24 91 19 for snow reports in English and Spanish.

Festivals

Valor: 'Moors and Christians' Festival, *Sept*. The events of the Moors' last stand are re-created each year.

Skiing

Up until recently the area was fairly inaccessible and the facilities pretty basic. But the place has come on in leaps and bounds, so much so that it was deemed good enough to host the 1995 World Skiing Championships. Most of what you'll need you can find here: ski hire shops rent out the entire kit (including clothes) for about €42. There is also what is reputed to be the biggest covered car park in Spain with space for almost 3,000 cars. Ski passes cost between €15 and €22 a day, depending on the season. Nearby are the lifts and cabins to the slopes. Seasoned Alpine skiers will not be hugely challenged by the slopes, but for the beginner the area is a dream, with plenty of wide gentle pistes. There is plenty to keep you occupied for two or three days, and the views from the top of Veleta, across to Morocco on clear days, are unsurpassable.

Where to Stay and Eat

Las Alpujarras

Lanjarón has most of the rooms; a score of good bargains (around €18–24) are to be found on or near the main road into town, Av. Andalucia and its continuation, the Av. de la Alpujarra. It also has the majority of what limited upmarket accommodation there is in the area. Elsewhere, you'll find acceptable rooms and food in **Orgiva**, **Pampaneira**, **Capileira** and **Ugíjar**. The area also abounds in self-catering apartments, *casas rurales* and privately rented houses for longer stays. You can pick up lists of these from the numerous tourist offices in the area, including Rustic Blue in Bubión (**t** 958 76 33 81, *www.rusticblue.com*) where English is spoken.

Lanjarón ✉ 18420, Orgiva ✉ 18400 and Ugíjar ✉ 18480

******Nuevo Palas**, Av. de Alpujarra 24, Lanjarón, **t** 958 77 00 86, **f** 958 77 01 11, *www.nuevopalas.com* (*moderate*). The best in town; recently refurbished, comfortable rooms with views, pool, gym, games room and a good restaurant.

★**España**, Av. Andalucía 44, Lanjarón, **t/f** 958 77 01 87 (*inexpensive*). Excellent value for what it has, which includes a pool and its own grounds. Situated in the fine-looking building on your left as you enter town on a street lined with other one- and two-star places that are all much of a muchness.

El Rincon de Jamon, along the main road just beyond the España, Lanjarón. For an altogether earthier experience, come here to enjoy a *copa* of *vino* and a few slices of *jamón* from Trevelez in spit-and-sawdust surroundings; it's also a good place to buy *embutidos*.

★★★**Taray**, Ctra Talbate-Albuñol Km18, Orgiva, **t** 958 78 45 25, **f** 958 78 45 31, *tarayalp@teleline.es* (*moderate*). On the road out of Orgiva, this is one of the best places to stay in the whole of this area: comfortable rooms in a *cortijo*-style hotel, set round a large pool, and with a bar and good restaurant.

Hs Vidaña, Ctra de Almería, Ugíjar, **t** 958 76 70 10 (*inexpensive*). Serves up humungous portions of delicious mountain fare, such as partridge, goat and rabbit; also provides basic accommodation.

Trevélez ✉ 18005

★★★**Alcazaba de Busquistar**, Ctra Orgiva-Láujar, Km37, **t** 958 85 86 87, **f** 958 85 86 93 (*moderate*). This is one of the best places to stay in the Alpujarras, despite the indifferent service. It is nowhere near Busquistar (but four kilometres beyond Trevélez). A new hotel with apartments and studios, all with log fires, kitchen, phone and satellite TV. There is also a heated indoor pool, squash court, an excellent **restaurant**, three cafés and games room.

★**La Fragua**, C/San Antonio 4 (in the Barrio del Medio), **t** 958 85 85 73 (*inexpensive*). The best in town, with warm rooms and a good **restaurant** specializing in mountain-cured ham (*moderate*).

The Hostal Mulhacén, Ctra Ugíjar, **t/f** 958 85 85 87 (*inexpensive*). Well situated for hill walks and the annual night pilgrimage up the mountain on 4 Aug. The *hostal* is also beside the river, where locals swim during the summer.

Mesón Haraiçel, **t** 958 85 85 30 (*inexpensive*). Serves Arab-influenced food with plenty of almond sauces and meat dishes. For dessert try a *soplillo* (honey and almond meringue).

La Fuente, in the main square, **t** 958 85 10 67 (*cheap*). The budget option, just round the corner from Gerald Brenan's house. Also rents apartments.

Solynieve (Pradollano) ✉ 18196

Most of the ski hotels close from June to December. Ask at the tourist office in Granada for what's available, or contact the Cetursa Reservation Centre in Pradollano, **t** 958 24 91 11. Among the five modern hotels in Pradollano, none particularly stands out; in the skiing season accommodation at these places (not including instruction) means a week's stay on half board for about €540–720 per person.

★★★**Kenia Nevada**, in town, **t** 958 48 09 11, **f** 958 48 08 07 (*expensive*). Alpine-style, with a Jacuzzi, pool, gym and sauna for those stiff days on the slopes.

★★★**Hotel Parador**, on the main highway, **t** 958 48 06 61, **f** 958 48 02 12 (*expensive–moderate*). A smaller, newer *parador* that remains open all year round.

★★★**Ziryab**, **t** 958 48 0512, **f** 958 48 1415 (*expensive–moderate*). A dramatically situated hotel on the main square, with big, comfortable rooms and lots of warm, chunky wood furniture. Right by the car park.

★**Telecabina**, Pza de Pradollano, **t** 958 24 91 20, **f** 958 24 91 22 (*moderate*). Offers pleasant but basic doubles. *Open summer only*.

★★**El Ciervo**, **t** 958 48 0409, **f** 958 48 0461, *www.eh.etursa.es* (*cheap*). A large *pensión*.

Albergue Universitario, Peñones de San Francisco, **t** 958 48 01 22 (*cheap*). Cheaper accommodation like this can be had in this village at the end of the bus route.

Most **restaurants** are open only in the skiing season, and most are a little pretentious.

Ruta de Veleta, **t** 958 48 12 28 (*moderate*). This restaurant in Edificio Bulgaria is worth a try.

Rincón de Pepe Reyes, in Pradollano (*inexpensive*). Has good *andaluz* cooking.

Borreguiles, halfway up Veleta, **t** 958 48 00 79. Take the cable car up to this frenetic and none-too-clean café and enjoy the view.

highest peak, **Mulhacén** (11,418ft), is less than 40 kilometres from the coast. Mulhacén and its sister peak **Veleta** (11,126ft) can be climbed without too much exertion.

Sierra Nevada

If you're adventurous, you can continue onwards from Veleta down into **Las Alpujarras**, a string of white villages along the valley of the Rio Guadalfeo, between the Sierra Nevada and the little Contraviesa chain along the sea coast. On the way, just outside Granada, you'll pass the spot called **Suspiro de Moro**, where poor Boabdil sighed as he took his last look back over Granada. His mother was less than sympathetic – 'Weep like a woman for what you were incapable of defending like a man', she told him. It gave Salman Rushdie the title for his novel *The Moor's Last Sigh* (1995). The last 33 kilometres of this route, where the road joins the Guadalfeo valley down to Motril, are some of the most scenic in Spain.

Lanjarón, a spa town and the principle tourist centre in the region, has been attracting visitors to its spas since Roman times. The ruined Moorish castle on the hill saw the Moors' last stand against the Imperial troops on 8 March 1500, but it is well and truly Catholic today; Lanjarón's *Semana Santa* celebrations are the most famous in the province. The biggest town in the province is **Orgiva**, and here you'll have a choice of keeping to the main road for **Ugíjar** or heading north through the highest and loveliest part of the region, with typical white villages climbing the hillsides under terraced fields. **Soportújar** is the first, followed by **Pampaneira**, and then **Bubión**; all beautiful and all within sight of each other on a short detour along the edge of the beautiful **Barranco de Poqueira**. The last village on the route over Mulhacén and Veleta is **Capileira**, north of which a tremendously scenic road takes you up across the Sierra Nevada and eventually to Granada. In winter this pass is snowbound, and even in summer you need to take extra care – it's steep and dangerous with precipitous drops down the ravines.

The road carries on, passing **Pórtugos** and **Busquistar** before arriving in **Trevélez**, on the slopes of Mulhacén. It is full of tour buses, and a string of ugly developments has removed any charm it once had. Climbers set off from here into the Sierra Nevada, but there's little to detain other visitors. The road slopes back down **Bérchules**, one of the villages where the tradition of carpet-weaving has been maintained since Moorish times. From there, the C332 takes you to **Yegen** which became famous as the long-time home of the writer Gerald Brenan. His house is still in the village – ask for 'El Casa del Inglés'. After that come more intensively farmed areas on the lower slopes, with oranges, vineyards and almonds; you can either hit Ugíjar or detour to the seldom-visited villages of **Laroles** and **Mairena** on the slopes of **La Ragua**, one of the last high peaks of the Sierra Nevada.

Around the Sierra Nevada

It's a better road entering Granada from the west than that leaving it to the east. Between the city and Murcia are some of the emptiest, bleakest landscapes in Spain. The poverty of this region has long forced many of its inhabitants to live in caves, and nowhere more so than in **Guadix**. Several thousand of this city's population, most of them gypsies, have homes – complete with whitewashed façades, chimneys and television aerials – built into the hillsides. The centre is dominated by a Moorish **Alcazaba**, largely rebuilt in the 16th century; near the arcaded central **Plaza Mayor** stands the huge **cathedral**, begun by Diego de Siloé and given its magnificent façade in the 1700s by Andalucía's great Rococo eccentric, Vicente Acero. There's not much else to distract you in this corner of Spain. If you're headed for Almería (N324), you'll pass near **La Calahorra**, with an unusual Renaissance castle with domed turrets.

Almería Province

The coastal road cuts between the sea and the plastic; not coastal development, but agricultural plastic, covering a good percentage of Europe's winter vegetables. At Adra you enter the province of Almería, the sunniest, driest and hottest little corner of all Europe. Until the 1970s the **Costa de Almería**, difficult of access and bereft of utilities and water, was untouched by tourism. Now, charter flights drop in from northern Europe, and hotels are sprouting up here and there – but compared with the region further west, it's pleasantly underwhelming.

Almería

Almería has been a genial, dusty little port since its founding by the Phoenicians, though for a short time in the 11th century, after the fall of the caliphate, it dominated this end of al-Andalus, rivalling Córdoba and Sevilla. The upper city, with its narrow streets, tiny pastel houses and whitewashed cave dwellings hugging the looming walls of the **Alcazaba** (*open daily 9–6.30*), has retained a fine Moorish feel to this day. Built by Caliph Abd ar-Rahman II in the 10th century, the Alcazaba was the most powerful Moorish fortress in Spain; today its great curtain walls and towers defend mostly market- and flower-gardens – nothing remains of the once-splendid palace. The main structure is joined to the northern hills by the **wall of Jayrán**, and between the two is the **Centre for the Rescue of Animals of the Sahara** (*C/General Segura 1, **t** 950 28 10 45*): before going up, get permission from the centre's headquarters off the Av. de Federico Garcia. Almería's **cathedral** (***t** 609 57 58 02; open Mon–Fri 10–4.30, Sat 10–1; closed Sun; adm*), begun in 1524, was built to defend marauding Berber pirates; its four mighty towers once held cannons. Prettier, and boasting a fine carving of St James (Santiago) Matamoros and a minaret-like tower, is **Santiago El Viejo**, just off the Puerta de Purchena near the top of Pso de Almería.

Around Almería

Adra was an ancient Phoenician town, and the last spot in Spain surrendered by the Moors at the moment Boabdil sailed from here to Africa. Though it's still basically a fishing and agricultural village, it has spawned **Almerimar**, a large new development of mostly villas and flats, with a marina and one of Spain's best golf courses. The resorts at **Roquetas de Mar** (more golfing) and **Aguadulce** (oldest and biggest course on the Almería coast) are easily reached from Almería by bus.

Getting Around

By Air

Almería's airport is 8km from the city on the road to Níjar, **t** 950 33 31 11, **f** 950 21 38 59. There are charters from London, and regular connections with Madrid, Barcelona and Melilla. A bus connects the airport with the town and runs every 30 mins: the No.14, which leaves for the airport from Av. Federico Garcia Lorca (next to Pizza Hut), **t** 950 22 14 22.

By Boat

Transmediterránea runs car ferries from Almería to Melilla on the North African coast at 11.30pm every day except Saturday, arriving the next morning. The return journey leaves Melilla at 2.30pm and arrives in Almería at 11.30pm. The ticket office is at Parque Nicolás Salmerón 19, **t** 950 23 69 56, **f** 950 25 73 90.

By Train

Almería's RENFE station is a block from the bus station, on Ctra Ronda, easy walking distance from the centre, **t** 950 25 11 35. The city office is at C/Alcalde Muñoz 1, **t** 950 23 18 22, **f** 950 23 12 07. There are daily trains and Talgos to Madrid, Barcelona and Valencia; you can go to Granada three times a day; or make an all-night journey across Andalucía, departures daily around 11pm, arriving in Córdoba at 7am, or Sevilla at 8am.

By Bus

The bus station, in the new part of town on the Pza Barcelona, **t** 950 21 00 29, has a daily service to the major cities of the Levante up to Barcelona; also to Madrid, Granada, Sevilla, Cádiz, Málaga and Algeciras. There are two buses daily to Adra; hourly connections to Aguadulce and Roquetas; five buses daily to Berja; at least three to Cabo de Gata, four to Mojácar, two each to Níjar and Tabernas and weekday connections to Jaén and Guadix.

Tourist Information

Almería: Parque de Nicolás Salmerón at Martínez Campos, **t** 950 27 23 55 (*open Mon–Fri 9–7, Sat and Sun 10–2*). Municipal Office Av. Federico Garcia Lorca. Internet Access: Cibereal, C/Real 80; Battlezone, C/de la Terriza 20; Cafe Granada, C/Granada.

Mojácar: Pza Nueva s/n, **t/f** 950 47 51 62 (*open Mon–Fri 10–2 and 5–7, Sat 10–1; closed Sun*).

Sorbas: C/Terraplén 9, **t** 950 36 44 76, **f** 950 36 40 01.

Tabernas: Pza Pueblo 1, **t** 950 36 53 39.

Many of the smaller villages have *puntos de informacion* kiosks on the beach in season.

Where to Stay and Eat

Almería ✉ 04000

******Gran Hotel Almería**, Av. Reina Regente 8, **t** 950 23 80 11, **f** 950 27 06 91 (*expensive*). When on location, Hollywood denizens have traditionally stayed here. Rooms are plush with a/c, and there's a pool and bingo hall.

Torreluz Hotel Complex, Pza de las Flores 1, **t/f** 950 23 43 99, *www.torreluz.com* (*expensive–inexpensive*). Another comfortable choice in town offering two-, three- and

East of Almería the road goes through the **Alhamilla** – one of the driest, most rugged and lunar of the Spanish sierras. Off the main N340 (on some maps marked as the A370) lies **Mini Hollywood** (*t 950 36 52 36, f 950 36 28 84; adm exp*), the town built by Sergio Leone for such classics as Clint Eastwood's first vehicle, *A Fistful of Dollars*, and subsequent spaghetti westerns. When filming was over, Leone's extras decided to buy the place and run it as a tourist attraction, maintaining it and re-enacting scenes from the films, with shootouts and mock hangings twice a day.

The main road east winds through the northern flanks of the sierra, passing through dusty **Tabernas**. The hanging houses of **Sorbas** are most impressive seen from the highway, but the edge of town affords some great views across this bizarre landscape, which forms part of the **Parque Natural de Karst En Yesos**.

four-star accommodation, all in the same pretty square. All three hotels offer parking, a/c, phone and TV; the four-star also has a pool. The hotels have an excellent **restaurant** attached, the Asador Torreluz, **t** 950 23 45 45.

★★★**Costasol**, Pso de Almería, 58, **t** 950 23 40 11 (*moderate*). The city's other quality choice, right where all the action is and with all three-star amenities.

★**Sevilla**, C/Granada, **t** 950 23 02 09 (*inexpensive*). The best in the range, just off the Puerta Purchena. It's been refurbished recently so each room is modern and smart, with en suite bathrooms, TV and phone.

Almería also has plenty of *hostales* around Puerta de Purchena and Pza San Sebastian.

The Bristol, Pza San Sebastian 8, **t** 950 23 15 95. In a good position, just off the top of the Pso de Almería; all rooms en suite.

The city has a numerous **tapas bars** and **restaurants**, many of which are detailed on a map available from the tourist office.

El Bello Rincón, Ctra Nacional 340, Km436, **t** 950 23 84 27 (*expensive*). Probably the best restaurant, with a beautiful vista over the sea and wonderfully fresh seafood. *Closed Mon, July and Aug*.

I Valentin, C/Tenor Iribarne 17, **t** 950 26 44 75 (*moderate*). One of the best places to eat in town, specializing in shellfish. Try the *rape a la cazuela* or – for a splurge – the lobster.

Casa Puga, C/Jovellanos 7. A family-run place, ancient, noisy and with a vast wine list.

Cerveceria La Estrella, Pza del Carmen, 12. By contrast, this *cerveceria* is stylish, modern and attracts a thirty-something crowd.

Bodeguilla Ramón, C/Padre Alonso Torres 4. Atmospheric place with bullfight pictures, *azulejos* and a wide range of reasonably priced tapas; try their grilled *chorizo*.

There are plenty of **bars and clubs** to check out in the streets to the west of Pso de Almería. However, do stick to the lit streets and note that the further west you go, the seedier it becomes.

Mojácar ✉ 04638

★★★★**Parador Reyes Católicos**, just over the road from the beach, **t** 950 47 82 50, **f** 950 47 81 83, *mojacar@parador.es* (*expensive*). Probably the best option, with a pool, tennis, a/c and rooms with balconies.

★★★**Indalo**, Pso del Mediterraneo 1, **t** 950 47 80 01, **f** 950 47 81 76 (*expensive–moderate*). Perhaps the next best option; much cheaper out of season, with all mod cons including pool, tennis and sea views.

★★**Virgen del Mar**, on the beach, **t** 950 47 22 22, **f** 950 47 22 11 (*moderate*). A good mid-priced option on the beach, but no pool. Good **restaurant** attached (*see* below).

Mamabel's, C/Embajadores 3, **t** 950 47 24 48 (*inexpensive*). A beach house owned by Belgian poet Jean-Marie Raths. Ask for Room No.1 – you're sure to like the view. Dinner is prepared here as well; seafood and couscous to order are served on Fridays.

Palacio, Pza del Caño, **t** 950 47 28 46 (*moderate*). The best restaurant in town, with excellent chocolate truffles.

Virgen del Mar, on the beach, **t** 950 47 22 22. Food on the beach is generally a sorry affair, with a rash of pizzerias and Chinese restaurants. However, this hotel restaurant with a lovely terrace and good fresh fish is an exception.

The Almería Coast

The coastal road struggles out to the **Cabo de Gata**, a natural park with pretty beaches, popular with divers. The area has two main resorts, the little town of Cabo de Gata itself and **San José**, beyond the lighthouse.

Isolated amidst the rugged mountains, on a hill two kilometres from the beach, trendy **Mojácar** has often been compared to a pile of sugar cubes. No town in Spain wears such a Moorish face, its flat-roofed houses stacked almost on top of one another. Most unusually, the old women in the village used to paint a symbol known as the *indalo* (a stick figure with outstretched arms, holding up an arc) on their doors as a charm against the evil eye and thunderbolts. No one knows when this practice originated, though in the nearby caves of **Vélez-Blanco** Neolithic drawings of *indalos* dating from 3000 BC have led anthropologists to the conclusion that this is one of the few cases of a prehistoric symbol being handed down in one place for thousands of years. The coast road north to **Garrucha** is now an almost continuous stream of *urbanizaciónes*; to the south it's bars, discos and English-run pubs. Northeast, there's nothing but empty space as far as the Andalucía/Murcia border.

Language

Castellano, as Spanish is properly called, was the first modern language to have a grammar written for it. When a copy was presented to Queen Isabel in 1492, she understandably asked what it was for. 'Your Majesty,' replied a perceptive bishop, 'language is the perfect instrument of empire.' In the centuries to come, this concise, flexible and expressive language would prove to be just that: an instrument that would contribute more to Spanish unity than any laws or institutions, while spreading itself effortlessly over much of the New World.

Among other European languages, Spanish is closest to Portuguese and Italian – and, of course, Catalan and Gallego. Spanish, however, may have the simplest grammar of any Romance language, and if you know a little of any one of these, you will find much of the vocabulary looks familiar. It's quite easy to pick up a working knowledge of Spanish; but Spaniards speak colloquially and fast, and in Andalucía they leave out half the consonants and add some strange sounds of their own. Expressing yourself may prove a little easier than understanding the replies. Spaniards will appreciate your efforts, and when they correct you, they're not being snooty; they simply feel it's their duty to help you learn.

There are dozens of language books and tapes on the market; one particularly good one is *Teach Yourself Spanish*, by Juan Kattán-Ibarra (Hodder & Stoughton, 1984). Note that the Spaniards increasingly use the familiar *tú* instead of *usted* even when addressing complete strangers.

Pronunciation

Pronunciation is phonetic though some consonants can be difficult to get the hang of for English speakers.

Vowels

a short *a* as in 'pat'
e short *e* as in 'set'
i as *e* in 'be'
o between long *o* of 'note' and short *o* of 'hot'
u silent after *q* and gue- and gui-; otherwise long *u* as in 'flute'
ü *w* sound, as in 'dwell'
y at end of word or meaning *and*, as **i**

Diphthongs

ai, ay as *i* in 'side'
au as *ou* in 'sound'
ei, ey as *ey* in 'they'
oi, oy as *oy* of 'boy'

Consonants

c before the vowels *i* and *e*, it's a *castellano* tradition to pronounce it as *th*; many Spaniards and all Latin Americans pronounce it in this case as an *s*
ch like *ch* in 'church'
d often becomes *th*, or is almost silent, at end of word
g before *i* or *e*, pronounced as **j** (*see* below)
h silent
j the *ch* in loch – a guttural, throat-clearing *h*
ll *y* or *ly* as in million
ñ *ny* as in canyon (the ~ is called a tilde)
q *k*
r usually rolled, which takes practice
v often pronounced as *b*
z *th*, but *s* in parts of Andalucía

Stress

If the word ends in a vowel, an *n* or an *s*, then the stress will fall on the penultimate syllable, otherwise stress will fall on the last syllable; any exceptions are marked with an accent.

If all this seems difficult, remember that English pronunciation is even worse for Spaniards.

Practise on some of the place names:
Madrid ma-DREED
León lay-OHN
Sevilla se-BEE-ah
Cáceres CAH-ther-es
Cuenca KWAYN-ka
Jaén ha-AIN
Sigüenza sig-WAYN-thah
Trujillo troo-HEE-oh
Jerez her-ETH
Badajóz ba-da-HOTH
Málaga MAHL-ah-gah
Alcázar ahl-CATH-ar
Valladolid ba-yah-dol-EED
Arévalo ahr-EB-bah-lo

Useful Words and Phrases

Hello *Holá*
Goodbye *Adios/Hasta luego*
Good morning *Buenos días*
Good afternoon *Buenas tardes*
Good night *Buenas noches*
Please *por favor*
Thank you (very much) *(muchas) gracias*
You're welcome *de nada*
Excuse me *Con permiso/¿Me permite?*
I am sorry (in apology) *Disculpe/Perdon*
I am sorry (in sympathy or regret) *Lo siento*
It doesn't matter *No importa/Es igual*
all right *está bien*
ok *vale*
yes *sí*
no *no*
nothing *nada*
I don't know *No sé*
I don't understand Spanish *No entiendo español*
Do you speak English? *¿Habla usted inglés?*
Does someone here speak English? *¿Hay alguien que hable inglés?*
Speak slowly *Hable despacio*
Can you help me? *¿Puede usted ayudarme?*
Help! *¡Socorro!*
It is urgent! *¡Es urgente!*
How do you do? *¿Cómo está usted?*
or more familiarly *¿Cómo estás? ¿Qué tal?*
Well, and you? *¿Bien, y usted?*
or more familiarly *¿Bien, y tú?*
What is your name? *¿Cómo se llama?*
or more familiarly *¿Cómo te llamas?*
My name is ... *Me llamo ...*
What is that? *¿Qué es eso?*
What ...? *¿Qué ...?*
Who ...? *¿Quién ...?*
Where ...? *¿Dónde ...?*
When ...? *¿Cuándo ...?*
Why ...? *¿Por qué ...?*
How ...? *¿Cómo ...?*
How much? *¿Cuánto/Cuánta?*
How many? *¿Cuántos/Cuántas?*
I am lost *Me he perdido*
I am hungry/thirsty *Tengo hambre/sed*
I am tired (man/woman) *Estoy cansado(a)*
I am ill *No siento bien*
good/bad *bueno(a)/malo(a)*
slow/fast *despacio/rápido(a)*
big/small *grande/pequeño(a)*
hot/cold *caliente/frío(a)*

Numbers

one *uno/una*
two *dos*
three *tres*
four *cuatro*
five *cinco*
six *seis*
seven *siete*
eight *ocho*
nine *nueve*
ten *diez*
eleven *once*
twelve *doce*
thirteen *trece*
fourteen *catorce*
fifteen *quince*
sixteen *dieciséis*
seventeen *diecisiete*
eighteen *dieciocho*
nineteen *diecinueve*
twenty *veinte*
thirty *treinta*
forty *cuarenta*
fifty *cincuenta*
sixty *sesenta*
seventy *setenta*
eighty *ochenta*
ninety *noventa*
one hundred *cien*
five hundred *quinientos*
one thousand *mil*
first *primero*
second *segundo*

third *tercero*
fourth *cuarto*
fifth *quinto*
tenth *décimo*

Time

What time is it? *¿Qué hora es?*
It is two o'clock *Son las dos*
... half past two *... las dos y media*
... a quarter past two *... las dos y cuarto*
... a quarter to three *... las tres menos cuarto*
month *mes*
week *semana*
day *día*
morning *mañana*
afternoon *tarde*
evening *noche*
today *hoy*
yesterday *ayer*
soon *pronto*
tomorrow *mañana*
now *ahora*
later *después*
early *temprano*
late *tarde*

Days

Monday *lunes*
Tuesday *martes*
Wednesday *miércoles*
Thursday *jueves*
Friday *viernes*
Saturday *sábado*
Sunday *domingo*

Months

January *enero*
February *febrero*
March *marzo*
April *abril*
May *mayo*
June *junio*
July *julio*
August *agosto*
September *septiembre*
October *octubre*
November *noviembre*
December *diciembre*

Shopping and Sightseeing

I would like... *Quisiera...*
Where is/are...? *¿Dónde está/están...?*
How much is it? *¿Cuánto vale eso?*
open/closed *abierto/cerrado*
cheap/expensive *barato/caro*
money *dinero*
Do you have any change? *¿Tiene cambio?*
bank *banco*
beach *playa*
booking/box office *taquilla*
church *iglesia*
department store *almacén*
hospital *hospital*
market *mercado*
museum *museo*
newspaper (foreign) *periódico (extranjero)*
pharmacy *farmacia*
police station *comisaría*
policeman *policía*
post office *correos*
postage stamp *sello*
sea *mar*
shop *tienda*
supermarket *supermercado*
telephone *teléfono*
theatre *teatro*
winery *bodega*
toilet/toilets *servicios/aseos*
men *señores/hombres/caballeros*
women *señoras/damas*

Accommodation

Where is the hotel? *¿Dónde está el hotel?*
Do you have a room? *¿Tiene usted una habitación?*
Can I look at the room? *¿Podría ver la habitación?*
How much is the room per day/week? *¿Cuánto cuesta la habitación por día/semana?*
... with two beds *con dos camas*
... with double bed *con una cama grande*
... with a shower/bath *con ducha/baño*
... for one person/two people *para una persona/dos personas*
... for one night/one week *una noche/una semana*
elevator *ascensor*
bathroom *servicio/cuarto de baño*

Driving

rent *alquilar*
car *coche*
motorbike/moped *moto/ciclomotor*
bicycle *bicicleta*
petrol *gasolina*
garage *garaje*
This doesn't work *Este no funciona*
road *carretera*
motorway *autopista*
Is the road good? *¿Es buena la carretera?*
breakdown *avería*
driving licence *carnet de conducir*
exit *salida*
entrance *entrada*
danger *peligro*
no parking *estacionament prohibido*
give way/yield *ceda el paso*
roadworks *obras*

Note: Most road signs will be in international pictographs

Transport and Directions

aeroplane *avión*
airport *aeropuerto*
bus/coach *autobús/autocar*
bus/railway station *estación*
bus stop *parada*
customs *aduana*
platform *andén*
port *puerto*
seat *asiento*
ship *buque/barco/embarcadero*
ticket *billete*
train *tren*
I want to go to... *Deseo ir a...*
How can I get to ...? *¿Cómo puedo llegar a ...?*
Where is ...? *¿Dónde está ...?*
When is the next (last)...? *¿Cuándo sale el próximo (último)...?*
What time does it leave (arrive)? *¿Parte (llega) a qué hora?*
From where does it leave? *¿De dónde sale?*
Do you stop at ... ? *¿Para en ... ?*
How long does the trip take? *¿Cuánto tiempo dura el viaje?*
I want a (return) ticket to ... *Quiero un billete (de ida y vuelta) a ...*
How much is the fare? *¿Cuánto cuesta el billete?*
here/there *aquí/allí*
close/far *cerca/lejos*
left/right *izquierda/derecha*
straight on *todo recto*
corner *esquina*
square *plaza*
street *calle*

Eating Out

See also 'Menu Decoder' in the **Food and Drink** chapter, pp.68–9.

menu *carta/menú*
bill/check *cuenta*
change *cambio*
set meal *menú del día*
waiter/waitress *camarero/a*
Do you have a table? *¿Tiene una mesa?*
... for one/two? *... ¿para uno/dos?*
Can I see the menu, please? *Déme el menú, por favor*
Do you have a wine list? *¿Hay una lista de vinos?*
Can I have the bill (check), please? *La cuenta, por favor*
Can I pay by credit card? *¿Puedo pagar con tarjeta de crédito?*

Some Useful Basque Words and Phrases

welcome *ongi-etorri*
danger, roadworks *kontuz, lanak*
beach *hondartza*
straight ahead *zuzen*
tourist office *turismo bulegoa*
closed *itxita*
train station *tren geltokia*
delay *atzerapena*
Hello, how are you? *Kaixo, zer moduz?*
a small beer *zuritoa*
a large beer *garagardoa*
some sardines, please *sardinak, mesedez*
men's *gizonak*
ladies' *emakumiak*
What is this? *zer da hau?*
yes *bai*
no *ez*
I don't understand *nik ez dut ulurtzen*
see you later *gero arte*

Glossary

ajimez: an arched double window (Moorish)
alameda: park or promenade
ayuntamiento: city hall
azulejo: painted glazed tiles, used in Moorish and *mudéjar* work and later architecture
baldachin: a canopy on posts over an altar or throne
barrio: city quarter or neighbourhood
calvario or **humilladero**: calvary, or stations of the Cross along a road outside town
castizo: anything purely Spanish (from the Castilian point of view)
castrum: Roman military camp
churrigueresque: florid Baroque style of late 17th and early 18th centuries, in the style of the architect and sculptor José Churriguera
converso: Jew who converted to Christianity
coro: walled-in choir a Spanish cathedral
corregidor: chief magistrate
cortes: Spanish Parliament
cortijo: Andalucían country house
custodia: tabernacle, where sacramental vessels are kept
diputación: seat of provincial government
esgrafiado: style of painting or etching designs in stucco, on a façade
estilo desornamentado: austere, heavy Renaissance style inaugurated by Juan de Herrera; sometimes described as Herreran
fandango: traditional dance and song, greatly influenced by the gypsies of Andalucía
feria: major festival or market
finca: farm, country house or estate
fuero: exemption or privilege of a town or region under medieval Spanish law
grandee: select member of Spain's nobility
hammam: Moorish bath
herreran: *see estilo desornamentado.*
hidalgo: literally, 'son of somebody': the lowest level of the nobility, just respectable enough for a coat-of-arms
homage tower: tallest tower of a fortification, sometimes detached from the wall
hórreo: Asturian/Galician granary or corn crib
Isabelline Gothic: late 15th-century style, roughly corresponding to the English Perpendicular style
judería: Jewish quarter
junta: council or, in specific terms, the regional government
kufic: angular style of Arabic calligraphy, often used as architectural ornamentation.
lonja: merchants' exchange.
majolica: porous pottery glazed with bright metallic oxides
mantilla: silk or lace scarf or shawl
medina: walled centre of a Moorish city
mezquita: mosque
mihrab: prayer niche facing Mecca, often elaborately decorated in a mosque
mirador: a scenic overlook or belvedere
modernista: Catalan Art Nouveau
monterías: hunting scenes (in art)
morisco: a Muslim who submitted to Christianization in order to remain in Spain after the Reconquista
mozarabic: referring to Christians under Muslim rule in Moorish Spain
mudéjar: Moorish-influenced architecture, characterized by decorative use of bricks and ceramics; Spain's 'national style' between the 12th and 16th centuries
muqarnas: hanging masonry effect created through multiple use of support elements
ogival: pointed (arches)
pallazo: circular, conical-roofed shepherd's hut in Asturias and Galicia
paseo: promenade, or evening walk along one
pazo: Galician manor house
plateresque: 16th-century style; heavily ornamented Gothic
pronunciamiento: a military coup
reja: iron grilles, either covering exterior windows, or decorative grilles in churches
retablo: carved or painted altarpiece
transitional: (in northern Spanish churches) referring to the transition between Romanesque and Gothic

Further Reading

Ball, Phil, *Morbo: The Story of Spanish Football* (When Saturday Comes). Brilliant examination into the history of Spanish football.

Borrow, George, *The Bible in Spain* (various editions, first in 1843). Jolly travel account by a preposterous Protestant Bible salesman in 19th-century Spain.

Boyle, Christine and Chris Nawrat, *The Traveller's Food and Wine Guide: Spain and Portugal* (Carberry). Pocket guide deciphering menus in Castilian and Catalan.

Brenan, Gerald, *Spanish Labyrinth* (Cambridge, 1943); *The Literature of the Spanish People* (Cambridge, 1951); *South from Granada* (Penguin). Classic works, treating respectively the origins of the Civil War, Spanish literature and life in Andalucía in the 1920s.

Fletcher, Richard, *Moorish Spain* (Phoenix Giant, 1994). A welcome new interpretation, particularly good on art and culture.

Calderon de la Barca, Pedro, *Life is a Dream* (Nick Hern). The Catholic *Hamlet*.

Casas, Penelope, *The Foods and Wines of Spain* (Penguin). The best Spanish cookbook written in English.

Castro, Américo, *The Structure of Spanish History* (E. L. King, 1954).

Cervantes, Miguel de, *Don Quixote* (Penguin and others). As great as its reputation.

Elliot, J. H., *Imperial Spain 1469–1714* (Pelican, 1983). Elegant proof that much of the best writing these days is in the field of history.

Epton, Nina, *Navarre: the Flea between Two Monkeys*, and *Grapes and Granite* (on Galicia). Good reads.

Ford, Richard, *Gatherings from Spain* (Everyman). A boiled-down version of the classic *A Handbook for Travellers in Spain* of 1845. Hard to find but worth the trouble.

Gibson, Ian, *The Assassination of Federico García Lorca* (Penguin); also *Fire in the Blood* (Faber). The latter is a fascinating introduction and analysis of New Spain and its spirit of *desfase* – happily unresolvable paradoxes.

Harrison, Richard J., *Spain at the Dawn of History* (Thames and Hudson). Spain before the Romans.

Harvey, L. P., *Islamic Spain, 1250–1500* (Chicago University Press). A thorough account.

Hamilton, R. and Janet Perry (translators), *The Poem of the Cid* (Penguin).

Hemingway, Ernest, *The Sun Also Rises* (Fiesta in the UK) and *Death in the Afternoon* (various editions).

Hooper, John, *The Spaniards* (Viking, 1993). A comprehensive account of modern Spanish life and politics.

Hughes, Robert, *Barcelona* (Harvill, Vintage). Fat, erudite and witty: one of the best tales of Barcelona and, in fact, of any city.

Irving, Washington, *Tales of the Alhambra* (various editions).

Keay, S. J., *Roman Spain* (British Museum/University of California). A lively account.

Lee, Laurie, *As I Walked Out One Midsummer Morning* and *A Rose for Winter*. Well-written adventures of a young man walking from Vigo to Málaga in 1936 and his return 20 years later.

Lorca, Federico García, *Three Tragedies and Five Plays* (Penguin). A good translation of his best works.

Morris, Jan, *Spain* (Penguin, 1982). Dubious ideas are sustained by crystalline prose.

Mitchell, David, *The Spanish Civil War* (Granada, 1982). Anecdotal; with wonderful photographs.

Mullins, Edwin, *The Pilgrimage to Santiago* (Secker & Warburg/Taplinger). One of the most colourful, wide-ranging accounts.

Orwell, George, *Homage to Catalonia* (Penguin). Fascinating first-hand account of the Civil War in and around Barcelona.

Pritchett, V. S., *The Spanish Temper* (Hogarth Press). Evocative account of Spain in the 1950s – another country altogether.

Thomas, Hugh, *The Spanish Civil War* (Penguin, 1977). The best general work.

Index

Main page references are in **bold**. Page references to maps are in *italics*.

About the Updaters

Kristina Cordero is 29 and lives in Madrid. She has written for Let's Go, Frommer's and various magazines. She is also a translator of Spanish and Latin American fiction, including novels by Alberto Fuguet, Jorge Volpi, Ray Loriga and Benjamin Prado.

Adam Coulter's first memory of Andalucía is of standing outside a tapas bar in Sevilla on a warm October night in 1989. He moved to Spain two years later, living in Oviedo and Madrid but frequently visiting the south. He now lives in London but returns to Spain whenever he can find a suitable excuse.

Mary-Ann Gallagher is a travel writer and editor. She has lived in New York, Japan, Spain and London, and has written and updated several titles for Cadogan Guides, as well as writing for other travel publications.

Susannah Sayler lives and works in New York. When she is not updating guidebooks or dreaming of Spain, she works as a private investigator and photographer.

David Stott and **Helen Laird** are 'slow drift' travellers; ten years combined wandering has taken them to nearly fifteen countries, most of them Latin. They have done anything and everything to survive, and now work as professional travel writers. David and Helen contributed a chapter to the Cadogan Guide *The Amazon*.

Catherine Weiss is an inveterate globetrotter and has lived in Argentina, Belgium, Portugal, Spain and the USA, in between bouts in England. She is also a passionate hispanophile, sallying south at the drop of a *sombrero*. Always the optimist, after dallying with City life, Catherine is now pursuing a future in human rights, yet more experimental cooking and, of course, more travels.

Acknowledgements

Mary-Ann Gallagher: A huge thanks to Adolfo and José for keeping me sane and showing me such a good time.

Catherine Weiss: *Muchísimas gracias* to everyone who gave a helping hand or made encouraging noises and especially to: the Spanish National Tourist Office in London and all the friendly, helpful local tourist offices; the exclusive Pensión Manglano in Madrid; Percival and Gonzalo; the Ferrando family, for their warm, Huescan welcome; Manolo in Aínsa; the guard who gave me such an inspired tour of San Juan de la Peña; Armen, for his inimitable humour, hospitality and birthday cake; the Valladolid police, for towing away my car and then being so apologetic; Philippa and Pani in Ciudad Rodrigo, for showing me the delights of the local Chinese; Mamen and the Família Montero, who spoilt me rotten; and to everyone at Cadogan, especially Justine.

The editor would like to thank Tori Perrot and Joss Waterfall for willing editorial assistance with even the dullest jobs, as well as Georgina Palffy, Claudia Martin, Linda McQueen and Christine Stroyan for help and advice whenever requested.

Also available from Cadogan Guides...

The Italy Series

Italy
The Bay of Naples and Southern Italy
Lombardy and the Italian Lakes
Tuscany, Umbria and the Marches
Tuscany
Umbria
Northeast Italy
Italian Riviera
Bologna and Emilia Romagna
Rome & the Heart of Italy
Sardinia
Sicily
Rome, Florence, Venice
Florence
Rome
Venice

The France Series

France
Dordogne & the Lot
Gascony & the Pyrenees
Brittany
The Loire
The South of France
Provence
Côte d'Azur
Corsica
Paris
Short Breaks in Northern France

The Spain and Portugal Series

Spain
Andalucía
Northern Spain
Bilbao and the Basque Lands
Granada, Seville, Cordoba
Madrid, Barcelona, Seville
Madrid
Barcelona

Portugal
Portugal: The Algarve
Madeira & Porto Santo

Spain touring atlas

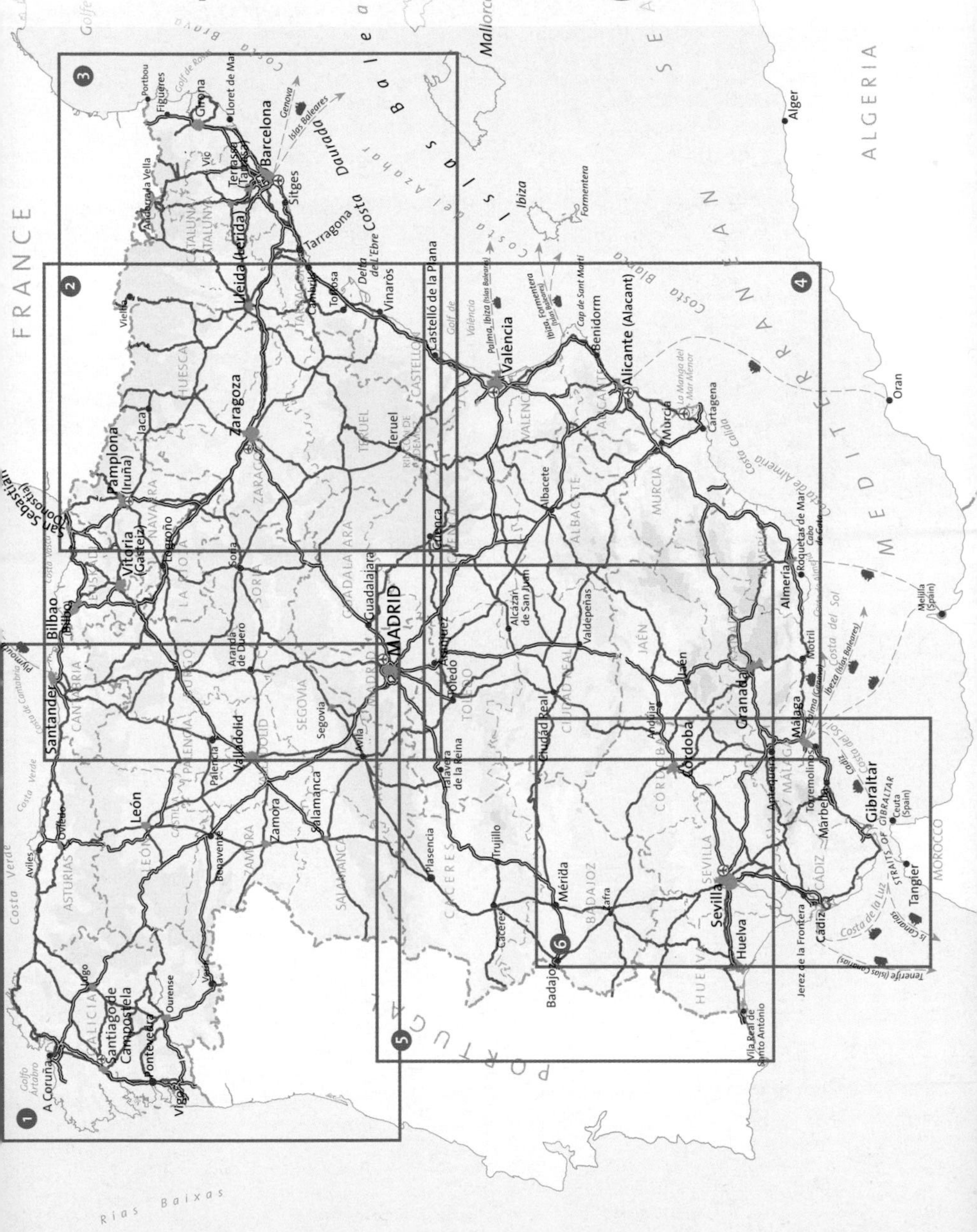

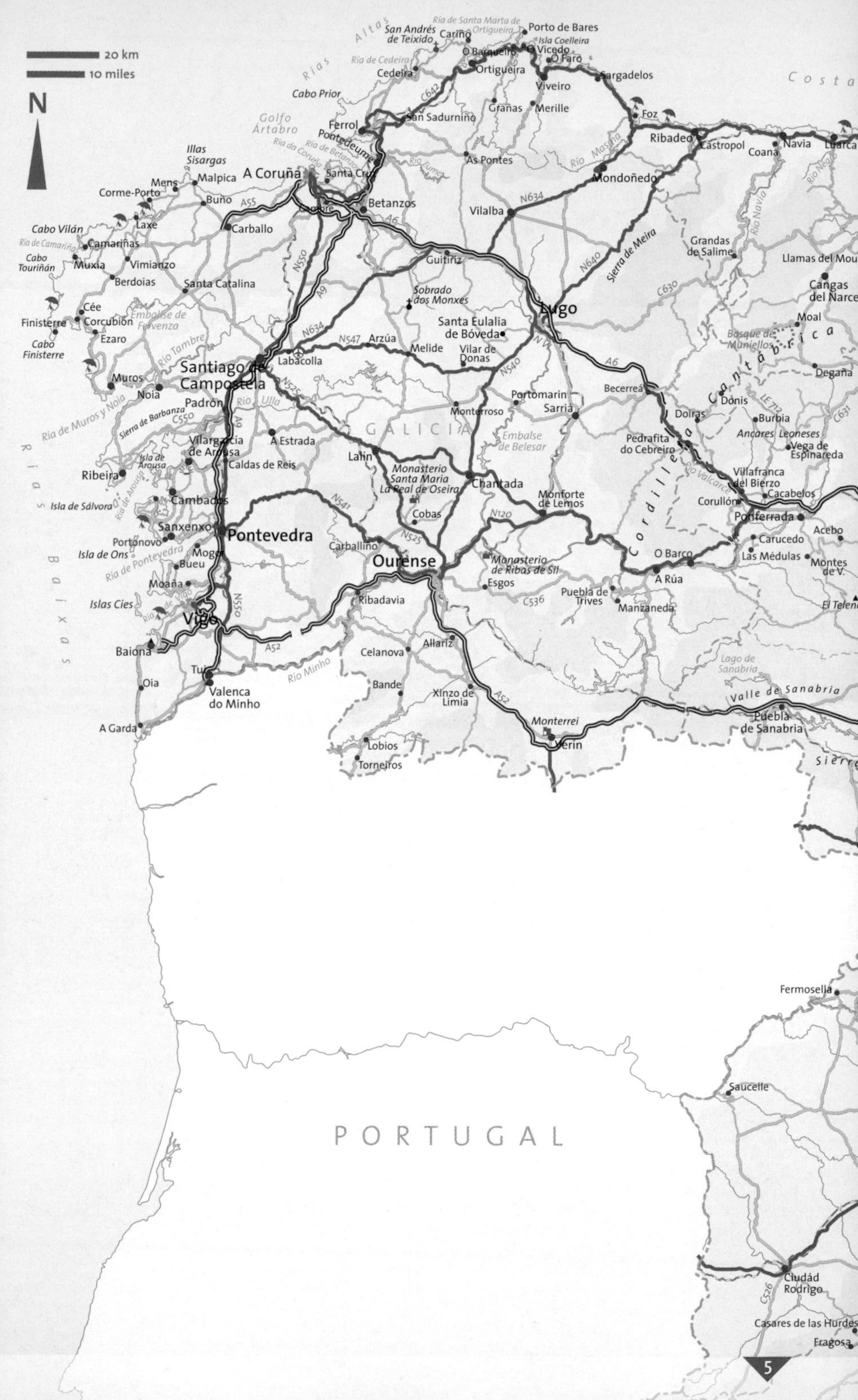

20 km
10 miles
N
Rías Altas
San Andrés de Teixido
Ría de Santa Marta de Ortigueira
Cariño
Porto de Bares
Isla Coelleira
O Barqueiro
O Vicedo
O Faro
Ría de Cedeira
Cedeira
Ortigueira
Sargadelos
Costa
Viveiro
Cabo Prior
C642
Grañas
Merille
Golfo Ártabro
Ferrol
San Sadurniño
Foz
Pontedeume
Ría de Betanzos
Ría da Coruña
Río Eume
As Pontes
Río Masma
Ribadeo
Castropol
Coaña
Navia
Luarca
Illas Sisargas
Malpica
A Coruña
Santa Cruz
Mondoñedo
Río Negro
Mens
Corme-Porto
Buño
A55
Betanzos
Vilalba
N634
Cabo Vilán
Laxe
Carballo
A6
Río Navia
Ría de Camariñas
Camariñas
Grandas de Salime
Cabo Touriñán
Muxia
Vimianzo
N550
Guitiriz
Sierra de Meira
N640
Llamas del Mour
Berdoias
Santa Catalina
A9
Sobrado dos Monxes
C630
Cangas del Narcea
Cée
Embalse de Fervenza
Lugo
Finisterre
Corcubión
N634
Santa Eulalia de Bóveda
Moal
Cabo Finisterre
Ezaro
Río Tambre
N547
Arzúa
Melide
Vilar de Donas
NVI
Bosque de Muniellos
Cordillera Cantábrica
Santiago de Compostela
Labacolla
N540
A6
Degaña
Muros
Noia
N525
Portomarín
Becerreá
Dónis
Padrón
Río Ulla
Monterroso
Sarria
LE 712
Ría de Muros y Noia
Sierra de Barbanza
C550
Doiras
Burbia
C631
GALICIA
Embalse de Belesar
Ancares Leoneses
Vilagarcía de Arousa
A Estrada
Pedrafita do Cebreiro
Vega de Espinareda
Isla de Arousa
Caldas de Reis
Lalín
Río Valcarce
Ribeira
Ría de Arousa
Monasterio Santa María La Real de Oseira
Chantada
Villafranca del Bierzo
Rías Baixas
Isla de Sálvora
Cambados
Monforte de Lemos
Cacabelos
N541
Cobas
Corullón
N120
Ponferrada
Sanxenxo
Pontevedra
N525
Acebo
Portonovo
Carballino
O Barco
Carucedo
Isla de Ons
Mogor
Ría de Pontevedra
Bueu
Ourense
Monasterio de Ribas de Sil
Las Médulas
Montes de V.
Esgos
A Rúa
Moaña
Ría de Vigo
Ribadavia
Puebla de Trives
C536
Islas Cíes
Manzaneda
El Teleno
Vigo
N550
Baiona
A52
Allariz
Celanova
Río Minho
Lago de Sanabria
Tui
Oia
Bande
Xinzo de Limia
A52
Valle de Sanabria
Valença do Minho
Puebla de Sanabria
A Garda
Monterrei
Verín
Lobios
Torneiros
Sierra
Fermoselle
Saucelle
PORTUGAL
Ciudad Rodrigo
C526
Casares de las Hurdes
Fragosa
5

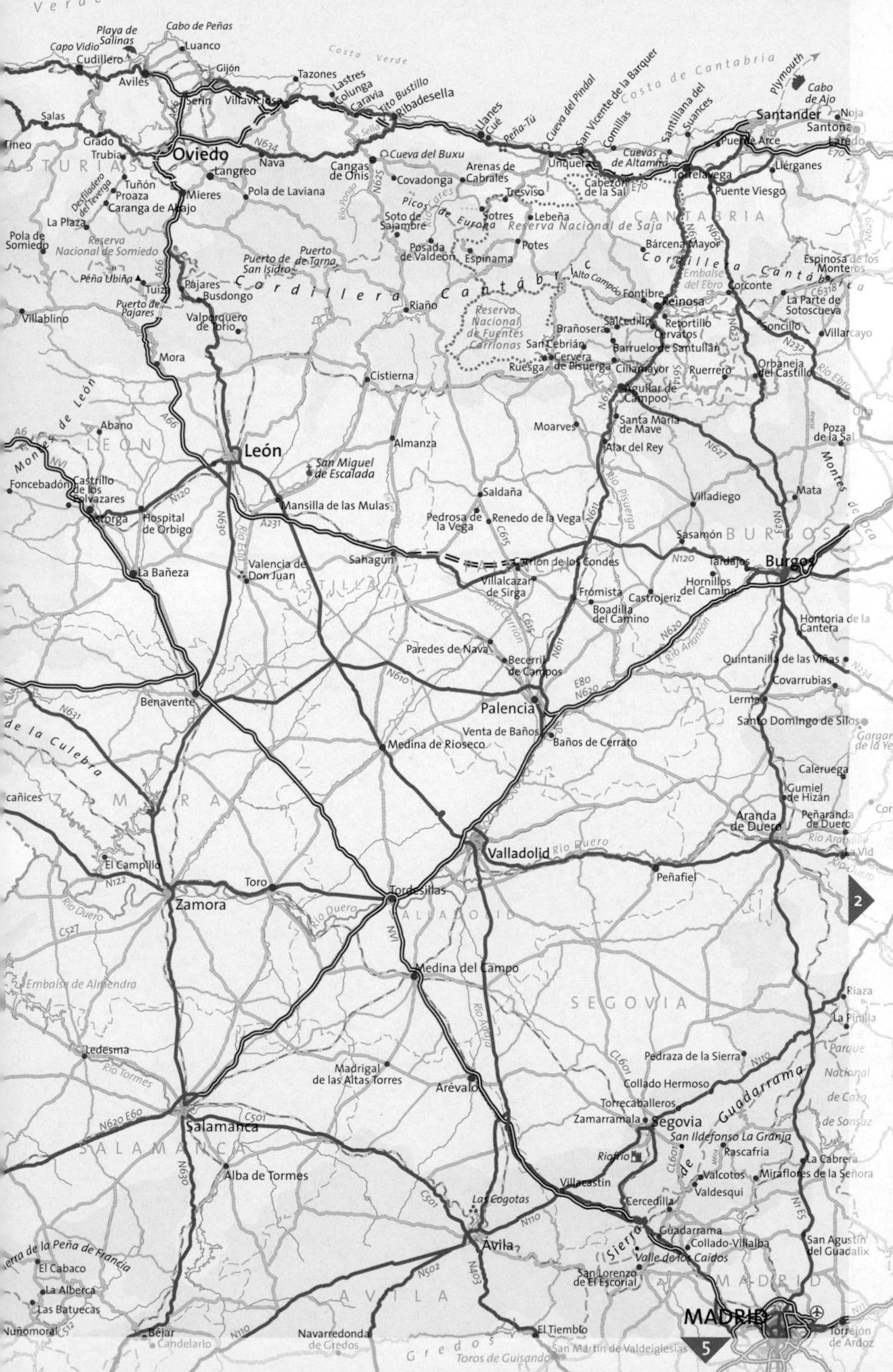
1
Verde
Playa de Salinas
Cabo de Peñas
Capo Vidio
Cudillero
Luanco
Costa Verde
Gijón
Tazones
Lastres
Colunga
Caravia
Tito Bustillo
Ribadesella
Avilés
Serín
Villaviciosa
Salas
Grado
Tineo
Trubia
Oviedo
N634
Nava
ASTURIAS
Langreo
Desfiladero del Teverga
Tuñón
Proaza
Caranga de Abajo
Mieres
Pola de Laviana
La Plaza
Pola de Somiedo
Reserva Nacional de Somiedo
Peña Ubiña
Tuiza
Puerto de Pajares
Pajares
Busdongo
Puerto de San Isidro
Puerto de Tarna
Villablino
Valporquero de Torio
Mora
Cangas de Onís
Cueva del Buxu
Covadonga
N625
Arenas de Cabrales
Picos de Europa
Soto de Sajambre
Posada de Valdeón
Espinama
Sotres
Tresviso
Lebeña
Potes
Cordillera Cantábrica
Riaño
Llanes
Cué
Peña-Tú
Cueva del Pindal
San Vicente de la Barquera
Costa de Cantabria
Comillas
Santillana del Mar
Suances
Unquera
Cuevas de Altamira
Cabezón de la Sal
E70
Torrelavega
Plymouth
Cabo de Ajo
Santander
Noja
Santoña
Puente Arce
Laredo
Liérganes
Puente Viesgo
CANTABRIA
Reserva Nacional de Saja
Bárcena Mayor
Cordillera Cantábrica
Embalse del Ebro
Corconte
Espinosa de los Monteros
C6318
La Parte de Sotoscueva
Alto Campóo
Fontibre
Reinosa
Salcedillo
Retortillo
Cervatos
Reserva Nacional de Fuentes Carrionas
Brañosera
San Cebrián
Cervera de Pisuerga
Ruesga
Barruelo de Santullán
Cillamayor
Ruerrero
Soncillo
Villarcayo
N232
Orbaneja del Castillo
Río Ebro
Oña
Aguilar de Campoo
N623
N627
Cistierna
Moarves
Santa María de Mave
Alar del Rey
Poza de la Sal
Montes de Oca
Abano
Montes de León
LEÓN
A66
León
San Miguel de Escalada
Almanza
Foncebadón
Castrillo de los Polvazares
Astorga
N120
Hospital de Orbigo
Mansilla de las Mulas
A231
N630
Río Esla
Saldaña
Pedrosa de la Vega
Renedo de la Vega
C615
Río Pisuerga
N611
Villadiego
Mata
Sasamón
BURGOS
La Bañeza
Valencia de Don Juan
CASTILLA
Sahagún
Carrión de los Condes
Villalcazar de Sirga
Río Carrión
Frómista
Boadilla del Camino
Castrojeriz
Tardajos
Hornillos del Camino
Burgos
Hontoria de la Cantera
N620
Río Arlanzón
A1
Paredes de Nava
Becerril de Campos
N610
Quintanilla de las Viñas
N234
Covarrubias
Lerma
Santo Domingo de Silos
Garganta de la Yecla
E80
Benavente
Palencia
Venta de Baños
Baños de Cerrato
N631
de la Culebra
Medina de Rioseco
Caleruega
Gumiel de Hizán
Alcañices
ZAMORA
Aranda de Duero
Peñaranda de Duero
Coruña
Río Arandilla
La Vid
Valladolid
Río Duero
Peñafiel
El Campillo
N122
Toro
Tordesillas
Zamora
Río Duero
VALLADOLID
C527
2
NVI
Medina del Campo
Embalse de Almendra
SEGOVIA
Río Adaja
Riaza
La Pinilla
Ledesma
Pedraza de la Sierra
Parque Nacional de Caza de Sonsaz
Río Tormes
Madrigal de las Altas Torres
Arévalo
CL601
Collado Hermoso
N110
Sierra de Guadarrama
Torrecaballeros
Zamarramala
Segovia
N620 E80
C501
Salamanca
San Ildefonso La Granja
SALAMANCA
Riofrío
Rascafría
La Cabrera
N630
Alba de Tormes
Valcotos
Miraflores de la Señora
Valdesqui
Villacastín
Las Cogotas
Cercedilla
N110
Guadarrama
Collado-Villalba
San Agustín del Guadalix
Sierra de la Peña de Francia
Ávila
Valle de los Caídos
N502
N403
El Cabaco
San Lorenzo de El Escorial
MADRID
La Alberca
AVILA
Las Batuecas
MADRID
Nuñomoral
Béjar
N110
Navarredonda de Gredos
El Tiemblo
Torrejón de Ardoz
Candelario
Gredos
Toros de Guisando
San Martín de Valdeiglesias
5

Costa de Cantabria
Llanes
Cué
Peña-Tú
Cueva del Pindal
San Vicente de la Barquera
Comillas
Santillana del Mar
Suances
Cabo Mayor
Plymouth
Santander
Cabo de Ajo
Noja
Santoña
Laredo
Castro-Urdiales
Bakio
Bermio
Mundaka
Lekeitio
Costa Vasca
San Sebastián (Donostia)
Cabo Higuer
Pasajes
Fuente
Unquera
Cuevas de Altamira
Puente Arce
Liérganes
Torrelavega
Cabezón de la Sal
Tresviso
Puente Viesgo
Plentzia
Getxo
Mungia
Gernika
Ondárroa
Zumaia
Getaria
Zarautz
Oiartzun
Irun
Bilbao (Bilbo)
VIZCAYA
Markina
Deba
Sotres
Lebeña
CANTABRIA
Reserva Nacional de Saja
Potes
Espinama
Bárcena Mayor
Cordillera Cantábrica
Espinosa de los Monteros
Bercedo
Vallejo de Mena
Durango
Elorrio
EUSKADI
GUIPÚZCOA
Azpeitia
Régil
Tolosa
Oñati
Betelu
Azpirotz
Leitza
Lekunberri
Zubieta
Alto Campóo
Fontibre
Embalse del Ebro
Corconte
Reinosa
La Parte de Sotoscueva
Soncillo
Villarcayo
Medina de Pomar
Embalse de Urrunaga
Aranzazu
Segura
Embalse de Ullivarri
Huarte Arakil
Altsasu
Reserva Nacional de Fuentes Carrionas
Brañosera
San Cebrián
Cervatos
Barruelo de Santullán
Puerto de Carrales
Ruesga
Cervera de Pisuerga
Cillamayor
Ruerrero
San Martín de Elines
Trespuentes
Gaceo
Vitoria (Gasteiz)
Aguilar de Campoo
Treviño
COUNTY OF TREVIÑO
Antoñana
Estella
Puente la Reina
Obanos
Moarves
Santa María de Mave
Alar del Rey
Oña
Frías
Poza de la Sal
Montes Obarenes
Pancorbo
Miranda de Ebro
Briñas
Montes
Briviesca
Haro
Biasteri
Los Arcos
Torres del Río
Viana
Artajona
Tafalla
Saldaña
Pedrosa de la Vega
Renedo de la Vega
Villadiego
Mata
Redecilla del Campo
Santo Domingo de la Calzada
Logroño
Osorno
PALENCIA
Grijalba
Sasamón
Tardajos
San Juan de Ortega
Nájera
Navarrete
Carrión de los Condes
Villalcazar de Sirga
Frómista
Castrojeriz
Burgos
Ezcaray
San Millán de la Cogolla
Valle de Iregua
LA RIOJA
Calahorra
Boadilla del Camino
Hontoria de la Cantera
Sierra de la Demanda
Arnedillo
Arnedo
Munilla
Préjano
Enciso
Becerril de Campos
Quintanilla de las Viñas
Reserva
Mansilla
Nacional de Cameros
Fitero
Cintruénigo
Covarrubias
Palencia
Venta de Baños
Lerma
Santo Domingo de Silos
Garganta de la Yecla
Laguna Negra de Urbión
Baños de Cerrato
Vinuesa
Caleruega
Peñalba de Castro
Cañon del Río Lobos
Numancia
Garray
Gumiel de Hizán
Coruña del Conte
Soria
Valladolid
Aranda de Duero
Peñaranda de Duero
Calatañazor
Río Duero
La Vid
El Burgo de Osma
SORIA
Peñafiel
VALLADOLID
Gormaz
Almazán
Berlanga de Duero
Casillas de Berlanga
Morón de Almazán
Tiermes
Ateca
Riaza
Villacadima
Campisábalos
SEGOVIA
La Pinilla
Albendiego
Atienza
Medinaceli
Monasterio de Piedra
Parque Nacional
Sierra de Alto Rey
Pedraza de la Sierra
Arévalo
de Caza
Carabias
Sigüenza
Barbatona
Collado Hermoso
Semillas
Torrecaballeros
Sierra de Guadarrama
Zamarramala
Segovia
de Sonsaz
Cogolludo
San Ildefonso La Granja
Rascafría
Montarrón
Jadraque
La Cabrera
Villacastín
Valcotos
Miraflores de la Señora
Valdesquí
Hita
Cifuentes
Las Cogotas
Cercedilla
Brihuega
GUADALAJARA
Guadarrama
Collado-Villalba
Ávila
San Agustín del Guadalix
Guadalajara
La Alcarria
Valle de los Caídos
San Lorenzo de El Escorial
Budia
MADRID
ÁVILA
Alcalá de Henares
Sacedón
San Miguel de las Victorias
Serranía de Cuenca
El Tiemblo
Torrejón de Ardoz
Mar de Castilla
Embalse de Buendía
Pastrana
San Martín de Valdeiglesias
Toros de Guisando
Arganda
Mondéjar
Sierra de Bascuñana
Villalba de la Sierra
Navalcarnero
La Ciudad Encantada
Illescas
Chinchón
TOLEDO
CUENCA
Cuenca
Río Tajo
Río Huécar
Sta Olalla
Aranjuez
Tarancón
Carrascosa del Campo
Las Torcas
Torrijos
1
4

2
20 km
10 miles
N
FRANCE
Urdazubi
Puerto de Izpegui
Elizondo
Puerto Ibañeta
Valcarlos
Burguete
Roncesvalles
Orhí
Pic d'Anie
Ochagavía
Pamplona (Iruña)
Zuriza
Isaba
Roncal
Puerto de Somport
Agoitz
Candanchú
Sallent de Gállego
Balneario de Panticosa
Anso
Siresa
Echo
Formigal
Panticosa
Noam
Hoz de Arbayún
Burgui
Navascues
Canfranc
Lumbier
Biescas
N260
Torla
Parque Nacional de Ordesa
Nerín
Valle de Pineta
Bielsa
Benasque
Cerler
Yesa
N240
Berdún
Jaca
Sangüesa
Javier
Embalse de Yesa
Santa Cruz de la Serós
Ujué
Olite
Sos del Rey Católico
Ainsa
Uncastillo
Loarre
Sierra de Guara
Ayerbe
Sádaba
Bárdenas Reales
Esquedas
Alquézar
Torreciudad
Graus
Embalse de Grado I
Ejea de los Caballeros
Las Cinco Villas
HUESCA
Huesca
Monasterio de Pueyo
Barbastro
Tudela
Sancho Abarca
Monzón
Tauste
Borja
Alagón
Zaragoza
ZARAGOZA
Río Ebro
Los Monegros
Lleida (Lerida)
Vall d'Aran
Vielha
Betrén
Salardú
Baquera
Arties
Los Montes Malditos
Túnel de Vielha
Caldes de Boí
Espot
Erill la Vall
Taüll
Parc Nacional d'Aiguestortes
La Pobla de Segur
Tremp
CATALUNA/CATALUNYA
3
Bellpuig
Fraga
La Almunia de Doña Godina
Quinto
Embalse de Mequinenza
Mequinenza
Monestir de Poblet
Calatayud
Cariñena
Belchite
Caspe
Cornudella
Prades
Scala Dei
Siurana
TARRAGONA
Falset
Hijar
Móra la Nova
Cambrils
Daroca
Gandesa
Alcañiz
El Pinell de Brai
Castillo Miravet
Miami Platja
Valderrobres
L'Ametlla de Mar
Tortosa
Delta de L'Ebre
Montalbán
Monreal del Campo
Parc Natural
Deltebre
Sorita
St Carles de la Ràpita
Port dels Alfacs
Villarluengo
Forcall
La Todolella
Morella
Maestrazgo
Mirambel
Muela
Vallivana
Traiguera
TERUEL
Cantavieja
Castellfort
Catí
Sant Mateu
Vinaròs
Benicarló
La Iglesuela del Cid
Ares del Maestrat
Vilafranca
Sierra de Gúdar
Valdelinares
Albarracín
Albocàsser
Benassal
Alcalà de Xivert
Peñíscola
Teruel
La Virgen de la Vega
Les Coves de Vinromà
Sierra de Irta
Castillo de Xivert
Montes Universales
CASTELLÓN
Rubielos de Mora
Arc de Cabanes
Vilafamés
Cabanes
Castielfabib
Orpesa del Mar
Montanejos
Benicàssim
Ademuz
RINCÓN DE ADEMUZ
Desert de les Palmes
Castelló de la Plana
4
Onda
El Grau de Castelló

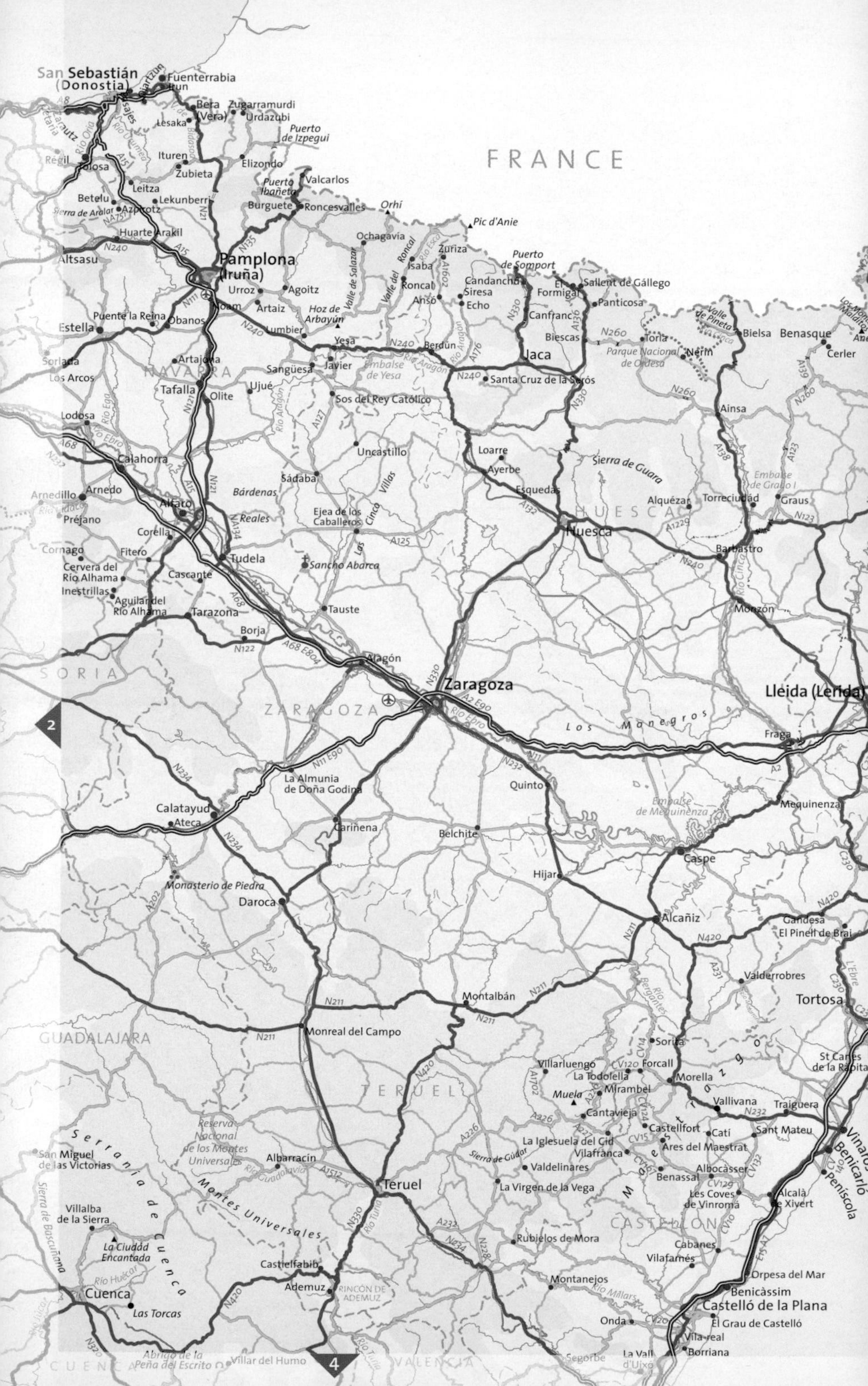

FRANCE
San Sebastián (Donostia)
Fuenterrabia
Irun
Bera (Vera)
Zugarramurdi
Urdazubi
Puerto de Izpegui
Lesaka
Régil
Tolosa
Ituren
Zubieta
Elizondo
Leitza
Puerto Ibañeta
Valcarlos
Betelu
Lekunberri
Sierra de Aralar
Azpirotz
Burguete
Roncesvalles
Orhí
Pic d'Anie
Huarte Arakil
Ochagavía
Zuriza
Altsasu
Pamplona (Iruña)
Isaba
Puerto de Somport
Urroz
Agoitz
Roncal
Candanchú
Siresa
El Formigal
Sallent de Gállego
Noam
Artaiz
Ansó
Echo
Panticosa
Puente la Reina
Obanos
Hoz de Arbayún
Canfranc
Valle de Pineta
Estella
Lumbier
Biescas
Torla
Bielsa
Benasque
Yesa
Berdún
Parque Nacional de Ordesa
Nerín
Cerler
Sorlada
Artajona
Sangüesa
Javier
Embalse de Yesa
Jaca
Los Arcos
NAVARRA
Ujué
Santa Cruz de la Serós
Tafalla
Olite
Sos del Rey Católico
Ainsa
Lodosa
Uncastillo
Loarre
Calahorra
Ayerbe
Sierra de Guara
Sádaba
Arnedillo
Arnedo
Bárdenas
Esquedas
Alquézar
Torreciudad
Graus
Alfaro
Reales
Ejea de los Caballeros
HUESCA
Préjano
Corella
Huesca
Cornago
Fitero
Tudela
Barbastro
Cervera del Río Alhama
Sancho Abarca
Cascante
Inestrillas
Aguilar del Río Alhama
Tarazona
Tauste
Monzón
Borja
Alagón
SORIA
Zaragoza
Lleida (Lerida)
ZARAGOZA
Los Monegros
Fraga
La Almunia de Doña Godina
Quinto
Calatayud
Ateca
Embalse de Mequinenza
Mequinenza
Cariñena
Belchite
Caspe
Monasterio de Piedra
Hijar
Daroca
Alcañiz
Gandesa
El Pinell de Brai
Valderrobres
Montalbán
Tortosa
Monreal del Campo
GUADALAJARA
Sorita
St Carles de la Ràpita
Villarluengo
Forcall
La Todolella
Morella
Muela
Mirambel
TERUEL
Vallivana
Traiguera
Cantavieja
Castellfort
Catí
Sant Mateu
Vinaròs
Serranía de Cuenca
Reserva Nacional de los Montes Universales
La Iglesuela del Cid
Vilafranca
Ares del Maestrat
Benicarló
San Miguel de las Victorias
Albarracín
Sierra de Gúdar
Valdelinares
Benassal
Albocàsser
Peñíscola
Montes Universales
Teruel
La Virgen de la Vega
Maestrazgo
Les Coves de Vinromà
Alcalà de Xivert
Villalba de la Sierra
Sierra de Bascuñana
CASTELLÓN
La Ciudad Encantada
Rubielos de Mora
Cabanes
Vilafamés
Castielfabib
Orpesa del Mar
Cuenca
Las Torcas
Ademuz
Rincón de Ademuz
Montanejos
Benicàssim
Castelló de la Plana
Onda
El Grau de Castelló
Vila-real
Borriana
CUENCA
Abrigo de la Peña del Escrito
Villar del Humo
VALENCIA
Segorbe
La Vall d'Uixó
2
4

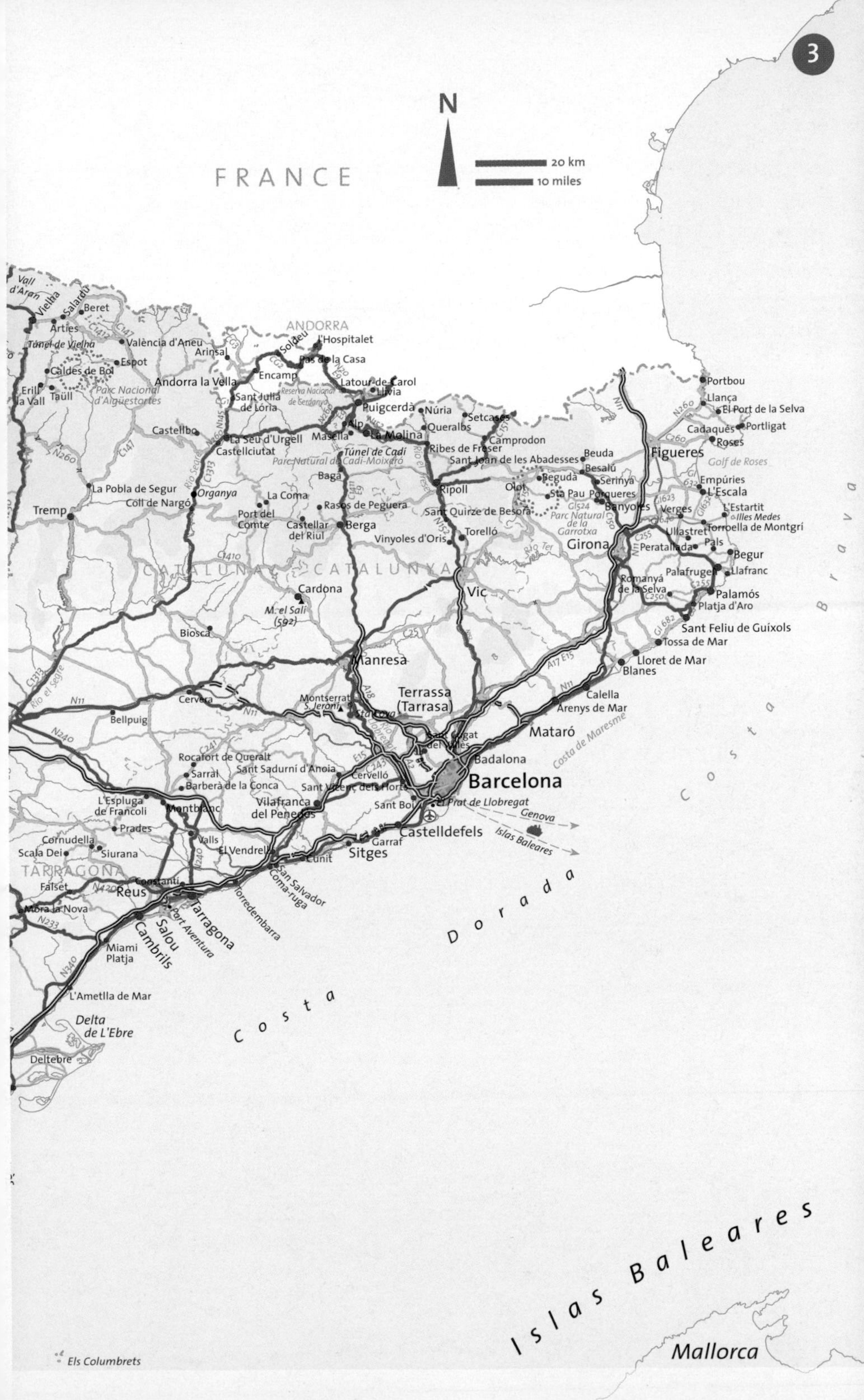

N
20 km
10 miles
FRANCE
ANDORRA
Vall d'Aran
Vielha
Salardú
Beret
Arties
Túnel de Vielha
València d'Aneu
Arinsal
Soldeu
l'Hospitalet
Pas de la Casa
Espot
Caldes de Boí
Encamp
Andorra la Vella
Erill la Vall
Taüll
Parc Nacional d'Aigüestortes
Sant Julià de Lória
Reserva Nacional de Cerdanya
Latour-de-Carol
Llívia
Puigcerdà
Núria
Setcases
Alp
Queralbs
Castellbò
La Seu d'Urgell
Castellciutat
Masella
La Molina
Camprodon
Túnel de Cadí
Ribes de Freser
Parc Natural de Cadí-Moixeró
Sant Joan de les Abadesses
Beuda
Figueres
Besalú
Baga
Ripoll
Olot
Beguda
Serinyà
Sta Pau
Porqueres
Banyoles
Parc Natural de la Garrotxa
La Pobla de Segur
Coll de Nargó
Organyà
La Coma
Rasos de Peguera
Port del Comte
Castellar del Riul
Berga
Sant Quirze de Besora
Vinyoles d'Oris
Torelló
Tremp
Girona
Río Ter
CATALUÑA
CATALUNYA
Cardona
M. el Sali (592)
Vic
Biosca
Manresa
Portbou
Llança
El Port de la Selva
Cadaqués
Portligat
Roses
Golf de Roses
Empúries
L'Escala
Verges
L'Estartit
Illes Medes
Torroella de Montgrí
Ullastret
Peratallada
Pals
Begur
Palafrugell
Llafranc
Romanyá de la Selva
Palamós
Platja d'Aro
Sant Feliu de Guíxols
Tossa de Mar
Lloret de Mar
Blanes
Calella
Arenys de Mar
Mataró
Costa de Maresme
Costa Brava
Río el Segre
Cervera
Bellpuig
Montserrat
S. Jeroni
Sta Cova
Terrassa (Tarrasa)
Sant Cugat del Vallès
Río Llobregat
Rocafort de Queralt
Sarral
Sant Sadurní d'Anoia
Barberà de la Conca
Cervelló
Badalona
Barcelona
Sant Vicenç dels Horts
L'Espluga de Francolí
Montblanc
Vilafranca del Penedès
Sant Boi
El Prat de Llobregat
Genova
Islas Baleares
Prades
Castelldefels
Cornudella
Siurana
Scala Dei
Valls
El Vendrell
Garraf
Sitges
Cunit
TARRAGONA
Constantí
Falset
Reus
Móra la Nova
San Salvador
Coma-ruga
Torredembarra
Tarragona
Salou
Port Aventura
Cambrils
Miami Platja
L'Ametlla de Mar
Delta de L'Ebre
Deltebre
Costa Dorada
Islas Baleares
Mallorca
Els Columbrets

2
Cuenca
Río Huécar
Río Tajo
NV E90
Sta Olalla
Barcience
Torrijos
Aranjuez
Tarancón
Carrascosa del Campo
Las Torca
Ocaña
NIV E5
NIII E901
Río Júcar
CUENCA
N320
N403
Gudamur
Toledo
Ruinas Romanas de Segóbriga
Nuestra Señora de Melque
TOLEDO
Tembleque
Mora
Orgaz
La Almarcha
N301
Quintanar de la Orden
Belmonte
Motilla del Palancar
Alarcón
El Toboso
Mota del Cuervo
CM400
N401
CM3103
Consuegra
Montes de Toledo
Alcázar de San Juan
Campo de Criptana
San Clemente
5
Puerto-Lápice
N420
Socuéllamos
Villarrobledo
La Roda
Parque Nacional de las Tablas de Daimiel
La Mancha
Tomelloso
N310
N430
Río Guadiana
Daimiel
Ciudad Real
Manzanares
Ruidera
Lagunas de Ruidera
N322
CIUDAD REAL
Almagro
Parque Natural de las Lagunas de Ruidera
Campo de Calatrava
CM412
ALBACETE
Almodóvar del Campo
Puertollano
Valdepeñas
Villanueva de Los Infantes
Santuario Nuestra Señora de Cortés
Convento Castillo de Calatrava la Nueva
Santa Cruz de Mudela
Alcaraz
Sierra de Alcaraz
Desfiladero de Despeñaperros
Elche de la Sierra
Sierra Morena
Parque Natural de la Sierra de Andújar
Yeste
Villanueva de Córdoba
A420
Cardeña
La Carolina
Parque Natural de la Sierra de Cardeña
NIV-E5
Hornos
Baños de la Encina
JAÉN
Coto Nacional de Cazorla
Sierra de Segura
Embalse del Guadalmellato
Montoro
Bailén
Linares
NIV
Canena
Torreperogil
Andújar
Baeza
Úbeda
C330
Sierra de Cazorla
Cazorla
La Iruela
N323-E902
Jódar
6
CÓRDOBA
A316
Jaén
N432
Martos
C3221
Sierra de la Pandera
Vélez Blanco
Vélez Rubio
Baena
Embalse del Negratín
Doña Mencía
Sierra de las Estancias
Cabra
Alcalá la Real
Baza
A92N
Priego de Córdoba
Huércal Overa
Parque Natural de la Sierra Subbética
Guadix
Embalse de Iznájar
GRANADA
Sierra de los Filabres
Granada
Calahorra
ALMERÍA
Loja
A92
Archidona
Sierra Nevada
Gérgal
Sorbas
A359
Parque Natural de la Sierra Nevada
Pico Veleta
Mulhacén
Puerto del Suspiro del Moro
A370
Tabernas
Antequera
Trevélez
Válor
Laroles
Mini Hollywood
Sierra Alhamilla
Alhama de Granada
Villanueva de la Concepción
El Torcal
Pampaneira
Bérchules
Yegen
Ugíjar
Níjar
Reserva Nacional de Sierra de Tejeda
Lanjarón
Orgiva
A347
A344
Parque Natural de Cabo de Gata-Níjar
Garganta del Chorro
A335
Cómpeta
Las Alpujarras
A346
Berja
Almería
Frigiliana
MÁLAGA
Vélez Málaga
Torrox
A340
Aguadulce
Cabo de Gata
Motril
Málaga
Nerja
Adra
Roquetas de Mar
Torre del Mar
Torrox Costa
Almuñécar
Salobreña
Almerimar
Costa de Almería
Melilla
Torremolinos
Costa del Sol

4
3
TERUEL
CASTELLÓN
Ademuz
RINCÓN DE ADEMUZ
Montanejos
Benicàssim
Castelló de la Plana
El Grau de Castelló
Onda
Vila-real
Borriana
Els Columbrets
Villar del Humo
Segorbe
La Vall d'Uixó
Platja de Nules
Almenara
Sagunt
El Port de Sagunt
Golf de València
Llíria
El Puig
Utiel
Manises
Alboraia
Palma, Ibiza (Islas Baleares)
Requena
Chiva
València
Buñol
El Saler
Cofrentes
VALENCIA
El Palmar
El Perelló
Cullera
Costa del Azahar
Albacete
Cueva de la Vieja
Xàtiva
Gandia
Oliva
Ibiza, Formentera (Islas Baleares)
Rugat
Dénia
Almansa
Cap de Sant Antoni
Xàbia
Cap de Sant Martí
Teulada
Moraira
Alcoi
Guadalest
Parc Natural de la Font Roja
Callosa d'en Sarrià
Calp
Penyal d'Ifac
Yecla
Villena
Biar
Ibi
Port de la Carrasqueta
Altea
Tobarra
Xixona
Sax
Benidorm
Busot
La Vila Joiosa
Hellín
ALICANTE
Jumilla
Platja de Sant Joan
Alicante (Alacant)
L'Altet
Golf d'Alacant
Elche
Santa Pola
Oran
Illa de Tabarca
Calasparra
Moratalla
Caravaca de la Cruz
Cehegín
La Marina del Pinet
Guardamar del Segura
Orihuela
Costa Blanca
MURCIA
Torrevieja
Murcia
Parque Natural de la Sierra de España
Platjas de Orihuela
Sierra de España
Alhama de Murcia
San Pedro del Pinatar
San Javier
Santiago de la Ribera
Totana
Los Alcázares
La Manga del Mar Menor
Lorca
Los Nietos
Cartagena
Cabo de Palos
Mazarrón
Bolnuevo
Puerto de Mazarr
El Hornillo
Costa Calida
Garrucha
Mojácar
Costa de Almería
MEDITERRANEAN SEA
N
20 km
10 miles

20 km
10 miles
N
SALAMANCA
1
La Alberca
Casares de las Hurdes
Las Batuecas
Fragosa
Béjar
Caminomorisco
Las Hurdes
Candelario
Pinofranqueado
Embalse de Gabriel y Galán
Hervás
Zarza de Granadilla
Jarandilla de la Vera
Losar de la Vera
Cuacos de Yuste
Valverde de la Vera
Coria
Plasencia
Torrejoncillo
Villareal de San Carlos
Parque Natural de Monfragüe
Palancar
Cañaveral
Embalse de Alcántara
Alcántara
Garrovillas
Río Tajo
CÁCERES
Cáceres
Trujillo
Valencia de Alcántara
Sierra de Guadalupe
Alburquerque
PORTUGAL
Medellín
Badajoz
Mérida
Río Guadiana
Olivenza
Almendralejo
Terra de Barros
BADAJOZ
Barcarrota
Zafra
Jerez de los Caballeros
Peñarroya-Pueblonuevo
Fregenal de la Sierra
Llerena
Azuaga
Fuente Obejuna
Rosal de la Frontera
Parque Natural de la Sierra de Aracena
Aroche
Jabugo
Galaroza
Cortegana
Aracena
Sierra Morena
Cazalla de la Sierra
Almonaster la Real
Sierra de Aracena
HUELVA
Nerva
Palma del Río
Las Nieves
Villanueva de los Castillejos
Valverde de Camino
Coto Nacional de la Pata del Caballo
Canal del Bajo Guadalquivir
Río Guadiana
Santiponce
Carmona
Olivares
Huelva
Sevilla
SEVILLA
Ayamonte
Moguer
Palos de la Frontera
El Arahal
Vila Real de Santo António
Isla Cristina
La Antilla
El Rompido
Punta Umbría
Mazagón
Marismas del Guadalquivir
El Rocío
Utrera
Playa de Mazagón
Morón de la Frontera
Matalascañas
6
Parque Nacional del Coto Doñana

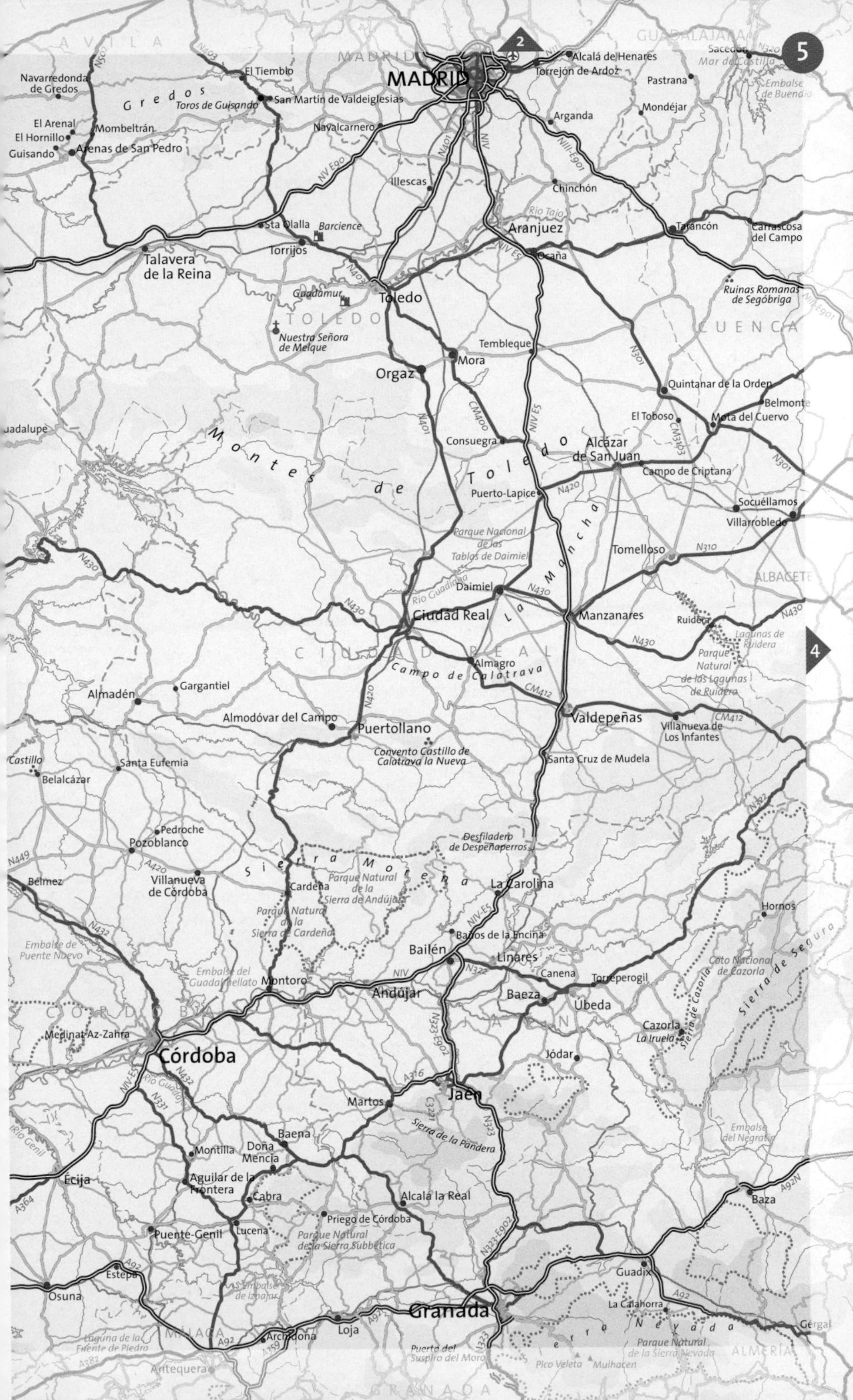

5
4
2
MADRID
Alcalá de Henares
Torrejón de Ardoz
Sacedón
Mar de Castilla
Embalse de Buendía
Pastrana
Mondéjar
Arganda
Chinchón
Río Tajo
Aranjuez
Tarancón
Carrascosa del Campo
Ocaña
Ruinas Romanas de Segóbriga
CUENCA
GUADALAJARA
AVILA
Navarredonda de Gredos
Gredos
Toros de Guisando
El Tiemblo
San Martín de Valdeiglesias
Navalcarnero
El Arenal
El Hornillo
Guisando
Mombeltrán
Arenas de San Pedro
Illescas
Sta Olalla
Barcience
Torrijos
Talavera de la Reina
Guadamur
Toledo
TOLEDO
Nuestra Señora de Melque
Tembleque
Mora
Orgaz
Quintanar de la Orden
Belmonte
El Toboso
Mota del Cuervo
Consuegra
Montes de Toledo
Alcázar de San Juan
Campo de Criptana
Puerto-Lapice
Socuéllamos
Villarrobledo
Parque Nacional de las Tablas de Daimiel
Tomelloso
La Mancha
Daimiel
Río Guadiana
Ciudad Real
Manzanares
Ruidera
Lagunas de Ruidera
Parque Natural de las Lagunas de Ruidera
ALBACETE
CIUDAD REAL
Almagro
Campo de Calatrava
Guadalupe
Almadén
Gargantiel
Almodóvar del Campo
Puertollano
Valdepeñas
Villanueva de Los Infantes
Convento Castillo de Calatrava la Nueva
Santa Cruz de Mudela
Castillo
Santa Eufemia
Belalcázar
Pedroche
Pozoblanco
Desfiladero de Despeñaperros
Sierra Morena
Belmez
Villanueva de Córdoba
Cardeña
Parque Natural de la Sierra de Andújar
Parque Natural de la Sierra de Cardeña
La Carolina
Baños de la Encina
Hornos
Embalse de Puente Nuevo
Bailén
Linares
Coto Nacional de Cazorla
Sierra de Segura
Embalse del Guadalmellato
Montoro
Andújar
Canena
Torreperogil
Baeza
Úbeda
CÓRDOBA
JAÉN
Sierra de Cazorla
Cazorla
La Iruela
Medinat-Az-Zahra
Córdoba
Jódar
Río Guadalquivir
Río Genil
Jaén
Martos
Sierra de la Pandera
Embalse del Negratín
Baena
Montilla
Doña Mencía
Écija
Aguilar de la Frontera
Cabra
Alcalá la Real
Baza
Priego de Córdoba
Puente-Genil
Lucena
Parque Natural de la Sierra Subbética
Guadix
Estepa
Osuna
Embalse de Iznájar
La Calahorra
Granada
Sierra Nevada
Loja
Gérgal
Laguna de la Fuente de Piedra
MÁLAGA
Archidona
Puerto del Suspiro del Moro
Parque Natural de la Sierra Nevada
Pico Veleta
Mulhacén
ALMERÍA
Antequera
GRANADA

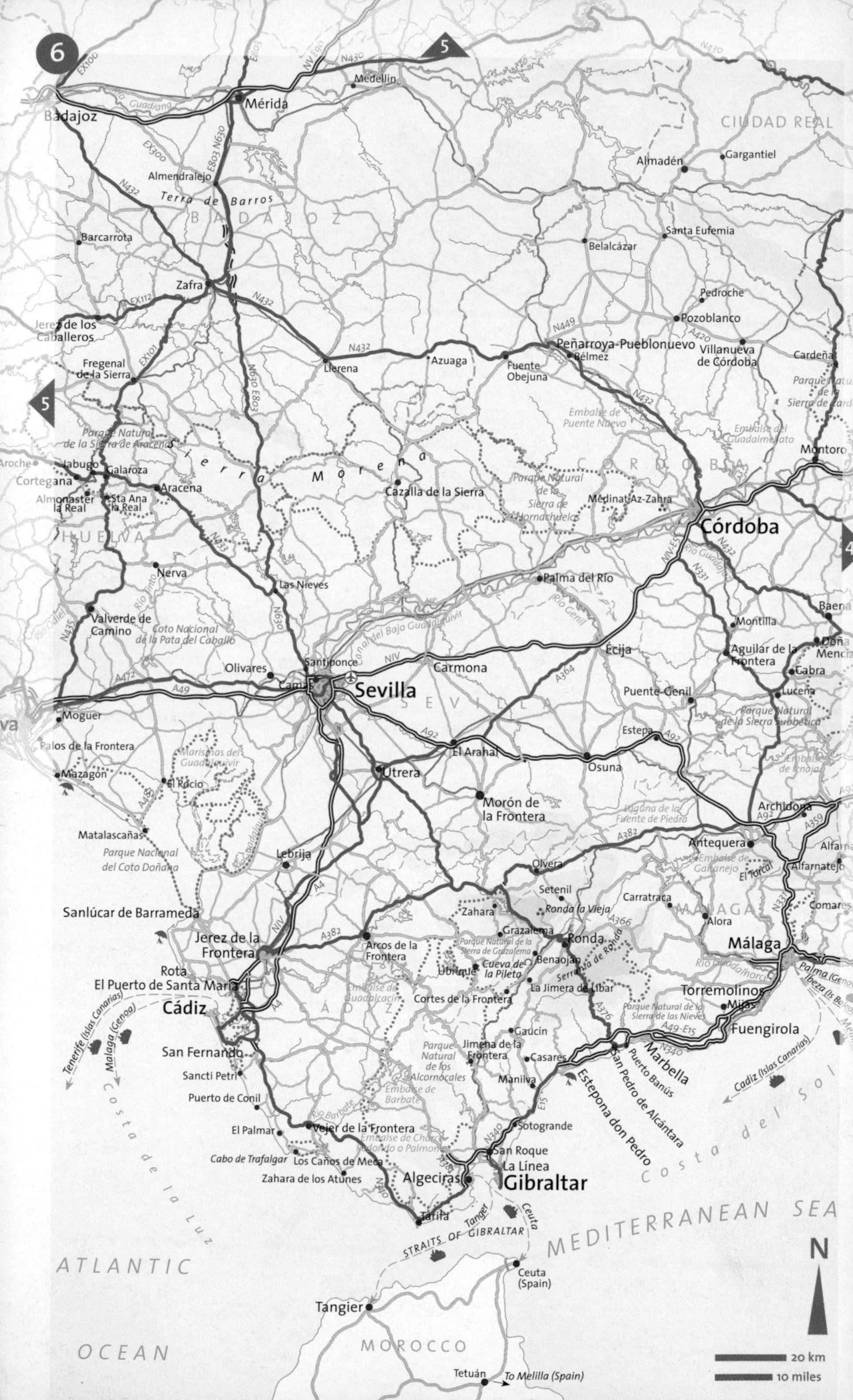

6
5
4
Badajoz
Mérida
Medellín
Almendralejo
Terra de Barros
BADAJOZ
Barcarrota
Zafra
Jerez de los Caballeros
Fregenal de la Sierra
Llerena
Azuaga
Fuente Obejuna
Peñarroya-Pueblonuevo
Bélmez
CIUDAD REAL
Almadén
Gargantiel
Santa Eufemia
Belalcázar
Pedroche
Pozoblanco
Villanueva de Córdoba
Cardeña
Montoro
Embalse de Puente Nuevo
Parque Natural de la Sierra de Aracena
Sierra Morena
Aroche
Jabugo
Galaroza
Cortegana
Almonaster la Real
Sta Ana la Real
Aracena
Cazalla de la Sierra
Parque Natural de la Sierra de Hornachuelos
Medinat Az-Zahra
CÓRDOBA
Córdoba
HUELVA
Nerva
Las Nieves
Palma del Río
Río Genil
Valverde de Camino
Coto Nacional de la Pata del Caballo
Canal del Bajo Guadalquivir
Montilla
Baena
Aguilar de la Frontera
Doña Mencía
Cabra
Lucena
Olivares
Santiponce
Camas
Sevilla
Carmona
Écija
Puente-Genil
Parque Natural de la Sierra Subbética
Moguer
Palos de la Frontera
Marismas del Guadalquivir
SEVILLA
El Arahal
Estepa
Osuna
Mazagón
El Rocío
Utrera
Morón de la Frontera
Matalascañas
Parque Nacional del Coto Doñana
Laguna de la Fuente de Piedra
Archidona
Antequera
Alfarnatejo
Embalse de Guadalteba
El Torcal
Lebrija
Olvera
Setenil
Ronda la Vieja
Carratraca
Álora
MÁLAGA
Comares
Sanlúcar de Barrameda
Zahara
Grazalema
Parque Natural de la Sierra de Grazalema
Ronda
Serranía de Ronda
Jerez de la Frontera
Arcos de la Frontera
Benaoján
Ubrique
Cueva de la Pileta
La Jimera de Líbar
Málaga
Rota
El Puerto de Santa María
Cádiz
Embalse de Guadalcacín
CÁDIZ
Cortes de la Frontera
Torremolinos
Mijas
Parque Natural de la Sierra de las Nieves
Fuengirola
Tenerife (Islas Canarias)
Malaga (Genoa)
San Fernando
Sancti Petri
Puerto de Conil
Parque Natural de los Alcornocales
Gaucín
Jimena de la Frontera
Casares
Manilva
Marbella
Puerto Banús
San Pedro de Alcántara
Estepona don Pedro
Palma (Genova)
Ibeza (Is Baleares)
Cadiz (Islas Canarias)
Costa del Sol
El Palmar
Vejer de la Frontera
Embalse de Barbate
Sotogrande
San Roque
La Línea
Gibraltar
Cabo de Trafalgar
Los Caños de Meca
Zahara de los Atunes
Algeciras
Tarifa
Costa de la Luz
MEDITERRANEAN SEA
STRAITS OF GIBRALTAR
Tanger
Ceuta
ATLANTIC OCEAN
Ceuta (Spain)
Tangier
MOROCCO
Tetuán
To Melilla (Spain)
N
20 km
10 miles